Theme Index

Critical Thinking

What's the Evidence

A Step Further

Evaluation of Evidence/ Questioning Assertions/ Critical Thinking

Try It Yourself

Online

Applied Psychology

Controversial Topics

Cultural and Ethnic Influences

To my family

James W. Kalat (rhymes with ballot) is Professor of Psychology at North Carolina State University, where he teaches introduction to psychology and biological psychology. Born in 1946, he received an AB degree summa cum laude from Duke University and a Ph.D. in psychology from the University of Pennsylvania, under the supervision of Paul Rozin. He is also the author of *Biological Psychology, Eighth Edition* (Belmont, CA: Wadsworth, 2004). In addition to textbooks, he has written journal articles on taste-aversion learning, the teaching of psychology, and other topics. A remarried widower, he has three children, two stepsons, and two grandchildren.

Brief Contents

Contents

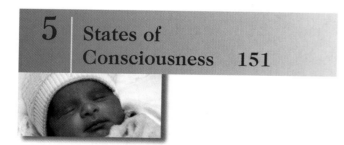

5 | States of Consciousness 151

6 | Learning 189

7 | Memory 231

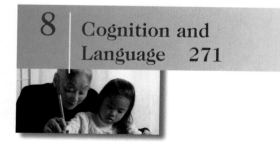

8 | Cognition and Language   271

11 | Motivation   405

14 | Social Psychology   531

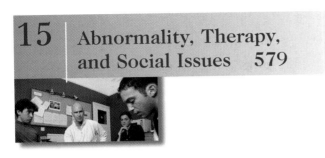

15 | Abnormality, Therapy, and Social Issues 579

16 | Specific Disorders and Treatments 613

Preface to the Instructor

A couple of years ago, I was on a plane that had to turn around shortly after takeoff because one of its two engines had failed. When we were told to get into crash position, the first thing I thought was, "I don't want to die yet! I was looking forward to writing the next edition of my textbook!" True story.

I enjoy writing textbooks, and I hope the students enjoy reading them. However, even under the best of circumstances, students will remember only a limited amount of material from any course. I know I have forgotten many of the facts I learned in college years ago. When I was recently looking over copies of tests I gave at the start of my college teaching career, I discovered that I have forgotten some of the facts that I used to *teach*. Learning facts should not be the goal anyway. Especially in psychology, I hope the field will continue to progress so that many of the facts we now teach will be supplanted by new research.

Ideally, a course or textbook in psychology should accomplish two goals. The first is to instill a love of learning, so that our graduates will continue to update their education. I fantasize that some of my former students occasionally pick up copies of *Scientific American, American Scientist, Cerebrum,* or similar publications and read about psychological research. The second goal is to teach people skills of evaluating evidence and questioning assertions, so that when they do read or hear about some newly reported discovery, they will ask the right questions and draw the appropriate conclusions (or lack of them).

Throughout this text I have tried to model the habit of critical thinking or evaluating the evidence, particularly in the **What's the Evidence** features, which describe research studies in some detail. I have pointed out the limitations of the evidence and the possibilities for alternative interpretations. The goal is to help students ask their own questions, distinguish between good and weak evidence, and ultimately, appreciate the excitement of psychological inquiry.

Approaches, Features, and Student Aids

Many years ago I read in an educational psychology textbook that children with certain learning disabilities and attention problems learn best from specific, concrete examples. I remember thinking, "Wait a minute. Don't we *all* learn best from specific, concrete examples?" It is for this reason that science classes use laboratories: to let students try demonstrations and experiments. Few introductory psychology classes offer laboratories, but we can nevertheless encourage students to try certain procedures that require little or no equipment. At various points the text describes simple **Try It Yourself** exercises, such as negative afterimages, binocular rivalry, encoding specificity, and the Stroop effect. The CD-ROM that accompanies this text offers additional **Online Try It Yourself** activities, which use sound or movement to illustrate points that a printed text cannot. These activities are also available on the companion Web site at **http://psychology.wadsworth. com/kalat_intro7e/.** Students who try these activities will understand and remember the concepts far better than if they read about them only in abstract terms. A few of the online activities even enable students to collect and report their own data.

Reading the material is good, but using it is better. The **Concept Checks** pose questions that attentive readers should be able to answer, with a little thought. The answers are available at the end of each chapter's modules. Students who answer correctly can feel encouraged; those who miss a question should use the feedback to reread the relevant passages. Questions marked **A Step Further** are more challenging and a possible basis for class discussion or short extra-credit papers. Because these questions invite creativity, none has a single "correct" answer; nevertheless, the Instructor's Resource Guide provides my attempt to answer them.

Education has long been a very traditional field in which the procedures had hardly changed since the invention of chalk and desks. Recently, however, educators have been learning to use the power of new technologies, and this text offers several important technological enhancements. The Web site mentioned above includes the Online Try It Yourself exercises as well as flash cards, quizzes, an online glossary, and links to other interesting sites related to each chapter. However, the links may differ from the text as we try to keep the list up-to-date. It also includes a new "virtual study center" in which a student answers questions and then receives a personalized Self-Study Assessment and study plan. The new vMentor option enables students to obtain live tutoring from an experienced instructor.

The **Try It Yourself CD-ROM** *with Critical Thinking Video Exercises* accompanies this text and includes a series of short videos, with accompanying questions to encourage critical thinking. Video topics include neural networks, addiction, and weight loss. On the CD you will also find the Online Try It Yourself exercises as well as a convenient portal to the Web site. *PsychNow!* 2.0 is another optional CD-ROM with a series of fascinating interactive presentations.

Each chapter of this text is divided into two to five modules, each with its own "In Closing" section and Summary. Modules provide flexibility for the instructor who wishes to take sections in a different order—for example, operant conditioning before classical conditioning—or who wishes to omit some section altogether. Modular format also breaks up the reading assignments so that a student reads one or two modules for each class. Key terms are listed and defined at the end of each chapter. At the end of the text, a combined Subject Index and Glossary provides definitions of key terms as well as page references for those terms and others.

What's New in the Seventh Edition

Does psychology really change fast enough to justify a new edition of an introductory text every 3 years? Some areas of psychology admittedly do not. For example, I don't have much new to say about Freud, classical conditioning, or the gross anatomy of the brain. (The anatomy of the brain hasn't changed much in the last 3 years. Evolution is very slow!) Other areas do change. This edition has almost 550 new references from 2001 or later, including many in the areas of cognition, emotion, and abnormal psychology. A few entirely new topics have emerged, such as research on the effectiveness of psychological profiling of criminals (Chapter 13, Personality). Even in topics where the content has not changed much, an author always finds many small ways to clarify the discussion, and my publisher has improved or replaced many of the photographs and figures. Throughout the text you can find many new Concept Checks, Try It Yourself exercises, and What's the Evidence sections. There are also new Online Try It Yourself activities to supplement the ones already available for the previous edition. Each of these activities is referenced in the text.

The main organizational change in this edition is the relocation of genetics. In the previous edition, genetics constituted the first module of Chapter 3 (Biological Psychology). Several reviewers commented that the result was a very long chapter on biology. Several also said they preferred to treat genetics as the start of developmental psychology. So, heeding all this advice, I have moved the genetics module to the start of Chapter 10 (Human Development). Genetic issues do show

up in some earlier chapters, especially Chapter 9 (Intelligence); however, it is possible to deal with those issues without a detailed background in genetics.

Chapters 7 (Memory) and 12 (Emotions, Stress, and Health) have been greatly reorganized. In Chapter 11 (Motivation), the old module on Achievement Motivation was replaced with a new one on Work Motivation, focusing more heavily on issues of industrial/organizational psychology. Here is a chapter-by-chapter list of major changes:

Chapter 1 (What Is Psychology?)

- Forensic psychologist added to the list of service-provider specialties.

Chapter 2 (Scientific Methods in Psychology)

- New introductory section, including clarification of the idea of falsifiability.
- New discussion of *burden of proof*, the idea that in science, as well as law or debate, someone advocating a position that should be demonstrable (if it is true) is obligated to demonstrate it.
- New examples of coincidence; influence of the wording of a survey; positive, negative, and zero correlations; correlation and causation; and random assignment.
- Replaced What's the Evidence section on the effects of media violence with new evidence on the same issue—an experiment by Zillman and Weaver (1999) and an analysis of correlational evidence by Huesmann, Moise-Titus, Podolski, and Eron (2003).

Chapter 3 (Biological Psychology)

- The major change is the movement of the genetics module from Chapter 3 to the start of Chapter 10 (Development).
- Updated discussion of the binding problem—the question of how activity in disparate brain areas produces a unified experience.

Chapter 4 (Sensation and Perception)

- Many new and improved figures. See especially Figures 4.16 (color constancy), 4.62, and 4.63 (optical illusions).
- New research reports that some people have as many as three times as many optic nerve axons as others do; the result is major variations in their ability to perceive weak or brief visual stimuli.
- New section on culture and color terms. One hypothesis for why many cultures in tropical areas lack a separate word for *blue* is that extensive exposure to the sun accelerates aging of the lens, impairing the ability to see short-wavelength light.
- New brief discussion of pitch recognition and tone deafness.
- New discussion of the sensation of itch. It is conducted by a separate pathway in the spinal cord and is independent of pain.

Chapter 5 (States of Consciousness)

- New introductory sections for the chapter as a whole and the first module.
- Hypnosis: Emphasized new evidence that hypnotizability closely matches suggestibility without hypnosis.
- Updated the discussion of marijuana. Recent evidence ties the cellular mechanisms of marijuana to stimulating negative-feedback receptors on the presynaptic neuron. That is, marijuana decreases the release of both excitatory and inhibitory neurotransmitters.

Chapter 6 (Learning)

- Changed the terms unconditioned reinforcer and conditioned reinforcer to primary reinforcer and secondary reinforcer.
- New What's the Evidence section on the possibility of conditioning emotional reactions without awareness.
- Shortened and simplified the section on contiguity and contingency.
- Reorganized the order of presentation in the Operant Conditioning module.
- Added a discussion of the controversy on whether physical punishment of children is always bad.

Chapter 7 (Memory)

- This chapter has been greatly reorganized. The second and third modules now focus on storage and retrieval.
- Expanded the discussion of suspect lineups and how psychological research has improved police investigations.
- New: Emphasis on the value of practicing something in varied ways.
- A new study is highlighted in a What's the Evidence section dealing with false memory. Seeing a photograph from early childhood increases the likelihood of endorsing a false memory from that age.
- Added a discussion of Alzheimer's disease.
- Update on infant amnesia. A fascinating new study reports that infants who learn a new skill can display it months later in their actions but cannot describe it with words they did not know at the time of original learning.

Chapter 8 (Cognition and Language)

- The first module has been extensively reorganized.
- A new What's the Evidence section on cultural differences in categorization. Although the Spanish word *botella* translates as the English word *bottle*, not everything called a bottle is also called a botella. However, people speaking English and Spanish have about the same ideas of which bottle-type objects are similar to each other.
- Major revision of the section on attention, with a new discussion of change blindness.

- New material on overconfidence and on generalizing solutions to new problems.
- Discussion of the positive features of heuristic reasoning. For example, the heuristic "a city I've heard of is probably bigger than one I haven't heard of" usually works.
- Deleted the section on gambling, moving parts of it to other places.
- New section on limits of our language understanding. For example, doubly embedded sentences are virtually incomprehensible, and sentences with negatives or double negatives are often confusing.

Chapter 9 (Intelligence)

- Changed order of presentation in first module, discussing the IQ tests before the theories that are based on them. Also some reordering in the second module.
- Added criticisms of Sternberg's triarchic theory of intelligence.
- Added discussion of "multiplier" effect that shows how environmental influences can magnify what was originally a small genetic influence.
- New evidence that heritability of IQ is much lower among impoverished families.

Chapter 10 (Human Development)

- Reorganization: The module on genetics was shortened, revised, and transferred from Chapter 3 to Chapter 10 where it introduces the discussion of heritability and early development. Genetics is combined with part of what used to be the first module, but the section on object permanence, previously in the first module, is now in the second as part of the discussion on Piaget's sensorimotor stages.
- The discussion of cross-sectional and longitudinal research methods was moved from the third module to the second to introduce research on age differences. Added a discussion of sequential designs, which are preferable to both cross-sectional and longitudinal.
- Several topics moved within Module 10.2 on cognitive development.
- Reorganized and simplified discussion of the limitations of Kohlberg's approach to moral reasoning.
- Material on self-esteem was moved to Chapter 13 (Personality).

Chapter 11 (Motivation)

- Deleted section on primary and secondary motives and Maslow's hierarchy of needs.
- Added a new section on delay of gratification.
- Reorganized the hunger module, starting with the physiology and ending with food selection, including cultural influences.

- Revisions of anorexia/bulimia section include interesting new research that compares bulimia nervosa to drug addiction.
- Preliminary evidence from a large, new cross-cultural survey of sexual behavior.
- Replaced old Module 10.4 (Achievement Motivation) with a new module (Work Motivation). It overlaps the old module somewhat but includes much new information from an industrial/organizational perspective.
- Added a new What's the Evidence section on the value of deadlines. Students who were required to meet evenly spaced deadlines for writing papers, or who chose to set evenly spaced deadlines, did better than those who chose to set later, more lenient deadlines for themselves.

Chapter 12 (Emotions, Stress, and Health)

- The first two modules have been vastly rewritten and reorganized, with much new research. The first is now The Nature of Emotion, and the second is A Survey of Emotions.
- Revised description of the James-Lange theory, with supporting evidence.
- New discussion of methods of measuring emotion and the limitations of each.
- New discussion of the role of emotion in moral decisions.
- Greatly revised and expanded discussion of emotional intelligence.
- New discussion of sadness, crying, and depressive realism.
- Schachter and Singer experiment is now presented as a What's the Evidence section.

Chapter 13 (Personality)

- New research shows that acting extraverted makes people feel happy, even if they are ordinarily introverted.
- Added a new section, Issues in Personality Measurement, which includes a discussion of research on self-esteem. Many of the reported conclusions about self-esteem depend on the method of measurement, which varies from study to study.
- New section on personality profiling of criminals, highlighting the weakness of the evidence for any usefulness of this procedure.

Chapter 14 (Social Psychology)

- New material on implicit measures of stereotypes and prejudice.
- Expanded previous brief discussion into a new section on Cultural Differences in Attribution and Related Matters.
- Added a new section on Cultural Differences in Conformity, which challenges the common characterization of southern Asian cultures as "collectivist."

- Several revisions in the section on Trying to Save a Marriage.
- New brief discussion of Zimbardo's old prison study, at start of section on Obedience to Authority.

Chapter 15 (Abnormality, Therapy, and Social Issues)

- Added a short section on historical trends in psychotherapy.
- Added a section on attention-deficit disorder/attention-deficit hyperactivity disorder, with a new Online Try It Yourself activity demonstrated to be sensitive to impulsiveness.

Chapter 16 (Specific Disorders and Treatments)

- A modified introduction to the chapter acknowledges major overlap among many disorders.
- New research on why obsessive-compulsive patients distrust their own memory: The act of repeated checking makes the most recent check less salient.
- New section on the motivations behind addiction: Is the goal to gain pleasure, to avoid withdrawal symptoms, or to produce a reduction of stress?
- New evidence indicates identified genes increase the depression-inducing effects of stress. Neither the genes nor the stress alone produces depression.
- Antidepressant effects have been demonstrated for aerobic exercise, regular sleep habits, and just "doing something."
- Interesting finding: Just encouraging depressed people to be more active produces as much antidepressant effect as a full psychotherapy regimen.
- Added cautions about diagnosing schizophrenia from occasional hallucinations or apparent delusions.
- Recent data indicate that schizophrenia has become more common and more serious among men than women.
- Added reasons to be skeptical of reported relationships between schizophrenia and genetics and brain damage. Some of the reported brain abnormalities may be due to alcohol abuse and not to schizophrenia itself.
- Expressed emotion looks less convincing than before as a cause of schizophrenia relapse. A parent's expressed emotion correlates better with the patient's previous behavior than with future behavior.

Teaching and Learning Supplements

You're familiar with those television advertisements that offer something, usually for $19.95, and then say,

"But wait, there's more!" Same here. In addition to the text, the publisher offers many supplements:

Study Guide, by Mark Ludorf, Stephen F. Austin State University, provides learning objectives, chapter outlines, other study aids and practice test items, with an explanation of why each wrong answer is wrong. It also includes a language-building component by Eric Bohman, William Rainey Harbor College.

Test Bank, by Peter Miene, Winona State University, includes some items from the previous edition, some items contributed by James Kalat, and many new ones by Peter Miene. That bank is also available in ExamView® electronic format. Many of the items have already been tested with classes at North Carolina State University, and the Test Bank indicates the percentage correct and point biserial. Note also that the Test Bank includes a special file of items that cut across chapters, intended for a comprehensive final exam.

Instructor's Resource Guide, by Nancy Melucci, Long Beach City College, is both thorough and creative. It includes suggestions for class demonstrations and lecture material; it also contains the author's suggested answers to the Step Further questions in this text.

Multimedia Manager Instructor's Resource CD-ROM, by Nancy Melucci, Long Beach City College, is designed to facilitate an instructor's assembly of PowerPoint® or similar demonstrations.

Self-Study Assessments, a new feature, were developed and written by Jori Reijonen, Kalamazoo Valley Community College. Students can take a pretest, and the program will develop a personalized Self-Study Assessment based on their answers. The Self-Study Assessments are available for all students on the companion site: **http://psychology.wadsworth.com/kalat_intro7e/**

PsychStudy, the enhanced version, comes with an instructor grade book and integrated learning modules and is available as a free bundle option.

Try It Yourself CD-ROM *with Critical Thinking Video Exercises* offers videos designed to promote critical thinking about various topics in the text as well as the interactive Online Try It Yourself exercises.

Theme Index (located at the front of the text) directs you to pages where important issues, such as applied psychology and gender and culture influences on behavior, are discussed.

PsychNow! 2.0 is an enjoyable interactive CD designed to help with the difficult concepts in psychology. At the end of each chapter, you can find suggestions of where to look on this disc for relevant material.

Acknowledgments

To begin the job of writing a textbook, a potential author needs self-confidence bordering on arrogance and, to complete it, the humility to accept criticism of favorite ideas and carefully written prose. A great many people provided helpful suggestions that made this a far better text than it would have been without them.

In preparing this edition, I was fortunate to work with very skilled and dedicated people. Vicki Knight, my acquisitions editor, provided consistent encouragement, friendship, support, and wise advice. Kate Barnes, my developmental editor, offered intelligent and sane advice on content, wording, organization, and illustrations. I have been delighted to work with both of them.

Jennifer Wilkinson did a tireless job of supervising all the supplements. Frank Hubert was one of the quickest and most cooperative copy editors I have dealt with in my two decades of textbook writing. Monica Sarmiento secured numerous quality peer reviews throughout the entire project. Paul Wells and Nancy Shammas did a marvelous job of supervising the production and keeping everyone on schedule, a most complicated task with a book such as this. Vernon Boes, who designed the cover and managed the design development, Lisa Torri, who managed the art development, and Tani Hasegawa, who designed the interior, had the patience and artistic judgment to counterbalance their very nonartistic author. Darin Derstine did a wonderful job creating an entirely new technology package. Kiely Sexton accomplished the nearly impossible task of managing all the permissions requests. Chris Caldeira planned and executed the marketing strategies. Terri Wright, the photo researcher, found an amazing variety of photographs. To each of these, my thanks and congratulations.

My wife, Jo Ellen Kalat, not only provided support and encouragement, but also listened to my attempts to explain concepts and offered many helpful suggestions and questions. I thank my department head, David Martin, and my N.C. State colleagues Lynne Baker-Ward, Bart Craig, Amy Halberstadt, Paul Thayer, and Larry Upton for their encouragement, ideas, and free advice.

I also thank the following for their helpful comments and suggestions: Stephen L. Black, Bishop's University, Lennoxville, QC, Canada; R. B. Lotto and Dale Purves, Duke University; and Elizabeth Sherwin, Georgia Southern University.

Many students who read the previous edition sent me letters with helpful comments and suggestions. I especially thank Terry Fidler, University of Victoria.

I thank the following people for their helpful reviews of all or part of this new edition:

Mark Affeltranger
University of Pittsburgh

Susan Anderson
University of South Alabama

Michael Brislawn
Bellevue Community College

Delbert Brodie
St. Thomas University

John Broida
University of Southern Maine

Katherine Demitrakis
Albuquerque Technical Vocational Institute

Kimberly Duff
Cerritos College

Joe Grisham
Indian River Community College

Debra Hollister
Valencia Community College

Charles Huffman
James Madison University

Linda Jackson
Michigan State University

Robert Jensen
California State University, Sacramento

Arthur Kemp
Central Missouri State University

Martha Kuehn
Central Lakes College

Mark Ludorf
Stephen F. Austin State University

Christopher Mayhorn
North Carolina State University

Gale Miller
Texas A&M University

Caryn Meade
North Carolina State University

Mary Meiners
San Diego Miramar College

Gerald Peterson
Saginaw Valley State University

Brady Phelps
South Dakota State University

Shane Pitts
Birmingham Southern College

Catherine Sanderson
Amherst College

Michele N. Shiota
University of California, Berkeley

Robert Stawski
Syracuse University

Patricia Toney
Sandhills Community College

Michael Walraven
Jackson Community College

I would also like to thank the following reviewers who have contributed their insight to previous editions: Bob Arkin, Ohio State University; Susan Baillet, University of Portland; Cynthia Bane, Denison Universtiy; Joe Bean, Shorter College; Bethany Neal-Beliveau, Indiana University Purdue University at Indianapolis; Mark Bodamer, John Carroll University; Gordon Brow, Pasadena City College; Gregory Bushman, Beloit College; James Calhoun, University of Georgia; Bernardo Carducci, Indiana University Southeast; Mar Casteel, Pennsylvania State University, York Campus; Karen Couture, Keene State College; Patricia Deldin, Harvard University; Janet Dizinno, St. Mary University; Susan Field, Georgian Court College; Deborah Frisch, University of Oregon; Gabriel Frommer, Indiana University; Rick Fry, Youngstown, State University; Robe Gehring, University of Southern Indiana; Judy Gentry, Columbus State Community College; Joel Grace, Mansfield University; Richard Hanson, Fresno City College; Richard Harris, Kansas State University; W. Bruce Haslam, Weber State University; Debra Hollister, Valencia Community College; Charles Huffman, James Madison University; James Johnson, Illinois State University; Craig Jones, Arkansas State University; Lisa Jordan, University of Maryland; Dale Jorgenson, California State University, Long Beach; Jon Kahane, Springfield College; Peter Kaplan, University of Colorado, Denver; Cindy J. Lahar; University of Calgary; Chris Layne, University of Toledo; Cynthia Ann Lease, Virginia Polytechnic Institute and State University; Chantal Levesque, University of Rochester; John Lindsay, Georgia College and State University; Mary Livingston, Louisiana Technical University; Sanford Lopater, Christopher Newport University; Steve Madigan, University of Southern California; Don Marzolf, Louisiana State University; Michael McCall, Ithaca College; Dianne Mello-Goldner, Pine Manor College; Rowland Miller, Sam Houston State University; Gloria Mitchell, De Anza College; Jeffrey Nagelbush, Ferris State University; Jan Ochman, Inver Hills Community College; Paul Moore, Quinnipiac University; Wendy Palmquist, Plymouth State College; Elizabeth Parks, Kennesaw State University; David Reitman, Louisiana State University; Thomas Rieg, Winona State University; Jeffrey Rudski, Muhlenberg College; Richard Russell, Santa Monica College; Mark Samuels, New Mexico Institute of Mining and Technology; Kim Sawrey, University of North Carolina at Wilmington; Noam Shpancer, Purdue University; James Spencer, West Virginia State College; Whitney Sweeney, Beloit College; Alan Swinkels, St. Edward's University; Stavros Valenti, Hofstra University; Douglas Wallen, Mankato State

University; Donald Walter, University of Wisconsin-Parkside; Jeffrey Weatherly, University of North Dakota; Fred Whitford, Montana State University; Don Wilson, Lane Community College; David Woehr, Texas A & M University; Jay Wright, Washington State University.

I also thank the following for their helpful comments and suggestions: Lynn Friedman, Carnegie Mellon University; G. William Domhoff, University of California, Santa Cruz; Janet Gebelt, University of Portland; Kenneth Gahagan, North Carolina State University; Timothy Gorrill, SUNY Buffalo; Kristen Kling, St. Cloud State University; Richard Pisacreta, Ferris State University; Edward Pollak, West Chester University; Dale Purves, Duke University; R. B. Lotto, Duke University; Ruth Schiller, Normandale Community College; Lisa Solberg, Santa Monica College; Larry Upton, North Carolina State University; Anthony Wagner, Harvard and Stanford Universities; Kathleen Vohs, Case Western Reserve University.

A great many students who read the previous editions sent me letters and comments. I thank Kenneth Gahagan, North Carolina State University; Timothy Gorrill, SUNY Buffalo; Catherine Heither, Normandale Community College; Naomi Huber, North Carolina State University; Futoshi Kobayashi, University of Texas at Austin; and Lisa Soldberg, Santa Monica College.

James Kalat

Preface to the Student

Welcome to introductory psychology! I hope you will enjoy reading this text as much as I enjoyed writing it. When you finish, I hope you will write your comments on the comments page, cut the page out, and mail it to the publisher, who will pass it along to me. If you are willing to receive a reply, please include a return address.

The first time I taught introductory psychology, several students complained that the book we were using was interesting to read but impossible to study. What they meant was that they had trouble finding and remembering the main points. I have tried to make this book interesting and as easy to study as possible.

Features of This Text

Modular Format

Each chapter is divided into two or more modules so that you can study a limited section at a time. Each chapter begins with a table of contents to orient you to the topics considered. At the end of each module is a summary of some important points, with page references. If a point is unfamiliar, you should reread the appropriate section. At the end of a chapter, you will find suggestions for further reading, a few Internet sites to visit, and a list of important terms.

Key Terms

When an important term first appears in the text, it is highlighted in **boldface** and defined in *italics*. All the boldface terms reappear in alphabetic order with definitions at the end of the chapter and again in the combined Subject Index and Glossary at the end of the book. You might want to find the Subject Index and Glossary right now and familiarize yourself with it. You can also consult or download a list of key terms with their definitions from this Internet site: http://psychology.wadsworth.com/kalat_intro7e/

I sometimes meet students who think they have mastered the course because they have memorized all the definitions. You do need to understand the defined words, but don't waste time memorizing definitions word for word. It would be better to try to use each word in a sentence or think of examples of each term. Better yet, when appropriate, think of evidence for or against the concept that the term represents.

Questions to Check Your Understanding and Go Further

When you read a text, you should want to find out how well you understand it. At various points in this text are Concept Checks, questions that ask you to use or apply the information you just read. Try to answer each of them and then turn to the indicated page to check your answer. If your answer is correct, you can feel encouraged. If it is incorrect, you should reread the section.

You will also find an occasional item marked A Step Further . . . Here you are asked to go beyond the text discussion and think about possible answers to a more challenging or speculative question. I hope you will spend time with these questions, perhaps talk about them with fellow students, and maybe ask your instructor for his or her opinion. (Instructors can check for my own answers in the Instructor's Resource Guide. But to these items, there is no single right answer.)

Try It Yourself Activities

The text includes many items marked Try It Yourself. Most of these can be done with little or no equipment in just a minute or two. You will understand and remember the text far better if you do try these exercises. In some cases you will understand the text *only* if you try them. I recall a couple of test questions that were answered correctly by almost all of my students who tried a particular Try It Yourself exercise and missed by almost everyone else. A word to the wise . . .

Also available are 19 Online Try It Yourself activities. These interactive exercises can be accessed through your CD-ROM or at:
http://psychology.wadsworth.com/kalat_intro7e/
The purpose of these is the same as the Try It Yourself activities in the text; the difference is that online activities can include sounds and motion. Often, the description of some research study will be easier to understand after you have experienced it yourself. You will also remember it better.

What's the Evidence Sections

Every chapter except the first includes a section titled What's the Evidence? These sections highlight research studies in more than the usual amount of detail, specifying the hypothesis (idea being tested), research methods, results, and interpretation. In some cases the discussion also mentions the limitations of the study. The purpose of these sections is to provide examples of how to evaluate evidence.

CD-ROM

Accompanying every new copy of the text is a CD-ROM. The main feature on this disc is a series of videos illustrating important points in psychology and inviting critical thinking about the meaning of various findings. The CD-ROM also includes a convenient portal to the book's Internet site.

Internet Site

The text Web site is:
http://psychology.wadsworth.com/kalat_intro7e/.
This site offers flash cards, quizzes, interactive art, an online glossary, and links to other interesting Web sites related to each chapter. It also includes a "virtual study center," in which you answer questions and then receive a personalized Self-Study Assessment and study plan. The site also includes Online Try It Yourself activities. In addition, it includes a new vMentor opportunity, in which you can ask questions and receive live tutoring from an experienced instructor during certain hours. To do so, go to your companion Web site and follow the links to the vMentor virtual classroom. All of these opportunities are highly recommended; please explore them.

Indexes and Reference List

In the front of your text note the Theme Index, which directs you to pages where general issues are discussed, such as the influences of gender and culture on behavior. A list of all the references cited in the text is at the back of the book in case you want to check something for more details. The combined Subject Index and Glossary defines key terms and indicates where in the book to find more information.

Optional Study Guide

Also available is a Study Guide to accompany this text, written by Mark Ludorf of Stephen F. Austin State University. It provides detailed chapter outlines, learning objectives, study hints, and other helpful information. The most valuable part for most students is the sample test questions, with an answer key that explains not only which answer is right but why each of the others is wrong. The Web site also offers sample questions, but not as many. The Study Guide also includes a language-building component by Eric Bohman, William Rainey Harbor College. The Study Guide is recommended for students who have not had much success with multiple-choice tests in the past,

and who are willing to spend some time in addition to reading the book and studying lecture notes. If your bookstore does not stock the Study Guide, you can ask them to order a copy. The ISBN is 0-534-62463-4.

Answers to Some Frequently Asked Questions

Do you have any useful suggestions for improving study habits? Whenever students ask me why they did badly on the last test, I ask, "When did you read the assignment?" Some answer, "Well, I didn't exactly read *all* of the assignment," or "I read it the night before the test." If you want to learn the material well, read it before the lecture, review it again after the lecture, and quickly go over it again a few days later. Then reread the textbook assignments and your lecture notes before a test. Memory researchers have clearly established that you will understand and remember something better by studying it several times spread out over days than by studying the same amount of time all at once. Also, of course, the more total time you spend studying, the better.

When you study, don't just read the text but stop and think about it. The more actively you use the material, the better you will remember it. One way to improve your studying is to read by the SPAR method: **S**urvey, **P**rocess meaningfully, **A**sk questions, **R**eview.

Survey: Know what to expect so that you can focus on the main points. When you start a chapter, first look over the outline to get a preview of the contents. When you start a new module, turn to the end and read the summary.

Process meaningfully: Read the chapter carefully, stopping to think from time to time. Tell your roommate something you learned. Think about how you might apply a concept to a real-life situation. Pause when you come to the Concept Checks and try to answer them. Do the Try It Yourself exercises. Try to monitor how well you understand the text and adjust your reading accordingly. Good readers read quickly through easy, familiar content but slowly through difficult material.

Ask questions: When you finish the chapter, try to anticipate what you might be asked later. You can use questions in the Study Guide or on the Web site or compose your own. Write out the questions and think about them, but do not answer them yet.

Review: Pause for a few hours or more. Now return to your questions and try to answer them. Check your answers against the text or the answers in the Study Guide. Reinforcing your memory a day or two after you first read the chapter will help you retain the material longer and deepen your understanding. If you study the same material several times at lengthy intervals, you increase your chance of remembering it long after the course is over.

What do those parentheses mean, as in "(Bushman & Anderson, 2001)"? Am I supposed to remember the names and dates? Psychologists generally cite references in the text in parentheses rather than in footnotes. "(Bushman & Anderson, 2001)" refers to an article written by Bushman and Anderson, published in 2001. All the references cited in the text are listed in alphabetical order (by the author's last name) in the References section at the back of the book.

You will also notice a few citations that include two dates separated by a slash, such as "(Wundt, 1862/1961)." This means that Wundt's document was originally published in 1862 and was republished in 1961.

No, you should not memorize the parenthetical source citations. They are provided so you can look up the source of a statement and check for further information. The names that *are* worth remembering, such as B. F. Skinner, Jean Piaget, and Sigmund Freud, are emphasized in the discussion itself.

Can you help me read and understand graphs? The graphs in this book are easy to follow. Just take a minute or so to study them carefully. You will encounter four kinds: pie graphs, bar graphs, line graphs, and scatter plots. Let's look at each kind.

Pie graphs show how a whole is divided into parts. Figure 1 shows that more than one third of all psychologists take a starting job with a college or some other educational institution. Another one third work in hospitals, clinics, and businesses. The total circle represents 100% of all psychologists.

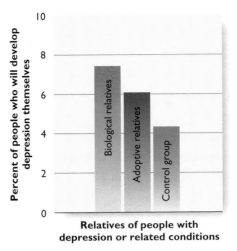

FIGURE 2

Bar graphs show how often events fall into one category or another. Figure 2 shows the percentage of relatives of people with depression or related disorders who develop depression as well.

Line graphs show how one variable is related to another variable. In Figure 3 you see that to memorize a list of 7 or fewer nonsense syllables, one reading was usually enough. To memorize a longer list took more repetitions.

Scatter plots are similar to line graphs, with this difference: A line graph shows averages, whereas a scatter plot shows individual data points. By looking at a scatter plot (Figure 4), we can see how much variation occurs among individuals.

To prepare a scatter plot, we make two observations about each individual. In Figure 4 each student is represented by one point. If you take that point and

FIGURE 1

FIGURE 3

FIGURE 4

scan down to the *x*-axis, you find that student's score on the first test. If you scan across the y-axis you find that student's score on the final exam. A scatter plot shows whether two variables are closely or only loosely related.

We may have to take multiple-choice tests on this material. How can I do better on those tests?

1. Read each choice carefully. Do not choose the first answer that looks correct; first make sure that the other answers are wrong. If two answers seem reasonable, decide which of the two is better.

2. If you don't know the correct answer, make an educated guess. Eliminate answers that are clearly wrong. An answer that includes absolute words such as *always* or *never* is probably wrong; don't choose it unless you have a good reason to support it. Also eliminate any answer that includes unfamiliar terms. If you have never heard of something, it is probably not the right answer.

3. After you finish a test, go back and check your answers and rethink them. You have probably heard the advice, "Don't change your answers; stick with your first impulse." No matter how often you have heard that advice, it is wrong. J. J. Johnston (1975) tested it by looking through the answer sheets of a number of classes that had taken a multiple-choice test. He found that of all the students who changed one or more answers, 71 students improved their scores by doing so and only 31 lowered their scores. Similar results have been reported in a number of other studies. Your reconsidered answer might be better than the first for a variety of reasons. Sometimes when you read the questions that appear later in a test, one of them may remind you of something that helps you correct an earlier answer. Sometimes you reread a question and realize that you misunderstood it the first time.

Why, then, do so many students (and professors) believe that it is a mistake to change an answer? Think of what happens when you get a test paper back. When you look it over, which items do you examine most carefully? The ones you got wrong, of course. You may notice three items that you originally answered correctly and then changed. You overlook the five other items you changed from wrong to right.

Last Words Before We Start . . .

Most of all, I hope you enjoy the text. I have tried to include the liveliest examples I can find. The goal is not just to teach you some facts but to teach you a love of learning so that you will continue to read more and educate yourself about psychology long after your course is over.

James Kalat

What is Psychology?

Who has the correct answers? None of us do, at least not always. Even when people we trust seem very confident of their opinions, we should ask for their evidence or reasoning.

If you are like most students, you start off assuming that just about everything you read in your textbooks and everything your professors tell you must be true.

But what if it isn't? Suppose that a group of impostors has replaced the faculty of your college. They pretend to know what they are talking about and they all vouch for one another's competence, but in fact they are all unqualified. They have managed to find textbooks that support their own prejudices, but the information in the textbooks is all wrong too. If that happened, how would you know?

As long as we are entertaining such skeptical thoughts, why limit ourselves to colleges? When you read advice columns in the newspaper, read books about how to invest money, or listen to political commentators, how do you know who has the right answers?

The answer is that *no one* has the right answers all of the time. Professors, textbook authors, advice columnists, politicians, and others have strong reasons for some beliefs and weak reasons for others, and sometimes they think they have strong reasons but discover to their embarrassment that they were wrong. I don't mean to imply that you should disregard everything you read or hear. But you should expect people to tell you the reasons for their conclusions and then draw your own conclusions. At least if you make a mistake, it will be your own and not someone else's.

You have just encountered the theme of this book: Evaluate the evidence. You have heard and you will continue to hear all sorts of claims concerning psychology. Some are valid, some are wrong, many are partly valid under certain conditions, and some are too vague to be either right or wrong. When you finish this book, you will be in a better position to examine evidence and to judge for yourself which claims to take seriously.

The Goals of Psychologists

What is psychology?

What philosophical questions motivate psychologists?

What do various kinds of psychologists do?

Should you consider majoring in psychology?

The term *psychology* derives from the Greek roots *psyche,* meaning "soul" or "mind," and *logos,* meaning "word"; thus, psychology is literally the study of the mind or soul. In the late 1800s and early 1900s, psychology was defined as the scientific study of the mind. Around 1920 psychologists became disenchanted with the idea of studying the mind. First, mind is private and not easily available to scientific study. Second, talking about "the mind" seemed to imply that mind is a "thing" as opposed to a series of processes. At any rate, through the middle 1900s, psychologists defined their field simply as the study of behavior.

However, people care about what they see, hear, and think, not just about what they do. When you look at this optical illusion and say that the horizontal part of the top line looks longer than that of the bottom line (although really they are the same), we want to know why it *looks* longer to you, not just why you *said* it looks longer. So for a compromise, let's define **psychology** as *the systematic study of behavior and experience.* The word *experience* lets us discuss your perceptions without implying a mind that exists independently of your body.

The kind of psychologist familiar to most people is a clinical psychologist—that is, a psychologist who tries to help worried, depressed, or otherwise troubled people. The last two chapters of this book will deal with abnormal behavior and its treatment, but that field is only part of psychology. Psychology also includes research on sensation and perception, learning and memory, hunger and thirst, sleep, attention, child development, and more. You might expect that a course in psychology will teach you to "analyze" people, to understand hidden aspects of their personality, perhaps even to use psychology to control them. It will not. You will learn to understand some aspects of behavior, but you will gain no dazzling powers. Ideally, you will learn to be more skeptical of those who claim to analyze people's hidden personality from small samples of their behavior.

Psychology and Common Sense

Almost everyone tries to understand why people act the way they do, and every culture has developed a "folk psychology" to try to explain people's feelings and actions. Much of folk psychology is at least good enough to be useful, and common sense is usually more accurate about psychology than it is about, say, physics. But your common sense is not the same as someone else's, especially someone from a different culture, and when we carefully evaluate our common-sense ideas, we find that some are correct, some are partly correct, and others are wrong. Psychological researchers collect systematic data to try to improve upon common sense. People also have many beliefs that are not quite common sense, but are based on statements they have heard and accepted without questioning. Let's try a few questions about psychology. Choose an answer for each item:

1. Typically, we use only 10% of our brains.
    true   uncertain   false
2. Alcoholism is a disease.
    true   uncertain   false
3. A drink of alcohol kills about 5,000 brain cells.
    true   uncertain   false
4. People will not do anything under hypnosis that they would refuse to do otherwise.
    true   uncertain   false
5. People often dream they are flying, but they never dream they hit the ground. If you did dream you hit the ground, you would die.
    true   uncertain   false
6. If you want to change people's behavior, first you have to change their attitudes.
    true   uncertain   false
7. A polygraph test can reveal whether or not a person is telling the truth.
    true   uncertain   false
8. Acts of violence are more common on nights of a full moon.
    true   uncertain   false

Try It Yourself

3

9. After finishing a test, you should:
   a. go back, rethink your answers, and consider changing some of them.
   b. stick with your first impulse.
10. Infants can recognize their own mother's voice on the day of birth.
    true   uncertain   false

Finished? Okay, now here are the answers that the research supports:

1. **Typically, we use only 10% of our brains.** *False.* I have heard this statement many times, and you probably have too. Does it mean that you could lose 90% of your brain and still do what you do now? If so, it's false. Does it mean that only 10% of your brain cells are active at any time? If so, again it's false.

   Granted, each of us could probably do much more with our brains than we are doing now, but that doesn't mean we use only part of our brains. I'm a poor athlete, but that's not because I use only 10% of my muscles. I use them all, just not very skillfully. Chapter 3 discusses brain functioning in detail.

2. **Alcoholism is a disease.** Here the best answer is *uncertain.* It depends on what you mean by "disease." Alcoholism resembles medical diseases in some ways but not others, and medical treatment for alcoholism is not consistently effective. We consider this issue further in Chapter 15.

3. **A drink of alcohol kills about 5,000 brain cells.** Again, the best answer is *uncertain.* The next time you hear someone say that an alcoholic drink kills some number of brain cells, ask, "Who counted?" We do know that people who drink enormous amounts of alcohol over many years lose brain cells, but part of their brain damage is due to poor diet. We shall consider brain functioning in Chapter 3, alcohol abuse in Chapter 16.

4. **People will not do anything under hypnosis that they would refuse to do otherwise.** Again, the best answer is *uncertain.* Hypnotized people will sometimes do some odd, even dangerous acts, but so do people who are not hypnotized, especially if they know they are in an experiment. That is, it's hard to find anything that we are sure people would "refuse to do otherwise"! Chapter 5 elaborates on this point.

5. **People often dream they are flying, but they never dream they hit the ground. If you did dream you hit the ground, you would die.** If this were true, how would anyone know? At best this statement is *uncertain,* but some people say they have dreamt they hit the ground (and they sur-

vived), so let's call this one *false.* Chapter 5 considers the research on dreaming.

6. **If you want to change people's behavior, first you have to change their attitudes.** *False.* As we'll see in Chapter 14, sometimes it's pretty easy to change people's behavior, and then they change their attitudes to match their behavior.

7. **A polygraph test can reveal whether or not a person is telling the truth.** *It depends.* ("It depends" is frequently a good answer in psychology.) Here it depends on how much accuracy you expect from the test. If you have to decide whether someone is lying, a polygraph is more accurate than flipping a coin, but it makes many mistakes. Chapter 12 goes into more detail.

8. **Acts of violence are more common on nights of a full moon.** *False.* Although many people believe this statement, research studies have consistently failed to support it. This is an "illusory correlation," as discussed in Chapter 2.

9. **After finishing a test, you should: (a) go back, rethink your answers, and consider changing some of them or (b) stick with your first impulse.** *Go back and consider changing your answers.* If you missed this one, you should go back and read the Preface to the Student.

10. **Infants can recognize their own mother's voice on the day of birth.** *True.* After all those false or uncertain statements, I thought I should give you one that's true. It probably doesn't sound like it would be true, and you might wonder how anyone could know. If you can't contain your curiosity, look ahead to Chapter 10.

Note that sometimes the best answer was "uncertain" or "it depends." If uncertainty makes you uncomfortable and you insist on statements that are definitely right or wrong, I suggest you consider a career in mathematics, not psychology. In psychology most answers are tentative.

Also note the range of questions we just considered, from brain mechanisms to the treatment of alcoholism. You can consider this little quiz a preview of the breadth of psychology. Psychologists want to understand why we think and act the way we do—and that task is a big one.

Major Philosophical Issues in Psychology

Many psychological concerns date back to the philosophers of ancient Greece. Although psychology has moved away from philosophy in its methods, it continues to be motivated by some of the same questions. Three of the most profound are free will versus determinism, the mind–brain problem, and the nature–nurture issue.

Free Will Versus Determinism

One of the key points of the scientific approach is seeking the *immediate* causes of an event (what led to what) instead of the *final* causes (the purpose of the event in an overall plan). That is, scientists act on the basis of **determinism,** *the assumption that everything that happens has a cause, or determinant, in the observable world.*

Is the same true for human behavior? We are, after all, part of the physical world, and our brains are made of chemicals. According to the *determinist* assumption of human behavior, everything we do has causes. This view seems to conflict with the impression all of us have that "*I* make the decisions about my actions. Sometimes when I am making a decision, like what to eat for lunch or which sweater to buy, I am in doubt right up to the last second. The decision could have gone either way. I wasn't controlled by anything, and no one could have predicted what I would do." *The belief that behavior is caused by a person's independent decisions* is known as **free will.**

Some psychologists argue that free will is an illusion (Wegner, 2002): What you call a decision is really more a prediction than a cause of your behavior. When you have the conscious experience of "deciding" to move a finger, the behavior is already starting to happen. What you feel as your "will" or "intention" is the result of many forces within you, of which you are unaware; it is not the cause of anything.

Other psychologists and philosophers reply that yes, of course, in a sense you *do* make decisions. A person walking down a mountainside is not like a rock bouncing down the same path. When you order soup and salad for lunch, the decision was a product of forces within you. The kind of person you are also determines what career you will choose, how hard you will work at it, how kind you will be to others, and so forth. However, your behavior is still a product of cause and effect. The "you" that makes all these decisions is itself a product of your heredity and all the events of your life until now. (You did not create yourself.) In this sense, yes, you have a will, and you might even call it "free" will depending on what you mean by "free" (Dennett,

2003). If you mean uncaused or random, some of the events of subatomic particles are apparently random, but at the scale of visible events, the random subatomic events cancel out. Furthermore, you probably wouldn't want to have a random will. You would prefer for it to be "determined" by the kind of person you are.

The test of determinism is ultimately empirical: If everything we do has a cause, our behavior should be predictable. In some cases it definitely is. For example, if you hear a sudden, unexpected, extremely loud noise, I can predict that, unless you are deaf, in a coma, or paralyzed, you will tense your muscles. I can even be more precise and predict you will tense your neck muscles within a quarter of a second.

In other cases psychologists' predictions are more like those of a meteorologist. A meteorologist who wants to predict tomorrow's weather for some city will want to know the location and terrain of that city, today's weather, and so forth. Even with all that information, the meteorologist will predict something such as, "High temperature around 30, low temperature around 20, with a 10% chance of precipitation." The lack of precision and occasional errors do not mean that the weather is "free" but only that it is subject to so many influences that no one can predict it exactly.

Similarly, a psychologist trying to predict your behavior for the next few days will want to know as much as possible about your past behavior, that of your friends and family, your current health, your genetics, where you live, and a great deal more. Even with all that information, the psychologist cannot predict perfectly.

Determinists are unembarrassed; after all, human behavior is subject to a great many influences, including many that are difficult to measure. Still, the more knowledge we gain, the better predictions we can make. Anyone who rejects determinism must insist that predictions of behavior could *never* become accurate, even with *complete* information about the person and the situation. To that idea a determinist replies that the only way to find out is to try.

Let's note an important point here: The assumption that behaviors follow cause and effect seems to work, and anyone planning to do research on behav-

Behavior is guided by external forces, such as waves, and by forces within the individual. According to the determinist view, even those internal forces follow physical laws.

ior is almost forced to start with this assumption. Still, to be honest, it is an assumption, not a certainty.

What kind of evidence, if any, would support the concept of free will? To support the concept of free will, one would need to demonstrate that no conceivable theory could make correct predictions about some aspect of behavior. Should a psychologist who believes in free will conduct the same kind of research that determinists conduct, a different kind, or no research at all?

The Mind–Brain Problem

Everything we experience or do depends on the physics and chemistry of the nervous system. Then what, if anything, is the mind? The *philosophical question of how experience is related to the brain* is the **mind–brain problem** (or mind–body problem). In a universe composed of matter and energy, why is there such a thing as a conscious mind? One view, called **dualism,** holds that *the mind is separate from the brain but somehow controls the brain and therefore the rest of the body.* The problem is that dualism contradicts the law of conservation of matter and energy, one of the cornerstones of physics. According to that law, the only way to influence any matter or energy, such as the matter and energy that compose your body, is to act on it with other matter or energy. That is, if the mind isn't composed of matter and energy, it can't *do* anything. For that reason nearly all brain researchers favor **monism,** *the view that conscious experience is inseparable from the physical brain.* That is, either the mind is something the brain produces (perhaps accidentally), or mind and brain activity are just two terms for the same thing.

As you can imagine, the mind–brain problem is a thorny philosophical issue, but it does lend itself to research. The research may not answer the question, but it can at least nibble away at it, determining what

FIGURE 1.1 PET scans show the brain activity of normal people engaged in different activities. Left column: Brain activity with no special stimulation, while passively watching something or listening to something. Center column: Brain activity while listening to music, language, or both. Right column: Brain activity during performance of a cognitive task, an auditory memory task, and the task of moving the fingers of the right hand. Red indicates the highest activity, followed by yellow, green, and blue. Arrows indicate the most active areas. *(Courtesy of Michael E. Phelps and John C. Mazziotta, University of California, Los Angeles, School of Medicine)*

Resting state

Music

Cognitive

Visual

Language

Memory

Auditory

Language and music

Motor

aspects of brain activity are necessary for consciousness (Crick & Koch, 2003). For example, participants in one study watched as words were flashed on a screen for a mere 29 milliseconds each. Sometimes they could identify a word consciously and say it; other times they reported only a blur or nothing at all. Brain scans demonstrated that all the flashed words activated the same brain areas but activated them more strongly on occasions when people could identify the words consciously (Dehaene et al., 2001). That is, consciousness has something to do with the total amount of brain stimulation.

The photos in Figure 1.1 show brain activity while a person is engaged in nine different tasks, as measured by a technique called positron-emission tomography (PET). Red indicates the highest degree of brain activity, followed by yellow, green, and blue. As you can see, the various tasks increase activity in different brain areas, although all areas show some activity at all times (Phelps & Mazziotta, 1985). Data such as these show a close relationship between brain activity and psychological events. You might well ask: Did the brain activity cause the thoughts, or did the thoughts cause the brain activity? Most brain researchers reply that neither brain activity nor mental activity "causes" the other; rather, brain activity and mental activity are the same thing (see Dennett, 1991).

Even if we accept this position, we are still far from understanding the mind–brain relationship. Is mental activity associated with all brain activity or just certain types? Why does conscious experience exist at all? Could a brain get along without it? Research studies are not about to resolve these questions and put philosophers out of business. But re-

search results do constrain the philosophical answers that we can seriously consider. The hope of learning more about the mind–brain relationship is one of the ultimate goals for many psychologists, especially those whose work we shall study in Chapters 3 and 4.

CRITICAL THINKING:
A STEP FURTHER
Mind and Brain

One way to think about the mind–brain relationship is to ask whether something other than a brain—a computer, for example—could have a mind. How would we know? What if we built a computer that could perform all the intellectual functions that humans perform? Could we then decide that the computer is conscious, as human beings are?

The Nature–Nurture Issue

Why do most little boys spend more time than little girls do with toy guns and trucks and less time with dolls? Are such behavioral differences mostly the result of genetic differences between boys and girls, or are they mostly the result of differences in how society treats boys and girls?

Alcohol abuse is a big problem in some cultures and a rare one in others. Are these differences entirely a matter of social custom, or do genes influence alcohol use also?

Certain psychological disorders are more common in large cities than in small towns and in the

▌ Why do different children develop different interests? They may have had different hereditary tendencies, but they have also experienced different environmental influences. Separating the roles of nature and nurture can be difficult.

countryside. Does life in crowded cities somehow cause psychological disorders? Or do people develop such disorders because of a genetic predisposition and then move to big cities in search of jobs, housing, and welfare services?

Each of these questions is related to the **nature–nurture issue**: *How do differences in behavior relate to differences in heredity and environment?* The nature–nurture issue shows up from time to time in practically all fields of psychology, and it seldom has a simple answer.

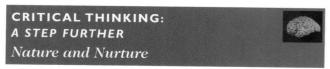

CRITICAL THINKING:
A STEP FURTHER
Nature and Nurture

Suppose researchers found that alcohol abuse is uncommon in Turkey because of Turkey's strict legal sanctions against alcohol use. Should we then assume that the differences in alcohol use among people in other countries is also due to nongenetic causes?

CONCEPT CHECK ☑

1. In what way does all scientific research presuppose determinism?
2. What is one major objection to dualism? (Check your answers on page 16.)

What Psychologists Do

We have considered some major philosophical issues related to the entire field of psychology. However, psychologists usually deal with smaller, more answerable questions.

Psychology is an academic discipline that includes many branches and specialties, ranging from the helping professions to research on brain functions. The educational requirements for becoming a psychologist vary from one country to another (Newstead & Makinen, 1997). In the United States and Canada, a psychologist starts with a bachelor's degree (usually requiring 4 years of college) and then probably a PhD degree (at least another 4 or 5 years, often more). Some people practice psychology with a master's degree (intermediate between a bachelor's and a doctorate), and a growing number have a PsyD (doctor of psychology) degree, which generally requires less research experience than a PhD but a similar period of training. Any psychologist specializes in a particular branch of psychology, such as experimental, developmental, clinical, or industrial.

Psychologists work in many occupational settings, as shown in Figure 1.2. The most common settings are

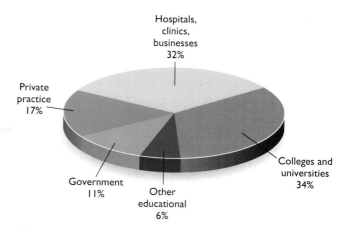

FIGURE 1.2 More than one third of psychologists work in academic institutions; the remainder find positions in a variety of settings. *(Based on data of Chamberlin, 2000)*

colleges and universities, private practice, hospitals and mental health clinics, and government agencies.

Psychologists in Teaching and Research

Many psychologists, especially those who are not clinical psychologists, have positions in colleges and universities where they teach and do research that will ideally lead to a greater understanding of behavior and experience and perhaps have useful applications. A small percentage of psychologists work in full-time research institutions. Here we preview a few major categories of psychological research.

Biological Psychology

A **biopsychologist (or behavioral neuroscientist)** *tries to explain behavior in terms of biological factors, such as electrical and chemical activities in the nervous system, the effects of drugs and hormones, genetics, and evolutionary pressures.* For example, the evidence suggests that certain genes influence the probability that someone will develop schizophrenia, depression, or alcoholism. However, the behavioral outcome depends on experiences as well as genetics.

Biopsychologists also study the effects of brain damage. Brain damage can result from such things as a sharp blow to the head, a ruptured blood vessel in the brain, an interruption of oxygen supply, prolonged malnutrition, or exposure to toxic chemicals. The effects of brain damage on behavior depend on the location and extent of the damage, as well as the age and overall health of the person.

Another research interest is the effects of drugs. For example, drugs such as amphetamine and cocaine usually increase activity levels, whereas heroin or morphine decrease them. Biopsychologists try to explain those effects. They have traced most drug effects to the chemical communication between one neuron and another at junctions called *synapses*.

So, according to biopsychologists, people differ from one another because they have different genes, different brain anatomies, and different hormonal patterns. Some have suffered brain damage. Others are under the influence of drugs or of nutritional deficiencies that affect the brain. Anything that affects the body, especially the brain, will also affect behavior. Chapter 3 provides much more information about biological psychology.

Evolutionary Psychology

An **evolutionary psychologist** *tries to explain behavior in terms of the evolutionary history of the species, including reasons evolution might have favored a tendency to act in particular ways.* It offers explanations such as, "The animal behaves this way because previous members of the species that behaved this way managed to survive and reproduce, whereas those that behaved another way were less successful." With nonhuman species we are accustomed to the idea that evolution has molded both behavior and appearance in ways that promote survival and reproduction. For example, the reptile in Figure 1.3 has evolved an appearance that blends in with its environment but also has evolved behaviors that get it into the position shown. In addition it has evolved a tendency to remain motionless for long periods; the lack of motion is critical to its camouflage.

Evolutionary psychologists apply the same kind of explanations to any behavior that is widespread within a species. In some cases the explanations are just as convincing for humans as for any other species. For example, humans have reflexes and built-in behavior tendencies (e.g., sleeping and yawning) that serve adaptive functions, even if we do not fully understand those functions. Presumably, we evolved these mechanisms because they aid us in survival and reproduction. However, although some evolutionary explanations of behavior are persuasive, others are uncertain or doubtful (de Waal, 2002). For one example of a controversial proposal,

FIGURE 1.3 This species of gecko (a kind of lizard) blends in so well with its environment that a potential predator could easily miss it. However, behavior is an important part of the camouflage. The gecko remains motionless in this position for long times; any quick movement will destroy the illusion that it is part of the plant.

Michael & Patricia Fogden/Minden Pictures

men tend to show more sexual jealousy than women do when a partner is suspected of being unfaithful. The strength of that tendency varies from one culture to another, but no culture is known in which women are more jealous than men. Evolutionary psychologists have argued that a woman always knows her baby is her own, but a man does not know his wife's baby is his, unless he is the only man who had sex with her (Buss, 2000). Therefore, throughout human evolutionary history, men were more likely to pass on their genes if they prevented their wives from having sex with other men; women gained less from being similarly jealous.

Not everyone finds this explanation convincing. Granted, evolution molds the brain as much as any other organ, and therefore also behavior. The question is whether evolution has micromanaged our behavior. Do we have (or need?) a specific mechanism in the brain that tells men to guard their girlfriends and wives jealously? Even when a general trend in behavior occurs in cultures throughout the world, it remains possible that people learned similar behaviors. For example, people throughout the world clean their food before eating it, but we do not assume they have a gene for food-cleaning. We shall return to evolutionary issues in several later chapters, especially Chapter 14.

Learning and Motivation

The research field of **learning and motivation** studies *how behavior depends on the outcomes of past behaviors and on current motivations.* How often we engage in any particular behavior depends on the results of that behavior in the past. For example, you undoubtedly have a friend whose interests differ from yours. One of you likes dancing, and the other likes painting, or one likes to play the guitar, and the other is politically active. The one who likes dancing may have received praise for dancing or may experience some good bodily sensations while dancing. The one who enjoys painting may once have tripped while dancing and therefore sought something else to do. Our current behavior depends on our past experiences.

Researchers in this field (most of whom call themselves *behaviorists*) study how the consequences of an action modify future behavior. For example, what are the effects of a payoff (money, praise, etc.) if it is infrequent and inconsistent? If someone were expecting a large payoff and instead got a smaller one, what would be the effect? What are the effects of punishment? Notice the theoretical orientation: The behaviorist studies what the person *does* as a result of the consequences of past actions, not what the person *thinks*. Because of this emphasis on actions instead of thoughts, behaviorists can conduct many of their studies on nonhuman animals. We shall consider this approach more thoroughly in Chapter 6.

Cognitive Psychology

Cognition refers to *thinking and acquiring knowledge.* A **cognitive psychologist** *studies those processes.* (The root *cogn-* also shows up in the word *recognize,* which literally means "to know again.") As a rule cognitive psychologists do not simply ask people to describe their thought processes. (If people thoroughly understood their own thoughts, there would be less need for psychologists!) Cognitive psychologists conduct experiments to infer what people know, how they came to know it, and how they use their knowledge to solve new problems. Some cognitive psychologists develop computer models of how people think.

One typical question for a cognitive psychologist is: What do experts know or do that sets them apart from other people? Much of the answer is simply that the expert knows more facts. Consider a subject on which you are an expert: how to find your way around your college campus. A fellow student asks you, "How do I get from here to the biology building?" To answer, you draw on the knowledge you share with the other student: "It's between the library and the math building." That communication works because you and the other student share a good deal of knowledge about the campus.

Now consider how you communicate with a visitor to the campus. You say, "Go over toward the library . . . " "Wait, where's the library?" "Well, go out this door, make a right, go to the next street . . . " Someone with little or no previous knowledge needs much more detailed instructions (Isaacs & Clark, 1987). Cognitive psychology is the focus of Chapters 7 and 8.

Developmental Psychology

Developmental psychologists *study the behavioral capacities typical of different ages and how behavior changes with age,* "from womb to tomb." In a typical study, developmental psychologists examine a particular behavior across a certain age span, such as language from age 2 to 4 or memory from age 60 to 80.

▌ Developmental psychologists study the behavioral differences among people of different ages.

The first question is: What do people do at one age that they do *not* do at another age? The second question is: Why? Was the change due to a biological process, to changes in experience, or to a complex combination of both? Developmental psychologists frequently deal with the nature–nurture issue. Because everything we do develops, developmental psychology is central to psychology and overlaps all other subdisciplines. Chapter 10 deals with developmental psychology.

Social Psychology

Social psychologists *study how an individual influences other people and is influenced by them.* When we are with other people, we tend to take our cues from them about what we should do. Suppose you arrive at a party and notice that the other guests are walking around, talking, and helping themselves to snacks. You do the same. When you go to a religious service or an art museum, you again notice how other people are acting and conform your behavior to theirs. Certainly, if you had grown up in a different country, you would have developed vastly different customs. Even within a given culture, though, individuals acquire different behaviors because of the people around them. If you had made friends with a different set of people in high school, how would you be different today?

According to social psychologists, people are also greatly influenced by other people's expectations. For example, parents often intentionally or unintentionally convey expectations that boys will be more competitive and girls will be more cooperative or that teenagers will be immature and 25-year-olds will be responsible. At least to some extent, people's behavior tends to live up to—or down to—the expectations of others. In Chapter 14 we deal with social psychology in more detail.

CONCEPT CHECK ☑

3. a. Of the kinds of psychological research just described—biological psychology, learning and motivation, cognitive psychology, developmental psychology, and social psychology—which field concentrates most on children?
   b. Which is most concerned with how people behave in groups?
   c. Which concentrates most on thought and knowledge?
   d. Which is most interested in the effects of brain damage?
   e. Which is most concerned with studying the effect of a reward on future behavior? (Check your answers on page 16).

Service Providers to Individuals

When most people hear the term *psychologist*, they first think of *clinical psychologists*, who constitute one type of mental health professionals. Clinical psychologists deal with problems ranging from depression, anxiety, and substance abuse to marriage conflicts, difficulties making decisions, or even the mere feeling that "I should be getting more out of life." Some clinical psychologists are college professors and researchers, but most are full-time practitioners.

It is important to distinguish among several types of mental health professionals. The term *therapist* itself has no precise meaning, and in many places even untrained, unlicensed people can hang out a shingle and call themselves therapists. Some of the main kinds of service providers for people with psychological troubles are clinical psychologists, psychiatrists, social workers, and counseling psychologists.

Clinical Psychology

Clinical psychologists *have an advanced degree in psychology, with a specialty in understanding and helping people with psychological problems.* Most have a PhD, which requires research training and the completion of a substantial research dissertation, or a PsyD, which places less emphasis on research. Also, as part of their training, clinical psychologists undergo at least a year of supervised clinical work called an *internship*.

Clinical psychologists can base their work on any of various theoretical viewpoints, or they can use a pragmatic, trial-and-error approach. They try, in one way or another, to understand why a person is having difficulties and then help that person overcome the difficulties.

Psychiatry

Psychiatry is a *branch of medicine that deals with emotional disturbances.* To become a psychiatrist, someone first earns an MD degree and then takes an additional 4 years of residency training in psychiatry. Psychiatrists and clinical psychologists provide similar services for most clients: They listen, ask questions, and try to help. Psychiatrists, however, are medical doctors and can therefore prescribe drugs, such as tranquilizers and antidepressants, whereas in most places psychologists cannot. Some states now permit psychologists with additional specialized training to prescribe drugs.

Does psychiatrists' ability to prescribe drugs give them an advantage over psychologists in places where psychologists cannot prescribe them? Sometimes but not always. Some psychiatrists habitually treat anxiety and depression with drugs, whereas psychologists treat problems by changing the person's way of living. Drugs can be useful, but relying on them too extensively can be a hazard.

Some Other Mental Health Professionals

Several other kinds of professionals also provide help and counsel. **Psychoanalysts** are *therapy providers who rely heavily on the theories and methods pioneered by the early 20th-century Viennese physician Sigmund Freud and later modified by others.* Freud and his followers attempted to infer the hidden, unconscious, symbolic meaning behind people's words and actions, and in various ways psychoanalysts today continue that effort.

There is some question about who may rightly call themselves psychoanalysts. Some people apply the term to anyone who attempts to uncover unconscious thoughts and feelings, perhaps even including followers of Carl Jung or others who broke away from Freud's views in significant ways. Others apply the term only to graduates of a 6- to 8-year program at an institute of psychoanalysis. These institutes admit only people who are already either psychiatrists or clinical psychologists. Thus, people completing psychoanalytic training will be at least in their late 30s.

A **clinical social worker** is *similar to a clinical psychologist but with different training.* In most cases a clinical social worker has a master's degree in social work with a specialization in psychological problems. A master's degree takes less education than a doctorate and requires much less research experience. In many cases health maintenance organizations (HMOs) steer most of their clients toward clinical social workers instead of psychologists or psychiatrists because the social workers, with less formal education, charge less per hour. Some psychiatric nurses (nurses with additional training in psychiatry) provide similar services.

Counseling psychologists *help people with educational, vocational, marriage, health-related, and other decisions.* A counseling psychologist has a doctorate degree (PhD, PsyD, or EdD) with supervised experience in counseling. The activities of a counseling psychologist overlap those of a clinical psychologist, but the emphasis is different. Whereas a clinical psychologist deals mostly with anxiety, depression, and other emotional distress, a counseling psychologist deals mostly with important life decisions and family or career readjustments, which, admittedly, can cause anxiety or depression! Counseling psychologists work in educational institutions, mental health centers, rehabilitation agencies, businesses, and private practice.

You may also have heard of **forensic psychologists,** *those who provide advice and consultation to police, lawyers, courts, or other parts of the criminal justice system.* Forensic psychologists are, in nearly all cases, trained as clinical or counseling psychologists with additional training in legal issues. They help with such decisions as whether a defendant is mentally competent to stand trial and whether someone eligible for parole is dangerous (Otto & Heilbrun, 2002). Several popular films have depicted forensic psychologists helping police investigators develop a "psychological profile" of a serial killer. That may sound like an exciting, glamorous profession, but bear in mind that very few psychologists engage in such activities (and the accuracy of their profiles is uncertain). We shall consider psychological profiling in Chapter 13.

Table 1.1 compares various types of mental health professionals.

CONCEPT CHECK ☑️

4. Can psychoanalysts prescribe drugs? (Check your answer on page 16.)

Service Providers to Organizations

Psychologists also work in business, industry, and school systems in some capacities that might be unfamiliar to you, doing things you might not think of as psychology. The job prospects in these fields have been good, however, and you might find these fields interesting.

Industrial/Organizational Psychology

The psychological study of people at work is known as **industrial/organizational (I/O) psychology.** It deals with issues you might not think of as psychology, such as matching the right person with the right job, training people for jobs, developing work teams, determining salaries and bonuses, planning an organizational

TABLE 1.1 Several Types of Mental Health Professionals

Type of Therapist	Education
Clinical psychologist	PhD with clinical emphasis or PsyD plus internship. Ordinarily, 5+ years after undergraduate degree.
Psychiatrist	MD plus psychiatric residency. Total of 8 years after undergraduate degree.
Psychoanalyst	Psychiatry or clinical psychology plus 6–8 years in a psychoanalytic institute. Many others who rely on Freud's methods also call themselves psychoanalysts.
Psychiatric nurse	From 2-year (AA) degree to master's degree plus supervised experience.
Clinical social worker	Master's degree plus 2 years of supervised experience. Total of at least 4 years after undergraduate degree.
Counseling psychologist	PhD, PsyD, or EdD plus supervised experience in counseling.
Forensic psychologist	Doctorate, ordinarily in clinical psychology or counseling psychology, plus additional training in legal issues.

structure, and organizing the workplace so that workers will be both productive and satisfied. I/O psychologists study the behavior of both the individual and the organization, including the impact of economic conditions and governmental regulations. We shall consider work motivation in Chapter 11.

Here's an example of a concern for industrial/organizational psychologists (Campion & Thayer, 1989): A company that manufactures complex electronic equipment needed to publish reference and repair manuals for its products. The engineers who designed the devices did not want to spend their time writing the manuals, and none of them were skilled writers anyway. So the company hired a technical writer to prepare the manuals. After a year she received an unsatisfactory performance rating because the manuals she wrote contained too many technical errors. She countered that, when she asked various engineers in the company to check her manuals or to explain technical details to her, they were always too busy. She found her job complicated and frustrating; her office was badly lit, noisy, and overheated; and her chair was uncomfortable. Whenever she mentioned any of these problems, however, she was told that she "complained too much."

In a situation such as this, an industrial/organizational psychologist can help the company evaluate the problem and develop possible solutions. Maybe the company hired the wrong person for this job. If so, they should fire her and hire some expert on electrical engineering who is also an outstanding writer and *likes* a badly lit, noisy, overheated, uncomfortable office. However, if the company cannot find or afford such a person, then it needs to improve the working conditions and provide the current employee with more training or more help with the technical aspects of the job.

In other words, when a company criticizes its workers, I/O psychologists try to discover whether the problem is poor workers or a difficult job. Depending on the answer, they then try to improve the hiring decisions or improve the working conditions.

CRITICAL THINKING:
A STEP FURTHER
I/O Psychology

I/O psychologists usually consult with business and industry, but suppose they were called on to help a university where certain professors had complained that "the students are too lazy and stupid to understand the lectures." How might the I/O psychologists react?

Ergonomics

Many years ago my son Sam, then about 16 years old, turned to me as he rushed out the door and asked me to turn off his stereo. I went to the stereo in his room and tried to find an on–off switch or a power switch. No such luck. I looked in vain for the manual. Finally, in desperation I had to unplug the stereo.

Learning to operate our increasingly complex machinery is one of the perennial struggles of modern life. Sometimes the consequences can be serious. Imagine an airplane pilot who intends to lower the landing gear and instead raises the wing flaps. Or a worker in a nuclear power plant who fails to notice a warning signal. In one field of psychology, an **ergonomist, or human factors specialist,** *attempts to facilitate the operation of machinery so that ordinary people can use it efficiently and safely.* The term *ergonomics* is derived from Greek roots meaning "laws of work." Ergonomics was first used in military settings, where complex technologies sometimes required soldiers to spot nearly invisible targets, understand speech through deafening noise, track objects in three dimensions while using two hands, and make life-or-death decisions in a split second. The military turned to psychologists to determine what skills their personnel could master and to redesign the tasks to fit those skills.

Ergonomists soon applied their experience not only to business and industry but also to everyday devices. As Donald Norman (1988) pointed out, many intelligent and educated people find themselves un-

❙ Ergonomists help redesign machines to make them easier and safer to use. An ergonomist uses principles of both engineering and psychology.

able to use all the features on a camera or a microwave oven; some even have trouble setting the time on a digital watch.

At various universities the ergonomics program is part of the psychology department, engineering, or both. Regardless of who administers the program, ergonomics necessarily combines features of psychology, engineering, and computer science. It is a growing field with many jobs available.

School Psychology

Many if not most children have academic problems at one time or another. Some children have trouble sitting still or paying attention. Others get into trouble for misbehavior. Others have specialized problems with reading, spelling, arithmetic, or other academic skills. Other children master their schoolwork very quickly and become bored. They too need special attention.

School psychologists are *specialists in the psychological condition of students,* usually in kindergarten through the 12th grade. Broadly speaking, school psychologists identify the educational needs of children, devise a plan to meet those needs, and then either implement the plan themselves or advise teachers how to implement it.

School psychology can be taught in a psychology department, a branch of an education department, or a department of educational psychology. In some countries it is possible to practice school psychology with only a bachelor's degree. In the United States the minimum is usually a master's degree, but job opportunities are much greater for people with a doctorate degree, and a doctorate may become necessary in the future. Job opportunities in school psychology have been strong and continue to grow. Most school psychologists

TABLE 1.2 Some Major Specializations in Psychology

Specialization	General Interest	Example of Interest or Research Topic
Biopsychologist	Relationship between brain and behavior	What body signals indicate hunger and satiety?
Clinical psychologist	Emotional difficulties	How can people be helped to overcome severe anxiety?
Cognitive psychologist	Memory, thinking	Do people have several kinds of memory?
Community psychologist	Organizations and social structures	Would improved job opportunities decrease psychological distress?
Counseling psychologist	Helping people make important decisions	Should this person consider changing careers?
Developmental psychologist	Changes in behavior over age	At what age can a child first distinguish between appearance and reality?
Educational psychologist	Improvement of learning in school	What is the best way to test a student's knowledge?
Environmental psychologist	How noise, heat, crowding, etc. affect behavior	What building design can maximize the productivity of the people who use it?
Ergonomist	Communication between person and machine	How can an airplane cockpit be redesigned to increase safety?
Evolutionary psychologist	Evolutionary history of behavior	Why do men generally show more sexual jealousy than women?
Industrial/organizational psychologist	People at work	Should jobs be made simple and foolproof or interesting and challenging?
Learning and motivation specialist	Learning in humans and other species	What are the effects of reinforcement and punishment?
Personality psychologist	Personality differences	Why are certain people shy and others gregarious?
Psychometrician	Measuring intelligence, personality, interests	How fair are current IQ tests? Can we devise better tests?
School psychologist	Problems that affect schoolchildren	How should the school handle a child who regularly disrupts the classroom?
Social psychologist	Group behavior, social influences	What methods of persuasion are most effective for changing attitudes?

work for a school system; others work for mental health clinics, guidance centers, and other institutions.

Table 1.2 summarizes some of the major fields of psychology, including several that have not been discussed.

Should You Major in Psychology?

Can you get a job if you major in psychology? Psychology is one of the most popular majors in the United States, Canada, and Europe. So if psychology majors cannot get jobs, a huge number of people are going to be in trouble!

The bad news is that very few jobs specifically advertise for college graduates with a bachelor's degree in psychology. The good news is that an enormous variety of jobs are available for graduates with a bachelor's degree, not specifying any major. Therefore, if you earn a degree in psychology, you will compete with history majors, English majors, astronomy majors, phys ed majors, and everyone else for jobs in government, business, and industry. According to one survey, only 20 to 25% of people who graduated with a degree in psychology took a job closely related to psychology, such as personnel work or social services (Borden & Rajecki, 2000). Still, many other jobs were good ones, even if they were not exactly in psychology.

Even if you get a job that seems remote from psychology, your psychology courses will have taught you much about how to evaluate evidence, organize and write papers, handle statistics, listen carefully to what people say, understand and respect cultural differences, and so forth. You will, of course, also gain useful background in your other courses. Regardless of your major, you should develop your skills in communication, mathematics, and computers. (If you don't have those skills, you will work for someone who does!)

Psychology also provides a good background for people entering professional schools. Many students major in psychology and then apply to medical school, law school, divinity school, or other programs. Find out what coursework is expected for the professional program of your choice and then compare the coursework required for a psychology major. You will probably find that the psychology major is compatible with your professional preparation.

If you want a career as a psychologist, you should aspire to an advanced degree, preferably a doctorate. A doctorate will qualify you to apply for positions as a college professor or, depending on your area of specialization, jobs in hospitals, clinics, private practice, school systems, or research. An increasing percentage of doctorate-level psychologists now work in business, industry, and the military doing research related to practical problems. If you are a first- or second-year college student now, it is hard to predict what the job market will be by the time you finish an advanced degree. If you are just looking for a safe, secure way to make a living, psychology offers no guarantees. A career in psychology is for those whose excitement about the field draws them irresistibly to it.

For more information about majoring in psychology, prospects for graduate school, and a great variety of jobs for psychology graduates, visit either of these Internet sites:

www.drlynnfriedman.com/

www.apa.org/students/

The types of people majoring in psychology have become more diverse over the years. Today, women receive about two thirds of the psychology PhDs in North America and most of those in Europe also (Newstead & Makinen, 1997; Sanderson & Dugoni, 1999). In some subfields such as developmental psychology, women receive as much as 80% of the new PhD degrees. Women are about as likely as men to assume leadership in the major psychological organizations and editorship of the major journals.

Minorities constitute a growing percentage of psychologists, although the total number is still small. Figure 1.4 shows the distribution for PhD degrees in psychology granted in 1996 in the United States

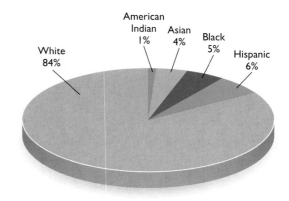

FIGURE 1.4 New psychology PhDs by race/ethnicity.

(Sanderson & Dugoni, 1999). Universities have been actively seeking more applications from minorities who are interested in graduate studies.

IN CLOSING

Types of Psychologists

An experimental psychology researcher, a clinical psychologist, an ergonomist, and an industrial/organizational psychologist are all psychologists, even though their daily activities have little in common. What does unite psychologists is a dedication to progress through research.

I have oversimplified this discussion of the various psychological approaches in several ways. First, biological psychology, cognitive psychology, social psychology, and the other fields all have their own specialized interests and questions, but they also constitute different ways of approaching many of the same questions. Furthermore, the various approaches overlap significantly. Nearly all psychologists combine insights and information gained from a variety of approaches. To understand why one person differs from another, psychologists combine information about biology, learning experiences, social influences, and much more.

As we proceed through this book, we shall consider one type of behavior at a time and, generally, one approach at a time. That is simply a necessity; we cannot talk intelligently about many topics at once. But bear in mind that all these processes do ultimately fit together; what you do at any given moment depends on a great many influences acting together.

Summary

The page number after an item indicates where the topic is first discussed.

- *What is psychology?* Psychology is the systematic study of behavior and experience. Psychologists deal with both theoretical and practical questions. (page 3)

- *Determinism/free will.* Determinism is the view that everything that occurs, including human behavior, has a physical cause. That view is difficult to reconcile with the conviction that humans have free will—that we deliberately, consciously decide what to do. (page 5)
- *Mind–brain.* The mind–brain problem is the question of how conscious experience is related to the activity of the brain. (page 6)
- *Nature–nurture.* Behavior depends on both nature (heredity) and nurture (environment). Psychologists try to determine the influence of these two factors on differences in behavior. The relative contributions of nature and nurture vary from one behavior to another. (page 7)
- *Research fields in psychology.* Psychology as an academic field has many subfields, including biological psychology, learning and motivation, cognitive psychology, developmental psychology, and social psychology. (page 8)
- *Psychology and psychiatry.* Clinical psychologists have either a PhD, PsyD, or master's degree; psychiatrists are medical doctors. Both clinical psychologists and psychiatrists treat people with emotional problems, but only psychiatrists can prescribe drugs and other medical treatments. Counseling psychologists help people deal with difficult decisions; they sometimes but less often also deal with psychological disorders. (page 11)

- *Service providers to organizations.* Nonclinical fields of application include industrial/organizational psychology, ergonomics, and school psychology. (page 12)
- *Job prospects.* People with a bachelor's degree in psychology enter a wide variety of careers or continue their education in professional schools. Those with a doctorate in psychology have additional possibilities depending on their area of specialization. In psychology, as in any other field, job prospects can change between the start and finish of one's education. (page 14)

Answers to Concept Checks

1. Any attempt to make discoveries about nature presupposes that we live in a universe of cause and effect. (page 8)
2. Dualism conflicts with the principle of the conservation of matter and energy. A nonmaterial mind could not influence anything in the universe. (page 8)
3. **a.** Developmental psychology. **b.** Social psychology. **c.** Cognitive psychology. **d.** Biological psychology. **e.** Learning and motivation. (page 11)
4. Most psychoanalysts can prescribe drugs because most are psychiatrists, and psychiatrists are medical doctors. However, psychoanalysts who are psychologists are not medical doctors and therefore cannot prescribe drugs. (page 12)

How did psychology get started?

What were the interests of psychologists in the early days?

How has psychology changed over the years?

Imagine yourself as a young scholar in about 1880. Enthusiastic about the new scientific approach in psychology, you have decided to become a psychologist yourself. Like other early psychologists, you have a background in either biology or philosophy. You are determined to apply the scientific methods of biology to the problems of philosophy.

So far, so good. But what questions will you address? A good research question is both interesting and answerable. (If it can't be both, it should at least be one or the other!) In 1880 how would you choose a research topic? You cannot get research ideas from a psychological journal because the first issue won't be published until next year. (And incidentally, it will be all in German.) You cannot follow in the tradition of previous researchers because there haven't *been* any previous researchers. Thus, you are on your own.

Furthermore, in the late 1800s and early 1900s, psychologists were not yet sure which questions were answerable. Sometimes they are still unsure: Should we try to study the nature of consciousness, or should we concentrate entirely on observable behavior? Many of the changes that have occurred during the history of psychology have been changes in investigators' decisions about which questions are answerable.

In the next several pages, we shall explore some of these changes in psychological research questions, including projects that dominated psychology for a while and then faded from interest. We shall discuss additional historical developments in later chapters, especially those that stood the test of time and continue to be highly influential today. Figure 1.5 outlines some major historical events inside and outside psychology. For additional information about the history of psychology, visit either of these Internet sites:

www.cwu.edu/warren/today.html

www.uakron.edu/ahap

The Early Era

At least since Aristotle (384–322 B.C.), philosophers and fiction writers have debated why people act the way they do, why they have the experiences they do,

and why one person is different from another. Without discounting the importance of these great thinkers, several 19th-century scholars wondered whether a scientific approach would be fruitful. They were impressed by the great strides made in physics, chemistry, and biology; they believed that similar progress could be made in psychology if evidence were collected and evaluated scientifically.

Wilhelm Wundt and the First Psychological Laboratory

The origin of psychology as we now know it is generally dated to 1879, when medical doctor and sensory researcher Wilhelm Wundt (pronounced "voont") set up the first psychology laboratory in Leipzig, Germany. Wundt and others had conducted psychological experiments before, but this was the first time anyone had established a laboratory exclusively for psychological research.

Wundt's broad interests ranged from the physiology of the sense organs to cultural differences in behavior, with emphases on motivation, voluntary control, and cognitive processes (Zehr, 2000). One of Wundt's fundamental questions was: What are the components of experience, or mind? He proposed that experience is composed of elements and compounds, like those of chemistry. Psychology's elements were, he maintained, sensations and feelings (Wundt, 1896/1902).[1] So at any particular moment, you might experience the taste of a fine meal, the sound of good music, and a certain degree of pleasure. These would merge into a single experience (a compound), but that experience would still include the separate elements. Furthermore, Wundt maintained, your experience is partly under your voluntary control; you can shift your attention from one element to another and get a different experience.

Wundt's question about the components of experience was a philosophical one, but Wundt, unlike the philosophers, tried to test his opinions by collecting data. He presented various kinds of lights, textures, and sounds and asked subjects to report the intensity

---

[1] A reference containing a slash between the years, such as this one, refers to a book originally published in the first year (1896) and reprinted in the second year (1902). All references are listed at the end of the book.

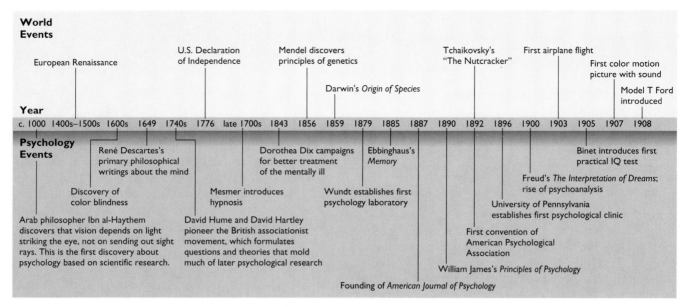

World Events

European Renaissance | U.S. Declaration of Independence | Mendel discovers principles of genetics | Tchaikovsky's "The Nutcracker" | First airplane flight | First color motion picture with sound | Model T Ford introduced

Darwin's *Origin of Species*

Year

c. 1000 1400s–1500s 1600s 1649 1740s 1776 late 1700s 1843 1856 1859 1879 1885 1887 1890 1892 1896 1900 1903 1905 1907 1908

Psychology Events

René Descartes's primary philosophical writings about the mind

Dorothea Dix campaigns for better treatment of the mentally ill

Ebbinghaus's *Memory*

Binet introduces first practical IQ test

Discovery of color blindness

Mesmer introduces hypnosis

Wundt establishes first psychology laboratory

Freud's *The Interpretation of Dreams*; rise of psychoanalysis

University of Pennsylvania establishes first psychological clinic

Arab philosopher Ibn al-Haythem discovers that vision depends on light striking the eye, not on sending out sight rays. This is the first discovery about psychology based on scientific research.

David Hume and David Hartley pioneer the British associationist movement, which formulates questions and theories that mold much of later psychological research

First convention of American Psychological Association

William James's *Principles of Psychology*

Founding of *American Journal of Psychology*

FIGURE 1.5 Dates of some important events in psychology and elsewhere. *(Based partly on Dewsbury, 2000a)*

and quality of their sensations. That is, he asked them to **introspect**—*to look within themselves.* He measured the changes in people's experiences as he changed the stimuli.

Wundt also demonstrated that it was possible to conduct meaningful psychological experiments. For example, in one of his earliest studies, he set up a pendulum that struck metal balls and made a sound at two points on its swing (points b and d in Figure 1.6). People would watch the pendulum and indicate where it appeared to be when they heard the sound. Often,

the pendulum appeared to be slightly in front of or behind the ball when people heard the strike. The apparent position of the pendulum at the time of the sound differed from its actual position by an average of $1/_8$ of a second (Wundt, 1862/1961). Apparently, the time we think we see or hear something is not the same as when the event occurred. Wundt's interpretation was that a person needs about $1/_8$ of a second to shift attention from one stimulus to another. (The same idea has been rediscovered in other contexts, as we shall see in Chapter 8.)

FIGURE 1.6 (Left) In one of Wilhelm Wundt's earliest experiments, the pendulum struck the metal balls (b and d), making a sound each time. To an observer, however, the ball appeared to be somewhere else at the time of the sound, generally the distance that it would travel in about $1/_8$ of a second. Wundt inferred that a person needs about $1/_8$ of a second to shift attention from one stimulus to another. (Right) The Walt Disney studios rediscovered Wundt's observation decades later: The character's mouth movements seem to be in synchrony with the sounds if the movements precede the sounds by $1/_8$ to $1/_6$ of a second.

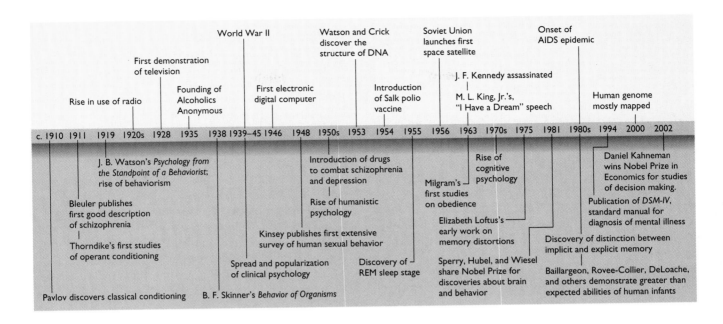

Wundt and his students were prolific investigators; the brief treatment here does not do him justice. He wrote more than 50,000 pages about his research, but his most lasting impact came from setting the precedent of studying psychological questions by collecting scientific data.

Edward Titchener and Structuralism

At first most of the world's psychologists received their education from Wilhelm Wundt himself. One of Wundt's students, Edward Titchener, came to the United States in 1892 as a psychology professor at Cornell University. Like Wundt, Titchener believed that the main question of psychology was the nature of mental experiences.

Titchener (1910) typically presented a stimulus and asked his subject to analyze it into its separate features—for example, to look at a lemon and de-

scribe its yellowness, its brightness, its shape, and so forth. He called his approach **structuralism,** *an attempt to describe the structures that compose the mind,* particularly sensations, feelings, and images. Later researchers were more interested in what those elements *do* (their functions).

If you asked psychologists today whether they thought Titchener correctly described the structures of the mind, you would probably get blank looks or shoulder shrugs. After Titchener died in 1927, psychologists virtually abandoned his research methods and even his questions. Why? Remember that a good scientific question is both interesting and answerable. Regardless of whether Titchener's questions about the elements of the mind were interesting, they appeared to be unanswerable.

For example, imagine you are the psychologist: I look at a lemon and tell you my experience of its brightness is totally separate from my experience of its yel-

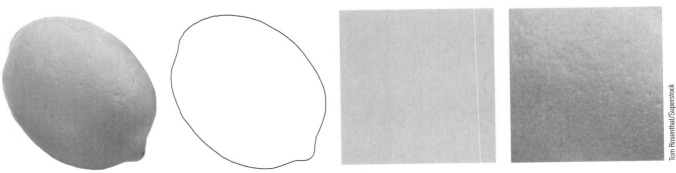

■ Edward Titchener asked subjects to describe their sensations. For example, they might describe their sensation of shape, their sensation of color, and their sensation of texture while looking at a lemon. Titchener had no way to check the accuracy of these reports, however, so later psychologists abandoned his methods.

lowness. How do you know whether I am lying, telling you what I think you want me to say, or even deceiving myself? Psychologists' frustration with Titchener's approach eventually turned many of them against studying the mind and toward studying observable behaviors.

William James and Functionalism

Almost simultaneously with the work of Wundt and Titchener, Harvard University's William James articulated some of the major issues of psychology and won eventual recognition as the founder of American psychology. James's book *The Principles of Psychology* (1890) defined the questions that dominated psychology for years afterward and even to a large extent today.

James had little patience with any search for the elements of the mind. He focused on the actions that the mind *performs* rather than what the mind *is*. That is, instead of trying to isolate the elements of consciousness, he preferred *to learn how people produce useful behaviors*. For this reason we call his approach **functionalism**. He suggested the following examples of good psychological questions (James, 1890):

- How can people strengthen good habits?
- Can someone attend to more than one item at a time?
- How do people recognize that they have seen something before?
- How does an intention lead to action?

James proposed possible answers but did little research of his own. His main contribution was to inspire later researchers to address the questions that he posed.

Studying Sensation

One of early psychologists' main research topics was the relationship between physical stimuli and psychological sensations. To a large extent, the study of

sensation *was* psychology. The first English-language textbook of the "new" scientifically based psychology devoted almost half of its pages to a discussion of the senses and the related topic of attention (Scripture, 1907). By the 1930s standard psychology textbooks devoted less than 20% of their pages to these topics (Woodworth, 1934), and today, it is down to about 5 to 10%. Why were early psychologists so interested in sensation?

One reason was philosophical: They wanted to understand mental experience, and experience consists of sensations. The other reason was strategic: A scientific psychology had to begin with answerable questions, and questions about sensation are more answerable than those about, say, personality.

Early psychologists discovered that what we see, hear, and otherwise sense is not the same as what is actually there. For example, the *perceived* intensity of a stimulus is not directly proportional to the *actual* physical intensity of the stimulus: A light that is twice as intense as another one does not look twice as bright. Figure 1.7 shows the relationship between the intensity of light and its perceived brightness. *The mathematical description of the relationship between the physical properties of a stimulus and its perceived properties* is called the **psychophysical function** because it relates psychology to physics. Such research demonstrated that, at least in the study of sensation, scientific methods can provide nonobvious answers to psychological questions.

CONCEPT CHECK ☑

5. What topic was the main focus of research for the earliest psychologists, and why?
6. What was the difference between structuralists and functionalists? (Check your answers on page 25.)

FIGURE 1.7 This graph of a psychophysical event shows the perceived intensity of light versus its physical intensity. When a light becomes twice as intense physically, it does not seem twice as bright. *(Adapted from Stevens, 1961)*

Darwin and the Study of Animal Intelligence

Charles Darwin's theory of evolution by natural selection (Darwin, 1859, 1871) had an enormous impact on psychology as well as biology. Darwin argued that humans and other species share a remote common ancestor. This idea implied that each species has specializations adapted to its own way of life, but also that all vertebrate species have many basic features in common. It further implied that nonhuman animals should exhibit varying degrees of human characteristics, including intelligence.

Based on this last implication, early **comparative psychologists,** *specialists who compare different animal species,* did something that seemed more reasonable at first than it did later: They set out to measure animal intelligence. They apparently imagined that they could rank-order animals from the smartest to the dullest. Toward that goal they set various species to such tasks as the delayed-response problem and the detour problem. In the *delayed-response problem,* an animal was given a signal indicating where it could find food. Then the signal was removed, and the animal was restrained for a while (Figure 1.8) to see how long it could remember

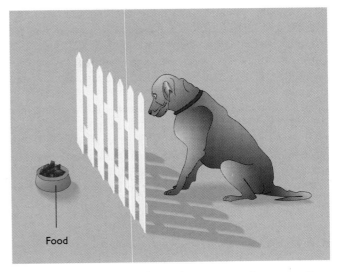

FIGURE 1.9 Another task popular among early comparative psychologists was the detour problem. An animal needed to first go away from the food in order to move toward it.

FIGURE 1.8 Early comparative psychologists assessed animal intelligence with the delayed-response problem. A stimulus was presented and a delay ensued; then the animal was expected to respond to the remembered stimulus. Variations on this delayed-response task are still used today.

the signal. In the *detour problem,* an animal was separated from food by a barrier (Figure 1.9) to see whether it would take a detour away from the food in order to get to it.

However, measuring animal intelligence turned out to be more difficult than it sounded. Too often a species seemed dull-witted on one task but brilliant on another. For example, zebras are generally slow to learn to approach one pattern instead of another for food, unless the patterns happen to be narrow stripes versus wide stripes, in which case they suddenly excel (Giebel, 1958) (see Figure 1.10). Rats seem unable to find food hidden under the object that looks different from the others, but they easily learn to choose the object that *smells* different from the others (Langworthy & Jennings, 1972).

Eventually, psychologists realized that the relative intelligence of nonhuman animals was a difficult

FIGURE 1.10 Zebras learn rapidly when they have to compare stripe patterns (Giebel, 1958). How "smart" a species is perceived to be depends in part on what ability or skill is being tested.

and probably meaningless question. The study of animal learning can illuminate general principles of learning and perhaps shed light on evolutionary questions (Papini, 2002), but because each species has somewhat different strengths, no one measurement applies to all.

Psychologists today do study animal learning and intelligence, but the emphasis has changed. The question is no longer simply which animals are the smartest, but "What can we learn from animal studies about the mechanisms of intelligent behavior?" and "How did each species evolve the behavioral tendencies it shows?"

Measuring Human Intelligence

While some psychologists studied animal intelligence, others pursued human intelligence. Francis Galton, a cousin of Charles Darwin, was among the first to try to measure intelligence and to ask whether intellectual variations were based on heredity. Galton was fascinated with trying to measure almost everything (Hergenhahn, 1992). For example, he invented the weather map, measured degrees of boredom during lectures, suggested the use of fingerprints to identify individuals, and—in the name of science—attempted to measure the beauty of women in different countries.

In an effort to determine the role of heredity in human achievement, Galton (1869/1978) examined whether the sons of famous and accomplished men tended to become eminent themselves. (Women in 19th-century England had little opportunity for fame.) Galton found that the sons of judges, writers, politicians, and other noted men had a high probability of similar accomplishment themselves. He attributed this edge to heredity. (I'll leave this one for you to judge: Did he have adequate evidence for his conclusion? If the sons of famous men become famous themselves, is heredity the only explanation?)

Galton also tried to measure intelligence using simple sensory and motor tasks, but his measurements were unsatisfactory. In 1905 a French researcher, Alfred Binet, devised the first useful intelligence test, which we shall discuss further in Chapter 9. At this point just note that the idea of testing intelligence became popular in the United States and other Western countries. Psychologists, inspired by the popularity of intelligence tests, later developed tests of personality, interests, and other psychological characteristics. Note that measuring human intelligence faces some of the same problems as animal intelligence: People have a great many intelligent abilities, and it is possible to be more adept at one than another. However, a great deal of research has been done to try to make tests of intelligence fair and accurate.

The Rise of Behaviorism

Earlier in this chapter, I casually defined psychology as "the systematic study of behavior and experience." For a substantial period of psychology's history, most experimental psychologists would have objected to the words "and experience." Some psychologists still object today, though less strenuously. From about 1920 to 1960 or 1970, most researchers described psychology as the study of behavior, period. These researchers had little to say about minds, experiences, or anything of the sort. (According to one quip, psychologists had "lost their minds.") What did psychologists have against mind or experience?

Recall the failure of Titchener's effort to analyze experience into its components. Most psychologists concluded that questions about the mind were unanswerable. Instead, they addressed questions about observable behaviors: What do people and other animals do and under what circumstances? How do changes in the environment alter what they do? What is learning and how does it occur? These questions were clearly meaningful and answerable, although the answers might be complex.

John B. Watson

Many regard John B. Watson as the founder of **behaviorism,** *a field of psychology that concentrates on observable, measurable behaviors and not on mental processes.* Watson was not the first behaviorist—it is uncertain who was the first—but he systematized the approach, popularized it, and stated its goals and assumptions (Watson, 1919, 1925). Here are two quotes from Watson:

> Psychology as the behaviorist views it is a purely objective experimental branch of natural science. Its theoretical goal is the prediction and control of behavior. (1913, p. 158)

> The goal of psychological study is the ascertaining of such data and laws that, given the stimulus, psychology can predict what the response will be; or, on the other hand, given the response, it can specify the nature of the effective stimulus. (1919, p. 10)

Studies of Learning

Inspired by Watson, many researchers set out to study animal behavior, especially animal learning. One advantage of studying nonhuman animals is that the researcher can control the animals' diet, waking–sleeping schedule, and so forth far more completely than with humans. The other supposed advantage was that nonhuman learning might be simpler to understand. Many psychologists optimistically expected to discover simple, basic laws of behavior, more or less the same from one species to another and from one situation to another. Just as physicists could study gravity by dropping any object in any location, many psychologists in the mid-1900s thought they could learn all about behavior by studying rats in mazes. One highly influential psychologist, Clark Hull, wrote, "One of the most persistently baffling problems which confronts modern psychologists is the finding of an adequate explanation of the phenomena of maze learning" (1932, p. 25). Another wrote, "I believe that everything important in psychology (except perhaps . . . such matters as involve society and words) can be investigated in essence through the continued experimental and theoretical analysis of the determiners of rat behavior at a choice-point in a maze" (Tolman, 1938, p. 34).

As research progressed, however, psychologists found that even the behavior of a rat in a maze was more complicated than they had expected, and such research declined in popularity. Just as psychologists of the 1920s abandoned Titchener's structuralist approach to the mind, later psychologists abandoned the hope that studying rats in mazes would uncover universal principles of behavior. Other approaches based on animal research have, however, remained influential. In Chapter 6 we shall consider the important ideas of B. F. Skinner.

The behaviorist emphasis continues to be highly influential, however, as we shall see especially in Chapter 6 (learning) and also in Chapters 15 and 16 (abnormal behavior and therapy). Many successful forms of therapy focus on describing problematic behaviors and then changing them through learning.

From Freud to Modern Clinical Psychology

In the early 1900s, clinical psychology was a small field devoted largely to visual, auditory, movement, and memory disorders (Routh, 2000). The treatment of psychological disorders (or mental illness) was mostly the province of psychiatry, a branch of medicine. The Austrian psychiatrist Sigmund Freud revolutionized and popularized psychotherapy with his methods of analyzing patients' dreams and memories. He tried to trace current behavior to early childhood experiences, including children's sexual fantasies. We shall examine Freud's theories in much more detail in Chapter 13. Here let me foreshadow that discussion by saying that Freud's influence has decreased sharply over the years. Freud was a very persuasive speaker and writer, but the evidence he proposed for his theories was extremely weak. In fact he changed his theory several times and often cited the same observations to support a new theory that he previously had cited as evidence to support the old theory! In other

Early behaviorists studied rats in mazes, hoping to find general laws of behavior. As they discovered that this apparently simple behavior was very complicated, their interest declined and they turned to other topics.

words his theories did not follow from his observations; he reinterpreted the observations to fit the theories. Nevertheless, Freud's influence was enormous, and by the mid-1900s, most psychiatrists in the United States and Europe were following his methods, at least in part.

During World War II more people wanted help, especially soldiers traumatized by war experiences. Because psychiatrists could not keep up with the need, psychologists began providing therapy. Clinical psychology became a much more popular field and much more similar to psychiatry, except without the license to prescribe drugs. Research began to compare the effectiveness of different methods, and new methods have taken the place of Freud's procedures, as we shall see in Chapters 15 and 16.

More Recent Trends in Psychology

The rest of this book will focus on the current era in psychology, with occasional flashbacks on the history of particular topics. Psychology today is an extremely diverse field, ranging from the study of simple visual processes to interventions intended to change whole communities. Recall that some of the earliest psychological researchers wanted to study the conscious mind, but the introspective methods of Titchener led nowhere. Since the mid-1960s, cognitive psychology (the study of thought and knowledge) has risen in prominence as psychologists found that they could indeed collect meaningful data about thought and knowledge (Robins,

Gosling, & Craik, 1999). Instead of asking people about their thoughts, today's cognitive psychologists carefully measure the accuracy and speed of responses under various circumstances to draw inferences about the underlying processes. They also use brain scans to determine what happens in the brain while someone is performing some task. Cognitive psychologists study human information processing in much the same way they would the information processing of a computer.

New fields of application have also arisen. For example, health psychologists study how people's health is influenced by their behaviors, such as smoking, drinking, sexual activities, exercise, diet, and reactions to stress. They also try to help people change their behaviors to promote better health. Sports psychologists apply psychological principles to helping athletes set goals, train, concentrate their efforts during a contest, and so forth.

Psychologists today have also broadened their scope to include more of human diversity. In its early days, around 1900, psychology was more open to women than most other academic disciplines, but even so, the opportunities for women were limited (Milar, 2000). Mary Calkins (Figure 1.11), an early memory researcher, was described as the best graduate student the Harvard psychology department had had to that point, but she was denied a PhD because Harvard insisted on its tradition of granting degrees to men only (Scarborough & Furomoto, 1987). She did, however, serve as president of the American Psychological Association, as did Margaret Washburn, another important woman in the early days of psychology.

Early psychological researchers tended not only to be men but also to focus their research attention

FIGURE 1.11 Mary Calkins, one of the first prominent women in U.S. psychology.

Wellesley College Archives © Notman

on the limited population of people around them. For certain purposes it is reasonable to conduct research on "just anybody"—college students, for example. In fact many of the general principles of vision, hearing, and nervous system functioning are so widespread that we can learn about them by studying laboratory animals. However, many principles of cognition, motivation, and social behavior differ from one culture to another, and the results from a study in the United States may not apply in China, for example (Nisbett, Peng, Choi, & Norenzayan, 2001). Psychologists have become more aware of cultural influences, and cross-cultural research has become more prominent than in the past.

What will psychology be like in the future? We don't know, of course, but we assume it will reflect the changing needs of humanity. A few likely trends are foreseeable. Advances in medicine have enabled

▌ We can learn much about what is or is not a stable feature of human nature by comparing people of different cultures.

© Bob Daemmrich/Stock Boston

© Kersten Geier/Gallo Images/CORBIS

people to live longer, while advances in technology have enabled them to build where there used to be forests and wetlands, heat and cool their homes, travel by car or plane to distant locations, and buy and discard enormous numbers of products. In short, we are quickly destroying our environment, using up natural resources, and polluting our air and water. Sooner or later it will become necessary either to decrease the population or to decrease the average person's use of resources (Howard, 2000). Convincing people to change their behavior is partly a political matter, but likely it will also be partly a task for psychologists.

IN CLOSING

Psychology Through the Years

Throughout the early years of psychology, many psychologists went down blind alleys, devoting enormous efforts to projects that produced disappointing results. Not all the efforts of early psychologists were fruitless by any means; in later chapters you will encounter some classic studies that have withstood the test of time. Still, if psychologists of the past spent countless years on fashionable projects, only to decide later that their efforts were misguided, how do we know that many psychologists aren't on the wrong track right now?

We don't, of course. In later chapters you will read about careful, cautious psychological research that has amassed what seems in many cases to be strong evidence, but you are welcome to entertain doubts. Maybe some psychologists' questions are not as simple as they seem; perhaps some of their answers are not very solid; perhaps you can think of a better way to approach certain topics. Psychologists have better data and firmer conclusions than they used to, but still they admit they do not have all the answers.

But that is not a reason for despair. Much like a rat in a maze, researchers make progress by trial and error. They pose a question, try a particular research method, and discover what happens. Sometimes the results support fascinating and important conclusions; other times they lead to rejections of old conclusions and therefore a search for replacements. In either case the experience leads ultimately to better questions and better answers. ∎

Summary

- *Choice of research questions.* During the history of psychology, researchers have several times changed their opinions about what constitutes an interesting, important, answerable question. (page 17)
- *First experiments.* In 1879 Wilhelm Wundt established the first laboratory devoted to psychological research. He demonstrated the possibility of psychological experimentation. (page 17)

- *Limits of self-observation.* One of Wundt's students, Edward Titchener, attempted to analyze the elements of mental experience, relying on people's own observations. Other psychologists became discouraged with this approach. (page 19)
- *The founding of American psychology.* William James, generally considered the founder of American psychology, focused attention on how the mind guides useful behavior rather than on the contents of the mind. By doing so James paved the way for the rise of behaviorism. (page 20)
- *Early sensory research.* In the late 1800s and early 1900s, many researchers concentrated on studies of the senses, partly because they were more likely to find definite answers on this topic than on other topics. (page 20)
- *Darwin's influence.* Charles Darwin's theory of evolution by natural selection influenced psychology in many ways; it prompted some prominent early psychologists to compare the intelligence of different species. That question turned out to be more complicated than anyone had expected. (page 21)
- *Intelligence testing.* The measurement of human intelligence was one concern of early psychologists that has persisted through the years. (page 22)
- *The era of behaviorist dominance.* As psychologists became discouraged with their attempts to analyze the mind, they turned to behaviorism. For many years psychological researchers concentrated on behavior, especially animal learning, to the virtual exclusion of mental experience. (page 22)
- *Maze learning.* Clark Hull exerted great influence for a number of years. Eventually, his approach became less popular because rats in mazes did not seem to generate simple or general answers to major questions. (page 22)
- *Psychological research today.* Today, psychologists study a wide variety of topics. Still, we cannot be certain that we are not currently going down some blind alleys, just as many psychologists did before us. (page 23)

Answers to Concept Checks

5. Early psychological research focused mainly on sensation, because sensation is central to experience and because the early researchers believed that sensation questions were answerable. (page 20)
6. Structuralists wanted to understand the components of the mind. They based their research mainly on introspection. Functionalists wanted to explore what the mind could *do,* and they focused mainly on behavior. (page 20)

CHAPTER ENDING

Key Terms and Activities

Key Terms

You can check the page listed for a complete description of a term. You can also check the glossary/index at the end of the text for a definition of a given term, or you can download a list of all the terms and their definitions for any chapter at this Web site:

http://psychology.wadsworth.com/kalat_intro7e/

behaviorism: a field of psychology that concentrates on observable, measurable behaviors and not on mental processes (page 22)

biopsychologist (or behavioral neuroscientist): a specialist who tries to explain behavior in terms of biological factors, such as electrical and chemical activities in the nervous system, the effects of drugs and hormones, genetics, and evolutionary pressures (page 8)

clinical psychologist: someone with an advanced degree in psychology, with a specialty in understanding and helping people with psychological problems (page 11)

clinical social worker: a person with a degree in social work instead of psychology, who helps people with psychological problems in ways similar to those of a clinical psychologist (page 11)

cognition: thinking and acquiring knowledge (page 10)

cognitive psychologist: a specialist who studies thought processes and the acquisition of knowledge (page 10)

comparative psychologist: a specialist who compares different animal species (page 21)

counseling psychologist: someone trained to help people with educational, vocational, marriage, health-related, and other decisions (page 12)

determinism: the assumption that all behavior has a cause, or *determinant,* in the observable world (page 5)

developmental psychologist: a specialist who studies the behavioral capacities of different ages and how behavior changes with age (page 10)

dualism: the view that the mind is separate from the brain (page 6)

ergonomist (or human factors specialist): a psychologist with engineering skills who works to facilitate the operation of machinery so that the average person can use it as efficiently and as safely as possible (page 13)

evolutionary psychologist: one who tries to explain behavior in terms of the evolutionary history of the species, including reasons evolution might have favored a tendency to act in particular ways (page 9)

forensic psychologist: one who provides advice and consultation to police, lawyers, courts, or other parts of the criminal justice system (page 12)

free will: the doctrine that behavior is caused by a person's independent decisions, not by external determinants (page 5)

functionalism: an attempt to understand how mental processes produce useful behaviors (page 20)

industrial/organizational (I/O) psychology: the psychological study of people at work (page 12)

introspection: looking within oneself (page 18)

learning and motivation: the study of how behavior depends on the outcomes of past behaviors and on current motivations (page 9)

mind–brain problem: the philosophical question of how the conscious mind is related to the physical nervous system, including the brain (page 6)

monism: the view that consciousness is inseparable from the physical brain (page 6)

nature–nurture issue: the question of the relative roles played by heredity (nature) and environment (nurture) in determining differences in behavior (page 8)

psychiatry: a branch of medicine that deals with emotional disturbances (page 11)

psychoanalyst: a psychotherapist who relies heavily on the theories of Sigmund Freud (page 11)

psychology: the systematic study of behavior and experience (page 3)

psychophysical function: the mathematical description of the relationship between the physical properties of a stimulus and its perceived properties (page 20)

school psychologist: a specialist in the psychological condition of students (page 13)

social psychologist: a specialist who studies how an individual influences others and is influenced by other people (page 10)

structuralism: an attempt to describe the structures that compose the mind (page 19)

Suggestions for Further Reading

Sechenov, I. (1965). *Reflexes of the brain.* Cambridge, MA: MIT Press. (Original work published 1863). One of the first attempts to deal with behavior scientifically and still one of the clearest statements of the argument for determinism in human behavior.

 Book Companion Web Site

Need help studying? Go to

http://psychology.wadsworth.com/kalat_intro7e/

for a virtual study center. You'll find a personalized Self-Study Assessment that will provide you with a study plan based on your answers to a pretest. Also study using flashcards, quizzes, interactive art, and an online glossary.

Check out interactive **Try It Yourself** exercises on the companion site! These exercises will help you put what you've learned into action.

Your companion site also has direct links to the following Web sites. These links are checked often for changes, dead links, and new additions.

Careers in Psychology

www.drlynnfriedman.com/

Clinical psychologist Lynn Friedman offers advice on majoring in psychology, going to graduate school, and starting a career.

Nontraditional Careers in Psychology

www.apa.org/students

Advice and information for students from the American Psychological Association.

Today in the History of Psychology

www.cwu.edu/~warren/today.html

Warren Street, at Central Washington University, offers a sample of events in the history of psychology for every day

of the year. Pick a date, any date (as they say), from the History of Psychology Calendar and see what happened on that date. The APA sponsors this site, which is based on Street's book, *A Chronology of Noteworthy Events in American Psychology.*

More About the History of Psychology

www.uakron.edu/ahap

The University of Akron has assembled a museum of old psychology laboratory equipment and other mementos from psychology's past.

What Else Would You Like to Know?

www.psywww.com

www.psychology.org

Both of these sites provide annotated links to a vast array of information about psychology.

 Try It Yourself CD-ROM
with Critical Thinking Video Exercises

Use your CD to access **videos** related to activities designed to help you think critically about the important topics discussed. You'll also find an easy portal link to the book companion site where you can access your personalized **Self-Study Assessments** and interactive Try It Yourself exercises.

PsychNow! 2.0

PsychNow! is a fun interactive CD designed to help you with the difficult concepts in psychology. Check out the Accessing Psychology section for the following topics that relate to this chapter:

Study Skills: learning styles video, study habit lesson, and printable schedule.

Psychology and its History: quizzes, historical facts, timeline.

Scientific Methods in Psychology

A few years ago, I was watching a Discovery Channel nature documentary about elephants. After the narrator discussed the enormous amount of food elephants eat, he started on their digestive system. He commented that the average elephant passes enough gas in a day to propel a car for 20 miles (32 km). I thought, "Wow, isn't that an amazing fact!" and I told a couple of other people about it.

A while later I started to think, "Wait a minute. *Who measured that? And how?* Did someone really attach a balloon to an elephant's rear end and collect gas for 24 hours? And then put it into a car to see how far they could make the car go? Was that a full-sized car or an economy car? City

traffic or highway? How do they know they measured a typical elephant? Maybe they chose an extra gassy one. Did they determine the mean for a broad sample of elephants?" The more I thought about it, the more I doubted the claim about propelling a car on elephant gas.

"Oh, well," you might say. "Who cares?" You're right; how far you could propel a car on elephant gas doesn't matter. However, my point is not to ridicule the makers of this documentary but to ridicule *me*. Remember, I said I told two people about this claim before I started to doubt it. For decades I have been teaching students to question assertions, evaluate the evidence, and think critically, and here I was, uncritically accepting a silly statement about elephants and even telling other people, who for all I know, may have gone on to tell other people who told still other people until someday it might become part of our folklore: "*They say* that you can propel a car 20 miles on a day's worth of elephant gas!" The point is that all of us yield to the temptation to accept unsupported claims, and we all need to discipline ourselves to question the evidence, especially for the interesting or exciting claims that we would most like to believe. This chapter concerns the evaluation of evidence in psychology.

Thinking Critically and Evaluating Evidence

induction - the process of absolute center - conclusion

How do scientists evaluate theories?

Why are most scientists so skeptical of theories and claims that contradict our current understanding?

The American comedian and politician Will Rogers once said that what worried him was not the things that people don't know but the things they *think* they know that really aren't so. You have heard people make countless claims about psychology, medicine, politics, religion, and so forth. But frequently, one confident claim contradicts another, so someone must be believing something that isn't true. How can you know what is true?

One way is to rely on logical deduction. Here is an example:

Premise 1. All human beings are mortal.
Premise 2. You are a human being.
Conclusion. Therefore, you are mortal.

Logical deduction gives us an absolutely certain conclusion, but only if the premises are true. How do we know that you are a human being? And how do we know that all humans are mortal? Premises like these cannot come from deduction, but only from **induction**, *the process of inferring a general principle from observations.* For example, we infer that "all human beings are mortal" because so far every human who has lived has been mortal, and we infer that you are a human being because you resemble other human beings. But can we be sure? Induction cannot lead to certainty (Pigliucci, 2003). For example, the fact that a flipped coin has come up "heads" 20 times in a row does not prove that it is a two-headed coin that will always come up heads. The fact that anything has happened many times in the past does not logically guarantee that it will happen again in the future. For that reason most scientists avoid the word *prove,* which sounds too final, except when they are talking about mathematical proofs. By avoiding the word *prove,* they affirm the possibility of altering a conclusion in the light of new evidence.

The lack of absolute certainty, however, does not mean that "you may as well believe anything you want" or that "anything has as much chance of being true as anything else." What it does mean is that people should always try to state the evidence behind the conclusion and not just the conclusion itself.

CONCEPT CHECK ☑

1. What is the difference between induction and deduction? (Check your answer on page 39.)

Evidence and Theory in Science

People sometimes say "I have a theory . . ." when they mean they have a guess. A scientific **theory** is far more than a guess; it is *an explanation or model induced from a great many observations and capable of making valid predictions.* A good theory is useful because of its ability to summarize existing observations and predict new ones. But can we ever be sure it is "true"? The philosopher Karl Popper argued that because no observation can prove a theory to be correct, the only purpose of research is to find which theories are *incorrect.* That is, the point of research is to *falsify* the incorrect theories, and a good theory is one that withstands all attempts to falsify it. In other words it wins by a process of elimination.

A well-formed theory, therefore, is **falsifiable** that is, *stated in such clear, precise terms that we can see what evidence would count against it* (if, of course, such evidence existed). For example, no number of confirming observations could prove the law of gravity true, so researchers can only try to show it is false. Because all attempts to disconfirm it have failed, we have high confidence that it is correct.

This point is worth restating because many find it confusing. It sounds as if "falsifiable" would be a bad thing. But falsifiable does not mean we actually have evidence against a theory. (If we did, it would be falsified.) Falsifiable means we can imagine what would be evidence against the theory. The theory of gravity is a well-formed theory because it makes precise predictions and any observation that did not match the predictions would contradict the theory.

A theory that is vague or badly stated is not falsifiable because we cannot even imagine evidence that would count against it. For example, Sigmund Freud claimed that all dreams are motivated by wish fulfillment, although they are disguised by a "censor" in the head. If you object that many of your dreams are unpleasant or frightening, Freud would reply that in those dreams the censor failed to disguise the wish properly. What about repetitive nightmares by someone who has endured some horrible traumatic experience? Freud (1933/1973) admitted that those dreams were not wish fulfillments but nevertheless claimed that "the exception does not overturn the rule" (p. 29). As Domhoff (2003) has pointed out, Freud stated his theory in such a way that any possible observation counted as evidence for it or at least not against it. If no conceivable evidence counts against it, nothing is impressive evidence for it either.

On the other hand, contrary to what Karl Popper wrote, science is not entirely a matter of falsifying theories, and some scientific statements can be verified but not falsified. It depends on how the statement is phrased. "All objects fall" (the law of gravity) is falsifiable. "Some objects fall," a much weaker statement, is not falsifiable. (Even if it were false, you could not demonstrate it to be false!) You also could not falsify the statement, "There is a monster in Loch Ness, Scotland." No matter how many times observers fail to find a monster there, we can't be sure. Similarly, consider the statement, "Some people have psychic powers that enable them to get information that did not pass through their senses." No matter how many people fail to show psychic powers, the possibility remains that someone else under other conditions might be different. In short, we cannot ask anyone to falsify this claim.

So, instead of insisting that all research is an effort to falsify some theory, a better idea is to use a phrase popular among debaters and lawyers: **Burden of proof** is *the obligation to present evidence to support one's claim.* In a criminal trial, the burden of proof is on the prosecution. If the prosecution does not make a convincing case, the defendant is set free. The reason is that if the defendant is guilty, it should be possible for the state to find good evidence, but it is not always possible to find evidence of innocence.

Similarly in science, the burden of proof is on anyone who makes a claim that should be possible to demonstrate if it is true. A claim that "some objects fall" or "some people have psychic powers" should be demonstrable. A claim that "*every* object falls" cannot be demonstrated, so the burden of proof is on anyone who doubts it.

CRITICAL THINKING:
A STEP FURTHER
Burden of Proof

If one person claims that intelligent life exists in outer space and someone else denies it, which side has the burden of proof? When finding evidence to support either view is difficult, what is a reasonable conclusion?

Steps for Gathering and Evaluating Evidence

The word *science* derives from a Latin word meaning "knowledge." Scientific reasoning is the same as any other kind of problem solving, but it is usually based on more information that is observed and recorded carefully (Klahr & Simon, 2001). Science is distinguished from most other human endeavors by the fact that scientists generally agree on how to evaluate theories. Most people can hardly imagine any evidence that would cause them to change their religious or political views. Scientists, however, generally agree about what would constitute evidence for or against any theory, and they sometimes do abandon theories in the light of new evidence.

In that sense psychologists—most of them, anyway—follow the scientific method. Obviously, our knowledge of psychology lacks the precision of physics, chemistry, and biology. But like physicists, chemists, and biologists, psychologists do generally agree on what constitutes good evidence.

The simplest kind of evidence is careful observation. The sciences of astronomy and anatomy are based almost entirely on observation and description. In psychology too we observe what people do and under what circumstances, and how people differ from one another. For example, Robert Provine (2000) simply recorded who laughed and when in shopping malls and similar places.

Ultimately, we want to go beyond observations to find explanations and to compare one explanation against another. Much of scientific argument consists of evaluating which explanation best fits the results we already have (Proctor & Capaldi, 2001). When a dispute is indecisive, researchers collect new data, guided by a **hypothesis,** which is *a clear predictive statement.* Research designed to test hypotheses goes through the series of steps described in the following four sections (see also Figure 2.1). Articles in scientific publications generally follow this sequence too. In each of the remaining chapters of this book, you will find at least one example of a psychological study described in a section entitled "What's the Evidence?" In this chapter the example concerns the question of how televised violence relates to aggressive behavior.

Hypothesis

A hypothesis can be based on preliminary observations, such as noticing that some children who watch much violence are themselves aggressive. It can also be based on a larger theory, such as "children tend to imitate the behavior they see, so those who watch a great deal of violence on television will themselves become more violent." A hypothesis can also emerge

FIGURE 2.1 An experiment tests the predictions that follow from a hypothesis. Results either support the hypothesis or indicate a need to revise or abandon it.

from trends in society. It has been estimated that the average child, before graduating from elementary school, will have watched 8,000 murders and 100,000 other violent acts on television (Bushman & Anderson, 2001) in addition to countless violent acts in video games (Anderson & Bushman, 2001). Presumably, all those experiences must produce *some* effect.

Method

Any hypothesis could be tested in many ways, and almost any method has its strengths and weaknesses. One way to test the effects of violent television shows would be to examine whether children who watch more violent programs engage in more violent behavior. The main limit of this approach is that we cannot conclude cause and effect: Watching violence may lead to violence, but it is also likely that people who are already violent like to watch violence. Another method is to see whether violent behavior increases in some geographical region after an increase in the availability of televised violence. However, other social, economic, and political events may occur at the same time, and we cannot separate the effects of televised violence from the other factors. A third method is to take a set of children, such as those attending a summer camp, let some watch violent programs while others watch nonviolent programs, and see whether the two groups differ in their violent behaviors. That kind of study can justify a cause-and-effect conclusion if indeed the groups differ, as often they do (Parke, Berkowitz, Leyens, West, & Sebastian, 1977). The limitation is that the results concern only short-term exposure. The programs children watch for a week or two are a drop in the bucket compared to many years of television watching.

Because any method has strengths and weaknesses, researchers try to use a variety of methods. A conclusion based on several different kinds of studies is more certain than one based on a single method.

Results

Fundamental to any research is measuring the outcome. A phenomenon such as "violent behavior" can be especially tricky to measure. (How do we decide what is *real* violence and what is just playfulness? Do threats count? Does verbal abuse?) It is important for an investigator to follow clear rules for making measurements. After making the measurements, the investigator must determine whether the results are impressive enough to call for an explanation.

Interpretation

The final task is to determine what the results mean. If they clearly contradict the hypothesis, researchers should either abandon or modify the original hypothesis. (Maybe it applies only to certain kinds of people or only under certain circumstances.) If the results match the prediction, investigators gain confidence in their hypothesis, but they also need to consider possible weaknesses in the study and other possible hypotheses consistent with the results.

Replicability

Most scientific researchers are scrupulously honest in reporting their results. Distortions of data are rare and scandalous. However, despite their customary honesty, scientists do not accept the statement "trust me" or "take my word for it." Anyone who reports a result in a scientific article also reports the methods in enough detail that someone else could repeat the study, and those who doubt the result are invited to do so. If they get the same results, they presumably will be convinced. But if they cannot, they should reject the original finding and base no theory upon it. Indeed, one reason most scientists are so honest is that they know that if they are not, anyone attempting to repeat their study will catch the error.

Replicable results are *those that anyone can obtain, at least approximately, by following the same procedures,* and scientists insist on replicable results. Let's consider an example of a nonreplicable result. In 1993 a team of researchers had several groups of young people listen to a Mozart sonata, a "relaxation tape," or silence and then take some psychological tests. They reported that the people who listened to Mozart performed better than the others on a test of spatial reasoning (Rauscher, Shaw, & Ky, 1993). The implication was that listening to music with a particular level of complexity might promote ideal brain functioning.

Wouldn't it be great if we could increase people's intelligence that easily? Unfortunately, the effect has not been replicable. Several other studies using virtually the same method as the original one found either no difference or a trivially small difference between the Mozart listeners and the other groups (Chabris, 1999; Steele, Bass, & Crook, 1999). Two studies found mild improvements after any pleasant experience but no evidence that Mozart's music was special (Nantais & Schellenberg, 1999; W. F. Thompson, Schellenberg, & Husain, 2001).

So, what conclusion should we draw? When the results are inconsistent, we draw no conclusions at all. Until or unless someone finds conditions under which the phenomenon is replicable (consistently repeatable), we do not take it seriously. This rule may seem harsh, but it is our best defense against error.

Sometimes, however, an effect is small but real. In education one method of presenting the material might work better than another, but the effect is small and has to compete with many other influences, so we might not see it in every study. The same is true for research on how to run an organization, how to deliver psychotherapy, and many other complex human behaviors. When we are looking at small trends in the data, we can combine the results of many studies to get an approximate measure of the size of the effect. A **meta-analysis** *combines the results of many studies and analyzes them as though they were all one very large study.* In most cases a meta-analysis will also determine which variations in procedure increase or decrease the effects.

Criteria for Evaluating Scientific Theories

After investigators collect mounds of evidence and identify the replicable findings, what do they do with the results?

One goal of scientific research is to establish theories. A good theory starts with as few assumptions as possible and leads to as many predictions as possible. In that way it reduces the amount of information we must remember. The periodic table in chemistry is a good example: From the information about the elements, we can predict the properties of an enormous number of compounds.

One important criterion for a good theory is that it should make accurate predictions. It is easy to come up with a "theory" to explain events in history or other facts that we already know. The real test is whether the theory predicts new observations. The more precise and accurate those predictions, the more impressive.

What do we do if we encounter several theories that fit the known facts about equally well? For example, suppose you don't wake up at your usual time, and several friends offer these competing explanations:

- Your alarm clock didn't work.
- You slept through the alarm.
- You were kidnapped by space aliens and then returned to your room after the alarm had shut off.

All three explanations fit the observation that you overslept, but we don't consider them on an equal basis. *When given a choice among theories that all seem to fit the facts, we should prefer the one whose assumptions are fewer, simpler, or more consistent with other well-established theories.* This principle is known as the principle of **parsimony** (literally "stinginess") or *Occam's razor* (after the philosopher William of Occam). The principle of parsimony is a conservative idea: We stick with ideas that work, and we don't introduce major new assumptions (e.g., space aliens) unless we have strong, unambiguous evidence to support them.

Parsimony and Degrees of Open-Mindedness

The principle of parsimony tells us to adhere as much as possible to what we already believe. You might protest: "Shouldn't we remain open-minded to new possibilities?" Yes, if open-mindedness means a willingness to consider proper evidence, but not if it means the assumption that "anything has as much chance of being true as anything else." The stronger the reasons behind our current opinion, the more evidence we should need before replacing it. Consider two examples:

Visitors from outer space. Many, probably most, physicists and astronomers doubt that visitors from other planets have ever landed on Earth or ever will. (To get from one solar system to another in less than thousands of years, you need to travel at nearly the speed of light. At that speed a collision with even a dust particle would be catastrophic.) However, we could imagine alien life forms whose biology enables them to survive a journey of thousands of years or whose technology permits greater speed than seems possible for the kind of travel we know. So we can remain open-minded to new evidence. If weird-looking beings stepped out of an odd-looking spacecraft, we should consider the possibility of a hoax by other people, but solid evidence could persuade us of real visitors from outer space.

Perpetual motion machines. A "perpetual motion machine" is one that generates more energy than it uses. For centuries people have attempted and failed to develop such a machine. (Figure 2.2 shows one example.) The U.S. Patent Office is officially closed-minded on this issue, refusing even to consider patent applications for such machines, because a perpetual motion machine violates what physicists call *the second law of thermodynamics.* According to that law, within a closed system, entropy (disorder) can never decrease. A more casual statement of the law is that any work wastes energy. That is, we need to keep adding energy to a machine to keep it going. Could the second law of thermodynamics be wrong? I recommend only the slightest amount of open-mindedness. It is supported by an enormous amount of data plus logical arguments about why it must be true. If someone shows you what appears to be a perpetual motion machine, look carefully for a hidden battery or other power source—that is, some simple, parsimonious explanation. Even if you don't find a hidden power source, it is more likely that you overlooked one than that the second law of thermodynamics is wrong. A claim as extraordinary as a perpetual motion machine requires extraordinary evidence.

What does all this discussion have to do with psychology? Sometimes people claim spectacular results that would seem impossible according to everything we know or think we know. Although it is only fair to examine the evidence behind such claims, it is also reasonable to maintain a skeptical attitude and to look as closely as possible for a simple, parsimonious explanation of the results. Let us consider two examples from psychology.

Applying Parsimony: Clever Hans, the Amazing Horse

Early in the 20th century, Mr. von Osten, a German mathematics teacher, set out to prove that his horse, Hans, had great intellectual abilities, particularly in arithmetic. To teach Hans arithmetic, he first showed him a single object, said "one," and lifted Hans's foot once. Then he raised Hans's foot twice for two objects and so on. Eventually, when von Osten presented a group of objects, Hans learned to tap his foot by himself, and with practice he managed to tap the correct number of times. With more practice it was no longer

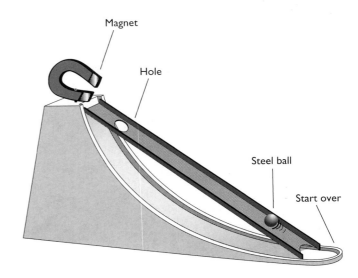

FIGURE 2.2 A proposed perpetual motion machine: The magnet pulls the metal ball up the inclined plane. When the ball reaches the top, it falls through the hole and returns to its starting point, from which the magnet will again pull it up. Can you see why this device is sure to fail? (See answer A on page 39.)

necessary for Hans to see the objects. Von Osten would just call out a number, and Hans would tap the appropriate number of times.

Mr. von Osten moved on to addition and then to subtraction, multiplication, and division. Hans caught on quickly, soon responding with 90 to 95% accuracy. Then von Osten began touring Germany; he asked questions and Hans tapped out the answers. Hans's abilities grew until he could add fractions, convert fractions to decimals or vice versa, do simple algebra, tell time to the minute, and give the values of all German coins. Using a letter-to-number code, he could spell out the names of objects and even identify musical notes such as B-flat. (Evidently, Hans had perfect pitch.) He responded correctly even when questions were put to him by people other than von Osten, in unfamiliar places, with von Osten nowhere in sight.

Given this evidence, many people were ready to believe that Hans had great intellectual powers. But others sought a more parsimonious explanation. Enter Oskar Pfungst. Pfungst (1911) discovered that Hans could not answer a question correctly unless the questioner had calculated the answer first. Apparently, the horse was somehow getting the answers from the questioner. Next Pfungst learned that, when the questioner stood in plain sight, Hans's accuracy was 90% or better, but when he could not see the questioner, his answers were almost always wrong.

Eventually, Pfungst observed that anyone who asked Hans a question would lean forward to watch Hans's foot. Hans had simply learned to start tapping whenever someone stood next to his right forefoot and leaned forward. As soon as Hans had given the correct number of taps, the questioner would give a slight upward jerk of the head and change facial expression in anticipation that this might be the last tap. (Even skeptical scientists who tested Hans did this involuntarily. After all, they thought, wouldn't it be exciting if Hans got it right?) Hans simply continued tapping until he received that cue.

In short, Hans was indeed a clever horse, but we do not believe that he understood mathematics. Note that Pfungst did not demonstrate that Hans *didn't* understand mathe-matics. Pfungst merely demonstrated that he could explain Hans's behavior in the simple, parsimonious terms of responses to facial expressions, and therefore, no one needed to assume that Hans had any more complicated abilities. The same principle applies for psychology in general: If we can find a simple explanation for some result, we prefer it to an explanation that requires new as-sumptions. Any extraordinary claim requires extraordi-nary evidence.

After Pfungst, 1911, in Fernald, 1984

▌ Clever Hans and his owner, Mr. von Osten, demonstrated that the horse could answer complex mathematical questions with great accuracy. The question was, "How?"

Applying Parsimony: Extrasensory Perception

The possibility of **extrasensory perception (ESP)** has long been controversial in psychology. Supporters of extrasensory perception claim that *at least some peo-ple, at least some of the time, can acquire informa-tion without using any sense organ and without re-ceiving any form of physical energy.* For example, a person gifted with ESP might identify another person's thoughts (via telepathy) even when the two are sepa-rated by a thick lead barrier that would block the transmission of almost any form of energy. Supporters of this view claim that people with telepathic powers can identify thoughts just as accurately from a great distance as from an adjacent room, in apparent viola-tion of the inverse-square law of physics, and that the accuracy is not diminished by a lead shield that would interrupt any known form of energy. Some ESP sup-porters also claim that certain people can perceive inanimate objects that are hidden from sight (clair-voyance), predict the future (precognition), and influ-ence such physical events as a roll of dice by sheer mental concentration (psychokinesis).

Acceptance of any of these claims would require us not only to overhaul some major concepts in psychol-ogy but also to discard the most fundamental tenets of physics, even the idea that we live in a universe of mat-ter and energy. What evi-dence is there for ESP?

Anecdotes

One kind of evidence con-sists of anecdotes—people's reports of isolated events, such as an amazing coinci-dence or a dream or hunch that comes true. Such experi-ences may seem impressive, but they are not scientific ev-idence. Consider the possi-bility of coincidence. Sooner or later, occasional bizarre coincidences are almost sure to occur. For example, as you have probably heard, people have found many parallels between the lives of Presidents Abraham Lincoln and John Kennedy, including the following:

- Lincoln was elected to Congress in 1846 and elected president in 1860; Kennedy was elected to Congress in 1946 and elected president in 1960.
- The names Lincoln and Kennedy each contain seven letters.
- Both Lincoln and Kennedy were shot in the head on a Friday, while seated next to their wives.
- Lincoln was shot in the Ford theater, and Kennedy was shot while in a Ford Lincoln.
- Both were succeeded in office by a southerner named Johnson.

The problem is, if you try hard enough, you can find parallels for many pairs of people. Consider Attila the Hun and former U.S. President Harry S Truman:

- Attila the Hun was king of the Huns from 445 until 453; Harry S Truman was president of the United States from 1945 until 1953.
- Both Attila and Truman took office upon the death of the previous leader; both were succeeded in of-fice by a military general.
- The initials for "The Hun" are T. H. The initials for "Harry Truman" are H. T.
- Both the name Attila the Hun and Harry S Truman consist of 12 letters and 2 spaces.
- Both had a middle name that is meaningless out of context ("The" and "S").

Pick two people in history, or two people you know, and see how many "uncanny" similarities you can find.

Furthermore, we tend to remember and talk about the hunches and dreams that *do* come true and to forget the others. People hardly ever say, "Strangest thing! I had a dream, but then nothing like it actually happened!" People often exaggerate the coincidences that occur and probably even misremember them. We could evaluate anecdotal evidence only if people recorded their hunches and dreams *before* the predicted events and then determined how many unlikely predictions actually came to pass.

Sometime you might try keeping track of psychics' predictions in tabloid newspapers for the new year. By the end of the year, how many came true? How many would you expect to come true just by chance? (The latter number is, of course, difficult to estimate.)

You may have heard of the "prophet Nostradamus," a 16th-century French writer who allegedly predicted many events of later centuries. Figure 2.3 presents four samples of his writings. All of his "predictions" are at this level of vagueness. After something happens, people imaginatively reinterpret his writings to fit the event. (If we don't know what a prediction means until *after* it occurs, is it really a prediction?)

CONCEPT CHECK ☑

2. How could someone scientifically evaluate the accuracy of Nostradamus's predictions? (Check your answer on page 39.)

Master magician Lance Burton can make people and animals seem to suddenly appear, disappear, float in the air, or do other things that we know are impossible. Even if we don't know how he accomplishes these feats, we take it for granted that they are magic tricks, based on methods of misleading the audience. The same assumption should apply when someone claims to be using psychic powers.

Professional Psychics

Various stage performers claim to read other people's minds and to perform other psychic feats. Two of the most famous are Uri Geller and The Amazing Kreskin. Actually, Kreskin has consistently denied doing anything supernatural; he prefers to talk of his "extremely sensitive" rather than "extrasensory" perception (Kreskin, 1991). Still, part of Kreskin's success as a performer comes from allowing people to believe he has mental powers that defy explanation.

After carefully observing Geller, Kreskin, and others, David Marks and Richard Kammann (1980) concluded that they used the same kinds of deception commonly employed in magic acts. For example, Kreskin sometimes begins his act by asking the audience to read his mind.

Let's try to duplicate this trick right now: Try to read my mind. I am thinking of a number between 1 and 50. Both digits are odd numbers, but they are not the same. For example, it could be 15 but it could not be 11. (These are the instructions Kreskin gives.) Have you chosen a number? Please do.

1. The great man will be struck down in the day by a thunderbolt. An evil deed, foretold by the bearer of a petition. According to the prediction another falls at night time. Conflict at Reims, London, and pestilence in Tuscany.

2. When the fish that travels over both land and sea is cast up on to the shore by a great wave, its shape foreign, smooth, and frightful. From the sea the enemies soon reach the walls.

3. The bird of prey flying to the left, before battle is joined with the French, he makes preparations. Some will regard him as good, others bad or uncertain. The weaker party will regard him as a good omen.

4. Shortly afterwards, not a very long interval, a great tumult will be raised by land and sea. The naval battles will be greater than ever. Fires, creatures which will make more tumult.

FIGURE 2.3 According to the followers of Nostradamus, each of these statements is a specific prophecy of a 20th-century event (Cheetham, 1973). Can you figure out what the prophecies mean? Compare your answers to answer B on page 39.

All right, my number was 37. Did you think of 37? If not, how about 35? You see, I started to think 35 and then changed my mind, so you might have got 35.

If you successfully "read my mind," are you impressed? Don't be. At first, it seemed that you had a lot of numbers to choose from (1 to 50), but by the end of the instructions, you had only a few. The first digit had to be 1 or 3, and the second had to be 1, 3, 5, 7, or 9. You had to eliminate 11 and 33 because both digits are the same, and you probably eliminated 15 because I cited it as a possible example. That leaves only seven possibilities. Most people like to stay far away from the example given and tend to avoid the highest and lowest possible choices. That leaves 37 as the most likely choice and 35 as the second most likely.

Second act: Kreskin asks the audience to write down something they are thinking about while he walks along the aisles talking. Then, back on stage, he "reads people's minds." He might say something like, "Someone is thinking about his mother . . ." In any large crowd, someone is bound to shout, "Yes, that's me. You read my mind!" On occasion he describes something that someone has written out in great detail. That person generally turns out to be someone sitting along the aisle where Kreskin was walking.

After a variety of other tricks (see Marks & Kammann, 1980), Kreskin goes backstage while the local mayor or some other dignitary hides Kreskin's paycheck somewhere in the audience. Then Kreskin comes back, walks up and down the aisles and across the rows, and eventually shouts, "The check is here!" The rule is that if he guesses wrong, then he does not get paid. (He hardly ever misses.)

This is an impressive trick, and even more impressive if you're part of the audience. How does he do it? Very simply, it is a Clever Hans trick. Kreskin studies people's faces. Most people want him to find the check, so they get more excited as he gets close to it and more disappointed or distressed if he moves away. In effect they are saying, "Now you're getting closer" and "Now you're moving away." At last he closes in on the check.

Of course, someone always objects, "Well, maybe you've explained what some professional psychics do. But there's this other guy you haven't investigated yet. Maybe he really does possess psychic powers." Well, maybe. But until there is solid evidence to the contrary, it is simpler (more parsimonious) to assume that other performers are also using illusion and deception.

Experiments

Because stage performances and anecdotal events always take place under uncontrolled conditions, we cannot determine the probability of coincidence or the possibility of deception. Laboratory experiments provide the only evidence about ESP worth serious consideration.

For example, consider the *ganzfeld* procedure (from German words meaning "entire field"). A "sender" is given a photo or film, selected at random from four possibilities, and a "receiver" in another room is asked to describe the sender's thoughts and images. Typically, the receiver wears half Ping-Pong balls over the eyes and listens to static noise through earphones to minimize normal stimuli that might overpower the presumably weaker extrasensory stimuli (Figure 2.4). Later a judge examines a transcript of what the receiver said and compares it to the four photos or films, determining which one it matches most closely. On the average it should match the target about one in four times. If a receiver "hits" more often than one in four, we can calculate the probability of accidentally doing that well. (ESP researchers, or parapsychologists, use a variety of other experimental procedures, but in each case the goal is to determine whether someone can gain more information than could be explained by chance without using his or her senses.)

Over the decades ESP researchers reported many apparent examples of telepathy or clairvoyance, none of which were replicable under well-controlled conditions. In the case of the ganzfeld studies, one review reported that 6 of the 10 laboratories using this method found positive results (Bem & Honorton, 1994); the authors suggested that here was, at last, a replicable phenomenon.

However, since then 14 studies from 7 laboratories failed to find evidence that the receiver chose the target stimulus any more often than one would expect

Photo by Dr. Elmar R. Gruber

FIGURE 2.4 In the ganzfeld procedure, a "receiver," who is deprived of most normal sensory information, tries to describe the photo or film that a "sender" is examining.

by chance (Milton & Wiseman, 1999). In short, the ganzfeld phenomenon, like other previous claims of ESP, is nonreplicable.

The lack of replicability is one major reason to be skeptical of ESP, but it is not the only one. The other is parsimony. If someone claims that a horse does mathematics or a person reads the minds of other people far away, we should search thoroughly for a simpler explanation and adopt a radically new explanation only if the evidence compels us. Even then we cannot accept a new explanation until someone specifies it clearly. Saying that some result demonstrates "an amazing ability that science cannot explain" is not a testable theory.

Would you like to test your own ability to find a parsimonious explanation for apparent mind reading? Go to

http://psychology.wadsworth.com/kalat_intro7e

Navigate to the student Web site, then to the Online Try It Yourself section, and click on Psychic Phenomenon.

IN CLOSING

Scientific Thinking in Psychology

What have we learned about science in general? Science does not deal with proof or certainty. All scientific conclusions are tentative and are subject to revision. The history of any scientific field contains examples of theories that were once widely accepted and were later revised. Nevertheless, this tentativeness does not imply a willingness to abandon well-established theories without excellent reasons.

Scientists always prefer the most parsimonious theory. Before they will accept any claim that requires a major new assumption, they insist that it be supported by replicable experiments that rule out simpler explanations and by a new theory that is clearly superior to the theory it replaces.

Summary

- *Uncertainty in science.* Neither deduction nor induction can give us completely certain information about the real world. Therefore, scientific conclusions are tentative, and one should always explain the reasons for a conclusion and not just the conclusion itself. (page 31)
- *Burden of proof.* In any dispute the side that should be capable of presenting clear evidence has the obligation to do so. (page 32)
- *Scientific approach to psychology.* Although psychology does not possess the same wealth of knowledge as other sciences, it shares with other scientific fields a commitment to scientific methods,

including a set of criteria for evaluating theories. (page 32)
- *Steps in a scientific study.* A scientific study goes through the following sequence of steps: hypothesis, method, results, interpretation. Because almost any study is subject to more than one possible interpretation, we base our conclusions on a pattern of results from many studies. The results of a given study are taken seriously only if other investigators can replicate them. (page 32)
- *Criteria for evaluating theories.* A good theory agrees with observations and leads to correct predictions of new information. All else being equal, scientists prefer the theory that relies on simpler assumptions. (page 34)
- *Skepticism about extrasensory perception.* Claims of the existence of extrasensory perception are scrutinized very cautiously because the evidence reported so far has been unreplicable and because the scientific approach includes a search for parsimonious explanations. (page 36)

Answers to Concept Checks

1. Induction is the process of inferring a general principle from a series of observations, such as "Every dropped object falls." Deduction is the process of deriving a conclusion from premises already given or assumed, such as "If A, then B. If B, then C. Therefore, if A, then C." (page 31)
2. To evaluate Nostradamus's predictions, we would need to ask someone to tell us precisely what his predictions mean before the events they supposedly predict had transpired. Then we would ask someone else to estimate the likelihood of those events. Eventually, we would compare the accuracy of the predictions to the advance estimates of their probability. (For example, if someone says that Nostradamus predicted violence in the Middle East next year, we need not be impressed if that prediction comes true.) (page 37)

Answers to Other Questions in the Module

A. Any magnet strong enough to pull the metal ball up the inclined plane would not release the ball when it reached the hole at the top. (page 35)
B. The prophecies of Nostradamus, as interpreted by Cheetham (1973), refer to the following: (1) the assassinations of John F. Kennedy and Robert F. Kennedy, (2) Polaris ballistic missiles shot from submarines, (3) Hitler's invasion of France, and (4) World War II. (page 37)

How do psychological researchers study processes that are difficult to define?

How do they design their research, and what special problems can arise?

How do researchers confront the ethical problems of conducting research using both human and nonhuman species?

A radio talk show once featured two psychologists as guests. The first argued that day care was bad for children because she had seen in her clinical practice many clients who had been left in day care as children and grew up to be sadly disturbed adults. The second psychologist, researcher Sandra Scarr (1997), pointed out that the clinician had no way of knowing about the children left in day care who became healthy, well-adjusted adults. (Well-adjusted people seldom consult a therapist.) Scarr then described the eight best research studies, concerning thousands of children in four countries, each of which found no evidence that day care produced any long-term undesirable consequences.

Which of these types of evidence strikes you as stronger? I hope you would conclude that day care is probably okay. To Scarr's dismay, however, the people who called in to the program seemed just as convinced by the anecdotes of disturbed people as by the extensive research studies, and several callers described anecdotes of their own.

Psychology, like any other field, can make progress only by distinguishing between strong evidence and weak evidence. Furthermore, psychological research can be tricky; sometimes even a careful investigation runs into unexpected difficulties. In this module we consider some of the special problems encountered when applying scientific methods to psychological phenomena.

General Principles of Psychological Research

The primary goal of this module is not to prepare you to conduct psychological research, but to help you be an intelligent interpreter of research. When you hear about some new study, you should be able to ask pertinent questions to decide how good the evidence is and what conclusion (if any) it justifies.

Operational Definitions

Suppose a physicist asks you to measure the effect of temperature on the length of an iron bar. You ask, "What do we *really mean* by temperature?" The physicist might reply, "Don't worry about it. Just measure it with this thermometer. Temperature *really is* the rate of motion of molecules, but for practical purposes what I mean by temperature is the reading on the thermometer."

We need the same strategy in psychology. If we want to measure the effect of hunger on students' ability to concentrate, we could spend hours attempting to define what hunger and concentration really are, or we could say, "Let's measure hunger by the hours since the last meal and concentration by the length of time that the student continues reading without stopping to do something else." By doing so we would be using an **operational definition,** *a definition that specifies the operations (or procedures) used to produce or measure something, a way to give it a numerical value.* An operational definition is not like a dictionary definition. You might object that "time since the last meal" is not what hunger really *is*. Of course not, but the reading on a thermometer is also not what temperature really is. An operational definition does not try to tell you what something is; it just tells you how to measure it. It enables us to get on with research.

Suppose that someone wants to investigate whether children who watch violence on television are likely to behave aggressively themselves. In this case the investigator needs operational definitions for *televised violence* and *aggressive behavior.* For example, the investigator might define *televised violence* as "the number of acts shown in which one person physically injures or attempts to injure another person." According to this definition, a 20-minute stalking scene would count as much as a quick attack. Just talking about a murder would not count. An unsuccessful attempt to injure someone would count, but verbal insults would not (because they would not inflict "physical" injury). This definition might not be the best, but at least it states how one investigator measures violence so that other people could try to replicate the results. If researchers using this definition cannot get consistent results, then they can try some other operational definition.

Similarly, the investigator needs an operational definition of *aggressive behavior.* To define it as "the number of murders or criminal assaults committed within 24 hours after watching a particular television program" would be an operational definition but not a practical one because (we hope!) almost everyone would have a score of zero. A better operational definition of *aggressive behavior* specifies more likely acts. For example, the experimenter might place a large plastic doll in front of a young child and record how often the child punches it.

Consider another example: What is love? Never mind what it *really is*. If we want to study it, we need to measure it, and therefore, we need an operational definition. One possibility would be "how many hours you are willing to spend with another person who asked you to stay nearby."

CONCEPT CHECK ☑

3. Which of the following is an operational definition of intelligence?
   a. the ability to comprehend relationships,
   b. a score on an IQ test,
   c. the ability to survive in the real world, or
   d. the product of the cerebral cortex of the brain.
4. What would you propose as an operational definition of friendliness? (Check your answers on page 55.)

Population Samples

The **population** is *the entire group of individuals to be considered.* Researchers generally wish to draw conclusions that apply to a large population, such as all 3-year-olds or all people with depression or even all human beings. Because it is not practical to examine everyone in the population, researchers study a small number of people, a *sample,* and assume that the results for the sample apply to the whole population.

For example, pollsters ask 1,000 or so voters which candidate they support and then project the probable result for the entire city, state, or country. Of course, the prediction can go wrong if some event changes many people's voting decision at the last moment or if the ballot is confusing.

In some cases almost any sample is satisfactory. For example, investigators interested in basic sensory processes need not worry too much about sampling problems. The eyes, ears, and other sense organs operate on the same principles for all people (with obvious exceptions of those with visual or hearing impairments). Similarly, many of the principles of learning, memory, hunger, thirst, sleep, and so forth are similar enough among all people that an investigator can do research with almost any group—students in an introductory psychology class, for example. We refer to *a group chosen because of its ease of study* as a **convenience sample.**

Even with fairly simple behaviors, however, we can add to our understanding by studying a more diverse sample. For example, we can establish general principles about sleep by studying college students, or even a group of laboratory rats, but those studies will not tell us how age affects sleep or whether people who are depressed have sleep problems. With other issues a convenience sample becomes increasingly inappropriate. For example, if you want to study how men's behavior differs from women's, it is important to examine multiple societies to see which differences are widespread and which ones are limited to certain societies (Wood & Eagly, 2002). Even within a society, to study a behavior that varies from one person to another, we need either a representative sample or a random sample of the population.

A **representative sample** *closely resembles the population in its percentage of males and females, Blacks and Whites, young and old, city dwellers and farmers, or whatever other characteristics are likely to affect the results.* To get a representative sample of the people in a given region, an investigator would first determine what percentage of the residents belong to each category and then select people to match those percentages. Of course, a sample that is representative in some regards might not be representative in other ways, such as religion or education.

In a **random sample,** *every individual in the population has an equal chance of being selected.* For example, to produce a random sample of Toronto residents, an investigator might start with a map of Toronto and select a certain number of city blocks at random, randomly select one house from each of those blocks, and then randomly choose one person from each of those households. Truly random sampling is difficult. Even after the difficult process of choosing a random sample, not everyone we choose will agree to participate. However, a random sample has one big advantage: The larger a random sample, the smaller the probability that its results differ substantially from the whole population.

What if we want to draw generalizations about all humans, not only those in one country? If you imagine trying to get a random or representative sample of all the people on the planet, you will quickly realize the impracticality. Nevertheless, although we cannot expect to study people from all cultures, it can be useful to study **cross-cultural samples,** *groups of people from at least two cultures,* preferably cultures that differ substantially. For example, consider questions about human nature: Do people learn facial expressions of emotions or are the expressions built-in? Is a financially prosperous society necessarily a happy society? Are people biologically predisposed to marriage? Cross-cultural data are critical for dealing with issues such as these. Table 2.1 reviews the major types of samples.

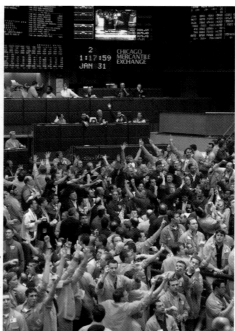

▌ A psychological researcher can test generalizations about human behavior by comparing people from different cultures.

Cross-cultural sampling is difficult, however (Matsumoto, 1994). Obvious problems include the expense, language barriers, and convincing members of another culture to answer personal questions and cooperate with unfamiliar kinds of tests. Also, imagine trying to compare "typical" behaviors between two cultures. There may be so much diversity within each that the comparison between them becomes almost meaningless.

 CONCEPT CHECK ☑

5. Suppose I compare the interests and abilities of male and female students at my university. If I find a consistent difference, can I assume that it represents a difference between men and women in general? (Obviously, the answer is no, or else I would not have asked the question.) Why not? (Check your answer on page 55.)

Eliminating the Influence of Expectations

People participating in psychological research almost always know they are being studied. Ethically, not much research can be done on people without getting their permission first. But once they know they are in an experiment, their behavior is influenced by what they expect and what they think the experimenters expect. The experimenters are human beings too, and how they record the data may reflect their own expectations. Good research requires finding ways to reduce the influence of all these expectations.

Experimenter Bias and Blind Studies

Experimenter bias is *the tendency of an experimenter (unintentionally, in most cases) to distort or misperceive the results of an experiment based on the expected outcome.* Imagine that you, as a psychological investigator, are testing the hypothesis that left-handed children are more creative than right-handed children. (I don't know why you would be testing this silly hypothesis, but suppose you are.) If the results support your hypothesis, you expect to be on your way to fame and success as a psychology researcher. Now you see a left-handed child do something and you are trying to decide whether it counts as "creative." You want to be fair. You don't want your hypothesis to influence your decision about whether to consider the act creative. Just try to ignore your hypothesis.

To overcome the potential source of error in an investigator's bias, psychologists prefer to use a **blind observer**—that is, *an observer who can record data*

TABLE 2.1 Types of Samples

Sample	Individuals Included	Advantages and Disadvantages
Convenience sample	Anyone who is available	Easiest to get, but results may not generalize to the whole population
Representative sample	Same percentage of male/female, White/Black, etc. as the whole population	Results probably similar to whole population, although sample may be representative in some ways and not others
Random sample	Everyone in population has same chance of being chosen	Difficult to get this kind of sample, but it is the best suited for generalizing to the whole population
Cross-cultural sample	People from different cultures	Difficulties include language barriers, cooperation problems, etc., but essential for studying many issues

without knowing what the researcher has predicted. For example, we might ask someone to record creative acts by a group of children without any hint that we are interested in the effects of handedness. Because blind observers do not know what hypothesis is being tested, they can record their observations more fairly.

Ideally, the experimenter will conceal the procedure from the participants as well. For example, suppose experimenters gave one group of children a pill that was supposed to increase their creativity. If those children knew the prediction, maybe they would act differently just because of their expectation. Or maybe the children not receiving the pill would be disappointed and therefore not try hard.

The best solution, therefore, is to give the drug to one group and a **placebo** (*a pill with no known pharmacological effects*) to another group, without telling the children which pill they are taking or what results the experimenter expects. The advantage of this kind of study is that any difference between the two groups cannot be due to their expectations.

In a **single-blind study,** *either the observer or the participants are unaware of which participants received which treatment* (Table 2.2). In a **double-blind study,** *both the observer and the participants are unaware.* Of course, the experimenter who organized the study would need to keep records of which participants received which procedure. (A study in which *everyone* loses track of the procedure is known jokingly as "triple blind.")

Demand Characteristics

Many people who know they are part of an experiment figure out, or think they have figured out, what is going to happen in the experiment. Sometimes those expectations produce big effects.

To illustrate, in some well-known studies on sensory deprivation that were popular in the 1950s, people were placed in an apparatus that minimizes vision, hearing, touch, and other sensory stimulation (Figure 2.5). Within hours many participants reported hallucinations, anxiety, and difficulty concentrating. Now suppose you have heard about these studies, and you agree to participate in an experiment described as a study of "meaning deprivation." The experimenter asks

FIGURE 2.5 In experiments on sensory deprivation, someone who is deprived of most sensory stimulation reports disorientation and sometimes hallucinations. But might these results depend partly on people's expectations of distorted experience?

you about your medical history and then asks you to sign a form agreeing not to sue if you have a bad experience. You see an "emergency tray" containing medicines and instruments, which the experimenter assures you is there "just as a precaution." Now you enter an "isolation chamber," which is actually an ordinary room with two chairs, a desk, a window, a mirror, a sandwich, and a glass of water. You are shown a microphone you can use to report any hallucinations or other distorted experiences and a "panic button" you can press for escape if the discomfort becomes unbearable.

Staying in a room by yourself for a few hours should hardly be a traumatic experience. But all the preparations suggested that terrible things were about to happen, so when this study was conducted, several students reported that they were hallucinating "multicolored spots on the wall," that "the walls of the room are starting to waver," or that "the objects on the desk are becoming animated and moving about." Some complained of anxiety, restlessness, difficulty concentrating, and spatial disorientation. One pressed the panic button to demand release (Orne & Scheibe, 1964).

Students in a control group were led to the same room, but they were not shown the "emergency tray," were not asked to sign a release form, and were given no other indication that anything unusual was likely to happen. They in fact reported no unusual experiences.

Sensory deprivation probably does influence behavior. But as this experiment illustrates, sometimes

TABLE 2.2 Single-Blind and Double-Blind Studies

Who is aware of which participants are in which group?		
	Experimenter Who Organized the Study	Observer	Participants
Single-blind	aware	unaware	aware
Single-blind	aware	aware	unaware
Double-blind	aware	unaware	unaware

what appears to be the influence of sensory deprivation (or any other influence) might really be the result of people's expectations. Martin Orne (1969) defined **demand characteristics** as *cues that tell a participant what is expected of him or her and what the experimenter hopes to find.* To minimize demand characteristics, many experimenters take elaborate steps to conceal the purpose of the experiment. A double-blind study serves the purpose: If two groups share the same expectations but behave differently because of some treatment, then the differences in behavior are presumably not the result of their expectations.

Observational Research Designs

The general principles that we just discussed apply to many kinds of research. Psychologists use various methods of investigation, and each has its own advantages and disadvantages. Most research in any field starts with description: What happens and under what circumstances? Let's first examine several kinds of observational studies. Later we shall consider experiments, which have a much greater ability to illuminate cause-and-effect relationships.

Naturalistic Observations

A **naturalistic observation** is *a careful examination of what happens under more or less natural conditions.* For example, biologist Jane Goodall (1971) spent years observing chimpanzees in the wild, recording their food habits, their social interactions, their gestures, and their whole way of life (Figure 2.6).

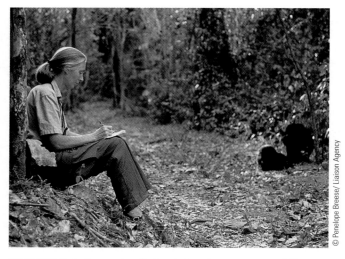

FIGURE 2.6 In a naturalistic study, observers record the behavior of people or other species in their natural settings. Here noted biologist Jane Goodall records her observations on chimpanzees. By patiently staying with the chimps, Goodall gradually won their trust and learned to recognize individual animals. In this manner she was able to add enormously to our understanding of chimpanzees' natural way of life.

Similarly, psychologists sometimes try to observe human behavior "as an outsider." A psychologist might observe what happens when two unacquainted people get on an elevator together: Do they stand close or far apart? Do they speak? Do they look toward each other or away? Does it matter whether they are both men, both women, or a man and a woman? Do Japanese people act the same as Brazilians?

Case Histories

Some fascinating conditions are rare. For example, some people have amazingly good or poor memories. People with Williams syndrome are mentally retarded in many ways but have impressive language abilities (Bellugi, Wang, & Jernigan, 1994). A psychologist who encounters someone with a rare condition may report a **case history**, *a thorough description of the person, including the person's abilities and disabilities, medical condition, life history, unusual experiences, or whatever else seems relevant.* It is, of course, possible to report a case history of any person, not just the unusual, but the unusual cases attract more attention. A case history is a kind of naturalistic observation; we distinguish it because it focuses on a single individual.

A case history can be extremely valuable, but it runs the risk of being just an anecdote. Unless other observers can interview and examine this special person or someone else who is very similar, we are at the mercy of the original investigator. Any individual investigator has some foibles or biases and will emphasize some points while omitting others. A good case history can be a guide for further research but by itself is usually not a basis for drawing any conclusion.

Surveys

A **survey** is *a study of the prevalence of certain beliefs, attitudes, or behaviors based on people's responses to specific questions.* Surveys are widespread in Western society. In fact no matter what your occupation, at some time you will probably conduct a survey of your employees, your customers, your students, your neighbors, or fellow members of an organization. You will also frequently read survey results in the newspaper or hear them reported on television. Thus, you should be aware of the difficulties of survey research and the ways in which the results can be misleading.

Sampling

Getting a random or representative sample is important in research, particularly with surveys. In 1936 the *Literary Digest* mailed 10 million postcards, asking people their choice for president of the United States. Of the 2 million responses, 57% preferred the Republican candidate, Alfred Landon.

Some odd survey results merely reflect the fact that people did not take the questions seriously or did not understand the questions. (© *Zits Partnership. Reprinted with special permission of King Features Syndicate.*)

Landon later lost by a wide margin to the Democratic candidate, Franklin Roosevelt. The problem was that the *Literary Digest* had selected names from the telephone book and automobile registration lists. In 1936, at the end of the Great Depression, few poor people (who were mostly Democrats) owned telephones or cars.

The Seriousness of Those Being Interviewed

When you answer a survey, do you carefully think about your answer to every question, or do you answer some of them impulsively? In one 1997 survey, only 45% of the respondents said they believed in the existence of intelligent life on other planets. However, a few questions later on the survey, 82% said they believed the U.S. government was "hiding evidence of intelligent life in space" (Emery, 1997). Did 37% of the people *really* think that the U.S. government is hiding evidence of something that doesn't exist? More likely, they were answering without much thought.

Here's another example: Which of the following programs would you most like to see on television reruns? Rate your choices from highest (1) to lowest (10). (Please fill in your answers, either in the text or on a separate sheet of paper, before continuing to the next paragraph.)

___South Park   ___Xena, Warrior Princess
___Thirtysomething   ___The X-Files
___Cheers   ___Teletubbies
___Seinfeld   ___Space Doctor
___I Love Lucy   ___Homicide

When I conducted this survey with my own students at North Carolina State University, nearly all did exactly what I asked—they gave every program a rating, including *Space Doctor*, a program that never existed. More than two thirds rated it either seventh, eighth, or ninth—it usually beat *Teletubbies*—but more than 10% rated it in the top five, and a few ranked it as their top choice. (This survey was inspired by an old *Candid Camera* episode in which interviewers asked people their opin-

ions of the nonexistent program *Space Doctor*, and recorded very confident, and therefore amusing, replies.)

Students who rated *Space Doctor* did nothing wrong, of course. I asked them to rank all of the programs and they did. The fault lies with anyone who interprets such survey results as if they represented informed opinions. This exercise demonstrates that people frequently express opinions even when they have no idea what they are talking about. (The same is true of political surveys.)

The Wording of the Questions

Let's start with a little demonstration. Please answer these two questions:

1. How often do you get headaches, backaches, toothaches, and muscle pains? (Circle one.)

| almost never | a few times a year | once or twice a month | more than twice a month |

2. Your college has just received a huge contribution, which it can spend any way it chooses. The administration has decided to poll students and faculty for their opinions. What percentage should it reserve for the following purposes? (Percentages should add to 100%.)
   ___% Improvements to buildings
   ___% All other purposes

Now cover up those answers and reply to these similar questions:

3. How often do you get headaches, backaches, toothaches, and muscle pains? (Circle one.)

| less than twice a month | less than once a day | about once a day | several times a day |

4. Your college has just received a huge contribution, which it can spend any way it chooses. The administration has decided to poll students and faculty for their opinions. What percentage should it reserve for the following purposes? (Percentages should add to 100%.)

   ___% Financial aid for needy students
   ___% Increased faculty salaries
   ___% Additions to the library
   ___% Better parking facilities
   ___% Improvements to buildings
   ___% Increased campus security
   ___% All other purposes

On questions such as these, most people answer differently based on the choices available (N. Schwarz, 1999). (You may not have if you thought about your answers to the first two questions while you were answering the next two.) On a question about aches and pains, most people pick an answer in the middle of whatever the scale is. So if "more than twice a month" is the highest answer, they report aches less than twice a month. But if "less than twice a month" is the lowest answer, they report aches more than that often. On the question about spending the money, most people feel obligated to devote some money to everything on the list, and many people divide it equally or almost equally among the choices. If "improvements to buildings" is the only option listed, the average student (in my classes) offers that option about 40% of the money. If it has to compete against five other choices (plus "all other purposes"), then building improvement gets only about 15% of the money. (Students generally vote the largest share to "financial aid for needy students.")

The point of all this is simple: The next time you hear that "38% of the people surveyed replied that . . . ," ask how the question was worded and what choices were offered. Even a slightly different wording could yield a different percentage.

Surveyor Biases

Sometimes a survey is sponsored by an organization that words the questions to encourage the answers they hope to receive. Here is an example: According to a 1993 survey, 92% of high school boys and 98% of high school girls claimed to have been victims of sexual harassment (Shogren, 1993). Shocking, isn't it? However, perhaps the designers of the survey *wanted* to show that sexual harassment is rampant. The survey defined sexual harassment by a long list of acts ranging from serious offenses (e.g., having someone rip your clothes off in public) to minor annoyances. For example, if you didn't like the sexual graffiti on the rest room wall, you could consider yourself sexually harassed. If you tried to make yourself look sexually attractive (as most teenagers do, right?) and then attracted a suggestive look from someone you *didn't* want to attract, that stare would count as sexual harassment. (It makes me wonder about those who said they *weren't* sexually harassed. They liked *all* the graffiti on the rest room walls? No one *ever* looked at them in a sexual way?) Sexual harassment is, of course, a serious problem, but a survey that combines major and minor offenses is likely to mislead.

Figure 2.7 shows the results for two surveys conducted on similar populations at about the same time. The issue is whether stem cells derived from aborted fetuses can be used in medical research. The question on the left was written by an organization opposed to abortion and stem cell research. The question on the right was worded by an organization that is either neutral or favorable to stem cell research (Public Agenda, 2001). As you can see, changes in the wording of the question led to very different distributions of answers.

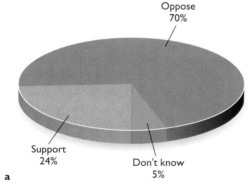

Stem cells are the basic cells from which all of a person's tissues and organs develop. Congress is considering whether to provide federal funding for experiments using stem cells from human embryos. The live embryos would be destroyed in their first week of development to obtain these cells. Do you support or oppose using your federal tax dollars for such experiments?

Oppose 70%
Support 24%
Don't know 5%

a

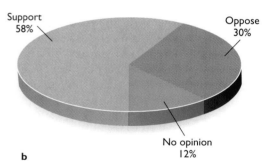

Sometimes fertility clinics produce extra fertilized eggs, also known as embryos, that are not implanted in a woman's womb. These extra embryos either are discarded, or couples can donate them for use in medical research called stem cell research. Some people support stem cell research, saying it's an important way to find treatments for many diseases. Other people oppose stem cell research, saying it's wrong to use any human embryos for research purposes. What about you — do you support or oppose stem cell research?

Support 58%
Oppose 30%
No opinion 12%

b

FIGURE 2.7 The question on the left, written by opponents of stem cell research, led most people to express opposition. The question on the right, worded differently, led most people to express support. *(a: From Public Agenda Copyright © 2004. Compiled from data from ICR/National Conference of Catholic Bishops, August 2001. Used with permission; b: From Public Agenda Copyright © 2004. Compiled from data from ABC News/Belletnet, June 2001. Used with permission.)*

Correlational Studies

Another type of research is a correlational study. A **correlation** is *a measure of the relationship between two variables.* (A variable is anything measurable that can differ among individuals. Height and weight are variables; so are years of education and reading speed.) A **correlational study** is *a procedure in which investigators measure the correlation between two variables without controlling either of them.* For example, investigators have observed correlations between people's height and weight, simply measuring them without attempting to influence anything. Similarly, one can find a correlation between scores on personality tests and how many friends someone has.

The Correlation Coefficient

Some correlations are stronger than others. For example, we would probably find a strong positive correlation between hours per week spent reading novels and scores on a vocabulary test. We would observe a lower correlation between hours spent reading novels and scores on a chemistry test.

The standard way to measure the strength of a correlation is known as a **correlation coefficient**, *a mathematical estimate of the relationship between two variables. The coefficient can range from +1 to –1.* A correlation coefficient indicates how accurately we can use a measurement of one variable to predict another. A correlation coefficient of +1, for example, means that as one variable increases, the other increases also. A correlation coefficient of –1 means that as one variable increases, the other decreases. A correlation of either +1 or –1 enables us to make perfect predictions of one variable from measurements of the other one. (In psychology you probably will never encounter a perfect +1 or –1 correlation coefficient.) A negative correlation is just as useful as a positive correlation and can indicate just as strong a relationship. For example, the more often people practice golf, the lower their golf scores, so golf practice is negatively correlated with scores.

A 0 correlation indicates that measurements of one variable have no linear relationship to measurements of the other variable. That is, as one variable goes up, the other does not consistently go up or down. A 0 or very low correlation can mean that two variables really are unrelated or that one or both of them were poorly measured. (If something is inaccurately measured, we can hardly expect it to predict anything else accurately.)

Figure 2.8 shows scatter plots for three correlations (real data). In each graph each dot represents one student in an introductory psychology class. The value for that student along the *y*-axis (vertical) in each case rep-

resents percent correct on the final exam. In the first graph, values along the *x*-axis (horizontal) represent scores on the first test in the course. Here the correlation is +.72, indicating a fairly strong relationship. That is, with a few exceptions, the students who did well on the first test also did well on the final, and those who did poorly on the first test also did poorly on the final. In the second graph, the *x*-axis represents times absent out of 38 class meetings. Here you see a correlation of –.44. This negative correlation indicates that, in general, those with more absences had lower final exam scores. The third graph in Figure 2.8 shows how the final exam scores related to the last three digits of each student's social security number. We would not expect any meaningful relationship, and the data confirm that expectation. The correlation is –.08, close to 0. The small negative correlation in the actual data represents a random fluctuation; if we examined the data for larger and larger populations of students, the correlation would no doubt come closer and closer to 0.

CONCEPT CHECK ☑

6. Identify each of these as a positive, zero, or negative correlation:
   a. The more crowded a neighborhood, the lower the income.
   b. People with high IQ scores are neither more nor less likely than other people to have high telephone numbers.
   c. People who awaken frequently during the night are more likely than other people to feel depressed.
7. Which indicates a stronger relationship between two variables, a +.50 correlation or a –.75 correlation?
8. The correlation between students' grades and their scores on a self-esteem questionnaire is very low, not much above 0. Why might that be? (Check your answers on page 55.)

FIGURE 2.8 Scatter plots for three correlations. (a) Scores on first test and scores on final exam (correlation = +.72). (b) Times absent and scores on final exam (correlation = –.44). (c) Last three digits of social security number and scores on final exam (correlation = –.08). (This kind of graph is called a scatter plot. Each dot represents the measurements of two variables for one person.)

Illusory Correlations

Sometimes with unsystematic observations we "see" a correlation that doesn't really exist. For example, many parents (and others) believe that consuming sugar makes children hyperactive or hyperactive children even more hyperactive. However, extensive research has found little effect of sugar on activity levels, and some studies even find that sugar *calms* behavior (Milich, Wolraich, & Lindgren, 1986; Wolraich et al., 1994). How, then, do we handle reports that sugar makes children hyperactive? Researchers watched two sets of mothers with their 5- to 7-year-old sons after telling one group that they had given the sons sugar and the other that they had given the sons a placebo. In fact they had given both a placebo. The mothers who *thought* their sons had been given sugar rated their sons as being hyperactive during the observation period, whereas the other mothers did not (Hoover & Milich, 1994). That is, people see what they expect to see.

When people expect to see a connection between two events (e.g., sugar and activity levels), they remember the cases that support the connection and disregard the exceptions, thus perceiving an **illusory correlation,** *an apparent relationship based on casual observations of unrelated or weakly related events.*

As another example of an illusory correlation, consider the widely held belief that a full moon affects human behavior. For hundreds of years, many people have believed that crime and various kinds of mental disturbance are more common under a full moon than at other times. In fact the term *lunacy* (from the Latin word *luna,* meaning "moon") originally meant mental illness caused by the full moon. Some police officers claim that they receive more calls on nights with a full moon, and some hospital workers say they have more emergency cases on such nights.

These reports, however, are based on what people recall rather than on carefully analyzed data. Careful reviews of the data have concluded that the phase of the moon has no measurable effect on crime or mental illness (Raison, Klein, & Steckler, 1999; Rotton & Kelly, 1985). Why, then, does this belief persist? It may have been true long ago, before the onset of arti-

People's expectations and faulty memories produce illusory correlations, such as between the full moon and abnormal behavior.

© Herman Eisenbeis/ Photo Researchers Inc.

ficial lights. But once the belief became widespread, it could persist without being true. People remember the occasions that fit the belief and disregard those that do not.

Correlation and Causation

A correlation tells us whether two variables are related to each other and, if so, how strongly. It does not tell us *why* they are related. If two variables—let's call them A and B—are positively correlated, it could be that A causes B, B causes A, or some third variable, C, causes both of them. Therefore, a correlational study does not justify a cause-and-effect conclusion.[1]

For example, there is a strong positive correlation between the number of books people own about chess and how good they are at playing chess. Does owning chess books cause someone to become a good chess player? Obviously not. Does being a good chess player cause someone to buy chess books? Not exactly. Rather, people who start to like chess usually buy chess books, which help them improve their game. As they get better, they become even more interested, buy more books, and play the game even better. But neither the chess books nor the skill causes the other.

"Then what good is a correlation?" you might ask. The simplest answer is that correlations help us make useful predictions. For example, if your friend has just challenged you to a game of chess, you can quickly scan your friend's bookshelves and estimate your chances of winning.

Here are three more examples to illustrate why we cannot draw conclusions regarding cause and effect from correlational data (see also Figure 2.9):

- *Unmarried men are more likely than married men to spend time in a mental hospital or prison.* That is, for men marriage is negatively correlated with mental illness and criminal activity. Does the corre-

[1] Exceptions to this rule arise under special circumstances. For example, you probably find a correlation between sunny weather and feeling a good mood, cloudy weather and a bad mood. It's pretty obvious that the weather influences your mood; your mood doesn't change the weather. However, in most cases we can imagine alternative explanations for a correlation and therefore cannot draw a cause-and-effect conclusion.

lation mean that marriage leads to mental health and good social adjustment? Or does it mean that the men in mental hospitals and prisons are unlikely to marry? (The second conclusion is certainly true; the first may be also.)

- *According to one study, people who sleep about 7 hours a night are less likely to die within the next few years than those who sleep either more or less* (Kripke, Garfinkel, Wingard, Klauber, & Marler, 2002). It's easy to believe that sleep deprivation could impair your health, but should we really conclude (as some people did from this evidence) that sleeping too much can also impair your health? Or can we imagine some other plausible explanation for this correlation? How about this: People who already have cancer or other life-threatening illnesses tend to sleep more than healthy people. So perhaps illness causes extra sleep, rather than extra sleep causing illness. Or perhaps advancing age increases the probability of both illness and extra sleep. (The study included people ranging from young adulthood through age 101!)

- *On the average, people who use large amounts of sunscreen are more likely than others to get skin cancer.* Does this correlation indicate that sunscreen causes skin cancer? Conceivably, but the more likely explanation is that the people who use the most sunscreen are those who spend the most time in the sun, and it is sun exposure that causes skin cancer (as well as increasing the use of sunscreen).

To repeat: A correlation does not tell us about causation. To determine causation an investigator needs to manipulate one of the variables directly through a research design known as an *experiment*. When an investigator manipulates one variable and then observes corresponding changes in another variable, a conclusion about causation can be justified, presuming, of course, that the experiment is well designed.

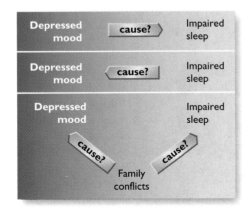

FIGURE 2.9 A strong correlation between depression and impaired sleep does not tell us whether depression interferes with sleep, poor sleep leads to depression, or whether another problem leads to both depression and sleep problems.

CONCEPT CHECK ✓

9. Suppose we find a .8 correlation between students' reported interest in psychology and their grades on a psychology test. What conclusion can we draw? (Check your answer on page 55.)

Experiments

An **experiment** is *a study in which the investigator manipulates at least one variable while measuring at least one other variable.* A before-and-after study can be an experiment, but it is generally not the best kind. Consider this example: Researchers give a rat a saccharin-flavored solution to drink for 15 minutes. They remove the solution, wait 30 minutes, and then inject the rat with a chemical that causes nausea. The next day they offer it the saccharin solution again and note that the rat does not drink it. Evidently, the rat blamed its illness on what it drank and now avoids that taste. Right? Well, maybe, but maybe the rat is still so sick the next day that it can't drink. There have been better experiments on this question, as we shall see in Chapter 6, and rats (and others) really do avoid tastes that are followed by illness. The point here is that a before-and-after study is difficult to interpret; behavior can change over time for reasons other than the one we wish to study.

A better design is to compare two groups: The investigator assembles a suitable sample of people or animals, divides them randomly into two groups, and then conducts some procedure with one group (the *experimental group*) and not the other (the *control group*). Someone, preferably a blind observer, records the behavior of the two groups. If the behavior of the two groups differs in some consistent way, then the difference is probably the result of the experimental procedure. Table 2.3 contrasts experiments with observational studies.

Sometimes people go astray in their conclusions if they forget about the need for a control group or if they don't use an appropriate control group. Sometimes on March 21 or September 21, you will hear someone say that because it is the equinox (when the length of the day equals that of the night), it is possible to balance an egg on its end, as in Figure 2.10. People will try and some will succeed, to their amazement. Should we conclude that something is special about the equinox? Hardly. The "research" is incomplete unless we also try balancing an egg on other days of the year. (It works just as well at any time.)

I shall describe psychological experiments and some of their special difficulties. To illustrate let's use

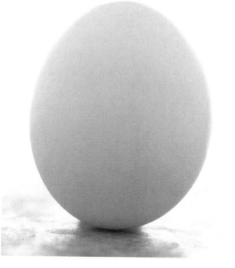

FIGURE 2.10 Can you get an egg to balance on a day of the equinox? Maybe. But it's equally possible on other days.

FoodPix/Getty Images

TABLE 2.3 Comparison of Five Methods of Research

Observational Studies	
Case Study	Detailed description of single individual; suitable for studying rare conditions.
Naturalistic Observation	Description of behavior under natural conditions.
Survey	Study of attitudes, beliefs, or behaviors based on answers to questions.
Correlation	Description of the relationship between two variables that the investigator measures but does not control; determines whether two variables are closely related but does not address questions of cause and effect.

Experiment	
	Determination of the effect of a variable controlled by the investigator on some other variable that is measured; the only method that can inform us about cause and effect.

the example of experiments conducted to determine whether watching violent television programs leads to an increase in aggressive behavior.

Independent Variables and Dependent Variables

An experiment is an attempt to measure how changes in one variable affect one or more other variables. The **independent variable** is *the item that an experimenter changes or controls—for example, the amount of violent television that people are permitted to watch.* (It could be measured in terms of hours of programs, number of violent acts, or any other operational definition.) *The **dependent variable** is the item that an experimenter measures to determine how it was affected.* In our example the experimenter measures the amount of aggressive behavior that the participants exhibit. If the procedure causes different groups to behave differently, you can think of the independent variable as the cause and the dependent variable as the effect (see Figure 2.11).

Experimental Group, Control Group, and Random Assignment

An **experimental group** *receives the treatment that an experiment is designed to test.* In a study of the effects of violence on aggressive behavior, the ex-

FIGURE 2.11 An experimenter manipulates the independent variable (in this case the programs people watch) so that two or more groups experience different treatments. Then the experimenter measures the dependent variable (in this case pulse rate) to see how the independent variable affected it.

perimental group would watch televised violence. The **control group** is *a set of individuals treated in the same way as the experimental group except for the procedure that the experiment is designed to test.* People in the control group would watch only nonviolent television programs (Figure 2.12). (The type of television program is the independent variable; the resulting behavior is the dependent variable.)

In principle this procedure sounds easy, although difficulties arise in practice. For example, if we are studying a group of teenagers with a history of violent behavior, it may be difficult to find nonviolent programs that hold their attention. As their attention wanders, those who were watching the nonviolent programs start picking fights with one another, and suddenly, the results of the experiment look very odd indeed.

Suppose we conduct a study inviting young people to watch either violent or nonviolent programs, and then we discover that those who watched violent programs act more aggressively. What conclusion could we draw? None, of course. Those who chose to watch violence were probably different from those who chose the nonviolent programs. Any good experiment has **random assignment** of participants to groups: *The experimenter uses a chance procedure, such as drawing names out of a hat, to make sure that every participant has the same probability as any other participant of being assigned to a given group.*

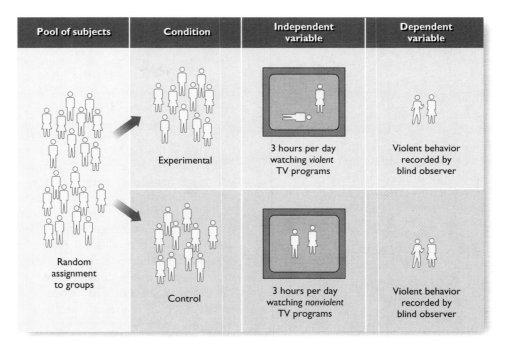

Pool of subjects	Condition	Independent variable	Dependent variable

FIGURE 2.12 Once researchers decide on the hypothesis they want to test, they must design the experiment. These procedures test the effects of watching televised violence. An appropriate, accurate method of measurement is essential.

CONCEPT CHECK ✓

10. You read (p. 49) a description of an unsatisfactory before-and-after study of rats getting sick after drinking a saccharin solution. Propose a better experiment using an experimental group and a control group.

11. Which of the following would an experimenter try to minimize or avoid?
    falsifiability, independent variables, dependent variables, blind observers, demand characteristics.

12. An instructor wants to find out whether the frequency of testing in an introductory psychology class has any effect on students' final exam performance. The instructor gives weekly tests in one class, just three tests in a second class, and only a single midterm exam in the third class. All three classes are given the same final exam, and the instructor then compares their performances. Identify the independent variable and the dependent variable. (Check your answers on page 55.)

CRITICAL THINKING:
WHAT'S THE EVIDENCE?
Effects of Watching Violence on Aggressive Behavior

We have talked in general terms about how to measure the effects of watching violent programs. The controversy is an old one. In the 1930s and 1940s, people worried about whether listening to crime programs on the radio was harmful to young people (Dennis, 1998), and way back in the time of Plato and Aristotle, people worried whether it was dangerous for children to listen to certain kinds of storytellers (Murray, 1998). Let's consider some research in detail. The first is an experiment; the second is an analysis of correlations.

FIRST STUDY (Zillman & Weaver, 1999)

Hypothesis People who have watched violent films will engage in more hostile behaviors than people who watched nonviolent films.

Method The study had two parts: (a) first watching violent or nonviolent films and (b) being "provoked" and then given an opportunity to retaliate in a hostile (though not violent) way.

Film-watching: Ninety-three college students agreed to be randomly assigned to watch different kinds of films on Monday through Thursday evenings. One group was asked to watch four extremely violent films; the other group watched films that had been about equally popular at the theaters but which included nothing more violent than occasional shouting or shoving.

Provocation with opportunity to retaliate: On Friday evening the students all participated in what appeared to them an unrelated study: A graduate-student researcher gave them a series of face photographs and asked them to identify the emotions expressed in each. The faces were in fact ambiguous, so none of the students could be sure of their answers. After they filled out the answer booklets, the researcher left, marked the booklets, and returned them with written comments. Half of the students were told they had done well; the others were told their performance had been "terrible." The researcher further wrote, "I certainly wouldn't hire you." Later, after the experimenter had left, someone else asked the students to evaluate this graduate student. In particular they were to indicate whether they thought this student should receive financial support while in graduate school on a scale from 0 (not at all deserving) to 10 (extremely deserving).

Results To no one's great surprise, students who had been told their performance was "terrible" did not like the experimenter and gave at best a mediocre rating to how well he or she deserved financial support. The more interesting result is that students who had spent the previous four nights watching violent films gave lower ratings than those who watched nonviolent films:

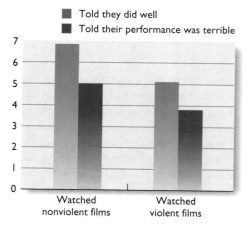

Interpretation Watching violence made people more likely to behave in a hostile manner (giving someone a low rating for getting financial support). This is just one of many experiments that have shown some increase in hostility after watching violent films. What makes this study particularly interesting is that the hostile act occurred a day after the last violent film. That is, the effect is not extremely brief; it can last at least one day and presumably longer.

Any study has its limitations. One limitation of this study is that the "hostile" response was just giving someone a low rating on worthiness for financial support. That is a long way from serious physical attacks. A second limitation is that the study provided only four evenings of violent films, by no means an insignificant amount but small compared to watching violence frequently over many years. Of course, no experimenter could control people's viewing habits for months or years. The best way to get around the limitations of this experiment is to try other research methods. Next is a very different kind of study.

SECOND STUDY (Huesmann, Moise-Titus, Podolski, & Eron, 2003)

Hypothesis Children who watch violent programs frequently, beginning when they are young, will become more violent over time, in contrast to similar children who watch less violence.

Method In 1977 researchers collected information from more than 500 children, ages 6 to 9, both male and female, concerning how frequently they watched various television programs. Other people rated the various programs on a scale from "not violent" to "very violent." For example, certain police dramas were rated very violent, as were *Roadrunner* cartoons. Researchers also got ratings of these children's aggressive behaviors by interviewing other children in their class. Fifteen to eighteen years later, the researchers reinterviewed more than 80% of these young people, asking about their current television watching and their current aggressive behaviors. They also checked police arrest records.

Results The amount of violent television watching in childhood correlated about .2 with measures of adult aggressive behavior. That is not a very high correlation, but the correlation between child violent television watching and adult aggression was *higher* than the correlation between child violent television and child aggressive behavior or adult violent television and adult aggressive behavior.

Interpretation Apparently, watching violent television predicts future violence more than it depends on current violent behavior. Another study with a similar design obtained similar results: The amount of violence that people watched during adolescence predicted the amount of violent behavior in adulthood, 17 years later, independently of the adolescents' current aggressive behavior (J. G. Johnson, Cohen, Smailes, Kasen, & Brook, 2002).

The combined conclusion from this study and the first one is firmer than we could draw from either study alone. Watching televised violence does not *cause* people to be violent; obviously, many other influences operate and some people are more easily influenced than others. Still, it appears that extensive viewing of violence tends to increase the likelihood of aggressive behavior.

Ethical Considerations in Research

In any experiment psychologists manipulate a variable to determine how it affects behavior. Perhaps you object to the idea of someone trying to alter your behavior. If so, consider that every time you talk to people you are trying to alter their behavior at least slightly. Most experiments in psychology are no more disruptive than a conversation. Still, some experiments do raise difficult issues, and researchers are bound by both law and conscience to treat their research participants ethically.

Ethical Concerns with Humans

In this chapter I discussed experiments on the effects of televised violence. If psychologists believed that watching violent programs might really transform viewers into murderers, then it would be unethical to conduct experiments to find out for sure. It would also be unethical to perform procedures likely to cause significant pain or embarrassment or any other harmful effects.

The central ethical principle is that experiments should include only procedures that people would agree to experience. Therefore, psychologists ask prospective participants to give their **informed consent** before proceeding, *a statement that they have been told what to expect and that they agree to continue.* When experimenters post a sign-up sheet asking for volunteers, they give at least a brief statement of what will occur. At the start of the experiment itself, they provide still more detail. In most studies the procedures are innocuous, such as watching a computer screen and pressing a button when a certain pattern appears or filling out a questionnaire. Occasionally, however, the procedure includes something that some people would not wish to do, such as drinking concentrated sugar water. Participants are told they have the right to quit immediately or to quit at any point in the study if they find it too disagreeable.

Most of the time, getting people's informed consent means that the study is safe and ethical. Problems do arise, however, with children, people who are mentally retarded, or anyone else who does not understand the instructions (Bonnie, 1997). Individuals with severe depression pose a special problem (Elliott, 1997): Some seem to have lost all interest in protecting their own welfare. In such cases researchers either consult the person's guardian or nearest relative or simply decide not to proceed.

Experiments conducted at a college or at any other reputable institution must first be approved by an institutional review board. Such a committee judges whether the proposed studies include procedures for informed consent and whether they safeguard each participant's confidentiality. The committee also tries to prevent risky procedures. For example, the committee would not approve a proposal to use large doses of cocaine, regardless of how many people were ready to give their informed consent.

The committee also judges procedures in which investigators want to deceive participants temporarily to hide the purpose of the study. For example, suppose researchers want to test whether it becomes more difficult to persuade people when they know someone is trying to persuade them. The researchers want to use two groups of people—one group that has been informed of the upcoming persuasion and one that does not know what to expect. The second group might even be misinformed about the intent of the study. If the researchers fully informed people about the procedures, the experiment would lose its whole point. Most people see little objection to this temporary deception, but the institutional committee would have to review the procedures and give its permission before the study could proceed.

Finally, the American Psychological Association, or APA (1982), publishes a booklet detailing the proper ethical treatment of volunteers in experiments. Any member who disregards these principles may be censured or expelled from membership in the APA.

Ethical Concerns with Nonhumans

Some psychological research deals with nonhuman animals, especially in research on basic processes such as how the eyes and ears work, the functions of sleep, and the effects of rewards on the rates of behaviors (Figure 2.13). Researchers are especially likely to turn to nonhumans if they want to control aspects of life that people will not let them control (e.g., who mates with whom), if they want to study behavior continuously over months or years (longer than people are willing to participate), or if the research poses health risks. Animal research has long been essential for preliminary testing of most new drugs, surgical procedures, and methods of relieving pain. People with untreatable illnesses argue that they have the right "to hope for cures or relief from suffering through research using animals" (Feeney, 1987). Even outside the medical field, much of our current knowledge in psychology either began with animal research or made use of animal studies at some point.

Nevertheless, some people oppose much or all animal research. Animals, after all, cannot give informed consent. Some animal rights supporters insist that animals should have the same rights as humans, that keeping animals (even pets) in cages is nothing short of slavery, and that killing any animal is murder. Others oppose some kinds of research but are willing to compromise about others.

Psychologists too vary in their attitudes. Most support at least some kinds of animal research, but almost all would draw a line somewhere separating acceptable from unacceptable research (Plous, 1996). Naturally, different psychologists draw that line at different places.

In this debate, as in so many other political controversies, one common tactic is for each side to crit-

FIGURE 2.13 One example of animal research: A mirror mounted on a young owl's head enables investigators to track the owl's head movements and thereby to discover how it localizes sounds with one ear plugged. The findings may help researchers understand how blind people use their hearing to compensate for visual loss.

icize the most extreme actions of its opponents. For example, animal rights advocates point to studies that exposed monkeys or puppies to painful procedures that seem difficult to justify.

On the other hand, researchers point to protesters who have distorted facts, vandalized laboratories, and even threatened to kill researchers and their children—and in one case, oddly enough, threatened to kill the researcher's pet dog. Some protesters have even stated that they would oppose the use of any AIDS medication if its discovery came from research with animals. Unfortunately, when both sides concentrate on criticizing their most extreme opponents, they trivialize the real issues and make points of agreement harder to find.

One careful study by a relatively unbiased outsider concluded that the truth is messy: Some research is painful to the animals *and* nevertheless valuable for advancing our understanding of important scientific or medical issues in ways that we could not otherwise achieve (Blum, 1994). In other words we cannot remain innocent of harming animals and still make the scientific and medical progress that we value.

If we cannot simply choose between progress and protecting animals, we must find a compromise. Professional organizations such as the Neuroscience Society and the American Psychological Association publish guidelines for the proper use of animals in research. Colleges and other research institutions maintain laboratory animal care committees to ensure that laboratory animals are treated humanely, that their pain and discomfort are kept to a minimum, and that experimenters consider alternatives before they impose potentially painful procedures on animals. Be-

cause such committees must deal with competing values, their decisions are never beyond dispute.

How can we determine in advance whether the value of the expected experimental results (which are hard to predict) will outweigh the pain the animals will endure (which is hard to measure)? As is so often the case with ethical decisions, reasonable arguments can be raised on both sides of the question, and no compromise is fully satisfactory.

> ### IN CLOSING
> ## *Psychological Research*

I mentioned at the beginning of this chapter that most scientists avoid the word *prove*. Psychologists certainly do. (The joke is that psychology courses don't have true–false tests, just maybe–perhaps tests.) The most complex, and therefore most interesting, aspects of human behavior are products of genetics, a lifetime of experiences, and countless current influences. Given the practical and ethical limitations, it might seem that the whole idea of psychological research is doomed from the start. However, largely because of these difficulties, many psychologists have been highly inventive in designing complex ways to isolate the effects of certain influences. A single study rarely answers a question decisively, but many studies can converge to increase our total understanding.

Summary

- *Operational definitions.* For many purposes psychologists prefer operational definitions, which state how to measure a given phenomenon or how to produce it. (page 40)

- *Sampling.* Psychologists hope to draw conclusions that apply to a large population and not just to the small sample they have studied, so they try to select a sample that resembles the total population. They may select either a representative sample or a random sample. To apply the results to people worldwide, they need a cross-cultural sample. (page 41)

- *Experimenter bias and blind observers.* An experimenter's expectations can influence the interpretations of behavior and the recording of data. To ensure objectivity investigators use blind observers, who do not know what results are expected. In a double-blind study, neither the observer nor the participants know the researcher's predictions. Researchers try to minimize the effects of demand characteristics, which are cues that tell participants what the experimenter expects them to do. (page 42)

- *Naturalistic observations.* Naturalistic observations provide descriptions of humans or other species under natural conditions. (page 44)

- *Case histories.* A case history is a detailed research study of a single individual, generally someone with unusual characteristics. (page 44)
- *Surveys.* A survey is a report of people's answers on a questionnaire. It is easy to conduct a survey and, unfortunately, very easy to conduct one badly. (page 44)
- *Correlations.* A correlational study is a study of the relationship between variables that are outside the investigator's control. The strength of this relationship is measured by a correlation coefficient, which ranges from 0 (no relationship) to plus or minus 1 (a perfect relationship). (page 46)
- *Illusory correlations.* Beware of illusory correlations—relationships that people think they observe between variables after mere casual observation. (page 48)
- *Inferring causation.* A correlational study cannot uncover cause-and-effect relationships, but an experiment can. (page 48)
- *Experiments.* Experiments are studies in which the investigator manipulates one variable to determine its effect on another variable. The manipulated variable is the independent variable. Changes in the independent variable may lead to changes in the dependent variable, the one the experimenter measures. (page 49)
- *Random assignment.* An experimenter should randomly assign individuals to form experimental and control groups. That is, all individuals should have an equal probability of being chosen for the experimental group. (page 50)
- *Ethics of experimentation.* Experimentation on either humans or animals raises ethical questions. Psychologists try to minimize risk to their participants, but they cannot avoid making difficult ethical decisions. (page 52)

Answers to Concept Checks

3. A score on an IQ test is an operational definition of intelligence. (Whether it is a particularly *good* operational definition is a different question.) None of the other definitions tells us how to measure or produce intelligence. (page 41)
4. Many operational definitions are possible for "friendliness," such as "the number of people that someone speaks to within 24 hours" or "the percentage of people one smiles at while walking down the street." You might think of a better operational definition. Remember that an operational definition specifies a clear method of measurement. (page 41)

5. Clearly not. It is unlikely that the men at a given college are typical of men in general or that the women are typical of women in general. Moreover, at some colleges the men are atypical in some respects and the women atypical in different ways. (page 42)
6. **a.** Negative correlation between crowdedness and income. **b.** Zero correlation between telephone scores and IQ. **c.** Positive correlation between awakenings and depression. (page 47)
7. The −.75 correlation indicates a stronger relationship—that is, a greater accuracy of predicting one variable based on measurements of the other. A negative correlation is just as useful as a positive one. (page 47)
8. One possibility is that happiness is unrelated to self-esteem. Another possibility is that we have used an inaccurate measurement of either self-esteem or happiness or both. If anything is measured poorly, it cannot correlate strongly with anything else. (page 47)
9. We can conclude only that if we know either someone's interest level or test score, we can predict the other with reasonably high accuracy. We *cannot* conclude that an interest in psychology will help someone learn the material or that doing well on psychology tests increases someone's interest in the material. Either conclusion might be true, of course, but neither conclusion follows from these results. A correlational study cannot demonstrate a cause-and-effect relationship. (page 49)
10. Here's one possibility: The experimental group of rats drinks saccharin and later is made sick. The control group drinks nothing but is made sick. Perhaps another control group drinks saccharin and is not made sick. The next day all groups are offered a choice between saccharin and water. If the first group learned an association between saccharin and illness, it should show the lowest saccharin preference. (page 51)
11. Of these, only demand characteristics are to be avoided. If you did not remember that falsifiability is a good feature of a theory, check page 31. Every experiment must have at least one independent variable (what the experimenter controls) and at least one dependent variable (what the experimenter measures). However, a study with many independent or dependent variables might become too complicated. Blind observers provide an advantage. (page 51)
12. The independent variable is the frequency of tests during the semester. The dependent variable is the students' performance on the final exam. (page 51)

Measuring and Analyzing Results

How can the "average" results in a study be described?

How can we describe the variations among individuals?

How can a researcher determine whether the results represent something more than just chance fluctuations?

Some years ago a television program about the alleged dangers of playing the game Dungeons and Dragons reported 28 known cases of D&D players who had committed suicide. Alarming, right?

Not necessarily. At that time at least 3 million young people played the game regularly. The reported suicide rate among D&D players—28 per 3 million—was considerably *less* than the suicide rate among teenagers in general.

So do these results mean that playing D&D *prevents* suicide? Hardly. The 28 reported cases are probably an incomplete count of all suicides by D&D players. Besides, no matter what the correlation between playing D&D and committing suicide, it could not tell us about cause and effect. Maybe the kinds of young people who play D&D are simply different from those who do not.

Then what conclusion should we draw from these data? *None.* When the data are incomplete or the method flawed, no conclusion follows. (Even when the data are acceptable, people sometimes present them in a confusing or misleading manner, as shown in Figure 2.14.)

Let's consider some proper ways of analyzing and interpreting results.

Descriptive Statistics

To explain the meaning of a study, an investigator must summarize the results in an orderly fashion. If a researcher observes 100 people, we do not want all the details about every person. We want the general trends or averages. We might also want to know whether most people were similar to the average or whether they varied a great deal. An investigator presents the answers to those questions through **descriptive statistics,** which are *mathematical summaries of results,* such as measures of the average and the amount of variation. The correlation coefficient, discussed earlier in this chapter, is an example of a descriptive statistic.

Measures of the Central Score

There are three ways of representing the central score: mean, median, and mode. The **mean** is *the sum of all the scores divided by the total number of scores.* Generally, when people say "average," they refer to the mean. For example, the mean of 2, 10, and 3 is 5 (15 ÷ 3). The mean is especially useful if the scores approximate the **normal distribution** (or normal curve), *a symmetrical frequency of scores clustered around the mean.* A normal distribution is often described as a bell-shaped curve. For example, if we measure how long it takes various students to memorize a poem, these times will probably follow a pattern similar to the normal distribution.

a   b

FIGURE 2.14 Statistics can be misleading: Both graphs present the same data, an increase from 20 to 22 over 1 year's time. But graph (b) makes that increase look more dramatic by ranging only from 20 to 22 (rather than from 0 to 22). *(After Huff, 1954)*

The mean can be misleading, however, if the distribution is far from normal. For example, one survey asked people how many sex partners they hoped to have, ideally, over the next 30 years. The mean for women was 2.8 and the mean for men was 64.3 (L. C. Miller & Fishkin, 1997). But those means are extremely misleading. Almost two thirds of women and about half of men replied "1." That is, they wanted a loving relationship with just one partner. Most of the others said they wanted more than one, but still just a few partners during their lifetime; however, a small number of men said they hoped for hundreds, or thousands, or tens of thousands of partners.

I have repeated this survey with my own classes, and I find that some men even use scientific notation to express huge numbers, such as 3.5×10^5. Others give nonnumerical answers such as "as many as possible" or "all of them" (whatever that means). If we take many, many small numbers (e.g., 1) and only a couple of huge numbers (e.g., 3.5×10^5), the mean can be misleading.

When the population distribution is extremely abnormal, we can better represent the typical individual with the median instead of the mean. To determine the **median**, *we arrange all the scores in order from the highest score to the lowest score. The middle score is the median.* For example, for the set of scores 2, 10, and 3, the median is 3. For the set of scores 1, 1, 1, and 3.5×10^5, the median is 1. In short, extreme scores greatly affect the mean but not the median.

The third way to represent the central score is the **mode**, *the score that occurs most frequently.* For example, in the distribution of scores 2, 2, 3, 4, and 10, the mode is 2. The mode is seldom useful except under special circumstances. Suppose we asked college students how much they study and gathered the results shown in Figure 2.15. Half of the students at this college study a great deal, and half study very little. The mean for this distribution is 4.28 hours per day, a very misleading number because all the students study either much more or much less than that. The median is no better as a representation of these results: Because we have an even number of students, there is no middle score. We could take a figure midway between the two scores nearest the middle, but in this case those scores are 2 and 7, so we would compute a median of 4.5, again misleading. A distribution like this is called a *bimodal distribution* (one with two common scores); the researcher might simply describe the two modes and not even mention the mean or the median.

To summarize: The mean is what most people intend when they say "average." It is the sum of the scores divided by the number of scores. The median is the middle score after the scores are ranked from highest to lowest. The mode is the most common score (Figure 2.16).

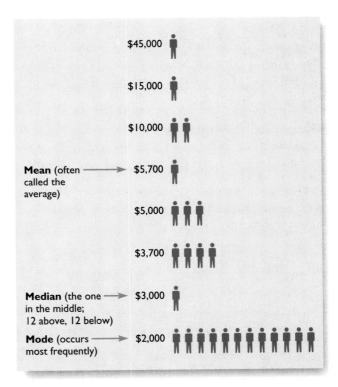

FIGURE 2.16 The monthly salaries of the 25 employees of company X, showing the mean, median, and mode. *(After Huff, 1954)*

FIGURE 2.15 Results of an imaginary survey of study habits at one college. This college apparently has two groups of students—those who study much and those who study little. In this case both the mean and the median are misleading. This distribution is bimodal; its two modes are 0 and 8.

CONCEPT CHECK ✓

13. a. For the following distribution of scores, determine the mean, the median, and the mode: 5, 2, 2, 2, 8, 3, 1, 6, 7.
    b. Determine the mean, median, and mode for this distribution: 5, 2, 2, 2, 35, 3, 1, 6, 7. (Check your answers on page 61.)

Measures of Variation

Figure 2.17 shows two distributions of test scores. Suppose that these represent scores on two introductory psychology tests. Both tests have the same mean, 70, but different distributions. If you had a score of 80, you would beat only 75% of the other students on the first test, but with the same score, you would beat 95% on the second test.

To describe the difference between Figure 2.17a and b, we need a measurement of the variation (or spread) around the mean. The simplest such measurement is the **range** of a distribution, *a statement of the highest and lowest scores.* The range in Figure 2.17a is 38 to 100, and in Figure 2.18b it is 56 to 94.

The range is a simple calculation, but it is not very useful because it reflects only the extremes. Statisticians need to know whether most of the scores are clustered close to the mean or scattered widely. The most useful measure is the **standard deviation (SD)**, *a measurement of the amount of variation among scores in a normal distribution.* In the appendix to this chapter, you will find a formula for calculating the standard deviation. For present purposes you can simply remember that when the scores are closely clustered near the mean, the standard deviation is small; when the scores are more widely scattered, the standard deviation is large.

As Figure 2.18 shows, the Scholastic Assessment Test (SAT) was designed to produce a mean of 500 and a standard deviation of 100. Of all people taking the test, 68% score within 1 standard deviation above or below the mean (400–600); 95% score within 2 standard deviations (300–700). Only 2.5% score above 700; another 2.5% score below 300.

Standard deviations provide a useful way of comparing scores on different tests. For example, if you scored 1 standard deviation above the mean on the SAT, you tested about as well as someone who scored 1 standard deviation above the mean on another test, such as the American College Test. We would say that both of you had a deviation score of +1.

CONCEPT CHECK ☑

14. Suppose that you score 80 on your first psychology test. The mean for the class is 70, and the standard deviation is 5. On the second test, you receive a score of 90. This time the mean for the class is also 70, but the standard deviation is 20. Compared to the other students in your class, did your performance improve, deteriorate, or stay the same? (Check your answers on page 61.)

FIGURE 2.17 These two distributions of test scores have the same mean but different variances and different standard deviations.

FIGURE 2.18 In a normal distribution of scores, the amount of variation from the mean can be measured in standard deviations. In this example scores between 400 and 600 are said to be within 1 standard deviation from the mean; scores between 300 and 700 are within 2 standard deviations.

Evaluating Results: Inferential Statistics

Suppose researchers conducted a study comparing two kinds of therapy to help people quit smoking cigarettes. At the end of 6 weeks of therapy, people who have been punished for smoking average 7.5 cigarettes per day, whereas those who have been rewarded for not smoking average 6.5 cigarettes per day. Presuming that the smokers were randomly assigned to the two groups, is this the kind of difference that might easily arise by chance? Or should we take this difference seriously and recommend that therapists use rewards and not punishment?

To answer this question, we obviously need to know more than just the numbers 7.5 and 6.5. How many smokers were in the study? (10 in each group? 100? 1,000?) Also, how much variation occurred within each group? Are most people's behaviors close to the group means, or are there a few extreme scores that distort the averages?

One way to deal with these issues is to present the means and 95% confidence intervals for each, as

shown in Figure 2.19. The **95% confidence interval** is *the range within which the true population mean lies, with 95% certainty.*

"Wait a minute," you protest. "We already know the means: 7.5 and 6.5. Aren't *those* the 'true' population means?" No, those are the means for particular samples of the population. Someone who studies another group of smokers may not get the same results. What we care about is the mean for all smokers. It is impractical to measure that mean, but if we know the sample mean, the size of the sample, and the standard deviation, we can estimate how close the sample mean is likely to be to the population mean. Figure 2.19 presents two possibilities.

a   **b**

FIGURE 2.19 The vertical lines indicate 95% confidence intervals. The pair of graphs in part a indicate that the true mean has a 95% chance of falling within a very narrow range. The graphs in part b indicate a wider range and therefore suggest less certainty that reward is a more effective therapy than punishment.

In part a the 95% confidence intervals are small; in other words the standard deviations were small, the samples were large, and the sample means are almost certainly close to the true population means. In part b the confidence intervals are larger, so the numbers 7.5 and 6.5 are just rough approximations of the true population means. Presenting data with confidence intervals can enable readers to decide for themselves how large and impressive the difference is between two groups (Hunter, 1997; Loftus, 1996).

A 95% confidence interval is one kind of **inferential statistic,** which is a *statement about a large population based on an inference from a small sample.* One alternative to the 95% confidence interval is a test that determines the probability that purely chance variation would achieve a difference as large as the observed one.

For example, if we compared two groups of smokers who were treated the same way, what would be the chance that the groups would differ by as much as the difference between 7.5 and 6.5? The result is summarized by a *p* (as in *probability*) value. For example,

p <.05 indicates that *the probability that randomly generated results would resemble the observed results is less than 5%.* The smaller the *p* value, the more impressive the results.

The usual agreement is that, if *p* is less than .05, researchers consider the results **statistically significant** or **statistically reliable**—that is, *unlikely to have arisen by chance.* A more cautious researcher might consider the results significant or reliable only if *p* were less than .01 or even .001. The appendix at the end of this chapter gives an example of a statistical test that can be used to determine a *p* value. Statistical significance depends on three factors: the size of the difference between the groups, the number of research participants in each group, and the amount of variation among individuals within each group (Figure 2.20).

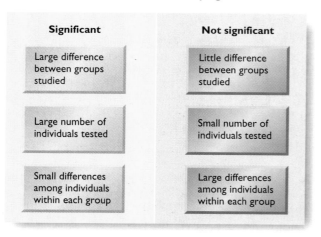

Factors that lead to a conclusion of "statistically significant" or "not statistically significant"

Significant	Not significant
Large difference between groups studied	Little difference between groups studied
Large number of individuals tested	Small number of individuals tested
Small differences among individuals within each group	Large differences among individuals within each group

FIGURE 2.20 Researchers say that results are *statistically significant* if they calculate that chance variations in data would be unlikely to produce a difference between groups as large as the one that the researchers actually observed.

If the results are not statistically significant, what then? Simply, we should not draw a conclusion. In particular we should *not* conclude that the hypothesis was *wrong* or that the procedure had no effect. Sometimes a hypothesis is correct but difficult to demonstrate, and sometimes a procedure appears to be ineffective just because our measurements are inaccurate (Kluger & Tikochinsky, 2001). Of course, the more often researchers have failed to find a significant effect, the more skeptical we should become.

CONCEPT CHECK ☑

15. Should we be more impressed with results when the 95% confidence intervals are large or small? Should we be more impressed if the *p* value is large or small? (Check your answer on page 61.)

Statistics and Conclusions

Sometimes psychological researchers get consistent, dependable effects, and they do not even have to consider statistics: Turn out the lights in a sealed room; people will no longer be able to see. Add sugar to your iced tea; it tastes sweet. The bigger the effect, the less we need to rely on complicated statistical tests. We pay more attention to statistics when we measure smaller effects: Does a change in wording alter people's responses to a survey? Does the use of an electronic study guide improve students' test scores? Does family therapy provide better results than individual therapy to treat alcohol and drug abuse? Many psychological researchers deal with small, fragile effects and therefore need a solid understanding of statistics.

Examining the statistics is only the first step toward drawing a conclusion. To say that an experiment has statistically reliable results means only that we would be unlikely to get such results merely by chance. If not by chance, then how? At that point psychologists use their knowledge to try to determine the most likely interpretation of the results.

Summary

- *Mean, median, and mode.* One way of presenting the central score of a distribution is via the mean, determined by adding all the scores and dividing by the number of individuals. Another way is the median, which is the middle score after all the scores have been arranged from highest to lowest. The mode is the score that occurs most frequently. (page 56)
- *Standard deviation (SD).* To indicate whether most scores are clustered close to the mean or whether they are spread out, psychologists report the range of scores, called the standard deviation. If we know that a given score is a certain number of standard deviations above or below the mean, then we can determine what percentage of other scores it exceeds. (page 58)
- *Inferential statistics.* Inferential statistics are attempts to deduce the properties of a large population based on the results from a small sample of that population. (page 59)
- *Probability of chance results.* The most common use of inferential statistics is to calculate the probability that a given research result could have arisen by chance. That probability is low if the difference between the two groups is large, if the variability within each group is small, and if the number of individuals in each group is large. (page 59)

- *Statistical significance.* When psychologists say $p < .05$, they mean that the probability that accidental fluctuations could produce the kind of results they obtained is less than 5%. They generally set a standard of 5% or less. If the results meet that standard, they are then said to be statistically significant or reliable. (page 60)

Answers to Concept Checks

13. a. Mean = 4; median = 3; mode = 2. **b.** Mean = 7; median = 3; mode = 2. Note that changing just one number in the distribution from 8 to 35 greatly altered the mean without affecting the median or the mode. (page 57)

14. Even though your score rose from 80 on the first test to 90 on the second, your performance actually deteriorated in comparison to other students' scores. A score of 80 on the first test was 2 standard deviations above the mean, better than 98% of all other students. A 90 on the second test was only 1 standard deviation above the mean, a score that beats only 84% of the other students. (page 58)

15. In both cases smaller. A small 95% confidence interval indicates high confidence in the results. A small p value indicates a low probability of getting such a large difference merely by chance. (page 60)

CHAPTER ENDING

Key Terms and Activites

Key Terms

95% confidence interval: the range within which the true population mean lies, with 95% certainty (page 59)

blind observer: an observer who can record data without knowing what the researcher has predicted (page 42)

burden of proof: the obligation to present evidence to support one's claim (page 32)

case history: a thorough description of a single individual, including information on both past experiences and current behavior (page 44)

control group: a group treated in the same way as the experimental group except for the procedure that the experiment is designed to test (page 50)

convenience sample: a group chosen because of its ease of study (page 41)

correlation: a measure of the relationship between two variables, which are both outside the investigator's control (page 46)

correlation coefficient: a mathematical estimate of the relationship between two variables, ranging from +1 (perfect positive relationship) to 0 (no linear relationship) to –1 (perfect negative relationship) (page 47)

correlational study: a procedure in which investigators measure the correlation between two variables without controlling either of them (page 46)

cross-cultural samples: groups of people from at least two cultures (page 41)

demand characteristics: cues that tell a subject what is expected of him or her and what the experimenter hopes to find (page 44)

dependent variable: the item that an experimenter measures to determine how changes in the independent variable affect it (page 50)

descriptive statistics: mathematical summaries of results such as measures of the average and the amount of variation (page 56)

double-blind study: a study in which neither the observer nor the subjects know which subjects received which treatment (page 43)

experiment: a study in which the investigator manipulates at least one variable while measuring at least one other variable (page 49)

experimental group: the group that receives the treatment that an experiment is designed to test (page 50)

experimenter bias: the tendency of an experimenter to unintentionally distort procedures or results based on the experimenter's own expectations of the outcome of the study (page 42)

extrasensory perception (ESP): the alleged ability of certain people to acquire information without using any sense organ and without receiving any form of physical energy (page 36)

falsifiable: (with reference to a theory) making sufficiently precise predictions that we can at least imagine evidence that would contradict the theory (if anyone had obtained such evidence) (page 31)

hypothesis: a clear predictive statement (page 32)

illusory correlation: an apparent relationship based on casual observations of unrelated or weakly related events (page 48)

independent variable: in an experiment the item that an experimenter manipulates to determine how it affects the dependent variable (page 50)

induction: the process of inferring a general principle from observations (page 31)

inferential statistics: statements about large populations based on inferences from small samples (page 59)

informed consent: a subject's agreement to take part in an experiment after being told what to expect (page 53)

mean: the sum of all the scores reported in a study divided by the total number of scores (page 56)

median: the middle score in a list of scores arranged from highest to lowest (page 57)

meta-analysis: a procedure that combines the results of many studies and analyzes them as though they were all one very large study (page 34)

mode: the score that occurs most frequently in a distribution of scores (page 57)

naturalistic observation: a careful examination of what many people or nonhuman animals do under natural conditions (page 44)

normal distribution (or normal curve): a symmetrical frequency of scores clustered around the mean (page 56)

operational definition: a definition that specifies the operations (or procedures) used to produce or measure something, a way to give it a numerical value (page 40)

p < .05: an expression meaning that the probability of accidentally achieving results similar to the reported results is less than 5% (page 60)

parsimony: (literally, stinginess) scientists' preference for the theory that explains the results using the simplest assumptions (page 34)

placebo: an inactive pill that has no known pharmacological effect on the subjects in an experiment (page 43)

population: the entire group of individuals to be considered (page 41)

random assignment: a chance procedure for assigning subjects to groups so that every subject has the same probability as any other subject of being assigned to a particular group (page 50)

random sample: a group of people picked in random fashion so that every individual in the population has an equal chance of being selected (page 41)

range: a statement of the highest and lowest scores in a distribution of scores (page 58)

replicable result: a result that can be repeated (at least approximately) by any competent investigator who follows the same procedures used in the original study (page 34)

representative sample: a selection of the population chosen to match the entire population with regard to specific variables (page 41)

single-blind study: a study in which either the observer or the subjects are unaware of which subjects received which treatment (page 43)

standard deviation (SD): a measurement of the amount of variation among scores in a normal distribution (page 58)

statistically significant (or statistically reliable) results: effects that have a low probability of having arisen by chance (page 60)

survey: a study of the prevalence of certain beliefs, attitudes, or behaviors based on people's responses to specific questions (page 44)

theory: a comprehensive explanation of observable events (page 31)

Suggestions for Further Reading

Martin, D. (2004). *Doing psychology experiments* (6th ed.). Belmont, CA: Wadsworth. A discussion of all aspects of research, including methods of conducting research and statistical analyses of results.

Stanovich, K. E. (2004). *How to think straight about psychology* (7th ed.). Boston: Pearson, Allyn & Bacon. An excellent discussion of how to evaluate evidence in psychology and how to avoid pitfalls.

Book Companion Web Site

Need help studying? Go to

http://psychology.wadsworth.com/kalat_intro7e/

for a virtual study center. You'll find a personalized Self-Study Assessment that will provide you with a study plan based on your answers to a pretest. Also study using flashcards, quizzes, interactive art, and an online glossary.

Check out interactive **Try It Yourself** exercises on the companion site! For example, the Psychic Phenomenon exercise ties to what you've learned in this chapter.

Your companion site also has direct links to the following Web sites. These links are checked often for changes, dead links, and new additions.

HyperText Psychology_BASICS

www.science.wayne.edu/~wpoff/basics.html

This site walks you through the basics of research: social science methods; field studies, surveys, and experiments; and the use of statistics in interpreting results.

Statistical Assessment Service (STATS)

www.stats.org/

Here you'll learn how statistical and quantitative information and research are represented (and misrepresented) by the media and how journalists can learn to convey such material more accurately and effectively.

Psychological Research Opportunities

http://psychexps.olemiss.edu/

The psychology department at the University of Mississippi invites you to participate in some of their research projects online.

Try It Yourself CD-ROM
with Critical Thinking Video Exercises

Use your CD to access **videos** related to activities designed to help you think critically about the important topics discussed. You'll also find an easy portal link to the book companion site where you can access your personalized **Self-Study Assessments** and interactive **Try It Yourself** exercises.

PsychNow! 2.0

PsychNow! is a fun interactive CD designed to help you with the difficult concepts in psychology. Check out the Accessing Psychology section for the following topics that relate to this chapter:

Research Methods: methods video and review and application of dependent and independent variables.
Critical Thinking in Psychology: association of sugar and hyperactivity with critical thinking lesson and application.
InteractNOW! Online Collaborative Lab: Critical Thinking and Evaluating Evidence

APPENDIX TO CHAPTER 2
Statistical Calculations

This appendix shows you how to calculate a few of the statistics mentioned in Chapter 2. It is intended primarily to satisfy your curiosity. Ask your instructor whether you should use this appendix for any other purpose.

Standard Deviation

To determine the standard deviation (SD):

1. Determine the mean of the scores.
2. Subtract the mean from each of the individual scores.
3. Square each of those results, add the squares together, and divide by the total number of scores.

The result is called the *variance.* The standard deviation is the square root of the variance. Here is an example:

Individual scores	Each score minus the mean	Difference squared
12.5	−2.5	6.25
17.0	+2.0	4.00
11.0	−4.0	16.00
14.5	−0.5	0.25
16.0	+1.0	1.00
16.5	+1.5	2.25
17.5	+2.5	6.25
105		36.00

The mean is 15.0 (the sum of the first column, divided by 7). The variance is 5.143 (the sum of the third column, divided by 7). The standard deviation is 2.268 (the square root of 5.143).

A Typical Statistical Test: The *t*-Test

Statistical tests are available to suit different kinds of data. Suppose we test many people's memory twice, once on a day when they are well rested and once after a night of little or no sleep. Imagine that scores on this test range from 0 to 25. For each person we determine the difference between performance on the 2 days. For example:

Well-rested performance	Nonrested performance	Difference
17	14	+3
23	14	+9
15	18	−3
25	24	+1
21	16	+5
19	17	+2
22	14	+8
24	19	+5
		30

We then determine X_D, the mean of the differences (30 ÷ 8 = 3.75) and σ, the standard deviation of the differences (3.63). We enter those into this formula for *t*, along with *N*, the number of people tested (which is 8):

$$t = \frac{X_D}{\sigma/\sqrt{N-1}} = \frac{3.75}{3.63/2.64} = 2.73$$

The larger the value of *t*, the less likely that the difference between the two groups is due to chance. The value of *t* will be high if the difference between the two scores (X_D)

is large, if the standard deviation (σ) is small relative to the mean, and if the number of individuals (N) is large. Statistics books contain tables to show the likelihood of a given t value. In this case, with a group of eight people and a t value of 2.73, $p < .05$. That is, the probability of getting such a large difference between the two sets of scores by chance (if sleeplessness really had no effect on performance) is less than 5%.

Correlation Coefficients

To determine the correlation coefficient, we designate one of the variables x and the other one y. We obtain pairs of measures, x_i and y_i. Then we use the following formula:

$$r = \frac{[(\Sigma x_i y_i) - n \cdot \bar{x} \cdot \bar{y}]}{n \cdot sx \cdot sy}$$

In this formula $(\Sigma x_i y_i)$ is the sum of the products of x and y. For each pair of observations (x, y), we multiply x times y and then add together all the products. The term $n \cdot \bar{x} \cdot \bar{y}$ means n (the number of pairs) times the mean of x times the mean of y. The denominator, $n \cdot sx \cdot sy$ means n times the standard deviation of x times the standard deviation of y.

Web/Technology Resources

Introductory Statistics: Concepts, Models, and Applications

www.psychstat.smsu.edu/introbook/sbk00.htm

You can read an entire statistics textbook by David W. Stockburger, Southwest Missouri State University, on the Web or download it, free!

Biological Psychology

It is easy to look at a human brain, which weighs only 1.2 to 1.4 kg (2.5 to 3 lb), and marvel at its abilities. A bee's brain is microscopically small, but even a bee has amazingly complex behaviors. It locates flowers, finds food in the flowers, evades predators, finds its way back to the hive, and then does a dance that tells other bees where it found the food. When necessary, it also takes care of the queen bee, protects the hive against intruders, and so forth. Not bad for a microscopic brain.

Understanding brain processes is a daunting challenge. Researchers necessarily proceed piecemeal, first answering the easiest questions. We now know a great deal about how nerves work and how brains record sensory experiences. What we understand least is why and how brain activity produces conscious experience. (Philosopher David Chalmers calls this "the hard problem.")

Will we someday understand nerves well enough to "read minds" or understand the origins of consciousness? Maybe, maybe not, but the fascination of the mind–brain question motivates many researchers to tireless efforts.

Biological explanations will play a key role in many chapters and are hardly limited to this one. One major biological influence is genetics, and research on genetics plays an increasingly central role in psychology. We shall consider genetics more systematically in Chapter 10 (Development). In this chapter we focus on the cells of the nervous system and the overall structure of the nervous system.

▮ A bee has amazingly complex behavior, but we have no way to get inside the bee's experience to know what (if anything) it feels like to be a bee.

Neurons and Behavior

Can we explain our experiences and our behavior in terms of the actions of single cells in the nervous system?

One highly productive strategy in science is *reductionism*—the attempt to explain complex phenomena by reducing them to combinations of simpler components. Biologists explain breathing, blood circulation, and metabolism in terms of chemical reactions and physical forces. Chemists explain chemical reactions in terms of the properties of the elements and their atoms. Physicists explain the properties of the atom in terms of a few fundamental forces.

How well does reductionism apply to psychology? Can we explain human behavior and experience in terms of chemical and electrical events in the brain? The only way to find out is to try. Here we explore efforts to explain behavior based on single cells of the nervous system.

Nervous System Cells

You experience your "self" as a single entity that senses, thinks, and remembers. And yet neuroscientists have found that the nervous system responsible for your experiences consists of an enormous number of separate cells. The brain processes information in **neurons** (NOO-rons), or *nerve cells*. Figure 3.1 shows estimates of the numbers of neurons in various parts of the human nervous system (R. W. Williams & Herrup, 1988). The nervous system also contains another kind of cells called **glia** (GLEE-uh), *which support the neurons in many ways such as by insulating them and removing waste products.* The glia are about one tenth the size of neurons but about 10 times more numerous.

How do so many separate neurons and glia combine forces to produce the single stream of experiences that is you? The secret is communication. Each neuron receives information and transmits it to other cells by conducting electrochemical impulses. Sensory neurons carry information from the sense organs to the central nervous system, where neurons process the information, compare it to past information, and exchange information with other neurons, and ultimately, motor neurons send commands to the muscles and glands.

To understand our nervous system, we must first understand the properties of both the individual neurons and the connections among them. Neurons have

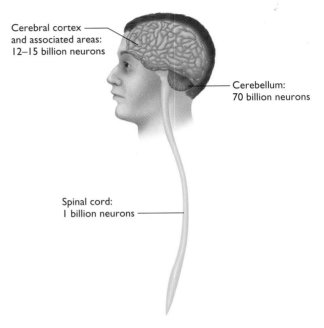

FIGURE 3.1 Estimated distribution of the neurons in the adult human central nervous system. No one has attempted an exact count, and the number varies substantially from one person to another. *(Based on data of R. W. Williams & Herrup, 1988).*

Cerebral cortex and associated areas: 12–15 billion neurons

Cerebellum: 70 billion neurons

Spinal cord: 1 billion neurons

a variety of shapes depending on whether they receive information from a few sources or many and whether they send impulses over a short or a long distance (Figure 3.2).

A neuron consists of three parts: a cell body, dendrites, and an axon (Figure 3.3). The **cell body** *contains the nucleus of the cell.* The **dendrites** (from a Greek word meaning "tree") are *widely branching structures that receive transmissions from other neurons.* The **axon** is a *single, long, thin, straight fiber with branches near its tip.* Some vertebrate axons are covered with *myelin,* an insulating sheath that speeds up the transmission of impulses along an axon. As a rule an axon transmits information to other cells, and the dendrites or cell body of each cell receives that information. That information can be either excitatory or inhibitory; that is, it can increase or decrease the probability that the next cell will send a message of its own. Inhibitory messages are important for many purposes. For example, during a period of painful stimulation, your brain has mechanisms to inhibit further sensation of pain.

FIGURE 3.2 Neurons, which vary enormously in shape, consist of a cell body and branched attachments called axons (coded blue for easy identification) and dendrites. The neurons in (a) and (b) receive input from many sources, the neuron in (c) from only a few sources, and the neuron in (d) from an intermediate number of sources. The sensory neurons (e) carry messages from sensory receptors to the brain or spinal cord. Inset: Electron micrograph showing cell bodies in brown and axons and dendrites in green. The color was added artificially; electron micrographs are made with electron beams, not light, and therefore, they show no color.

CONCEPT CHECK ☑

1. Which part of a neuron receives input from other neurons? Which part sends messages to other cells? (Check your answers on page 77.)

The Action Potential

Axons are specialized to convey information over distances ranging to a meter or more. Imagine what would happen if they relied on electrical conduction: Electricity is extremely fast, but with a poor conductor such as any part of an animal body, electrical impulses weaken noticeably as they travel. The farther from your brain some information started, the less you would feel it. Short people would feel a pinch on their toes more intensely than tall people would . . . if indeed either felt their toes at all.

Instead, axons convey information by a special combination of electrical and chemical processes called an **action potential,** *an excitation that travels along an axon at a constant strength, no matter how far it must travel.* An action potential is a yes/no or on/off message, like a standard light switch. (Most switches don't let you make the light dimmer or brighter. It's either on or off.) This principle is known as the *all-or-none law.*

The advantage of an action potential over simple electrical conduction is that action potentials from distant places like your toes reach your brain at full strength. The disadvantage is that action potentials are slower than electrical conduction. Your knowledge of what is happening to your toes is at least a twentieth of a second out of date. A twentieth of a second is seldom worth worrying about, but your information

about different body parts is out of date by different delays. Consequently, if you are touched on two or more body parts at almost the same time, your brain cannot accurately gauge which touch came first.

Here is a quick description of how the action potential works:

1. When the axon is not stimulated, its membrane has a **resting potential,** *an electrical polarization across the membrane (or covering) of an axon, with a negative charge inside the axon.* A typical value is –70 millivolts on the inside relative to the outside. The resting potential depends largely on negatively charged proteins inside the axon. In addition a mechanism called the sodium-potassium pump pushes sodium ions out of the axon while pulling potassium ions in. In Figure 3.4 the sodium ions are marked Na^+, and the potassium ions are marked K^+, their chemical symbols. Both have a charge of +1 unit. The result of the sodium-potassium pump is that sodium ions are more concentrated outside the axon and potassium ions are more concentrated inside.

2. An action potential starts in either of two ways: First, many axons produce spontaneous activity. Second, input from other axons can excite a neuron's membrane. In either case, when the action potential starts, sodium gates open and allow sodium ions to enter (Figure 3.5). As the sodium ions enter the axon, they drive the inside of the cell to a slightly positive charge. Whenever that charge is great enough to reach the *threshold* of the axon, it opens narrow channels that permit still more sodium ions to enter, bringing with them their positive charges. This influx of positively charged sodium ions is the action potential.

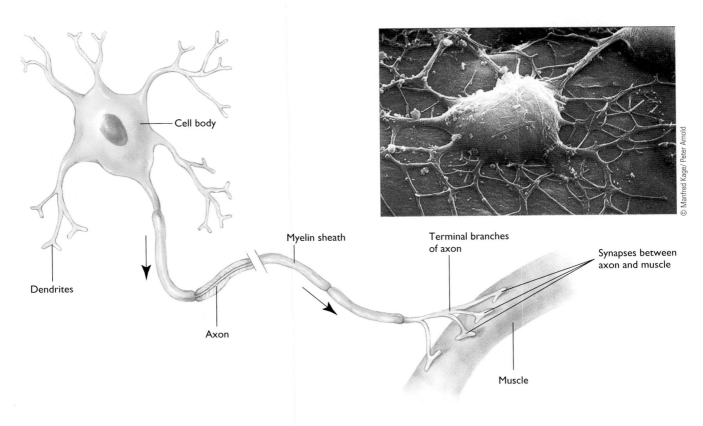

FIGURE 3.3 The generalized structure of a motor neuron shows the dendrites, the branching structures that receive transmissions from other neurons, and the axon, a single, long, thin, straight fiber with branches near its tip. Inset: A photomicrograph of a neuron.

3. After the sodium gates have been open for barely an instant, they snap shut. Then potassium gates open to allow potassium ions to leave the axon. The potassium ions each carry a positive charge, so their exit drives the inside of the axon back to its original resting potential (Figure 3.6b).

4. Eventually, the sodium-potassium pump removes the invading sodium ions and recaptures the escaping potassium ions.

You will recall that the axon does not conduct like an electrical wire. The action potential travels down the axon like a wave of energy, and the stimulation at each point excites the next point along the axon. You could imagine it like a fire burning along a string: The fire at each point ignites the next point, which in turn ignites the

FIGURE 3.4 The sodium and potassium distribution for a resting membrane. Sodium ions (Na$^+$) are concentrated outside the neuron; potassium ions (K$^+$) are concentrated inside. Because of negatively charged proteins inside the neuron, the inside of the cell is negatively charged relative to the outside. Protein and chloride ions (not shown) bear negative charges inside the cell. At rest very few sodium ions cross the membrane except by the sodium-potassium pump. Potassium tends to flow into the cell because it is attracted by the negative charge inside the cell. It tends to flow out because it is more concentrated inside than outside.

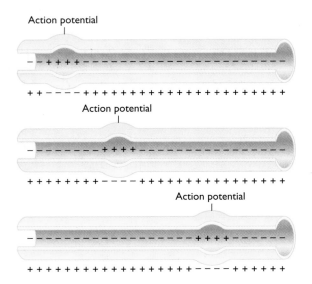

FIGURE 3.5 Ion movements conduct an action potential along an axon. At each point along the membrane, sodium ions enter the axon and alter the distribution of positive and negative charges. As each point along the membrane returns to its original state, the action potential flows to the next point.

next point. That is, after sodium ions enter some point along an axon, some of them diffuse to the neighboring portion of the axon and thereby excite that part of the membrane enough to open its own sodium gates. The action potential spreads to this next area and so on down the axon, as shown in Figure 3.6. In this manner the action potential re-

mains equally strong all the way to the end of the axon.

All of this information is clearly important to investigators of the nervous system, but why should a psychology student care? First, it explains why sensations on points on your fingers and toes do not fade away by the time they reach your brain. Second, an understanding of action potentials is one step toward understanding the communication between one neuron and the next. Third, certain drugs operate by blocking action potentials. For example, anesthetic drugs (e.g., Novocain) silence neurons by clogging the sodium gates. When your dentist drills a tooth, the receptors in your tooth send out the message "Pain! Pain! Pain!" But that message does not get through to the brain because a shot of Novocain has blocked the sodium gates and thereby halted the sensory messages.

CONCEPT CHECK ✓

2. If a mouse and a giraffe both get pinched on the toes at the same time, which will respond faster? Why?
3. Fill in these blanks: When the axon membrane is at rest, the inside has a _____ charge relative to the outside. When the membrane reaches its threshold, ____ ions enter from outside to inside, bringing with them a _____ charge. That flow of ions constitutes the ____ _____ of the axon. (Check your answers on page 77.)

Synapses

Communication between one neuron and the next is not like transmission along an axon. At a **synapse** (SIN-aps), *the specialized junction between one neuron and another* (Figure 3.7), *a neuron releases a chemical that either excites or inhibits the next neuron.* That is, the chemical can make the next neuron either more or less likely to produce an action potential. At other kinds of synapses, a neuron releases a chemical that excites a muscle or gland. The events at synapses are central to everything that your nervous system does because synapses determine which cells will be active at any moment.

FIGURE 3.6 (a) During an action potential, sodium gates in the neuron membrane open, and sodium ions enter the axon, bringing a positive charge with them. (b) After an action potential occurs at one point along the axon, the sodium gates close at that point and open at the next point along the axon. When the sodium gates close, potassium gates open, and potassium ions flow out of the axon, carrying a positive charge with them. *(Modified from Starr & Taggart, 1992)*

© Omikron / Photo Researchers, Inc.

FIGURE 3.7 The tips of axons swell to form terminal boutons, which form synapses onto the surface of another cell, as shown in this electron micrograph.

charged or negatively charged ions to enter. The postsynaptic neuron produces an action potential of its own if the total excitation at any moment outweighs the total inhibition coming from a variety of synapses. The process resembles making a decision: When you are trying to decide whether to do something, you weigh all the pluses and minuses and act if the pluses are stronger.

Inhibition is not the absence of excitation; it is like stepping on the brakes. For example, when a pinch on your foot causes you to raise it, thus contracting one set of muscles, inhibitory synapses in your spinal cord block activity in the muscles that would move your leg in the opposite direction. Those inhibitory synapses prevent messages from trying to raise your leg and extend it at the same time.

After a neurotransmitter excites or inhibits a receptor, it separates from the receptor, terminating the

A typical axon has several branches, each ending with a little bulge called a *presynaptic ending,* or **terminal bouton** (or **button**), as shown in Figure 3.8. When an action potential reaches the terminal bouton, it releases molecules of a **neurotransmitter,** *a chemical that has been stored in the neuron and that can activate receptors of other neurons* (Figure 3.8). Several dozen chemicals are used as neurotransmitters in various brain areas, although any given neuron releases only one or a few of them. The neurotransmitter molecules diffuse across a narrow gap to the **postsynaptic neuron,** *the neuron on the receiving end of the synapse.* There the neurotransmitter molecules attach to receptors on the neuron's dendrites or cell body (or for special purposes on the tip of its axon). The neural communication process is summarized in Figure 3.9.

Depending on the neurotransmitter and the type of receptor, the attachment can either excite or inhibit the postsynaptic neuron. That is, it enables either positively

FIGURE 3.8 The synapse is the junction of the presynaptic (message-sending) cell and the postsynaptic (message-receiving) cell. At the end of the presynaptic axon is the terminal bouton, which contains many molecules of the neurotransmitter. The thick, dark area at the bottom of the cell is the synapse.

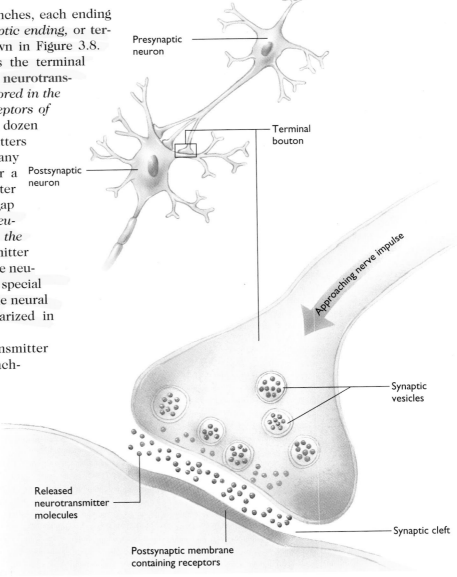

Presynaptic neuron

Terminal bouton

Postsynaptic neuron

Approaching nerve impulse

Synaptic vesicles

Synaptic cleft

Released neurotransmitter molecules

Postsynaptic membrane containing receptors

Action potential

Synapse

Postsynaptic cell

Axon

Axon

Dendrite

Action potential travels down the axon toward the synapse.

Transmitter substance

Presynaptic terminal bouton

Synaptic vesicles

Synaptic cleft

Postsynaptic dendrite

At the synapse, the transmitter substance is released.

Receptor

The transmitter crosses the synaptic cleft, where it binds to the receptors on the surface of the postsynaptic cell, usually on its dendrites, though not necessarily.

Sodium ions⁺

If binding of the transmitter to the receptor cell opens gates for positively charged sodium ions to enter the cell, the cell will produce more action potentials. This is an *excitatory synapse.*

produces more action potentials excitatory synaps.

Potassium ions⁺

Chloride ions⁻

If binding of the transmitter to the receptor cell opens gates for positively charged potassium ions to leave the cell or negatively charged chloride ions to enter the cell, the cell will produce fewer action potentials. This is an *inhibitory synapse.*

produce few action potentials inhibitory synaps.

FIGURE 3.9 The complex process of neural communication takes only 1–2 milliseconds.

message. From that point on, the fate of the receptor molecule varies. It could become reabsorbed by the axon that released it (through a process called *reuptake)*; it could diffuse away, get metabolized, and eventually show up in the blood or urine; or it could bounce around for a moment, return to the postsynaptic receptor, and reexcite it. Many antidepressant drugs act by blocking reuptake and therefore prolonging the effects of one transmitter or another.

Different neurotransmitters are associated with different functions, although it is misleading to as-

sign a specific behavior (e.g., sleep or pleasure) to a specific transmitter. Any complex behavior depends on many transmitter systems, and each transmitter contributes to many aspects of behavior. Still, an alteration of a particular kind of synapse will affect some behaviors more than others. For that reason it is possible to develop drugs that decrease depression, anxiety, appetite, and so forth by increasing or decreasing activity of a certain type of synapse. However, because each transmitter has several behavioral functions, drugs intended for one purpose almost always have other results, referred to as "side effects."

[handwritten margin notes: PRESY. — releases neurotrans. post synaptic — activating excitory or inhibit. receptors]

CONCEPT CHECK ☑

4. What is the difference between the presynaptic neuron and the postsynaptic neuron?
5. GABA is a neurotransmitter that inhibits postsynaptic neurons. If a drug were injected to prevent GABA from attaching to its receptors, what would happen to the postsynaptic neuron? (Check your answers on page 77.)

CRITICAL THINKING:
WHAT'S THE EVIDENCE?
Neurons Communicate Chemically

You have just learned that neurons communicate by releasing chemicals at synapses. Perhaps you are perfectly content to take my word for it and go on with something else. Still, it is advisable to pause and contemplate the evidence responsible for an important conclusion.

Today, neuroscientists have a wealth of evidence that neurons release chemicals at synapses. They can radioactively trace where chemicals go and what happens when they get there; they also can inject purified chemicals at a synapse and use extremely fine electrodes to measure the response of the postsynaptic neuron. But scientists of the 1920s had no fancy equipment, yet they still managed to establish that neurons communicate with chemicals.

Otto Loewi conducted a simple, clever experiment, as he later described in his autobiography (Loewi, 1960).

Hypothesis   If a neuron releases chemicals, an investigator should be able to collect some of those chemicals, transfer them from one animal to another, and thereby get the second animal to do what the first animal had been doing. Loewi had no method of collecting chemicals released within the brain itself, so he worked with axons communicating with the heart muscle. (The communication between a neuron and a muscle is similar to that between neurons.)

Method   Loewi began by electrically stimulating some axons connected to a frog's heart. These particular axons slowed down the heart rate. As he continued to stimulate those axons, he collected some of the fluid on and around that heart and transferred it to the heart of a second frog.

Results   When Loewi transferred the fluid from the first frog's heart, the second frog's heart rate also slowed (Figure 3.10).

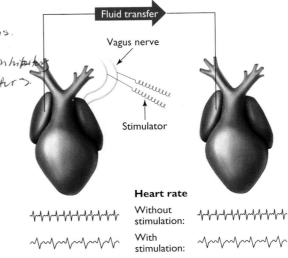

FIGURE 3.10 Otto Loewi demonstrated that axons release chemicals that can affect other cells. Using a frog, he electrically stimulated a set of axons known to decrease the heart rate. Then he collected some fluid from around the heart and transferred it to the surface of another frog's heart. When that heart slowed its beat, Loewi concluded that the axons in the first heart must have released a chemical that slows the heart rate.

Interpretation   Evidently, the stimulated axons had released a chemical that slows heart rate. At least in this case, neurons send messages by releasing chemicals.

Loewi eventually won a Nobel Prize in physiology for this and related experiments. Even outstanding experiments have limitations, however. In this case the main limitation was the uncertainty about whether axons release chemicals at most synapses, all, or only a few. Answering *that* question required technologies not available until several decades later. (The answer is that *most* communication by neurons depends on chemicals; a few synapses use electrical communication.)

Neurotransmitters and Behavior

The use of drugs that affect neurotransmitters has already revolutionized psychiatry, and investigating the role of these neurotransmitters has produced major theoretical implications for psychology. The brain has dozens of neurotransmitters, and each activates many kinds of receptors. For example, serotonin activates at least 15 kinds, probably more (Roth, Lopez, & Kroeze, 2000). Each receptor type controls somewhat different aspects of behavior. For example, serotonin type 3 receptors are responsible for nausea, and this fact makes it possible to develop drugs that block nausea without major effects on other aspects of behavior (Perez, 1995).

Any drug that increases or decreases the activity of a particular type of receptor produces specific ef-

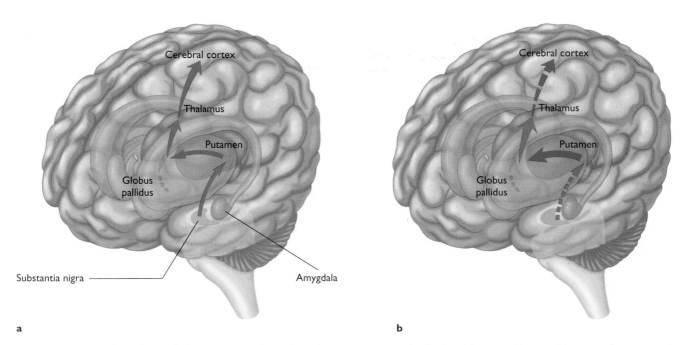

FIGURE 3.11 With Parkinson's disease, axons from the substantia nigra gradually die. (a) Normal brain. (b) Brain of person with Parkinson's disease. Green = excitatory path; red = inhibitory.

fects on behavior. One hypothesis, therefore, is that any unusual behavior is due to an excess or deficiency of some kind of synaptic activity. One example is **Parkinson's disease,** *a condition that affects about 1% of people over the age of 50. The main symptoms are difficulty in initiating voluntary movement, slowness of movement, tremors, rigidity, and depressed mood.* All of these symptoms can be traced to a gradual decay of a pathway of axons that release *the neurotransmitter* **dopamine** (DOPE-uh-meen) (Figure 3.11). One common treatment is the drug L-dopa, which enters the brain, where neurons convert it into dopamine. The effectiveness of this treatment for most people with mild cases of Parkinson's disease supports our beliefs about the link between the transmitter and the disease.

An example that shows more of the difficulty of interpreting results is **attention deficit disorder (ADD),** *a condition marked by impulsive behavior and short attention span.* ADD is usually treated with amphetamine or methylphenidate (Ritalin), and researchers know how these drugs work: Both prevent presynaptic neurons from reabsorbing (and thus recycling) the neurotransmit-

ters dopamine and serotonin after releasing them (Volkow et al., 1998). Amphetamine also increases the release of dopamine (Giros, Jaber, Jones, Wightman, & Caron, 1996). So both drugs prolong the activity of dopamine and serotonin at their synaptic receptors. It might seem, therefore, that the underlying problem in ADD is either a deficiency of those transmitters or an abnormality of their receptors. However, most people with ADD have normal dopamine release and receptors, and many people with abnormal dopamine receptors do not have ADD (Faraone & Biederman,

Former boxing champion Muhammad Ali developed symptoms of Parkinson's disease.

1998; Swanson et al., 2000). Perhaps understanding the drugs that relieve the problem doesn't tell us what caused the problem. One study found that methylphenidate improves attention even for normal healthy children, who presumably have normal dopamine activity (Zahn, Rapoport, & Thompson, 1980).

As we shall see in Chapter 16, drugs that alleviate depression and schizophrenia also act on dopamine and serotonin synapses, but again the relationship between the neurotransmitters and the behavior is complex. We still have much to learn about the relationship between the elements of the nervous system and their behavioral outcomes.

CONCEPT CHECK ☑

6. People suffering from certain disorders are given haloperidol, a drug that blocks activity at dopamine synapses. How would haloperidol affect someone with Parkinson's disease? (Check your answer on this page.)

IN CLOSING

Neurons and Behavior

Here is an imperfect analogy for the nervous system: At U.S. high school or college football games, one section of the stands is sometimes set aside for fans holding large cards. When their leader calls out a signal, such as "16," each of them holds up the appropriate card. If you were one of the fans, your card 16 might be all red, providing no clue about what the overall message might be. But the pattern provided by a few hundred fans might spell "Go, State." The message of neurons is a little like that because the activity or inactivity of any cell or synapse is part of a large overall pattern. The analogy is imperfect because the card message tells something to viewers on the other side of the field, whereas nothing reads the message of the neurons, except for the neurons themselves. However, the analogy works in some regards: Each neuron conveys a message that means nothing by itself but becomes part of an important message in context. Also, a mistake by one cardholder or one neuron is not too costly, and the overall message still gets through. Only a systematic mistake by a whole group of individuals (neurons) could garble the message.

Summary

- *Neuron structure.* A neuron, or nerve cell, consists of a cell body, dendrites, and an axon. The axon conveys information to other neurons. (page 69)
- *The action potential.* Information is conveyed along an axon by an action potential, which is regenerated without loss of strength at each point along the axon. (page 70)
- *Mechanism of the action potential.* An action potential depends on the entry of sodium into the axon. Anything that blocks this flow will block the action potential. (page 70)
- *How neurons communicate.* A neuron communicates with another neuron by releasing a chemical called a neurotransmitter at a specialized junction called a synapse. A neurotransmitter can either excite or inhibit the next neuron. (page 72)
- *Neurotransmitters and behavioral disorders.* An excess or a deficit of a particular neurotransmitter can lead to abnormal behavior, such as that exhibited by people with Parkinson's disease. However, understanding what happens at some kind of synapse is far removed from understanding the entire behavior pattern. (page 75)

Answers to Concept Checks

1. Dendrites receive input from other neurons. Axons send messages. (page 70)
2. The mouse will react faster because the action potentials have a shorter distance to travel in the mouse's nervous system than in the giraffe's. (page 72)
3. negative . . . sodium . . . positive . . . action potential (page 72)
4. The presynaptic neuron releases a neurotransmitter that travels to the postsynaptic neuron, where it activates an excitatory or inhibitory receptor. (page 75)
5. Under the influence of a drug that prevents GABA from attaching to its receptors, the postsynaptic neuron will receive less inhibition than usual. If we presume that the neuron continues to receive a certain amount of excitation, it will then produce action potentials more frequently than usual. (page 75)
6. Haloperidol would increase the severity of Parkinson's disease. In fact large doses of haloperidol can induce symptoms of Parkinson's disease in anyone. (page 77)

The Nervous System and Behavior

If you lose part of your brain, do you also lose part of your mind?

Why should psychologists care about the brain and the effects of brain damage? The reasons are both practical and theoretical. A practical reason is to distinguish between people who act strangely because of bad experiences and people who have brain disorders. There's no point in talking to someone about deep-seated psychological conflicts if the real problem is a brain tumor.

A theoretical reason is that studying the brain helps explain the organization of behavior. In some manner behavior must be made up of component parts, but what are they? Is behavior composed of ideas? Sensations? Movements? Personality characteristics? And how do the various components combine to produce the overall pattern? One way to answer such questions is to take behavior apart, one piece at a time, and brain damage does exactly that.

A related reason is that studying the brain sheds light on the mind–brain relationship discussed in Chapter 1. According to brain researchers, the mind *is* brain activity. But what exactly does that statement mean? And if it is so, why is it so? And how does brain activity produce experience? We cannot answer these questions, but studies of the brain at least help us come closer to an understanding.

The Major Divisions of the Nervous System

Psychologists and biologists distinguish between the central nervous system and the peripheral nervous system.

The **central nervous system** consists of *the brain and the spinal cord.* The central nervous system communicates with the rest of the body by the **peripheral nervous system,** which is composed of *bundles of axons between the spinal cord and the rest of the body.* The *peripheral nerves that communicate with the skin and muscles* are collectively called the **somatic nervous system.** Those that control the heart, stomach, and other organs are called the *autonomic nervous system.* Figure 3.12 summarizes these major divisions of the nervous system.

Early in its embryological development, the central nervous system of vertebrates, including humans, is a tube with three lumps, as shown in Figure 3.13. These lumps develop into the *forebrain,* the *midbrain,* and the *hindbrain;* the rest of the tube develops into the spinal cord (Figure 3.14). The forebrain, which contains the cerebral cortex and other struc-

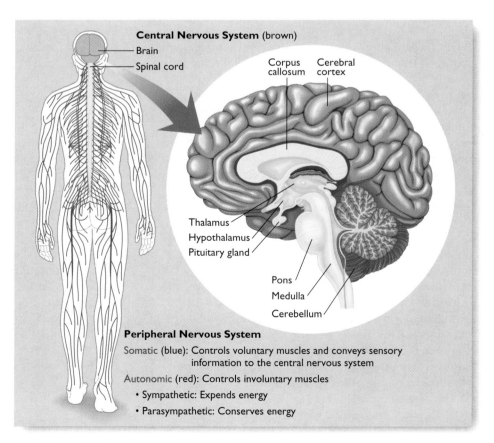

Central Nervous System (brown)
- Brain
- Spinal cord

Corpus callosum — Cerebral cortex

Thalamus
Hypothalamus
Pituitary gland

Pons
Medulla
Cerebellum

Peripheral Nervous System

Somatic (blue): Controls voluntary muscles and conveys sensory information to the central nervous system

Autonomic (red): Controls involuntary muscles
- Sympathetic: Expends energy
- Parasympathetic: Conserves energy

FIGURE 3.12 The nervous system has two major divisions: the central nervous system and the peripheral nervous system. Each of these has major subdivisions, as shown.

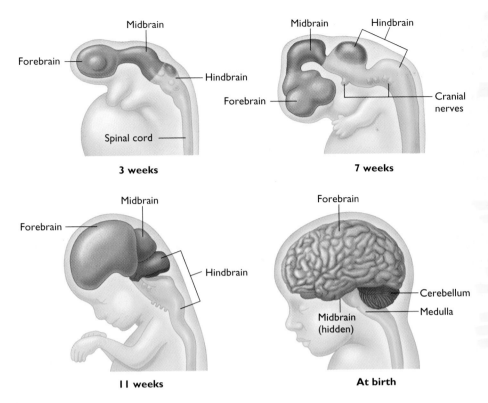

FIGURE 3.13 The human brain begins development as three lumps. By birth the forebrain has grown much larger than either the midbrain or the hindbrain, although all three structures perform essential functions.

tures, is by far the dominant portion of the brain in mammals, especially in humans.

The Forebrain

The forebrain consists of two **hemispheres,** *the left and right halves* (Figure 3.15). Each hemisphere is responsible for sensation and motor control on the opposite side of the body. Why does each hemisphere control the opposite side instead of its own side? People have speculated, but no one knows. We shall consider the differences between the left and right hemisphere in more detail later in this chapter.

The *outer covering of the forebrain,* known as the **cerebral cortex,** is especially prominent in humans. You have probably heard people talk about "having a lot of gray matter." Gray matter is composed of cell bodies and dendrites, which are grayer than the axons, and the cerebral cortex is by far your biggest area of gray matter. The interior of the forebrain beneath the cerebral cortex consists of axons, many of them covered with *myelin,* a white insulation. You can see areas of gray matter and white matter in Fig-

ure 3.16. If you would like to compare the brain anatomy of humans and many other mammalian species, see this Web site:

www.brainmuseum.org/sections/ index.html

For the sake of convenience, we describe the cortex in terms of four *lobes:* occipital, parietal, temporal, and frontal, as shown in Figure 3.17. The **occipital lobe,** *at the rear of the head, is specialized for vision.* People with damage in this area have *cortical blindness:* They have no conscious vision, no object recognition, and no visual imagery (not even in dreams), although they still have visual reflexes, such as eye blinks, that do not depend on the cerebral cortex. They also tend to set their wake–sleep cycles so they wake up in the day and get sleepy at night, again because this aspect of behavior depends on subcortical brain areas, not the cerebral cortex.

The **parietal lobe,** *just anterior (forward) from the occipital lobe, is specialized for the body senses, including touch, pain, temperature, awareness of the location of body parts, and perception of location of the body in space.* The **primary somatosensory** (body-sensory) **cortex,** *a strip in the anterior portion of the parietal lobe, has neurons*

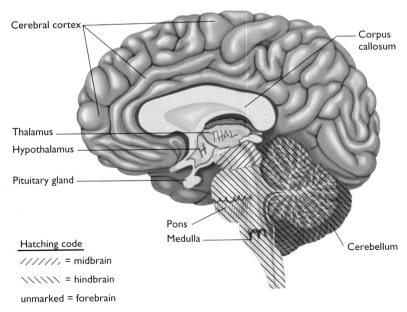

FIGURE 3.14 The major divisions of the human central nervous system, as seen from the midline.

FIGURE 3.15 The human cerebral cortex: (a) left and right hemispheres; (b) inside view of a complete hemisphere. The folds greatly extend the brain's surface area.

sensitive to touch in different body areas, as shown in Figure 3.18. Note that in Figure 3.18a larger areas are devoted to touch in the more sensitive parts of the body, such as the lips and hands, than to less sensitive areas, such as the abdomen and the back. Damage to any part of the somatosensory cortex will impair sensation from the corresponding part of the body. Extensive damage here also interferes with spatial attention. After parietal damage,

people see something but cannot decipher where it is relative to their body; consequently, they have trouble reaching toward it, walking around it, or shifting attention from one object to another. Because they cannot locate objects in space, they often confuse two objects. While looking at a yellow lemon and a red tomato, they might report seeing a yellow tomato and no lemon at all (Robertson, 2003). Most intact people can hardly imagine what the world must look like after parietal damage.

The **temporal lobe** of each hemisphere, *located toward the left and right sides of the head, is the main processing area for hearing and some of the complex aspects of vision.* People with damage to small areas of the temporal lobe show striking and specialized deficits, such as an inability to recognize faces and other complex patterns (Tarr & Gauthier, 2000); difficulty perceiving visual motion (Zihl, von Cramon, & Mai, 1983); or difficulty recognizing melodies and other complex sounds. One area in the temporal lobe of the left hemisphere is important for language comprehension. Damage in this area produces *Wernicke's aphasia,* characterized by trouble remembering the names of objects and understanding speech, although these people do a little better if someone speaks slowly. Their own speech, largely lacking nouns and verbs, is hard to understand, and they resort to made-up expressions, as do normal people if they are pressured to talk faster than they can think of the correct words (Dick et al., 2001).

Other parts of the temporal lobe are critical for certain aspects of emotion. The *amygdala* (Figure 3.19), a structure within the temporal lobe, responds strongly to emotional situations and to facial expressions that convey emotion. People with damage to the amygdala are slow to process emotional information (Baxter & Murray, 2002). Apparently, their problem is not that they cannot feel fear, for example, but that they are not sure when to feel fear. If you were driving down a steep, winding mountain road and suddenly discovered that your brakes weren't working, how frightened would you be? On a scale from 0 to 9, almost everyone rates this situation as 9, but someone with amygdala damage rates it about 6 (Adolphs, Russell, & Tranel, 1999).

FIGURE 3.16 (a) This cross section of a human brain shows gray matter (mostly cell bodies and dendrites) and white matter (axons). The whiteness comes from myelin, a fatty sheath that surrounds many axons. (b) The H-shaped structure in the center of the spinal cord is gray matter, composed largely of cell bodies. The surrounding white matter consists of axons. *(Source: Manfred Kage/Peter Arnold, Inc.)*

In later chapters we shall return to examine some of the structures that you see in Figure 3.19. The hippocampus is a key topic in Chapter 7 (Memory), and the hypothalamus and amygdala are important for emotional and motivated behaviors (Chapters 11 and 12).

The **frontal lobe,** *at the anterior (forward) pole of the brain,* includes the primary motor cortex, *a structure that is important for the planned control of fine movements,* such as moving one finger at a time. As with the primary somatosensory cortex, each area of the primary motor cortex controls a different part of the body, and larger areas are devoted to precise movements of the tongue and fingers than to, say, the shoulder and elbow muscles. The *anterior sections of the frontal lobe,*

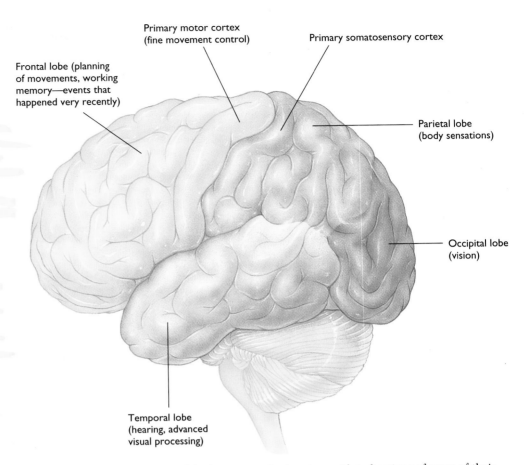

FIGURE 3.17 The four lobes of the human cerebral cortex, with indications of some of their major functions.

(a) Somatosensory cortex

(b) Motor cortex

FIGURE 3.18 (a) The primary somatosensory cortex and (b) the primary motor cortex, illustrating which part of the body each brain area controls. Larger areas of the cortex are devoted to body parts that need to be controlled with great precision, such as the face and hands. *(Parts a and b adapted from* The Cerebral Cortex of Man *by W. Penfield and T. Rasmussen, Macmillan Library Reference. Reprinted by permission of Gale, a division of Thomson Learning.)*

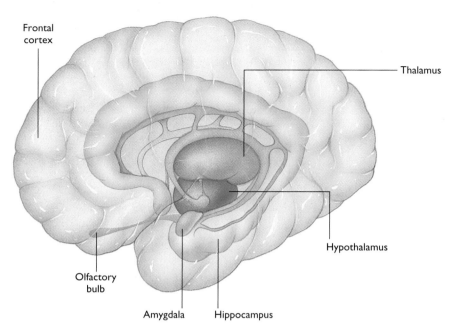

Frontal cortex

Thalamus

Olfactory bulb

Hypothalamus

Amygdala   Hippocampus

FIGURE 3.19 A view of the forebrain, showing internal structures as though the cerebral cortex were transparent.

sends information that eventually reaches the **thalamus,** *a forebrain area that relays information to the cerebral cortex* (Figure 3.19). Vision, hearing, and taste information also goes through several synapses before reaching the thalamus and then the cerebral cortex.

The cerebral cortex does not directly control the muscles. It sends information to the **pons** and **medulla,** *which control the muscles of the head* (e.g., for chewing, swallowing, and breathing), and the **spinal cord,** *which controls the muscles from the neck down* (Figures 3.14 and 3.20). The spinal cord also controls many reflexes that do not require the forebrain. A **reflex** is *a rapid, automatic response to a stimulus,* such as unconscious adjustments of your legs while you are walking or quickly jerking your hand away from something hot.

The medulla, pons, and midbrain also contain the *reticular formation* and several other systems that send messages throughout the forebrain to regulate its arousal (Young & Pigott, 1999). A malfunction in these systems, depending on its nature and location, can render someone either persistently sleepy or persistently aroused.

called the **prefrontal cortex,** contribute to the organization and planning of movements and to certain aspects of memory. Indeed, planning a movement depends on memory. Recall, for example, the delayed-response task (Chapter 1): The individual must remember a signal during a delay and then make the appropriate movement. Certain areas in the left frontal lobe are essential for producing language.

CONCEPT CHECK ☑

7. The following five people are known to have suffered damage to the cerebral cortex. From their behavioral symptoms, state the probable location of each one's damage:
    a. impaired touch sensations and spatial localization
    b. impaired hearing and some changes in emotional experience
    c. inability to make fine movements with the right hand
    d. loss of vision in the left visual field
    e. poor performance on a delayed-response task, indicating difficulty remembering what has just happened. (Check your answers on page 91.)

How the Cerebral Cortex Communicates with the Body

The only sensory information that goes directly to the cerebral cortex is olfaction (the sense of smell). Touch, pain, and other skin senses enter the spinal cord, which

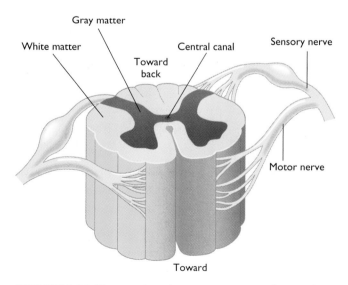

Gray matter

White matter

Central canal

Sensory nerve

Toward back

Motor nerve

Toward

FIGURE 3.20 The spinal cord receives sensory information from all parts of the body except the head. Motor nerves in the spinal cord send messages to control the muscles and glands.

The **cerebellum** (Latin for "little brain"), *another part of the hindbrain,* is important for any behavior that requires aim or timing, such as tapping out a rhythm, judging which of two visual stimuli is moving faster, and judging whether the delay between one pair of sounds is shorter or longer than the delay between another pair (Ivry & Diener, 1991; Keele & Ivry, 1990). It is also essential to learned responses that require precise timing (Krupa, Thompson, & Thompson, 1993).

CONCEPT CHECK ☑

8. People who have become intoxicated on alcohol have slow, slurred speech and cannot walk a straight line. From these observations which part of the brain would you think the alcohol has most greatly impaired? (Check your answer on page 91.)

The Autonomic Nervous System and Endocrine System

The **autonomic nervous system,** closely associated with the spinal cord, *controls the internal organs such as the heart.* The term *autonomic* means involuntary, or automatic, in the sense that we have little voluntary control of it. We are generally unaware of its activity, although it does receive information from, and sends information to, the brain and the spinal cord.

The autonomic nervous system has two parts: (a) The *sympathetic nervous system,* controlled by a chain of neurons lying just outside the spinal cord, increases heart rate and breathing rate and readies the body for vigorous fight-or-flight activities. (b) The *parasympathetic nervous system,* controlled by neurons at the very top and very bottom levels of the spinal cord, decreases heart rate, increases digestive activities, and in general promotes activities of the body that take place during rest (Figure 3.21). We shall return to this topic in more detail in the discussion of emotions (Chapter 12).

The autonomic nervous system has some control over the **endocrine system,** *a set of glands that produce hormones and release them into the blood.* Hormones controlled by the hypothalamus and pituitary gland also regulate the endocrine system. Figure 3.22 shows some of the major endocrine glands. **Hormones** are *chemicals released by glands and conveyed via the blood to alter activity in various organs.* Hormones' effects resemble those of neurotransmitters. The difference is that a neurotransmitter is released immediately adjacent to a synapse, whereas a hormone flows with the blood. Some hormonal effects are brief, such as

Sympathetic system	Parasympathetic system
Uses much energy	**Conserves energy**
• Pupils open	• Pupils constrict
• Saliva decreases	• Saliva flows
• Pulse quickens	• Pulse slows
• Sweat increases	• Stomach churns
• Stomach less active	
• Epinephrine (adrenaline) secreted	

FIGURE 3.21 The sympathetic nervous system prepares the body for brief bouts of vigorous activity; the parasympathetic nervous system promotes digestion and other nonemergency functions. Although both systems are active at all times, the balance can shift from a predominance of one to a predominance of the other.

changes in blood pressure, but others can last months, such as preparation for migration or hibernation.

CONCEPT CHECK ☑

9. Just after a meal, the pancreas produces increased amounts of the hormone insulin, which increases the conversion of the digested food into fats in many cells throughout the body. How is a hormone more effective for this purpose than a neurotransmitter would be? (Check your answer on page 91.)

Measuring Brain Activity

Up to this point, you have been reading about the functions of various brain areas, as well as those of endocrine organs and so forth. But how did we learn about these functions? For many years nearly all the conclusions came from studies of medical patients, especially brain-damaged patients, but their brain damage could not be examined until after death. Researchers can now supplement such evidence with modern techniques that examine brain anatomy and activity in living people.

An **electroencephalograph (EEG)** *uses electrodes on the scalp to record rapid changes in brain electrical activity* (Figure 3.23). A similar method is a **magnetoencephalograph (MEG),** *which records magnetic changes.* Both of these methods provide data on a millisecond-by-millisecond basis, so they can measure people's reactions to lights and sounds, as well as how reactions depend on instructions, previous experience, and so forth. However, because EEG and MEG record from the surface of the scalp, they provide little detail about the location of the brain activity.

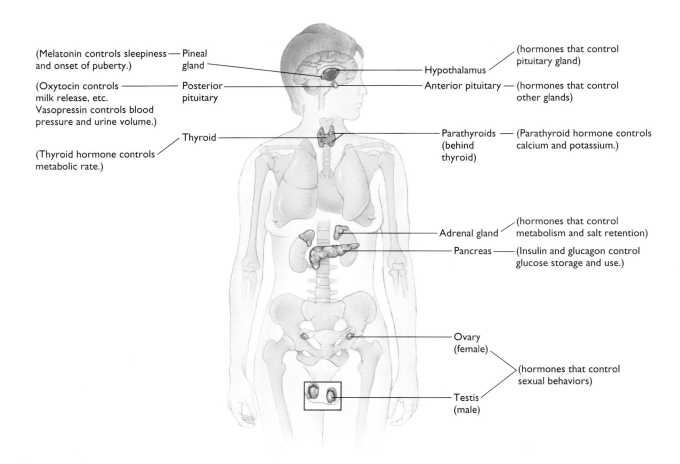

(Melatonin controls sleepiness and onset of puberty.) — Pineal gland

(Oxytocin controls milk release, etc. Vasopressin controls blood pressure and urine volume.) — Posterior pituitary

(Thyroid hormone controls metabolic rate.) — Thyroid

Hypothalamus — (hormones that control pituitary gland)

Anterior pituitary — (hormones that control other glands)

Parathyroids (behind thyroid) — (Parathyroid hormone controls calcium and potassium.)

Adrenal gland — (hormones that control metabolism and salt retention)

Pancreas — (Insulin and glucagon control glucose storage and use.)

Ovary (female)

(hormones that control sexual behaviors)

Testis (male)

FIGURE 3.22 Glands in the endocrine system produce hormones and release them into the bloodstream. This figure shows only some of the endocrine glands and some of their most abundant hormones.

Another method offers much better anatomical localization, with information on a minute-by-minute basis: **Positron-emission tomography (PET)** *records radioactivity of various brain areas emitted from injected chemicals* (Phelps & Mazziotta, 1985). First someone receives an injection of a radioactively labeled compound such as glucose. Glucose, a simple sugar that is the brain's main fuel (almost its only fuel), is absorbed mainly in the most active brain areas. Therefore, radioactivity comes primarily from those areas. Detectors around the head record the amount of radioactivity coming from each brain area and send that information to a computer, which generates an image such as the one in Figure 3.24. Red indicates areas of greatest activity, followed by yellow, green, and blue. Unfortunately, PET scans are expensive and require exposing the brain to radioactivity, a risky procedure, especially with repeated use.

Another technique, **functional magnetic resonance imaging (fMRI),** *uses magnetic detectors outside the head to compare the amounts of hemoglobin with and without oxygen in different brain areas* (J. D. Cohen, Noll, & Schneider, 1993). (Adding or removing oxygen changes the response of hemoglobin to a magnetic field.) Highly active brain areas use much oxygen and therefore decrease the oxygen bound to hemoglobin in the blood. The fMRI technique thus indicates which brain areas are currently the most active, as in Figure 3.25. For more detail about brain scan techniques, see this Web site:

http://www.musc.edu/psychiatry/fnrd/primer_index.htm

Brain scans are a potentially powerful research tool, but interpreting the results requires careful research. For example, suppose we want to determine which brain areas are important for recent memory. We record activity while someone is engaged in a memory task and compare that activity to times when the person is doing . . . what? Doing nothing? That comparison wouldn't work; the memory task presumably includes sensory stimuli, motor responses, attention, and other processes besides memory. Researchers must design a comparison task that requires

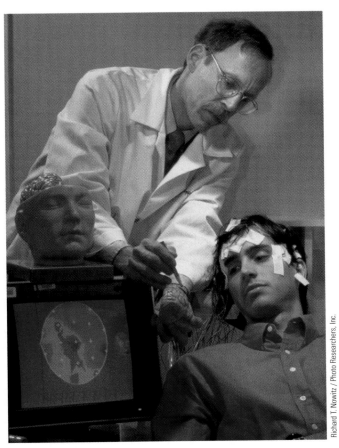

FIGURE 3.23 An EEG records momentary changes in electrical potential from the scalp, revealing an average of the activity of brain cells beneath each electrode.

FIGURE 3.24 A PET scan of the human brain. Red shows areas of most-increased activity during some task, yellow shows areas of next most-increased activity.

attention to the same sensory stimuli, the same hand movements, and so forth as the memory task.

CRITICAL THINKING:
A STEP FURTHER
Testing Psychological Processes

Suppose you want to determine which brain areas are active during recent memory. Try to design some task that requires memory and a comparison task that is similar in every other way except for the memory requirement.

Effects of Experience on Brain Structure

Several illustrations in this text have been labeled "the" human nervous system. We do not need to specify whose nervous system because the gross structure is about the same from one person to another anywhere in the world. The detailed anatomy does vary,

however. For example, brain volume tends to shrink in old age (Sowell et al., 2003), and it declines sharply with Alzheimer's disease and other medical conditions. The brain also shows small beneficial changes as a result of experience. Both axons and dendrites almost constantly withdraw old branches and grow new ones, producing a periodic turnover of synapses. Dendritic changes and synaptic renewal are particularly common in young animals (and presumably humans also) and become progressively less vigorous with advancing age (Grutzendler, Kasthuri, & Gan, 2002).

Can you improve your brain functioning by "exercising" your brain, as you can with your muscles? People have long assumed so. In former times students were taught ancient Latin and Greek on the assumption that they would acquire mental discipline that would make them more accomplished in whatever other tasks they undertook. Today, a similar argument is sometimes offered for why students should study Shakespeare or calculus. But is it true? There is such a thing as learning to study, but otherwise, it is difficult to demonstrate that studying one topic carries over to unrelated topics (Barnett & Ceci, 2002). For example, practicing chess would make you better at chess but not at anything else.

When we look at brain anatomy, the result is that practicing a particular skill expands the dendritic spread and probably the cell bodies of the brain areas

© Wagner, Desmond, Demp, Glover & Gabrieli

Courtesy of Drs. Scott T. Grafton and John D Van Horn, Dartmouth Brain Imaging Center, Dartmouth College

FIGURE 3.25 (a) This brain scan was made with functional magnetic resonance imaging (fMRI). Participants looked at words or pictures and judged whether each item was abstract or concrete, living or nonliving. Yellow shows the areas most activated by this judgment; red shows areas less strongly activated. *(From Wagner, Desmond, Demb, Glover, & Gabrieli, 1997. Photo courtesy of Anthony D. Wagner)* (b) A male volunteer, using his dominant right hand, was either rotating a small cylinder or resting in alternating 30-second intervals during a 5-minute fMRI scan, yielding six perspectives in which motor areas of the left brain are highlighted.

relevant to that skill. For example, professional musicians have a larger than average auditory cortex (Schneider et al., 2002) and expansions of several other brain areas important for timing and other musical processes (Gaser & Schlaug, 2003). The brain area representing the fingers expands in people who spend much time reading Braille (Pascual-Leone, Wasserman, Sadato, & Hallett, 1995). The longer someone has been a London taxi driver, the larger the posterior hippocampus, a brain area important for spatial memory (Maguire et al., 2000).

The hypothesis that using your brain in general expands your brain in general is harder to demonstrate. Rats that live in large cages with other rats do show brain enlargement relative to those in small individual cages (Greenough, 1975), but much or all of that effect can be attributed to increased physical activity, which increases blood flow to the head (van Praag, Kempermann, & Gage, 2000). Physical activity also benefits human brain size, especially in old age (Colcombe et al., 2003). Brain autopsies have shown that people with more education or greater mental activity in their daily lives tend to have greater branching in their dendrites (Jacobs, Schall, & Scheibel, 1993). However, we cannot draw a cause-and-effect conclusion. It is possible that education and mental activity promote brain growth but also possible that people who started with more dendritic branching succeeded well in their education and were drawn to more intellectual activities. In short, no evidence available so far indicates unambiguously that "exercising" your brain expands it anatomically.

For many decades researchers believed that all neurons formed before birth or early after it, so that beyond early infancy one could only lose neurons and never gain new ones. However, later researchers found that in a few brain areas, it is possible for *undifferentiated cells called* **stem cells** to develop into additional neurons (Gage, 2000; Graziadei & deHan, 1973; Song, Stevens, & Gage, 2002). Development of new neurons is well established in rats and songbirds, although not yet clear in humans, as the studies in humans may not have distinguished adequately between new neurons and new glia cells (Eriksson et al., 1998; Rakic, 2002). At most, however, new neurons form slowly, sporadically, and only in certain brain areas. It is not a routine matter like growing new skin cells or blood cells.

CONCEPT CHECK ☑

10. Under some conditions the axons and dendrites of a neuron increase their branching. Will the number of synapses change? (Check your answer on page 91.)

The "Binding Problem"

As researchers answered certain questions about brain function, a new one arose: One part of your brain is responsible for hearing, another for touch, several other areas for various aspects of vision, and so forth, and those areas have few if any direct connections with one another. So how do you get the experience of being a single "self"? If you shake a baby's toy rattle, how do you know that the object you see is also what you hear and feel? *The question of how separate brain areas combine forces to produce a unified perception of a single object* is the **binding problem** (Treisman, 1999). The binding problem is at the heart of the profound and difficult mind–brain problem mentioned in Chapter 1.

A naive explanation would be that all the various parts of the brain funnel their information to a "little person in the head" who puts it all together. Although no one takes that concept seriously, the underlying idea is hard to abandon, and brain researchers have sometimes imagined a "master area" of the brain that would serve the same purpose. Research on the cerebral cortex, however, has found no master area or central processor. Few neurons receive a combination of visual and auditory information or visual and touch information.

In fact the mystery deepens: Even in vision, different brain areas specialize in different aspects of the stimulus, such as shape, color, and movement. When you see a brown rabbit hopping, one brain area is most sensitive to the shape, another most sensitive to the movement, and another most sensitive to the brownness. The division of labor is not complete, but it is enough to make researchers wonder how we combine the different aspects, or "bind" them into a single object (Gegenfurtner, 2003).

The answer is not fully known, but part of the answer lies with the parietal cortex, important for spatial perception. Go back to shaking a toy rattle: If you can identify the location of your hand, the location of the rattle you see, and the location of the sound source, you probably can link the sensations together. If, like someone with parietal cortex damage, you cannot locate anything in space, you probably won't bind sensations into a single experience (Robertson, 2003). We also know that binding occurs only for precisely simultaneous events. Have you ever watched a film or television show in which the soundtrack is noticeably ahead of or behind the picture? If so, you knew that the sound wasn't coming from the performers on screen. You get the same experience watching a

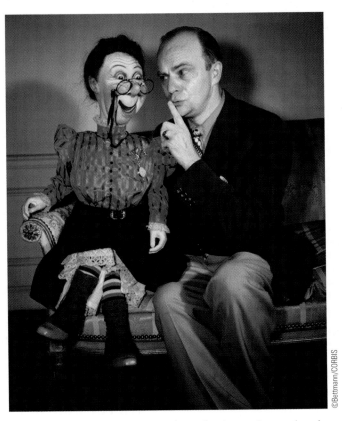

We hear the sound as coming from the dummy's mouth only if sound and movements are synchronized. In general, binding depends on simultaneity of two kinds of stimuli.

poorly dubbed foreign-language film. However, when you watch a ventriloquist, the motion of the dummy's mouth simultaneous with the sound causes you to perceive the sound as coming from the dummy.

We also know that binding takes time. If you see a brief flash on the screen showing a red circle and a green square, you might see red, green, circle, and square but not be sure which color went with which shape. The more complex the stimulus, the longer it takes to bind its elements into a whole (Holcombe & Cavanagh, 2001). People with parietal lobe damage have trouble binding a stimulus even with prolonged exposure (Treisman, 1999; Wheeler & Treisman, 2002).

The Corpus Callosum and the Split-Brain Phenomenon

What would happen if the two hemispheres of your brain could not communicate with each other? Such a situation occurs after damage to the **corpus callosum**, *a set of axons connecting the cerebral cortex of the left and right hemispheres* (Figure 3.26). Corpus callosum damage prevents someone from comparing sights seen on the left to those on the right and from comparing something felt with the left hand to something in the right. In some ways the person now has two half-brains side by side, and maybe even two spheres of consciousness.

Occasionally, brain surgeons cut the corpus callosum in an effort to relieve **epilepsy,** *a condition in which neurons somewhere in the brain emit abnormal rhythmic, spontaneous impulses.* Depending on where the abnormal impulses start and spread, epilepsy can produce varied effects. Most people with epilepsy respond well to antiepileptic drugs and live normal lives. A few, however, continue to have frequent major seizures. When all else fails, surgeons sometimes recommend cutting the corpus callosum. The original idea was that epileptic seizures would be limited to one hemisphere and therefore less incapacitating.

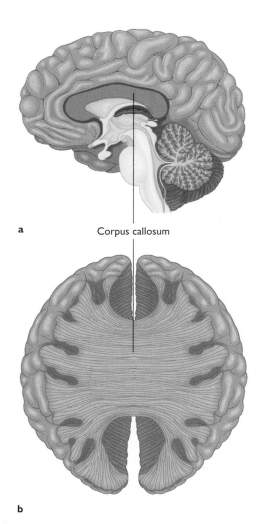

a   Corpus callosum

b

FIGURE 3.26 The corpus callosum is a large set of axons that convey information between the two hemispheres of the cerebral cortex. (a) A midline view showing the location of the corpus callosum. (b) A horizontal section showing how each axon of the corpus callosum links one spot in the left hemisphere to a corresponding spot in the right hemisphere.

The operation was more successful than expected. Not only are the seizures limited to one side of the body, but they also become less frequent. A possible explanation is that the operation interrupts the feedback loop between the two hemispheres that allows an epileptic seizure to echo back and forth. However, although these split-brain patients resume a normal life, they have some interesting behavioral effects. First, we need to consider some anatomy.

Connections Between the Eyes and the Brain

Note: This section presents a concept that is contrary to most people's expectations, and the left-right–right-left connections can be confusing. So please read carefully!
Because each hemisphere of the brain controls the muscles on the opposite side of the body, each half of the brain needs to see the opposite side of the

world. This does *not* mean that your left hemisphere sees with the right eye or that your right hemisphere sees with the left eye.

Convince yourself: Close one eye, then open it, and close the other. Note that you see almost the same view with both eyes. You see each half of the world with part of your left eye and part of your right eye.

Figure 3.27, which shows the human visual system, warrants careful study. Light from each half of the world strikes receptors on the opposite side of *each* retina. (The retina is the lining in the back of each eye. The retina is lined with receptors.) Information from the left half of each retina travels via the *optic nerves* to the left hemisphere of the cerebral cortex; information from the right half of each retina travels via the optic nerves to the right hemisphere.

Here is one way to remember this material: *Light from each side of the world strikes the opposite side of the retina. The brain is connected to the eyes so that each hemisphere sees the opposite side of the world.* If you remember those two statements, you should be able to deduce that each hemisphere is connected to the half of each retina *on the same side,* as shown in Figure 3.27. You might also draw the diagram for yourself.

What about the very center of the retina? The cells in a thin strip down the center of each retina send axons to both sides of the brain.

Effects of Severing the Corpus Callosum

For almost all right-handed people and about 60% of left-handed people, parts of the left hemisphere control speech. For most other left-handers, both hemispheres control speech. Complete right-hemisphere control of speech is rare. The right hemisphere is critical for understanding the emotional aspects of speech, however, as we shall see later.

Assuming you have left-hemisphere control of speech, can you talk about something you feel with the left hand or see in the left visual field? Yes, easily, if your brain is intact: The information enters your right hemisphere but then passes quickly across the corpus callosum to your left hemisphere.

The result is different if the corpus callosum is severed. A split-brain patient (someone whose corpus callosum has been cut) feels something with the left hand but cannot describe it because the information goes to the right (nonspeech) hemisphere (Nebes, 1974; Sperry, 1967). If asked to point to it, the person points correctly only with the left hand. In fact, while correctly pointing with the left hand, the person might say, "I have no idea what it was. I didn't feel anything." Evidently, the right hemisphere can understand the in-

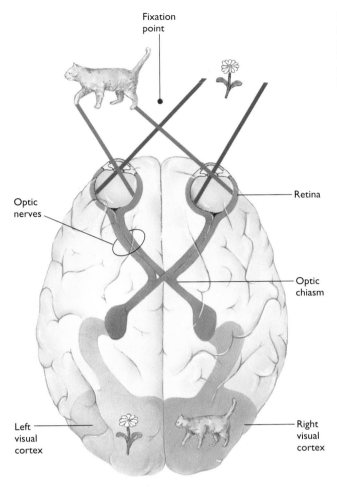

Fixation point

Optic nerves

Retina

Optic chiasm

Left visual cortex

Right visual cortex

FIGURE 3.27 In the human visual system (viewed here from above), light from either half of the world crosses through the pupils to strike the opposite side of each retina. Axons from the left half of each retina travel to the left hemisphere of the brain; axons from the right half of each retina travel to the right hemisphere of the brain.

in the middle of the screen. The investigator flashes a word such as *hatband* on the screen for a split second, too briefly for an eye movement, and asks for the word. The reply is, "band," which is what the left hemisphere saw. (Information from the right side, you will recall, goes to the left side of each retina and from there to the left hemisphere.) To the question of what *kind* of band it might be, the reply is, "I don't know. Jazz band? Rubber band?" However, the left hand points to a hat (which the right hemisphere saw).

Split-brain people get along reasonably well with common behaviors such as walking or even tying shoes because well-practiced behaviors don't need much input from the cerebral cortex anyway. The problem comes with unfamiliar behaviors. Two split-brain people were asked "pretend you're threading a needle" and "pretend you're attaching a fishhook to a line." The two behaviors require almost the same movements. The person who had frequently threaded a needle before the operation had no trouble threading an imaginary needle but couldn't show how to attach a fishhook. Another who had previously attached many fishhooks but never used a sewing needle had the opposite results (Franz, Waldie, & Smith, 2000).

In special circumstances the two hemispheres cooperate in clever ways. One split-brain person was looking at pictures flashed on a screen, as in Figure 3.28a. He could seldom name the objects flashed in the left visual field, but after some delay, he could name simple shapes. Here is how he did it: After seeing the object in the left visual field (with the right hemisphere), he let his eyes move around the room. (Both hemispheres control the eye muscles.) When the right hemisphere

structions and answer with the hand it controls, but it cannot talk.

Now consider what happens when a split-brain patient sees something (Figure 3.28). Ordinarily, the person moves the eyes and sees the same thing in both hemispheres. In the laboratory, however, researchers can flash information faster than the eyes can move. The person in Figure 3.28 focuses the eyes on a point

a

b

c

FIGURE 3.28 (a) When the word hatband is flashed on a screen, a split-brain patient reports only what the left hemisphere saw, *band* and (b) writes *band* with the right hand. However, (c) the left hand (controlled by the right hemisphere) points to a hat, which is what the right hemisphere saw.

saw something with the same shape as the object it had just seen, it would stop moving the eyes. The left hemisphere just waited for the eyes to stop moving and then called out the shape of the object it saw.

CONCEPT CHECK ☑

11. Light from the left side of the world strikes the _____ side of each retina, which sends information to the _____ side of the brain.
12. After damage to the corpus callosum, a person can describe some of what he or she sees, but not all. Where must the person see something to describe it in words? That is, which half of each retina? Which visual field? (Check your answers on page 91.)

The Right and Left Hemispheres

How does the right hemisphere differ from the left? The right hemisphere does not speak, but it understands language, especially with short words and simple grammar. It is especially important for understanding the emotional content of speech; people with right-hemisphere damage often can't tell when a speaker is being sarcastic, and they frequently don't understand jokes (Beeman & Chiarello, 1998). The right hemisphere is also better than the left for recognizing and understanding facial expressions (Stone, Nisenson, Eliassen, & Gazzaniga, 1996) and for tasks that are hard to put into words, such as drawing pictures or arranging puzzle pieces.

Let me describe an interesting study. It will seem that I am changing the subject, but later you will see that I am not. People watched a videotape that showed each of 10 people speaking twice. In one speech they described themselves honestly, and in the other case they told nothing but lies. Do you think you could tell when someone was telling the truth? The average for MIT undergraduates was 47% correct, slightly *less* than they should have done by random guessing. Other groups did about equally badly, except for one group that managed to get 60% correct. (That's not great, but it's better than anyone else did.) Guess who could tell lies from truth. They were people with left-hemisphere brain damage! They could understand almost nothing of what people were saying, so they relied on gestures and facial expressions—which the right hemisphere understands quite well (Etcoff, Ekman, Magee, & Frank, 2000).

Split-brain surgery is rare. We study such patients not because you are likely to meet one but because they teach us something about brain organization: Although we cannot fully explain our experience of a unified consciousness, we see that it depends on communication across brain areas. If communication be-

tween the two hemispheres is lost, then each hemisphere becomes partly independent of the other.

Before closing this section, I want to caution you about a common misunderstanding. The left hemisphere is specialized for language and the right hemisphere for emotional perception and complex visuospatial tasks. Some writers have gone beyond this generalization to claim that the left hemisphere is logical and the right hemisphere is creative, so logical people are left brained and creative people are right brained. Some have even suggested that we could all become more creative if we could find a way to exercise the right hemisphere.

In fact, although certain tasks activate one hemisphere more than the other, complex tasks require both. What's the evidence that some people are left brained or that others are right brained? We have *no* evidence, except in the rare cases of people who have had damage to one hemisphere or the other. Nevertheless, the hypothesis is popular. Some people excuse themselves for thinking illogically by saying, "I'm a right-brained person," with the implication that *because* they are illogical, *therefore* they are creative!

IN CLOSING

Brain and Self

One of the persistent issues of brain science has been whether the brain operates as a whole or as a collection of independent parts. This in turn has implications for psychology. Are you a single thinking, behaving individual or a collection of pieces?

The correct answer is probably somewhere in between. After localized brain damage, a person will lose one kind of behavior (e.g., face recognition) more than others, but in no case does someone lose one function completely without any loss of other functions. No brain area is so specialized that it contributes to just one behavior. Similarly, no behavioral skill is totally independent of the others.

Summary

- *Central and peripheral nervous systems.* The central nervous system consists of the brain and the spinal cord. The peripheral nervous system consists of nerves that communicate between the central nervous system and the rest of the body. (page 78)
- *The cerebral cortex.* The four lobes of the cerebral cortex and their primary functions are: occipital lobe, vision; temporal lobe, hearing and some aspects of vision; parietal lobe, body sensations; frontal lobe, preparation for movement. Damage in the cerebral cortex can produce specialized deficits depending on the location of damage. (page 79)

- *Communication between the cerebral cortex and the rest of the body.* Information from the cerebral cortex passes to the medulla and then on into the spinal cord. The medulla and spinal cord have axons that receive sensory input from the periphery and other axons that send output to the muscles and glands. (page 82)
- *Autonomic nervous system and endocrine system.* The autonomic nervous system controls the body's organs, preparing them for emergency activities or for vegetative activities. The endocrine system consists of organs that release hormones into the blood. (page 83)
- *Imaging brain activity.* Modern technology enables researchers to develop images showing the structure and activity of various brain areas in living, waking people. (page 83)
- *Experience and brain structure.* The anatomy of the nervous system is constantly in flux in small ways. Extensive practice of a behavior can modify brain structure, especially if the practice begins early in life. (page 85)
- *The binding problem.* Brain researchers cannot yet explain how we develop a unified experience of an object even though our registers of hearing, touch, vision, and so forth occur in different brain areas that do not connect directly to one another. Even different aspects of vision depend on different brain areas. (page 86)
- *Corpus callosum.* The corpus callosum is a set of axons through which the left and right hemispheres of the cortex communicate. If the corpus callosum is damaged, information that reaches one hemisphere cannot be shared with the other. (page 87)
- *Connections from eyes to brain.* In humans information from the *left* visual field strikes the *right*

half of both retinas, from which it is sent to the *right* hemisphere of the brain. Information from the *right* visual field strikes the *left* half of both retinas, from which it is sent to the *left* hemisphere. (page 88)
- *Split-brain patients.* The left hemisphere is specialized for language in most people, so split-brain people can describe information only if it enters the left hemisphere. Because of the lack of direct communication between the left and right hemispheres in split-brain patients, such people show signs of having separate fields of awareness. (page 88)

Answers to Concept Checks

7. **a.** parietal lobe; **b.** temporal lobe; **c.** primary motor cortex of the left frontal lobe; **d.** right occipital lobe; **e.** prefrontal cortex. (page 82)
8. Alcohol impairs the cerebellum faster and more visibly than most other brain areas. Many of the common symptoms of alcohol intoxication are due to suppressed activity in the cerebellum. (page 83)
9. Hormones have prolonged effects in widespread areas of the body, whereas a neurotransmitter affects cells close to its point of release. (page 83)
10. Increased branching of axons and dendrites makes it possible for them to form more synapses. (page 86)
11. right . . . right. (page 90)
12. To describe something, a person must see it with the left half of the retina of either eye. The left half of the retina sees the right visual field. (page 90).

CHAPTER ENDING

Key Terms and Activites

Key Terms

action potential: an excitation that travels along an axon at a constant strength, no matter how far it must travel (page 70)

attention deficit disorder (ADD): a condition marked by impulsive behavior and short attention span (page 76)

autonomic nervous system: a system of neurons that controls the internal organs such as the heart (page 83)

axon: a single, long, thin, straight fiber that transmits information from a neuron to other neurons or to muscle cells (page 69)

binding problem: the question of how separate brain areas combine forces to produce a unified perception of a single object (page 87)

cell body: the part of the neuron that contains the nucleus of the cell (page 69)

central nervous system: the brain and the spinal cord (page 78)

cerebellum: (Latin for "little brain") a hindbrain structure that is active in the control of movement, especially for complex, rapid motor skills and behaviors that require precise timing (page 83)

cerebral cortex: the outer surface of the forebrain (page 79)

corpus callosum: a large set of axons connecting the left and right hemispheres of the cerebral cortex and thus enabling the two hemispheres to communicate with each other (page 87)

dendrite: one of the widely branching structures of a neuron that receive transmissions from other neurons (page 69)

dopamine: a neurotransmitter that promotes activity levels and facilitates movement (page 76)

electroencephalograph (EEG): a device that uses electrodes on the scalp to record rapid changes in brain electrical activity (page 83)

endocrine system: a set of glands that produce hormones and release them into the bloodstream (page 83)

epilepsy: a condition characterized by abnormal rhythmic activity of brain neurons (page 87)

frontal lobe: a portion of each cerebral hemisphere at the anterior pole, with sections that control movement and certain aspects of memory (page 81)

functional magnetic resonance imaging (fMRI): a technique that uses magnetic detectors outside the head to measure the amounts of hemoglobin, with and without oxygen, in different parts of the brain and thereby provides an indication of current activity levels in various brain areas (page 84)

glia: a cell of the nervous system that insulates neurons, removes waste materials (e.g., dead cells), and performs other supportive functions (page 69)

hemisphere: the left or right half of the brain; each hemisphere is responsible for sensation and motor control on the opposite side of the body (page 79)

hormone: a chemical released by glands and conveyed by the blood to other parts of the body, where it alters activity (page 83)

magnetoencephalograph (MEG): a device that records rapid magnetic changes during brain activity (page 83)

medulla: a structure that is located in the hindbrain and is an elaboration of the spinal cord; controls many muscles in the head and several life-preserving functions, such as breathing (page 82)

neuron: a cell of the nervous system that receives information and transmits it to other cells by conducting electrochemical impulses (page 69)

neurotransmitter: a chemical that is stored in the terminal of an axon and that, when released, activates receptors of other neurons (page 73)

occipital lobe: the rear portion of each cerebral hemisphere, critical for vision (page 79)

parietal lobe: a portion of each cerebral hemisphere; the main receiving area for the sense of touch and for the awareness of one's own body and perception of location of the body in space (page 79)

Parkinson's disease: a condition that affects about 1% of people over the age of 50; the main symptoms are difficulty in initiating voluntary movement, slowness of movement, tremors, rigidity, and depressed mood (page 76)

peripheral nervous system: the bundles of axons that convey messages between the spinal cord and the rest of the body (page 78)

pons: a structure adjacent to the medulla that receives sensory input from the head and controls many muscles in the head (page 82)

positron-emission tomography (PET): a technique that provides a high-resolution image of brain activity by recording radioactivity emitted from injected chemicals (page 84)

postsynaptic neuron: a neuron on the receiving end of a synapse (page 73)

prefrontal cortex: an area in the anterior portion of the frontal lobes, critical for planning movements and for certain aspects of memory (page 82)

primary motor cortex: a strip in the posterior (rear) part of the frontal cortex that controls fine movements, such as hand and finger movements (page 81)

primary somatosensory cortex: a strip in the anterior (forward) part of the parietal lobe that receives most touch sensations and other information about the body (page 79)

reflex: a rapid, automatic response to a stimulus (page 82)

resting potential: electrical polarization that ordinarily occurs across the membrane of an axon that is not undergoing an action potential (page 70)

somatic nervous system: peripheral nerves that communicate with the skin and muscles (page 78)

spinal cord: that part of the central nervous system that communicates with sensory neurons and motor neurons below the level of the head (page 82)

stem cells: undifferentiated cells (page 86)

synapse: the specialized junction between one neuron and another; at this point one neuron releases a neurotransmitter, which either excites or inhibits the next neuron (page 72)

temporal lobe: a portion of each cerebral hemisphere; the main processing area for hearing, complex aspects of vision, and certain aspects of emotional behavior (page 80)

terminal bouton (or button): a bulge at the end of an axon from which the axon releases a chemical called a neurotransmitter (page 73)

thalamus: a forebrain area that relays information to the cerebral cortex (page 82)

Suggestions for Further Reading

Kalat, J. W. (2004). *Biological psychology* (8th ed.). Belmont, CA: Wadsworth. Chapters 1 through 4 deal with the material discussed in this chapter in more detail.

Klawans, H. L. (1996). *Why Michael couldn't hit.* New York: Freeman. Informative and entertaining account of how the rise and fall of various sports heroes relates to what we know about the brain.

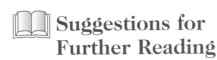 # Book Companion Web Site

Need help studying? Go to

http://psychology.wadsworth.com/kalat_intro7e/

for a virtual study center. You'll find a personalized Self-Study Assessment that will provide you with a study plan based on your answers to a pretest. Also study using flashcards, quizzes, interactive art, and an online glossary.

Check out interactive **Try It Yourself** exercises on the companion site! For example, the Illustration of Binding and Hemisphere Control exercises tie to what you've learned in this chapter.

Your companion site also has direct links to the following Web sites. These links are checked often for changes, dead links, and new additions.

The Whole Brain Atlas

www.med.harvard.edu/AANLIB/home.html

Stunning photographs of both normal and abnormal brains.

Brain Scans

www.biophysics.mcw.edu

Click various links to see images and movies of the three-dimensional structure of the brain.

Brain Images

http://www.musc.edu/psychiatry/fnrd/primer_index.htm

Extensive detail about PET scans and other ways of forming images of living human brains.

Brain Anatomy of Various Species

www.brainmuseum.org/sections/index.html

Compare the brains of humans, chimpanzees, dolphins, weasels, hyenas, polar bears, and a great many other mammals.

 # Try It Yourself CD-ROM
with Critical Thinking Video Exercises

Use your CD to access **videos** related to activities designed to help you think critically about the important topics discussed. For example, the video about neural networks ties to what you've learned in this chapter. You'll also find an easy portal link to the book companion site where you can access your personalized **Self-Study Assessments** and interactive **Try It Yourself** exercises.

PsychNow! 2.0

PsychNow! is a fun interactive CD designed to help you with the difficult concepts in psychology. Check out the Accessing Psychology section for the following topics that relate to this chapter:

Neurons and Synaptic Transmission: neuron concentration game, parts of the neuron, 3-D virtual brain animation, and quiz.

Brain and Behavior: explore potassium depletion, cerebral cortex and subcortex lesson, and a brain and behavior review. *ExperimentNOW! Research Experiments:* Neurocognition— Brain Asymmetry

© Lynn Rogers

Sensation and Perception

When my son Sam was 8 years old, he asked me, "If we went to some other planet, would we see different colors?" He did not mean a new mixture of familiar colors. He meant colors that were as different from familiar colors as yellow is from red or blue. I told him that would be impossible, and I tried to explain why.

No matter where we go in outer space, no matter what unfamiliar objects or atmospheres we might encounter, we could never experience a color or a sound or any other sensation that would be fundamentally different from what we experience on Earth. Different combinations, perhaps. But fundamentally different sensory experiences, no.

■ No matter how exotic some other planet might be, it could not have colors we do not have here. The reason is that our eyes can see only certain wavelengths of light, and color is the experience our brains create from those wavelengths.

Three years later, Sam told me he wondered whether people who look at the same thing are all having the same experience: When different people look at something and call it "green," how can we know whether they are all seeing the same "green"? I agreed that there is no way of knowing for sure.

Why am I certain that colors on a different planet would look the same as they do here on Earth and yet uncertain whether colors look the same to different people here? The answer may be obvious to you. If not, I hope it will be after you have read this chapter.

Sensation is the *conversion of energy from the environment into a pattern of response by the nervous system.* It is the registration of information. **Perception** is *the interpretation of that information.* For example, light rays striking your eyes give rise to sensation. When you conclude from that sensation, "I see my roommate," you are expressing your perception. (In practice the distinction between sensation and perception is often difficult to make.)

Vision

How do our eyes convert light energy into something that we can experience?

How do we perceive colors?

We are constantly surrounded by **stimuli**—*energies that affect what we do.* Our eyes, ears, and other sensory organs are packed with **receptors**—*specialized cells that convert environmental energies into signals for the nervous system.* We see, hear, and so forth because stimuli activate receptors, which in turn send messages to the brain, which eventually uses this information to guide our behavior.

You have probably already learned this account in a high school or even elementary school science class. But did you believe it? Evidently, not everyone does. One survey posed the questions, "When we look at someone or something, does anything such as rays, waves, or energy go out of our eyes? Into our eyes?" Among first graders (about age 6), 49% answered (incorrectly) that energy went out of the eyes, and 54% answered that energy came into the eyes. (It was possible to say *yes* to both.) Among college students, 33% said that energy went out of the eyes; 88% said that energy came in (Winer & Cottrell, 1996).

Follow-up studies revealed that the students did not simply misunderstand the question. They really believed that their eyes sent out rays and that those rays were essential to vision. Even after reading a textbook chapter that explained vision, they did no better. After a psychologist patiently explained that the eyes do *not* send out sight rays, most answered correctly, but when asked again a few months later, almost half had gone back to believing their eyes sent out sight rays (Winer, Cottrell, Gregg, Fournier, & Bica, 2002). (It is hard to imagine a more discouraging comment on the ineffectiveness of education.)

Many people have additional misconceptions about vision. We are often led astray because we imagine that what we see is a copy of the outside world, but it is not. For example, color is not a property of objects; it is something your brain creates in response to light of different wavelengths. Brightness is not the same as the intensity of the light. (Light that is twice as intense does not appear twice as bright.) Our experiences *translate* the stimuli of the outside world into very different representations.

The Detection of Light

What we call *light* is just one part of the electromagnetic spectrum. As Figure 4.1 shows, the **electromagnetic spectrum is** *the continuum of all the frequencies of radiated energy*—from gamma rays and x-rays with very short wavelengths, through ultraviolet, visible light, and infrared to radio and TV transmissions with very long wavelengths.

FIGURE 4.1 Visible light, what human eyes can see, is only a small part of the entire electromagnetic spectrum. While experimenting with prisms, Isaac Newton discovered that white light is a mixture of all colors, and color is a property of light. A carrot looks orange because it reflects orange light and absorbs all the other colors.

What makes "visible light" visible? The answer is our receptors, which are equipped to respond to wavelengths from 400 to 700 nanometers (nm). With different receptors we might see a different range of wavelengths. Some species—bees, for example—respond to wavelengths shorter than 350 nm, which are invisible to humans.

The Structure of the Eye

When we see an object, light reflected from that object passes through the **pupil,** *an adjustable opening in the eye through which light enters.* The **iris** is the *colored structure on the surface of the eye, surrounding the pupil.* It is the structure we describe when we say someone has brown, green, or blue eyes. When the light is dim, muscles widen the pupil to let in more light. When the light is bright, muscles narrow the pupil.

After light passes through the pupil, it travels through the *vitreous humor* (a clear jellylike substance) and strikes the retina at the back of the eyeball. The **retina** is a *layer of visual receptors covering the back surface of the eyeball* (Figure 4.2). As light passes through the eye, the cornea and the lens focus the light on the retina as shown. The **cornea,** *a rigid transparent structure on the outer surface of the eyeball,* always focuses light in the same way. The **lens** is

a *flexible structure that can vary in thickness,* enabling the eye to **accommodate,** that is, *to adjust its focus for objects at different distances.* When we look at a distant object, for example, our eye muscles relax and let the lens become thinner and flatter, as shown in Figure 4.3a. When we look at a close object, our eye muscles tighten and make the lens thicker and rounder (Figure 4.3b).

The **fovea** (FOE-vee-uh), *the central area of the human retina,* is adapted for highly detailed vision (Figure 4.2). Of all retinal areas, the fovea has the greatest density of receptors; also, more of the cerebral cortex is devoted to analyzing input from the fovea than input from other areas. If you want to see something in detail, such as letters of the alphabet, you focus it on the fovea.

Hawks, owls, and other predatory birds have a greater density of receptors on the top of the retina (for looking down) than on the bottom of the retina

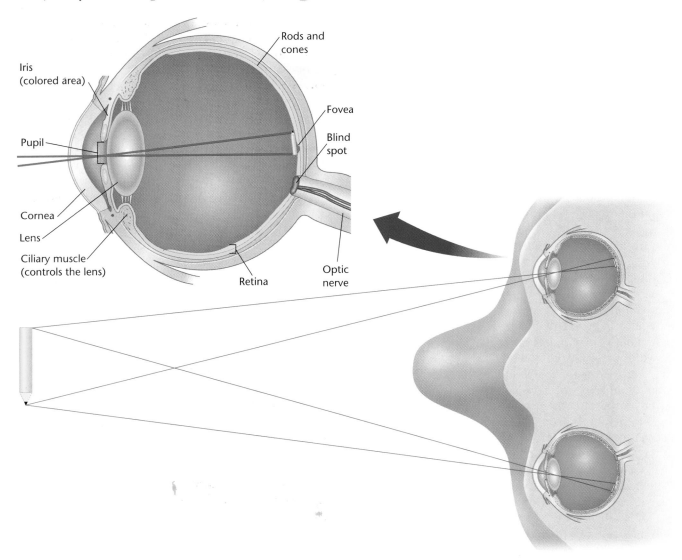

FIGURE 4.2 The lens gets its name from Latin for *lentil,* referring to its shape—an appropriate choice, as this cross section of the eye shows. The names of other parts of the eye also refer to their appearance.

a

Cornea

Lens

Focus on distant object
(lens thin)

b

Cornea

Lens

Focus on close object
(lens thick)

FIGURE 4.3 The flexible, transparent lens changes shape so that objects (a) far and (b) near can come into focus. The lens bends entering light rays so that they fall on the retina. In old age the lens becomes rigid, and people find it harder to focus on nearby objects.

(for looking up). When these birds are flying, this arrangement enables them to see the ground beneath them in detail. When they are on the ground, however, they have trouble seeing above themselves (Figure 4.4).

© Swift Photography/Chase Swift

FIGURE 4.4 The consequence of having receptors mostly on the top of the retina: Birds of prey, such as these owlets, can see down much more clearly than they can see up. In flight that arrangement is helpful. On the ground they have to turn their heads almost upside down to see above them.

Some Common Disorders of Vision

As people grow older, they gradually develop **presbyopia,** *decreased flexibility of the lens and therefore inability to focus on nearby objects.* (The Greek root *presby* means "old." This root also shows up in the word *presbyterian,* which means "governed by the elders.") Many people's eyes are not quite spherical. A person whose eyeballs are elongated, as shown in Figure 4.5a, can focus well on nearby objects but has difficulty focusing on distant objects. Such a person is said to be *nearsighted,* or to have **myopia** (mi-O-pee-ah). About half of all 20-year-olds are nearsighted and must wear glasses or contact lenses to see well at a distance. An older person with both myopia and presbyopia needs bifocal glasses to help with both near focus and distant focus. A person whose eyeballs are flattened, as shown in Figure 4.5b, has **hyperopia, or** *farsightedness.* Such a person can focus well on distant objects but has difficulty focusing on close objects.

Two other common visual disorders are glaucoma and cataracts. **Glaucoma** is a *condition characterized by increased pressure within the eyeball;* the result can be damage to the optic nerve and therefore a progressive loss of peripheral vision ("tunnel vision"). A **cataract** is a *disorder in which the lens becomes cloudy.* People with severe cataracts can have the lens surgically removed and replaced with a contact lens. Because the normal lens filters out more blue and ultraviolet light than other light, people with artificial lenses sometimes report seeing blue more clearly and distinctly than they ever had before (Davenport & Foley, 1979). They do, however, suffer increased risk of damage to the retina from ultraviolet light.

CONCEPT CHECK ☑

1. Suppose you have normal vision and you try on a pair of glasses made for a person with myopia. How will the glasses affect your vision? (Check your answer on page 110.)

The Visual Receptors

The visual receptors of the eye, specialized neurons in the retina at the back of the eyeball, are so sensitive to light that they are capable of responding to a single photon, the smallest possible quantity of light. There are two types of visual receptors: cones and rods, which differ in appearance, as Figure 4.6 shows, and in function. The **cones** are *receptors adapted for color vision, daytime vision, and detailed vision.* The **rods** are *receptors adapted for vision in dim light.*

About 5 to 10% of all the visual receptors in the human retina are cones. Most birds have at least that high a proportion of cones and correspondingly have good color vision. Species that are active mostly at

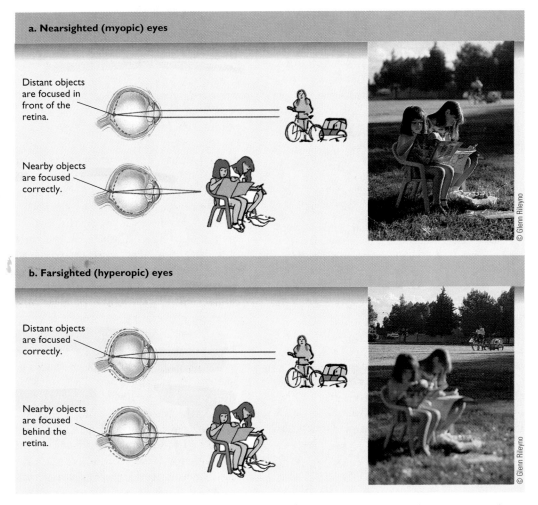

a. Nearsighted (myopic) eyes

Distant objects are focused in front of the retina.

Nearby objects are focused correctly.

© Glenn Rileyno

b. Farsighted (hyperopic) eyes

Distant objects are focused correctly.

Nearby objects are focused behind the retina.

© Glenn Rileyno

FIGURE 4.5 The structure of (a) nearsighted and (b) farsighted eyes distorts vision. Because the nearsighted eye is elongated, light from a distant object focuses in front of the retina. Because the farsighted eye is flattened, light from a nearby object focuses behind the retina. (The dashed line shows the position of the normal retina in each case.)

night—rats and mice, for example—have mostly rods and thus good perception in faint light.

The proportion of cones is highest toward the center of the retina. The fovea consists solely of cones (Figure 4.2). Away from the fovea, the proportion of cones drops sharply. For that reason you are colorblind in the far periphery of your eye.

Try this experiment: Hold several pens or pencils of different colors behind your back. (Any objects will work as long as they have about the same size and shape and approximately the same brightness.) Pick one at random without looking at it. Hold it behind your head and bring it very

FIGURE 4.6 Rods and cones seen through a scanning electron micrograph. The rods, which number over 120 million in humans, provide vision in dim light. The 6 million cones in the retina can distinguish gradations of color in bright light; they enable us to see that roses are red, magenta, ruby, carmine, cherry, vermilion, scarlet, and crimson—not to mention pink, yellow, orange, and white.

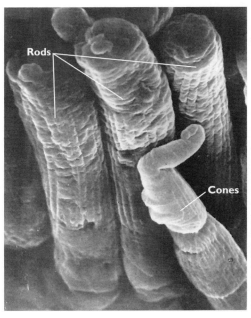

Rods

Cones

© E.R. Lewis, F.S. Werb, & Y.Y. Zeevi

slowly into your field of vision. When you just barely begin to see it, you will probably not be able to tell what color it is. (If glaucoma or another medical problem has impaired your peripheral vision, you will have to bring the object closer to your fovea before you can see it at all, and then you will see its color at once.) Go to http://psychology.wadsworth.com/kalat_intro7e. Navigate to the student Web site, then to the Online Try it Yourself section, and click on Blindness in Visual Periphery.

The rods are more effective than the cones for detecting dim light for two reasons: First, a rod is slightly more responsive to faint stimulation than a cone is. Second, the rods pool their resources. Only a few cones converge their messages onto the next cell, called a *bipolar cell,* whereas many rods converge their messages. In the far periphery of the retina, more than 100 rods send messages to a bipolar cell (see Figure 4.7). Table 4.1 summarizes some of the key differences between rods and cones.

FIGURE 4.7 Because so many rods converge their input into the next layer of the visual system, known as bipolar cells, even a small amount of light falling on the rods stimulates the bipolar cells. Thus, the periphery of the retina, with many rods, readily detects faint light. However, because bipolars in the periphery get input from so many receptors, they have only imprecise information about the location and shape of objects.

CONCEPT CHECK ☑

2. Why is it easier to see a faint star in the sky if you look slightly to the side of the star instead of straight at it? (Check your answer on page 110.)

Dark Adaptation

Suppose you go into a basement at night trying to find your flashlight. The only light bulb in the basement is burned out. A little moonlight comes through the basement windows, but not much. At first you can hardly see anything. A minute or two later, you are beginning to see well enough to find your way around, and eventually, you can see well enough to find the flashlight. This *gradual improvement in the ability to see in dim light* is called **dark adaptation.**

The mechanism behind dark adaptation is this: Exposure to light causes a chemical change in certain molecules called *retinaldehydes,* thereby stimulating the visual receptors. (Retinaldehydes are derived from vitamin A.) Under normal (moderate) light, the receptors *regenerate* (rebuild) the molecules about as fast as the light alters them, and the person maintains about a constant level of visual sensitivity. In darkness or very dim light, however, the receptors can regenerate their molecules without interruption, so the person gradually becomes better able to detect faint lights.

The cones and rods adapt to the dark at different rates. During the day our vision ordinarily relies overwhelmingly on cones. When we enter a dark place, our cones regenerate their retinaldehydes faster than the rods do, but by the time the rods finish their regeneration, they are far more sensitive to faint light than the cones are. At that point we are seeing mostly with rods.

Here is how a psychologist demonstrates this process of dark adaptation (E. B. Goldstein, 1989): You are taken into a room that is completely dark except for one tiny flashing light. You have a knob that

TABLE 4.1 Differences Between Rods and Cones

	Rods	Cones
Shape	Nearly cylindrical	Tapered at one end
Prevalence in human retina	90–95%	5–10%
Abundant in	All vertebrate species	Species active during the day (birds, monkeys, apes, humans)
Area of the retina	Toward the periphery	Toward the fovea
Important for color vision?	No	Yes
Important for detail?	No	Yes
Important in dim light?	Yes	No
Number of types	Just one	Three types

controls the intensity of the light; you are told to make the light so dim that you can barely see it. Over the course of 3 or 4 minutes, you will gradually decrease the intensity of the light, as shown in Figure 4.8a. Note that a decrease in the intensity of the light indicates an increase in the sensitivity of your eyes. If you stare straight at the point of light, your results will demonstrate the adaptation of your cones to the dim light. (You have been focusing the light on your fovea, which has no rods.)

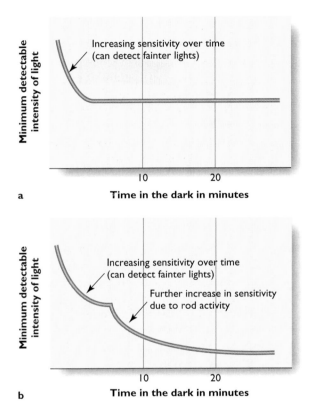

a
Time in the dark in minutes

b
Time in the dark in minutes

FIGURE 4.8 These graphs show dark adaptation to (a) a light you stare at directly, using only cones, and (b) a light in your peripheral vision, which you see with both cones and rods. *(Based on E. B. Goldstein, 1989)*

Now the psychologist repeats the study with one change in procedure: You are told to stare at a very faint light while another light flashes somewhat to the side of the fovea, where it stimulates both rods and cones. You turn a control knob until the flashing light in the periphery is just barely visible. (Figure 4.8b shows the results.) During the first 7 to 10 minutes, the results are the same as before. But then your rods become more sensitive than your cones, and you begin to see even fainter lights. Your rods continue to adapt to the dark over the next 20 minutes or so.

To demonstrate dark adaptation for yourself without any apparatus, try this: At night turn on one light in your room. Close one eye and cover it tightly with your hand for at least 1 minute, preferably longer. Your covered eye will adapt to the dark while your open eye remains adapted to the light. Next turn off your light and open both eyes. You will see better with your dark-adapted eye than with the light-adapted eye. (This instruction assumes you still have some faint light coming through the window. In a *completely* dark room, of course, you will see nothing with either eye.)

CONCEPT CHECK ✓

3. You may have heard people say that cats can see in total darkness. Is that possible?
4. After you have thoroughly adapted to extremely dim light, will you see more objects in your fovea or in the periphery of your eye? (Check your answers on pages 110, 111.)

The Visual Pathway

If you or I were designing an eye, we would probably run the axons of the cones and rods straight to the brain. Nature chose a different method. The visual receptors send their impulses *away from* the brain, toward the center of the eye, where they make synaptic contacts with other neurons called bipolar cells. The bipolar cells in turn make contact with still other neurons, the **ganglion cells,** which are *neurons that receive their input from the bipolar cells.* The *axons from the ganglion cells join to form* the **optic nerve,** *which turns around and exits the eye,* as Figures 4.2 and 4.9 show. Half of each optic nerve crosses to the opposite side of the brain at the optic chiasm (KI-az-m). Axons from the optic nerve then separate and go to several locations in the brain. In humans most go to the thalamus, which then sends information to the primary visual cortex in the occipital lobe. People vary in the number of axons they have in the optic nerve; some have up to three times as many as others. Those with the thickest optic nerves can see fainter or briefer lights and can detect smaller amounts of movement (Andrews, Halpern, & Purves, 1997; Halpern, Andrews, & Purves, 1999).

The *retinal area where the optic nerve exits* is called the **blind spot.** There is no room for receptors here because the exiting axons take up all the space. Ordinarily, you are unaware of your blind spot.

To illustrate, cover your left eye and stare at the center of Figure 4.10; then slowly move the page forward and backward. When your eye is about 25 to 30 cm

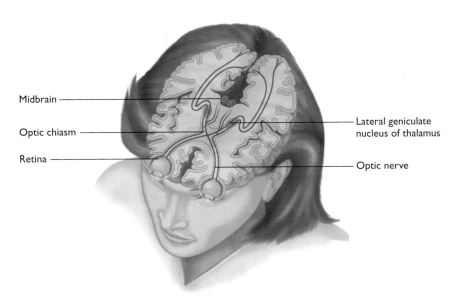

Midbrain

Optic chiasm

Retina

Lateral geniculate
nucleus of thalamus

Optic nerve

FIGURE 4.9 Axons from cells in the retina depart the eye at the blind spot and form the optic nerve. In humans about half the axons in the optic nerve cross to the opposite side of the brain at the optic chiasm. Some optic nerve axons carry information to the midbrain; others carry it to the thalamus, which relays information to the cerebral cortex.

some large blood vessels, and many receptors in the retina fall in the shadow of these blood vessels. We do not notice them, however, as our brain fills in the gaps with what "must" be there (Adams & Horton, 2002).

Information from the left and right eyes remains separate until it reaches the visual cortex. Each cell in the visual cortex receives input from one part of the left retina and a corresponding part of the right retina—that is, two retinal areas that ordinarily focus on the same point in space. Under normal conditions the input coming from the left retina is almost the same as that coming from the right retina, and the two effects summate. However, examine Figure 4.11 to see what happens if the retinal images conflict.

(10 to 12 inches) away from the page, the lion disappears because it falls into your blind spot. In its place you perceive a continuation of the circle. Go to http://psychology.wadsworth.com/kalat_intro7e. Navigate to the student Web site, then to the Online Try it Yourself section, and click on Filling in the Blind Spot.

Online Try It Yourself

In fact we have little "blind spots" throughout the retina. The retina has

FIGURE 4.10 Close your left eye and focus your right eye on the animal trainer. Move the page toward your eyes and away from them, until you find the point where the lion on the right disappears. At that point the lion is focused on the blind spot of your retina, where you have no receptors. What you see there is not a blank spot but a continuation of the circle.

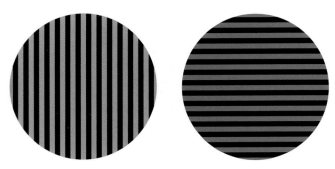

FIGURE 4.11 To produce binocular rivalry, move your eyes toward the page until the two circles seem to merge. You will alternate between seeing red lines and green lines.

Look at the two circles in Figure 4.11 and bring the page so close to your eyes that your nose touches or almost touches the page. At this point the two circles seem to merge. Some of the neurons in your visual cortex respond to vertical lines. When you merge the two circles, those cells are stimulated by the green and black vertical stripes and inhibited by the red and black horizontal stripes. For a short while, the stimulation dominates, but then for a while, the inhibition dominates. Meanwhile, inhibition and stimulation are also alternating for cells that respond to horizontal lines. The net effect is that you see green lines, then red lines, then green lines again, and so forth. With effort you can voluntarily direct attention toward the red lines or the green lines, but you cannot maintain control for long; soon the other pattern emerges again (Blake & Logothetis, 2002). The *alternation between seeing the pattern in the left retina and the pattern in the right retina* is known as **binocular rivalry.**

We become aware of visual information only after it reaches the cerebral cortex. Someone who has intact eyes but a damaged visual cortex is blind and even loses visual imagery. However,

someone with damaged eyes and an intact brain can at least imagine visual scenes. One laboratory has developed a way to bypass damaged eyes and send visual information directly to the brain. As shown in Figure 4.12, a camera attached to a blind person's sunglasses sends messages to a computer, which then sends messages to electrodes that stimulate appropriate spots in the person's visual cortex (Dobelle, 2000). After hours of practice, such people can see well enough to find their way around, to identify simple shapes, and to count how many fingers someone holds up. The goal is a more elaborate array of electrodes that might be more useful than a guide dog without being much more expensive.

Color Vision

As Figure 4.1 shows, different colors of light correspond to different wavelengths of electromagnetic energy. (White light consists of an equal mixture of all the visible wavelengths.) How does the visual system convert these wavelengths into our perception of color? The process begins with three kinds of cones, which respond to different wavelengths of light. Later cells in the visual path code this wavelength information in terms of pairs of opposites— roughly, red versus green, yellow versus blue, and white versus black. Finally, cells in the cerebral cortex compare the input from various parts of the visual field to synthesize a color experience for each object. We shall examine these three stages in turn.

The Trichromatic Theory

Thomas Young was an English physician of the 1700s who, among other accomplishments, helped to decode the Rosetta stone (making it possible to understand Egyptian hieroglyphics), introduced the modern concept of energy, revived and popularized the wave theory of light, showed how to calculate annuities

FIGURE 4.12 William Dobelle has developed an apparatus that takes an image from a camera attached to a blind person's sunglasses, transforms it by a computer, and sends a message to electrodes in the visual cortex. By this means someone with damaged eyes regains some vision.

for insurance, and offered the first theory about how people perceive color (Martindale, 2001). His theory, elaborated and modified by Hermann von Helmholtz in the 1800s, came to be known as the **trichromatic theory** or the **Young-Helmholtz theory**. It is called *trichromatic* because it claims that our receptors respond to three primary colors. In modern terms we say that *color vision depends on the relative rate of response by three types of cones.* Each type of cone is most sensitive to a particular range of light wavelengths (Figure 4.13). One type is most sensitive to short wavelengths (which we generally see as blue), another to medium wavelengths (seen as green), and another to long wavelengths (red). Each wavelength prompts varying levels of activity in the three types of cones. So, for example, green light excites mostly the medium-wavelength cones, red light excites mostly the long-wavelength cones, and yellow light excites the medium-wavelength and long-wavelength cones about equally. Every wavelength of light produces its own distinct ratio of responses by the three kinds of cones. White light excites all three kinds of cones equally.

Young and Helmholtz proposed their theory long before experiments confirmed the existence of these three types of cones (Wald, 1968). They relied entirely on a behavioral observation: Observers can take three different colors of light and then, by mixing them in various proportions, match all other colors of light. (Note that mixing light of different colors is not the same as mixing paints of different colors. Mixing yellow and blue *paints* produces green; mixing yellow and blue *lights* produces white.)

The short-wavelength cones, which respond most strongly to blue, are less numerous than the other two types of cones, especially in the fovea. Consequently, a tiny blue point may look black. For the retina to detect blueness, the blue must extend over a moderately large area.

Figure 4.14 illustrates this effect. Count the red spots and then the blue spots. Then stand farther away and count the spots again. You will probably see as many red spots as before but fewer blue spots.

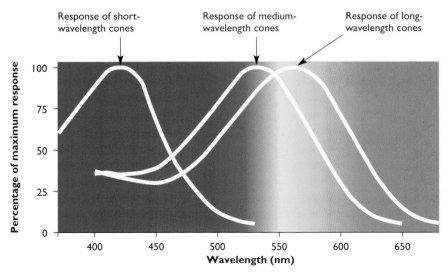

FIGURE 4.14 Blue spots look black unless they cover a sizable area. Count the red dots; then count the blue dots. Try again while standing farther away from the page.

CONCEPT CHECK ☑

5. According to the trichromatic theory, how does our nervous system tell the difference between bright yellow-green and dim yellow-green light? (Check your answer on page 111.)

The Opponent-Process Theory

Young and Helmholtz were right about how many cones we have, but our perception of color has some complicated features that the trichromatic theory cannot easily handle. For example, four colors, not three, *seem* primary or basic to most people: red, green, yellow, and blue. Yellow simply does not seem like a mixture of reddish and greenish experiences, nor is green a yellowish blue. More important, if you stare for a minute or so at something red and look away, you see a green afterimage. If you stare at something green, yellow, or blue, you see a red, blue, or yellow afterimage. The trichromatic theory provides no easy explanation for these afterimages.

Therefore, a 19th-century scientist, Ewald Hering, proposed the **opponent-process theory** of color vision: *We perceive color not in terms of independent colors but in terms of a system of paired opposites—red versus green, yellow versus blue, and white versus black.* This idea is best explained with an example.

FIGURE 4.13 Sensitivity of three types of cones to different wavelengths of light. *(Based on data of Bowmaker & Dartnall, 1980)*

Response of short-wavelength cones

Response of medium-wavelength cones

Response of long-wavelength cones

Percentage of maximum response

100
75
50
25
0

400 450 500 550 600 650

Wavelength (nm)

Stare at one of Daffy's pupils near the center of the Figure 4.15 for a minute or so under a bright light without moving your eyes or your head. Then look at a plain white or gray background. *Do this now.*

Try It Yourself

1999

© USPS 1998

AP/Wide World Photos

FIGURE 4.15 Use this image to see the negative afterimages of opposite colors, which rebound after sufficient stimulation. Stare at one of Daffy's pupils for a minute or more; then focus on a white background.

When you looked away, you saw the cartoon in its normal coloration. After staring at something blue, you get a yellow afterimage. Similarly, after staring at yellow, you see blue; after red, you see green; after green, you see red; after white, black; and after black, white. These *experiences of one color after the removal of another* are called *negative afterimages.*

Presumably, the explanation depends on cells somewhere in the nervous system that maintain a spontaneous rate of activity when unstimulated, increase their activity in the presence of, say, green, and decrease it in the presence of red. After prolonged green stimulation fatigues them, they become less active than usual—in other words responding as if in the presence of red. Similarly, other cells would be excited by red and inhibited by green, excited by yellow and inhibited by blue, and so forth. Patterns of this type have been found in many neurons at various locations in the visual parts of the nervous system (DeValois & Jacobs, 1968; Engel, 1999).

CONCEPT CHECK ☑

6. Which theory most easily explains negative color afterimages?
7. The negative afterimage that you created by staring at Figure 4.15 may seem to move against the background. Why doesn't it stay in one place? (Check your answers on page 111.)

The Retinex Theory

The opponent-process theory accounts for many phenomena of color vision but overlooks an important one. Suppose you look at a large white screen illuminated entirely with green light in an otherwise dark room. How would you know whether this is a white screen illuminated with green light or a green screen illuminated with white light? Or a blue screen illuminated with yellow light? (The possibilities go on and on.) The answer is, you wouldn't know. But now someone wearing a brown shirt and blue jeans stands in front of the screen. Suddenly, you see the shirt as brown, the jeans as blue, and the screen as white, even though all the objects are reflecting more green light than anything else. The point is that we do not ordinarily perceive the color of an object in isolation. We perceive color by comparing the light an object reflects to the light that other objects in the scene reflect. As a result we can perceive blue jeans as blue and bananas as yellow regardless of the type of light. This *tendency of an object to appear nearly the same color under a variety of lighting conditions* is called **color constancy** (see Figure 4.16).

In response to such observations, Edwin Land (the inventor of the Polaroid Land camera) proposed the **retinex theory.** According to this theory, *we perceive color through the cerebral cortex's comparison of various retinal patterns.* (*Retinex* is a combination of the words *retina* and *cortex.*) The cerebral cortex compares the patterns of light coming from different areas of the retina and synthesizes a color perception for each area (Land, Hubel, Livingstone, Perry, & Burns, 1983; Land & McCann, 1971).

As Figure 4.16 emphasizes, it is wrong to call short-wavelength light "blue" or long-wavelength light "red" as the text implied a few pages ago. In Figure 4.16 a gray pattern looks blue in one context and yellow in another (Lotto & Purves, 2002; Purves & Lotto, 2003). The "color" is a construction by our brain, not a property of the light itself, and which color our brain constructs depends on multiple circumstances.

In the 1800s the trichromatic theory and the opponent-process theory were considered rival theories, but vision researchers today consider both of them, as well as the retinex theory, correct statements that address different aspects of vision. The trichromatic theory is certainly correct in stating

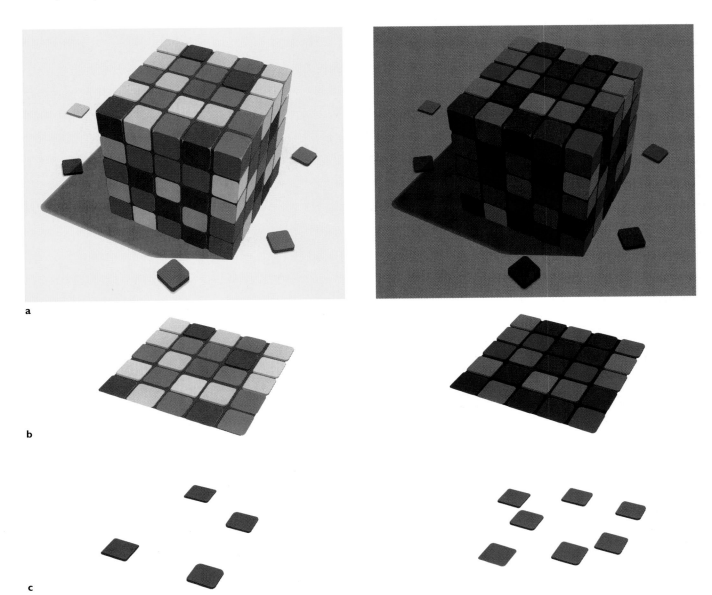

a

b

c

FIGURE 4.16 (a) When the block is under yellow light (left) or blue light (right), you can still recognize individual squares as blue, yellow, white, red, and so forth. However, the actual light reaching your eyes is different in the two cases. Parts b and c show the effects of removing more and more of the background: The squares that appear blue in the left half of part a are actually grayish; so are the squares that appear yellow in the right half. (*Why We See What We Do, by D. Purves and R. B. Lotto, figure 6.10, p. 134. Copyright 2003 Sinauer Associates, Inc. Reprinted by permission.*)

that human color vision starts with three kinds of cones. The opponent-process theory explains how the bipolar cells and later cells organize color information. The retinex theory adds the final touch, noting that the cerebral cortex compares color information from various parts of the visual field.

CRITICAL THINKING:
A STEP FURTHER
Color Afterimages

If you stare for a minute at a small green object on a white background and then look away, you will see a red afterimage. But if you stare at a green wall nearby so that you see nothing but green in all directions, then when you look away, you do not see a red afterimage. Why not?

Color Vision Deficiency

For a long time, people apparently assumed that anyone with normal vision could see and recognize colors (Fletcher & Voke, 1985). Then during the 1600s, the phenomenon of color vision deficiency (or colorblindness) was unambiguously recognized. Here was the first clue that color vision is a function of our eyes and brains and not just of the light itself.

The older term color-*blindness* is misleading because very few people are totally unable to distinguish one color from another. However, about 8% of men and less than 1% of women have difficulty distinguishing red from green and distinguishing either one from yellow (Bowmaker, 1998). The ultimate cause is a recessive gene on the X chromosome. Because men have only one X chromosome, they need just one gene to become red-green color deficient. Women need two such genes to develop the condition because they have two X chromosomes. The result is either a lack of long-wavelength or medium-wavelength cones or a decreased responsiveness of one of those cone types (Fletcher & Voke, 1985). A much smaller number of people have trouble distinguishing yellow from blue, caused by a lack of short-wavelength cones.

Figure 4.17 gives a crude but usually satisfactory test for red-green color vision deficiency. What do you see in each part of the figure? (To interpret your answers, refer to answer A on page 111.)

How does the world look to people who are colorblind? They describe the world with all the usual color words: Roses are red, violets are blue, bananas are yellow, grass is green. But their answers do not mean that they perceive colors the same as other people do. Can they tell us what a "red" rose actually looks like? In most cases no. Certain rare individuals, however, are red-green colorblind in one eye but have normal vision in the other eye. Because they know what the

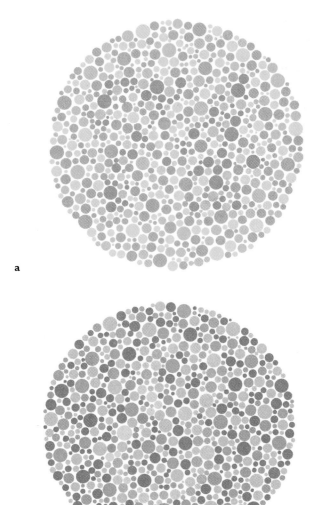

a

b

FIGURE 4.17 These items provide an informal test for red-green color vision deficiency, an inherited condition that mostly affects men. What do you see? Compare your answers to answer A on page 111. *(Reproduced from Ishihara's Test for Color Blindness. Kanehara & Co., Ltd., Tokyo, Japan. A test for color blindness cannot be conducted with this material. For accurate testing, the original plate should be used. Reprinted with permission.)*

color words really mean (from experience with their normal eye), they can tell us what their colorblind eye sees. They say that objects that look red or green to the normal eye look yellow or yellow-gray to the colorblind eye (Marriott, 1976).

If you have normal color vision, Figure 4.18 will show you what it is like to be red-green colorblind. First, cover part b, a typical item from a colorblindness test, and stare at part a, a red field, under a bright light for about a minute. (The brighter the light and the longer you stare, the greater the effect will be.) Then look at part b. Staring at the red field has fatigued your red cones, so you will now have only a weak sensation of red. As the red cones recover, you will see part b normally.

Now stare at part c, a green field, for about a minute and look at part b again. Because you have fatigued your green cones, the figure in b will stand out even more strongly than usual. In fact, certain people with red-green colorblindness may be able to see the number in b only after staring at c. (Refer to answer B on page 111.)

a   b   c

FIGURE 4.18 Adaptation to these stimuli temporarily alters sensitivity to reds and greens. First, stare at pattern (a) under bright light for about a minute and then look at (b). What do you see? Next stare at (c) for a minute and look at (b) again. Now what do you see? Compare your answer to answer B on page 111. *(Reproduced from Ishihara's Test for Color Blindness. Kanehara & Co., Ltd., Tokyo, Japan. A test for color blindness cannot be conducted with this material. For accurate testing, the original plate should be used. Reprinted with permission.)*

Color Vision, Color Words, and Culture

Some languages have more color words than others. For example, English has many words for shades of red, including carnation, crimson, maroon, ruby, and scarlet. Some languages do not even have a word for blue. They either use the same word for blue as for green (think of it as something like "grue") or a single word that means either blue or dark. Can we find any explanation behind this cultural difference? That is, *why* do some cultures have a separate word for blue whereas others do not?

One interesting speculation is based on the pattern shown in Figure 4.19. Many cultures in the tropics lack a separate word for blue, whereas those in more temperate climates have a word for blue. In general, temperate climates (e.g., Europe) have higher literacy rates, and written languages accumulate more words. However, consider another possibility: People in tropical climates generally have greater exposure to direct sunlight, and exposure to the sun accelerates aging of the lens of the eye. The more time someone spends in bright sunlight, the yellower the lens gets and therefore the harder it is to see short-wavelength (blue) light. As the lens ages, what used to appear as blue becomes greenish or dark. The suggestion is that physiological changes in the eye make it difficult for many tropical people to see blue, and consequently, they do not use a word for blue (Lindsey & Brown,

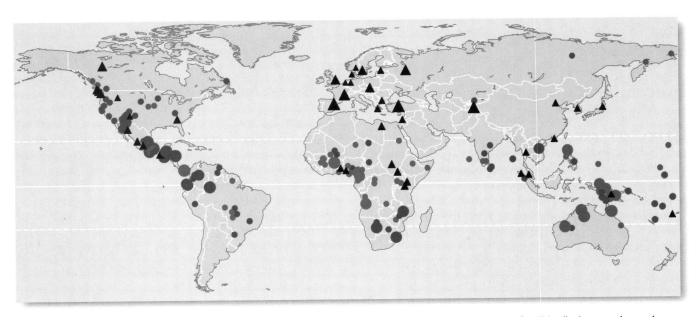

FIGURE 4.19 Each symbol represents one culture. Those with a blue triangle have a separate word for "blue"; those with a red circle have a word meaning "green or blue." Those with a green circle refer to blue objects using the same word as "dark." Note that the cultures lacking a separate word for "blue" are concentrated mostly in or near the tropics. *(Lindsey, D. T., and Brown, A. M., "Color naming and the phototoxic effects of sunlight on the eye," Psychological Science, 13, 506–512. Figure 2, p. 508. Reprinted with permission.)*

2002). (As I said, this explanation is speculative. Can you imagine a good way to test it?)

In the introduction to this chapter, I suggested that we would see no new colors on another planet and that we cannot be certain that different people on Earth really have the same color experiences. Now try to explain the reasons behind those statements.

IN CLOSING

How We See

Before there were any people or other color-sighted animals, was there any color on Earth? *No.* There was light, to be sure, and different objects reflected different wavelengths of light, but color exists only in brains, not in the objects themselves. Our vision is not just a copy of the outside world; it is a construction that enables us to interact with the world to our benefit.

To many readers vision and our other senses seem more complicated than some of the later topics in this book, such as motivation or emotion. It seems that way because researchers have learned so much more about the senses. The more we learn about any topic, the more sophisticated questions we can ask. (If we understand something poorly, neither the questions nor the answers can be very complicated.) The complexity of what we now know about vision is a tribute to many generations of researchers.

Summary

- *Common misconceptions.* The eyes do not send out "sight rays," nor does the brain build little copies of the stimuli it senses. It converts or translates sensory stimuli into an arbitrary code that represents the information. (page 97)
- *Focus.* The cornea and lens focus the light that enters through the pupil of the eye. If the eye is not spherical or if the lens is not flexible, corrective lenses may be needed. (page 98)
- *Cones and rods.* The retina contains two kinds of receptors: cones and rods. Cones are specialized for detailed vision and color perception. Rods detect dim light. (page 99)
- *Blind spot.* The blind spot is the area of the retina through which the optic nerve exits; this area has no visual receptors and is therefore blind. (page 102)
- *Binocular rivalry.* Under normal circumstances the two retinas receive similar information patterns and provide the brain with information for three-dimensional perception. If the two retinas receive incompatible patterns, we experience a competition in which one pattern or the other dominates at any given moment. (page 104)
- *Color vision.* Color vision depends on three types of cones, each most sensitive to a particular range of light wavelengths. The cones transmit messages so that the bipolar and ganglion cells in the visual system are excited by light of one color and inhibited by light of the opposite color. Then the cerebral cortex compares the responses from different parts of the retina to determine the color of light coming from each area of the visual field. (page 104)
- *Color vision deficiency.* Complete colorblindness is rare. Certain people have difficulty distinguishing reds from greens; in rare cases some have difficulty distinguishing yellows from blues. (page 108)

Answers to Concept Checks

1. If your vision is normal, then wearing glasses intended for a myopic person will make your vision blurry. Such glasses alter the light as though they were bringing the object closer to the viewer. Unless the glasses are very strong, you may not notice much difference when you are looking at distant objects because you can adjust the lens of your eyes to compensate for what the glasses do. However, nearby objects will appear blurry in spite of the best compensations that the lenses of your eyes can make. (page 99)
2. The center of the retina consists entirely of cones. If you look slightly to the side, the light falls on an area of the retina that consists partly of rods, which are more sensitive to faint light. (page 101)
3. As do people, cats can adapt well to dim light. No animal, however, can see in complete darkness. Vision is the detection of light that strikes the eye. (Similarly, the x-ray vision attributed to the comic book character Superman is impossible. Even if he could send out x-rays, he would not see anything unless those x-rays bounced off an object and back into his eyes.) (page 102)

4. You will see more objects in the periphery of your eye. The fovea contains only cones, which cannot become as sensitive as the rods do in the periphery. (page 102)

5. Although bright yellow-green and dim yellow-green light would evoke the same ratio of activity by the three cone types, the total amount of activity would be greater for the bright yellow-green light. (page 105)

6. The opponent-process theory most easily explains negative color afterimages because it assumes that we perceive colors in terms of paired opposites, red vs. green and yellow vs. blue (as well as white vs. black). (page 106)

7. The afterimage is on your eye, not on the background. When you try to focus on a different part of the afterimage, you move your eyes and the afterimage moves with them. (page 106)

Answers to Other Questions in the Module

A. In Figure 4.17a a person with normal color vision sees the numeral 74; in Figure 4.17b the numeral 8.

B. In Figure 4.18b you should see the numeral 29. After you have stared at the red circle in part a, the 29 in part b may look less distinct than usual, as though you were red-green colorblind. After staring at the green circle, the 29 may be even more distinct than usual. If you do not see either of these effects at once, try again, but this time stare at part a or c a little longer and continue staring at part b a little longer. The effect does not appear immediately, only after a few seconds.

How do hearing, the vestibular sense, skin senses, pain, taste, and smell work?

Consider these common expressions:

- I *see* what you mean.
- I *feel* your pain.
- I am deeply *touched* by everyone's support and concern.
- The Senate will *hold* hearings on the budget proposal.
- She is a person of fine *taste*.
- He was *dizzy* with success.
- The policies of this company *stink*.
- That *sounds* like a good job offer.

Each sentence expresses an idea in terms of sensation, though we know that these terms are not meant to be taken literally. If you compliment people on their "fine taste," you are not referring to their tongues.

The broad metaphorical use of terms of sensation is not accidental. Our thinking and brain activity deal mostly, if not entirely, with sensory stimuli. Perhaps you doubt that assertion: "What about abstract concepts?" you might object. "Sometimes I think about numbers, time, love, justice, and all sorts of other nonsensory concepts." Yes, but how did you learn those concepts? Didn't you learn numbers by counting objects you could see or touch? Didn't you learn about time by observing changes in sensory stimuli? Didn't you learn about love and justice from specific events that you saw, heard, and felt? Could you explain any abstract concept without referring to something you detect through your senses?

We have already considered how we detect light. Now let's discuss how we detect sounds, head tilt, skin stimulation, and chemicals.

Hearing

What we familiarly call the "ear" is a fleshy structure technically known as the *pinna*. It serves to funnel sounds to the inner ear, where the receptors lie. The mammalian ear converts sound waves into mechanical displacements that a row of receptor cells can detect. **Sound waves** are *vibrations of the air or of another medium*. They vary in both frequency and amplitude (Figure 4.20). The frequency of a sound wave is the number of *cycles (vibrations) that it goes through per second*, designated **hertz (Hz)**. **Pitch** is a *perception closely related to frequency*. We perceive a high-frequency sound wave as high pitched and a low-frequency sound as low pitched.

Loudness is a *perception that depends on the amplitude of sound waves*—that is, their intensity. Other things being equal, the greater the amplitude of a sound, the louder it sounds. Because pitch and loudness are psychological experiences, however, they are influenced by factors other than the physical frequency and amplitude of sound waves. For example, tones of different frequencies may not sound equally loud, even though they have the same physical amplitude.

The ear, a complicated organ, converts relatively weak sound waves into more intense waves of pressure in the *fluid-filled canals of the snail-shaped organ* called the **cochlea** (KOCK-lee-uh), *which contains the receptors for hearing* (Figure 4.21). When

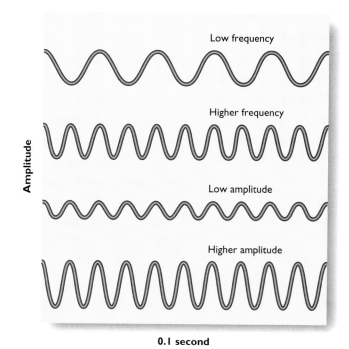

FIGURE 4.20 The period (time) between the peaks of a sound wave determines the frequency of the sound; we experience frequencies as different pitches. The vertical range, or amplitude, of a wave determines the sound's intensity and loudness.

sound waves strike the eardrum, they cause it to vibrate. The eardrum is connected to three tiny bones: the hammer, the anvil, and the stirrup (also known by their Latin names: malleus, incus, and stapes). As the weak vibrations of the large eardrum travel through these bones, they are transformed into stronger vibrations of the much smaller stirrup. The stirrup in turn transmits the vibrations to the fluid-filled cochlea, where the vibrations displace hair cells along the basilar membrane in the cochlea. These hair cells, which act much like touch receptors on the skin, are connected to neurons whose axons form the auditory nerve. The auditory nerve transmits impulses to the brain areas responsible for hearing.

Our knowledge of the mechanisms of hearing enables us to understand and explain hearing loss. One kind of hearing loss is **conduction deafness**, which *results when the bones connected to the eardrum fail to transmit sound waves properly to the cochlea.* Surgery can sometimes correct conduction deafness by removing whatever is obstructing the bones' movement. Someone with conduction deafness can still hear his or her own voice because it is conducted through the skull bones to the cochlea, bypassing the eardrum altogether. The other type of hearing loss is **nerve deafness**, which *results from damage to the cochlea, the hair cells, or the auditory nerve.* Nerve deafness can result from heredity, disease, or prolonged exposure to loud noises. Surgery cannot correct nerve deafness. Hearing aids can compensate for hearing loss in most people with either type of deafness (Moore, 1989). Hearing aids merely increase the intensity of the sound, however, so they are of little help in cases of severe nerve deafness.

Many people have hearing impairments for only certain frequencies. For example, people with damage to certain parts of the cochlea have trouble hearing high frequencies or medium-range frequencies. Modern hearing aids can be adjusted to intensify only the frequencies that a given person has trouble hearing.

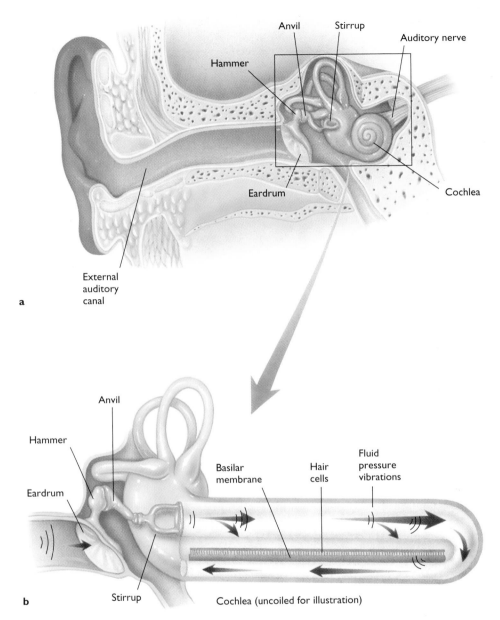

FIGURE 4.21 When sound waves strike the eardrum (a), they cause it to vibrate. The eardrum is connected to three tiny bones—the hammer, anvil, and stirrup—that convert the sound wave into a series of strong vibrations in the fluid-filled cochlea (b). These vibrations displace the hair cells along the basilar membrane in the cochlea, which is aptly named after the Greek word for snail. Here the dimensions of the cochlea have been changed to make the general principles clear.

▌ Hearing is the sensing of vibrations. Evelyn Glennie, profoundly deaf since childhood, has become a famous percussionist. Although she cannot hear her music, she detects the vibrations through her stocking feet.

Pitch Perception

Adult humans can hear sound waves from about 15–20 hertz to about 15,000–20,000 Hz (cycles per second). The low frequencies are perceived as low pitch; the high frequencies are perceived as high pitch, but frequency is not the same as pitch. (For example, doubling the frequency doesn't make the pitch seem twice as high; it makes it one octave higher.) The upper limit of hearing declines with age and also after exposure to loud noises. Thus, children hear higher frequencies than adults do.

We hear pitch by different mechanisms at different frequencies. At low frequencies (up to about 100 Hz), *a sound wave through the fluid of the cochlea vibrates all the hair cells, which produce action potentials in synchrony with the sound waves.* This is the **frequency principle.** For example, a sound with a frequency of 50 Hz makes each hair cell send the brain 50 impulses per second.

Beyond about 100 Hz, hair cells cannot keep pace. (A neuron never fires more than about 1,000 action potentials per second, and it cannot maintain that rate for long.) Even so, each sound wave excites at least a few hair cells, and *"volleys" of them (groups) respond to each vibration by producing an action potential* (Rose, Brugge, Anderson, & Hind, 1967). This is known as the **volley principle.** Thus, a tone at 1000 Hz might send 1,000 impulses to the brain per second, even though no single neuron was firing that rapidly. Volleys can keep up with most speech and music sounds up to about 4000 Hz. (The highest note on a piano is 4224 Hz.)

At still higher frequencies, we must rely on a different mechanism. At each point along the cochlea, the hair cells are tuned resonators that vibrate only for sound waves of a particular frequency. That is, *the highest frequency sounds vibrate hair cells near the stirrup end and lower frequency sounds (down to about 100–200 Hz) vibrate hair cells at points farther along the membrane* (Warren, 1999). This is the **place principle.** Note that tones less than about 100 Hz excite all the hair cells equally, and we hear them by the frequency principle. We identify tones from 100 to 4000 Hz by a combination of the volley principle and the place principle. Beyond 4000 Hz we identify tones only by the place principle. Figure 4.22 summarizes the three principles of pitch perception.

CONCEPT CHECK ☑

8. Suppose a mouse emits a soft high-frequency squeak in a room full of people. Which kinds of people are least likely to hear the squeak?
9. When hair cells at one point along the basilar membrane produce 50 impulses per second, we hear a tone at 5000 Hz. What do we hear when the same hair cells produce 100 impulses per second? (Check your answers on page 124.)

You have heard of people who can listen to a note and identify its pitch by name: "Oh, that's a C-sharp." That ability, called absolute pitch or perfect pitch, is found mostly in people with extensive musical training beginning in childhood (Takeuchi & Hulse, 1993).

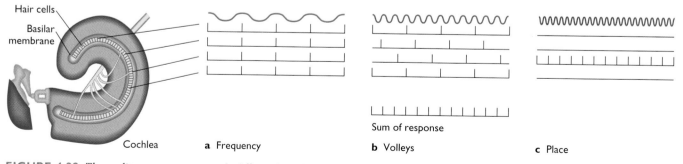

FIGURE 4.22 The auditory system responds differently to low-, medium-, and high-frequency tones. (a) At low frequencies hair cells at many points along the basilar membrane produce impulses in synchrony with the sound waves. (b) At medium frequencies different cells produce impulses in synchrony with different sound waves, but a volley (group) still produces one or more impulses for each wave. (c) At high frequencies only one point along the basilar membrane vibrates; hair cells at other locations remain still.

If you are amazed at absolute pitch, your own ability to recognize (though not name) a specific pitch might surprise you. In one study 48 college students with no special talent or training listened to 5-second segments from television theme songs, played either in their normal key or one-half or one note higher or lower. The students usually could choose which version was correct *if* they had repeatedly watched the program but not if they were unfamiliar with the program (Schellenberg & Trehub, 2003). That is, they remembered the familiar pitches.

You probably also have heard of people who are "tone-deaf." Anyone who was *completely* tone-deaf would be unable even to understand speech, as slight pitch changes differentiate one speech sound from another. However, for unknown reasons, some people are greatly impaired at detecting pitch changes. The result is that any melody sounds the same as any other, and music is no more pleasant than random noise (Peretz et al., 2002).

Localization of Sounds

What you hear is a stimulus in your ear, but you experience the sound as "out there," and you can generally estimate its approximate place of origin. What cues do you use?

The auditory system determines the direction of a source of sound by comparing the messages coming from the two ears. If a sound is coming from a source directly in front, the messages will arrive at the two ears simultaneously with equal loudness. If it comes from the left, however, it will arrive at the left ear slightly before the right ear, and it will be louder in the left ear (Figure 4.23). The timing is important for localizing low-frequency sounds; intensity is the cue for localizing high-frequency sounds.

The auditory system can also detect the approximate distance of a sound source. If a sound grows louder, you interpret it as coming closer. If two sounds differ in pitch, you assume the one with more high-frequency tones is closer. (Low-frequency tones carry better over distance, so if you can hear a high-frequency tone, its source is probably close.) However, loudness and frequency tell

you only the *relative* distances of sound sources, not the *absolute* distance. The only cue for absolute distance is the amount of reverberation (Mershon & King, 1975). In a closed room, you first hear the sound waves coming directly from the source and a little later the waves that reflected off the walls, floor, ceiling, or other objects. If you hear many reflected sounds (echoes), you judge the source of the sound to be far away. In a noisy room, the echoes are hard to hear, so people have trouble localizing sound sources; because they hear few echoes, all sounds seem nearby (McMurtry & Mershon, 1985).

CONCEPT CHECK ☑

10. Why is it difficult to tell whether a sound is coming from directly in front of or directly behind you?

11. If someone who needs hearing aids in both ears wears one in only the left ear, what will be the effect on sound localization?

12. Suppose you are listening to a monaural (nonstereo) radio. Can the station play sounds that you will localize as coming from different directions, such as left, center, and right? Can it play sounds that you will localize as coming from different distances? Why or why not? (Check your answers on page 124.)

FIGURE 4.23 The ear located closest to the sound will receive the sound waves first. That cue is important for localizing low-frequency sounds.

The Vestibular Sense

In the inner ear on each side of the head, adjacent to the structures responsible for hearing, is a structure called the *vestibule*. The **vestibular sense** that it controls *tells us the direction of tilt and amount of acceleration of the head and the position of the head with respect to gravity.* It plays a key role in posture and balance and is responsible for the sensations we experience when we are riding on a roller coaster or sitting in an airplane during takeoff. Intensive vestibular sensations are responsible for the phenomenon of motion sickness.

The vestibular sense also enables us to keep our eyes fixated on a target when our head is moving. When you walk down the street, you can keep your eyes fixated on a distant street sign, even though your head is bobbing up and down. The vestibular sense detects each head movement and controls the movement of your eyes to compensate for it.

To illustrate, try to read this page while you are jiggling the book up and down and from side to side, keeping your head steady. Then hold the book steady and move your head up and down and from side to side. You probably will find it much easier to read when you are moving your head than when you are jiggling the book. The reason is that your vestibular sense keeps your eyes fixated on the print during head movements. People who have suffered injury to

❚ The vestibular sense plays a key role in posture and balance as it reports the position of the head.

© Julie Lemberger/CORBIS

their vestibular sense report that their vision is blurry while they are walking. To read street signs, they must come to a stop.

The vestibular system is composed of three semicircular canals, oriented in three separate directions, and two otolith organs (Figure 4.24b). The *semicircular canals* are lined with hair cells and filled with a jellylike substance. When the body accelerates in any direction, the jellylike substance in the corresponding semicircular canal pushes against the hair cells, which send messages to the brain. The two *otolith organs* shown in Figure 4.24b also contain hair cells (Figure 4.24c), which lie next to the *otoliths* (calcium carbonate particles). Depending on which way the head

tilts, the particles excite different sets of hair cells. The otolith organs report the direction of gravity and therefore which way is up.

If the otoliths provide unreliable information, we can use vision instead. For astronauts in the zero-gravity environment of outer space, the otoliths cannot distinguish up from down; indeed, the up–down dimension is almost meaningless. Instead, they learn to rely entirely on visual signals, such as distance and direction to the walls of the ship (Lackner, 1993).

The Cutaneous Senses

What we commonly think of as the sense of touch consists of several partly independent senses: pressure on the skin, warmth, cold, pain, vibration, movement across the skin, and stretch of the skin. These sensations depend on several kinds of receptors, as Figure 4.25 shows (Iggo & Andres, 1982). A pinprick on the skin feels different from a light touch, and both feel different from a burn, because each excites different receptors. Collectively, these sensations are known as the **cutaneous senses,** meaning the *skin senses.* Although they are most prominent in the skin, we also have them in our internal organs, enabling us to feel internal pain, pressure, and temperature. Therefore, the cutaneous senses are sometimes known as the *somatosensory system,* meaning *body-sensory system.*

One way of studying the cutaneous senses is to examine people who have suffered impairments. After certain kinds of nervous-system damage, people sometimes lose one kind of touch sensation while keeping others. One patient lost the connections of light touch to the primary somatosensory part of his cerebral cortex. He could still feel pain and temperature but had very little sensation from soft touch. For example, if someone stroked a brush across his skin, he reported a "pleasant" sensation, but he could not describe the sensation further and could not tell which direction the brush went (Olausson et al., 2002).

Have you ever wondered about the sensation of itch? Is it a kind of touch or pain or what? The receptors have not been identified, but we know they are stimulated by histamine, a chemical released by injured tissues. When a mosquito bites you or when you are recovering from a wound, released histamines cause an itching sensation. It is definitely unlike pain; in fact it is inhibited by pain (Andrew & Craig, 2001).

FIGURE 4.25 Cutaneous sensation is the product of many kinds of receptors, each sensitive to a particular kind of information.

FIGURE 4.24 (a) Location of and (b) structures of the vestibule. (c) Moving your head or body displaces hair cells that report the tilt of your head and the direction and acceleration of movement.

When you scratch an itchy spot, your scratching has to produce some pain to relieve the itch. For example, if a dentist anesthetizes one side of your mouth prior to dental surgery, as the anesthesia wears off, the itch receptors sometimes recover before the pain and touch receptors. At that point you can scratch the itchy spot, but you don't feel the scratch and it does not relieve the itch.

Tickle is another kind of cutaneous sensation. Have you ever wondered why you can't tickle yourself? Actually, you can, a little, but it's not the same as when someone else tickles you. The reason is that when you are about to touch yourself, certain parts of your brain build up an anticipation response that is quite similar to the result of the actual stimulation (Carlsson, Petrovic, Skare, Petersson, & Ingvar, 2000). That is, when you try to tickle yourself, the sensation comes as no surprise.

Pain

Pain is a cutaneous sensation of obvious importance in medicine and a topic of interest to psychologists as well because of its relation to depression and anxiety. The experience of pain is a complicated mixture of sensation (the information about tissue damage) and emotion (the unpleasant reaction). The sensory and emotional qualities are governed by different brain areas (Craig, Bushnell, Zhang, & Blomqvist, 1994; Fernandez & Turk, 1992). The brain area responsive to the emotional aspect of pain—the *anterior cingulate cortex*—also responds to the emotional "pain" of feeling rejected by other people (Eisenberger, Lieberman, & Williams, 2003). Telling people to expect pain or distracting them from the pain changes the emotional response, including the activity in the anterior cingulate cortex, but does not change the sensation itself (Ploghaus et al., 1999).

The Gate Theory of Pain

You visit a physician because of severe pain, but as soon as the physician tells you the problem is nothing to worry about, the pain starts to subside. Have you ever had such an experience? Pain can increase or decrease greatly because of expectations.

Recall the term *placebo* from Chapter 2: A placebo is a drug or other procedure that has no important effects other than those that result from people's expectations; researchers ordinarily give placebos to control groups. Placebos have little effect on most medical conditions, but they sometimes relieve pain, or at least the emotional distress of pain, quite impressively (Hróbjartsson. & Gøtzsche, 2001). Even the effects of the drug itself depend partly on expectations. When people have a catheter in their arm and receive painkilling medicine without knowing it, the drug is less effective than when people know they are receiving it (Amanzio, Pollo, Maggi, & Benedetti, 2001).

In one experiment college students had a smelly brownish liquid rubbed onto one finger. It was in fact just a placebo, but they were told that it was a painkiller. Then they were given a painful pinch stimulus to that finger and a finger of the other hand. They consistently reported less pain on the finger with the placebo (Montgomery & Kirsch, 1996). How placebos work is far from clear, but these results eliminate mere relaxation, which would presumably affect both hands equally.

Because of observations such as these, Ronald Melzack and P. D. Wall (1965) proposed the **gate theory** of pain, the idea that *pain messages must pass through a gate, presumably in the spinal cord, that can block the messages.* For example, if you injure yourself, rubbing the surrounding skin sends inhibitory messages to the spinal cord, closing the pain gates. Pleasant or distracting events also send inhibitory messages. The gate can also enhance the pain messages; for example, inflamed skin (e.g., after sunburn) increases sensitivity of the spinal cord neurons so that almost any stimulation becomes painful (Malmberg, Chen, Tonegawa, & Basbaum, 1997). In short, the activities of the rest of the nervous system can facilitate or inhibit the transmission of pain messages (Figure 4.26).

Mechanisms of Decreasing Pain

Some people are completely insensitive to pain. Before you start to envy them, consider: They often burn themselves by picking up hot objects, scald their tongues on hot coffee, cut themselves without realizing it, and bite

their tongues hard, possibly even biting off the tip. They sit in a single position for hours without growing uncomfortable, thereby damaging their bones and tendons (Comings & Amromin, 1974).

Although it would be a mistake to rid ourselves of pain altogether, we would like to limit it. One way is to provide distraction. For example, postsurgery patients in a room with a pleasant view complain less about pain, take less painkilling medicine, and recover faster than do patients in a windowless room or a room with a poor view (Ulrich, 1984).

Several other methods depend on medications. *Pain stimuli cause the nervous system to release a neurotransmitter,* called **substance P,** for intense pains and another transmitter, glutamate, for all pains including mild ones. Mice that lack substance P receptors react to all painful stimuli as if they were mild (DeFelipe et al., 1998). Another set of neurons release **endorphins,** *neurotransmitters that inhibit the release of substance P and thereby weaken pain sensations* (Pert & Snyder, 1973) (see Figure 4.27). The term *endorphin* is a combination of the terms *endogenous* (self-produced) and *morphine*. The drug morphine, which stimulates endorphin synapses, has

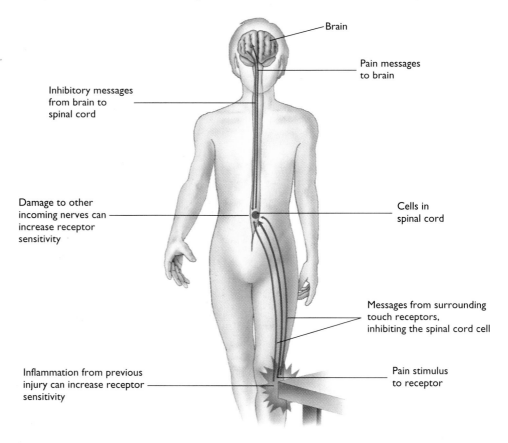

Inhibitory messages from brain to spinal cord

Damage to other incoming nerves can increase receptor sensitivity

Inflammation from previous injury can increase receptor sensitivity

Brain

Pain messages to brain

Cells in spinal cord

Messages from surrounding touch receptors, inhibiting the spinal cord cell

Pain stimulus to receptor

FIGURE 4.26 Pain messages from the skin are relayed from spinal cord cells to the brain. According to the gate theory of pain, those spinal cord cells serve as a gate that can block or enhance the signal. The proposed neural circuitry is simplified in this diagram. Green lines indicate axons with excitatory inputs; red lines indicate axons with inhibitory inputs.

FIGURE 4.27 Substance P is the neurotransmitter most responsible for pain sensations. Endorphins are neurotransmitters that block the release of substance P, thereby decreasing pain sensations. Opiates decrease pain by imitating the effects of endorphins.

long been known for its ability to inhibit dull, lingering pains. Endorphins are also released by pleasant experiences, such as sexual activity or thrilling music (A. Goldstein, 1980). (That effect may help to explain why a pleasant view helps to ease postsurgical pain.) In short, endorphins are a powerful method of closing pain gates.

Paradoxically, another method of decreasing pain begins by inducing it. The *chemical* **capsaicin** *stimulates receptors that respond to painful heat* (Caterina, Rosen, Tominaga, Brake, & Julius, 1999) and thereby *causes the release of substance P.* Capsaicin is the chemical that makes jalapeños and similar peppers taste hot. Injecting capsaicin or rubbing it on the skin produces a temporary burning sensation (Yarsh, Farb, Leeman, & Jessell, 1979). However, after that burning sensation subsides, the skin becomes less sensitive to pain than usual. Several skin creams intended for the relief of aching muscles contain capsaicin. One reason capsaicin decreases pain is that it releases substance P faster than the neurons can resynthesize it. However, that explanation cannot be complete because rapid repetition of capsaicin (which should deplete substance P even more) increases the pain instead of decreasing it (B. G. Green, 1996).

CONCEPT CHECK ☑

13. Naloxone, a drug used as an antidote for an overdose of morphine, is known to block the endorphin synapses. How could we use naloxone to determine whether a pleasant stimulus releases endorphins?
14. Psychologist Linda Bartoshuk recommends candies containing moderate amounts of jalapeño peppers as a treatment for people with pain in the mouth. Why? (Check your answers on page 124.)

Phantom Limbs

A particularly fascinating phenomenon is the **phantom limb,** *a continuing sensation of an amputated body part.* For example, someone might report occasional feelings of touch, tingling, or pain from an amputated hand, arm, leg, foot, or any other amputated part. The phantom sensation might last only days or weeks after the amputation, but it sometimes lasts years or even a lifetime (Ramachandran & Hirstein, 1998).

Physicians and psychologists have long wondered about the cause of phantom sensations. Some believed

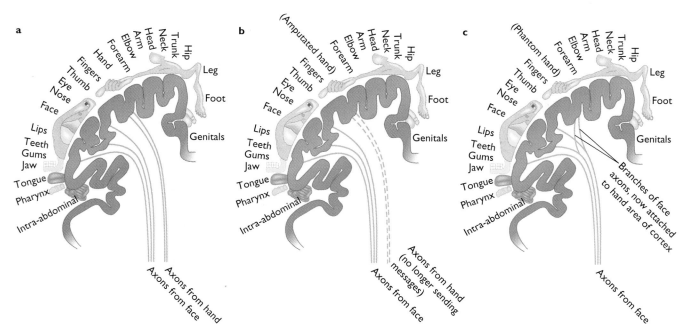

FIGURE 4.28 (a) Each area in the somatosensory cortex gets its input from a different part of the body. (b) If one body part, such as the hand, is amputated, its part of the cortex no longer gets its normal input. (c) However, the axons from a neighboring area, such as the face, can branch out to excite the vacated area or strengthen existing synapses. Now any stimulation of the face will excite both the face area and the hand area. But when it stimulates the hand area, it feels like the hand, not the face.

it was an emotional reaction, and others believed it began with irritation of nerves at the stump where the amputation occurred. Research in the 1990s established that the problem lies within the brain.

In the last chapter, Figure 3.18 shows how each part of the somatosensory cortex gets its input from a different body area. Figure 4.28a repeats part of that illustration. Part b shows what happens immediately after an amputation of the hand: The hand area of the cortex becomes inactive because the axons from the hand are inactive. (You might think of the neurons in the face area of the cortex as "widows" that have lost their old partners and are signaling their eagerness for new partners.) As time passes, axons from the face, which ordinarily excite only the face area of the cortex, form (or strengthen) branches to the hand area of the cortex, which is adjacent to the face area. So any stimulation of the face continues to excite the face area but now also excites the hand area. When it stimulates the hand area, it produces a hand experience—in other words a phantom limb (Flor et al., 1995; Ramachandran & Blakeslee, 1998).

One way is known to relieve phantom sensations: Individuals with amputations who learn to use an artificial limb gradually lose their phantoms (Lotze et al., 1999). Evidently, the hand and arm areas of their

cortex start experiencing the artificial limb (!), and this sensation displaces the abnormal sensation coming from the face.

CONCEPT CHECK

15. A phantom hand sensation is greater at some times than others. When should it be strongest? (Check your answer on page 124.)

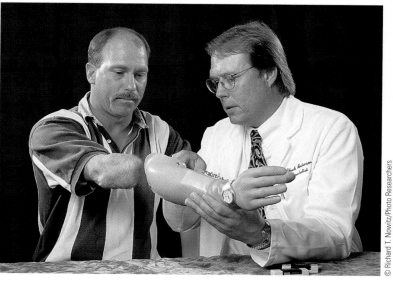

▌ After a person with an amputation gains experience using an artificial limb, phantom limb sensations fade or disappear altogether.

The Chemical Senses

Many textbooks on sensation ignore taste and smell or mention them only briefly. If rats or raccoons wrote sensation textbooks, however, they would probably devote as much coverage to taste and smell as they would to hearing and mention vision only briefly. Many invertebrates have no vision or hearing at all, surviving with only chemical senses and touch.

Taste

Vision and hearing enable humans to find food and water, avoid danger, keep our balance, and find suitable mates. The sense of **taste**, which *detects chemicals on the tongue,* serves just one function: It governs our eating and drinking.

The *taste receptors are* in the **taste buds,** *located in the folds on the surface of the tongue,* almost exclusively along the outside edge of the tongue in adults (Figure 4.29). (Children's taste buds are more widely scattered.)

Try this demonstration (based on Bartoshuk, 1991): Soak something small (a cotton swab will do) in sugar water, salt water, or vinegar. Then touch it to the center of your tongue, not too far back. You will feel it but taste nothing. Then slowly move the soaked substance toward the side or front of your tongue. Suddenly, you taste it.

If you go in the other direction (first touching the side of the tongue and then moving toward the center), you will continue to taste the substance even when it reaches the center of your tongue. The explanation is not that you suddenly grew new taste buds.

Rather, your taste buds tell you nothing about location. Once you have stimulated any taste buds, you will continue tasting the substance, but the taste receptors do not tell you *where* you are tasting the substance. If you now stimulate *touch* receptors elsewhere on your tongue, your brain interprets the taste perception as coming from the spot you are touching, even though the taste sensation is in fact coming from somewhere else.

Different Types of Taste Receptors

Researchers now have a reasonably clear understanding of how taste receptors work (Lindemann, 1996). Traditionally, Western cultures have talked about four primary tastes: sweet, sour, salty, and bitter. However, the taste of monosodium glutamate (MSG), common in many Asian cuisines, cannot be fully described in terms of those four primaries (Kurihara & Kashiwayanagi, 1998; Schiffman & Erickson, 1971), and researchers have found a taste receptor specific to MSG (Chaudhari, Landin, & Roper, 2000). So it may be better to talk about five primary tastes. English has never had a word for the taste of MSG (similar to the taste of unsalted chicken soup), so researchers have adopted the Japanese word *umami.*

Bitter taste is hard to explain because such diverse chemicals taste bitter. About the only thing they have in common is that most bitter substances are poisonous or at least harmful in large amounts. How could such diverse chemicals all excite the same receptor? The answer is that they don't. We have a large number of different bitter receptors—about 40 to 80—each sensitive to different types of chemicals (Adler et al., 2000; Matsunami, Montmayeur, & Buck, 2000). Any chemical that excites any of these receptors produces the same

Tongue surface

Dendrite of sensory neuron

a   b   c

FIGURE 4.29 (a) Taste buds, which react to chemicals dissolved in saliva, are located along the edge of the tongue in adult humans but are more widely distributed in children. (b) A cross section through part of the surface of the tongue showing taste buds. (c) A cross section of one taste bud. Each taste bud has about 50 receptor cells within it.

bitter sensation. One consequence is that a wide variety of harmful chemicals taste bitter. Another consequence is that we do not always detect low concentrations of bitter chemicals; with so many different kinds of bitter receptors, we do not have many of any one kind.

Individual Differences

Researchers in the 1930s discovered that the chemical phenothiocarbamide (PTC) tasted bitter to some people but was tasteless to others. Later researchers traced the difference to a single gene (Kim et al., 2003). Most people who are insensitive to PTC, called *nontasters,* have less than average sensitivity to other tastes as well. Another group of people, called *supertasters,* have more than the usual number of taste buds, again for genetic reasons, and detect most tastes extremely strongly. Most supertasters dislike black coffee, black breads, hot peppers, sour fruits such as grapefruit, and strong-tasting vegetables such as radishes and Brussels sprouts (Bartoshuk, Duffy, Lucchina, Prutkin, & Fast, 1998; Drewnowski, Henderson, Short, & Barratt-Fornell, 1998). They also tend to be content with smaller portions of food, and most of them are relatively thin. In short, genes can affect food intake by altering taste receptors.

Taste sensitivity also depends on other factors (Yamauchi, Endo, & Yoshimura, 2002): It declines with age, especially after age 70. Cigarette smokers have decreased sensitivity, especially for bitter tastes. After about age 20, women have greater taste sensitivity than men, apparently as a result of estrogens (female-typical hormones). Women's taste sensitivity fluctuates over the monthly cycle and reaches a peak early in pregnancy (Prutkin et al., 2000).

Smell

The *sense of smell* is known as **olfaction.** The olfactory receptors, located on the mucous membrane in the rear air passages of the nose (Figure 4.30), detect the presence of certain airborne molecules. Chemically, these receptors are much like synaptic receptors, but they are stimulated by chemicals from the environment instead of chemicals released by other neurons. The axons of the olfactory receptors form the olfactory tract, which extends to the olfactory bulbs at the base of the brain.

How many kinds of olfactory receptors do we have? Until 1991 researchers had virtually no idea. In principle researchers could determine the number of receptor types with behavioral data. With color vision, for example, the researchers of the 1800s established that people can mix three colors of light in various amounts to match any other color. Therefore, even before the technology existed to examine the cones in the retina, researchers had reason to believe that the retina had three kinds of cones. Regarding olfaction, however, no one reported such behavioral results. Can people match all possible odors by mixing appropriate amounts of three, four, seven, or ten, or however many primary odors?

Perhaps it is just as well that no one spent a lifetime trying to find out. Linda Buck and Richard Axel (1991) used modern biochemical technology to demonstrate that the human nose has at least 100 types of olfactory receptors, and later research put the number at several hundred, whereas rats and mice

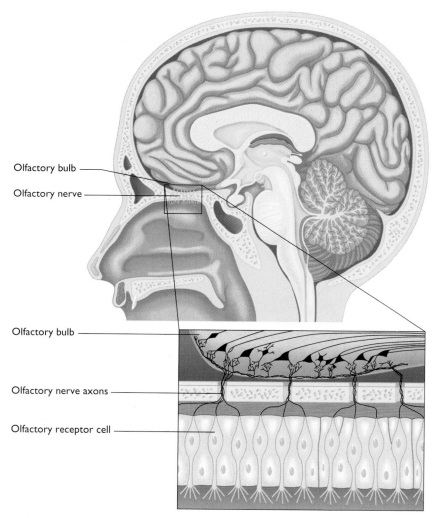

FIGURE 4.30 The olfactory receptor cells lining the nasal cavity send information to the olfactory bulb in the brain. There are at least 100 types of receptors with specialized responses to airborne chemicals.

have about 1,000 (Zhang & Firestein, 2002). Each olfactory receptor can detect only a small group of closely related chemicals (Araneda, Kini, & Firestein, 2000). Such extreme specificity is rare in the body; the only other example is the immune system.

Much remains to be learned about olfaction. Of course it depends on stimulation of the receptors in the nose, but the brain processes the information further (Figure 4.31). For example, you will find it easier to distinguish one smell from another if both are familiar to you than if either is new (Stevenson & Boakes, 2003).

Olfaction is particularly important for food selection. Neurons in the prefrontal cortex receive both taste and olfactory information, producing the combined sensation that we call *flavor*. These cells also receive input that indicates hunger, and they respond vigorously to the flavor of a food only when the individual is hungry (Rolls, 1997).

Olfaction also serves social functions, especially in nonhuman mammals that identify one another by means of **pheromones,** which are *chemicals they release into the environment.* Nearly all nonhuman mammals rely on pheromones for sexual communication. For example, a female dog in her fertile and sexually responsive time of year emits pheromones that attract every male dog in the neighborhood that is free to move. Pheromones act primarily on the vomeronasal organ, a set of receptors near, but separate from, the standard olfactory receptors (Monti-Bloch, Jennings-White, Dolberg, & Berliner,

Professional deodorant tester: That's a career option you probably never considered. U.S. industries spend millions of dollars to eliminate the kinds of personal odors that are essential to other mammalian species.

1994). Each of those receptors responds to one and only one chemical, and they respond to it even at extremely low concentrations (Leinders-Zufall et al., 2000).

Humans prefer *not* to recognize one another by smell. The deodorant and perfume industries exist for the sole purpose of removing and covering up human odors. But perhaps we respond to pheromones anyway, unconsciously. For example, young women who are in frequent contact, such as roommates in a college dormitory, tend to synchronize their menstrual cycles, probably as a result of pheromones they secrete (McClintock, 1971).

One study examined women in Bedouin Arab families. The advantages of studying that culture are that the mother and sisters within a family have extensive daily contact, unmarried women have almost no contact with men, and very few women use oral contraceptives. Thus, pheromones have a maximum opportunity to show their effects. The results showed that the women in most families were at least partly synchronized; they might not begin to menstruate on exactly the same day, but they were close (Weller & Weller, 1997).

IN CLOSING

Sensory Systems

The world as experienced by a bat (which can hear frequencies of 100,000 Hz) or a dog (which can discriminate odors that you and I would never notice) or a mouse (which depends on its whiskers when exploring the world) is in many ways a different world from the one that people experience. The function of our senses is not to tell us about everything in the world, but to alert us to the information we are most likely to use, given our way of life.

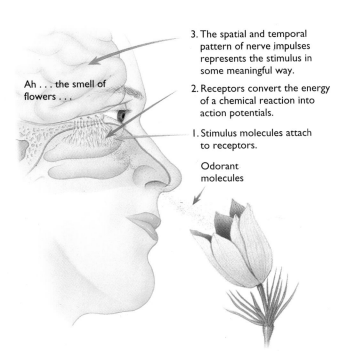

Ah . . . the smell of flowers . . .

3. The spatial and temporal pattern of nerve impulses represents the stimulus in some meaningful way.

2. Receptors convert the energy of a chemical reaction into action potentials.

1. Stimulus molecules attach to receptors.

Odorant molecules

FIGURE 4.31 Olfaction, like any other sensory system, converts physical energy into a complex pattern of brain activity.

Summary

- *Pitch.* At low frequencies of sound, we identify pitch by the frequency of vibrations of hair cells. At intermediate frequencies, we identify pitch by volleys of responses from many neurons. At high frequencies, we identify pitch by the location where the hair cells vibrate. (page 114)

- *Localizing sounds.* We localize the source of a sound by detecting differences in the time and loudness of the sounds our two ears receive. We localize the distance of a sound source mostly by the amount of reverberation, or echoes, following the main sound. (page 115)

- *Vestibular system.* The vestibular system tells us about the movement of the head and its position with respect to gravity. It enables us to keep our eyes fixated on an object while the rest of our body is in motion. (page 115)

- *Cutaneous receptors.* We experience many types of sensation on the skin, each dependent on different receptors. Itch is a sensation based on tissue irritation, inhibited by pain. Tickle depends on the unpredictability of the stimulus. (page 116)

- *Pain.* The experience of pain can be greatly inhibited or enhanced by other simultaneous experiences, including touch to surrounding skin or the person's expectations. Pain depends largely on stimulation of neurons that are sensitive to the neurotransmitter substance P, which can be inhibited by endorphins. (page 117)

- *Phantom limbs.* After an amputation the corresponding portion of the somatosensory cortex stops receiving its normal input. Soon axons from neighboring cortical areas form branches that start exciting the silenced areas of cortex. When they receive the new input, they react the old way, producing a phantom sensation. (page 119)

- *Taste receptors.* Even before researchers identified the taste receptors, they knew that there must be at least four kinds because certain procedures affect one taste quality (e.g., sweetness) without affecting the others. An adult human has taste receptors only along the edges of the tongue. (page 121)

- *Olfactory receptors.* The olfactory system—the sense of smell—depends on at least 100 types of receptors, each with its own special sensitivity. Olfaction is important for many behaviors, including food selection and (especially in nonhuman mammals) identification of potential mates. (page 122)

Answers to Concept Checks

8. Obviously, the people farthest from the mouse are least likely to hear it. In addition older people would be less likely than young people are to hear the squeak because the ability to hear high frequencies declines in old age. Another group unlikely to hear the squeak are those who have had repeated exposure to loud noises. For this reason you should avoid attending loud rock concerts and listening to recorded music played at a loud volume. You could damage your hearing in the long run, even if you do not realize it now. (page 114)

9. We still hear a tone at 5000 Hz, but it is louder than before. For high-frequency tones the pitch we hear depends on which hair cells are most active, not how many impulses per second they fire. (page 114)

10. We localize sounds by comparing the input into the left ear with the input into the right ear. If a sound comes from straight ahead or from directly behind us (or from straight above or below), the input into the left ear will be identical with the input into the right ear. (page 115)

11. Sounds will be louder in the left ear than in the right, and therefore, they may seem to be coming from the left side even when they aren't. (However, a sound from the right will still strike the right ear before the left, so time of arrival at the two ears will compete against the relative loudness.) (page 115)

12. Various sounds from the radio cannot seem to come from different directions because your localization of the direction of a sound depends on a comparison between the responses of the two ears. However, the radio can play sounds that seem to come from different distances because distance localization does not depend on a difference between the ears. It depends on the amount of reverberation, loudness, and high-frequency tones, all of which can be varied with a single speaker. Consequently, the radio can easily give an impression of people walking toward you or away from you, but not of people walking left to right or right to left. (page 115)

13. First determine how much the pleasant stimulus decreases the experience of pain for several people. Then give half of them naloxone and half of them a placebo. Again measure how much the pleasant stimulus decreases the pain. If the pleasant stimulus decreases pain by releasing endorphins, then naloxone should impair its painkilling effects. (page 119)

14. The capsaicin in the jalapeño peppers will release substance P faster than it can be resynthesized, thus decreasing the later sensitivity to pain in the mouth. (page 119)

15. The phantom hand sensation should be strongest when something is rubbing against the face. (page 120)

The Interpretation of Sensory Information

What is the relationship between the real world and the way we perceive it?

Why are we sometimes wrong about what we think we see?

No doubt you have heard the expression "a picture is worth a thousand words." If so, what is one one-thousandth of a picture worth? One word? Perhaps not even that.

Printed photographs, such as the one on page 123, are composed of a great many dots. Ordinarily, you will be aware of only the overall patterns and objects, but if you magnify a photo, as in Figure 4.32, you can see the individual dots. Although one dot by itself tells us almost nothing, the pattern of dots as a whole constitutes a meaningful picture.

Actually, our vision is like this all the time. Your retina includes about 126 million rods and cones, each of which sees one dot of the visual field. What you perceive is not dots, however, but lines, curves, and complex objects. In a variety of ways, your nervous system starts with an array of details and extracts the meaningful information.

Perception of Minimal Stimuli

Some of the very earliest psychological researchers asked, "What is the weakest sound, the weakest light, the weakest touch, and so forth that a person can de-

tect?" They assumed that this question would be easy to answer and therefore a good starting point for further research. As is often the case, however, a question that appeared simple became more complicated.

Sensory Thresholds and Signal Detection

Imagine a typical experiment to determine the threshold of hearing—that is, the minimum intensity that one can hear: Participants are presented with tones of varying intensity in random order, and sometimes no tone occurs at all. Each time, the participants are asked to say whether they heard anything. Figure 4.33 presents typical results. Notice that no sharp line separates sounds that people hear from sounds they do not. Researchers therefore define an **absolute sensory threshold** as the *intensity at which a given individual can detect a stimulus 50% of the time.* Note, however, that people sometimes report stimuli below the threshold or fail to report stimuli above it. Note also that people sometimes report hearing a tone when none was present. We should not be surprised. Throughout the study they have been listening to faint tones and saying "yes" when they heard almost nothing. The difference between nothing and almost nothing is pretty slim.

FIGURE 4.32 Although this photograph is composed entirely of dots, we see objects and patterns. The principles at work in our perception of this photograph are at work in all our perceptions.

© Louis Psihoyos/Contact Press Images/Colorific!

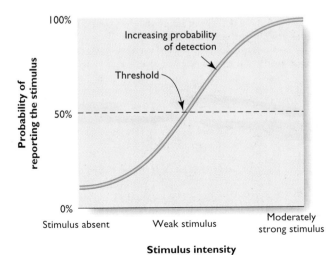

FIGURE 4.33 Typical results of an experiment to measure an absolute sensory threshold. There is no sharp boundary between stimuli that you can perceive and stimuli that you cannot perceive.

125

Your threshold can change drastically from one time to another. For example, if you have been outdoors on a bright, sunny day and you now walk into a darkened movie theater, you will have trouble seeing the seats at first. After a few minutes, your threshold drops (i.e., your sensitivity increases) and you can see better. Your threshold would drop still further in a completely darkened room.

When people try to detect weak stimuli, they can be correct in two ways: reporting the presence of a stimulus (a "hit") and reporting its absence (a "correct rejection"). They can also be wrong in two ways: failing to detect a stimulus when present (a "miss") and reporting a stimulus when none was present (a "false alarm"). Figure 4.34 outlines these possibilities.

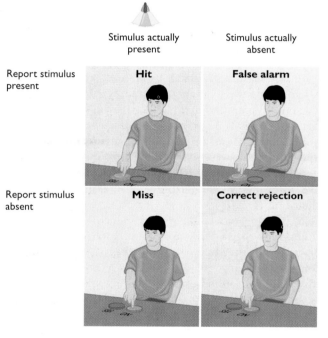

FIGURE 4.34 People can make two kinds of correct judgments (green backgrounds) and two kinds of errors (red backgrounds). Someone who too readily reports the stimulus present would get many hits but also many false alarms.

Signal-detection theory is the *study of people's tendencies to make hits, correct rejections, misses, and false alarms* (D. M. Green & Swets, 1966). (Signal-detection theory originated in engineering, where it is applied to such matters as detecting radio signals in the presence of interfering noise.) In signal-detection studies, we compare responses for stimulus-present and stimulus-absent trials. For example, suppose that someone reports a stimulus present on 80% of the trials when it is actually present. That statistic is meaningless unless we also know how often the person said it was present when it was not. For example, the person might have reported a stimulus present on 80% of trials when it was absent. In that case we would conclude that

the person can't tell the difference between stimulus-present and stimulus-absent.

In a signal-detection experiment, people's responses depend on their willingness to risk a miss or a false alarm. (When in doubt, you have to risk one or the other.) Suppose you are the participant and I tell you that you will receive a 10-cent reward whenever you correctly report that a light is present, but you will be fined 1 cent if you say "yes" when it is absent. When you are not sure, you will probably guess "yes," and the results will resemble those in Figure 4.35a. Then I change the rules: You will receive a 1-cent reward for correctly reporting the presence of a light, but you will suffer a 10-cent penalty and an electrical shock if you report a light when none was present. Now you will say "yes" only when you are certain, and the results will look like those in Figure 4.35b. In short, people's answers depend on the instructions they receive and the strategies they use, not just what their senses tell them.

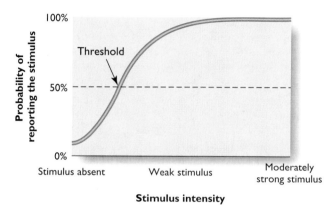

Instructions: You will receive a 10-cent reward for correctly reporting that a light is present. You will be penalized 1 cent for reporting that a light is present when it is not.

a

Instructions: You will receive a 1-cent reward for correctly reporting that a light is present. You will be penalized 10 cents *and* subjected to an electric shock for reporting that a light is present when it is not.

b

FIGURE 4.35 Results of experiments to measure a sensory threshold using two different sets of instructions.

People become cautious about false alarms for other reasons too. In one experiment participants were asked to read words that were flashed on a screen for a split second. They performed reasonably well with ordinary words such as *river* or *peach*. For emotionally loaded words such as *penis* or *bitch*, however, they generally said they were not sure what they saw. Several explanations are possible (e.g., G. S. Blum & Barbour, 1979); one is that participants hesitate to blurt out an emotionally charged word unless they are certain they are right.

The signal-detection approach is useful in many settings remote from a psychologist's laboratory. For example, the legal system is also a signal-detection situation. When we examine the evidence and try to decide whether someone is guilty or innocent, we can be right in two ways and wrong in two ways:

	Defendant is actually guilty	Defendant is actually innocent
Jury votes "guilty"	Hit	False alarm
Jury votes "not guilty"	Miss	Correct rejection

Most people agree it is more important to avoid false alarms (finding an innocent person guilty). Therefore, we insist on convincing evidence before convicting someone of a crime.

CONCEPT CHECK ☑

16. Suppose we find that nearly all alcoholics and drug abusers have a particular pattern of brain waves. Can we now use that pattern as a way to identify people with an alcohol or drug problem? (Check your answer on page 145.)

Subliminal Perception

You have probably heard of **subliminal perception,** the idea that *a stimulus can influence our behavior even when it is presented so faintly or briefly or along with such strong distracters that we do not perceive it consciously.* (*Limen* is Latin for "threshold"; thus, subliminal means "below the threshold.") Generally, the operational definition of "not perceived consciously" is that the person reports not seeing it. Is subliminal perception powerful, meaningless, or something in between?

What Subliminal Perception Cannot Do

Many years ago claims were made that subliminal messages could control people's buying habits. For example, an unscrupulous theater owner might insert a single frame, "EAT POPCORN," in the middle of a film. Customers who were not consciously aware of the message could not resist it, so they would flock to the concession stand to buy popcorn. Despite many tests of this claim, no one found any evidence to support it (Bornstein, 1989).

Another claim is that certain rock-'n'-roll recordings contain "satanic" messages that were recorded backward and superimposed on the songs. Some people allege that listeners unconsciously perceive these messages and then follow the evil advice. The issue for psychologists is not whether any rock band ever inserted such a message. (There are a lot of rock bands, after all.) The issue is whether a backward message has any influence. If people hear a backward message, can they understand it? Even if they don't, does it influence their behavior? Researchers have recorded various messages (nothing satanic) and asked people to listen to them backward. So far, no one listening to a backward message has been able to discern what it would sound like forward, and listening to it has not influenced behavior in any detectable way (Vokey & Read, 1985). In other words even if certain music does contain messages recorded backward, we have no evidence that the messages matter. (To hear some examples of backward speech, although not necessarily a scientific interpretation of them, visit this Web site: **www.reversespeech.com/.**)

A third unsupported claim: "Subliminal audiotapes" can help you improve your memory, quit smoking, lose weight, raise your self-esteem, and so forth. In one study psychologists asked more than 200 volunteers to listen to a popular brand of audiotape. But they intentionally mislabeled some of the tapes. That is, some tapes with self-esteem messages were labeled "memory tapes," and some tapes with memory messages were labeled "self-esteem tapes." After 1 month of listening, most who *thought* they were listening to self-esteem tapes said they had greatly improved their self-esteem; those who *thought* they were listening to memory tapes said their memory had greatly improved. What they actually heard made no difference. In other words the memory improvement was a result of people's expectations, not the tapes themselves (Greenwald, Spangenberg, Pratkanis, & Eskanazi, 1991).

What Subliminal Perception Can Do

Subliminal messages do produce effects, although they are in most cases brief, subtle, and hard to measure. For example, people in one study viewed a happy, neutral, or angry face flashed on a screen for less than one thirtieth of a second, followed immediately by a neutral face. Under these conditions no one reports seeing a happy or angry face, and even if asked to guess, people do no better than chance. However, when they see a happy face, they slightly and briefly move their facial muscles in the direction of a smile; after seeing an angry face, they tense their muscles slightly and briefly in the direction of a frown (Dimberg, Thunberg, & Elmehed, 2000).

In another study students watched a screen where they saw a word flash for one third of a second, followed by a 133-millisecond response window in which they were supposed to press one computer key if they saw a "pleasant" word (e.g., HAPPY or WARM) and a different key if they saw an "unpleasant" word (e.g., SCUM or KILL). They do see the word, but because they are forced to respond so quickly, they find the task difficult and make many mistakes. The additional element of this procedure is that prior to the flashed word, another word was also flashed *very* briefly, under conditions that made it impossible for anyone to identify it consciously. That is, it was subliminal. The full procedure is outlined as follows:

1 Blank screen	**2** Masking stimulus such as KQHYTPDQFPBYL for 150 milliseconds
3 Subliminal stimulus such as FRIEND for 50 ms	**4** Another interfering stimulus for 17 ms
5 Target stimulus such as HAPPY for 333 ms	**6** Response window for 133 ms

Although none of the participants could identify any of the subliminal words (step 3), or even noticed them at all, they responded more accurately to the target stimulus (step 5) if both the subliminal and target stimuli were pleasant, or both were unpleasant, than if one was pleasant and the other unpleasant. In other words a pleasant subliminal word (step 3) primed them to respond better to a pleasant target word (step 5), and an unpleasant subliminal word primed them to respond to an unpleasant target word (Abrams, Klinger, & Greenwald, 2002). Other research has indicated that unpleasant subliminal words have a slightly stronger effect than pleasant ones (Dijksterhuis & Aarts, 2003).

The fact that subliminal perception affects behavior at all is theoretically interesting. It shows that we are not consciously aware of all the information we process or all the events that influence us (Greenwald & Draine, 1997). However, notice that what has been demonstrated is a small, brief facilitation of one response or another, and researchers have to average results over many participants and many trials to demonstrate any effect at all. The evidence does not indicate any powerful or long-lasting subliminal influences.

Perception and the Recognition of Patterns

How do you know what you're looking at? Take what seems like a very simple example: When you look at something, how does your brain decide how bright it is? We might guess that the answer would be simply that the more intense the light, the brighter the appearance.

However, perceived brightness depends on comparison to the surrounding objects. **Brightness contrast** *is the increase or decrease in an object's apparent brightness because of the effects of objects around it.* Consider Figure 4.36. Compare the pink bars in the middle left section to those in the middle right. The ones on the right probably look darker, but in fact they are the same. Then examine Figure 4.37.

Compare the little square in the center of the upper face of the cube to the one in the center of the front face. The one on the top face looks brown, whereas the one on the front face looks yellow or orange. Amazingly, they are physically the same (Lotto & Purves, 1999). Don't believe it? Cover everything on the page except those two squares and then compare them. Go to http://psychology.wadsworth.com/ kalat_intro7e. Navigate to the student Web site, then to the Online Try it Yourself section, and click on Brightness Contrast.

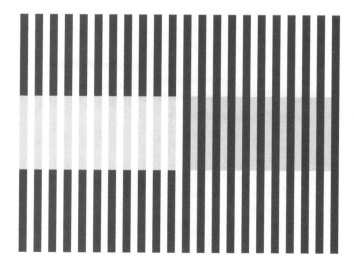

FIGURE 4.36 Because pink bars appear to lie above the dark bars on the left and below them on the right, we see a contrast between pink and dark red on the left, pink and white on the right. Therefore, we see the pink bars on the right as darker, even though they are actually the same shade as the others.

FIGURE 4.37 The little squares in the center of the top and front faces of the left cube look very different, but they are physically identical. The cube on the right has those same squares, but the context has been removed. Try covering everything on the left cube except the two central squares, or fold the page so you can match the squares of the right cube with those of the left. *(From Lotto & Purves, 1999)*

If two spots on the page reflect light the same way, why don't we see them the same? Apparently, when the brain sees something, it uses its past experience to calculate how that pattern of light probably was generated (Lotto & Purves, 1999). In Figure 4.37 the context clearly indicates that the top face is in bright light, whereas the front face is in a shadow. The square you see in the top face is seen as a dark object, brown in color. The square you see in the front face is rather bright considering that it's in a shadow, and therefore, it looks yellow or orange. Your brain calculates what the object probably *is*, not just what light strikes your retina.

Similarly, in Figure 4.36 we see what appears to be a partly clear white bar covering the center of the left half of the grid, and the pink bars look very light. The corresponding section to the right also has pink bars, but these appear to be under the red bars and on top of a white background; here the pink looks much darker. As you will have guessed by now, the pink bars on the left are the same brightness and color as those on the right.

CONCEPT CHECK ☑

17. Of the three theories of color vision discussed earlier in this chapter (trichromatic, opponent-process, and retinex), which one best accounts for your perception of Figure 4.37? (Check your answer on page 145.)

If just perceiving brightness is that complicated, imagine how hard it is to explain something like face recognition. People are amazingly good at recognizing faces, though inept at explaining how they do it. When you someday attend your 25th high school reunion, you will probably recognize many people despite major changes in their appearance.

Can you match the high school photos in Figure 4.38 with the photos of the same people as they looked 25 years later? Probably not, but other people who had attended that high school succeeded with a respectable 49% accuracy (Bruck, Cavanagh, & Ceci, 1991). Go to http://psychology. wadsworth.com/kalat_intro7e. Navigate to the student Web site, then to the Online Try it Yourself section, and click on Matching High School Photos.

We recognize faces by whole patterns, and certain areas in the temporal lobe of the brain appear to be specialized for facial recognition (Farah, 1992; Kanwisher, 2000). Changing even one feature can sometimes make a face hard to recognize. Perhaps you have had the experience of seeing people who have just changed their hair style and for a moment you cannot recognize them. Can you identify the person in Figure 4.39?

The Feature-Detector Approach

Even explaining how we recognize a simple letter of the alphabet is difficult enough. According to one explanation, we begin recognition by breaking a com-

High-school photos

a   b   c   d   e

25 years later

1   2   3   4   5

6   7   8   9   10

M. Bruck, P. Cavanagh & S.J. Ceci "Fortysomething: Recognizing Faces at One's 25th Reunion," in *Memory & Cognition*, 19:221–228, 1991. Reprinted by permission of M. Bruck.

FIGURE 4.38 High school photos and the same people 25 years later. Can you match the photos in the two sets? (Check your answers by going online for a drag and drop version of this figure or check answer C on page 145.)

plex stimulus into its component parts. For example, when we look at a letter of the alphabet, *specialized neurons in the visual cortex*, called **feature detectors**, *respond to the presence of certain simple features, such as lines and angles.* That is, one neuron might

become active only when you are looking at a horizontal line in a particular location. That feature detector would be detecting the feature "horizontal line." Other neurons might detect horizontal lines in other locations, vertical lines, and so forth.

FIGURE 4.39 Who is this? We recognize people partly by hair as well as facial features. If you're not sure who it is, check answer D, page 145.

© San Francisco Exploratorium

CRITICAL THINKING: WHAT'S THE EVIDENCE?
Feature Detectors

What evidence do we have for the existence of feature detectors in the brain? We have two kinds of evidence: one from laboratory animals and one from humans.

EXPERIMENT I

Hypothesis Neurons in the visual cortex of cats and monkeys will respond specifically when light strikes the retina in a particular pattern.

Method Two pioneers in the study of the visual cortex, David Hubel and Torsten Wiesel (1981 Nobel Prize winners in physiology and medicine), inserted thin electrodes into cells of the occipital cortex of cats and monkeys and then recorded the activity of those

FIGURE 4.40 Hubel and Wiesel implanted electrodes to record the activity of neurons in the occipital cortex of a cat. Then they compared the responses evoked by various patterns of light and darkness on the retina. In most cases a neuron responded vigorously when a portion of the retina saw a bar of light oriented at a particular angle. When the angle of the bar changed, that cell became silent but another cell responded.

cells when various light patterns struck the animals' retinas. At first they used mere points of light; later they tried lines (Figure 4.40).

Results   They found that each cell responds best in the presence of a particular stimulus (Hubel & Wiesel, 1968). Some cells become active only when a vertical bar of light strikes a given portion of the retina. Others become active only when a horizontal bar strikes the retina. In other words such cells appear to act as feature detectors. In later experiments Hubel and Wiesel and other investigators found cells that respond to other kinds of features, such as movement in a particular direction.

Interpretation   Hubel and Wiesel reported feature-detector neurons in both cats and monkeys. If the organization of the occipital cortex is similar in species as distantly related as cats and monkeys, it is likely (though not certain) to be similar in humans.

A second line of evidence is based on the following reasoning: If the human cortex does contain feature-detector cells, one type of cell should become fatigued after we stare for a time at the features that excite it. When we look away, we should see an aftereffect created by the inactivity of that type of cell. (Recall the negative afterimage in color vision, as shown by Figure 4.15.) Try the Online Try It Yourself activity. Go to   http://psychology.wadsworth. com/kalat_intro7e. Navigate to the student Web site, then to the Online Try It Yourself section, and click on Motion Aftereffect.

One example of this phenomenon is the waterfall illusion: *If you stare at a waterfall for a minute or more and then turn your eyes to some nearby cliffs, the cliffs will appear to flow upward.* By staring at the waterfall, you fatigue the neurons that respond to downward motion. When you look away, those neurons become inactive, but others that respond to upward motion continue their normal activity. Even though the motionless cliffs stimulate those neurons only weakly, the stimulation is enough to produce an illusion of upward motion. For another example here is a demonstration that you can perform yourself.

EXPERIMENT 2

Hypothesis   After you stare at one set of vertical lines, you will fatigue the feature detectors that respond to lines of a particular width. If you then look at lines slightly wider or narrower than the original ones, they will appear to be even wider or narrower than they really are.

Method   Cover the right half of Figure 4.41 and stare at the little rectangle in the middle of the left half for at least 1 minute. (Staring even longer will increase the effect.) Do not stare at just one point; move your focus around within the rectangle. Then look at the square in the center of the right part of the figure and compare the spacing between the lines of the top and bottom gratings (Blakemore & Sutton, 1969). Try the Online Try it Yourself activity. Go to http://psychology.wadsworth.com/ kalat_intro7e. Navigate to the student Web site, then to the Online Try it Yourself section, and click on Afterimage.

Results   What did you perceive in the right half of the figure? People generally report that the top lines look narrower and the bottom lines look wider, even though they are the same.

Interpretation   Staring at the left part of the figure fatigues neurons sensitive to wide lines in the top part of the figure and neurons sensitive to narrow lines in the bottom part. Then, when you look at lines of medium width, the fatigued cells become inactive.

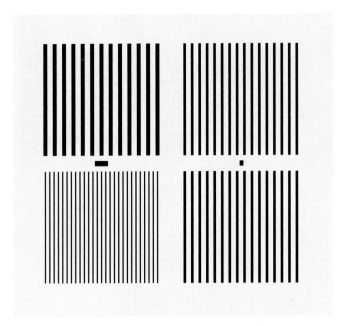

FIGURE 4.41 Use this display to fatigue your feature detectors and create an afterimage. Follow the directions in Experiment 2. *(From Blakemore & Sutton, 1969)*

Therefore, your perception is dominated by cells sensitive to narrower lines in the top part and to wider lines in the bottom part.

To summarize, we have two types of evidence for the existence of visual feature detectors: (a) The brains of other species contain cells with the properties of feature detectors, and (b) after staring at certain patterns, we see aftereffects that can be explained as fatigue of feature-detector cells in the brain.

The research just described was only the start of an enormous amount of activity by laboratories throughout the world; later results have led to revised views of what the earlier results mean. For example, even though certain neurons respond better to a single vertical line

than to points or lines of other orientations, the vertical line may not be the best stimulus for exciting those neurons. Most respond even more strongly to a sine-wave grating of lines:

Thus, the feature that such cells detect is probably more complex than just a line. Furthermore, because each cell responds to stimuli as different as a line and a group of lines, obviously no one cell provides an unambiguous message about what someone is seeing at any moment.

One important point about scientific advances: A single line of evidence—even excellent, Nobel Prize-winning evidence—seldom provides the final answer to any question. We should always look for multiple ways to test a hypothesis; even if several kinds of evidence support a conclusion, a great many unanswered questions can still remain.

CONCEPT CHECK ☑

18. What is a feature detector, and what evidence supports the idea of feature detectors? (Check your answer on page 145.)

Do Feature Detectors Explain Perception?

The neurons I have just described are active during the early stages of visual processing. Do we simply add up the responses of a great many feature detectors so that the sum of enough feature detectors constitutes your perception of, say, your psychology professor's face?

No, feature detectors cannot provide a complete explanation even for how we perceive letters, much less faces. For example, we perceive the words in Figure 4.42a as CAT and HAT, even though the A in CAT is identical to the H in HAT, and therefore, both of them stimulate the same feature detectors. Likewise, the character in the center of Figure 4.42b can be read as either the letter B or the number 13. The early stages of visual perception use feature detectors, but the perception of a complex pattern requires more.

a　　　　　　　　b

FIGURE 4.42 We perceive elements differently depending on their context. In (a) the A in CAT is the same as the H in HAT, but we perceive them differently. In (b) the central character can appear to be a B or the number 13 depending on whether we read horizontally or vertically. *(Part b from Inversions, by S. Kim. W. H. Freeman and Company. Copyright © 1989 by Scott Kim.)*

© Courtesy of McDonnell Douglass

FIGURE 4.43 According to Gestalt psychology, the whole is different from the sum of its parts. Here we perceive an assembly of several hundred people as an airplane.

Gestalt Psychology

Figure 4.43, which we see as the overall shape of an airplane, is a photo of several hundred people. The plane is the overall pattern, not the sum of the parts. Recall also Figure 4.32 from earlier in this chapter: The photograph is composed of dots, but we perceive a face, not just dots.

Such observations derive from **Gestalt psychology**, a field that focuses on our ability to perceive overall patterns. *Gestalt* (geh-SHTALT) is a German word translated as "overall pattern or configuration." The founders of Gestalt psychology rejected the idea that a perception can be broken down into its component parts. A melody broken up into individual notes is no longer a melody. Their slogan was, "The whole is different from the sum of its parts." According to Gestalt psychologists, visual perception is an active creation, not just the adding up of lines, dots, or other pieces. We considered an example of this principle in Figure 4.42. Here are some further examples.

In Figure 4.44 you may see animals or you may see meaningless black and white patches. You might see only patches for a while, and then one or both animals suddenly emerge. (If you give up, check answer E on page 145.) To perceive the animals, you must separate **figure and ground**—that is, you must distinguish the *object from the background.* Ordinarily, you make that distinction almost instantly; you become aware of the process only when it is difficult (as it is here).

Figure 4.45 contains five **reversible figures,** *stimuli that can be perceived in more than one way.* In effect we test hypotheses: "Is this the front of the object or is that the front? Is the object facing left or right? Is this section the foreground or the background?" In Figure 4.45 part a is called the *Necker cube,* after the psychologist who first called

a

b

FIGURE 4.44 Do you see an animal in each picture? If not, check answer E on page 145. *(Part b from Dallenbach, 1951)*

attention to it. Which is the front face of the cube? If you look long enough, you will see it two ways. You can see part b either as a vase or as two profiles.

a   b   c   d   e

FIGURE 4.45 Reversible figures: (a) The Necker cube. Which is the front face? (b) Faces or a vase. (c) A sax player or a woman's face ("Sara Nader"). (d) An old woman or a young woman. (e) A face or what? (*Part c from Shepard, 1990; part d from Boring, 1930*)

In part c, with a little imagination, you might see a woman's face or a man blowing a horn. (If you need help, check answer F on page 145.) Part d shows both an old woman and a young woman. Almost everyone sees one or the other immediately, but many people lock into one perception so tightly that they cannot see the other one. Part e was drawn by an 8-year-old girl who intended it as the picture of a face. Can you find another possibility? (If you have trouble with parts d or e, check answers G and H on page 145.) Overall, the point of the reversible figures is that we perceive by imposing order on an array, not just by adding up lines and points.

CONCEPT CHECK ☑

19. In what way does the phenomenon of reversible figures conflict with the idea that feature detectors explain vision? (Check your answer on page 145.)

The Gestalt psychologists described several principles of how we organize perceptions into meaningful wholes, as illustrated in Figure 4.46. **Proximity** is the *tendency to perceive objects that are close together as belonging to a group.* The objects in part a form two groups because of their proximity. The *tendency to perceive objects that resemble each other as forming a group* is called **similarity.** The objects in part b group into Xs and Os because of similarity. When lines are interrupted, as in part c, we may perceive **continuation,** *a filling in of the gaps.* You probably perceive this illustration as a rectangle covering the center of one very elongated hot dog.

When a familiar figure is interrupted, as in part d, we perceive a **closure** of the figure; that is, *we imagine the rest of the figure.* The figure we imagine completes what we already see in a way that is simple, symmetrical, or consistent with our past experience (Shimaya, 1997). For example, you probably see the following as an orange rectangle overlapping

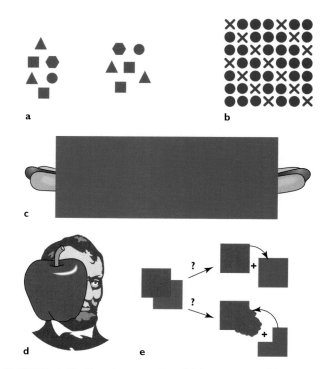

a   b

c

d   e

FIGURE 4.46 Gestalt principles of (a) proximity, (b) similarity, (c) continuation, (d) closure, and (e) good figure.

a blue diamond, although you don't really know what, if anything, is behind the rectangle:

Of course, the principle of closure is similar to that of continuation. With a complicated pattern, however, closure takes into account more than a continuation of the lines. For example, in Figure 4.46c you fill in the gaps to perceive one long hot dog. With some additional context, you would probably perceive the same pattern as two shorter hot dogs:

Yet another Gestalt principle is **common fate:** *We perceive objects as being part of the same group if they change or move in similar ways at the same time.* Suppose you see an array of miscellaneous objects differing in shape, size, and color. If some of them move in the same direction and speed, we see them as a related group. Also if some of them grow brighter or darker together, again we see them as related (Sekuler & Bennett, 2001).

In everyday life the principle of common fate is a useful tool. Imagine you see a snake's head sticking out of one hole in the ground and a tail sticking out of another. When the head starts moving forward, if the tail also moves down into the ground, you perceive it as all one snake. If the head moves and the tail doesn't, you see that you have two snakes to deal with.

Finally, when possible, we tend to perceive a **good figure**—*a simple, familiar, symmetrical figure.* Many important, familiar objects in the world are geometrically simple or close to it: The sun and moon are round, tree trunks meet the ground at almost a right angle, faces and animals are nearly symmetrical, and so forth. When we look at a complex pattern, we tend to focus on regular patterns. If we can see something as a circle, square, or straight line, we do. In Figure 4.46e the part on the left could represent a red square overlapping a green one or a green backward L overlapping a red object of irregular shape. We are powerfully drawn to the first interpretation because it includes "good," regular, symmetrical objects.

In Figure 4.47a we perceive a white triangle overlapping three ovals (Singh, Hoffman, & Albert, 1999). That perception is so convincing that you may have to look carefully to persuade yourself that there is no line establishing a border for the triangle. However, if we tilt the black objects slightly, as in Figure 4.47b, the illusion of something lying on top of them disappears. We "see" the overlapping object only if it is a symmetrical, good figure.

FIGURE 4.47 In (a) we see a triangle overlapping three irregular ovals. We see it because triangles are "good figures" and symmetrical. If we tilt the ovals, as in (b), they appear as irregular objects, not as objects with something on top of them. *(From "Contour Completion and Relative Depth: Petter's Rule and Support Ratio," by M. Singh, D. D. Hoffman and M. K. Albert, Psychological Science, 1999, 10, 423-428. Copyright © 1999 Blackwell Publishers Ltd. Reprinted by permission.)*

Similarities Between Vision and Hearing

The perceptual organization principles of Gestalt psychology apply to hearing as well as to vision. There are reversible figures in sound, just as there are in vision. For instance, you can hear a clock going "tick, tock, tick, tock" or "tock, tick, tock, tick." You can hear your windshield wipers going "dunga, dunga" or "gadung, gadung."

The Gestalt principles of continuation and closure work best when we see something that has interrupted something else. For example, consider Figure 4.48. In parts c and d, the context suggest objects partly blocking our view of a three-dimensional cube. In parts

FIGURE 4.48 (a) and (b) appear to be arrays of flat objects. Introducing a context of overlapping lines causes a cube to emerge in (c) and (d). *(From Organization in Vision: Essays on Gestalt Perception, by Gaetano Kanizsa, pp. 7-9. Copyright © 1979 by Gaetano Kanizsa. Reproduced with permission of Greenwood Publishing Group, Westport, CT.)*

a and b, we are much less likely to see a cube, as nothing suggests an object occluding our view. Similarly, in Figure 4.49a we see a series of meaningless patches. In Figure 4.49b the addition of some black glop helps us see these patches as the word *psychology* (Bregman, 1981). We get continuation or closure

FIGURE 4.49 Why is the word "psychology" easier to read in (b) than in (a)? *(After Bregman, 1981)*

mainly when we see that something has blocked the presumed object in the background.

The same is true in hearing. If a speech or song is broken up by periods of silence, we do not fill in the gaps and we find the utterance hard to understand. However, if the same gaps are filled by noise, we "hear" what probably occurred during those gaps; in other words we apply continuation and closure (C. T. Miller, Dibble, & Hauser, 2001; Warren, 1970).

Feature Detectors and Gestalt Psychology

The Gestalt approach to perception does not conflict with the feature-detector approach as much as it might seem. The feature-detector approach describes the first stages of perception—how the brain takes individual points of light and connects them into lines and then into more complex features. According to the feature-detector approach, the brain says, "I see these points here, here, and here, so there must be a line. I see a line here and another line connecting with it here, so there must be a letter L." The Gestalt approach describes how we combine visual input with our knowledge and expectations. According to the Gestalt interpretation, the brain says, "I see what looks like a circle, so the missing piece must be part of a circle too."

Which view is correct? Both, of course. Our perception must assemble the individual points of light or bits of sound, but once it forms a tentative interpretation of the pattern, it uses that interpretation to organize or reorganize the information.

Perception of Movement and Depth

As an automobile drives away from us, its image on the retina grows smaller, yet we perceive it as moving, not as shrinking. That perception illustrates **visual constancy**— *our tendency to perceive objects as keeping their shape, size, and color, even though what actually strikes our retina changes from time to time.* Figure 4.50 shows examples of two visual constancies: shape constancy and size constancy. Constancies depend on our familiarity with objects and on our ability to estimate distances and angles of view. For example, we know that a door is still rectangular even when we view it from an odd angle. But to recognize that an object keeps its shape and size, we have to perceive movement or changes in distance. How do we do so?

Perception of Movement

Moving objects capture our attention, and for a good reason. A moving object could be a person or animal, something people have made (e.g., a car), something thrown, or something that has fallen. In any case it is more likely to require our immediate attention than something stationary.

The detection of motion raises some interesting issues, including how we distinguish between our own movement and the movement of objects. Try this simple demonstration: Hold an object in front of your eyes and then move it to the right. Now hold the object in front of your eyes and move your eyes to the

FIGURE 4.50 (a) Shape constancy: We perceive all three doors as rectangles. (b) Size constancy: We perceive all three hands as equal in size.

left. The image of the object moves across your retina in the same way when you move the object or move your eyes. Yet you perceive the object as moving in one case but not in the other. Why?

The object looks stationary when you move your eyes for two reasons. One is that the vestibular system informs the visual areas of the brain about your head movements. When your brain knows that your eyes have moved to the left, it interprets a change in what you see as being a result of that movement. One man

with a rare kind of brain damage could not connect his eye movements with his perceptions. Whenever he moved his head or eyes, the world appeared to be moving, and frequently, he became dizzy and nauseated (Haarmeier, Thier, Repnow, & Petersen, 1997).

The second reason that the object does not appear to move is that we perceive motion when an object moves *relative to the background* (Gibson, 1968). For example, when you walk forward, stationary objects in your environment move across your retina. If something fails to move across your retina, you perceive it as moving in the same direction as you are.

What do we perceive when an object is stationary and the background is moving? That seldom happens, but when it does, we may *incorrectly perceive the object as moving against a stationary background*, a phenomenon called **induced movement**. For example, when you watch clouds moving slowly across the moon, you might perceive the clouds as stationary and the moon as moving. Induced movement is a form of *apparent movement*, as opposed to *real movement*.

You have already read about the waterfall illusion (page 131), another example of apparent movement. Yet another is **stroboscopic movement**, an *illusion of movement created by a rapid succession of stationary images*. When a scene is flashed on a screen and is followed a split second later by a second scene slightly different from the first, you perceive the objects as having moved smoothly from their location in the first scene to their location in the second scene (Figure 4.51). Motion pictures are actually a series of still photos flashed on the screen.

We also experience an *illusion of movement created when two or more stationary lights separated by a short distance blink on and off at regular intervals*. Your brain creates the sense of motion in what is called the **phi effect**. You may have noticed signs in front of restaurants or motels that use this effect. As the lights blink on and off, an arrow seems to move and invite you in.

Our ability to detect visual movement played an interesting role in the history of astronomy. In 1930 Clyde Tombaugh was searching the skies for a possible undiscovered

FIGURE 4.51 A movie consists of a series of still photographs flickering at 86,400 per hour. You perceive moving objects, however, not a series of stills. Here you see a series of stills spread out in space instead of time.

planet beyond Neptune. He photographed each region of the sky twice, several days apart. A planet, unlike a star, moves from one photo to the next. However, how would he find one dot that moved among all the countless unmoving dots in the sky? He put each pair of photos on a machine that would flip back and forth between one photo and the other. When he came to the correct pair of photos, the machine flipped back and forth between them, and he immediately noticed the one moving dot (Tombaugh, 1980). We now know that little dot as the planet Pluto (Figure 4.52).

FIGURE 4.53 Convergence of the eyes as a cue to distance. The more this viewer must converge her eyes toward each other to focus on an object, the closer the object must be.

FIGURE 4.52 Clyde Tombaugh photographed each area of the sky twice, several days apart. Then he used a machine to flip back and forth between the two photos of each pair. When he came to one part of the sky, he immediately noticed one dot that moved between the two photos. That dot was the planet Pluto.

Perception of Depth

Although we live in a world of three dimensions, our retinas are in effect two-dimensional surfaces. **Depth perception,** our *perception of distance,* enables us to experience the world in three dimensions. This perception depends on several factors.

One factor is **retinal disparity**—*the difference in the apparent position of an object as seen by the left and right retinas.* Try this: Hold one finger at arm's length. Focus on it with one eye and then with the other. Note that the apparent position of your finger shifts with respect to the background. Now hold your finger closer to your face and repeat the experiment. Notice that the apparent position of your finger shifts even more. The discrepancy between the slightly different views the two eyes see becomes greater as the object comes closer. We use the amount of discrepancy to gauge distance. If you watch a three-dimensional movie while wearing special glasses, the principle is that the lenses enable your two eyes to see different views of the same scene.

A second cue for depth perception is the **convergence** of the eyes—that is, the *degree to which they turn in to focus on a close object* (Figure 4.53). When you focus on a distant object, your eyes are looking in

almost parallel directions. When you focus on something close, your eyes turn in, and you sense the tension of your eye muscles. The more the muscles pull, the closer the object must be.

Retinal disparity and convergence are called **binocular cues** because they *depend on the action of both eyes.* **Monocular cues** enable a person to *judge depth and distance with just one eye* or when both eyes see the same image, as when you look at a picture, such as Figure 4.54. The ability to use these monocular cues to interpret an illustration depends on our experience, including specifically experiences

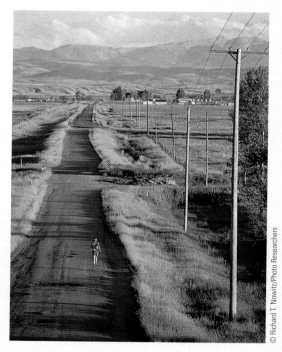

FIGURE 4.54 We judge depth and distance in a photograph using monocular cues (those that would work even with just one eye): (a) Closer objects occupy more space on the retina (or in the photograph) than do distant objects of the same type. (b) Nearer objects show more detail. (c) Closer objects overlap certain distant objects. (d) Objects in the foreground look sharper than objects do on the horizon.

FIGURE 4.55 Which animal is the hunter attacking? Most readers of this text, using monocular cues to distance, will reply that the hunter is attacking the antelope. However, many African people unfamiliar with drawings thought he was attacking a baby elephant because the hunter is physically closer to the elephant in the drawing. *(From Hudson, 1960)*

with photographs and drawings. For example, in Figure 4.55, does it appear to you that the hunter is aiming his spear at the antelope? When this drawing was shown to African people who had seldom seen drawings, many said the hunter was aiming at a baby elephant (Hudson, 1960). Clearly, people have to learn how to judge depth in drawings.

Let's consider some of the monocular cues we use to perceive depth:

Object size: Other things being equal, a nearby object produces a larger image than a distant one. However, this cue is useful only for objects of known sizes. For example, the jogger in Figure 4.54 produces a larger image than do any of the houses, which we know are actually larger. So we see the jogger as closer. However, the mountains in the background differ in actual as well as apparent size, so we cannot assume the ones that look bigger are closer.

Linear perspective: As parallel lines stretch out toward the horizon, they come closer and closer together. Examine the road in Figure 4.54. At the bottom of the photo (close to the viewer), the edges of the road are far apart; at greater distances they come together.

Detail: We see nearby objects, such as the jogger, in more detail than objects in the distance.

Interposition: A nearby object interrupts our view of a more distant object. For example, the closest telephone pole (on the right) interrupts our view of the closest tree, so we see that the telephone pole is closer than the tree.

Texture gradient: Notice the distance between one telephone pole and the next. At greater distances the poles come closer and closer together. The "packed together" appearance of objects gives us another cue to their approximate distance.

Shadows: Shadows help us gauge sizes as well as relative locations of objects.

Accommodation: The lens of the eye *accommodates*—that is, it changes shape—to focus on nearby objects, and your brain detects that change and thereby infers the distance to an object. Accommodation could help tell you how far away the photograph itself is, although it provides no information about the relative distances of objects in the photograph.

Motion parallax: Another monocular cue helps us perceive depth while we are moving, although it does not help with a photograph. When we are walking or riding in a car, close objects seem to pass by swiftly, while distant objects seem to pass by very slowly. *The faster an object passes by, the closer it must be.* This is the principle of motion parallax. Television and film crews use this principle. If the camera moves very slowly, you see closer objects move more than distant ones and get a good sense of depth.

▌ If you were a passenger on this train, the ground beside the tracks would appear to pass by more quickly than the more distant elements in the landscape. In this photo's version of motion parallax, the ground is blurred and more distant objects are crisp.

© Steve McCurry/Magnum Photos

20. Which monocular cues to depth are available in Figure 4.55?
21. With three-dimensional photography, cameras take two views of the same scene from different locations through lenses with different color filters or with different polarized-light filters. The two views are then superimposed. The viewer looks at the composite view through special glasses so that one eye sees the view taken with one camera and the other eye sees the view taken with the other camera. Which depth cue is at work here? (Check your answers on page 145.)

Optical Illusions

Many people claim to have seen ghosts, flying saucers, the Loch Ness monster, Bigfoot, or people floating in the air. Maybe they are lying, maybe they did see something extraordinary, or maybe they saw something ordinary but misinterpreted it. An **optical illusion** is a *misinterpretation of a visual stimulus.* Figure 4.56 shows a few examples. Also see the Online Try It Yourself called Muller-Lyer Illusion. For more, visit: www.exploratorium.edu/exhibits

Psychologists would like to develop a single explanation for all optical illusions. (Remember the principle of parsimony from Chapter 2.) They can explain many, though not all, optical illusions from the relationship between size perception and depth perception.

The Relationship Between Depth Perception and Size Perception

If you can estimate the size of an object, you can deduce its distance. If you can estimate its distance, you can deduce its size. Figure 4.57 shows that a given image on the retina may represent either a small, close object or a large, distant object.

Watch what happens when you take a single image and change its apparent distance: Stare at Figure 4.15 again to form a negative afterimage. First examine the afterimage while you are looking at the wall across the room. Then look at the afterimage against a sheet of paper. Suddenly, the image becomes smaller. As you move the paper backward and forward, you can make the apparent size change.

In the real world, we usually have many cues for judging the size and distance of objects. However, when you have fewer cues, you can become confused (Figure 4.58). I once saw an airplane overhead and was unsure whether it was a small, remote-controlled toy airplane or a distant, full-size airplane. Airplanes come in many sizes, and the sky has few cues to distance.

A similar issue arises in reported sightings of UFOs. When people see an unfamiliar object in the

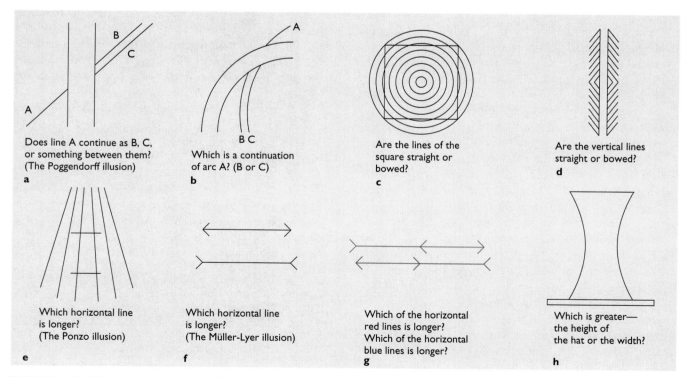

FIGURE 4.56 These geometric figures illustrate optical illusions. Answers (which you are invited to check with ruler and compass): (a) B, (b) B, (c) straight, (d) straight, (e) equal, (f) equal, (g) equal, (h) equal.

FIGURE 4.57 The trade-off between size and distance: A given image on the retina can indicate either a small, close object or a large, distant object.

sky, they can easily misjudge its distance. If they overestimate its distance, they also will overestimate its size and speed.

What does all this have to do with optical illusions? Whenever we misjudge distance, we misjudge size as well. For example, Figure 4.59a shows people in the Ames room (named for its designer, Adelbert Ames). The room is designed to look like a normal rectangular room, though its true dimensions are as shown in Figure 4.59b.

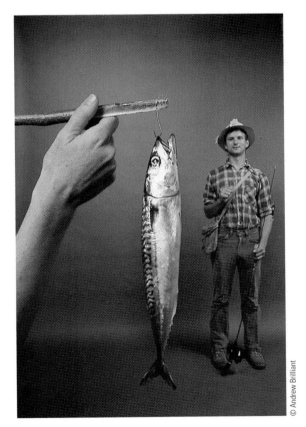

FIGURE 4.58 Because fish come in many sizes, we can estimate the size of a fish only if we know how far away it is or if we can compare its size to other nearby objects. See what happens when you cover the man and then cover the hand.

The right corner is much closer than the left corner. The two young women are actually the same height. If we eliminated all the background cues, we would correctly perceive the women as being the same size but at different distances. However, the apparently rectangular room provides such powerful (though misleading) cues to distance that the women appear to differ greatly in height.

Even a two-dimensional drawing on a flat surface can offer cues that lead to erroneous depth perception. People who have had much experience with photos and drawings tend to interpret two-dimensional drawings as if they were three-dimensional. Figure 4.60 shows a bewildering two-prong/three-prong device and a round staircase that seems to run uphill all the way clockwise or downhill all the way counterclockwise. Both drawings puzzle us because we try to interpret them as three-dimensional objects.

In Figure 4.61 linear perspective suggests that the right of the picture is farther away than the left. We therefore see the cylinder on the right as being the farthest away. If it is the farthest away and still produces the same size image on the retina as the other two, then it would have to be the largest. In short, by perceiving two-dimensional representations as if they were three-dimensional, we misjudge distance and consequently misjudge size. When we are somehow misled by the cues that ordinarily ensure constancy in size and shape, we experience an optical illusion (Day, 1972).

We can experience an *auditory illusion* by a similar principle: If we misestimate the distance to a sound source, we misestimate the intensity of the sound. That is, if you hear a sound that you think is coming from a distant source, you hear it as loud. (It would have to be for you to hear it so well from a distance.) If you hear the same sound but think it is coming from a source near you, it sounds softer (Kitigawa & Ichihara, 2002; Mershon, Desaulniers, Kiefer, Amerson, & Mills, 1981).

Further Evidence Linking Illusions to Depth Perception

The illusions occur because your brain does its best to judge distances and depths and then constructs an image of what the objects it sees *really are* (as opposed to what pattern of light strikes the retina). Let's belabor this point with two more examples.

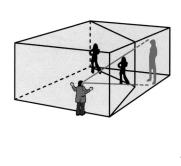

FIGURE 4.59 The Ames room is a study in deceptive perception, designed to be viewed through a peephole with one eye. **(a)** Both of these people are actually the same height. We are so accustomed to rooms with right angles that we can't imagine how this apparently ordinary room creates this optical illusion. **(b)** This diagram shows the positions of the people in the Ames room and demonstrates how the illusion of distance is created. *(Part b from J. R. Wilson et al., 1964)*

FIGURE 4.60 These two-dimensional drawings puzzle us because we try to interpret them as three-dimensional objects.

The first, shown in Figure 4.62, is the tabletop illusion (Shepard, 1990). Here, almost unbelievably, the vertical dimension of the blue table equals the horizontal dimension of the yellow table, and the horizontal dimension of the blue table equals the vertical dimension of the yellow table. (Take measurements at the center of each table. The shapes

FIGURE 4.61 Many optical illusions depend on misjudging distances. The jar on the right seems larger because the context makes it appear farther away.

of the two tables are not exactly the same.) The blue table appears long and thin compared to the yellow one because we interpret it in depth. In effect your brain constructs what each table would have to really *be* in order to look this way (Purves & Lotto, 2003).

Now consider the Poggendorff illusion, first shown in Figure 4.56a, with a modified version in Figure 4.63. A diagonal line interrupted by something else appears to be not quite straight, not quite continuous. Branka Spehar and Barbara Gillam (2002) have suggested an explanation: When we see a diagonal line, we ordinarily interpret it as a line receding into the distance, such as a path moving away from us toward the horizon. In Figure 4.63a the object that interrupts a diagonal line is consistent with that interpretation and even encourages it. In that case the illusion weakens or disappears; we see each line on the right as a continuation of the correct line on the left. However, in part b the bar provides a context that conflicts with the idea of a receding line, and we have more trouble processing the information.

The Moon Illusion

To most people, the *moon close to the horizon appears about 30% larger than it appears when it is higher in the sky.* This **moon illusion** is so convincing that some people have tried to explain it by referring to the bending of light rays by the atmosphere or another physical phenomenon. The explanation, however, must depend on the observer, not the light rays. If you measure the moon image with navigational or photographic equipment, you will find that it is the same size at the horizon as it is higher in the sky. For example, Figure 4.64 shows

FIGURE 4.62 The tabletop illusion. The blue table is as wide as the yellow table is long, and as long as the yellow table is wide, if you measure in the middle of each table. The parts below show rotation of the blue table to overlap the yellow one.

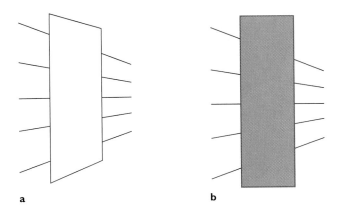

FIGURE 4.63 Variations of the Poggendorff illusion. If the interrupting bar encourages the perception of a line receding into the distance, we see the lines as continuous and straight. However, if the bar suggests the line has not receded, the lines appear distorted. *(From Spehar & Gillam, 2002)*

the moon at two positions in the sky; you can measure the two images to demonstrate that they are really the same size. (The atmosphere's bending of light rays makes the moon look orange near the horizon, but it does not increase the size of the image.) However, photographs do not capture the full strength of the moon illusion as we see it in real life. In Figure 4.64 (or any similar pair of photos), the moon looks almost the same at each position; in the actual night sky, though, the moon looks enormous at the horizon.

One explanation is that the vast terrain between the viewer and the horizon provides a basis for size comparison. When you see the moon at the horizon, you can compare it to other objects you see at the horizon, which look tiny. By contrast the moon looks

FIGURE 4.64 Ordinarily, the moon looks much larger at the horizon than it does overhead. In photographs this illusion disappears almost completely, but the photographs do serve to demonstrate that the physical image of the moon is the same in both cases. The moon illusion requires a psychological explanation, not a physical one.

large. When you see the moon high in the sky, however, it is surrounded only by the vast, featureless sky, so in contrast it appears smaller (Baird, 1982; Restle, 1970).

A second explanation is that the terrain between the viewer and the horizon gives an impression of great distance. When the moon is high in the sky, we have no basis to judge distance, and perhaps we unconsciously see the overhead moon as closer than when it is at the horizon. If we see the "horizon moon" as more distant, we will perceive it as larger (Kaufman & Rock, 1989; Rock & Kaufman, 1962). This explanation is appealing because it relates the moon illusion to our misperceptions of distance, a factor already accepted as important for many other illusions.

Many psychologists are not satisfied with this explanation, however, primarily because they are not convinced that the horizon moon looks farther away than the overhead moon. If we ask people which looks farther away, many say they are not sure. If we insist on an answer, most say the horizon moon looks *closer,* contradicting the theory. Some psychologists reply that the situation is complicated: We unconsciously perceive the horizon as farther away; consequently, we perceive the horizon moon as very large; then, because of the perceived large size of the horizon moon, we secondarily and consciously say it looks closer, although we continue to unconsciously perceive it as farther (Rock & Kaufman, 1962).

One major message arises from work on optical illusions and indeed from all the research on visual perception: What we perceive is not the same as what is "out there." Our visual system does an amazing job of providing us with useful information about the world around us, but under unusual circumstances we can be very wrong about what we think we see.

IN CLOSING

Making Sense Out of Sensory Information

You have probably heard the expression, "Seeing is believing." The saying is true in many ways, including that what you believe influences what you see. Perception is not just a matter of adding up all the events striking the retina; we look for what we expect to see, we impose order on haphazard patterns, we see three dimensions in two-dimensional drawings, and we see optical illusions. The brain does not simply compute what light is striking the retina, but what objects probably exist "out there" and what they are doing.

Summary

- *Perception of minimal stimuli.* There is no sharp dividing line between sensory stimuli that can be perceived and sensory stimuli that cannot be perceived. (page 125)

- *Signal detection.* To determine how accurately someone can detect a signal or how accurately a test diagnoses a condition, we need to consider not only the ratio of hits to misses when the stimulus is present but also the ratio of false alarms to correct rejections when the stimulus is absent. (page 126)

- *Subliminal perception.* Under some circumstances a weak stimulus that we do not consciously identify can influence our behavior, at least weakly or briefly. However, the evidence does not support claims of powerful effects. (page 127)

- *Face recognition.* People are amazingly good at recognizing faces. (page 129)

- *Detection of simple visual features.* In the first stages of the process of perception, feature-detector cells identify lines, points, and simple movement. Visual afterimages can be interpreted in terms of fatiguing certain feature detectors. (page 129)

- *Perception of organized wholes.* According to Gestalt psychologists, we perceive an organized whole by identifying similarities and continuous patterns across a large area of the visual field. (page 133)

- *Visual constancies.* We ordinarily perceive the shape, size, and color of objects as constant, even though the pattern of light striking the retina varies from time to time. (page 136)

- *Motion perception.* We perceive an object as moving if it moves relative to its background. We can generally distinguish between an object that is actually moving and a similar pattern of retinal stimulation that results from our own movement. (page 136)

- *Depth perception.* To perceive depth, we use the retinal discrepancy between the views that our two eyes see. We also learn to use other cues that are just as effective with one eye as with two. (page 138)

- *Optical illusions.* Many, but not all, optical illusions result from interpreting a two-dimensional display as three-dimensional or from other faulty estimates of depth. (page 140)

- *The size-distance relationship.* Our estimate of an object's size depends on our estimate of its distance from us. If we overestimate its distance, we will also overestimate its size. (page 140)

Answers to Concept Checks

16. We have been told the hit rate, but we cannot evaluate it unless we also know the false alarm rate. That is, how many people without any alcohol or drug problem have this same pattern of brain waves? If that percentage is large, the test is useless. The smaller that percentage is, the better. (page 127)

17. The retinex theory is the only one that accounts for your perception of Figure 4.37. According to the retinex theory, your cortex compares your input in various parts of the retina to synthesize a perception of each part based on the whole context. (page 129)

18. A feature detector is a neuron in the visual system of the brain that responds mostly in the presence of a particular feature, such as a straight horizontal line. One kind of evidence is that recordings from neurons in laboratory animals indicate increased response of different cells to different visual stimuli. Another line of evidence is that people who have stared at one kind of stimulus become temporarily less sensitive to that kind of stimulus, as if the feature detectors for that stimulus have become fatigued. (page 132)

19. Feature detectors cannot fully explain how we see a reversible figure in two or more ways. If vision were simply a matter of stimulating various line detectors and adding up their responses, then a given display would always produce the same perceptual experience. (page 134)

20. Object size and linear perspective are cues that the elephant must be far away. (page 140).

21. Retinal disparity. (page 140)

Answers to Other Questions in the Module

C. a. **7.** b. **1.** c. **5.** d. **9.** e. **4.**

D.

E.

F.

G.

Young woman   Old woman

H.

I. Line d is the same length as the one on the right. (Check it with a ruler.)

CHAPTER ENDING

Key Terms and Activities

Key Terms

absolute sensory threshold: the intensity at which a given individual can detect a sensory stimulus 50% of the time; a low threshold indicates the ability to detect faint stimuli (page 125)

accommodation of the lens: an adjustment of the thickness of the lens to focus on objects at different distances (page 98)

binocular cues: visual cues that depend on the action of both eyes (page 138)

binocular rivalry: the alteration between seeing the pattern in the left retina and the pattern in the right retina (page 104)

blind spot: the area where the optic nerve exits the retina (page 102)

brightness contrast: an increase or decrease in an object's apparent brightness because of the effects of objects around it (page 128)

capsaicin: a chemical that stimulates the release of substance P (page 119)

cataract: a disorder in which the lens of the eye becomes cloudy (page 99)

closure: in Gestalt psychology the tendency to imagine the rest of an incomplete, familiar figure (page 134)

cochlea: the snail-shaped, fluid-filled structure that contains the receptors for hearing (page 112)

color constancy: the tendency of an object to appear nearly the same color under a variety of lighting conditions (page 107)

common fate: the tendency to perceive objects as being part of the same group if they change or move in similar ways at the same time (page 135)

conduction deafness: a hearing loss that results when the bones connected to the eardrum fail to transmit sound waves properly to the cochlea (page 113)

cone: the type of visual receptor that is adapted for color vision, daytime vision, and detailed vision (page 99)

continuation: in Gestalt psychology the tendency to fill in the gaps in an interrupted line (page 134)

convergence: the degree to which the eyes turn in to focus on a close object (page 138)

cornea: a rigid, transparent structure on the surface of the eyeball (page 98)

cutaneous senses: the skin senses, including pressure on the skin, warmth, cold, pain, vibration, movement across the skin, and stretch of the skin (page 116)

dark adaptation: a gradual improvement in the ability to see in dim light (page 101)

depth perception: the perception of distance, which enables us to experience the world in three dimensions (page 138)

electromagnetic spectrum: the continuum of all the frequencies of radiated energy (page 97)

endorphin: any of the neurotransmitters that decrease the perception of pain (page 118)

feature detector: a neuron in the visual system of the brain that responds to the presence of a certain simple feature, such as a horizontal line (page 130)

figure and ground: an object and its background (page 133)

fovea: the central part of the retina that has a greater density of receptors, especially cones, than any other part of the retina (page 98)

frequency principle: the identification of pitch by the frequency of action potentials in neurons along the basilar membrane of the cochlea, synchronized with the frequency of sound waves (page 114)

ganglion cells: neurons in the eye that receive input from bipolar cells, which in turn receive their input from the visual receptors (page 102)

gate theory: the proposal that pain messages must pass through a gate, probably in the spinal cord, that can block these messages (page 118)

Gestalt psychology: an approach to psychology that seeks to explain how we perceive overall patterns (page 133)

glaucoma: a condition characterized by increased pressure within the eyeball, resulting in damage to the optic nerve and therefore a loss of vision (page 99)

good figure: in Gestalt psychology the tendency to perceive simple, symmetrical figures (page 135)

hertz (Hz): a unit of frequency representing one cycle (vibration) per second (page 112)

hyperopia: farsightedness; the inability to focus on nearby objects (page 99)

induced movement: a perception that an object is moving and the background is stationary when in fact the object is stationary and the background is moving (page 137)

iris: the colored structure on the surface of the eye, surrounding the pupil (page 98)

lens: a flexible structure that can vary its thickness to enable the eye to focus on objects at different distances (page 98)

loudness: a perception that depends on the amplitude of a sound wave (page 112)

monocular cues: visual cues that are just as effective with one eye as with both (page 138)

moon illusion: the apparent difference between the size of the moon at the horizon and its size when viewed higher in the sky (page 142)

motion parallax: the apparently swift motion of objects close to a moving observer and the apparently slow motion of objects farther away (page 139)

myopia: nearsightedness; the inability to focus on distant objects (page 99)

negative afterimage: a color that a person sees after staring at its opposite color for a while (page 106)

nerve deafness: a hearing loss that results from damage to the cochlea, the hair cells, or the auditory nerve (page 113)

olfaction: the sense of smell; the detection of chemicals in contact with the membranes inside the nose (page 122)

opponent-process theory: the theory that we perceive color in terms of a system of paired opposites: red versus green, yellow versus blue, and white versus black (page 105)

optic nerve: a set of axons that extend from the ganglion cells of the eye to the thalamus and several other areas of the brain (page 102)

optical illusion: a misinterpretation of a visual stimulus as being larger or smaller, or straighter or more curved, than it really is (page 140)

perception: the interpretation of sensory information (page 96)

phantom limb: a continuing sensation of an amputated body part (page 119)

pheromone: an odorous chemical, released by an animal, that changes how other members of the species respond to that animal socially (page 123)

phi effect: the illusion of movement created when two or more stationary lights separated by a short distance flash on and off at regular intervals (page 137)

pitch: a perception closely related to the frequency of sound waves (page 112)

place principle: the identification of pitch by determining which auditory neurons, coming from which part of the basilar membrane, are most active (page 114)

presbyopia: a decreased flexibility of the lens and therefore the inability to focus on nearby objects (page 99)

proximity: in Gestalt psychology the tendency to perceive objects that are close together as belonging to a group (page 134)

pupil: the adjustable opening in the eye through which light enters (page 98)

receptor: a specialized cell that converts environmental energies into signals for the nervous system (page 97)

retina: a layer of visual receptors covering the back surface of the eyeball (page 98)

retinal disparity: the difference in the apparent position of an object as seen by the left and right retinas (page 138)

retinex theory: the theory that color perception results from the cerebral cortex's comparison of various retinal patterns (page 107)

reversible figure: a stimulus that you can perceive in more than one way (page 133)

rod: the type of visual receptor that is adapted for vision in dim light (page 99)

sensation: the conversion of energy from the environment into a pattern of response by the nervous system (page 96)

signal-detection theory: the study of people's tendencies to make hits, correct rejections, misses, and false alarms (page 126)

similarity: in Gestalt psychology the tendency to perceive objects that resemble each other as belonging to a group (page 134)

sound waves: vibrations of the air or of another medium (page 112)

stimulus: energy in the environment that affects what we do (page 97)

stroboscopic movement: an illusion of movement created by a rapid succession of stationary images (page 137)

subliminal perception: the ability of a stimulus to influence our behavior even when it is presented so faintly or briefly or along with such strong distracters that we do not perceive it consciously (page 127)

substance P: a neurotransmitter responsible for much of the transmission of pain information in the nervous system (page 118)

taste: the sensory system that responds to chemicals on the tongue (page 121)

taste bud: the site of the taste receptors, located in one of the folds on the surface of the tongue (page 121)

trichromatic theory (or Young-Helmholtz theory): the theory that color vision depends on the relative rate of response of three types of cones (page 105)

vestibular sense: a specialized sense that detects the direction of tilt and amount of acceleration of the head and the position of the head with respect to gravity (page 115)

visual constancy: the tendency to perceive objects as unchanging in shape, size, and color, despite variations in what actually reaches the retina (page 136)

volley principle: the identification of pitch by groups of hair cells responding to each vibration by producing an action potential (page 114)

waterfall illusion: a phenomenon in which prolonged staring at a waterfall and then looking at nearby cliffs causes those cliffs to appear to flow upward (page 131)

Suggestions for Further Reading

Purves, D., & Lotto, R. B. (2003). *Why we see what we do.* Sunderland, MA: Sinauer Associates. Insightful and creative account of human perception.

Ramachandran, V. S., & Blakeslee, S. (1998). *Phantoms in the brain.* New York: Morrow. Fascinating explanation of phantom limbs and related phenomena.

Warren, R. M. (1999). *Auditory perception: A new analysis and synthesis.* Cambridge, England: Cambridge University Press. Superb treatment of hearing, with a CD-ROM disk that includes demonstrations of auditory phenomena.

 # Book Companion Web Site

Need help studying? Go to

http://psychology.wadsworth.com/kalat_intro7e/

for a virtual study center. You'll find a personalized Self-Study Assessment that will provide you with a study plan based on your answers to a pretest. Also study using flashcards, quizzes, interactive art, and an online glossary.

Check out interactive **Try It Yourself** exercises on the companion site! For example, the Motion Aftereffect, Brightness Contrast, Blind Spot, and Matching High School Photos exercises are pulled directly from sections in this chapter.

Your companion site also has direct links to the following Web sites. These links are checked often for changes, dead links, and new additions.

More Illusions

www.exploratorium.edu/exhibits

Here are wonderful illusions, both visual and auditory. Enjoy.

Seeing, Hearing, and Smelling

www.hhmi.org/senses/

Elaborate psychological and medical information, courtesy of the Howard Hughes Medical Institute.

Smells and Flavors

http://www.leffingwell.com/

Rich source of information about olfaction, ranging from the chemistry of perfumes to the olfactory receptors and how our brains handle olfaction.

Reverse Speech Home Page

www.reversespeech.com/

You've heard that particular recordings contain hidden messages that can be heard only if the material is played backward. One person had the time and patience to research such claims. You will need the RealAudio plug-in, available for free at

www.realaudio.com/products/player/index.html.

Can you provide a better explanation for the reversed messages?

 Try It Yourself CD-ROM
with Critical Thinking Video Exercises

Use your CD to access **videos** related to activities designed to help you think critically about the important topics discussed. For example, the video about visual impairment relates to what you've learned in this chapter. You'll also find an easy portal link to the book companion site where you can access your personalized **Self-Study Assessments** and interactive **Try It Yourself** exercises.

PsychNow! 2.0

PsychNow! is a fun interactive CD designed to help you with the difficult concepts in psychology. Check out the Accessing Psychology section for the following topics that relate to this chapter:

Vision and Hearing: roller coaster video, lesson about the path from stimulus to brain, and a transduction path quiz.

Chemical and Somesthetic Senses: muscular directionality exercise, kinesthesia, balance, smell, taste, and touch lesson as well as a chemical and somesthetic sense video.

Perception: interactive 3-D "Magic Eye" image, vision cues lesson, interactive Escher drawing to show perception.

InteractNOW! Online Collaborative Lab: Perception and Motion Aftereffects

ExperimentNOW! Research Experiments: Perception—Apparent motion, attention blink, signal detection, visual search, and the Stroop effect

States of Consciousness

One of the great philosophical issues of psychology is the relationship between mind and brain. Why, in a universe composed of matter and energy, is there such a thing as consciousness? One reason this issue is so difficult is that no one can specify exactly what we mean by consciousness or mind. As William James (1892/1961) said about consciousness, "Its meaning we know so long as no one asks us to define it" (p. 19).

Sleep and dreams are an alteration of consciousness. People who have trouble sleeping at night are likely to have difficulties the next day.

Let's make at least a feeble attempt to define it. Defining consciousness in terms of synonyms like *awareness* accomplishes nothing unless we can define *awareness*. For some purposes we can use an operational definition such as "you are conscious of something if you can describe it in words." That definition helps distinguish conscious stimuli from subliminal ones, as in the last chapter, but it is not suitable overall. Surely, we do not assume that toddlers are unconscious until they learn to talk!

Consciousness relates closely to sensory experience, with an emphasis on the private, subjective aspect. That is, when you and I look at something and both call it red, we cannot be sure that your conscious experience of it is the same as mine. Consciousness also relates closely to perception *of ourselves*. That is, you perceive your own body and you perceive yourself as the thing that perceives other objects. Antonio Damasio (2003) defined consciousness as "the process whereby a mind is imbued with a reference we call self, and is said to know of its own existence and the existence of objects around it" (p. 184). We might simplify the definition of **consciousness** as *the subjective experience of perceiving oneself and other entities.*

Feel free to argue with that definition, but even without a satisfactory definition, perhaps we can agree on one fact about consciousness: It varies. When you are alert, you notice and remember many things, although hardly everything that you see or hear. You notice and remember less when you are drowsy and still less when asleep. Even people who are anesthetized or in a coma occasionally respond briefly to salient events and occasionally report them afterward. In short, consciousness is not an all-or-none process. In this chapter we study some of the ways it varies.

Sleep and Dreams

Why do we sleep?

What accounts for the content of our dreams?

Consciousness and alertness cycle daily between wakefulness and sleep. During sleep we become less aware of our surroundings, though not totally unresponsive. During dreams we live in a fantasy world where many impossible events seem possible. Why do we have these periods of altered consciousness?

Our Circadian Rhythms

Sleep is not the only important biological cycle. Consider hibernation. Ground squirrels hibernate during the winter, when they would have trouble finding food. The females awaken in spring as soon as food becomes available. The males also need to awaken in time to eat, but they have another reason to awaken: The females are ready to mate as soon as they come out of their winter burrows, and each female mates only once a year. Any male who awakens later than the females pays for his extra rest by missing his only mating opportunity for the *entire year*. So males don't take any chances; they all awaken from hibernation a full week before the females do. And then they sit around waiting . . . with no females, nothing to eat, and little to do except fight with one another (French, 1988).

The point is that animals have evolved internal timing mechanisms to prepare them for predictable needs. Male ground squirrels awaken not in response to their current situation but in preparation for what will happen a few days later. Similarly, most migrating birds start south in the fall well before their northern homes become inhospitable.

Humans also have mechanisms that prepare us for activity during the day and for sleep at night. Each species generates a **circadian rhythm,** a *rhythm of activity and inactivity lasting about 1 day.* (The term *circadian* comes from the Latin roots *circa* and *dies,* meaning "about a day.") The rising and setting of the sun provide cues to reset our rhythm each day. In an environment with no cues for time, such as polar regions in winter, most people generate a waking–sleeping rhythm a little longer than 24 hours, although it gradu-

ally drifts out of phase with the clock and sleeping becomes irregular (Palinkas, 2003). The best current estimate is that our spontaneous circadian rhythm lasts about 24.2 hours (Czeisler et al., 1999), although the exact length depends on the brightness and timing of light (Campbell, 2000).

The genes that control circadian rhythms vary, like any other gene. Some people have a mutated gene that causes their circadian rhythm to run faster than normal (Toh et al., 2001). They consistently go to sleep hours earlier than other people and wake up hours earlier. Most people see weekends and vacations as an opportunity to stay up later than usual and sleep later than usual in the morning. But people with these fast-running rhythms enjoy the opportunity to go to sleep even earlier than usual and awaken even earlier than usual!

©Jeff Greenberg/The Image Works

❚ The rising and setting of the sun do not directly produce our daily rhythm of wakefulness and sleepiness, but they synchronize that rhythm. We adjust our internally generated cycles so that we feel alert during the day and sleepy at night.

One of the earliest demonstrations of humans' circadian rhythms was a study of two people who spent a few weeks in a remote part of Mammoth Caves in Kentucky (Kleitman, 1963). For 24 hours per day, the temperature was a constant 12° Celsius (54°F), and the relative humidity was 100%. They saw no light except from lamps that they controlled themselves, and they heard no noises except their own. Any decisions about when to sleep and when to awaken had to come from within, not from the environment. Yet they went to sleep and awoke at about the same time every day.

Sleepiness and alertness depend strongly on one's position within the circadian rhythm. If you have ever gone all night without sleep—as most college students do at one time or another—you probably grew very sleepy between about 2 and 5 A.M. But if you were still awake at 7 or 8 A.M., you began feeling less sleepy, not more. You became more alert because of your circadian rhythm, even though your sleep deprivation had continued.

In one study volunteers went without sleep for three nights. An experimenter periodically took their temperature and measured their performance on logical reasoning tasks. Both temperature and logical reasoning declined during the first night and then increased the next morning. During the second and third nights, temperature and reasoning decreased more than they had the first night, but they increased again the next day (Figure 5.1). Thus, sleep deprivation produces a pattern of progressive deterioration superimposed on the normal circadian cycle of rising and falling body temperature and alertness (Babkoff, Caspy, Mikulincer, & Sing, 1991). In short, sleepiness apparently depends partly on how long one has gone without sleep and partly on the time of day (i.e., one's circadian rhythm).

Morning People and Evening People

Our circadian rhythms do not affect us all in exactly the same way. "Morning people" awaken easily, full of energy, and do their best work before noon; "evening people" take longer to warm up in the morning (literally as well as figuratively) and do their best work in the afternoon or evening (Horne, Brass, & Pettitt, 1980). Most people are pretty consistent, and you probably know whether you are a morning person, evening person, or somewhere in between.

The morning person/evening person distinction is particularly relevant for research on aging. Most young adults are either evening people or neutral (about equally alert at all times), whereas nearly all people over age 65 are morning people. For many years researchers reported substantial declines in memory with older people. But who did most of this research? Graduate students. How old are graduate students? Most are in their 20s. What time do graduate students choose to conduct their research? Late afternoon or evening, a fine time for most graduate students but not for the elderly. Researchers in one study compared the memories of young adults (18–22 years old) and older adults (66–78 years old) at different times of day. Early in the morning, the older adults did about as well as the younger ones. However, as the day went on, the

FIGURE 5.1 Cumulative effects of three nights without sleep: Both body temperature and logical reasoning decrease each night and increase the next morning. They also deteriorate from one day to the next. (*From "Monotonic and Rhythmic Influences: A Challenge for Sleep Deprivation Research," by H. Babkoff, T. Caspy, M. Mikulincer, & H. C. Sing, Psychological Bulletin, 1991, 109, pp. 411–428. Copyright © 1991 American Psychological Association. Reprinted with permission.*)

younger adults either remained steady or improved, whereas the older adults deteriorated steadily (May, Hasher, & Stoltzfus, 1993). Figure 5.2 shows the results of this study. The deterioration over the day represents a loss of alertness, and older people can recover their performance in the afternoon or evening by drinking caffeinated coffee (Ryan, Hatfield, & Hofstetter, 2002).

Incidentally, the relationship between age and morning or evening arousal is apparently not specific to our culture or even our species. Young rats are about equally able to perform difficult tasks at all times of day, but aged rats do best shortly after they wake up and then deteriorate as the day goes on (Winocur & Hasher, 1999).

FIGURE 5.2 If tested early in the morning, older people perform as well as younger people on memory tasks. As the day progresses, young people improve and older people deteriorate.

Are most college classes offered in the early morning or late afternoon? Is that because *you* want to take them at that time or because your aging professors want to schedule them then?

Shifting Sleep Schedules

Ordinarily, the light of early morning resets the body's clock each day to keep it in synchrony with the outside world. If you travel across time zones, the light in your new location will eventually reset your clock to the new time, but until it does, your internal rhythms will be out of phase with your new environment. For example, if you travel from California to France, it will be 7 A.M. (time to get up) when your body says it is 10 P.M. (getting close to bedtime). You will experience jet lag, *a period of discomfort and inefficiency while your internal clock is out of phase with your new surroundings.*

Most people find it easier to adjust when flying west, where they go to bed later, than when flying east, where they go to bed earlier. Thus, east-coast people adjust to west-coast time faster than west-coast people adjust to east-coast time (Figure 5.3). Most of us simply find it easier to stay up later than to go to bed earlier.

It is possible to have an experience like jet lag without leaving town. Suppose you stay up late on Friday night and wake up late on Saturday morning—a common practice for young adults. Then you stay up late again on Saturday and wake up late on Sunday. By Monday morning, your circadian rhythm has reset, so when your clock says 7 A.M. and time to wake up, your internal clock thinks you are somewhere west and the time is about 5 A.M.

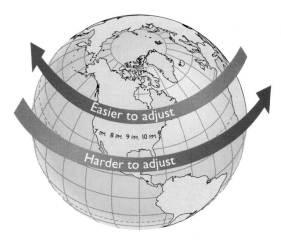

FIGURE 5.3 People traveling east suffer more serious jet lag than people traveling west.

Companies that keep their factories going nonstop run three work shifts, such as midnight–8 A.M., 8 A.M.–4 P.M., and 4 P.M.–midnight. Because few people want to work regularly on the midnight–8 A.M. shift, many companies rotate their workers among the three shifts. Suppose that you worked the 8 A.M.–4 P.M. shift today but tomorrow you are scheduled for midnight–8 A.M. You can't get to sleep at 4 in the afternoon, so you show up for work at midnight without having slept. You are likely to make many mistakes during the night, and when you drive home the next morning, you will be as impaired as if you were legally drunk (Dawson & Reid, 1997). Even people who work the night shift month after month may continue feeling groggy on the job and sleeping fitfully during the day.

There are two ways for employers to ease this burden on their workers: First, when they transfer workers from one shift to another, they should transfer workers to a *later* shift (Czeisler, Moore-Ede, & Coleman, 1982) (Figure 5.4). That is, someone working the 8 A.M.–4 P.M. shift should switch to the 4 P.M.–midnight shift (equiva-

Easier to adjust

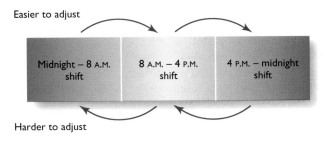

Harder to adjust

FIGURE 5.4 The graveyard shift is aptly named: Serious industrial accidents usually occur at night, when workers are least alert. Night-shift jobs providing emergency services are essential. But few people want to work permanently at night, so workers rotate among three shifts. As in jet lag, the direction of change is critical. Moving forward—clockwise—is easier than going backward.

lent to traveling west) instead of the midnight–8 A.M. shift (equivalent to traveling east).

Second, employers can help workers adjust to the night shift by providing bright lights that resemble sunlight. In one study young men exposed to very bright lights at night adjusted well to working at night and sleeping during the day. Within 6 days their circadian rhythms had shifted to the new schedule. Another group of men who worked the same schedule under dimmer lights showed no indications of altering their circadian rhythms (Czeisler et al., 1990).

CONCEPT CHECK

1. Suppose you are the president of a company in the United States. You are negotiating a difficult business deal with someone from the opposite side of the world. Should you prefer a meeting place in Europe or on an island in the Pacific Ocean? (Check your answer on page 168.)

CRITICAL THINKING:
A STEP FURTHER
Sleep Cycles

Imagine someone who cannot get to sleep until 3 A.M.; for months she has been trying to get to bed earlier but failing. What advice would you offer? (Hint: Remember that our internal clocks can shift more easily to a later time than to an earlier time.)

Brain Mechanisms of Circadian Rhythms

The circadian rhythm of sleep and wakefulness is generated by a tiny structure at the base of the brain known as the *suprachiasmatic nucleus.* If that area of the brain is damaged, the body's activity cycles become erratic (Rusak, 1977). If cells from that area are kept alive outside the body, they generate a circadian rhythm on their own (Earnest, Liang, Ratcliff, & Cassone, 1999; Inouye & Kawamura, 1979). Cells in other body areas also produce daily rhythms, but those in the suprachiasmatic nucleus are sufficient, by themselves, to produce daily rhythms of activity and inactivity (Sujino et al., 2003). In short, this brain area is the body's clock (see Figure 5.5).

The suprachiasmatic nucleus exerts its control partly by regulating the pineal gland's secretions of the hormone *melatonin,* which induces drowsiness. Ordinarily, the human pineal gland starts increasing its release of melatonin at about 8 to 10 P.M., so people find it easy to fall asleep about 2 or 3 hours later. If you take a melatonin pill in the evening, you will notice little if any effect because you were already producing increased

melatonin at that time. However, if you have just flown a few time zones east and want to get to bed in a couple of hours, but you're not sleepy yet, then a melatonin pill can be helpful indeed (Deacon & Arendt, 1996).

CONCEPT CHECK

2. Suppose you are required to work the midnight–8 A.M. shift, and you would like to go to sleep at 4 P.M. to be well rested before starting work. Would a melatonin pill help? If so, when should you take it? (Check your answer on page 168.)

Why We Sleep

We would not have been born with a mechanism that forces us to sleep for 8 hours or so out of every 24 unless sleep did us some good. But what good does sleep do? Scientists have proposed two theories.

The Repair and Restoration Theory

According to the **repair and restoration theory,** *the purpose of sleep is to enable the body to recover from the exertions of the day.* We undeniably need sleep, and we suffer if we do not get it. If you are not doing well in school or if you are frequently ill, consider the possibility that you are not sleeping enough. Sleep deprivation leads to irritability, impairs attention, and weakens the immune system (Dement, 1972; Everson, 1995; Rechtschaffen & Bergmann, 1995). People who are sleep deprived make poor decisions, especially when faced with unexpected events (Harrison & Horne, 2000). Many people's alertness and performance deteriorate even within a day, and a short nap can restore good performance (Mednick et al., 2002). After awakening from sleep, people sometimes have insightful restructuring of previous experiences, seeing complex patterns that had previously eluded them (Wagner, Gais, Haider, Verleger, & Born, 2004).

However, most of the restorative functions that occur during sleep—such as digestion and protein synthesis—also occur during quiet waking periods. That is, we do need sleep, but it is possible to imagine evolving the ability to perform the restorative functions without setting aside a part of the day for sleep. The following list highlights facts that do not fit well with the repair and restoration theory:

- People need only a little more sleep after a day of extreme physical or mental activity than after a day of inactivity (Horne & Minard, 1985).
- Some people get by with much less than the typical 7.5 to 8 hours of sleep per day. One extreme case was a healthy 70-year-old woman who slept only about 1 hour each night (Meddis, Pearson, & Langford, 1973).

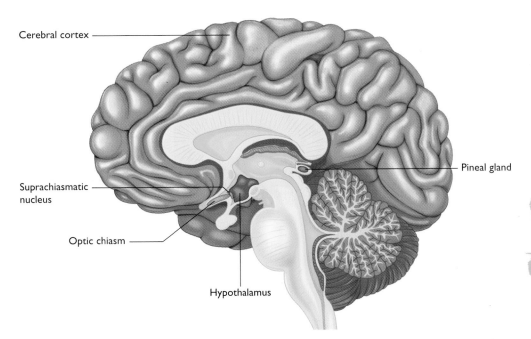

Cerebral cortex

Suprachiasmatic
nucleus

Optic chiasm

Hypothalamus

Pineal gland

FIGURE 5.5 The suprachiasmatic nucleus, a small area at the base of the brain, produces the circadian rhythm. Information from the optic nerves resets the circadian rhythm but is not necessary for its generation. Cells in the suprachiasmatic nucleus can generate approximately a 24-hour rhythm of activity on their own, even if they are separated from the rest of the body.

The Evolutionary, or Energy-Conservation, Theory

If we built a robot to explore another planet, we would probably program it to shut down most of its activities at night. According to the *evolutionary, or energy-conservation, theory of sleep, evolution equipped us with a regular pattern of sleeping and waking for the same reason—to conserve fuel and to prevent us from walking into dangers* (Kleitman, 1963; Webb, 1979). Humans and other highly visual species are relatively inefficient at night. Throughout our evolutionary history, until the invention of electric lights, moving around at night was unhelpful and probably dangerous. By sleeping we could decrease our energy use by 10 to 25%. When food is scarce, people conserve even more energy by sleeping

- Some people fare better than we would have expected after a week or more of sleep deprivation (Figure 5.6). In 1965 a San Diego high school student, Randy Gardner, stayed awake for 264 hours and 12 minutes—11 days—in a project for a high school science fair and suffered no serious psychological consequences (Dement, 1972). On the last night, he played about 100 arcade games against sleep researcher William Dement and won every game. Just before the end of the 264 hours, he held a television press conference and handled himself well. He then slept for 14 hours and 40 minutes and awoke refreshed.

If a torturer prevented you from sleeping for the next 11 days, would you do as well as Randy Gardner? Probably not, for two reasons: First, Gardner knew he could quit if necessary. A sense of control makes any experience less stressful. Second, people vary in their ability to tolerate sleep deprivation. We heard about Gardner only because he tolerated it so well. We have no idea how many other people tried to deprive themselves of sleep for many days but gave up.

The summary evaluation of the repair and restoration theory is that the body does do restorative functions during sleep, and sleep deprivation *is* harmful. However, each of us has an urge to sleep, even a need to sleep, at a certain time of day, regardless of how active or inactive we have been during the day. Therefore, it is possible that sleep serves other functions as well, such as simply saving energy.

FIGURE 5.6 Even near the end of Randy Gardner's 264 consecutive hours without sleep, he was able to perform tasks requiring strength and skill. Here observers dutifully record his every move.

FIGURE 5.7 Many birds sleep with one eye open, unless they are sitting next to another bird that might be keeping watch. Humans too sleep less well if they are in an unfamiliar or possibly dangerous place.

longer or lowering their body temperature even more than usual during sleep (Berger & Phillips, 1995).

However, sleep protects us only from the troubles we might walk into, not from trouble that comes looking for us! So we sleep well in a familiar, safe place, but not when we fear that burglars will break into the house or that bears will nose into our tent. Animals in danger of being attacked during sleep rouse quickly at any noise. Birds that are surrounded by others of their species sleep more soundly, presumably secure that the others will squawk if they spot danger. However, a bird at the end of the line spends much of the night with one eye open (Rattenborg, Lima, & Amlaner, 1999) (see Figure 5.7).

The evolutionary theory accounts for differences in sleep among species (Campbell & Tobler, 1984). For example, why do cats sleep so much and horses so little? First, cats can afford to have long periods of inactivity because they eat one or two large meals per day; horses need to spend most of the day grazing. Second, cats are seldom attacked while they sleep, whereas horses must always be ready to run away (Figure 5.8). (Woody Allen once said, "The lion and the calf shall lie down together, but the calf won't get much sleep.")

Which of these two theories regarding sleep is correct? To a large degree, both are. Supporters of the repair and restoration theory concede that the timing and even the amount of sleep depend on when the animal is least efficient. Supporters of the evolu-tionary theory concede that, during the time that evolution has set aside for an animal to conserve energy, the animal takes that opportunity to perform repair and restoration functions.

Stages of Sleep

In the mid-1950s American and French researchers independently discovered a stage of sleep called *paradoxical sleep,* or rapid eye movement (REM) sleep (Dement & Kleitman, 1957a, 1957b; Jouvet, Michel, & Courjon, 1959). *During this stage of sleep, the sleeper's eyes move rapidly back and forth under the closed lids.* (All other stages of sleep are known as non-REM, or NREM, sleep.) A paradox is an apparent contradiction; REM sleep is also called paradoxical because it is light in some ways and deep in others. It is light because the brain is active and the body's heart rate, breathing rate, and temperature fluctuate substantially (Parmeggiani, 1982). It is deep because the large muscles of the body that control posture and locomotion are deeply relaxed. Indeed, the nerves to those muscles are virtually paralyzed at this time. REM also has some features that are hard to classify as

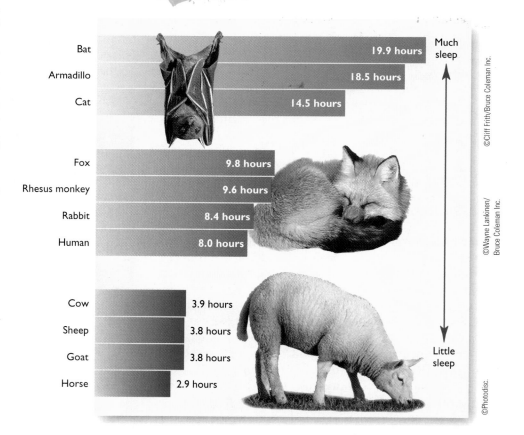

FIGURE 5.8 Predatory mammals sleep many hours. They get all the energy they need in a short feeding time, and they are seldom attacked while sleeping. Prey species sleep less; they need to spend many hours each day eating, and they need to arouse quickly to avoid being attacked in their sleep. *(Based on data from Zepelin & Rechtschaffen, 1974)*

deep or light, such as penis erections and vaginal lubrication.

William Dement's early research indicated that people who were awakened during REM sleep usually reported they had been dreaming, but people who were awakened during any other period seldom reported dreaming. So at first REM sleep was thought to be almost synonymous with dreaming. Later research has weakened that link, however. Adults who are awakened during REM sleep report dreams about 85 to 90% of the time, whereas those awakened during NREM sleep report dreams on 50 to 60% of occasions (Foulkes, 1999). REM dreams are on the average more complicated and more visual, but not always. People sometimes have complex, highly visual dreams during NREM sleep also, especially toward the end of the night. Furthermore, some people with brain damage have REM sleep but no dreams, and others have dreams but no REM sleep (Solms, 1997). Thus, REM is not synonymous with dreaming (Domhoff, 1999).

Sleep Cycles During the Night

Sleep researchers distinguish among stages of sleep by recording brain waves with electrodes attached to the scalp (Figure 5.9). *A device* called an **electroencephalograph (EEG)** *measures and amplifies slight electrical changes on the scalp that reflect patterns of activity in the brain.* Sleep researchers *combine an EEG measure with a simultaneous measure of eye movements to produce a* **polysomnograph** (literally,

FIGURE 5.9 Electrodes monitor the activity in a sleeper's brain, and an EEG then records and displays brain-wave patterns.

"many-sleep measure"), as shown in Figure 5.10. Upon falling asleep one enters non-REM stage 1, when the eyes are nearly motionless and the EEG shows many short, choppy waves, as shown in Figure 5.10a. These small waves indicate a fair amount of brain activity, with brain cells firing out of synchrony with one another. Because they are out of synchrony, their activities nearly cancel each other out, like people in a crowd talking at the same time.

As sleep continues a person progresses into non-REM stages 2, 3, and 4, as shown in Figure 5.10b–e. These stages are most easily distinguished by the number of long, slow waves; stage 1 has the fewest, and stage 4 has the most. These large waves indicate synchrony among neurons, which occurs during *decreased* brain activity. The waves grow larger from one stage to the next because the brain has little stimulation, so the little activity that does occur drives many neurons in synchrony. (Note that the eyes remain mostly inactive in each of these stages.)

After stage 4 a sleeper gradually moves back through stages 3 and 2. After stage 2, however, the sleeper enters REM sleep, not stage 1. That is, REM sleep replaces most of stage 1 except for the first episode of the night. In Figure 5.10f the EEG in REM sleep resembles that of stage 1, but the eyes are moving more extensively and more regularly than they do during other stages. At the end of REM sleep, the sleeper cycles through stages 2, 3, 4 and then back to 3, 2, and REM again. In a healthy young adult, each cycle lasts 90 to 100 minutes on average. As shown in Figure 5.11, the cycles continue throughout the night, but as the night progresses, the duration of stages 3 and 4 gets shorter and the duration of REM and stage 2 increases. Figure 5.11 represents sleep under quiet, undisturbed conditions; someone who sleeps in an uncomfortable room will have many awakenings and very little stage 3 or 4 sleep (Velluti, 1997).

Sleep Stages and Dreaming

The interest in REM sleep prompted sleep investigators to awaken people during REM sleep and ask for dream reports in an attempt to answer some very basic questions. For example, does everyone dream? Adults who claim they do not dream have been taken into the laboratory and attached to a polysomnograph, which revealed normal periods of REM sleep. When these people were awakened during a REM period, they usually reported dreaming (to their own surprise). Apparently, they dream normally but forget their dreams quickly. However, children younger than 5 years old seldom report dreams, even if awakened during REM sleep (Foulkes, 1999).

Another question: How long do dreams last? William Dement and Edward Wolpert (1958) awakened

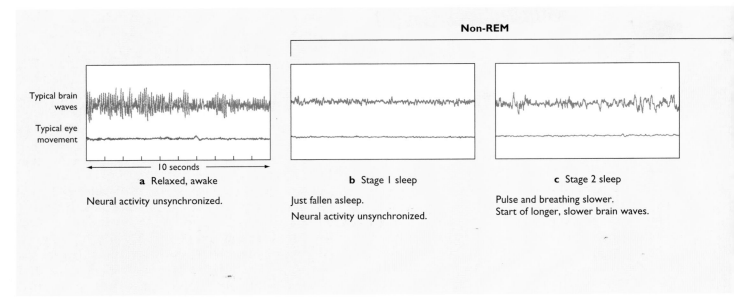

FIGURE 5.10 During sleep people progress through stages of varying brain activity. The blue line indicates brain waves, as shown by an EEG. The red line shows eye movements. Note that REM sleep resembles stage 1 sleep, except for the addition of rapid eye movements. *(Courtesy of T. E. Le Vere)*

FIGURE 5.11 This fairly typical sleeper had five cycles of REM and non-REM sleep and awakened (A) briefly three times during the night. Note that stage 4 occupies much time early in the night but less later; REM sleep becomes more and more prevalent as the night progresses. *(From Dement, 1972)*

people after REM periods of various durations and asked them to describe their dreams. Someone awakened after 1 minute of REM sleep would usually tell a brief story; a person awakened after 5 minutes of REM sleep would usually tell a story about 5 times as long and so on. Evidently, dreams take place in "real time." That is, a dream is not over in a split second; if a dream seemed to last several minutes, it probably did.

CONCEPT CHECK ☑

3. Is dreaming more common toward the end of the night's sleep or toward the beginning? (Check your answer on page 168.)

The Functions of REM Sleep

Given that people spend 20 to 25% of an average night in REM sleep, it presumably serves an important function, but what? The most direct way to approach this question is to deprive people of REM

sleep and study how this deprivation affects their health or behavior.

In one study William Dement (1960) monitored the sleep of eight young men for seven consecutive nights and awakened them for a few minutes whenever their EEG and eye movements indicated the onset of REM sleep. He awakened the members of a control group equally often but at random times so that he did not necessarily interrupt their REM sleep. Over the course of 1 week, Dement found it harder and harder to prevent REM sleep in the experimental group . . . and harder to keep them from quitting the experiment. On the first night, the average participant had to be awakened 12 times; by the seventh night, 26 times. During the day REM-deprived participants experienced anxiety, irritability, and impaired concentration. On the eighth night, all were permitted to sleep without interruption.

Most showed a "REM rebound," spending 29% of the night in REM sleep compared with 19% before the experiment began. People in the control group, who had not been deprived of REM sleep, showed no such REM

Non-REM

d Stage 3 sleep

Pulse, breathing, and brain activity slower yet.

Neural activity more synchronized.

Stages 3 and 4 dominate first half of night.

e Stage 4 sleep

Pulse, breathing, and brain activity slowest.

Brain waves highly synchronized, indicating low overall neuron activity.

f REM (paradoxical) sleep

Eyes move back and forth.

Dreams more frequent, vivid, complex.

Brain waves desynchronized.

Postural muscles most relaxed.

Duration gets longer toward morning.

Typical brain waves

Typical eye movement

rebound. So evidently, REM sleep does satisfy a need, and the body will work to catch up on at least some of the REM sleep it has missed. However, in this and related studies, the effects of REM deprivation were not catastrophic, so the question of why we need REM sleep remains.

A second approach is to determine which people get more REM sleep than others. One clear pattern is that infants get more REM sleep than children and children more than adults. From that observation many researchers have inferred that REM sleep serves a function that is more acute in younger people. However, infants not only get more REM sleep but also more total sleep (Figure 5.12). If we compare species, we find that the species that get the most sleep (e.g., cats) also generally have the greatest percentage of REM sleep.

Among adult humans, those who sleep 9 or more hours per night spend a large percentage of that time in REM sleep; those who sleep 6 hours or less also get less REM sleep. In short, those who sleep the most spend the greatest percentage of that time in REM. It is as

Awake
Asleep

Newborn

One year old

Four years old

Ten years old

Adult

6 A.M.   Noon   6 P.M.   Midnight

FIGURE 5.12 Newborns' sleep alternates between wakefulness and naps throughout the day. Within a few months, infants consolidate most of their sleep into one longer period at night, although they continue having one or two naps during the day. As people grow older, the amount of sleep per day decreases. (*Based on Kleitman, 1963*) though a certain amount of *non*-REM sleep is necessary each night, and additional amounts of REM sleep can be added if sleep continues long enough (Horne, 1988).

A long controversy has concerned the role of REM in memory. If you learn something today, your memory of it will improve tomorrow *if* you get a good night's sleep (Fenn, Nusbaum, & Margoliash, 2003; Stickgold, Whidbee, Schirmer, Patel, & Hobson, 2000). Even a 60- to 90-minute nap helps (Mednick, Nakayama, & Stickgold, 2003). However, these findings indicate the value of sleep in general, not specifically REM. Some studies have found that when people learn a difficult new task, the brain areas active during the learning also become activated during REM sleep that night (Maquet et al., 2000). However, other studies have failed to replicate this finding (Siegel, 2001). Also, some studies have found that on a day with unusual learning experiences, REM increases that night, but again other studies have failed to replicate this tendency (Siegel, 2001). Even when REM does increase after a day with much learning, it is possible that the increase depends on stress, not learning. Furthermore, drugs that block REM do not impair memory (Parent, Habib, & Baker, 1999).

Even if REM sleep does help consolidate memories, memory may not be its original or primary function. For example, what are the uses of computers? The answers include e-mail, Internet use, writing papers, and playing video games. But the *original* function of computers was mathematical calculations; all other uses came later. Similarly, REM's original function might not be something we notice most prominently today. One speculation is that its original function was simply to move the eyes around after prolonged sleep. The corneas of the eyes (see Figure 4.2) usually get most of their oxygen directly from the air; they also get some from the fluid behind them. During sleep the eyelids are shut, and they no longer get oxygen from the air. After several hours of sleep, the fluid behind the cornea can become so stagnant that the cornea would get little oxygen from that source either, unless the eyes shook back and forth to get the fluid moving. REM is in fact more common after prolonged sleep and more common in species with large eyes, for whom stagnation of the fluid is most likely to be a problem. It is therefore conceivable that REM evolved originally as a means of getting oxygen to the corneas (Maurice, 1998).

Abnormalities of Sleep

Comedian Steven Wright says that someone asked him, "Did you sleep well last night?" He replied, "No, I made a few mistakes."

We laugh because sleep isn't the kind of activity on which a person makes mistakes; sleep just happens. Sometimes, however, sleep doesn't happen or it happens at the wrong time or it does not seem restful or we have bad dreams. We would not call these unpleasant experiences "mistakes," but in one way or another, our sleep is not what we wanted it to be.

For more information in general about sleep disorders, visit this Web site: **www.thesleepsite.com/**

Insomnia

Insomnia literally means "lack of sleep." However, we cannot usefully define insomnia in terms of the number of hours of sleep. Some people feel well rested after fewer than 6 hours of sleep per night; others feel poorly rested after 9 hours. A complaint of insomnia indicates that *the person feels poorly rested* the next *day.* By this definition about one third of all adults have occasional insomnia and about one tenth have serious or chronic insomnia (Lilie & Rosenberg, 1990). Most of those with serious insomnia have other medical or psychological disorders as well, such as anxiety disorders or depression (Ohayon, 1997). People sometimes have trouble sleeping because of noise, worries, indigestion, uncomfortable temperatures, use of alcohol or caffeine, and other miscellaneous problems.

Sleep Apnea

One of the causes of insomnia is known as sleep apnea (AP-nee-uh). *Apnea* means "no breathing." Many people have either irregular breathing or occasional periods of 10 seconds or so without breathing during their sleep. People with sleep apnea, however, may *fail to breathe for a minute or longer and then wake up gasping for breath.* When these people do manage to breathe during their sleep, they generally snore. They

▌Insomnia is identified not by how many hours one sleeps at night but by how sleepy the person is the following day.

may lie in bed for 8 to 10 hours per night but sleep less than half that time. During the following day, they are likely to feel sleepy and they may have headaches.

Although some cases of sleep apnea are due to brain abnormalities, the most common cause is obstructions in the breathing passages. When someone with a very large abdomen—usually a middle-aged man—lies on his back, the abdomen's weight interferes with the diaphragm muscles that control breathing (Mezzanotte, Tangel, & White, 1992). Sleep apnea is reported in about 8% of adult men, 4% of adult women, and 2 or 3% of children (Moorcroft, 2003).

Narcolepsy

People who experience *sudden attacks of extreme, even irresistible, sleepiness in the middle of the day* are said to have **narcolepsy.** Narcolepsy affects about one person per 5,000 (Moorcroft, 2003). Such people may also experience sudden attacks of muscle weakness or paralysis. Sometimes they have vivid dreamlike experiences while awake. Each of these symptoms could be interpreted as a sudden intrusion of REM sleep into the waking period of the day (Guilleminault, Heinzer, Mignot, & Black, 1998).

Most people with narcolepsy have no relatives with similar problems. Narcolepsy also occurs in dogs, for whom it has a strong genetic basis. Researchers who located the gene responsible for narcolepsy in dogs discovered that it controls the brain receptors for a chemical called *hypocretin* or *orexin* (Lin et al., 1999). Other researchers found that preventing production of that chemical can cause narcolepsy in mice, which do not ordinarily get it (Chemelli et al., 1999). People with narcolepsy have fewer than normal of the kind of neurons that produce hypocretin/orexin (Thanickal et al., 2000). The reason for the deficiency is unknown. Focusing on this chemical should speed the search for better treatments for narcolepsy and perhaps also for other sleep disorders.

Sleep Talking, Sleepwalking, Nightmares, and Night Terrors

Many people, whether or not they suffer from insomnia, nevertheless have unsettling experiences during their sleep. Sleep talking is the most common and least troublesome. Most people talk in their sleep more often than they realize because they do not remember sleep talking themselves and usually no one else is awake to hear them. Sleep talking is most common during stage 2 sleep but can occur during any stage (Moorcroft, 2003). It ranges from a single indistinct word to a clearly articulated paragraph. Sleep talkers sometimes pause between utterances, as if they were carrying on a conversation with someone else. In fact it is possible to engage some sleep talkers in a dialogue. Sleep talking is nothing to worry about. It is not related to any mental or emotional disorder, and sleep talkers rarely say anything that they would be embarrassed to say when awake.

Sleepwalking tends to run (walk?) in families. True sleepwalking occurs mostly in children during stage 4 sleep and lasts fewer than 15 minutes. Few children hurt themselves when sleepwalking, and most children outgrow it (Dement, 1972). It also occurs in some adults, mostly during the first half of the night's sleep. Apparently, the brain arouses partly from sleep but not fully. The person engages in clumsy, apparently purposeless movements with only limited responsiveness to surroundings. It is not necessarily harmful to awaken a sleepwalker, but it is not easy either, nor particularly helpful (Moorcroft, 2003). A better idea is just to guide the person gently back to bed.

Other concerns include nightmares and night terrors. Nightmares are merely unpleasant dreams, which all people have occasionally. A night terror, however, causes someone to awaken in a state of extreme panic, screaming and sweating with a heart rate up to triple the normal rate. Night terrors occur during stage 3 or stage 4 sleep, not during REM sleep, and their content is usually rather simple, like a single image rather than a complex story. Sometimes people report no dream content at all. Night terrors are fairly common in young children but uncommon in adults (Salzarulo & Chevalier, 1983). They are more frequent when people have a fever and among people who have been under much stress.

Leg Movements While Trying to Sleep

Have you ever lain in bed, trying to fall asleep, when suddenly one of your legs kicked? An occasional leg jerk while trying to fall asleep is a common experience and no cause for concern. In contrast some people have *prolonged "creepy-crawly" sensations in their legs, accompanied by repetitive leg movements strong enough to awaken the person, especially during the first half of the night* (Moorcroft, 1993). This condition, known as **periodic limb movement disorder** (or more informally, as restless leg syndrome), is a common cause of poor sleep in people over the age of 50. Sufferers can stop the leg kicks by standing and walking, but by doing so they of course interrupt their sleep. The causes of this disorder are unknown, and the best advice is to avoid factors that can make the condition worse, such as caffeine, stress, or fatigue. Tranquilizers suppress these leg movements in some people (Schenck & Mahowald, 1996).

CONCEPT CHECK

4. Why would it be unlikely, if not impossible, for sleepwalking to occur during REM sleep? (Check your answer on page 168.)

Hypersomnia

Finally, consider the opposite of insomnia: A small number of people suffer from **hypersomnia,** *excessive but unrefreshing sleep.* The person sleeps 8 or 9 hours per day during the week, plus an afternoon nap, and then "catches up" by sleeping longer on weekends, sometimes as much as 18 to 22 hours per day. Even after this much sleep, the person has trouble awakening and feels confused and poorly rested. In some cases the disorder can be traced to a history of head trauma, viral infection, or mood disorder, but in many cases the cause is unknown (Bassetti & Aldrich, 1997).

If You Have Trouble Sleeping . . .

Insomnia can be a brief, minor annoyance or a sign of a potentially serious disorder. If you experience persistent difficulties sleeping, consult a physician, but for occasional or minor insomnia, you can try a few things yourself (Hauri, 1982; Lilie & Rosenberg, 1990):

- Try to associate your bed with sleeping, not with lying awake. If you find that you just can't get to sleep, get up, do something else, and return to bed when you start to feel sleepy.

▌ One recommended strategy if you have trouble sleeping: Don't just lie in bed worrying about your lack of sleep. Get up, do something else, and try going back to sleep later.

©Patrick Coughlin/ Getty Images

- Try to keep a regular schedule of when you go to bed and when you wake up each day.
- Avoid caffeine, nicotine, and other stimulants, especially in the evening.
- Avoid habitual use of alcohol or sleeping pills. (Either may help you get to sleep occasionally, but they become counterproductive after repeated use. Also, alcohol decreases REM sleep.)
- Keep your bedroom cool and quiet.
- Get a consistent amount of exercise daily, but don't exercise shortly before bedtime.

The Content of Our Dreams

Even a saint is not responsible for what happens in his dreams.
—St. Thomas Aquinas

What do we dream about and why? People once believed that dreams foretold the future. Occasionally, of course, they do—either by coincidence or because the dreamer had a reason to expect some outcome. Today, psychologists do not expect dreams to tell us about the future, but some do look to dreams to tell us something about the dreamer. Even that effort is controversial, however.

Freud's Approach

The Austrian physician and founder of psychoanalysis, Sigmund Freud, maintained that dreams reveal the dreamer's unconscious thoughts and motivations. To understand a dream, he said, one must probe beneath the surface to find a hidden symbolic meaning. Each dream has a **manifest content**—*the content that appears on the surface*—and a **latent content**—*the hidden content that is represented symbolically in the dream experience.*

To illustrate, Freud (1900/1955) once dreamed that one of his friends was his uncle. He worked out the following associations: Both this friend and another one had been recommended for an appointment as professor at the university. Both had been turned down, probably because they were Jews. Freud himself had been recently recommended for the same appointment, but he feared that he too would be rejected for the same reason. Freud's only uncle had once been convicted of illegal business dealings. Freud's father had said, however, that the uncle was not bad, but just a simpleton.

What was the relationship between the two friends and the uncle? One of the friends was in Freud's judgment a bit simpleminded. The other had once been accused of sexual misconduct, although he was not convicted. By linking these two friends to his uncle, Freud interpreted the dream as meaning, "Maybe they didn't get the university appointment because one was a simpleton (like my uncle) and the other was regarded as a criminal (like my uncle). If so, my being Jewish might not stop me from getting the appointment."

In some cases Freud relied on individual associations, as in the dream just described, but in other cases he assumed that certain elements had predictable meanings, regardless of whether the dreamer agreed. For example, he claimed that the number three in a dream represented a man's penis and testes. The penis alone was represented by anything long, such as a stick or pole; anything that could penetrate the body, such as a knife or gun; anything from which water flows; anything that can be lengthened; almost any tool; and anything that can fly or float—because rising is like an erection (Freud, 1935). He admitted that if you dream about a knife or an airplane, you really might be dreaming about a knife or airplane instead of a penis, but he was confident that a skilled psychoanalyst could tell the difference (even if the dreamer could not).

Freud's approach to dream analysis became popular for many years, although it is now on the decline. The problem lies in how to test such interpretations (Domhoff, 2003). When people doubt or challenge a dream interpretation, psychoanalysts offer no evidence to back their conclusions and no way to check their accuracy other than trusting their expertise.

One of Freud's most famous dream analyses concerned a man who reported remembering a dream from when he was 4 years old (!) in which he saw six or seven white dogs with large tails sitting motionless in a tree outside his window. (The actual dream was of spitz dogs, although Freud's writings described them as wolves.) After a laborious line of reasoning, Freud concluded that the child had dreamed about his parents in their bedclothes (presumably white, which is why the dogs or wolves were white). The motionless dogs represented the opposite—frantic sexual activity. The big tails also represented their opposite—the boy's fear of having his penis cut off. In short, said Freud, the boy had dreamed about watching his parents have sex . . . doggy style. Decades later researchers actually located the man who had told this dream to Freud. He reported that (a) he regarded Freud's interpretation of his dream as far-fetched and (b) Freud's treatment did him no apparent good, as he spent many later years in continued treatment (Esterson, 1993).

Regardless of whether Freud himself offered far-fetched interpretations, the important question is whether *anyone* can listen to dreams and determine hidden aspects of the dreamer's motivations and past experience. That question is difficult to answer. Undoubtedly, many therapists do offer dream interpretations that their clients find meaningful. The problem

is the serious risk of going astray with confident, persuasive, but misleading analyses.

CONCEPT CHECK ☑

5. Are Freud's ideas on dreaming falsifiable in the sense described in Chapter 2? (Check your answer on page 168.)

The Activation-Synthesis Theory

An important contemporary theory relates dream content to spontaneous activity that arises in the brain during REM sleep. According to the **activation-synthesis theory of dreams,** *input arising from the pons (see Figure 3.14) activates the brain during REM sleep. The cortex takes that haphazard activity plus whatever stimuli strike the sense organs and does its best to synthesize a story to make sense of all this activity* (Hobson & McCarley, 1977). The activation-synthesis theory does not necessarily imply that our dreams are meaningless. Even if they begin with more or less random activity in various brain areas, the dreamer's interpretations of this activity depend on his or her personality, motivations, and previous experiences. Still, Freud saw the meaning as the cause of the dream; in the activation-synthesis theory, the meaning occurs only as a by-product of other processes.

Many kinds of dreams do appear to relate to the spontaneous activity of the brain during REM sleep. For a most basic example, input from the pons activates the visual areas of the brain during REM sleep, especially during the first minutes of a REM period, and nearly all dreams include visual content (Amzica & Steriade, 1996). Also, many people occasionally dream of flying or falling, probably because the vestibular system detects the body's horizontal position and the brain interprets this sensation as floating or flying (Hobson & McCarley, 1977; Velluti, 1997).

Have you ever dreamed that you are trying to walk or run away but you cannot move? One explanation is that the major postural muscles are really paralyzed during REM sleep. Thus, your brain could send messages telling your muscles to move but then receive sensory feedback indicating that they have not moved at all.

The main problem with the activation-synthesis theory is that it does not make clear, testable predictions. For example, people almost always sleep horizontally but only occasionally dream of flying or falling. Why not always? Our muscles are always paralyzed during REM sleep. Why don't we always dream that we can't move? *After* a dream the activation-synthesis theory can provide explanations, but it offers only vague predictions of who will dream about what and when. Recall from Chapter 2 that a good theory should make clear, precise predictions. The one prediction the theory makes is that sounds and other stimuli in the room might be incorporated into the dream, but in fact few dreams have an apparent connection to any stimulation present at the time.

The Neurocognitive Theory

Sometimes you may have a dream that strikes you as so strange that you never would have thought of such a thing in waking life. Nevertheless, you did think of it while dreaming. The **neurocognitive theory** *treats dreams as a kind of thinking that occurs under special conditions* (Domhoff, 2001; Foulkes, 1999; Solms, 2000). These conditions include:

- persisting activity of much of the cortex
- great reduction of sensory stimulation, including reduced activity in the primary sensory areas of the brain
- loss of voluntary self-control of thinking

The result is that the brain is active enough to engage in imagination, but the images are not overridden by sensory information or intentional control. According to this theory, REM sleep is not necessary for dreaming, although the arousal associated with REM tends to intensify dreams. The arousal of emotional areas of the brain, especially in the temporal lobe, adds an emotional content to many dreams (Maquet et al., 1996).

Researchers working within this framework have attempted to describe people's dreams. Sometimes people keep dream diaries; sometimes they report the most recent dream they can remember; sometimes researchers awaken them in the laboratory and ask for immediate dream reports (Domhoff, 2003). Table 5.1 lists the themes reported by the largest number of U.S. college students and the corresponding percentages for Japanese college students (Griffith, Miyagi, & Tago, 1958). Note that the same dreams are common in both cultures. Note also that many dreams deal with "things that could go wrong," such as falling, being chased, or being unable to do something. The most common emotion in adult dreams is apprehension or fear; dreams include more misfortune than good fortune; and the dreamer is more often the victim of aggression than the cause of it (Domhoff, 1996; Hall & Van de Castle, 1966). People occasionally awaken with disappointment that it was only a dream, but more often with relief. Curiously, 11- to 13-year-olds have more happy dreams than people of any other age (Foulkes, 1999).

Although some of the most memorable dreams are bizarre, most are commonplace and not much different from everyday thinking (Domhoff, 1996; Hall & Van de Castle, 1966). For example, preteens seldom dream about the opposite sex, but teenagers do (Strauch & Lederbogen, 1999). Blind people frequently dream about difficulties in locomotion or transportation (Hurovitz, Dunn, Domhoff, & Fiss, 1999). In one study young adults checked off from a list the topics (e.g., marriage, family, friends, and hobbies) those that were "concerns" to them and others that were matters of indifference. Then they reported their dreams over three nights. They frequently dreamed of the concerns and very rarely of the nonconcerns (Nikles, Brecht, Klinger, & Bursell, 1998). However, how we spend our day is not necessarily a focus of dreams: People rarely dream about reading, writing, using a computer, or watching television (Schredl, 2000). Of course, even when awake, those are things we do, not things we fantasize about doing. For the best research on the content of dreams, visit this Web site: www.dreamresearch.net/.

The ability to dream requires cognitive maturity (Foulkes, 1999). Even infants have a great deal of REM sleep, but a child younger than 5 years old who is awakened during REM sleep seldom reports an experience that we could call a dream. It is hard to know whether young children don't have dreams or just can't report them. However, even somewhat older children report dreams in fewer than half of their REM awakenings, and at those ages only children with strong visuospatial abilities (e.g., the ability to solve puzzles) often report clear dreams. Evidently, the stronger one's imagination during wakefulness, the greater the chance of dreaming when asleep. The dreams that young children report

TABLE 5.1 Percentages of College Students in Two Cultures Who Reported Remembering Certain Kinds of Dreams

Dream Topic	U.S. Students	Japanese Students
Falling	83%	74%
Being attacked or pursued	77%	91%
Trying to do something again and again	71%	87%
School work	71%	86%
Sex	66%	68%
Arriving too late	64%	49%
Eating delicious food	62%	68%
Frozen with fright	58%	87%
Loved one dying	57%	42%

Based on Griffith et al. (1958).

are mostly of unmoving images. Table 5.2 outlines stages of the development of dreaming in children.

You might try keeping a dream diary and checking the content of your dreams. Do you in fact dream mostly about the topics that you think about or fantasize about while you are awake?

Many other questions about dreaming remain unanswerable, however. For example, how accurately do we remember our dreams? Well, how would we find out? With real events we can compare people's memories to what actually happened, but we have no way to compare reported dreams to the originals. Or consider this apparently simple question: Do we dream in color? The fact that people ask this question reveals why it is difficult to answer: They ask because they do not remember whether their dreams were in color. But how could an investigator de-termine whether people dream in color except by asking them to remember? The best evidence we have is that, when people are awakened during REM sleep, when their recall should be as sharp as possible, they report color at least half of the time (Herman, Roffwarg, & Tauber, 1968; Padgham, 1975). This result does not necessarily mean that their other dreams are in black and white; it may mean only that the colors in those dreams were not memorable.

TABLE 5.2 Stages in the Development of Dreaming in Children

Age	Frequency of Dream Reports if Awakened During REM Sleep	Median Length of Dream Report	Typical Dream Content
3-5 years	15%, including many questionable reports	14 words	A single motionless image; many reports of animals; almost none about the self; almost no emotions
5-7 years	31%	41 words	Simple event with some motion; self seldom does anything
7-9 years	43%	72 words	More complex stories, including many with active self; mostly happy with some fear

Based on Foulkes (1999).

These comic strips represent actual dreams as described to the artist. Dreams often mix possible with impossible events and frequently explore the theme of "things that could go wrong." (Cartoons reprinted with permission of Jesse Reklaw.)

You might wonder whether people who are blind have visual dreams. The answer depends on when and how someone became blind. People who experienced eye damage after about age 5 to 7 continue to have visual dreams, and some have them quite often. However, people who were born blind or who became blind in early childhood have no visual imagery in their dreams; instead, they dream of sounds, touch, smells, and taste (Hurovitz et al., 1999). People who are sighted dream of smells or tastes only rarely (Zadra, Nielsen, & Donderi, 1998). People who become blind because of damage to the visual cortex lose visual dreaming as well as visual imagery.

CONCEPT CHECK ☑

6. According to the neurocognitive theory of dreaming, how does dreaming differ from other thinking? (Check your answer on this page.)

IN CLOSING

The Mysteries of Sleep and Dreams

Sleep and dreams are unlike wakefulness in some ways, but they are not a state of complete unconsciousness. For example, a parent will awaken at the sound of a child softly crying. The brain is never completely off duty, never completely relaxed.

Although our understanding of sleep and dreams continues to grow, several major questions remain. Even such basic issues as the function of REM sleep remain in doubt. People have long found their dreams a source of wonder, and researchers continue to find much of interest and mystery.

Summary

- *Circadian rhythms.* Sleepiness depends on the time of day. Even in an unchanging environment, people become sleepy in cycles of approximately 24 hours. (page 153)
- *Theories about our need for sleep.* Several repair and restoration functions take place during sleep. Sleep also serves to conserve energy at times of relative inefficiency. (page 156)

- *REM sleep.* A special stage known as REM sleep replaces many of the stage 1 periods. REM sleep is characterized by rapid eye movements, a high level of brain activity, and relaxed muscles. People usually dream during this stage but can dream in other stages also. The function of REM sleep is still uncertain. (page 158)
- *Sleep stages.* During sleep people cycle through sleep stages 1 through 4 and back through stages 3 and 2 to 1 again. The cycle beginning and ending with stage 1 lasts about 90 to 100 minutes. (page 159)
- *Insomnia.* Insomnia—subjectively unsatisfactory sleep—can result from many influences, including sleep apnea and narcolepsy. (page 162)
- *The content of dreams.* Freud proposed that dreams are the product of unconscious wishes. The activation-synthesis theory claims that dreams are an accidental by-product of random arousal during REM sleep. The neurocognitive theory states that dreaming is just thinking, except that it occurs under conditions of low sensory input and no voluntary control of thinking. (page 164)

Answers to Concept Checks

1. You should prefer to schedule the meeting on a Pacific island so that you will travel west and the other person will travel east. (page 156)
2. Try a melatonin pill 2 or 3 hours before your desired bedtime—in this case about 1 to 2 P.M. (page 156)
3. REM sleep and dreaming are more common toward the end of the night's sleep. (page 160)
4. During REM sleep the major postural muscles of the body are completely relaxed. (page 164)
5. No. A falsifiable theory makes specific predictions so that we could imagine evidence that would contradict it. Freud's theories attempt to interpret reported dreams; they make no clear predictions. (page 165)
6. According to the neurocognitive theory, dreaming is like other thinking, except that it occurs during a time of decreased sensory input and loss of voluntary control of thinking. (page 168)

Hypnosis

What can hypnosis do?

What are its limitations?

Truth is nothing but a path traced between errors. *
—Franz Anton Mesmer

If a hypnotist told you that you were 4 years old and you suddenly starting acting like a 4-year-old, we would say that you are a good hypnotic subject. If the hypnotist said that you see your cousin sitting in the empty chair in front of you, and you agreed that you see her, then again we would remark on the depth of your hypnotism.

But what if you had *not* been hypnotized and you suddenly started acting like a 4-year-old or insisted that you saw someone in that empty chair? In this case psychologists would suspect that you were suffering from a serious psychological disorder. Hypnosis induces a temporary state that is sometimes bizarre; no wonder we find it so fascinating.

Hypnosis is *a condition of increased suggestibility that occurs in the context of a special hypnotist–subject relationship.* The term *hypnosis* comes from Hypnos, the Greek god of sleep, although the similarity between hypnosis and sleep is superficial. People in both states close their eyes and lose initiative, and hypnotized people, like dreamers, accept contradictory information without protest. Hypnotized people, however, can walk around and respond to objects in the real world. Also, their EEG is not like that of sleepers. It resembles that of any other waking person, except for increased activity in the visual cortex and a few other brain areas (Rainville, Hofbauer, Bushnell, Duncan, & Price, 2002).

Hypnosis was first practiced by an Austrian philosopher and physician, Franz Anton Mesmer (1734–1815). When treating certain medical problems, Mesmer would pass a magnet back and forth across the patient's body to redirect the flow of blood, nerve activity, and certain undefined "fluids." Some patients reported dramatic benefits. Later, Mesmer discovered that he could dispense with the magnet and use only his hand. From this observation you or I would conclude that magnetism was unimportant and that the phenomenon was related to the power of sug-

gestion. Mesmer, however, drew the quirky conclusion that he did not need a magnet because *he himself* was a magnet. With that claim he gave us the term "animal magnetism."

After his death, others studied "animal magnetism" or "Mesmerism," eventually calling it "hypnotism." But by that time, many physicians and scientists associated hypnosis with eccentrics, charlatans, and hocus-pocus. Even today, some stage performers use hypnosis for entertainment. We should carefully distinguish the exaggerated claims from the legitimate use of hypnosis by licensed therapists.

Ways of Inducing Hypnosis

Mesmer thought hypnosis was a power that emanated from his own body. If so, only special people could hypnotize others. Today, we believe that becoming a successful hypnotist requires practice but no unusual powers or personality.

▌ Although Mesmer is often depicted as irresistibly controlling people, psychologists now recognize that hypnosis reflects a willingness by the hypnotized person.

*Does this sound profound? Or is it nonsense? Many statements sound profound until we try to figure out exactly what they mean.

The first step toward being hypnotized is simply agreeing to give it a try. Contrary to what you may have seen in the movies or on television, no one can hypnotize an uncooperative person. The hypnotist tells you, for example, to sit down and relax, and you do so because you would like to experience hypnosis. The whole point of hypnosis is doing what the hypnotist suggests, and by sitting down and relaxing, you are already starting to follow suggestions.

A hypnotist might then monotonously repeat something like, "You are starting to fall asleep. Your eyelids are getting heavy. Your eyelids are getting very heavy. They are starting to close. You are falling into a deep, deep sleep." In another technique (Udolf, 1981) the hypnotist suggests, "After you go under hypnosis, your arm will begin to rise automatically." (Some people, eager for the hypnosis to succeed, shoot their arm up immediately and have to be told, "No, not yet. Just relax; that will happen later.") Then the hypnotist encourages you to relax and suggests that your arm is starting to feel lighter, as if it were tied to a helium balloon.

Later, the hypnotist suggests that your arm is beginning to feel a little strange and is beginning to twitch. The timing of this suggestion is important because when people stand or sit in one position long enough, their limbs really do begin to feel strange and twitch. If the hypnotist's suggestion comes at just the right moment, you think, "Wow, that's right. My arm does feel a little strange. This is really starting to work!" Believing that you are being hypnotized is a big step toward actually being hypnotized.

▌ A hypnotist induces hypnosis by repeating suggestions, relying on the hypnotized person's cooperation and willingness to accept suggestions. No one can force hypnosis on an unwilling person.

The Uses and Limitations of Hypnosis

Hypnosis can produce relaxation, concentration, changes in behavior, and sometimes changes that persist beyond the end of the hypnotic state. Some people can be hypnotized more deeply than others; in other

words they follow more suggestions. Hypnotizability is a stable individual trait; if you respond well to hypnotic suggestions today, you probably will again tomorrow or 3 years from now. However, hypnotizability is almost the same as ordinary suggestibility. If I asked you to imagine a bright, sunny day, you almost certainly would, even without being hypnotized. If I asked you to please stand and put your hands on your head, you probably would (if I asked nicely), again without being hypnotized. If I asked you to stand, flap your arms, and cluck like a chicken, you might or might not. People vary in how far they will follow suggestions without hypnosis, and suggestibility without hypnosis matches almost perfectly suggestibility with hypnosis. You might follow suggestions a little more with hypnosis than without, but only a little (Kirsch & Braffman, 2001). If you are highly hypnotizable and highly suggestible, you probably also respond strongly to well-made films, reacting emotionally almost as if the film events were really happening. That is, hypnotizability is just a variation on people's normal suggestibility.

What Hypnosis Can Do

One well-established effect of hypnosis is to inhibit pain. Some people can undergo medical or dental surgery with just hypnosis and no anesthesia. The benefits of hypnosis are most easily demonstrated for acute (sudden) pains, but hypnosis can help with chronic pains too if carefully administered (Patterson & Jensen, 2003). Hypnosis is particularly helpful for people who react unfavorably to anesthetic drugs and those who have developed a tolerance for painkilling opiates.

▌ Some dentists have used hypnosis as a means of relieving pain, even for tooth extractions and root canal surgery.

Recall from Chapter 4 that pain has both sensory and emotional components. Hypnosis alters mostly the emotional components. Even when a hypnotized person says that he or she feels no pain, the heart rate and blood pressure still shoot up as much as they do in nonhypnotized people (Hilgard, 1973). Under hypnotic suggestion to feel no unpleasantness, a person subjected to painful stimuli will have high arousal in the parietal cortex areas responsive to body sensations but not in the frontal cortex areas responsive to unpleasant emotions (Rainville, Duncan, Price, Carrier, & Bushnell, 1997) (see Figure 5.13).

Another potentially constructive use of hypnosis is the **posthypnotic suggestion,** *a suggestion to do or experience something particular after coming out of hypnosis.* For example, people who are told to forget what happened during hypnosis often do forget, although careful testing can reveal that the memory is not completely obliterated (David, Brown, Pojoga, & David, 2000). People also respond to posthypnotic suggestions to change their behavior.

In one study adults already known to be easily hypnotized were randomly assigned to different groups. One group was handed a stack of 120 addressed stamped postcards and asked (without being hypnotized) to mail one back each day until they exhausted the stack. Another group was given a posthypnotic suggestion to mail one card per day. The nonhypnotized group actually mailed back more cards, but they reported the experience differently. The nonhypnotized people said they had to remind themselves each day to mail a card. Those given the posthypnotic suggestion said they never made a deliberate effort, but the idea of mailing a card just "popped into mind" and then they felt a sudden compulsion to mail one (Barnier & McConkey, 1998).

Can one put posthypnotic suggestions to practical use? Many therapists have given cigarette smokers a posthypnotic suggestion that they will not want to smoke. The results here are mixed. Some studies do report benefits, although generally they are small and not always greater than the effects of placebos (J. P. Green & Lynn, 2000). That is, a hypnotist who convinces someone that the treatment will work may in fact produce benefits, but based more on expectations than on the hypnosis itself.

Distortions of Perception Under Hypnosis

A few people report visual or auditory **hallucinations** (*sensory experiences not corresponding to reality*) under hypnosis, and many report touch hallucinations after suggestions such as "your nose itches" or "your left hand feels numb" (Udolf, 1981). When hypnotized people report hallucinations, are they telling the truth or are they just saying what the hypnotist wants them to say?

At least in some cases, people's reports are correct. In one study researchers performed brain scans while people listened to sounds, imagined sounds, or hallucinated them under hypnotic suggestion. The hypnotic suggestion activated some of the same brain areas as actual sounds did, but imagining sounds did not activate those areas (Szechtman, Woody, Bowers, & Nahmias, 1998). Evidently, hypnotic hallucinations are more like real experiences than like imagination.

However, when hypnotized people claim that they don't see or hear something, careful testing can demonstrate that the information did register at least in some ways. In one study people who were highly susceptible to hypnosis looked at the optical illusion shown in Figure 5.14a. Like other people, they reported that the top horizontal line looked longer than the bottom horizontal line. Then they were hypnotized and told not to see the radiating lines but to see only the two horizontal ones. Those who said that they no longer saw the radiating lines still perceived the top line as longer than the bottom one (R. J. Miller, Hennessy, & Leibowitz, 1973). If the radiating lines had truly disappeared, then they would have seen something like Figure 5.14b, where the horizontal lines look equal. So these people did see the radiating lines, at least at some level, even though they reported that they did not.

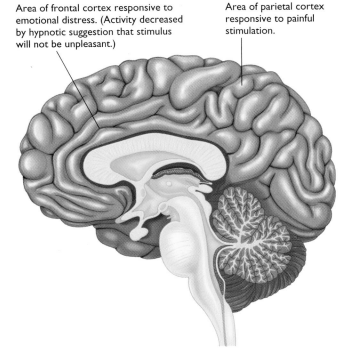

Area of frontal cortex responsive to emotional distress. (Activity decreased by hypnotic suggestion that stimulus will not be unpleasant.)

Area of parietal cortex responsive to painful stimulation.

FIGURE 5.13 Hypnotic suggestions to experience less pain can decrease the emotional intensity but generally have less effect on the sensation itself. The hypnotic suggestion that a stimulus will not be unpleasant decreases activity in the frontal cortex areas associated with emotional distress but has little effect on the sensory area in the parietal cortex.

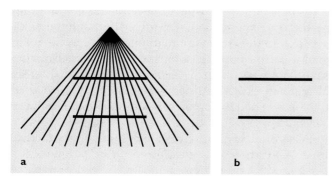

FIGURE 5.14 Horizontal lines of equal length in (a) the Ponzo illusion and (b) without the optical illusion. Researchers employ such visual stimuli to determine how hypnosis may alter sensory perception.

What Hypnosis Cannot Do

Most of the spectacular claims made for the power of hypnotic suggestion turn out to be less impressive on closer scrutiny. For instance, as in Figure 5.15, people under hypnosis can become as stiff as a board so that they can balance their head and neck on one chair and their feet on another chair and even allow someone to stand on their body! Amazing? Not really. It's easier than it looks, with or without hypnosis. Give it a try, though you shouldn't invite someone to stand on you. (Someone who does not balance correctly could injure you.)

Many people have attempted to use hypnosis to enhance memory. For example, a distressed person tells a psychotherapist, "I don't know why I have such troubles. Maybe I had some really bad experience when I was much younger, but I just can't remember." Or a witness to a crime says, "I saw the culprit for a second or two, but now I can't give you a good description." Therapists and police officers have sometimes turned to hypnotism in the hope of uncovering lost memories. However, hypnotized people are highly suggestible. Even when they are given an innocent suggestion such as "you will remember more than you told us before," many hypnotized people reply with incorrect information. If they are also asked misleading questions, such as "Did the woman have one or two children?" (when in fact she had none), hypnotized people are easily influenced into reporting false information (Scoboria, Mazzoni, Kirsch, & Milling, 2002). Let's consider one typical study.

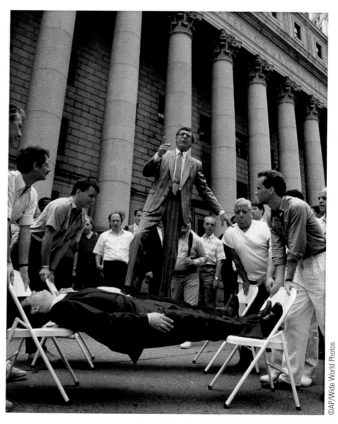

FIGURE 5.15 The U.S. Supreme Court ruled in 1987 that criminal defendants may testify about details they recalled under hypnosis. Its decision sparked this protest by the magician known as The Amazing Kreskin, who borrowed a stunt commonly used to demonstrate the power of hypnosis—standing on a person suspended between two chairs.

people under hypnosis and other people without hypnosis to see how the hypnosis changes their memory (Dywan & Bowers, 1983).

Hypothesis People will remember some of the material without hypnosis and then will remember more of it after hypnosis.

Method Fifty-four people looked at a series of 60 slides of black-and-white drawings of simple objects (e.g., pencil, hammer, or bicycle) presented one every 3.5 seconds. Then they were given a sheet with 60 blank spaces and asked to recall as many of the items as possible. The slides were presented a second and third time, and after each session, the participants had another chance to recall items. Each day for the next week, they again wrote a list of all the items they could remember (but without seeing the slides again). Finally, a week after the original slide sessions, they returned to the laboratory. Half of them (selected at random) were hypnotized and the others were just told to relax; then all were asked to recall as many of the drawings as possible.

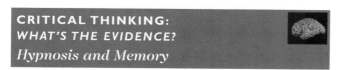

CRITICAL THINKING:
WHAT'S THE EVIDENCE?
Hypnosis and Memory

The design of this study and many like it is simple: The experimenter presents a large array of material, tests people's memory of it, and then retests some

Results Figure 5.16 shows the means for the two groups. The hypnotized people did report some new memories that they had not recalled before and more than the nonhypnotized group did. However, both groups reported more incorrect items than correct items, and the hypnotized group reported more incorrect items than the nonhypnotized group did.

Interpretation These results show no evidence that hypnosis improves memory. Rather, it may decrease people's usual hesitance about reporting uncertain or doubtful memories. It may also cause people to confuse imagination with reality.

You might note that this study is an example of the signal-detection issue discussed in Chapter 4 (page 126): A reported new memory is a "hit," but the number of hits, by itself, is useless information unless we also know the number of "false alarms"—reported memories that are incorrect.

Many other studies have produced similar conclusions: Hypnosis sometimes does increase the number of correct items recalled, but it also increases the number of incorrect items recalled, and people who have been hypnotized continue to report both the correct and incorrect items with high confidence, even after the hypnotic session (Steblay & Bothwell, 1994). Typically, hypnotized people are more confident than nonhypnotized people in both their correct and incorrect reports (Fligstein, Barabasz, Barabasz, Trevisan, & Warner, 1998).

In response to such findings, a panel appointed by the American Medical Association (1986) recommended that courts of law should refuse to admit any testimony that was elicited under hypnosis, although hypnosis might occasionally be used as an investigative tool if all else fails. (For example, if a hypnotized witness reports a license plate number, and the police track down the car and find blood on it, the blood is certainly admissible evidence, even if the hypnotized report is not. Success stories of that type are rare.)

However, professional hypnotists have objected to having their work rejected by the courts, and some judges do admit hypnotically induced testimony, provided that the hypnotic session was fully recorded so that opposing attorneys could watch it. The result is sometimes, shall we say, questionable. In one case a truck crashed into a car in an intersection, killing the driver and seriously wounding a passenger in the backseat, whose head injury left him dazed and confused at the time and unable to remember anything afterward. Three eyewitnesses testified, and the police agreed, that the car had entered the intersection on a red light and that the truck driver was not to blame. *After* the backseat passenger collected damages from the driver's insurance company, and almost 2 years after the accident, he contacted a hypnotist to help him remember more of how the accident happened. Under hypnosis he reported that just before the accident he leaned forward and saw that the light was green, thus implying that the accident was the truck driver's fault. Although it is extremely doubtful that hypnosis could reinstate a 2-year-old memory of an event that caused head injury and confusion, the judge ruled that because the hypnotic session had been carefully recorded, it could be admitted as evidence. A few days later, the truck company settled the suit for hundreds of thousands of dollars (Karlin, 1997).

An even more doubtful claim is that hypnosis can help people recall their early childhood. A hypnotist might say, "You are getting younger. It is now the year . . . ; now it is . . . ; now you are only 6 years old." A hypnotized person may act like a young child, playing with teddy bears and blankets (Nash, Johnson, & Tipton, 1979). But is he or she reliving early experiences? Evidently not.

- The childhood "memories," such as the names of friends and teachers and the details of birthday parties, are generally inaccurate according to records that parents or others have kept (Nash, 1987).
- Someone who has presumably regressed under hypnosis to early childhood retains spelling and other skills learned later in life. When asked to draw a picture, he or she does not draw as children draw but as adults imagine that children draw (Orne, 1951) (see Figure 5.17).
- Hypnotized subjects will respond just as well to suggestions that they are growing older as to suggestions that they are growing younger. They give as convincing a performance of being an older per-

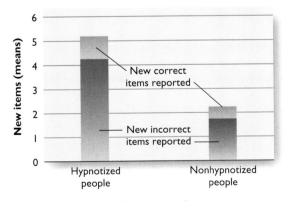

FIGURE 5.16 Items recalled 1 week after viewing a series of slides and *not* recalled before that. Hypnosis did increase people's recall of items they had not recalled before. However, most of the new "memories" they confidently reported were incorrect. *(Reprinted with permission from "The Use of Hypnosis to Aid Recall," by J. Dywan & K. Bowers,* Science, *1983, 222, 184-185. Copyright © 1983 American Association for the Advancement of Science.)*

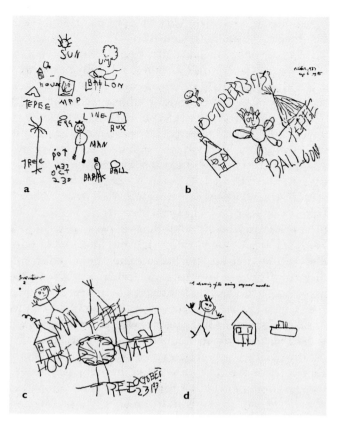

FIGURE 5.17 Regression or role-playing? One person made drawing (a) at age 6 and the other three drawings (b, c, & d) as a college student under hypnosis. While under hypnosis the person was asked to regress to age 6. The drawings created while under hypnosis are not like drawings done in childhood. Orne (1951) concluded that the hypnotized students played the role of a 6-year-old and drew as they thought a child would.

son as of being a younger person (Rubenstein & Newman, 1954). Because their reports of the future can only be imagination, we should assume the same for their past.

You may even encounter the astounding claim that hypnosis can help someone recall memories from a previous life. Hypnotized young people who claim to be recollecting a previous life most often describe the life of someone similar to themselves and married to someone remarkably similar to their current boyfriend or girlfriend. If they are asked whether their country (in their past life) is at war or what kind of money is in use, their guesses are seldom correct (Spanos, 1987–1988).

CONCEPT CHECK ✓

7. List two practical uses of hypnosis that the evidence supports and one that it does not. (Check your answer on page 177.)

(Check your answer on page 177.)

CRITICAL THINKING:
WHAT'S THE EVIDENCE?
Hypnosis and Risky Acts

Most hypnotists agree about one of the limits of hypnosis: "You don't have to worry," a hypnotist will reassure you. "People will not do anything under hypnosis that they would ordinarily refuse to do." That reassurance is an important strategy in getting you to agree to hypnosis. But is it true? And how would anyone know? Do you suppose that hypnotists frequently ask clients to perform criminal or immoral acts and meet with repeated refusals and then report these unethical experiments in professional journals? Not likely. Furthermore, when investigators have in fact asked hypnotized people to perform dangerous acts, the results have been hard to interpret. Here is one example.

Hypothesis Hypnotized people will sometimes perform acts that nonhypnotized people would refuse to do.

Method Eighteen college students were randomly assigned to three groups. The investigator hypnotized those in one group, instructed the second group to pretend they were hypnotized, and merely asked the third group to participate in the study, without mentioning hypnosis. Each student was then asked to perform three acts: First, go to a box and pick up a poisonous snake. The snake really was poisonous, and anyone who got too close was restrained at the last moment. Second, reach into a vat of fuming nitric acid to retrieve a coin (which was already starting to dissolve). Here there was no last-second restraint. Anyone who followed the instructions was told to wash his or her hands in warm soapy water immediately afterward. (Today's ethical procedures would prevent this study.) Third, throw the nitric acid into the face of the hypnotist's assistant. Unnoticed, the researcher had swapped the container of nitric acid for a container of water, but the participant had no way of knowing that.

Results Five of the six hypnotized students followed all three directions (Orne & Evans, 1965). Moreover, so did all six of those who were pretending to be hypnotized! So did two of the six who were just told to take these actions as part of an experiment, with no mention of hypnosis. (Nonhypnotized subjects did, however, hesitate much longer than the hypnotized subjects.)

Why would people do such extraordinary things? They explained that they simply trusted the experimenter: "If he tells me to do something, it can't really be dangerous."

Interpretation Many hypnotized people *will* do some strange and dangerous acts. However, many nonhypnotized people will as well if they are asked by someone they consider reputable.

■ Will hypnotized people do anything that they would otherwise refuse to do? The problem with answering this question is that nonhypnotized people will sometimes perform some strange and dangerous acts, either because an experimenter asked them to or on their own.

In short, we simply do not have adequate evidence to decide whether people under hypnosis will do anything that they would utterly refuse to do otherwise because it is difficult to find anything that people will refuse to do!

There is a message here about the importance of control groups: We cannot simply assume what people would do without hypnosis; we need to test them.

Is Hypnosis an Altered State of Consciousness?

If a hypnotist tells you, "Your hand is rising; you can do nothing to stop it," your hand might indeed rise. If you were later asked why, you might reply (as many do) that you lost control over your own behavior. Still, you were not a puppet. Was the act voluntary, involuntary, or something in between? To put the question differently, is hypnosis really anything different from normal wakefulness?

At one extreme, some psychologists regard hypnosis as a special state of consciousness characterized by greatly increased suggestibility. At the other extreme, some psychologists emphasize the similarities between hypnosis and normal wakeful consciousness, including the fact that people who respond well to hypnosis also respond strongly to suggestions without hypnosis. Most psychologists take intermediate positions, noting that hypnotized people are neither "pretending to be hypnotized"

nor under a hypnotist's control. That is, hypnosis is a special state in some ways but not others (Kirsch & Braffman, 2001; Kirsch & Lynn, 1998).

One way to determine whether hypnosis is a special state of consciousness is to find out whether unhypnotized people can do everything that hypnotized people do. That is, if you agreed to pretend that you were hypnotized, could you act exactly like a hypnotized person?

How Well Can a Nonhypnotized Person Pretend to Be Hypnotized?

In several experiments some college students were hypnotized and others were told to pretend they were hypnotized. An experienced hypnotist then examined them and tried to determine which ones were really hypnotized.

Fooling the hypnotist turned out to be easier than expected. The pretenders were able to tolerate sharp pain without flinching and could pretend to recall old memories. They made their bodies as stiff as a board and lay rigid between two chairs. When standing people were told to sit down, they did so immediately (as hypnotized people do) without first checking to make sure there was a chair behind them (Orne, 1959, 1979). When told to experience anger or another emotion, they exhibited physiological changes such as increased heart rate and sweating, just as hypnotized people do (Damaser, Shor, & Orne, 1963). Not even highly experienced hypnotists could accurately identify the pretenders.

However, a few differences between the hypnotized people and pretenders did emerge (Orne, 1979). The pretenders failed to match some of the behaviors of hypnotized people—not because they couldn't do them but because they did not know how a hypnotized subject would act. For instance, when the hypnotist suggested, "You see Professor Schmaltz sitting in that chair," people in both groups reported seeing the professor. Some of the hypnotized subjects, however, said they were puzzled. "How is it that I see the professor there, but I can also see the entire chair?" Pretenders never reported seeing this "double reality." At that point in the experiment, Professor Schmaltz actually walked into the room. "Who is that entering the room?" asked the hypnotist. The pretenders would either say they saw no one, or they would identify Schmaltz as someone else. The hypnotized subjects would say, "That's Professor Schmaltz." Some then said that they were confused by seeing the same person in two places at the same time. For some of them, the hallucinated professor faded at that moment, whereas others continued to accept the double image.

One study reported a way to distinguish hypnotized people from pretenders more than 90% of the time. But it might not be the way you would expect. Simply ask people how deeply hypnotized they thought they were, how relaxed they were, and whether they were aware of their surroundings while hypnotized. People who rate themselves as "extremely" hypnotized, "extremely" relaxed, and so forth are almost always pretenders. Those who rate themselves as only mildly influenced were really hypnotized (Martin & Lynn, 1996).

So, what is our conclusion? Is hypnosis an altered state, or are hypnotized people just playing a role? Apparently, people pretending to be hypnotized can mimic almost any effect of hypnosis that they know about. However, hypnosis is ordinarily not just role-playing (Hilgard, 1971). The effects that role-players learn to imitate happen spontaneously for the hypnotized people.

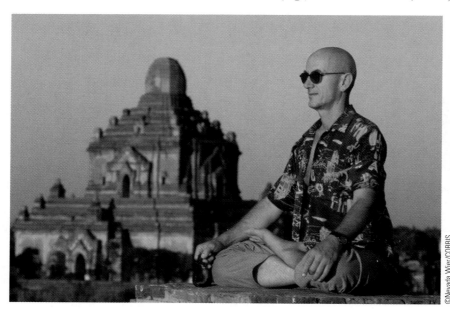
❙ Meditation excludes the worries and concerns of the day and thereby induces a calm, relaxed state.

©Nevada Wier/CORBIS

CONCEPT CHECK ☑

8. Does hypnosis give people the power to do anything they could not do otherwise? Does it cause them to do anything they would be unwilling to do otherwise? (Check your answers on page 177.)

Meditation: In Some Ways Like Hypnosis

Hypnosis is not the only method of inducing a relaxed and possibly altered state of consciousness. **Meditation,** *a method of inducing a calm, relaxed state through the use of special techniques,* follows a tradition that has been practiced in various parts of the world for thousands of years. For example, one may sit quietly while repeating a sound (e.g., "om") for 15 to 20 minutes twice a day. The point is "to empty one's mind"—that is, to expel all the worries, troubles, and doubts that otherwise intrude into our thoughts. In that respect meditation has some similarities to the relaxed, passive state of hypnosis. However, it in-

cludes no hypnotist or suggestions.

Many studies document that meditation decreases physiological arousal as measured by heart rate, breathing rate, blood pressure, EEG patterns, and so forth (e.g., Travis & Wallace, 1999). These benefits do not necessarily confirm the claims that meditation performs a special transcendental or spiritual function, however. Most studies that have compared meditation with relaxation have found little difference in results between the two groups (Holmes, 1987). The point is not that meditation is useless, but only that it is a way to relax, and relaxation of any kind is helpful. As with hypnosis, it is important to separate the real phenomenon from the exaggerated claims.

IN CLOSING

The Nature of Hypnosis

Researchers have still not reached a consensus on exactly what hypnosis is. They do agree on a few general points, however: Hypnosis is not faking or pretending to be hypnotized, and it does not give people mental or physical powers that they otherwise lack. Hypnosis merely enables people to relax, concentrate, and follow suggestions better than they usually do. Be skeptical of anyone who claims much more than that for hypnosis.

Summary

* *Nature of hypnosis.* Hypnosis is a condition of increased suggestibility that occurs in the context of a special hypnotist–subject relationship. Psychologists try to distinguish the genuine phenomenon, which deserves serious study, from exaggerated claims. (page 169)

* *Hypnosis induction.* To induce hypnosis a hypnotist asks a person to concentrate and then makes repetitive suggestions. The first steps toward being

hypnotized are the willingness to be hypnotized and the belief that one is becoming hypnotized. (page 169)

- *Uses.* Hypnosis can alleviate pain, and through posthypnotic suggestion, it can help people combat bad habits. (page 170)
- *Sensory distortions.* Hypnosis can induce hallucinations and other sensory distortions. However, when hypnotized people are told not to see something, even when they claim not to see it, enough aspects of the information get through to the brain to influence other perceptions. (page 171)
- *Nonuses.* Hypnosis does not give people special strength or unusual powers. Most of the new "memories" evoked under hypnosis are false. (page 172)
- *Uncertain limits.* Although many hypnotists insist that hypnotized people will not do anything that they would refuse to do when not hypnotized, there is little solid evidence to back up this claim. (page 174)
- *Hypnosis as an altered state.* Controversy continues about whether hypnosis is a special state of consciousness and, indeed, what we mean by an altered state. (page 175)
- *Meditation.* Meditation can induce a relaxed condition that one might regard as an altered state of consciousness. (page 176)

Answers to Concept Checks

7. Supported by the evidence: Hypnosis can decrease pain. Weakly supported by the evidence: Posthypnotic suggestions can sometimes help people break bad habits. Not supported: Hypnosis does not improve people's memories. (Nor does it give them added strength.) (page 174)

8. No evidence indicates that hypnosis empowers people to do anything they could not do otherwise if sufficiently motivated. That is, people pretending to be hypnotized can imitate all the things hypnotized people do, and the only exceptions are things that the imitators did not know about. As to whether hypnosis can make people do something they would ordinarily refuse to do, we simply do not know. In certain experiments hypnotized people have done some strange things, such as attempting to pick up a poisonous snake or putting their hand into a vat of concentrated acid. However, some nonhypnotized people did too. It is hard to find an act that people will refuse to do, especially if they know they are in an experiment. (page 176)

Drugs and Their Effects

What experiences do abused drugs produce?

Why do people experiment with such drugs?

Considering all the people who tell us (with good reason), "Don't use drugs" and all the reports about people who have ruined their health or wasted their lives by using drugs, why would anyone nevertheless use drugs? No doubt you can generate many explanations, but one reason is simple curiosity. Just as people like to visit other countries, sample a variety of foods, or try unusual forms of entertainment, we are curious what it would be like to *feel* different. What would it feel like to be a bird, for example? We can't answer that, but it is possible to find out what it feels like to drink a couple glasses of wine.

Unfortunately, as you well know, after people have tried a drug once or twice, some find it difficult to stop. The abuse of alcohol and other drugs is a widespread problem, which we shall consider in Chapter 16. Here our focus is on the experiences associated with some commonly abused drugs. In the study of drug effects, it is more difficult than usual to separate fact from fiction and sometimes difficult to find unbiased information. Many people who are trying to discourage drug use exaggerate the dangers and their warnings become hard to believe. At the opposite extreme, many other people seriously understate the dangers. As with other topics, we should be skeptical of claims that go beyond the evidence.

A Survey of Abused Drugs and Their Effects

Some abused drugs, such as alcohol and opiates, have predominantly calming effects. Others, such as amphetamines and cocaine, are known for their stimulating effects. Still others, such as LSD, produce hallucinations. What do they have in common that would account for their tendency to be abused? Nearly all abused or addictive drugs increase the activity at dopamine synapses in the brain, especially at particular types of dopamine receptors known as types D2, D3, and D4 (Maldonado et al., 1997). They can do so by a variety of means, including increased release of dopamine, blocking the mechanisms that remove dopamine from the synapse after its release, stimulating neurons that release dopamine, or inhibiting neurons that inhibit release of dopamine. The addictive actions of dopamine (and therefore of abused drugs) depend largely on a tiny brain area called the *nucleus accumbens,* apparently a central area for attention and perhaps habit formation (Berridge & Robinson, 1998). Figure 5.18 shows the location of the nucleus accumbens. Table 5.3 lists some of the commonly abused drugs and their most prominent effects.

However, we should not expect to find all the answers to addiction in the chemistry of the drugs. People can also become addicted to gambling and even to

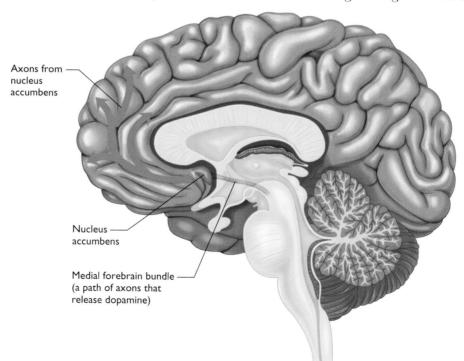

Axons from nucleus accumbens

Nucleus accumbens

Medial forebrain bundle (a path of axons that release dopamine)

FIGURE 5.18 The nucleus accumbens is a small brain area that is critical for the motivating effects of many experiences, including drugs, food, and sex. Most abused drugs increase the activity of the neurotransmitter dopamine in this area.

TABLE 5.3 Commonly Abused Drugs and Their Effects

Drug Category	Effects on the Nervous System	Effects on Behavior
Stimulants		
Amphetamine	Increases release of dopamine and decreases reuptake, prolonging effects	Increases energy and alertness
Cocaine	Decreases reuptake of dopamine, prolonging effects	Increases energy and alertness
Methylphenidate (Ritalin)	Decreases reuptake of dopamine, but with slower onset and offset than cocaine	Increases alertness; much milder withdrawal effects than cocaine
Caffeine	Blocks a chemical that inhibits glutamate synapses	Increases energy and alertness
Nicotine	Stimulates some acetylcholine synapses; stimulates some neurons that release dopamine	Increases arousal; abstention by a habitual smoker produces tension and depression
Depressants		
Alcohol	Facilitates effects of GABA, an inhibitory neurotransmitter	Relaxation, reduced inhibitions, impaired memory and judgment
Benzodiazepine tranquilizers	Facilitate effects of GABA, an inhibitory neurotransmitter	Relaxation, decreased anxiety, sleepiness
Narcotics		
Morphine, heroin, other opiates	Stimulate endorphin synapses	Decrease pain; withdrawal from interest in real world; unpleasant withdrawal effects during abstention
Marijuana		
Marijuana	Excites negative feedback receptors of both excitatory and inhibitory transmitters	Decreases pain and nausea; distorted sense of time
Hallucinogens		
LSD	Stimulates serotonin type 2 receptors at inappropriate times	Hallucinations, sensory distortions
MDMA ("ecstasy")	Stimulates neurons that release dopamine; at higher doses also stimulates neurons that release serotonin	At low doses increases arousal; at higher doses hallucinations; can damage or destroy axons
Phencyclidine (PCP or "angel dust")	Inhibits one type of glutamate receptor	Intoxication, slurred speech; at higher doses hallucinations, thought disorder, impaired memory and emotions

some extent videogame playing, even though these addictions do not include any "substance." Videogame playing, and presumably gambling as well, can increase the release of dopamine in the nucleus accumbens *in those people who have developed a strong habit* (Koepp et al., 1998).

Stimulants

Stimulants are *drugs that boost energy, heighten alertness, increase activity, and produce a pleasant feeling.* Two powerful stimulants are amphetamine and cocaine. Methylphenidate (Ritalin) is another

drug with the same type of effects, but it acts more slowly. Ritalin and other stimulant drugs benefit some children with attention deficit disorder.

Amphetamine, cocaine, and methylphenidate all prevent neurons from reabsorbing the dopamine they have released; they thereby prolong the effects of the dopamine (Volkow, Wang, & Fowler, 1997; Volkow, Wang, Fowler, et al., 1998). Amphetamine not only causes the membrane to stop reabsorbing released dopamine but also increases the release (Giros, Jaber, Jones, Wightman, & Caron, 1996; Paladini, Fiorillo, Morikawa, & Williams, 2001). Because each of these drugs also increases the activity at norepinephrine and serotonin synapses, their effects on behavior are complex and far-reaching, including increases in heart rate, blood pressure, and body temperature.

Cocaine has long been available in the powdery form of cocaine hydrochloride, which can be sniffed. Its stimulant effects increase gradually over a few minutes and then decline gradually over about half an hour. It also anesthetizes the nostrils (because cocaine resembles Novocain) and can in some cases damage the lungs. Sniffed cocaine hydrochloride is only moderately habit-forming. Before 1985 the only way to get a more intense effect from cocaine hydrochloride was to treat it with ether to convert it into *freebase cocaine*—cocaine with the hydrochloride removed. Smoking freebase cocaine enables a high percentage of it to enter the body rapidly and thereby enter the brain rapidly. The faster a drug enters the brain, the more intense the resulting experience will be.

The drug known as *crack cocaine* first became available in 1985. Crack is cocaine that has already been converted into freebase rocks, ready to be smoked (Brower & Anglin, 1987; Kozel & Adams, 1986). It is called "crack" because it makes popping noises when smoked. Crack produces a rush of potent effects within a few seconds, much faster than other forms of cocaine. The effects are generally described as pleasant, although some people report intense anxiety instead, and other people suffer heart attacks or other severe medical complications. Long-term use can lead to a sore throat, mental confusion, lung diseases, and other serious problems. It is also habit-forming, although the habit forms so slowly that frequent users may lull themselves into a false sense of security: "I can take it or leave it" (Gawin, 1991). While someone is using cocaine, the drug experience itself becomes the focus of so much attention that the person neglects usual activities such as eating, sleeping, going to work, or taking care of family members.

Coffee, tea, and many soft drinks contain caffeine, which is also a stimulant, though less powerful and less dangerous than amphetamine or cocaine. Habitual coffee drinkers can become dependent on it, and abstaining from it can cause headaches and drowsiness (Hughes et al., 1991). Surgical patients sometimes report distress that people assume stems from the operation but really is a result of caffeine withdrawal.

Tobacco delivers nicotine, which stimulates acetylcholine receptors, thereby increasing wakefulness and arousal. Some of those acetylcholine receptors stimulate neurons that increase the release of dopamine in the nucleus accumbens (Pich et al., 1997). Thus, nicotine's effects overlap those of amphetamines, cocaine, and other addictive drugs.

Although nicotine is generally classed as a stimulant, most smokers say it relaxes them. The research points to an explanation for this paradox. As people smoke more and more, their stress levels and tension *increase,* and habitual smokers experience greater stress levels than nonsmokers. However, a habitual smoker who goes even a short time between cigarettes begins to feel withdrawal symptoms, including nervousness and unhappy mood. Smoking another cigarette relieves the withdrawal symptoms and restores the usual mood, which is slightly tense but not as bad as the withdrawal state (Parrott, 1999). Quitting altogether would lead to a temporary unpleasant withdrawal state and to an eventual state of reduced stress. We shall consider nicotine addiction again in Chapter 16.

CONCEPT CHECK ☑

9. A drug called AMPT (alpha-methyl-para-tyrosine) prevents the body from making the transmitter dopamine. If someone took a large dose of AMPT, how would it affect that person's later responsiveness to cocaine, amphetamine, or methylphenidate? (Check your answer on page 185.)

■ Because crack is smoked, it reaches the brain in 8 seconds, much faster than other forms of cocaine. All else being equal, the faster a drug reaches the brain, the more intense the experience will be and the greater the probability of addiction.

Depressants

Depressants are *drugs that predominantly decrease arousal.* Two common types of depressants are alcohol and tranquilizers. When archeologists unearthed a Neolithic village in Iran's Zagros Mountains, they found a jar that had been constructed about 5500–5400 B.C., one of the oldest human-made crafts ever found (Figure 5.19). Inside the jar, especially at the bottom, the archeologists found a yellowish residue. They were curious to know what the jar had held, so they sent some of the residue for chemical analysis. The unambiguous answer came back: The jar had been a wine vessel (McGovern, Glusker, Exner, & Voigt, 1996).

©University of Pennsylvania Museum

FIGURE 5.19 This jar, dated about 5500–5400 B.C., is one of the oldest human crafts ever found. It was used for storing wine.

Clearly, the use of alcohol is a tradition that has stood the test of time. **Alcohol** is a *class of molecules that includes methanol, ethanol, propyl alcohol (rubbing alcohol), and others. Ethanol is the type that people drink;* the others are toxic if consumed. Alcohol acts primarily as a relaxant. Moderate use of alcohol serves as a tension reducer. In greater amounts it can increase aggressive and risk-taking behaviors, mainly by depressing the fears and anxieties that ordinarily inhibit such activities. In still greater amounts, as in binge drinking, it leads to unconsciousness and even death.

Excessive use can damage the liver and other organs, aggravate or prolong many medical conditions, and impair memory and motor control. A woman who drinks alcohol during pregnancy risks impairing her baby's brain development, health, and appearance (see Chapter 10).

Alcohol abuse is a worldwide problem, although it is more common in some populations than others. Within the United States, alcohol abuse is more common among Native Americans than among other ethnic groups and least common among those of Asian ancestry. The reasons are not well understood, but it is not true (as many have supposed) that Native Americans get drunk more easily than others. If anything, they are *less* affected than others by moderate amounts of alcohol (Garcia-Andrade, Wall, & Ehlers, 1997). Whatever the explanation, the ethnic differences are worth taking seriously; many observers believe that differences in alcohol use constitute a major reason for ethnic differences in life span (Rivers, 1994).

Another type of depressant drugs, **tranquilizers,** *help people to relax and to fall asleep; they can also decrease muscle tension and suppress epileptic seizures.* Barbiturates, once a common type of tranquilizer, proved to be highly habit-forming and life-threatening in large doses. Today, the most common tranquilizers are chemicals called *benzodiazepines,* which include the drugs diazepam (Valium) and alprazolam (Xanax). Benzodiazepines can also be habit-forming, although less so than barbiturates. Thousands of tons of these pills are taken every year in the United States.

Benzodiazepines exert their calming effects by facilitating transmission at synapses that use the neurotransmitter GABA. Alcohol facilitates transmission at the same synapses, though by a different mechanism (Sudzak et al., 1986). Taking alcohol and tranquilizers together can be dangerous because the combination increases GABA transmission so profoundly that it suppresses the brain areas that control breathing and heartbeat.

One benzodiazepine drug, flunitrazepam (Rohypnol), has attracted attention as the "date rape drug." Flunitrazepam dissolves quickly in water; it has no color, odor, or taste; and it can therefore be easily slipped into a drink without the drinker realizing it. The effects of this drug, like those of other tranquilizers, include drowsiness, poor muscle coordination, and memory impairment—including impaired ability to describe the attack later (Anglin, Spears, & Hutson, 1997; Woods & Winger, 1997). A hospital that suspects someone has been given this drug can run a simple urine test to determine its presence.

Narcotics

Narcotics are *drugs that produce drowsiness, insensitivity to pain, and decreased responsiveness to events.* The classic examples of narcotics, **opiates,** are *either natural drugs derived from the opium poppy* *or synthetic drugs with a chemical structure similar to that of natural opiates.* An opiate drug makes people feel happy, warm, and content, with little anxiety or pain. Unpleasant consequences include nausea and withdrawal from the real world. Once the drug·has left the brain, the affected synapses become understimulated, and the user then enters withdrawal. Elation gives way to anxiety, pain, and hyperresponsiveness to sounds and other stimuli.

Morphine (named after Morpheus, the Greek god of dreams) has important medical use as a painkiller. When used for that purpose, morphine is almost never habit-forming. (No drug is automatically habit-forming. The probability of abuse or habit formation depends on a variety of circumstances, including dose and social setting.)

Opiate drugs such as morphine, heroin, methadone, and codeine bind to a specific set of neurotransmitter receptors in the brain (Pert & Snyder, 1973). The discovery of neurotransmitter receptors prompted neuroscientists to look for naturally occurring brain chemicals that bind to those receptors because it hardly seemed likely that evolution would equip us with receptors to respond only to extracts of the opium poppy. Researchers found that the brain produces several chemicals, called **endorphins,** that *bind to the opiate receptors* (Hughes et al., 1975), as mentioned in Chapter 4. Endorphins serve to inhibit chronic pain. They also inhibit neurons that inhibit the release of dopamine (North, 1992); by this double negative, they increase dopamine release and therefore produce reinforcing effects.

Marijuana

Marijuana (*cannabis*) is difficult to classify. It is certainly not a stimulant. It often has a calming effect but not like that of alcohol or tranquilizers. It softens pain but not as powerfully as opiates. It produces some sensory distortions, especially an illusion that time is passing more slowly than usual, but such distortions are not much like the hallucinations that accompany LSD use. Because marijuana does not closely resemble any other drug, it is discussed here separately.

The disadvantageous effects of marijuana include memory impairments and decreased drive. Most studies reporting memory problems in marijuana users are hard to interpret. Does marijuana impair memory or do people with memory problems like to use marijuana? As always, correlation does not indicate causation. However, one study found that a few months after people quit using marijuana, their memory improved (Pope, Gruber, Hudson, Huestis, & Yurgelun-Todd, 2001). This result strongly suggests that poor memory was a result of marijuana use, not a lifelong characteristic of those who chose to use marijuana.

Marijuana has several potential medical uses. It reduces nausea, suppresses tremors, reduces pressure in the eyes, and decreases cell loss in the brain just after a stroke (Glass, 2001; Panikashvili et al., 2001). Because of legal restrictions in the United States, not much research has been done on the possible medical uses of marijuana. On the negative side, marijuana increases the risk of Parkinson's disease (Glass, 2001), and long-term use probably increases the risk of lung cancer, as tobacco cigarettes do.

You may have heard that marijuana is dangerous as a "gateway drug"; that is, many people who go on to use heroin or cocaine used marijuana first. True, but they also used cigarettes and alcohol first, and many had risky sexual experiences and so forth. It is unclear that marijuana "leads to" the use of heroin or other dangerous drugs any more than tobacco, alcohol, or anything else does.

Although people are aware of marijuana's effects for no more than 2 or 3 hours after using it, it dissolves in the fats of the body, so traces of it can be found for weeks after the drug has been used (Dackis, Pottash, Annitto, & Gold, 1982). One consequence is that someone can "test positive" for marijuana use long after quitting it.

The active ingredient in marijuana is THC, or tetrahydrocannabinol. THC attaches to receptors that are abundant throughout the brain (Herkenham, Lynn, deCosta, & Richfield, 1991), especially in the hippocampus (an important brain area for memory) and brain areas important for the control of movement (Herkenham et al., 1990). The presence of

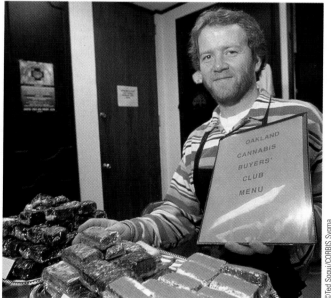

After California legalized marijuana for medical uses, many clubs and stores opened for the sale and distribution of the drug.

those receptors implies that the brain produces some THC-like chemical of its own. Researchers first discovered a brain chemical that they named *anandamide* (from *ananda*, the Sanskrit word for "bliss") which attaches to the same receptors as THC (Devane et al., 1992). However, the brain does not have much anandamide. A more prevalent compound that attaches to the same receptors has the not very catchy name *sn-2* arachidonylglycerol, abbreviated 2-AG (Stella, Schweitzer, & Piomelli, 1997). Receptors for these chemicals are widespread in most brain areas. However, the medulla—the brain area that controls heart rate and breathing—has many opiate receptors but few marijuana-type receptors (Herkenham et al., 1990). So a large dose of heroin or morphine produces a life-threatening decrease in breathing and heart rate, but marijuana does not.

Unlike the more familiar kinds of neurotransmitter receptors, those for anandamide and 2-AG (and therefore also for marijuana) are located on the *presynaptic* neuron. When the presynaptic neuron releases a transmitter, such as glutamate or GABA, the postsynaptic (receiving) cell releases anandamide or 2-AG, which returns to the presynaptic cell to inhibit further release (Kreitzer & Regehr, 2001; R. I. Wilson & Nicoll, 2001, 2002). In effect it tells the presynaptic cell, "I received your signal. You can slow down on sending any more of it." Marijuana, by resembling these natural reverse transmitters, has the same effect. Because it slows the release of both excitatory and inhibitory neurotransmitters, it is itself neither a stimulant nor a depressant. Perhaps we should call it a neural "leveler-outer"?

Hallucinogens

Drugs that induce sensory distortions are called **hallucinogens** (Jacobs, 1987). Most of these drugs are derived from certain mushrooms or other plants; some are manufactured. Hallucinogenic drugs such as LSD distort sensations and sometimes produce a dreamlike state or an intense mystical experience. Peyote, a hallucinogen derived from a cactus plant, has a long history of use in Native American religious ceremonies (see Figure 5.20).

LSD attaches mainly to one kind of brain receptor sensitive to the neurotransmitter serotonin (Jacobs, 1987). It stimulates those receptors at irregular times and prevents neurotransmitters from stimulating them at the normal times. We have an interesting gap in our knowledge at this point: We know that LSD's disruption of certain kinds of serotonin receptors leads to hallucinogenic experiences, but we do not understand *how* altering those receptors leads to the resulting experiences.

©Archives for Research in Archetypical Symbolism, San Francisco

FIGURE 5.20 Tablas, or yarn paintings, created by members of the Huichol tribe (Mexico) evoke the beautiful lights, vivid colors, and "peculiar creatures" experienced after the people eat the hallucinogenic peyote cactus in highly ritualized ceremonies.

The drug MDMA (methylenedioxymethamphetamine), better known as "ecstasy," produces stimulant effects similar to amphetamine at low doses and hallucinogenic effects similar to LSD at higher doses. Of all abused drugs, this is the one for which the evidence of brain damage is strongest. Use of MDMA stimulates dopamine and serotonin axons, thus producing the stimulant and hallucinogenic effects, but in the process damages or destroys those axons (McCann, Lowe, & Ricaurte, 1997). Perhaps for this reason, many users report that their first use was intense and pleasant, the next occasion less pleasant, and so forth.

One study reported that heavy users of MDMA showed memory losses that persisted even a year after they quit using the drug (Reneman et al., 2001). Conceivably, those people may have had the memory problems before they started using MDMA, but the pattern of results suggests danger. The drug also sometimes induces people to prolonged dancing or other activity to the point of severe dehydration, a serious and sometimes fatal problem.

Yet another hallucinogen, phencyclidine (PCP, or "angel dust") acts by inhibiting receptors for the neurotransmitter glutamate. At low doses PCP's effects resemble those of alcohol. At higher doses it produces hallucinations, thought disorder, memory loss, and loss of emotions.

Figure 5.21 diagrams the effects of several drugs.

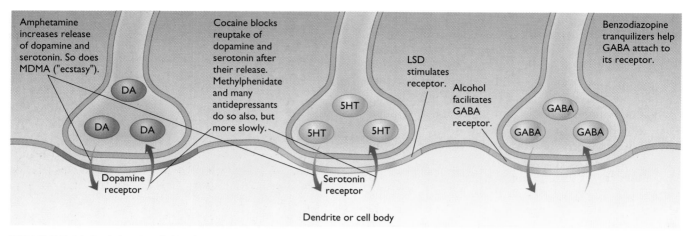

FIGURE 5.21 Both legal and illegal drugs operate at the synapses. Drugs can increase the release of neurotransmitters, block their reuptake, or directly stimulate or block their receptors.

Chronic Drug Effects

Initially, any drug produces some presumably desirable effect such as excitement, relaxation, or a distortion of experience. As the drug leaves the brain and the effects wear off, the person experiences **withdrawal effects**, which are generally *the opposite of the initial effects*. For example, a few hours after taking cocaine or amphetamine, someone becomes inactive and depressed. Furthermore, after someone has taken a drug repeatedly, its effects grow weaker and weaker, unless the person increases the dosage. This *decrease in effect* is called **tolerance**. Drug users often seek the drug partly to combat the withdrawal effects, increasing their dosage to compensate for the tolerance. That is, withdrawal effects and tolerance tend to promote increased use of a drug.

Drug Withdrawal

When habitual users suddenly stop using a drug, they gradually enter a state of withdrawal. With alcohol the typical withdrawal symptoms are sweating, nausea, sleeplessness, and in severe cases hallucinations and seizures (Mello & Mendelson, 1978). With opiate drugs the typical withdrawal symptoms are anxiety, restlessness, loss of appetite, vomiting, diarrhea, sweating, and gagging (Mansky, 1978). People who quit using tranquilizers can experience sleeplessness and nervousness. Someone who *feels compelled to use a drug to reduce unpleasant withdrawal symptoms* is said to have a **physical dependence** on the drug.

We distinguish between physical dependence and **psychological dependence**, which is a *strong repetitive desire for something without any accompanying physical symptoms of withdrawal*. For example, habitual gamblers have a psychological dependence on placing bets, even though they can abstain from gam-

bling without undergoing withdrawal symptoms (at least not in the usual sense). A psychological dependence can be extremely insistent, and in many cases it is pointless to try to decide whether someone's dependence is physical or psychological. (For example, someone who quits using cocaine experiences mostly "psychological" effects such as a lack of pleasure, with only brief physiological effects. So is the dependence physiological or psychological?)

Drug Tolerance

People who take a drug repeatedly develop a tolerance to its effects. To achieve the desired high, drug users must repeatedly increase the dose. Some longtime users inject more heroin or morphine into their veins than it would take to kill a nonuser.

What brings about drug tolerance? It may result in part from automatic chemical changes that occur in cells throughout the body to counteract the drug's effects (Baker & Tiffany, 1985). It may also result in part from psychological causes. For example, alcohol impairs the coordination of rats as well as that of humans. If rats are simply injected with alcohol every day for 24 days, they show no apparent tolerance for alcohol, as indicated by a coordination test given on the last day. However, if their coordination is tested after each of the 24 injections, each test session offers the rats an opportunity to practice their coordination, so their performance steadily improves (Wenger, Tiffany, Bombardier, Nicholls, & Woods, 1981). In other words, by practicing coordination while under the influence of alcohol, the rats develop a tolerance to alcohol. Similarly, people who use stimulant drugs as appetite suppressants start to develop a tolerance to the effects after a few meals. We shall discuss drug tolerance in more detail in the next chapter.

CONCEPT CHECK ☑

10. In what ways do withdrawal effects and tolerance tend to increase drug use? (Check your answer on this page.)

IN CLOSING

Drugs and Awareness

If you were to change a few of a computer's connections at random, you could produce an "altered state," which would almost certainly not be an improvement. Giving drugs to a human brain is a little like changing the connections of a computer, and almost any drug at least temporarily impairs brain functioning in some way. By examining both the desirable and undesirable effects of drugs on the brain, we can gain greater insight into the brain's normal processes and functions.

One message of this chapter is that altered states of consciousness are not vast alterations. Dreaming is much like other thinking, and people usually dream about the same topics they fantasize about when awake. Hypnosis makes people more suggestible, but the effects are usually mild. Drugs also alter behavior, but the result depends on the person's personality as well as the nature of the drug itself. Even an "altered" consciousness has much in common with your normal state.

Summary

- *Stimulants.* Stimulant drugs such as amphetamines and cocaine increase activity levels and pleasure. Compared to other forms of cocaine, crack produces more rapid effects on behavior, greater risk of addiction, and greater risk of damage to the heart and other organs. (page 179)
- *Alcohol.* Alcohol, the most widely abused drug in our society, relaxes people and relieves their inhibitions. It can also impair judgment and reasoning. (page 181)

- *Tranquilizers.* Benzodiazepine tranquilizers, widely used to relieve anxiety, can also relax muscles and promote sleep. (page 181)
- *Opiates.* Opiate drugs bind to endorphin receptors in the nervous system. The immediate effect of opiates is pleasure and relief from pain. (page 181)
- *Marijuana.* Marijuana's active compound, THC, acts on abundant receptors, found mostly in the hippocampus and certain brain areas important for the control of movement. Marijuana acts on receptors on the presynaptic neuron, putting the brakes on release of both excitatory and inhibitory transmitters. (page 182)
- *Hallucinogens.* Hallucinogens induce sensory distortions. LSD acts at one type of serotonin synapse; we do not yet know why activity at that type of synapse should produce these effects. MDMA produces stimulant effects at low doses, hallucinogenic effects at higher doses, and a risk of brain damage. (page 183)
- *Withdrawal.* After using a drug, the user enters a rebound state known as withdrawal. Drug users often crave drugs as a way of decreasing their withdrawal symptoms. (page 184)
- *Tolerance.* People who use certain drugs repeatedly become less and less sensitive to them over time. (page 184)

Answers to Concept Checks

9. Someone who took AMPT would become much less responsive than usual to amphetamine, cocaine, or methylphenidate. These drugs increase the release of dopamine or prolong its effects, but if the neurons haven't been able to make dopamine, they cannot release it. (page 180)
10. Habitual users take drugs partly to avoid withdrawal effects. Because tolerance reduces the effect of a given dose, users increase the dose to try to achieve the original effect. (page 185)

Key Terms and Activities

Key Terms

activation-synthesis theory of dreams: the theory that parts of the brain are spontaneously activated during REM sleep and that a dream is the brain's attempt to synthesize these sensations into a coherent pattern (page 165)

alcohol: a class of molecules that includes methanol, ethanol, propyl alcohol (rubbing alcohol), and others (page 181)

circadian rhythm: a rhythm of activity and inactivity lasting approximately 1 day (page 153)

consciousness: the subjective experience of perceiving oneself and other entities (page 152)

depressant: drugs that predominantly decrease arousal (page 180)

electroencephalograph (EEG): a device that measures and amplifies slight electrical changes on the scalp that reflect brain activity (page 159)

endorphins: chemicals produced by the brain that have effects resembling those of opiates (page 182)

evolutionary theory (or energy-conservation theory) of sleep: the theory that sleep evolved primarily as a means of forcing animals to conserve their energy when they are relatively inefficient (page 157)

hallucination: a sensory experience not corresponding to reality, such as seeing or hearing something that is not present or failing to see or hear something that is present (page 171)

hallucinogens: drugs that induce sensory distortions (page 183)

hypersomnia: excessive but unrefreshing sleep (page 164)

hypnosis: a condition of increased suggestibility that occurs in the context of a special hypnotist–subject relationship (page 169)

insomnia: a failure to get enough sleep at night to feel well rested the next day (page 162)

jet lag: the discomfort and inefficiency that travelers experience in a new time zone because their internal clocks are out of phase with the light–dark cycle of their new environment (page 155)

latent content: the hidden content that is represented symbolically in a dream experience, according to Freud (page 164)

manifest content: the content that appears on the surface of a dream, according to Freud (page 164)

meditation: a method of inducing a calm, relaxed state through the use of special techniques (page 176)

narcolepsy: a condition characterized by suddenly falling asleep, or at least feeling very sleepy, during the day (page 163)

narcotics: drugs that produce drowsiness, insensitivity to pain, and decreased responsiveness to events (page 181)

neurocognitive theory: the approach that treats dreams as just another example of thinking, except that they occur under special conditions (page 166)

opiates: either drugs derived from the opium poppy or synthetic drugs that produce effects similar to those of opium derivatives (page 181)

periodic limb movement disorder: a condition that occurs during sleep, marked by unpleasant sensations in the legs and many repetitive leg movements strong enough to interrupt sleep (page 163)

physical dependence: a condition whereby a habitual drug user is driven to seek the drug to escape or avoid the unpleasant withdrawal effects that occur during abstention from the drug (page 184)

polysomnograph: a device that measures sleep stages using a combination of EEG and eye-movement records (page 159)

posthypnotic suggestion: a suggestion made to hypnotized subjects that they will do or experience something particular after coming out of hypnosis (page 171)

psychological dependence: a strong repetitive desire for something without any physical symptoms of withdrawal (page 184)

rapid eye movement (REM) sleep: a stage of sleep characterized by rapid eye movements, a high level of brain activity, and deep relaxation of the postural muscles; also known as paradoxical sleep (page 158)

repair and restoration theory: the theory that the purpose of sleep is to enable the body to recover from the exertions of the day (page 156)

sleep apnea: a condition causing a person to have trouble breathing while asleep (page 162)

stimulants: drugs that boost energy, heighten alertness, increase activity, and produce a pleasant feeling (page 179)

tolerance: the weakened effect of a drug after repeated use (page 184)

tranquilizers: drugs that help people to relax (page 181)

withdrawal effects: experiences that occur as a result of the removal of a drug from the brain (page 184)

Suggestions for Further Reading

Domhoff, G. W. (2003). *The scientific study of dreams.* Washington, DC: American Psychological Association. A review of the best research on dreams.

Moorcroft, W. (2003). *Understanding sleep and dreaming.* New York: Kluwer. An excellent review of research on many aspects of sleep and dreams.

Book Companion Web Site

Need help studying? Go to

http://psychology.wadsworth.com/kalat_intro7e/

for a virtual study center. You'll find a personalized Self-Study Assessment that will provide you with a study plan based on your answers to a pretest. Also study using flashcards, quizzes, interactive art, and an online glossary.

Check out interactive **Try It Yourself** exercises on the companion site! These exercises will help you put what you've learned into action.

Your companion site also has direct links to the following Web sites. These links are checked often for changes, dead links, and new additions.

Sleep Disorders

www.thesleepsite.com/

Learn more about sleep disorders and treatment.

Dream Research

www.dreamresearch.net

The best scientific work on the content of dreams.

Sleep Research

www.sleepfoundation.org/

Links to all kinds of information about sleep.

Web of Addictions

www.well.com/user/woa/

Andrew L. Homer and Dick Dillon provide factual information about alcohol and other abused drugs. Fact sheets and other material are arranged by drug, with links to Net resources related to addictions, in-depth information on special topics, and a list of places to get help with addictions.

National Clearinghouse for Alcohol and Drug Information

www.health.org/newsroom/

News reports about drug and alcohol abuse, with links to many other sites.

Try It Yourself CD-ROM
with Critical Thinking Video Exercises

Use your CD to access **videos** related to activities designed to help you think critically about the important topics discussed. For example, the video about sleep deprivation relates to what you've learned in this chapter. You'll also find an easy portal link to the book companion site where you can access your personalized **Self-Study Assessments** and interactive **Try It Yourself** exercises.

PsychNow! 2.0

PsychNow! is a fun interactive CD designed to help you with the difficult concepts in psychology. Check out the Brain & Consciousness section for the following topics that relate to this chapter:

Sleep and Dreaming: Facts about sleep, sleep video, and quiz.

Psychoactive Drugs: Drug names exercise, drug lesson, and applied simulated courtroom scene.

InteractNOW! *Online Collaborative Lab:* Consciousness and Stress

Learning

Learning is a change in behavior, or the potential for future behavior, as a result of experience.[1] Suppose we set up a simple experiment on animal learning. We put a monkey midway between a green wall and a red wall. If it approaches the green wall, it receives a few raisins; if it approaches the red wall, it gets nothing. After a few trials, the monkey consistently approaches the green wall. After it has made the correct choice, say, 12 times in a row, we are satisfied that the monkey has learned something.

Now imagine the same experiment with an alligator. We use the same procedure, but the alligator strains our patience, sitting motionless for hours at a time. When it finally does move, it is as likely to approach one wall as the other. Eventually, *we* learn something: not to go into the alligator-training business! But we see little evidence that the alligator has learned anything.

Should we conclude that alligators are slow learners? Not necessarily. Maybe they are not hungry. Maybe they can't see the difference between red and green. Maybe they learn but also forget quickly, so they cannot put together a long streak of consecutive correct approaches. Maybe they learn poorly in this situation but well in some other.

Similar problems arise when we evaluate human learning. If little Joey is having academic troubles, should we consider him a "slow learner"? Not necessarily. Like the alligator, perhaps he is not motivated, or he may have visual or hearing problems. Maybe he is distracted by his emotional troubles at home. (That's a possibility we probably wouldn't consider with the alligator.)

Psychologists have devoted an enormous amount of research to learning. One key finding is how important it is to consider all the influences that might interfere with learned performance. Psychologists have developed and polished many of their research skills by conducting experiments on learning.

▌ Understanding how an animal learns or why it fails to learn requires careful testing of all the factors that can influence behavior.

This chapter is about the procedures that produce changes in behavior—why you lick your lips at the sight of tasty food, why you turn away from a food that once made you sick, why you get nervous if a police car starts to follow you, and why you shudder at the sight of a ferocious person charging toward you with a chain saw. This chapter is also about why you persevere longer at some tasks than others. In Chapter 7 we proceed to the topic of memory. Obviously, any change in behavior implies some sort of memory, and any memory implies previous learning. Still, the study of learning is based on a different research tradition from that of memory.

[1] A better definition of learning would limit the term to just certain kinds of experience. For example, spending an hour on a sunny beach without sunglasses will weaken your sensitivity to faint light and therefore change certain aspects of your behavior temporarily, but we would not call that change learning. However, a "better" definition of learning would be neither brief nor simple.

Behaviorism

How and why did the behaviorist viewpoint arise?

What is its enduring message?

A monitor lizard eats smaller lizards. When it sees one of the small lizards, instead of chasing it at once, the monitor heads for the nearest pile of rocks, which is the only place the smaller lizard might be able to escape. The small lizard, now with no place to go, is easy prey (Sweet & Pianka, 2003). Should we describe this as intelligent, insightful behavior by the monitor lizard? Or does it reflect simple trial-and-error learning, where the monitor has simply learned to obtain food by going first to the rocks?

A case like this can ultimately be decided by extensive research—if anyone cares to spend the necessary effort—but psychologists differ in their initial inclinations as to what is a likely explanation. The study of learning, especially animal learning, has been dominated by **behaviorists,** *psychologists who insist that psychologists should study only observable, measurable behaviors, not mental processes.* Their inclination has been overwhelmingly to assume the simplest possible explanation for behavior and to resist interpretation in terms of understanding or insight. At least, they insist, we should exhaust attempts at simple explanations before we adopt more complex ones. You will recognize this idea as the principle of parsimony from Chapter 2.

The term *behaviorist* applies to theorists and researchers with quite a range of views (O'Donohue & Kitchener, 1999). Two major categories are *methodological behaviorists* and *radical behaviorists.* **Methodological behaviorists** *study only the events that they can measure and observe*—in other words the environment and the individual's actions—*but they sometimes use those observations to make inferences about internal events* (Day & Moore, 1995). For example, depriving an animal of food, presenting it with very appealing food, or making it exercise will increase the probability that the animal will eat food, work for food, and so forth. From such observations a psychologist can infer an **intervening variable,** *something that we cannot directly observe but that links a variety of procedures to a variety of possible responses.* In this case the intervening variable is *hunger:*

Similarly, one could use other kinds of observations to infer different intervening variables, such as

Operation	Intervening Variable	Observable Response
Food deprivation Prolonged exercise Presence of other animals that are eating Presence of highly appealing food Certain medical conditions	Any of these can increase → Hunger (an intervening variable) → Increases any of these	Increased protein intake Increased carbohydrate intake Increased fat intake Increased work on tasks that have previously produced food

thirst, sex drive, anger, fear, and so forth. Note that any of these intervening variables is inferred from behavior, never observed directly. The important point is that a methodological behaviorist will use such terms only after anchoring them firmly to observable procedures and responses—that is, after giving them a clear operational definition (as discussed in Chapter 2). Many psychological researchers are methodological behaviorists, even if they do not use that term.

CRITICAL THINKING: A STEP FURTHER
Intervening Variables

Choose an intervening variable, such as fear or anger, and describe what measurements you could use to infer it. In the process do you in fact establish an operational definition?

Radical behaviorists do not deny that private events such as hunger or fear exist, and they agree it is possible to study the circumstances that cause people to *say,* "I am hungry," "I am frightened," and so forth. The distinguishing feature of radical behaviorists is that they *deny that hunger, fear, or any other internal, private event causes behavior* (Moore, 1995). For example, they would say if food deprivation leads to hunger and hunger leads to eating, why not just say that food deprivation leads to eating? What do we gain by introducing the word *hunger?* According to radical behaviorists, any internal state is

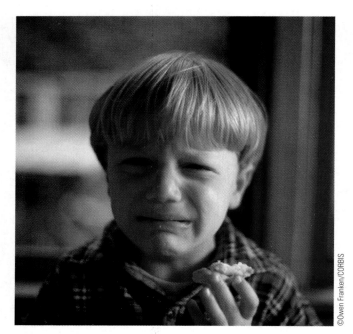

Behaviorists agree that all psychological investigations should be based on behavioral observations. A methodological behaviorist might use observations of, say, facial expressions to make inferences about such processes as "sadness." A radical behaviorist, however, would study the facial expressions themselves, but not as a means of inferring something else.

protest movement against structuralism. Behaviorists insisted that it is useless to ask people to report their own private experiences. For example, if someone says, "My idea of roundness is stronger than my idea of color," we have no way to check the accuracy of the report. We are not even certain what it means. If psychology is to be a scientific enterprise, behaviorists insisted, it must deal with only observable, measurable events—that is, behavior and its relation to the environment.

To avoid any mention of the mind, thoughts, or knowledge, some behaviorists went to the opposite extreme. One of the forerunners of behaviorism, Jacques Loeb (1918/1973), argued that much of animal behavior, and perhaps human behavior as well, could be described in terms of simple responses to simple stimuli—for example, approaching light, turning away from strong smells, clinging to hard surfaces, walking toward or away from moisture, and so forth (see Figure 6.1). Complex behavior, he surmised, is just the result of adding together many changes of speed and direction elicited by various stimuli. Loeb's view of behavior was an example of **stimulus–response psychology**, *the attempt to explain behavior in terms of how each stimulus triggers a response.*

caused by an event in the environment (or by the individual's genetics), and therefore, the ultimate cause of any behavior lies in the observable events that led up to the behavior, not the internal states.

According to this point of view, discussions of mental events are just sloppy language. For example, as B. F. Skinner (1990) argued, when you say, "I *intend* to . . . ," what you really mean is "I am about to . . . " or "In situations like this, I usually . . . " or "This behavior is in the preliminary stages of happening . . . ." That is, any statement about mental experiences can be converted into a description of behavior.

CONCEPT CHECK ☑

1. How does a radical behaviorist differ from a methodological behaviorist? (Check your answer on page 194.)

The Rise of Behaviorism

Behaviorism should be understood within the historical context in which it arose. During the early 1900s, one highly influential group within psychology, the *structuralists* (see Chapter 1), studied people's thoughts, ideas, and sensations by asking people to describe them. The early behaviorists began as a

FIGURE 6.1 Jacques Loeb, an early student of animal behavior, argued that much or all of invertebrate behavior could be described as responses to simple stimuli, such as approaching light, turning away from light, or moving opposite to the direction of gravity.

Although the term *stimulus–response psychology* was appropriate for Loeb, it is a misleading description of today's behaviorists. Behaviorists believe that behavior is a product of not only the current stimuli but also the individual's history of stimuli and responses and their outcomes, plus the internal state of the organism, such as wakefulness or sleepiness (Staddon, 1999).

If behaviorists are to deal successfully with complex behaviors, they must be able to explain changes in behavior. The behaviorist movement became the heir to a tradition of animal learning research that had begun for other reasons. Charles Darwin's theory of evolution by natural selection inspired many early psychologists to study animal learning and intelligence (Dewsbury, 2000b). At first they were interested in comparing the intelligence of various species. By about 1930, however, most had lost interest in that topic because it seemed unanswerable. (A species that seems more intelligent on one task can be less intelligent on another.) Nevertheless, the behaviorists carried forth the tradition of experiments on animal learning, although they asked different questions.

If nonhumans learn in more or less the same way as humans do, behaviorists reasoned, then it should be possible to discover the basic laws of learning by studying the behavior of a convenient laboratory animal, such as a pigeon or a rat. This enterprise was ambitious and optimistic; its goal was no less than to determine the basic laws of behavior, analogous to the laws of physics. Most of the rest of this chapter will deal with behaviorists' research about learning.

The Assumptions of Behaviorism

Behaviorists make several assumptions, including determinism, the ineffectiveness of mental explanations, and the power of the environment to select behaviors (Moore, 1995). Let's consider each of these points.

Determinism

Behaviorists assume that we live in a universe of cause and effect; in other words they accept the idea of *determinism* as described in Chapter 1. Given that our behavior is part of the universe, it too must have causes that can be understood through scientific methods. That is, behavior follows laws, and if we determine those laws and learn enough about an individual, we should be able to predict that individual's

behavior. (Of course, it is impractical to predict behavior completely, just as it is with the weather.)

Here is one simple example of a behavioral law: An individual deprived of food will increase the rate of any behavior that leads to food. Behaviorists seek more and more detailed laws of behavior, and they test their understanding by trying to predict or control behavior.

❚ Behaviorists emphasize the role of experience in determining our actions—both our current experience and our past experiences in similar situations.

The Ineffectiveness of Mental Explanations

In everyday life we commonly refer to our motivations, emotions, and mental state. However, behaviorists insist that such statements explain nothing:

Q. Why did she yell at that man?
A. She yelled because she was angry.
Q. How do you know she was angry?
A. We know she was angry because she was yelling.

Here the reference to mental states lured us into circular reasoning. Behaviorists, especially radical behaviorists, avoid mental terms as much as possible. B. F. Skinner, the most famous and influential behaviorist, resisted using even apparently harmless words such as *hide* because they imply an intention (L. D. Smith, 1995). Skinner preferred simply to describe what the individuals *did* instead of inferring what they were *trying* to do.

The same insistence on description is central to the British and American legal systems: A witness is asked, "What did you see and hear?" An acceptable answer would be, "The defendant was sweating and trembling, and his voice was wavering." A witness should not say, "The defendant was nervous and worried," because that statement requires an inference that the witness is not entitled to make. (Of course, the jury might draw an inference.)

The Power of the Environment to Mold Behavior

Behaviors produce outcomes. Eating your carrots has one kind of outcome; insulting your roommate has another. The outcome determines how often the behavior will occur in the future. In effect our environment selects successful behaviors, much as evolution selects successful animals.

Behaviorists have sometimes been accused of believing that the environment controls practically all aspects of behavior. The most extreme statement of environmental determinism came from John B. Watson, one of the founders of behaviorism, who said, "Give me a dozen healthy infants, well-formed, and my own specified world to bring them up in and I'll guarantee to take any one at random and train him to become any type of specialist I might select—doctor, lawyer, artist, merchant-chief, and yes, even beggar-man thief—regardless of his talents, penchants, tendencies, abilities, vocations, and race of his ancestors. I am going beyond my facts and I admit it, but so have the advocates of the contrary" (1925, p. 82).

Today, few psychologists would claim that variations in behavior depend entirely on the environment (or that they depend entirely on heredity, for that matter). Although behaviorists do not deny the importance of heredity, they do not generally emphasize it. Their research focuses on how the environment selects one behavior over another, and their explanations of individual differences concentrate on how different people's behaviors emerge from different learning histories.

CONCEPT CHECK ☑

2. Why do behaviorists reject explanations in terms of thoughts? (Check your answer on this page.)

IN CLOSING

Behaviorism as a Theoretical Orientation

Many students quickly dismiss behaviorism because, at least at first glance, it seems so ridiculous: "What do you *mean,* my thoughts and beliefs and emotions don't cause my behavior?!" The behaviorists' reply is, "Exactly right. Your thoughts and other internal states do not cause your behavior because events in your present and past environment caused those thoughts.

The events that caused the thoughts are therefore the real causes of your behavior, and psychologists should spend their time trying to understand the influence of the events, not trying to analyze your thoughts." Don't be too quick to agree or disagree. Just contemplate this: If you believe that your thoughts or other internal states cause behaviors *independently* of your previous experiences, what evidence could you provide to support your claim?

Summary

* *Range of positions among behaviorists.* Behaviorists insist that psychologists should study behaviors and their relation to observable features of the environment. Methodological behaviorists use these observations to draw inferences about internal states. Radical behaviorists insist that internal states are of little scientific use and that they do not control behavior. The causes of the internal states themselves, as well as of the behaviors, lie in the environment. (page 191)

* *The origins of behaviorism.* Behaviorism began in part as a protest against structuralists, who asked people to describe their own mental processes. Behaviorists insisted that the structuralist approach was futile and that psychologists should study observable behaviors. (page 192)

* *Behaviorists' interest in learning.* Before the rise of the behaviorist movement, other psychologists had studied animal intelligence. Behaviorists adapted some of the methods used in previous studies but changed the questions, concentrating on the basic mechanisms of learning. (page 193)

* *Behaviorists' assumptions.* Behaviorists assume that all behaviors have causes (determinism), that mental explanations are unhelpful, and that the environment acts to select effective behaviors and suppress ineffective ones. (page 193)

Answers to Concept Checks

1. All behaviorists insist that conclusions must be based on measurements or observations of behavior. However, a methodological behaviorist will sometimes use behavioral observations to make inferences about motivations or other internal states. A radical behaviorist avoids discussion of internal events as much as possible and insists that internal events are never the cause of behavior. (page 192)

2. We cannot directly observe or measure thoughts or other internal events. We infer them from observed behaviors, and therefore, it is circular to use them as an explanation of behavior. (page 194)

Classical Conditioning

When we learn a relationship between two stimuli, what happens?

Do we start responding to one stimulus as if it were the other?

Or do we learn how to use information from one stimulus to predict something about the other?

You are sitting in your room when your roommate flicks a switch on the stereo. Your experience has been that the stereo is set to a deafening level. You flinch not because of the soft flicking sound of the switch itself but because of the loud noise it predicts.

Many aspects of our behavior consist of learned responses to signals. However, even apparently simple responses to simple stimuli no longer seem as simple as they once did. Psychologists' efforts to discover what takes place during learning have led them to conduct thousands of experiments on both humans and nonhumans.

For certain kinds of learning, such as birdsong learning, the results depend heavily on which species is being studied, but for many other kinds of learning, the similarities among species are more impressive than the differences. Even insects learn in ways that are surprisingly similar to our own (Giurfa, Zhang, Jennett, Menzel, & Srinivasan, 2001). In some ways it is easier to study nonhumans because a researcher can better control what and when they eat and many other variables likely to influence performance.

Pavlov and Classical Conditioning

Aristotle explained falling objects by saying that objects sought the ground, which was their natural resting place. Later explanations of falling objects, first by Newton and then by Einstein, eliminated the "seeking" and explained falling objects in purely mathematical terms.

The behaviorists tried to do the same for learning. If a cat claws at the refrigerator and meows, you might say that it "expects" food or "knows" food is in the refrigerator, but behaviorists would not. Instead, they sought simple mechanical explanations.

Therefore, the mood of the time was ready for the simple theories of Ivan P. Pavlov, a Russian physiologist who had won a Nobel Prize in physiology in 1904 for his research on digestion. As Pavlov continued his research, one day he noticed that a dog would salivate or secrete stomach juices as soon as it saw the lab worker who customarily fed the dogs. Because this secretion undoubtedly depended on the dog's previous experiences, Pavlov called it a "psychological" secretion. Pavlov enlisted the help of other specialists, who then discovered that "teasing" a dog with the sight of food produced salivation that was as predictable and automatic as any reflex. Pavlov adopted the term *conditional reflex,* implying that he only *conditionally* (or tentatively) accepted it as a reflex (Todes, 1997). However, the term has usually been translated into English as *conditioned reflex,* and that term is now well established in the literature.

▌ Ivan P. Pavlov (with the white beard) with students and a dog. Pavlov focused on limited aspects of the dog's behavior—primarily salivation—and devised some apparently simple principles to describe that behavior.

©Sovfoto/Eastfoto

Pavlov's Procedures

Pavlov guessed that animals are born with certain *automatic connections*—we call them **unconditioned reflexes**—*between a stimulus such as food and a response such as secreting digestive juices.* He conjectured that animals acquire new reflexes by transferring a response from one stimulus to another. For example, if a neutral stimulus (e.g., a buzzer) always preceded food, an animal might begin to respond to the buzzer as it responds to food. Thus, the buzzer would also elicit digestive secretions.

The *process by which an organism learns a new association between two paired stimuli—a neutral stimulus and one that already evokes a reflexive response*—has come to be known as **classical conditioning, or Pavlovian conditioning.** (It is called classical because it has been known and studied for a long time.)

Pavlov used an experimental setup like the one in Figure 6.2 (Goodwin, 1991). First, he selected dogs with a moderate degree of arousal. (Highly excitable dogs would not hold still long enough, and highly inhibited dogs would fall asleep.) Then he attached a tube to one of the salivary ducts in the dog's mouth to measure salivation. He could have measured stomach secretions, but it was easier to measure salivation.

Pavlov found that, whenever he gave a dog food, saliva flowed in the dog's mouth. The food → salivation connection was automatic, requiring no training. Pavlov called the food the unconditioned stimulus, and he called the salivation the unconditioned response. The **unconditioned stimulus (UCS)** is *an event that consistently, automatically elicits an un-*

FIGURE 6.2 Pavlov used dogs for his experiments on classical conditioning and salivation. The experimenter can ring a buzzer (CS), present food (UCS), and measure the responses (CR and UCR). Pavlov himself collected saliva with a simple measuring pouch attached to the dog's cheek; his later colleagues used a more complex device.

conditioned response, and the **unconditioned response (UCR)** is *an action that the unconditioned stimulus automatically elicits.*

Next Pavlov introduced a new stimulus, such as a metronome. Upon hearing the metronome, the dog lifted its ears and looked around but did not salivate, so the metronome was a neutral stimulus with regard to salivation. Then Pavlov sounded the metronome a couple of seconds before giving food to the dog. After a few pairings of the metronome with food, the dog began to salivate as soon as it heard the metronome (Pavlov, 1927/1960).

We call the metronome the **conditioned stimulus (CS)** because the dog's *response to it depended on the preceding conditions*—that is, the pairing of the CS with the UCS. The salivation that followed the sounding of the metronome was the **conditioned response (CR)**. The conditioned response is simply *whatever response the conditioned stimulus begins to elicit as a result of the conditioning (training) procedure.* At the start of the conditioning procedure, the conditioned stimulus does *not* elicit a conditioned response. After conditioning, it does.

In Pavlov's experiment the conditioned response (salivation) closely resembled the unconditioned response (also salivation). However, in some cases it is quite different. For example, the unconditioned response to an electric shock includes shrieking and jumping or at least flinching. The conditioned response to a stimulus paired with shock (i.e., a warning signal for shock) is a tensing of the muscles and lack of activity (e.g., Pezze, Bast, & Feldon, 2003).

To summarize, the *unconditioned stimulus (UCS),* such as food, automatically elicits the *unconditioned response (UCR),* such as salivating. A neutral stimulus, such as a sound, that is paired with the UCS becomes a *conditioned stimulus (CS).* At first this neutral stimulus elicits either no response or some irrelevant response, such as just looking around. After some number of pairings of the CS with the UCS, the conditioned stimulus elicits the *conditioned response (CR),* which usually resembles the UCR. The key difference between the CR and UCR is that the CS (conditioned stimulus) elicits the CR (conditioned response) and the UCS (unconditioned stimulus) elicits the UCR (unconditioned response). Figure 6.3 diagrams these relationships.

All else being equal, conditioning occurs more rapidly if the conditioned stimulus is unfamiliar. For example, if you heard a tone many times (followed by nothing) and then started hearing the tone followed by a puff of air to your left eye, you would be slow to show signs of conditioning. Similarly, imagine two people who are bitten by a snake. One has never been close to a snake before; the other has spent years tending snakes at the zoo. You can guess which one will develop a fear of snakes.

At first,

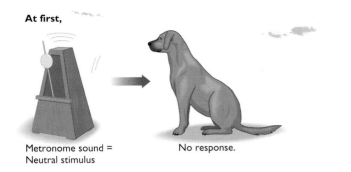

Metronome sound =
Neutral stimulus

No response.

FIGURE 6.3 With classical conditioning a conditioned stimulus is followed by an unconditioned stimulus. At first the conditioned stimulus elicits no response, and the unconditioned stimulus elicits the unconditioned response. After sufficient pairings the conditioned stimulus begins to elicit the conditioned response, which can resemble the unconditioned response.

During training,

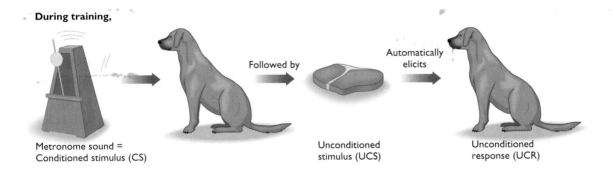

Metronome sound =
Conditioned stimulus (CS)

Followed by

Unconditioned stimulus (UCS)

Automatically elicits

Unconditioned response (UCR)

After some number of repetitions,

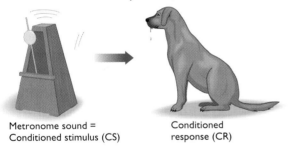

Metronome sound =
Conditioned stimulus (CS)

Conditioned response (CR)

More Examples of Classical Conditioning

Here are some other examples of classical conditioning:

- You hear a tone and then you get a puff of air to your eyes. After a few repetitions, hearing the tone makes you blink your eyes.

| Unconditioned stimulus | = air puff | → | Unconditioned response | = eye blink |
| Conditioned stimulus | = tone | → | Conditioned response | = eye blink |

- Your alarm clock makes a faint clicking sound a couple of seconds before the alarm goes off. At first the click by itself does not awaken you, but the alarm does. After a week or so, however, you awaken as soon as you hear the click.

| Unconditioned stimulus | = alarm | → | Unconditioned response | = awakening |
| Conditioned stimulus | = click | → | Conditioned response | = awakening |

- You hear the sound of a dentist's drill shortly before the unpleasant experience of the drill on your teeth. From then on the sound of a dentist's drill arouses anxiety.

| Unconditioned stimulus | = drilling | → | Unconditioned response | = tension |
| Conditioned stimulus | = sound of the drill | → | Conditioned response | = tension |

- A nursing mother responds to her baby's cries by putting the baby to her breast, stimulating the flow of milk. After a few days of repetitions, the sound of the baby's cry is enough to start the milk flowing.

| Unconditioned stimulus | = baby sucking | → | Unconditioned response | = milk flow |
| Conditioned stimulus | = baby's cry | → | Conditioned response | = milk flow |

Note the usefulness of classical conditioning in each of these cases: It prepares an individual for likely events. In some cases, however, the effects can be unwelcome.

For example, many cancer patients who have had repeated chemotherapy treatments become nauseated when they approach or even imagine the building where they received treatment (Dadds, Bovbjerg, Redd, & Cutmore, 1997).

Form an image of a lemon, a nice fresh juicy one. You cut it into slices and then suck on a slice. And then another slice. Imagine that sour taste. As you imagine the lemon, do you notice yourself salivating? If so, your imagination produced enough resemblance to the actual sight and taste of a lemon to serve as a conditioned stimulus.

CONCEPT CHECK ✓

3. At the start of training, the CS elicits ___ and the UCS elicits ___. After many repetitions of the CS followed by the UCS, the CS elicits ___ and the UCS elicits ___.

4. In this example identify the CS, UCS, CR, and UCR: Every time an army drill sergeant calls out "Ready, aim, fire," the artillery shoots, making a painfully loud sound that causes you to flinch. After a few repetitions, you tense your muscles after the word "fire," before the shot itself. (Check your answers on page 204.)

The Phenomena of Classical Conditioning

We start by discussing mostly laboratory studies but later come to an application of classical conditioning to some human experiences. The *process that establishes or strengthens a conditioned response* is known as *acquisition*. Figure 6.4 shows how the strength of a conditioned response increases after pairings of the conditioned and unconditioned stimuli. Acquisition is not the end of the story, however, because any response that can be learned can also be unlearned.

Once Pavlov had demonstrated how classical conditioning occurs, curious psychologists wondered what would happen after various changes in the procedures. Their investigations have extended our knowledge of classical conditioning. Here are a few of the main phenomena.

Extinction

Suppose I sound a buzzer and then blow a puff of air into your eyes. After a few repetitions, you will start to close your eyes as soon as you hear the buzzer (Figure 6.5). Now I sound the buzzer repeatedly without the puff of air. What do you do?

You will blink your eyes the first time and perhaps the second and third times, but before long you will stop. This decrease of the conditioned response is called **extinction** (see Figure 6.4). *To extinguish a classically conditioned response, repeatedly present the conditioned stimulus (CS) without the unconditioned stimulus (UCS).* That is, acquisition of a response (CR) occurs if the CS predicts the UCS; extinction occurs if the CS no longer predicts the UCS.

Extinction is not the same as forgetting. Both weaken a learned response, but they arise in different ways. Forgetting occurs when we have no opportunity to practice a certain behavior over a period of time. Extinction occurs as the result of a specific experience—the presentation of the conditioned stimulus without the unconditioned stimulus.

Extinction does not erase the original connection between the CS and the UCS. You might think of acquisition as learning to do a response and extinction as learning to inhibit it. For example, suppose you have gone through original learning in which a tone regularly preceded a puff of air to your eyes. You learned to blink your eyes at the tone. Then you went through an extinction process in which you heard the tone many times but received no air puffs. You extinguished, so the tone no longer elicited a blink. Now, without warning, you get another puff of air to your eyes. As a result, the next time you hear the tone, you will blink your eyes. Extinction inhibited your response to the CS (here, the tone), but a sudden puff of air weakens that inhibition (Bouton, 1994).

Phase:	Before training	Acquisition		Extinction		Pause	Spontaneous recovery
Conditioned stimulus		♪ ♪ ♪ ♪ ♪ ♪ ♪		♪ ♪ ♪ ♪ ♪ ♪ ♪ ♪ ♪ ♪			♪ ♪ ♪ ♪ ♪
Unconditioned stimulus	👁👁 👁	👁👁👁👁 👁👁					
Response	💧 💧 💧	💧 💧 💧 💧 💧 💧		💧 💧 💧 💧 💧			💧 💧

FIGURE 6.4 If the conditioned stimulus regularly precedes the unconditioned stimulus, acquisition occurs. If the conditioned stimulus is presented by itself, extinction occurs. A pause after extinction yields a brief spontaneous recovery.

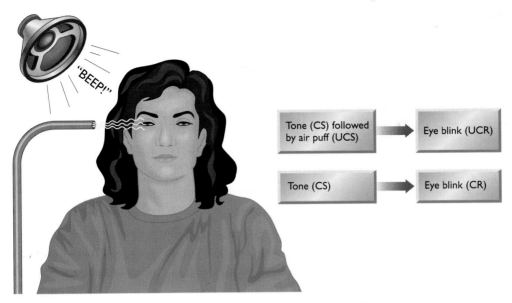

FIGURE 6.5 The procedure for classical conditioning of the eye-blink response.

Spontaneous Recovery

Suppose you are in a classical conditioning experiment. At first you repeatedly hear a buzzer sound (CS) that is always followed by a puff of air to your eyes (UCS). Then the buzzer stops predicting an air puff, and after a few trials, your response to the buzzer extinguishes. Now suppose you sit there for a long time with nothing happening and then suddenly you hear another buzzer sound. What do you suppose you will do? Chances are that you will blink your eyes at least slightly. Spontaneous recovery is *this temporary return of an extinguished response after a delay* (see Figure 6.4). Spontaneous recovery requires no additional CS–UCS pairings.

Why does spontaneous recovery take place? Think of it this way: At first the buzzer predicted a puff of air to your eyes, and then it didn't. You behaved in accordance with the more recent experiences. Hours later neither experience is much more recent than the other, and the effects of the original acquisition are almost as strong as those of extinction.

CONCEPT CHECK ☑

5. In Pavlov's experiment on conditioned salivation in response to a buzzer, what procedure could you use to produce extinction? What procedure could you use to produce spontaneous recovery? (Check your answers on page 204.)

Stimulus Generalization

Suppose your alarm clock makes a faint clicking sound (CS) a few seconds before the alarm (UCS), and you have learned to awaken as soon as you hear the

click. What if you now buy a new alarm clock? It makes a different clicking sound before the alarm goes off. Will the click awaken you?

It probably will. The closer the sound of the new click is to the original one, the more likely you are to respond by awakening (Figure 6.6). Stimulus generalization is the *extension of a conditioned response from the training stimulus to similar stimuli*.

This definition may sound pretty straightforward, but in fact psychologists find it difficult to specify exactly what "similar" means (Pearce, 1994). For example, if you hear a clicking sound somewhere other than in your bedroom or at a time other than your usual awakening time, it may be ineffective. So your response at any moment depends on how similar the total configuration of stimuli is to the set on which you were trained, and that similarity is hard to measure.

Discrimination

Suppose your alarm clock makes one kind of click when the alarm is about to ring but occasionally makes a different kind of click at other times. Eventually, you will learn to discriminate between these two clicks: You will *respond differently to the two stimuli*

FIGURE 6.6 Stimulus generalization is the process of extending a learned response to new stimuli that resemble the one used in training. As a rule a stimulus similar to the training stimulus elicits a strong response; a less similar stimulus elicits a weaker response.

because they predicted different outcomes. You will awaken when you hear one click but not when you hear the other. Similarly, you learn that one bell signals that it is time for class to start, and a different bell signals a fire.

CRITICAL THINKING:
A STEP FURTHER
Discrimination

We can easily determine how well human subjects discriminate between two stimuli. We can simply ask, "Which note has the higher pitch?" or "Which light is brighter?" How could we determine how well a non-human can discriminate between two stimuli?

CRITICAL THINKING:
WHAT'S THE EVIDENCE
Emotional Conditioning Without Awareness

In many situations conditioning occurs fastest when people are aware of the connection between the CS and UCS (Knuttinen, Power, Preston, & Disterhoft, 2001). (With laboratory animals, it is hard to ask!) However, several studies indicate that emotional responses sometimes become conditioned without awareness. If so, the implications are far-reaching. We shall examine one study in detail. In some ways this discussion will seem out of place: The whole idea of discussing attitudes, emotions, and so forth is contrary to the customs of radical behaviorism. Nevertheless, we see here how other psychologists have taken the idea of classical conditioning and applied it more broadly.

Hypothesis People will form favorable attitudes toward items paired with something they like and unfavorable attitudes toward items paired with something they dislike, even if they are not aware of the connection (Olson & Fazio, 2001).

Method Forty-five female college students viewed a series of slides. Most included a Pokemon image, as shown in Figure 6.7, although a few were blank. Most of those with a Pokemon also included another picture or a word. Each student's task was to look for a particular "target" Pokemon and press a computer key whenever she saw it, ignoring all the other pictures and words. One of the "other" nontarget Pokemon images was always paired with something likable, such as a picture of tasty food or the word "excellent." Another nontarget Pokemon image was always paired with something negative, such as a picture of a cockroach or the word "terrible." Still other Pokemon images were paired with neutral or varying words and pictures. After viewing all the slides repeatedly, each student was asked to look at all the Pokemon images (by themselves) and rate how pleasant or unpleasant they were. They were also asked whether they remembered what other items had paired with each Pokemon.

FIGURE 6.7 One Pokemon was the target, and the participant was to press a key whenever she saw it. Among the others, which she was to ignore, one was always paired with a pleasant word or image, another was always paired with something unpleasant, and still others were not consistently paired with anything either pleasant or unpleasant.

Results On the average the women gave a higher pleasantness rating to the Pokemon that had been associated with favorable words and pictures and lower ratings to the one associated with unfavorable words and pictures. However, they did not remember what words or pictures had been associated with each Pokemon. (They hadn't been told to pay attention to those pairings, and they didn't.)

Interpretation The attitudes that people express ("I like it" or "I don't like it") presumably reflect emotional responses. These results show classical conditioning of attitudes or emotional responses based on pairings of words and images, even though people did not notice them enough to report explicit memories.

Drug Tolerance as an Example of Classical Conditioning

Classical conditioning sometimes occurs in surprising ways. One example is **drug tolerance:** *Users of certain drugs experience progressively weaker effects after taking the drugs repeatedly.* Consequently, the users crave ever larger amounts of the drug.

Drug tolerance depends partly on classical conditioning. Consider: When drug users inject themselves with morphine or heroin, the drug injection procedure is an elaborate stimulus that includes the time and place as well as the needle injection itself. This total stimulus reliably predicts a second stimulus, the drug's entry into the brain, which triggers a variety of body defenses against its effects—for example, changes in hormone secretions, heart rate, and breathing rate.

First stimulus → Second stimulus → Automatic response
(Injection   (Drug enters   (Body's defenses)
procedure)   brain)

Whenever one stimulus predicts a second stimulus that produces an automatic response, the conditions are present for classical conditioning. The first stimulus becomes the CS, the second becomes the UCS, and its response is the UCR. So we can relabel as follows:

Conditioned → Unconditioned → Unconditioned
stimulus   stimulus   response
(Injection   (Drug enters   (Body's defenses)
procedure)   brain)

If conditioning occurs here, what would be the consequences? Suppose the CS (drug injection) produces a CR that resembles the UCR (the body's defenses against the drug). The result is that as soon as the person starts injecting the drug, before it even enters the body, the body is already mobilizing its defenses against the drug. Therefore, the drug will have less effect. In other words the body develops tolerance. Shepard Siegel (1977, 1983) has confirmed that classical conditioning occurs during drug injections. That is, after many drug injections, the injection procedure by itself evokes the body's anti-drug defenses:

Conditioned stimulus   →   Conditioned response
(Injection procedure)   (Body's defenses)

One prediction was as follows: If the injection procedure serves as a conditioned stimulus, then the body's defense reactions should be strongest if the drug is administered in the usual way, in the usual location, with as many familiar stimuli as possible. (The whole experience constitutes the conditioned stimulus.)

The evidence strongly supports this prediction for a variety of drugs (Marin, Perez, Duero, & Ramirez, 1999; Siegel, 1983). For example, a rat that is repeatedly injected with alcohol develops a tolerance, improving its balance while intoxicated. But if it is now tested in the presence of loud sounds and strobe lights, its balance suffers. Conversely, if it had practiced its balance while intoxicated in the presence of loud sounds and strobe lights, its balance suffers if it is tested *without* those stimuli (Larson & Siegel, 1998). In short, the tolerance depends on learning.

Why do some people die of a drug overdose that is no larger than the dose they normally tolerate? They probably took the fatal overdose in an unfamiliar setting. For example, someone who is accustomed to taking a drug at home in the evening could suffer a fatal reaction from taking it at a friend's house in the morning. Because the new setting did not serve as a CS, it failed to trigger the usual drug tolerance.

CONCEPT CHECK ☑

6. When an individual develops tolerance to the effects of a drug injection, what are the conditioned stimulus, the unconditioned stimulus, the conditioned response, and the unconditioned response?
7. Within the classical-conditioning interpretation of drug tolerance, what procedure should extinguish tolerance? (Check your answers on page 204.)

Explanations of Classical Conditioning

What is classical conditioning, really? As is often the case, the process appeared at first to be fairly simple, but later investigation found it to be a more complex and indeed more interesting phenomenon.

Pavlov noted that conditioning depended on the timing between CS and UCS, as shown here:

Forward (delayed) conditioning: CS comes first, but continues until US.
Conditioning occurs readily.

Forward (trace) conditioning: CS comes first, ends before start of US.
Conditioning occurs readily, but response is sometimes weak.

Forward (trace) conditioning with longer delay:
Conditioning is weaker.

Simultaneous conditioning: In most cases, conditioning is weak or hard to demonstrate.

Backward conditioning: After a few repetitions, CS becomes inhibitory— that is, a signal for a time of *absence* of the US.

In these displays read time left to right. Pavlov surmised that presenting the CS and UCS at nearly the same time caused the growth of a connection in the brain so that the animal treated the CS as if it were the UCS. Figure 6.8a illustrates the connections before the start of training: The UCS excites a UCS center in the brain, which immediately stimulates the UCR center. Figure 6.8b illustrates connections that develop during conditioning: Pairing the CS and UCS causes the development of a connection between their brain representations. After this connection develops, the CS excites the CS center, which excites the UCS center, which excites the UCR center and produces a response.

Later studies contradicted that idea. For example, a shock (UCS) causes rats to jump and shriek, but a conditioned stimulus paired with shock makes rats freeze in position. They react to the conditioned stimulus as a danger signal, not as if it were itself a shock. Also, in delay conditioning (Figure 6.8), where a delay separates the end of the CS from the start of the UCS, the animal does not make a conditioned response immediately after the conditioned stimulus, but instead waits until almost the end of the usual delay between CS and UCS. Again, it is not treating the CS as if it were the UCS; it is using it as a predictor, a way to prepare for the UCS (Gallistel & Gibbon, 2000).

It is true, as Pavlov suggested, that the longer the delay between the CS and the UCS, the weaker the conditioning, all other things being equal. However, just having the CS and UCS close together in time is

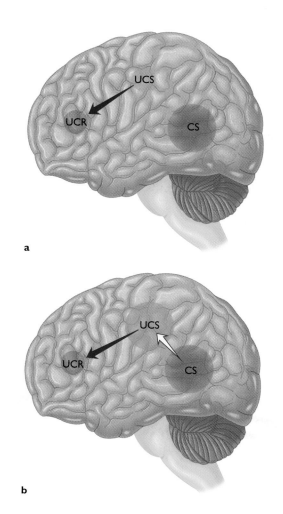

FIGURE 6.8 Pavlov believed that conditioning depended on presenting the CS and UCS at nearly the same time: (a) At the start of conditioning, activity in the UCS center automatically causes activation of the UCR center. At this time activity of the CS center does not affect the UCS center. (b) After sufficient pairings of the CS and UCS, their simultaneous activity causes the growth of a connection between the CS and UCS centers. Afterward, activity in the CS center will flow to the UCS center and therefore excite the UCR center.

not enough. What is essential is for them to occur more often together than they occur apart. That is, there must be some contingency or predictability between them. Consider this experiment: For rats in both Group 1 and Group 2, every presentation of a CS is followed shortly thereafter by a UCS, as shown in Figure 6.9. However, for Group 2, the UCS also appears at many other times, without the CS. In other words, for this group, the UCS is going to happen every few seconds anyway, and it isn't much more likely with the CS than without it. Group 1 learns a strong response to the CS; Group 2 does not (Rescorla, 1968, 1988).

Group 1

Group 2

FIGURE 6.9 In Rescorla's experiment the CS was always followed by the UCS in both groups, but Group 2 received the UCS frequently at other times also. Group 1 developed a strong conditioned response to the CS; Group 2 did not.

CONCEPT CHECK ✓

8. If classical conditioning depended *entirely* on presenting the CS and UCS at nearly the same time, what result should the experimenters have obtained in this experiment? (Check your answer on page 205.)

Also consider this experiment: One group of rats receives a light (CS) followed by shock (UCS) until

they respond consistently to the light. (The response is to freeze in place.) Then they get a series of trials with both a light and a tone, again followed by shock. Do they learn a response to the tone? No. The tone always precedes the shock, but the light already predicted the shock, and the tone adds nothing new. The same pattern occurs with the reverse order: First rats learn a response to the tone and then they get light–tone combinations before the shock. They continue responding to the tone, but not to the light, again because the new stimulus predicted nothing that wasn't already predicted (Kamin, 1969) (see Figure 6.10). These results demonstrate the **blocking effect:** *The previously established association to one stimulus blocks the formation of an association to the added stimulus.* Again, it appears that conditioning depends on more than presenting two stimuli together in time; learning occurs only when one stimulus predicts another.

Group 1

Group 2

FIGURE 6.10 Each rat first learned to associate either light or sound with shock. Then it received a compound of both light and sound followed by shock. Each rat continued to show a strong response to the old stimulus (which already predicted shock) but little to the new one.

9. Suppose you have already learned to flinch when you hear the sound of a dentist's drill. Now your dentist turns on some soothing background music at the same time as the drill. The background music is paired with the pain just as much as the drill sound is. Will you learn to flinch at the sound of that background music? (Check your answer on page 205.)

IN CLOSING

Classical Conditioning Is More Than Drooling Dogs

People sometimes use the term "Pavlovian" to mean simple, mechanical, robotlike behavior. But Pavlovian or classical conditioning is not a mark of stupidity: It is a way of responding to relationships among events, a way of preparing us for what is likely to happen. Classical conditioning requires processing a fair amount of information.

Classical conditioning is important for some aspects of our behavior but less important for others. It alters our motivational or emotional reactions to stimuli, including responses related to fear, preparations for eating, preparations for a drug injection, and so forth. But it does not control walking toward or away from various stimuli. That is, classical conditioning might tell us to be afraid, but it does not tell us how to avoid the frightening item. It might tell us to salivate in preparation for eating, but it does not tell us how to find food. Other types of learning can answer these other questions, as we shall see in the next module.

Summary

- *Classical conditioning.* Ivan Pavlov discovered classical conditioning, the process by which an organism learns a new association between two stimuli that have been paired with each other—a neutral stimulus (the conditioned stimulus) and one that initially evokes a reflexive response (the unconditioned stimulus). The organism displays this association by responding in a new way (the conditioned response) to the conditioned stimulus. (page 195)

- *Extinction.* After classical conditioning has established a conditioned response to a stimulus, the response can be extinguished by repeatedly presenting that stimulus by itself. (page 198)

- *Spontaneous recovery.* If the conditioned stimulus is not presented at all for some time after extinction and is then presented again, the conditioned response may return to some degree. That return is called spontaneous recovery. (page 199)

- *Stimulus generalization.* An individual who learns to respond to one stimulus will respond similarly to similar stimuli. However, it is difficult to specify how we should measure similarity. (page 199)

- *Discrimination.* If one stimulus is followed by an unconditioned stimulus and another similar stimulus is not, the individual will come to discriminate between these two stimuli. (page 199)

- *Emotional conditioning without awareness.* In many situations conditioning is strongest if the learner is aware of the CS–UCS connection. However, some subtle emotional responses can be conditioned even if the learner is not aware of the connection or even not aware of the CS at all. (page 200)

- *Drug tolerance.* Drug tolerance is partly a form of classical conditioning in which the drug administration procedure comes to evoke defensive responses by the body. (page 201)

- *Basis for classical conditioning.* Pavlov believed that conditioning occurred because presenting two stimuli close to each other in time caused the growth of a connection between their representations in the brain. Later research showed that animals do not treat the conditioned stimulus as if it were the unconditioned stimulus. Also, being close in time is not enough; learning requires that the first stimulus predict the second stimulus. (page 201)

Answers to Concept Checks

3. No response (or at least nothing of interest) . . . the UCR . . . the CR . . . still the UCR. (page 198)

4. The conditioned stimulus is the sound "Ready, aim, fire." The unconditioned stimulus is the artillery shot. The unconditioned response is flinching; the conditioned response is tensing. (page 198)

5. To bring about extinction, present the buzzer repeatedly without presenting any food. To bring about spontaneous recovery, first bring about extinction; then wait hours or days and present the buzzer again. (page 199)

6. The conditioned stimulus is the injection procedure. The unconditioned stimulus is the entry of the drug into the brain. Both the conditioned response and the unconditioned response are the body's defenses against the drug. (page 201)

7. To extinguish tolerance, present the injection procedure (conditioned stimulus) without injecting the drug (unconditioned stimulus). Instead,

inject just water or salt water. Siegel (1977) demonstrated that repeated injections of salt water do reduce tolerance to morphine in rats. (page 201)

8. If classical conditioning depended entirely on presenting the CS and UCS at nearly the same time, the rats in both groups would have responded equally to the conditioned stimulus, re-gardless of how often they received the unconditioned stimulus at other times. (page 203)

9. No, you will not learn to flinch at the sound of the background music. Because the drill sound already predicted the pain, the new stimulus is un-informative and will not be strongly associated with the pain. (page 204)

Operant Conditioning

How do the consequences of our behaviors affect future behaviors?

Sometimes a simple idea, or at least one that sounds simple, can be amazingly powerful. In this module we consider the simple but powerful idea that behaviors become more likely or less likely because of their consequences. In other words we either repeat a behavior or cease it depending on the outcome.

Thorndike and Operant Conditioning

Shortly before Pavlov's research, Edward L. Thorndike (1911/1970), a Harvard graduate student, began training some cats in a basement. Saying that earlier experiments had dealt only with animal intelligence, never with animal stupidity, he devised a simple behavioristic explanation of learning. Thorndike put cats into puzzle boxes (Figure 6.11) from which they could escape by pressing a lever, pulling a string, or tilting a pole. Sometimes he placed food outside the box. (Usually, though, cats worked just to escape from the box.) The cats learned to make whatever response opened the box, especially if the box opened immediately.

The learning was strictly trial and error. When a cat had to tilt a pole to escape from the box, it would first paw or gnaw at the door, scratch the walls, or

FIGURE 6.11 Each of Thorndike's puzzle boxes had a device that could open it. Here tilting the pole will open the door. *(Based on Thorndike, 1911/1970)*

pace back and forth. Eventually, it would bump against the pole by accident and the door would open. The next time, the cat would go through the same repertoire of behaviors but might bump against the pole a little sooner. Over many trials the time it took the cat to escape grew shorter in a gradual and irregular fashion. Figure 6.12 shows a learning curve to represent this behavior. A **learning curve** is *a graph of the changes in behavior that occur over the course of learning.*

FIGURE 6.12 As the data from one of Thorndike's experiments show, the time that a cat needs to escape from a puzzle box decreases gradually, but in an irregular manner. Thorndike concluded that the cat did not at any point "suddenly get the idea." Instead, reinforcement gradually increased the probability of the successful behavior.

Had the cat "figured out" how to escape? Had it come to "understand" the connection between bumping against the pole and opening the door? No, said Thorndike. If the cat had gained a new insight at some point, its speed of escaping would have increased suddenly at that time. Instead, the cat's performance improved slowly and inconsistently, suggesting no point of insight or understanding.

Thorndike concluded that learning occurs only when certain behaviors are strengthened at the expense of others. An animal enters a given situation with a certain repertoire of responses such as pawing the door, scratching the walls, pacing, and so forth (labeled R_1, R_2, R_3, . . . in Figure 6.13). First, the animal engages in its most probable response for this situation (R_1). If nothing special happens, it proceeds to other responses, eventually reaching a response that opens the door—for example, bumping against the pole (R₇ in this example). The opening of the door serves as a reinforcement.

A **reinforcement** is *an event that increases the future probability of the most recent response.* Thorndike said that it "stamps in," or strengthens, the response. The next time the cat is in the puzzle box, it has a slightly higher probability of bumping the lever; after each succeeding reinforcement, the probability goes up another notch until it becomes the most probable response and the cat escapes quickly (Figure 6.13c).

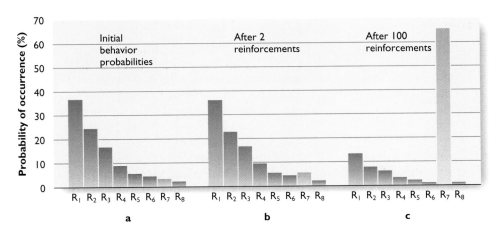

FIGURE 6.13 According to Thorndike, a cat starts with a large set of potential behaviors in a given situation. When one of these, such as bumping against a pole, leads to reinforcement, the future probability of that behavior increases. We do not need to assume that the cat understands what it is doing or why.

Thorndike summarized his views in the **law of effect** (Thorndike, 1911/1970, p. 244): *"Of several responses made to the same situation, those which are accompanied or closely followed by satisfaction to the animal will, other things being equal, be more firmly connected with the situation, so that, when it recurs, they will be more likely to recur."* In other words the animal becomes more likely to repeat the responses that led to favorable consequences even if it does not understand why. In fact it doesn't need to "understand" anything at all. A fairly simple machine could produce responses at random and then repeat the ones that led to reinforcement.

Thorndike revolutionized the study of animal learning, substituting experimentation for the collection of anecdotes. He also demonstrated the possibility of simple explanations for apparently complex behaviors (Dewsbury, 1998). On the negative side, he set the example of studying animals in contrived laboratory situations unrelated to their normal way of life (Galef, 1998).

The kind of learning that Thorndike studied is known as **operant conditioning** (because the subject *operates* on the environment to produce an outcome), or **instrumental conditioning** (because the subject's behavior is *instrumental* in producing the outcome). Operant or instrumental conditioning is *the process of changing behavior by following a response with reinforcement.* The defining difference between operant conditioning and classical conditioning is the procedure: *In operant conditioning the subject's behavior determines an outcome and is affected by the outcome. In classical conditioning the subject's behavior has no effect on the outcome (the presentation of either the CS or the UCS).* For example, in classical conditioning the experimenter (or the world) presents two stimuli at particular times, regardless of what the individual does or doesn't do. In operant conditioning the individual has to make some response before the reinforcement can occur.

In general the two kinds of conditioning also differ in the behaviors they affect. Classical conditioning applies primarily to **visceral** responses (i.e., *responses of the internal organs*), such as salivation and digestion, whereas operant conditioning applies primarily to **skeletal** responses (i.e., *movements of leg muscles, arm muscles, etc.*). However, this distinction sometimes breaks down. For example, if a tone is consistently followed by an electric shock (a classical-conditioning procedure), the tone will make the animal freeze in position (a skeletal response) as well as increase its heart rate (a visceral response).

CONCEPT CHECK ☑

10. When I ring a bell, an animal sits up on its hind legs and drools; then I give it some food. Is the animal's behavior an example of classical conditioning or operant conditioning? So far, you do not have enough information to answer the question. What else would you need to know before you could answer? (Check your answer on page 219.)

Reinforcement and Punishment

What constitutes reinforcement? From a practical standpoint, a **reinforcer** is *an event that follows a response and increases the later probability or fre-*

Items that serve as reinforcers for one person might not for another. Lucy Pearson (left) has collected over 110,000 hubcaps. Jim Hambrick (right) collects Superman items.

quency of that response. However, from a theoretical standpoint, we would like to have some way of predicting what would be a reinforcer and what would not. We might guess that reinforcers are biologically useful to the individual, but in fact many are not. For example, saccharin, a sweet but biologically useless chemical, can be a reinforcer. For many people alcohol and tobacco are stronger reinforcers than vitamin-rich vegetables. So biological usefulness doesn't define reinforcement.

In his law of effect, Thorndike described reinforcers as events that brought "satisfaction to the animal." That definition won't work, either. We do not know what brings "satisfaction," and more important, we see that people will work very hard for a paycheck, a decent grade in a course, or other outcomes that don't produce clear evidence of pleasure (Berridge & Robinson, 1995).

David Premack (1965) proposed a simple rule, now known as the **Premack principle:** *The opportunity to engage in frequent behavior* (e.g., eating) *will be a reinforcer for any less frequent behavior* (e.g., lever pressing). A great strength of this idea is that it recognizes that what is a reinforcer for one individual may not be for another and what works at one time may not work at another. For example, if you ordinarily spend more time reading than watching television, someone could increase your television watching by reinforcing you with books. For someone else it might be possible to reinforce reading by opportunities to watch television.

The limitation of the Premack principle is that we are sometimes reinforced by opportunities for uncommon behaviors. For example, if we watched how often people did various acts, we might not guess that someone who almost never had sex would be strongly reinforced by an opportunity for sex. Also, how much time do you spend clipping your toenails during an average week? Almost none? Still, if you are badly overdue for

clipping them, an opportunity to do so would be reinforcing. So the key is not how often you do something, but whether you have recently been doing it less often than you would like. According to the **disequilibrium principle** of reinforcement, *each of us has a normal, or "equilibrium," state. When at equilibrium, we divide our time among activities in a preferred way, and if we are removed from that state, a return to it will be reinforcing* (Farmer-Dougan, 1998; Timberlake & Farmer-Dougan, 1991). For example, suppose that if you had no one telling you what to do, you would spend 30% of your day sleeping, 10% eating, 12% exercising, 11% reading, 9% talking with friends, 3% grooming, 3% playing the piano, and so forth. If you have been forced to spend less than this amount of time on one of those activities, then the opportunity to engage in that activity will be reinforcing to you.

CONCEPT CHECK ✓

11. Suppose you want to reinforce a child for doing chores around the house, and you don't know what would be a good reinforcer. According to the disequilibrium principle, how should you proceed? (Check your answer on page 219.)

Primary and Secondary Reinforcers

Psychologists distinguish between **primary reinforcers** (or *unconditioned reinforcers*), *which are reinforcing because of their own properties,* and **secondary reinforcers** (or *conditioned reinforcers*), *which became reinforcing because of previous experiences.* Food and water are primary reinforcers. Coins and bills (secondary reinforcers) become reinforcing because they can be exchanged for food or other primary reinforcers. A student learns that good grades will win the approval of parents and teachers;

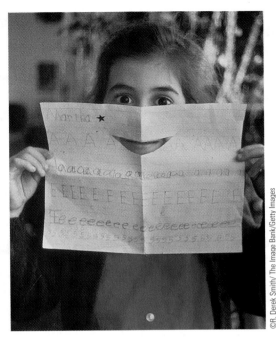

❙ Many conditioned reinforcers are surprisingly powerful. Consider, for example, how hard some children will work for a little gold star that the teacher pastes on an assignment.

an employee learns that increased sales will win the approval of an employer. In this case secondary just means learned; do not by any means assume that secondary reinforcers are weak. We spend most of our time working for secondary reinforcers.

Punishment

In contrast to a *reinforcer,* which increases the probability of a response, a **punishment** is *an event that decreases the probability of a response.* A reinforcer can be either the presentation of something (like food) or the removal of something (like pain). A punishment can be either the presentation of something (like pain) or the removal of something (like food).

In some cases punishment or the threat of punishment is ineffective. You already know that from human behavior; if the threat of punishment were always effective, we wouldn't have to worry about crime. B. F. Skinner (1938) also showed punishment to be ineffective in a famous laboratory study. He first trained food-deprived rats to press a bar to get food and then stopped reinforcing their bar presses. For the first 10 minutes, some rats not only failed to get food but had the bar slap their paws every time they pressed it. The punished rats temporarily suppressed their bar-pressing, but in the long run, they made as many presses as did the unpunished rats. Skinner concluded that punishment temporarily suppressed behavior but produced no long-term effects.

That conclusion, however, is an overstatement (Staddon, 1993). A better conclusion would have been that punishment does not greatly weaken a response when no other response is available. Skinner's food-deprived rats had no other way to seek food. Similarly, if someone punished you for breathing, you would continue breathing, but not because you were a slow learner.

Is physical punishment of children, such as spanking, a good or bad idea? Most American parents spank their children at times, whereas spanking is uncommon or even illegal in many other countries. Many psychologists recommend against it, although the research findings are marred by several difficulties. Researchers almost always have to rely on parents' self-reports, which no doubt misstate the amount of spanking. Also, many studies do not distinguish adequately between mild spanking and physical abuse.

A review of the literature found that physical punishment had one clear benefit, which was immediate compliance. That is, if you want your child to stop doing something at once, a quick spank or slap on the hand will work (Gershoff, 2002). Punishment produces compliance especially if it is quick and predictable. If you *might* get punished a long time from now, the effects are weak and variable. The threat of punishment for crime is often ineffective because the punishment is uncertain and long delayed.

On the negative side, however, children who are spanked tend to be more aggressive than other children, more prone to antisocial and criminal behavior in both adolescence and later adulthood, and less healthy mentally. On the average they have a worse relationship with their parents, and they are more likely than others later to become abusive toward their own children or spouse (Gershoff, 2002).

Now, can we draw the conclusion that physical punishment leads to all these undesirable consequences? I hope you see immediately that we cannot. A quick summary of the results is that parents who spank their children are more likely than others to have ill-behaved children. Sure, it is possible that spanking *caused* children to become violent and poorly adjusted, but it is also possible that being violent and poorly adjusted led to the spankings (Baumrind, Larzelere, & Cowan, 2002).

Psychologists are virtually unanimous in recommending against severe punishment or any physical punishment before age 18 months or after the onset of puberty (Baumrind et al., 2002). On the issue of mild physical punishment for children between 18 months and puberty, the research data are not conclusive. (You might contemplate the difficulty of obtaining conclusive results, given the ethical impossibility of randomly assigning children to spanking or non-spanking groups.)

12. The U.S. government imposes strict punishments for selling illegal drugs. Based on what you have just read, why are those punishments ineffective for many people? (Check your answer on page 219.)

Categories of Reinforcement and Punishment

As mentioned, a reinforcement can be either the onset of something like food or the removal of something like pain. Of course, what works as a reinforcer for one person at one time may not for another person or at another time. A punishment also can be either the onset or offset of something. Psychologists use different terms to distinguish these possibilities, as shown in Table 6.1.

Note that the upper left and lower right of the table both show reinforcement; either gaining food or preventing pain will *increase* the behavior. The items in the upper right and lower left are both punishment; preventing food or gaining pain will *decrease* the behavior. Food and pain are, of course, just examples; many other events serve as reinforcers or punishers. Let's go through these terms and procedures, beginning in the upper left of the table and proceeding clockwise.

Positive reinforcement is the *presentation of an event* (e.g., food or money) *that strengthens or increases the likelihood of a behavior.*

Punishment occurs when a response is followed by an event such as pain; the frequency of the response then decreases. For example, you put your hand on a hot stove and burn yourself, and you learn to stop doing that. Punishment is also called **passive**

avoidance learning because *the individual learns to avoid an outcome by being passive* (e.g., by *not* putting your hand on the stove).

Try not to be confused by the term negative reinforcement. Remember that **negative reinforcement is** *a kind of reinforcement (not a punishment), and therefore it increases the frequency of a behavior. It is "negative" in the sense that the reinforcement is the absence of something.* For example, you learn to apply sunscreen to avoid skin cancer, and you learn to brush your teeth to avoid tooth decay. With negative reinforcement the behavior increases and the outcome deceases. Negative reinforcement is also known as **avoidance learning** *if the response prevents the outcome altogether* or **escape learning** *if it makes some outcome stop after it has already begun.* Most people find the terms "escape learning" and "avoidance learning" less confusing than "negative reinforcement" (see Kimble, 1993), but you should understand all of these terms.

If reinforcement by avoiding something bad is negative reinforcement, then *punishment by avoiding something good is* **negative punishment.** If your parents punished you by taking away your allowance, your television privileges, or your travel privileges ("grounding you"), they were using negative punishment. Another example is a teacher punishing a child by a "time out" session away from classmates. Although this practice is common, the term negative punishment is not widely used. The practice is usually known simply as punishment or as **omission training** *because the omission of the response leads to restoration of the usual privileges.*

Classifying some procedure in one of these four categories is sometimes tricky. If you are told you

TABLE 6.1 Four Categories of Operant Conditioning

	Event Such as Food	Event Such as Pain
Behavior leads to the event	**Positive Reinforcement** *Result:* Increase in the behavior, reinforced by presentation of food. *Example:* "If you clean your room, I'll get you a pizza tonight."	**Punishment = Passive Avoidance Learning** *Result:* Decrease in the behavior, and therefore a decrease in pain. *Example:* "If you insult me, I'll slap you."
Behavior avoids the event	**Negative Punishment = Omission Training** *Result:* Decrease in the behavior, and therefore food continues to be available. *Example:* "If you hit your little brother again, you'll get no dessert."	**Negative Reinforcement = Escape or Avoidance Learning** *Result:* Increase in the behavior, and therefore a decrease in pain. *Example:* "If you go into the office over there, the doctor will remove the thorn from your leg."

can be suspended from school for academic dishonesty, you can think of it as being honest in order to stay in school (positive reinforcement), being honest in order to avoid suspension (negative reinforcement or avoidance learning), decreasing dishonesty in order to avoid suspension (punishment or passive avoidance), or decreasing dishonesty in order to stay in school (negative punishment or omission training). Sorry about that. Just attend to how something is worded: Are we talking about increasing or decreasing some behavior, and increasing or decreasing some outcome? Practice with the concept check that follows.

CONCEPT CHECK ☑

13. Identify each of the following examples using the terms in Table 6.1:
    a. Your employer gives you bonus pay for working overtime.
    b. You learn to stop playing your accordion at 5 A.M. because your roommate threatens to kill you if you do it again.
    c. You turn off a dripping faucet, ending the "drip drip drip" sound.
    d. You learn to drink less beer than you once did because you have felt sick after drinking too much.
    e. Your swimming coach says you cannot go to the next swim meet (which you are looking forward to) if you break a training rule.
    f. If you get a speeding ticket, you will temporarily lose the privilege of driving the family car.
    g. You learn to come inside when a storm is brewing to avoid getting wet. (Check your answers on page 219.)

CRITICAL THINKING:
A STEP FURTHER
Using Reinforcement

Your local school board proposes to improve class attendance by lowering the grades of any student who misses a certain number of classes. Might the board achieve the same goal more effectively by using positive reinforcement?

Additional Phenomena of Operant Conditioning

Recall the concepts of extinction, generalization, and discrimination in classical conditioning. The same concepts apply to operant conditioning, although the procedures are a little different.

Extinction

No doubt you are familiar with the saying, "If at first you don't succeed, try, try again." Better advice is, "Try again, but differently!" After all, you may be doing something wrong.

In operant conditioning **extinction** *occurs if responses stop producing reinforcements*. For example, you were once in the habit of asking your roommate to join you for supper. The last five times you asked, your roommate said no, so you stop asking. In classical conditioning extinction is achieved by presenting the CS without the UCS; in operant conditioning, the procedure is response without reinforcement. Table 6.2 compares classical and operant conditioning.

TABLE 6.2 Classical Conditioning and Operant Conditioning

	Classical Conditioning	Operant Conditioning
Terminology	CS, UCS, CR, UCR	Response, reinforcement
Behavior	Does not control UCS	Controls reinforcement
Paired during acquisition	Two stimuli (CS and UCS)	Response and reinforcement (in the presence of certain stimuli)
Responses	Mostly visceral (internal organs)	Mostly skeletal muscles
Extinction procedure	CS without UCS	Response without reinforcement

Generalization, Discrimination, and Discriminative Stimuli

Someone who receives reinforcement for a response in the presence of one stimulus will probably make the same response in the presence of a similar stimulus. *The more similar a new stimulus is to the original reinforced stimulus, the more likely the same response.* This phenomenon is known as **stimulus generalization.** For example, you might reach for the turn signal in a rented car in the same place you would find it in your own car.

If reinforcement occurs for responding to one stimulus and not another, the result is a **discrimination** between them and *a response to one stimulus and not the other.* For example, you walk toward a parked car that you think is yours, but then you realize it is not. After several such experiences, you learn to identify your own car from a distance.

A *stimulus that indicates which response is appropriate or inappropriate* is called a **discriminative**

animals in an operant-conditioning chamber. When the light above the bar is on, pressing the bar is reinforced. A food pellet rolls out of the storage device (left) and down the tube into the cage.

Does that definition make sense? Skinner's reply was that it did because it led to consistent results in his research. Skinner's procedures became standard

food. Then it is put on the intermediate platform with a ladder in place leading to the top platform. The rat learns to climb the ladder. After it has done so repeatedly, it is placed again on the intermediate platform, but this time the ladder is not present. It must learn to pull a string to raise the ladder so that it can climb to the top platform. Then the rat is placed on the bottom platform (Figure 6.16a). It

stimulus. A great deal of our behavior is governed by discriminative stimuli. For example, you learn ordinarily to be quiet in class but to talk when the professor encourages discussion. You learn to drive fast on some streets and slow on others. Throughout your day one stimulus after another signals which behaviors will yield reinforcement, punishment, or neither. *The*

However, belongingness may not be the whole explanation for why Thorndike's cats were slow to associate scratching themselves with escaping from a box: Perhaps a cat scratches itself only when it itches (Charlton, 1983). Suppose someone said you could win a large prize if you finished first in a rapid saliva-swallowing contest. (Why not? People compete at

now has to learn to climb the ladder to the intermediate platform, pull a string to raise the ladder, and then climb the ladder again. We could, of course, extend the chain still further. Each behavior is reinforced with the opportunity for the next behavior, except for the final behavior, which is reinforced with food.

People learn to make chains of responses too. First, you learned to eat with a fork and spoon. Later, you learned to put your own food on the plate before eating. Eventually, you learned to plan a menu, go to the store, buy the ingredients, cook the meal, put it on the plate, and then eat it. Each behavior is reinforced by the opportunity to engage in the next behavior.

To show how effective shaping and chaining can be, Skinner performed this demonstration: First, he trained a rat to go to the center of a cage. Then he trained it to do so only when he was playing a certain piece of music. Next he trained it to wait for the music, go to the center of the cage, and sit up on its hind legs. Step by step, he eventually trained the rat to wait for the music (which happened to be the "Star-Spangled Banner"), move to the center of the cage, sit up on its hind legs, put its claws on a string next to a pole, pull the string to hoist the U.S. flag, and then salute it. Only then did the rat get its reinforcement. Needless to say, a display of patriotism is not part of a rat's usual repertoire of behavior.

A   B   C

D   E   F

©TIME Inc./Robert Kelly, Life Magazine

FIGURE 6.16 Chaining is a procedure in which the reinforcement for one behavior is the opportunity to engage in the next behavior. To reach food on the top platform, this rat must climb a ladder (a, b) and pull a string to raise the ladder (c, d) so that it can climb up again (e, f). The final behavior is reinforced by food.

Schedules of Reinforcement

The simplest procedure in operant conditioning is to provide reinforcement every time the correct response occurs. **Continuous reinforcement** refers to *reinforcement for every correct response.* As you know, not every response in the real world leads to reinforcement.

Reinforcement for some responses and not for others is known as **intermittent reinforcement.** We behave differently when we learn that only some of our responses will be reinforced. Psychologists have investigated the effects of many **schedules of reinforcement,** which are *rules or procedures for the delivery of reinforcement.* Four schedules for delivery of intermittent reinforcement are fixed ratio, fixed interval, variable ratio, and variable interval (see

TABLE 6.3 Some Schedules of Reinforcement

Type	Description
Continuous	Reinforcement for every response of the correct type
Fixed ratio	Reinforcement following completion of a specific number of responses
Variable ratio	Reinforcement for an unpredictable number of responses that varies around a mean value
Fixed interval	Reinforcement for the first response that follows a given delay since the previous reinforcement
Variable interval	Reinforcement for the first response that follows an unpredictable delay (varying around a mean value) since the previous reinforcement

Table 6.3). A ratio schedule provides reinforcements depending on the number of responses. An interval schedule provides reinforcements depending on the timing of responses.

Fixed-Ratio Schedule

A **fixed-ratio schedule** *provides a reinforcement only after a certain (fixed) number of correct responses have been made*—after every sixth response, for example. We see similar behavior among pieceworkers in a factory whose pay depends on how many pieces they turn out or among fruit pickers who get paid by the bushel.

The response rate for a fixed-ratio schedule tends to be rapid and steady. Researchers sometimes graph the results with a *cumulative record,* in which each response is noted by a movement upward that is added to the previous level. That is, the line is flat when the animal does not respond; it moves up with each response. For a fixed-ratio schedule, a typical result would look like this:

However, if the schedule requires a large number of responses for reinforcement, there may be a temporary interruption after each reinforced response. For example, if you have just completed 10 calculus problems, you may pause briefly before starting your French assignment; after completing 100 problems, you would pause even longer.

Variable-Ratio Schedule

A **variable-ratio schedule** is similar to a fixed-ratio schedule except that *reinforcement is provided after a variable number of correct responses.* For example, reinforcement may come after an average of six responses but may come after just one or two and sometimes after twenty or more. Variable-ratio schedules generate steady response rates.

Variable-ratio schedules, or reasonable approximations of them, occur whenever each response has about an equal probability of success. For example,

when you apply for a job, you might or might not get it. The more times you apply, the better your chances, but you cannot predict how many applications you need to submit before receiving a job offer.

Fixed-Interval Schedule

A **fixed-interval schedule** *provides reinforcement for the first response made after a specific time interval.* For instance, an animal might get food for only the first response it makes after each 15-second interval. Then it would have to wait another 15 seconds before another response would be effective. Animals (including humans) on such a schedule usually learn to pause after each reinforcement and begin to respond again only as the end of the time interval approaches. The cumulative record would look like this:

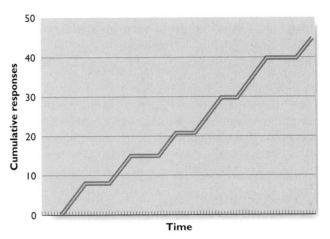

Checking your mailbox is an example of behavior on a fixed-interval schedule. If your mail is delivered at about 3 P.M., you will get no reinforcement for checking your mailbox at 2 P.M. If you are eagerly awaiting an important package, you might begin to check around 2:30 and continue checking every few minutes until it arrives.

Variable-Interval Schedule

In a **variable-interval schedule,** *reinforcement is available after a variable amount of time has elapsed.* For example, reinforcement may come for the first response after 2 minutes, then for the first response after the next 7 seconds, then after 3 minutes 20 seconds, and so forth. There is no way to know how much time will pass before the next response is reinforced. Consequently, responses on a variable-interval schedule occur at a slow but steady rate. Checking your e-mail is an example: A new message could appear at any time, so you check occasionally but not constantly.

Stargazing is also reinforced on a variable-interval schedule. The reinforcement for stargazing—finding a comet, for example—appears at irregular, unpredictable intervals. Consequently, both professional and amateur astronomers scan the skies regularly.

Extinction of Responses Reinforced on Different Schedules

Suppose you and a friend go to a gambling casino and bet on the roulette wheel, choosing bets with an almost 50% chance of winning, such as "red." Amazingly, your first 8 bets are all winners. Your friend wins 8 times out of the first 16 tries. Then both of you go into a prolonged losing streak. Presuming that the two of you have the same amount of money available and no unusual personality quirks, which of you is likely to continue betting longer?

Your friend is, even though you had a more favorable early experience. Extinction of responses is slower after a schedule of intermittent reinforcement (either a ratio schedule or an interval schedule) than after continuous reinforcement (reinforcement for every response). One explanation is that the lack of reinforcement is nothing new for someone who has been responding for intermittent reinforcement. Someone who has had continuous reinforcement can immediately notice the change.

CONCEPT CHECK ☑

14. Identify which schedule of reinforcement applies to each of the following examples:
    a. You attend every new movie that appears at your local theater, although you enjoy about one fourth of them.
    b. You phone your best friend and hear a busy signal. You don't know how soon your friend will hang up, so you try again every few minutes.
    c. You tune your television set to an all-news cable channel, and you look up from your studies to check the sports scores every 30 minutes.
15. Stargazing in the hope of finding a comet was cited as an example of a variable-interval schedule. Why is it *not* an example of a variable ratio?
16. A novice gambler and a longtime gambler both lose 20 bets in a row. Which one is more likely to continue betting? Why? (Check your answers on page 219.)

Applications of Operant Conditioning

Although operant conditioning arose from purely theoretical concerns, it has a long history of applications. Here are four examples.

Animal Training

Most animal acts are based on training methods similar to Skinner's. To induce an animal to perform a trick, the trainer first trains it to perform a simple act similar to its natural behavior. Then the trainer shapes the animal to perform more complex behaviors. Most animal trainers rely on positive reinforcement and seldom use punishment.

▌ Monkeys can be trained to help the disabled. (a) Monkeys are proving useful for indoor tasks for people with limited mobility. (b) This monkey is being trained to retrieve objects identified with a laser beam. Such training relies on shaping—building a complex response by reinforcing sequential approximations to it.

Sometimes what an animal learns is not exactly what the trainer intended (Rumbaugh & Washburn, 2003). Once some psychologists tried to teach a chimpanzee to urinate in a pan instead of on the floor. They gave her some chocolate candy every time she used the pan. Quickly, she learned to urinate just a few drops at a time, holding out her hand for candy each time. When at last she could urinate no more, she *spat* into the pan and again held out her hand for candy!

Persuasion

How could you persuade someone to do something that he or she did not want to do? To use an extreme example, how could you convince a prisoner of war to cooperate with the enemy?

The best way is to start by reinforcing a slight degree of cooperation and then working up to the goal little by little. This principle has been applied by people who had probably never heard of B. F. Skinner, positive reinforcement, or shaping. During the Korean War, the Chinese Communists forwarded some of the letters written home by prisoners of war but intercepted others. (The prisoners could tell from the replies which letters had been forwarded.)

The prisoners began to suspect that they would have better luck getting their letters through if they said something mildly favorable about their captors. So from time to time, they would include a brief remark that the Communists were not really so bad, that certain aspects of the Chinese system seemed to work pretty well, or that they hoped the war would end soon.

After a while the Chinese devised essay contests, offering a little extra food or other privileges to the soldier who wrote the best essay (in the captors' opinion). Most of the winning essays contained a statement or two that complimented the Communists on minor matters or admitted that "the United States is not perfect." Gradually, more and more soldiers started to include such statements. Then the Chinese might ask, "You said the United States is not perfect. We wonder whether you could tell us some of the ways in which it is not perfect, so that we can better understand your system." Then they would ask the soldier to read aloud the lists of what was wrong with the United States. Gradually, without torture and with only modest reinforcements, the Chinese induced prisoners to make public statements denouncing the United States, make false confessions, inform on fellow prisoners, and even reveal military secrets (Cialdini, 1993).

The point is clear: Whether we want to get rats to salute the flag or soldiers to denounce it, the most effective training technique is to start with easy behaviors, reinforce those behaviors, and then gradually shape more complex behaviors.

Applied Behavior Analysis/ Behavior Modification

In one way or another, people are almost constantly trying to influence other people's behavior. Psychologists have developed influence procedures based on operant conditioning.

In **applied behavior analysis,** also known as **behavior modification,** a *psychologist first determines the reinforcers that sustain an unwanted behavior and then tries to alter that behavior by reducing the reinforcers for the unwanted behavior and providing suitable reinforcers for more acceptable behaviors.* For example, one mentally retarded man had a habit of "inappropriate" speech, including lewd sexual comments. Psychologists found that telling him not to say such things actually increased their frequency; getting people's attention was reinforcing. So they switched to ignoring his inappropriate comments and responding attentively to all acceptable comments. The result was increased appropriate and decreased inappropriate comments (Dixon, Benedict, & Larson, 2001).

Another example: Many children get injured on playgrounds, often by using equipment improperly, such as going down the slide head first. The reinforcement for such risky behavior is simply the thrill of it. To stop such behavior, a safety officer talked to elementary school classes about playground safety and offered rewards to the whole class if everyone shifted to safer playground behaviors. College students observed the children in the playground and reported instances of risky behavior. The reinforcements here were almost trivial, such as a blue ribbon for every student or a colorful poster for the door. Nevertheless, the result was decreased head-first sliding and other risky behaviors, and the improved safety continued for weeks afterward (Heck, Collins, & Peterson, 2001).

CONCEPT CHECK ☑

17. Of the procedures characterized in Table 6.1, which one applies to giving more attention to someone's appropriate speech? Which one applies to decreasing attention to inappropriate speech? (Check your answers on page 219.)

Breaking Bad Habits

Some people learn to conquer their own bad habits by means of reinforcements. Nathan Azrin and Robert Nunn (1973) recommend this three-step method:

1. Become more aware of your bad habit. Interrupt the behavior and isolate it from the chain of normal activities. Then you might imagine an association between the behavior and something re-

pulsive. For example, to break a nail-biting habit, imagine your fingernails covered with sewage.

2. If no one else will reinforce you for making progress, provide your own reinforcements. For example, buy yourself a special treat after you have abandoned your bad habit for a certain period of time.

3. Do something incompatible with the offending habit. For example, if you have a nervous habit of hunching up your shoulders, practice depressing your shoulders.

Figure 6.17 shows an example of a college student setting up a list of reinforcements and punishments to support her goal of decreasing her smoking. If she successfully limits her smoking, she will treat herself to a movie. If she breaks the vow, she must clean the room by herself on the weekend. If you decide to try this approach, set clear goals, choose realistic reinforcers, and keep track of your successes and failures. Telling your roommate or someone else about the plan, as in this example, makes the plan work better. (It's harder for you to give up on it.)

Date: January 1, 2004

Goal: <u>To cut down on my smoking</u>

<u>What I will do</u>: For the first month I will smoke no more than one cigarette per hour. I will not smoke immediately after meals. I will not smoke in bed. In February I will cut back to one every other hour.

<u>What others will do</u>: My roommate Rebecca will keep track of how many cigarettes I smoke by counting cigarettes in the pack each night. She will keep records of any cigarettes I smoke after meals or in bed.

<u>Rewards if contract is kept</u>: I will treat myself to a movie every week if I stick to the contract.

<u>Consequences if contract is broken</u>: If I break the contract, I have to clean the room by myself on the weekend.

Signatures:

Sarah Self
Rebecca Roommate

FIGURE 6.17 Sometimes people try to change their own behavior by setting up a system of reinforcements and punishments.

Operant Conditioning and Human Behavior

Suppose one of your instructors announced that everyone in the class would receive the same grade at the end of the course, regardless of performance on tests and papers. Would you study hard in that course? Probably not. Or suppose your employer said that all raises and promotions would be made at random, with no regard to how well you do your job. Would you work as hard as possible? Not likely. Our behavior depends on its consequences, just like that of a rat, pigeon, or any other animal. That is the main point of operant conditioning.

Summary

- *Reinforcement.* Edward Thorndike introduced the concept of reinforcement. A reinforcement increases the probability that the preceding response will be repeated. (page 207)

- *Operant conditioning.* Operant conditioning is the process of controlling the rate of a behavior through its consequences. (page 207)

- *The nature of reinforcement.* The opportunity to engage in a more probable behavior will reinforce a less probable behavior. Something that an individual can exchange for a reinforcer becomes a reinforcer itself. (page 207)

- *Reinforcement and punishment.* Behaviors can be reinforced (strengthened) by presenting favorable events or by omitting unfavorable events. Behaviors can be punished (suppressed) by presenting unfavorable events or by omitting favorable events. (page 210)

- *Extinction.* In operant conditioning a response becomes extinguished if it is no longer followed by reinforcement. (page 211)

- *Shaping.* Shaping is a technique for training subjects to perform difficult acts by reinforcing them for successive approximations to the desired behavior. (page 213)

- *Schedules of reinforcement.* The frequency and timing of a response depend on the schedule of reinforcement. In a ratio schedule of reinforcement, an individual is given reinforcement after a fixed or variable number of responses. In an interval schedule of reinforcement, an individual is given reinforcement after a fixed or variable period of time. (page 214)

- *Applications.* People have applied operant conditioning to animal training, persuasion, applied behavior analysis, and the breaking of bad habits. (page 216)

Answers to Concept Checks

10. You would need to know whether the bell was always followed by food (classical conditioning) or whether food was presented only if the animal sat up on its hind legs (operant conditioning). (page 207)

11. Begin by determining how this person spends his or her time—for example, exercising, reading, watching television, visiting with friends. Then determine something that he or she has recently not had much opportunity to do. Activities for which one has only limited opportunities become good reinforcers. (page 208)

12. To be effective, punishments must be quick and predictable. Punishments for drug dealing are neither. Furthermore, punishment most effectively suppresses a response when the individual has alternative responses that can gain reinforcements. Many people who gain enormous profits by selling drugs have no alternative way to gain similar profits. (page 210)

13. **a.** positive reinforcement; **b.** punishment or passive avoidance; **c.** escape learning or negative reinforcement; **d.** punishment or passive avoidance; **e.** omission training or negative punishment; **f.** omission training or negative punishment; **g.** avoidance learning or negative reinforcement. (page 211)

14. **a.** variable ratio. (You will be reinforced for about one fourth of your entries to the theater but on an irregular basis.) **b.** variable interval. (Calling will become effective after some interval of time, but the length of that time is unpredictable.) **c.** fixed interval. (page 216)

15. In a variable-ratio schedule, the number of responses matters, but the timing does not. If you have already checked the stars tonight and found no comets, checking three more times tonight will probably be fruitless. Checking at a later date gives you a better chance. (page 216)

16. The longtime gambler will continue longer because he or she has a history of being reinforced for gambling on a variable-ratio schedule, which retards extinction. (For the same reason, an alcoholic who has had both good experiences and bad experiences while drunk is likely to keep on drinking even after several bad experiences.) (page 216)

17. Increasing attention for appropriate speech is positive reinforcement. Decreasing attention for inappropriate speech is omission training or negative punishment. (If you called it "lack of positive reinforcement," you would not be wrong, and calling it simply "punishment" is acceptable for most purposes.) (page 217)

Other Kinds of Learning

What kinds of learning do not fit neatly into the categories of classical or operant conditioning?

How do we learn from the successes and failures of others without trying every response ourselves?

Operant and classical conditioning both depend on an association between a first event (response or CS) and a second event (reinforcement or UCS). The main difference is that in operant conditioning the first event is something the individual does, whereas in classical conditioning the first event is a stimulus in the outside world. It might seem that all possible examples of learning would fall into either of these two categories; several, however, are difficult to classify or require special treatment.

Conditioned Taste Aversions

If you eat something with an unfamiliar flavor and then feel ill, you will quickly learn to avoid that flavor. The same process works in rats and every other species researchers have tested. Most psychologists describe this process as classical conditioning, with the taste as CS and illness as US. In fact, however, because it occurs after just one trial, its classification is ambiguous: Do you (or a rat) associate the *taste* with illness or do you associate your *response* (eating or drinking that substance) with illness? If the illness depends on your response, then we should call it operant conditioning. In any case this type of learning has several special features.

An *association between eating something and getting sick* is **conditioned taste aversion**, first documented by John Garcia and his colleagues (Garcia, Ervin, & Koelling, 1966). One of its special features is the fact that

it occurs reliably after a single pairing of food with illness, even with a long delay between them. For example, a rat is drinking a saccharin solution, which it has never tasted before. Saccharin tastes sweet, and in moderate amounts it is neither healthful nor harmful. After the rat has drunk for a few minutes, the experimenter removes the bottle, waits minutes or even hours, and then injects a small amount of poison, making the rat moderately ill. The experimenter then waits long enough for the rat to recover and offers it a choice between the saccharin solution and unflavored water. The rat will strongly prefer the unflavored water (Garcia et al., 1966). In contrast, rats that have not been poisoned, or that have been poisoned after drinking something else, strongly prefer the saccharin solution. In most other cases of either classical or operant conditioning, learning is greatest with a 1- or 2-second delay between the events to be associated and hard to demonstrate at all with delays over 20 seconds (Kimble, 1961).

An animal that learns a conditioned taste aversion to a particular food treats that food as if it tasted bad (Figure 6.18) (Garcia, 1990). Some ranchers in the western United States have used this type of learning to deter coyotes from eating sheep. They offer the coyotes sheep meat containing enough lithium salts to produce nausea but not enough to be dangerous. Afterward, the coyotes become less likely to attack sheep, although they continue to hunt rabbits and other prey. One study reported that this method reduced coyotes' sheep kills to about half of what had occurred the previous year (Gustavson, Kelly, Sweeney, & Garcia, 1976). This technique has the potential of protecting sheep without killing the coyotes, which are a threatened species.

©Stuart Ellins

FIGURE 6.18 This coyote previously fell ill after eating sheep meat containing a mild dose of lithium salts. Now it reacts toward both live and dead sheep as it would toward bad-tasting food.

Conditioned taste aversions are probably responsible for some of our choices of food and beverage. Mice that have trouble metabolizing alcohol get sick after drinking it and learn to avoid it or anything else they tasted prior to consuming it (Broadbent, Muccino, & Cunningham, 2002). Similarly, people who have trouble metabolizing alcohol also get sick after they drink it and learn to avoid it (Tu & Israel, 1995). Many women who get nauseated during pregnancy learn aversion to the foods they have been eating (Crystal, Bowen, & Bernstein, 1999), and many cancer patients learn aversions to foods they ate just prior to chemotherapy or radiation therapy (Bernstein, 1991).

Conditioned taste aversions are special in another regard as well: Recall that an animal can associate a food with feeling ill hours later. No doubt the animal had many other experiences between the food and the illness. Nevertheless, animals are predisposed to associate illness mostly with what they eat. In one classic experiment (Garcia & Koelling, 1966), rats were allowed to drink saccharin-flavored water from tubes that were set up so that, whenever the rats licked the water, they turned on a bright light and a loud noise. Some of the rats were exposed to x-rays (which can induce nausea) while they drank. Others were given electric shocks to their feet 2 seconds after they started drinking. After the training was complete, each rat was tested separately with a tube of saccharin-flavored water and a tube of unflavored water that produced lights and noises. (Figure 6.19 illustrates the experiment.)

The rats that received x-rays avoided the flavored water. The rats that received shocks avoided the tube that produced lights and noises. Evidently, rats (and other species) have a built-in predisposition to associate illness mostly with what they eat or drink. They associate skin pain mostly with what they see or hear. (This tendency is an example of preparedness, mentioned earlier in this chapter.) Such predispositions are presumably beneficial because foods are more

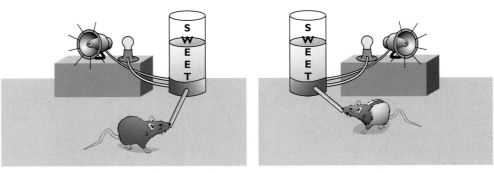

Rats drink saccharin-flavored water. Whenever they make contact with the tube, they turn on a bright light and a noisy buzzer.

Then

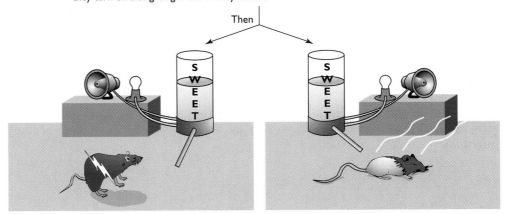

Some rats get electric shock.

Some rats are nauseated by x-rays.

Next day: Rats are given a choice between a tube of saccharin-flavored water and a tube of unflavored water hooked up to the light and the buzzer.

Rats that had been shocked avoid the tube with the lights and noises.

Rats that had been nauseated by x-rays avoid the saccharin-flavored water.

FIGURE 6.19 An experiment by Garcia and Koelling (1966): Rats "blame" an illness on what they ate; they blame pain on what they saw or heard or where they were.

likely to cause internal events, and lights and sounds are more likely to signal external events.

One problem remains with all of this: I have described associations between food and "illness," but some drugs that make the animal very ill produce only weak learned aversions, and some procedures such as x-rays that hardly make the animal ill at all (and produce only slight nausea in humans) produce powerful aversions to recently eaten foods. Rats will work for an opportunity to get into a running wheel, and they prefer to be in a distinctive cage associated with a running wheel instead of other cages. Nevertheless, running evidently produces some mild stomach distress (probably analogous to riding a roller coaster), and rats learn to avoid the taste of anything they drank just before getting into the running wheel (Lett, Grant, Koh, & Smith, 2001). The fact that running in a wheel can simultaneously increase preference for the cage while decreasing preference for a food indicates that conditioned taste aversion is a special kind of learning. It also indicates that a single event can be reinforcing for one response and punishing for another!

A male white-crowned sparrow learns his song in the first months of life but does not begin to sing it until the next year.

©Joe McDonald/CORBIS

CONCEPT CHECK ☑

18. Which kind of learning takes place despite a long delay between the events to be associated?
19. What evidence indicates that conditioned taste aversion is different compared to other kinds of learning? (Check your answers on page 226.)

Birdsong Learning

Birdsongs brighten the day for people who hear them, but they are earnest business for the birds themselves. For most species only males sing, and they sing only in spring, the mating season. As a rule a song indicates, "Here I am. I am a male of species ___. If you're a female of my species, please come closer. If you're a male of my species and you can hear me, you're too close. If I find you, I'll attack."

(Among the delights of birdsongs are the exceptions to the rule. Mockingbirds copy all the songs they hear and defend their territory against intruders of all species—sometimes even squirrels, cats, people, and automobiles. Carolina wrens sing male-and-female

duets throughout the year. Woodpeckers don't sing, but rely on the rhythm and loudness of their pecks to signal others. That woodpecker banging on the metal siding of your house in spring is *trying* to make a racket to impress the females. But on to more relevant matters.)

If you were to rear an infant songbird in isolation from others of its species, would it develop a normal song on its own? Maybe or maybe not depending on its species. Some species have to learn their song. For example, in several sparrow species, a male develops a normal song only if he hears the song of his own species. He *learns most readily during a* **sensitive period** *early in his first year of life*. The young bird learns better from a live tutor, such as his father, than from a tape-recorded song in a laboratory (Baptista & Petrinovich, 1984; Marler & Peters, 1987, 1988). It will not learn at all from the song of another species. Evidently, a fledgling sparrow is equipped with mechanisms to produce approximately the right song and ways of identifying which songs to imitate (Marler, 1997).

Birdsong learning resembles human language learning in that both take place in a social context, both occur most easily in early life, both start with babbling and gradually improve, and both deteriorate gradually if the individual becomes deaf later (Brainard & Doupe, 2000). Song learning differs, however, from standard examples of classical and operant conditioning. During the sensitive period, the infant bird only listens. We cannot call the song he hears an unconditioned stimulus because it elicits no apparent response. At no time in this sensitive period does the bird receive any apparent reinforcement.

Nevertheless, he learns a representation of how his song should sound, even though we cannot classify the learning as either classical or operant. The following spring, when the bird starts to sing, we see a trial-and-error process with a strange form of operant conditioning. At first his song is a disorganized mixture of sounds, somewhat like a babbling human infant. As time passes he eliminates some sounds and rearranges others until he matches the songs he heard the previous summer (Marler & Peters, 1981, 1982). But there is no external reinforcer; the only reinforcer is somehow "knowing" that he has sung correctly.

The point is that the principles of learning vary from one situation to another. If a situation poses special problems (e.g., food selection, song learning in birds, probably language learning in humans), we can expect to find that species have evolved their own special ways of learning (Rozin & Kalat, 1971).

CONCEPT CHECK ☑

20. What aspects of birdsong learning set it apart from classical and operant conditioning? (Check your answer on page 226.)

Social Learning

According to the **social-learning approach** (Bandura, 1977, 1986), *we learn about many behaviors before we try them the first time. Much learning, especially in humans, results from observing the behaviors of others and from imagining the consequences of our own behavior.* For example, if you want to learn how to swim, paint pictures, or drive a car, you *could* try to learn strictly by trial and error, but you would probably start by watching someone who is already skilled. When you do try the task yourself, your attempt will be subject to reinforcement and punishment; therefore, it falls into the realm of operant conditioning. However, because you will be facilitated by your observations of others, we treat social learning as a special case.

"Social-learning theory" is not a *theory* in the sense described in Chapter 2. The social-learning approach is more a field of emphasis, with a focus on observation, imitation, setting goals, and self-reinforcement.

According to the social-learning approach, we learn many behaviors by observing what others do, imitating behaviors that are reinforced, and avoiding behaviors that are punished.

Modeling and Imitation

If you visit another country with customs unlike your own, you may find yourself bewildered about things you used to take for granted. Ordering food in a restaurant is not done the way you did it back home; paying for the meal is done differently too. A hand

gesture such as [hand gesture] is considered friendly in some countries but rude and vulgar in others. Many visitors to Japan are confused by the toilets. With effort you learn foreign customs either because someone explains them to you or because you watch and copy. We say that you *model* your behavior after others or *imitate* others. On a smaller scale, you also model or imitate the customs of a religious organization, a fraternity or sorority, a new place of employment, or any other group you join.

Albert Bandura, Dorothea Ross, and Sheila Ross (1963) studied the role of imitation for learning aggressive behavior. They asked two groups of children to watch films in which an adult or a cartoon character violently attacked an inflated "Bobo" doll. Another group watched a film in which the adult or character did not attack the doll. They then left the children in a room with a Bobo doll. Only the children who had watched films with attacks on the doll attacked the doll themselves, using many of the same movements they had just seen (Figure 6.20). The clear implication is

A Japanese toilet is a hole in the ground with no seat. Western visitors usually have to ask how to use it. (You squat.)

FIGURE 6.20 A child will mimic an adult's behavior even when neither one is reinforced for the behavior. This girl attacks a doll after seeing a film of a woman hitting it. People who witness violent behavior, including violence at home, may be more prone than others to turn to violent behavior themselves.

that children copy the aggressive behavior they have seen in others.

CONCEPT CHECK

21. Many people complain that they cannot find much difference between the two major political parties in the United States because so many American politicians campaign using similar styles and take similar stands on the issues. Explain this observation in terms of social learning. (Check your answer on page 226.)

Vicarious Reinforcement and Punishment

Six months ago, your best friend quit a job with Consolidated Generic Products to open a restaurant. Now you are considering quitting your job and opening your own restaurant. How do you decide what to do?

You would probably start by asking how successful your friend has been. You imitate behavior that apparently has been reinforcing to someone else. In other words you learn by **vicarious reinforcement** or **vicarious punishment**—that is, by *substituting someone else's experience for your own.*

Whenever a new business venture succeeds, other companies copy it. For example, the first few successful Internet companies were followed by a horde of imitators. When a sports team wins consistently, other teams

copy its style of play. When a television program wins high ratings, other producers are sure to present look-alikes the following year. Advertisers depend heavily on vicarious reinforcement; they show you happy, successful people using their product, with the implication that if you use their product, you too will be happy and successful. The people promoting state lotteries show the ecstatic winners—never the losers!—suggesting that if you try the lottery, you too can win a fortune.

Might vicarious learning lead to monotony of behavior and excessive conformity? How can we learn vicariously without becoming just like everyone else?

Although we can think of many examples of vicarious reinforcement, vicarious punishment seems less effective. If someone gets caught cheating, either in a classroom or in business, or if someone goes to prison for a crime, do other people quit those behaviors? Not necessarily. We are often reminded of the health risks associated with cigarette smoking, overweight, risky sex, lack of exercise, or failure to wear seat belts, but many people ignore the dangers. Even the death penalty, an extreme example of vicarious punishment, does not demonstrably lower the murder rate.

Why is vicarious punishment often so ineffective? One explanation is

▌ States that sponsor lotteries provide publicity and an exciting atmosphere for each big payoff. They hope that this publicity will provide vicarious reinforcement to encourage other people to buy lottery tickets.

that we are influenced by vicarious reinforcement or punishment to someone we consider to be like ourselves. Most of us think of ourselves as successful people and therefore unlike the "loser" who is being punished.

Self-Efficacy in Social Learning

We primarily imitate people we regard as successful. So, when you watch an Olympic diver win a gold medal for a superb display of physical control, do you then go out and try to imitate those dives? Probably not. People imitate someone else's behavior only if they have a sense of **self-efficacy**—*the perception that they themselves could perform the task successfully.* You observe your past successes and failures, compare yourself to the successful person, and estimate your chance of success.

We see this effect in children's life aspirations. Nearly anyone would like a high-paying, high-prestige profession, but many think they could never rise to that level, so they don't try (Bandura, Barbaranelli, Caprara, & Pastorelli, 2001). One reason for trying to get more women and minorities into high-visibility leadership jobs in business, education, and government is to provide role models—that is, to show young people that the gates are not closed, and strong effort can be rewarded.

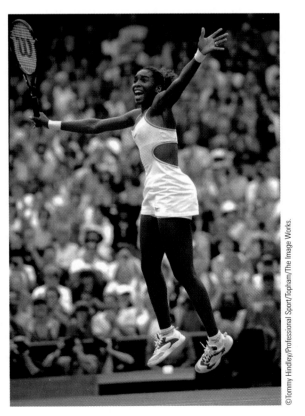

▌ We tend to imitate the actions of successful people, but only if we feel self-efficacy, a belief that we could perform the task well.

Sometimes people know that they cannot do much themselves but gain confidence in what they can do with a group effort (Bandura, 2000). Even groups differ in their feeling of efficacy or nonefficacy; a group with confidence in its abilities accomplishes much more than a group with doubts.

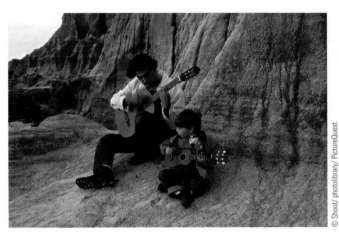

▌ We acquire a sense of self-efficacy mainly through our own successes but also partly by watching and identifying with role models.

Self-Reinforcement and Self-Punishment in Social Learning

We learn by observing others who are doing what we would like to do. If our sense of self-efficacy is strong enough, we try to imitate their behavior. But actually succeeding often requires prolonged efforts. People typically set a goal for themselves and monitor their progress toward that goal. They even provide reinforcement or punishment for themselves, just as if they were training someone else. They say to themselves, "If I finish this math assignment on time, I'll treat myself to a movie and a new magazine. If I don't finish on time, I'll make myself clean the stove and the sink." (Nice threat, but people usually forgive themselves and don't impose the punishment.)

Some therapists teach clients to use self-reinforcement. One 10-year-old boy had a habit of biting his fingernails, sometimes down to the skin and even drawing blood. He learned to keep records of how much nail-biting he did in the morning, afternoon, and evening, and then he set goals for himself. If he met the goals by reducing his nail-biting, he wrote compliments such as "I'm great! I did wonderful!" The penalty for doing worse was that he would return his weekly allowance to his parents. An additional reinforcement was that his father promised that if the son made enough progress, he would let the son be the "therapist" to help the father quit smoking. Over several weeks the boy quit nail-biting altogether (Ronen & Rosenbaum, 2001).

One amusing anecdote shows how self-reinforcement and self-punishment can fail: Psychologist Ron Ash (1986) tried to teach himself to stop smoking by smoking only while he was reading *Psychological Bulletin* and other highly respected but tedious publications. He hoped to associate smoking with boredom. Two months later he was smoking as much as ever, but he was starting to *enjoy* reading *Psychological Bulletin*!

IN CLOSING

Why We Do What We Do

Almost everything you have done today was a learned behavior—from getting dressed and combing your hair this morning to reading this chapter right now. In fact you would have trouble listing much you did that was not learned. Even your bad habits were learned.

One point that I hope has emerged is that learning takes many forms. Classically conditioned salivation, operantly conditioned movements, conditioned taste aversions, and socially learned behaviors occur under diverse circumstances. The underlying mechanisms in the brain may or may not be the same, but at a descriptive level, these types of learning differ in some important ways. In short, your behavior is subject to a wide variety of learned influences.

Summary

- *Conditioned taste aversions.* Animals, including people, learn to avoid foods, especially unfamiliar ones, if they become ill afterward. This type of learning occurs reliably after a single pairing, even with a delay of hours between the food and the illness. Animals are predisposed to associate illness with what they eat or drink, not with other events. (page 220)
- *Birdsong learning.* Infant birds of some species must hear their songs during a sensitive period in the first few months of life if they are to develop a fully normal song the following spring. During the early learning, the bird makes no apparent response and receives no apparent reinforcement. (page 222)

- *Learning by observation.* We learn much by observing what other people do and what consequences they experience. (page 223)
- *Vicarious reinforcement and punishment.* We tend to imitate behaviors that have led to reinforcement for other people. We are less consistent in avoiding behaviors that have led to punishment. (page 224)
- *Self-efficacy.* Whether we decide to imitate a behavior depends on whether we believe we are capable of duplicating it and whether we believe we would be reinforced for it. (page 225)
- *Self-reinforcement and self-punishment.* Once people have decided to try to imitate a certain behavior, they set goals for themselves and may even provide their own reinforcements and punishments. (page 225)

Answers to Concept Checks

18. Conditioned taste aversions develop despite a long delay between food and illness. (page 222)
19. In addition to the fact that conditioned taste aversion occurs over long delays, animals are predisposed to associate foods and not other events with illnesses. Also, an event such as running in a wheel can be reinforcing for other responses but simultaneously decrease preference for a taste associated with it. (page 222)
20. The most distinctive feature is that birdsong learning occurs during a time when the learner makes no apparent response and receives no apparent reinforcement. Also, at least in certain sparrow species, birdsong learning occurs most readily during an early sensitive period, and the bird is capable of learning its own species' song but not the song of another species. (page 223)
21. One reason that most American politicians run similar campaigns and take similar stands is that they all tend to copy the same models—candidates who have won recent elections. Another reason is that they all pay attention to the same public opinion polls. (page 224)

Key Terms and Activities

Key Terms

acquisition: the process by which a conditioned response is established or strengthened (page 198)

applied behavior analysis (or behavior modification): a procedure for determining the reinforcers that sustain an unwanted behavior and then reducing the reinforcements for the unwanted behavior and providing suitable reinforcers for more acceptable behaviors (page 217)

avoidance learning: learning to make a response that avoids pain or some similar outcome (page 210)

behaviorist: a psychologist who insists that psychologists should study only observable, measurable behaviors, not mental processes (page 191)

belongingness: the concept that certain stimuli are readily associated with each other and that certain responses are readily associated with certain outcomes (page 212)

blocking effect: the tendency of a previously established association to one stimulus to block the formation of an association to an added stimulus (page 203)

chaining: a procedure for developing a sequence of behaviors in which the reinforcement for one response is the opportunity to engage in the next response (page 213)

classical conditioning (or Pavlovian conditioning): the process by which an organism learns a new association between two paired stimuli—a neutral stimulus and one that already evokes a reflexive response (page 196)

conditioned response (CR): whatever response the conditioned stimulus begins to elicit as a result of the conditioning procedure (page 196)

conditioned stimulus (CS): a stimulus that comes to evoke a particular response after being paired with the unconditioned stimulus (page 196)

conditioned taste aversion: the tendency to avoid eating a substance that has been followed by illness when it was eaten in the past (page 220)

continuous reinforcement: reinforcement for every correct response (page 214)

discrimination: (1) in classical conditioning making different responses to different stimuli that have been followed by different outcomes (page 199); (2) in operant conditioning learning to respond in one way to one stimulus and in a different way to another stimulus (page 211)

discriminative stimulus: a stimulus that indicates on which occasion a response will produce a certain consequence (page 211)

disequilibrium principle: the principle that an opportunity to engage in any deprived activity will be a reinforcer because it restores equilibrium (page 208)

drug tolerance: the progressively weaker effects of a drug after repeated use (page 201)

escape learning: learning to escape from an event such as shock (page 210)

extinction: (1) in classical conditioning the dying out of the conditioned response after repeated presentations of the conditioned stimulus without the unconditioned stimulus (page 198); (2) in operant conditioning the weakening of a response after a period without reinforcement (page 211)

fixed-interval schedule: a rule for delivering reinforcement for the first response that the subject makes after a specified period of time has passed (page 215)

fixed-ratio schedule: a rule for delivering reinforcement only after the subject has made a specific number of correct responses (page 215)

intermittent reinforcement: reinforcement for some responses and not for others (page 214)

intervening variable: something that we infer without directly observing it and that links a variety of procedures to a variety of possible responses (page 191)

law of effect: Thorndike's theory that a response followed by favorable consequences becomes more probable and a response followed by unfavorable consequences becomes less probable (page 207)

learning curve: a graphical representation of the changes in behavior that occur over the course of learning (page 206)

methodological behaviorist: a psychologist who studies only measurable, observable events but sometimes uses those observations to make inferences about internal events (page 191)

negative punishment: a decrease in the future probability of a response because it led to the absence of something such as food (page 210)

negative reinforcement: an increase in the future probability of a response because it led to the *absence* of something such as pain (page 210)

omission training: learning to suppress a behavior that would lead to the omission of an event such as food (page 210)

operant conditioning (or instrumental conditioning): the process of changing behavior by following a response with reinforcement (page 207)

passive avoidance learning: learning to avoid an outcome such as shock by being passive—that is, by inhibiting a response that would lead to the outcome (page 210)

positive reinforcement: strengthening a behavior through the presentation of an event such as food (page 210)

Premack principle: the principle that the opportunity to engage in a frequent behavior will reinforce a less frequent behavior (page 208)

primary reinforcer: an event that is reinforcing because of its own properties (page 208)

punishment: an event that decreases the probability that a response will be repeated (page 209)

radical behaviorist: a behaviorist who denies that internal, private events are causes of behavior (page 191)

reinforcement: an event that increases the future probability of the most recent response (page 207)

reinforcer: an event that follows a response and increases the later probability or frequency of that response (page 207)

schedule of reinforcement: a rule or procedure linking the pattern of responses to the reinforcements (page 214)

secondary reinforcer: an event that becomes reinforcing because it has previously been associated with a primary reinforcer (page 208)

self-efficacy: the perception of one's own ability to perform a task successfully (page 225)

sensitive period: a time early in life during which some kind of learning occurs most readily (page 222)

shaping: a technique for establishing a new response by reinforcing successive approximations (page 213)

skeletal responses: movements of the muscles that move the limbs, trunk, and head (page 207)

social-learning approach: the view that people learn by observing and imitating the behavior of others and by imagining the consequences of their own behavior (page 223)

spontaneous recovery: the temporary return of an extinguished response after a delay (page 199)

stimulus control: the ability of a stimulus to encourage some responses and discourage others (page 212)

stimulus generalization: (1) in classical conditioning the extension of a conditioned response from the training stimulus to similar stimuli (page 199); (2) in operant conditioning the tendency to make a similar response to a stimulus that resembles one that has already been associated with reinforcement (page 211)

stimulus–response psychology: a field that attempts to explain behavior in terms of how each stimulus triggers a response (page 192)

unconditioned reflex: an automatic connection between a stimulus and a response (page 196)

unconditioned response (UCR): an automatic response to an unconditioned stimulus (page 196)

unconditioned stimulus (UCS): a stimulus that automatically elicits an unconditioned response (page 196)

variable-interval schedule: a rule for delivering reinforcement after varying amounts of time (page 215)

variable-ratio schedule: a rule for delivering reinforcement after varying numbers of correct responses (page 215)

vicarious reinforcement (or vicarious punishment): the observed reinforcement or punishment experienced by someone else (page 224)

visceral responses: activities of the internal organs (page 207)

📖 Suggestions for Further Reading

Bandura, A. (1986). *Social foundations of thought and action.* Upper Saddle River, NJ: Prentice Hall. A review of social learning by its most influential investigator.

Staddon, J. (1993). *Behaviorism.* London: Duckworth. A critique of both the strengths and weaknesses of Skinner's views.

Book Companion Web Site

Need help studying? Go to

http://psychology.wadsworth.com/kalat_intro7e/

for a virtual study center. You'll find a personalized Self-Study Assessment that will provide you with a study plan based on your answers to a pretest. Also study using flashcards, quizzes, interactive art, and an online glossary.

Check out interactive **Try It Yourself** exercises on the companion site! These exercises will help you put what you've learned into action.

Your companion site also has direct links to the following Web sites. These links are checked often for changes, dead links, and new additions.

Positive Reinforcement

server.bmod.athabascau.ca/html/prtut/reinpair.htm

Lyle K. Grant of Athabasca University helps students understand what does and what does not constitute positive reinforcement. Be sure you understand the examples before you begin the practice exercise.

Dr. P's Dog Training

www.uwsp.edu/psych/dog/dog.htm

Mark Plonsky of the University of Wisconsin discusses applications of operant conditioning to obedience competition, K9 training, assistance dogs, and working dogs.

Albert Bandura

www.ship.edu/~cgboeree/bandura.html

C. George Boeree of Shippensburg University provides a short biography of Albert Bandura, a leading pioneer in the field of social learning.

 ## Try It Yourself CD-ROM
with Critical Thinking Video Exercises

Use your CD to access **videos** related to activities designed to help you think critically about the important topics discussed. You'll also find an easy portal link to the book companion site where you can access your personalized **Self-Study Assessments** and interactive **Try It Yourself** exercises.

PsychNow! 2.0

PsychNow! is a fun interactive CD designed to help you with the difficult concepts in psychology. Check out the Learning & Cognition section for the following topics that relate to this chapter:

Classical Conditioning: stimuli video, a stimulus and response lesson, and a CS and CR exercise.

Operant Conditioning: explore operant conditioning with explanation and take a quiz.

Observational Learning: Skinner and a rat video, TV violence video, Bandura and observational learning lesson and quiz.

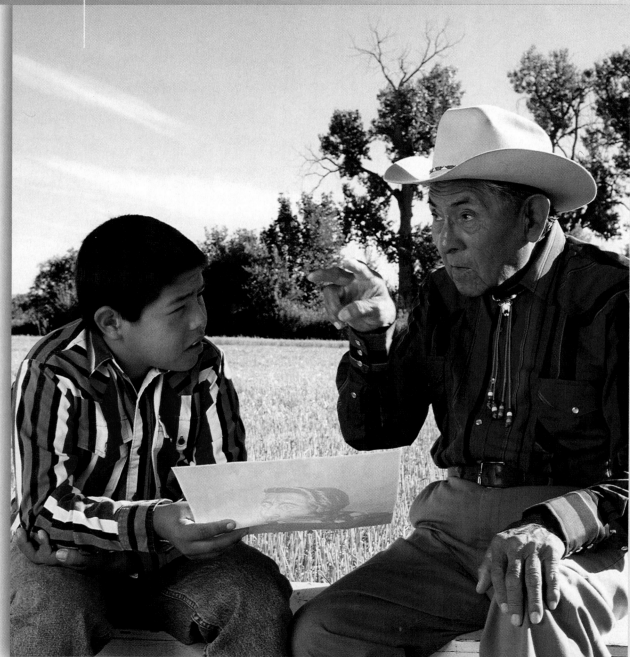

Memory

Suppose I offer you—for a price—an opportunity to do absolutely anything you want for a day. You will not be limited by the usual physical constraints. You can travel in a flash from one place to another, visiting as many places as you wish, even in outer space. You can travel forward and backward through time, finding out what the future holds and witnessing the great events of the past. (You will not be able to alter history.) Anything you want to do—just name it and it is yours. Furthermore, I guarantee your safety: No matter where you choose to go or what you choose to do, you will not get hurt.

How much would you pay for this once in a lifetime opportunity? Oh, yes, I should mention, there is one catch. When the day is over, you will completely forget everything that happened. Any notes or photos will vanish. And anyone else who takes part in your special day will forget it too.

Now how much would you be willing to pay? Much less, no doubt, and perhaps nothing. Living without remembering is hardly living at all: Our memories are almost the same as our selves.

❙ With a suitable reminder, you will find that you remember some events quite distinctly, even after a long delay. Other memories, however, are lost or distorted.

Types of Memory

Do we have different kinds of memory?

If so, what is the best way to describe those differences?

Every year people compete in the World Memory Championship in Britain. (If you would like to read about it, visit this Web site: **http://www.worldmemorychampionship.com/**). One event is speed of memorizing a shuffled deck of 52 cards. (The all-time record is 34.03 seconds.) Other events include rapidly memorizing long lists of numbers and words. Dominic O'Brien, the eight-time world champion, set an all-time record by memorizing a 316-digit number in 5 minutes. However, he admits that one time while he was practicing his card memorization, an irate friend called to complain that O'Brien had forgotten to meet him at the airport. O'Brien apologized and drove to London's Gatwick Airport, practicing card memorization along the way. When he arrived, he remembered that his friend's flight arrived at Heathrow, London's other major airport (Johnstone, 1994).

Anyone—you, me, or Dominic O'Brien—remembers some items and forgets others. Let's define memory broadly. **Memory refers to** *the process of retaining information and to the information retained.* Memory includes skills, such as how to ride a bicycle or how to eat with chopsticks. It also includes facts that never change (your birthday), facts that seldom change (your mailing address), and facts that frequently change (where you last parked your car). You remember repeated events (the changing seasons of the year), many important events (your last day of high school or first day of college), and some of the less important events. You remember many of the most interesting and important facts you were taught in school and a few of the less useful ones. (I remember learning that "Polynesians eat poi and breadfruit," although I seldom meet a Polynesian person, and I wouldn't recognize poi or breadfruit if I saw it.)

Human memory is not much like that of a computer (Bjork & VanHuele, 1992). If you hit the "store" key, your computer will store the information without pausing to consider whether it is "boring." If you try to retrieve it later, the computer will give it to you precisely. In contrast, if you try to recall an old event yourself, you remember better at some times than others, and you remember some parts correctly while losing or distorting others. You might even claim to remember events that never happened.

Ebbinghaus's Pioneering Studies of Memory

Suppose you wanted to study memory, but no one had ever done memory research before, so you couldn't copy anyone else's procedure. Where would you start? Some of the earliest psychological researchers simply asked people to describe their memories. The obvious problem was that the researchers did not know when the memories had formed, how many times they had been rehearsed, or even whether they were correct. German psychologist Hermann Ebbinghaus (1850–1909) got around these problems by an approach that was completely original at the time, although we now take it for granted: He taught new material, so that he knew exactly what someone had learned and when, and then measured memory after various delays. To be sure the material was totally new, he used lists of nonsense syllables, such as GAK or JEK. He wrote out 2,300 such syllables, assembled them randomly into

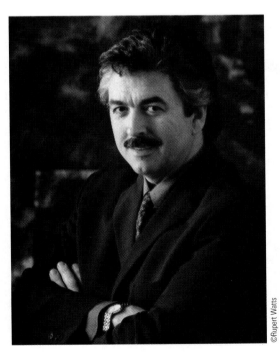

©Rupert Watts

❙ Dominic O'Brien, eight-time winner of the World Memory Championship and author of several books on training your memory, admits he sometimes forgets practical information, such as promising to meet a friend at Heathrow Airport.

233

FIGURE 7.1 Hermann Ebbinghaus pioneered the scientific study of memory by observing his own capacity for memorizing lists of nonsense syllables.

lists (Figure 7.1), and then set out to study memorization. He had no cooperative introductory psychology students to enlist for his study nor friends eager to spend many hours memorizing nonsense, so he ran all the tests on himself. Over about 6 years, he memorized thousands of lists of nonsense syllables. (He was either very dedicated to his science or uncommonly tolerant of boredom.)

Many of his findings were hardly surprising. For example, as shown in Figure 7.2, the longer a list of nonsense syllables, the more slowly he memorized it. "Of course!" you might scoff. But Ebbinghaus was not just demonstrating the obvious; he measured *how much* longer it took to memorize a longer list. You might similarly object to the law of gravity: "Of course the farther something falls, the longer it takes to hit the ground!" Nevertheless, measuring the exact acceleration of gravity was essential to progress in physics. In the same way, measuring how long it takes to learn

FIGURE 7.2 Ebbinghaus counted how many times he had to read a list of nonsense syllables before he could recite it once correctly. For a list of seven or fewer, one reading was usually enough. Beyond seven, the longer the list, the more repetitions he needed. *(From Ebbinghaus, 1885/1913)*

a list enables researchers to compare learning under different conditions: Do adults learn faster than children? Do we learn some kinds of lists faster than others? And so forth. Ebbinghaus's approach led to all the later research on memory, including findings that were not so obvious.

Methods of Testing Memory

Nearly everyone occasionally has a tip-of-the-tongue experience (Brown & McNeill, 1966). You are trying to think of someone's name, and all you can think of is some similar name that you know isn't right. You will probably think of the correct name later, and you are sure you would recognize it if you heard it.

In other words memory is not an all-or-none thing. You might seem to remember or seem to forget depending on how someone tests you. Let's survey the main ways of testing memory.

Free Recall

The simplest method for the tester (though not for the person tested) is to ask for free recall. To recall something is *to produce a response, as you do on essay tests or short-answer tests*. For instance, "Please name all the children in your third-grade class." You probably will not name many, partly because you confuse the names of the children in your third-grade class with those you knew in other grades.

Cued Recall

You will do better with cued recall, in which you *receive significant hints about the material*. For example, a photograph of the children in your third-grade class (Figure 7.3) or a list of their initials will

FIGURE 7.3 Can you recall the names of the students in your third-grade class? Trying to remember without any hints is *free recall*. Using a photo or a list of initials is *cued recall*.

help you remember many names. Try this: Cover the right side of Table 7.1 with a piece of paper and try to identify the authors of each book on the left. (This method is recall.) Then uncover the right side, revealing each author's initials, and try again. (This method is cued recall.)

TABLE 7.1 The Difference Between Free Recall and Cued Recall

Instructions: First try to identify the author of each book listed in the left column while covering the right column (free recall method). Then expose the right column, which gives each author's initials, and try again (cued recall).

Book	Author
Moby Dick	H. M.
Emma and *Pride and Prejudice*	J. A.
Hercule Poirot stories	A. C.
Sherlock Holmes stories	A. C. D.
I Know Why the Caged Bird Sings	M. A.
War and Peace	L. T.
This textbook	J. K.
The Canterbury Tales	G. C.
The Origin of Species	C. D.
Gone with the Wind	M. M.
Les Miserables	V. H.

(For answers, see page 244, answer A.)

Recognition

With **recognition**, a third method of testing memory, someone is *offered several choices and asked to select the correct one.* People usually recognize more items than they recall. For example, I might give you a list of 60 names and ask you to check off the correct names of children in your third-grade class. Multiple-choice tests use the recognition method.

Savings

A fourth method, the **savings method** (also known as the **relearning method**), detects weak memories *by comparing the speed of original learning to the speed of relearning.* Suppose you cannot name the children in your third-grade class and cannot even pick out their names from a list of choices. You would nevertheless learn a correct list of names faster than a list of people you had never met. That is, you save time when you relearn material that you learned in the past. The amount of time saved (time needed for original learning minus the time for relearning) is a measure of memory.

Implicit Memory

Free recall, cued recall, recognition, and savings are all tests of **explicit** (or **direct**) memory—*someone who states an answer regards it as a product of his or her memory.* In **implicit memory** (or **indirect memory**), *an experience influences something you say or do even though you might not be aware of the influence.* If you find that definition unsatisfactory, you are not alone (Frensch & Rünger, 2003). Defining something in terms of a vague concept like "awareness" is not a good habit. Regard the current definition as tentative until we can develop a better one.

Probably the best way to explain implicit memory is by example: Suppose you are having one discussion while other people in the room are having another. You ignore the other conversation, but occasionally, words from that background conversation creep into your own. You do not even notice the influence, although an observer might.

Here is a demonstration of implicit memories. For each of the following three-letter combinations, fill in additional letters to make any English word:

CON___   DIS___
SUP___   PRO___

You could have thought of any number of words—the dictionary lists well over 100 familiar CON___ words alone. Did you happen to write any of the following: *conversation, suppose, discussion,* or *probably?* Each of these words appeared in the paragraph before this demonstration. *Reading or hearing a word temporarily* primes *that word and increases the chance that you will use it yourself,* even if you are not aware of the influence (Graf & Mandler, 1984; Schacter, 1987). However, this demonstration works better if you listen to spoken words than if you read them. To get a better sense of priming, go to http://psychology.wadsworth.com/kalat_intro7e. Navigate to the student Web site, then to the Online Try It Yourself section, and click on Implicit Memories. Table 7.2 contrasts the various memory tests.

Procedural memories, *memories of motor skills,* are also generally considered implicit memories. If you try to explain to someone how to ride a bicycle or how to use in-line skates or almost any other complex motor task, you will discover how difficult it is to put into words and how much you do without thinking about it verbally. The brain stores procedural memories differently from **declarative memories**, *memories we can readily state in words* (Schacter & Badgaiyan, 2001). People who seem to have forgotten everything—even their name—can still remember how to walk, talk, eat, use the toilet, and so forth.

TABLE 7.2 Several Ways to Test Memory

Title	Description	Example
Recall	You are asked to say what you remember.	Name the Seven Dwarfs.
Cued recall	You are given significant hints to help you remember.	Name the Seven Dwarfs. Hint: One was always smiling, one was smart, one never talked, one always seemed to have a cold . . .
Recognition	You are asked to choose the correct item from among several items.	Which of the following were among the Seven Dwarfs: Sneezy, Sleazy, Dopey, Dippy, Hippy, Happy?
Savings (relearning)	You are asked to relearn something: If it takes you less time than when you first learned that material, some memory has persisted.	Try memorizing this list: Sleepy, Sneezy, Doc, Dopey, Grumpy, Happy, Bashful. Can you memorize it faster than this list: Sleazy, Snoopy, Duke, Dippy, Gripey, Hippy, Blushy?
Implicit Memory	You are asked to generate words, without necessarily regarding them as memories	You hear the story "Snow White and the Seven Dwarfs." Later you are asked to fill in these blanks to make any words that come to mind: _ L _ _ P _ _ N _ _ Z _ _ _ C _ O _ E _ Y _ R _ _ P _ _ _ P P _ _ A _ H _ U _

CONCEPT CHECK ☑

1. For each of these examples, identify the method of measuring memory.
   a. Although you thought you had completely forgotten your high school French, you do better in your college French course than your roommate, who never had French in high school.
   b. You don't have a telephone directory and are trying to remember the phone number of the local pizza parlor.
   c. You hear a song on the radio without paying much attention to it. Later, you find yourself humming a melody, but you don't know what it is or where you heard it.
   d. You forget where you parked your car, so you scan the parking lot hoping to pick yours out among all the others.
   e. Your friend asks, "What's the name of our chemistry lab instructor? I think it's Julie or Judy something."
2. Is remembering how to tie your shoes a procedural memory or a declarative memory? Is remembering the color of your shoes a procedural or a declarative memory? (Check your answers on page 244.)

Application: Suspect Lineups as Recognition Memory

Suppose you witness a crime, and now the police would like you to identify the guilty person. They ask you to look at a few suspects in a lineup or to examine a book of photos. Your task is a clear example of recognition memory; you are trying to identify the correct item among a group of distracters.

The task raises a problem, which is familiar to you from your own experience. When you take a multiple-choice test—another clear example of recognition memory—you pick the best available choice. Sometimes you are not sure that any of the choices are quite right, but you can eliminate some as obviously wrong, and you settle on what seems the best of the others. Now imagine you do the same with a book of photos. You look through the choices, eliminate some, and pick the one that looks most like the perpetrator of the crime. You tell the police you think suspect 42 is the guilty person. "Think?" the police ask. "Your testimony won't be worth much in court unless you're sure." You look again. You would like to cooperate, and after all you're *pretty* sure. Finally, you say yes, you're sure. The police say, "Good, that's the person we thought did it," and with that confirmation you now become confident. You testify in court, and the suspect is convicted. But is justice done? Since the advent of DNA testing, investigators have identified many innocent people who were convicted by the testimony of a confident witness.

Memory researchers have proposed ways to improve suspect lineups, and most U.S. police investigators now follow these recommendations. One is to avoid hinting which person the police actually suspect and to avoid any sign of agreeing with a tentative choice (Wells, Olson, & Charman, 2003; Zaragoza, Payment, Ackil, Drivdahl, & Beck, 2001). Another is to record the witness's confidence *immediately* at the time of initial identification, before the witness has heard of any other evidence against that suspect

(Wells, Olson, & Charman, 2002). Also, the lineup should be done sequentially—that is, one suspect at a time (Wells et al., 2000). For each suspect the witness says "yes" or "no." As soon as the witness says yes, the procedure is finished; after all, there is no point in looking at additional suspects if the witness has already decided. Most important, the witness should have no opportunity to go back and reexamine photos after rejecting them. The witness's decision should be certain, not just the best of the available choices.

CRITICAL THINKING:
A STEP FURTHER
Lineups and Multiple-Choice Testing

What would happen if classroom multiple-choice tests were done with sequential answers? That is, after each question you would have to say yes or no to each answer before reading the next answer.

The Information-Processing View of Memory

Over the years psychologists have repeatedly tried to explain the mechanisms of behavior by analogy to the technologies of their time. In the early 1900s, psychologists suggested that learning and thinking worked like a telephone switchboard, unplugging old connections and making new ones. Later, they compared behavior mechanisms to a computer. A computer has three kinds of memory. First, if you type letters faster than they can appear on the screen, the computer will store a few letters in a temporary buffer until it can display them. (Older computers showed this effect more often than today's faster models.) Second, the material you have written without saving it is in random access memory (RAM). RAM is vulnerable, as you learned if you ever had a power outage while writing something. Finally, you can save something to a disk. A hard disk or set of CDs or floppies can store vastly more information than RAM and is less vulnerable.

According to the **information-processing model** of memory, human memory resembles that of a computer: *Information enters the system, is processed, coded, and then stored* (Figure 7.4). According to a popular version of this model, information first enters a sensory store (like the computer's buffer). Some of that information is stored in short-term memory (like RAM), and some short-term memory is transferred into long-term memory (like a hard disk). Eventually, a cue from the environment causes the system to retrieve information from storage (Atkinson & Shiffrin, 1968). We shall examine each portion of this model.

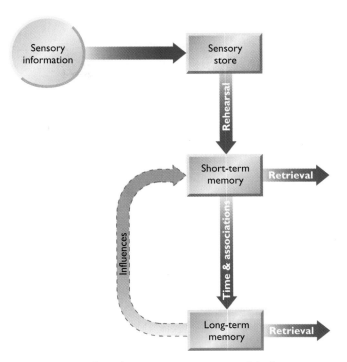

FIGURE 7.4 The information-processing model of memory resembles a computer's memory system, including temporary and permanent memory.

The Sensory Store

Close your eyes and turn your head. Then quickly blink your eyes open and shut. You will have a sudden impression that you can still "see in your mind's eye" a great deal of detail from what you just saw. However, you could not describe it all, mainly because the image fades faster than you can describe it. (It fades even faster if you look at something else instead of keeping your eyes shut.)

▮ A bolt of lightning flashes through the sky for a split second, but you can visualize it in detail for a short time afterward. That image is held momentarily in your sensory store.

Medium tone

LJ68

Stimulus array flashed on
screen for 0.05 seconds

Tone within the next 0.3 seconds
indicates which row to speak

Participant says the correct row

FIGURE 7.5 George Sperling (1960) flashed arrays like this on a screen for 50 milliseconds. After the display went off, a signal told the viewer which row to recite.

This *very brief storage of sensory information* is called the **sensory store,** also known as iconic memory (for visual information) and echoic memory (for auditory). George Sperling (1960) found a way to demonstrate visual sensory store. He flashed an array like the one shown in Figure 7.5 onto a screen for 50 milliseconds. When he asked viewers to report what they saw, he found that they could recall a mean of only about four items. If he had stopped his experiment at that point, he might have concluded that viewers stored only a little of the array. However, he surmised that the sensory store was probably fading while people were describing it. So he told viewers he would ask them to report only one row of the array, a different row each time.

After flashing an array on the screen, he immediately used a high, medium, or low tone to signal which row to recall. Frequently, people could name all the items in whichever row he indicated. Evidently, the whole array was briefly available to memory. When he waited for even 1 second before signaling which row to recall, though, recall was poor. That is, for the sensory store, "use it or lose it," and you had better use it fast.

You can try a version of Sperling's experiment online. Go to http://psychology. wadsworth.com/kalat_intro7e. Navigate to the student Web site, then to the Online Try It Yourself section, and click on Sperling Effect. However, this is a fragile effect (as opposed to a robust effect, which would occur under a variety of circumstances). The effect improves with practice; it also varies from one person to another and even from one computer to another depending on their speed. Give it a try, but don't be too dismayed if your results don't match the predictions.

Is the sensory store really memory, or is it perception? It is a little of both. Not everything falls neatly into our human-made categories.

Online
Try It
Yourself

CONCEPT CHECK ☑️

3. Would viewers probably remember as many items if Sperling had flashed pictures of objects instead of numbers and letters? (Check your answer on page 244)

CRITICAL THINKING:
A STEP FURTHER
Sensory Storage

Sperling demonstrated the capacity of the sensory store for visual information. How could you demonstrate the capacity of the sensory store for auditory information?

Short-Term and Long-Term Memory

Of all the vast information that passes through our sensory store, most fades quickly, we deal with a little of it for temporary use, and we store even less for permanent reference. According to the traditional version of information-processing theory, we distinguish between **short-term memory,** *temporary storage of recent events,* and **long-term memory,** *a relatively permanent store.* For example, while you are playing tennis, the current score is in your short-term memory, and the rules of the game are in your long-term memory.

Psychologists distinguish two major types of long-term memory: semantic and episodic. **Semantic memory** is *memory of general principles,* and **episodic memory** is *memory for specific events in a person's life* (Tulving, 1989). For example, your memory of the rules of tennis is a semantic memory; your memory of the time you beat your roommate at tennis is an episodic memory.

Most episodic memories are more fragile than semantic memories. For example, even if you don't play tennis again for a few years, you will remember most of the rules, but you will forget most of the specific times you played tennis. Older people are especially likely to retain semantic memories but forget specific episodes (Piolino, Desgranges, Benali, & Eustache, 2002).

People also frequently remember something they have heard (a semantic memory) but forget where they heard it (an episodic memory). Therefore, they confuse reliable information with the unreliable. ("Did I hear this idea from my professor or was it on *South Park*? Did I read about brain transplants in *Scientific American* or in the *National Enquirer*?") As a result you might dismiss an idea at first because you know it came from an unreliable source, but later remember it, forget where you heard it, and start to take it seriously (Johnson, Hashtroudi, & Lindsay, 1993; Riccio, 1994). In Chapter 14 we shall again discuss this phenomenon, known as the *sleeper* effect.

Psychologists have traditionally drawn several distinctions between short- and long-term memory, including capacity, dependence on retrieval cues, and decay over time. However, on closer examination we can find exceptions at least to the latter two. Let us consider these comparisons between short- and long-term memory (see also Table 7.3).

Differences in Capacity

Long-term memory has a vast, hard-to-measure capacity. Asking how much information you could store in long-term memory is like asking how many books you could fit into a library; the answer depends on how big the books are, how you arrange them, and so forth. Short-term memory in contrast has a small, easily measured capacity. Read each of the following sequences of letters and then look away and try to repeat them from memory. Or read each aloud and ask a friend to repeat it.

Try It Yourself

E H G P H
J R O Z N Q
S R B W R C N
M P D I W F B S
Z Y B P I A F M O

Most normal adults can repeat a list of approximately seven letters, numbers, or words. Some can re-

TABLE 7.3 Comparison of Sensory Store, Short-Term Memory, and Long-Term Memory

	Sensory Store	Short-Term Memory	Long-Term Memory
Capacity	Whatever you see or hear at one moment	7 ± 2 items in healthy adults	Vast, uncountable
Duration	Fraction of a second	A period of seconds if not rehearsed	Perhaps a lifetime
Example	You see something for an instant and then recall a detail about it	You look up a telephone number, remember it long enough to dial it	You remember the house where you lived when you were 7 years old

member eight or nine; others, only five or six. George Miller (1956) referred to the short-term memory capacity as "the magical number seven, plus or minus two." When people try to repeat a longer list, however, they may fail to remember even the first seven items. It is somewhat like trying to hold objects in one hand: If you try to hold too many, you drop them all.

The limit of short-term memory depends partly on how long it takes to say a word. If you were equally fluent in English and Welsh, you would seem to have a greater short-term memory for

▌ Short-term memory is like a handful of eggs; it can hold only a limited number of items at a time.

numbers when tested in English, just because you can say English numbers like *five* and *seven* faster than Welsh numbers like *pedwar* and *chwech* (Ellis & Hennelley, 1980). For the same reason, you would have a greater short-term memory for numbers in Chinese than in German (Lüer et al., 1998). Of

▌ Kutbidin Atamkulov travels from one Central Asian village to another singing from memory the tale of the Kirghiz hero, Manas. The song, which lasts 3 hours, has been passed from master to student for centuries.

course, if you were more fluent in one language than the other, you would show less short-term memory in your second language.

You can also store more information in short-term memory by coding it efficiently through a process called chunking—*grouping items into meaningful sequences or clusters* (see Figure 7.6). For example, the sequence "ventysi" has seven letters, at the limit of most people's short-term memory capacity. However, "seventysix" has three additional letters, but can be easily remembered as "76," a two-digit number. "Seventeenseventysix" is even longer, but if you think of it as 1776, one important date in history, it now is just a single item to store.

One college student in a lengthy experiment initially could repeat about seven digits at a time, the same as average (Ericsson, Chase, & Faloon, 1980). Over a year and a half, working 3 to 5 hours per week, he gradually improved until he could repeat 80 digits, as shown in Figure 7.7, by using extraordinary strategies for chunking. He was a competitive runner, so he might store the sequence "3492 . . ." as "3 minutes, 49.2 seconds, a near world-record time for running a mile." He might store the next set of numbers as a good time for running a kilometer, a mediocre marathon time, or a date in history. With practice he started recognizing larger and larger chunks. However, when he was tested on his ability to remember a list of letters, his performance was only average because he had not developed any chunking strategies for letters.

One cautionary point before we proceed: We talk about "storing" a memory and sometimes even compare the process to holding objects in your hand or placing books on the shelf of a library. These are only loose analogies. The brain does not store a memory like an object in one place; memory representation is a diffuse set of changes in synapses spread out over a huge population of cells.

FIGURE 7.7 Most people can repeat a list of about seven numbers. One college student gradually increased his ability to repeat a list of numbers over 18 months of practice. He greatly expanded his short-term memory for digits but not for letters or words. *(Reprinted with permission from "Acquisition of a Memory Skill," by K. A. Ericsson, W. G. Chase, and S. Faloon, Science, 1980, 208, 1181-1182. Copyright © 1980 American Association for the Advancement of Science.)*

Dependence on Retrieval Cues

When you store something in long-term memory and try to find it later, you need a retrieval cue (*associated information that might help you regain the memory*). For example, if someone asks you what *demand characteristics* are, you might say you have no idea. Then the person says, "I think they have something to do with research methods in psychology." Still you don't remember. "Do you remember something about an experiment in which people were really in an ordinary room, but they thought they were in sensory depriva-

FIGURE 7.6 We overcome the limits of short-term memory through chunking. You probably could not remember the 26-digit number in (a), but by breaking it up into a series of chunks, you can remember it and dial the number correctly.

tion, so they reported hallucinations and . . . ?" Suddenly, you remember the concept.

Traditionally, psychologists have regarded retrieval cues as irrelevant to short-term memory. For example, if you fail to recall a telephone number that you heard a few seconds ago, it is presumably "gone" and no reminder will help. The results are different, though, for more meaningful materials. Suppose you hear a list of words, including "closet," and then recall as many of the words as you can. If you don't recall "closet," but someone gives you the reminder "broom . . . ," you might say, "Oh, yes, 'closet.'" So retrieval cues are helpful for some short-term memories, even if not for all (Nelson & Goodmon, 2003).

Decay of Memories Over Time

A well-learned memory can last a lifetime. Harry Bahrick (1984) found that people who had studied Spanish in school 1 or 2 years ago remembered more than those who had studied it 3 to 6 years ago, but beyond 6 years the retention appeared to be stable (Figure 7.8). If you ask your grandparents to get out an old photo scrapbook, they will recall events they had not thought about in decades. Although the photographs may have faded, it is not certain that the memories themselves fade. They gradually become harder to retrieve, but mainly because of interference from other memories.

Short-term memories do seem to fade, however. In fact neuroscientists have identified a protein that the brain makes after an experience that weakens or destroys the memory trace, presumably to avoid permanently storing unimportant information (Genoux et al., 2002). Obviously, the effects of that protein can be canceled if the information is repeated. It can also be canceled by emotional arousal, which mobilizes epi-

nephrine (adrenalin) and thereby strengthens memory formation (LaLumiere, Buen, & McGaugh, 2003).

Here is the classic behavioral demonstration of the fading of short-term memories: Lloyd Peterson and Margaret Peterson (1959) wanted to present a meaningless sequence of letters, like HOXDF, and then test people's memory after various delays. However, people who expect to be tested spend the delay rehearsing "HOXDF, HOXDF . . ." To prevent rehearsal, the experimenters gave a competing task. They simultaneously presented the letters and a number, such as 231. The instruction was to start with that number and count backward by threes, such as "231, 228, 225, 222, 219 . . ." until the end of the delay and then say the letters.

Figure 7.9 shows the results. Note that only about 10% of the participants could recall the letters after 18 seconds. In other words an unrehearsed short-term memory decays rapidly. You can demonstrate this phenomenon online. Go to http://psychology.wadsworth.com/kalat_intro7e. Navigate to the student Web site, then to the Online Try It Yourself section, and click on Decay of Short-Term Memory.

Online Try It Yourself

However, do not take that figure of 18 seconds too seriously. Peterson and Peterson were dealing with nonsense information, such as HOXDF. They presented a long series of trials, and the answer to each one would interfere with the others. Under other circumstances people can remember meaningful short-term memories for much longer. Certainly, you should

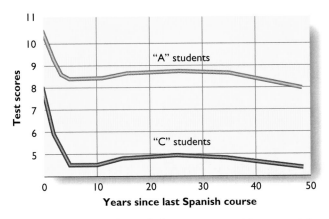

FIGURE 7.8 Spanish vocabulary as measured by a recognition test shows a rapid decline in the first few years but then long-term stability. The students who received an "A" had a better performance at the start, but both groups showed similar rates of forgetting. (*"Semantic Memory Content in Permastore: Fifty Years of Memory for Spanish Learned in School,"* by H. P. Bahrick, Journal of Experiential Psychology: General, *1984, 113, 1–29. Copyright © 1984 by the American Psychological Association. Reprinted with permission of the author.*)

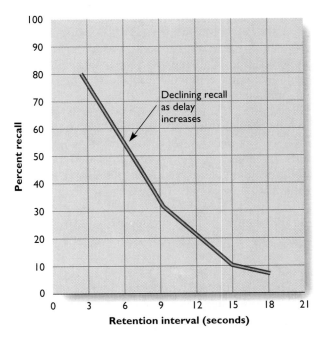

FIGURE 7.9 In a study by Peterson and Peterson (1959), people remembered a set of letters well after a short delay, but their memory faded greatly over 18 seconds if they were prevented from rehearsing during that time.

not imagine that every memory either fades within 18 seconds or so (short-term memory) or lasts a lifetime (long-term). You have many memories that you keep as long as they are current, updating them with new information as often as necessary (Altmann & Gray, 2002). For example, if you are playing basketball, you remember the score, approximately how much time is left in the game, what defense your team is using, what offense, how many fouls you have committed, and so forth. You won't (and wouldn't want to) remember all that information for the rest of your life, but you also don't need to rehearse it constantly to prevent it from fading within 18 seconds. Similarly, right now you may remember approximately how much money is in your wallet, what you plan to do next weekend, and a great deal of other information you need to store as long as it is current, until you update it with new information. So not all memories fade at the same rate.

CONCEPT CHECK ☑

4. Is your memory of your current mailing address a semantic memory or an episodic memory? What about your memories of the day you moved to your current address?
5. How does the capacity of short-term memory compare with that of long-term memory? (Check your answers on page 244.)

Working Memory

Originally, psychologists described short-term memory as the way you store something while you are moving it into long-term storage. Eventually, problems accumulated for that idea. One problem is that *how long* information remains in short-term memory is a poor predictor of whether it will become a long-term memory. For example, you might watch a hockey game in which the score remains the same for 2 hours, but you don't remember that score permanently. In contrast, if someone tells you something important, like "Your sister just had a baby," you can form a lasting memory quickly.

Today, most researchers emphasize temporary memory storage as the information you are working with at the moment, regardless of whether you ever store it as a more permanent memory. To emphasize this different perspective, they speak of *working memory* instead of short-term memory.

Working memory is *a system for processing or working with current information*. It is almost synonymous with someone's current sphere of attention. Different psychologists have used the term in different ways, and some have broadened the term until it is al-

most synonymous with intelligence (Oberauer, Süss, Wilhelm, & Wittman, 2003).

Working memory includes at least three major components (Baddeley, 2001; Baddeley & Hitch, 1994):

- A *phonological loop*, which stores and rehearses speech information. The phonological loop, similar to the traditional view of short-term memory, enables us to repeat seven or so items immediately after hearing them. It is probably essential for anyone first learning a language (Baddeley, Gathercole, & Papagno, 1998). It is also essential for understanding a long sentence; you have to remember the words at the start of the sentence long enough to connect them to the words at the end.
- A *visuospatial sketchpad*, which stores and manipulates visual and spatial information, providing for vision what the phonological loop provides for speech (Luck & Vogel, 1997). You would use this process for recognizing pictures or for imagining what an object looks like from another angle.

  Researchers distinguish between the phonological and visuospatial stores because you can do an auditory word task and a visuospatial task at the same time without much interference but not two auditory tasks or two visuospatial tasks (Baddeley & Hitch, 1974; Hale, Myerson, Rhee, Weiss, & Abrams, 1996). People presumably have additional stores for touch, smell, and taste, but so far researchers have concentrated on the auditory and visual stores.
- A *central executive*, which governs shifts of attention. The hallmark of good working memory is the ability to shift attention as needed among different tasks. Imagine a hospital nurse who has to keep track of the needs of several patients, sometimes interrupting the treatment of one patient to take care of an emergency and then returning to complete the first patient. Also imagine yourself driving a car, watching the oncoming traffic, the cars in front of you and behind, the gauges on your dashboard, sometimes a map, and possibly a conversation with a passenger.

Psychologists are not precisely what they mean by "central executive" or "shifting attention," so it is not easy to find a perfect measure of it (Logan, 2003). (The same issue arises for "intelligence" in the next chapter, as well as many other terms in psychology.) Here is one simple way to measure shifting attention: Recite aloud some poem, song, or other passage that you know well. (If you can't think of a more interesting example, you can recite the alphabet.) Time how long it takes. Then measure how long it takes you to say the same thing silently. Finally, time how long it takes you to alternate—the first word aloud, the second silent, the third aloud, and so forth. Alternating takes longer because you have to keep shifting attention.

Here is another way to measure executive processes: You hear a list of words such as *maple, elm, oak, hemlock, chestnut, birch, sycamore, pine, redwood, walnut, dogwood, hickory.* After each word you are supposed to say the *previous* word. So after "maple, elm," you should say "maple." After "oak" you reply "elm." If you do well on that task, you proceed to a more difficult version: You should repeat what you heard *two* words ago. So you wait for "maple, elm, oak" and reply "maple." Then you hear "hemlock" and reply "elm." Note how you need to shift back and forth between listening to the new word and repeating something from memory.

Another example: An investigator flashes on the screen a simple arithmetic question and a word, such as

$$(2 \times 3) + 1 = 8? \text{ SPRING}$$

As quickly as possible, you should read the arithmetic question, answer it yes or no, and then say the word. As soon as you do, you will see a new question and word; again you answer the question and say the word. After a few such items, the investigator stops and asks you to say all the words in order. To do well you have to shift your attention between doing the arithmetic and memorizing the words. This is a difficult task. Some people have trouble remembering even two words under these conditions; remembering five or six is an excellent score.

People who do well on this task (who are considered to have a "high capacity" of working memory) also do well on a variety of other tasks, including intelligence tests (Engle, Tuholski, Laughlin, & Conway, 1999; Süss, Oberauer, Wittman, Wilhelm, & Schulze, 2002). They do better than most other people at suppressing unwanted thoughts (Brewin & Beaton, 2002). They are more likely than other people to prefer a large reward later instead of a smaller reward now (Hinson, Jameson, & Whitney, 2003). They also excel at naming as many animals as possible in 10 minutes and learning several consecutive word lists without confusing one with another. Interestingly, if people have to perform an additional constantly distracting task, such as tapping a rhythm with their fingers, everyone's performance suffers, but those with the best working memory suffer the most (Kane & Engle, 2000; Rosen & Engle, 1997). They still perform better than people with less working memory but not by as much as usual. Of course, one reason is that those with poor working memory weren't doing well anyway, so they had less room to get worse. Another explanation is that people with good working memory usually do well because they direct their attention to the important aspects of the task. With a constant distracter, they lose that advantage.

CONCEPT CHECK ☑

6. Some students like to listen to music while studying. Is the music likely to help or impair their study? (What might the answer depend on?) (Check your answer on page 244.)

IN CLOSING

Varieties of Memory

Although researchers still disagree with one another on many points about memory, they do agree about what memory is *not*: Memory is not a single store into which we simply dump things and later take them out. When Ebbinghaus conducted his studies of memory in the late 1800s, he thought he was measuring the properties of memory, period. We now know that the properties of memory depend on the type of material being memorized, the individual's experience with similar materials, the method of testing, and the recency of the event. Memory is not one process, but many.

Summary

- *Ebbinghaus's approach.* Hermann Ebbinghaus pioneered the experimental study of memory by testing his own ability to memorize and retain lists of nonsense syllables. (page 233)
- *Methods of testing memory.* The free recall method reveals only relatively strong memories. Progressively weaker memories can be demonstrated by the cued recall, recognition, and savings methods. Implicit memories are changes in behavior under conditions in which the person cannot verbalize the memory or is unaware of the influence. (page 234)
- *Suspect lineups.* Suspect lineups are an example of the recognition method of testing memory. Unfortunately, witnesses sometimes choose the best available choice and then decide they are sure. Psychologists have recommended ways of improving lineups to decrease inaccurate identifications. (page 236)
- *The information-processing model.* According to the information-processing model of memory, information first enters a sensory store, then becomes a short-term memory, and finally, a long-term memory. (page 237)
- *Differences between short-term and long-term memory.* Long-term memory requires elicitation by a retrieval cue, whereas short-term memory does not. Short-term memory has a capacity of only about seven items in normal adults, although

chunking can enable us to store much information in each item. Long-term memory has a very large, not easily measured capacity. Short-term memories fade over time if not rehearsed, whereas some long-term memories last a lifetime. (page 239)

- *Working memory.* As an alternative to the traditional description of short-term memory, current researchers identify working memory as a system for dealing with current information, including the ability to shift attention back and forth among several tasks as necessary. (page 242)

Answers to Concept Checks

1. **a.** savings; **b.** recall; **c.** implicit; **d.** recognition; **e.** cued recall. (page 236)
2. Remembering how to tie your shoes is a procedural memory. Remembering their appearance is a declarative memory (one you could express in words). (page 236)
3. If we assume that it would take longer to name objects than numbers or letters, people would probably name fewer. The longer it takes for people to answer, the more their sensory store fades. (page 238)

4. Your memory of your current address is a semantic memory. Your memory of the events of moving day is an episodic memory. (page 242)
5. Short-term memory has a capacity limited to only about seven items in the average adult, whereas long-term memory has a huge, difficult-to-measure capacity. (page 242)
6. If the music requires any attention at all or evokes any response, such as occasionally singing along, it will impair attention. The difference will be most noticeable for the best students. However, background music with no words and no tendency to evoke responses is probably a slight benefit if it prevents the student from noticing other sounds that might be more distracting. (page 243)

Answers to Other Questions in the Module

A. Herman Melville, Jane Austen, Agatha Christie, Arthur Conan Doyle, Maya Angelou, Leo Tolstoy, James Kalat, Geoffrey Chaucer, Charles Darwin, Margaret Mitchell, Victor Hugo. (page 235)

Long-Term Memory Storage

How can we improve our memories?

There you are, taking a geography test, unable to remember the major rivers of Africa. You remember reviewing that section in your book last night; you even remember that it was on the upper left side of the page, and there was a map to the right. You remember the cappuccino you were sipping. And the time was 9:30 P.M. You just don't remember the names of the rivers.

How can we improve our memory? The main point of this module is simple: To improve your memory, improve the way you store the material in the first place.

Meaningful Storage and Levels of Processing

If you want to memorize a definition, what would you do? Repeat it over and over? Repetition does help, other things being equal, but repetition by itself is a poor study method.

To illustrate, examine Figure 7.10, which shows a real U.S. penny and 14 fakes. If you live in the United States, you have seen pennies countless times, but can you now identify the real one? Most U.S. citizens guess wrong (Nickerson & Adams, 1979). (If you do not have a penny in your pocket, check answer B on

■ Most actors preparing for a play spend much time thinking about the meaning of what they say (a deep level of processing) and only a little time simply repeating the words.

page 251. If you are not from the United States, try drawing the front or back of a common coin in your own country.) In short, mere repetition, such as looking at a coin many times, does not guarantee a strong memory.

Suppose you read two articles of equal length from the sports pages of a newspaper. One is about a sport you follow closely, and the other is about a sport that has never interested you. Even though you spend the same amount of time reading each article, you will remember more from the article you care about. The more you already know about any topic, the easier it is to learn still more (Hambrick & Engle, 2002). The important points stand out, and you quickly associate the details to other facts you already know.

According to the **levels-of-processing principle** (Craik & Lockhart, 1972), *how easily we can retrieve a memory depends on the number and types of associations we form.* The associations establish retrieval cues. By analogy, a librarian who places a new book on the shelf also enters information into the retrieval system so that anyone who knows the title, author, or topic can find the book. The more items the librarian enters, the easier it will be for someone to find that book later. The same is true of your memory.

When you read something—this chapter, for example—you might simply read over the

FIGURE 7.10 Can you spot the genuine penny among 14 fakes? If you're not sure (and you don't have a penny with you), check answer B on page 251. (*"Long-term Memory for a Common Object,"* by R.S. Nickerson and M.J. Adams, Cognitive Psychology, 1979, 11, 287–307. Copyright © 1979 Academic Press. Reprinted with permission.)

TABLE 7.4 Levels-of-Processing Model of Memory

Superficial processing	Simply repeat the material to be remembered: "Hawk, Oriole, Tiger, Timberwolf, Blue Jay, Bull."
Deeper processing	Think about each item. Note that two start with T and two with B.
Still deeper processing	Note that three are birds and three are mammals. Also, three are major league baseball teams and three are NBA basketball teams. Use whichever associations mean the most to you.

words, giving them little thought. We call that kind of study "shallow processing," and you will remember almost nothing at test time. Alternatively, you might stop and consider various points that you read, relate them to your own experiences, and think of your own examples of the principles. The more ways you think about the material, the "deeper" your processing is and the more easily you will remember later. Table 7.4 summarizes this model.

Imagine several groups of students who study a list of words in different ways. One group simply reads the list over and over, and a second counts the letters in each word. Both procedures yield poor recall later. A third group tries to think of a synonym for each word or tries to use each word in a sentence. These students form many associations and later recall the words better than the first two groups. Students in the fourth group ask about each word, "How does it apply to some experience in my own life?" This group does even better than the third group. For a while psychologists thought that relating words to yourself produces a special kind of strengthening, but later research found equally strong memories in students who tried to relate each word to their mothers (Symons & Johnson, 1997). The conclusion is that memory grows stronger when people elaborate and organize the material and relate it to anything they know and care about.

You can improve your level of processing in two ways (Einstein & Hunt, 1980; McDaniel, Einstein, & Lollis, 1988): First, you can think about the items on the list one by one. Second, you can look for relationships among them. You might notice, for example, that a list consists of five animals, six foods, four methods of transportation, and five wooden objects. One of the skills we gain through education is learning to organize material in this way. According to one study of the Kpelle people in West Africa, teenage children who had gone to school organized a list of words into categories and remembered the list well. Unschooled children did not sort the list into categories and did not remember it well (Scribner, 1974).

CONCEPT CHECK

7. Many students who get the best grades in a course read the assigned text chapters more slowly than average. Why? (Check your answer on page 251.)

Encoding Specificity

If encoding something in a variety of ways leads to easy recall under varied circumstances, then encoding it in just one way means that only a few retrieval cues will stimulate the memory later. Those few cues, however, can be highly effective.

According to the **encoding specificity principle** (Tulving & Thomson, 1973), *the associations you form at the time of learning will be the most effective retrieval cues* (Figure 7.11). Here is an example (modified from Thieman, 1984). First, read the pairs of words (which psychologists call *paired associates*) in Table 7.5a. Then turn to Table 7.5b on page 248. For each of the words on that list, try to recall a related word on the list you just read. *Do this now.* (The answers are on page 251, answer C.)

Most people find this task difficult. Because they initially coded the word *cardinal* as a type of clergyman, for example, they do not think of it when they see the retrieval cue *bird*. If they had thought of it as a bird, then *clergyman* would not have been a good reminder.

The principle of encoding specificity extends to other aspects of experience at the time of storage. For example, if you return to a place where you haven't

FIGURE 7.11 According to the principle of encoding specificity, the way we code a word during original learning determines which cues will remind us of that word later. For example, when you hear the word *queen*, you may think of that word in any of several ways. If you think of *queen bee*, then the cue *playing card* will not remind you of it later. If you think of the *queen of England*, then *chess piece* will not be a good reminder.

TABLE 7.5a

Clergyman—Cardinal	Geometry—Plane
Trinket—Charm	Tennis—Racket
Type of wine—Port	Music—Rock
U.S. politician—Bush	Magic—Spell
Inch—Foot	Envelope—Seal
Computer—Apple	Graduation—Degree

been in years, you may remember events that happened there. In one study college students who were fluent in both English and Russian were given a list of words such as *summer, birthday,* and *doctor,* some in English and some in Russian. For each word they were asked to describe any related event they remembered. In response to Russian words, they recalled mostly events that happened when they were speaking Russian. In response to English words, they recalled mostly events when they were speaking English (Marian & Neisser, 2000).

More examples: If you experience something while you are sad, you will remember it better when you are sad again (Eich & Macaulay, 2000). If you learn something while frightened, you will remember it better when you are frightened again, and if you learn while calm, you will remember better when calm (Lang, Craske, Brown, & Ghaneian, 2001). Strong drugs can induce this effect also. State-dependent memory is *the tendency to remember something better if your body is in the same condition during recall as it was during the original learning.* State-dependent memory, however, is a small effect that is often difficult to demonstrate (Eich, 1995).

The encoding specificity principle has a couple of clear implications. First, if you want to remember something at a particular time and place, make your study conditions similar to the conditions when you will try to remember. On the other hand, if you want to remember the material for life, under a wide variety of conditions, then you should vary your study habits.

CONCEPT CHECK ☑

8. Suppose someone cannot remember what happened at a party last night. What steps might help improve the memory? (Check your answer on page 251.)

The Timing of Study Sessions

If you need to take a test on some topic, should you study a little at a time or wait until shortly before the test? Even if you sometimes do wait until just before

the test, you probably know how risky this strategy is. On the day before the test, some unforeseen event might arise that prevents you from studying at all. Also, if the material is complicated, you might not be able to understand it all in one reading.

But let's change the question in a way that makes the answer less obvious: Suppose you don't wait until the day before the test, but you nevertheless study the material all at once on a day when you have plenty of time and no distractions. Will your result be better, worse, or about the same as if spread out your study over days or weeks?

The answer is that studying all at once is worse, for a variety of reasons. One is that if you study all at once, you are not sure when you have studied "enough." Most students overestimate how well they understand something, and below-average students are especially likely to overestimate (Dunning, Johnson, Ehrlinger, & Kruger, 2003). If you overestimate your understanding, you stop studying too soon. However, if you spread out your study over days, then when you return after an absence, you notice how much you have forgotten, and therefore study it again.

Imagine yourself in the following study: A three-letter combination appears on a computer screen. It might be a word like BUG or a meaningless combination like FXH. You are instructed to study it for as long as you want—absolutely no rush—until you are sure you will be able to recall it later. There will be 27 such three-letter combinations. Take your time with each one. Don't proceed until you are sure you have

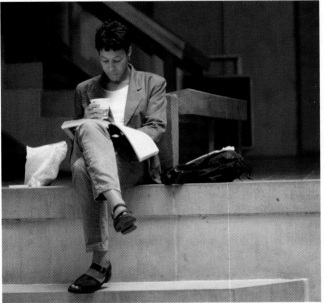

❙ People need to monitor their understanding of a text to decide whether to continue studying or whether they already understand it well enough. Most readers have trouble making that judgment correctly.

TABLE 7.5b

Instructions: For each of these words, write one of the second of the paired terms from the list in Table 7.5a.

Animal—	Stone—
Part of body—	Personality—
Transportation—	Write—
Temperature—	Bird—
Crime—	Harbor—
Shrubbery—	Fruit—

learned it well, and then press the key to move on to the next item. At the end, theoretically, you should get them all correct. However, when this study was actually conducted, the average student recalled only 49% of them (Nelson & Leonesio, 1988). Two conclusions follow: (a) It is hard to judge how well you have learned something if you haven't waited long enough to see whether you will forget (Maki & Serra, 1992; Weaver & Kelemen, 1997). (b) Studying something once is seldom effective, even if you study it very hard that one time.

A second reason for spreading out your study is that if you study under a variety of conditions, you will establish a wide variety of retrieval cues and therefore remember under a variety of conditions. Psychologist Harry Bahrick and members of his family studied foreign language vocabulary, varying the frequency of study. Some had a study session every 2 weeks; others studied the same number of hours but spread out over longer times, such as once every 8 weeks. The result: More frequent study led to faster learning, but less frequent study led to better long-term retention, as measured years later (Bahrick, Bahrick, Bahrick, & Bahrick, 1993).

Results of many other studies confirm the same general principle: If you want to remember something under a variety of conditions, practice it under a variety of conditions (Schmidt & Bjork, 1992). Varying the conditions may actually slow down the original learning and make the task seem more difficult, but in the long run it helps. In one experiment a group of 8-year-old children practiced throwing a small beanbag at a target on the floor 3 feet away. Another group practiced with a target sometimes 2 feet away and sometimes 4 feet away, but never 3 feet away. Then both groups were tested with the target 3 feet away. The children who had been practicing with the 3-foot target missed it by a mean of 8.3 inches. The children who had been practicing with 2-foot and 4-foot targets actually did better, missing by a mean of only 5.4 inches, even though they were aiming at the 3-foot target for the first time (Kerr & Booth, 1978). In another experiment young adults

practiced a technique for mentally squaring two-digit numbers—for example, $23 \times 23 = 529$. Those who practiced with just a small range of numbers learned the technique quickly but also forgot it quickly; those who practiced with a wider range of numbers learned more slowly but remembered better at a later time and applied the technique better to a new set of problems (Sanders, Gonzalez, Murphy, Pesta, & Bucur, 2002).

The SPAR Method

One systematic way to organize your study is the SPAR method:

Survey. Get an overview of what the passage is about. Scan through it; look at the boldface headings; try to understand the organization and goals of the passage.

Process *meaningfully.* Read the material carefully. Think about how you could use the ideas or how they relate to other things you have read. Evaluate the strengths and weaknesses of the argument. The more actively you think about what you read, the better you will remember the material.

Ask questions. If the text provides questions, like the Concept Checks in this text, try to answer them. Then pretend you are the instructor; write the questions you would ask on a test and answer them yourself. In the process you will discover which sections of the passage you need to reread.

Review. Wait a day or so and then retest your knowledge. Spreading out your study over time increases your ability to remember it over the long term.

CONCEPT CHECK ☑

9. If you want to do well on the final exam in this course, what should you do now—review this chapter or review the first three chapters in the book?

10. How does the advice to spread out your study over a long time instead of doing it all at one sitting fit or contrast with the encoding specificity principle? (Check your answers on page 251.)

Emotional Arousal and Memory Storage

People usually remember emotionally arousing events. Chances are you vividly remember your first day of college, your first kiss, the time your team won the big game, and times you were extremely frightened.

The effects of arousal on memory have been known for centuries. In England in the early 1600s, when people sold land, they did not yet have the custom of recording the sale on paper. (Paper was expensive and few people could read anyway.) Instead, local residents would gather around while someone announced the sale and instructed everyone to remember it. Of all those present, whose memory of the sale was most important? The children because they would live the longest. And of all those present, who were least interested? Right, again, it's the children. To increase the chances that the children would remember, the adults would kick them while telling them about the business deal. The same idea persisted in the custom, still common in the early 1900s, of slapping schoolchildren's hands with a stick to make them pay attention.

However, although emotional arousal enhances memory, what you remember may not be what you want to remember. Furthermore, your "flashbulb" memories of where you were, what you were doing, and so forth when you heard some shocking news may be emotionally intense but not necessarily accurate. In one study Israeli students were interviewed 2 weeks after the assassination of Israel's Prime Minister, Itzhak Rabin, and again 11 months later. About 36% of the emotionally intense memories they reported at the later time differed from what they had reported earlier (Nachson & Zelig, 2003). In another study U.S. students reported their memories of where they were, what they were doing, and so forth at the time of hearing about the terrorist attacks on September 11, 2001. They reported their memories on the day after the attacks and then again weeks or months later. Over time the students continued to report high vividness of the memories and high confidence in them, but the accuracy of their memory reports gradually declined, just as do any other memories (Talarico & Rubin, 2003).

■ Do you remember the first time you saw a comet? Most people recall emotionally arousing events, sometimes in great detail, although not always accurately.

Advertisers try to get you to remember their product by making their ads exciting or (for television ads) by airing them on exciting programs. However, excitement from one event doesn't always carry over to memory for another. For example, an ad featuring attractive people in skimpy bathing suits may get you excited, but you may or may not remember the product. If it is an ad for swimsuits, sunscreen, or something else related to beaches, then yes. However, a sexually exciting ad won't help you remember an ad for kitchen appliances or farm equipment. Similarly, watching a violent television program is emotionally arousing, but it actually decreases memory of the products advertised, which are generally unrelated to violence (Bushman & Phillips, 2001). The best advice for advertisers is to get the viewer or listener excited about the product itself or to advertise on an exciting program related to the product. Similarly, the advice for a student is that if you want to remember something, get excited about the content itself. Find some way to see it as interesting.

Why are emotionally arousing events generally so memorable? The physiological explanation is that emotional arousal increases the release of the hormones cortisol and epinephrine (adrenaline) from the adrenal gland. Some of the cortisol reaches the brain, and the epinephrine stimulates peripheral nerves that extend into the brain. The net effect is increased excitation of the *amygdala* and other brain areas that enhance memory storage (Cahill & McGaugh, 1998; Williams, Men, Clayton, & Gold, 1998).

CONCEPT CHECK ☑

11. Most people with posttraumatic stress disorder have lower than normal levels of cortisol. What would you predict about their memory? (Check your answer on page 251)

Mnemonic Devices

If you needed to memorize something lengthy and not especially exciting—for example, a list of all the bones in the body—how would you do it? One effective strategy is to attach systematic retrieval cues to each term so that you can remind yourself of the terms when you need them.

A **mnemonic device** is *any memory aid that relies on encoding each item in a special way.* The word *mnemonic* (nee- MAHN-ik) comes from a Greek root meaning "memory." (The same root appears in the word *amnesia,* "lack of memory.") Some mnemonic devices are simple, such as "Every Good Boy Does Fine" to remember the notes EGBDF on the treble clef in music. If you have to remember the functions of various brain areas, you might try links like those shown in Figure 7.12 (Carney & Levin, 1998).

A parachute lets you coast down slowly, like the parasympathetic nervous system.

If the symphony excites you, it arouses your sympathetic nervous system.

FIGURE 7.12 A simple mnemonic device is to think of a short story or image that will remind you of what you need to remember. Here you might think of images to help remember functions of different brain areas.

Suppose you had to memorize a list of Nobel Peace Prize winners (Figure 7.13). You might try making up a little story: "Dun (Dunant) passed (Passy) the Duke (Ducommun) of Gob (Gobat) some cream (Cremer). That made him internally ILL (Institute of In-

Nobel Peace Prize Winners

1901	H. Dunant and F. Passy
1902	E. Ducommun and A. Gobat
1903	Sir W. R. Cremer
1904	Institute of International Law
1905	Baroness von Suttner
1906	T. Roosevelt
1907	E. T. Moneta and L. Renault
1908	K. P. Arnoldson and F. Bajer
1909	A. M. F. Beernaert and Baron d'Estournelles de Constant

1990	M. Gorbachev
1991	A. S. Suu Kyi
1992	Rigoberta Menchú
1993	Nelson Mandela and Frederik W. de Klerk
1994	Yasir Arafat, Yitzhak Rabin, and Shimon Peres
1995	Joseph Rotblat and Pugwash Conferences on Science and World Affairs
1996	Carlos Felipe Ximenes Belo and José Ramos-Horta
1997	Jody Williams and International Committee to Ban Landmines
1998	John Hume and David Trimble
1999	Doctors Without Borders
2000	Kim Dae Jung
2001	Kofi Annan
2002	Jimmy Carter, Jr.
2003	Shirin Ebadi

FIGURE 7.13 A list of Nobel Peace Prize winners: Mnemonic devices can be useful when people try to memorize long lists like this one.

ternational Law). He suited (von Suttner) up with some roses (Roosevelt) and spent some money (Moneta) on a Renault (Renault) . . ." You'd still have to study the names, but your story might help.

Another mnemonic device is the **method of loci** (method of places). *First, you memorize a series of places, and then you use a vivid image to associate each of these locations with something you want to remember.* For example, you might start by memorizing every location along the route from your dormitory room to, say, your psychology classroom. Then you link the locations, in order, to the names.

Suppose the first three locations you pass are the desk in your room, the door to your room, and the corridor. To link the first Nobel Peace Prize winners, Dunant and Passy, to your desk, you might imagine a Monopoly game board on your desk with a big sign "DO NOT (Dunant) PASS (Passy) GO." Then you link the second pair of names to the second location, your door: A DUKE student (as in Ducommun) is standing at the door, giving confusing signals. He says "DO COME IN (Ducommun)" and "GO BACK (Gobat)." Then you link the corridor to Cremer, perhaps by imagining someone has spilled CREAM (Cremer) all over the floor (Figure 7.14). You continue in this manner until you have linked every name to a location. Now, if you can remember all those locations in order and if you have good visual images for each one, you will be able to recite the list of Nobel Peace Prize winners.

How useful are elaborate mnemonic devices? Few people find mnemonics useful for everyday tasks such as remembering where you parked your car, but mnemonics can be helpful in their proper place. For

FIGURE 7.14 The method of loci is one of the oldest mnemonic devices. First, learn a list of places, such as "my desk, the door of my room, the corridor, . . ." Then link each of these places to the items on a list of words or names, such as a list of the names of Nobel Peace Prize winners.

example, you might find mnemonics useful for remembering people's names (e.g., you might remember someone named Harry Moore by picturing him as "more hairy" than everyone else).

IN CLOSING

Improving Your Memory

You have probably heard of people taking gingko biloba or other herbs or drugs to try to improve their memory. These chemicals do produce small but measurable memory benefits for patients with impaired blood flow to the brain (Gold, Cahill, & Wenk, 2002; McDaniel, Maier, & Einstein, 2002). However, no one has demonstrated any benefits for healthy people. Some people do remember better than others, even when they have studied equally, and someday—who knows—perhaps researchers will find "the secret" to improving overall memory. Until then, by far the best strategy is to think carefully about anything you want to remember, study it under a variety of conditions, and review frequently.

Summary

* *Levels-of-processing principle.* According to the levels-of-processing principle, a memory becomes stronger (and easier to recall) if we think about the meaning of the material and relate it to other material. (page 245)
* *Encoding specificity.* When we form a memory, we store it with links to the way we thought about it at that time. When we try to recall the memory, a cue

is most effective if it is similar to the links we formed at the time of storage. (page 246)
* *Timing of study.* If you study all at one time, you cannot be sure how much you have learned and how much you will forget. It is best to spread out the study, and the more you spread it out, the longer you are likely to remember it. (page 247)
* *Emotional arousal.* Emotionally exciting events tend to be remembered vividly if not always accurately. (page 248)
* *Mnemonics.* Specialized techniques for establishing systematic retrieval cues can help people remember ordered lists of names or terms. (page 249)

Answers to Concept Checks

7. Students who read slowly and frequently pause to think about the meaning of the material are engaging in deep processing and are likely to remember the material well, probably better than those who read through the material quickly. (page 246)
8. Sometimes someone who claims not to remember simply does not want to talk about it. However, presuming the person really wants to remember, it would help to return to the place of the party, with the same people present, perhaps even at the same time of day. If he or she used alcohol or other drugs, take them again. The more similar the conditions of original learning and later recall, the better the probability of remembering. (page 247)
9. To prepare well for the final exam, you should review all the material at irregular intervals. Thus, you might profit by skimming over Chapters 2 and 3 right now. Of course, if you have a test on Chapter 7 in a day or two, your goal is different and your strategy should be different. (page 248)
10. If you study all at one sitting, the memory will be encoded specifically to what you are thinking about at that time. If you study at several times, the memory will attach to a greater variety of retrieval cues instead of being specific to just one set. (page 248)
11. Because of the lower cortisol levels, they should have trouble storing memories and therefore report frequent memory lapses. (page 249)

Answers to Other Questions in the Module

B. The correct coin is A. (page 245)
C. Animal—Seal; Part of body—Foot; Transportation—Plane; Temperature—Degree; Crime—Racket; Shrubbery—Bush; Stone—Rock; Personality—Charm; Write—Spell; Bird—Cardinal; Harbor—Port; Fruit—Apple. (page 248)

Retrieval of Memories

Why is memory retrieval sometimes difficult?

Why do we sometimes report confident but inaccurate memories?

Imagine that you have written a term paper on your computer, and when you click the icon to retrieve it, the computer gives you this error message: "I know it's around here somewhere, but I just can't find it. Try asking me again in a few hours." Or suppose it displays, not the correct term paper, but another one that you wrote the previous semester. Or odder yet, it prints out an elaborate, complicated term paper that you never wrote!

A computer doesn't make those errors (unless it has a virus or some other strange problem). Human memory does, however. This module is titled "Retrieval of Memories," but in fact much of the discussion focuses on failures and errors of retrieval.

Retrieval and Interference

A moment ago I said a computer would not make the mistake of displaying the wrong material. That is true for its internal memory, but when a computer searches for something on the Internet, it will often display the wrong material. When you look for a particular Web site, your search engine may display hundreds of others that resemble it.

Human memory also makes mistakes by confusing the sought material with similar information. If you want to recall a particular memory, then the more often you have learned something similar, the harder it will be to recall the correct information. The first experimental demonstration of this principle was accidental. Remember Hermann Ebbinghaus, who pioneered experimental research on memory. Ebbinghaus measured how long he could remember various lists of 13 nonsense syllables each. The results appear as the blue line on Figure 7.15. On the average he forgot more than half of each list within the first hour (Ebbinghaus, 1885/1913). What a discouraging graph! If people typically forget that fast, then education would seem pointless. However, later replications of this procedure with college students produced the red line of Figure 7.15. Note that most students remembered nearly 90% of the list 24 hours later (Koppenaal, 1963).

Why do you suppose most college students remember a list so much better than Ebbinghaus did? You may be tempted to say that college students are

Ebbinghaus could learn new lists of nonsense syllables, but he forgot them quickly because of interference from all the previous lists he had learned. People who memorize many similar lists start to confuse them with one another.

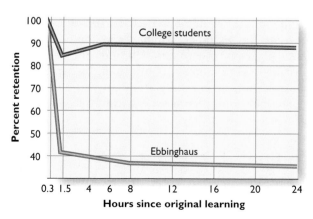

FIGURE 7.15 Blue line: Recall of lists of syllables by Ebbinghaus (1885/1913) after delays of various lengths. Red line: Recall of lists by college students after delays of various lengths. Ebbinghaus learned as fast as other people but forgot faster. *(Based on Koppenaal, 1963).*

very intelligent. Well, yes, but Ebbinghaus was no dummy either. Or you might suggest that college students "have had so much practice at memorizing nonsense." (Sorry if you think so.) But the explanation is the opposite: Ebbinghaus had memorized *too much* nonsense—thousands of lists of syllables. If you memorize large amounts of similar material, your memory becomes like a cluttered room: The clutter doesn't prevent you from bringing in still more clutter, but it makes it harder to find the item you want. Ebbinghaus forgot new lists quickly because of interference from older lists.

If you learn several sets of related materials, the old interferes with the new and the new interferes with the old. The *old materials increase forgetting of the new materials* through **proactive interference** (acting forward in time); the *new materials increase forgetting of the old materials* through **retroactive interference** (acting backward in time). Figure 7.16 shows the distinction between these two kinds of interference.

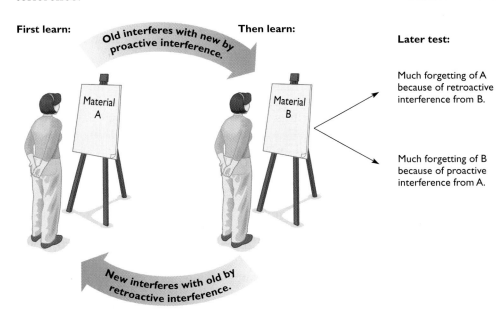

FIGURE 7.16 When someone learns two similar sets of materials, each interferes with retrieval of the other.

Interference is a major cause of forgetting. You may forget where you parked your car because of proactive interference from all the previous times you parked in the same lot. You may forget last week's French vocabulary list because of retroactive interference from this week's list.

CONCEPT CHECK ✓

12. Professor Tryhard learns the names of his students every semester. After several years he learns them as quickly as ever but forgets them

faster. Does he forget because of retroactive interference or proactive interference?

13. Remember the concept of spontaneous recovery from Chapter 6, page 199? Can you explain it in terms of proactive interference? (Hint: Original learning comes first and extinction comes second. What would happen if the first interfered with the second?) (Check your answers on page 262.)

Distinctiveness

Let's consider an application of this idea of interference. Read the following list and then recall, in any order, as many items as you can:

Brussels, Oslo, Bangkok, Calcutta, Kyoto, chocolate, Buenos Aires, Tripoli, Johannesburg, Istanbul

In this list of world cities, the word *chocolate* stands out as different, and you are therefore likely to remember it. If one of the cities had been printed in large purple letters, you would probably remember that one too. When many items are similar and one is different, the similar items interfere with one another, and the distinctive item is easier to retrieve.

Similarly, we tend to remember unusual people and those with unusual names. If you meet several men of ordinary appearance and similar names, like John Stevens, Steve Johnson, and Joe Stevenson, you will have trouble learning their names. You will more quickly remember a 7-foot-tall, redheaded man named Stinky Rockefeller.

Let's reconsider a classic study from the first module of this chapter: Peterson and Peterson demonstrated decay of short-term memories over 18 seconds. For example, if you read the letters BKLRE and then count backward by 3s from 228, you probably will forget the letters within 18 seconds. That result is correct if we take the average over many trials, but it is *not* true on the first trial. On the first trial, you have no interference from previous letter sequences, and you probably will remember for well beyond the usual time (Keppel & Underwood, 1962). Evidently, short-term memories

Bob Williams was one of 40 aging former paratroopers who reenacted his parachute jump on the 50th anniversary of D-day. We forget most events from 50 years ago but remember the distinctive ones.

fade fast only because of proactive interference from similar materials.

Serial Order and Retrieval

In addition to the most distinctive items on a list (e.g., *chocolate* among a list of world cities), we are also particularly likely to remember the items at the beginning and end of a list. This tendency, known as the serial-order effect, includes two aspects: *The primacy effect is the tendency to remember well the first items, partly because of the lack of proactive interference. The recency effect is the tendency to remember the final items, partly because of the lack of retroactive interference.*

The primacy and recency effects are consistent and robust and occur for many reasons. If you try to list all the people you have ever dated, all the long-distance trips you have ever taken, or all the teachers you have ever had, you will almost certainly include the most recent ones and probably the earliest ones too.

CONCEPT CHECK ☑

14. If you memorize a list of words, which ones are you most likely to remember well? How does interference explain your answer? (Check your answers on page 262.)

Reconstructing Past Events

If you try to retrieve a memory of some experience, you will start with the details that you remember clearly and reconstruct the rest to fill in the gaps: *During an original experience, we construct a memory. When we try to retrieve that memory, we reconstruct an account based partly on surviving memories and partly on our expectations of what must have happened.* For example, you might recall studying in the library three nights ago. With a little effort, you might remember where you sat, what you were reading, who sat next to you, and where you went for a snack afterward. If you aren't quite sure, you fill in the gaps with what usually happens during an evening at the library. Within weeks you gradually will forget that evening, and if you try to remember it, you will rely more and more on "what must have happened" with a consequent decline in accuracy of details (Schmolck, Buffalo, & Squire, 2000). However, if you happen to fall in love with the person who sat next to you that evening, the events will become a lifetime memory. Still, when you try to recall it, you will have to reconstruct the details. You might remember where you went for a snack and some of what the two of you said, but if you wanted to recall the book you were reading, you would have to reason it out: "Let's see, that semester I was taking a chemistry course that took a lot of study, so maybe I was reading a chemistry book. No, wait, I remember. When we went out to eat, we talked about politics. So maybe I was reading my political science text."

Reconstruction and Inference in List Memory

Try this demonstration: Read the words in list A once; then turn away from the list, pause for a few seconds, and write as many of the words as you can remember. Repeat the same procedure for lists B and C. *Please do this now, before reading the following paragraph.*

List A	List B	List C
bed	candy	fade
rest	sour	fame
weep	sugar	face
tired	dessert	fake
dream	salty	date
wake	taste	hate
snooze	flavor	late
keep	bitter	mate
doze	cookies	rate
steep	fruits	
snore	chocolate	
nap	yummy	

After you have written out your lists, check how many of the words you got right. If you omitted many, you are normal. The point of this demonstration is not how many you got right, but whether you included *sleep* on the first list, *sweet* on the second, or *fate* on the third. Many people include one or more of these (which are not on the lists), and some do so with great confidence (Deese, 1959; Roediger & McDermott, 1995). Apparently, while learning the individual words, people also learn the gist of what they are all about, and when they are trying to retrieve the list later, they reconstruct a memory of a word that the list implied (Seamon et al., 2002). This powerful effect occurs under a wide variety of conditions, even if people are warned about it before they hear the list (Roediger & McDermott, 2000). Evidently, we reconstruct what "must have" been on the list.

In list B *sweet* is related to the other words in meaning; in list C *fate* resembles the others in sound. In list A *sleep* is related to most of the words in meaning, but the list also includes three words that rhyme with sleep (*weep, keep,* and *steep*). This combined influence is even more effective, producing false recall in a higher percentage of people. With a still longer list that includes an equal number of similar-meaning and similar-sounding words, up to 65% of people report the implied but absent word (Watson, Balota, & Roediger, 2003).

If you did not include *sleep, sweet,* or *fate,* try the Online Try It Yourself activity. Go to http://psychology. wadsworth.com/kalat_intro7e. Navigate to the student Web site, then to the Online Try It Yourself section, and click on False Memory. Hearing a list (as you can with the online demonstration) produces a bigger effect than reading a list.

The effect occurs mostly when people have neither a strong nor a very weak memory, but something inter-

mediate. If a list is short or if you have a chance to learn it well, you are unlikely to infer an extra word not on the list. On the other hand, if you had such a defective memory that you could not remember any of the words on the list, you could not use them to infer another word on the list, and again you would not show a false memory (Schacter, Verfaellie, Anes, & Racine, 1998). As people grow old, their ability to remember the correct words on the list becomes less reliable, and they compensate for their loss of detailed memory by relying on gist, therefore becoming more likely to report words implied but not actually on a list (Lövdén, 2003).

CONCEPT CHECK ☑

15. If you studied a list such as "candy, sour, sugar, dessert, salty, taste . . . " thoroughly instead of hearing it just once, would you be more likely or less likely to include "sweet," which isn't on the list? Why? (Check your answers on page 262.)

Reconstructing Stories

Suppose you listen to a story about a teenager's day, including a mixture of normal events (watching television) and oddities (clutching a teddy bear and parking a bicycle in the kitchen). Which would you remember better—the normal events or the oddities? You might expect to remember the unusual and distinctive events, and you would be right—*if* you are tested while your memory is still strong. However, if you start forgetting the story, you probably will reconstruct a more typical day for the teenager, recalling the normal events, omitting the unlikely ones, and adding other likely events that the story omitted, such as "the teenager went to school in the morning." In short, the less certain your memory is, the more you rely on your expectations (Heit, 1993; Maki, 1990). If you retell something several times over a period of time—either a story you heard or an event from your own experience—the retellings gradually become more coherent and make more sense (Ackil, Van Abbema, & Bauer, 2003; Bartlett, 1932). They make more sense because you rely more on the gist, keeping the details that fit the overall theme and omitting or distorting those that do not.

In a study that highlights the role of expectations, U.S. and Mexican adults tried to recall three stories. Some were given U.S. versions of the stories; others were given Mexican versions. (For example, in the "going on a date" story, the Mexican version had the man's sister go along as a chaperone.) On the average U.S. participants remembered the U.S. versions better, whereas the Mexicans remembered the Mexican versions better (R. J. Harris, Schoen, & Hensley, 1992).

16. When you read an account of history, it often seems that one event led to another in a logical order, whereas in everyday life events often seem illogical, unconnected, and unpredictable. Why? (Check your answer on page 262.)

Hindsight Bias

Let's try another demonstration. First read the following paragraph and then answer the question that follows:

> For some years after the arrival of Hastings as governor general of India, the consolidation of British power involved serious war. The first of these wars took place on the northern frontier of Bengal where the British were faced by the plundering raids of the Gurkas of Nepal. Attempts had been made to stop the raids by an exchange of lands, but the Gurkas would not give up their claims to country under British control, and Hastings decided to deal with them once and for all. The campaign began in November, 1814. It was not glorious. The Gurkas were only some 12,000 strong; but they were brave fighters, fighting in territory well-suited to their raiding tactics. The older British commanders were used to war in the plains where the enemy ran away from a resolute attack. In the mountains of Nepal it was not easy even to find the enemy. The troops and transport animals suffered from the extremes of heat and cold, and the officers learned caution only after sharp reverses. Major-General Sir D. Octerlony was the one commander to escape from these minor defeats. (Woodward, 1938, pp. 383–384)

Question

In light of the information in this passage, what was the probability of each of the four possible outcomes listed below? (The probabilities should total 100%.)

a. a British victory ___%
b. a Gurka victory ___%
c. military stalemate with no peace settlement ___%
d. military stalemate with a peace settlement ___%

Note that each of these possible outcomes seems possible, given what you have read. Now that you have made your estimates of the probabilities, I can tell you what really happened: The two sides reached a military stalemate without any settlement. The British had the advantages of superior numbers and superior equipment, but the Gurkas knew the territory and refused to give up, so battles continued indecisively for years. Now that you know the outcome, would you like to revise your estimates of the probabilities? Perhaps if you reread the paragraph, you will decide that you had overestimated the probabilities of some outcomes and underestimated others.

Subjects in one experiment read the preceding passage about the British and the Gurkas. Some were told which outcome "actually occurred" (although some were misinformed); all were then asked to estimate the probabilities of the four possible outcomes. Each group listed a high estimated probability for the "actual" outcome they had been given (Fischhoff, 1975). That is, once they knew what "really" happened (or incorrectly *thought* they knew), they reinterpreted the information with extra emphasis on the facts that fit the eventual (supposed) outcome (Figure 7.17). Their behavior illustrates **hindsight bias,** *the tendency to mold our recollection of the past to fit how events later turned out.* Something happens and we then say, "I *knew* that was going to happen!" (Oh, incidentally, I lied about the outcome of the British–Gurkas war. Actually, the British won. Would you like to reevaluate your estimates *again*?)

In another study, three weeks before the impeachment trial of U.S. President Clinton in 1999, college students were asked to predict the outcome. On the average they estimated the probability of a conviction at 50.5%. A week and a half after Clinton was not convicted, they were asked, "What would you have said 4 ½ weeks ago was the chance [of a conviction]?" On the average, they reported a 42.8% estimate (Bryant & Guilbault, 2002).

Hindsight bias is not altogether irrational. When you are making a prediction, you receive a huge array of information, some of it unimportant or even wrong. When you get the final outcome, you quite reasonably conclude that the information that had pointed in the correct direction was the best. You want to focus on that information so you can pay more attention to it in the future (Hoffrage, Hertwig, & Gigerenzer, 2000). In the process you may accidentally convince yourself that you were already strongly influenced by that information.

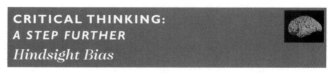

CRITICAL THINKING:
A STEP FURTHER
Hindsight Bias

Can you interpret people's beliefs that they had a "psychic hunch" in terms of hindsight bias?

The "Recovered Memory" Versus "False Memory" Controversy

Occasionally, someone tells a therapist about vague unpleasant feelings, and the therapist replies, "Symptoms like yours are usually found among people who were abused, especially sexually abused, in childhood. Do you think you were?" In some cases the client says

a Subjects told outcome was a British victory

b Subjects told outcome was a Gurka victory

c Subjects told outcome was a stalemate without settlement

d Subjects told outcome was a stalemate with settlement

FIGURE 7.17 People who thought the British had won said that under the circumstances the British had a very high probability of victory. Those who thought the Gurkas had won said that was the most likely outcome under the circumstances and so forth. *(Based on data of Fischhoff, 1975)*

"no," but the therapist persists: "The fact that you can't remember doesn't mean that it didn't happen. It may have been so painful that you repressed it." The therapist may then recommend hypnosis, repeated attempts to remember, or other techniques. Several ses-

sions later the client may say, "It's starting to come back to me. . . . I think I do remember. . . . " Most therapists would not use such aggressive techniques to try to recover old memories, but some do. *Reports of long-lost memories, prompted by clinical techniques, are known as* **recovered memories.**

Sexual abuse in childhood does occur, and no one knows how often. Some abused children do develop long-lasting psychological scars. But when people claim to recover long-forgotten memories, has the therapist uncovered the truth, distorted the truth, or convinced the client to believe something that never happened? Since the early 1990s, this issue has been one of the most heated debates in psychology. When a commission of respected therapists and researchers met to consider the evidence, they found that they disagreed on many points and had to issue competing reports (Alpert, Brown, & Courtois, 1998; Ornstein, Ceci, & Loftus, 1998).

Some reports are bizarre. In one case two sisters accused their father of raping them many times, both vaginally and anally; bringing his friends over on Friday nights to rape them; and forcing them to participate in satanic rituals that included cannibalism and the slaughter of babies (L. Wright, 1994). The sisters had not remembered any of these events until repeated sessions with a therapist. In another case a group of 3- and 4-year-old children, after repeated urgings from a therapist, accused their Sunday school teacher of sexually abusing them with a curling iron, forcing them to drink blood and urine, hanging them upside down from a chandelier, dunking them in toilets, and killing an elephant and a giraffe during Sunday school class (M. Gardner, 1994). There was no physical evidence to support the claims, such as scarred tissues or giraffe bones.

Even when recovered-memory claims are much less bizarre, their accuracy is uncertain. If a 30-year-old woman claims that her father sexually abused her when she was 8, that she had not told anyone about it at the time, and in fact had forgotten it until now, how could anyone check her accuracy? One might consult old school records for any mention of physical and emotional scars, but even the best of such records are incomplete.

Some related questions are, however, testable: When people have abusive experiences, are they likely to forget them for years? And is it possible to persuade someone to "remember" an event that never actually happened just by suggesting it?

Memory for Traumatic Events

Sigmund Freud, whom we shall consider more fully in Chapter 13, introduced the term **repression** as *the process of moving an unbearably unacceptable memory or impulse from the conscious mind to the unconscious mind.* Although many therapists continue to use the concept of repression, the research on memory has found no clear, unambiguous support for the idea (Holmes, 1990). Experiments that were designed to demonstrate repression have produced small effects that one could explain without the concept of repression. Many clinicians now prefer the term dissociation, referring to *memory that is stored but cannot be retrieved* (Alpert et al., 1998). However, most of the doubts about the term *repression* also apply to the similar concept of *dissociation*.

Do people forget traumatic events? It depends. (Almost always a good answer in psychology.) Partly it depends on what we mean by "forget." Someone with a painful memory might avoid thinking or talking about it and might say "I don't remember" to avoid talking about it (Pope, Hudson, Bodkin, & Oliva, 1998).

In general, however, people seldom forget traumatic events. One study examined 16 children who had witnessed the murder of one of their parents. All had recurring nightmares and haunting thoughts of the experience; none had forgotten (Malmquist, 1986). Other studies have examined prisoners of war who had been severely mistreated (Merckelbach, Dekkers, Wessel, & Roefs, 2003), children who had been kidnapped or forced to participate in pornographic movies (Terr, 1988), and others who had additional horrible experiences. People almost always remembered the events, or they forgot only about as much as one might expect for very old events. Evidently, if repression of traumatic experiences occurs at all, it does so only under rare and undefined circumstances.

Memory for a traumatic experience depends on someone's age at the time of the event, its severity, and the reaction of other family members. In one study investigators interviewed 129 young adult women who had been brought to a hospital emergency ward because of sexual assault at ages 1 to 12 years. Most reported remembering the sexual assault, although 38% did not (L. M. Williams, 1994). Generally, those who were at least 7 years old at the time of the attack remembered better than those who were younger. In a similar study, researchers interviewed 168 young adults who had been victims of criminally prosecuted child sexual abuse. Of these, 142 reported the sexual abuse during a telephone conversation, and 12 more reported it in a follow-up mailing or face-to-face interview, leaving only 14 (8%) who did not report it at all (Goodman et al., 2003). Recall was more likely among those who were older at the time of the offense, those who had more severe or repeated abuse, and those who received more family support and encouragement. Better memory by those who were older is unsurprising; people almost always remember later events better than those of early childhood. Better recall for more severe and repeated abuse is important: It is what we would expect based on memory research—

greater recall of stronger, repeated, more important events. The result, however, is contrary to what one would predict based on the idea of repression: Theoretically, people should repress the more severely distressing experiences. In short, the results suggest that early traumatic memories are similar to other memories and are not likely to be lost.

Areas of Agreement and Disagreement

Psychologists agree that some people have had abusive childhood experiences that they later cannot remember. However, these cases are not common, except among those who were very young at the time of the abuse. Even when someone does forget a horrible experience, the question is why. Many clinicians believe that repression or dissociation is a possible explanation; if so, then attempts to recover the memory are at least a theoretical possibility (Alpert et al., 1998). (Whether recovering them would be *beneficial* is, however, not at all certain.) The alternative view, favored by most memory researchers, is that traumatic memories are like other memories: If we don't think about something for a long time, we find them harder to retrieve, and if we try to reconstruct them later, the result will be an uncertain mixture of truth and distortion.

CONCEPT CHECK ☑

17. Based on material earlier in this chapter, why should we expect traumatic events to be remembered better than most other events? (Check your answer on page 262.)

CRITICAL THINKING:
WHAT'S THE EVIDENCE?
Suggestions and False Memories

Critics of attempts to help people recover lost memories have suggested that a therapist who repeatedly encourages a client to recall lost memories can unintentionally implant a false memory (or false report), *a report that someone believes to be a memory but that does not correspond to real events* (Lindsay & Read, 1994; Loftus, 1993). We shall examine three representative experiments.

EXPERIMENT I

Hypothesis If people are asked questions that suggest or presuppose a certain fact, many people will later report remembering that "fact," even if it never happened.

Method Elizabeth Loftus (1975) asked two groups of students to watch a videotape of an automobile accident. Then she asked one group but not the other, "Did you see the children getting on the school bus?" In fact the videotape did not show a school bus. A week later she asked both groups 20 new questions about the accident, including this one: "Did you see a school bus in the film?"

Results Of the first group (those who were asked about seeing children get on a school bus), 26% reported that they had seen a school bus; of the second group, only 6% said they had seen a school bus.

Interpretation The question "Did you see the children getting on the school bus?" implies that there *was* a school bus. Some of the students who heard that question reconstructed events by combining what they actually saw, what they believed must have happened, and what the researcher suggested afterward.

EXPERIMENT 2

The first experiment demonstrated that a suggestion can distort memories of something that people watched. But could a suggestion implant a memory of an experience that never really occurred?

Hypothesis If people are told about a childhood event by a trusted person, they will come to remember it as something they experienced, even if in fact they did not.

Method The participants, aged 18 to 53, were told that the study concerned their memories of childhood. Each participant was given four paragraphs, and each paragraph described a different event. Three of the events had actually happened. (The experimenters had contacted parents to get descriptions of childhood events.) A fourth event was a plausible story about getting lost, which had not happened. An example for one Vietnamese woman: "You, your Mom, Tien, and Tuan, all went to the Bremerton Kmart. You must have been 5 years old at the time. Your Mom gave each of you some money to get a blueberry ICEE. You ran ahead to get into the line first, and somehow lost your way in the store. Tien found you crying to an elderly Chinese woman. You three then went together to get an ICEE." After reading the four paragraphs, each participant was asked to write whatever additional details he or she could remember of the event. Participants were asked to try again 1 week later and then again after another week (Loftus, Feldman, & Dashiell, 1995).

Results Of 24 participants, 6 reported remembering the suggested (false) event. Participants generally described the false memories in fewer words than the correct memories, but some did provide a fair amount of additional detail. The woman in the foregoing example said, "I vaguely remember walking around Kmart crying and looking for Tien and Tuan. I thought I was lost forever. I went to the shoe department, because we always spent a lot of time there. I went to the handkerchief place because we were there last. I circled all over the store it seemed 10 times. I just remember walking around crying. I do not remember the Chinese woman, or the ICEE (but it would be raspberry ICEE if I was getting an ICEE) part. I don't even remember being found."

Interpretation A simple suggestion can provoke some people to recall a personal experience in moderate detail, even though the event never happened. Granted, the suggestion influenced fewer than half of the people tested, and most of them reported only vague memories. Still, the researchers achieved this effect after only a single brief suggestion. In a similar study, 13 of 47 participants reported detailed false memories of getting lost or getting attacked by an animal or another child, and 18 more participants reported partial recollection (Porter, Birt, Yuille, & Lehman, 2000).

One objection is that perhaps this "false" memory was not entirely false. Maybe this young woman *was* lost at some point—if not in a Kmart at age 5, then somewhere else at some other age. Some later studies tried to establish memories of virtually impossible events. In one study college students read fake advertisements for Disneyland that depicted people meeting and shaking hands with Bugs Bunny (a Warner Brothers character who would *never* appear at Disneyland). About 30% of those who read this ad later reported that they too had met Bugs Bunny at Disneyland. Some reported touching his ears or tail (Loftus, 2003). In another study British students who were asked to imagine certain experiences later reported that they actually remembered those experiences, including "having a nurse remove a skin sample from my little finger"—a procedure that never occurs in Britain (Mazzoni & Memon, 2003). In short, suggestions can lead people to report memories of events that we can be confident never happened.

EXPERIMENT 3

Some therapists recommend that their clients examine photographs from their childhood to help evoke old memories. They are certainly right that old photographs do bring back memories. The question, however, is whether looking at old photographs might also increase the report of false memories.

Hypothesis A false suggestion about a childhood event will evoke memory reports more readily if people have examined photographs from when they were that age.

Method The researchers contacted the parents of 45 college students and asked each to provide a report of some event that happened while these students were in third or fourth grade and another that happened in fifth or sixth grade. Both were supposed to be events that the student might or might not remember, not an event that the family had repeatedly discussed. The researchers also asked the parents to confirm that the following "false memory" event—the one they planned to suggest—had *not* happened: In the first grade, the child took a "Slime" toy to school, and then she and another child slid it into the teacher's desk and received a mild punishment. Finally, the researchers asked the parents for copies of class photographs from first grade, third or fourth, and fifth or sixth.

After all these preparations, they brought in the students and briefly described for each student the two correct events (provided by the parents) and the one false event. For each they asked the students to provide whatever additional information they remembered. Half of them (randomly selected) were shown their class photographs and half were not. At the end of the session, they were asked to think about the first-grade event for the next week and try to remember more about it. Those in the photograph group took the photo with them. A week later the students returned and again reported whatever they thought they remembered (Lindsay, Hagen, Read, Wade, & Garry, 2003).

Results Most students reported clear memories of the two real events. For the false event of first grade, Figure 7.18 shows the percentage of students who reported some memory of the event in the first and second sessions. Memories increased from the first to the second session, and students who saw the pho-

tographs reported more memories than those who did not see photographs. By the second session, almost two thirds of the students who saw a class photograph reported some memory of the false event.

At the end of the study, the researchers explained that the first-grade event did not really happen. Many of the students expressed surprise, such as "No way! I remember it! That is so weird!" (Lindsay et al., 2004, page 153).

Interpretation   Examining an old photograph evokes old memories, but it also increases suggestibility about false memories. Looking at the photo helps the person remember, "Oh, yes, that's what my first grade teacher looked like. And that was my closest friend back then . . ." If the person tries to remember acting with a friend to pull a prank on the teacher, the visual image becomes more vivid and therefore more convincing. At any rate the message is that combining a suggestion about a possible memory with a photograph from that time is risky; it may strengthen false memories as well as real ones.

The question still remains, however, about clinicians' reports of recovering lost memories of early trauma. Many clinicians object that the kinds of false memories implanted in research settings (being lost in a mall, first-grade mischief, etc.) are different from emotionally intense memories of sexual abuse. To this criticism researchers reply that, ethically, they could not try to implant painful memories of traumatic abuse just to demonstrate the possibility.

If someone reports remembering some event after many years of not remembering it, we may never know whether the event actually happened. No one recommends disbelieving all such reports (Pope, 1996). The recommendation is to withhold judgment about the accuracy of a "recovered" memory unless someone has independent evidence to support it. Furthermore, the more suggestions someone was given prior to the recall, the more skeptical we should be.

CONCEPT CHECK ☑

18. In what way is hindsight bias similar to an implanted "false memory"? (Check your answer on page 262.)

Children as Eyewitnesses

Finally, should we trust the reports of young children who are witnesses or victims of a crime? On the one hand, if we routinely disregard their testimony, anyone who abuses children can be sure of avoiding prosecution. On the other hand, we know that young chil-

FIGURE 7.18 More students who saw a first-grade class photograph reported remembering the suggested (false) event. The percentage of recall increased from the first session to the second, a week later, especially among those who saw the photograph. *("Recall of False Event," by D.S. Lindsay, L. Hagen, J.D. Read, K.A. Wada, and M. Garry. True Photographs and False Memories. Psychological Science. Copyright 2004 Blackwell Publishing. Reprinted with permission.)*

dren sometimes confuse fantasy with reality or say what they think someone wants them to say.

Research here can be tricky. No ethical researcher would abuse children or tell children they had been abused. A better approach is to ask children to recall a medical or dental examination, where a stranger probed various parts of a child's body. How well can the child report what happened?

In such studies researchers found that children as young as 3 years old report accurately under proper conditions. Children 3 to 5 years old volunteer very little when asked, "Tell me what happened." However, they do answer correctly to specific questions such as, "Did the doctor shine a light in your eyes?" We might worry that the children were responding to suggestions or agreeing to whatever someone asked them. However, they consistently respond "no" to questions about acts that did not happen, such as, "Did the doctor cut your hair?" Children's accuracy is reasonably good even 6 weeks after the physical exam (Baker-Ward, Gordon, Ornstein, Larus, & Clubb, 1993). However, after persistent questioning and prodding, young children do start reporting elaborate false memories (Ceci, 1995).

Several factors influence the accuracy of children's reports:

- **The delay between event and questioning.** If 4- to 6-year-old children are asked about a likely event that did *not* occur in the most recent physical exam, they correctly deny it if they are asked within 6 weeks but report it if asked later. Evidently, they start to confuse the most recent exam with the usual exam (Ornstein et al., 1998).
- **Suggestive questions.** To an invitation such as, "Tell me what happened," a young child's answer is usually short but accurate. To a suggestive question such as, "Did he touch you under your clothing?" the probability of a false report increases (Lamb & Fauchier, 2001).
- **The understandability of the questions.** Three-year-olds who understand a question will usually answer correctly. When they don't understand, instead of saying they don't understand, they usually answer "yes" (Imhoff & Baker-Ward, 1999).

  Sometimes a questioner thinks a child understands, but the child does not. Once my son and his family were on a trip, and the parents told my granddaughter, then 3 years old, that they would stop at a barbecue restaurant for dinner. She was so excited that she could hardly wait. She spent most of the trip asking, "Now how long till barbecue?" As they finally approached the restaurant, she asked, "Will other children be there too, with their Barbies?"
- **Repetition of the question.** A 3-year-old who is asked the same question twice within a single session is likely to answer differently the second time (Poole & White, 1993). Evidently, the child assumes that the first answer must have been wrong. However, asking the question every few days helps the child remember, and that persistence is important if a child has to testify in court at a later date (Poole & White, 1995).
- **Use of doll props.** We might imagine that children's reports are limited by their small vocabulary. Some psychologists try to help them by providing anatomically detailed dolls and asking them to act out what happened. The idea sounds reasonable, but when researchers ask children to act out a doctor's exam (where we know what actually happened), they act out many events that did not happen (Greenhoot, Ornstein, Gordon, & Baker-Ward, 1999). If a child acts out a sexual contact, we cannot assume that the child was sexually molested. In fact, if you point to a child's elbow and then ask the child to find the doll's elbow, many young children cannot. Interpreting a child's doll play is a very uncertain matter (Ceci, 1995; Koocher et al., 1995).

The general recommendations for children's eyewitness testimony are simple: If a child is asked simple questions, without suggestions or pressure and reasonably soon after the event, even children as young as 3 can be believable (Ceci & Bruck, 1993). However, a young child can be highly influenced by suggestions.

CRITICAL THINKING:
A STEP FURTHER
Unlikely Memory Reports

Some people claim to have been abducted by aliens from another planet. Apparently, most of these people are neither mentally ill nor deliberately lying (Banaji & Kihlstrom, 1996). Presuming that they were not actually abducted by aliens, how might we explain their reports?

IN CLOSING

Memory Distortions

Memory distortions are sometimes a serious problem, but they are the by-product of a useful process. That process is our ability to focus on the essential gist. When we are reasoning and making decisions, we need to focus on trends and general principles, and depending on the question, we may or may not need the details (Brainerd & Reyna, 2002). The older some experience is, the less likely we are to need its details. If we do need the details, we can usually reason them out well enough for most purposes. So memory distortions are not evidence of something going wrong. They are a necessary consequence of the way our memory normally works. The following dialogue captures well our tendency to forget details:

He: We met at nine.
She: We met at eight.
He: I was on time.
She: No, you were late.
He: Ah, yes! I remember it well. We dined with friends.
She: We dined alone.
He: A tenor sang.
She: A baritone.
He: Ah, yes! I remember it well. That dazzling April moon!
She: There was none that night. And the month was June.
He: That's right! That's right!
She: It warms my heart to know that you remember still the way you do.
He: Ah, yes! I remember it well.
　　—"I Remember It Well" from the musical *Gigi* by Alan Jay Lerner and Frederick Loewe

Summary

- *Interference.* When someone learns several similar sets of material, the earlier ones interfere with retrieval of later ones by proactive interference. The later ones interfere with earlier ones by retroactive interference. (page 252)
- *Distinctiveness and serial order.* It is easiest to remember items that are least blocked by interference, such as the first and last items on a list and any unusual items. (page 253)
- *Reconstruction.* When remembering stories or events from their own lives, people recall some of the facts and fill in the gaps based on logical inferences of what must have happened. They rely particularly heavily on inferences when their memory of the details is weak. (page 254)
- *Reconstructions from a word list.* If people read or hear a list of related words and try to recall them, they are likely to include closely related words that were not on the list. They have remembered the gist and reconstructed what else must have been on the list. (page 254)
- *Story memory.* Someone who tries to retell a story after memory of the details has faded will rely on the gist and therefore leave out some details that seemed irrelevant and add or change other facts to fit the logic of the story. (page 255)

- *Hindsight bias.* People often revise their memories of what they previously expected, saying that how events turned out was what they had expected all along. (page 256)
- *The "recovered memory" vs. "false memory" debate.* Some therapists have used hypnosis or suggestive lines of questioning to try to help people remember painful experiences. Suggestions can induce people to distort memories or report events that did not happen. It is difficult to distinguish accurate memories from distorted or false ones. (page 256)
- *Children as eyewitnesses.* Even children 3 to 5 years old can correctly report events if they are asked simple questions without pressure soon after the event. However, suggestive questions can lead them astray. (page 260)

Answers to Concept Checks

12. It is due to proactive interference—interference from memories learned earlier. Much of the difficulty of retrieving long-term memories is due to proactive interference. (page 253)
13. First, someone learns the response; the second learning is the extinction of the response. If the first learning proactively interferes with the later extinction, spontaneous recovery will result. (page 253)
14. It will be easiest to remember the first, last, and most unusual items on the list. The first is spared from proactive interference; the last is spared from retroactive interference; and an unusual item is not greatly weakened by either kind of interference. However, low interference is not the only explanation for the serial order effect. (page 254)
15. You would be less likely to add a word not on the list. We rely on inferences mostly when the actual memory is weak. (page 255)
16. Long after the fact, a historian puts together a coherent story based on the gist of events, emphasizing details that fit the pattern and omitting others. In your everyday life, you are aware of all the facts, including those that do not fit any pattern. (page 256)
17. Emotionally arousing memories are usually more memorable than other events. Any emotionally arousing event stimulates cortisol release and in other ways activates the amygdala, a brain area that helps store memories. (page 258; see also page 249)
18. In a case of hindsight bias, something that you learn later operates like a suggestion, so that when you try to remember what you previously thought, you are influenced by that suggestion and change your reported memory to fit it. (page 260)

Amnesia

| *Why do some people have severe memory problems?*

Imagine you defied the advice given to computer owners and passed your computer through a powerful magnetic field. Chances are you would erase all the memory, but suppose you found that you had erased only the text files and not the graphics files. Or suppose the old memories were intact but you could no longer store new ones. From the damage you would gain hints about how your computer's memory works.

The same is true of human memory. Various kinds of brain damage impair one kind of memory and not another, enabling us to draw inferences about how memory is organized.

Normal forgetting depends largely on interference from similar memories. It also depends on the absence of appropriate retrieval cues. For example, if you learn something in a particular place, time, and state of mind, you may forget it in another. In addition to these normal mechanisms of forgetting, some people have more serious problems.

Amnesia After Damage to the Hippocampus

Amnesia is a *loss of memory*. Even in the most severe cases, people don't forget everything they ever learned. For example, they don't forget how to walk, talk, or eat.

(If they did, we would call it *dementia,* not amnesia.) Amnesia can result from many kinds of brain damage, including damage to the hippocampus.

In 1953 a man with the initials H. M. was suffering from many small daily epileptic seizures and about one major seizure per week. He did not respond to any antiepileptic drugs, so in desperation, surgeons removed most of his **hippocampus,** *a large forebrain structure in the interior of the temporal lobe* (Figure 7.19), where they believed his epileptic seizures were originating. They also removed some surrounding brain areas. At the time researchers knew very little about the hippocampus and did not know what to expect. Had they known the behavioral outcome, H. M. almost certainly would have preferred to continue having epileptic seizures instead of undergoing this operation.

The surgery did greatly decrease the frequency and severity of H. M.'s seizures. His personality remained the same, but he became more passive (Eichenbaum, 2002). His IQ score increased slightly, presumably because of the decreased epileptic interference. However, he suffered severe memory problems (Corkin, 1984; Milner, 1959). H. M. suffered a massive **anterograde** (ANT-eh-ro-grade) **amnesia,** *inability to store new long-term memories.* For years after the operation, he cited the year as 1953 and his own age as 27. Later, he took wild guesses (Corkin, 1984). He would read the same issue of a

Corpus callosum

Prefrontal cortex

Temporal lobe

Hippocampus

a

b

©Suzanne Corkin, Psychology Dept., MIT

FIGURE 7.19 (a) The hippocampus is a large subcortical structure of the brain. (b) After damage to the hippocampus and related structures, patient H. M. had great difficulty storing new long-term memories. The photo shows a scan of the brain of H. M. formed by magnetic resonance imaging. The asterisk indicates the area from which the hippocampus is missing. The arrow indicates a portion of the hippocampus that is preserved. *(Photo courtesy of Suzanne Corkin and David Amaral)* magazine repeatedly without recognizing it. He could not even remember where he had lived. He also suffered a moderate **retrograde amnesia,** *loss of memory for events that occurred shortly before the brain damage* (see Figure 7.20). That is, he had some trouble recalling events that had happened within the last 1 to 3 years before the operation. Any loss of consciousness, such as after a concussion or excessive alcohol intake, can produce retrograde amnesia, although seldom as extensive as 1 to 3 years (Riccio, Millin, & Gisquet-Verrier, 2003).

FIGURE 7.20 Brain damage induces retrograde amnesia (loss of old memories) and anterograde amnesia (difficulty storing new memories).

H. M. could form normal short-term memories, such as repeating a short list of words or numbers, and he could retain them as long as he kept rehearsing them. However, a brief distraction would eliminate the memory. For example, he might tell the same person the same story several times within a few minutes, each time forgetting that he had told it before (Eichenbaum, 2002).

Like Rip van Winkle (the story character who slept for 20 years and awakened to a vastly changed world), H. M. became more and more out of date with each passing year (Gabrieli, Cohen, & Corkin, 1988; M. L. Smith, 1988). He did not recognize the names or faces of people who became famous after the mid-1950s. He could not name the president of the United States even when Ronald Reagan was president, although he remembered Reagan as an actor. He did not understand the meaning of words and phrases that entered the English language after his surgery. For example, he treated *Jacuzzi* and *granola* as non-words (Corkin, 2002). He guessed that *soul food* means "forgiveness" and that a *closet queen* might be "a moth" (Gabrieli et al., 1988). Seldom-used words like *squander* gradually slipped out of his vocabulary (James & McKay, 2001).

In spite of H. M.'s massive memory difficulties, he could still acquire and retain new skills. Recall the distinction between procedural memory (skills) and declarative memory (facts). H. M. learned to read material written in mirror fashion (N. J. Cohen & Squire, 1980), such as shown at top right. However, he could not remember having learned this skill or any of the

others he acquired, and always expressed surprise at his success.

.siht ekil ,sdrawkcab nettirw secnetnes daer dluoc eH

The results for H. M. led researchers to study both people and laboratory animals with similar damage. The following points have emerged:

- The hippocampus is important for storing most long-term memories.
- Although H. M. and others with damage to the hippocampus can still retrieve old memories, an intact hippocampus is ordinarily active during retrieval (Maguire & Frith, 2003).
- Other things being equal, the more difficult a memory task, the more it depends on the hippocampus (Reed & Squire, 1999).
- The hippocampus is less important for implicit than explicit memory (Ryan, Althoff, Whitlow, & Cohen, 2000), perhaps because tests of implicit memory can detect weaker memories.
- The hippocampus is important for remembering details. One man with hippocampal damage could sketch the general layout of his home neighborhood but could not identify photos of houses and other landmarks within the neighborhood (Rosenbaum et al., 2000).

CONCEPT CHECK ☑

19. Which kinds of memory are most impaired in H. M.? Which kinds are least impaired? (Check your answers on page 268.)

Amnesia After Damage to the Prefrontal Cortex

Amnesia can also arise after damage to the prefrontal cortex (see Figure 7.19). Because the prefrontal cortex receives extensive input from the hippocampus, the symptoms of prefrontal cortex damage overlap those of hippocampal damage. However, some special deficits also arise.

Prefrontal cortex damage can be the result of a stroke, trauma to the head, or **Korsakoff's syndrome,** *a condition caused by a prolonged deficiency of vitamin B_1 (thiamine), usually as a result of chronic alcoholism.* This deficiency leads to widespread loss or shrinkage of neurons, especially in the prefrontal cortex and areas connected to it. Patients suffer apathy, confusion, and severe amnesia, both retrograde and anterograde (Squire, Haist, & Shimamura, 1989). If given a long list of words to remember, they forget those at the beginning of the list before they reach the end and soon forget those at the end also (Stuss et al., 1994).

Patients with prefrontal cortex damage answer many questions with **confabulations,** which are *attempts to fill in the gaps in their memory.* Most confabulations include out-of-date information, indicating a failure to suppress inappropriate memories (Schnider, 2003). For example, a hospitalized dentist might insist that patients are waiting for his or her attention, or an aged woman might insist that she had to go home to feed her baby. Confabulations are not exactly attempts to hide their inability to answer a question, as they almost never confabulate on a question such as "Where is Premola?" or "Who is Princess Lolita?" (Schnider, 2003). That is, if they never knew the answer, they freely admit not knowing. The following interview is a typical example (Moscovitch, 1989, pp. 135–136). Note the mixture of correct information, confabulations that were correct at some time in the past, and imaginative attempts to explain the discrepancies between one answer and another:

Psychologist: How old are you?
Patient: I'm 40, 42, pardon me, 62.
Psychologist: Are you married or single?
Patient: Married.
Psychologist: How long have you been married?
Patient: About 4 months.
Psychologist: What's your wife's name?
Patient: Martha.
Psychologist: How many children do you have?
Patient: Four. (He laughs.) Not bad for 4 months.
Psychologist: How old are your children?
Patient: The eldest is 32; his name is Bob. And the youngest is 22; his name is Joe.
Psychologist: How did you get these children in 4 months?
Patient: They're adopted.
Psychologist: Who adopted them?
Patient: Martha and I.
Psychologist: Immediately after you got married you wanted to adopt these older children?
Patient: Before we were married we adopted one of them, two of them. The eldest girl Brenda and Bob, and Joe and Dina since we were married.
Psychologist: Does it all sound a little strange to you, what you are saying?
Patient: I think it is a little strange.
Psychologist: I think when I looked at your record it said that you've been married for over 30 years. Does that sound more reasonable to you if I told you that?
Patient: No.
Psychologist: Do you really believe that you have been married for 4 months?
Patient: Yes.

Patients with prefrontal cortex damage confidently defend their confabulations and often maintain the same confabulation from one time to the next. Actually, the same is true of normal people when they learn something poorly. In one study college students listened to complicated 2-minute descriptions of topics they knew little about and then answered detailed questions. Once a week for the next 4 weeks, the process repeated; they heard the complicated description and answered the same questions. Generally, they repeated the same incorrect guesses from one week to the next (Fritz, Morris, Bjork, Gelman, & Wickens, 2000).

Why do people with prefrontal damage confabulate so much more than the rest of us? According to Morris Moscovitch (1992), the prefrontal cortex is necessary for *working with memory,* the strategies we use to reconstruct memories that we cannot immediately recall. For example, if you are asked what is the farthest north that you have ever traveled or how many salads you ate last week, your answer requires reasoning. People with prefrontal cortex damage have difficulty making reasonable inferences.

People who spend many hours playing the game Tetris report seeing images of Tetris blocks, especially as they are falling asleep. So do people with severe amnesia, even though they don't remember playing the game.

Despite their impoverished memory in other regards, people with brain damage are nearly normal on most tests of implicit memory. For example, after hearing a list of words, a patient may not be able to say any of the words on the list and may not even remember that there was a list. However, when given a set of three-letter stems such as CON— and TRA—, the patient completes them to make words that were on the list (Hamann & Squire, 1997).

Another example: After patients repeatedly practiced playing the video game Tetris, they said they did not remember playing the game before, although they did improve from one session to the next. When they closed their eyes to go to sleep at night, they said they saw little images of blocks but did not know what they were (Stickgold, Malia, Maguire, Roddenberry, & O'Connor, 2000).

One important conclusion emerges from all the studies of brain damage and amnesia: We have several different types of memory. It is possible to impair one type, such as explicit and declarative, without equally damaging another type, such as implicit and procedural.

CONCEPT CHECK

20. Although confabulation is a kind of false memory, how does it differ from the suggested false memories discussed in the previous module? (Check your answer on page 268.)

Memory Impairments in Alzheimer's Disease

A more common cause of memory loss is **Alzheimer's** (AHLTZ-hime-ers) **disease**, *a condition occurring mostly in old age, characterized by increasingly severe memory loss, confusion, depression, disordered thinking, and impaired attention.* Several genes have been found that lead to an onset of Alzheimer's disease before age 60 (Goate et al., 1991; Murrell, Farlow, Ghetti, & Benson, 1991; Schellenberg et al., 1992; Sherrington et al., 1995). However, more than 99% of the people with Alzheimer's disease have a later onset, and most cases of the late-onset form are not linked with any identified gene. Moreover, the effects of these genes are not inevitable. The genes linked to Alzheimer's disease in the United States are also found among the Yoruba people of Nigeria (Hendrie, 2001), but the Yoruba almost never get Alzheimer's disease. Which aspect of their culture shields them from Alzheimer's is uncertain, although diet is a likely candidate.

Alzheimer's disease is marked by a gradual accumulation of harmful proteins in the brain and deterioration of brain cells, leading to a loss of arousal and attention. The memory problem is broad, including both anterograde and retrograde amnesia. Alzheimer's patients have deficits in semantic memory as well as episodic memory (Beauregard, Chertkow, Gold, & Bergman, 2001). As a rule they can learn new skills and other implicit memories much better than new explicit memories. For example, they can be taught to use a mobile phone (Lekeu, Wojtasik, Van der Linden, & Salmon, 2002). However, even their implicit memory is deficient in some cases (McGeorge, Taylor, Della Sala, & Shanks, 2002). Like Korsakoff's patients, they often confabulate (Nedjam, Dalla Barba, & Pillon, 2000). This mixture of memory problems should not be surprising, given the overall decrease of arousal and attention. Weak arousal and impaired attention cause problems for almost any aspect of memory.

CONCEPT CHECK ☑

21. What evidence indicates that Alzheimer's disease is not strongly dependent on genetic influences? (Check your answer on page 268.)

Infant Amnesia

Can you recall events from when you were 8 years old? How about age 6? Age 4? Most people report a cutoff somewhere around age 5. The exact age varies, but before the cutoff age, one has few if any memories. The *near absence of early declarative memories* is known as **infant amnesia,** or **childhood amnesia.** (People retain procedural memories from early childhood, such as memory of how to walk, but of course they practiced those skills from then on.) Although psychologists have proposed many theories of infant amnesia, none are fully persuasive (Howe & Courage, 1997).

In what may have been the earliest proposal on this issue, Sigmund Freud suggested that children go through emotionally difficult experiences at ages 4 to 5 that are so disturbing that a child represses everything experienced at that time or before. However, neither Freud nor anyone else has ever offered any evidence to support this idea.

A more modern proposal is that the hippocampus, known to be important for memory, is slow to mature, so memories from the first few years are not well stored (Moscovitch, 1985). A weakness of that suggestion is that young children do form long-term memories. A typical 4-year-old can accurately describe experiences from ages 2 and 3, such as birthday parties, holiday celebrations, and visits to grandparents (Bauer, 1996). Even 2-year-olds remember events that happened months ago, although we have to test them in nonverbal ways to demonstrate the memories (Bauer, 2002; Liston & Kagan, 2002). In short, young children establish long-term memories, but those memories last only months or years, not a lifetime as later memories do.

Another proposal is that a permanent memory of an experience requires a "sense of self" that develops between ages 3 and 4 (Howe & Courage, 1993). A difficulty with this idea is that rats, pigeons, and other nonhuman species develop long-lasting memories. If we want to avoid saying that rats have a "sense of self" and 3-year-old children do not, we could argue that rats' memories aren't the same as the kind of memory we are discussing for adult humans. However, at best, this idea is not yet convincing.

Another possibility is that after we come to rely on language, we lose access to memories encoded earlier, nonverbally. That idea will not explain why a 4-year-old can describe what happened at age 3, whereas a 7-year-old cannot. Still, some interesting research supports the onset of language as one factor in infant amnesia: Psychologists let some 3-year-olds play with a "magic shrinking machine." A child could place a large toy into a slot, crank a handle, and then see a smaller version of the same toy come out, as if the machine had shrunk the toy. When the children returned 6 months or a year later, they clearly remembered the machine and how to work it. However, when they were asked to describe how the machine worked or to name the toys that it shrank, the children described their experience using only the words they had known at the time they originally played with the machine (Simcock & Hayne, 2002). For example, a child who knew the word "teddy bear" at age 3 would use it later, but a child who did not know the term at age 3 would not (even after learning it in the meantime).

One more possibility is that infant amnesia relates to encoding specificity (page 246). If we learn something in one time, place, physiological condition, or state of mind, we remember it more easily under the same or similar conditions. Maybe we forget our early years just because we don't have enough of the right retrieval cues to find those infant memories.

At this point none of these hypotheses is well established. Infant amnesia probably has several explanations, not just one.

CONCEPT CHECK ☑

22. What evidence indicates that infant amnesia is not due to a failure to establish long-term memories? (Check your answer on page 268.)

IN CLOSING

The Complexities of Amnesia

Some degree of memory loss is normal and even healthy (Schacter, 1999). If you remembered everything that ever happened to you, and none of those memories faded for even a moment, you would be overwhelmed with more and more information, most of it useless.

However, people with amnesia forget useful information, sometimes even information about themselves. We still have much to learn about amnesia. In this module the emphasis has been on brain damage (or brain maturation, in the case of infants), but the situation is often more complex. Almost every patient with severe amnesia has some degree of brain damage, but in some cases the person has relatively mild brain damage and additional problems in handling emotions and life events (M. D. Kopelman, 2000). Emotional problems by themselves seldom if ever cause prolonged amnesia, but they do compound and magnify organic problems. Important psychological phenomena seldom have a single, simple explanation.

Summary

- *Amnesia after damage to the hippocampus.* H. M. and other patients with damage to the hippocampus have great difficulty storing new long-term declarative memories, although they form normal short-term, procedural, and implicit memories. (page 263)
- *Damage to the frontal lobes.* Patients with damage to the frontal lobes fail to suppress old, irrelevant information and therefore give confident wrong answers, known as confabulations. (page 264)
- *Alzheimer's disease.* Patients with Alzheimer's disease, a condition that occurs mostly after age 60 to 65, have a variety of memory problems, although implicit and procedural memory are more intact than explicit, declarative memory. Their problems stem largely from impairments of arousal and attention. (page 266)
- *Lessons from amnesia.* Studies of people with brain damage demonstrate the value of distinguishing among different types of memory, such as declarative and procedural or explicit and implicit. (page 266)
- *Infant amnesia.* Most people remember little from early childhood, even though preschoolers have clear recollections of experiences that happened months or even years ago. No one explanation is fully convincing. However, research shows that as children develop language, they do not apply their newly learned words to old memories. (page 266)

Answers to Concept Checks

19. H. M. is greatly impaired at forming new declarative memories. His short-term memory is intact, as is his memory for events long before the operation and his ability to form new procedural memories. (page 264)

20. Most confabulated statements were true at one time, though not now. Also, people with brain damage seldom confabulate answers to questions they never could have answered in the past. That is, they seldom make up totally new information. (page 266)

21. Identified genes have been linked to early-onset Alzheimer's disease but not to many people with the more common late-onset type. Also, even the genes that do lead to Alzheimer's disease fail to do so in some cultures, indicating that environmental influences alter the effects of the genes. (page 266)

22. Young children remember events that happened months or even years ago. However, a few years later, they lose those memories. (page 267)

CHAPTER ENDING

Key Terms and Activities

Key Terms

Alzheimer's disease: a condition occurring mostly in old age, characterized by increasingly severe memory loss, confusion, depression, and disordered thinking (page 266)

amnesia: the severe loss or deterioration of memory (page 263)

anterograde amnesia: the inability to store new long-term memories (page 263)

chunking: the process of grouping digits or letters into meaningful sequences (page 240)

confabulations: attempts made by amnesic patients to fill in the gaps in their memory, mostly with out-of-date information (page 265)

cued recall: a method of testing memory by asking someone to remember a certain item after being given a hint (page 234)

declarative memory: the recall of factual information (page 235)

dissociation: a condition in which memory is stored but cannot be retrieved (page 258)

encoding specificity principle: the tendency for the associations formed at the time of learning to be more effective retrieval cues than other associations (page 246)

episodic memory: a memory for specific events in a person's life (page 238)

explicit memory (or direct memory): a memory that a person can state, generally recognizing that it is the correct answer (page 235)

false memory: a report that someone believes to be a memory but that does not actually correspond to real events (page 258)

free recall: a method of testing memory by asking someone to produce a certain item (e.g., a word) without substantial hints, as on an essay or short-answer test (page 234)

hindsight bias: the tendency to mold our recollection of the past to fit how events later turned out (page 256)

hippocampus: a forebrain structure in the interior of the temporal lobe that is important for storing certain kinds of memory (page 263)

implicit memory (or indirect memory): a memory that influences behavior without requiring conscious recognition that one is using a memory (page 235)

infant amnesia (or childhood amnesia): a relative lack of declarative memories from early in life (page 266)

information-processing model: the view that information is processed, coded, and stored in various ways in human memory as it is in a computer (page 237)

Korsakoff's syndrome: a condition caused by a prolonged deficiency of vitamin B_1, which results in both retrograde amnesia and anterograde amnesia (page 264)

levels-of-processing principle: the concept that the number and types of associations established during learning determine the ease of later retrieval of a memory (page 245)

long-term memory: a relatively permanent store of information (page 238)

memory: the process of retaining information or the information retained (page 233)

method of loci: a mnemonic device that calls for linking the items on a list with a memorized list of places (page 250)

mnemonic device: any memory aid that is based on encoding each item in a special way (page 249)

priming: the temporarily increased probability of using a word as a result of recently reading or hearing it (page 235)

proactive interference: the hindrance that an older memory produces on a newer one (page 253)

procedural memory: the retention of learned skills (page 235)

recognition: a method of testing memory by asking someone to choose the correct item from a set of alternatives (page 235)

reconstruction: putting together an account of past events, based partly on memories and partly on expectations of what must have happened (page 254)

recovered memory: a report of a long-lost memory, prompted by clinical techniques (page 257)

repression: according to Freudian theory, the process of moving a memory, motivation, or emotion from the conscious mind to the unconscious mind (page 257)

retrieval cue: information associated with remembered material, which can be useful for helping to recall that material (page 240)

retroactive interference: the impairment that a newer memory produces on an older one (page 253)

retrograde amnesia: the loss of memory for events that occurred before the brain damage (page 264)

savings method (or relearning method): a method of testing memory by measuring how much faster someone can relearn something than learn something for the first time (page 235)

semantic memory: memory of general principles (page 238)

sensory store: a very brief storage of sensory information (page 238)

serial-order effect: the tendency to remember the items near the beginning and end of a list better than those in the middle (page 254)

short-term memory: a temporary storage of a limited amount of information (page 238)

SPAR method: a systematic way to monitor and improve understanding of a text by surveying, processing meaningfully, asking questions, and reviewing (page 248)

state-dependent memory: the tendency to remember something better if your body is in the same condition during recall as it was during the original learning (page 247)

working memory: a system that processes and works with current information, including three components—a central executive, a phonological loop, and a visuospatial sketchpad (page 242)

Suggestion for Further Reading

Schacter, D. L. (1996). *Searching for memory*. New York: Basic Books. Discusses current theories and research in an accessible manner.

 ## Book Companion Web Site

Need help studying? Go to

http://psychology.wadsworth.com/kalat_intro7e/

for a virtual study center. You'll find a personalized Self-Study Assessment that will provide you with a study plan based on your answers to a pretest. Also study using flashcards, quizzes, interactive art, and an online glossary.

Check out interactive **Try It Yourself** exercises on the companion site! For example, the Sperling Effect, Decay of Short-Term Memory, and False and Implicit Memories exercises tie to what you've learned in this chapter.

Your companion site also has direct links to the following Web sites. These links are checked often for changes, dead links, and new additions.

The Magic Number Seven, Plus or Minus Two

www.well.com/user/smalin/miller.html

This is George Miller's classic article about the limits of short-term memory, complete with graphs and references, as it originally appeared in the *Psychological Review* in 1956.

 ## Try It Yourself CD-ROM
with Critical Thinking Video Exercises

Use your CD to access **videos** related to activities designed to help you think critically about the important topics discussed. You'll also find an easy portal link to the book companion site where you can access your personalized **Self-Study Assessments** and interactive **Try It Yourself** exercises.

PsychNow! 2.0

PsychNow! is a fun interactive CD designed to help you with the difficult concepts in psychology. Check out the Learning & Cognition section for the following topics that relate to this chapter:

Memory Systems: "Lost in a Shopping Mall" video with researcher Elizabeth Loftus, memory flowchart lesson, permanent short-term memory loss video.

Forgetting: repeating musical notes in order, memory interference lesson and quiz.

InteractNOW! Online Collaborative Lab: Memory and the *ExperimentNOW! Research Experiment:* Memory—Brown-Peterson, false memory, memory span, partial report, serial position, Sternberg search

ExperimentNOW! Research Experiment: Imagery—Mental rotation

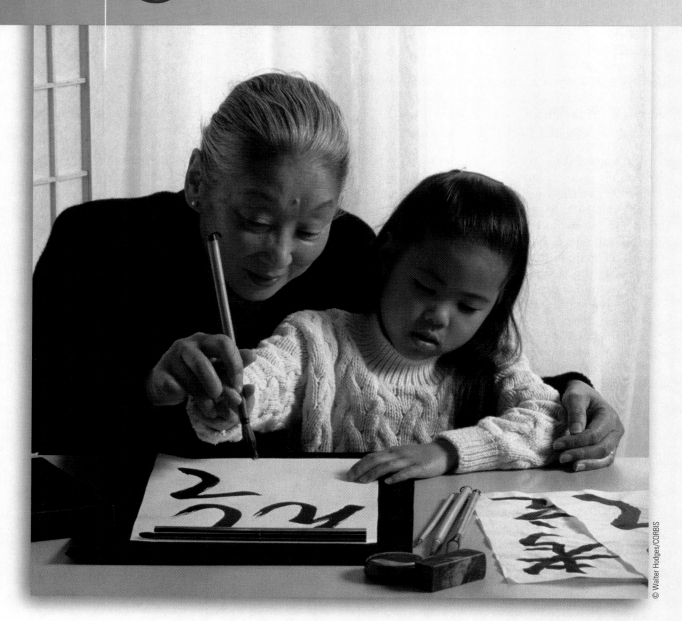

© Walter Hodges/CORBIS

Cognition and Language

onsider the statement, "This sentence is false." Is the statement itself true or false? Declaring the statement true agrees with its own assessment that it is false. But declaring it false would make its assessment correct. A sentence about itself, called a *self-referential* sentence, can be utterly confusing, like the one above, or true (like this one!). It can also be false ("Anyone who reads this sentence will be transported suddenly to the planet Neptune"), untestable ("Whenever no one is reading this sentence, it changes into the passive voice"), or amusing ("This sentence no verb" or "This sentence sofa includes an unnecessary word").

In this chapter you will be asked to think about thinking, talk about talking, and read about reading. Doing so is self-referential, and if you try to "think about what you are thinking now," you can easily go into a confusing loop like the one in "This sentence is false." Psychological researchers focus as much as possible on results obtained from carefully controlled experiments, not just on what people say that they think about their own thought processes. They also try to understand how we use our thought processes to produce language.

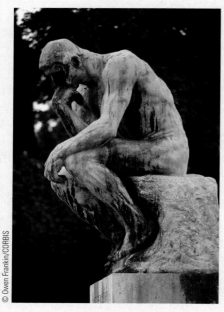

▮ Cognitive psychology studies how people think and what they know.

Categorization and Attention

What are concepts and attention? How can we measure them?

Cognition means *thinking, gaining knowledge, and dealing with knowledge.* Cognitive psychologists study how people think, how they acquire knowledge, what they know, how they imagine, and how they solve problems. They also deal with how people organize their thoughts into language and communicate with others.

Cognitive psychology increased in popularity after computers became popular. Although brains and computers do not work the same way, computers provide a valuable way of modeling theories of cognitive processes. A researcher may say, "Imagine that cognitive processes work as follows. . . . Now let's program a computer to go through those same steps. If we then give the computer the same information that a human has, will it draw the same conclusions and make the same errors as a human?" In short, computer modeling provides a way to test theories of cognition. Today, cognitive psychologists use a variety of methods to measure mental processes and to test theories about what we know and how we know it.

Methods of Research in Cognitive Psychology

Perhaps it seems that cognitive psychology should be simple. "If you want to find out what people think or what they know, why not ask them?" Sometimes psychologists do ask, but people can't always describe their own thought processes (Kihlstrom, Barnhardt, & Tataryn, 1992). Recall, for example, implicit memory as discussed in Chapter 7: Sometimes you see or hear something that influences your behavior without your realizing it. Similarly, we sometimes solve a problem without knowing how we did it.

Also, consider visual imagery. People often claim that they have a clear mental image of some object but then cannot correctly answer simple questions about it. To illustrate, imagine a simple cube balanced with one point (corner) on the table and the opposite point straight up. Imagine that you are holding the highest point with one finger. Now, using a finger of the opposite hand, point to all the remaining corners

of the cube (not counting the one touching the table). How many corners do you touch?

You probably will say that you answered this question by "picturing" a cube in your mind as if you were actually seeing it. However, most people answer the question incorrectly, and few get it right quickly (Hinton, 1979). (Check answer A on page 284.)

In short, we cannot simply accept people's self reports about their thinking. So how *can* we measure thinking, a process that we obviously cannot observe? Physicists don't directly observe magnetic fields or electrical currents either. In each case researchers infer the unobservable processes from their effects. To illustrate, let's consider one of the classic experiments in cognitive psychology, which demonstrated a way to measure a mental process.

CRITICAL THINKING: *WHAT'S THE EVIDENCE?* *Mental Imagery*

Roger Shepard and Jacqueline Metzler (1971) studied how humans solve visual problems. They reasoned that if people visualize mental images, then the time it takes them to rotate a mental image should be similar to the time needed to rotate a real object.

Hypothesis When people have to rotate a mental image to answer a question, the farther they have to rotate it, the longer it will take them to answer the question.

Method Participants examined pairs of drawings of three-dimensional objects, as in Figure 8.1, and indicated whether the two drawings represented one object and a rotated view of it or different objects. (Try to answer this question yourself before reading further. Then check answer B on page 284.)

People pulled one lever to indicate *same* and another lever to indicate *different*. When the correct answer was *same*, someone might determine that answer by rotating a mental image of the first picture until it matched the second. If so, the delay should depend on how far the image had to be rotated.

Results Participants answered almost 97% of the items correctly. As predicted, their reaction time

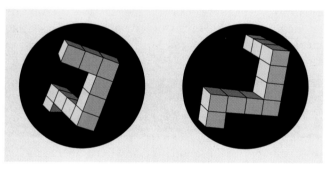

FIGURE 8.1 Examples of pairs of drawings used in an experiment by Shepard and Metzler (1971). Do the drawings for each pair represent the same object being rotated, or are they different objects? (See answer B on page 284.) (*Reprinted with permission from "Mental Rotation of Three-Dimensional Objects," by R. N. Shepard and J. N. Metzler,* Science, *1971, 171, 701-703. Copyright © 1980 American Association for the Advancement of Science.*)

when they responded *same* depended on the angular difference in orientation between the two views. For example, if the first image of a pair had to be rotated 30 degrees to match the second image, people needed a certain amount of time to pull the *same* lever. If an image had to be rotated 60 degrees to match the other, they took twice as long to pull the lever. In other words they reacted as if they were watching a model of the object rotate; the more the object needed to be rotated, the longer they took to determine the answer.

Interpretation First, viewing a mental image is at least partly like real vision. So, in this case common sense appears to be correct. Second, it is possible for researchers to infer thought processes from someone's delay in answering a question.

Some people report that they have auditory images as well as visual images. They "hear" words or songs "in their head." What kind of evidence would we need to test this claim?

Categorization

An ancient Greek philosopher once said that you cannot step into the same river twice. He referred to the fact that the river changes, but in fact you change too from one time to the next. Nothing stays the same, and almost every concept refers to items that differ from one another. Nevertheless, to make reasonable decisions, we have to treat similar objects similarly. A major part of thinking is the formation of categories or concepts.

Ways of Describing a Category

Do we look up our concepts in a mental dictionary to determine their meaning? A few words have simple, unambiguous definitions. For example, we think of the term *bachelor* as an unmarried male. Because we would not ordinarily apply the term bachelor to a young child or to a Catholic priest, we might refine the definition to "a male who has not yet married but could." That definition pretty well explains the concept.

Many concepts are harder to define, however. Try defining *country music,* for example. Also, imagine a man who loses one hair from his head. Is he bald? Of course not. Then he loses one more hair, then another and another. Eventually, he *is* bald, so was there some point at which losing one more hair made him bald? We are forced to that absurdity if we use baldness as a yes/no category. (Similar problems arise if we try to classify everyone as depressed or not, schizophrenic or not, and alcoholic or not. Almost everything comes in degrees.)

Eleanor Rosch (1978; Rosch & Mervis, 1975) argued that many categories are best described by *familiar or typical examples* called **prototypes.** We decide whether an object belongs to a category by determining how much it resembles the prototypes of that category. For example, we define the category "vehicle" by examples: *car, bus, train, airplane, boat, truck.* Is a *blimp* also a vehicle? What about an *elevator* or *water skis*? These other items resemble the prototypes in some ways but not others, so they are marginal members of the category, which has fuzzy boundaries.

However, some categories cannot be described by prototypes (Fodor, 1998). For example, we can talk and think about "bug-eyed monsters from outer space" without ever encountering a single prototype of that category.

Conceptual Networks and Priming

Choose any concept and try to think about only it and nothing else. It's impossible. You can't really think about something without relating it to something else. When you think about some concept, for example *bird,* you link it to more specific terms, such as *sparrow,* more general terms, such as *animals,* and related terms such as *flight* and *eggs.*

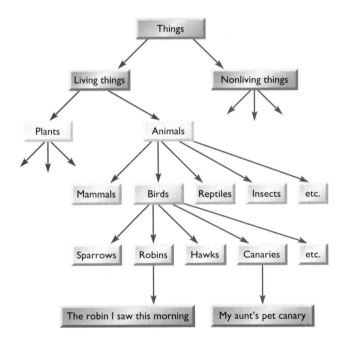

We naturally organize items into hierarchies, such as animal as a higher level category, bird as intermediate, and sparrow as a lower level category. Researchers demonstrate the reality of this kind of hierarchy by measuring the delay for people to answer various questions (A. M. Collins & Quillian, 1969, 1970). Answer the following true/false questions as quickly as possible:

- Canaries are yellow.
- Canaries sing.
- Canaries lay eggs.
- Canaries have feathers.
- Canaries have skin.

Presumably you answered "true" to all five items, but you may have answered some faster than others. Most people answer fastest on the *yellow* and *sing* items, slightly slower on the *eggs* and *feathers* items, and still slower on the *skin* item. Why? It is because yellowness and singing are distinctive char-

acteristics of canaries. You probably do not think of eggs or feathers specifically as canary features; instead you reason (quickly), "Canaries are birds, and birds lay eggs. So canaries must lay eggs." Skin is not even distinctive of birds, so you have to reason, "Canaries are birds and birds are animals. Animals have skin, so canaries must have skin." Even though this way of categorizing things delays you slightly in answering whether canaries have skin, it saves you enormous effort overall. When you learn some new fact about birds or animals in general, you don't have to learn it again separately for every individual species. Reasoning in terms of categories and subcategories simplifies our memory.

CONCEPT CHECK ☑

1. Which would people answer faster: whether politicians give speeches or whether they sometimes eat spaghetti? Why? (Check your answers on page 284.)

We also link a word or concept to other concepts related to it. Figure 8.2 shows a possible network of conceptual links that someone might have at a par-

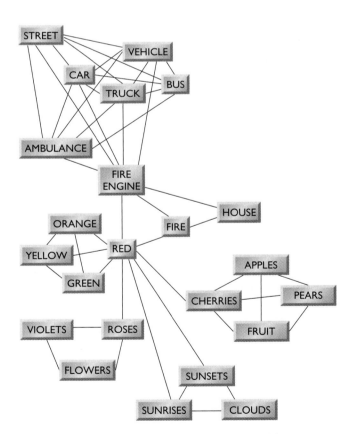

FIGURE 8.2 We link each concept to a variety of other related concepts. Any stimulus that activates one of these concepts will also partly activate (or "prime") the ones that are linked to it. *(From A. M. Collins & Loftus, 1975)*

ticular moment (A. M. Collins & Loftus, 1975). Suppose this network describes your own concepts. *Thinking about one of the concepts shown in this figure will activate, or prime, the concepts linked to it* (A. M. Collins & Loftus, 1975). This process is called **spreading activation**. For example, if you hear *flower*, you are primed to think of *rose, violet,* and various other flowers. If you also hear *red*, the combination of *flower* and *red* strongly primes you to think of *rose*. You might think of the word spontaneously, and you would recognize it more easily than usual if it were flashed briefly on a screen or spoken very softly.

Priming is important during reading. When you come to a difficult word that you barely know, you find it easier to understand if the preceding sentences were about closely related concepts (Plaut & Booth, 2000). In effect they provide hints about the meaning of the new word.

Here is an illustration that can be explained in terms of a spreading activation model. Quickly answer each of the following questions (or ask someone else):

1. How many animals of each kind did Moses take on the ark?
2. What was the famous saying uttered by Louis Armstrong when he first set foot on the moon?
3. Some people pronounce St. Louis "saint loo-iss" and some pronounce it "saint loo-ee." How would you pronounce the capital city of Kentucky?

The answers are in the footnote on this page.[1] Many people miss these questions and are then embarrassed or angry. Figure 8.3 offers an explanation in terms of spreading activation (Shafto & MacKay, 2000): The question about Louis Armstrong activates a series of sounds and concepts that are linked to one another and to other items. The sound *Armstrong* and the ideas *first astronaut on the moon* and *famous sayings* are all linked to "One small step for a man . . ."

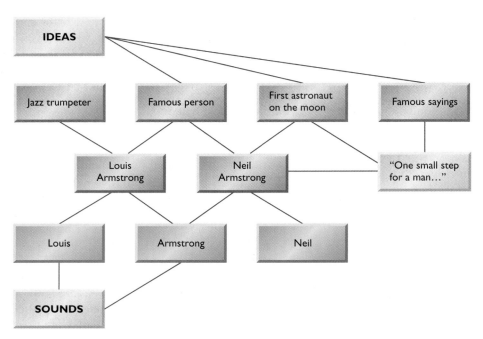

FIGURE 8.3 According to one explanation, the word *Armstrong* and the ideas *astronaut, first person on the moon,* and *famous sayings* all activate the linked saying "One small step for a man . . ." Even the word *Louis* contributes, because both Louis Armstrong and Neil Armstrong were famous people.

Even the name *Louis Armstrong* is loosely linked to *Neil Armstrong* because both are famous people. (You probably would not respond the same way to a question about "What was the famous line uttered by Jennifer Armstrong . . . ?") The combined effect of all these influences automatically triggers the answer, "One small step for a man . . ."

CONCEPT CHECK ☑

2. Suppose someone says "cardinal" and then flashes the word *bird* on a screen very briefly. Some viewers identify the word correctly, suggesting priming, and some do not. Considering both priming and the encoding specificity idea from Chapter 7, how might you explain why some people and not others identified the word *bird*? (Check your answer on page 284.)

Cross-Cultural Studies of Concepts

When you and I use the same term—river, vehicle, free will, or anything else—do we really have the same concept? Do people of different cultures and languages have the same concepts? People fluent in two languages sometimes remark that something gets lost in translation; a translated statement doesn't mean in English exactly the same as what it meant in Russian.

[1]Answers: 1. None. Moses didn't have an ark; Noah did. 2. Louis Armstrong never set foot on the moon; it was Neil Armstrong. 3. The right pronunciation of Kentucky's capital is "frank-furt." (Not "loo-ee-ville"!)

Let's start with one line of research that measures differences in meaning for what are regarded as equivalent words in different languages.

Hypothesis   Even though a word in one language is considered a translation of a word in another language, people will use them in different ways. For example, the English word *bottle* is considered a translation of the Spanish word *botella,* and the English word *jar* is translated as the Spanish word *frasco.* Nevertheless, they might not apply to all the same objects.

Method   Researchers showed English-, Argentinean Spanish-, and Chinese-speaking people a large array of objects, including those shown in Figure 8.4. Researchers asked them what word they would use for each. They also asked people to arrange pictures of the objects into groups of "similar" objects.

Results   U.S. English speakers used seven words for the various objects—*jar, bottle, container, can, jug, tube,* and *box.* Argentinean Spanish speakers used fifteen words for the same objects, and Chinese speakers used five. Of the sixteen objects called *bottle* in English, many were called *botella* in Spanish, but a total of six other names were given to some of them. One Chinese term applied to all the objects called *jar* in English but also applied to some of the objects considered *bottles* or *containers.*

However, when people were asked to arrange pictures of objects into groups of similar items, users of the three languages made remarkably similar categories. That is, people might put several objects into the same group, even though they gave them different names (Malt, Sloman, & Gennari, 2003; Malt, Sloman, Gennari, Shi, & Wang, 1999).

Interpretation   The simple conclusion is that words don't translate exactly. Generally, the items that English-speakers considered good examples (prototypes) of *bottle* were also considered good examples of *botella* in Spanish and so forth. However, people disagreed about how to label many marginal cases. On the other hand, differences in what people called objects had little apparent influence on which objects they considered similar. So, in this case the results suggest that people speaking different languages do not think very differently. (Obviously, we should not generalize too far based on this one example.)

Attention

You are constantly bombarded with sights, sounds, smells, and other kinds of sensation. **Attention** is *your tendency to respond to some stimuli more than others at any given time or to remember some more than others.* Attention can shift or select. That is, you attend to different items at different times.

To illustrate, recall from Chapter 4 that the fovea of your retina receives the most detail. Ordinarily, you remember mainly what was in your fovea, and that information has the biggest impact on your behavior. However, it is possible to direct your attention elsewhere. For example, you might not want someone to know that you are watching him or her, so you look off to the side, but you nevertheless concentrate on that person. You can demonstrate your ability to shift attention with the following. Fixate your eyes on the x in the center, and then without moving your eyes, read the letters in the circle around it clockwise:

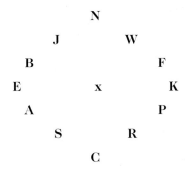

As you see, focusing your attention away from the center of your vision is difficult but possible. You can even attend to two nonadjacent spots at once—for example, the places occupied by **A** and **F** in the display above. When you increase your attention to something in your visual field, the part of your visual cortex sensitive to that area becomes more active and receives more blood flow (Müller, Malinowski, Gruber, & Hillyard, 2003). Also, if you try to pay extra attention to the color or motion of the next object to be shown on the screen, then the brain areas sensitive to color or motion become more active, even before the object appears (Driver & Frith, 2000). So attention is a process of increasing the brain's response to certain classes of stimuli. Nevertheless, explaining exactly how all this happens is a major challenge.

Preattentive and Attentive Processes

In the example just described, you deliberately shifted your attention from one letter to another. Often, however, objects grab your attention automatically when they start to move (Abrams & Christ, 2003) or because

FIGURE 8.4 What word would you use for each of these objects? Would all the objects you call *bottle* translate as *botella* in Spanish? *(From Malt, Sloman, Gennari, Shi, & Wang, "Knowing vs. Naming: Similarity and the Linguistic Categorization of Artifacts," Journal of Memory and Language, 40, 230–262, 1999.)*

a shopping mall, but not quite so easy at a beach and not at all at a nudist beach. Our attention is drawn to the unusual, but what is unusual depends on the context. Ordinarily, we notice something that is flashing on and off, but if almost everything is flashing on and off, our attention is drawn to the one thing that isn't (Pashler & Harris, 2001).

To illustrate how an unusual object draws attention, look at Figure 8.5, which shows a huge flock of sandhill cranes plus one whooping crane. Find the whooping crane—the one that's different. That was easy, wasn't it? When an object differs drastically from those around it in size, shape, or color, we find it by a **preattentive process,** *meaning that it stands out immediately; we don't have to shift attention from one object to another.* Because the distinctive item jumps out preattentively, the number of sandhill cranes is irrelevant. Even if someone added or subtracted a few, you would find the whooping crane just as fast.

Contrast that task with Figure 8.6. Here the photo shows a flock of marbled godwits. Most of them are facing to your left; your task is to find the one that is facing to your right. Now you have to check each one separately, and the more birds present, the longer you will need, on the average, to find the one you are looking for. (You might find it quickly if you are lucky enough to start your search in the correct corner of the photograph.) You had to rely on an **attentive process**—*one that requires searching through the items in series* (Enns & Rensink, 1990; Treisman & Souther, 1985). (The *Where's Waldo* books are an excellent example of a task requiring an attentive process.) Studies of brain activity confirm that when we are searching through a complex display for an item that is hard to find, we are shifting attention (and the brain's responsiveness) from one area to another (Woodman & Luck, 2003).

The distinction between attentive and preattentive processes has practical applications. Imagine yourself as an ergonomist (human factors psychologist) designing machinery with several gauges. When the apparatus is running safely, the first gauge should read about 70, the second 40, the third 30, and the fourth 10, and any reading far from these normal values is dangerous. If

they are brightly colored or surprising in some way. I once watched an unusual costume contest. People were told to dress so distinctively that their friends or family could find them in a crowd as quickly as possible. The winner was a young man who came onto the stage naked. Although I concede that he earned the prize, there is a problem with this contest: The most distinctive clothing (or lack of it) depends on what everyone else is wearing. A naked person would be easy to spot in

FIGURE 8.5 Demonstration of preattentive processes: Find the one whooping crane among the sandhill cranes. It stands out immediately. You would find the whooping crane just as fast in a much larger or much smaller flock of sandhill cranes.

© Michael Forsberg/www.michaelforsberg.com

© Wendy Shattil and Bob Rozinski

FIGURE 8.6 Demonstration of attentive processes: Find the marbled godwit that is facing to the right. In this case you need an attentive process, checking the birds one at a time.

you arrange the gauges as in the top row of Figure 8.7, then people using this machine must check each gauge separately to find anything dangerous. Note how the bottom row of Figure 8.7 simplifies the process: All the gauges are arranged so that the safe range is on the right. Now someone can glance at the display and quickly (preattentively) notice anything out of position.

CONCEPT CHECK ☑

3. Suppose you are in a field full of brownish bushes and one motionless brown rabbit. Will you find the rabbit by attentive or preattentive processes? If the field has many motionless rabbits and one that is hopping, will you find the active one by attentive or preattentive processes? (Check your answers on page 284.)

The Stroop Effect

Here is another example of something that grabs our attention automatically: Read the following instructions and then examine Figure 8.8:

Notice the blocks of color at the top of the figure. Scanning from left to right, give the name of each color as fast as you can. Then notice the nonsense syllables printed in different colors in the center of the figure. Don't try to pronounce them; just say the color of each one as fast as possible. Then turn to the real words at the bottom. Don't read them; quickly state the color in which each one is printed.

Most people find it very difficult to ignore the words at the bottom of the figure. After all of your years of reading, you can hardly bring yourself to look at RED and say "green." *The tendency to read the word, instead of saying the color of ink as instructed,* is known as the **Stroop effect,** after the psychologist who discovered it.

One explanation of the Stroop effect that we can discard is the idea that words always take priority over colors. Try the following: Go back to

Figure 8.8 and notice the red, green, blue, and yellow patches at the four corners. This time, instead of saying anything, point to the correct color patch. First, try pointing to the color patch corresponding to the color of the ink; that is, when you come to RED, point to the blue patch in the lower left. Then try it again but point to the color corresponding to the meaning of the word. That is, when you come to RED, point to the red patch in the upper left. Try it now.

You probably found it easy to point to the patch that matches the color of the ink and harder to point to the color matching the word meaning (Durgin, 2000). When you are speaking, you are primed to read the words you see, but when you are pointing, you are more primed to attend to something nonverbal, such as ink color. In either case one response dominates, and it interferes with the less dominant response.

FIGURE 8.7 Each gauge represents a measurement of a different variable in a machine, such as an airplane. The top row shows one way of presenting the information. The operator must check each gauge one at a time to find out whether the reading is within the safe range for that variable. The bottom row shows the information represented in a way that is easier to read. The safe range for each variable is rotated to the same visual position. At a glance the operator can detect any reading outside the safe zone.

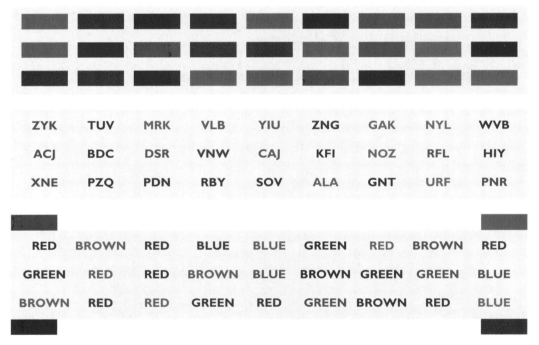

FIGURE 8.8 Read (left to right) the color of the ink in each part. Try to ignore the words themselves.

Attention Limits over Space and Time

How much can you hold in your attention at once? For example, imagine yourself in the control room of the Three Mile Island nuclear power plant, the site of a nearly disastrous accident in 1979. Figure 8.9 shows a small portion of the room as it appeared then. You notice immediately the enormous number of knobs and gauges for what is, after all, a complicated system. What you cannot see in the picture is that in certain cases the knob controlling something and the gauge measuring it were in different places.

© GPU Nuclear Corp.

FIGURE 8.9 The Three Mile Island TMI-2 nuclear power plant had a complex and confusing control system, a small portion of which is shown here. Some of the important gauges were not easily visible, some were poorly labeled, and many alarm signals had ambiguous meanings. After the accident in 1979, the control system was redesigned and simplified.

Since then the controls have been redesigned to simplify the task. Designing good controls is a challenge for engineers and psychologists with a combination of theoretical and applied interests. One of the main issues they face is understanding the limits of human attention.

Change Blindness

If you look out your window, you see a scene with many objects. Do you see the whole scene at once? Recall the concept of *sensory store* from Chapter 7 (p. 237): If a display disappears but a signal immediately calls your attention to one part of the display, you can say what had been there. So, in a sense you did see the whole scene. However, if nothing calls your attention to a particular spot, then how much did you see and how well could you recall it? If you have scanned around the scene, briefly fixating practically everything, do you now know everything in the scene?

Most people think they do, and they believe they would notice anything that changed. However, movie

directors discovered long ago that they could shoot different parts of a story segment on different days, and few viewers would notice that some of the actors had changed clothes, that some of the props had moved, or that the extra actors in the background were different people (Simons & Levin, 2003).

Psychologists have named this phenomenon **change blindness**—*the frequent failure to detect changes in parts of a scene.* If anything moves or changes its appearance suddenly in any way, it automatically draws your attention. However, if a similar change occurs slowly or during an instant you are not watching, you might not notice. Have you ever seen one of those puzzles that ask you to "find ten differences between these two pictures"? The difficulty of finding them all indicates that you don't exactly "see" everything you look at. You can experience this effect yourself. Go to http://psychology.wadsworth.com/kalat_intro7e. Navigate to the student Web site, then to the Online Try It Yourself section, and click on Change Blindness.

In one experiment people looked at a screen that alternated between two views of a scene, as shown in Figure 8.10. Each view appeared for 560 milliseconds (ms), followed by a blank screen for 80 ms, and then the other view for 560 ms, with the sequence repeating until the viewer detected how the two scenes differed. Generally, viewers found differences in important features of the scene faster than changes in less central details, but on the average they took almost 11 seconds to find a difference. On some pairs of pictures the average viewer needed more than 50 seconds (Rensink, O'Regan, & Clark, 1997).

CONCEPT CHECK ☑

4. Did viewers in this study detect the changes by a preattentive or an attentive mechanism? (Check your answer on page 284.)

Even without an intervening blank screen, people often fail to detect a change in the scene if the change happens while they are blinking their eyes or even while moving their eyes to focus on a different area (Henderson & Hollingworth, 2003b). They are more likely to notice a changed object if their eyes were moving toward that object than if moving away (Henderson & Hollingworth, 2003a).

Would viewers notice a change in a display even if they had already paid attention to every part of the display? In one experiment students looked at a circular array of one-digit numbers, as shown in Figure 8.11, for 2 seconds. During that time they had to attend to each digit to answer a question such as, "What is the

a Change in marginal interest (MI)

b Change in central interest (CI)

FIGURE 8.10 Viewers' task was to detect what was different between the two scenes, which were presented in alternation. The top scene has a change in a usually unattended detail; the lower scene has a change in a more important feature. If you can't find the changes, check answer C, page 284. *(Rensink, R.A., O'Regan, J.K., and Clark, J.J. (1997). "To see or not to see: The need for attention to perceive changes in scenes."* Psychological Science, 8, 368–373. Figure 2, p. 370. Reprinted with permission of Blackwell Publishing.)

highest digit included?" or "What is the lowest digit *not* included?" Then the display went blank for 150 milliseconds and reappeared. The viewers' task was to say whether any of the digits had changed. They detected a change only about one third of the time (Becker & Pashler, 2002).

In sound we have change deafness, analogous to change blindness. In one study students tried to re-

FIGURE 8.11 In the experiment by Becker and Pashler (2002), people saw a circular array of numbers for 2 seconds and then, after a 150 millisecond delay, saw the same or a changed array. People usually failed to detect the change.

peat the words they heard someone speak, as quickly as possible. After a 1-minute rest break, the procedure continued, but in some cases with a new voice speaking the words. Only about half of the students noticed the change (Vitevitch, 2003).

Overall, the apparent conclusion is that you do not maintain a detailed representation of what you have seen or heard. You hold a few details, but which details you hold vary from one time to another. (That's what we mean by attention.) You do retain the gist of the rest of the scene but not in detail (Becker & Pashler, 2002; Tatler, Gilchrist, & Rusted, 2003). Recall a similar conclusion about story memory from Chapter 7: We ordinarily remember a few details and only the gist of the rest of the story.

Shifting Attention

Paying attention to one thing detracts from attention to something else (Pashler, 1994). Can you do two things at once? Yes, you can *do* two things at once, especially if one of them is simple or highly practiced. However, you cannot *plan* two actions at once. For example, if you have to respond to one signal that tells you something to say and another signal that tells you which computer key to press, you can't make both responses as fast as you could make just one or the other (Ruthruff, Pashler, & Hazeltine, 2003; Ruthruff, Pashler, & Klaassen, 2001).

Many years ago, when automobile radios were introduced, people worried that listening to the radio would distract drivers and cause accidents. We no longer worry about radio, but we do worry about drivers using cell phones, and some states and countries have outlawed driving while holding a cell phone. Even if you don't have to hold the phone, listening with a phone on one ear tends to shift your attention toward that side of the body instead of straight ahead (Spence & Read, 2003). Also, conversations require more attention than radio, and a cell-phone conversation is more distracting than one with a passenger in the car because most passengers pause a conversation when they see that driving conditions are difficult. Research on simulated driving finds that a cell-phone conversation decreases a driver's attention to signs and increases the risk of accidents (Stayer, Drews, & Johnston, 2003).

The way you divide your attention among tasks is not fixed from birth; you can change it—perhaps unintentionally. For example, the research indicates that people who spend much time playing complex action video games learn to divide their attention widely over the video screen. That division of attention helps while playing the games, and probably in some real-life situations too, but on the other hand, it impairs the ability to concentrate on just one item. That is, habitual video game players tend to be distracted by irrelevant stimuli in their peripheral vision that most other people ignore (C. S. Green & Bavelier, 2003). Not much is known yet about this process, but it opens the way for further research: Might certain kinds of video games be either helpful or harmful to people with, say, attention deficit disorder?

The Attentional Blink

Just as we don't attend equally to every point in space, we also don't attend equally at all points in time. It takes time to shift attention from one item to another.

The demonstration of this point is called the **attentional blink:** *During a brief time after perceiving one stimulus, it is difficult to attend to something else.* Just as you don't see anything during a brief blink of the eyes, you don't attend to something during the attentional "blink." For example, suppose you watch a screen that displays a series of letters, one at a time for 90 ms each. Every series includes one letter in blue ink, and it may or may not include the letter T. Your task is to name the blue letter and say whether or not a T appeared. Here are two series and their correct answers:

D S R B J A O E C V "B, no."
Y L H F X G W K T Q "G, yes."

Most people miss the T (and say "no") if the T appears during a period about 100 to 700 ms after the blue letter. Similar results occur with many other kinds of stimuli and several variations of this procedure (Visser, Bischof, & DiLollo, 1999). It is an interesting demonstration theoretically and also a useful way of measuring how quickly various people can switch attention. For example, people with attention deficit disorder—known for their difficulty in controlling attention—have an unusually long attentional blink and often miss a target letter (T in the preceding example) even a full second after the blue letter (Hollingsworth, McAuliffe, & Knowlton, 2001). One exception: You might not notice most words if they are presented during the attentional blink, but you do notice your own name (K. L. Shapiro, Caldwell, & Sorensen, 1997).

Note that calling this phenomenon the attentional blink does not explain it. Why do we not notice a second stimulus 100 to 700 ms after the first one? "Be-

cause of the attentional blink." How do we know there is such a thing as an attentional blink? "Because we ignore a second stimulus 100 to 700 ms after the first one." Among several possible explanations that psychologists have been considering, one is that while the brain is "binding" the first stimulus into a single object, it cannot bind the second one and therefore does not fully perceive it (Raymond, 2003). Clearly, much more research is needed here.

CONCEPT CHECK ☑

5. Suppose you are playing a video game and you see two signals, about a quarter-second apart, telling you to do two things. You respond to the first one but not to the second. Why? (Check your answer on page 284.)

CRITICAL THINKING:
A STEP FURTHER
The Attentional Blink

When you read or listen to someone talk, one word or syllable follows another with very short delays. Why doesn't the attentional blink stop you from hearing or reading some of the words?

IN CLOSING

Thinking About Concepts and Attention

Behaviorists have traditionally avoided the topic of cognition because thinking and knowledge are unobservable. Although I hope this module has demonstrated that scientific research on cognition is possible and leads to new understanding, I also hope you see that the behaviorists' objections were not frivolous. Research on cognition is difficult, and each advance requires many experiments to check and recheck each conclusion and compare alternative explanations. The task is not purely theoretical; the better we can specify what we mean by "attention," for example, the better we can deal with those who have deficits in it.

Summary

- *Research methods in cognitive psychology.* Researchers cannot directly observe thinking or knowledge, but they can make inferences from observations such as people's delays in answering various questions. (page 273)

- *Mental imagery.* Mental images resemble vision in certain respects. For example, the time required to answer questions about a rotating object depends on how far the object would actually rotate between one position and another. (page 273)
- *Categorization.* People use many categories that are hard to define; we determine whether something fits the category by how closely it resembles familiar examples. Many items are marginal examples of a category, so we cannot insist on a yes/no decision. (page 274)
- *Conceptual networks.* We represent words or concepts with links to related concepts. Hearing or thinking about one concept will temporarily prime the linked concepts, and hearing several concepts can strongly prime another. (page 275)
- *Cross-cultural studies of concepts.* A word in one language may not correspond exactly to a word in another language; however, the similarities people see across objects do not depend on the words they use to name them. (page 276)
- *Attentive and preattentive processes.* We notice unusual items or items that have started to move almost at once, preattentively, regardless of potential distracters. Noticing less distinct items requires more careful attention to one possible target after another. (page 277)
- *The Stroop effect.* Sometimes it is difficult to avoid attending to certain stimuli; for example, it is difficult to state the color of the ink in which words are written while ignoring the words themselves (especially if they are color names). (page 279)
- *Attention limits.* Ordinarily, we notice only a small portion of a scene, perceiving and remembering just a vague gist of the rest. We often fail to detect changes in a scene if they occur slowly or during an eye blink or eye movement. We also frequently fail to detect a stimulus that appears 100 to 700 ms after a first stimulus that required some attention. (page 280)
- *Shifting attention.* Attending to one stimulus or activity detracts from attention to another. However, repeated practice, such as from playing video games, alters the degree to which someone divides attention across objects. (page 282)

Answers to Concept Checks

1. It would take longer to answer whether politicians sometimes eat spaghetti. Giving speeches is a distinctive feature of politicians; eating spaghetti is not. To answer the second question, you have to reason that politicians are people, and most people sometimes eat spaghetti. (page 275)

2. People who heard "cardinal" and thought of it as a bird would have spreading activation to prime the word *bird*. However, other people who thought of "cardinal" as an officer in the Catholic church would have spreading activation to prime a very different set of words, and not *bird*. (page 276)

3. Finding a motionless brown rabbit in a field full of brown objects will require attentive processes, but you could use preattentive processes to find a hopping rabbit in a field where nothing else is moving. (For this reason small animals in danger of predation stay motionless when they can.) (page 279)

4. The changes did not jump out by a preattentive mechanism. People had to use an attentive process to check each part of the scene one at a time. (page 281)

5. The second signal arrived during the attentional blink while you were still processing the first stimulus. (page 283)

Answers to Other Questions in the Module

A. The cube has six (not four) remaining corners. (page 273)

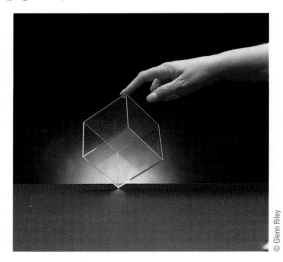

© Glenn Riley

B. The objects in pair a are the same; in b they are the same; and in c they are different. (page 274)
C. In the top scene, a horizontal bar along the wall has changed position. In the lower scene, the location of the helicopter has changed. (page 282)

Problem Solving, Expertise, and Error

How does someone become an expert?

What are some common errors of thinking?

On a college physics exam, a student was asked how to use a barometer to determine the height of a building. He answered that he would tie a long string to the barometer, go to the top of the building, and carefully lower the barometer until it reached the ground. Then he would cut the string and measure its length.

When the professor marked this answer incorrect, the student asked why. "Well," said the professor, "your method would work, but it's not the method I wanted you to use." When the student objected, the professor offered as a compromise to let him try again.

"All right," the student said. "Take the barometer to the top of the building, drop it, and measure the time it takes to hit the ground. Then, from the formula for the speed of a falling object, using the gravitational constant, calculate the height of the building."

"Hmmm," replied the professor. "That too would work. And it does make use of physical principles. But it still isn't the answer I had in mind. Can you think of another way?"

"Another way? Sure," he replied. "Place the barometer next to the building on a sunny day. Measure the height of the barometer and the length of its shadow. Also measure the length of the building's shadow. Then use the formula

> height of barometer ÷ height of building = length of barometer's shadow ÷ length of building's shadow

The professor was impressed but still reluctant to give credit, so the student persisted with another method: "Measure the barometer's height. Then walk up the stairs of the building, marking it off in units of the barometer's height. At the top take the number of barometer units and multiply by the height of the barometer to get the height of the building."

The professor sighed: "Give me one more way—any other way—and I'll give you credit, even if it's not the answer I wanted."

"Really?" asked the student with a smile. *"Any other way?"*

"Yes, any other way."

"All right," said the student. "Go to the man who owns the building and say, 'Hey, buddy, if you tell me how tall this building is, I'll give you this cool barometer!'"

Whenever we face a new problem, we must devise a new solution instead of relying on a memorized or practiced solution. Sometimes people develop creative, imaginative solutions like the ones that the physics student proposed. Sometimes they offer less imaginative but reasonable solutions or something quite illogical or no solution at all. Psychologists study problem-solving behavior partly to understand the thought processes behind it and partly to look for ways to help people reason more effectively.

▌ How would you carry 98 water bottles—all at one time, with no vehicle? When faced with a new problem, sometimes people find a novel and effective solution, and sometimes they do not.

Expertise

People vary in their performance on problem-solving and decision-making tasks. In the barometer story just described, we would probably talk about the student's creativity; in other cases we might talk of expertise. Expertise is a high level of thinking and knowledge in a particular field and therefore an example of outstanding cognition.

If you want to become an expert on something, what would you have to do? Above all, you would have to learn facts . . . many, many facts. Computer programmers realized that need when they tried to develop software to answer people's questions (C. Thompson, 2001). For example, if a Web site is to advise someone on travel plans, it should be able to say, "Because you are claustrophobic, you should avoid taking the Channel Tunnel from England to France." But to do so, the program needs to be told that:

- Claustrophobic people dislike long tunnels.
- The Channel Tunnel is 31 miles long.

285

- In this context anything more than 50 feet is considered "long."
- 31 miles is longer than 50 feet.

To get a Web site to answer various other questions, programmers had to provide the following information:

- Water is wet.
- Every person has a mother.
- You should carry a glass of water open end up.
- When people die, they stay dead.
- If you melt a statue, it is no longer a statue.

These facts are so obvious that stating them seems humorous. The point is that even the simplest decisions require a huge array of facts, and expert decisions require even more.

Practice Makes (Nearly) Perfect

Expert performance can be extremely impressive. An expert crossword puzzle solver not only completes *The New York Times* Sunday crossword—an impressive feat in itself—but tries to make it more interesting by racing against someone else. An expert bird watcher can look at a blurry photo of a bird and identify not only the species but also sometimes the subspecies and whether the bird is male or female, juvenile or adult, and in summer or winter plumage.

It is tempting to assume that experts were born with a special talent or great intelligence. Not so, say psychologists who have studied expertise. Remember the World Memory Championship from the start of Chapter 7? Winning contestants memorize a shuffled deck of cards in less than 40 seconds or a 300-digit number in 5 minutes. Psychologists tested 10 of the top memory performers and found that their mean IQ score was 111, as compared to a mean of 100 for the whole population (Maguire, Valentine, Wilding, & Kapur, 2003). A score of 111 is above average but hardly unusual. These people had developed their skills mainly by practicing the method of loci (page 250). They were no better than anyone else at remembering a series of photographs—a memory task they had not practiced because it is not part of the contest.

Similarly, in fields ranging from chess to sports to violin playing, the rule is that expertise requires about 10 years of concentrated practice (Ericsson & Charness, 1994; Ericsson, Krampe, & Tesch-Römer, 1993). The top violin players say they have practiced 3 to 4 hours every day since early childhood. A world-class tennis player spends hours working on backhand shots; a golfer works on chip shots. American writer John Irving is dyslexic and says it always took him longer than others to complete reading and writing assignments in school. By his own assessment, he is not a "talented" writer; he succeeded only because of

long, hard work and a willingness to undertake many revisions (Amabile, 2001). In short, experts are made, not born, and they are extremely impressive only in their area of specialization. In fact, the very brightest people—the top 1% of the top 1%—seldom become experts at anything because they get bored with the repetition and want to move on to something else.

Hungarian author Laszlo Polgar set out to demonstrate his conviction that almost anyone can achieve expertise with sufficient effort. He allowed his three young daughters to explore several fields; when they showed an interest in chess, he devoted enormous efforts to nurturing their chess skills. All three became outstanding chess players, and one, Judit, was the first woman and the youngest person ever to reach grand master status.

Some psychologists have argued that expertise depends *entirely* on practice, regardless of inborn predispositions. That claim is almost certainly an overstatement (H. Gardner, 1995). For obvious examples, short slow people will not become basketball stars, no matter how hard they practice, and blind people will not be-

❚ Judit Polgar confirmed her father's confidence that prolonged effort could make her an expert in her chosen field, chess. By reaching the status of grand master at age 15 years and 5 months, she beat Bobby Fisher's previous record for being the youngest.

come expert photographers. Also, in any field those who show early success are most likely to devote the necessary effort to achieve expertise. The main point, however, is that even someone born with "talent" or "potential" (whatever that means) needs years of hard work to achieve expertise on any complicated task.

Would you like to become an expert at something? In fields as competitive as chess, violin, or basketball, nearly all the great performers started young. Still, you have a choice among many other fields. (For example, if you want to be an expert psychologist, you won't have to worry about competing against people who started in childhood.) However, do not underestimate the effort required. Judit Polgar became a grand master by practicing chess about 8 hours a day from age 5 to 15, missing nearly all of the usual childhood activities. Thomas Young, a great 19th-century scientist, worked 16 hours a day, 7 days a week, including the day he died. His wife complained that she could not get pregnant because her husband almost never found time for sex (Martindale, 2001).

Expert Pattern Recognition

What exactly do experts do that other people do not? One important characteristic is that experts can look at a pattern and recognize its important features quickly.

In a typical experiment (de Groot, 1966), chess experts and beginners were shown pieces on a chessboard, as in Figure 8.12, for 5 seconds, and then asked to recall the positions of all the pieces. When the pieces were arranged as they might be in an actual game, expert players recalled 91% of the positions correctly, whereas novices recalled only 41%. When the pieces were arranged randomly, however, the expert players did no better than the novices. That is, on the average, expert chess players recognize the common chessboard patterns, but they do not have a superior overall memory. They still have to reason out the best move in a less-than-familiar situation, and even top chess players make occasional blunders when rushed for time (Chabris & Hearst, 2003), but recognizing common patterns is a huge head start.

a   b

FIGURE 8.12 Pieces arranged on a chessboard as they might actually occur in a game (a) and in a random manner (b). Master chess players can memorize the realistic pattern much better than others can, but they are no better than average at memorizing the random pattern.

In a wide variety of other areas from bird identification to reading x-rays to judging gymnastic competitions, experts recognize key patterns that other observers overlook (Murphy & Medin, 1985; Ste-Marie, 1999). They also know the difference between relevant and irrelevant information (Proffitt, Coley, & Medin, 2000).

Here is a quick demonstration, introduced by Herbert Simon, to show what happens when you develop expertise on a simple task where you do not need 10 years of practice. First, play this game with someone: The two of you take turns choosing a number from the set 1-2-3-4-5-6-7-8-9. When one of you chooses a number, scratch it out so that the other can't choose the same number. Continue until one of you has a set of three numbers that add to 15. For example, the combination 2, 4, 9 would win because 2 + 4 + 9 = 15. After you have tried this game two or three times, turn to answer D on page 300.

Problem Solving

Problem solving can be described in terms of four phases (Polya, 1957): (a) understanding the problem, (b) generating hypotheses, (c) testing the hypotheses, and (d) checking the result (Figure 8.13). We shall discuss these four phases in detail.

FIGURE 8.13 Four steps to solving a problem.

Understanding and Simplifying a Problem

Sometimes a problem is easy to solve once we recognize it as a problem. For years airport terminals listed incoming and outgoing flights in order of time. You can imagine the struggle to find your flight: You might remember that it was supposed to depart somewhere

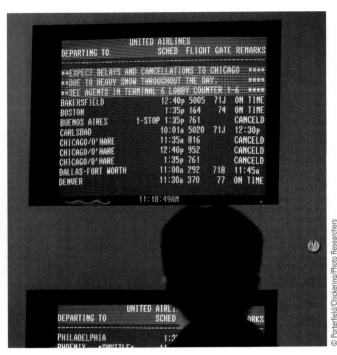

FIGURE 8.14 Switching airport terminal displays from listings by times (the old way) to listings by destinations (the new way) took little effort and had clear advantages.

between 10 and 10:30, but you didn't remember exactly when (and planes seldom leave exactly on time anyway), so you would have to sort through listings of many irrelevant flights to find the right one. Eventually, someone recognized the problem: People look for "the flight to San Jose," not "the flight at 10:27." Once the problem was recognized, the solution was obvious (Figure 8.14). (And then people wondered why they had overlooked the obvious for so long.)

When we recognize a problem but don't know how to solve it, a good strategy is to start with a simpler version. For example, here is what may appear to be a difficult, even impossible, problem: A professor hands back students' test papers at random. On the average how many students will accidentally receive their own paper?

Note that the problem does not specify how many students are in the class. If you don't see how to approach the problem, try the simplest cases: How many students will get their own paper back if there is only one student in the class? One, of course. What if there are two students? There is a 50% chance that both will get their own paper back and a 50% chance that neither will, for an average of one student getting the correct paper. What if there are three students? Each student then has one chance in three of getting his or her own paper. A one-third chance times three students means that on the average one student will get the correct paper. Already the pattern is clear: If there are n students, each student has one chance in n of getting his or her own paper back. No matter how many

students are in the class, on the average one student will get his or her own paper back.

Generating Hypotheses

After you have simplified a problem, you generate *hypotheses*—preliminary interpretations that you can evaluate or test. In some cases you can test every possible hypothesis. For example, suppose you want to connect your television set to a pair of stereo amplifiers, a VCR, and a DVD player, but you have lost the instruction manuals. You have several cables to attach, and each device has input and output channels. You could simply connect the cables by trial and error, testing every possibility until you find one that works. *A mechanical, repetitive procedure for solving a problem or testing every hypothesis* is called an **algorithm.** The rules for alphabetizing a list are one example; you check every possible item to see which one goes first, then check them all for which goes second, and so forth. You can also learn an algorithm for how to win, or at least tie, every time you play tick-tack-toe.

In many situations, however, the possible hypotheses are too numerous or vague to apply any algorithm. Consider the question, "What should I do with my life?" You could not consider every possible choice, and even if you did, you would not be sure how to evaluate them. **Heuristics** are *strategies for simplifying a problem or for guiding an investigation.* For the question about your future, you might restrict your attention to a few possible careers and then learn whatever you can about them.

▌ To find the right way to connect the lines, you could use the simple algorithm of trying every possible combination, one after the other.

To illustrate the contrast between algorithms and heuristics, consider chess. At a typical point in a game of chess, a player has about 25 legal moves, and the opponent has about 25 legal replies to each of them. To choose your best move by an algorithm, you would consider each of your possible moves, each of your opponent's possible replies, each of your next moves, and so forth, as many moves ahead as possible. Finally, you would select the move that gives you the best result, assuming that your opponent made the best possible reply at each point. Computerized chess programs do use algorithms, but human memory is more limited, so you simplify the task with heuristics: On each move you select just a few possible moves for serious consideration. You consider just a few of your opponent's likely responses, a few of your possible next moves, and so forth.

CONCEPT CHECK ☑

6. Suppose you are a traveling salesperson. You must start from your home city, visit each of several other cities, and then return home. Your task is to find the shortest route. What would be the appropriate algorithm? What would be a possible heuristic for simplifying the problem? (Check your answers on page 300.)

Testing Hypotheses and Checking the Results

If you think you have solved a problem, test whether your idea works. Many people who think they have a great idea never bother to try it out, even on a small

FIGURE 8.15 What is wrong with this perpetual motion machine?

scale. One inventor applied for a patent on the "perpetual motion machine" shown in Figure 8.15. Rubber balls, being lighter than water, rise in a column of water and flow over the top. The balls are heavier than air, so they fall, thus moving a belt and generating energy. At the bottom they reenter the water column. Do you see why this system could never work? You would if you tried to build it. (Check answer E on page 300.)

Even if you can't physically check your idea, consider whether it is realistic. One article published in 1927 claimed that a deer botfly has a speed of 800 miles per hour (almost 1,300 kilometers per hour). Some books and Internet sources to this day list that speed as the record for the fastest species on earth. One physicist calculated that an object moving that fast would generate more than enough air pressure to squash the fly. A fly striking you at that speed would pierce you like a bullet. And the energy to move that fast would require the fly to eat 1.5 times its weight in food *per second* (May, 1999).

Generalizing Solutions to Similar Problems

You might imagine that people who had just solved one problem would quickly recognize how to solve a similar problem (see Figure 8.16). Often, they do not. For example, if you have learned to use a formula in

FIGURE 8.16 The computer mouse was invented by a computer scientist who was familiar with an engineering device called a planimeter that he believed could be modified for use with computers. Such insights are unusual; most people do not generalize a solution from one task to another.

mathematics, you probably won't recognize that the same formula applies to some problem in a physics class, unless someone points out the similarity (Barnett & Ceci, 2002; Gick & Holyoak, 1980). You probably would learn faster in the new situation, so the previous training was not worthless (De Corte, 2003), but still it is noteworthy how often people apply a principle in one situation but not another.

For an example of failure to transfer principle, consider Figure 8.17a, which shows a coiled garden hose. When the water spurts out, what path will it take? (Draw it.) Figure 8.17b shows a curved gun barrel. When the bullet comes out, what path will it take? (Draw it.)

Almost everyone draws the water coming straight out of the garden hose, but most draw a bullet coming out of a gun in a curved path, as if the bullet remembered the curved path it had just taken (Kaiser, Jonides, & Alexander, 1986). The physics is the same in both situations: Except for the effects of gravity, both the water and the bullet will follow a straight path.

Here is another example in which people answer correctly one version of the problem but not another. Let's start with the harder version: You will be presented with a series of cards, each of which has a letter on one side and a number on the other. Your task is to test the hypothesis that "any card that has a vowel on one side has an even number on the other." The cards are shown below. Which cards do you need to turn over to test the hypothesis?

| A | T | 4 | 7 |

One choice is easy (if you understand the instructions): You have to turn over the card with an A. Most people, however, turn over the card with a 4, which is unnecessary. (Either a vowel or a consonant on the back of the 4 would be okay, according to the hypothesis.) But a vowel on the back of the 7 would contradict the hypothesis, and most people do not check the 7 (Wason, 1960).

Change the task, however, and it becomes easy. Now you are told that each card represents a person. One side indicates the person's age and the other is what kind of beverage the person is drinking. You are supposed to test the hypothesis that everyone under age 21 is drinking nonalcoholic beverages. Here are the cards; which ones do you need to turn over to check the hypothesis?

FIGURE 8.17 (a) Draw the trajectory of water as it flows out of a coiled garden hose. (b) Draw the trajectory of a bullet as it leaves a coiled gun barrel.

| Age 18 | Age 30 | Drinking Ginger Ale | Drinking Wine |

With this version the answer is obvious: Check the 18-year-old and the person drinking wine but not the other two (Cosmides, 1989).

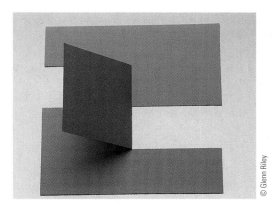

FIGURE 8.18 This object was made by cutting and folding an ordinary piece of cardboard with nothing left over. How was it done?

CRITICAL THINKING:
A STEP FURTHER
Logical Reasoning

Why was this version so much easier than the first? Some psychologists believe we are specialized to think more clearly about human social situations than about anything else. Try writing the question in some other way that pertains to realistic nonhuman events. Is your phrasing as easy as the human drinking example, as difficult as the letter–vowel example, or intermediate?

Why do we sometimes solve one problem and not another, even though they are logically similar? Part of the answer is that we sometimes apply a principle in one situation without fully understanding it or mastering it. After you have applied an approach in a few situations, you more quickly recognize its usefulness in still others (Gick & Holyoak, 1983). (This finding resembles the encoding specificity principle of memory: If you study something in just one situation, you remember it well in that one situation but probably not in others. If you study in several contexts, you remember in many.)

The other part of the answer is that, bluntly, we usually don't rely much on logical reasoning (Evans, 2002). We answer impulsively, or we look for evidence to support what we have already decided (Brownstein, 2003). In some cases people's intuitions are so strong that even solid evidence and logic fail to persuade them (Arkes, 2003; Krauss & Wang, 2003).

There is also a general point that will arise again in Chapter 10: A concept isn't something you either have or don't have. You can have it to a greater or lesser degree, find it easy or difficult to use, and use it frequently or infrequently (Siegler, 2000).

Special Features of Insight Problems

In "insight" or "aha!" problems, the correct answer occurs to you suddenly or not at all. Here is an example (M. Gardner, 1978): Figure 8.18 shows an object that was made by cutting and bending an ordinary piece of cardboard. How was it made? If you think you know, take a piece of paper and try to make it yourself. (The solution is on page 301, answer F.)

Sudden or Gradual Insights?

Solving insight problems differs from solving, say, algebra problems. Most people can look at an algebra problem and predict how quickly they will solve it if at all. As they work on it, they estimate how close they are to a solution. With insight problems, however—like the paper-folding problem just presented—people often think they are making no progress and then suddenly solve it (Metcalfe & Wiebe, 1987). Does the answer really come as suddenly as it seems?

If you were groping your way around in a dark room, you would have no idea how soon you were going to find the door, but nevertheless, you were making progress. You would have learned much about the room, including where the door was *not*. So maybe people are making more progress than they realize on insight problems. To test this possibility, psychologists gave students problems with the following form:

The following three words are all associated with one other word. What is that word? color numbers oil

In this case the intended answer is paint, although you might be able to defend some other answers. As with other insight questions, participants who solved it said the answer came to them suddenly. Then the experimenters gave the students paired sets of three words each, like those shown here in Sets 1 and 2, to examine for 12 seconds. In each pair one set had a correct answer (like paint in the example just given). The other set had no correct answer. Students were asked to generate a correct answer if they could, but if not, at least to guess which set had a correct answer. Examples:

Set 1

| playing | credit | report | *or* | still | pages | music |

Set 2

| town | root | car | *or* | ticket | shop | broker |

(You can check your answers on page 301, answer G.)

The main result: Even students who did not know the correct answer usually guessed correctly which set had an answer (Bowers, Regehr, Balthazard, & Parker, 1990). Even when they said they had "no confidence" in their guesses, they were still right more often than not. In short, people often make progress on insight problems without realizing it.

The Characteristics of Creativity

Why are some people more creative than others? Creativity is not the same as expertise. An expert gymnast goes through the same motions every time, and an expert chess player may use the same strategy in game after game, but a writer, composer, or painter who kept doing the same thing again and again would not be considered creative. One hallmark of creative people is a willingness to take risks. For example, painter Claude Monet deliberately varied the style and content of his paintings instead of just producing a series of successful but similar paintings (Stokes, 2001).

Creative writers, composers, and scientists have certain features in common, such as nonconformity, risk-taking, willingness to tolerate rejection, openness to new experiences, and at least moderate intelligence (Simonton, 2000b). However, it is misleading to talk about "creative people" as if certain people are creative in everything they do. People have to know a field well before they can make creative contributions to it. That is, don't expect a creative poet to offer creative solutions to an auto-mechanics problem.

Howard Gardner (1993) studied creativity by examining the lives of seven 20th-century people who are widely regarded as creative in very different fields: Sigmund Freud (psychology), Albert Einstein (physics), Pablo Picasso (painting), Igor Stravinsky (musical composition), T. S. Eliot (poetry), Martha Graham (dance),

⦚ Creative problem solving, evident in this temporary bridge made of old railroad cars, has two elements: novelty and social value.

and Mahatma Gandhi (political resistance and spirituality). Gardner found a few patterns that these people had in common, including the following:

- They worked in an atmosphere of moderate tension, sensing that the old ways of doing things were not quite right.
- They had enough background in their fields to feel confident but not so much experience that they became trapped into traditional habits.
- Early in life, each relied heavily on one or a few close friends for advice and encouragement.
- Each threw him- or herself wholeheartedly into the work, at the expense of family and friendships. Even Gandhi, a famous advocate for love and justice, had trouble developing close relationships.

⦚ Howard Gardner studied the lives of seven highly creative people, including political and spiritual leader Mahatma Gandhi and dance pioneer Martha Graham, to find the features that promote creativity.

Creative careers, however, are extremely variable (Simonton, 1997). As a rule poets are recognized for their greatness early in life, generally in their 20s, whereas the greatest, most creative historians seldom do their best work before their 40s or 50s. Within any field some people start early and quit early and others bloom late. Some—such as Bach, Picasso, and Edison—produce enormous quantities of good work, whereas others produce only one or two great works.

CONCEPT CHECK ☑

7. Great creative poets die younger on the average than equally recognized historians. Why? (Hint: Imagine the distribution of ages at death for both groups.) (Check your answer on page 300.)

Reasoning by Heuristics

Heuristics, you will recall, are methods of simplifying a problem. We all have limited knowledge, limited memory, and limited time to collect information and reason out an answer. Frequently, we have to make very quick decisions with almost no time to weigh the evidence and consider alternatives. Therefore, heuristics are often an excellent guide, if not a necessity.

Furthermore, simple heuristics sometimes produce surprisingly good results. For example, people are given pairs of U.S. cities, such as San Diego and San Antonio, and pairs of German cities, such as Munich and Cologne. For each pair they are asked to pick the one with the larger population. Oddly, Americans guess more accurately with the German cities and Germans guess more accurately with American cities (Goldstein & Gigerenzer, 2002). Almost everyone relies on the heuristic, "The city I've heard of probably has more people." That heuristic works fine for a country you know a little about, but less well for your own country, where both cities are familiar. So the heuristic works best if you don't know too much!

However, heuristics can lead us astray if we use them habitually even when we have an opportunity to weigh the evidence logically. Economists generally assume that people are more or less rational. That is, they follow their own best interests as well as they can; they make decisions based on the facts; and they buy and sell products at prices that match their real values. In 2002 Daniel Kahneman won the Nobel Prize for Economics for research demonstrating that people often make illogical decisions based on heuristics, emotions, and biases.

∎ In 2002 Princeton psychologist Daniel Kahneman (left) won the Nobel Prize for Economics. (There is no Nobel Prize in psychology.) Although others have won Nobel Prizes for research related to psychology, Kahneman was the first winner who had a PhD in psychology.

The Representativeness Heuristic and Base-Rate Information

Perhaps you have heard the saying: "If something looks like a duck, waddles like a duck, and quacks like a duck, chances are it's a duck." This saying is an example of the **representativeness heuristic,** *the tendency to assume that, if an item resembles members of a particular category, it is probably a member of that category itself.*

The assumption is usually correct, but research by Kahneman and others has shown how it leads us astray when we deal with uncommon events. For example, if you see something that looks, walks, and sounds like some rare bird, you may indeed have found a rarity, but you should check carefully to make sure it isn't some similar, more common species. In general, to decide whether something belongs in one category or another, you should consider how closely it resembles the two categories but also the **base-rate information**—that is, *how common the two categories are.*

When people apply the representativeness heuristic, they frequently overlook base-rate information. For example, consider the following question (modified from Kahneman & Tversky, 1973):

Psychologists have interviewed 30 engineers and 70 lawyers. One of them, Jack, is a 45-year-old married man with four children. He is generally conservative, cautious, and ambitious. He shows no interest in political and social issues and spends most of his free time on home carpentry, sailing, and solving mathematical puzzles. What is the probability that Jack is one of the 30 engineers in the sample of 100?

Most people estimate a rather high probability—perhaps 80 or 90%—because the description sounds more representative of engineers than lawyers. That estimate isn't really wrong, as we have no logical way to determine the true probability. The interesting point is that if some people are told the sample included 30 engineers and 70 lawyers, and others are told it included 70 engineers and 30 lawyers, both groups make about the same estimate for Jack (Kahneman & Tversky, 1973). Certainly, the base-rate information should have some influence.

Here is another example of misuse of the representativeness heuristic. Read the following description and then answer the questions following it:

Linda was a philosophy major. She is 31, bright, outspoken, and concerned about issues of discrimination and social justice.

What would you estimate is the probability that Linda is a bank teller? What is the probability that she is a feminist bank teller? (Answer before you read on.)

The true probabilities, hard to estimate, are not the point. The interesting result is that most people estimate a higher probability that Linda is a *feminist* bank teller than the probability that she is a bank teller (A. Tversky & Kahneman, 1983). However, she could clearly not be a feminist bank teller without being a bank teller. Apparently, people regard this description as fairly typical for a feminist and thus for a feminist bank teller (or feminist anything else) but not typical for bank tellers in general (Shafir, Smith, & Osherson, 1990).

CONCEPT CHECK ☑

8. A device was built to protect airplanes by detecting explosives that people might have in their luggage. The device detects 95% of bombs and has a false alarm (saying there is a bomb when there is none) only 5% of the time. Is this device good enough to use? (Hint: Think about the base-rate probability of the presence of a bomb.) (Check your answer on page 300.)

The Availability Heuristic

When we estimate how common something is, we generally start by trying to think of examples. Try this question: In the English language, are there more words that start with *k* or more words with *k* as the third letter? Most people guess that more words start with *k*. They start by trying to think of words that start with *k*: "king, kitchen, kangaroo, key, knowledge, . . ." Those were pretty easy. Then they try to think of words with *k* as the third letter: "ask, ink, . . . uh . . ." They rely on the **availability heuristic,** *the strategy of assuming that how easily one can remember examples of some kind of event indicates how common the event itself is* (Table 8.1). Because it is easier to think of words that start with *k* than words with *k* as the third letter, people assume that more words start with *k*. In fact, however, many more words have *k* as the third letter.

Because the news media tend to emphasize the spectacular, our use of the availability heuristic leads us to overestimate some dangers and underestimate others. For example, would you guess that more people die from tornadoes or lightning? From diabetes or homicide? From stomach cancer or automobile accidents? A tornado that kills 10 people gets national publicity, whereas a bolt of lightning that kills one person may not even make the local news show. Therefore, we assume tornado deaths are more common, although in fact lightning kills more people. Similarly, diabetes and stomach cancer kill far more people than homicide or automobile accidents but get little publicity. If you guessed that homicide and automobile accidents kill more, probably you were using the availability heuristic (Ruscio, 2000).

Another example: Would you rate yourself a better than average, average, or worse than average driver? Most people rate themselves above average, although statistically it is impossible for more than half to be above

TABLE 8.1 **The Representativeness Heuristic and the Availability Heuristic**

	A Tendency to Assume That	Leads Us Astray When	Example of Error
Representativeness Heuristic	An item that resembles members of a category probably belongs to that category.	Something resembles members of a rare category.	Something looks like it might be a UFO, so you decide it is.
Availability Heuristic	The more easily we can think of members of a category, the more common the category is.	One category gets more publicity than another or is more memorable.	You remember more reports of airplane crashes than car crashes so you think air travel is more dangerous.

average. When people try to imagine other people's driving, it is easy to remember times when you saw someone driving extremely badly—much worse than you ever would, right?—but hard to remember anyone driving especially better than you. Similarly, almost all people say they have less than average racial prejudice. Extremely prejudiced people stand out in your memory more than people with less prejudice.

Other Common Errors in Human Cognition

Common human errors include inappropriate use of the representativeness heuristic and availability heuristic but also include many other tendencies. Although we humans pride ourselves on our intelligence and our ability to solve problems, we sometimes make embarrassing mistakes. For decades college professors have talked about the importance of **critical thinking,** *the careful evaluation of evidence for and against any conclusion.* However, even the sincerest advocates of critical thinking sometimes find that they have been repeating nonsense that they should have questioned. For example, I myself used to repeat the rumors—only I didn't know they were rumors; I thought they were facts—that "glass flows as a very slow liquid," that "when the lemming population gets very high, some of them jump off cliffs," and that "Thomas Crapper invented the flush toilet." I later learned that all these claims were false. (The story about Thomas Crapper was started by Wallace Reyburn, who wrote the book *Flushed with Pride,* a partly true, partly fictitious biography of Crapper, who manufactured toilets, but didn't invent them. Everyone might have continued to believe Reyburn's hoax if he hadn't followed it with a less plausible book, *Bust Up,* a biography of Otto Titzling, allegedly the inventor of the bra!)

Why do intelligent people sometimes come to false conclusions or accept conclusions without adequate evidence? The reasons are many; here we consider just a few.

Overconfidence

Let's start with a demonstration. Ten questions follow. Few people know any of the answers exactly, but I'm asking for only an approximation. For each question answer with a 90% confidence range; that is, give a range within which you are 90% sure the correct answer lies. For example, consider this question: In the 2000 summer Olympics in Sydney, Australia, how many silver medals did China win? You might decide that you would be surprised if they won fewer than 5 or more than 25, so you guess "5 to 25."

If so, you would be right because China won 16 silver medals. Okay, that's the idea. Now fill in your answers:

Your estimate (as a 90% confidence range)

1. How old was Martin Luther King, Jr., at the time of his death?   — to —
2. How long is the Nile River?   — to —
3. How many countries belong to OPEC?   — to —
4. How many books are in the Old Testament?   — to —
5. What is the diameter of the moon?   — to —
6. What is the weight of an empty Boeing 747?   — to —
7. In what year was Mozart born?   — to —
8. What is the gestation period of an Asian elephant? (in days)   — to —
9. How far is London from Tokyo?   — to —
10. What is the deepest known point in the ocean? (in feet or meters)   — to —

Now turn to answer H on page 301 to check your answers (Plous, 1993). How many of your ranges included the correct answer? Because you said you were 90% confident of each answer, you should be right on about nine of ten. However, most people miss more than half. That is, they were **overconfident;** *they believed their estimates were more accurate than they actually were.* These were, of course, very difficult questions. On extremely easy questions, the trend is reversed and people tend to be underconfident (Erev, Wallsten, & Budescu, 1994; Juslin, Winman, & Olsson, 2000). You can try additional items with the Online Try It Yourself exercise. Go to http://psychology.wadsworth.com/kalat_intro7e. Navigate to the student Web site, then to the Online Try It Yourself section, and click on Overconfidence.

Philip Tetlock (1994) conducted a study of government officials and consultants, foreign policy professors, newspaper columnists, and others who make their living by analyzing and predicting world events. He asked them to predict world events over the next several years—such as what would happen in Korea, the Middle East, Eastern Europe, and Cuba—and to state their confidence in their predictions (such as 70%). Five years later he compared predictions to actual results and found very low accuracy, especially among those who were the most confident and those with a strong liberal or conservative point of view. That is, those who saw both sides of a question were more likely to be right.

Most people are overconfident of their understanding of complex physical processes. In one study college students were asked to rate how well they understood how various devices work, including a speedometer, zipper, flush toilet, cylinder lock, helicopter, quartz watch, sewing machine, and others. Then the researchers asked them in fact to explain four of the devices and answer questions about them, such as "How could someone pick a cylinder lock?" and "How does a helicopter go from hovering to forward flight?" After producing what were obviously weak answers, nearly all students lowered their ratings of understanding for these four phenomena (Rozenblit & Keil, 2002). However, curiously, some insisted that except for the four devices that the experimenters happened to choose, they really did understand all the other devices pretty well!

CONCEPT CHECK ☑

9. When students estimate their grades for the coming semester or athletic coaches estimate their teams' success for the coming year, what mistake is likely? (Check your answer on page 300.)

Attractiveness of Valuable but Very Unlikely Outcomes

If people are faced with choices A and B, and on the average A is worth $1 and on the average B is also worth $1, then theoretically, people should like both choices equally. In reality, people don't behave that way.

Which would you rather have:

- $100,000 for sure or a 10% chance of winning $1 million?
- $10,000 or a 1% chance at $1 million?
- $1,000 or a 0.1% chance at $1 million?
- $100 or a 0.01% chance at $1 million?
- $10 or a 0.001% chance at $1 million?
- $1 or a 0.0001% chance at $1 million?

If you are like most people, you chose the $100,000 over a 10% chance at a million and $10,000 over a 1% chance. But at some point, you switched from the sure profit to the gamble. Especially if the sure profit is $10 or less, most people prefer a chance at winning a million. In fact almost half of college students said they would forego $10 to have even one chance in a million of winning a million—a gamble of very bad odds (Rachlin, Siegel, & Cross, 1994). A later study, using an Internet sample of thousands of people from 44 countries, confirmed this tendency to prefer a long-shot bet over a small but sure gain (Birnbaum, 1999), so it is not something unique to one culture.

Why do people prefer a slim chance at a fortune to a small but sure gain? First, for most people $10 is not going to raise your standard of living. A million dollars would. Second, although you understand the difference between a 10% chance and a 1% chance, it is hard to grasp the difference between a 0.001%

chance and a 0.0001% or even a 0.000001% chance. They blur together as "unlikely but not impossible," and we think, "Someone is going to win, and it might be me." In fact the unlikeliness of winning is part of the appeal: People report more pleasure from a surprising gain than from one they expected (Mellers, Schwartz, Ho, & Ritov, 1997). That is, a surprising gambling win is a bigger thrill than money you knew you were going to gain.

Confirmation Bias

Often, we make mistakes by *accepting one hypothesis and then looking for evidence to support it, instead of considering other possibilities.* This tendency is known as the **confirmation bias.** For example, examine the poorly focused photo in Figure 8.19a and guess what it depicts. Then see Figures 8.19b and 8.19c on the following pages. Many people find that seeing the extremely out-of-focus photo makes it harder to identify the items in the better focused photo. When they saw the first photo, they formed a hypothesis, probably a wrong one, which interfered with correctly perceiving the later photo (Bruner & Potter, 1964).

Peter Wason (1960) asked students to discover a certain rule he had in mind for generating sequences of numbers. One example of the numbers the rule might generate, he explained, was "2, 4, 6." He told the students that they could ask about other se-

FIGURE 8.19a People who form a hypothesis based on the first photo look at succeeding photos to find evidence that they are right. Because their first guess is generally wrong, they don't do as well as people who look at the later photos before making any preliminary guesses. Try to guess what this shows. Then examine parts b and c on pages 298 and 300.

© Susan Ashukian

quences, and he would tell them whether or not those sequences fit his rule. They should tell him as soon as they thought they knew the rule.

Most students started by asking, "8, 10, 12?" When told "yes," they proceeded with "14, 16, 18?" Each time, they were told, "Yes, that sequence fits the rule." Soon most of them guessed, "The rule is three consecutive even numbers." "No," came the reply. "That is not the rule." Many students persisted, trying "20, 22, 24?" "26, 28, 30?" "250, 252, 254?" Note that they were testing sequences that fit their rule, ignoring other possibilities. The rule Wason had in mind was, "Any three positive numbers of increasing magnitude." For instance, 1, 2, 3, would be acceptable, and so would 21, 25, 24, 601.

A special case of confirmation bias is **functional fixedness,** *the tendency to adhere to a single approach or a single way of using an item.* Here are three examples:

1. You are provided with a candle, a box of matches, some thumbtacks, and a tiny piece of string, as shown in Figure 8.20. Using no other equipment, find a way to mount the candle to the wall so that it could be lit.

FIGURE 8.20 You are provided with a candle, a box of matches, some thumbtacks, and a tiny piece of string. What is the best way, using no other equipment, to attach the candle to a wall so that it could be lit?

2. Consider an array of nine dots:

Connect all nine dots with a series of connected straight lines, such that the end of one line is the start of the next. For example, one way would be:

But use the fewest lines possible.

3. There are some students in a room. All but two of them are psychology majors, all but two are chemistry majors, and all but two are history majors. How many students are in the room, and what are their majors? (If your first impulse is to say "two of each," try it out: It doesn't work.) Now here's the interesting part: There are two possible solutions. After you have found one solution, discard it and find another. After you have either found solutions to these questions or given up, check answer I on page 301. (Solve these problems before reading further.)

Question 1 was difficult because most people think of the matchbox as simply a container for matches, not as a potential tool on its own. The box is "functionally fixed" for one way of using it. Question 2 was difficult because most people assume that the lines must remain within the area defined by the nine dots. On question 3 it is difficult to think of even one solution, and after thinking of it, it is hard to abandon it to think of an entirely different approach.

Framing Questions

A truly logical person would give the same answer to a question no matter how it was worded. In fact most people answer questions differently depending on how they are phrased, as you may recall from the discussion of surveys in Chapter 2.

For example, answer the following: "What's the probability that Sunday will be hotter than every other day next week?" (Please answer before you read on.)

Many people answer "50%" because it seems there are two possibilities—it will be hotter, or it won't. But now consider this rewording: "What's the probability that next week, the hottest day of the week will be Sunday?" With this wording, most people switch to the correct answer, one seventh, because they see that there are seven days with an equal chance of being the hottest (Fox & Rottenstreich, 2003).

For another example, suppose you have been appointed head of the Public Health Service, and you need to choose a plan to deal with a disease that has endangered the lives of 600 people. If you adopt plan A, you will save the lives of 200 people. If you adopt plan B, there is a 33% chance that you will save all 600 and a 67% chance that you will save no one. *Choose plan A or B before reading further.*

Now another disease breaks out; again you must choose between two plans. If you adopt plan C, 400 people will die. If you adopt plan D, there is a 33% chance that no one will die and a 67% chance that 600 will die. *Choose plan C or D now.*

Figure 8.21 shows the choices that more than 150 people made. Most chose A over B and D over C. However, note that plan A is exactly the same as C (200 live, 400 die), and plan B is exactly the same as D. Why then did so many people choose both A and D? The reason, according to Tversky and Kahneman (1981), is that most people avoid taking a risk to gain something (like saving lives) but willingly take a risk to avoid loss (like not letting people die). *The tendency to answer a question differently when it is framed (phrased) differently* is called the **framing effect.** For an additional example of the framing effect go to http://psychology.wadsworth.com/kalat_intro7e. Navigate to the student Web site, then to the Online Try It Yourself section, and click on Framing Questions.

Plan	How question was framed	Plan preferred by	Outcome
A	Save 200 people	72%	
C	400 people will die	22%	200 live, 400 die
B	33% chance of saving all 600; 67% chance of saving no one	28%	
D	33% chance no one will die; 67% chance all 600 will die	78%	33% chance 600 live or 67% chance 600 die

FIGURE 8.21 Most people chose plan A over B, and D over C, although A produces the same result as C and B produces the same result as D. Amos Tversky and Daniel Kahneman (1981) proposed that most people play it safe to gain something but accept a risk to avoid a loss.

CONCEPT CHECK ☑

10. Someone says, "More than 90% of all college students like to watch late-late-night television, whereas only 20% of older adults do. Therefore, most watchers of late-late-night television are college students." What error in thinking has this person made?

11. Someone tells me that if I say "abracadabra" every morning, I will stay healthy. I say it daily and, sure enough, I stay healthy. I conclude that saying this magic word really does ensure health. What error of thinking have I made?

12. Which of the following offers by your professor would probably be more persuasive? (a) "If you do this extra project, there's a small chance I will add some points to your grade." (b) "I'm going to penalize this whole class for being inattentive today, but if you do this extra project, there's a chance I won't subtract anything from your grade." (Check your answers on page 300.)

FIGURE 8.19b

The Sunk Cost Effect

The sunk cost effect is a special case of the framing effect, but let's start with some examples:

- You have bought a $200 plane ticket to Wonderfulville and a $500 ticket to Marvelousville. Too late, you realize that they are both for the same weekend, and both are nonrefundable. You think you would prefer Wonderfulville, but you paid more for the ticket to Marvelousville. Where will you go?
- Months ago you bought an expensive ticket to a football game, but the game is today and the weather is miserably cold. You wish you hadn't bought the ticket. Do you go to the game?

Many people say they would go to Marvelousville instead of Wonderfulville because the Marvelousville ticket was more expensive and they don't want to waste the money. Many also say they will go to the football game in the bad weather, again because they don't want to waste the money. These examples illustrate the **sunk cost effect,** *the willingness to do something we wouldn't otherwise choose to do because of money or effort already spent* (Arkes & Ayton, 1999). This tendency arises in many situations. Someone gambles weekly on the state lottery, losing huge sums, but keeps betting because to quit without winning it back would admit that all the previous bets were a mistake. A company invests vast amounts of money in a project that now appears to be a mistake but doesn't want to cancel the project and admit it has wasted so much money. A professional sports team gives someone a huge signing bonus, and later finds the player's performance disappointing, but keeps using that player anyway to avoid wasting the money.

Curiously, young children never show the sunk cost effect. The fact that they have already wasted much time or money doesn't induce them to waste still more. No one has ever demonstrated the sunk cost effect in nonhuman animals either in spite of repeated efforts (Arkes & Ayton, 1999). Apparently, you have to be fairly intelligent to do something this stupid.

CRITICAL THINKING:
A STEP FURTHER
Framing a Question

Recall the discussion on page 297 about how the phrasing of a question influences people's answers. For example, most people will take more risks to avoid a loss than to increase a gain. Can you use this principle to explain why many gamblers on a losing streak will continue betting, sometimes increasing their bets? Is there a different way to think about the situation to decrease the temptation to continue gambling?

IN CLOSING
Successful and Unsuccessful Problem Solving

In this module we have considered thinking at its best and worst—expertise and error. Experts polish their skills through extensive practice. Of course, all of us have to make decisions about topics in which we are far from being experts, and we cannot expect perfect decisions. However, without insisting on perfection, we can at least hold ourselves to the standard of not doing anything foolish. We often make mistakes even when we have enough information, time, and skill to make a better decision. Perhaps if we become more aware of common errors, we can be more alert to avoid them.

Summary

- *Becoming an expert.* Experts are made, not born. Becoming an expert requires years of practice and effort. (page 285)
- *Expert pattern recognition.* Experts recognize and memorize familiar and meaningful patterns more rapidly than less experienced people do. (page 287)
- *Steps for solving a problem.* Problem solving can be described as a series of steps: understanding the problem, generating hypotheses, testing the hypotheses, and checking the result. (page 287)
- *Algorithms and heuristics.* People solve problems by using algorithms (repetitive means of checking every possibility) or heuristics (ways of simplifying the problem to get a reasonable solution). (page 288)
- *Generalizing.* People who have learned how to solve a problem often fail to apply that solution to a similar problem. (page 289)
- *Insight.* With insight problems people have trouble estimating how close they are to a solution. However, they may be making more progress than they realize. (page 291)
- *Creativity.* Creative people work in a field in which they have knowledge and self-confidence; no one is creative in all fields. Many highly creative people go through a period in which they rely on a small group of friends, perhaps just one, for support and encouragement. They dedicate their lives to their work, often to the exclusion of all else. (page 292)
- *Thinking by heuristics.* Heuristics simplify complex problems and help us find quick answers that are correct most of the time. However, overreliance on them or inappropriate use of them can lead to errors. (page 293)
- *Representativeness heuristic and base-rate information.* If something resembles members of some

category, we usually assume it too belongs to that category. However, that assumption is risky if the category is a rare one. (page 293)

- *Availability heuristic.* We generally assume that the more easily we can think of examples of some category, the more common that category is. However, some rare items are easy to think of because they get much publicity or because they stand out emotionally. (page 294)

- *Critical thinking.* Even people who try conscientiously to evaluate the evidence for every claim sometimes find themselves repeating a nonsensical statement that they know they should have doubted. (page 295)

- *Reasons for errors.* People tend to be overconfident about their own judgments, especially on difficult questions. They are attracted to high-payoff gambles even when the chance of winning is extremely low. They tend to look for evidence that supports their hypothesis instead of evidence that might reject it. They answer the same question differently when it is phrased differently. They sometimes take unpleasant actions to avoid admitting that previous actions were a waste of time or money. (page 295)

Answers to Concept Checks

6. An algorithm would check each possible route: For your home city (H) and three other cities (1, 2, and 3), the possible routes would be H-1-2-3-H, H-1-3-2-H, and H-2-1-3-H. (Three other routes that you could generate would be the mirror images of these three and therefore are not necessary to consider.) As the number of cities increases, the number of possible routes rises rapidly. If you had to visit 10 cities, your algorithm would have to consider almost 2 million routes. One possible heuristic would be to consider only those routes that led you from any city to one of the two cities closest to it. Another would be to consider only those routes that did not require you to cross a path already taken. (page 289)

7. Because many poets are recognized for their greatness while they are still young, it is possible to be a great poet and die young. Most historians are in their 40s or later when they do their first outstanding work; therefore, it is almost impossible to be recognized as a great historian and die young. (page 293)

8. A false-alarm rate of 5% is far too high. Imagine a plane with 100 innocent passengers, each checking two bags. Of the 200 innocent bags, this device will identify 5%—that is, 10 bags—as containing a bomb! Speer (1989) estimated that this device (which the Federal Aviation Administration actu-

ally considered using) would have 5 million false alarms for every bomb it found. (page 294)

9. Both are likely to overestimate their success. Generally, the weakest students are most likely to overestimate their success. However, the straight-A students can hardly overestimate and are therefore more likely to underestimate. (page 296)

10. Failure to consider the base rate: 20% of all older adults is a larger number than 90% of all college students. (page 298)

11. Premature commitment to one hypothesis without testing the hypothesis that one could stay healthy without the magic word. (page 298)

12. Probably (b). People are generally more willing to take a risk to avoid losing something than to gain something. (page 298)

Answers to Other Questions in the Module

D. At first you probably had no idea what strategy to use. As shown below, the game is equivalent to tick-tack-toe. If you know the correct strategy for tick-tack-toe, you now know what strategy to use for the numbers-adding-to-15 game. (page 287)

2	7	6
9	5	1
4	3	8

E. The water in the tube would leak out of the hole in the bottom. Any membrane heavy enough to keep the water in would also keep the rubber balls out. (page 289)

© Susan Ashukian

FIGURE 8.19c

F. This illustration shows how to cut and fold an ordinary piece of paper or cardboard to match the figure with nothing left over. (page 291)

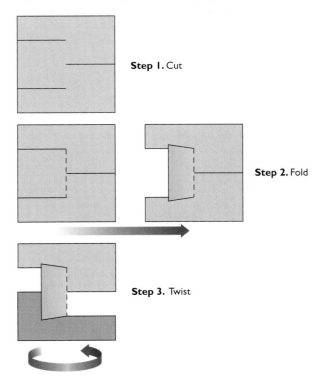

Step 1. Cut

Step 2. Fold

Step 3. Twist

G. Set 1: The words *playing, credit,* and *report* are all associated with *card.* Set 2: The words *ticket, shop,* and *broker* are all associated with *pawn.* (page 291)

H. (1) 39 years. (2) 4,187 miles, or 6,738 kilometers. (3) 13 countries. (4) 39 books. (5) 2,160 miles, or 3,476 kilometers. (6) 390,000 pounds, or 177,000 kilograms. (7) 1756. (8) 645 days. (9) 5,959 miles, or 9,590 kilometers. (10) 36,198 feet, or 11,033 meters. (page 295)

I. (1) The best way to attach the candle to the wall is to dump the matches from the box and thumbtack the side of the box to the wall, as shown in this picture. The tiny piece of string is irrelevant.

(2) The dots can be connected with four lines:

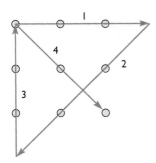

(3) One answer is three students: one psychology major, one chemistry major, and one history major. The other possibility is two students who are majoring in something else—music, for example. (If there are two music majors, all but two of them are indeed majoring in psychology etc.) (page 297)

How do we learn language?

Language is a complicated and impressive product of human cognition. It enables us to learn from the experiences of people who lived at other times and places and thereby enables education and advances in technology. Thinking and language are not synonymous, but they are certainly related closely. It sometimes seems that people speak without thinking, but presumably, their speech represented *some* kind of thinking, even if it wasn't careful thinking. Furthermore, when adult humans think about something, they usually do so in words.

Language is an extremely versatile system. Other species signal one another in various ways, but only human languages have the property of **productivity,** *the ability to express new ideas.* Every day we say and hear a few stock sentences like "Nice weather we're having," or "I can't find my keys," but we also invent new sentences that no one has ever said before. The productivity of language enables humans to communicate an ever-changing array of ideas.

You might ask, "How do you know that no one has ever said that sentence before?!" Well, of course, no one can be certain that a particular sentence is new, but we can be confident that many sentences are new (without specifying which ones) because of the vast number of possible ways to rearrange words. Imagine this exercise (but don't really try it unless you have nothing else to do with your life): Pick a sentence of more than 10 words from any book you choose. How long would you need to keep reading, in that book or any other, until you found the exact same sentence again?

In short, we do not memorize all the sentences we use. Not even infants do. Instead, we learn rules for making and understanding sentences. The famous linguist Noam Chomsky (1980) described those rules as a **transformational grammar,** *a system for converting a deep structure into a surface structure.* The deep structure is the underlying logic or meaning of a sentence. The surface structure is the sequence of words as they are actually spoken or written (Figure 8.22). According to this theory, whenever we speak, we transform the deep structure of the language into a surface structure.

Two surface structures can resemble each other without representing the same deep structure, or conversely, they can represent the same deep structure without resembling each other. For example, "John is

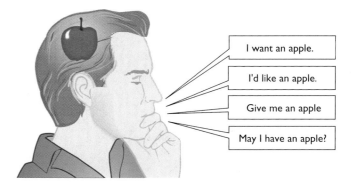

FIGURE 8.22 According to transformational grammar, we can transform a sentence with a given deep structure into any of several other sentences with different surface structures.

easy to please" has the same deep structure as "pleasing John is easy" and "it is easy to please John." These sentences all represent the same underlying idea.

In contrast consider the sentence, "Never threaten someone with a chain saw." The surface structure of that sentence maps into two quite different deep structures, as shown in Figure 8.23.

Language researcher Terrence Deacon once presented a brief talk about language to his 8-year-old's elementary school class. One child asked whether other

Deep Structure No. 1: You are holding a chain saw. Don't threaten to use it to attack someone!

Deep Structure No. 2: Some deranged person is holding a chain saw. Don't threaten him!

FIGURE 8.23 The sentence "Never threaten someone with a chain saw" has one surface structure but two deep structures, corresponding to different meanings.

animals have their own languages. Deacon explained that other species communicate but without the productivity of human language. The child persisted, asking whether other animals had at least a *simple* language, perhaps one with only a few words and short sentences. No, he replied, they do not have even a simple language.

Then another child asked, "Why not?" (Deacon, 1997, p. 12). Deacon paused, and then paused some more. Why not, indeed. He realized that this 8-year-old had asked a profound question. If language is so extremely useful to humans, why haven't other species evolved at least a little of it? And what makes humans so good at learning language?

Nonhuman Precursors to Language

One way to examine humans' language specialization is to ask how far another species could progress toward language with sufficient training. Beginning in the 1920s, several psychologists reared chimpanzees in their homes and tried to teach them to talk. The chimpanzees learned many human habits (Figure 8.24) but understood only a little of language.

Chimpanzees' vocal cords are poorly adapted to making voice sounds. The sounds they do make are mostly during inhaling, not exhaling. (Try to speak

a

b

c

d

e

FIGURE 8.24 Psychologists have tried to teach chimpanzees to communicate with gestures or visual symbols. (a) One of the Premacks' chimps arranges plastic chips to request food. (b) Viki in her human home, helping with the housework. After years with the Hayeses, she could make only a few sounds similar to English words. (c) Kanzi, a bonobo, presses symbols to indicate words. Among the primates bonobos have shown the most promising ability to acquire language. (d) A chimp signing *toothbrush*. (e) Roger Fouts with Alley the chimp, who is signing *lizard*.

while inhaling!) However, chimpanzees do make hand gestures in nature. R. Allen Gardner and Beatrice Gardner (1969) taught a chimpanzee named Washoe to use the sign language of the American deaf (Ameslan). Washoe eventually learned the symbols for about 100 words.

How much do these gestures resemble language? Washoe and other chimpanzees trained in this way used their symbols almost exclusively to make requests, not to describe, and rarely in new, original combinations (Pate & Rumbaugh, 1983; Terrace, Petitto, Sanders, & Bever, 1979; C. R. Thompson & Church, 1980). By contrast a human child with a vocabulary of 100 words or so starts linking them into original combinations and short sentences and frequently uses words to describe.

The results have been different, however, for another species, *Pan paniscus,* sometimes known as the pygmy chimpanzee (a misleading term because these animals are almost as large as common chimpanzees) and sometimes known as the bonobo. Bonobos' social behavior resembles that of humans in several regards: Males and females form strong attachments; females are sexually responsive throughout the month, not just during their fertile period; males contribute to infant care; and adults often share food with one another.

Several bonobos have used symbols in impressive ways. They occasionally use the symbols to name and describe objects that they are not requesting. They sometimes use the symbols to describe past events. (One with a cut on his hand explained that his mother had bit him.) Also, they frequently make original, creative requests, such as asking one person to chase another.

The most proficient bonobos seem to comprehend symbols about as well as a 2- to 2 ½-year-old child understands language (Savage-Rumbaugh et al., 1993). They have also shown considerable understanding of spoken English, following even such odd commands such as "bite your ball" and "take the vacuum cleaner outside" (Savage-Rumbaugh, 1990; Savage-Rumbaugh, Sevcik, Brakke, & Rumbaugh, 1992). They also passed the test of responding to commands issued over earphones, eliminating the possibility of unintentional "Clever Hans"-type signals, as discussed in Chapter 2 (Figure 8.25).

The explanation for this impressive success pertains partly to species differences: Apparently, bonobos have greater language capacities than common chimpanzees. Another part of the explanation pertains to the method of training: Learning by observation and imitation promotes better understanding than the formal training methods that were used in previous studies (Savage-Rumbaugh et al., 1992). People, after all, learn language by imitation. Finally, the bonobos began their language experi-

FIGURE 8.25 Kanzi, a bonobo, points to answers on a board in response to questions he hears through earphones. Experimenter Rose Sevcik sits with him but does not hear the questions, so she cannot signal the correct answer.

ence early in life. Humans learn language more easily when they are young, and the same may be true for bonobos.

CONCEPT CHECK ☑

13. Based on the studies with bonobos, can you offer advice about how to teach language to children with impaired language learning? (Check your answer on page 316.)

Human Specializations for Learning Language

Is the glass half full or half empty? Should we be impressed that bonobos understand language almost as well as a 2½-year-old child or wonder why they do not progress further? Humans are clearly specialized to learn language in a way that no other species can.

Language and General Intelligence

Did we evolve language as an accidental by-product of evolving big brains and great intelligence? The idea sounds appealing, but several observations argue strongly against it. Dolphins and whales have larger brains than humans have but do not develop language. (Yes, they communicate, but not in a flexible system resembling human language.) Some people with massive brain damage have less total brain mass than a chimpanzee but continue to speak and understand language.

Also, people in one family, all having a particular gene, develop normal intelligence except for language (Fisher, Vargha-Khadem, Watkins, Monaco, & Pembrey, 1998; Lai, Fisher, Hurst, Vargha-Khadem, & Monaco, 2001). Their pronunciation is poor and they do not fully master even simple rules, such as how to form plurals of nouns. So normal human brain size and normal intelligence do not automatically produce language.

At the opposite extreme, consider **Williams syndrome**, *a genetic condition characterized by mental retardation in most regards but skillful use of language.* Before the discovery of Williams syndrome, psychologists would have confidently said that good language was impossible without normal intelligence. One 14-year-old with Williams syndrome could write good creative stories and songs, but in other ways she performed like a 5- to 7-year-old and could not be left alone without a baby-sitter. Another child with Williams syndrome, when asked to name as many animals as he could think of, started with "ibex, whale, bull, yak, zebra, puppy, kitten, tiger, koala, dragon . . ." Another child could sing more than 1,000 songs in 22 languages (Bellugi & St. George, 2000). However, these children prefer 50 pennies to 5 dollars and, when asked to estimate the length of a bus, give answers such as "3 inches or 100 inches, maybe" (Bellugi, Lichtenberger, Jones, Lai, & St. George, 2000). Again, the conclusion is that language ability is not synonymous with overall intelligence.

Language Learning as a Specialized Capacity

Susan Carey (1978) calculated that children between the ages of 1½ and 6 learn an average of nine new words per day. But how do they infer the meanings of all those words? Suppose you are in Japan and someone points to a pillow and says "makura." You therefore conclude that *makura* is the Japanese word for *pillow.* But logically, it could have meant "soft thing," "throwable thing," or even *this particular* pillow. How did you make the correct inference that the word probably referred to the category *pillow*? More important, how did you know it meant anything at all? All you observed was that someone made a sound and pointed; you inferred the intention to communicate. That inference comes naturally to humans, but not to other species.

Noam Chomsky has argued that people learn language so easily that they must not be learning in the usual way. Children must begin with some preconceptions. The simplest and perhaps most important is the idea that words *mean* something. Children also make essential distinctions, such as between actors and actions (i.e., nouns and verbs), actors and recipients of

action, singular and plural, same and different, and so forth. They have to learn how to express those relationships in their particular language, but they do not have to learn concepts like singular and plural themselves. Chomsky and his followers therefore suggest that people are born with a **language acquisition device** or "language instinct," *a built-in mechanism for acquiring language* (Pinker, 1994).

Doubts and controversies remain, however, about exactly what is built in. Are we really born with concepts, distinctions, and a primitive grammar, or just with the ability to learn them? If we are born with a predisposition to learn language, what is the nature of that predisposition? The predisposition could be far removed from the details of language itself (Deacon, 1997; Seidenberg, 1997).

Here is one study suggesting an innate predisposition: Adult German speakers were asked to learn a little of Italian or Japanese, which were unfamiliar to them before the experiment. In all cases the experimenters used real Italian or Japanese words, but they taught some people real grammatical rules (which are unlike those of German) and other people some made-up rules unlike those of any known language. For example, one made-up rule was, "to make a sentence negative, add the negative word (*no* in Italian, *nai* in Japanese) after the third word of the sentence, whatever that word may be." Another fake rule was "to make a statement into a question, say the words in reverse order." So, "*Paolo mangia la pera*" (the Italian for "Paul eats the pear") would become "*Pera la mangia Paolo?*" ("Does Paul eat the pear?"). Those who learned either Italian or Japanese with real grammar showed increased activity in the brain areas usually associated with language. Those learning with the fake rules showed increased activity in other brain areas but not in the circuits usually important for language (Musso et al., 2003). Evidently, some grammars seem "natural" even when they are unfamiliar, whereas other grammars are recognized as "not real language."

But what conclusion do we draw? It would be a vast overstatement to say that we are literally born knowing the grammars of all possible languages. A more reasonable conclusion is that we are predisposed to learn some relationships more easily than others (Saffran, 2003). For example, making interrogatives by inverting the order of entire sentences would be difficult. Learning the rule itself would be easy, but applying it would be a difficult memory task when dealing with a long sentence.

Is it possible that infants learn all the complexities of word meanings and grammar from the apparently meager information they receive? Perhaps the information is better than we imagined. Parents throughout the world simplify the language-learning task by speaking to their infants in "parentese." I am not talking about silly "goo-goo" baby talk, but a pattern of speech that emphasizes and prolongs the vowels, making clearer than usual the difference between words such as *cat* and *cot* (Kuhl et al., 1997). Infants listen more intently to parentese than to normal speech and learn more from it. We also speak slowly, distinctly, and in simple words to someone who barely understands our language. To those who know the language well, we can speak rapidly, mumble, or speak in a noisy environment and still expect decent understanding (Calvin & Bickerton, 2000).

Several studies have found that even infants younger than 1 year old detect the regularities of the language they hear (Marcus, Vijayan, Rao, & Vishton, 1999; Saffran, 2003). For example, when adults speak they usually run all their words together without pausing between them: "Lookattheprettybaby." The infant detects which sounds go together as words by statistical relations. For example, the infant frequently hears the two-syllable combination "pre-tty" and frequently hears "ba-by" but less often hears the combination "ty-ba" and concludes that the word break comes between *pretty* and *baby*. We can infer that infants draw this conclusion because infants react to "ty-ba" as a new, attention-getting sound and don't react the same way to "pretty" or "baby" (Saffran, Aslin, & Newport, 1996). In short, infants learn the basics of language from regularities in what they hear.

Adults go through much the same process when trying to learn a foreign language (Cutler, Demuth, & McQueen, 2002). If you heard someone say, "vogubarilatusomatafikogovogurasu . . ." you would infer that the first word is either "vo," "vog," "vogu," or something longer because no word in any language is shorter than one syllable. (Whether we are born with that assumption or learn it is not known.) Because "vogu" was repeated already, but "voguba" was not, you would probably infer that "vogu" is one word of this language.

Language and the Human Brain

What aspect of the human brain enables us to learn language so easily? Studies of people with brain damage have long pointed to two brain areas as particularly important for language. People with damage in the frontal cortex, including *Broca's area* (Figure 8.26), develop **Broca's aphasia,** *a condition characterized by inarticulate speech and by difficulties with both using and understanding grammatical devices—prepositions, conjunctions, word endings, complex sentence structures, and so forth.* For example, one patient who was asked about a dental appointment slowly mumbled, "Yes . . . Monday . . . Dad and Dick . . . Wednesday nine o'clock . . . 10 o'clock . . . doctors . . . and . . . teeth" (Geschwind, 1979, p. 186). These people do not really

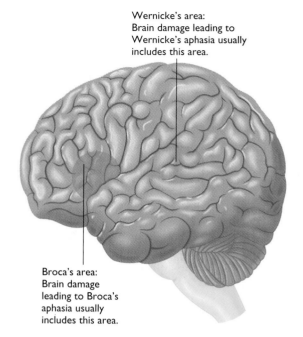

Wernicke's area: Brain damage leading to Wernicke's aphasia usually includes this area.

Broca's area: Brain damage leading to Broca's aphasia usually includes this area.

FIGURE 8.26 Brain damage that produces major deficits in language usually includes the left-hemisphere areas shown here. However, the deficits are severe only if the damage is more extensive, including these areas but extending to others as well. Many areas of the human brain contribute to language comprehension and production.

lose all grammatical understanding; they merely find it much more difficult to use and understand language, much as other people do when they are extremely distracted (Blackwell & Bates, 1995).

People with damage in the temporal cortex, including *Wernicke's area* (Figure 8.26), develop **Wernicke's aphasia,** *a condition marked by difficulty recalling the names of objects and impaired comprehension of language.* Because these people do not remember names, their speech is nonsensical even when it is grammatical. For example, one patient responded to a question about his health, "I felt worse because I can no longer keep in mind from the mind of the minds to keep me from mind and up to the ear which can be to find among ourselves" (Brown, 1977, p. 29).

However, language did not evolve simply by adding a language module to a chimpanzee brain. The brain areas important for language are critical for many other processes as well, including music (Patel, 2003) and some aspects of memory (Tyler et al., 2002). Brain damage that seriously impairs language always extends well beyond Broca's or Wernicke's area. Indeed, the nature of the language deficit varies from one person to another, and the location of the damage does accurately predict the language problems. Evidently, each person's language cortex is organized somewhat differently from everyone else's. Furthermore, PET scans or other brain recordings show widespread activation during speech (Just, Carpenter, Keller, Eddy, & Thulborn, 1996). It is hardly an exaggeration to say that the whole human brain is specialized to make language possible.

Stages of Language Development

Table 8.2 lists the average ages at which children reach various stages of language ability (Lenneberg, 1969; Moskowitz, 1978). Progression through these stages depends largely on maturation, not just extra experience (Lenneberg, 1967, 1969). Parents who expose their children to as much language as possible find that they can increase the children's vocabulary, but they hardly affect the rate of progression through language stages (Figure 8.27). At the other extreme, hearing children of deaf parents are exposed to much less spoken language, and at first they start "babbling" with rhythmic hand gestures (Petitto, Holowka, Sergio, & Ostry, 2001), but with even modest exposure to spoken language, their language development progresses on schedule.

Deaf infants babble as much as hearing infants do for about the first 6 months and then start to decline. At first, hearing infants babble only haphazard sounds, but soon they start repeating the sounds that are common in the language they have been hearing. Thus, a 1-year-old babbles a variety of sounds that resemble French, Chinese, or whatever other language the family speaks (Locke, 1994).

One of the first sounds an infant can make is *muh*, and *muh, muh-muh,* or something similar has been adopted by most of the world's languages to mean "mother." Infants also make the sounds *duh, puh,* and

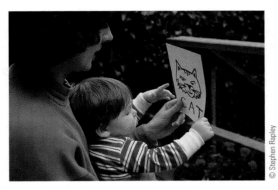

FIGURE 8.27 Some overeager parents try to teach their children language at a very early age. The child may enjoy the attention, but the activity is unlikely to accelerate the child's progress in language development.

buh. In many languages the word for father is similar to *dada* or *papa*. *Baba* is the word for grandmother in several languages. In effect infants tell their parents what words to use for important concepts. Indeed, Deacon (1997) has argued that children do not evolve to learn language; languages evolve to be easy for children to learn.

By age 1½ most toddlers have a vocabulary of about 50 words, but they seldom link words together. Thus, a toddler will say "Daddy" and "bye-bye" but not "Bye-bye, Daddy." In context parents can usually discern considerable meaning in these single-word utterances. *Mama* might mean, "That's a picture of Mama," "Take me to Mama," "Mama went away and left me here," or "Mama, I'm hungry." At this age toddlers understand language far better than they can produce it. In a sense they "learn how to learn" the meanings of words. If they are given careful practice with the idea that names refer to the shapes of objects—for example, being taught that *box* always refers to a particular shape, regardless of the color or size—they start increasing their vocabulary faster, particularly their vocabulary of the names of objects (L. B. Smith, Jones, Landau, Gershkoff-Stowe, & Samuelson, 2002).

By age 2, children start producing "telegraphic" phrases of two or more words, including combinations such as "more page," "allgone sticky," and "allgone outside" to indicate "read some more," "my hands are now clean," and "someone has closed the door," respectively. Note the originality of such phrases; it is unlikely that the parents ever said "allgone sticky"!

By age 2½ to 3 years, most children are generating full sentences, though each child maintains a few peculiarities. For example, many young children have their own rules for forming negative sentences. A common one is to add *no* or *not* to the beginning or end of a sentence, such as, "No I want to go to bed!" One little girl formed her negatives just by saying something louder and at a higher pitch; for instance, if she shrieked, "I

TABLE 8.2
Stages of Language Development

Age	Typical Language Abilities (Much Individual Variation)
3 months	Random vocalizations.
6 months	More distinct babbling.
1 year	Babbling that resembles the typical sounds of the family's language; probably one or more words including "mama"; language comprehension much better than production.
1½ years	Can say some words (mean about 50), mostly nouns; few or no phrases.
2 years	Speaks in two-word phrases.
2½ years	Longer phrases and short sentences with some errors and unusual constructions. Can understand much more.
3 years	Vocabulary near 1,000 words; longer sentences with fewer errors.
4 years	Close to adult speech competence.

want to share my toys!" she really meant, "I do *not* want to share my toys." Presumably, she had learned this "rule" by remembering that people screamed at her when they told her not to do something. My son Sam made negatives for a while by adding the word *either* to the end of a sentence: "I want to eat lima beans either." Apparently, he had heard people say, "I don't want to do that either" and had decided that the word *either* at the end of the sentence made it an emphatic negative.

Young children act as if they were applying grammatical rules. (I say "as if" because they cannot state the rules. By the same token, baseball players chasing a high fly ball act "as if" they understood calculus.) For example, a child may learn the word *feet* at an early age and then, after learning other plurals, abandon *feet* in favor of *foots*. Later, the child begins to compromise by saying "feets," "footses," or "feetses" before eventually returning to "feet." Children at this stage say many things they have never heard anyone else say, such as "the womans goed and doed something." Clearly, they are applying rules for how to form plurals and past tenses, although they *overregularize* or *overgeneralize* the rules. My son David invented the word *shis* to mean "belonging to a female." (He had apparently generalized the rule "He–his, she–shis.") Note that all these inventions imply that children are learning rules, not just repeating word combinations.

The progression of language stages suggests that language is a developmental process that unfolds, much like growth. Do we have a "critical period" for learning language early in life? Adults can learn the vocabulary of a second language faster than children can, but children learn the pronunciation better, as well as difficult aspects of the grammar. Even those who overheard another language in childhood without paying much attention to it learn it more easily later in life (Au, Knightly, Jun, & Oh, 2002). However, researchers find no sharp age cutoff for when language becomes more difficult. That is, starting a second language is easier for 2-year-olds than 4-year-olds, but also somewhat easier for 13-year-olds than 16-year-olds (Hakuta, Bialystok, & Wiley, 2003; Harley & Wang, 1997). So the results do not support a "critical period" with a cutoff date; we have a gradual tendency toward learning quicker when younger and gradually worsen with age (as with many other kinds of learning as well).

CONCEPT CHECK ☑

14. At what age do children begin to string words into combinations that they have never heard before? Why do psychologists believe that even very young children learn some of the rules of grammar? (Check your answers on page 316.)

Children Exposed to No Language or Two Languages

Would children who were exposed to no language at all make up their own? In rare cases an infant who was accidentally separated from other people grew up in a forest without human contact until discovered years later. Such children not only fail to show a language of their own but also fail to learn much language after they are given the chance (Pinker, 1994). However, their development is so abnormal and their early life so unknown that we should hesitate to draw conclusions.

The best evidence comes from studies of children who are deaf. Children who cannot hear well enough to learn speech and who are not taught sign language invent their own sign language, which they teach to other deaf children and so far as possible to their parents. As they grow older, they make the system more complex, linking signs together into sentences with fairly consistent word order and grammatical rules—for example, "Mother, twist open the jar, blow a bubble, so I can clap it" (Goldin-Meadow, McNeill, & Singleton, 1996; Goldin-Meadow & Mylander, 1998). Observations of sign language in Nicaragua found that the language had evolved over the decades, becoming more complex and richer in information. Thus, the younger deaf people, who had learned the richer language from their early childhood, had in many ways more expressive signs than older deaf people, who had originally learned the less complex version (Senghas & Coppola, 2001).

Although each deaf child invents a different system, most systems share some interesting similarities. For example, most include some sort of marker to indicate the difference between a subject that is doing something to an object ("the mouse eats the cheese") and a subject that is doing something without an object ("the mouse is moving"). The sign languages invented by children in Taiwan resemble those of children in the United States, even though the spoken languages of those countries—Chinese and English—have very different grammars (Goldin-Meadow & Mylander, 1998).

If a deaf child starts to invent a sign language and no one responds to it, because the child meets no other deaf children and the adults fail to or refuse to learn, the child gradually abandons it and becomes totally without language. If such a child is exposed to sign language much later, such as age 12, he or she struggles to develop even weak signing skills and never catches up with those who started earlier (Harley & Wang, 1997; Mayberry, Lock, & Kazmi, 2002). This observation is our best evidence for the importance of early development in language learning: A child who doesn't learn a language while young is permanently impaired at learning one.

Some children grow up in a **bilingual** environment, *learning two languages about equally well.* Bilingualism is especially common among immigrant children, who are generally bicultural as well, learning both their parents' customs and those of their new country. The areas of brain activity during language use are the same in bilingual people as in those with only one language (Paradis, 1990; Solin, 1989). If the brain representations are so similar, how do bilingual people keep their two languages separate? The answer is that they do not, at least not completely (Francis, 1999).

Bilingualism has two disadvantages: Children take longer to master two languages than to master one (of course), and even adult bilinguals occasionally confuse words from the two languages. The primary advantage is obvious: If you learn a second language, you can communicate with more people. A second advantage is subtle: A bilingual person gains extra cognitive flexibility by learning that there are different ways of expressing the same idea. For example, children younger than 6 years old who speak only one language apparently believe that every object has only one name. If an adult gestures toward a cup and a gyroscope and says, "Please bring me the gyroscope," a child who knows the word *cup* will immediately bring the gyroscope, assuming that if one object is the cup, the other one must be the gyroscope. But the child would also fetch the gyroscope if asked to bring the *vessel,* the *chalice,* or any other synonym for *cup* that the child did not know. A bilingual child, however, is more likely to hesitate or to ask for help, understanding that an unfamiliar word could refer to the cup just as easily as the other object (Davidson, Jergovic, Imami, & Theodos, 1997).

CONCEPT CHECK ☑

15. What is the most convincing evidence that early exposure to language is necessary for language development? (Check your answer on page 316.)

Understanding Language

On a trip to Norway some years ago, I consulted my Norwegian phrase book and asked directions to the men's room: "Hvor er toalettet?" When the man answered—in Norwegian, of course—I suddenly realized the problem: It doesn't do me any good to speak the language unless I understand the answers!

Understanding a Word

We customarily describe the word *cat* as being composed of three sounds, *kuh, ah,* and *tuh.* However, the first sound in *cat* is not quite the same as the consonant sound in *kuh;* the *a* and *t* sounds are changed also. Each letter changes its sound depending on the other sounds that precede and follow it. What we hear also depends on the context and our expectations. For example, a researcher computer-modified a sound to be halfway between a normal *s* sound and a normal *sh* sound. When this intermediate sound replaced the *s* sound at the end of the word *embarrass,* people heard it as an *s* sound, but when the same sound replaced the *sh* at the end of *abolish,* people heard the same sound as *sh* (Samuel, 2001).

We also use lipreading more than we realize to understand what we hear. If lip movements do not match the sound, we sometimes "hear" something that is neither what we saw nor what we heard, but a compromise between them (McGurk & MacDonald, 1976). To experience this phenomenon go to http://psychology. wadsworth.com/kalat_intro7e. Navigate to the student Web site, then to the Online Try It Yourself section, and click on McGurk Effect.

In another study students listened to a tape recording of a sentence with one sound missing (Warren, 1970). The sentence was, "The state governors met with their respective legislatures convening in the capital city." However, the sound of the first *s* in the word *legislatures,* along with part of the adjacent *i* and *l,* had been replaced by a cough or a tone. The students were asked to listen to the recording and try to identify the location of the cough or tone. None of the 20 students identified the location correctly, and half thought the cough or tone interrupted one of the other words on the tape. They all claimed to have heard the *s* plainly. In fact even those who had been told that the *s* sound was missing still insisted that they had heard the sound. Apparently, the brain uses the context to fill in the missing sound.

Many English words have different meanings in different contexts. *Rose* can refer to a flower, or it can be the past tense of the verb *to rise. Dove* can refer to a bird related to pigeons, or it can be the past tense of the verb *to dive.* Consider the word *mean* in this sentence: "What did that mean old statistician mean by asking us to find the mean and mode of this distribution?" Just as we hear the word *legislatures* as a whole, not as a string of separate letters, we interpret a sequence of words as a whole, not one at a time. For example, suppose you hear a tape-recorded word that is carefully engineered to sound halfway between *dent* and *tent.* If you simply hear it and are asked to say what you heard, you might reply "dent," "tent," or "something sort of intermediate between dent and tent." But now suppose you hear that same sound in context:

1. When the *ent in the fender was well camouflaged, we sold the car.
2. When the *ent in the forest was well camouflaged, we began our hike.

Most people who hear sentence 1 report the word *dent.* Most who hear sentence 2 report *tent.* Now consider two more sentences:

3. When the *ent was noticed in the fender, we sold the car.
4. When the *ent was noticed in the forest, we stopped to rest.

For sentences 3 and 4, the context comes too late to help. People are as likely to report hearing *dent* in one sentence as in the other (Connine, Blasko, & Hall, 1991). Think for a moment what this means: In the first two sentences, the fender or forest showed up three syllables after *ent. In the second pair, the fender or forest appeared six syllables later. Evidently, when you hear an ambiguous sound, you can hold it in a temporary "undecided" state for about three syllables for the context to help you understand it. Beyond that point it is too late; you hear it one way or the other and stick with your decision, regardless of the later context.

Although a long-delayed context cannot help you hear an ambiguous word correctly, it can help you understand its meaning. Consider the following sentence from Karl Lashley (1951):

> Rapid righting with his uninjured hand saved from loss the contents of the capsized canoe.

If you hear this sentence spoken aloud, so that spelling is not a clue, you are likely at first to interpret the second word as *writing,* until you reach the final two words of the sentence. Suddenly, the phrase *capsized canoe* changes the whole scenario; now we understand that *righting* meant "pushing with a paddle." In summary only the immediate context can influence what you hear, but even a delayed context can change the word's meaning.

Understanding Sentences

Making sense of language requires knowledge about the world. For example, consider the following sentences (from Just & Carpenter, 1987):

- That store sells horse shoes.
- That store sells alligator shoes.

You interpret *horse shoes* to mean "shoes for horses to wear," but you don't interpret *alligator shoes* as "shoes for alligators to wear." Your understanding of the sentences depended on your knowledge of the world, not just the syntax of the sentences.

Here is another example:

- I'm going to buy a pet hamster at the store, if it's open.
- I'm going to buy a pet hamster at the store, if it's healthy.

Nothing about the sentence structure told you that *it* refers to the store in the first sentence and the hamster in the second sentence. You understood because you know that stores but not hamsters can be open, whereas hamsters but not stores can be healthy.

In short, you don't base your sentence understanding just on the sentence itself. Language comprehension depends on your knowledge of the world and all the assumptions that you share with the speaker or writer of the sentence. Sometimes you even have to remember where you are because the meaning of a word differs from one place to another (Figure 8.28).

FIGURE 8.28 In England a *football coach* is a bus full of soccer fans. In the United States it's the person who directs a team of American football players.

Now consider this sentence: *While Anna dressed the baby played in the crib.* Quickly: Whom did Anna dress? And who played in the crib? The addition of a comma would simplify the sentence, but even without it, English grammar prohibits "baby" from being both the object of *dressed* and the subject of *played.* If the baby played in the crib (as you no doubt answered), Anna must have dressed herself. Nevertheless, many people misunderstand and think Anna dressed the baby (Ferreira, Bailey, & Ferraro, 2002). Remember the example from earlier in the chapter about how many animals Moses took on the ark? That was another example in which many people overlook the details of the sentence and construct a "good enough" interpretation of the sentence's meaning based on their knowledge and reasonable expectations. That strategy occasionally misleads us, but it proves valuable in far more cases, such as those about the alligator shoes or buying a hamster at the store.

Limits to Our Language Understanding

Some sentences that follow the rules of grammar are nevertheless nearly incomprehensible. One example is a doubly embedded sentence—a sentence within a sentence within a sentence. A singly embedded sentence is understandable, though not simple:

The dog the cat saw chased a squirrel.
The squirrel the dog chased climbed the tree.

In the first sentence, "the cat saw the dog" is embedded within "the dog chased a squirrel." In the second, "the dog chased the squirrel" is embedded within "the squirrel climbed the tree." So far, so good, but now consider a doubly embedded sentence:

The squirrel the dog the cat saw chased climbed the tree.

Doubly embedded sentences overburden our memory. In fact, if your memory is already burdened with other matters, you may have trouble understanding even a singly embedded sentence (Gordon, Hendrick, & Levine, 2002).

Double negatives are also difficult to understand. "I would not deny that . . ." means that I agree. "It is not false that . . ." means that something is true. People can understand such sentences, but with difficulty. Have you ever seen a multiple-choice test item that asks "Which of the following is not true . . ." and then one of the choices has a *not* in it? When that happens, confusion is almost certain.

Triple negatives are, of course, still worse. Consider the following sentence, which includes *four* (!) negatives (emphasis added): "If you do *not* unanimously find from your consideration of all the evidence that there are *no* mitigating factors sufficient to *preclude* the imposition of a death sentence, then you should sign the verdict requiring the court to impose a sentence *other than* death." In Illinois a judge reads those instructions to a jury in a capital punishment case to explain how to decide between a death penalty and life in prison. (Do you think many jurors will understand?)

Even single negatives are sometimes confusing. Suppose you are trying to decide whether to buy a product at the supermarket. You notice on the package, "Contains no cyanide or rat pieces!" Does that notice encourage you to buy the product? Hardly! It is as if you do not fully believe the "no." (After all, why would the manufacturer even mention the absence of something unless it might be present?) I was once on an airplane that turned around shortly after departure because one of its two engines failed. The attendant told the passengers what was happening, but until she said "Please don't panic," we didn't realize there was any reason to panic.

In one clever experiment, students watched an experimenter pour sugar into two jars. The students were then told to label one jar "sucrose, table sugar" and the other "not sodium cyanide, not poison." Then the experimenter made two cups of Kool-Aid, one from each jar of sugar, and asked the students to choose one cup to drink (Figure 8.29). Of those who expressed a preference, 35 of 44 wanted Kool-Aid made from the jar marked "sucrose," not from the one that denied cyanide and poison (Rozin, Markwith, & Ross, 1990).

FIGURE 8.29 Most students preferred Kool-Aid made with sugar labeled "sugar" instead of sugar labeled "not cyanide," even though they had placed the labels themselves. Evidently, people do not fully believe the word "not." *(Based on results of Rozin, Markwith, & Ross, 1990)*

Monitoring Understanding

Earlier, we encountered the sentence "Never threaten someone with a chain saw." Another ambiguous sentence is "The daughter of the man and the woman arrived." Who arrived—one person (the man and woman's daughter)—or two people (the man's daughter plus some other woman)? If you said something like this, you would presumably know which meaning you intended, and your listener might know too because of the context or because of your pauses, intonations, and gestures. But might you overestimate your listener's understanding?

In one study people were asked to read aloud a series of ambiguous sentences, such as, "The daughter of the man and the woman arrived." In each case the speaker was told which of the two meanings was correct and was instructed to say the sentence to convey that meaning. After each sentence the speaker estimated the probability that a listener would correctly understand. On the average, speakers estimated correct understanding 72% of the time, whereas the listeners understood only 61% (Keysar & Henly, 2002). Remember from earlier in this chapter people's general tendency to be overconfident of themselves (page 295). Here we see another example.

Good writers try to avoid ambiguous or confusing sentences, and their copy editors try to catch any confusion the writer hadn't noticed. Still, some badly worded sentences make it to print. For example, a student newspaper once included this gem of a sentence: *He said Harris told him she and Brothers told French that grades had been changed.* When good readers find a sentence like that, they stop and reread it until they understand. Poorer readers tend to read everything at about a steady speed, regardless of how confusing it is.

Reading

As you will recall from earlier in this chapter, expertise achieved after 10 or so years of intensive practice enables one to recognize complex patterns at a glance. You have intensively practiced reading for more than the last 10 years, so in that regard you qualify as an expert reader. You may not think of yourself as an expert because we usually reserve the term *expert* for someone who is far more skilled than others. Nevertheless, your years of reading enable you to recognize words instantaneously, like an expert who recognizes chess patterns at a glance.

Word Recognition

Consider the following experiment: The investigator flashes one letter on a screen for less than a quarter of a second and then shows an interfering pattern and asks,

FIGURE 8.30 Either a word or a single letter flashed on a screen and then an interfering pattern. The observers were asked, "Which was presented: *C* or *J*?" More of them identified the letter correctly when it was part of a word.

"Was the letter C or J?" Then the experimenter flashes an entire word on the screen for the same length of time and asks, "Was the first letter of the word C or J?" (Figure 8.30). Which question do you think would be easier to answer? Most people can *identify the letter more accurately when it is part of a whole word than when it is presented by itself* (Reicher, 1969; Wheeler, 1970). This is known as the **word-superiority effect.** You can experience it yourself. Go to http://psychology.wadsworth. com/kalat_intro7e. Navigate to the student Web site, then to the Online Try It Yourself section, and click on Word Superiority Effect.

In further research James Johnston and James McClelland (1974) briefly flashed words on the screen and asked students to identify one letter (whose position was marked) in each word (Figure 8.31). On some trials the experimenters told the students to focus on the center of the area where the word would appear and to try to see the whole word. On other trials they showed the students exactly where the critical letter would appear on the screen and told them to focus on that spot and ignore the rest of the screen. Most students identified the critical letter more successfully when they looked at the whole word than when they focused on just the letter itself. This benefit occurs only with a real word, like COIN, not with a nonsense combination, like CXQF (Rumelhart & McClelland, 1982).

You may have experienced the word-superiority effect yourself. To pass time on long car trips, people sometimes try to find every letter of the alphabet on the billboards. It is usually easier to spot a letter by reading complete words than by checking letter by letter.

What accounts for the word-superiority effect? According to one model (J. L. McClelland, 1988;

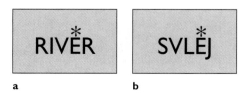

FIGURE 8.31 Students identified an indicated letter better when they focused on an entire word (a) than on a single letter in a designated spot (b).

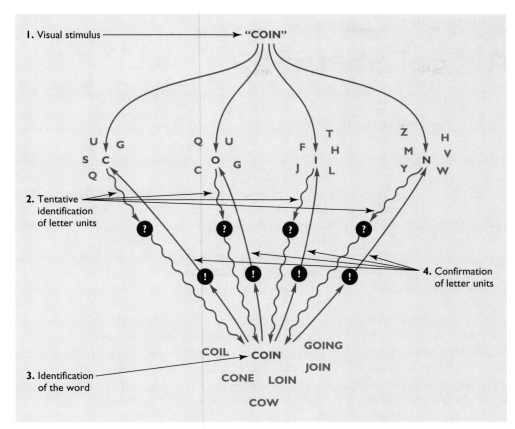

FIGURE 8.32 According to one model, a visual stimulus activates certain letter units, some more strongly than others. Those letter units then activate a word unit, which in turn strengthens the letter units that compose it. For this reason we recognize a whole word more easily than a single letter.

Rumelhart, McClelland, & the PDP Research Group, 1986), our perceptions and memories are represented by vast numbers of connections among "units," presumably corresponding to sets of neurons. Each unit is connected to other units (Figure 8.32). Each unit, when activated, excites some of its neighbors and inhibits others. Suppose that, at a given moment, units corresponding to the letters C, O, I, and N are moderately active. They excite a higher order unit corresponding to the word COIN. Although none of the four letter units sends a strong message by itself, the collective impact is strong (J. L. McClelland & Rumelhart, 1981). This higher level perception COIN then feeds excitation back to the individual letter-identifying units and confirms their tentative identifications.

This model helps explain our perception of Figure 8.33. Why do you see the top word in that figure as *RED* instead of *PFB*? After all, in the other words, those letters do look like *P, F,* and *B.* But in the top word, one ambiguous figure activates some *P* units and some *R* units; the next figure activates *E* and *F* units, and the third figure activates *D* and *B* units. All of those units in turn activate other more complex units corresponding to *RFB, PFB, PFD,* and *RED.* As

you tentatively perceive the word as *RED* (the only English word among those choices), the feedback strengthens the activity of the *R, E,* and *D* units.

Reading and Eye Movements

In an alphabetical language such as English, the printed page consists of letters that form familiar clusters that in turn form words and sentences. One kind of cluster is a **phoneme,** *a unit of sound.* A phoneme can be a single letter (such as *f*) or a combination of letters (such as *sh*). Good reading requires mastering phonics—the relationship between letters and sounds (Rayner, Foorman, Perfetti, Pesetsky, & Seidenberg, 2001). Another kind of cluster is a **morpheme,** *a unit of meaning.* For example, the noun *thrills* has two morphemes (*thrill* and *s*). The final *s* is a unit of meaning because it indicates that the noun is plural (see Figure 8.34).

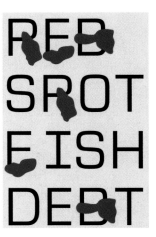

FIGURE 8.33 The combination of possible letters enables us to identify a word; word recognition in turn helps to confirm the letter identifications. Although each of the letters in the top word is ambiguous, a whole word—RED—is perceived. *("Parallel Distributed Processing: Explorations in the Microstructures of Cognition," Vol. 1: Foundations by David E. Rumethan et al., p. 8, figure 2. Series in Computational Models of Cognition and Perception. Copyright 1986 by MIT Press. Used with permission of the publisher.)*

Phonemes
(units of sound):

Morphemes
(units of meaning):

FIGURE 8.34 The word *shamelessness* has nine phonemes (units of sound) and three morphemes (units of meaning).

CONCEPT CHECK ☑

16. How many phonemes are in the word *thoughtfully*? How many morphemes? (Check your answers on page 316.)

When we read, do we ordinarily read one letter, one phoneme, one morpheme, or one or more words at a time? And do we move our eyes in a steady or jerky fashion? The movements are fast, and we are ordinarily not aware of them. Psychologists have arranged devices to monitor eye movements during reading. Their first discovery was that a reader's eyes move in a jerky fashion. You can move your eyes steadily to follow a moving object, but when you are scanning a stationary object, such as a page of print, you alternate between **fixations,** *when your eyes are stationary,* and *quick eye movements called* **saccades** (sa-KAHDS) *that take your eyes from one fixation point to another.*

You read during your fixations but you are virtually blind during the saccades. To illustrate this point, try the following demonstration: Look at yourself in the mirror and focus on your left eye. Then move your focus to the right eye. Can you see your eyes moving in the mirror? (Go ahead; try it.) People generally agree that they do not see their eyes move.

"Oh, but wait," you say. "That movement in the mirror was simply too quick and too small to be seen." Wrong. Try again, but this time get someone else to look at your left eye and then shift his or her gaze to your right eye. Now you do see the other person's eye movement, so the movement itself is not too fast or too small to be seen. Go back and try your own eyes in the mirror again and observe the difference. You can see someone else's eyes moving, but you cannot see your own eyes moving in the mirror.

There are two explanations: First, certain areas in the parietal cortex monitor impending eye movements and send a message to the primary visual cortex, in effect telling the visual cortex, "The eyes are about to move, so shut down activity for a moment." Even if you are in total darkness, the visual cortex decreases its activity during saccadic eye movements (Burr,

Morrone, & Ross, 1994; Paus, Marrett, Worsley, & Evans, 1995). Second, the stationary view at the end of a saccade interferes with the blurry view you saw during the saccade (Matin, Clymer, & Matin, 1972).

The consequence is that we see during fixations and not during saccades. An average adult reading a magazine article fixates on each point for about 200 to 250 milliseconds (ms). Good readers generally have briefer fixations than poor readers do, and everyone has briefer fixations on familiar words like *girl* than on harder words like *ghoul.* We also tend to pause a little longer on words with more than one meaning, like *bark* or *lie* (Rodd, Gaskell, & Marslen-Wilson, 2002). After each fixation, the next saccade lasts 25 to 50 ms. Thus, most readers have about four fixations per second (Rayner, 1998).

(In the attentional blink experiments discussed earlier, a letter that is flashed on the screen interferes with another letter that is flashed 200 ms later. So why doesn't one fixation interfere with another one when you are reading? The main explanation is that the flashes are very brief in the attentional blink experiments. The other explanation relates to the word-superiority effect: It is easier to read whole words in a meaningful context than to identify isolated letters.)

How much can a person read during one fixation? Many people believe they see quite a bit of the page at each instant. However, research indicates that we read only about 11 characters—one or two words—at a time. To demonstrate this limitation, focus on the letter *i* marked by an arrow (↓) in the two sentences below.

↓
1. This is a sentence with no misspelled words.
↓
2. Xboc tx zjg rxunce with no mijvgab zucn.

If you permit your eyes to wander back and forth, you quickly notice that sentence 2 is mostly gibberish. But as long as you dutifully keep your eyes on the fixation point, the sentence looks all right. You can read the letter on which you fixated plus about three or four characters (including spaces) to the left and about seven to the right; the rest is a blur. Therefore, you see —*ce with no m*—, or possibly —*nce with no mi*—.

This limit of about 11 letters depends partly on the lighting; in faint light your span decreases to as little as 1 or 2 letters, and your reading ability suffers accordingly (Legge, Ahn, Klitz, & Luebker, 1997). The limit does not depend on how much fits into the fovea of your eyes. In the following display, again focus on the letter *i* in each sentence and check how many letters you can read to its left and right:

This is a sentence with no misspelled words.

This is a sentence with no misspelled words.

is a sentence with no misspelled

If your reading span were limited by how many letters can fit into the fovea of your retina, you should be able to read more letters in the top sentence and fewer as the letters get larger. In fact you do at least as well, maybe even better, with a larger print sentence (up to a point).

What we can see at a glance also depends on our habits of reading. In Japanese, where each character conveys more information than English letters do, readers see fewer letters per fixation (Rayner, 1998). And in Hebrew and Farsi, which are written right to left, readers read more letters to the left of fixation and fewer to the right (Brysbaert, Vitu, & Schroyens, 1996; Faust, Kravetz, & Babkoff, 1993; Malamed & Zaidel, 1993).

Often, our 11-character window of reading includes one word plus a fragment of another. For example, suppose you have fixated on the point shown by an arrow in the following sentence:

The government made serious mistakes.

Readers can see the word *serious* plus about the first three letters of *mistakes*. Three letters do not identify the word; from what the reader knows, the next word could be *misspellings, misbehavior, missiles, mishmash,* or any of a number of other *mis*-things that a government might make.

Does the preview of the next word facilitate reading? Yes. In one study college students again read passages on a computer screen while a machine monitored their eye movements. The computer correctly displayed the word the student fixated on plus the next zero, three, or four letters. So the display might look like this:

made
serious
mistakes.

or like this:

made ser
serious mis
mistakes.

Students who could preview the first three or four letters of the next word read significantly faster than those who could not (Inhoff, 1989). Evidently, while we are reading one word, we are previewing the next. Our preview helps guide the next eye movement and gives us a head start on identifying the next word (Inhoff, Radach, Eiter, & Juhasz, 2003).

You might wonder what speed-readers do differently from normal readers. An average adult reader has about four or five fixations per second with occasional backtracks, for an overall rate of about 200 words per minute. Speed-readers have briefer fixations with fewer backtracks. With practice people can double or triple their reading speed with normal comprehension. Some claim that they see more than 11 characters per fixation, and unfortunately, researchers haven't done enough studies to test this possibility. However, unless they increase their span enormously, reading speed has some physical limits. Each saccadic eye movement lasts 25 to 50 ms, and reading does not occur during saccades. Thus, it would be impossible to exceed 20 to 40 fixations per second, even if each fixation lasted no time at all! If we make the generous estimate that people might be able to average 2 words per fixation, the theoretical maximum would be 20 to 80 words per second, or 1,200 to 4,800 words per minute. And remember, this calculation unrealistically assumes a fixation time of zero. Yet some people claim to read 5,000 to 10,000 words per minute. In fact they are fixating on some words and guessing the rest. A combination of reading and guessing can produce very fast reading and adequate comprehension of books with predictable content, like a James Bond novel. However, the speed-reader does miss details. When speed-readers read college textbooks, they either slow their reading (Just & Carpenter, 1987) or fail the tests (Homa, 1983).

CONCEPT CHECK

17. Why can we sometimes read two or three short words at a time, whereas we need a saccade or two to read the same number of longer words?
18. If a word is longer than 11 letters, will a reader need more than one fixation to read it? (Check your answers on page 316.)

IN CLOSING

Language and Humanity

At the start of this module, we considered the question, "If language is so extremely useful to humans, why haven't other species evolved at least a little of it?" None of the research directly answers this question, but we can speculate. Certain adaptations are much more useful on a large scale than on a small scale. For example, skunks survive because they are very stinky; being just slightly stinky wouldn't help much. Porcupines survive because they have long, sharp quills; having a few short quills might be slightly helpful, but not very. Similarly, a little language might be slightly helpful (like a little stink or a few short quills), but better developed language is vastly more useful. A little bit of language development is probably an unstable condition, evolutionarily speaking. Once a species such as humans had evolved a little language, those individuals with still better language abilities would have a huge selective advantage over the others.

Summary

- *Language productivity.* Human languages enable us to create new words and phrases to express new ideas. (page 302)
- *Language training in nonhumans.* Bonobos, and to a lesser extent other chimpanzees, have learned certain aspects of language. Human evolution evidently elaborated on potentials found in our apelike ancestors but developed that potential further. (page 303)
- *Language and intelligence.* It is possible to have intelligence without language or language without other aspects of intelligence. Therefore, many psychologists regard language as a specialized capacity, not just a by-product of overall intelligence. (page 304)
- *Rapid language learning in children.* Children learn language at an amazing rate, considering the unsystematic training they receive. In some way children are born with a predisposition to learn language easily. (page 305)
- *Brain organization and aphasia.* Brain damage, especially in the left hemisphere, can impair people's ability to understand or use language. However, many brain areas contribute to language in varied ways. (page 306)
- *Stages of language development.* Children advance through several stages of language development, probably reflecting maturation of brain structures necessary for language and not just the total amount of experience. From the start children's language is creative, using the rules of language to make new word combinations and sentences. (page 307)
- *Children exposed to no language or two.* If deaf children are not exposed to language, they invent a sign language of their own. However, a deaf child who has no opportunity to use sign language in childhood will be impaired on learning it or any

other language later. Children in a bilingual environment sometimes have trouble keeping the two languages separate but gain the ability to converse with many people and in certain ways show extra cognitive flexibility. (page 308)
- *Understanding language.* Much of speech is ambiguous; we understand words and sentences in context by applying the knowledge we have about the world in general. (page 309)
- *Limits to our language understanding.* Many sentences are difficult to understand, especially those with embedded clauses or more than one negative. Difficult grammar places a burden on our working memory. (page 311)
- *Reading.* When we read, we have fixation periods separated by eye movements called saccades. We read during the fixations, not the saccades. Even good readers can read only about 11 letters per fixation; people increase their speed of reading by increasing the number of fixations per second. (page 312)

Answers to Concept Checks

13. Start language learning when a child is young. Rely on imitation as much as possible, instead of providing direct reinforcements for correct responses. (page 304)
14. Children begin to string words into novel combinations as soon as they begin to speak two words at a time. We believe that they learn rules of grammar because they overgeneralize those rules, creating such words as *womans* and *goed*. (page 308)
15. Deaf children who cannot learn spoken language and who have no opportunity to communicate with signs early in life are permanently disadvantaged in learning sign language. (page 309)
16. *Thoughtfully* has seven phonemes: th-ough-t-f-u-ll-y. (A phoneme is a unit of sound, not necessarily a letter of the alphabet.) It has three morphemes: thought-ful-ly. (Each morpheme has a distinct meaning.) (page 314)
17. Two or three short words can fall within the window of about 11 letters that we can fixate at one time. If the words are longer, it may be impossible to see them all at once. (page 315)
18. Sometimes but not always. Suppose your eyes fixate on the fourth letter of *memorization*. You should be able to see the three letters to its left and the seven to its right—in other words all except the final letter. Because there is only one English word that starts *memorizatio-*, you already know the word. (page 315)

Key Terms and Activities

Key Terms

algorithm: a mechanical, repetitive procedure for solving a problem (page 288)

attention: the tendency to respond to some stimuli more than others or to remember some more than others (p. 277)

attentional blink: a brief period after perceiving a stimulus, during which it is difficult to attend to another stimulus (page 283)

attentive process: a procedure that extracts information from one part of the visual field at a time (page 278)

availability heuristic: the strategy of assuming that how easily one can remember examples of some kind of event indicates how common the event actually is (page 294)

base-rate information: data about the frequency or probability of a given item (page 293)

bilingual: able to use two languages about equally well (page 309)

Broca's aphasia: a condition characterized by inarticulate speech and by difficulties with both using and understanding grammatical devices—prepositions, conjunctions, word endings, complex sentence structures, and so forth (page 306)

change blindness: the tendency to fail to detect changes in any part of a scene to which we are not focusing our attention (page 281)

cognition: the processes of thinking, gaining knowledge, and dealing with knowledge (page 273)

confirmation bias: the tendency to accept one hypothesis and then look for evidence to support it, instead of considering other possibilities (page 296)

critical thinking: the careful evaluation of evidence for and against any conclusion (page 295)

fixation: a period when the eyes are steady (page 314)

framing effect: the tendency to answer a question differently when it is framed (phrased) differently (page 298)

functional fixedness: the tendency to adhere to a single approach to a problem or a single way of using an item (page 297)

heuristics: strategies for simplifying a problem or for guiding an investigation (page 288)

language acquisition device: a built-in mechanism for acquiring language (page 305)

morpheme: a unit of meaning (page 313)

overconfidence: the belief that one's opinions or predictions are highly correct when in fact they are not (page 295)

phoneme: a unit of sound (page 313)

preattentive process: a procedure for extracting information automatically and simultaneously across a large portion of the visual field (page 278)

productivity: the ability to express new ideas (page 302)

prototype: a familiar or typical example of a category (page 274)

representativeness heuristic: the tendency to assume that, if an item is similar to members of a particular category, it is probably a member of that category itself (page 293)

saccade: a quick jump in the focus of the eyes from one point to another (page 314)

spreading activation: the process by which the activation of one concept also activates or primes other concepts that are linked to it (page 276)

Stroop effect: the tendency to read a word, especially if it is a color name, in spite of instructions to disregard the word and state the color of the ink in which it is printed (page 279)

sunk cost effect: the willingness to do something we wouldn't otherwise choose to do because of money or effort already spent (page 299)

transformational grammar: a system for converting a deep structure of a language into a surface structure (page 302)

Wernicke's aphasia: a condition marked by difficulty recalling the names of objects and impaired comprehension of language (page 306)

Williams syndrome: a genetic condition characterized by mental retardation in most regards but skillful use of language (page 305)

word-superiority effect: identifying a letter with greater ease when it is part of a whole word than when it is presented by itself (page 312)

Suggestion for Further Reading

Pinker, S. (1999). *Words and rules: The ingredients of language.* New York: Basic Books. A discussion of language by a writer with a keen eye for excellent examples.

Book Companion Web Site

Need help studying? Go to

http://psychology.wadsworth.com/kalat_intro7e/

for a virtual study center. You'll find a personalized Self-Study Assessment that will provide you with a study plan based on your answers to a pretest. Also study using flashcards, quizzes, interactive art, and an online glossary.

Check out interactive **Try it Yourself** exercises on the companion site! For example, the Work-Superiority Effect and Overconfidence exercises relate to what you've learned in this chapter.

Your companion site also has direct links to the following Web sites. These links are checked often for changes, dead links, and new additions.

Preattentive Processes

www.csc.ncsu.edu/faculty/healey/PP/Interfere.html

A description of preattentive processes with interesting demonstrations.

Human Language

http://www.ilovelanguages.com

This site has links to many sources of information about languages.

Try It Yourself CD-ROM
with Critical Thinking Video Exercises

Use your CD to access **videos** related to activities designed to help you think critically about the important topics discussed. You'll also find an easy portal link to the book companion site where you can access your personalized **Self-Study Assessments** and interactive **Try It Yourself** exercises.

PsychNow! 2.0

PsychNow! is a fun interactive CD designed to help you with the difficult concepts in psychology. Check out the Learning & Cognition section for the following topics that relate to this chapter:

Cognition and Language: framing pretest, interactive risk/outcome scenarios, apply solution to the pretest.

Problem Solving nd Creativity: pretests, creativity and problem solving lesson, and an animated solution to the pretest.

ExperimentNOW! Concepts: Lexical decisions and prototypes

Intelligence

The famous mathematician Alan Turing bicycled to and from work each day. Occasionally, the chain fell off his bicycle and he had to replace it. Eventually, Turing kept records and noticed that the chain fell off at regular intervals, after exactly a certain number of turns of the front wheel. He calculated that this number was the product of the number of spokes in the front wheel times the number of links in the chain, times the number of cogs in the pedal. He deduced that the chain came loose whenever a particular link in the chain came in contact with a particular bent spoke on the wheel. He identified that spoke, repaired it, and never again had trouble with his bicycle (I. Stewart, 1987).

Turing's solution to his problem is impressive, but hold your applause. Your local bicycle mechanic could have solved the problem quickly without using mathematics at all. So, you might ask, what's my point? Was Turing unintelligent? Of course not. If you have a complicated, unfamiliar problem to solve, you should take it to someone like Turing, not your local bicycle mechanic. The point is that intelligence includes both general abilities and practiced skills. The term *intelligence* can refer to the highly practiced skills shown by a good bicycle mechanic, a Micronesian sailor, a hunter-gatherer of the Serengeti Plain, or anyone else with extensive experience. Intelligence also refers to the generalized problem-solving ability that Turing showed. But even that sort of ability develops gradually, reflecting many kinds of experience.

▌ To repair a bicycle, you could use general problem-solving skills or specific expertise about bicycles. Either approach qualifies as a kind of intelligence.

Intelligence and Intelligence Tests

What do we mean by "intelligence"? Is there more than one kind of intelligence?

You might imagine that people would first develop a theoretical understanding of intelligence and then find a way to measure it. In fact the order was reversed: The tests came first, with purely practical intentions, and psychologists continue to try to develop a theoretical basis. The same, actually, was true in physics: People measured gravity, magnetism, and other variables long before they had a reasonable theoretical understanding of them.

Consider this analogy: You have just been put in charge of choosing the members of your country's next Olympic team. However, the Olympic rules have been changed: Each country will send only 30 men and 30 women, and each athlete must compete in every event. Furthermore, the Olympic committee will not announce what those events are until all the athletes have been chosen. Clearly, you cannot hold the usual kind of tryouts, but neither will you choose people at random. How will you proceed?

Your best bet would be to devise a test of "general athletic ability." You might measure the abilities of applicants to run, jump, change direction, maintain balance, throw and catch, kick, lift weights, respond rapidly to signals, and perform other athletic feats. Then you would choose the applicants with the best scores.

No doubt, your test would be imperfect. Any test would be. But if you want your team to do well, you need some way to measure athletic ability. Later, other people begin to use your test also. Does its wide acceptance imply that athletic ability is a single quantity, like speed or weight? Of course not. You found it useful to treat athletic ability as a single quantity, but you know that great basketball players are not necessarily great swimmers or gymnasts. Does your test imply that athletic ability reflects innate talent? No, it merely measures athletic skills, without any implication of how they developed.

What Is Intelligence?

Intelligence tests resemble our imaginary test of athletic ability. If you were in charge of choosing which applicants a college should admit, you would want to select those who would learn the most. Because students may be studying subjects that they have never studied before, it makes sense to measure a range of skills, not just knowledge of a single topic.

Originally, the goal of intelligence tests was to identify the *least* capable children, who could not learn from ordinary schooling. Later, the tests were used also to identify the best students, who would profit from accelerated classes. The tests were based on no theory of intelligence, and many test administrators have been content to define intelligence as the ability to do well in school. Given that definition, IQ tests do measure intelligence. Of course, by that definition so do grades in school.

For theoretical purposes, however, "ability to do well in school" is hardly a satisfactory definition. What would be a better one? Here are some of the ways that psychologists have defined intelligence (Sternberg, 1997; Wolman, 1989):

- The mental abilities that enable one to adapt to, shape, or select one's environment.
- The ability to judge, comprehend, and reason.
- The ability to understand and deal with people, objects, and symbols.
- The ability to act purposefully, think rationally, and deal effectively with the environment.

Note that these definitions use such terms as *judge, comprehend, understand,* and *think rationally*—terms that are themselves just as poorly defined as intelligence. To clarify the meaning of intelligence, psychologists have conducted research on the relationship among various "intelligent" abilities. Note also that these definitions focus strictly on cognitive intelligence. In Chapter 12 we shall consider the possibility of emotional intelligence, the ability to perceive people's emotions and handle emotional situations.

People say, "Don't put the cart before the horse." Here, I need to discuss intelligence tests and theories of intelligence, but which is the cart and which is the horse? It seems logical to discuss what intelligence is before how to test it, but all the theories of intelligence are based on the intelligence tests or criticisms of them. Let us therefore begin with examples of IQ tests, which will show what the theories are trying to explain.

IQ Tests

It would be hard to estimate how much time you have already spent taking tests. Some teachers give so many tests that they hardly have any time to teach. Still, a college or medical school that cannot admit every applicant needs some way to select those who are likely to do the best work. A school that wants to provide accelerated classes needs a way to identify students who would profit from them. Teachers' recommendations are useful up to a point, but teachers have their own quirks and biases, and objective measures help compare students from different classes and different schools.

Intelligence quotient (IQ) tests attempt to *measure an individual's probable performance in school and similar settings.* (The term *quotient* dates from when IQ was determined by dividing mental age by chronological age and then multiplying by 100. For example, an 8-year-old who performed like an average 10-year-old would have a mental age of 10, a chronological age of 8, and an IQ of $10 / 8 \times 100 = 125$. That method is now obsolete, but the term remains.) Two French psychologists, Alfred Binet and Theophile Simon (1905), devised the first IQ tests. The French Ministry of Public Instruction wanted a fair way to identify children who had such serious intellectual deficiencies that they should not be placed in the same classes with other students. The task of identifying such children had formerly been left to medical doctors, but the school system wanted an impartial test. Binet and Simon's test measured the skills that children need for success in school, such as understanding and using language, computational skills, memory, and the ability to follow instructions.

Their test and others like it do make reasonably accurate predictions. But suppose that a test correctly predicts that one student will perform better than another in school. Can we then say that the first student did better in school *because of* a higher IQ score? No. Consider this analogy: Suppose we ask why some basketball player misses most of his shots. Someone answers, "Because he has a low shooting average." Clearly, that explains nothing. (The reason for his low shooting average is that he misses so many shots.) Similarly, saying that a student does poorly in school because of a low IQ score isn't much of an explanation; after all, the IQ test was designed to measure the skills that schoolwork requires. An IQ score measures performance; it does not explain it.

The Stanford-Binet Test

The test that Binet and Simon designed was later modified for English speakers by Lewis Terman and other Stanford psychologists and published as the **Stanford-Binet IQ test.** School psychologists are carefully trained on how to administer the test items and score the answers. The test's items are designated by age (see Table 9.1). An item designated as "age 8," for example, will be answered correctly by 60 to 90% of 8-year-olds. (A higher percentage of older children answer it correctly and a lower percentage of younger children.)

A psychologist testing an 8-year-old might start with the items designated for 7-year-olds. Unless the child missed many of the 7-year-old items, the psychologist would simply give credit for all the 6-year-old items without testing them. If the child answered most of the 7-year-old items correctly, the psychologist would proceed to the items for 8-year-olds, 9-year-olds, and so forth, until the child began to miss most items. At that point the psychologist would end the test. (This method is known as *adaptive testing.*) Individuals proceed at their own pace, usually finishing in somewhat over an hour (McCall, Yates, Hendricks, Turner, & McNabb, 1989).

Stanford-Binet IQ scores are computed from tables set up to ensure that a given IQ score means the same at different ages. The mean IQ at each age is

TABLE 9.1 Examples of the Types of Items on the Stanford-Binet Test

Age	Sample Test Item
2	Test administrator points at pictures of everyday objects and asks, "What is this?" "Here are some pegs of different sizes and shapes. See whether you can put each one into the correct hole."
4	"Why do people live in houses?" "Birds fly in the air; fish swim in the ____."
6	"Here is a picture of a horse. Do you see what part of the horse is missing?" "Here are some candies. Can you count how many there are?"
8	"What should you do if you find a lost puppy?" "Stephanie can't write today because she twisted her ankle. What is wrong with that?"
10	"Why should people be quiet in a library?" "Repeat after me: 4 8 3 7 1 4."
12	"What does *regret* mean?" "Here is a picture. Can you tell me what is wrong with it?"
14	"What is the similarity between high and low?" "Watch me fold this paper and cut it. Now, when I unfold it, how many holes will there be?"
Adult	"Make up a sentence using the words *celebrate*, *reverse*, and *appointment.*" "What do people mean when they say, 'People who live in glass houses should not throw stones' "?

Source: Modified from Nietzel and Bernstein, 1987.

100. A 6-year-old with an IQ score of, say, 116, has performed better on the test than 84% of other 6-year-olds; similarly, an adult with an IQ score of 116 has performed better than 84% of other adults. The Stanford-Binet also provides subscores reflecting visual reasoning, short-term memory, and other specialized skills (Daniel, 1997; McCall et al., 1989).

In Table 9.1 note that the Stanford-Binet test has questions for children as young as 2 years old. However, scores below age 4 or 5 fluctuate markedly (Honzik, 1974; Morrow & Morrow, 1974). You no doubt have your good days and your bad days, but when much is at stake, you probably can force yourself to make an effort even if you don't feel like it. Preschoolers who don't feel like trying perform badly. Their test scores should be interpreted very cautiously.

The Wechsler Tests

Two IQ tests devised by David Wechsler, known as the **Wechsler Adult Intelligence Scale–Third Edition (WAIS–III)** and the **Wechsler Intelligence Scale for Children–Fourth Edition (WISC–IV),** produce the same average, 100, and almost the same distribution of scores as the Stanford-Binet. The WISC is given to children up to age 16; the WAIS is for everyone older. As with the Stanford-Binet, the Wechsler tests are administered to one person at a time.

A Wechsler test provides an overall score and several subscores representing presumed components of intelligence. For example, the WISC–IV has four composite scores. One is the Verbal Comprehension Index, based on such items as "Define the word *letter*" and "How are a peach and a plum similar?" A second part is the Perceptual Reasoning Index, which calls for nonverbal answers. For example, the examiner might arrange four blocks in a particular pattern and then ask the child to arrange four other blocks to match the pattern (Figure 9.1).

A third part, the Working Memory Index, includes such items as "Listen to these numbers and then repeat them: 3 6 2 5" and "Listen to these numbers and repeat them in reverse order: 4 7 6." The fourth part is Processing Speed. An example of an item is "Here is a page full of shapes.

△ ○ □ ▱ ○ △ ▱ □ ○

Put a slash (/) through all the circles and an X through all the squares." In this case the task itself is simple; the question is how much of the page a child can complete within a short time limit.

Each part of the WISC–IV or the WAIS–III begins with the simplest questions and progresses to increasingly difficult ones. The inclusion of several subscores calls attention to someone's specific strengths and weaknesses. For example, an immigrant child who learned

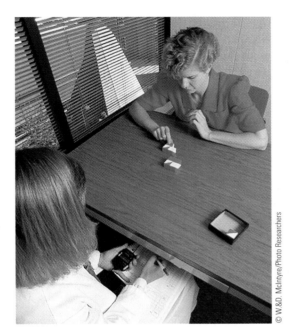

FIGURE 9.1 Both the WISC–IV and the WAIS–III include many nonverbal items. For example, in the Block Design task, the instruction is to match a pattern of blocks as arranged by the examiner.

English as a second language might do poorly on the Verbal Comprehension Index but much better on Perceptual Reasoning and Processing Speed, which do not require verbal answers. People with certain disabilities perform slowly on the Processing Speed tasks but do well on other parts of the test. Sometimes a low score on one part of the WISC helps identify a problem for which teachers can provide help or special consideration.

Culture-Reduced Testing

The Stanford-Binet and Wechsler tests, though useful for many purposes, have one major limitation: Because they require use and comprehension of the English language, they are unfair to immigrants, people with hearing impairments, and anyone else who does not speak English well. "Why not simply translate the tests into other languages, including sign language?" you might ask. Psychologists sometimes do, but a translated item may be easier or harder than the original. For example, one part of the Stanford-Binet presents words and asks for words that rhyme with them. Generating rhymes is moderately easy in English, even easier in Italian, but reportedly almost impossible in Zulu (M. W. Smith, 1974).

To overcome such problems, psychologists have tried to devise a culture-fair or culture-reduced test. No task is free of cultural influences (Rosselli & Ardila, 2003). However, a test with no language is at least fairer to more people, including immigrants and people who are deaf, than are most other tests. *The most widely used culture-reduced test* is the **Progressive Matrices** test devised by John C. Raven. These matrices, which *progress* gradually from easy to difficult items, attempt to measure abstract reasoning. To answer the questions, a person must generate hypotheses, test them, and infer rules (Carpenter, Just, & Shell, 1990). Figure 9.2 presents three matrices similar to those on this test. The first is relatively easy, the second is harder, and the third is harder still.

The Progressive Matrices test requires no verbal responses or factual information, and the instructions are simple. It therefore gives a non-English speaker a better opportunity than most other IQ tests do. The main disadvantage is that this test provides only a single overall score, instead of identifying an individual's strengths and weaknesses.

How culture-fair is the Progressive Matrices test? It requires less information than the Wechsler or Stanford-Binet tests, but it does assume familiarity with pencil-and-paper, multiple-choice tests and other Western customs. For example, children from some cultures have been taught not to express their own opinions without first checking with their parents or not to speak to unfamiliar adults, including the person administering the test (Greenfield, 1997). In short, the Progressive Matrices test has less cultural content than the other tests, but any test contains elements that are more familiar in some cultures than others.

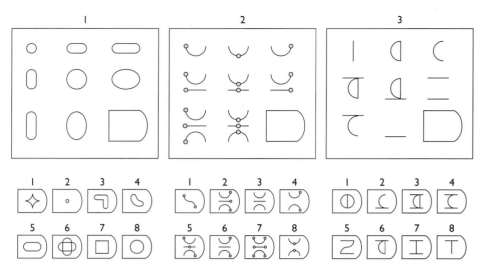

FIGURE 9.2 Items similar to those in Raven's Progressive Matrices test. The instructions are: "Each pattern has a piece missing. From the eight choices provided, select the one that completes the pattern, both going across and going down." (You can check your answers against answer A on page 331.)

CONCEPT CHECK ☑

1. What is one advantage of the Wechsler IQ tests over Raven's Progressive Matrices? What is an advantage of the Progressive Matrices? (Check your answers on page 331.)

The Relationship Between IQ Tests and Intelligence

Do the IQ tests measure intelligence? That question sounds reasonable, but it assumes that intelligence is a single something and that we know what that something is. Better, at least more answerable, questions are, "What do the intelligence tests measure?" and "What do the test results tell us, if anything, about the nature of intelligence?"

Spearman's Psychometric Approach and the g Factor

Among the earliest research studies in psychology, one of the most influential was Charles Spearman's (1904) **psychometric approach** to intelligence, based on *the measurement of individual differences in performance.* Spearman began by measuring how well various people performed various tasks, such as following directions, judging musical pitch, matching colors, and doing arithmetic. He found that performance on any of his tasks correlated positively with performance on any of the others. He therefore inferred that all the tasks must have something in common. To perform well on any test of mental ability, Spearman argued, people need a certain *"general"* ability, which he called *g*. (The symbol *g* is italicized and always lowercase, like the mathematical terms *e* and *i*.)

To account for the fact that performances on various tasks do not correlate perfectly, Spearman suggested that each task requires the use of a *"specific" ability,* **s,** in addition to the general ability *g* that all tasks require (Figure 9.3). Thus, intelligence consists of a general ability plus an unknown number of specific abilities, such as mechanical, musical, arithmetical, logical, and spatial abilities. Spearman called his theory a "monarchic" theory of intelligence because it included a dominant ability, or monarch (*g*), which ruled over the lesser abilities.

Later researchers have confirmed that scores on virtually all kinds of cognitive tests correlate positively with one another under nearly all circum-

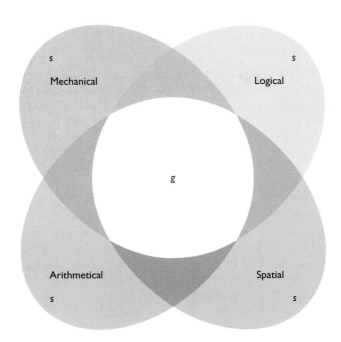

FIGURE 9.3 According to Spearman (1904) all intelligent abilities have an area of overlap, which he called *g* (for "general"). Each ability also depends partly on an *s* (for "specific") factor.

stances. You have probably noticed this trend yourself: A student who does well in one course probably will also do well in other courses. Researchers have reported the same trend even in mice: The mice that learn well in one situation generally also learn quickly in another, even with different responses, different reinforcers, and different kinds of stimuli (Matzel et al., 2003). Only under special conditions do individuals perform well on one test and poorly on another. For example, if we gave English-language and Spanish-language IQ tests to some people who spoke only English and some who spoke only Spanish, then those who did well on one test would do poorly on the other. Similarly, in one study rural Kenyan children who did the best on an academic test did poorly on a test of knowledge about traditional herbal medicines, and those who did best on the test of herbal medicines did poorly on the academic test (Sternberg et al., 2001). Presumably, the two groups of children had been exposed to different sets of experiences and information.

Possible Explanations for g

The observations underlying *g* indicate that whatever causes people to do well on one test also increases their probability of doing well on almost any other test. But what is that "something" that contributes to good performance on so many kinds of tests? The simplest and most popular interpretation is that all the tasks measure a single underlying ability. Consider the fol-

lowing analogy: First, consider the high correlation among the tasks shown in Figure 9.4: Most people who excel at running a 100-meter race also do well at the high jump and the long jump. We can hardly imagine an outstanding high jumper who could not manage a decent long jump. The reason for this high correlation is that all three events depend on the same leg muscles. An injury that impaired performance on one event would impair performance on all three.

Similarly, people might perform well on a variety of intellectual tests because all the tests depend on the same underlying skill. What might that underlying skill be? One possibility is that all intellectual tests depend on "mental speed" (Luo, Thompson, & Detterman, 2003). Another is that *g* represents how easily one's neurons change in response to altered experiences (Garlick, 2003). Other possibilities include attentional resources and speed of visual pro-

FIGURE 9.4 Measurements of sprinting, high jumping, and long jumping correlate with one another because they all depend on the same leg muscles. Similarly, the *g* factor that emerges in IQ testing could reflect a single ability.

cessing. Performance on IQ tests correlates strongly with the kinds of working memory tasks described in Chapter 7 (Gray, Chabris, & Braver, 2003; Süss, Oberauer, Wittman, Wilhelm, & Schulze, 2002). However, many psychologists remain skeptical that any one ability accounts for all of *g* (Kray & Frensch, 2002; Posthuma, Neale, Boomsma, & de Geus, 2001).

An alternative explanation for *g* is that we have several "intelligent" abilities that correlate because they grow in the same ways (Petrill, Luo, Thompson, & Detterman, 1996). That is, the "something" that contributes to all forms of intelligence is that they all depend on good health, good nutrition, and so forth.

By analogy consider the lengths of three body parts—the left leg, the right arm, and the left index finger: As a rule these three measurements correlate strongly with one another. That is, most people with a long left leg also have a long right arm and left index finger. Obviously, the three lengths do not measure the same thing. (Amputating one of them would not affect the others.) Lengths of leg, arm, and finger correlate because all the factors that cause any to grow also cause the others to grow. Similarly, all forms of intelligence depend on health, nutrition, education, and probably genetics; most people who have good support for developing one intellectual skill also have good support for developing others.

Which of these examples is more like intelligence? Do the various intellectual skills correlate with one another because they all measure a single underlying ability (like running and jumping, which require good leg muscles) or because they all grow together (like your arms, legs, and fingers)?

To some extent both are probably correct. Many intellectual tasks activate the same areas of the frontal cortex, which are regarded as essential to attention and working memory (Duncan et al., 2000). So those brain areas might be central to *g*. On the other hand, the genes, nutrition, health, and other factors that cause any brain area to grow have the same effects on other areas, so independent brain functions could correlate with one another for reasons of health, nutrition, and so forth. Even across species, if you know the size of one brain area, you can predict the size of other brain areas with remarkable accuracy (Clark, Mitra, & Wang, 2001).

CONCEPT CHECK ☑

2. What evidence did Spearman have in favor of the concept of *g*?
3. What are two possible explanations for *g*? (Check your answers on page 331.)

Fluid Intelligence and Crystallized Intelligence

Raymond Cattell (1987) proposed an important modification to the concept of general intelligence by distinguishing two components: fluid intelligence and crystallized intelligence. The analogy is to water: Fluid water can fit into a container of any shape, whereas an ice crystal fits only one shape. **Fluid intelligence** is *the power of reasoning and using information.* It includes the ability to perceive relationships, solve unfamiliar problems, and gain new knowledge. **Crystallized intelligence** consists of *acquired skills and knowledge and the ability to apply that knowledge in specific situations.* For example, fluid intelligence is the ability to learn new skills in a new job, whereas crystallized intelligence includes the job skills that someone has acquired over years. Expertise, as discussed in Chapter 8, is mostly crystallized intelligence; it requires many years of study and practice. Even memory experts—those who win competitions for memorizing shuffled decks of cards or long numbers—achieve that expertise through practice at specific skills, not through a high overall *g* (Maguire, Valentine, Wilding, & Kapur, 2003).

Standard IQ tests try to focus mainly on fluid intelligence because each person has a different kind of crystallized intelligence, and no test could do justice to that variety. However, an employer might use a test of crystallized intelligence specific to a given job. For example, an airline would want to know about applicants' specific skills in piloting an airplane.

Fluid intelligence reaches its peak before age 20, remains nearly steady for decades, and declines on the average in old age, although much more in some people than others (Horn, 1968). Crystallized intelligence, on the other hand, continues to increase as long as people are active and alert (Cattell, 1987; Horn & Donaldson, 1976). A 20-year-old may be more successful than a 65-year-old at solving a new, unfamiliar problem, but the 65-year-old will excel on problems in his or her area of specialization. However, the distinction between fluid and crystallized intelligence is sharper in theory than in practice. Any task taps both crystallized and fluid intelligence to some extent.

CONCEPT CHECK ☑

4. Was Alan Turing's solution to the slipping bicycle chain, from the introduction to this chapter, an example of fluid or crystallized intelligence? Would the solution provided by a bicycle mechanic be an example of fluid or crystallized intelligence? (Check your answers on page 331.)

Gardner's Theory of Multiple Intelligences

The concept of *g* is based on the fact that scores on mathematical, verbal, and other tests correlate positively with one another, usually rather highly. Critics argue that the scores correlate only because the tests measure similar processes. Perhaps we have some "intelligent" processes that do not correlate with the others, and *g* appears only because the tests ignore these other kinds of intelligence.

For example, Howard Gardner (1985) has claimed that people have **multiple intelligences**—*numerous unrelated forms of intelligence,* including language, musical abilities, logical and mathematical reasoning, spatial reasoning, body movement skills, self-control and self-understanding, and sensitivity to other people's social signals. He argues that people can be outstanding in one type of intelligence but not others. For example, an athlete can excel at body movement skills but lack musical abilities, an outstanding musician can be insensitive to other people, and so forth. Someone who seems intelligent in one way may be mediocre or worse in another.

Gardner certainly makes the important point that each person has different valuable skills. However, not much research has addressed the two most basic theoretical questions: (a) How independent are these skills? For example, do musical abilities correlate positively with language and mathematical skills? It is one thing to suggest that various performances are independent, but another to demonstrate their independence. (b) To the extent that skills are different, do they represent separate underlying *abilities* or separate kinds of *crystallized* intelligence? If you are better at music than you are at mathematics, for example, one likely explanation is that you have spent more time practicing music. Even social sensitivity is

In Garrison Keillor's fictional *Lake Wobegon,* "all the children are above average." Although that description sounds impossible, in one sense it is true: Everyone is above average at something. A given individual may excel at mathematics, dancing, piano playing, juggling, poetry, cooking, or whatever.

largely a learned, or crystallized, skill (Lee, Wong, Day, Maxwell, & Thorpe, 2000). The fluid versus crystallized distinction already acknowledges that people can be good at one skill and not so good at another because of practice.

Sternberg's Triarchic Theory of Intelligence

Regardless of exactly why *g* emerges or what it means, we often need to know about more than general overall ability. For example, many children labeled "learning disabled" have serious difficulties on one or two kinds of skills while performing at an average or above-average level on others. To help these children, psychologists and teachers want to determine exactly

According to Howard Gardner, we have many intelligences, including mathematical ability, artistic skill, muscle skills, and musical abilities.

why a child is struggling (Conners & Schulte, 2002; Das, 2002).

Spearman's concept of intelligence has been called "monarchic" because it proposes *g* as a "monarch" that rules over the more specialized abilities. Robert Sternberg (1985) attempted to go beyond this view by proposing a **triarchic theory** that deals with *three aspects of intelligence: (a) cognitive processes, (b) identifying situations that require intelligence, and (c) using intelligence in the external world.* He tried to analyze the cognitive processes into smaller components. For example, he suggested that when solving certain kinds of problems we go through several stages, including encoding the information, drawing inferences, mapping relationships, and applying the knowledge. If so, it might make sense for intelligence tests to measure each of these processes separately. The goal was an intelligence test that had some theoretical relationship to cognitive psychology. Unfortunately, when Sternberg tried to develop tests of encoding, inferring, mapping, and so forth, he found that all the measures correlated fairly highly with each other (Deary, 2002). In other words he had rediscovered *g*.

Since then, Sternberg has explored other possible distinctions among types of intelligence. He has argued that we have at least three types of intelligence: *analytical* (or academic), *creative* (planning approaches to new problems), and *practical* (actually doing something). He has criticized standard IQ tests for concentrating only on analytical intelligence. Sternberg has tried to develop new tests that tap creative and practical aspects as well. An example of an item to measure practical intelligence would be, "Which of the following steps would be most likely to help a young person advance in his or her career . . . ?"

Such items clearly vary from situation to situation and from culture to culture. For example, one test Sternberg and his colleagues (2001) devised for use in rural Kenya included an item about why your baby brother might be crying and suffering from a stomachache. One of the acceptable ("correct") answers is that maybe one of your father's other wives gave your brother the "evil eye"!

Controversy persists regarding the status of creative and practical intelligence. On the one hand, we can all think of people we have known who seem high in academic intelligence but not in creativity or practical intelligence. On the other hand, thinking of a few such examples is not enough; the ques-

tion is whether *in general* analytical intelligence is strongly or weakly correlated with creativity and practical intelligence. Furthermore, measuring creativity and practical intelligence is easier said than done. Consider the example just given about why your baby brother is sick, in which evil eye is an acceptable answer. Sternberg and colleagues call this a test of practical intelligence; others might say it is merely another test of facts that someone has been taught. The difference is that it's a *different* set of facts taught by someone other than a schoolteacher. We would presumably classify it as crystallized intelligence.

Sternberg and his colleagues have argued that their tests of creative and practical intelligence are better predictors of intelligence in everyday life than are standard IQ tests (Sternberg, 2002). However, many other researchers remain unconvinced, arguing as follows (Brody, 2003; Gottfredson, 2003):

- The tests that claim to measure analytical, creative, and practical intelligence produce scores that correlate highly with one another, so it is not clear that they are measuring different processes. Sternberg may have rediscovered *g* again.
- The scores on analytical, creative, and practical tests also correlate highly with the scores on more traditional IQ tests.
- The analytical scores (similar to standard IQ tests) predict people's creative and practical behaviors about as well as scores on the creative and practical tests do. Again, what are claimed to be three different kinds of tests seem to be measuring the same processes.

Table 9.2 summarizes four theories of intelligence.

CONCEPT CHECK ☑

5. What evidence would we need to determine whether music, mathematics, social sensitivity, and so forth are really different kinds of intelligence or just different aspects of a single type? (Check your answer on page 331.)

TABLE 9.2 Four Theories of Intelligence

Theory	Theorist	Key Ideas and Terms
Psychometric approach	Charles Spearman	*g* factor: general reasoning ability *s* factor: specific ability required for a given task
Fluid and crystallized intelligence	Raymond Cattell	Fluid intelligence: solving unfamiliar problems Crystallized intelligence: highly practiced skills
Multiple intelligences	Howard Gardner	Music, social attentiveness, dancing, mathematics, and all other skills that society values
Triarchic theory	Robert Sternberg	Analytical, creative, and practical intelligence

Measuring Something We Don't Fully Understand

The standard IQ tests were devised by trial and error long before most of the discoveries about memory and cognition that we discussed in the last two chapters. We still have only a limited theoretical understanding of intelligence. Can we measure intelligence without understanding it? Possibly so; physicists measured gravity and magnetism long before they understood them theoretically. Maybe psychologists can do the same with intelligence.

Or maybe not. Physicists of the past measured not only gravity and magnetism but also "phlogiston," a substance that they later discovered does not exist. Measuring a poorly understood phenomenon is risky. Many psychologists who are dissatisfied with the current tests are striving toward better ones. However, producing a significantly improved IQ test is not as easy as it may sound.

In the meantime the current tests have both strengths and weaknesses. An IQ test, like any other tool, can be used in constructive or destructive ways. The next module explores ways of evaluating IQ tests and their uses.

Summary

- *Defining intelligence.* The designers of the standard IQ tests defined intelligence simply as the ability to do well in school. Psychologists with a more theoretical interest have defined intelligence by listing the abilities that it includes. (page 323)
- *IQ tests.* The Stanford-Binet and other IQ tests were devised to predict the level of performance in school. (page 324)
- *Wechsler IQ tests.* The Wechsler IQ tests measure separate abilities and therefore identify one's strengths and weaknesses. (page 325)
- *Culture-reduced tests.* Culture-reduced tests such as Raven's Progressive Matrices can be used to test people who are unfamiliar with English. However, every test is based on familiarity with some customs that are more common in one culture than in another. (page 325)
- *g factor.* People's scores on almost any test of "intelligent" abilities correlate positively with scores on other tests. The overlap among tests is referred to as *g*, meaning the general factor in intelligence. (page 326)
- *Possible explanations for g.* Many psychologists believe the *g* factor corresponds to an ability that underlies all kinds of intelligence, such as mental speed or working memory. Another possibility is that all kinds of intellectual abilities correlate with one an-

other because the same growth factors that promote any one of them also support the others. (page 327)
- *Fluid and crystallized intelligence.* Psychologists distinguish between fluid intelligence (a basic reasoning ability that can be applied to any problem, including unfamiliar ones) and crystallized intelligence (acquired abilities to solve familiar types of problems). (page 328)
- *Abilities that make up intelligence.* Psychologists have drawn up different lists of the abilities that make up intelligence. Some define intelligence fairly narrowly in terms of academic skills; others include such abilities as social attentiveness, musical abilities, and motor skills. According to the theory of multiple intelligences, people possess many independent types of intelligence. (page 329)
- *Triarchic theory.* According to Sternberg's triarchic theory, intelligence consists of analytical, creative, and practical abilities. However, testing creative and practical intelligence is difficult, and so far the scores on those kinds of tests seem closely related to analytical intelligence. (page 329)

Answers to Concept Checks

1. The Wechsler tests provide separate scores for different tasks and therefore identify someone's strengths and weaknesses. Raven's Progressive Matrices are fairer for someone who is not a native speaker of English. (page 326)
2. Scores on many different kinds of tests correlate positively with one another. (page 328)
3. Different kinds of intellectual tests may all tap the same underlying ability, such as working memory. Or they may depend on different abilities that tend to develop together because they all depend on the same influences, including health, nutrition, education, and genetics. (page 328)
4. Turing's solution reflected fluid intelligence, a generalized ability that could apply to any topic. The solution provided by a bicycle mechanic reflected crystallized intelligence, an ability developed in a particular area of experience. (page 328)
5. We would need to determine whether ability at each kind of intelligence correlates highly with the others. If they all correlate highly with one another, they are simply different aspects of *g*. If they do not, and if the differences reflect more than just different amounts of practice at different skills, then they are separate kinds of intelligence. (page 330)

Answers to Other Questions in the Module

A. 1. (8); 2. (2); 3. (4) (page 326)

Evaluation of Intelligence Tests

How accurate, useful, and fair are the IQ tests?

Why do some people score higher than others?

Edward Thorndike, a pioneer in the study of both animal and human learning, is often quoted as saying, "If something exists, it exists in some amount. If it exists in some amount, it can be measured." Douglas Detterman (1979) countered, "Anything which exists can be measured incorrectly."

Both quotes apply well to intelligence: If intelligence exists at all, it must be measurable, but it can also be measured incorrectly. The challenge is to evaluate the accuracy, usefulness, and fairness of IQ tests. Because much is at stake here, the conclusions are often controversial.

The Standardization of IQ Tests

In the first module, we considered some of the current IQ tests. To evaluate them, we need to go beyond impressions of whether they look like reasonable tests. To evaluate any test—of IQ, personality, or anything else—we need extensive information about what the test scores mean. This evaluation begins with **standardization,** *the process of establishing rules for administering a test and interpreting the scores.* One of the main steps is to find the **norms,** which are *descriptions of how frequently various scores occur.* Psychologists try to standardize a test on a large sample of people who are as representative as possible of the entire population.

The Distribution of IQ Scores

Binet, Wechsler, and the other pioneers who devised the first IQ tests chose items and arranged the scoring method to establish the mean score at 100, with a standard deviation of 15 for the Wechsler test, as Figure 9.5 shows, and 16 for the Stanford-Binet. (Recall from Chapter 2 that the standard deviation measures the variability of performance. It is small if most scores are close to the mean and large if scores vary widely.) The scores of almost any population approximate a *normal distribution,* or bell-shaped curve, as shown in Figure 9.5; the distribution is symmetrical and most scores are close to the mean.

In any normal distribution, 68% of all people fall within 1 standard deviation above or below the mean

and about 95% are within 2 standard deviations. Someone with a score of 115 on the Wechsler test exceeds the scores of people within 1 standard deviation from the mean, plus all of those more than 1 standard deviation below the mean—a total of 84%, as shown in Figure 9.5. We say that such a person is "in the 84th percentile." Someone with an IQ score of 130 is in the 98th percentile, with a score higher than those of 98% of others.

Psychologists sometimes refer to people more than 2 standard deviations above the mean as "gifted." The cutoff line is arbitrary, as someone with an IQ of 129 is virtually the same as one with an IQ of 130. Indeed, anyone's score fluctuates from one test administration to another, so you might have a gifted score one day and not another. Still, regardless of where we draw the line, some people do stand out as

FIGURE 9.5 The scores on an IQ test form an approximately bell-shaped curve. The curve shown here represents scores on the Wechsler IQ test, with a standard deviation of 15 (15 points above and below the mean, which is 100). The results on the Stanford-Binet test are very similar, except that the standard deviation is 16, so the spread is slightly wider.

exceptionally bright. They learn rapidly without much help, seek to master knowledge, ask deep philosophical questions, and develop new ideas (Winner, 2000).

Psychologists classify people more than 2 standard deviations below the mean as "retarded," "mentally challenged," or some other synonym. Again, the cutoff is arbitrary and many people with lower scores do not seem intellectually impaired. In the United States, the Individuals with Disabilities Education Act requires public schools to provide "free and appropriate" education for all children, regardless of their limitations. Children with mild physical or intellectual disabilities are "mainstreamed" as much as possible—that is, placed in the same classes as other children but given special consideration. The results of mainstreaming have been mixed. On the plus side, some studies have found that children included in mainstream classes develop better language abilities than those in classes limited to children with disabilities (Laws, Byrne, & Buckley, 2000). However, most children with disabilities have few friends, especially as they advance to the later grades (Hall & McGregor, 2000). Unfortunately, we do not know as much as we would like about how to educate people with special needs (Detterman & Thompson, 1997).

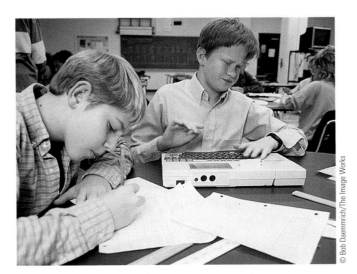

❚ Many children with very low IQ scores can be mainstreamed in regular classes; those with more severe disabilities are taught in special classes.

Restandardizations and the Flynn Effect

Over the years the norms for any test eventually become obsolete. In 1920 a question that asked people to identify Mars was considered difficult because most people knew little about the planets. Today, the same question is easy. Every test needs to be restandardized periodically to make sure it has not become easier or harder.

Those who restandardized the IQ tests eventually realized that they were consistently making the questions more difficult to keep the mean score from rising. That is, *decade by decade, generation by generation, people's raw scores on IQ tests have gradually increased, and test makers have had to make the tests harder to keep the mean score at 100.* This tendency is known as the **Flynn effect,** after the psychologist who first called attention to it (Flynn, 1984, 1999). The results vary among tests, but on some the Flynn effect averages almost 6 IQ points per 10 years. So if you took the same IQ test as your parents, then (assuming your parents are about 25 years older than you) your score might be 15 points higher than theirs. If people of your generation took an IQ test from your grandparents' era, most of you would score in or near the gifted range.

Another consequence is that if you take an older form of an IQ test and then take a new, revised form, your IQ will probably drop! You didn't actually decline; you are just being compared to a higher standard. For most people a few points more or less on an IQ test won't make much difference, but for people at the lower end of the distribution, the loss of a few points might qualify them as mentally retarded, and therefore eligible for government help, but also stick them with an unwanted label (Kanaya, Scullin, & Ceci, 2003).

The Flynn effect—increase in IQ scores over generations—is an amazingly robust effect. It has been reported for a wide variety of IQ tests, including the Wechsler tests (Kaufman, 2001), Raven's Progressive Matrices (Pind, Gunnarsdóttir, & Jóhannesson, 2003), and others (Colom & García-López, 2003). It has occurred in all ethnic groups (Raven, 2000), in every decade since the tests were devised in the early 1900s, and in every country for which we have data, including the United States, Canada, Britain, all of continental Europe, Australia, New Zealand, Israel, Japan, and urban areas of Brazil and China (Flynn, 1998). It has occurred even in rural Kenya, where people live mainly by subsistence farming (Daley, Whaley, Sigman, Espinosa, & Neumann, 2003).

What accounts for the Flynn effect? No one explanation is convincing. Evolution is not a plausible candidate for such a rapid change. Another implausible hypothesis is that people have been getting better at taking tests. The improvement on test scores amounts to almost 30 IQ points over 50 years, and no amount of test-taking practice produces that much benefit. Besides, the IQ improvement is evident in 6-year-old children, who have not had much practice at taking tests, and in rural Kenya, where these kinds of tests are unfamiliar (Daley et al., 2003).

A stronger hypothesis is improved health and nutrition (Lynn, 1998; Sigman & Whaley, 1998). After all, people have been getting taller over the years, presumably because of advances in health and nutrition. However, the improving IQ trends have continued during recent decades, even though many researchers question whether nutrition has continued to improve (Martorell, 1998).

Another possible explanation is better education (W. M. Williams, 1998). However, the IQ gains have been greatest on Raven's Progressive Matrices and other nonverbal tests; they have been weak or nonexistent on the topics taught in school, such as vocabulary, knowledge, and arithmetic (Flynn, 1999). Yet another possibility is exposure to increasing technology, beginning with movies and radio in the early 1900s and progressing through television, video games, and the Internet. These kinds of experience probably stimulate good visuospatial thinking (Neisser, 1997). Even in rural Kenya, the least technological place in which the Flynn effect has been demonstrated, some homes now have television and newspapers (Daley et al., 2003).

The Flynn effect is difficult to explain because it has been so widespread. If we could contrast the times and places where it occurred to others where it did not, we might see a pattern. But if an effect occurs everywhere at all times, finding the cause is difficult.

Another major question is that although IQ test performance has been increasing, actual intelligence may not have been. It is possible to argue that young adults today are somewhat smarter than young adults of previous generations (Howard, 1999; Schooler, 1998). However, a mean increase of 30 IQ points over 50 years is huge. If people really are that much smarter, teachers should have noticed that their classes are full of creative geniuses. Most teachers in Western-culture countries report that today's students seem no more intelligent than those of the past, although a survey reported that teachers in South Korea and Singapore consider their current students more intelligent (Cocodia et al., 2003).

Conversely, if the people of 50 years ago really were the equivalent of those with an IQ of 70 today, then most people back then could barely have taken care of themselves without supervision, and most could not have understood the rules of a sport like baseball or basketball. Flynn (1998) therefore argues that we have seen an increase in IQ scores, but not intelligence, over time. If so, what exactly do IQ scores mean? At a minimum we should beware of comparing two people's scores unless they grew up in the same era and took the same test at about the same time.

Evaluation of Tests

Have you ever complained about a test in school that seemed unfair? *Seeming* unfair doesn't necessarily make a test unfair (and seeming fair doesn't necessarily make it fair). When psychologists want to evaluate the accuracy or fairness of a test, they examine specific kinds of evidence. The main ways of evaluating any test are to check its reliability and validity.

Reliability

The **reliability** of a test is defined as *the repeatability of its scores* (T. B. Rogers, 1995). A reliable test produces consistent, repeatable results. To determine the reliability of a test, psychologists calculate a correlation coefficient. (Recall from Chapter 2 that a correlation coefficient measures how accurately we can use one measurement to predict another.) Psychologists may test the same people twice, either with the same test or with equivalent versions of it, and compare the two sets of scores. Or they may compare the scores on the first and second halves of the test or the scores on the test's odd-numbered and even-numbered items. If all items measure approximately the same thing, one set of scores should correlate highly with the other set. Any correlation coefficient can theoretically range from +1 to –1. In the real world, however, a reliability coefficient is always either zero or positive. A negative reliability would mean that most people who score high the first time they take the test do worse than average the second time. That pattern simply never happens. Figure 9.6 illustrates **test–retest reliability**, *the correlation between scores on a first test and a retest.*

FIGURE 9.6 On a test with high reliability, people who score high the first time will score high when they take the test again. On a test with low reliability, scores fluctuate randomly.

If a test's reliability is perfect (+1), the person who scores the highest on the first test will also score highest on the retest, the person who scores second highest on the first test will also score second highest on the retest, and so forth. If the reliability is 0, scores vary randomly from one test to another. The reliability of the WISC–III has been measured at .96 (Wechsler, 1991), and the reliabilities of the Stanford-Binet, Progressive Matrices, and other commonly used intelligence tests are also above .9.

Whatever it is that IQ tests measure, it is reasonably stable over time for most individuals. Many studies have found correlations over .9 for people taking the same test at two times 10 years apart, and one study found that IQ scores at age 11 correlate .63 with scores at age 77 (Deary, Whalley, Lemmon, Crawford, & Starr, 2000).

CRITICAL THINKING:
A STEP FURTHER
Reliability

Try to imagine a test with 0 reliability. What kind of questions would such a test include?

CONCEPT CHECK

6. I have just devised a new "intelligence test." I measure your intelligence by dividing the length of your head by its width and then multiplying by 100. Would that test be reliable?

7. Most students find that their scores on any standardized test increase the second time they take it. Does the improvement indicate that the test is unreliable? (Check your answers on page 346.)

Validity

A test's **validity** is *a determination of how well it measures what it claims to measure.* One type of validity is **content validity.** We say that a test has high content validity if *its items accurately represent the information that the test is meant to measure.* For example, a test for a driver's license has content validity if it includes important laws and regulations that pertain to driving. A licensing examination for psychologists would have high content validity if it tested information that a practicing psychologist needs to know. If you took a test in class that concentrated on material that was included in neither the lectures nor the reading, that test would have low content validity.

A second type of validity is **construct validity.** A test has construct validity if *what it measures corresponds to a theoretical construct.* For an IQ test to have construct validity, older children should as a rule answer more questions correctly than younger children do. It should also have the property of being independent of eyesight and motor coordination; people with physical limitations should be able to get scores similar to other people. A test of anxiety would have construct validity if the scores increased in situations likely to make people nervous. In short, a test has good construct validity if the scores depend on factors we believe to be important and not on factors we regard as unimportant (Messick, 1995).

Predictive validity, a third type, is *the ability of a test's scores to predict some real-world performance.* An IQ test has predictive validity if it correctly predicts how well a student will perform in school. As with reliability, psychologists measure predictive validity by a correlation coefficient. To determine the predictive validity of an IQ test, psychologists determine how well the scores predict students' grades. A validity of +1 would mean that the scores perfectly predicted performance, and a validity of 0 would mean that the scores were worthless as predictors. A major problem in predicting school performance is that our measure of school performance—grades—is itself an inaccurate measurement of performance. The less reliable the grading system, the harder it is for anything else to correlate with it.

The predictive validities of most IQ tests range from about .3 to .6, varying from one school to another (Anastasi, 1988; Siegler & Richards, 1982). As a rule Raven's Progressive Matrices scores predict mathematics grades better than language grades (Pind et al., 2003). However, success in school depends not only on students' academic skills but also on their motivation, persistence, and other personality attributes

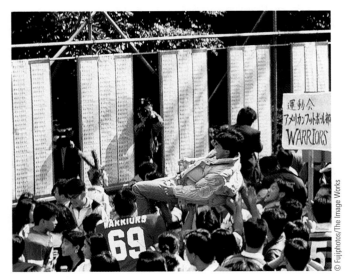

▮ In some countries test scores determine a student's future almost irrevocably. Students who perform well are almost assured of future success; those who perform poorly will have very limited opportunities.

that are hard to measure—as well as what courses they take and what standards their teachers use. IQ scores (as well as SAT scores) correlate fairly well with grades for students in a particular course with a particular instructor, but if we combine results for students in different courses, graded by different standards, IQ scores no longer make useful predictions (Humphreys & Stark, 2002).

Validity of Test Scores for Other Purposes

IQ tests were designed to predict school performance. Later results showed that they predicted other outcomes as well, to the surprise of almost everyone, including the authors of the tests.

Critics of IQ tests have argued that the tests measure only "book learning" that has little or no relevance to real life. Of course, if book learning really had no important relevance to real life, there would be no point in education. IQ scores correlate positively with more aspects of life than one might guess. People with high scores on standard intelligence tests average fewer automobile accidents than others do (O'Toole, 1990) and are less likely to suffer posttraumatic stress disorder (Vasterling et al., 2002). They do better than others at reading maps, understanding order forms, reading a bus schedule, and taking their medicines correctly (Gottfredson, 2002a). Many of these correlations are only small to moderate; nevertheless, *g* correlates at least somewhat with a wide variety of important outcomes.

(As always, we should hesitate about reaching conclusions from correlational data. For example, do people with high IQ scores avoid automobile accidents by driving "intelligently," or do high IQ scores help them get better jobs so they drive safer cars?)

IQ tests also have some validity for predicting success on a variety of jobs, and if combined with other information, such as a structured interview or a work sample, they produce a validity greater than .6 (Schmidt & Hunter, 1998). According to Linda Gottfredson (2002b, pp. 25, 27), "The general mental ability factor—*g*—is the best single predictor of job performance . . . [It] enhances performance in all domains of work." According to Frank Schmidt and John Hunter (1981, p. 1128), "Professionally developed cognitive ability tests are valid predictors of performance on the job . . . for all jobs . . . in all settings." That is probably an overstatement. (It could hardly be an understatement!) For example, if you wanted to predict who would have a successful career as a singer or professional athlete, I doubt you would bother to give applicants an IQ test. For some aspects of job performance, personality factors such as conscientiousness are important predictors, although difficult to measure (Wagner, 1997). Still, for many jobs, using some type of cognitive test score to select employees

increases the chances that those who are hired will learn their jobs quickly and succeed at them.

The problem for society is that, on the average, people of European or Asian ancestry get higher test scores than those of African ancestry, so relying heavily on test scores conflicts with the goals of diversity in the workplace and equal employment opportunity for all groups. Employers have tried many strategies to deal with this issue, such as other types of tests, but so far no test has appreciably decreased the ethnic difference in scores while maintaining high validity for predicting performance. Giving some coaching on test-taking skills has narrowed the ethnic difference in some studies and deserves further research (Sackett, Schmitt, Ellingson, & Kabin, 2001).

Special Problems in Measuring Validity

Measuring the validity of a test can be tricky. For example, consider data for the Graduate Record Examination (GRE), a test taken by applicants to most graduate schools in the United States. Grades for first-year graduate students in physics correlated .13 with their GRE quantitative scores and .19 with their verbal scores. That is, their verbal scores were better predictors than their quantitative scores. For first-year students in English, the pattern was reversed. Their grades correlated .29 with their quantitative scores and .23 with their verbal scores (Educational Testing Service, 1994). These scores surprise most people because physics is such a quantitative field and English is such a verbal field.

How can we explain the results? Simply. Almost all graduate students in physics have about the same (very high) score on the quantitative test, and almost all English graduate students have the same (very high) score on the verbal test. If almost all the students in a department have nearly the same score, their scores cannot predict which students will succeed. A test has a high predictive validity only for a population whose scores vary over a substantial range.

CONCEPT CHECK ☑

8. Can a test have high reliability and low validity? Can a test have low reliability and high validity?

9. If physics graduate departments tried admitting some students with low quantitative scores on the GRE and English departments tried admitting some students with low verbal scores, what would happen to the predictive validity of the tests?

10. Would you expect the SAT scores to show higher predictive validity at a college with extremely competitive admissions standards or at a college that admits almost every applicant? (Check your answers on page 346.)

TABLE 9.3 Evaluating Intelligence Tests

Reliability	Validity	Utility	Bias
How consistent are the same person's scores?	How well does the test measure what it claims to measure?	How useful is the test for a particular purpose?	Do test scores make equally accurate predictions for all groups?
	Content: Do the test items represent the pertinent information?		
	Construct: Do the results match theoretical expectations?		
	Prediction: Do the test scores predict real-world performance?		

Utility

In addition to reliability and validity, a good test should have utility. **Utility** is defined as *usefulness for a practical purpose.* In other words "is it worth the bother?" A test can be reliable and valid but still not be very useful. For example, one college required all applicants to take both the general part of the Scholastic Assessment Test (SAT) and the SAT achievement tests. Grades correlated with both of the scores (indicating validity), but because the two scores correlated highly with each other, it was possible to predict grades just as well from one as from a combination of both (Baron & Norman, 1992). If, for example, the college required the achievement tests, then the general test had no utility.

Table 9.3 summarizes the criteria for evaluating intelligence tests, including bias, which we consider later in this chapter.

Interpreting Fluctuations in Scores

Suppose on the first test in your psychology course you get 94% correct. On the second test (which was equally difficult), your score is only 88%. Does that score indicate that you studied harder for the first test than for the second test? Not necessarily. Whenever you take tests that are not perfectly reliable, your scores are likely to fluctuate. The lower the reliability, the greater the fluctuation.

When people lose sight of this fact, they sometimes draw unwarranted conclusions. In one study Harold Skeels (1966) tested infants in an orphanage and identified those with the lowest IQ scores. He then had those infants transferred to an institution that provided more personal attention. Several years later, most of them showed major increases in their IQ scores. Should we conclude, as many psychologists did, that the extra attention improved the children's IQ performances? Not necessarily (Longstreth, 1981). IQ tests for infants have low reliability. In other words the scores fluctuate widely from one time to another,

even from one day to the next. If someone selects infants with low scores and retests them later, their mean IQ score is almost certain to improve simply because the scores had nowhere to go but up.

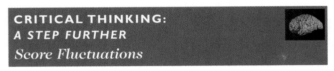

CRITICAL THINKING: A STEP FURTHER
Score Fluctuations

What would be the proper control group for the study by Skeels?

Heredity, Environment, and IQ Scores

Why do some people score higher than others on IQ tests? The two obvious possibilities are differences in heredity and environment. The British scholar Francis Galton (1869/1978)[1] was the first to argue for the importance of heredity. His evidence was that politicians, judges, and other eminent and distinguished people generally had distinguished relatives. I assume you will quickly see why this evidence does not justify a conclusion about the importance of genetics.

Let's consider the evidence we have today. Although the evidence is certainly stronger than it was in Galton's time, it still is not overwhelming.

Family Resemblances

Figure 9.7, based on a literature review by Thomas Bouchard and Matthew McGue (1981), shows the correlations of IQ scores for people with various degrees of genetic relationship. These data are based mostly on middle-class European American families.

---

[1]Remember, a slash like this indicates original publication date and the date of a revised printing. It does not represent Galton's birth and death dates.

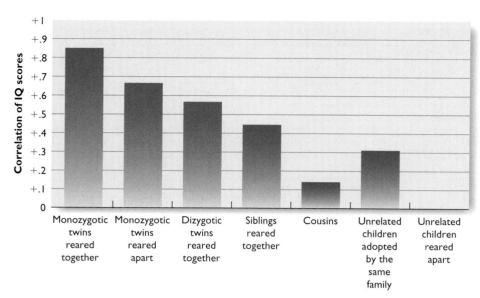

FIGURE 9.7 Mean correlations for the IQs of children with various degrees of genetic and environmental similarity. (Siblings are nontwin children in the same family.) *(Reprinted with permission from "Familial Studies of Intelligence: A Review," by T. Bouchard and M. McGue, Science, 1981, 212, 1055-1059. Copyright © 1981 American Association for the Advancement of Science.)*

Because no IQ test has perfect reliability, someone taking the test on two occasions will get slightly different scores. The scores of monozygotic (identical) twins correlate with each other about .85, not much less than the reliability of the test (McGue & Bouchard, 1998). Monozygotic twins resemble each other not only in overall IQ but also in tests of more specific skills such as working memory and processing speed (Luciano et al., 2001); they continue to resemble each other throughout life, even beyond age 80 (Petrill et al., 1998). Fraternal twins and nontwin siblings also resemble each other, but not as closely as monozygotic twins (Bishop et al., 2003). The greater similarity between monozygotic twins implies a probable genetic basis.

Identical Twins Reared Apart

In Figure 9.7 note the high correlation between identical twins reared apart. That is, identical twins who have been adopted by different parents and reared in separate environments strongly resemble each other in IQ scores (Bouchard & McGue, 1981; Farber, 1981). That resemblance implies a genetic contribution to IQ.

However, the results may overstate the genetic contribution. Consider this athletic analogy: Suppose identical twins separated at birth both show some athletic ability early in life for genetic reasons. Because of their early success, other people encourage them to develop their skills, they become even more successful, receive even more coaching and encouragement, and so on.

Eventually, they might both emerge as great athletes, and their similar outcomes would imply a strong genetic basis. Indeed, there was a genetic basis at first, but the environment magnified it (Dickens & Flynn, 2001). The same holds for intelligence: Twins who show early promise will receive encouragement that magnifies that promise, so what appears to be a hereditary effect also depends on the environment.

A further problem is that most twin studies rely primarily on data from middle-class families. Studies of impoverished families find much less evidence for a genetic influence; that is, identical twins in those families resemble each other no more than fraternal twins do (Turkheimer, Haley, Waldron, D'Onofrio, & Gottesman, 2003). The probable meaning is this: As far as IQ development goes, the difference between a pretty good environment and a very good one has only a small influence. However, the difference between a pretty bad environment and a very bad one has a powerful influence. When children grow up in a terrible environment, their genetics may not matter; their chance for intellectual success is limited.

Twins and Single Births

In Figure 9.7 notice that fraternal twins resemble each other more closely than single-birth siblings do. This finding, consistent across several studies but not all (Bishop et al., 2003), suggests an influence from being born at the same time. Presumably, twins have extra resemblance because they shared a greater amount of their environment, including their prenatal environment. Sharing prenatal environment means having the same nutrition, body temperature, alcohol or tobacco effects, and so forth during key moments in brain development (Devlin, Daniels, & Roeder, 1997).

Adopted Children

In Figure 9.7 note the positive correlation between unrelated children adopted into the same family. This correlation indicates an influence from their shared environment. However, because this correlation is lower than the correlation between siblings (brothers or sisters), the resemblances among siblings must be due partly to genetics (or prenatal environment), not just to growing up together.

The IQs of adopted children correlate moderately well with those of their adoptive parents while the children are young. As they grow older, their IQ scores gradually correlate more with those of their biological parents and less with those of their adoptive parents (Loehlin, Horn, & Willerman, 1989; Plomin, Fulker, Corley, & DeFries, 1997) (see Figure 9.8).

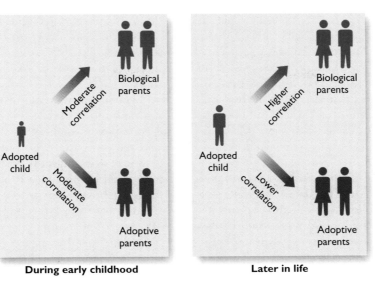

FIGURE 9.8 As adopted children grow older, their IQs begin to correlate more strongly with those of their biological parents.

These results seem to imply a genetic influence from the biological parents. However, another interpretation is possible. Many of the low-IQ parents who put their children up for adoption probably do not provide good prenatal care. The mother may not get good prenatal nutrition, may smoke and drink, and may in other ways put her infant at risk for low IQ for reasons other than genetics. If so, the child's IQ could resemble the biological mother's IQ for nongenetic reasons.

CONCEPT CHECK ✅

11. What are the main types of evidence supporting a genetic contribution to individual differences in IQ scores? What are some reasons to suspect that the evidence overstates the role of genetics? (Check your answers on page 347.)

Gene Identification

The strongest line of evidence would be a demonstration that different forms of particular genes are associated with higher or lower IQ scores. The Human Genome Project and related research now make it possible to seek exactly that kind of evidence.

The outline of the research is to compare people varying in their intellectual performances and determine whether any gene is more common among those with higher scores. Similar research has been done with laboratory animals, comparing fast learners to slow learners. Dozens of genes have been found to correlate with human performance, and dozens in mice, some of them the same genes that were identified in humans. However, each of the identified genes has only a small effect (Goldberg et al., 2003; Morely & Montgomery,

2001; Plomin et al., 2001). So far no researcher has found a "genius" gene, and it appears that intelligence depends on the combined influence of many genes, as well as of course environmental influences. The task now is to learn more about *how* various genes contribute and *which* environmental influences are most important.

The heritability of variations in IQ scores does not mean that people are somehow limited by the abilities they had at birth. Obviously, if we gave every child either an extremely good or extremely bad environment, we could raise or lower all their IQ scores. The Flynn effect, regardless of its cause, indicates that some influence has raised IQ performances for a whole generation of people. Positive heritability of IQ scores merely means that if children grow up in the same environment, some do better than others, and part of that difference relates to genetics.

A variety of programs have attempted to take children from extremely deprived homes and give them special intervention to improve their intellectual development. People who hoped that a brief intervention might lead to huge long-term gains have been disappointed. Just as no one gene produces a huge effect, no single environmental intervention does either. However, intensive programs occupying many hours per week for several years do produce significant, lasting benefits (Ramey & Ramey, 1998).

Gender and Ethnic Differences in IQ Scores

Binet and the other pioneers in IQ testing discovered that girls tend to do better than boys on certain kinds of language tasks, especially verbal fluency. Boys, however, tend to do better than girls on visuospatial rotations. By loading the test with one type of item, they could have produced results showing that girls are smarter than boys or that boys are smarter than girls. Instead, they balanced these two types of items to ensure that the mean scores of both females and males would be 100, and they continue to be equal today (Colom, Juan-Espinosa, Abad, & Garciá, 2000).

Males show greater individual variability. Thus, the data on a variety of intellectual measures, especially relating to mathematics, show a higher percentage of males than females at the very top of the range but also at the very bottom, even though the averages for males and females are about the same (Halpern, 1997; Hedges & Nowell, 1995). (*Why* males are more variable, we do not know.)

Ethnic groups in the United States also differ in their mean performances on IQ tests (Herrnstein & Murray, 1994). One problem when dealing with these data is that any group—such as African Americans—includes a diverse population who vary among themselves both genetically and environmentally. Ordinarily, researchers classify people simply by asking them how they classify themselves, and the resulting categories are at best only partly satisfactory from either a biological or sociological standpoint. Furthermore, a growing number of Americans describe themselves as ethnically "mixed."

With these limitations in mind, here are the data for people in the United States (Neisser et al., 1996; Suzuki & Valencia, 1997): *Please bear in mind that all these data reflect the means for entire populations. Each ethnic group includes many individuals with extremely high and low scores. The data do not justify prejudices or assumptions about any given individual.*

The mean score of European Americans as a whole is about 100, with the Jewish subpopulation averaging a few points higher. The mean score for Latinos/Latinas is in the 90s, but many of them are first-generation immigrants to the United States who are hampered by language problems. The means for East Asians (those of Japanese, Chinese, or Korean descent) vary from one sample to another, either about 100 or a few points higher. The mean for African Americans used to be 85 but has risen over the last several decades to about 90. From about 1970 to 1990, African Americans' SAT scores, vocabulary scores, and other achievement scores increased dramatically, cutting the gap by about one third between African Americans and European Americans (Grissmer, Williamson, Kirby, & Berends, 1998; Hauser, 1998; Huang & Hauser, 1998). The reasons are unknown, but possibilities include improved socioeconomic status, better health and nutrition, better education of both children and their parents, smaller family size, and possibly decreased smoking and drinking by the mothers during pregnancy.

Are IQ Tests Biased?

One often-proposed explanation for group differences in IQ scores is that the tests are biased. That is, ethnic groups do not actually differ; they just appear to differ because of unfair or inappropriate tests. Presumably, according to this viewpoint, a better test would indicate no group differences.

The first point to emphasize is a difficult one: The fact that one group tends to do better than another on some test does not, by itself, demonstrate that the test is biased. Possibly the test is biased, but maybe the groups really do differ. If a test correctly reports a real difference, we should not blame the test.

Bias means a distortion or inaccuracy of evaluation. To determine whether or not a test is **biased** against a group, psychologists determine *whether the test underestimates the group's performance.* Consider two examples in which a test does show bias: First, the Stanford-Binet and Wechsler IQ tests *are* biased against non-English speaking immigrants to the United States. In the long run, after immigrants have learned the language, they usually succeed beyond what their initial test scores would indicate. That is, the test scores underestimate their eventual performance.

As a second example, women who enter college or graduate school after age 25 generally receive better

▮ Many immigrants to the United States settle in ethnic neighborhoods where they can use their original language. Most first-generation immigrants do not score highly on English-language intelligence tests; as a rule their children and grandchildren get higher scores.

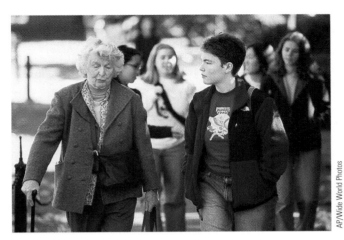

▌ Women who return to school after age 25 usually get better grades than their test scores would predict. That is, the tests are "biased" against them in the technical sense. The test scores underpredict their performance.

grades than their test scores predict (Swinton, 1987). Therefore, the tests are biased against them, even though in fact their test scores are usually pretty good. To say that the tests are biased against them means that a given test score means something different for a 25-year-old woman than for a 20-year-old. Why do the older women get better grades than their test scores predict? Here are three hypotheses: (a) Because they have been away from school for a while, their test-taking skills are rusty. (b) Anyone who returns to school at that point must have strong motivation, whereas some younger students do not. (c) A few extra years of experiences give them some advantages.

Repeating for emphasis: To determine whether a test is biased against any group, psychologists must find out whether such people perform better in school or college than the test scores predict. Psychologists try to identify bias both in individual test items and in the test as a whole.

Evaluating Possible Bias in Single Test Items

An individual item on a test is considered biased if it is among the easiest for one group but relatively difficult for another (Schmitt & Dorans, 1990). That pattern would suggest the item tapped information that was more readily available for one group than the other. For example, Figure 9.9, an item that once appeared on the Scholastic Assessment Test (SAT), diagrams an American football field and asks for the ratio of the distance between the goal lines to the distance between the sidelines. For men this was one of the easiest items on the test. In contrast many women missed it, including some of the brightest women who missed almost no other questions.

The reason was that some women had so little interest in football that they did not know which were the goal lines and which were the sidelines. Therefore, the publishers of the SAT removed the item from the test. Standardized tests such as the SAT are routinely purged of any items with demonstrable bias against a particular group.

Evaluating Possible Bias in a Test as a Whole

By definition a biased test is one that systematically underestimates (underpredicts) the performance of a group. If an IQ test is indeed biased against African Americans, for example, then African Americans who score, say, 100 really deserve better than the score indicates and will do better in school than European Americans with the same score.

However, the evidence indicates that African American students with a given IQ score generally do about the same in school as do European Americans with the same score (Jensen, 1980). The same is true for SAT scores (McCornack, 1983). A few exceptions have been reported, but

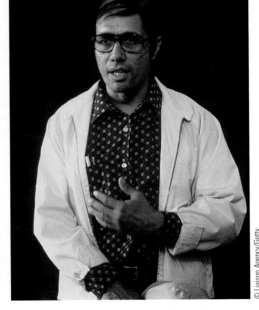

▌ "Students will rise to your level of expectation," says Jaime Escalante (left), the high school teacher portrayed by Edward James Olmos (right) in *Stand and Deliver*. The movie chronicles Escalante's talent for inspiring average students to excel in calculus.

The diagram above represents a football field. What is the ratio of the distance between the goal lines to the distance between the sidelines?

a. 1.89
b. 1.53
c. 0.53
d. 5.3
e. 53

FIGURE 9.9 This item was eliminated from the SAT when researchers determined that it was biased against women. Some women who did very well on the rest of the test did not know which were the goal lines and which were the sidelines.

only with small samples (Lawlor, Richman, & Richman, 1997). The unpleasant fact is that over many years European American students have usually had better grades in school than African Americans. The difference in IQ scores correlates with that difference in performance.

In recent decades African American students have been doing somewhat better than before on the tests and getting better grades also (Grissmer et al., 1998; Hauser, 1998). The fact that grades and test scores improved simultaneously supports the idea that the tests are predicting performance validly.

Saying the tests are unbiased does *not* imply that the differences are rooted in genetics. It merely implies that whatever causes African American students to do less well in school also leads them to do less well on the standardized tests. Researchers still need to uncover the underlying reasons.

CONCEPT CHECK ☑

12. A test of driving skills includes items requiring good vision. People with visual impairments score lower than people with good vision. Is the test therefore biased against people with visual impairments?

13. Suppose that on some new IQ test tall people generally get higher scores than short people. How could we determine whether this test is biased against short people? (Check your answers on page 347.)

Test Anxiety and Stereotype Threat

Many explanations have been proposed for the ethnic difference in test scores. Poverty is no doubt one contributor, but it cannot be the only one. That is, on the average, impoverished European Americans score higher than impoverished African Americans, and middle-class European Americans score higher than middle-class African Americans (Herrnstein & Murray, 1994). (There is also the difficulty of determining to what extent poverty leads to low IQ and to what extent low IQ leads to poverty.) The ethnic difference is also not attributable to specific kinds of information. The ethnic difference is at least as large on the Raven's Progressive Matrices, a nonverbal test, as on more fact-loaded tests such as the Wechsler or Stanford-Binet (Flynn, 1999).

A more promising hypothesis is that many participants are nervous about the testing procedure. In some studies (though not all), children scored somewhat higher if they were tested by an interviewer of their own ethnic group (Kim, Baydar, & Greek, 2003). Because most of the psychologists administering IQ tests are European Americans, many African American students may feel uncomfortable or may not put out a full effort.

Claude Steele introduced the concept of **stereotype threat**, *people's perceived risk that they might do something that supports an unfavorable stereotype about their group.* African American students who take an IQ test may fear not only that a poor score would reflect badly on themselves personally but also that it may support prejudices against African Americans in general. They may become distracted and upset, or they may decide not to try. Studies have found that African American students perform worse if they are told that a test measures intellectual ability than if they are told it is just an exploratory study unrelated to their abilities (Steele & Aronson, 1995). Three later studies found that calling the attention of Asian American girls or women to their status as females slightly depressed their performance on a math test, presumably because of the stereotype that females are not strong at math. However, focusing their attention on being Asian (who stereotypically do well at math) improved their math performance in two of the three studies (Ambady, Shih, Kim, & Pittinsky, 2001; Cheryan & Bodenhausen, 2000; Shih, Pittinsky, & Ambady, 1999).

Genetics?

The measurable effects of poverty, test anxiety, and stereotype threat on IQ performance are real but not large enough to account for the entire ethnic difference, at least not convincingly. The most controversial hypothesis is that the difference between European Americans and African Americans might relate partly to genetic differences. On the one hand, it seems worthwhile to discuss this issue to show the possibility of evaluating the evidence carefully, even on a difficult, emotionally charged question. Also, whether we discuss the issue or not, many people do form strong opinions, and if you are going to have an opinion, you should know the relevant evidence. On the other hand, unfortunately, there *isn't* much good evidence on this issue, and much of the evidence that does exist is old.

In a controversial book, *The Bell Curve,* Richard Herrnstein and Charles Murray (1994) made the arguments listed below. Other distinguished investigators largely concur with the first four points; the main disagreement is how likely they consider the fifth point (Arvey et al., 1994; Neisser et al., 1996).

1. IQ tests, imperfect as they are, reliably measure *something*, regardless of whether we choose to call it intelligence.
2. Whatever that something is, it is neither all-important nor trivial. It correlates positively, though not always highly, with many valued outcomes. That is, the IQ tests have some validity.
3. Measured differences among groups are not illusions that we can attribute to faulty tests. So far no one has developed a valid IQ test that does not show a gap between African Americans and European Americans.
4. Within the European or European American population, where most of the research has concentrated, genetic differences appear responsible for *some* of the variance in IQ scores, although *how much* is uncertain. Important environmental influences include the obvious ones such as education but also early nutrition, exposure to lead and other toxins, and whether the mother drank alcohol during pregnancy.
5. IQ differences among ethnic groups may also reflect a combination of environmental and genetic differences.

The fifth point, if taken literally, should hardly be a point of disagreement: The ethnic differences *may* reflect some combination of environmental and genetic differences. (After all, they *must* reflect at least one or the other!) However, Herrnstein and Murray implied, without actually saying so, that they suspected genetic influences account for a significant portion of the ethnic difference. Many other psychologists disagree. The fact that genetic factors account for some of the IQ variation within the middle-class European American population implies nothing about the difference between European Americans and African Americans. After all, remember the Flynn effect: Variations in test performance among people of a

particular generation have something to do with genetics, but the difference between one generation and the next, though large, is *not* due to genetics.

Let's consider two of the best-designed studies concerning ethnic differences in IQ test performance.

CRITICAL THINKING:
WHAT'S THE EVIDENCE?
Environmental Contributors to Ethnic Differences

If the gap between African American and European American IQ scores depends on the difference in environment, then children of different ethnic backgrounds growing up in the same environment should do equally well. Researchers examined African American children who were adopted by European American families. (European American children are very rarely adopted by African American families.) Do African American and European American children adopted in the same family really have "the same" environment? In some ways they do but in other ways they do not. We shall return to this issue after examining the results.

Hypothesis If the IQ differences between groups is partly due to environmental differences, then African American children reared by European American families should perform better on IQ tests than do most other African American children.

Method Sandra Scarr and Richard Weinberg (1976) studied European American families in Minnesota that had adopted African American children or ethnically mixed children (one African American and one European American parent).

Many of the adopting parents also had biological children of their own, and many had adopted other children of various ethnic backgrounds. The investigators tested the IQs of the children and the adopting parents and tested them again 10 years later (Scarr & Weinberg, 1976; Weinberg, Scarr, & Waldman, 1992).

Results Figure 9.10 shows the mean scores for only those individuals who were tested both times. All the means were lower at the second test because of changes in the IQ test itself. (As mentioned earlier, psychologists restandardize the test every few years, consistently making it more difficult.)

Interpretation The key data are the mean scores for the adopted children. The adopted European American children scored higher than ethnically mixed adopted children, who in turn scored higher than adopted children with two African American parents. However, the ethnically mixed adopted children scored near 100 (slightly higher on the first test and

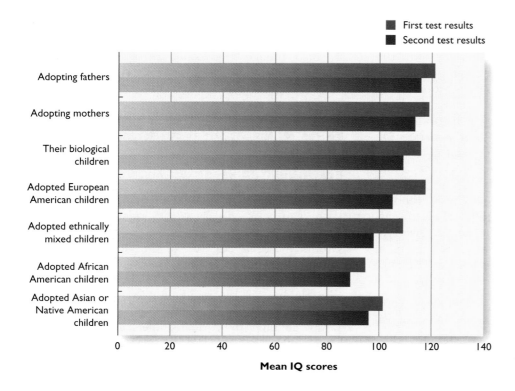

■ First test results
■ Second test results

Adopting fathers

Adopting mothers

Their biological children

Adopted European American children

Adopted ethnically mixed children

Adopted African American children

Adopted Asian or Native American children

0   20   40   60   80   100   120   140

Mean IQ scores

FIGURE 9.10 During childhood African American children adopted by upper-middle-class European American families showed IQ scores well above the national average for African Americans, but 10 years later they showed only small benefits.

slightly lower on the second). Adopted children with two African American parents scored a mean of 95 on the first test and 89 ten years later.

These results are not easy to interpret (e.g., Levin, 1994; Waldman, Weinberg, & Scarr, 1994). Rearing African American children in upper-middle-class European American families may have raised their IQs in childhood, but not much by adolescence. (The

■ If ethnic differences in IQ are largely the result of environmental differences, African American children adopted by middle-class European American families should score higher on average than similar children reared in African American homes. The results of research have been hard to interpret because many of the children studied were adopted relatively late.

mean IQ for African Americans in Minnesota at the time was about 88.)

If these data suggest only a small environmental influence, we need to ask again, "Do children of different ethnic backgrounds growing up in the same family have the same environment?" In two major ways they do not: First, they had different prenatal and early postnatal environments, and many of the biological mothers may not have provided good nutrition and health care. Second, African American children, even those adopted in European American families, are probably not treated the same as European American children by their teachers, schoolmates, and others. In short, although this study found little evidence for the importance of living with a European American middle-class family, it does not consider the role of other environmental influences.

CRITICAL THINKING:
WHAT'S THE EVIDENCE?
Hereditary Contributors to Ethnic Differences

Whereas the first study set out to demonstrate environmental influences, the second was an attempt to measure genetic influences.

Hypothesis Few African Americans have 100% African ancestry. If heredity is responsible for any part of the race difference in IQ performance, then

▌ Variations in skin darkness are an inaccurate indicator of degree of African ancestry. Blood-typing provides a somewhat better indicator, although it is also far from certain.

Blacks with more European ancestry should obtain higher IQ scores than those with less.

Method   Determining a child's ethnic ancestry is difficult. Most family trees do not go back far enough, and skin color is not a good indicator. (Even in Africa skin darkness varies from one region to another.) Blood-typing provides a better estimate, although it is still far from perfect.

The investigators (Scarr, Pakstis, Katz, & Barker, 1977) examined 362 African American children in Philadelphia, testing different blood factors such as the familiar ABO blood types, the Rh factor, the Duffy factor, and 11 others. Certain blood factors are more common in Europe than in Africa, and vice versa. For example, type B blood is present in only 9% of Europeans but in 21% of Africans. Few if any Europeans have Duffy type A– B– blood, whereas 94% of Africans do. By comparing each child's blood factors to the frequency of those blood factors in both Europe and Africa, the investigators estimated the degree of European ancestry for each child. Then the investigators correlated their estimates of European ancestry with the children's performances on Raven's Progressive Matrices and four other tests.

Results   The investigators tried several methods of weighting the importance of various blood factors to estimate European and African ancestry. Regardless of which method they used, however, they found virtually a zero correlation between estimates of European ancestry and measures of performance.

Interpretation   If hereditary factors were a major contributor to ethnic differences in IQ scores, we would predict that the greater the amount of European ancestry, the higher the IQ scores. The absence of such a correlation indicates that heredity contributes either nothing to the ethnic differences or too little to measure by this method.

Where does all this information leave us with regard to ethnic differences in IQ scores? These two studies, well designed and with reasonably large samples, found little clear evidence for environmental influences (first study) and no evidence for genetic influences (second study). Both studies are decades old now, and no one has reported any attempt to replicate either of them. Given the weakness of the evidence, it seems fair to say that those who express strong opinions on this issue probably formed those opinions on some basis other than scientific evidence.

As James Flynn (1999) has pointed out, people in general have improved their IQ test performance by about 30 points over the last 50 years, and we cannot explain that difference. So we should not be too amazed that we have not yet explained the smaller differences among ethnic groups.

CONCEPT CHECK ☑

14. Suppose the researchers had found that those African American children with higher amounts of estimated European ancestry had higher IQ scores than other African American children. What conclusion would those data have supported? (Check your answer on page 347.)

IN CLOSING

Difficult Issues

This chapter began with an analogy between testing intelligence and testing athletic ability. Intelligence testing began for practical purposes and continues, despite its difficulties, for practical purposes. Just as a coach tries to choose the best players for an athletic team, colleges and employers try to choose the applicants who will learn the fastest. If people are going to make those judgments—as they no doubt will—we want them to evaluate intelligence accurately and fairly. For that reason psychological researchers carefully standardize tests and measure their reliability and validity. Further research can lead to better tests; in the meantime researchers identify the strengths, weaknesses, and limitations of currently available tests.

The most heated controversies relate to ethnic differences in performance. Research on this topic has not been popular. Some psychologists avoid it because they fear that their results might support racism or other undesirable ends (Reiss, 2000). Others avoid it because the research is difficult, probably more difficult than it is worth. However, some closely related topics do deserve attention. First, if genes do have an influence, *how* do they exert their influence? For example, as we shall consider at the start of the next chapter, genes that cause you to be tall or good-looking alter other people's reactions to you, and their behavior changes your behavior. Genes that control your skin color also change other people's reactions to you. Thus, a gene could influence your behavior by changing your social environment. For this and many other reasons, it is impossible to draw a firm distinction between genetic and environmental influences.

We also need a better understanding of the environmental influences on intelligence, ranging from prenatal health and nutrition to the expectations that teachers and others unintentionally express. If we can identify the factors that promote intellectual development, we might accomplish something to benefit everyone.

Summary

- *Standardization.* To determine the meaning of a test's scores, the authors of a test determine the mean and the distribution of scores for a random or representative sample of the population. IQ tests are revised periodically. (page 332)

- *Distribution of IQ scores.* IQ tests have a mean of 100 and a standard deviation of about 15 or 16, depending on the test. (page 332)

- *The Flynn effect.* To keep the mean score at 100, authors of the IQ tests have had to revise the tests periodically, always making them more difficult. That is, raw performance has been increasing steadily. The reasons for this trend are unknown. (page 333)

- *Reliability, validity, and utility.* Tests are evaluated in terms of reliability, validity, and utility. Reliability is a measure of the repeatability of a test's scores. Validity is a determination of how well a test measures what it claims to measure. Utility is a decision of whether the test scores are sufficiently helpful to be worth using. (page 334)

- *Hereditary and environmental influences.* To determine the contribution of heredity to the variations in scores on IQ tests, investigators compare identical twins and fraternal twins, study identical twins reared apart, compare adopted children with their biological and adoptive parents, and examine chromosomes to see whether higher performing people have different genes from lower performing people. Much evidence implies some genetic contribution to IQ differences, but the strength of that contribution is still uncertain. (page 337)

- *Test bias.* Psychologists try to remove from a test any item that tends to be easy for one group of people to

answer but difficult for another. They also try to evaluate the possible bias of a test as a whole. Bias is defined as an incorrect estimation of how well some group of people will perform. By that definition IQ tests are biased against immigrants but apparently not against racial minorities; they predict the school performance of African American students about as accurately as that of European Americans. (page 340)

- *Test anxiety and stereotype threat.* Many African American students perform worse on tests when they are aware they are being evaluated and fear that a poor performance might reflect badly on their group. (page 342)

- *The controversy concerning ethnic differences in IQ.* Ethnic groups differ on the average in IQ performance, although the group mean scores cannot tell us what to expect from each individual. Not much research has been done on this issue, and much of what has been done is old and not conclusive. (page 343)

Answers to Concept Checks

6. Yes! To say that a test is "reliable" is simply to say that its scores are repeatable—that and only that. My test would give perfectly reliable (repeatable) measurements. True, they would be utterly useless, but reliability is not a measure of usefulness. (page 335)

7. No. An individual's score may be higher on the retest either because of practice at taking the test or because of additional months of education. But the rank order of scores does not change much. That is, if some people retake the test, all of them are likely to improve their scores, but those who had the highest scores the first time will probably still have the highest scores the second time. (page 335)

8. Yes, a test can have high reliability and low validity. A measure of intelligence determined by dividing head length by head width has high reliability (repeatability) but presumably no validity. A test with low reliability cannot have high validity, however. Low reliability means that the scores fluctuate randomly. If the test scores cannot even predict a later score on the same test, then they can hardly predict anything else. (page 336)

9. The predictive validity of the tests would increase. The predictive validity tends to be low when almost all students have practically the same score; it is higher when students' scores are highly variable. (page 336)

10. The predictive validity of SAT scores will be higher at the university that admits almost any-

one. At the university with extremely competitive admissions standards, almost all students have nearly the same SAT scores, and the slight variation in scores cannot predict which students will get the best grades. (page 336)

11. One type of evidence is that identical twins resemble each other in IQ more than fraternal twins do. However, this observation may overstate the role of genetics because twins that show early talent in some area such as academics (possibly for genetic reasons) will receive encouragement to develop that ability, so environmental factors strengthen the early tendency. Also, most data deal with middle-class families, and environmental variations are more extreme among low-income families. A second type of evidence is that IQs of adopted children correlate significantly with those of their biological parents. The limitation here is that the biological mother provides the prenatal environment as well as genetics. (page 339)

12. No, this test is not biased against people with visual impairments. It correctly determines that they are likely to be poor drivers. A *difference* between groups does not constitute bias; only an *inaccurate* difference in scores constitutes bias. (page 342)

13. We would need to determine whether the test accurately predicts the school performances of both short and tall people. If short people with, say, an IQ score of 100 perform better in school than tall people with the same score, then the test is underpredicting the short people's performances, and we can conclude that this test is biased. (The mere fact that tall people do better on this test is not *in itself* evidence of bias.) (page 342)

14. If African American children with more European ancestry had higher IQ scores, the data would have implied a genetic contribution to the ethnic difference in IQ. The near-zero correlation between European ancestry and IQ scores implied the lack of a significant genetic contribution. (page 345)

CHAPTER ENDING

Key Terms and Activities

Key Terms

bias: the tendency for test scores to exaggerate a difference between groups or to report a nonexistent difference (page 340)

construct validity: the correspondence of a test's measurements to a theoretical construct (page 335)

content validity: the similarity between the items in a test and the information that the test is meant to measure (page 335)

crystallized intelligence: acquired skills and knowledge and the application of that knowledge to the specific content of a person's experience (page 328)

fluid intelligence: the basic power of reasoning and using information, including the ability to perceive relationships, solve unfamiliar problems, and gain new types of knowledge (page 328)

Flynn effect: the tendency for people's performance on IQ tests to improve from one decade or generation to the next (page 333)

g: Spearman's "general" factor which all IQ tests and all parts of an IQ test are believed to have in common (page 326)

intelligence quotient (IQ): a measure of an individual's probable performance in school and in similar settings (page 324)

multiple intelligences: Gardner's theory that intelligence is composed of numerous unrelated forms of intelligent behavior (page 329)

norms: a description of the frequencies of occurrence of particular scores (page 332)

predictive validity: the ability of a test's scores to predict some real-world performance (page 335)

Progressive Matrices: an IQ test that attempts to measure abstract reasoning without the use of language or recall of facts (page 326)

psychometric approach: the measurement of individual differences in abilities and behaviors (page 326)

reliability: the repeatability of a test's scores (page 334)

s: a "specific" factor that is more important for performance on some portions of an intelligence test than it is for others (page 326)

standardization: the process of establishing rules for administering a test and for interpreting the scores (page 332)

Stanford-Binet IQ test: a test of intelligence; the first important IQ test in the English language (page 324)

stereotype threat: people's perceived risk that they might do something that supports an unfavorable stereotype about their group (page 342)

test–retest reliability: the correlation between scores on a first test and on a retest (page 334)

triarchic theory: Sternberg's theory that intelligence has three aspects: the cognitive processes that occur within the individual, the situations that require intelligence, and how intelligence relates to the external world (page 330)

utility: the usefulness of a test for a practical purpose (page 337)

validity: the determination of how well a test measures what it claims to measure (page 335)

Wechsler Adult Intelligence Scale–Third Edition (WAIS–III): an IQ test originally devised by David Wechsler, commonly used with adults (page 325)

Wechsler Intelligence Scale for Children–Fourth Edition (WISC–IV): an IQ test originally devised by David Wechsler, commonly used with children (page 325)

Suggestion for Further Reading

Neisser, U., et al. (1996). Intelligence: Knowns and unknowns. *American Psychologist, 51,* 77–101. Although much dispute surrounds the meaning of IQ scores and the reasons individuals differ, psychologists have also found areas of agreement. This article describes the consensus of most psychologists, the evidence behind their conclusions, and the questions that still remain unanswered.

Book Companion Web Site

Need help studying? Go to

http://psychology.wadsworth.com/kalat_intro7e/

for a virtual study center. You'll find a personalized Self-Study Assessment that will provide you with a study plan based on your answers to a pretest. Also study using flashcards, quizzes, interactive art, and an online glossary.

Check out interactive **Try It Yourself** exercises on the companion site! These exercises will help you put what you've learned into action.

Your companion site also has direct links to the following Web sites. These links are checked often for changes, dead links, and new additions.

Sample IQ Tests

2h.com/

Take a variety of IQ and personality tests. Some are serious and some are obviously fake. None of these are the best established tests, and their reliability and validity are unknown; still, you might find them interesting.*

The Flynn Effect

http://pespmc1.vub.ac.be/FLYNNEFF.html

Read about research concerning the Flynn effect, including data from various countries.

---

*Note: Any psychological test that is readily available to the public, while entertaining and possibly informative, should not be used to make important decisions. The most powerful, valid, and reliable psychological assessment devices are usually kept under the tight control of their creators or copyright holders.

The Bell Curve

apa.org/journals/bell.html

Two noted psychologists present reviews with very different conclusions concerning the controversial book *The Bell Curve*.

Try It Yourself CD-ROM
with Critical Thinking Video Exercises

Use your CD to access **videos** related to activities designed to help you think critically about the important topics discussed. For example, the video about different views on intelligence enhancement relates to what you've learned in this chapter. You'll also find an easy portal link to the book companion site where you can access your personalized **Self-Study Assessments** and interactive **Try It Yourself** exercises.

PsychNow! 2.0

PsychNow! is a fun interactive CD designed to help you with the difficult concepts in psychology. Check out the Personality and Abnormal Psychology section for the following topic that relates to this chapter:
Assessment: interactive reaction time and intelligence tests, quiz, and test scores.

© Joel Gordon

Human Development

Suppose you buy a robot. When you get home, you discover that it does nothing useful. It cannot even maintain its balance. It makes irritating, high-pitched noises, moves its limbs haphazardly, and leaks. The store you bought it from refuses to take it back. And for some reason you cannot turn it off. So you are stuck with this useless machine.

A few years later, your robot can walk and talk, read and write, draw pictures, and do arithmetic. It follows your directions (usually) and sometimes even finds useful things to do without being told. It often beats you at checkers and almost always at memory games.

How did all this happen? After all, you knew nothing about how to program a robot. Did your robot have some sort of built-in programming that simply took a long time to phase in? Or was it programmed to learn all these skills?

Children are a great deal like that robot. Nearly every parent wonders, "How did my children get to be the way they are?" The goal of developmental psychology is to understand everything that influences human behavior "from womb to tomb."

▌As we grow older, we change in many ways—we gain in some ways and lose in others. Developmental psychologists seek to understand the changes in our behavior and the reasons behind these changes.

Getting Started: From Genetics Through Infancy

How do genes influence behavior?

How can we infer the sensation, memory, and other capacities of an infant?

Identical, or monozygotic (one egg), **twins** *develop from a single fertilized egg and therefore have identical genetics.* **Fraternal,** or dizygotic (two eggs), **twins** *develop from two eggs and share only half their genes, like brother and sister* (Figure 10.1). Many studies of nature and nurture focus on comparing the two kinds of twins, especially if the twins grew up in separate environments. When twins are put up for adoption today, adoption agencies place them both in one family, but many years ago it was common for twins to be adopted separately. One pair of identical twins who were separated at birth and reared in different western Ohio cities were reunited in adulthood (Figure 10.2). They quickly discovered that they had much in common:

Both had been named Jim by their adoptive parents. Each liked carpentry and drafting, had built a bench around a tree in his yard, and worked as a deputy sheriff. Both chewed their fingernails, gained weight at the same age, smoked the same brand of cigarettes, drove Chevrolets, and took their vacations in western Florida. Each married a woman named Linda, divorced her, and married a woman named Betty. One had a son named James Alan and the other a son named James Allen; both had a pet dog named Toy.

Undoubtedly, some of these similarities are mere coincidences. Lots of people drive Chevrolets, for example, and many people from western Ohio vacation in western Florida. It's hard to believe that they had genes causing them to marry a Linda and divorce her to marry a Betty. (If they lived in some other country, they would have had trouble finding either a Linda or a Betty. And did these women have genes that attracted them to men named Jim?)

All right, but let's consider other identical twins separated at birth. One pair of women each wore rings on seven fingers. A pair of men discovered that they used the same brands of toothpaste, shaving lotion, hair tonic, and cigarettes. When they sent each other a birthday present, their presents crossed in the mail and each discovered that he had received the same present he had sent. Another pair reported that whenever they went to the beach, they waded into the water backward and only up to their knees (Lykken, McGue, Tellegen, & Bouchard, 1992).

Researchers have examined up to 100 pairs of twins, some identical and

Identical twins

One sperm, one egg → Zygote divides → Two zygotes with identical chromosomes → Same sex only

Fraternal twins

Two sperm, two eggs → Two zygotes with different chromosomes → Same or opposite sex

FIGURE 10.1 Identical (monozygotic) twins develop from the same fertilized egg. Fraternal (dizygotic) twins grow from two eggs fertilized by different sperm.

FIGURE 10.2 Identical twins Jim Lewis and Jim Springer were separated at birth, reared in separate cities of western Ohio, and reunited in adulthood.

others fraternal, who were reared in separate homes and then reunited as adults. The identical twins resembled each other more than did the fraternal pairs with regard to hobbies, vocational interests, consumption of coffee and fruit juices, preference for awakening early in the morning or staying up late at night, answers on personality tests, and political beliefs (DiLalla, Carey, Gottesman, & Bouchard, 1996; Hur, Bouchard, & Eckert, 1998; Hur, Bouchard, & Lykken, 1998; Lykken, Bouchard, McGue, & Tellegen, 1993; McCourt, Bouchard, Lykken, Tellegen, & Keyes, 1999). Evidently, genetic factors influence a wide range of behaviors.

But *how* do genes influence behavior? We discussed some of the issues and controversies in the last chapter with regard to intelligence. The same issues arise in almost any discussion of developmental psychology. You developed your personality, your social behavior, and all your other characteristics through a complex combination of heredity and environmental influences. But the role of heredity varies from one behavior to another. Let's first take a quick survey of genes and what they do. Then we shall explore the application of genetics to human behavior.

Genetic Principles

If you have already studied genetics in a biology class, much of this discussion will be a review. Skim what you already know and concentrate on unfamiliar material.

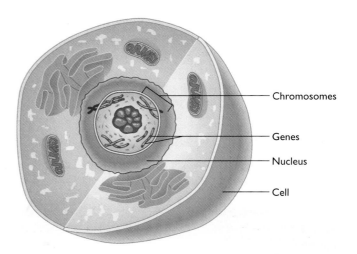

FIGURE 10.3 Genes are sections of chromosomes in the nuclei of cells. (Scale is exaggerated for illustration purposes.)

Except for your red blood cells, all of your cells contain a nucleus, which includes *strands of hereditary material* called chromosomes (Figure 10.3). Chromosomes provide the chemical basis of heredity. Humans have 23 pairs of chromosomes, except in egg or sperm cells, which have 23 unpaired chromosomes. At fertilization the 23 chromosomes from an egg cell combine with the 23 of a sperm to form 23 pairs for the new person (Figure 10.4).

Sections along each chromosome are known as genes, *which control the chemical reactions that direct development*—for example, determining proba-

FIGURE 10.4 The nucleus of each human cell contains 46 chromosomes, 23 from the sperm and 23 from the ovum, united in pairs.

ble height or hair color. They can influence behavior by changes in the brain or sense organs or indirectly by changes in other body parts.

Genes are composed of the chemical DNA, which controls the production of other chemicals called RNA, which among other functions control the production of proteins. The proteins either become part of the body's structure or control the rates of chemical reactions in the body.

Because chromosomes come in pairs (one from the mother and one from the father), you have two of almost all genes. (The exception: Men have one X chromosome and one Y chromosome and therefore have unpaired genes on their X and Y chromosomes.) To explain the concept of genes, educators often use an example such as eye color. If you have either one or two genes for brown eyes, you will have brown eyes because the brown-eye gene is dominant. The gene for blue eyes is recessive, so you can have blue eyes only if you have two genes for blue eyes. A behavioral example is the ability to curl your tongue lengthwise (Figure 10.5). If you have this dominant gene, you can curl your tongue, and if you don't have it, you can't. (You will be seldom inconvenienced.)

FIGURE 10.5 A single gene determines whether you can curl your tongue.

However, examples like this are misleading. First, they imply that each gene has only one effect, whereas most genes have many. Second, they imply that a gene completely controls something so that there is nothing you could do about it. Most genes' effects vary with your age, diet, health, and other factors. Many genes increase or decrease the probability of some behavior, but the outcome depends on other influences also.

CONCEPT CHECK ☑

1. If two parents cannot curl their tongues, what can you predict about their children? (Check your answer on page 363.)

Sex-Linked and Sex-Limited Genes

One pair of chromosomes is known as **sex chromosomes** because they *determine whether an individual develops as a male or as a female*. Mammals' sex chromosomes are known as X and Y (Figure 10.6). *A female has two X chromosomes in each cell; a male has one X chromosome and one Y chromosome*. The mother contributes an X chromosome to each child, and the father contributes either an X or a Y.

FIGURE 10.6 An electron micrograph of X and Y chromosomes shows the difference in length. *(From Ruch, 1984)*

Genes located on the X chromosome are known as X-linked or **sex-linked genes**. A sex-linked recessive gene shows its effects more often in men than in women. For example, the most common type of color vision deficiency depends on a sex-linked recessive gene. A man with that gene on his X chromosome will be colorblind because he has no other X chromosome. A woman with that gene probably has a gene for normal color vision on her other X chromosome. Conse-

▌ Albinos occur in many species, always because of a recessive gene. (a) Striped skunk. (b) American alligator. (c) Mockingbird.

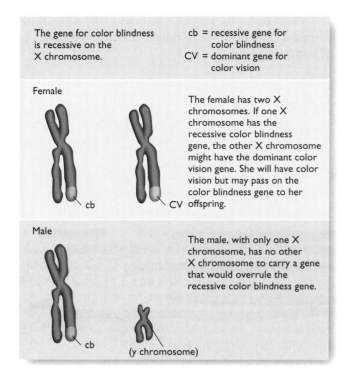

The gene for color blindness is recessive on the X chromosome.

cb = recessive gene for color blindness

CV = dominant gene for color vision

Female

The female has two X chromosomes. If one X chromosome has the recessive color blindness gene, the other X chromosome might have the dominant color vision gene. She will have color vision but may pass on the color blindness gene to her offspring.

cb   CV

Male

The male, with only one X chromosome, has no other X chromosome to carry a gene that would overrule the recessive color blindness gene.

cb   (y chromosome)

FIGURE 10.7 Why males are more likely than females to be colorblind.

quently, far more men than women have color vision deficiency (Figure 10.7).

A **sex-limited gene** occurs *equally in both sexes but exerts its effects in one but not the other* (or only slightly in the other). For example, both men and women have the genes for facial hair, but men's hormones activate those genes. Similarly, both men and women have the genes for breast development, but women's hormones activate those genes.

CONCEPT CHECK ☑

2. Suppose a father has color vision deficiency and a mother has two genes for normal color vision. What sort of color vision will their children have? (Check your answer on page 363.)

Identifying and Localizing Genes

Modern technology has enabled researchers to identify genes that increase the risk of Alzheimer's disease and other diseases. Some genes increase the risk only slightly, and others more substantially. You could (for a price) have someone examine your chromosomes and tell you which diseases you are likely to get, how likely you are to get them, and in some cases how soon you will get them (Gusella & MacDonald, 2000).

As research progresses, the possibilities for prediction will grow even stronger.

Would you want to know this information? Your answer probably depends on what you could do with it. For example, learning that you were predisposed to alcoholism might lead you to take precautions, such as not joining a fraternity or sorority with a reputation for heavy drinking. On the other hand, learning that you were likely to develop Alzheimer's disease in old age might be useless information, unless researchers found some way to prevent the disease. The following Web site documents research on the identification of human genes:

www.ornl.gov/TechResources/
Human_Genome/home.html

Estimating Heritability in Humans

You might hear someone ask whether some behavior depends on heredity or environment. That question is meaningless as it is phrased. (Take away either your heredity or your environment and there is no "you" left!) However, a change in wording makes the question meaningful: Does a given *difference* in behavior (e.g., the difference between an alcoholic and a non-alcoholic) depend more on *differences* in heredity or *differences* in environment? That is, if we want to predict who will become alcoholics, how well could we succeed if we knew their heredity, and how well if we knew their environment?

The answer to a question like this is summarized by the term **heritability,** *an estimate of the variance within a population that is due to heredity.* Heritability ranges from 1, indicating that heredity controls all the variance, to 0, indicating that it controls none of it. For example, tongue curling has a heritability of almost 1.

For an example of a condition with virtually 0 heritability, consider which language someone speaks. If you want to predict whether a child will speak English, Greek, or Bengali, you should ask which language the child's parents and community speak. Examining the child's genes will not help.

To estimate the heritability of a behavior, researchers rely on the following types of evidence (Segal, 1993):

- Do identical twins resemble each other more closely than fraternal twins do? Identical twins have the same genes; fraternal twins resemble each other genetically only as much as a brother and sister do. If fraternal twins resemble each other as much as identical twins do, then heritability is low.

If identical twins resemble each other more than fraternal twins do, a genetic influence is likely but not certain. Most identical twins share a single amniote before birth, whereas fraternal twins have separate amniotes (Figure 10.8). Therefore, identical twins have more similarities in prenatal (before-birth) influences, and what appears to be evidence for a genetic influence might also reflect similar prenatal environments (Phelps, Davis, & Schartz, 1997). Also, because of their nearly identical appearance, identical twins tend to be treated more alike after birth.

- Do twins who are adopted by separate families and reared apart resemble each other more closely than we would expect by chance? If so, again genetic similarity is a likely explanation.
- To what extent do adopted children resemble their adoptive and biological parents? Any resemblance of adopted children to their biological parents probably reflects a genetic influence, although again we should consider prenatal influences.

A low correlation with the adoptive parents can also be misleading. Recall from Chapter 2 that two variables are highly correlated if we can use measurements of one to predict the other accurately. Imagine trying to predict which adopted children will become alcoholics by examining the alcohol habits of their adoptive parents. You can't make much of a prediction because adoption agencies almost never let alcoholics adopt children. The low correlation between adopted child and adoptive parent doesn't tell us the possible effect of a severely alcoholic family (Stoolmiller, 1999).

The point is that accurately measuring heritability is difficult. Better evidence will emerge from new biochemical methods of determining which identified genes are associated with one behavior or another.

CONCEPT CHECK ☑

3. If our society changed so that an equally good environment was provided for all children, would the heritability of behaviors increase or decrease? (Check your answer on page 363.)

How Genes Influence Behavior

Based on studies of twins and adopted children, researchers have found at least moderate heritability for almost every behavior they have examined. For example, adopted children resemble their birth parents with regard to how much time they spend watching television (Plomin, Corley, DeFries, & Fulker, 1990). Monozygotic twins reared apart resemble each other in their religious devoutness (Waller, Kojetin, Bouchard, Lykken, & Tellegen, 1990). (Their religious affiliation, however, depends on the adoptive family. There is no gene for Presbyterian.) The evidence also indicates moderate heritability for loneliness (McGuire & Clifford, 2000), neuroticism (Lake, Eaves, Maes, Heath, & Martin, 2000), and a host of other variables. How could genes affect such complicated characteristics?

Direct and Indirect Influences

Genes control maturation of brain structures, production of neurotransmitters, and production of neurotransmitter receptors. However, genes can also influence behaviors indirectly. For example, imagine a gene that makes you tall. If you live where people play basketball, you are more likely than shorter people to spend much of your time playing basketball and, therefore less time playing chess, writing poetry, and so forth.

Or imagine genes that cause you to be especially good-looking. Many people will smile at you, invite you to parties, and try to become your friend. You

a   b

FIGURE 10.8 (a) Fraternal twins develop with separate amniotes and therefore separate blood supplies. (b) Most monozygotic (identical) twins develop with a single amniote and therefore the same blood supply, the same hormone levels, and so forth.

may develop increased self-confidence and a number of other subtle changes in personality. The genes changed your behavior by changing the way your environment treated you.

Also consider dietary choices: Almost all infants can digest *lactose,* the sugar in milk. As they grow older, most Asian children and many non-Asian children lose the ability to digest it. (They lose that ability even if they drink milk frequently. The loss depends on genes.) They can still enjoy a little milk, and more readily enjoy cheese, yogurt, and other easy-to-digest dairy products, but they get gas and cramps from consuming too much milk or ice cream (Flatz, 1987; Rozin & Pelchat, 1988). Figure 10.9 shows how the ability to digest dairy products varies from one part of the world to another. The point is that a gene can affect behavior—in this case consumption of dairy products—by altering chemical reactions outside the brain itself.

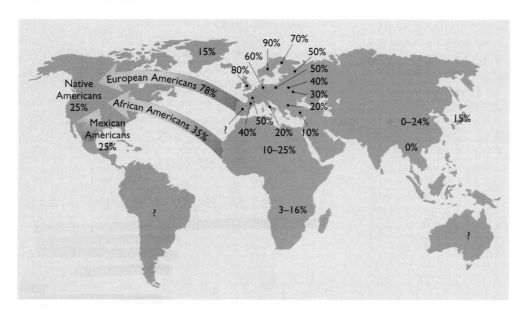

FIGURE 10.9 Adult humans vary in their ability to digest lactose, the main sugar in milk. The numbers refer to the percentage of each population's adults that can easily digest lactose. In Asian countries and other locations where most adults cannot digest lactose, cooks seldom use dairy products. *(Based on Flatz, 1987; Rozin & Pelchat, 1988)*

Phenylketonuria: Modifying Genetic Effects Through Diet

Some people assume that if something is under genetic control, we can't do anything about it. Nonsense. For example, you might have genes for straight black hair, but you could curl it, dye it blonde, or shave it off.

Here is a stronger example: **Phenylketonuria (PKU)** is *an inherited condition that, if untreated, leads to mental retardation.* About 2% of people with European or Asian ancestry, and virtually no one of African ancestry, has one copy of the recessive gene

that leads to PKU, but one copy produces no apparent harm. People who have two copies, one on each chromosome, cannot metabolize *phenylalanine,* a common constituent of proteins. On an ordinary diet, an affected child accumulates phenylalanine in the brain and becomes mentally retarded; however, following a diet low in phenylalanine protects the brain. Thus, a controlled diet prevents a disorder that is "under genetic control." One hope is that research on genetics may help us control undesirable genetic effects.

The Fetus and the Newborn

Genes control development of the body, which in turn provides for behavior. A course in psychology emphasizes behavior. However, because this chapter covers development over the life span, let's focus briefly on early physical development.

During prenatal development, everyone starts as a *fertilized egg cell,* or **zygote,** which develops through its first few stages until it is identified as a **fetus** *about 8 weeks after conception.* Even as soon as 6 weeks after conception, the brain is mature enough to produce the first few movements. By the 36th week, the brain can turn the head and eyes in response to sounds and proceeds through recognizable stages of waking, sleeping, and REM sleep (Joseph, 2000). None of this behavior requires the cerebral cortex, which matures more slowly than other brain areas.

The growing body receives nutrition from the mother. If she eats little, the baby receives little nourishment. If she takes drugs, the baby gets them too. Undernourished mothers generally give birth to small babies (Figure 10.10), and investigators have long known that newborns weighing less than about 1,750–2,000 grams (4 pounds) are at high risk of dying in infancy (Kopp, 1990). Those that survive have an increased risk of conduct problems and poor academic performance (H. G. Taylor, Klein, Minich, & Hack, 2000). These facts are beyond dispute, but their meaning is less certain.

FIGURE 10.10 Low-birthweight babies are susceptible to many physical and behavioral difficulties later in life; however, we cannot be sure that low birthweight causes the problems. Many of these babies are born to mothers who are poorly nourished, who take illegal drugs, or who fail to obtain good nutrition and care.

The apparently obvious interpretation is that low birthweight leads to impaired brain development and thus to later academic and behavior problems. However, many low-birthweight babies are born with low birthweights because their mothers were poorly nourished, unhealthy, victims of family violence, possibly smoking or drinking during pregnancy, and not receiving medical care (Garcia Coll, 1990; McCormick, 1985). In short, many low-birthweight babies have other problems as well (Brooks-Gunn & Furstenberg, 1989; Zeanah, Boris, & Larrieu, 1997).

One way to study the effect of low birthweight separately from other problems is to examine pairs of twins where one twin was born much heavier than the other. In most cases the low birthweight infant develops about as well as the heavier twin (R. S. Wilson, 1987). In short, low birthweight *by itself* is not necessarily a serious problem; it correlates with developmental difficulties partly because many low-birthweight babies have other disadvantages.

A more severe risk arises if the fetus is exposed to alcohol or other substances. *If the mother drinks alcohol during pregnancy,* the infant may develop signs of **fetal alcohol syndrome,** *a condition marked by stunted growth of the head and body; malformations of the face, heart, and ears; and nervous system damage, including seizures, hyperactivity, learning disabilities, and mental retardation* (Streissguth, Sampson, & Barr, 1989). In milder cases children appear normal but have moderate deficits in language, memory, and coordination (Mattson, Riley, Grambling, Delis, & Jones, 1998). The more alcohol the mother drinks during pregnancy, the greater the risk to the fetus (see Figure 10.11).

The reason for the nervous system damage is now understood: Developing neurons require persistent excitation to survive. Without it, they activate a self-destruct program. Alcohol facilitates the main inhibitory neurotransmitter of the brain (known as GABA) and interferes with the main excitatory neurotransmitter (glutamate). It therefore decreases neurons' arousal and leads them to self-destruct (Ikonomidou et al., 2000). An implication is that pregnant women should minimize the use of tranquilizers and anesthetics because they also inhibit neuronal activity.

Women who smoke during pregnancy have an increased probability that their babies will have health problems early in life. They also run an increased risk that their children, especially sons, eventually will develop *conduct disorder,* a condition marked by discipline problems both at school and at home and potentially even criminal behavior in adulthood. Conduct disorder has been found to correlate more strongly with the mother's smoking during pregnancy than with the father's antisocial behavior, the family's

FIGURE 10.11 (a) The more alcohol a woman drinks during pregnancy, the more likely her baby is to have anomalies of the head, face, and organs. *(Based on data of Ernhart et al., 1987)* (b) A child with fetal alcohol syndrome: Note the wide separation between the eyes, a common feature of this syndrome.

economic status, lack of child supervision, or excessive punishment (Wakschlag et al., 1997). To be safe, pregnant women should avoid alcohol and tobacco and should get a physician's advice before taking any medications.

Still, it is remarkable that an occasional "high-risk" child—small at birth, perhaps exposed to alcohol or other drugs before birth, perhaps from an impoverished or turbulent family—overcomes all odds and becomes a healthy, productive, outstanding person. Resilience (the ability to overcome obstacles) is poorly understood and difficult to study (Luthar, Cicchetti, & Becker, 2000). However, the more positive influences one has in life, the easier it is to overcome negative ones. That is, most people who overcome disadvantages have some special source of strength such as a close relationship with one or more supporting people, an effective school, a strong faith, some special skill, or just a naturally easygoing disposition (Masten & Coatsworth, 1998).

CONCEPT CHECK ☑

4. Why should a pregnant woman avoid taking large amounts of tranquilizers? (Check your answer on page 363.)

Behavioral Capacities of the Newborn

Even at birth, each infant differs from others in many ways. For example, some are calm whereas others are easily aroused. The differences relate to genetics and prenatal environment. From birth onward infants begin interacting with a much wider environment and trying to make sense of it.

Studying the infant's early attempts to understand the world is both fascinating and frustrating. A newborn is like a computer that is not attached to a monitor or printer: No matter how much information it processes, it cannot tell us about it. The challenge of studying the newborn is to figure out how to attach some sort of "monitor" to find out what is going on inside.

Newborns have little control of their muscles. At first they cannot keep their head from flopping over, and their arms and legs flail about aimlessly. They gradually gain muscle control

through a combination of maturation and practice. For example, babies who are too young to support their own weight flail their arms and legs in varied and haphazard ways; as soon as they can support their weight, they quickly abandon most of their varied movement patterns and settle on the standard patterns and rhythms of human crawling (Freedland & Bertenthal, 1994).

About the only useful movements that newborns can make are eye and mouth movements, especially sucking. As the months pass, and as their control spreads from the head muscles downward, they make progressively finer movements, eventually including single finger movements.

If we want to test infants' sensory and learning abilities, we must test the responses that they can control, such as eye or head movements. If we try to train them to reach out and grab something, we will certainly underestimate their capacities.

Newborns' Vision

William James, the founder of American psychology, once said that as far as an infant can tell, the world is a "buzzing confusion," full of meaningless sights and sounds. Since James's time, psychologists have substantially increased their estimates of infants' vision.

One research method is to record the infant's eye movements. In general, infants direct their eyes toward the same kinds of objects that attract adults' attention. For example, even 2-day-old infants spend more time looking at drawings of human faces than at other patterns with similar areas of light and dark (Fantz, 1963) (see Figure 10.12).

By the age of 5 months or so, infants have had extensive visual experience but almost no experi-

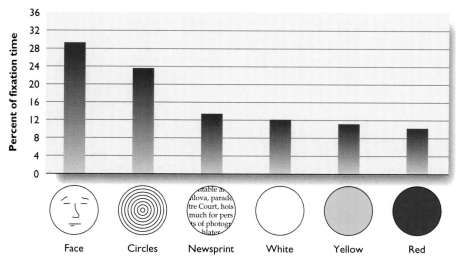

FIGURE 10.12 Infants pay more attention to faces than to other patterns. These results suggest that infants are born with certain visual preferences. *(Based on Fantz, 1963)*

ence at crawling or reaching for objects. Over the next several months, they increase their control of arm and leg movements. They learn to reach out to pick up toys, crawl around objects, avoid crawling off ledges, and in other ways coordinate what they see with what they do. Apparently, they need experience of controlling their own movements before they show a fear of heights. Infants usually take a tumble or two before they develop a fear of heights (Adolph, 2000). Those who crawl early develop a fear of heights early; those who are late to crawl are also late to develop a fear of heights (Campos, Bertenthal, & Kermoian, 1992).

Newborns' Hearing

It might seem difficult to measure newborns' responses to sounds because we cannot observe anything like eye movements. However, infants suck more vigorously when they are aroused, and certain sounds arouse them more than others do.

In one study the experimenters played a brief sound and noted how it affected an infant's sucking rate (Figure 10.13). On the first few occasions, the sound increased the sucking rate. A repeated sound produced less and less effect. We say that the infant became *habituated* to the sound. **Habituation** is *decreased response to a repeated stimulus.* When the experimenters substituted a new sound, the sucking rate increased. Evidently, the infant was aroused by the unfamiliar sound. *When a change in a stimulus produces an increase in a previously habituated response,* we say that the stimulus produced **dishabituation**.

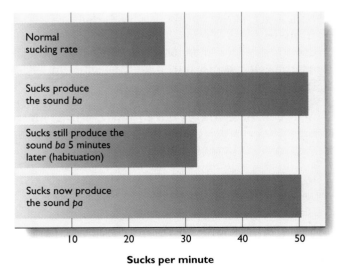

FIGURE 10.13 After repeatedly hearing a *ba* sound, the infant's sucking habituates. When a new sound, *pa*, follows, the sucking rate increases, an indication that infants hear a difference between the sounds. *(Based on results of Eimas, Siqueland, Jusczyk, & Vigorito, 1971)*

Psychologists use this technique to determine whether infants hear a difference between two sounds. For example, infants who have become habituated to the sound *ba* will increase their sucking rate when they hear the sound *pa* (Eimas, Siqueland, Jusczyk, & Vigorito, 1971). Apparently, even month-old infants can tell the difference between *ba* and *pa*, an important distinction for later language comprehension.

Similar studies have shown that infants who have habituated to hearing one language, such as Dutch, dishabituate when they hear a different language, such as Japanese. At first they show no response to a shift between Dutch and English, presumably because the sounds and rhythms are fairly similar. By age 5 months, however, they dishabituate when they hear a change from a British accent to an American accent (Jusczyk, 2002). Studies of this sort show that children can discriminate relevant language sounds long before they know what any of the words mean.

CONCEPT CHECK ☑

5. Suppose an infant habituates to the sound *ba*, and when we substitute the sound *bla*, the infant fails to increase its sucking rate. What interpretation would be likely? (Check your answer on page 363.)

Infants' Learning and Memory

Infants certainly cannot describe their memories to us. But if they respond differently to a stimulus because of previous experience with it, we can infer a memory.

Several studies have begun with the observation that infants learn to suck harder on a nipple if their sucking turns on a sound. Investigators then tried to determine whether infants work to turn on certain sounds more than others. In one study 26 babies younger than 3 days old could turn on a tape recording of their mother's voice by sucking on a nipple at certain times or at certain rates. By sucking at different times or at different rates, they could turn on a tape recording of another woman's voice. When their sucking produced their own mother's voice, they sucked more frequently (DeCasper & Fifer, 1980). They did not suck much to produce a different voice. Apparently, even very young infants recognized their own mother's voice and preferred it to an unfamiliar voice. Because they showed this preference so early—in some cases on the day of birth—developmental psychologists believe that the infants display a memory of what they heard before birth.

6. Suppose a newborn sucks to turn on a tape recording of its father's voice. Eventually, the baby habituates and the sucking frequency decreases. Now the experimenters substitute the recording of a different man's voice. What would you conclude if the sucking frequency increased? What if it remained the same? What if it decreased? (Check your answers on page 363.)

Using somewhat older infants, Carolyn Rovee-Collier (1997, 1999) demonstrated an ability to learn a response and remember it for days. In one series of studies, she attached a ribbon to an ankle so that an infant could activate a mobile by kicking with one leg (Figure 10.14). Two-month-old infants quickly learned this response and generally kept the mobile going nonstop for a full 45-minute session. (Earlier, I said infants cannot control their leg muscles, but they didn't need much control to keep the mobile going.) Once they have learned, they quickly remember what to do when the ribbon is reattached several days later—to the infants' evident delight. Six-month-old infants remembered the response for 2 weeks. Even after forgetting it, they could relearn it in 2 minutes and then retain it for an additional month or more (Hildreth, Sweeney, & Rovee-Collier, 2003).

In another series of studies, Rovee-Collier and her colleagues found that 9-month-olds can learn to press a lever to make a toy train go around a track. In both the mobile studies and the train studies, older infants remembered the response longer than younger ones (Hartshorn et al., 1998).

FIGURE 10.14 Two-month-old infants rapidly learn to kick to activate a mobile attached to their ankles with a ribbon. They remember how to activate the mobile when tested days later. *(From Hildreth, Sweeney, & Rovee-Collier, 2003)*

IN CLOSING

Getting Started in Life

Physicists say that the way the universe developed depended on its "initial conditions"—the array of matter and energy a fraction of a second after the start of the "big bang." The outcome of any experiment in physics or chemistry depends on the initial conditions—the type of matter, its temperature and pressure, and so forth. You had initial conditions too—your genetics and prenatal environment. Understanding those initial conditions is critical to understanding your special characteristics. However, you also have "conditions added later." At any point in your life, your behavior depends on a complex combination of your predispositions, the effects of past experiences, and all aspects of the current environment.

Research on infants' sucking, kicking, and other simple responses has enabled psychologists to infer the thoughts and perceptions of infants too young to talk. As research methods have advanced, the trend has been a steady increase in our estimation of infants' capacities. Are we now at risk of jumping from underestimates of infants' abilities to overestimates? You can see the fascination of this research topic.

Summary

- *Genes.* Genes, which are segments of chromosomes, control heredity. (page 354)
- *Sex-linked and sex-limited genes.* Genes on the X chromosome are sex linked. A sex-linked recessive gene will show its effects more frequently in males than in females. A sex-limited gene is present in both sexes, but it affects one more than the other. (page 355)
- *Locating genes.* In some cases researchers can locate specific genes linked to a specific outcome. (page 356)
- *Evidence for genetic influences.* Researchers estimate genetic contributions to behavior by comparing identical twins to fraternal twins, by comparing twins reared in separate environments, and by examining how adopted children resemble their biological and adoptive parents. However, each kind of research has limitations. (page 356)
- *How genes affect behavior.* Genes can affect behaviors indirectly, by influencing some aspect of the body that in turn influences behavior. (page 357)
- *Influence of the environment on gene expression.* It is possible to control a genetically influenced condition by changing the environment. One example is the use of a low-phenylalanine diet to prevent the mental retardation associated with phenylketonuria. (page 358)

- *Prenatal development*. Although the cerebral cortex is slow to mature, the rest of the brain begins to produce movements long before birth. Exposure to drugs such as alcohol decreases brain activity and releases neurons' self-destruct programs. (page 358)
- *Inferring infant capacities*. We easily underestimate newborns' capacities because they have so little control over their muscles. With careful testing procedures, we can demonstrate that newborns can see, hear, and remember more than we might have supposed. (page 360)
- *Infant vision and hearing*. Newborns stare at some visual patterns longer than others. Newborns habituate to a repeated sound but dishabituate to a slightly different sound, indicating that they hear a difference. (page 360)
- *Infant memory*. Newborns increase or alter their rate of sucking if a particular pattern of sucking turns on a recorded voice. They suck more vigorously to turn on a recording of their own mother's voice than some other woman's voice, indicating a memory of the sound of the mother's voice. Infants just 2 months old can learn to kick to move a mobile and remember how to do it several days later. (page 361)

Answers to Concept Checks

1. Both parents must lack the dominant gene that controls the ability to curl their tongues. Therefore, they can transmit only "noncurler" genes, and their children will be noncurlers also. (page 355)

2. The woman will pass a gene for normal color vision to all her children, so they will all have normal color vision. The man will pass a gene for deficient color vision on his X chromosome, so his daughters will be carriers for color deficiency. (page 356)

3. If all children had equally supportive environments, the heritability of behaviors would *increase*. Remember, heritability refers to how much of the difference among people is due to hereditary variation. If the environment is practically the same for all, then environmental variation cannot account for much of the variation in behavior. Whatever behavioral variation still occurs would be due mostly to hereditary variation. (Note one implication: Any estimate of heritability applies only to a given population. In another population the heritability could be much different.) (page 357)

4. Tranquilizers decrease brain stimulation, and neurons that fail to receive enough stimulation self-destruct. Tranquilizers during pregnancy therefore provide the same risk as alcohol. (page 360)

5. Evidently, the infant does not hear a difference between *ba* and *bla*. (This is a hypothetical result; the study has not been done.) (page 361)

6. If the frequency increased, we would conclude that the infant recognizes the difference between the father's voice and the other voice. If the frequency remained the same, we would conclude that the infant did not notice a difference. If it decreased, we would assume that the infant preferred the sound of the father's voice. (page 362)

How do children's thought processes differ from adults'?

The artwork of young children is amazingly inventive and revealing. One toddler, 1½ years old, showed off a drawing that consisted only of dots on a sheet of paper. Puzzled adults did not understand. It is a rabbit, the child explained, while making more dots: "Look: hop, hop, hop . . . ." (Winner, 1986). When my daughter, Robin, was 6 years old, she drew a picture of a boy and a girl drawing pictures (Figure 10.15). The overall drawing has features that may not be clear; for example, both children are wearing Halloween costumes. For the little girl's drawing, Robin pasted on some wildlife photos. This array, she maintained, was what the little girl had drawn. Now look at the little boy's drawing, which is just a scribble. When I asked why the little girl's drawing was so much better than the little boy's, Robin replied, "Don't make fun of him, Daddy. He's doing the best he can."

miss the highly expressive drawings of her early childhood. The point is this: As we grow older, we gain many new abilities and skills. But we lose something too.

Studying the abilities of young children is challenging. Often, they misunderstand our questions or we misunderstand their answers. Developmental psychologists have made progress by devising increasingly careful methods of measurement.

Research Designs for Studying Development

Comparing people of different ages may sound easy, but any research method has limitations. Two major research designs are cross-sectional studies and longitudinal studies. A **cross-sectional study** *compares groups of individuals of different ages all at the same time.* For example, we could compare the drawing abilities of 6-year-olds, 8-year-olds, and 10-year-olds. The main weakness of cross-sectional studies is the difficulty of obtaining equivalent samples at different ages. For example, suppose you want to compare 20-year-olds and 60-year-olds. You might study a sample of 20-year-olds from the local college, but how will you find a comparable group of 60-year-olds?

A **longitudinal study** *follows a single group of individuals as they develop.* For example, we could study one group of children as they age from, say, 6 to 12. Table 10.1 contrasts the two kinds of studies. Longitudinal studies face practical difficulties. A longitudinal study necessarily takes years, and not everyone who participates the first time is willing and available later.

FIGURE 10.15 A drawing of two children drawing pictures, courtesy of 6-year-old Robin Kalat.

© Courtesy of Robin Kalat

Sometimes, as in this case, a child's drawing can tell us a great deal about the child's worldview. As children grow older, their art changes. Robin Kalat, now an adult, draws with skill that I envy. Still, I sometimes

As we grow older, we mature in our social and emotional behaviors. However, many revert quickly to childlike behaviors in situations where such behavior is acceptable.

Furthermore, those who leave a study may differ in important ways from those who continue. Suppose a creature from outer space observes humans and discovers that about 50% of young adults are males but that only 10 to 20% of 90-year-olds are males. The creature concludes that, as humans grow older, most males transform into females. You know why that conclusion is wrong. Males—with a few exceptions—do not change into females, but on the average they die earlier, leaving a greater percentage of older females. **Selective attrition** is *the tendency for some kinds of people to be more likely than others to drop out of a study.* Psychologists can compensate by reporting the data for only the people who stayed to the end of the study.

A longitudinal study also faces the difficulty of separating the effects of age from the effects of changes in society. For example, if people change their political views over the years, we do not know whether they changed because they grew older or because of changes in the world situation.

Despite these difficulties, certain questions logically require a longitudinal study. For example, to study the effects of divorce on children, researchers compare how each child reacts at first with how that same child reacts later. To study whether happy children are likely to become happy adults, we would follow a single group of people over time.

Sequential Designs

A sequential (or "cross-sequential") design combines the advantages of both cross-sectional and longitudinal designs. In a **sequential design**, *researchers start*

TABLE 10.1 Cross-Sectional and Longitudinal Studies

	Description	Advantages	Disadvantages	Example
Cross-sectional	Several groups of subjects of various ages studied at one time	1. Quick 2. No risk of confusing age effects with effects of changes in society	1. Risk of sampling error by getting different kinds of people at different ages 2. Risk of cohort effects	Compare memory abilities of 3-, 5-, and 7-year-olds
Longitudinal	One group of subjects studied repeatedly as the members grow older	1. No risk of sampling differences 2. Can study effects of one experience on later development 3. Can study consistency within individuals over time	1. Takes a long time 2. Some participants quit 3. Sometimes hard to separate effects of age from changes in society	Study memory abilities of 3-year-olds, and of the same children again 2 and 4 years later

with groups of people of different ages, studied at the same time, and then study them again at one or more later times. For example, imagine we study the drawings of 6-year-olds and 8-year-olds and then examine the drawings by those same children 2 years later:

First Study	2 Years Later
Group A, age 6 years	Group A, now 8 years old
Group B, age 8 years	Group B, now 10 years old

If Group A at age 8 years resembles Group B at age 8 years, we can feel confident that the groups are comparable. We can then compare Group A at 6 years, both groups at 8 years, and Group B at 10 years.

Cohort Effects

Sometimes people differ not because of age but because of the era in which they were born. Consider: On the average who knows more about the Vietnam War, current 20-year-olds or current 60-year-olds? Who knows more about computers, 20-year-olds or 60-year-olds? Presumably, you answered *60-year-olds* to the first question and *20-year-olds* to the second. People born in a given era share life experiences with those born at the same time, and they differ in many ways from people born in other eras. Psychologists call these differences *cohort effects* (Figure 10.16). **A cohort is** *a group of people born at a particular time or a group of people who entered an organization at a particular time.*

Indeed, the era in which you grew up is one of the most important influences on your behavior. For example, people whose youth spanned the Great Depression and World War II learned to save money and to sacrifice their own pleasures for the needs of society as a whole. Even after the war was over and prosperity reigned, most remained thrifty and cautious (Rogler, 2002). In contrast the generation who lived their youth in the 1990s and early 2000s has had a great deal of leisure time to spend on television and video games (Larson, 2001). They are more extraverted than previous generations but also more depressed and prone to anxiety (Twenge, 2002).

CONCEPT CHECK

7. Suppose you study the effect of age on artistic abilities, and you want to be sure that any apparent differences are due to age and not to cohort effects. Which should you use, a longitudinal study or a cross-sectional study?
8. Suppose you want to study the effect of age on choice of clothing. What problems would arise with either a longitudinal study or a cross-sectional study?
9. At Santa Enigma College, the average first-year student has a C-minus average, and the average senior has a B-plus average. An observer concludes that, as students progress through college, they improve their study habits. Based on the idea of selective attrition, propose another possible explanation. (Check your answers on page 382.)

Jean Piaget's Views of Development

Attending a political rally can have a profound effect on a young adult, less effect on a preteen, and none at all on an infant. However, playing with a pile of blocks will be a more stimulating experience for a young child than for anyone older. The effect of any experience depends on a person's maturity and previous experiences. The theorist who made this point most influentially was Jean Piaget (pee-ah-ZHAY) (1896–1980).

Early in his career, Piaget administered IQ tests to French-speaking children in Switzerland. He grew bored with the tests but was fascinated by children's incorrect answers. Piaget concluded that children and adults use qualitatively different thought processes. This view contrasts with the approach of most cognitive researchers, who describe age differences as quantitative changes in memory storage, speed of pro-

FIGURE 10.16 Children of the 1920s, 1960s, and 1990s differed in their behavior because they grew up in different historical eras, with different education, nutrition, and health care. Differences based on such influences are called *cohort effects.*

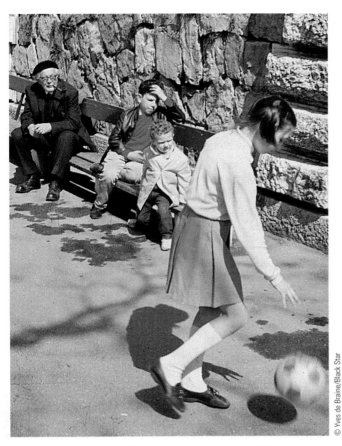

▎ Jean Piaget (on the left) demonstrated that children with different levels of maturity react differently to the same experience.

cessing, and so forth. Piaget supported his conclusion with extensive studies of children, especially his own, relying mainly on description and not on quantitative measurements.

CRITICAL THINKING:
A STEP FURTHER
Children's Thinking

How could we know whether the difference in adult and child thought processes is qualitative or quantitative? Consider: A modern computer differs from an old one in purely quantitative ways—speed of processing and amount of memory. The basic principles of computing are the same. Yet the new computer runs programs that the old one cannot—a qualitative difference in results. Could the differences between child and adult thinking reflect just speed of processing and amount of memory?

According to Piaget a child's intellectual development is not merely an accumulation of experience or a maturational unfolding. Rather, the child constructs

new mental processes as he or she interacts with the environment.

In Piaget's terminology behavior is based on schemata (the plural of *schema*). A **schema** is *an organized way of interacting with objects in the world.* For instance, infants have a grasping schema and a sucking schema. Older infants gradually add new schemata to their repertoire and adapt their old ones. The adaptation takes place through the processes of assimilation and accommodation.

Assimilation means *applying an old schema to new objects or problems.* For example, a child who observes that animals move on their own may believe that the sun and moon are alive because they seem to move on their own. (Many ancient adult humans believed the same thing.) **Accommodation** means *modifying an old schema to fit a new object or problem.* For example, a child may learn that "only living things move on their own" is a rule with exceptions and that the sun and moon are not alive.

Infants shift back and forth between assimilation and accommodation. **Equilibration** is *the establishment of harmony or balance between the two,* and according to Piaget equilibration is the key to intellectual growth. A disturbance or discrepancy occurs between the child's current understanding and some evidence to the contrary. That disturbance leads to assimilation and accommodation and then to equilibration at a higher level of functioning.

The same processes occur in adults. When you are given a new mathematical problem to solve, you try several methods until you hit upon one that works. In other words you assimilate the new problem to your old schema. However, if the new problem is different from any problem you have ever solved before, you modify (accommodate) your schema until you work out a solution. Through processes like these, said Piaget, intellectual growth occurs.

Piaget contended that children progress through four major stages of intellectual development:

1. *The sensorimotor stage* (from birth to almost 2 years)
2. *The preoperational stage* (from just before 2 to 7 years)
3. *The concrete operations stage* (from about 7 to 11 years)
4. *The formal operations stage* (from about 11 years onward)

The ages are variable, and not everyone reaches the formal operations stage. However, apparently everyone progresses through the stages in the same order. We shall encounter the same principle in other theories about stages of human development: Speed of progress through the stages varies, but order is con-

FIGURE 10.17 If someone places a bit of unscented rouge on a child's nose, a 2-year-old shows self-recognition by touching his or her own nose. A younger child ignores the red spot or points at the mirror.

stant. Let us consider children's capacities at each of Piaget's stages.

Piaget's Sensorimotor Stage

Piaget called the first stage of intellectual development the sensorimotor stage because *at this early age (birth to almost 2 years) behavior is mostly simple motor responses to sensory stimuli*—for example, the grasp reflex and the sucking reflex. According to Piaget infants respond only to what they see and hear right now.

Infants nevertheless notice relationships among their experiences. For example, even young infants can figure out which person in the room is talking, based on lip movements and the sound of the voice, and then look at the talking person (Lickliter & Bahrick, 2000).

As children progress through the sensorimotor stage of development, they appear to gain some concept of "self." The data are

as follows: A mother puts a spot of unscented rouge on an infant's nose and then places the infant in front of a mirror. Infants younger than 1½ years old either ignore the red spot they see on the baby in the mirror or reach out to touch the red spot. At some point after age 1½ years, infants in the same situation touch themselves on the nose, indicating that they recognize themselves in the mirror (Figure 10.17). Infants show this sign of self-recognition at varying ages; the age when they start to show self-recognition is about the same as when they begin to act embarrassed (Lewis, Sullivan, Stanger, & Weiss, 1991). That is, they show a sense of self either in both situations or in neither.

CRITICAL THINKING: WHAT'S THE EVIDENCE?
The Infant's Thought Processes About Object Permanence

A central point of Piaget's concept of the sensorimotor period was that infants respond only to what they see, not to what they remember. In fact he argued that infants in the first few months of life lack the concept of object permanence, *the idea that objects continue to exist even when we do not see or hear them.* That is, infants not only ignore what they don't see; they don't even know the objects still exist. How could Piaget know what an infant thinks? Obviously, he could only infer.

Piaget drew his inferences from observations of this type: Place a toy in front of a 6-month-old infant, who reaches out and grabs it. Later, place a toy in the same place, but before the infant has a chance to grab it, cover it with a clear glass. No problem; the infant removes the glass and takes the toy. Now repeat that procedure, but this time cover the toy with an opaque

FIGURE 10.18 (a) A 6- to 9-month-old child reaches for a visible toy, but not one that is hidden behind a barrier (b) even if the child sees someone hide the toy. According to Piaget this observation indicates that the child hasn't yet grasped the concept of object permanence.

(nonclear) glass. The infant, who watched you place the glass over the toy, makes no effort to remove the glass and obtain the toy. Or place a thin barrier between the infant and the toy. An infant who cannot see at least part of the toy does not reach for it (Piaget, 1937/1954) (see Figure 10.18). Even at 9 months, a child who has repeatedly found a toy in one location will reach there again after watching you hide it in a neighboring location.

Why not? According to Piaget the infant *does not know* that the hidden toy is there. However, one can imagine other possible explanations. A study by Renee Baillargeon (1986) suggests that infants do show signs of understanding object permanence when they are tested differently.

Hypothesis An infant who sees an event that would be impossible (if objects are permanent) will be surprised and therefore will stare longer than will an infant that sees a similar but possible event.

Method Infants aged 6 or 8 months watched a series of events staged by the researcher. First, the child watched the experimenter raise a screen to show nothing behind it and then watched a toy car go down a slope and emerge on the other side, as shown in the drawing below. This was called a "possible" event.

Possible event. The block appears to be behind the track, and the car passes by the block.

The researchers measured how long the child stared after the car went down the slope. They repeated the procedure until the child decreased his or her staring time for three trials in a row (showing habituation).

Then the experimenters presented two kinds of events. One kind was the possible event as just described; the other was an impossible event like this:

Impossible event. The raised screen shows a box on the track right where the car would pass. After the screen lowers, the car goes down the slope and emerges on the other side.

In an impossible event, the raised screen showed a box that was on the track, right where the car would pass. After the screen lowered, the car went down the slope and emerged on the other side. (The experimenters had pulled the box off the track after lowering the screen.) The experimenters measured each child's staring times after both kinds of events. They repeated both events two more times, randomizing the order of events.

Results Figure 10.19 shows the mean looking times. Infants stared longer after seeing an impossible event than after seeing a possible event. They also stared longer during the first pair of events than after the second pair and longer after the second than the third (Baillargeon, 1986).

Interpretation Why did the infants stare longer at the "impossible" event? The inference—and admittedly only an inference, not a certainty—is that the infants found the impossible event surprising. To be surprised, the infants had to expect that the box would continue to exist where it was hidden and that a car could not go through it. If this inference is correct, even 6-month-old infants have some understanding of the permanence of objects, as well as elementary physics. A later study with a slightly different method again measured how long infants stared at

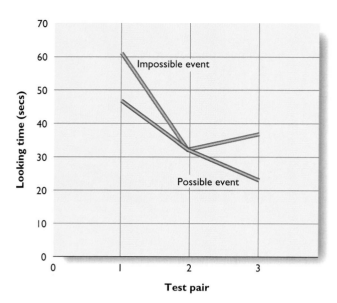

FIGURE 10.19 Mean looking times of 6- and 8-month-old infants after they had watched either possible or impossible events. *(Baillargeon, R. "Representing the existence and the location of hidden objects: Object permanence in 6- and 8-month-old infants." Cognition, 23, 21-41. Copyright 1986. Reprinted with permission from Elsevier.)*

possible and impossible events and demonstrated object permanence in infants as young as 3½ months (Baillargeon, 1987).

Still, remember that 9-month-olds failed Piaget's object permanence task of reaching out to pick up a hidden object. Do infants have the concept of object permanence or not? Perhaps there is something wrong with the question. It is possible to have a concept but use it in some situations and not others (Munakata, McClelland, Johnson, & Siegler, 1997). Even college students can pass a physics test and then fail to apply the laws of motion in a new situation or state a rule of grammar and yet make grammatical errors.

The important point is this: When dealing with infants or anyone else whose thought processes are likely to be different from our own, we should be cautious about inferring what they can or cannot do. The results may vary depending on the exact procedures.

CRITICAL THINKING:
A STEP FURTHER
Inferring "Surprise"

Suppose we play a series of musical notes and an infant stares longer toward the source of *do-re-mi-fa-so-la-ti* than *do-re-mi-fa-so-la-ti-do*. Should we infer that the infant is "surprised" by the absence of the final *do*?

Piaget's Preoperational Stage

By or before age 2, most children are learning to speak; within a few years, they will have nearly mastered their language. When a child asks for a toy, there is no longer any doubt that the child understands the concept of object permanence. Nevertheless, at this age children's understanding is not like that of adults. For example, they have difficulty understanding that a mother can be someone else's daughter. A boy with one brother will assert that his brother has no brother. Piaget refers to this period as the **preoperational stage** because *the child lacks operations, which are reversible mental processes.* For example, for a boy to understand that his brother has a brother, he must be able to reverse the concept of "having a brother." According to Piaget three typical aspects of preoperational thought are egocentrism, difficulty distinguishing appearance from reality, and lack of the concept of conservation.

Egocentrism: Understanding Other People's Thoughts

According to Piaget young children's thought is **egocentric.** By this term Piaget did *not* mean that children are selfish; instead, he meant that *a child sees the world as centered around himself or herself and cannot easily take another person's perspective.* If you and a preschooler sit on opposite sides of a complicated pile of blocks and you ask the child to draw or describe what the blocks would look like from your side, the child draws or describes them as they look from the child's side.

Another example: Young children hear a story about a little girl, Lucy, who wants her old pair of red shoes. Part way through the story, Lucy's brother Linus comes into the room, and she asks him to bring her red shoes. He goes and brings back her new red shoes, and she is angry because she wanted the old red shoes. Young children are often surprised that he brought the wrong shoes because *they* knew which shoes she wanted (Keysar, Barr, & Horton, 1998). In this and other studies, children up to 4, 5, or 6 years old (depending on the details) seem to assume that whatever *they* know, other people will know too (Birch & Bloom, 2003).

Unfortunately, none of us completely outgrow this tendency. In one study adults heard a story in which Jane recommends a restaurant to David. He goes there and dislikes it. Later, she asks him how he liked the restaurant, and he replies, ". . . it was marvelous, just marvelous." Adults who knew he disliked it are surprised that Jane didn't realize he was being sarcastic. Like the children, the adults were egocentric by assuming that what they knew other people would know also (Keysar et al., 1998).

FIGURE 10.20 Sometimes a child saw that the adult could see two glasses; other times it was clear that the adult could see only one. If two glasses were visible, the child usually told the adult which glass to pick up, instead of just saying "pick up the glass." *(From Nadig, A. S., & Sedivy, J. S.,"Evidence of Perspective-Taking Constraints in Children on line Reference Resolution" American Psychological Society, Vol. 13, No. 4, July 2002. Photo reprinted with the permission of the author and publisher.)*

Furthermore, even young children are able to understand another person's perspective some of the time if the task is simple. In one study 5- and 6-year-old children had to tell an adult to pick up a particular glass. If a child saw that the adult could see two glasses, the child usually said to pick up the "big" or "little" glass, so the adult could get the right one. If the child saw that the adult could see only one glass, the child was more likely just to say "the glass" (Nadig & Sedivy, 2002) (see Figure 10.20).

CONCEPT CHECK ☑

10. Which of the following is the clearest example of egocentric thinking?
    a. A writer who uses someone else's words without giving credit.
    b. A politician who blames others for everything that goes wrong.
    c. A professor who gives the same complicated lecture to a freshman class that she gives to a convention of professionals. (Check your answer on page 382.)

To say that a child is egocentric is to say that he or she has trouble understanding what other people know and don't know. Psychologists say that a young child lacks, but gradually develops, **theory of mind,** which is *an understanding that other people have a mind too and that each person knows some things that other people don't know.* How can we know whether a child has this understanding? Here is one example of a research effort.

CRITICAL THINKING: WHAT'S THE EVIDENCE?
Children's Understanding of Other People's Knowledge

How and when do children first understand that other people have minds and knowledge? Researchers have developed some clever experiments to answer this difficult question.

Hypothesis A child who understands that other people have minds will distinguish between someone who knows something and someone who could not.

Method A 3- or 4-year-old child sat in front of four cups (Figure 10.21) and watched as one adult hid a candy or toy under one of the cups, although a screen prevented the child from seeing which cup. Then another adult entered the room. The "informed" adult pointed to one cup to show where he or she had just hidden the surprise; the "uninformed" adult pointed to one of the other cups. The child was then given an opportunity to look under one cup for the surprise.

This procedure was repeated 10 times for each child. The two adults alternated roles, but on each trial one or the other hid the surprise while the other was absent. That is, one was in a position to know where the surprise was hidden and the other was not.

Results Of the 4-year-olds, 10 of 20 consistently chose the correct cup (the one indicated by the informed adult). That is, many of them showed that they understood who had the relevant knowledge and who did not. However, the 3-year-olds were just as likely to follow the lead of the uninformed adult as that of the informed adult (Povinelli & deBlois, 1992).

Interpretation Evidently, 4-year-olds are more likely than 3-year-olds to understand other people's knowledge (or lack of it).

Other experiments, using a somewhat different procedure, have yielded similar results. For example, children in one study watched a dramatization where a girl who had a marble in her basket left the room temporarily. During her absence a second girl moved the marble from the first girl's basket to her own basket. When the first girl returned to the room, the children were asked "Where is the marble?" and "Where will the first girl look for it?" Most 4-year-olds answered that she would look in her own basket, but younger children thought she would look in the second girl's basket (Wimmer & Perner, 1983). As in the previous study, 4-year-olds inferred what various people might or might not know.

Although these are important results, we should avoid concluding that children at some point suddenly understand that other people have minds. Children sometimes act as if they understand and sometimes not depending on the situation (Yirmiya, Erel, Shaked, & Solomonica-Levi, 1998). Gaining a concept is seldom an all-or-none process.

Distinguishing Appearance from Reality

Piaget and many other psychologists have contended that children in the early preoperational stage do not distinguish clearly between appearance and reality. For example, a child who sees you put a white ball behind a blue filter will say that the ball is blue. When you ask, "Yes, I know the ball *looks* blue, but what color is it *really*?" the child replies that it really *is* blue (Flavell,

FIGURE 10.21 A child sits in front of a screen covering four cups and watches as one adult hides a surprise under one of the cups. Then that adult and another (who had not been present initially) point to one of the cups to signal where the surprise is hidden. Many 4-year-olds consistently follow the advice of the informed adult; 3-year-olds do not.

1986). Similarly, a 3-year-old who encounters a sponge that looks like a rock probably will say that it really is a rock, but a child who says it is a sponge will also insist that it *looks like* a sponge. Children have to grow a year or two older before they say that something looks like one thing but really is another.

However, other psychologists have argued that the 3-year-old's difficulty is more with language than with understanding the appearance–reality distinction. (After all, 3-year-olds do play games of make-believe, so they sometimes do distinguish appearance from reality.) In one study psychologists showed 3-year-olds a sponge that looked like a rock and let them touch it. When the investigators asked what it looked like and what it was *really*, most of the children said either "rock" both times or "sponge" both times. However, if the investigators asked, "Bring me something so I can wipe up some spilled water," the children brought the sponge. And when the investigators asked, "Bring me something so I can take a picture of a teddy bear with something that looks like a rock," they again brought the sponge. So evidently, they did understand that something could be a sponge and look like a rock, even if they didn't say so (Sapp, Lee, & Muir, 2000).

Also consider the following experiment: A psychologist shows a child a playhouse room that is a scale model of a full-size room. Then the psychologist hides a tiny toy in the small room (while the child watches) and explains that a bigger toy just like it is "in the same place" in the bigger room. (For example, if the little toy is behind the sofa in the little room, the big toy is behind the sofa in the big room.) Then the psychologist asks the child to find the big toy in the big room. Most 3-year-olds look in the correct place and find the toy immediately (DeLoache, 1989). Adult chimpanzees solve a similar problem (Kuhlmeier & Boysen, 2002). Most 2½-year-old children, however, search haphazardly (see Figure 10.22a). If the experimenter shows the child the big toy in the big room and asks the child to find the little toy "in the same place" in the little room, the results are the same: Most 3-year-olds find it, but most 2½-year-olds cannot (DeLoache, 1989).

Before we speak too confidently about what a 2½-year-old cannot do, however, consider this clever follow-up study: The psychologist hides a toy in the small room while the child watches. Then both step out of the room, and the psychologist shows the child a "machine that can make things bigger." The psychologist aims a beam from the machine at the room and takes the child out of the way. They hear some chunkata-chunkata-clunkata-clunkata sounds, and then the psychologist shows the

a A 2½-year-old is shown small room where stuffed animal is hidden.

Child is unable to find the stuffed animal in the larger room.

b Child is shown small room where stuffed animal is hidden.

Child is told that the machine expands the room. Child stands out of the way during some noises and then returns.

Child is able to find the stuffed animal in the "blown-up" room.

FIGURE 10.22 If an experimenter hides a small toy in a small room and asks a child to find a larger toy "in the same place" in the larger room, most 2½-year-olds search haphazardly. (a) However, the same children know where to look if the experimenter says this is the same room as before, except that a machine has expanded it (b).

full-sized "blown-up" room and asks the child to find the hidden toy. Even 2½-year-olds go immediately to the correct location (DeLoache, Miller, & Rosengren, 1997) (see Figure 10.22b). Evidently, they can use one room as a "map" of the other *if* they think of them as "the same room." (Incidentally, hardly any of the children doubted that the machine had actually expanded the room, and many continued to believe it even after the psychologist tried to explain what had really happened!) The overall conclusion is that a child can appear to have an ability or to lack it depending on how we ask the question.

Developing the Concept of Conservation

According to Piaget preoperational children lack the concept of **conservation.** They fail to *understand that objects conserve such properties as number, length, volume, area, and mass after changes in the shape or arrangement of the objects*. They cannot perform the mental operations necessary to understand such transformations. (Table 10.2 shows some typical conservation tasks.) For example, if we set up two glasses of the same size containing the same amount of water and then pour the contents of one glass into a taller, thinner glass, preoperational children will say that the second glass contains more water (Figure 10.23).

I once doubted whether children really believed what they were saying in such a situation. I thought perhaps the phrasing of the questions somehow tricks them into saying something they do not believe. If you have these same doubts, borrow someone's 6-year-old child and try it yourself with your own wording. Here's my own experience: Once when I was discussing Piaget in my introductory psychology class, I invited my son Sam, then 5½ years old, to take part in a class demonstration. I started with two glasses of water, which he agreed contained equal amounts of water. Then I poured the water from one glass into a wider glass, lowering the water level. When I

asked Sam which glass contained more water, he confidently pointed to the tall, thin one. After class he complained, "Daddy, why did you ask me such an easy question? Everyone could see that there was more water in that glass! You should have asked me something harder to show how smart I am!" The following year I brought Sam to class again for the same demonstration. He was now 6½ years old, about the age when children make the transition from preoperational thinking to the next stage. This time I poured the water from one of the tall glasses into a wider one and asked him which glass contained more water. He looked and paused. His face got red. Finally, he whispered, "Daddy, I don't know!" After class he complained, "Why did you ask me such a hard question? I'm never coming back to any of your classes again!" The question that used to be embarrassingly easy had become embarrassingly difficult.

The next year, when he was 7½, I tried again (at home). This time he answered confidently, "Both glasses have the same amount of water, of course. Why? Is this some sort of trick question?"

TABLE 10.2 Typical Tasks Used to Measure Conservation

Conservation of number
Preoperational children say that these two rows contain the same number of pennies.
Preoperational children say that the second row has more pennies.

Conservation of volume
Preoperational children say that the two same-size containers have the same amount of water.

250 cc   250 cc

Preoperational children say that the taller, thinner container has more water.

250 cc   250 cc

Conservation of mass
Preoperational children say that the two same-size balls of clay have the same amount of clay. Preoperational children say that a squashed ball of clay contains a different amount of clay than the same-size round ball of clay.

FIGURE 10.23 Preoperational children, usually younger than age 7, don't understand that the volume of water remains constant despite changes in its appearance. During the transition from preoperational thinking to concrete operations, a child finds conservation tasks difficult and confusing.

Piaget's Concrete Operations Stage and Formal Operations Stage

At about the age of 7, children enter the stage of concrete operations and begin to understand the conservation of physical properties. This transition is not sudden, however. For instance, a 6-year-old child may understand that squashing a ball of clay will not change its weight but may not realize until years later that squashing the ball will not change the volume of water it displaces when it is dropped into a glass.

According to Piaget, during the **stage of concrete operations,** *children can perform mental operations on concrete objects but still have trouble with abstract or hypothetical ideas.* For example, ask this question: "How could you move a 4-mile-high mountain of whipped cream from one side of the city to the other?" Older children think of imaginative answers, but children in the concrete operations stage are likely to complain that the question is silly.

Or ask, "If you could have a third eye anywhere on your body, where would you put it?" Children in this stage generally respond immediately that they would put it right between the other two, on their foreheads. Older children suggest more imaginative ideas such as on the back of their heads, in the stomach (so they could watch food digesting), or on the tip of a finger (so they could peek around corners).

Finally, in Piaget's **stage of formal operations,** children develop *the mental processes that deal with abstract, hypothetical situations. Those processes demand logical, deductive reasoning and systematic planning.* According to Piaget children reach the

stage of formal operations at about age 11. Later researchers found that many people take longer to reach this stage, and some never reach it.

Suppose we ask three children, ages 6, 10, and 14, to arrange a set of sticks in order from the longest to the shortest. The 6-year-old (preoperational) child fails to order the sticks correctly. The 10-year-old (concrete operations) eventually gets them in the right order but only after prolonged trial and error. The 14-year-old (formal operations) holds the sticks upright with their bottom ends on the table and then removes the longest one, the second longest, and so forth.

A second example: We set up five bottles of clear liquid and explain that it is possible to mix some combination of them to produce a yellow liquid. The task is to find that combination. Children in the concrete operations stage plunge right in with no plan. They try combining bottles A and B, then C and D, then perhaps A, C, and E. Soon they have forgotten which combinations they've already tried. If they do stumble onto the correct combination, it is mostly by luck.

Children in the formal operations stage approach the problem more systematically. They may first try all the two-bottle combinations: AB, AC, AD, AE, BC, and so forth. If those fail, they try three-bottle combinations: ABC, ABD, ABE, ACD, and so on. By trying every possible combination only once, they are sure to succeed.

Children do not reach the stage of formal operations any more suddenly than they reach the concrete operations stage. Reasoning logically about a particular problem requires some experience with it. A 9-year-old chess hobbyist reasons logically about chess problems and plans several moves ahead but reverts to concrete reasoning when faced with an unfamiliar problem. Table 10.3 summarizes Piaget's four stages.

TABLE 10.3 Summary of Piaget's Stages of Cognitive Development

Stage and Approximate Age	Achievements and Activities	Limitations
Sensorimotor (birth to 1½ years)	Reacts to sensory stimuli through reflexes and other responses	Little use of language; seems not to understand object permanence in the early part of this stage
Preoperational (1½ to 7 years)	Develops language; can represent objects mentally by words and other symbols; can respond to objects that are remembered but not present	Lacks operations (reversible mental processes); lacks concept of conservation; focuses on one property at a time (such as length or width), not on both at once; still has trouble distinguishing appearance from reality
Concrete operations (7 to 11 years)	Understands conservation of mass, number, and volume; can reason logically with regard to concrete objects that can be seen or touched	Has trouble reasoning about abstract concepts and hypothetical situations
Formal operations (11 years onward)	Can reason logically about abstract and hypothetical concepts; develops strategies; plans actions in advance	None beyond the occasional irrationalities of all human thought

CONCEPT CHECK ☑

11. You are given the following information about four children. Assign each of them to one of Piaget's stages of intellectual development.
    a. Child has mastered the concept of conservation; has trouble with abstract and hypothetical questions.
    b. Child performs well on tests of object permanence; has trouble with conservation.
    c. Child has schemata; does not speak in complete sentences; fails tests of object permanence.
    d. Child performs well on tests of object permanence, conservation, and hypothetical questions. (Check your answers on page 382.)

Are Piaget's Stages Distinct?

According to Piaget the four stages of intellectual development are distinct, and a transition from one stage to the next requires a major reorganization of the child's thinking, almost as a caterpillar metamorphoses into a chrysalis and then the chrysalis metamorphoses into a butterfly. In other words intellectual growth is marked by periods of revolutionary reorganization.

Later research has cast much doubt on this conclusion. If it were true, then a child in a given stage of development—say, the preoperational stage—should perform consistently at that level. In fact children's performance fluctuates as a task is made slightly more or less difficult. For example, consider the conservation-of-number task, in which an investigator presents two rows of seven or more objects and then spreads out one row and asks which row "has more." Preoperational children reply that the spread-out row has more. However, when Rochel Gelman (1982) presented two rows of only three objects each (Figure 10.24) and then spread out one of the rows, even 3- and 4-year-old children usually answered that the rows had the same number of items. After much practice with short rows, most of the 3- and 4-year-olds also answered correctly that a spread-out row of eight items had the same number of items as a tightly packed row of eight.

FIGURE 10.24 (a) With the standard conservation-of-number task, preoperational children answer that the lower row has more items. (b) With a simplified task, the same children say that both rows have the same number of items.

Whereas Piaget believed children made distinct jumps from one stage to another, most psychologists today see development as gradual and continuous (Courage & Howe, 2002). That is, the difference between older children and younger children is not so much a matter of *having* or *lacking* an ability. Rather, younger children use their abilities only in simpler situations.

Differing Views: Piaget and Vygotsky

One implication of Piaget's findings is that children must discover certain concepts, such as the concept of conservation, mainly on their own. Teaching a concept means directing children's attention to the key aspects and then letting them discover the concept for themselves.

Another implication frequently drawn from Piaget's work is that teachers should determine a child's level of functioning and then teach material appropriate to that level. For example, teachers should not introduce abstract concepts to children who are at the concrete operations stage of development. They should wait for children to discover many concepts on their own.

In contrast Russian psychologist Lev Vygotsky (1978) argued that educators cannot wait for children to rediscover the principles of physics and mathematics. Indeed, he argued, the distinguishing characteristic of human thought is that it is based on language and symbols that enable each generation to profit from the experience of the previous ones.

However, when Vygotsky said that adults should teach children, he did not mean that adults should ignore the child's developmental level. Rather, every child has a **zone of proximal development**, which is *the distance between what a child can do alone and what the child can do with help*. Instruction should remain within that zone. For example, one should not try to teach a 4-year-old the concept of conservation of volume, and it would be a waste of time to try to teach it to an 8-year-old who understands it already. But a child around 6 years old who does not yet understand the concept might learn it

with help and guidance. Similarly, children improve their recall of a story when adults provide appropriate hints and reminders, and they can solve more complicated math problems with help than without it. Vygotsky compared this help to *scaffolding*, the temporary supports that builders use during construction: After the building is complete, the scaffolding is removed. Good advice for an educator, therefore, is to be sensitive to a child's zone of proximal development and attempt to detect how much further the child can be pushed.

CONCEPT CHECK ☑

12. What would be the opinions of Piaget and Vygotsky about the feasibility of teaching the concept of conservation? (Check your answer on page 382.)

The Development of Moral Reasoning

Just as people gradually develop their understanding of the physical world, they also gradually develop their understanding of right and wrong.

Kohlberg's Measurements of Moral Reasoning

Psychologists once regarded morality as a set of arbitrary, learned rules, such as driving on the right or left side of the road depending on the country. Lawrence Kohlberg (1969; Kohlberg & Hersh, 1977) proposed instead that moral reasoning is a process that naturally matures through a series of stages. For example, children younger than about 6 years old say that accidentally breaking something valuable is worse than intentionally breaking something of less value; older children and adults attend more to people's intentions. Although Kohlberg's stages of moral reasoning are analogous to Piaget's stages, someone might progress more rapidly through Piaget's stages than Kohlberg's, or the reverse.

Kohlberg argued that moral reasoning should not be evaluated according to someone's de-

▌ Lev Vygotsky called attention to a child's zone of proximal development: the gap between what a child can do alone and what the child can do with help. Education within that zone advances a child's reasoning abilities.

© Laura Dwight /PhotoEdit

▌ A real-life moral dilemma: Michigan physician Jack Kevorkian developed a device to help terminally ill patients kill themselves painlessly. Is it morally right or wrong to aid in someone else's suicide? According to Kohlberg the morality of an act depends on the reasoning behind it.

cisions but according to the reasons behind them. For example, do you think that designing nuclear bombs is a moral way to make a living? According to Kohlberg the answer depends on one's reasons for taking the job. Hugh Gusterson (1992) interviewed nuclear bomb designers at the Lawrence Livermore National Laboratory. When he asked them about the morality of their actions, nearly everyone said something like, "You're lucky you chose me to interview, because I, unlike all the others, think deeply about these matters." Nearly all insisted that the weapons' only function was to threaten an enemy and thereby prevent wars. If you doubt that assumption, you might disagree with the morality of the bomb designers' *actions,* but you could still respect their moral *reasoning.*

To measure the maturity of someone's moral judgments, Kohlberg devised a series of **moral dilemmas**— *problems that pit one moral value against another.* Each dilemma is accompanied by a question such as, "What should this person do?" or "Did this person do the right thing?" Kohlberg was not concerned about the choices people make because well-meaning people disagree on the right answer. More revealing is their explanations, which are categorized into six stages, grouped into three levels (see Table 10.4). Because few people respond consistently at stage 6, many authorities combine stages 5 and 6. To emphasize: Kohlberg's stages do not represent moral or immoral decisions but only moral and less moral *reasons* for a decision.

CRITICAL THINKING:
A STEP FURTHER
Kohlberg's Stages

Suppose a military junta overthrows a democratic government and sets up a dictatorship. In which of Kohlberg's stages of moral reasoning would you classify the members of the junta? Would your answer depend on their reasons for setting up the dictatorship?

People begin at Kohlberg's first stage and then progress through the others in order, although few reach the highest stages. (The order of progression is an important point: If people were just as likely to progress in the order 3-5-4 as in the order 3-4-5, then we would have no justification for calling one stage higher than the other.) People seldom skip a stage or revert to an earlier stage after reaching a higher one. People do fluctuate from one time to another. Nevertheless, we can classify people in terms of the usual or average level of their answers. Figure 10.25 shows that most 10-year-olds' judgments are at Kohlberg's first or second stage, but 13- and 16-year-olds progress to higher levels. Kohlberg suggests that this rather swift development results from cognitive growth: 16-year-olds are capable of more mature reasoning than 10-year-olds.

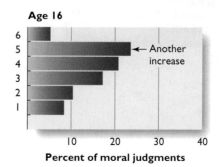

FIGURE 10.25 Most younger adolescents give answers corresponding to Kohlberg's earlier moral stages. By age 16 most of their answers are at higher levels. *(Based on Kohlberg, 1969)*

TABLE 10.4 Responses to One of Kohlberg's Moral Dilemmas by People at Six Levels of Moral Reasoning

The dilemma: Heinz's wife was near death from cancer. A druggist had recently discovered a drug that might be able to save her. The druggist was charging $2000 for the drug, which cost him $200 to make. Heinz could not afford to pay for it, and he could borrow only $1000 from friends. He offered to pay the rest later. The druggist refused to sell the drug for less than the full price paid in advance: "I discovered the drug, and I'm going to make money from it." Late that night, Heinz broke into the store to steal the drug for his wife. Did Heinz do the right thing?

Level/Stage	Typical Answer	Basis for Judging Right from Wrong	Description of Stage
The Level of Preconventional Morality			
1. Punishment and obedience orientation	"No. If he steals the drug, he might go to jail." "Yes. If he can't afford the drug, he can't afford a funeral, either."	Wrong is equated with punishment. What is good is whatever is in the man's immediate self-interest.	Decisions are based on their immediate consequences. Whatever is rewarded is "good" and whatever is punished is "bad." If you break something and are punished, then what you did was bad.
2. Instrumental relativist orientation	"He can steal the drug and save his wife, and he'll be with her when he gets out of jail."	Again, what is good is whatever is in the man's own best interests, but his interests include delayed benefits.	It is good to help other people, but only because they may one day return the favor: "You scratch my back and I'll scratch yours."
The Level of Conventional Morality			
3. Interpersonal concordance, or "good boy/nice girl" orientation	"People will understand if you steal the drug to save your wife, but they'll think you're cruel and a coward if you don't."	Public opinion is the main basis for judging what is good.	The "right" thing to do is whatever pleases others, especially those in authority. Be a good person so others will think you are good. Conformity to the dictates of public opinion is important.
4. "Law and order" orientation	"No, because stealing is illegal." "Yes. It is the husband's duty to save his wife even if he feels guilty afterward for stealing the drug."	Right and wrong can be determined by duty or by one's role in society.	You should respect the law—simply because it *is* the law—and work to strengthen the social order that enforces it.
The Level of Postconventional or Principled Morality			
5. Social-contract legalistic orientation	"The husband has a right to the drug even if he can't pay now. If the druggist won't charge it, the government should look after it."	Laws are made for people's benefit. They should be flexible. If necessary, we may have to change certain laws or allow for exceptions to them.	The "right" thing to do is whatever people have agreed is the best thing for society. As in stage 4, you respect the law, but in addition recognize that a majority of the people can agree to change the rules. Anyone who makes a promise is obligated to keep the promise.
6. Universal ethical principle orientation	"Although it is legally wrong to steal, the husband would be morally wrong not to steal to save his wife. A life is more precious than financial gain."	Right and wrong are based on absolute values such as human life. Sometimes these values take precedence over human laws.	In special cases it may be right to violate a law that conflicts with higher ethical principles, such as justice and respect for human life. Among those who have obeyed a "higher law" are Jesus, Mahatma Gandhi, and Martin Luther King, Jr.

Source: Kohlberg, 1981.

CONCEPT CHECK ☑

13. For the moral dilemma described at the top of Table 10.4, suppose someone says that Heinz was wrong to steal the drug to save his wife's life. Which level of moral reasoning is characteristic of this judgment? (Check your answer on page 382.)

Limitations of Kohlberg's Views

Kohlberg's theory is based on several uncertain assumptions. Let us consider two major issues: (a) justice versus caring orientations to morality and (b) the relationship between moral reasoning and behavior.

Are There Other Types of Moral Reasoning?

Kohlberg assumed that most judgments of right and wrong depend on "justice." In many non-Western cultures, such as the Hindu culture of India, people seldom talk about justice, laws, or personal happiness. They talk instead of a natural sense of duty toward others (Shweder, Mahapatra, & Miller, 1987). Even in Western cultures, we don't always reason in terms of justice. Carol Gilligan (1977, 1979) pointed out that we sometimes rely on a "caring" orientation—that is, what would help or hurt other people. She proposed alternative stages of moral development, as outlined in Table 10.5, ranging from preconventional (the least mature stage) to postconventional (the most mature). Gilligan initially argued that men rely more on a justice orientation and women rely more on caring. Later research found that this gender difference is small and inconsistent (Jaffee & Hyde, 2000). Nearly everyone shows some concern with both justice and caring. However, the key point is that the two orientations can be in conflict.

For example, at one point during the Vietnam War, a group of soldiers were ordered to kill a group of unarmed civilians. One soldier, who regarded the order as immoral, refused to shoot. In terms of "justice," he acted at a high moral level, following a "higher law" that required him not to kill. However, his actions

▌ Sometimes the two "voices" of moral reasoning—justice and caring—are in conflict with each other. From a caring standpoint, you want to help someone in distress. From a justice standpoint, you may think it wrong to encourage begging.

made no difference, as the other soldiers killed all the civilians. In terms of "caring," he would have been more moral if he had found a way to hide a few of the victims (Linn & Gilligan, 1990).

How Does Moral Reasoning Relate to Behavior?

The movie *Schindler's List* portrays a German man who risked his life to save Jewish people from the Nazi Holocaust. We all agree he did the right thing. But if you or I had been non-Jewish Germans at the time, what would we have done? I don't know. Stating the right thing to do is not the same as doing it.

Kohlberg's approach to morality has been criticized for both overestimating and underestimating people's moral behavior reasoning. I shall present both arguments and let you draw your own conclusions.

The first argument is as follows: Although many people give answers that qualify as stages 4, 5, and 6, moral *behavior* at those levels is less common, and we can understand why (Krebs, 2000). Behavior at stages 1, 2, and 3 benefits yourself: Seek rewards, avoid punishments, and cooperate with others who cooperate with you. ("You scratch my back and I'll scratch yours.") Behavior at stages 4, 5, and 6 benefits other people whom you will never meet.

On the other hand, maybe we underestimate the moral imperative. Most of us *want* to behave morally, even though we know that we often yield to temptations. Imagine the following: You and another student show up for psychological research. The researchers explain that two studies are available. One study sounds interesting and pleasant; the other is difficult and painful. You are invited to flip a coin and then announce who gets to be in the pleasant study.

TABLE 10.5 Carol Gilligan's Stages of Moral Development

Stage	Basis for Deciding Right from Wrong
Preconventional	What is helpful or harmful to myself?
Conventional	What is helpful or harmful to other people?
Postconventional	What is helpful or harmful to myself and others?

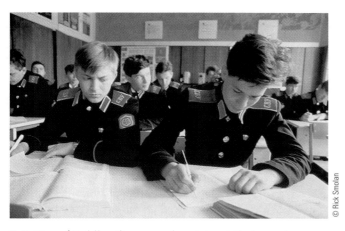

■ Critics of Kohlberg's approach point out that moral reasoning is not the same as moral action. This cadet at a Russian military academy (left) could probably explain why cheating is immoral, but he cheats nevertheless.

In this situation 85 to 90% of students claim they won the toss and get to be in the pleasant experiment. Obviously, many are lying. However, suppose you were asked whether you want to flip the coin and announce the results or let the experimenter do it. Now most people say "let the experimenter do it" (Batson & Thompson, 2001). They avoid putting themselves in a situation in which they know they will be tempted to lie.

IN CLOSING

Developing Cognitive Abilities

The universe is a complicated place, and none of us fully understands it. We should not be surprised that children misunderstand a great deal. For example, when a child fails to distinguish between appearance and reality—well, it's quite natural to assume that what you see is real.

Not only do young children often misunderstand the world; we adults often misunderstand children. They cannot express themselves clearly, and infants can't even control their muscles well. When an infant appears not to understand object permanence or when a toddler seems to have trouble understanding another person's point of view or when a child says it is wrong to do something "because you'll get punished," we are tempted to assume that what we see is real—that is, the child lacks certain ideas or abilities. Maybe so, but maybe not. More extensive testing sometimes reveals greater potentials than appeared at first. Children's development is complicated, and we should be humble enough to recognize the limits of our understanding.

Summary

- *Cross-sectional and longitudinal studies.* Psychologists study development by means of cross-sectional studies, which examine people of different ages at the same time, and by means of longitudinal studies, which look at a single group of people at various times as they grow older. A sequential design combines the main advantages of both methods. (page 364)
- *Cohort effects.* Many differences between young people and old people are not due to age but to time of birth. A group of people born in a particular era is called a cohort, and one cohort can differ from another in important ways. (page 366)
- *Piaget's view of children's thinking.* According to Jean Piaget, children's thought differs from adults' thought qualitatively as well as quantitatively. He believed children grew intellectually through accommodation and assimilation. (page 366)
- *Piaget's stages of development.* Children in the sensorimotor stage respond to what they see or otherwise sense at the moment. In the preoperational stage, according to Piaget, they lack reversible operations, such as the ability to understand that a mother could be someone else's daughter. In the concrete operations stage, children can reason about concrete problems but not abstractions. Adults and older children are in the formal operations stage, in which they can plan a strategy and can deal with hypothetical or abstract questions. (page 368)
- *Egocentric thinking.* Young children sometimes have trouble understanding other people's point of view. However, the results vary depending on the procedure. (page 370)
- *Appearance and reality.* Young children sometimes seem not to distinguish between appearance and reality. However, with a simpler task or different method of testing, they do distinguish. In many cases children do not fully have or lack a concept; they show the concept under some conditions and not others. (page 372)
- *Vygotsky.* Most psychologists now doubt that children go through distinct stages. Rather, one level of performance gradually blends into the next. According to Lev Vygotsky, children must learn new abilities from adults or older children; we cannot wait for them to make the discoveries by themselves. (page 377)
- *Kohlberg's view of moral reasoning.* Lawrence Kohlberg contended that moral reasoning matures naturally through stages. According to Kohlberg moral reasoning should be evaluated on the basis of the reasons someone gives for a decision rather than the decision itself. (page 377)

- *Challenges to Kohlberg's views.* Kohlberg concentrated on "justice," ignoring a "caring" orientation that sometimes gives a conflicting view. It has been argued both that people's actions are less moral than their answers to Kohlberg's questions and that their actions are in fact more moral than their answers imply. (page 380)

Answers to Concept Checks

7. Use a longitudinal study, which studies the same people repeatedly instead of comparing one cohort with another. (page 366)

8. With a longitudinal study, you would see clothing changes over time, but you would not know whether the changes were due to age or to changes in society. A cross-sectional study would be better, but you would have problems due to cohort effects. The older generation probably has always differed in its taste from the current younger generation. (page 366)

9. Another possible explanation is that the first-year students who have the lowest grades (and there-fore pull down the grade average for first-year students) do not stay in school long enough to become seniors. (page 366)

10. c is the clearest case of egocentric thought, a failure to recognize another person's point of view. (page 371)

11. **a.** concrete operations stage; **b.** preoperational stage; **c.** sensorimotor stage; **d.** formal operations stage. (page 376)

12. Piaget would recommend waiting for the child to discover the concept by himself or herself. According to Vygotsky the answer depends on the child's zone of proximal development. Some children could be taught the concept, and others are not yet ready for it. (page 377)

13. Not enough information is provided to answer this question. In Kohlberg's system any judgment can represent either a high or a low level of moral reasoning; we evaluate a person's moral reasoning by the explanation, not by the decision itself. (page 380)

Social and Emotional Development

How do we change, socially and emotionally, as we grow older?

You are a contestant on a new TV game show called *What's My Worry?* Behind the curtain is someone with an overriding concern. You are to identify that concern by questioning a psychologist who knows what it is. (You neither see nor hear the concerned person.) You must ask questions that can be answered with a single word or a short phrase. If you identify the worry correctly, you can win as much as $50,000.

Here's the catch: The more questions you ask, the smaller the prize. If you guess correctly after only one question, you win $50,000. After two questions, you win $25,000 and so on. It would therefore be poor strategy to keep asking questions until you are sure; instead, you should ask one or two questions and then make an educated guess.

What would your first question be? Mine would be: "How old is this person?" The principal worries of teenagers are different from those of most 20-year-olds, which in turn differ from those of still older people. Each age has its own characteristic concerns, opportunities, and pleasures.

Erikson's Description of Human Development

Erik Erikson divided the human life span into eight periods that he variously called ages or stages. At each stage of life, he said, people have specific tasks to master, and each generates its own social and emotional conflicts. Table 10.6 summarizes Erikson's stages, with the particular issues associated with each of them.

Erikson suggested that failure to master the task of a particular stage meant unfortunate consequences that would carry over to later stages. For example, the newborn infant deals with the issue of basic trust versus mistrust. An infant whose early environment is supportive, nurturing, and loving will form a strong attachment to the parents, and this attachment will positively influence future relationships with other people (Erikson, 1963). An infant who is mistreated will fail to form a close, trusting relationship with his or her parents and will have trouble developing close ties with anyone else later. This idea is, of course, testable, and later in this module, we shall consider some of the relevant research.

Consider also adolescence, with its issue of identity. Adolescents in Western societies have many options of how they will spend the rest of their lives. Most people consider many options before deciding, and it is possible to delay a decision or even to change one. Eventually, however, a decision becomes important. You can't work on achieving your plans until you have plans.

According to Erikson the key decision of young adulthood is intimacy or isolation—that is, sharing your life with someone else or living alone. Here is it pretty clear how a good decision can benefit the rest of your life and how a poor decision can hurt it.

If you live a full life span, you will spend about half your life in "middle adulthood," where the issue is

TABLE 10.6 Erikson's Stages of Human Development

Stages	Main Conflict	Typical Question
Infant	Basic trust versus mistrust	Is my social world predictable and supportive?
Toddler (ages 1–3)	Autonomy versus shame and doubt	Can I do things by myself or must I always rely on others?
Preschool child (ages 3–6)	Initiative versus guilt	Am I good or bad?
Preadolescent (ages 6–12)	Industry versus inferiority	Am I successful or worthless?
Adolescent (early teens)	Identity versus role confusion	Who am I?
Young adult (late teens and early 20s)	Intimacy versus isolation	Shall I share my life with another person or live alone?
Middle adult (late 20s to retirement)	Generativity versus stagnation	Will I succeed in my life, both as a parent and as a worker?
Older adult (after retirement)	Ego integrity versus despair	Have I lived a full life or have I failed?

© Bettmann/CORBIS

▌ Erik Erikson argued that each age group has its own special social and emotional conflicts.

generativity (producing something important, such as children or work) versus stagnation (not producing). If all goes well, you can take pride in your success. If not, then the difficulties and disappointments are almost certain to continue into old age.

Is Erikson's view of development accurate? This question is unanswerable. He provided a description, not an explanation. You might or might not find his description of development a useful way to describe life concerns, but it is not the kind of theory that one can test scientifically. However, two of his general points do seem valid: Each stage has its own special difficulties, and an unsatisfactory resolution to the problems of one stage of development will carry over as an extra difficulty in the next stage.

Now let's examine in more detail some of the major social and emotional issues that confront people at different ages. Beyond the primary conflicts that Erikson highlighted, development is marked by a succession of other significant problems.

CRITICAL THINKING:
A STEP FURTHER
Erikson's Stages

Suppose you disagreed with Erikson's analysis; for example, suppose you believe that the main concern of young adults is not "intimacy versus isolation" but "earning money versus not earning money" or "finding meaning in life versus meaninglessness." How might you determine whether your theory or Erikson's is more accurate?

Infancy and Childhood

An important aspect of human life at any age is **attachment**—*a long-term feeling of closeness toward another person*—and one of the most important events of early childhood is the formation of one's first attachments. John Bowlby (1973) developed a theoretical view that infants who develop one or more good attachments have a sense of security and safety. They can explore the world and return to their attachment figure when frightened or distressed. Those who do not develop strong early attachments will probably have trouble developing close relations later as well and need to cope with life's troubles without social support (Mikulincer, Shaver, & Pereg, 2003).

All that sounds fine in theory, but how can we measure strength of attachment to begin to test and extend the theory? Most work has used the **Strange Situation** (usually capitalized), pioneered by Mary Ainsworth (1979). In this procedure *a mother and her infant* (typically 12 or 18 months old) *come into a room with many toys. Then a stranger enters the room. The mother leaves and then returns. A few minutes later, both the stranger and the mother leave; then the stranger returns, and finally, the mother returns.* Through a one-way mirror, a psychologist observes the infant's reactions to each of these events. Observers classify infants' responses in the following categories. Of course, not all fit neatly into one category or another.

- *Securely attached.* The infant uses the mother as a base of exploration, often showing her a toy, cooing at her, or making eye contact with her. The infant shows some distress when the mother leaves but cries only briefly or not at all. When she returns, the infant goes to her with apparent delight, cuddles for a while, and then returns to the toys.
- *Anxious* (or *resistant*). Responses toward the mother fluctuate between happy and angry. The infant clings to the mother and cries profusely when she leaves, as if worried that she might not return. When she does return, the infant clings to her again but does not use her as a base to explore a room full of toys. A child with an anxious attachment typically shows many fears, including a strong fear of strangers.
- *Avoidant.* While the mother is present, the infant does not stay near her and does not interact much with her. The infant may or may not cry when she leaves and does not go to her when she returns.
- *Disorganized.* The infant seems not even to notice the mother or looks away while approaching her or covers his or her face or lies on the floor. The infant may alternate between approach and avoidance and shows more fear than affection.

The prevalence of the various attachment styles varies from one population to another, but these numbers are often cited as an approximation for North America: 65% secure, 10% anxious/resistant, 15% avoidant, 10% disorganized (Ainsworth, Blehar, Waters, & Wall, 1978). Of course, many children do not fit neatly into one category or another, so some who are classified as "secure" or "avoidant" are more secure or avoidant than others.

The Strange Situation also can be used to evaluate the relationship between child and father (Belsky, 1996), child and grandparent, or other relationships. As a rule the quality of one relationship correlates with the quality of others. For example, most children who have a good relationship with the mother also have a good relationship with the father, and chances are the parents are happy with each other as well (Elicker, Englund, & Sroufe, 1992; Erel & Burman, 1995). Beyond about age 18 months, the Strange Situation is no longer a useful tool, as children become much less distressed when they are left alone or with a stranger. The attachment patterns continue, though, and can be measured in other ways. For example, most infants who have a secure relationship with their parents at age 12 months continue to have a close relationship with them decades later (Waters, Merrick, Treboux, Crowell, & Albersheim, 2000). They are also likely to form close and mutually supportive relationships with friends and romantic partners, whereas those with anxious or avoidant attachments worry excessively about rejection or fail to seek others' support in times of distress (Mikulincer et al., 2003).

What influences a child's attachment pattern? That is, why do some children develop more secure attachments than others? One possibility is that children differ genetically in their tendency to fear the unfamiliar, and several studies with older children support this idea (McGuire, Clifford, Fink, Basho, & McDonnell, 2003; Schwartz, Wright, Shin, Kagan, & Rauch, 2003). However, much of the observed variance in attachment style depends on how responsive the parents are to the infants' needs, including such things as talking to the infant but also quite importantly holding and touching. Gentle touch can be very reassuring (Hertenstein, 2002). Programs that teach parents to be more responsive produce significant increases in secure attachments by the infants (Bakermans-Kranenburg, van IJzendoorn, & Juffer, 2003).

Extreme early experiences can also produce powerful effects. One study examined children adopted in Britain after living up to their first 2 years of life in Romanian orphanages where they had received little attention. Many of them did not even resemble any of the usual attachment styles. They

might approach and cling to the stranger instead of the parent. Some of them approached the stranger in a friendly way at first and then withdrew, unlike typical children who avoid a stranger at first and then become more friendly (O'Connor et al., 2003).

The patterns of attachment are somewhat consistent across cultures, but not entirely. For example, in most parts of the United States, most mothers encourage their infants to be independent from an early age, and mothers who exert much physical control over their infants tend to be less sensitive to their infants, leading to an avoidant attachment style. In Puerto Rico, however, most mothers exert much physical control while nevertheless being warm and sensitive, leading to a secure attachment style (Carlson & Harwood, 2003). In Asia most mothers hold their infants much of the day and keep them in bed with the parents at night. If an Asian mother is persuaded to leave her infant with a stranger in the Strange Situation, it may be the first time the infant has been away from its mother, and it cries loud and long. By Western standards these children qualify as "anxiously attached," but the behavior means something different in its cultural context (Rothbaum, Weisz, Pott, Miyake, & Morelli, 2000).

CONCEPT CHECK ☑

14. If a child in the Strange Situation clings tightly to the mother and cries furiously when she leaves, which kind of attachment does the child have? Does the child's culture affect the answer? (Check your answers on page 390.)

Social Development in Childhood and Adolescence

The social and emotional development of children depends in part on how successfully they form friendships with other children. "Popular" children have many friends and admirers. "Rejected" children are avoided by most other children. "Controversial" children who have some social skills but an aggressive streak are liked by some but rejected by others. In most cases a child's status as popular, rejected, or controversial is consistent from year to year (Coie & Dodge, 1983).

Adolescence begins when the body reaches *puberty,* the onset of sexual maturation. Adolescence merges into adulthood, and adulthood is more a state of mind than a condition of the body. Some 12-year-

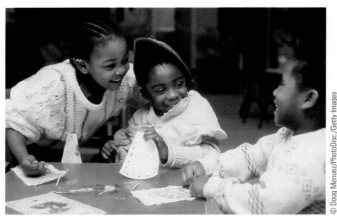

Children learn social skills by interacting with brothers, sisters, and friends close to their own age.

olds act like adults, and some 30-year-olds act like adolescents.

Adolescence has sometimes been portrayed as a period of "storm and stress," characterized by moodiness, conflict with parents, and risky behaviors. To some extent those trends reflect hormonal changes and brain maturation during adolescence. Even adolescent rats and other species show risky, sensation-seeking behaviors (Spear, 2000). However, the storm and stress vary substantially among individuals, families, and cultures (Arnett, 1999). For example, in Western societies the adolescent years are typically the time when people start dating, and the romantic relationships (or lack of

them) can be a source of either great pleasure or displeasure (Furman, 2002).

In many nontechnological societies, most teenagers are married and working. In effect they move directly from childhood into adulthood. In Western culture our excellent health and nutrition have gradually lowered the average age of puberty (Okasha, McCarron, McEwen, & Smith, 2001), but our economic situation encourages people to stay in school into their 20s and to postpone marriage, family, and career (Arnett, 2000). The consequence is a long period of physical maturity without adult status. Imagine that our society decided that people should stay in college until age 30, postponing marriage, children, and career decisions until even later. Would this policy bring out the best behavior in 25- to 30-year-olds?

Identity Development

As Erik Erikson pointed out, adolescence is a time of "finding yourself," of determining "who am I?" or "who will I be?" It is when most people first construct a coherent "life story" of how they got to be the way they are and how one life event led to another (Habermas & Bluck, 2000).

In some societies most people are expected to enter the same occupation as their parents and to live in the same town. The parents may even choose their children's marriage partners. Western society offers young people choices about education, career, marriage, political and religious affiliation, where to live, and activities regarding sex, alcohol, and drugs. Remember from Chapter 8 that, even when people are

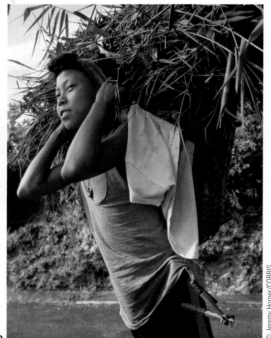

(a) American teenagers are financially dependent on their parents but have the opportunity to spend much time in whatever way they choose. (b) In many nontechnological societies, teenagers are expected to do adult work and accept adult responsibilities.

given all the information they need to answer a question, they sometimes still rely on inappropriate heuristics and make illogical decisions. With regard to life's most important choices, people almost never have all the information. Having a great deal of freedom to choose a life path can be invigorating, but it can also be more than a little frightening.

An adolescent's *concern with decisions about the future and the quest for self-understanding* has been called an **identity crisis**. The term *crisis* implies more emotional turbulence than is typical. Identity development has two major elements: whether one is actively exploring the issue and whether one has made any decisions (Marcia, 1980). We can diagram the possibilities using the following grid:

	Has explored or is exploring the issues	Has not explored the issues
Decisions already made	Identity achievement	Identity foreclosure
Decisions not yet made	Identity moratorium	Identity diffusion

Those who have not yet given any serious thought to making any decisions and who in fact have no clear sense of identity are said to have **identity diffusion**. People in this stage are not actively concerned with their identity and are waiting to clarify the issues. People in **identity moratorium** are *seriously considering the issues but have not yet made any decisions*. They experiment with various possibilities and imagine themselves in different roles before deciding which one is best.

Identity foreclosure is a state of *reaching firm decisions without much thought*. For example, a young man might be told that he is expected to go into the family business with his father, or a young woman might be told that she is expected to marry and raise children. Decrees of that sort were once common in North America and Europe, and they are still common in many other societies today. Someone who accepts such decisions has little reason to explore alternative possibilities.

Finally, **identity achievement** is *the outcome of having explored various possible identities and then making one's own decisions*. Identity achievement does not come all at once. For example, you might be fully decided about your career but not about marriage or about marriage but not a career. You might also reach identity achievement and then rethink some of those decisions years later.

The "Personal Fable" of Teenagers

Answer the following items true or false:

- Other people may fail to realize their life ambitions, but I will realize mine.
- I understand love and sex in a way that my parents never did.
- Tragedy may strike other people, but probably not me.
- Almost everyone notices how I look and how I dress.

According to David Elkind (1984), teenagers are particularly likely to harbor such beliefs. Taken together, he calls them the "personal fable," the conviction that "I am special—what is true for everyone else is not true for me." Up to a point, this fable can help us to maintain a cheerful, optimistic outlook on life, but it becomes dangerous when it leads people to take foolish chances.

For example, one study found that high school girls who were having sexual intercourse without contraception estimated that they had only a small chance of becoming pregnant through unprotected sex. Girls who were either having no sex or using contraception during sex estimated a much higher probability that unprotected sex would lead to pregnancy (Arnett, 1990). Because this was a correlational study, we do not know which came first—the girls' underestimation of the risk of pregnancy or their willingness to have unprotected sex. In either case the results illustrate the attitude, "it can't happen to me."

❚ Some teenagers seriously risk their health and safety. According to David Elkind, one reason for such risky behavior is the "personal fable," the secret belief that "nothing bad can happen to me."

This attitude is hardly unique to teenagers, however. Most middle-aged adults regard themselves as more likely than other people to succeed on the job and as less likely than average to have an injury or a serious illness (Quadrel, Fischhoff, & Davis, 1993). They also overestimate their own chances of winning a lottery, especially if they get to choose their own lottery ticket (Langer, 1975). That is, few people fully outgrow the personal fable.

Adulthood and the Midlife Transition

From their 20s until retirement, the main concern of most adults is, as Erik Erikson noted: "What will I achieve and contribute to society and my family? Will I be successful?" The young adult years begin with a flurry of major decisions about marriage, career, having children, where to live, and how to live. Whether middle age is a time of satisfaction depends on the quality of those decisions.

No doubt you have heard people talk about a "midlife crisis." Few people experience enough distress to call it a crisis, but many do experience *a reassessment of personal goals,* which we call a **midlife transition**. As people realize that their lives are about half over, they reconsider their careers and other choices.

Just as the adolescent identity crisis is a bigger issue in cultures that offer many choices, the same is true for the midlife transition. If you lived in a society that offered no choices, you would not worry about the paths not taken! People in Western society, however, enter adulthood with high hopes. While you are young, you dream of all the great things you will experience and accomplish. You plan to earn an advanced degree, work at a wonderful job, excel at it, marry a wonderful person, have marvelous children, become a leader in your community, run for political office, write a great novel, compose great music, travel the world . . . You know you are not working on all of your goals right now, but you can tell yourself, "I'll do it later." But at some point as you grow older, you realize that you are running out of "later." Even if some of your dreams are still achievable, time is passing: "What am I waiting for?"

People deal with their midlife transitions in many ways. Some abandon their unrealistic goals and set new goals more consistent with the direction their lives have taken. That is, they decide to do as well as possible at what they are already doing. Others decide that they have been ignoring dreams that they are not willing to abandon. They quit their jobs and go back to school, set up a business of their own, or try something else they had always wanted to do. In one study middle-aged women who made major changes in their lives were happier and more successful than those who didn't (Stewart & Ostrove, 1998). (Of course, we don't know whether the life changes made women happy and successful or whether happy, successful women are more likely than others to make changes.)

The least satisfactory outcome is to decide, "I can't abandon my dreams, but I can't do anything about them either. I can't take the risk of changing my life, even though I am dissatisfied with it." People with that attitude become frustrated, discouraged, depressed.

The advice is clear: To increase your chances of feeling good in middle age and beyond, make good decisions now. If there is something you really care about, such that you will regret not trying it, don't wait until you have a midlife crisis. Get started on it now. Take chances. If you fail, well, at least you won't always wonder what would have happened if you had tried. Besides, in the process of trying to do what you want, you might discover a related opportunity that you would not have found otherwise. And you never know: You might succeed.

CONCEPT CHECK ☑

15. How does a midlife transition resemble an adolescent identity crisis? (Check your answer on page 390.)

Old Age

People age in different ways. Some people, especially those with Alzheimer's disease or other serious ailments, deteriorate rapidly, both intellectually and physically. However, most people over 65 continue to work at full-time or part-time jobs, volunteer work, or other activities. Many remain active and alert well into their 80s and 90s. It is difficult to remain alert without remaining active; programs that increase older people's physical exercise lead to improvements in memory and cognition as well (Colcombe & Kramer, 2003).

Your satisfaction in old age will depend largely on how you live while younger. Some older people can say, "I hope to continue living many more years, but even if I don't, I have lived my life well. I did everything that I really cared about." Others say, "There is so much that I wanted to do but never did." Feeling dignity in old age also depends on how people are treated by their families, communities, and societies. Some cultures, including the people of Korea, observe a special ceremony to celebrate a person's retirement or 70th birthday (Damron-Rodriguez, 1991). African American and Native American families traditionally honor their elders, giving them a position of status in

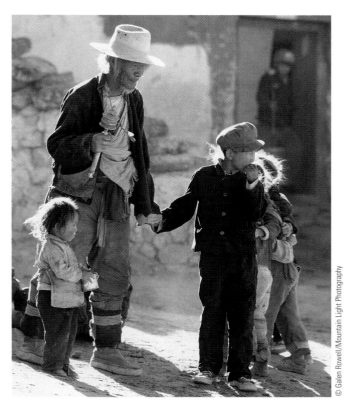

In Tibet and many other cultures, children are taught to treat old people with respect and honor.

© Galen Rowell/Mountain Light Photography

the family and calling on them for advice. Japanese families follow a similar tradition, at least publicly (Koyano, 1991).

Older people make some different choices than young people, but their differences are easy to understand. Suppose we ask young and old adults whether they would prefer to spend this weekend meeting interesting new people or with friends they have known for years. Young people generally opt for an exciting stranger, but older people strongly prefer longtime friends. Why? You can probably identify with the older people if we change the question slightly. You still have a choice between meeting exciting new people or visiting with longtime friends, except that you plan soon to move permanently to the other side of the world. Now whom do you want to visit? Almost certainly, you will want to use this last opportunity to visit your best friends (Carstensen & Charles, 1998).

Although an increasing percentage of people over 65 remain in the work force, most people eventually retire. Retirement decreases stress, but it also brings a sense of loss to those whose lives had centered around their work (Kim & Moen, 2001). Loss of control becomes a more serious issue still later if someone is in failing health. Consider someone who spent half a century running a business who now lives in a nursing home where staff members make all the decisions. Leaving even a few of the choices and responsi-

bilities to the residents improves their health, alertness, and memory (Rodin, 1986; Rowe & Kahn, 1987).

The Psychology of Facing Death

A man who has not found something he is willing to die for is not fit to live.
—Martin Luther King Jr. (1964)

This is perhaps the greatest lesson we learned from our patients: LIVE, so you do not have to look back and say, "God, how I have wasted my life!"
—Elisabeth Kübler Ross (1975)

The worst thing about death is the fact that when a man is dead it's impossible any longer to undo the harm you have done him, or to do the good you haven't done him. They say: live in such a way as to be always ready to die. I would say: live in such a way that anyone can die without you having anything to regret.
—Leo Tolstoy (1865/1978, p. 192)

We commonly associate death with older people, although people die at any age. Just thinking about the fact that you will eventually die evokes distress. According to **terror-management theory,** *we cope with our fear of death by avoiding thinking about death and by affirming a worldview that provides self-esteem, hope,*

© Ken Probst/CORBIS OUTLINE

Pedro Zamora worked to educate people about HIV prevention and AIDS after he learned he was HIV positive. He became famous when he appeared on MTV's *Real World* and later died of AIDS-related complications.

and value in life (Pyszczynski, Greenberg, & Solomon, 2000). If someone simply reminds you that you are mortal, your probable reactions include self-assurances that you have many years to live, that your health is good, and that you will quit smoking, lose weight, or do whatever else would improve your health. You probably also will increase your ambitions temporarily, talking about the high salary you will earn and the exciting things you will do during the rest of your life (Kasser & Sheldon, 2000).

Still, even excellent health merely postpones death, so a reminder of death also redoubles people's efforts to defend a belief that life is part of something eternal. People with strong religious beliefs may have faith in a continuation of their own lives after death. Others think in terms of how their lives contribute to their families, their countries, their professions, or something else that will continue after they are gone (Pyszczynski et al., 2000). Even a casual reference to death increases people's defenses of their beliefs, whatever those beliefs are.

IN CLOSING

Social and Emotional Issues Through the Life Span

Let's close by reemphasizing a key point of Erik Erikson's theory: Each age or stage builds on the previous ones. For example, the quality of your early attachments to parents and others correlates with your ability to form close, trusting relationships later. How well you handle the identity issues of adolescence affects your adult life. Certainly, your productivity during adulthood (generativity vs. stagnation) determines how satisfied you can feel with your life when you reach old age.

We could make a similar point for Piaget's cognitive stages or Kohlberg's stages of moral reasoning, discussed in the previous module: Each of us has to master the tasks of an earlier stage before we can deal effectively with those of the next stage. Life is a continuum, and the choices you make at any age are linked with those you made before and after.

Summary

* *Erikson's view of development.* Erik Erikson described the human life span as a series of eight ages or stages, each with its own social and emotional conflicts. (page 383)
* *Infant attachment.* Infants can develop several kinds of attachment to significant people in their lives, as measured in the Strange Situation. However, the results of studies in Western society do not apply equally well in other societies. (page 384)
* *Adolescent identity crisis.* Adolescents have to deal with the question "Who am I?" Many experiment with several identities before deciding. (page 386)
* *Adults' concerns.* One of the main concerns of adults is productivity in family and career. Many adults undergo a midlife transition when they reevaluate their goals. (page 388)
* *Old age.* Dignity and independence are key concerns of old age. (page 388)
* *Facing death.* People at all ages face the anxieties associated with the inevitability of death. A reminder of death influences people to set higher goals and to defend their worldviews. (page 389)

Answers to Concept Checks

14. In the United States, this pattern would indicate an anxious or insecure attachment. In Southeast Asia, however, this behavior is normal and we should beware of applying any labels that have been established for Western children. (page 385)

15. In both cases people examine their lives, goals, and possible directions for the future. (page 388)

Temperament, Family, Gender, and Cultural Influences

What factors influence development of personality and social behavior?

If you had to describe yourself briefly, what would you say? You probably would mention your age, your family, whether you are male or female, where you live, where you work or go to school, and your main interests and activities. You might mention your political or religious affiliation and possibly your nationality or ethnic identity.

The point is this: You are a unique individual and also a member of many groups. Your group memberships mold some of your thoughts about yourself and how other people treat you. You are a complex product of both what you bring to a situation (your personality and temperament) and how a situation affects you. Let's begin with temperament.

Temperament and Lifelong Development

People differ markedly in their temperament—their *tendency to be either active or inactive, outgoing or reserved, and to respond vigorously or quietly to new stimuli.* Would you rather go to a party where you will meet new people or spend a quiet evening with a few old friends? Would you try a risky activity or would you watch while someone else tries it? In general, are you more impulsive or more reserved than most of the people you know?

Now consider how you just described yourself: How long have you been like that? Were you at one time a great deal more outgoing and adventurous, or shyer and more reserved, than you are now?

To test the persistence of temperament, researchers have conducted studies lasting from infancy into adulthood. Infants who frequently kick and cry are termed "difficult" or "inhibited," whereas those who seldom kick or cry are called "easy" or "uninhibited" (Thomas & Chess, 1980; Thomas, Chess, & Birch, 1968). The inhibited infants have irregular eating and sleeping habits. As children they are frequently tense and hard to comfort (Kagan, 1989). They also contract contagious diseases more often than others (Lewis, Thomas, & Worobey, 1990). (Inhibited and uninhibited children are, of course, two ends of a continuum. Many children are intermediate.)

Jerome Kagan and Nancy Snidman (1991) identified some clearly inhibited and uninhibited 4-month-old infants and then tested them again a few months later in mildly frightening situations. For example, the experimenter might uncover a rotating toy, frown, and then scream a nonsense phrase. Infants who had been inhibited at age 4 months were in general easily frightened at 9 and 14 months. When they were tested again at 7½ years, they tended to be shy, nervous, and fearful (Kagan, Reznick, & Snidman, 1988). As adults they were tested with functional magnetic resonance imaging, a procedure that measures the activity of various brain areas. As shown in Figure 10.26, when inhibited people viewed photographs of unfamiliar people, they had higher than average activity in the *amygdala,* a brain area that processes anxiety-related information (Schwartz et al., 2003).

▌ Most people's temperaments remain fairly consistent over time. An outgoing, uninhibited child will probably continue to be outgoing and uninhibited for years, perhaps even into adulthood.

FIGURE 10.26 This horizontal section through an image of the human brain shows two areas that were more active in inhibited than uninhibited adults. Areas marked in red showed a large difference and those in yellow showed an even larger difference. "Amy" indicates the area of the amygdala (on each side of the brain). "OTC" indicates the occipital and temporal areas of the cortex.

Apparently, temperament depends at least partly on genetics. Identical twins resemble each other in temperament more than fraternal twins do (Matheny, 1989). Identical twins reared in separate and apparently rather different environments generally end up with similar temperaments (Bouchard, Lykken, McGue, Segal, & Tellegen, 1990). However, environmental factors must contribute also; otherwise, identical twins would always match each other exactly.

CONCEPT CHECK ☑

16. Were the studies of temperament over the years longitudinal or cross-sectional?
17. Why is it likely that temperament is one influence on behavior in the Strange Situation? (Check your answers on page 399.)

The Family

In early childhood our parents and other relatives are the most important people in our lives. How do those early family experiences mold our personality and social behavior?

Birth Order and Family Size

You have no doubt heard people say that first-born children are more successful in schoolwork and career accomplishments than later borns. First borns also rate themselves as more ambitious, honest, and conscientious (e.g., Paulhus, Trapnell, & Chen, 1999). On the other hand, later-born children are said to be more popular, more independent, less conforming, less neurotic, and possibly more creative.

Those generalizations are based on an enormous number of studies. However, most of those studies have used flawed research methods (Ernst & Angst, 1983; Schooler, 1972). The simplest and by far most common way to do the research is this: You ask some large number of people to tell you their birth order and something else about themselves, such as their grade point average in school. Then you measure the correlation between the measurements. Do you see any possible problem here?

The problem is that many first borns come from families with *only* one child, whereas (of course) later-born children all come from larger families. In general, highly educated and ambitious parents are more likely to have only one child and to provide that child with many advantages. Therefore, what appears to be a difference between first- and later-born children could be a difference between small and large families (Rodgers, 2001).

A better way to do the study is to compare first- versus second-born children in only families with at least two children, first- versus third-born children in only families with at least three children, and so forth. Figure 10.27 shows the results of one such study. As you can see, the average IQ is higher in small families

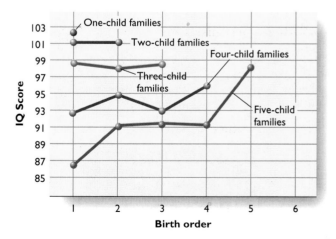

FIGURE 10.27 Children from small families tend to score higher on IQ tests than children from large families. However, within a family of a given size, birth order is not related to IQ. If we combine results for families of different sizes, first borns have a higher mean score, but only because many of them come from small families. *(Adapted from Rodgers et al., 2000)*

than in large families. However, within a family of any given size, first borns do no better than later borns on the average (Rodgers, Cleveland, van den Oord, & Rowe, 2000).

"But wait," you say. "The first born in my family does act different from the others, and most of the people I know see the same pattern in their own families." In a sense you are right: The first born takes more responsibility, identifies more with the parents, bosses the younger children around, and in many other ways, acts differently from the later-born children *while at home*. However, the way people act at home is not necessarily the way they act among friends at school (Harris, 2000).

CONCEPT CHECK ☑

18. Suppose someone found that last-born children (those with no younger brothers or sisters) do better in school than second-to-last borns. What would be one likely explanation? (Check your answer on page 400.)

Effects of Parenting Styles

If and when you have children of your own, will you be loving and kind or strict and distant? Will you give the children everything they want or make them work for rewards? Will you encourage their independence or enforce restrictions? Moreover, how much does your behavior matter?

Psychologists have done a great deal of research comparing parenting styles to the behavior and personality of the children. Much of this research is based on four parenting styles described by Diana Baumrind (1971):

Authoritative parents: These parents *set high standards and impose controls, but they are also warm and responsive to the child's communications.* They set limits but adjust them when appropriate; they encourage their children to strive toward their own goals.

Authoritarian parents: Like the authoritative parents, authoritarian parents set firm controls, but they tend to be *emotionally more distant from the child; they set rules without explaining the reasons behind them.*

Permissive parents: Permissive parents are *warm and loving but undemanding.*

Indifferent or uninvolved parents: These parents *spend little time with their children and do little more than provide them with food and shelter.*

Parenting styles are reasonably consistent within a family. For example, parents who are permissive with one child are usually permissive with the others too (Holden & Miller, 1999). The research has found small but reasonably consistent links between parenting style and children's behavior. For example, most children of authoritative parents are self-reliant, cooperate with others, and do well in school. Children of authoritarian parents tend to be law-abiding but distrustful and not very independent. Children of permissive parents are often socially irresponsible. Children of indifferent parents tend to be impulsive and undisciplined.

However, the interpretation of the results is not as easy as it may appear. Many psychologists have drawn cause-and-effect conclusions—for example, assuming that parental indifference *leads to* impulsive, out-of-control children. However, as Judith Rich Harris (1998) pointed out, other explanations are possible. Maybe impulsive, hard-to-control children cause their parents to withdraw into indifference. Or maybe the parents and children share genes that lead to uncooperative behaviors. Similarly, the kindly behaviors of authoritative parents could encourage well-mannered behaviors in their children, but it is also possible that these children were well behaved from the start, thereby encouraging kindly, understanding behaviors in their parents.

A better approach is to study adopted children, who are genetically unrelated to the parents rearing them. If their behavior depends on the parenting style or resembles the behavior of the parents in any way, we cannot explain the relationship in terms of shared genes. The results of such studies surprise most people: Most measures of personality show nearly a zero correlation between adoptive parents and their adopted children (Heath, Neale, Kessler, Eaves, & Kendler, 1992; Loehlin, 1992; Viken, Rose, Kaprio, & Koskenvuo, 1994). For this reason Harris (1995, 1998) has argued that family life has little lasting influence on most aspects of personality (except for what people do specifically at home). Much of personality variation depends on genetic differences, and the rest of the variation, she argues, depends mostly on peer influences—that is, the other children in the neighborhood. If a researcher picks two children at random from the same classroom, they are more likely than children from different schools to resemble each other in a wide variety of behaviors (Rose et al., 2003). In short, peer influences are strong. For more information visit this Web site:

home.att.net/~xchar/tna/

As you can imagine, not everyone happily accepted Harris's conclusion. Psychologists who had spent a career studying parenting styles were not pleased to be told that their results were inconclusive. Parents were not pleased to be told that they had less influence on their children than they had thought. Harris (2000), however, chose her words carefully. She did not say that it makes no difference how you treat your children. For one thing, obviously, if you treat your children badly, they won't like you!

Also, parents control where the children live and therefore influence their choice of peers, and parents influence some aspects of life that peers usually don't care about, such as religion, exposure to music lessons, and what spices to put on food. Parents have other influences too, and indeed, Harris may have overstated her case (Vandell, 2000). What is clear, however, is that previous psychologists had overstated their case even more. Parents do have an influence on their children's psychological development but not the huge effect we used to assume.

CONCEPT CHECK ☑

19. Why is a correlation between parents' behavior and children's behavior indecisive concerning how parents influence their children? Why would a correlation between adoptive parents' behavior and that of their adopted children provide more useful information? (Check your answers on page 400.)

Parental Employment and Child Care

Many people assume that the "normal" way to rear infants is for the mother to stay with them full time because that custom was prevalent in much of North America and Europe for many years. However, child-rearing customs vary greatly from one culture to another, one era to another, and even one social class to another.

In many subsistence cultures, a mother returns to her usual tasks of gathering food and so forth shortly after giving birth, leaving her infant most of the day with other women, relatives, and older children (McGurk, Caplan, Hennessy, & Moss, 1993). For example, in the Efe culture of Africa, a mother stays with her infant only about half of the day, but the infant is seldom alone. Within the first few months, the infant establishes strong attachments to several adults and children (Tronick, Morelli, & Ivey, 1992). In wealthy families in Europe, it has long been the custom for "nannies" (paid caregivers) to take care of the children for most of the day. In short, if we consider all the people who ever lived anywhere, it is a rarity for a child to be reared exclusively by the mother.

Still, many psychologists in Europe and North America developed a theoretical belief that healthy emotional development required an infant to establish a strong attachment to a single caregiver—ordinarily, the mother. When more and more families began placing infants in day care so that both parents could return to work shortly after their infant's birth, a question arose about the psychological effect on those children.

Many studies compared children who stayed with their mothers and those who entered day care early. The studies examined attachment (as measured by the Strange Situation or in other ways), adjustment and well-being, play with other children, social relations with other adults, and intellectual development. The results were that most children develop satisfactorily, both intellectually and socially, if they receive at least adequate day care (Scarr, 1998). One longitudinal study of 2,402 low-income families examined both preschoolers and older children before and after their mothers took jobs. The preschoolers showed no behavioral changes, and the older children showed slight benefits in some aspects of adjustment (Chase-Lansdale et al., 2003). One study showed a surprising result: Children who started day care before age 1 showed more favorable attachment behaviors than those who started after age 2½ (Erel, Oberman, & Yirmiya, 2000). Perhaps those who started day care early got used to it, whereas those who started later had more trouble adjusting to the change.

Undoubtedly, the quality of day care makes a difference to children's behavior, although most studies have found big differences only for children from disadvantaged homes. Evidently, development is satisfactory when either home life or day care is good; prob-

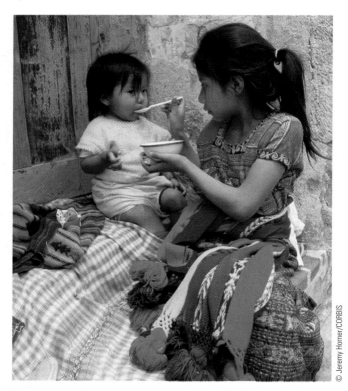

❙ In many cultures it has long been the custom for a mother to leave her infant for much of the day with friends, relatives, and other children.

❚ Many children today are reared by a single parent. Some are reared primarily by the father or grandparents. Some are reared by gay parents. The research says that who rears the child has little influence on long-term personality development if the caregivers are loving and dependable.

lems arise when both are bad. When children from disadvantaged homes experience good day care (with a consistent, affectionate staff and adequate facilities), they develop *better* than if they had stayed at home (McGurk et al., 1993; Scarr, Phillips, & McCartney, 1990). Children from deprived homes who experience poor day care, which is often all the parents can afford, are at a clear disadvantage.

Nontraditional Families

Western society has considered a "traditional" family to be a mother, a father, and their children. A "nontraditional" family is, therefore, anything else. Psychologists have studied the personalities of children who were reared by unmarried mothers (Weissman, Leaf, & Bruce, 1987), gay or lesbian couples (Patterson, 1994), and families where the mother works full time and the father stays home with the children (Parke, 1995). Parenting styles do differ; for example, fathers generally play with their children more, talk to them less, and tell them more facts with less praise (Leaper, Anderson, & Sanders, 1998). Single parents (usually mothers) often have trouble paying the bills, and their children have troubles resulting from poverty.

However, according to the available data, if we control for the effects of poverty, the other variables in family composition make little measurable difference. Researchers have found no consistent personality effects from being reared by one parent instead of two or mainly by the father instead of the mother or by gay or lesbian couples instead of a heterosexual couple (Golombok et al., 2003; Silverstein & Auerbach, 1999).

At least those are the conclusions from the available data. Not many studies have examined children reared mainly by fathers or by homosexual couples, and most of those studies have a small sample size and only a modest number of behavioral observations (Redding, 2001). More extensive studies would be a good idea.

Parental Conflict and Divorce

At an earlier time in the United States, divorce was unusual and considered shameful. When Adlai Stevenson was defeated in the presidential campaign of 1952, the fact that he was divorced was considered a major explanation. By 1980, when Ronald Reagan was elected president, voters hardly noticed his divorce and remarriage.

Most children who experience the divorce of their parents show a variety of academic, social, and emotional problems compared to other children. One reason is that the children of divorced families receive less attention and suffer greater economic hardship. Also, many children in divorced families endure prolonged hostility between their parents (Amato & Keith, 1991). If the divorce takes place while the children are still too young to realize what is happening, the effects are milder (Tschann, Johnston, Kline, & Wallerstein, 1990).

Mavis Hetherington and her associates have conducted longitudinal studies of middle-class children and their families following a divorce (Hetherington, 1989). Compared to children in intact families, those in divorced families are more likely to have conflicts with their parents and other children. They pout and seek attention, especially in the first year after a divorce. The boys in particular become aggressive, both at home and at school. Generally, distress is greatest if a mother who had not worked before the divorce takes a job immediately afterward—often by economic necessity. The children then feel that they have lost both parents.

▌Many sons of divorced parents go through a period when they act out their frustrations by starting fights.

In families where the mother remarried, the daughters were often indifferent or hostile to the step-father and showed poorer adjustment than children of mothers who did not remarry (Hetherington, Bridges, & Insabella, 1998). Many of the girls rejected every attempt by their stepfathers to establish a positive relationship until eventually the stepfather simply gave up (Hetherington, 1989).

"Complex" or "blended" stepfamilies are composed of parents and their children from previous marriages. Such families have special opportunities and difficulties. Interestingly, the children usually get along fairly well with their new step-brothers and sisters. They may, however, show resentment toward their parents (Hetherington, Henderson, & Reiss, 1999).

Hetherington's studies concentrated on European American middle-class children, and the results differ for other cultures. Divorce is more common in African American families but as a rule more accepted and less stressful (Fine & Schwebel, 1987). Many African American families ease the burden of single parenthood by having a grandmother or other relative help with child care. As in European American families, the more upset the mother is by the divorce, the more upset the children are likely to be (R. T. Phillips & Alcebo, 1986).

Exceptions can be found to almost any generalization about the effects of divorce on children (Hetherington, Stanley-Hagan, & Anderson, 1989). Some children show emotional distress for 1 or 2 years and then gradually feel better. Others remain depressed 5 or 10 years after the divorce. A few seem to do well for years but become more distressed during adolescence. Other children are amazingly resilient throughout their parents' divorce and afterward. They keep their friends, do all right in school, and maintain good relationships with both parents. In fact even some children who are seriously maltreated or abused develop far better than one might expect (Caspi et al., 2002).

Given the emotional trauma usually associated with divorce, should parents stay together for the children's sake? Not necessarily. Children do not fare well if their parents are constantly fighting. Indeed, most children (especially boys) begin to show signs of distress years *before* their parents' divorce, perhaps in response to the parental conflict they already see (Cherlin et al., 1991).

Gender Influences

How would you be different if you had been born female instead of male or male instead of female? Males and females differ, on the average, in many regards. Generally, men fight more often than women and with less provocation. Men also swear more. Men and women generally carry books and packages in different ways, men to the side and women in front. Men are generally more likely to help a stranger change a flat tire, but women are more likely to provide long-term nurturing support (Eagly & Crowley, 1986). When giving directions, men are more likely to use directions and distances—such as "go four blocks east . . ."—whereas women are more likely to use landmarks—such as "go until you see the library . . ." (Saucier et al., 2002). The more pairs of shoes you own, the higher is the probability that you are female. The list of miscellaneous differences could go on and on.

However, many of the differences vary across circumstances. For example, many tasks that are defined as "men's work" in some cultures are "women's work" in others. A few examples are building a fire, making leather products, weaving baskets, planting crops, and milking cows (Wood & Eagly, 2002). Generally, if a culture lives in conditions that require hunting, vigorous defense of resources, or other use of physical strength, men have much greater status and power than women. When food is abundant and enemies are few, men and women have more equal status. Of course, after a culture has adopted a certain set of values, they tend to continue long after the conditions that established them (D. Cohen, 2001).

Within the United States, the percentage of women pursuing careers has greatly increased since the 1950s, as has the percentage of men devoting substantial efforts to child care (Barnett & Hyde, 2001). More women than ever before hold positions of authority in business and industry, and their leadership style differs from men's in only small ways (Eagly, Johannesen-Schmidt, & van Engen, 2003). Thus, many of the male–female differences are more flexible than we once assumed.

Cognitive Differences

Two cognitive differences between the genders are reasonably consistent. First, beginning at an early age, females tend to perform better on certain aspects of language use, especially language fluency (Maccoby & Jacklin, 1974). Second, men generally do better on spatial tasks (Collins & Kimura, 1997). Men are more likely to enter careers in mathematics, physical sciences, and engineering, even in comparison to women of similar mathematical abilities (Benbow, Lubinski, Shea, & Efekhari-Sanjani, 2000).

You might try this task and compare results with your friends: Here is a drawing of a bottle half full of water and then the same bottle tilted. Draw the water level in the tilted bottle.

Most studies—although I have never been able to see this effect with my own students—report that most U.S. men draw the water level parallel to the ground, as shown below in the drawing on the left, whereas most women draw it partly or entirely parallel to the bottom of the bottle, as shown in the other two drawings (Vasta & Liben, 1996). (The one on the left is correct, of course.)

Many researchers have speculated that men evolved greater attention to spatial relationships because men in early hunter-gatherer societies had to find their way home from hunting, whereas women spent more time close to home (Silverman et al., 2000). However, we know little for sure about prehistoric human life. Also, it has been reported that male rats have better spatial learning abilities than female rats (Williams, Barnett, & Meck, 1990), so the difference is probably not specific to anything about early humans.

Differences in Social Behaviors

One idea you have encountered repeatedly is that the results of psychological research depend on details of the method. The same is true for gender differences. If you watch boys and girls at a playground, you see large, consistent differences in their play. Then you set up a laboratory test to measure those differences. You test boys and girls one at a time, and you are stunned to find almost no difference. Many of the differences between males and females emerge only in a social context

a   b

❚ One girl tested alone behaves about the same as one boy tested alone. But when boys play together, they show off to one another and to other observers (a); girls play more cooperatively (b).

(Maccoby, 1990). When boys get together with other boys or girls get together with other girls, the social influence magnifies tendencies that are hardly detectable if you examine each person individually.

Girls play competitive games too, but they are more likely than boys to play cooperatively. They take turns, present their desires as "suggestions" instead of demands, and (usually) avoid hurting each other's feelings. Boys compete with each other almost constantly, even when they are just talking: They shout orders, interrupt, threaten, boast, and insult one another.

What happens when boys and girls play together? If they are working on a task that requires cooperation, few sex differences are evident (Powlishta & Maccoby, 1990). However, in unsupervised situations the boys often dominate and intimidate the girls. In some cases the boys take control and the girls simply watch (Maccoby, 1990).

When boys grow up, they do not entirely change their ways. Deborah Tannen (1990) reports one episode at a college basketball game: At the University of Michigan at the time, the custom was for students to ignore the seat numbers on their tickets and take seats on a first-come, first-served basis. One night several men from the visiting team, Michigan State, tried to go to the seats listed on their tickets, only to find University of Michigan students, both men and women, already seated there. The Michigan State students asked the others to leave; the University of Michigan men replied rudely, and the dispute quickly escalated to insults. The women were mortified with embarrassment.

Within a few minutes, however, the Michigan State men settled into neighboring seats, and soon the two groups of men were happily discussing basketball strategies. The women didn't understand why the men had screamed insults in the first place or how they had become friends so quickly afterward.

Reasons Behind Gender Differences

It is easy to list differences between men and women but difficult to explain them. Opinions are often firmer than the evidence.

On the one hand, it is undeniable that adults treat little boys differently from little girls. In one fascinating study, researchers set up cameras and microphones to eavesdrop on 298 families who had brought a child (one child each) to a science museum. Boys and girls spent about equal time looking at each exhibit, and the parents spent about equal time telling boys or girls how to use each exhibit, but on the average they provided about three times as much scientific explanation to the boys as to the girls, regardless of how many questions the children themselves asked (Crowley, Callanen, Tenenbaum, & Allen, 2001).

On the other hand, the fact that we treat boys and girls differently does not negate the possibility that they also differ biologically. If nothing else, men are on the average taller and more muscular than women, and those differences are agreed to be biological in origin. The physical differences predispose to certain behavioral differences, and in turn those differences alter the way other people react, and other people's reactions alter further behavior. (Recall the "magnifier" effect mentioned in Chapter 9, page 338.) In short, neither biological nor cultural influences act in isolation, but only in combination with each other.

Ethnic and Cultural Influences

Membership in a minority group molds a child's development in two major ways: First, the customs of the minority group may differ from those of other groups. Second, members of a minority group are affected because other people treat them differently or expect certain behaviors from them.

Immigrants to any country undergo a period of **acculturation**, *a transition from feeling part of the culture of their original country to the culture of the country they enter.* Acculturation is gradual; people sometimes require a generation or more before they or their descendants feel fully comfortable in a new culture. Most recent immigrants to the United States have come from Latin America or Asia, and most of the children have been highly motivated to learn English and to achieve beyond the level of their parents. Delinquency, crime, and drug and alcohol abuse are less common in recent immigrants than in other U.S. residents (Fuligni, 1998).

Although most immigrant parents want their children to become successful members of their new culture, they also want them to maintain the best parts of their old cultures, such as values of hard work, cooperation, and generosity (Fuligni, 1998). The alternative to full assimilation is **biculturalism**, *the ability to alternate between membership in one culture and membership in another.* For example, people who settle in an Italian American community speak Italian and follow Italian customs in their home neighborhood but speak English and follow U.S. customs elsewhere.

The advantages of biculturalism resemble those of bilingualism: Someone who speaks two languages can communicate with more people and read a greater variety of literature than can a monolingual person. Also, bilingual people come to understand their primary language from a new perspective. Similarly, a bicultural person interacts with a great variety of other people and becomes aware of the strengths and weaknesses of each culture (Harrison, Wilson, Pine, Chan, & Buriel, 1990; LaFromboise, Coleman, & Gerton,

■ Many immigrants are bicultural, having reasonable familiarity with two sets of customs. These immigrant children attend middle school in Michigan.

1993). Many African Americans and Asian Americans identify with their ethnic groups, live in a neighborhood populated mostly by members of the same group, and rely on the help of an extended family but also join the melting pot culture at school, on the job, and in other settings.

At least to a small extent, nearly all of us learn to function in a variety of subcultures. Unless you live in a small town where everyone has the same background, religion, and customs, you have to learn to adjust what you say and do in different settings and with different groups of people. However, the transitions are more noticeable and more intense for ethnic minorities.

IN CLOSING

Understanding and Accepting Many Ways of Life

Each of us can easily fall into the trap of thinking that our own way of growing up and relating to other people is the "normal" way. In fact people differ substantially in their social development, and understanding psychology requires understanding that diversity. Developmental psychologists conduct extensive research to specify the influences behind that diversity, ranging from genetics and prenatal environment to the physical, familial, and cultural environment.

Summary

- *Temperament.* Even infants who are only a few months old differ in their characteristic way of reacting to experiences. Temperament remains fairly consistent as a person grows older. (page 391)

- *Birth order.* Most studies comparing first-born versus later-born children confound the effects of birth order with the effects of family size. If we disregard families with only one child, first borns and later borns behave about the same way when they are outside the home. (page 392)

- *Parenting styles.* Parenting style correlates with the behavior of the children. For example, caring, understanding parents tend to have well-behaved children. However, most studies do not separate the effects of social influences from genetics. Adopted children usually do not resemble their adoptive parents' personalities. Judith Rich Harris has therefore argued that personality and social behavior depend mostly on genetics and peer influences. (page 393)

- *Nontraditional child care.* Children who spend much time early in day care develop about the same as those reared at home by a parent. A child's normal personality and social development require at least one caring adult, but the number of caregivers and their gender and sexual orientation apparently matter little. (page 394)

- *Effects of divorce.* Children of divorced parents often show signs of distress, sometimes even before the divorce. The distress is generally more marked in European American families than in African American families. (page 395)

- *Gender influences.* Women tend to do better than men on certain aspects of language, whereas men tend to solve spatial problems better. Social differences between males and females are small on the average when people are tested one at a time but larger when tested in all-male or all-female groups. Individuals can differ greatly from the averages. (page 396)

- *Ethnic and cultural differences.* People also differ because of ethnic and cultural influences. Acculturation is the process of transition from one culture to another. Many people can function successfully as members of two or more cultures simultaneously. (page 398)

Answers to Concept Checks

16. Kagan and Snidman's study was longitudinal; they studied the same children at different ages. (page 392)

17. Temperament is a measure of how people react to novel stimuli, and the Strange Situation is also a test of reaction to novel stimuli. The difference is

that the Strange Situation focuses specifically on social stimuli, particularly the presence or absence of the mother or some other important person in a child's life. (page 392)

18. An only child is a last born as well as a first born. A large sample of last borns will include many children from single-child families, which are often characterized by high IQ and ambitions. Second-to-last borns necessarily come from larger families. (page 393)

19. Children can resemble their parents' behavior because of either genetics or social influences. Adoptive children do not necessarily resemble their adopted parents genetically, so any similarity in behavior would reflect environmental influences. Of course, the question would remain as to whether the parents influenced the children or the children influenced the parents. (page 394)

CHAPTER ENDING

Key Terms and Activities

Key Terms

accommodation: Piaget's term for the modification of an established schema to fit a new object or problem (page 367)

acculturation: a transition from feeling part of the culture of one's original country to the culture of the country that one enters (page 398)

assimilation: Piaget's term for the application of an established schema to new objects or problems (page 367)

attachment: a long-term feeling of closeness between people, such as a child and a caregiver (page 384)

authoritarian parents: those who exert firm controls on their children, generally without explaining the reasons for the rules and without providing much warmth (page 393)

authoritative parents: those who are demanding and impose firm controls, but who are also warm and responsive to the child's communications (page 393)

biculturalism: the ability to alternate between membership in one culture and membership in another (page 398)

chromosome: a strand of hereditary material found in the nucleus of a cell (page 354)

cohort: a group of people born at a particular time (as compared to people born at different times) (page 366)

conservation: the concept that objects retain their weight, volume, and certain other properties in spite of changes in their shape or arrangement (page 374)

cross-sectional study: a study of groups of individuals of different ages all at the same time (page 364)

dishabituation: an increase in a previously habituated response as a result of a change in the stimulus (page 361)

egocentric: the inability to take the perspective of another person; a tendency to view the world as centered around oneself (page 370)

equilibration: the establishment of harmony or balance between assimilation and accommodation (page 367)

fetal alcohol syndrome: a condition marked by stunted growth of the head and body; malformations of the face, heart, and ears; and nervous system damage, including seizures, hyperactivity, learning disabilities, and mental retardation (page 359)

fetus: an organism more developed than an embryo but not yet born (from about 8 weeks after conception until birth in humans) (page 358)

fraternal twins: twins who develop from two eggs (dizygotic) fertilized by two different sperm; they are no more closely related than are any other children born to the same parents (page 353)

gene: a segment of a chromosome that controls chemical reactions that ultimately direct the development of the organism (page 354)

habituation: a decrease in a person's response to a stimulus after it has been presented repeatedly (page 361)

heritability: an estimate of the variance within a population that is due to heredity (page 356)

identical twins: twins who develop from the same fertilized egg (monozygotic) and therefore have the same genes (page 353)

identity achievement: the outcome of having explored various possible identities and then making one's own decisions (page 387)

identity crisis: concerns with decisions about the future and the quest for self-understanding (page 387)

identity diffusion: the condition of having not yet given any serious thought to identity decisions and having no clear sense of identity (page 387)

identity foreclosure: the state of having made firm identity decisions without having thought much about them (page 387)

identity moratorium: the state of seriously considering one's identity without yet having made any decisions (page 387)

indifferent or uninvolved parents: those who pay little attention to their children beyond doing what is necessary to feed and shelter them (page 393)

longitudinal study: a study of a single group of individuals over time (page 364)

midlife transition: a time of goal reassessment (page 388)

moral dilemma: a problem that pits one moral value against another (page 378)

object permanence: the concept that objects continue to exist even when one does not see, hear, or otherwise sense them (page 368)

operation: according to Piaget a mental process that can be reversed (page 370)

permissive parents: those who are warm and loving but undemanding (page 393)

phenylketonuria (PKU): an inherited disorder in which a person lacks the chemical reactions that convert a nutrient called phenylalanine into other chemicals; unless the diet is carefully controlled, the affected person will become mentally retarded (page 358)

preoperational stage: according to Piaget the second stage of intellectual development, in which children lack operations (page 370)

schema (pl.: schemata): an organized way of interacting with objects in the world (page 367)

selective attrition: the tendency of some kinds of people to be more likely than others to drop out of a study (page 365)

sensorimotor stage: according to Piaget the first stage of intellectual development; an infant's behavior is limited to making simple motor responses to sensory stimuli (page 368)

sequential design: a procedure in which researchers start with groups of people of different ages, studied at the same time, and then study them again at one or more later times (page 365)

sex chromosomes: the pair of chromosomes that determine whether an individual will develop as a female or as a male (page 355)

sex-limited gene: a gene that affects one sex more strongly than the other, even though both sexes have the gene (page 356)

sex-linked gene: a gene located on the X chromosome (page 355)

stage of concrete operations: according to Piaget the ability to deal with the properties of concrete objects but not hypothetical or abstract questions (page 375)

stage of formal operations: according to Piaget the stage when children develop the ability to deal with abstract, hypothetical situations, which demand logical, deductive reasoning and systematic planning (page 375)

Strange Situation: a procedure in which a psychologist observes an infant's behavior in an unfamiliar room at various times as a stranger enters, leaves, and returns and the mother enters, leaves, and returns (page 384)

temperament: people's tendency to be either active or inactive, outgoing or reserved, and to respond vigorously or quietly to new stimuli (page 391)

terror-management theory: the proposal that we cope with our fear of death by avoiding thinking about death and by affirming a worldview that provides self-esteem, hope, and value in life (page 389)

theory of mind: an understanding that other people have a mind too and that each person knows some things that other people don't know (page 371)

X chromosome: a sex chromosome; females have two per cell and males have only one (page 355)

Y chromosome: a sex chromosome; males have one per cell and females have none (page 355)

zone of proximal development: the distance between what a child can do on his or her own and what the child can do with the help of adults or older children (page 377)

zygote: a fertilized egg cell (page 358)

Suggestions for Further Reading

Elkind, D. (1984). *All grown up and no place to go.* Reading, MA: Addison-Wesley. An account of the problems that teenagers and young adults face.

Tannen, D. (1990). *You just don't understand.* New York: William Morrow. A popular book that discusses the various reasons that men and women often fail to understand one another.

 Book Companion Web Site

Need help studying? Go to

http://psychology.wadsworth.com/kalat_intro7e/

for a virtual study center. You'll find a personalized Self-Study Assessment that will provide you with a study plan based on your answers to a pretest. Also study using flash cards, quizzes, interactive art, and an online glossary.

Check out interactive **Try It Yourself** exercises on the companion site! For example, the Genetic Generations exercise ties to what you've learned in this chapter.

Your companion site also has direct links to the following Web sites. These links are checked often for changes, dead links, and new additions.

Human Genome Project

www.ornl.gov/TechResources/Human_Genome/home.html

This is the definitive site for understanding the Human Genome Project, from the basic science to ethical, legal, and social considerations to the latest discoveries.

The Child Psychologist

www.childpsychology.com/

Rene Thomas Folse's site focuses on "Specific Disorders and Other Reasons for Concern" about the behavior of children and on "Treatment, Resources, and Remediation." There are links to information about several specific diagnostic tests used with children.

American Academy of Child and Adolescent Psychiatry

http://www.aacap.org

Check this site for information about common psychological disorders of children and teenagers.

The Nurture Assumption

home.att.net/~xchar/tna/

Judith Rich Harris maintains this Web page about her controversial book on the importance of peers and the relative unimportance of parenting styles.

The Child Artist Grown Up

www.robinka.com

Did you like Robin Kalat's drawing at the start of Module 10.2? Check out her adult art at this site.

Try It Yourself CD-ROM
with Critical Thinking Video Exercises

Use your CD to access **videos** related to activities designed to help you think critically about the important topics discussed. For example, the video about anxiety disorders in children relates to what you've learned in this chapter. You'll also find an easy portal link to the book companion site where you can access your personalized **Self-Study Assessments** and interactive **Try It Yourself** exercises.

PsychNow! 2.0

PsychNow! is a fun interactive CD designed to help you with the difficult concepts in psychology. Check out the Human Development section for the following topics that relate to this chapter:

Infant Development: explore children's drawings over time, infant development, and then guess developmental stages.

Child Development: learn about child development stages, Piaget's stages, and his conservation tasks.

Adolescent Development: define adolescence, explore the development of identity, and take an identity self-test.

Adult Development, Aging, and Death: test existing knowledge and watch videos of adults reflecting on their lives.

InteractNOW! Online Collaborative Lab: Development and the sensorimotor stage

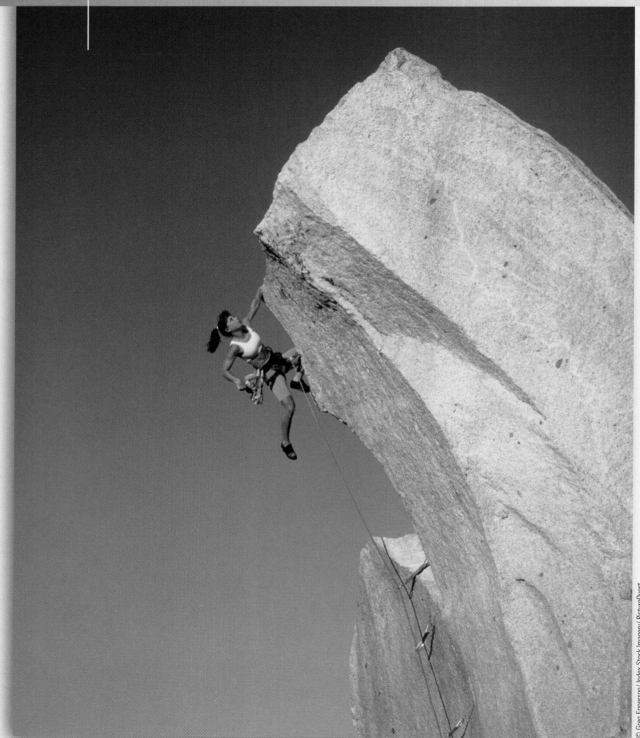

Motivation

During the summer of 1996, the proprietors of London's Kew Gardens announced that they had a most unusual plant, native to Sumatra and rarely cultivated elsewhere, that was about to bloom for the first time since 1963. If you had been in London then, with enough time available, would you have made a point of visiting Kew Gardens to witness this rare event? No? What if I told you that it was a truly beautiful flower? With a lovely, sweet smell? Still no?

Then what if I told you the truth—that it has the nastiest, most obnoxious smell of any flower on Earth—that the name of the flower is the *stinking lily* because it smells like a huge, week-old carcass of rotting meat or fish and that one whiff of it can make a strong person retch. Now would you want to visit the flower? If so, you would have to wait in line. When Kew Gardens announced that the stinking lily was about to bloom, an enormous crowd gathered, forming a line that stretched to the length of a soccer field (MacQuitty, 1996). (The first day that the flower bloomed, it had hardly begun to stink. Disappointed visitors vowed to return later.)

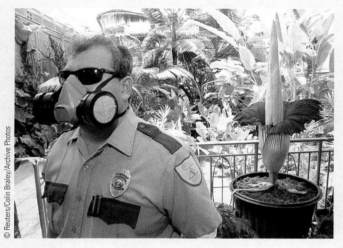

■ This flower is seldom cultivated, for good reasons. Would you stand in line to visit it?

Although the visitors' behavior may seem illogical and puzzling, it is not that unusual. People frequently seek new and interesting experiences, even when their only apparent motive is curiosity. Even motivations with obvious biological value, such as hunger and sex, sometimes produce puzzling behaviors. Researchers have nevertheless made clear progress in understanding many aspects of motivation. We begin this chapter with an overview of some general principles of motivation. Then we shall explore three representative and obviously important motivations: hunger, sexual activity, and work motivation.

General Principles of Motivation

What is motivation?

What is the difference between motivated and nonmotivated behaviors?

You are sitting quietly, reading a book, when suddenly you hear a loud noise. You jump a little and gasp. Was your action motivated? "No," you say. "I jumped involuntarily." Now I tell you that I want to do a little experiment. As soon as you hear me tap my pencil, you should try to jump and gasp just as you did the first time. I tap my pencil, and sure enough, you jump and gasp. Was that action motivated? "Yes," you reply.

So, what appears to be approximately the same behavior can be motivated at one time and unmotivated at another time. Can we trust people to tell us whether their behavior was motivated or unmotivated? Not always. Someone accused of murder says, "I didn't mean to kill. It was an accident." Your friend, who promised to drive you somewhere and then left without you, says, "I didn't do it on purpose. I just forgot." How can we determine whether a behavior is motivated or accidental? We need a clear understanding of how motivated behaviors differ from unmotivated behaviors.

Properties of Motivated Behavior

What, if anything, do various types of motivated behavior have in common? That is, what distinguishes a motivated act from a reflex? Motivated behaviors vary from time to time and from person to person. For example, on a hot day, you drink lemonade and get into a swimming pool; on a cold day, you drink hot chocolate and put on a heavy coat. Perhaps the foremost characteristic of motivated behaviors is that they are goal directed. If you are motivated to accomplish something, you try one approach after another until you succeed. If necessary, you set up subgoals you need to meet on your way to the final goal (Austin & Vancouver, 1996). For example, if you were motivated to improve your house, you might start by making a list of the items that need repair and the tools you will need.

These criteria are good in principle. However, nearly all behaviors are combinations of motivation and reflex. Even intentional acts such as walking depend on leg reflexes that maintain balance. Eating is motivated but requires reflexes of digestion. Fixating your eyes on a target is motivated but is also controlled by reflexive movements of eye muscles.

> **CRITICAL THINKING:**
> *A STEP FURTHER*
> *Motivations and Reflexes*
>
>
> A frog flicks its tongue at a passing insect, captures it, and swallows it. The behavior satisfies the frog's need for food, so we might guess that it is motivated. However, the behavior appears to be as constant as a reflex. How might you determine whether this behavior is motivated?

Views of Motivation

Like many other important terms in psychology, motivation is difficult to define. Let's consider several possibilities: "Motivation is what activates and directs behavior." That description fits many examples well enough, but it also fits some nonmotivational phenomena. For instance, light activates and directs the growth of plants, but we would hardly say that light motivates plants.

"Motivation is what makes our behavior more vigorous and energetic." The problem with that definition is that some people are strongly motivated to lie motionless for hours on end. Also, coffee can make you more energetic without changing your motives.

How about this: Based on the concept of reinforcement from Chapter 6, we could define **motivation as** *the process that determines the reinforcement value of an outcome.* For example, something to eat or drink is more reinforcing at some times than others; thus, we say that motivation for them has increased or decreased. You will note therefore the close relationship between learning and motivation.

That definition works as a description, although it offers no theory. Few psychologists today spend much time debating the true nature of motivation, but let's briefly consider a few influential theories, with their strengths and weaknesses.

Motivation as an Energy

Motivation, which comes from the same root as *motion,* is literally something that "moves" a person. So we might think of it as a type of energy. According to Konrad Lorenz (1950), a pioneer in the study of animal behavior, animals engage in instinctive acts when specific energies reach a critical level. For example, a male stickleback fish has no specific energy for mating outside the breeding season, so it will not respond sexually. At the start of the breeding season, it has a small amount of mating energy, and it will then court female stickleback fish and attack male stickleback fish. At the height of the breeding season, it has a great amount of mating energy, so it will court females vigorously; it may even respond sexually to a piece of wood painted to resemble a female of its species.

Figure 11.1 illustrates Lorenz's model. A specific kind of energy builds up in the reservoir and flows into the tray below. The outlets in that tray represent ways of releasing this energy. If conditions are right, the energy is released through the lowest outlet—for example, mating with a normal partner. If that outlet is blocked and energy continues to build up, the energy will spill through one of the higher, less preferred outlets. However, Lorenz's theories are based on the idea of specific energies for specific tasks—an idea that neuroscience research has disconfirmed. He believed that every impulse had to be carried out in some way (to use up the energy). We now know that an individual can simply inhibit an impulse.

Drive Theories

Related to the instinctive energy theories are theories that describe motivation as a **drive,** *a state of unrest*

FIGURE 11.1 According to Konrad Lorenz, energy (represented as a fluid) builds up in a "reservoir" in the brain and needs to be discharged. For example, you might build up a sexual-behavior–specific energy. If that energy cannot discharge through its normal outlets (because they are blocked), the energy builds up until it discharges through some other outlet. *(After Lorenz, 1950)*

or irritation that energizes one behavior after another until one of them removes the irritation (Hull, 1943). For example, when you get a splinter in your finger, the discomfort motivates you to try various actions until you remove the splinter.

According to the *drive-reduction theory* that was popular among psychologists of the 1940s and 1950s, humans and other animals strive to reduce their needs and drives as much as possible. They eat to reduce their hunger, drink to reduce their thirst, have sexual activity to reduce their sex drive, and so forth. This view implies that if we satisfy all our needs, we would then become inactive. People's search for new experiences—riding roller coasters or smelling odd flowers, for example—is a problem for this view.

Another flaw in drive theory is that it ignores the role of external stimulation. For example, your interest in food depends not only on hunger (an internal drive) but also on what foods are available. Similarly, interest in sex depends partly on an internal drive and partly on the presence of a suitable partner.

Homeostasis

One important advance upon the idea of drive reduction is the concept of **homeostasis,** *the maintenance of an optimum level of biological conditions within an organism* (Cannon, 1929). The idea of homeostasis recognizes that we are motivated to seek a state of equilibrium, which is not zero stimulation. For example, people maintain a nearly constant body temperature, resisting either an increase or decrease. We also work to maintain a fairly steady body weight, a nearly constant amount of water in the body, a moderate amount of sensory experience, and so on.

Unlike a rock, which remains static only because nothing is acting upon it, the homeostasis of the body is more like a spinning top; it needs additional energy from time to time to keep it spinning. For example, we maintain constant body temperature partly by shivering, sweating, and other involuntary physiological responses and partly by putting on extra clothing, taking off excess clothing, or finding a more comfortable location.

Human motivated behaviors differ from the actions of a thermostat in one important regard: Our behavior often anticipates future needs. For example, you might eat a large breakfast one morning even though you are not terribly hungry, just because you know you are going to be too busy to stop for lunch. If you are angry or frightened, you begin to sweat even before you begin the vigorous actions that might heat your body. (We call this phenomenon a "cold sweat.") Thus, a fruitful way of describing motivation is that it maintains current homeostasis and anticipates future needs to maintain future homeostasis (Appley, 1991).

Incentive Theories

The homeostasis concept of motivation overlooks the power of new stimuli to arouse behaviors. For example, why do you sometimes eat tasty-looking foods even when you are not hungry? Why do we seek opportunities to enjoy music and art? Many strong motivations correspond to no apparent need.

Evidently, motivation includes more than the internal forces that push us toward certain behaviors; it also includes incentives—*external stimuli that pull us toward certain actions.* Most motivated behaviors are controlled by a combination of drives and incentives. You eat because you are hungry (a drive) and because you see appealing food in front of you (an incentive). You jump into a swimming pool on a hot day to cool your body (a drive) and because you will enjoy splashing around in the water with friends (an incentive).

Intrinsic and Extrinsic Motivations

Similar to the distinction between drives and incentives, psychologists also distinguish between intrinsic and extrinsic motivations. An intrinsic motivation is *a motivation to do an act for its own sake;* an extrinsic motivation is *based on the reinforcements and punishments that the act may bring.* For example, reading a book because you enjoy it displays an intrinsic motivation; reading a book to pass a test depends on an extrinsic motivation. The two kinds of motivation frequently combine. For instance, an artist paints for the joy of creation (intrinsic) and for the hope of profit (extrinsic). Even if you read a book because it is assigned—this one, for example—you might also enjoy it. We seldom do anything for just one reason.

Does a combination of intrinsic and extrinsic motivations lead to more persistent and effective performance than, say, intrinsic motivation alone? Not always. In a classic study, researchers let mon-

FIGURE 11.2 Monkeys learned to remove the pin, hook, and hasp in that order to open this device. When they started receiving a raisin instead of opening it just for fun, their performance deteriorated.

keys play with a device like the one in Figure 11.2. To open it, a monkey had to remove the pin, lift the hook, and then lift the hasp. The monkeys played with the device over a period of 10 days. They played with it apparently just for the fun of it (an intrinsic motivation). Then the device was placed over a food well containing a raisin (an extrinsic motivation). If they opened the device, they could get the raisin. Suddenly, their ability to open the device deteriorated. Instead of patiently removing the pin, the hook, and the hasp as before, they attacked the hasp forcefully. They took longer to open the device for food than they did for play. Later, when they were offered the device by itself with no food available, they played with it less than before (Harlow, Harlow, & Meyer, 1950). Evidently, the device had become work, not play.

Does the same principle apply to human behavior? In a typical experiment, college students were asked to try to arrange seven plastic pieces with complex shapes to match figures in a drawing. At one point halfway through the experiment, students in the experimental group were paid $1 for each correct match. (Students in the control group did not know that the experimental group was being paid.) Later, the experiment continued without pay for anyone. After pay was suspended, the experimental group decreased their efforts (Deci, 1971). As with the monkeys, once you have been paid for doing something, it becomes work and not play.

▌ The artist who created this wooden cow probably hoped for recognition and money (an extrinsic motivation) but also must have enjoyed the creative process itself (an intrinsic motivation). The back of the cow folds out to reveal a desk.

Results such as these illustrate the **overjustification effect:** *When people are given more extrinsic motivation than necessary to perform a task, their intrinsic motivation declines.* The same principle works for both rewards and punishments. That is, you could work harder than usual to get a reward or to avoid a punishment. In either case, after you finished what you had to do, you probably would stop working on the task, even if it was something you previously enjoyed (Ryan & Deci, 2000).

One explanation for the overjustification effect is that after working extra hard on a task, you become tired of it. However, even after a rest period, people still often show a decreased interest in the task. According to another explanation, people ask themselves, "Why am I doing this?" They then answer, "It's not because I enjoy the task. It's because I'm being paid." (Or "Because I'll be punished if I stop.") Therefore, they no longer do it for the sheer joy of it.

The overjustification effect applies under some conditions but not others, and it is sometimes a weak effect (Eisenberger & Cameron, 1996). For example, would you guess that praising a child for work well done would strengthen intrinsic motivation, or would it act like a payment does and decrease intrinsic motivation? The results vary from one study to another (Henderlong & Lepper, 2002). As a rule praise helps if the recipient thinks the praise was deserved. If the praise appears to be insincere, it accomplishes nothing. Someone who is praised after a mediocre effort may conclude, "They expected very little of me."

Table 11.1 summarizes four views of motivation.

CONCEPT CHECK ☑

1. Suppose you want to encourage your younger cousin to continue taking piano lessons. Based on the overjustification effect, would it be wise to pay him for practicing? (Check your answer on page 411.)

Delay of Gratification

Often, a motivation requires you to choose a less pleasant behavior now to have a more pleasant opportunity later. For example, you might spend long hours studying when you would prefer to watch television or wake up and go to your job when you would prefer to stay asleep. You take the less preferred act now because of the probable payoff later.

People differ in how well they can *defer gratification*—that is, choose the action that produces the bigger payoff later instead of the smaller pleasure now (Simpson & Vuchinich, 2000). We can measure this aspect of personality with simple questions: Which would you prefer, $500 now or a promise of $1,000 next year? If you prefer the $500 now, how large would the promise have to be before you would switch to the delayed reward? If you prefer the $1,000, how much smaller could we make the delayed reward before you would switch to the $500 now? Most children prefer a small reward now to a larger one later. As people grow older, they become more likely to choose the delayed but larger reward (L. Green, Myerson, & Ostraszewski, 1999).

If you tend to prefer the immediate reward, one way to overcome that tendency is to commit yourself

TABLE 11.1 Four Views of Motivation

View	Basic Position	Major Weaknesses
Instinct Theories According to instinct theories, motivation is a kind of energy that builds up until it finds a release.	Motivations are energies that accumulate; each energy specifies a preferred action, although it might spill over into a less preferred outlet.	Based on obsolete view of the nervous system.
Drive Theories According to drive theories, motivation is an irritation that continues until we find a way to reduce it.	Motivations are based on needs or irritations that we try to reduce; they do not specify particular actions.	Implies that we always try to reduce stimulation, never to increase it. Also overlooks importance of external stimuli.
Homeostasis (plus anticipation) Homeostasis is the process of maintaining a variable such as body temperature within a set range.	Motivations tend to maintain body states near some optimum intermediate level. They may react to current needs and anticipate future needs.	Overlooks importance of external stimuli.
Incentive Theories Incentives are external stimuli that attract us even if we have no biological need for them.	Motivations are responses to attractive stimuli.	Incomplete theory unless combined with drive or homeostasis.

to an action well in advance. For example, suppose you know you generally choose $500 now over $1,000 a year later. For most people that is economically a poor choice, as 100% interest over one year is outstanding. You can probably make the economically wise decision if you choose far in advance. For example, which would you prefer, $500 a year from now or $1000 two years from now? You know that when you get to one year from now, you will wish you could have the $500 right away, but if you choose now, you can commit yourself to the better but more delayed reward.

Similarly, suppose someone offers to pay you some reasonable price to do a somewhat difficult or unpleasant job a year from now. This far in advance, you can agree to the deal. When you get close to the actual time, you start thinking more about the unpleasant details, and if you could make the decision anew, you probably would find plenty of excuses to refuse (Trope & Liberman, 2003). However, having already committed yourself, you probably keep the deal.

Although we generally prefer a reward now even to a bigger one later, the reverse occurs if the reward will be emotionally exciting. Most people would prefer to receive a passionate kiss from their favorite movie star a few days from now instead of right now (Loewenstein, 1987). Presumably, they enjoy the anticipation, the opportunity to look forward to an emotionally exciting event. Conversely, most would prefer to receive a painful, unavoidable shock today than 10 years from now. It feels better to get it over with than to have to dread it for so long. Similarly, most people don't object to waiting a couple of weeks to receive information that is sure to be reasonably good news. However, most people want to know bad news as quickly as possible (Lovallo & Kahneman, 2000). The period of dreading the bad news only makes it worse.

CONCEPT CHECK ☑

2. If you want to invite someone to be a guest speaker for your favorite organization, should you make the invitation long in advance or wait until close to the time of the talk? Why?

3. Can you explain why many people would prefer to bet on a lottery than a roulette wheel, which produces immediate results? (Check your answers on this page.)

IN CLOSING

Many Types of Motivation

People frequently puzzle over why a person did something that has no apparent benefit. For unusual behaviors like this, people seldom have just one motivation. More often, it is a combination: curiosity, the

desire to have something unusual to talk about with friends, perhaps even a desire for fame. As you will see in later modules of this chapter, even clearly adaptive behaviors such as hunger and sex are based on multiple and complex motives.

Summary

*   *Characteristics of motivated behaviors.* Motivated behaviors vary from time to time, from situation to situation, and from person to person. They persist until the individual reaches the goal. (page 407)
*   *Motivation as energy or drive reduction.* Viewing motivation as a type of energy is an analogy not to be taken too seriously. Some aspects of motivation can be described as drive reduction, but people strive for new experiences that do not reduce any apparent drive. (page 408)
*   *Motivation as a way of maintaining homeostasis.* Many motivated behaviors tend to maintain body conditions and stimulation at a near-constant, or homeostatic, level. This view of motivation can account for much behavior if we also assume that behaviors anticipate future needs instead of just responding to current needs. (page 408)
*   *Motivation as incentive.* Motivations are partly under the control of incentives—external stimuli that pull us toward certain actions. Both drives and incentives control most motivated behaviors. (page 409)
*   *Delayed gratification.* People vary in how well they can postpone pleasure, choosing a larger reward later over a smaller one now. It is often easier to make the economically logical decision if you make it far in advance. Although people usually prefer a reward now instead of later, they reverse that preference if the reward has high emotional value so they can enjoy the anticipation. (page 410)

Answers to Concept Checks

1. According to the overjustification effect, you should not pay him enough so that he starts practicing just for the reward. However, verbal praise would be good. (page 410)
2. Make the invitation far in advance. Far in advance, it is easy to see that the advantages of an action outweigh the disadvantages. When the time is close, the details of the task become more salient, and people will find an excuse for not participating. (page 411)
3. Someone who bets on a lottery can enjoy the long period of anticipation of how exciting the win might be. If the payoff (or loss) from a gamble comes quickly, that long anticipation is not possible. (page 411)

MODULE | 11.2 Hunger Motivation

How do we decide how much to eat and which foods to eat?

Small birds eat only what they need at the moment, storing almost no fat at all. The advantage is that they remain light and fast enough to escape predators. The disadvantage is that they starve to death if they have trouble finding food for even a short time. Bears follow a different strategy. They easily find food when nuts and berries are in season, but at other times they go days or even weeks with nothing to eat. Their evolved strategy is to eat as much as they can whenever they can and then live off their stored fat.

Few humans eat as gluttonously as bears, but we too have apparently evolved a strategy of eating more than we need at the moment in case food is scarce tomorrow, as it frequently has been during human history. Today, however, prosperous countries have abundant, tasty food every day, and the result is much overeating (Pinel, Assanand, & Lehman, 2000).

How much we eat and what and when also depend on social motives. Imagine that you visit your boyfriend or girlfriend's family and you want to make a good impression. "Dinner's ready!" someone calls. You go into the dining room and find a huge meal spread out before you, which your hosts clearly ex-

pect you to enjoy. Do you explain that you are not hungry because you already made a pig of yourself at lunch? Probably not.

The Physiology of Hunger and Satiety

Hunger is a partly homeostatic drive that keeps fuel available for the body. When supplies begin to drop, specialized mechanisms in your brain trigger behaviors that lead to eating. But how does your brain know how much fuel is available and how much more you should eat?

The problem is more complex than keeping enough fuel in your car's gas tank. When the fuel gauge shows that the tank is running low, you fill it with gas. By contrast keeping track of the fuel in your stomach does not tell you how much more you need. In addition to the fuel in your stomach and intestines, fuel is present in every cell of your body and more is circulating in your blood, ready to enter cells that need it. Fat cells and liver cells store still more fuel. If necessary, your body can break down muscle tissues for additional fuel.

How do you know how much to eat, considering that each meal has a different density of nutrients from any other? Fortunately, you don't have to get it exactly right. You have one set of mechanisms that control short-term changes in hunger and separate long-term mechanisms that correct for short-term fluctuations in your intake.

Short-Term Regulation of Hunger

Under most circumstances the main factor responsible for ending a meal is distension of the stomach and intestines; we feel full because the digestive system is literally full (Seeley, Kaplan, & Grill, 1995). With familiar foods we also calibrate approximately how much nutrition we are getting per amount swallowed (Deutsch & Gonzalez, 1980), and receptors in our intestines detect the sugars in the food (Lavin et al., 1996).

■ Mealtime is more than just an opportunity to satisfy hunger: It is an occasion to bring the family and sometimes friends together, to share a pleasant experience, to discuss the events of the day, and even to pass on cultural traditions from one generation to the next. We expect family members to participate in these meals, even if they are not hungry.

© Annie Griffiths Belt/CORBIS

The main factor responsible for the onset of hunger and the start of a meal is a drop in how much glucose enters the cells, but the control of glucose is a complicated story (Figure 11.3). Glucose, *the most abundant sugar in your blood, is an important source of energy for all parts of the body and almost the only source for the brain.* We could say, with only mild oversimplification, that hunger is a homeostatic mechanism that motivates you to provide enough glucose. The body can make glucose from almost any nutrient. If you eat too much, your body converts excess blood glucose into fats and other stored fuels. If you eat too little, you convert stored fuels back into blood glucose. The flow of glucose to or from the blood depends on two hormones released by the pancreas: insulin and glucagon.

The hormone insulin *increases the flow of glucose and several other nutrients into body cells.* At the beginning of a meal, before the nutrients have even started entering the blood, the brain sends messages to the pancreas to increase its secretion of insulin. Insulin promotes the movement of glucose and other nutrients out of the blood and into both the cells that need fuel and the cells that store the nutrients as fats and other supplies.

As the meal continues, the digested food enters the blood, but almost as fast as it enters, insulin helps to move excess nutrients out of the blood and into the liver or fat cells. In that manner the insulin holds down the surge of glucose and other nutrients in the blood (Woods, 1991). Later, long after the meal, when the nutrient supply in the blood starts to drop, the pancreas reduces its secretion of insulin and increases its secretions of glucagon, *a hormone that helps to convert stored energy supplies back into blood glucose.*

However, consider what happens if insulin levels stay constantly high or low: When insulin levels are consistently low, as with Type I diabetes (also known as insulin-dependent diabetes or juvenile-onset diabetes), nutrients enter the cells very slowly (Figure 11.4). People with untreated Type I diabetes eat without satisfying their hunger because so little glucose enters the cells. It does not even enter the fat cells, so people with diabetes eat a great deal but then excrete it and lose weight (Lindberg, Coburn, & Stricker, 1984). (People

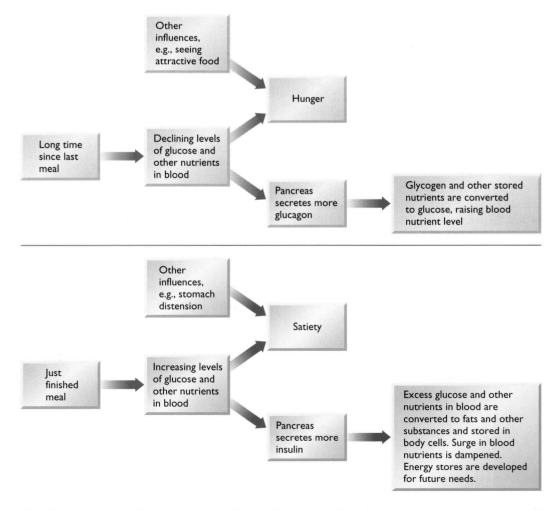

FIGURE 11.3 Varying secretions of the hormones insulin and glucagon regulate the flow of nutrients from the blood into the cells or from storage back into the blood.

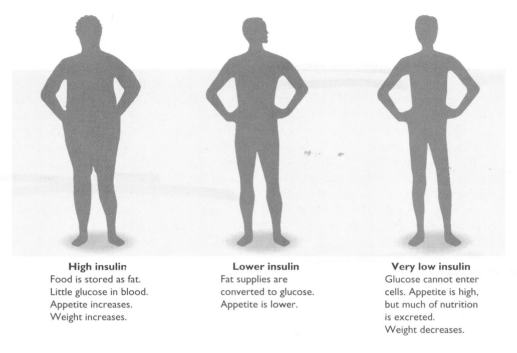

High insulin
Food is stored as fat.
Little glucose in blood.
Appetite increases.
Weight increases.

Lower insulin
Fat supplies are
converted to glucose.
Appetite is lower.

Very low insulin
Glucose cannot enter
cells. Appetite is high,
but much of nutrition
is excreted.
Weight decreases.

FIGURE 11.4 How insulin affects glucose, appetite, and weight.

with Type II diabetes have approximately normal insulin levels but their cells do not respond properly to it. They are overweight, but their extra weight is a cause of diabetes, not a result of it.)

At the opposite extreme, if insulin levels are consistently high, nutrients enter the cells easily, but most of the glucose is converted to fats and stored in fat cells. Because the insulin level remains high, the food stored in fat cells stays there longer instead of being mobilized back into blood glucose. Consequently, blood glucose levels begin to decline again soon after any meal *(hypoglycemia)* and appetite increases. (Figure 11.5 shows the relationship between glucose level

and food intake.) Note that if the insulin level is either consistently low or consistently high, the result will be an increased appetite; however, very low insulin levels lead to weight loss, whereas very high insulin levels lead to weight gain.

CONCEPT CHECK ☑

4. Insulin levels fluctuate cyclically over the course of a day. Would they be higher in the middle of the day, when people tend to be hungry, or late at night, when most are less hungry? (Check your answer on page 425.)

Long-Term Regulation of Hunger

Stomach distension and the other mechanisms for ending a meal are far from perfect. Depending on the caloric density of your next meal, you may eat a bit more or less than you need. If you misjudged in the same direction meal after meal, you would soon have a problem.

However, you have long-term mechanisms to correct short-term errors. If you overeat for several meals, you will feel less hungry until you get back to about your normal weight. Conversely, if you undereat for a few meals, you will start feeling hungrier than usual until you get back to normal. Most people's weight fluctuates from one day to the next but remains remarkably stable from month to month, even if they seldom check the scales.

| Lack of eating, empty digestive system |

↓

| Low blood insulin, so little glucose enters cells; appetite increases |

↓

| Eating fills digestive system, increases insulin level; more glucose enters cells |

↓

| Appetite decreases, digestive system empties |

FIGURE 11.5 A feedback system between eating and insulin levels maintains homeostatic control of nutrition.

FIGURE 11.6 For most people weight fluctuates around a set point, the way a diving board bounces up and down from a central position.

That mean weight is referred to as a **set point**—*a level that the body works to maintain* (Figure 11.6). The mechanism for this correction is now partly understood (J. M. Friedman, 2000). *The body's fat cells produce a hormone called* **leptin** *in amounts proportional to the total amount of fat.* When the body gains fat, the extra leptin alters activity in parts of the hypothalamus (an area of the brain), causing meals to satisfy hunger faster. That is, leptin is your fat cells' way of telling the brain "you have enough fat already, so stop eating." Among the many other effects of leptin, it triggers the start of puberty: When the body reaches a certain size and weight, the increased leptin levels combine with other forces to induce the hormonal changes of puberty (Chehab, Mounzih, Lu, & Lim, 1997).

Those few people who lack the genes to produce leptin do become obese (Farooqi et al., 2001). Their brains get no signals from their fat supplies, so they act as if they have no fat and are starving. They also fail to enter puberty (Clément et al., 1998). Injections of leptin greatly reduce obesity for these few people. However, most obese people produce large amounts of leptin; apparently, they just fail to respond to it. Injections of even larger amounts can decrease their appetite somewhat, but only at the risk of inducing Type II diabetes (B. Cohen, Novick, & Rubinstein, 1996).

CONCEPT CHECK ☑

5. What are two hormones that influence appetite, and which body parts release them? (Check your answer on page 425.)

Brain Mechanisms

The brain must monitor information from the blood, cells, and digestive system to determine when to eat and when to stop. Several brain areas, especially those in the hypothalamus (Figure 11.7), are especially important in this process.

The **lateral hypothalamus** appears to be *a critical area for starting meals.* It modulates other brain areas to increase the taste of foods, increase salivation and digestion, and increase the reward value of food (Hernandez, Murzi, Schwartz, & Hoebel, 1992; van den Pol, 1999).

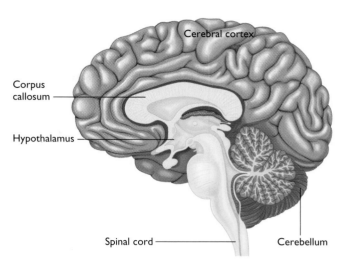

FIGURE 11.7 The hypothalamus, a small area on the underside of the brain, contains several subareas that contribute in various ways to eating, drinking, sexual behavior, and other motivated activities.

Two areas of the hypothalamus are important for ending meals. One is the **ventromedial hypothalamus.** *After damage that includes the ventromedial hypothalamus and the axons that pass nearby, an individual digests food more rapidly than usual and secretes more insulin.* The high insulin level causes a disproportionate amount of each meal to be stored as fat. Because the food passes quickly through the digestive system and into the fat cells where it stays, the individual becomes hungry again shortly after each meal (Hoebel & Hernandez, 1993). Figure 11.8 shows a rat with this kind of brain damage. One woman with a tumor in this area gained an average of more than 10 kg (20 lb) per month (Reeves & Plum, 1969).

Another area of the hypothalamus contributes to ending meals in a different way. *After damage to or*

FIGURE 11.8 An obese rat with a damaged ventromedial hypothalamus (left) can eat less than an ordinary rat (right) and still gain weight. This rat's excess fat prevents it from grooming its fur.

Reeves & Plum, "Hyperphagia, rage, and dementia accompanying a ventromedial hypothalamic neoplasm," *Archives of Neurology 1969*, Vol.20, no. 616-624.

chemical inhibition of the **paraventricular hypothalamus,** *meals are of normal frequency but each individual meal is enormous* (Leibowitz & Alexander, 1991; Leibowitz, Hammer, & Chang, 1981). An individual with such brain damage continues eating until the stomach and intestines are about to burst.

CONCEPT CHECK

6. Many young ballet dancers and other female athletes who exercise heavily and keep their weight low are slower to start puberty than most other girls. Why?

7. After damage to the ventromedial hypothalamus, an animal's weight eventually reaches a higher than usual level and then fluctuates around that amount. What has happened to the set point? (Check your answers on page 425.)

Social and Cultural Influences on Eating

Physiological mechanisms account for only part of our eating habits. In the United States, obesity is far more common today than it was two or three generations ago. People's physiology is the same as ever, but now we have easy-to-prepare high-calorie foods, all-you-can-eat buffets (sometimes called "all night" buffets), and sit-at-a-desk jobs.

Social factors significantly influence our eating. When you eat with friends, you linger over the meal. You eat a few more bites after you thought you were done, and later a few more. Someone wants to have dessert, so you have one too. On the average you will sit at the table two or three times as long with a group of friends as you would alone (Bell & Pliner, 2003), and you will eat almost twice as much food (de Castro, 2000).

Overeating has also spread in other cultures as they became, as some people put it, "Coca-Colonized" by the U.S. and similar cultures (J. M. Friedman, 2000). The strongest example comes from the Native American Pima of Arizona (Figure 11.9). Most Pima adults are seriously obese, probably because of several genes (Norman et al., 1998), and most also have high blood pressure and Type II diabetes. However, their ancestors—with the same genes—were not obese. They ate only the fruits and vegetables that grow in the Sonoran Desert, which are available only for brief seasons of the year. To survive, they had to eat as much as possible when food was available and conserve their energy as much as possible. Beginning in the 1940s, they switched to the same diet as other Americans, which is richer in calories and available year-round. The Pima still eat massive quantities and conserve their energy by being relatively inactive, and the result is weight gain. We see here a superb example of the combined influence of genetics and environment. The Pima became obese because of a combination of their genes and the change in diet; neither by itself would have this effect.

Eating Too Much or Too Little

Obesity has become widespread but not universal. Why do some people become obese whereas others do not? And at the other extreme, why do some people eat too little? The puzzles are great, and the answers are incomplete. One generalization that does emerge is

FIGURE 11.9 (a) Until the 1940s the Native American Pima ate their traditional diet of desert plants and remained thin. (b) Today, they eat the typical U.S. diet while remaining relatively inactive, and the result is high prevalence of obesity.

that abnormal eating reflects a combination of social and physiological influences.

Obesity

Obesity is *the excessive accumulation of body fat.* Physicians calculate a *body mass index,* defined as weight in kilograms divided by height in meters squared (kg/m²). A ratio over 25 is considered overweight; over 30, obese; over 40, extremely obese (National Institutes of Health, 2000). The current estimate is that 30% of U.S. adults are obese and another 35% are overweight (Marx, 2003). Obesity increases the risk of diabetes, coronary heart disease, certain kinds of cancer, sleep apnea (difficulty breathing while asleep), and several other diseases (Kopelman, 2000). For much information about obesity in general, visit this Web site:

www.obesity.org.

People become seriously overweight because they take in more calories than they use up. But *why* do they do that?

The Limited Role of Emotional Disturbances

One prevalent idea has been that anxiety, depression, or other emotional problems lead to overeating and weight gain. However, anxiety, depression, and other psychological concerns are not unusually common among obese people (Wadden & Stunkard, 1987), and there is no evidence that emotional problems cause obesity. Nevertheless, some obese people react strongly to the unfavorable way in which they are treated. Because prejudices against the obese are so common, many obese people have a restricted social life and have trouble getting a good job (M. A. Friedman & Brownell, 1996).

Although emotional distress does not cause obesity, it can produce temporary fluctuations in eating and body weight for almost anyone. In one survey of 100 adults (Edelman, 1981), 40 said that they overeat three or more times per month when they feel nervous, tired, lonely, or sorry for themselves. The eating binge enables them to focus their attention on eating and away from their other concerns (Heatherton & Baumeister, 1991). Such eating binges are most frequent and most extreme with people who have been dieting to lose weight (Greeno & Wing,

❚ Although obesity is not significantly linked with anxiety or depression, some obese people feel distressed and suffer from low self-esteem because of how other people treat them.

1994). Evidently, dieters actively inhibit their desire to eat until a stressful experience breaks these inhibitions and releases the pent-up desire to eat.

Genetics and Energy Output

Obesity tends to run in families, and studies of twins and adopted children indicate a fairly high heritability for obesity (Comuzzie & Allison, 1998). But how do those genes exert their effects?

Many overweight people who claim to eat only normal amounts of food eat more than they admit, maybe even more than they admit to themselves. In one admirably simple study, researchers collected the supermarket receipts and found that overweight families bought more food per person than average and especially more high-fat food (Ransley et al., 2003). However, in addition to consuming more energy, they also have low energy output, including a low metabolic rate.

One group of investigators compared the infants of twelve overweight mothers and six normal-weight mothers over their first year of life. All the babies weighed about the same at birth, but six of the babies of the overweight mothers were inactive compared to the other babies and became overweight within their first year. During their first 3 months, they expended about 20% less energy per day than the average for other babies (Roberts, Savage, Coward, Chew, & Lucas, 1988).

Low energy expenditure is a good predictor of weight gain in adults as well. Eric Ravussin and his associates (1988) found that the adults with the lowest energy expenditure over a 24-hour period were the most likely to gain weight over the next 2 to 4 years.

Losing Weight

People trying to lose weight have a conflict between the motive to enjoy eating now and the motive to feel good about losing weight later. Clinical psychologists who work with people trying to lose weight report frequent frustrations as people lose weight for a while and then relapse, lose again and relapse again, often blaming the therapist for their failure (Polivy & Herman, 2002). However, you probably know some people who did manage to diet and then keep to a moderate weight. The reason we hear about more dieting failures than successes is simple: Most of the people who lose weight and keep it off don't keep talking about it and seeking help (Schachter, 1982). The people who show up at one weight-loss clinic after another have repeatedly failed to lose weight, and so the difficult patients seem disproportionately common.

Many approaches are available for those seeking help in losing weight. A survey of weight-loss experts found that they disagreed about much but did agree on a few recommendations (Schwartz & Brownell, 1995):

- Almost anyone who needs to lose weight should include increased exercise as part of the strategy. The best advice is to set realistic exercise goals and stick to them.
- Only people with severe, life-threatening obesity should even consider surgical removal of fat.
- Programs such as Overeaters Anonymous (OA) help people who feel comfortable with the spiritual focus

and the emphasis on overeating as an addiction or disease. However, not everyone feels comfortable with this approach.
- Private counseling is useful mostly for people with other psychological problems in addition to their weight problem.

The advisability of weight-loss drugs is controversial. Medications are now available or are being researched to weaken hunger signals to the brain, block absorption of fat in the intestines, and increase metabolism (Bray & Tartaglia, 2000).

The Effect of Intentional Weight Loss on Appetite

Are you satisfied with your weight? In the United States, women in particular are unlikely to be satisfied with their own appearance, and the percentage of women expressing dissatisfaction has increased grad-

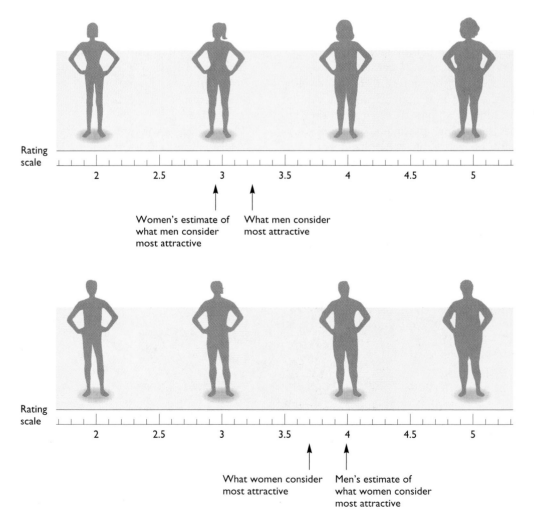

FIGURE 11.10 In a study by Fallon and Rozin (1985), women and men were asked which figure they considered most attractive and which figure they believed the opposite sex considered most attractive. Each sex misestimated the other's preferences.

ually over decades. Even unattractive men are likely to say they are satisfied with their appearance, and even attractive women say they are dissatisfied with their appearance (Feingold & Mazzella, 1998).

Dissatisfaction about one's body often translates into worries about eating, especially in the United States. Before we proceed try these questions. In each case circle one of the choices.

- *Ice cream* belongs
  best with: delicious   fattening
- *Chocolate cake* belongs
  best with: guilt   celebration
- *Heavy cream* belongs
  best with: whipped   unhealthy
- *Fried eggs* belong
  best with: breakfast   cholesterol

On questions like these, U.S. people, especially women, are more likely to circle *fattening, guilt, unhealthy,* and *cholesterol*—indicating food worries—whereas people in Japan, Belgium, and France are more likely to circle *delicious, celebration, whipped,* and *breakfast*. On a wide range of questions, U.S. people indicate great interest in getting highly healthful foods, and yet when they are asked whether they eat a healthy diet, the Americans mostly say "no" whereas the French say "yes" (Rozin, Fischler, Imada, Sarubin, & Wrzesniewski, 1999). Furthermore, the French eat a high-fat diet, which Americans consider unhealthy, and yet they have *less* cardiovascular disease than Americans do. Several explanations have been offered for the French people's health, including small portion sizes (Rozin, Kabnick, Pete, Fischler, & Shields, 2003), unhurried meals, and the benefits of drinking moderate amounts of wine. In addition, Rozin and colleagues (1999) suggest that another reason for the French people's surprisingly good health is that they worry less!

In the United States and other Western countries, slenderness is fashionable, especially for women. April Fallon and Paul Rozin (1985) asked women to indicate on a diagram which body figure they thought men considered most attractive. The investigators also asked men which female figure *they* considered most attractive. As Figure 11.10 shows, women thought that men preferred thinner women than most men actually do. (The same study also found that men thought women preferred heavier men than most women actually do.)

Given the social pressure to be thin, many normal-weight people deprive themselves of food they would like to eat. Doing so apparently requires considerable mental effort. Here is a somewhat complicated experiment to illustrate this point.

CRITICAL THINKING: WHAT'S THE EVIDENCE?
Dieting Requires Mental Energy

In this study dieters were exposed to the temptation to snack and then, after they resisted the temptation, were required to eat some ice cream in the second part of the study (Vohs & Heatherton, 2000).

Hypothesis   Dieters who have to fight a strong temptation to eat will be "mentally worn out" and therefore more likely to yield to the next temptation.

Method   Chronic dieters and nondieters participated in a two-part study. First, they watched a video and answered some questions about it. During the video an array of snacks (cheese-flavored corn chips, candies, and salted peanuts) was either next to them or 3 meters (10 feet) away. Half of each group were told not to touch the snacks (because they were for people in another study), and the other half were told to help themselves. That is, the study had eight groups of participants:

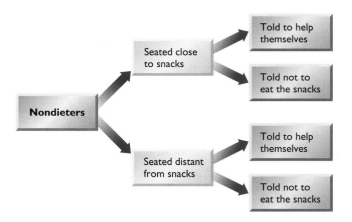

The key to the study was the results for dieters who were seated next to the snacks and told to help themselves. In fact they did not eat any snacks (because they were on a diet), but presumably (and according to their own reports), they were strongly tempted. Those who were told not to eat the snacks had less temptation, as did those who were seated far from the snacks. But imagine yourself on a diet sitting right next to appealing snacks and being told to help yourself. You fight the urge, but the resistance is not easy.

Next, participants were taken to another room where their task was to sample ice cream from three large containers and rate the taste of each. The experimenter left the room, remarking, "Help yourself to any ice cream you want; we have tons in the freezer." During this part even the dieters had no choice but to eat, although they could control how much they ate.

Results Of the eight groups in this study, the people who ate the most ice cream were the dieters who had been told "help yourself" to snacks in the first part of the study while being seated close to the snacks.

Interpretation According to the researchers, these results suggest that people have limited resources for self-regulation. After you have resisted temptation for a while (using up some self-regulation resources), your ability to regulate your behavior again weakens, leaving you vulnerable to the next temptation. The study has the interesting implication that you should try to avoid putting yourself into one tempting situation after another, especially within a short time. That conclusion probably applies to cigarettes, alcohol, or any other habit you are trying to break. The experiment is also interesting in showing that research procedures frequently require more than just an experimental group and a control group. Here we care about whether the results differ for dieters and nondieters, as well as the difference between various levels of temptations and kinds of instructions.

CONCEPT CHECK ☑

8. Which group in the experiment ate the most ice cream and why? (Check your answers on page 425.)

Anorexia Nervosa

The Duchess of Windsor once said, "You can't be too rich or too thin." She may have been right about too rich, but she was definitely wrong about too thin. Some people are so strongly motivated to be thin that they threaten their health.

Anorexia nervosa is *a condition in which someone refuses to eat enough to maintain a stable weight, intensely fears gaining weight, and misperceives his or her body as fatter than it actually is.* Most people with anorexia also exercise heavily. *Anorexia* means "loss of appetite," although the problem here is more a refusal to eat than a loss of appetite. *Nervosa* means "for reasons of the nerves" and distinguishes this condition from disorders of the digestive system. Anorexia nervosa occurs in about 0.3% of young women about age 15 to 24, with much lower incidence in men and older women (Hoek & van Hoeken, 2003). As with other psychological conditions, anorexia nervosa comes in all degrees, but in its most severe form, it can fatally damage the heart muscle.

The prevalence of anorexia seems to have increased over the last several decades, presumably in response to social pressures. However, the increase has been slow, and it is difficult to know how much of the increase is real and how much is due to increased recognition and improved recordkeeping (Lindberg & Hjern, 2003).

At the outset the person may have decided to lose weight for health reasons, to become a ballet dancer or model, or for some other reason. Unlike people who are food-deprived for other reasons, people with anorexia run long distances, compete at sports, work diligently on their school assignments, and sleep little. Most are perfectionists who take pride in the extreme self-control they demonstrate by refusing to eat (Halmi et al., 2000). The perfectionist personality probably contributes to anorexia, although it could hardly be the whole explanation.

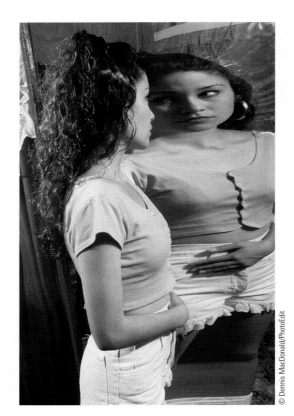

A fun house mirror causes a temporary distortion of everyone's appearance. People with anorexia nervosa report a similar distortion of body image at all times, describing themselves as much fatter than they really are.

The causes of anorexia are unknown. Many biochemical abnormalities have been demonstrated in the brains of anorexics, but the abnormalities are probably more the result than the cause of severe weight loss (Ferguson & Pigott, 2000). After weight returns to normal, most of the biochemical measures do too. Similarities between monozygotic twins imply a genetic contribution, although the route of the genes' effects is not yet known (Klump, Miller, Keel, McGue, & Iacono, 2001). Anorexia is reported more often in upper-middle-class families, although part of the explanation is that people from poorer families are less likely to get help, and therefore less likely to show up in the statistics (Becker, Franko, Speck, & Herzog, 2003). Anorexia is also somewhat more common among families with a psychiatrically disordered parent (Lindberg & Hjern, 2003). However, most people with anorexia have no psychiatric history themselves before the onset of anorexia.

One hypothesis is that anorexia reflects impairment of the brain's hunger mechanisms. However, most people with anorexia enjoy the taste of food and even enjoy preparing it. The problem is more a fear of eating than a lack of hunger. Some even refuse to lick postage stamps for fear that the glue might contain some tiny fraction of a calorie. People with anorexia usually deny or understate their problem. Even when they become dangerously thin, they often describe themselves as "looking fat" and "needing to lose weight."

Cultural influences are strong but not the whole story. Western culture today puts strong pressure, especially on young women, to be thin, and dieting in response to that pressure can lead to anorexia. However, society's pressure cannot be the complete explanation, as most women who go on severe diets do not develop anorexia. Anorexia is more common in cultures that emphasize thinness, such as the United States, Canada, and northern Europe. Immigrants from southern Europe, Africa, or the Arab countries have increased risk of anorexia after living in one of the cultures with higher incidence (Lindberg & Hjern, 2003). However, occasional cases of anorexia nervosa have been documented in non-Westernized cultures of Africa and Southeast Asia, as well as in Europe hundreds of years ago, long before the "thin is beautiful" emphasis (Keel & Klump, 2003). In some of those cases, society had other kinds of pressures, such as fasting for religious reasons. So cultural influences contribute to the onset of anorexia, but the nature of the cultural influence can vary, and we need to explain why some people react so much more strongly than others.

An interesting proposal compares anorexia nervosa to the behavior of elk and similar animals that sometimes migrate great distances in search of a better feeding ground. While they are migrating, they are

© Archive Photos/Express Newspapers

▌ While being treated at an anorexia clinic, this young woman was approached on an outing by someone who offered her a job as a model. Society's pressures on women to be ultrathin contribute to the anorexia problem.

highly active and ordinarily do not eat at all, even when they find little patches of food. Perhaps at some point in early human evolution, some people developed a similar mechanism, enabling them to react to food deprivation by traveling vigorously without eating. Now, when a genetically predisposed person loses weight rapidly—in response to dieting, for example—the sudden weight loss triggers this mechanism, provoking hyperactivity and loss of eating (Guisinger, 2003). This hypothesis potentially explains much, although it requires a series of untested assumptions. It merits further research.

CONCEPT CHECK ☑

9. In what way is a patient with anorexia strikingly different from typical starving people? (Check your answer on page 425.)

Bulimia Nervosa

Another eating disorder is **bulimia nervosa** (literally, "ox hunger"), in which people—again, mostly women—alternate *between self-starvation and frequent periods of excessive eating when they feel they have lost their ability to control themselves. To compensate for the overeating, they force themselves to vomit or use laxatives or enemas.* That is, they "binge and purge." In extreme eating binges, people consume up to 20,000 calories at a time (Schlesier-Stropp, 1984). A meal of a "regular size" cheeseburger, regular fries, and a milkshake constitutes about 1,000 calories, so imagine eating that meal 20 times at one sitting. However, the binges usually feature mainly sweets and fats with little protein (Latner, 2003), so a better illustration of 20,000 calories would be 10 liters of chocolate fudge topping.

In the United States, about 1% of adult women and about 0.1% of adult men have bulimia nervosa (Hoek & van Hoeken, 2003). Many others have occasional eating binges but not enough to qualify for a diagnosis of bulimia nervosa. One study found that, 6 years after women were treated for bulimia, 60% were fully recovered, 30% still had moderate problems, and 10% had serious disorders or were dead (Fichter & Quadflieg, 1997).

The incidence of bulimia nervosa has increased steadily over the last few decades. Whenever the numbers seem to go up or down, the question arises as to whether the actual incidence has changed or whether psychiatrists have changed their diagnoses. In this case, however, we have a special kind of evidence: The more recently a woman was born, the higher her risk of ever developing bulimia nervosa, even when all women are evaluated at the same time and according to the same criteria. That is, bulimia is more common among young women today than it is or ever was in their mothers' and grandmothers' generations (Kendler et al., 1991).

Culture is a major contributor to bulimia nervosa. Bulimia was rare and perhaps nonexistent until a few decades ago, and it has not been recorded in any cultures without a strong Western influence (Keel & Klump, 2003). Of course, it would be hard to have an eating binge except where huge amounts of tasty food are available.

The most spectacular example comes from the Fiji Islands, where women have traditionally been heavy but content with their bodies. The idea of dieting to lose weight was unknown until the introduction of television, with many American programs, in 1995. Since then, many have begun dieting, self-induced vomiting, and binge eating. Many said they were trying to lose weight to be more like the women they saw on television (Becker, Burwell, Gilman, Herzog, & Hamburg, 2002; Becker, Burwell, Navara, & Gilman, 2003).

One hypothesis has been that either anorexia or bulimia might result from sexual abuse early in life, low self-esteem, or depression (Bardone, Vohs, Abramson, Heatherton, & Joiner, 2000; Fairburn, Welch, Doll, Davies, & O'Connor, 1997). However, the research has found no consistent link between any of these factors and the onset of eating disorders (Stice, 2002). The disorders do tend to persist longer in depressed people (Stice, 2002).

Another hypothesis is that people with bulimia starve themselves for a while, fight their persistent feelings of hunger, and then go on an eating binge (Polivy & Herman, 1985). That idea may be on the right track, but it is incomplete. Of the people who starve themselves for days or weeks, some do develop eating binges, but others do not (Stice, 2002).

The results may depend on what someone eats after a period of deprivation. Whereas most people who end a fast begin the next meal with meat, fish, or eggs, people with bulimia start with dessert or snack foods (Latner, 2003). One hypothesis compares bulimia to drug addiction (Hoebel, Rada, Mark, & Pothos, 1999). Overeating can provide a "high" similar to that from drugs, and some drug users withdrawing from a drug turn to overeating as a substitute. Moreover, when an addict abstains from a drug for a while and then returns to it, the first new use of the drug can be highly reinforcing. By this reasoning the cycles of abstention and overeating become addictive because the first big meal after a period of abstention is extremely reinforcing.

To test this idea, researchers put laboratory rats on a regimen of no food for 12 hours, including the first 4 hours of their waking day, followed by a meal of a sweet, syrupy liquid. With each repetition of this schedule, the rats ate more and more of that rich meal. Furthermore, if they were then deprived of this accustomed meal, they shook their heads and chattered their teeth in a pattern much like that of rats going through morphine withdrawal (Colantuoni et al., 2001, 2002). Obviously, the rats in this study do not fully model the complexities of human bulimia, but they suggest that a pattern of deprivation followed by overeating can provide strong reinforcement that overwhelms other motivations.

CONCEPT CHECK ☑

10. Under what circumstances would an eating binge be likely to produce an experience similar to taking an addictive drug? (Check your answer on page 425.)

Motives in Food Selection

Up to this point, we have considered the decision of how much to eat, but an equally important decision is *which* foods to eat. Have you ever wondered how anyone first figured out which foods were edible? It was easy for you and me; our parents and other people told us what to eat, and we did not have to try all the weeds in the field to decide which ones were good. Our parents learned from their parents and they from their parents, but long ago somebody had to discover what was edible by trial and error. Moreover, people had to discover how to prepare many foods that are inedible when raw (Rozin, 1996). For example, cassava, a root native to South America, is poisonous unless someone washes and pounds it for 3 days. Can you imagine discovering that fact? Someone had to say, "So far, everyone who ate this plant died, but I bet that if I wash and pound it for 3 days, then it will be okay." Cashews are covered with a thin membrane that must be carefully removed; anyone who touches it will react as if he or she had touched poison ivy. American corn (maize) has a deficit of certain nutrients and beans are deficient in other nutrients, but corn and beans together make a good combination—as the Native Americans discovered long ago.

We learn our food choices largely by learning what *not* to eat. Toddlers around the age of 1 1/2 will try to eat almost anything they can fit into their mouths. Up to age 7 or 8, about the only reason children give for refusing to eat something is that they think it would taste bad (Rozin, Fallon, & Augustoni-Ziskind, 1986). As they grow older, they cite more and more reasons for accepting certain foods and rejecting others. As with other motivations, food selection depends on a combination of physiological, social, and cognitive factors.

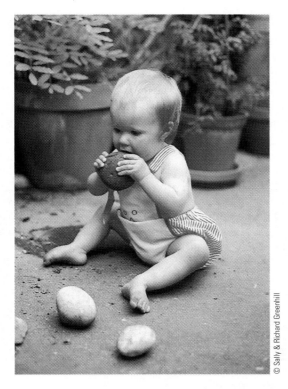

▌ Infants and young children will try to eat almost anything. As they grow older, they learn to avoid foods for reasons other than just taste.

Food Selection Based on Taste

Some taste preferences and aversions are present at birth. Infants readily consume sweet liquids but spit out anything sour or bitter. That predisposition is adaptive, as most sweets are nutritious and almost all bitter substances are poisonous (Scott & Verhagen, 2000). People also have temporary taste cravings, most of which we cannot explain. For example, about one fourth of women report a strong craving for sweets, especially chocolate, around the time of menstruation. We might guess the craving has something to do with hormones or discomfort, but hormonal treatments don't alter the craving and neither do tranquilizers (Michener, Rozin, Freeman, & Gale, 1999).

One craving that we can explain, at least in some cases, is the craving for salty tastes. Many years ago a young child showed a strong craving for salt. As an infant he licked the salt off crackers and bacon but refused to eat the food itself. One of the first words he learned was *salt*. He put a thick layer of salt on everything he ate, and sometimes he swallowed salt directly from the shaker. When deprived of salt, he stopped eating and began to waste away. At the age of 3 1/2, he was taken to the hospital and fed the usual hospital fare. He soon died of salt deficiency (Wilkins & Richter, 1940).

The reason was that he had defective adrenal glands. These glands secrete hormones that enable the body to retain salt (Verrey & Beron, 1996). He craved salt because it was being excreted so rapidly from his body. (We are often told to limit our salt intake for health reasons, but too little salt can also be dangerous.)

Research on animals confirms that as soon as animals, including humans, become salt deficient, they show a heightened preference for salty tastes (Rozin & Kalat, 1971). People who have lost large quantities of salt by bleeding or heavy sweating often express a craving for salt. Apparently, salty foods taste better to salt-deficient people and animals than they do to others (Jacobs, Mark, & Scott, 1988).

Preference for Familiar Foods

People from different parts of the world have different taste preferences. Contrast, for example, Greek, Mexican, and Chinese cuisines. Cultural differences in taste preferences evidently have nothing to do with differences in taste sensations, as taste buds are about the same throughout the world (Laing et al., 1993). Food preferences depend mainly on familiarity (Rozin, 1996).

Cuisine is one of the most stable and defining features of any culture. In one study researchers interviewed Japanese high school and college students who had spent a year in another country as part of an exchange program. The researchers asked the students how much they enjoyed their experience.

Their satisfaction had little relationship to the educational system, religion, family life, recreation, or dating customs of the host country. The main determinant was the food: Students who could sometimes eat Japanese food had a good time. Those who could not became homesick (Furukawa, 1997).

Learned Associations with Food

As mentioned in Chapter 6, laboratory animals associate foods with the gastrointestinal consequences that follow. If they eat something and then get sick, they avoid what they ate. The same is true of humans. When you eat something and later feel sick, you form a strong aversion to the food, especially if it was unfamiliar. It doesn't matter whether you consciously think the food made you ill. If you eat something at an amusement park and then go on a wild ride and get sick, you may never again like that food. Even though you know the ride was at fault, an area deep in your brain still associates the food with the sickness.

▌ People associate what they eat, especially unfamiliar foods, with the way they feel afterward. If you ate corn dogs and cotton candy and then got sick on a wild ride, something in your brain would blame the food, regardless of what you think consciously. Ordinarily, however, this kind of learning teaches us to avoid harmful substances.

People can also develop preferences by associating a food with another food that they already enjoy (Capaldi, 1996). For example, parents who want their child to learn to like broccoli might mix a little broccoli with cheese or some other food that the child already likes. Later, they could gradually reduce the amount of cheese.

People also reject safe foods because of the very idea of what they are (Rozin & Fallon, 1987; Rozin, Millman, & Nemeroff, 1986). In the United States, most people refuse to eat dog, cat, or horse meat. Many vegetarians consider any kind of meat disgusting and are distressed even to watch other people eat it. The longer

---

Crispy Cajun Crickets

Adapted from a recipe in the *Food Insects Newsletter*, March 1990

Tired of the same old snack food? Perk up your next party with Crispy Cajun Crickets ("pampered" house crickets, *Acheta domesticus*, available from Flucker's Cricket Farm, P.O. Box 378, Baton Rouge, LA 70821, 800-735-8537).

1 cup crickets
1 pinch oatmeal
4 ounces butter, melted
Salt
Garlic
Cayenne

1. Put crickets in a clean, airy container with oatmeal for food. After one day, discard sick crickets and freeze the rest.
2. Wash frozen crickets in warm water and spread on a cookie sheet. Roast in a 250-degree oven until crunchy.
3. Meanwhile heat butter with remaining ingredients and sprinkle this sauce on crickets before serving.

Yield: 1 serving

FIGURE 11.11 People avoid some potential foods because they are disgusted by the very idea of eating them. For example, most Westerners refuse to eat insects, despite assurances that most are nutritious and harmless.

people have been vegetarians, the more firmly they tend to regard meat-eating as not only undesirable but also immoral (Rozin, Markwith, & Stoess, 1997).

How would you like to try the tasty morsels described in Figure 11.11? Most people find the idea of eating insects repulsive, even if the insects were sterilized to kill all the germs (Rozin & Fallon, 1987). Would you be willing to drink a glass of apple juice after a dead cockroach had been dipped into it? What if the cockroach had been carefully sterilized? Many people not only refuse to drink that glass of apple juice but say they have lost their taste for apple juice in general (Rozin, Millman, & Nemeroff, 1986). Would you drink pure water from a brand-new, never-used toilet bowl? Would you eat a piece of chocolate fudge shaped like dog feces? If not, you are guided by the idea of the food, not its taste or safety.

▌ Different cultures have different taboos. Here is an assortment of insect and reptile dishes. (Yum, yum?)

11. Why do many menstruating women crave potato chips? (Check your answer on this page.)

IN CLOSING

The Complexities of Hunger

The research on nearly every topic in this module underscores the idea that our motivations are controlled by a complex mixture of physiological, social, and cognitive forces. For example, people become overweight (or falsely perceive themselves as overweight) for a variety of reasons relating to everything from genetics to culture, and they then try to lose weight mostly for social reasons, such as trying to look attractive. Sometimes the physiological factors and the social factors collide, as when normal-weight people try to make themselves thinner and thinner.

The overall point is this: All our motivations interact and combine. How much we eat and what and when we eat depend not only on our need for food but also on social needs and the need for self-esteem.

Summary

- *Short-term regulation of hunger.* Meals are ended by several mechanisms, principally distension of the stomach and intestines. Hunger resumes when the cells begin to receive less glucose and other nutrients. The hormones insulin and glucagon regulate the flow of nutrients from the blood to storage and from there back into the blood. (page 412)

- *Long-term regulation of hunger.* An individual meal can be larger or smaller than necessary to provide the energy that the body needs. The body's fat cells secrete the hormone leptin in proportion to their mass; an increase of leptin decreases hunger, and a decrease of leptin increases hunger. (page 414)

- *Causes of being overweight.* People become overweight for many reasons, but emotional difficulties are rarely a major factor. Some people are predisposed to obesity for genetic reasons; whether they become obese or how obese they become depends on the kinds and amounts of food available. (page 417)

- *Weight-loss techniques.* Many people resort to a variety of strategies to lose weight, ranging from dieting to surgery. Increased exercise is a good idea for almost anyone wishing to lose weight. Resisting the temptation to snack requires significant mental effort or resources. (page 417)

- *Anorexia nervosa and bulimia nervosa.* People suffering from anorexia nervosa deprive themselves of food, sometimes to the point of starvation. People suffering from bulimia nervosa alternate between periods of strict dieting and brief but spectacular eating binges. The cultural pressure to become thin is a contributor to both conditions but not a sufficient explanation of either. (page 420)

- *Food selection.* Food preferences can be altered by changes in body chemistry, such as a deficiency of salt. Other things being equal, we tend to prefer familiar foods. We avoid foods that have been associated with something nauseating or repulsive and prefer foods previously associated with other good-tasting foods. (page 422)

Answers to Concept Checks

4. Insulin levels are higher in the middle of the day (LeMagnen, 1981). As a result much of the food you eat is stored as fats, and you become hungry again soon. Late at night, when insulin levels are lower, some of your fat supplies are converted to glucose, which enters the blood. (page 414)

5. Leptin, released by fat cells, and insulin, released by the pancreas. (You could also mention glucagon, released by the pancreas.) (page 415)

6. By keeping their fat levels very low, they also keep their leptin levels low, and leptin is one of the triggers for puberty. (page 416)

7. The set point has increased. (page 416)

8. The group who were dieters seated next to the snacks in the first part of the study and told to "help yourself." These people had been more strongly tempted to snack than dieters who were seated far from the snacks or who were told not to eat them. Therefore, they had presumably exhausted much of their "self-restraint" reserves. (page 420)

9. Unlike typical starving people, those with anorexia have high levels of activity. Also, they refuse to eat in the presence of tasty foods. (page 421)

10. Eating a meal high in sweets and fats right after a deprivation period apparently produces an experience comparable to those produced by addictive drugs. (page 422)

11. It is possible to lose much blood and therefore salts during menstruation. The loss of salt triggers an increased preference for salty tastes, such as found with potato chips. (page 425)

What do people do sexually?

Why do some people's sexual interests differ from others'?

If you have any doubts about people's interest in sex, take a look at television listings, popular books and magazines, and films. Humans, unlike most other mammalian species, are interested in sex when a woman is unlikely to get pregnant. In fact people often take measures to prevent pregnancy.

Sexual motivation, like hunger, depends on both a physiological drive and available incentives. Also like hunger, the sex drive increases during times of deprivation, at least up to a point, and it can be inhibited for social and symbolic reasons, including religious ones. However, the sex drive differs from hunger in important ways. We do not need to be around food to feel hungry, but many people do need a partner to feel sexual arousal. We eat in public, but we have sexual activities in private.

Ultimately, of course, hunger and sex serve important biological functions that we ordinarily don't even think about during the acts themselves. We eat because we enjoy eating, and we evolved mechanisms that make us enjoy eating because eating keeps us alive. Similarly, we enjoy sex, and we evolved mechanisms that make sex feel good because it leads to reproduction. Several psychologists have further theorized that we have evolved mechanisms that lead men and women to different kinds of courtship and sexual behaviors because the effective reproductive strategies of men and women differ. We shall discuss those issues in Chapter 14 when we consider attraction.

What Do People Do, and How Often?

Researchers have many reasons for inquiring about the frequency of various sexual behaviors. For example, if we want to predict how fast and how far AIDS is likely to spread in the population, it is important to know how many people are having unsafe sex and with how many partners. In addition to the scientific and medical reasons for studying sexual behavior, let's admit it: Most of us are curious about what other people do. We would like to know, "Am I normal?" The answer depends on what we mean by "normal." If that term means "reasonably common in the population," then it is hard to think of anything you might be doing—or not doing—that would make you abnormal.

The Kinsey Survey

The first important survey of human sexual behavior was conducted by Alfred C. Kinsey, a shy insect biologist who once agreed to teach the biological portion of Indiana University's course on marriage. When he found that the library included very little information about human sexuality, he decided to conduct a survey. What he intended as a small-scale project for teaching purposes grew into a survey of 18,000 people.

Although Kinsey's sample was large, it was neither random nor representative. He obtained most of his interviews by going to organizations, ranging from fraternities to nunneries, and asking everyone in the organization to talk to him. He interviewed mostly midwestern European Americans who belonged to organizations that agreed to cooperate, and the percentages he reported do not generalize to other populations.

Alfred C. Kinsey, who pioneered survey studies of sexual behavior, was an outstanding interviewer. He put people at ease so that they could speak freely but was also alert to probable lies. His results should be interpreted cautiously, however, because he did not obtain a random or representative sample of the U.S. population.

▌ Sexual customs vary sharply from one society to another. At a Hmong Festival, unmarried women toss tennis balls to potential suitors.

Nevertheless, he did document that human sexual behavior is extremely variable (Kinsey, Pomeroy, & Martin, 1948; Kinsey, Pomeroy, Martin, & Gebhard, 1953). For example, he found some men and women who had rarely or never experienced orgasm. At the other extreme, he found one man who reported an average of four or five orgasms per day over the preceding 30 years (with a wide variety of male, female, and nonhuman partners) and several women who sometimes had 50 or more orgasms within 20 minutes.

Kinsey found that most people were unaware of the great variation in sexual behavior in the population at large. When he asked people whether they believed that "excessive masturbation" causes physical and mental illness, most said yes. (We now know it does not.) He then asked what would constitute "excessive." For each person "excessive" meant a little more than what he or she did. One young man who masturbated about once per month said he thought three times per month would cause mental illness. A man who masturbated three times per day said he thought five times per day would be excessive. (In reaction to these findings, Kinsey once defined a *nymphomaniac* as "someone who wants sex more than you do.")

Contemporary Surveys

Kinsey did not even try to interview a random sample of the population because he assumed that most people would refuse to cooperate and perhaps even take offense at being asked. He may have been right about people in the 1940s, but in the 1980s and beyond, researchers identified random samples and managed to get cooperation from most of the people they approached (Fay, Turner, Klassen, & Gagnon, 1989; Laumann, Gagnon, Michael, & Michaels, 1994).

(Some advice if anyone ever asks you to participate in a sex survey: Legitimate researchers carefully present their credentials to show their affiliation with a research institute. They also take precautions to guarantee the confidentiality of responses. If "researchers" who want to ask you about your sex life fail to show their credentials or seem unconcerned about your confidentiality, do not trust them. Be especially wary of sex surveys by telephone. Some sex researchers do conduct research by telephone, but it is hard to distinguish a legitimate telephone sex survey from a disguised obscene phone call.)

A survey of a random sample of almost 3,500 U.S. adults (Laumann et al., 1994) explored what people would *like* to be doing. Figure 11.12 shows the percentage of men and women who describe various sexual activities as "very appealing." The most popular sexual activity is vaginal intercourse, followed by watching one's partner undress and then by oral sex. Other possible options lag well behind. Note an ambiguity in certain responses: When 13% of men say they find group sex "very appealing," do they mean they have frequently enjoyed doing it or that they have fantasies about it?

Note that more men than women report enjoying every activity on the graph. Besides the differences shown in Figure 11.12, men are much more likely than women to masturbate frequently and to look forward to opportunities for casual sex (Oliver & Hyde, 1993). In general, men also have stronger preferences for what activities they want to do, how often, and with how much variety. A woman who changes partners is more likely to accept the preferences of her new partner than a man is to alter his pattern to suit a new female partner (Baumeister, 2000). Women are also more likely to switch between heterosexual and homosexual (in either direction) than men are (Peplau, 2003). Why women are more flexible remains unexplained.

In Figure 11.13 you see some preliminary results from the first large-scale international survey of sexual behavior, including 27,500 people in 30 countries throughout the world. Cultures vary in their customs about dating, marriage, and public display of near nudity, but a number of trends are remarkably similar across cultures. For example, as Figure 11.13 shows, sexual activity declines gradually with age, but even beyond age 70, about half remain sexually active (Gingell et al., 2002). Although these data are for men only, a previous study limited to the United States found parallel results for women (Laumann et al., 1994). Even in old age, most people remain interested in sex if they remain healthy and have a healthy, willing partner. However, as people age their frequency of sexual activity declines, and the probability of having more

FIGURE 11.12 The percentage of U.S. adults who rate various sexual activities as "very appealing" as opposed to "somewhat appealing," "not appealing," or "not at all appealing." *(Based on data of Laumann, Gagnon, Michael, & Michaels, 1994)*

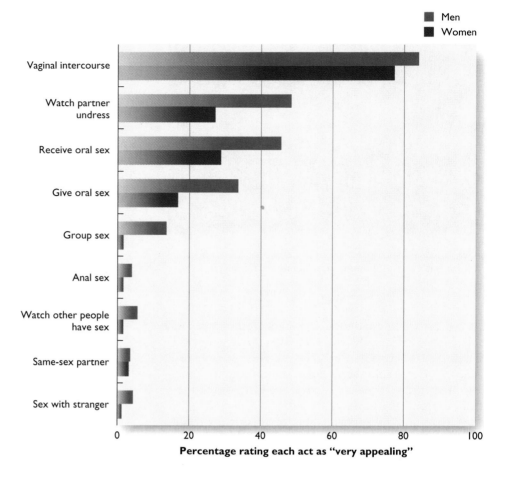

than one sex partner declines sharply (Laumann et al., 1994).

A survey conducted in the United States in the 1990s found the results shown in Figure 11.14. On the average, people in their 40s reported more sex partners in their lifetime than did people in their 50s. This is a cohort effect, like those described in Chapter 10: People who were in their 40s at the time of the survey had been young during an era of greater sexual freedom than that experienced by people born earlier.

CONCEPT CHECK ☑

12. Why did Kinsey's results differ from those of later surveys? (Check your answer on page 437.)

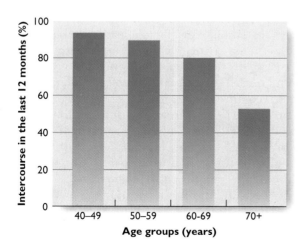

FIGURE 11.13 According to a worldwide study, the percentage of men reporting at least occasional sexual intercourse declines slowly with advancing age but remains around 50% even over age 70. *(From Gingell et al., for the GSSAB Investigator's Group. [2002, October 25–27]. "Sexual behaviors and functioning in mature men: Results of an international survey." Paper presented at the 2nd World Congress of Men's Health, Vienna, Austria.)*

Sexual Behavior in the Era of AIDS

During the 1980s a new factor entered into people's sexual motivations: the fear of **acquired immune deficiency syndrome (AIDS)**, *a sexually transmitted disease that gradually destroys the body's immune sys-*

FIGURE 11.14 The percentage of U.S. men and women reporting more than 10 or 20 sex partners in their lives. *(Based on data of Laumann et al., 1994)*

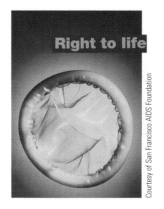

▮ AIDS is a preventable disease. Use condoms during sex and don't share injection needles with other people, and you greatly decrease the probability of transmitting or receiving the AIDS virus. Advertisements such as this one have prompted many people to change their behavior.

tem. For HIV (human immunodeficiency virus)—the virus that causes AIDS—to spread from one person to another, it must enter the other person's blood. (The virus does not survive long outside body fluids.) The three common routes of transmission are transfusions of contaminated blood, sharing needles used for intravenous injections of illegal drugs, and sexual contact. Of types of sexual contact, anal intercourse is the riskiest, but vaginal intercourse is risky also. Touching

and kissing do not spread the virus unless both people have open wounds that facilitate the exchange of blood.

For generations people have known how to avoid contracting syphilis, gonorrhea, and other sexually transmitted diseases: Don't have sex with someone who might be infected, or when in doubt, use a condom. If people had consistently followed this advice, we could have eliminated those diseases long ago. The same advice is now offered to combat AIDS, and the amount of compliance varies. Information campaigns have produced some benefits, but often less than we might hope.

AIDS spread first among male homosexuals and later among heterosexuals as well. In some parts of Africa, it affects one fifth or more of the adult population. One difficulty is that people remain symptom-free for years, so they can spread the virus long before they know they have it and before their partners have reason to suspect it.

▮ Different cultures have very different standards regarding public display of the human body and premarital sex.

Sexual Arousal

Sexual motivation depends on both physiological and cognitive influences—that is, not just the "plumbing" of the body but also the presence of a suitable partner, a willingness to be aroused, and a lack of anxiety. William Masters and Virginia Johnson (1966), who pioneered the study of human sexual response, discovered similarities in physiological arousal between men and women.

They observed hundreds of people masturbating or having sexual intercourse in a laboratory and monitored their physiological responses, including heart rate, breathing, muscle tension, blood engorgement of the genitals and breasts, and nipple erection. Masters and Johnson identified four physiological stages in sexual arousal (Figure 11.15).

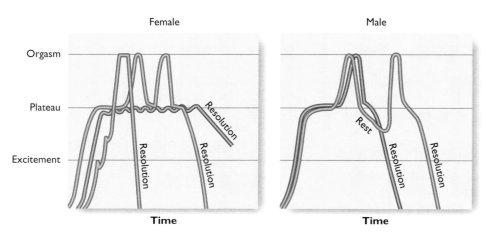

FIGURE 11.15 Sexual arousal usually proceeds through four stages—excitement, plateau, orgasm, and resolution. Each color represents the response of a different individual. Note the variation. Sexual experience varies from person to person and even from one time to another for a given individual. *(After Masters & Johnson, 1966)*

During the first stage, *excitement,* a man's penis becomes erect and a woman's vagina becomes lubricated. Breathing becomes rapid and deep. Heart rate and blood pressure increase. Many people experience a flush of the skin, which sometimes resembles a measles rash. Women's nipples become erect, and the breasts swell slightly for women who have not nursed a baby. Although this stage is referred to as excitement, nervousness interferes with it, as do stimulant drugs (even coffee).

During the second stage, called the *plateau,* excitement remains fairly constant. This stage lasts for varying lengths of time depending on the person's age and the intensity of the stimulation. Excitement becomes intense in the third stage, until a sudden release of tension known as *climax* or *orgasm,* which is felt throughout the entire body. During the fourth and final stage, *resolution,* the person returns to an unaroused state.

As Figure 11.15 shows, the pattern of excitation varies from one person to another. During a given episode, a woman may experience no orgasm, one, or many. Most men do not experience multiple consecutive orgasms, although they can achieve orgasm again following a rest (or refractory) period. Among individuals in both sexes, the intensity of the orgasm ranges from something like a sigh to an extremely intense experience.

Sexual Dysfunction

The pattern just described is common but hardly universal. Many people experience sexual difficulties of one sort or another at some point in life (Laumann et al., 2003). One problem, for example, is a decreased interest in sex. People with decreased interest miss an opportunity for pleasure in their own lives and risk jeopardizing their relationship with a partner.

Many people—more women than men—experience sexual arousal without orgasm. That is, they go through Masters and Johnson's first two stages without reaching the third. In some cases the lack of orgasm relates to psychological depression, but in most cases the cause is unknown (Laumann et al., 2003).

Some men cannot produce or maintain an erection. A man's erection requires relaxation of the smooth muscles controlling blood flow to the penis. The drug sildenafil (trade name Viagra) relaxes those muscles and thereby facilitates an erection (Rowland & Burnett, 2000). Other men, especially young men, have premature ejaculations, advancing from excitement to orgasm sooner than they or their partners wish. Unfortunately, most people hesitate to discuss sexual problems with their physicians (or anyone else), and physicians seldom ask about such problems. Consequently, most difficulties go untreated.

Sexual Anatomy and Identity

Gender identity (or sexual identity) is *the sex that a person regards him- or herself as being.* Most people have either male genitals and a male identity or female genitals and a female identity, but exceptions do occur.

In the earliest stages of development, the human fetus has a "unisex" appearance (Figure 11.16). One

Undifferentiated before sixth week

Genital tubercle
Urethral fold
Urethral groove
Genital fold
Anal pit

a

Seventh to eighth week

Male   **Female**

Glans
Area where foreskin (prepuce) forms
Urethral fold
Urogenital groove
Genital fold (becomes
shaft of penis or labia minora)
Labioscrotal swelling
(becomes scrotum or labia majora)
Anus

b

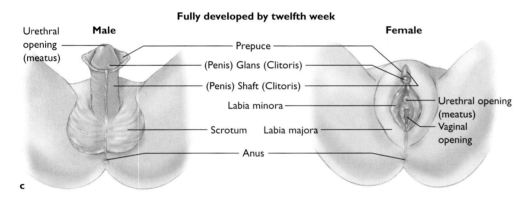

Fully developed by twelfth week

Urethral opening (meatus)   **Male**   **Female**

Prepuce
(Penis) Glans (Clitoris)
(Penis) Shaft (Clitoris)
Labia minora
Scrotum   Labia majora
Anus

Urethral opening (meatus)
Vaginal opening

c

FIGURE 11.16 The human genitals look the same in male and female fetuses for about the first 6 or 7 weeks after conception (a). Differences begin to emerge over the next couple of months (b) and are well developed at birth (c).

structure subsequently develops into either a penis or a clitoris; another structure develops into either a scrotum or labia. The direction this development takes depends on hormonal influences during prenatal development. Beginning in the seventh or eighth week after conception, genetic *male fetuses generally secrete higher levels of the hormone* **testosterone** *than do females* (although both sexes produce some), and over the next couple of months, the testosterone causes the tiny fetal structures to grow into a penis and a scrotum. In genetic female fetuses, with lower levels of testosterone, the structures develop into a clitoris and labia. Levels of *the hormone* **estrogen** *increase more in females than in males* at this time; estrogen is important for internal female development but has little effect on whether one develops a penis or a clitoris and a scrotum or labia.

Remember: In humans and other mammals, high testosterone levels produce a male anatomy; low testosterone levels produce a female anatomy. Within

normal limits the amount of circulating estrogen does not determine whether one develops a male or female appearance.

At least 1 child in 2,000 is born with genitals that are hard to classify as male or female, and 1 or 2 in 100 have an anatomy that is at least slightly ambiguous (Blackless et al., 2000). Some genetic female fetuses have overactive adrenal glands that secrete enough testosterone to partially masculinize development. The genetic female may then develop a sexual anatomy that looks intermediate between male and female (Money & Ehrhardt, 1972). In rarer cases a genetic male develops an intermediate appearance because of a gene that alters hormone receptors (Misrahi et al., 1997). *People with an anatomy that appears intermediate between male and female* are known as **intersexes** (Figure 11.17). The Intersex Society of North America (www.isna.org) is an organization devoted to increasing understanding and acceptance of people with ambiguous genitals.

FIGURE 11.17 External genitals of a 3-month-old genetic female who was masculinized before birth by excess androgens from the adrenal gland.

How should parents and others treat intersexed people? The main question is how people with ambiguous genitals can have a satisfactory status in society. For decades the standard medical recommendation has been, when in doubt, call the child female and perform surgery to make her anatomy look female. This surgery includes creating or lengthening a vagina and reducing the ambiguous penis/clitoris to the size of an average clitoris. Many cases require repeated surgery to obtain a satisfactory appearance.

■ A group of intersexed adults gathered to provide mutual support and protest against involuntary surgical intervention for intersexes. To emphasize that they do not consider intersexuality shameful, they requested that their names be used. Left to right: Martha Coventry, Max Beck, David Vandertie, Kristi Bruse, and Angela Moreno.

This recommendation has been based on the assumption that, if a child looks like a girl and is treated like a girl, she will develop psychologically as a girl. Physicians never had much evidence for their assumption. Later research found a variety of ways in which one person's brain differs from another, even at birth. Those differences are complex; one part of someone's brain might be "male-typical" whereas another is "female-typical" (Woodson & Gorski, 2000). Nevertheless, it is possible that different people come into life predisposed to react differently from one another in many ways, including perhaps some that are related to sexual development. Regardless of the explanation, some intersexed adults, in spite of a feminine appearance and rearing, develop a male identity.

Furthermore, a great many complain that genital surgery—reducing or removing the penis/clitoris—left them with greatly reduced sexual excitation and a feeling of mutilation. An artificial vagina may be satisfactory to a male partner, but it provides no sensation or pleasure to the woman, and it requires frequent attention to prevent scar tissue. Finally, intersexed individuals object that, in many cases, physicians lied to them about the surgery and the reasons for it. Today, more and more physicians recommend that parents raise the child as the gender the genitals most resemble and perform surgery—if at all—only when the child is old enough to make the decision. Many intersexed individuals prefer to remain as they are, without surgery (Dreger, 1998).

CONCEPT CHECK ☑

13. If a human fetus were exposed to very low levels of both testosterone and estrogen during prenatal development, how would the sexual anatomy appear?
14. If a human fetus were exposed to high levels of both testosterone and estrogen throughout prenatal development, how would the sexual anatomy appear? (Check your answers on page 437.)

Sexual Orientation

Sexual orientation is *a person's tendency to respond sexually to male or female partners (or both or neither).* People vary in their sexual orientations, just as they do in their food preferences and other motivations. Those who prefer partners of their own sex have a homosexual (gay or lesbian) orientation.

How many people have a homosexual orientation? You may have heard people confidently assert "10%." That number is derived from Kinsey's report that about 13% of the men and 7% of the women he in-

▌Attitudes toward homosexual relationships have varied among cultures and among historical eras. In the United States and Canada, many have come to accept, or at least consider, the idea of same-sex marriage.

Paul, & Herbison, 2003). Although most people cannot imagine switching between homosexual and heterosexual, some do switch, with higher frequency of switches among women (Cameron & Cameron, 2002; Diamond, 2003a; Dickson et al., 2003). It is especially common for people who consider themselves "bisexual" (attracted to both sexes) to switch between being predominantly one orientation and predominantly the other. Some people are even in love with a person of one sex while being sexually attracted to the other sex (Diamond, 2003b).

If you have frequently heard the prevalence of homosexual orientations estimated at 10%, you may be skeptical of the report that only 1 to 3% of people identify themselves as gay or lesbian. However, three other large surveys reported that 1 to 2%, 3%, or 6% of U.S. men were either gay or bisexual (Billy, Tanfer, Grady, & Klepinger, 1993; Cameron, Proctor, Coburn, & Forde, 1985; Fay et al., 1989). Exclusive homosexual behavior is less common among women, although bisexual attraction may be as common or more so in

terviewed in the 1940s and 1950s stated a predominantly homosexual orientation. The often-quoted figure of 10% is simply the mean of Kinsey's results for men and women. However, Kinsey's data were based on a nonrandom sample of the population.

According to a survey of a random sample of 3,500 U.S. adults, 2.8% of men and 1.4% of women describe themselves as having a homosexual (gay or lesbian) orientation (Laumann et al., 1994). More people describe a homosexual experience if they answer on a computer than if they fill out a piece of paper, presumably because the computer answer is more clearly anonymous (Turner et al., 1998). However, even with the greatest assurances of anonymity, the descriptions of homosexuality don't increase much.

As Figure 11.18 suggests, heterosexuality versus homosexuality is a continuum. Of those who regard themselves as gay or lesbian, most have had at least one or two heterosexual experiences (Diamond, 2000). Some people who consider themselves fully heterosexual report at least one adult homosexual experience, and if we expand the scope to include early adolescence, 9% of men report at least one homosexual experience (Laumann et al., 1994). Even higher percentages of both men and women say they have felt some attraction to a member of their own sex at some time in their life (Dickson,

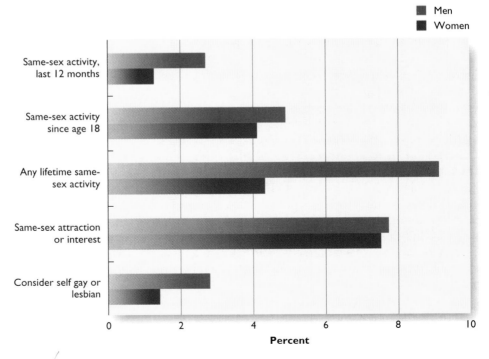

FIGURE 11.18 The percentages of U.S. adults who report sexual activity or interest in sexual activity with people of their own sex. *(Based on data of Laumann et al., 1994)*

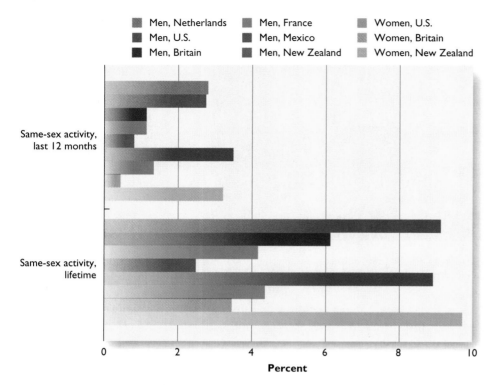

FIGURE 11.19 Comparisons of the results of surveys conducted in six countries, in which people were asked about homosexual experiences. *(Based on data of Dickson et al., 2003; Izazola-Licea, Gortmaker, Tolbert, De Gruttola, & Mann, 2000; Laumann, Gagnon, Michael, & Michaels, 1994; Sandfort, de Graaf, Bijl, & Schnabel, 2001; Spira et al., 1993; Wellings, Field, Johnson, & Wadsworth, 1994)*

women than in men. Surveys in other countries have reported similar or slightly lower percentages, as shown in Figure 11.19 (Izazola-Licea, Gortmaker, Tolbert, De Gruttola, & Mann, 2000; Sandfort, de Graaf, Bijl, & Schnabel, 2001; Spira et al., 1993; Wellings, Field, Johnson, & Wadsworth, 1994).

Society's attitudes toward homosexuality have changed repeatedly over time. As far as we can determine, the ancient Greeks and Romans considered it fairly typical for men to engage in occasional sexual activities with each other as well as with women (Boswell, 1990). (The Greek and Roman writers said little about women's sexual interests.) During a later era, Europeans regarded male homosexuality as sinful or criminal. By the early 20th century, the "enlightened" view was that homosexuality was not sinful but "merely" a sign of mental illness. That opinion, however, was based on a badly distorted sample: Psychiatrists and psychologists met only those homosexual people who sought help for psychological troubles. The prevalence of depression, anxiety, and substance abuse is indeed somewhat higher among homosexual than heterosexual people, but probably because of the frequent stresses of confronting prejudices and hostility (Meyer, 2003). However, studies of broader samples found that most homosexual people are well ad-justed (Siegelman, 1974), and therefore psychologists and psychiatrists today consider a homosexual orientation to be a natural variation in sexual motivation.

The origins and determinants of sexual orientation are not well understood. Most adults, especially males, report that their sexual orientation was apparent to them from as young as they can remember. The available research, based on only a few studies, suggests that genetic factors contribute toward sexual orientation for both men and women. Figure 11.20 shows the results of studies concerning homosexuality in twins and other relatives of adult gays and lesbians (Bailey & Pillard, 1991; Bailey, Pillard, Neale, & Agyei, 1993). Note that homosexuality is more prevalent in their identical twins than in their fraternal twins. Another study with a smaller sample showed the same trends (Kendler, Thornton, Gilman, & Kessler, 2000).

That trend suggests a genetic influence toward homosexuality, although a gene could hardly be the only factor. (If it were, then every pair of identical twins would match each other's sexual orientation.) Note also that homosexuality is more common among the fraternal twins of a homosexual person than among adopted brothers or sisters. That trend also suggests a genetic factor, although it could also indicate the influence of a factor in the prenatal environment shared by twins but not by boys who grow up in the same family.

If genes affect sexual orientation, they must do so by altering the development of some part of the body. The answer does *not* lie in adult hormone levels. On the average, adult homosexual people are similar to heterosexual people in their levels of testosterone and estrogen. Altering someone's testosterone or estrogen level can alter the strength of the sex drive, but it does not change the sexual orientation (Tuiten et al., 2000). By analogy changing your insulin or glucose levels can affect your hunger but has little effect on what you consider to be good food.

However, it is possible that prenatal sex hormones influence later sexual orientation (Lalumière, Blanchard, & Zucker, 2000). Presumably, if they do,

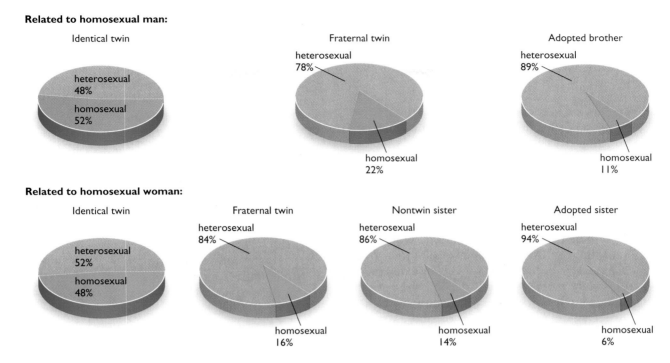

Related to homosexual man:

Identical twin

heterosexual 48%
homosexual 52%

Fraternal twin

heterosexual 78%
homosexual 22%

Adopted brother

heterosexual 89%
homosexual 11%

Related to homosexual woman:

Identical twin

heterosexual 52%
homosexual 48%

Fraternal twin

heterosexual 84%
homosexual 16%

Nontwin sister

heterosexual 86%
homosexual 14%

Adopted sister

heterosexual 94%
homosexual 6%

FIGURE 11.20 The probability of a homosexual orientation is higher among identical twins of adult homosexuals than among their fraternal twins. The probability is higher among fraternal twins than among adopted brothers or sisters who grew up in the same family. These data suggest a possible genetic role in the development of sexual orientation. *(Based on results of Bailey & Pillard, 1991; Bailey, Pillard, Neale, & Agyei, 1993)*

the main place to look for any anatomical differences is in the brain. One widely quoted and often misunderstood study reported a small but measurable difference between the brains of homosexual and heterosexual men. Let's examine the evidence.

CRITICAL THINKING:
WHAT'S THE EVIDENCE?
Sexual Orientation and Brain Anatomy

Animal studies have demonstrated that one section of the anterior hypothalamus is generally larger in males than in females. This brain area is necessary for the display of male-typical sexual activity in many mammalian species, and its size depends on prenatal hormones. Might part of the anterior hypothalamus differ between homosexual and heterosexual men?

Hypothesis   INAH3, a particular cluster of neurons in the anterior hypothalamus, will be larger on average in the brains of heterosexual men than in the brains of homosexual men or heterosexual women.

Method   Simon LeVay (1991) examined the brains of 41 adults who died at ages 26–59. AIDS was the cause of death for all 19 of the homosexual men in the study, 6 of the 16 heterosexual men, and 1 of the 6 heterosexual women. No brains of homosexual women were available for study. LeVay measured the sizes of four clusters of neurons in the anterior hypothalamus, including two clusters for which sex differences are common and two that do not differ between the sexes.

Results   LeVay found that three of the four neuron clusters did not consistently vary in size among the groups he studied. However, area INAH3 was on the average about twice as large in heterosexual men as it was in homosexual men and about the same size in homosexual men as in heterosexual women. Figure 11.21

a   b

FIGURE 11.21 One section of the anterior hypothalamus (marked by arrows) is larger on the average in the brains of heterosexual men (a) than in the brains of homosexual men (b) or heterosexual women. Review Figure 11.7 for the location of the hypothalamus. (© S. Levay, 1991, "A Difference in Hypothalamic Structure Between Heterosexual & Homosexual Men," Science 253, 1034-1037) shows results for two representative individuals. The size of this area was about the same in heterosexual men who died of AIDS as in heterosexual men who died of other causes, so AIDS probably did not control the size of this area.

Interpretation   These results suggest that the size of the INAH3 area of the anterior hypothalamus may be related to heterosexual versus homosexual orientation, at least for some individuals. Note, however, the variation within each group. The anatomy is not perfectly correlated with the behavior.

Like most studies, this one has its limitations: As with any study, we do not know whether the people that LeVay studied were typical of others. One later study found that the INAH3 of homosexual men was intermediate in size between that of heterosexual men and heterosexual women (Byne et al., 2001). That study extended our knowledge by finding that the INAH3 varied among people because of differences in the size of neurons there, not the number of neurons.

Another limitation is that LeVay's study does not tell us whether brain anatomy influenced people's sexual orientation or whether their sexual activities altered brain anatomy. As mentioned in Chapter 3, extensive experience can modify some aspects of brain anatomy, even in adults.

So, where do all these studies leave us? At this point the evidence suggest that certain genes predispose some people toward one sexual orientation or the other and that adult homosexual and heterosexual men differ on the average in at least one aspect of brain anatomy. We know little, however, about what kinds of experience influence sexual orientation, and we have no reason to assume that one explanation will apply to all people. We need to await additional studies before we can draw any confident conclusions. Uncertainty and tentative conclusions are not unusual in psychology. If you decide to become a psychologist, you will need to get used to the words "maybe" and "probably." As mentioned in Chapter 2, most psychologists avoid the word "prove"; results merely increase or decrease their confidence in a conclusion.

CONCEPT CHECK ☑

15. Most studies find that adult homosexual men have approximately the same levels of testosterone in their blood as heterosexual men of the same age. Do such results conflict with the suggestion that prenatal hormonal conditions can predispose certain men to homosexuality? (Check your answer on page 437.)

IN CLOSING

The Biology and Sociology of Sex

What do studies of sexual motivation tell us about motivation in general? One point is that important motives have multiple determinants, both biological and social. We engage in sexual activity because it feels good, and we have evolved mechanisms that make it feel good because sex leads to reproduction. On the other hand, often it makes good biological sense to postpone reproduction until a safer time, so it is no wonder that nervousness decreases sexual arousal. We also engage in sexual activity because it cements a relationship with another person. Sex is one of the most powerful ways of drawing people together or tearing their relationship apart.

Because of its power, society regulates sexual behavior strictly. The rules vary from one culture to another, but every culture has definite expectations about what people will do, when, and with whom. In short, we cannot make much sense of complex human behaviors without considering a range of biological and social influences.

Summary

- *Variability in human sexual behavior.* Alfred Kinsey, who conducted the first extensive survey of human sexual behavior, found that sexual activity varies more widely than most people realize. (page 426)

- *More recent surveys.* Both men and women choose vaginal intercourse as their most preferred sexual activity. On the average, men express a greater interest than women do in varied sexual practices and varied partners. Most people remain sexually active even into their 70s if they remain healthy and have a healthy, willing partner. (page 427)

- *Sexual arousal.* Sexual arousal proceeds through four stages: excitement, plateau, orgasm, and resolution. (page 430)

- *Development of genitals.* In the early stages of development, the human fetus possesses anatomical structures that may develop into either male genitals (if testosterone levels are high enough) or female genitals (if testosterone levels are lower). (page 430)

- *Prevalence of homosexuality.* According to surveys in several countries, about 2 to 4% of adult men and somewhat fewer women regard themselves as primarily or exclusively homosexual. Sexual orientation varies in degree from exclusively homosexual to exclusively heterosexual, with many intermediate gradations. (page 432)

- *Origins of sexual orientation.* The reasons for different sexual orientations remain unclear. Genetic influences can apparently alter the probability of a homosexual orientation, although these influences alone cannot account for all variations in sexual orientation. On the average, heterosexual and homosexual men differ in the size of one structure in the hypothalamus that contributes to certain aspects of sexual behavior. (page 435)

Answers to Concept Checks

12. Kinsey interviewed a nonrandom, nonrepresentative sample of people. (page 428)

13. A fetus exposed to very low levels of both testosterone and estrogen throughout prenatal development would develop a female appearance. (page 432)

14. A fetus exposed to high levels of both testosterone and estrogen would develop a male appearance. High levels of testosterone lead to male anatomy; low levels lead to female anatomy. The level of estrogen does not play a decisive role. (page 432)

15. Not necessarily. The suggestion is that prenatal hormones can alter early brain development. In adulthood hormone levels are normal, but certain aspects of brain development have already been determined. (page 436)

Why do some people try harder than others?

Most people like to compete against others, at least if they think they have a chance of winning. Archeologists once excavated an ancient human civilization from about 1400 B.C., where they discovered, to their surprise, a ball court complete with nets (Hill, Blake, & Clark, 1998). Clearly, the idea of competitive sports dates back a long time. People also strive to improve on their own previous performance. In effect they compete against themselves: Can I run farther, or bicycle faster, than last time?

Striving for excellence on the job resembles competing at sports: People will put out great efforts to outdo a competitor or to reach their own goals *if* they think they have a chance of succeeding. One of the key interests of both employers and industrial/organizational psychologists is to understand what motivates workers to put their full efforts into their jobs. We shall consider "work" and "jobs" broadly; although most research focuses on employment, the same principles apply to schoolwork.

Goals and Deadlines

If you did not have deadlines to meet, how hard would you work? For example, if one of your instructors said you could turn in your papers and take your tests "whenever you wanted," how would you react? Even when you have deadlines, do you sometimes wait until shortly before the deadline to start working in earnest? For example, are you reading this chapter now because you have to take a test on it tomorrow? (If so, don't feel too embarrassed. I wouldn't be sitting here revising this chapter late at night except for the deadline my publisher gave me! People never outgrow their need for deadlines.)

Procrastination (putting off work until tomorrow) is a problem for many students and for workers on the job as well. Here is an experiment that beautifully illustrates the phenomenon:

CRITICAL THINKING: WHAT'S THE EVIDENCE?
The Value of Deadlines

A professor set firm deadlines for one class and let the other class choose their own deadlines to see whether those with evenly spaced deadlines would outperform those who were exposed to the temptation to procrastinate (Ariely & Wertenbroch, 2002).

Hypothesis Students who are required, or who require themselves, to spread out their work over a semester will do better than those with an opportunity to wait until the end.

Method A professor taught two sections of the same course. Students were not randomly assigned to sections, but the students in the two sections had about equal academic records. The professor told one class that they had to write three papers, the first due after one third of the semester, the second after two thirds, and the third at the end of the semester. The other class was told that they could choose their own deadlines. They might make their papers due at one third, two thirds, and the end of the semester or all three at the end of the semester or whatever else they chose. However, they had to make a decision before the second day of class, and whatever deadlines they chose would be enforced. That is, a paper that missed a deadline would be penalized, even though the student could have chosen a later deadline.

At the end of the course, the professor graded all the papers, blind to when they had been submitted.

Results If you were in the class with a choice, what would you do? Twelve of the fifty-one students set all three deadlines on the final day of the semester. Presumably, they reasoned that they could still try to finish papers at one third, two thirds, and the end, but if for any reason they needed extra time, they would have as much as possible. That is, they gave themselves built-in extensions on their due dates. Other students, however, saw that if they set their deadlines at the end, they would expose themselves to a temptation that would be hard to resist, so they imposed earlier deadlines. Some spaced the deadlines evenly at one third, two thirds, and the end of the semester, whereas others compromised, setting deadlines for the first two papers later than one third and two thirds but not at the end of the semester.

On average the students in the section with assigned deadlines got better grades than those who were allowed to choose their own deadlines. Of those permitted to choose their own deadlines, those who set their deadlines at approximately one third, two thirds, and the end of the semester did about the same as those with assigned deadlines and much better than those who set all their deadlines at the end.

Interpretation By itself, the fact that those who spread out their deadlines over the semester did better than those who set late deadlines would tell us nothing. It could mean that early deadlines help, but it could also mean that better students set earlier deadlines. However, the early-deadline students merely matched the assigned-deadline students, whereas the late-deadline students did significantly worse. Therefore, the conclusion follows that setting deadlines does help. If you are required to do part of your work at a time, you manage your time to accomplish it. If your deadlines are all at the end, you face a powerful temptation to delay starting your work.

CONCEPT CHECK ☑

16. What conclusion would have followed if the early-deadline students did better than the late-deadline students but that class as a whole did as well as the assigned-deadline students? (Check your answer on page 443.)

High and Low Goals

If you are going to set goals for yourself or your employees, does it matter what kind of goals? Take an academic example: At the start of a semester, which of these goals would be best:

- I will work for an A in every course (a high goal).
- I will work for at least a C average (a low goal).
- I will do my best (a vague goal).

The research says that a vague "do your best" goal is no better than no goal at all. Although it sounds nice, you never know whether you are achieving it. You are never obviously behind schedule on achieving the goal, so it doesn't motivate extra work.

The most effective goal is one that is high but realistic (Locke & Latham, 2002). For example, a goal of an A in every course would be effective for someone who had a mix of As and Bs last semester but not for a student who is likely to become discouraged because the goal is way out of reach. A goal of a C average would be too low a goal for most students, but it might be appropriate for a student whose previous grades were well below that level.

The same principles apply at work. Suppose a company announces that it will provide a nice bonus for all employees if profits increase by 10% this year. The employees will work to reach that level if they see

a realistic chance of achieving it. If they think that the best they could do, even with extraordinary effort, would be a 7 or 8% increase, and that nothing less than 10% will qualify for the bonus, they are likely to give up. On the other hand, if business is booming and a 10% increase will be easy, again that goal won't motivate increased efforts.

For any goal to be effective, certain conditions are necessary (Locke & Latham, 2002). One is to take the goal seriously, preferably by committing to it publicly. If you want to get better grades next semester, tell your friends about it. If a company wants greater profits, it needs its employees to agree to the goal. Another condition for success is that you get frequent feedback about your progress. If you are aiming for all As and you get a B on a test in one course, you know you have to study harder in that course. If you want to increase profits by 10% and you learn that they are currently up 9%, you know you need to work just a little harder. One final condition is that you have to believe that the reward at the end will be worth your effort. Some students believe a high grade-point average is worth the effort; others don't. Some employees trust their bosses to pay the bonuses they promised; others consider their bosses lying, cheating scoundrels (Craig & Gustafson, 1998) (see Figure 11.22).

A word of caution about setting goals: When people work hard toward a goal, they subordinate everything else. In other words they stop doing activities that don't lead to the goal. If you own a store and you convince your sales staff to try to increase sales, they may spend *less* effort than before on cleaning the floor, neatly arranging the shelves, or anything else that does not immediately increase sales. In 1995 the Australian government set a goal for the faculty at the national universities. It said the faculty should increase their number of publications, and henceforth their salary increases would depend on the number of

Setting goals leads to vigorous activity if:

> The goal is realistic.

> A serious commitment is made, especially if it is made publicly.

> Feedback is received.

> Believe that achieving the goal will be worth the effort.

FIGURE 11.22 The conditions under which goals are most effective in motivating vigorous efforts.

professional publications. Can you guess what happened? Over the next few years, the Australian faculty members greatly increased their *number* of publications, not in prestigious journals like *Nature* and *Science,* but in seldom-read journals that were willing to publish minor findings (Butler, 2002). As the saying goes, be careful what you wish for, because you might get it.

CONCEPT CHECK ☑

17. Under what conditions would people be most likely to keep their New Year's resolutions? (Check your answer on page 443.)

Job Design and Job Satisfaction

People work harder, more effectively, and with more satisfaction at some jobs than at others. Why?

Two Approaches to Job Design

Imagine that you are starting up or reorganizing a company, and you must decide how to divide the workload. Should you make the jobs challenging and interesting at the risk of being difficult? Or should you make them simple and foolproof at the risk of being boring?

The answer depends on what you assume about the workers and their motivations. *According to the* **scientific-management** approach to job design, also known as *Theory X, most employees are lazy, indifferent, and uncreative.* Therefore, employers should make the work as foolproof as possible and supervise the workers to make sure they are doing each task the right way to save time and avoid injury (Figure 11.23). The employer leaves nothing to chance or to the worker's own initiative (McGregor, 1960).

According to an alternative view, the **human-relations** approach to job design, also known as *Theory Y, employees like variety in their job, a sense of accomplishment, and a sense of responsibility* (McGregor, 1960). Therefore, employers should enrich the jobs, giving each employee responsibility for meaningful tasks. For example, a financial services corporation that followed the scientific-management approach would have one employee keep a different kind of records, developing expertise at a narrow task. The same company, reorganized according to the human-relations approach, might put each employee in charge of particular clients, therefore keeping a variety of records, doing different things at various times, and seeing how all the pieces come together. Employees with enriched jobs generally report

greater satisfaction (Campion & McClelland, 1991). From the employer's standpoint, the enriched jobs have many advantages but two disadvantages: It takes longer to train the workers than it would with simpler jobs, and the workers performing enriched jobs expect to be paid more!

So, which approach is better? It depends. Consider an analogy to education: Professor X tells students exactly what to read on which day, what facts to study for each test, and precisely what to do to get a good grade. (This course is analogous to the scientific-management approach.) Professor Y outlines the general issues to be discussed, provides a list of suggested readings, lets the students control class discussion, and invites students to create their own ideas for projects. (This course is analogous to the human-relations approach, though perhaps more extreme.) Which class would you like better?

If you are highly interested in the topic and have ideas of your own, you would love Professor Y's course and would consider Professor X's course tedious and insulting. But if you are taking the course just to satisfy a requirement, you might appreciate the precise structure of Professor X's class. The same is true of jobs. Some workers, especially the younger and brighter ones, thrive on the challenge of an enriched job, but others prefer a simple, secure, stable set of tasks (Arnold & House, 1980; Campion & Thayer, 1985; Hackman & Lawler, 1971).

CONCEPT CHECK ☑

18. "I want my employees to enjoy their work and to feel pride in their achievements." Does that statement reflect a belief in the human-relations approach or the scientific-management approach? (Check your answer on page 443.)

FIGURE 11.23 Psychologists have conducted research to determine the best, safest, most efficient ways to perform even simple tasks. For example, the drawing on the left shows the right way to lift a brick, and the drawing on the right shows the wrong way, according to Gilbreth (1911).

Job Satisfaction

Your choice of career profoundly affects the quality of your life. Between the ages of 20 and 70, you will spend about half of your waking hours on the job. You will not want to spend it on work you find unimportant. In turn how much you like your job correlates moderately well with how well you perform it (Judge, Thoresen, Bono, & Patton, 2001). The causation probably goes in several directions: High job satisfaction improves performance, good performance improves job satisfaction, and qualities such as a conscientious personality improve job performance and also help develop a contented personality (Judge et al., 2001; Tett & Burnett, 2003).

Obviously, job satisfaction depends largely on the job itself, including the interest level, the pay, coworkers, and the management. Less obviously, it also depends on the worker's personality. Some people are just easier to please than others. Comparisons of identical and fraternal twins indicate that job satisfaction is highly heritable (Arvey, McCall, Bouchard, Taubman, & Cavanaugh, 1994). That is, if your close relatives say they are happy with their jobs, you probably will also, even though you have a different job. You don't inherit your job, but you inherit your disposition. Some people find things to like about their jobs, they like their lives, and they are easy to please in many ways. Others dislike almost everything and tend to complain about almost everything (Ilies & Judge, 2003; Judge & Larsen, 2001; Thoresen, Kaplan, Barsky, Warren, & de Chermont, 2003). People who are prone to unpleasant feelings become exhausted with their work faster than others do and are likely to complain of "job burnout" (Houkes, Janssen, de Jonge, & Nijhuis, 2001; Maslach, 2003).

On the average older workers express higher job satisfaction than younger workers do (Pond & Geyer, 1991) (see Figure 11.24). One possible explanation is that older workers have better, higher paying jobs. Another is that today's young people are harder to satisfy than past cohorts (Beck & Wilson, 2000). Another possibility is that many young workers start in the wrong job and find a more suitable one later on. Still another is that many young people are still considering the possibility of changing jobs. By middle age most people have reconciled themselves to whatever jobs they have.

Pay and Job Satisfaction

An employer who wants to keep workers satisfied must pay careful attention to the pay scale. Obviously, workers want to be paid well, and the more pay the better, but in addition they need to perceive the pay scale as fair. In one classic experiment, some workers were led to believe that they had been hired in spite of less-than-average qualifications for the job. They

Possible reasons why older workers report greater job satisfaction than younger workers

Better pay

Greater responsibility

Greater challenges

Comfort of status quo

Less perceived likelihood of getting a better job

Previous experience in less suitable jobs

FIGURE 11.24 Psychologists propose several reasons why most older workers report higher job satisfaction than younger workers do.

worked harder than average, apparently to convince the employer that they deserved the job, but perhaps also to convince themselves that they earned their pay (Adams, 1963).

Employees expect their bosses to be honest and open with them and to follow fair procedures in determining salaries. Those who perceive their bosses as operating unfairly often start looking for another job. They also stop doing the "good citizen" behaviors that help the company even though the worker isn't paid to do them, such as keeping the building tidy, helping other workers, attending extra meetings after working hours, and so forth (Simons & Roberson, 2003).

Apparently, even monkeys care about fair pay! An experimenter gave a monkey a pile of small rocks and taught her to trade them to the experimenter for a piece of cucumber. All went well until she saw the monkey in the adjoining cage trade similar rocks for a grape—a much preferred food. Suddenly, she refused to trade a rock for a cucumber. In effect she went "on strike" (Brosnan & de Waal, 2003).

Money is certainly part of anyone's work motivation. Presumably, you would quit your job if your employer stopped paying you. However, pay is not the whole motivation. Many people take a lower paying job because it offers a greater sense of accomplishment or more pleasant working conditions than some higher paying job. Even after people retire, many find that they miss the work. For many people work is an enjoyable, important part of who they are. As with other behaviors, we work because of multiple motives.

CONCEPT CHECK ☑

19. What are some factors that contribute to high job satisfaction? (Check your answer on page 443.)

Leadership

How hard you are motivated to work also depends on how you perceive the leadership of your organization. Some leaders inspire deep loyalties, such that their workers will go well beyond the call of duty to make the organization succeed. Others can barely get their workers to do the minimum. (The same is true of college professors.)

So far, so good, but can we measure the qualities of an effective leader or give advice on how to become one? It is certainly not easy. For example, industrial/organizational psychologists have been trying to measure "leader-member exchange," which more or less means trust, attention, and sensitivity by the leader toward subordinates. Over the years the questionnaires for measuring it have changed repeatedly, as has the description of exactly what the questionnaires are trying to measure, so it is difficult to compare any set of results to any other (Schriesheim, Castro, & Cogliser, 1999).

One of the interesting and prominent ideas is the distinction between transformational and transactional leadership styles. A **transformational leader** *articulates a vision of the future, intellectually stimulates subordinates, and motivates them to use their imagination to raise the organization to a new level.* A **transactional leader** *tries to make the organization more efficient at doing what it is already doing by providing rewards (mainly pay) for effective work.* A leader can, of course, be either of these, both, or neither. People who are perceived as transformational leaders are also perceived as effective in almost any organization (Lowe, Kroeck, & Sivasubramaniam, 1996). This result should not be surprising. You would hardly describe your leader as "a visionary who intellectually stimulates me and motivates me to reach my potential" if you also thought your leader were doing a bad job overall. Workers are more likely to describe their immediate supervisors—the people they contact every day—as transformational leaders than they are the top people in the organization, whom they seldom meet. Transactional leaders are effective also, under some circumstances, mainly in stable organizations where activities stay the same from year to year (Lowe et al., 1996).

CONCEPT CHECK ☑

20. Do transformational leaders emphasize intrinsic or extrinsic motivation? Which do transactional leaders emphasize? (Check your answer on page 443.)

IN CLOSING

Work as Another Kind of Motivation

In this chapter we have considered hunger, sex, and work. People have many other motivations, of course, but we can understand the basic principles without going through an exhaustive list of examples. Work motivation has important points in common with hunger, sex, and other motivations. For example, they are all marked by persistent and varied behaviors to reach a goal. However, work also has some special features. One is the aspect of striving for excellence. Work is often competitive in a way that eating and sex are not. (Oh, I suppose you could compete at eating or sex, but ordinarily, we don't.) Striving for excellence is never fully satisfied. Those who achieve their goals in business or other competitive endeavors usually respond by setting new, higher goals. In short, any kind of motivation requires a kind of striving, but each kind of striving has its own special features.

Summary

- *Deadlines.* In general, people who are forced to meet deadlines manage their time to do so. If it is possible to postpone all work until later, many find it hard to resist that temptation. Setting deadlines for parts of one's own work can help. (page 438)

- *Effectiveness of goal setting.* Setting a work goal motivates strong effort if the goal is high but realistic. Other important factors include making a serious commitment to the goal, receiving feedback on progress, and believing that the goal will bring a fair reward. (page 439)

- *Job design.* According to the scientific-management approach, jobs should be made simple and foolproof. According to the human-management approach, jobs should be made interesting enough to give workers a sense of achievement. (page 440)

- *Job satisfaction.* Job satisfaction is moderately correlated with good performance on the job for several reasons. People with a happy disposition are more likely than others to be satisfied with their jobs, as are older workers in general. Job satisfaction also requires a perception that the pay scale is fair. (page 441)

- *Leadership.* Leaders who are perceived as inspiring their associates to fulfill a vision are also perceived as effective in almost any organization. Those perceived as using rewards to get employees to do their work efficiently are effective in some situations, mainly when the business is stable. (page 442)

Answers to Concept Checks

16. If students in the two sections had equal performance overall, we could not conclude that deadlines help. Instead, the conclusion could be that brighter students tend to set earlier deadlines. (page 439)

17. A New Year's resolution is like any other goal: People are more likely to keep it if it is realistic, if they state the resolution publicly, and if they receive feedback on how well they are doing. (page 440)

18. It reflects the human-relations approach. (page 440)

19. Among factors associated with high job satisfaction are high ability to perform the job, a happy personality, perception that the pay scale is fair, and old age. (page 441)

20. A transformational leader emphasizes intrinsic motivation, the desire to achieve excellence. A transactional leader applies rewards to get workers to do their current jobs efficiently and so emphasizes extrinsic motivation. (page 442)

CHAPTER ENDING

Key Terms and Activities

Key Terms

acquired immune deficiency syndrome (AIDS): a disease often transmitted sexually that gradually destroys the body's immune system (page 428)

anorexia nervosa: a psychological condition in which a person refuses to eat adequate food and steadily loses weight (page 420)

bulimia nervosa: a condition in which a person alternates between self-starvation and excessive eating (page 421)

drive: an internal state of unrest or irritation that energizes one behavior after another until one of them removes the irritation (page 408)

estrogen: a hormone present in higher quantities in females than in males (page 431)

extrinsic motivation: a motivation based on the rewards and punishments that an act may bring (page 409)

gender identity: the sex that a person regards him- or herself as being (page 430)

glucagon: a hormone that the pancreas releases to convert stored energy supplies back into blood glucose (page 413)

glucose: the most abundant sugar in the blood (page 413)

homeostasis: the maintenance of biological conditions at an optimum level within an organism (page 408)

human-relations approach (also known as Theory Y): the view that employees like to take responsibility for their work, to enjoy some variety in their jobs, and to feel a sense of accomplishment (page 440)

incentive: an external stimulus that prompts an action to obtain the stimulus (page 409)

insulin: a hormone that the pancreas releases to increase the entry of glucose and other nutrients into the cells (page 413)

intersexes: people with external sexual anatomy that appears intermediate between male and female (page 431)

intrinsic motivation: a motivation to engage in an act for its own sake (page 409)

lateral hypothalamus: an area of the brain that contributes to the control of hunger (page 415)

leptin: a hormone released by fat cells; among other effects, it signals the brain to decrease meal size (page 415)

motivation: the process that determines the reinforcement value of an outcome (page 407)

obesity: the excessive accumulation of body fat (page 417)

overjustification effect: the tendency of people who are given more extrinsic motivation than necessary to perform a task to experience a decline in their intrinsic motivation (page 410)

paraventricular hypothalamus: an area of the brain in which damage leads to weight gain via an increase in the size of meals (page 416)

scientific-management approach (also known as Theory X): the view that most employees are lazy, indifferent, and uncreative, so jobs should be made simple and foolproof (page 440)

set point: a level of some variable (e.g., weight) that the body works to maintain (page 415)

sexual orientation: a person's tendency to react sexually toward either males or females (page 432)

testosterone: a hormone present in higher quantities in males than in females (page 431)

transactional leader: one who tries to make the organization more efficient at doing what it is already doing by providing rewards (mainly pay) for effective work (page 442)

transformational leader: one who articulates a vision of the future, intellectually stimulates subordinates, and motivates them to use their imagination to raise the organization to a new level (page 442)

ventromedial hypothalamus: an area of the brain in which damage leads to weight gain via an increase in the frequency of meals (page 415)

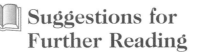

Suggestions for Further Reading

Capaldi, E. D. (Ed.). (1996). *Why we eat what we eat.* Washington, DC: American Psychological Association. A collection of articles about food selection and the regulation of hunger.

Diamond, J. (1997). *Why is sex fun?* New York: Basic Books. Exploration of the "why" of sex. Why did we evolve to reproduce sexually? Why is human sex in several ways different from that of other animals?

Book Companion Web Site

Need help studying? Go to

http://psychology.wadsworth.com/kalat_intro7e/

for a virtual study center. You'll find a personalized Self-Study Assessment that will provide you with a study plan based on your answers to a pretest. Also study using flash cards, quizzes, interactive art, and an online glossary.

Check out interactive **Try It Yourself** exercises on the companion site! These exercises will help you put what you've learned into action.

Your companion site also has direct links to the following Web sites. These links are checked often for changes, dead links, and new additions.

Obesity

www.obesity.org

Check all kinds of information about this serious eating disorder.

Sexual Behavior

www.indiana.edu/~kinsey/

See the latest research reports by the research institute that Kinsey founded.

Intersexes

www.isna.org/

Information from a support group for people with ambiguous genitalia.

Try It Yourself CD-ROM
with Critical Thinking Video Exercises

Use your CD to access **videos** related to activities designed to help you think critically about the important topics discussed. For example, the video about weight control ties to what you've learned in this chapter. You'll also find an easy portal link to the book companion site where you can access your personalized **Self-Study Assessments** and interactive **Try It Yourself** exercises.

PsychNow! 2.0

PsychNow! is a fun interactive CD designed to help you with the difficult concepts in psychology. Check out the Motivation & Emotion section for the following topics that relate to this chapter:

Motivation: play an interactive survey game and take a theory matching quiz.

Human Sexuality: test your sexual education and learn the sexual response cycles.

Emotions, Stress, and Health

Suppose you are the first astronaut to land on a planet where the inhabitants experience no emotions at all (but who conveniently speak English). They gather around and ask you, their first visitor from Earth, what *emotion* is. What do you tell them?

"Well," you might say, "emotion is how you feel when something surprisingly good or surprisingly bad happens to you." "Wait a minute," they reply. "We don't understand these words *feel* and *surprisingly.*" "All right, how about this: Emotions are experiences like anger, fear, happiness, sadness . . ." "*Anger, fear* . . . what do those terms mean?" they ask.

Could you explain them? Could you even explain how to measure emotions? (After all, you could show people who are blind how to measure color vision, even if they never had the experience themselves.) Emotions are hard to define except by showing examples, and the examples mean nothing to someone who does not experience emotions.

In this chapter we consider what psychologists have

▌Would you make more intelligent decisions if you could thoroughly suppress your emotions, like the fictional character Spock? Observations of individuals with brain damage indicate that people with impaired emotions make worse than average decisions.

learned so far about emotions, while leaving some major questions unanswered. We begin with general theories and principles. Later, we turn to the role of emotions in health and how people cope with the emotions associated with stress.

The Nature of Emotion

What is the relationship between arousal and emotion?

How many kinds of emotions do people have?

In what ways do emotions sometimes improve our decision making?

Imagine that you tried to keep track of all the emotions you felt during a day. At one time or another, you might feel frightened, angry, sad, joyful, disgusted, worried, bored, ashamed, frustrated, contemptuous, embarrassed, surprised, and confused. But before you put those all on your list, you should stop to consider which of those states are really emotions. You might also wonder which states are different emotions, as opposed to being different terms for approximately the same experience.

Psychologists also wonder about these questions. For a long time, most psychologists considered emotion too subjective or vague a topic for serious research. It has recently become a more popular research topic, but it's still a difficult one. Almost everyone agrees, however, that emotions are interesting and important. It is difficult to imagine what life would be like without them.

If you think you can define *emotion* clearly, you are welcome to try. Psychologists who have thought extensively about the topic find themselves drawn to rather complicated definitions that include four dimensions (Keltner & Shiota, 2003): physiology (e.g., increased heart rate), cognition (thoughts), phenomenology (feelings), and actions (running away, attacking, etc.). Note that motivations also include physiology, cognition, feelings, and action. It is difficult to distinguish firmly between motivations and emotions, and perhaps unnecessary. The two are closely related, as almost any emotional state motivates us to do something, and almost any motivation includes some emotional feeling.

Measuring Emotions

Psychologists measure emotions by self-reports, behavioral observations, and physiological measures. Each method has its strengths and weaknesses.

Self-Reports

Psychologists often measure emotions by asking people how happy they are, how nervous, and so forth. Self-reports are quick, easy, and almost the only choice for measuring something like happiness that is hard to observe. However, their accuracy is questionable. For example, if you rate your current anger 3 on a 1-to-7 scale, we can't assume it's the same as someone else's 3 or even the same as your own 3 from another time.

Behavioral Observations

Although we cannot observe emotion directly, we infer it from someone's behavior and its context. For example, if we see one person make a fist and another person shriek and run away, we infer that the second person is afraid. Indeed, when you were an infant, your parents must have inferred your emotions before you started to report them verbally. They had to, before they could teach you the words for emotions! At some point you screamed and someone said that you were "afraid," and at some other time you smiled and someone told you that you were "happy."

One behavior that we watch closely is facial expressions. People can smile or frown when they do not feel an emotion or suppress smiles and frowns when they do. However, *very brief, involuntary expressions of fear, anger, or other emotions*, called **microexpressions,** are harder to control. For example, someone who is pretending to be calm or happy may show occasional brief signs of anger, fear, or extreme sadness (Ekman, 2001). With practice (or a videotape that can be played slowly), psychologists can sometimes identify emotions that people would like to hide.

Physiological Measures

Originally, the term *emotion* referred to any sort of turbulent motion. Centuries ago, people described thunder as an "emotion of the atmosphere." Eventually, people limited the term to body motions and their associated feelings, but the idea still includes turbulence and vigorous arousal.

Any stimulus that arouses an emotion alters the activity of the **autonomic nervous system,** *the section of the nervous system that controls the functioning of the internal organs.* The word *autonomic* means independent; biologists once believed that the autonomic nervous system was independent of the brain and the spinal cord. We now know that the brain and spinal cord can alter the activity of the autonomic nervous system, but the term *autonomic* remains.

449

▌ Ordinarily, an emotional state elicits a tendency toward vigorous action, even if we suppress that tendency. Here, a soldier disarms a mine during the war in the former Yugoslavia.

The autonomic nervous system has two branches: the sympathetic and the parasympathetic nervous systems (Figure 12.1). *Two chains of neuron clusters just to the left and right of the spinal cord* make up the **sympathetic nervous system,** *which arouses the body for vigorous action.* Traditionally, it has been called the "fight-or-flight" system because it increases your heart rate, breathing rate, production of sweat, and flow of epinephrine (EP-i-NEF-rin; also known as adrenaline), thereby preparing you for intense activity. However, different situations activate different parts of the sympathetic nervous system to facilitate different kinds of intense activity.

The **parasympathetic nervous system** consists of *neurons whose axons extend from the medulla* (Figure 12.1) *and the lower part of the spinal cord to neuron clusters near the internal organs. The*

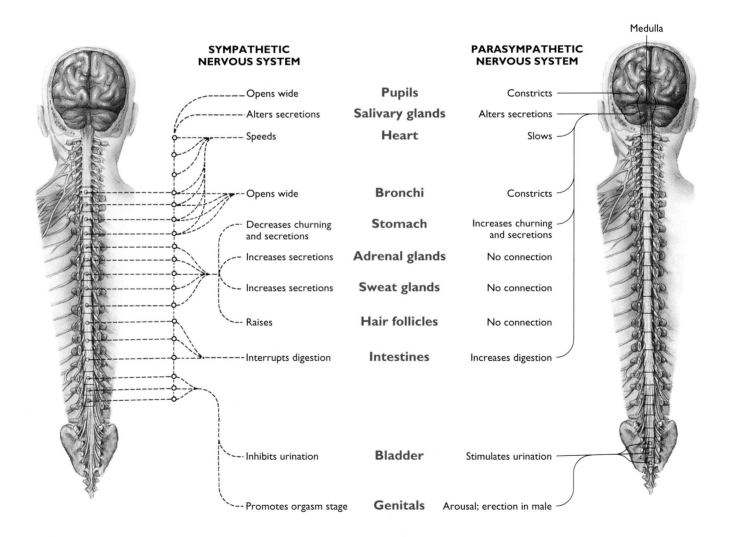

FIGURE 12.1 The autonomic nervous system consists of the sympathetic and parasympathetic nervous systems, which sometimes act in opposing ways and sometimes cooperate. The sympathetic nervous system readies the body for emergency action; the parasympathetic nervous system supports digestive and other nonemergency functions.

❚ The sympathetic nervous system prepares the body for a vigorous burst of activity.

parasympathetic nervous system decreases the heart rate, promotes digestion, and in general supports nonemergency functions. Both the sympathetic and parasympathetic systems send axons to the heart, the digestive system, and other organs. A few organs, such as the adrenal gland, receive input from only the sympathetic nervous system.

Both systems are constantly active, although one system can temporarily dominate. An emergency that demands a vigorous response activates mostly the sympathetic system, whereas a restful situation activates mostly the parasympathetic system. Many situations activate parts of both systems (Berntson, Cacioppo, & Quigley, 1993). For example, a frightening situation may increase your heart rate and sweating (sympathetic responses) and also promote bowel and bladder evacuation (parasympathetic responses). Do you remember ever being so frightened that you thought you might lose your bladder control?

Researchers often measure activity of the sympathetic nervous system as an indicator of emotional arousal. For example, moment-by-moment changes in the electrical conductivity across the skin indicate instantaneous changes in the amount of sweating, a sympathetic nervous system response that reflects emotional arousal. However, remember that the sympathetic nervous system is the fight-*or*-flight system, so its responses could indicate anger, fear, or any other intense emotion. Physiological measurements do not tell us *which* emotion someone is feeling.

Brain measurements are somewhat more specific, but not much. Figure 12.2 summarizes the results of many studies using PET and fMRI brain scans (see Chapter 3) to measure which brain areas

Happiness
Sadness
Disgust
Fear
Anger

FIGURE 12.2 Researchers aroused emotions in various ways and then used PET or fMRI scans to identify which brain areas became aroused. Certain areas were aroused in many studies, suggesting great importance for emotional processing. However, no brain area appears to be specific to just one type of emotion. *(From Phan, K.L., Wager, T., Taylor, S.F., & Liberzon, I., 2002. "Functional Neuroanatomy of Emotion: A Meta-analysis of Emotion Activation Studies in PET and fMRI," NeuroImage, 16, 331–348. Photo reprinted with the permission of the author and publisher.)*

became active when five different emotions were aroused in various ways (Phan, Wager, Taylor, & Liberzon, 2002). As you can see, the areas aroused by a given emotion are partly distinct but also largely overlap those aroused by other emotions. Thus, brain scans do not indicate for certain which emotion someone feels.

CONCEPT CHECK ☑

1. Why should we not insist on verbal reports to infer or measure emotions?
2. Why are physiological measurements more helpful for determining the intensity of an emotion than for identifying which emotion is present? (Check your answers on page 464.)

Emotion, Arousal, and Actions

If an emotion includes cognitions, feelings, behavior, and arousal, what is the relationship among those parts? William James, the founder of American psychology, put forth one of psychology's first theories, which concerned the nature of emotion.

The James-Lange Theory of Emotions

Common sense suggests that you feel sad and therefore you cry; you become afraid and therefore you tremble; you feel angry and therefore your heart beats faster and your face turns red. In 1884 William James and Carl Lange independently proposed to turn this concept around. According to the **James-Lange theory,** *your interpretation of a stimulus directly evokes autonomic changes and sometimes muscle actions; your perception of those changes is the feeling aspect of the emotion.* Actually, in James's original article, he said simply that the situation (e.g., the sight of a bear) gives rise to an action (e.g., running away), and your perception of the action is the emotion. That is, you don't run away because you are afraid; you feel afraid because you perceive yourself running away. In a later article in response to his critics, he clarified his view (James, 1894): Obviously, the sight of a bear doesn't automatically cause you to run away. You first appraise the situation. If it is a caged bear or a trained circus bear, you do not run. If it appears to be dangerous, you do. So your appraisal of the total situation is the cognitive aspect of the emotion. Your perception of yourself running away, with heart rate and breathing rate soaring, is what you *feel* as the emotion. That is,

Situation → Appraisal → Actions → Perception
　　　　　　　　　　　　　　　　　　　 of the Actions

　　　 = cognitive aspect　　 = feeling aspect
　　　 of the emotion　　　　 of the emotion

Given this interpretation, the James-Lange theory strikes many people as almost self-evident. Furthermore, much evidence supports it. The two main types of evidence are that people who perceive little reaction to an event feel little emotion, and people who are made to feel a stronger reaction feel an enhanced emotion.

Effects of Decreased Perceived Arousal

People with certain medical conditions feel little physiological arousal. One such condition is **pure autonomic failure,** *an uncommon condition with unknown cause in which the autonomic nervous system stops regulating the organs.* That is, nothing happening in the nervous system influences heart rate, breathing rate, and so forth. One effect is that if the person stands up quickly, none of the usual reflexes kick in to prevent gravity from drawing most of the blood from the head, and the person faints. With regard to emotions, affected people still recognize which situations call for anger, fear, sadness, and the like, but they report that their emotions feel much less intense than before (Critchley, Mathias, & Dolan, 2001). That is, the cognitive aspect of emotion remains, but the feeling aspect is weak, exactly as the James-Lange theory predicts.

Effects of Increased Perceived Arousal

Suppose some researcher induced you to attack someone. Would you then feel angry? Researchers steer away from anything so ethically doubtful, but milder ways are available to achieve almost the same effect. Suppose researchers molded your posture and breathing pattern into a pattern typical of a given emotion. Would you then feel that emotion? Have someone read these instructions to you, or read them to someone else and check what happens emotionally:

> Lower your eyebrows toward your cheeks. Sigh. Close your mouth and push your lower lip slightly upward. Sigh again. Sit back in your chair and draw your feet under the chair. Be sure you feel no tension in your legs or feet. Sigh again. Fold your hands in your lap, cupping one in the other. Drop your head, letting your rib cage fall, letting most of your body go limp, except for a little tension in the back of your neck and across your shoulder blades. Sigh again.

Most people holding this posture and repeatedly sighing report that they start to feel sad (Flack, Laird, & Cavallaro, 1999; Philippot, Chapelle, & Blairy, 2002). Instructions to hold the posture and breathing pattern characteristic of happiness, anger, or fear induce those emotions too, although the instructions for fear sometimes induce anger and those for anger sometimes induce fear. (Those two emotions are physiologically similar.)

One worry about studies of this type is that the participants may guess what the experimenter is trying to demonstrate. (Remember the issue of "demand characteristics" from Chapter 2.) One group of researchers found a clever way to conceal the purpose and expectation of the study. They told participants that the experiment related to how people learn to

a   b

FIGURE 12.3 Facial expression can influence mood. When people hold a pen with their teeth (a), they rate cartoons as funnier than when they hold it with their protruded lips (b).

write after amputation or paralysis of their arms. The participants were told to hold a pen either with their teeth or with their protruded lips, as Figure 12.3 shows. Then they were to use the pen in various ways, such as drawing lines between dots and making check marks to rate the funniness of cartoons.

When they held the pen with their teeth, their face was forced into a near smile and they rated the cartoons as very funny. When they held the pen with protruded lips, a smile was impossible and they rated the cartoons as less funny (Strack, Martin, & Stepper, 1988). Try holding a pen one way and then the other while reading newspaper cartoons. Do you notice any difference?

Try It Yourself

CONCEPT CHECK ☑

3. According to the James-Lange theory, do you run away from something because you are afraid of it?
4. What happens to emotions in people with medical conditions that weaken their autonomic and other responses to a situation? What happens when people adopt postures and breathing patterns characteristic of a particular emotion? How do these results relate to the James-Lange theory? (Check your answers on page 464.)

Schachter and Singer's Theory of Emotions

All right, once you get your body into a hunched-over posture with tension only in your neck and you are constantly sighing, you feel sad. But how did you get

into that posture in the first place? Your appraisal of the situation had to enter into the process somewhere.

Furthermore, how can you tell whether you are angry or frightened? As mentioned, the breathing pattern, heart rate pattern, and many other physiological activities are almost the same for anger and fear. Even extreme elation can elevate heart rate and produce other physiological changes that overlap those for anger and fear. Your autonomic changes tell you how strong your emotional feeling is, but the autonomic differences between one emotion and another are probably not strong enough to tell you which emotion you are experiencing (Lang, 1994).

Because of considerations like these, Stanley Schachter and Jerome Singer (1962) proposed a theory of how we identify one emotion from another. According to **Schachter and Singer's theory of emotions**, a physiological state is not the same as an emotion (see Figure 12.4). *The intensity of the*

FIGURE 12.4 According to Schachter and Singer's theory, physiological arousal determines the intensity of an emotion, but a cognitive appraisal determines which emotion one feels.

physiological state—that is, the degree of sympathetic nervous system arousal—determines the intensity of the emotion, but a cognitive appraisal of the situation identifies the type of emotion. That is, a given type of arousal might feel like fear, anger, euphoria (excited happiness), or none of these depending on the situation. Schachter and Singer saw their theory as an alternative to the James-Lange theory, but it really addresses a different question.

The ideal test of Schachter and Singer's theory would be to wire you to another person so that whenever the other person's heart rate, breathing rate, and so forth changed, yours would too, at the same time and to the same degree. Then when something caused the other person to feel some emotion, researchers would ask whether you feel it too. That procedure is impossible, at least with current technology, so Schachter and Singer (1962) tried a much simpler procedure.

CRITICAL THINKING:
WHAT'S THE EVIDENCE?
The Cognitive Aspect of Emotion

Hypothesis A drug that increases physiological arousal will enhance whatever emotion the situation arouses, but the type of emotion will depend on the situation.

Method The experimenters put college students into different situations but gave some of them injections of epinephrine (adrenalin) to induce (they hoped) the same physiological condition regardless of the situation. (Epinephrine mimics the effects of the sympathetic nervous system.) They tried to influence some participants to attribute their suddenly increased arousal to the situation and others to attribute it to the injection.

Specifically, the experimenters told some participants that the injections were vitamins that would have no easily noticed effects. These participants would presumably notice their arousal and attribute it to the situation, feeling intense emotions. Others were told to expect side effects, including increased heart rate, butterflies in the stomach, and so forth. When these people felt those changes, they would presumably attribute them to the injections and not consider them emotional experiences. Additional participants were given one set of instructions or the other but injected with a placebo instead of epinephrine.

Participants were then placed in different situations to elicit euphoria or anger. Each student in the euphoria situation was asked to wait in a room with a very playful young man who flipped paper wads into a trash can, sailed paper airplanes, built a tower with manila folders, shot paper wads at the tower with a rubber band, played with a Hula-Hoop, and tried to get the other student to join his play. Each participant in the anger situation was asked to fill out a questionnaire full of such insulting items as these:

Which member of your immediate family does not bathe or wash regularly?
With how many men (other than your father) has your mother had extramarital relationships?
4 or fewer   5–9   10 or more

Results Many students in the euphoria situation joined the playful partner (Figure 12.5). One jumped up and down on the desk, and another opened a window and threw paper wads at passersby. The anger situation was less effective than we might have expected, although a few students muttered angry comments or refused to complete the questionnaire.

Recall that some of the participants had been informed beforehand that the injections would produce certain autonomic effects, including tremors and increased heart rate. No matter which situation those participants were in, they showed only slight emotional responses. When they felt themselves sweating and their hands trembling, they said to themselves, "Aha! I'm getting the side effects, just as they said I would."

Interpretation Unfortunately, this experiment has some problems that limit the conclusions we can draw. Recall that some participants were given one set of instructions or the other and placed in one situation or the other, but injected with a placebo instead of epinephrine. These participants showed about as much euphoria in the euphoria situation and as much anger in the anger situation as did the participants injected with epinephrine. Therefore, the epinephrine injections apparently had nothing to do with the results. If we accept that possibility, we are left with this unexciting summary of the results: People in a situation designed to induce euphoria act happy; those in an anger situation act angry (Plutchik & Ax, 1967). However, if they attribute their arousal to an injection, their behavior is more restrained.

Despite the problems in Schachter and Singer's experiment, the idea behind it is reasonable, and other research since then has supported it in many though not all cases. That idea, to reiterate, is that the arousal you perceive in yourself determines the intensity of the emotion, although not the identity of the emotion itself. To illustrate with one example, young heterosexual men were asked to rate the attractiveness of each woman in the *Sports Illustrated* swimsuit issue. (They participated in the name of science, of course.) While they were viewing each photo, they heard sounds. Some were told (correctly) that they were listening to random sounds, and others were told (incorrectly) that they were hearing their own heartbeat. The rate of the sounds fluctuated haphazardly. The men who thought

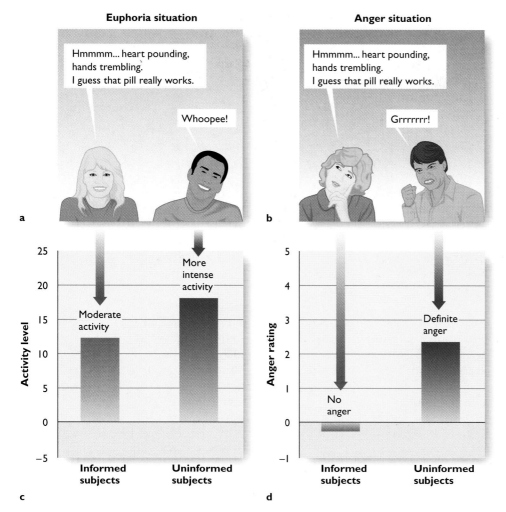

FIGURE 12.5 (a and b) In Schachter and Singer's experiment, people who were uninformed about the effects of epinephrine reported strong emotions appropriate to the situation. (c and d) According to Schachter and Singer, autonomic arousal controls the strength of an emotion, but cognitive factors tell us which emotion we are experiencing.

The Range of Emotions

How many different emotions do humans experience? Do we have a few "basic" emotions that combine to form other experiences, like the elements of chemistry? Or is the boundary between one emotion and another arbitrary? Do people's emotions vary from culture to culture, or do people throughout the world (and maybe even non-human animals) have the same emotions?

Psychologists have not yet agreed on a single list of basic emotions. Some psychologists have proposed a very short list, such as pain and pleasure, and others offer a longer list, such as happiness, sadness, anger, fear, disgust, surprise, contempt, and shame. Others add even more candidates, such as guilt, interest, hope, pride, relief, frustration, love, awe, boredom, jealousy, regret, or embarrassment (Keltner & Buswell, 1997). Japanese people list among the emotions *amae*, translated as "the pleasant feeling of depending on someone else," or "the feeling of comfort in another person's acceptance." The Japanese believe that people in other cultures have this emotion but fail to notice or emphasize it (Doi, 1981; Lambie & Marcel, 2002). Hindus include heroism, amusement, peace, and wonder (Hejmadi, Davidson, & Rozin, 2000). Still other theorists question whether it makes sense even to talk about basic emotions (e.g., Ortony & Turner, 1990; Russell, 2003). Perhaps it makes more sense to talk about continuous emotional dimensions, such as pleasant–unpleasant and engaged–disengaged (D. Watson, Wiese, Vaidya, & Tellegen, 1999).

How can we decide what is a basic emotion (if there is such a thing)? Psychologists have generally accepted the following criteria:

- Basic emotions should emerge early in life without requiring much experience. For example, nostalgia and pride emerge relatively slowly and therefore

they were hearing their own heartbeats gave very high ratings to whatever women they were examining when they thought their heartbeat was accelerating (Crucian et al., 2000). That is, when a man thought his heart was beating faster, he assumed it was because of his excitement over a particular woman. Experiments like this suggest that what emotion (if any) we perceive depends on a cognitive attribution we make based on the situation. However, results of such experiments vary depending on details of the procedure (Reisenzein, 1983).

CONCEPT CHECK ☑

5. You are going on a first date with someone you hope will find you exciting. According to Schachter and Singer's theory, should you plan a date walking through an art gallery or riding on roller coasters? (Check your answer on page 464.)

FIGURE 12.6 Chimpanzees and humans have very special facial expressions.

seem less basic than fear, anger, or joy (Lewis, 1995). The problem is that all emotional expressions emerge gradually over age. Infants' expressions at first do not distinguish among distress, anger, and fear (Messinger, 2002). They also do not smile or laugh in the first couple of months, although they open their eyes wider when a parent speaks in a happy tone of voice (Mastropieri & Turkewitz, 1999).

- Basic emotions should be similar across cultures. However, it is surprising how many emotions are recognizably similar throughout human cultures, so this criterion does not eliminate much.

- Each basic emotion should have its own biological basis and perhaps its own facial expression. We shall explore this point more fully.

Producing Facial Expressions

Does each emotion have its own special expression? And why do we have facial expressions of emotions anyway?

Quite simply, the function of facial expressions is communication. Primates (humans, apes, and monkeys) communicate their emotional states through gestures and facial expressions (Redican, 1982) (see Figure 12.6). Humans also rely on nonverbal expressions when we can. You wink, nod, or smile to show a possible romantic interest; you withhold such expressions to indicate a lack of interest. (You *could* tell a stranger "I find you sexually attractive" or "I find you boring," but facial expressions are at least as effective and much less risky.)

Facial expressions provide a kind of "truth in advertising." That is, your expression reflects your internal state and therefore tells other people whether you are likely to interact with them in a friendly or an

uncooperative manner (Buck, 1994). Emotional expressions occur mostly in a social context. For example, Olympic medal winners generally smile if they are waiting for the awards ceremony with others but not if they are waiting alone (Fernández-Dols & Ruiz-Belda, 1997). Even 10-month-old infants smile more when their mothers are watching than when they are not (S. S. Jones, Collins, & Hong, 1991). Laughter occurs mostly in social settings, and we laugh mostly when others are laughing. Robert Provine (2000) spent many hours in shopping malls and elsewhere recording and observing laughter. He found that people laughed almost entirely when they were with friends and that the speakers laughed more than the listeners. Most of the time people laughed while saying something that wasn't even funny, such as "Can I join you?" or "It was nice meeting you too." The laughter seemed to be simply a way of expressing friendliness.

Voluntary smiles, frowns, and other facial expressions seldom exactly match the appearance of spontaneous expressions. For example, the smile of a truly happy person includes movements of the mouth muscles and the muscles surrounding the eyes (Figure 12.7a). Voluntary smiles (Figure 12.7b) generally do not include the muscles around the eyes (Ekman & Davidson, 1993). *The full expression including the muscles around the eyes* is called the **Duchenne smile,** named after Duchenne de Boulogne, the first person to describe it.

Because the Duchenne smile is hard to produce voluntarily, it is a good indicator of someone's true feelings. Researchers have found that women with a Duchenne smile in their college yearbooks were more likely than other women to have happy, long-lasting marriages and to report feeling happy and competent decades after graduation from college (Harker & Keltner, 2001).

a   b

FIGURE 12.7 A spontaneous, happy smile (a) uses both the mouth muscles and the muscles surrounding the eyes. This expression is sometimes called the *Duchenne smile*. A voluntary smile (b) ordinarily includes only the mouth muscles. Most people cannot voluntarily activate the eye muscles associated with the Duchenne smile.

FIGURE 12.9 A boy who has been blind since birth covers his face in embarrassment. He prevents others from seeing his face, even though he has never experienced sight himself.

FIGURE 12.8 This laughing girl was born deaf and blind.

they saw. He reported that people everywhere had similar facial expressions, including expressions of grief, determination, anger, surprise, terror, and disgust. A century later Irenäus Eibl-Eibesfeldt (1973, 1974) photographed people in various cultures, documenting smiling, frowning, laughing, and crying throughout the world, even in children who were born deaf and blind (Figures 12.8 and 12.9). Evidently, at least some of our facial expressions develop without any need for imitation.

Eibl-Eibesfeldt also found that people everywhere expressed a friendly greeting by briefly raising their eyebrows (Figure 12.10). The mean duration of that expression is the same in all cultures: one third of a second from start to finish.

To move beyond naturalistic observations, researchers typically use photos of people showing the presumed "basic" facial expressions, as shown in Figure 12.11. Look at each face and try to name its expression. (Please try now.)

Understanding Facial Expressions

Do we learn how to make appropriate facial expressions, or are they part of our biological heritage? One way to approach this question is through naturalistic observations.

Charles Darwin (1872/1965) asked missionaries and other people in remote places to describe the facial expressions of the people

FIGURE 12.10 Like this man from New Guinea, people throughout the world raise their eyebrows as a greeting.

a b c

d e f

© P. Ekman & W. Friesen, "Unmasking the Face," 2nd Edition 1984. Used by permission of Ekman

FIGURE 12.11 Paul Ekman has used these faces in experiments testing people's ability to recognize emotional expressions. Can you identify them? Check answer A on page 464.

Then look at each and match the expressions to the following labels (one face per label): anger, disgust, fear, happiness, sadness, and surprise. Most people can match all six expressions to their labels.

Try It Yourself

After researchers translated the labels into other languages, people in other cultures also matched them, though somewhat less accurately (Ekman, 1992). What should we conclude? Evidently, these facial expressions have approximately the same meaning throughout the world (Ekman, 1994). The expressions do vary slightly, with differences that have been compared to regional "accents." That is, just as you understand the speech from your own region better than that of people from elsewhere, you recognize facial expressions a bit more accurately among people from your own culture or subculture (Marsh, Elfenbein, & Ambady, 2003). Still, most people can identify the expressions with better than chance accuracy even when looking at faces from a culture unfamiliar to them (Ekman & Friesen, 1984; Russell, 1994). For more go to http://psychology.wadsworth.com/kalat_intro7e. Navigate to the student Web site, then to Online Try It Yourself, and click on Universal Emotions.

Online Try It Yourself

The research has some difficulties, however, and the results may either overestimate or underestimate

how easy it is to recognize emotional expressions. Imagine yourself as the researcher. Suppose you show people the faces in Figure 12.11 and someone looks at the picture that is supposed to be "fear" and calls it "worry" or "distress." Do you call that answer right or wrong? To make the scoring more objective, you might list the six emotions and ask people to choose one. But then anyone who can identify five of them gets the sixth one by process of elimination. In fact someone who identifies even one or two faces for sure has an improved chance at guessing the others (Russell, 1994). So the matching method tends to overestimate people's accuracy.

On the other hand, asking people to identify emotions from a still photograph can underestimate their abilities. Ordinarily, we identify emotions from changing facial expressions, gestures, tone of voice, and the context (Edwards, 1998; Russell, 1997). Furthermore, the six faces in Figure 12.11 are all looking directly at the camera and, therefore, the viewer. From the standpoint of experimental design, putting all the faces in the same position seems to make sense. However, sad people almost always look down, not directly at you. Frightened people look directly at you only if they are afraid of *you,* and why would they be afraid of you . . . especially when you are sitting there calmly, as you probably are right now? Examine the photos in Figure 12.12. Which expression is easier to identify? Most observers identify sad, frightened, or angry expressions faster when they see someone looking away than looking directly at them

a Direct gaze   b Averted gaze

© Reginald Adams, Jr.

FIGURE 12.12 What emotions are these faces expressing? Most people identify fearful expressions more easily when the person is looking away.

(Adams & Kleck, 2003). In contrast happy and angry expressions are easier to identify if the person is looking directly forward.

CONCEPT CHECK

6. Researchers have often shown observers a set of still photographs and asked them to pair each with the name of an emotion. In what way might this procedure overestimate accuracy of recognizing emotions? In what way might it underestimate accuracy? (Check your answers on page 464.)

Do Facial Expressions Indicate Basic Emotions?

Let's return to the question of how many "basic" emotions people have. Suppose we shrug off the research problems and agree that people throughout the world do recognize facial expressions of joy, sadness, fear, anger, disgust, and surprise. Can we then conclude that people have six basic emotions? No. First, people can, with a little less accuracy but still better than chance, identify several other facial expressions too. Try to identify the expression in Figure 12.13, for ex-

FIGURE 12.13 Can you identify this emotional expression? Check answer B on page 464. *(From Rozin, P., Lowery, L., Imada, S., & Haidt, J. "The CAD triad hypothesis: A mapping between three moral emotions [contempt, anger, disgust] and three moral codes [community, autonomy, divinity],"* Journal of Personality & Social Psychology, 76, 574–586, 1999. *Photo reprinted with permission from author and publisher.)*

ample, and then check answer B on page 464. Also, from videotapes, though not from still photographs, most people can identify expressions of "peace" and "heroism," which Hindu people generally list as emotions (Hejmadi et al., 2000). So if the ability to identify an expression is evidence for a basic emotion, our list should grow.

Second problem: We readily identify the facial expression in Figure 12.14 as "sleepiness," although few people regard sleepiness as an emotion. We can also identify expressions of "confusion," although confusion is at best a debatable example of emotion (Keltner & Shiota, 2003; Rozin & Cohen, 2003). So the fact that we recognize facial expressions of surprise and disgust is not necessarily evidence that surprise and disgust are emotions.

© Michael Porsche/CORBIS

FIGURE 12.14 Simple point: We easily recognize expressions of sleepiness, although we do not regard sleepiness as an emotion. So recognizing expressions of disgust or surprise does not necessarily qualify them as emotions either.

Finally, not all psychologists are convinced that anger, fear, and so forth are psychological "elements." Just as water is a compound of hydrogen and oxygen, maybe what we describe as an emotion is a compound of several parts. For example, consider the expression of anger in Figure 12.15. Instead of calling it a single expression, we could describe it as a combination of components (Ortony & Turner, 1990): The widened eyes express surprise, a common component of anger but also a component of fear. The turned-down corners of the mouth indicate displeasure, a component of both anger and sadness. The furrowed eyebrows indicate a desire to change something about the situation. The raised fist indicates, of course, a potential to strike. In short, it is not obvious that the study of our ability to recognize facial expressions leads to a clear identification of "basic" emotions.

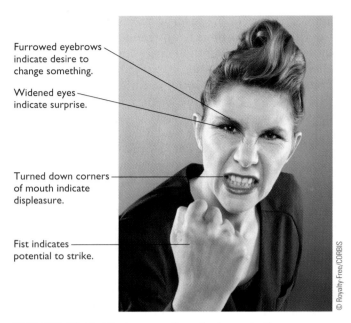

Furrowed eyebrows indicate desire to change something.

Widened eyes indicate surprise.

Turned down corners of mouth indicate displeasure.

Fist indicates potential to strike.

© Royalty-Free/CORBIS

FIGURE 12.15 What we usually regard as a single expression—in this case anger—may be analyzed as a compound of several parts.

Emotions and Moral Decisions

We enjoy having emotions, but are they *useful* for anything? When we are making important decisions, people often advise us "not to let our emotions get in the way." If emotions really were so harmful to decision making, presumably we would not have evolved the ability to feel them. Let's consider some of the ways that emotions—within moderate limits, of course—can aid us in decision making.

Let's begin with two moral dilemmas. Like Kohlberg's moral dilemmas described in Chapter 10, these are difficult decisions on which well-meaning people can disagree.

The Trolley Dilemma. A trolley car with defective brakes is coasting downhill toward five people standing on the tracks. You could throw a switch to divert the trolley onto a different track, where one person is standing. That is, if you flip the switch, the trolley will kill one instead of five. Should you do it?

The Footbridge Dilemma. Another trolley with defective brakes is coasting downhill toward five people who are sure to be killed. This time you are standing on a footbridge over the track. You see one way to save those five people: A fat person is standing with you, leaning over. You could push him off the bridge, so he would land on the track and block the

trolley. (You are, we shall assume, too thin to block it yourself.) So again your action would kill one to save five. Should you do it? (See Figure 12.16.)

Most people say *yes* to flipping the switch in the first dilemma, but either say *no* or hesitate for a long time in the second dilemma (J. D. Greene, Sommerville, Nystrom, Darley, & Cohen, 2001). Logically, the answer should be the same if in each case you kill one person to save five. Of course, the situations are not quite comparable. The instruction says you can save five people by pushing one man off a bridge, but you may not feel sure. What if you pushed him to his death and the trolley killed the others anyway? Or what if you pushed him and then the others jumped out of the way so that killing him was unnecessary? However, even if you were fully confident that pushing one man off a bridge would save five others, it would still be difficult to do. The idea of putting your hands on someone to push him to his death is emotionally repulsive. *And it should be!* In a bizarre case like this, maybe it does make sense to push a stranger off a bridge, but ordinarily, it does not, and your emotional reaction is a good, quick guide to making the decision that is almost always right.

Let's try another scenario. Here you don't have to make a decision; you just decide whether the decision two people already made is acceptable: Mark and Julie are brother and sister, both of them college students. During one summer they traveled together, and one night they stayed at a cabin in the woods. They decided it would be fun to have sex together, so they did.

a

b

FIGURE 12.16 Should you flip a switch so the trolley goes down a track with one person instead of five? Should you push a fat person off the bridge to save five people?

Julie was taking birth-control pills, but Mark used a condom anyway just to be sure. Both enjoyed the experience and neither felt hurt in any way. They decided not to do it again, but to keep it as their little secret. They feel even closer than ever as brother and sister. Was their action okay?

Almost everyone reacts vigorously and immediately that their decision was wrong. Why? They used two reliable methods of birth control, and both said they enjoyed the experience and neither was hurt. So if their act was wrong, why was it wrong? Regardless of whether you can state a logical reason, your real reason is probably that the idea of brother–sister sex *feels* wrong; it is emotionally repulsive (Haidt, 2001). Again, your emotions are a good guide to behavior. Even if Mark and Julie weren't hurt—and I understand if you doubt that claim!—they would be an extremely rare exception to a dependable rule.

Decisions by People with Impaired Emotions

Antonio Damasio (1994) described patients who suffered impoverished or inappropriate emotions following brain damage. One was the famous patient Phineas Gage, who survived an accident in 1848 in which an iron bar shot through his head. Nearly one-and-a-half centuries later, researchers examined his skull (which is still on display in a Boston museum) and reconstructed the route that the bar must have taken through his brain (Damasio, Grabowski, Frank, Galaburda, & Damasio, 1994). As you can see in Figure 12.17, the accident damaged part of his prefrontal cortex. As a result Gage often showed little emotion, and what emotion he did show was inappropriate. He seemed to lose his former values, becoming unreliable in both his work and his personal habits. He made rude sexual advances and used profanities that people had not heard him say before. He followed each whim of the moment, unable to carry out any long-term plans.

A more recent example is known to us as "Elliot" (Damasio, 1994). Elliot too suffered damage to his prefrontal cortex as a result of surgery to remove a brain tumor. After the operation he showed almost no emotional expression, no impatience, no frustration, no joy from music or art, and almost no anger. He described his brain surgery and the resulting deterioration of his life with calm detachment, as if describing events that happened to a stranger. Besides his impaired emotions, he had great difficulty making or following reasonable plans. If given an array of information, he discussed the probable outcome of each possible decision but still had trouble deciding. As a result Elliot could not keep a job, invest his money intelligently, or maintain normal friendships.

According to Damasio (1994), Elliot's impaired decision making stemmed from his weak emotions. Ordi-

© H. Damasio, T. Grabowski, R. Frank, A.M. Galabu & A.R. Damasio, "The Return of Phineas Gage: Clues about the Brain from the Skull of a Famous Patient," *Science 264*, 1994

FIGURE 12.17 In the 1990s researchers used modern technology to reconstruct the path that an iron bar must have made through the brain of Phineas Gage, who survived this injury in 1848. The damage impaired Gage's judgment and decision-making ability.

narily, when you or I consider possible decisions, we contemplate the possible outcomes and briefly experience how each outcome might feel. For example, if you consider a job offer from a company that recently fired your best friend, you imagine the unpleasant scene when you next face that friend, and you reject the offer. Elliot feels little emotion and cannot even imagine feeling good after one outcome or bad after another. If nothing feels good or bad, then it doesn't seem to matter what you do. As Damasio (1999, p. 55) said, "Emotions are inseparable from the idea of good and evil." If you cannot even imagine happiness or unhappiness, you are likely to make terrible decisions.

CONCEPT CHECK

7. In what way does prefrontal cortex damage interfere with decision making? (Check your answer on page 464.)

Emotional Intelligence

Is reasoning about emotional issues any different from reasoning about anything else? The observations on patient Elliot imply a difference, as he can answer questions normally as long as they have nothing to do with emotional consequences. Casual observations in everyday life also suggest that reasoning about emotional topics might be special. Some people usually seem to know the right thing to say to make someone else feel better. They notice subtle signals in people's facial expressions; they know who needs a pat on the back or a kind word. They can judge whether someone's smile is sincere or fake. They know whether their romantic attachments are going well or about to break up. Also, for every person you can think of who is good at these judgments, you can probably think of at least one who seems always to say the wrong thing.

Many psychologists therefore speak of **emotional intelligence,** *the ability to perceive, imagine, and understand emotions and to use that information in making decisions* (Mayer & Salovey, 1995, 1997). Part of emotional intelligence is detecting other people's emotions and knowing the right thing to say to manage emotional situations. Another aspect is being aware of one's own emotions, managing them, and expressing them or restraining them depending on the situation (Mayer, 2001; Swinkels & Giuliano, 1995).

The idea of emotional intelligence quickly became popular, both inside and outside psychology, although the evidence behind the idea is still not strong. If the concept is going to be useful, emotional intelligence has to have enough in common with other kinds of intelligence that it deserves to be called intelligence. For example, it should increase from childhood to adulthood, as academic intelligence does, and we should be able to measure emotional intelligence with reasonable reliability and validity. However, emotional intelligence should not overlap too heavily with academic intelligence, or we would have no reason to talk about it separately. To make any progress, the first step has to be finding a way to measure emotional intelligence.

As you will see in the next chapter, psychologists usually measure personality variables by asking people to rate themselves. For example, you might rate how extraverted you are or how conscientious. That method does not work well for emotional intelligence. If a question asks "how sensitive you are to other people's feelings," many people whom others regard as insensitive rate themselves as highly sensitive (Carney & Harrigan, 2003). Apparently, they do not even realize how insensitive they are.

Many psychologists therefore have been trying to measure emotional intelligence with pencil-and-paper tests. Here are examples of the questions, reworded slightly (Mayer, Caruso, & Salovey, 2000):

1. A middle-aged man has been so busy at work that he spends little time with his wife and daughter. He feels guilty for spending so little time with them, and they feel hurt. Recently a relative who lost his job moved in with them. A few weeks later they told him he had to leave because they needed their privacy.

On a scale from 1 to 5, where 5 is highest, rate how much this man feels:
Depressed _____
Frustrated _____
Guilty _____
Energetic _____
Liking _____
Joyous _____
Happy _____

2. A driver hit a dog that ran into the street. The driver and the dog's owner hurried to check on the dog.

On a scale from 1 to 5, where 5 means "extremely likely" and 1 means "extremely unlikely," how would the driver and the dog's owner probably feel?
The owner would feel angry at the driver _____
The owner would feel embarrassed at not training the dog better _____
The driver would feel guilty for not driving more carefully _____
The driver would feel relieved that it was a dog and not a child _____

3. Someone you know at work seems worried. You and he have lunch alone at a quiet restaurant. He confides in you that he lied on his application to get his job, and now he is afraid of getting caught.

What do you do?

These are reasonable questions, although you would no doubt prefer more information. You could judge better from people's tone of voice, facial expressions, the context, and maybe even smells, none of which can appear on a pencil-and-paper test. Still, you could do your best to answer. The problem then is . . . gulp . . . what are the correct answers? In fact, *are there* correct answers other than "it depends"? We can imagine several ways to determine the "right" answers, but none of them is perfect (Roberts, Zeidner, & Matthews, 2001).

One way is "consensus": Ask many people to answer and take the most common answer as correct. However, if we rely on consensus scoring, we cannot have any difficult questions to identify people with special talent. All we could do is identify people who fail to answer questions that most people get right. That by itself is worth something. People with certain kinds of brain damage or psychiatric disorder do poorly even on easy questions, such as looking at pictures of faces and identifying their emotional expressions (Adolphs, Baron-Cohen, & Tranel, 2002; Edwards, Jackson, & Pattison, 2002; Kornreich et al., 2001; Rosen et al., 2002; Townshend & Duka, 2003). So the test would identify "emotional stupidity," even if it didn't identify emotional intelligence.

An alternative is to ask experts to identify the correct answers. Tests of mathematics use that approach, of course. However, in mathematics it is easy to identify the experts. Who are the experts on emotional intelligence? If we assume that psychologists who have done years of research on emotion are experts on emotional intelligence, then according to the experts' scoring key, men on the average get higher emotional intelligence scores than women. That result should be surprising. Many studies show that from childhood on, girls and women are better than boys and men at detecting emotions from nonverbal signals (Chen & Haviland-Jones, 2000; Hall & Halberstadt, 1994; McClure, 2000). Most people informally agree that they can think of more women than men who seem to have good emotional intelligence. Guess what? All of the emotion researchers who determined the expert scoring key were men (Roberts et al., 2001). In a case like this, diversity is even more important than usual because we do not know whether one group of "experts" would agree with another. After all, perhaps the correct answers differ from one subculture to another.

In short, emotional intelligence is an interesting idea, but researchers have a long way to go. The currently available tests of emotional intelligence have decent reliability (Mayer, Salovey, Caruso, & Sitarenios, 2001), but little is known about their validity. Is a pencil-and-paper test even a reasonable idea, or should we use more complex stimuli, such as videotapes? We can expect to see interesting developments in this area in coming years.

CONCEPT CHECK ☑

8. How does consensus scoring differ from expert scoring? (Check your answer on page 464.)

IN CLOSING

Research on Emotions

Research on emotions is fascinating. It is also difficult. Of the various components of emotion, the cognitive and phenomenological (feeling) aspects are the hardest to measure. Behavioral and physiological measures are more objective but have their own problems. The best solution, therefore, is to approach each problem in multiple ways. Any one kind of study has flaws and limitations, but if several different kinds of research point to the same conclusion, we gain confidence in the overall idea. That principle is, indeed, important throughout psychology: Seldom is any study fully decisive, so we strive for independent lines of research, using different methods, that converge on the same conclusion.

Summary

- *Measuring emotions.* Emotions are inferred, not observed directly. Researchers rely on self-reports, observations of behavior, and measurements of physiological changes. (page 449)

- *Emotions and autonomic arousal.* Most emotions are associated with increased arousal of the sympathetic nervous system, although some parts of the parasympathetic nervous system increase their activity also. The sympathetic nervous system readies the body for emergency action. (page 449)

- *James-Lange theory.* According to the James-Lange theory of emotions, the feeling aspect of an emotion is the perception of a change in the body's physiological state. (page 452)

- *Evidence supporting the James-Lange theory.* People who lose control of their autonomic responses generally report weakened emotional feelings. Also, molding someone's posture and breathing pattern into the pattern typical for some emotion tends to elicit that emotion. (page 452)

- *Schachter and Singer's theory.* According to Schachter and Singer's theory, autonomic arousal determines the intensity of an emotion but does not determine which emotion occurs. We identify an emotion on the basis of how we perceive the situation. (page 453)

- *Range of emotions.* Psychologists do not fully agree on which emotions, if any, are basic. (page 455)

- *Facial expressions.* People produce facial expressions of emotion as a means of communicating their probable social behaviors. (page 456)

- *Understanding facial expressions.* Many human facial expressions have similar meanings in cultures throughout the world. (page 457)

- *Emotions and moral decisions.* When we face a moral decision, we often react emotionally for or against one of the choices. Those quick emotional feelings may be an evolved mechanism to steer our behavior toward what is usually the right choice. (page 460)

- *The usefulness of emotions.* We make many decisions by imagining the emotional consequences of the possible outcomes. People with brain damage that impairs their emotions have trouble making good decisions. (page 461)

- *Emotional intelligence.* People need special skills to judge other people's emotions and intentions and the probable emotional outcomes of their own possible behaviors. The ability to handle such issues may constitute an "emotional intelligence" that is related to but not identical to academic intelligence. However, much work needs to be done to improve our measurements of emotional intelligence. (page 461)

Answers to Concept Checks

1. It would be impossible to teach a child (or anyone else) the words for emotions unless we had already inferred the emotions from the individual's behavior. (page 452)

2. The sympathetic nervous system is aroused by either anger or fear (fight or flight), and therefore, its arousal indicates strength of one or the other but does not identify which one. Brain measurements show overlap among the various emotions; that is, the areas excited by one emotion can be aroused by other emotions as well. (page 452)

3. No. According to the James-Lange theory, you feel fear because you are running away. (page 453)

4. People with pure autonomic failure have no systematic autonomic changes, and their emotions feel weak. When people adopt the postures and breathing patterns characteristic of some emotion, they are more likely than usual to feel that emotion. These results confirm the predictions of the James-Lange theory. (page 453)

5. According to Schachter and Singer's theory, you should plan a date riding roller coasters. If your date gets emotionally excited, he or she may attribute the arousal to you. (page 455)

6. The matching procedure can overestimate accuracy because someone who identifies one or more correctly has an improved chance of guessing the others by the process of elimination. However, the use of still photographs underestimates people's accuracy because we ordinarily have many other cues, such as change over time, gestures, tone of voice, and context. Also, it is easier to recognize expressions of sadness and fear if the person looks down or to the side. (page 459)

7. People with damage to the prefrontal cortex cannot imagine feeling good or bad after various outcomes, and therefore, they see little reason to prefer one outcome over another. (page 461)

8. Consensus scoring takes the most common answer to the question as correct. Expert scoring uses the decision of a group of experts to determine the correct answer. (page 463)

Answers to Other Questions in the Module

A. faces express (a) happiness, (b) anger, (c) sadness, (d) surprise, (e) disgust, and (f) fear.

B. Most people describe this expression as "contempt."

What makes people happy, sad, frightened, or angry?

How do our emotions affect our actions?

The field of emotions includes difficult theoretical issues, such as whether each emotion is like an element or is like a compound of smaller parts. Fortunately, we do not have to wait until we answer these questions. We can proceed to issues of practical importance to almost everyone, especially clinical psychologists: How can we make ourselves happier or at least less sad, frightened, or angry?

Happiness, Joy, and Positive Psychology

Positive psychology is *the study of the features that enrich life, such as hope, creativity, courage, spirituality, and responsibility* (Seligman & Csikszentmihalyi, 2000). The meaning of an enriched life varies from one culture to another. For example, in many Asian cultures, people say their main goal in life is to fulfill their duties rather than to seek personal happiness (Heine, Lehman, Markus, & Kitayama, 1999). Still, if fulfilling one's duties brings a sense of satisfaction, presumably people of all cultures strive for at least that kind of positive emotion.

Research on the positive emotions, including happiness and joy, became common in psychology only since about the 1990s (Seligman & Csikszentmihalyi, 2000). One reason is the more practical need to understand fear, anger, and sadness, which are constant concerns in clinical psychology. Another reason is that fear and anger produce easily measured changes in behavior, and to some extent sadness does too. Happiness is harder to measure because it produces no obvious behavioral markers other than smiles, and even smiles are inconsistent. Happy people don't always smile, and smiling people aren't always happy.

Most researchers have resorted to asking people to rate their happiness or **subjective well-being,** *which is a self-evaluation of one's life as pleasant, interesting, and satisfying* (Diener, 2000). What factors influence happiness or subjective well-being? Pose these questions to your friends. You can ask everyone question 1, but for some people add just question 2 and for other people question 3. (Answering either question 2 or 3 alters people's answer to question 1.)

Try It Yourself

1. Rate your happiness on a scale where 0 means extremely unhappy and 10 means extremely happy.
2. What would make you happier than you are now?
3. What makes you happy?

On the first question, most American students rate themselves on the positive side of the scale, calling themselves happy. A longer questionnaire produces a more reliable measurement (Pavot & Diener, 1993), but the point remains that most people consider themselves happy, except those in countries overrun by poverty, war, or disease (Diener & Diener, 1996).

To the question of what would make you happier, most U.S. students mention money, a good job, more time to relax, or a boyfriend or girlfriend (or a "better" boyfriend or girlfriend). To the question of what makes you happy, common answers include relationships with friends and family, exercise, music, a sense of accomplishing something well, religious faith, and enjoyment of nature.

Influence of Wealth

Note that many people say more money would make them happier, but few say their money does make them happy. How important is money for happiness?

Within a country richer people on the average rate themselves only slightly happier than poorer people, except for those who are extremely poor. (Wealth can't make you happy, but extreme poverty can make you unhappy.) Comparisons across countries produce complex results (Myers, 2000). Figure 12.18 relates the average incomes in various countries to the average reported happiness (Inglehart, 1997). Note that the results fall into two clusters. People in the 19 more prosperous countries in the study generally rated themselves as happier than did those in the less prosperous countries. However, within either the more prosperous or the less prosperous cluster, wealth had little relationship to happiness. That is, wealth does not explain why people in Poland were happier than those in Russia or why people in Iceland were happier than those in Japan.

For more information about happiness research, including happiness ratings for various countries, visit this Web site:

www.eur.nl/fsw/research/happiness/index.htm

Whenever two variables are poorly correlated (e.g., wealth and happiness), one possible explanation is that

465

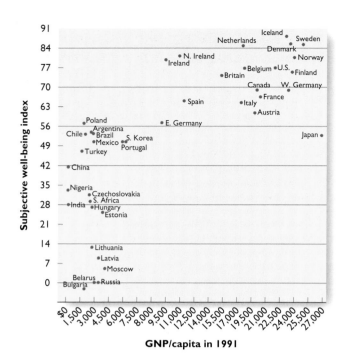

FIGURE 12.18 Each dot shows the mean data for one country. People in the wealthier cluster of countries are generally happier than those in the poorer countries, but wealth alone cannot account for all these data. *(From* Modernization and Postmodernization *by R. Inglehart, 1997. Copyright © 1997 by R. Inglehart. Reprinted by permission of Princeton University Press.)*

the relationship really is weak. Here that is a reasonable interpretation, as people's reported happiness in different countries correlates better with health, human rights, and high status of women than it does with income (Basabe et al., 2002). However, another explanation for any low correlation can be that one or both of the variables were measured poorly. (An unreliable measurement does not correlate highly with anything—not even with a second measurement of the same variable.)

Consider the cross-cultural data. In some low-income countries, many people have no money but enough land to grow food and feed their family. They may even have enough food to trade for other products. Little money passes through their hands, but a farmer with no money (and no bills) is not the same as a city-dweller with no money. So "average income" can be a misleading measurement when we compare different countries.

Happiness ratings are misleading for a different reason. Suppose two people both rate their happiness as 7. Does one person's 7 mean the same as the other person's? Consider this analogy: Some people have far more taste buds on their tongues than others. Those with the most taste buds ("supertasters") reject many foods; what an average person regards as slightly sour or bitter, a supertaster considers inedible. A supertaster is likely even to reject many sweets because they are excessively, sickeningly sweet. People at the opposite ex-

treme ("nontasters") seldom even detect bitterness (Bartoshuk, Duffy, Lucchina, Prutkin, & Fast, 1998). However, when various people rate "how strong" something tastes, on the average a nontaster rates most substances just as high as a supertaster! A nontaster who rates something 10 on a 1-to-10 scale means "it is as strong as tastes ever get . . . in my experience." A supertaster would also rate it 10, while having a much more intense experience (Bartoshuk, 2000).

The same principle applies to happiness surveys. If richer and poorer people rate themselves equally happy on some questionnaire, we cannot assume that they really are equally happy. One person's scale can be different from another's.

Another way to examine the effect of wealth on happiness is to interview people who recently gained much wealth. As you might guess, people who have just won a lottery call themselves very happy. As you might not guess, people who won a lottery a few months ago no longer rate themselves unusually happy (Diener, Suh, Lucas, & Smith, 1999; Myers, 2000). There are several possible explanations. First, maybe money really doesn't buy happiness. Second, lottery winners get used to a new level of happiness, so a given rating doesn't mean what it used to. Third, people are greedy. According to one newspaper survey, people earning $25,000 a year thought $50,000 a year would make them happy, but those earning $50,000 a year said they would need $100,000 a year, and those earning $100,000 a year wanted $200,000 (Csikszentmihalyi, 1999). Fourth, winning a lottery backfires for many people. Some lottery winners spend more than they won; many quit their jobs and lose all sense of accomplishment; and many encounter conflicts with relatives and friends who expect a share of the lottery winnings.

The overall conclusion is that many poor people are happy and many rich people are depressed. However, because of difficulties of measurement, we cannot say for sure how much influence wealth has on happiness.

CONCEPT CHECK ☑

9. According to one survey, most students in Michigan say they think they would be happier if they lived in a warmer climate, such as California, but on the average, students in California rate themselves no happier than students in Michigan (Schkade & Kahneman, 1998). How could we explain these results? (Check your answer on page 475.)

Other Influences

Considering how hard it is to measure happiness, you might be discouraged about finding anything that influences it. However, some factors do correlate fairly well. The more sloppily something is measured, the harder it is for anything else to correlate with it, so if an inaccurately measured variable does correlate with something else, the correlation *underestimates* the true strength of the relationship.

One of the strongest influences is people's temperament or personality. In one study more than 2,000 twins' ratings of happiness correlated slightly with their wealth, education, job prestige, and so forth, but in most cases either both twins were happy, both were neutral, or both were unhappy (Lykken & Tellegen, 1996). Some people tend to be gloomy and others tend to be cheerful, and most events shift the level of happiness only briefly. In other words how happy you are now is a pretty good predictor of how happy you will be years in the future (Pavot & Diener, 1993). A few major events are exceptions, however. For example, losing one's job is a major blow to life satisfaction, and many people do not fully recover (Lucas, Clark, Georgellis, & Diener, 2004). The same is true after death of a spouse and presumably other major losses.

Many aspects of life correlate somewhat with happiness or subjective well-being. In the following list, remember that in each case the link is based on a correlation, and correlations do not demonstrate causation, so alternative explanations are possible.

- Married people tend to be happier than unmarried people (DeNeve, 1999; Myers, 2000), and college students with close friendships and romantic attachments are usually happier than those without such attachments (Diener & Seligman, 2002). At least two explanations are likely. Social contacts, especially loving contacts, are helpful in many obvious ways. Lonely people are at risk for a wide variety of diseases (Cacioppo, Hawkley, & Berntson, 2003). Also, happy people are more likely than sad people to establish friendships and long-lasting love relationships. (After all, who would want a partner who is usually unhappy?)
- Happy people are more likely than unhappy people to have a goal in life, such as advancing the cause of peace and justice. The only kind of goal *not* correlated with happiness is the goal of making money (Csikszentmihalyi, 1999; Diener et al., 1999). One reason that goal does not lead to happiness is that most people who strive to be rich do not succeed! Those who do become rich are reasonably happy, but those who really care about wealth and fail to find it are decidedly unhappy (Nickerson, Schwarz, Diener, & Kahneman, 2003).
- Generally, health and happiness go together (DeNeve, 1999; Myers, 2000). It seems obvious that health improves happiness, and a happy disposition may also improve the chances of long-term health. Also, even when happy and unhappy people in fact have the same illness, the unhappy people complain more (Salovey & Birnbaum, 1989).

- People with religious faith are more likely to be happy than those without it (Myers, 2000). Again, alternative explanations are possible. Faith probably supports favorable attitudes, but in addition it is probable that happy people are more likely than unhappy people to believe that the universe follows a grand purpose.
- Happy people are more likely to trust others, to be emotionally stable, to be conscientious workers, and to enjoy being in control of a situation (DeNeve, 1999; DeNeve & Cooper, 1998). Again, you can no doubt imagine alternative explanations.

Sadness

If you ask people what makes them happy, you will get many answers, but if you ask what makes them sad, most answers fall into one pattern: People feel sad from a sense of loss. It could be death of a loved one, breakup of a romantic relationship, failure of health, or financial setbacks, but whatever someone has lost, there is little prospect of recovering it. (People who can still avoid the loss are more likely to express fear or anger.)

Crying

Severely sad people often react by crying. Just as cultures differ in their attitudes toward loud public laughter, they also differ in attitudes about adult crying. Adults in the United States cry—or at least admit to crying—far more often than those in China, for example. Women report crying more than men in each of the 30 cultures in one survey (Becht & Vingerhoets, 2002).

Many people say that crying relieves tension and makes them feel better, but the evidence says otherwise. While people are crying, sympathetic nervous system arousal and other signs of tension visibly increase. Relaxation occurs only when the person *stops* crying (Gross, Fredrickson, & Levenson, 1994). Even after they stop, they may be no more relaxed than if they had not cried at all. In one experiment one group was encouraged to cry and another was instructed to hold back their tears while watching a very sad film. Contrary to the idea that crying relieves tension, the two groups had equal tension at the end, and those who cried reported more depression (Kraemer & Hastrup, 1988). Certainly, if crying has any benefits, other than gaining the attention and sympathy of others, those benefits are not easy to demonstrate.

Crying is an interesting mystery in another regard too. Although many other species howl or whimper after an injury or during separation from their group, the shedding of tears seems to be a human specialization. Its function is not at all clear, unless it is simply to attract more attention and perhaps sympathy.

"Depressive Realism"

Presumably, we evolved the capacity to feel emotions because they are useful. The values of fear and anger, under appropriate circumstances, are obvious, but what could be the advantage of feeling sad?

One hypothesis is that sad people size up the situation realistically and act cautiously, thereby making good decisions under challenging circumstances. For example, most people overestimate how well they have done on a test, how well they will do on a future test, and how well other people like them (Robins & Beer, 2001). Sad or mildly depressed people are the exception to this rule. They tend to estimate their own performance, popularity, and so forth more accurately than others do. If anything, they slightly underestimate their own success (Stone, Dodrill, & Johnson, 2001).

People who are in a sad mood are also more likely than other people to weigh carefully the evidence before making a decision, according to most studies. For example, in one experiment students listened to two arguments concerning possible increases in student fees at their university. Students who were in a sad mood were more persuaded by the stronger, more factual argument, whereas students in a happy mood found both arguments about equally persuasive (Bless, Bohner, Schwarz, & Strack, 1990). Other studies found that students in a sad mood were more likely than others to give serious, principled explanations to their answers on Kohlberg's moral dilemmas (Chapter 10) and less likely than others to judge people according to stereotypes (Park & Banaji, 2000; Zarinpoush, Cooper, & Moylan, 2000).

Why might people in a sad mood evaluate the evidence more carefully? Perhaps the setbacks that make you feel sad also impair your self-confidence. Happy people are confident and therefore accept their first impulse. Sad people have more doubts and therefore delay making a decision until they have considered the facts more fully (Tiedens & Linton, 2001).

CONCEPT CHECK ☑

10. Does the evidence indicate that crying relieves tension?
11. What is one apparent "advantage" of feeling sad? (Check your answers on page 475.)

Fear and Anxiety

Fear and anxiety are virtually the same experience. *Fear* generally refers to the response to an immediate danger, whereas *anxiety* is a vague, long-lasting sense that "something bad might happen." Clinical psychol-ogists spend much of their time dealing with people's excessive anxieties.

Is there a "right" level of anxiety? Presumably, evolution enabled us to readjust our "anxiety thermostat" based on our experiences with danger. People who are surrounded by enemies and hazards increase their anxiety level and learn to flee at any warning.

Measuring Anxiety

Research on happiness and sadness relies heavily on self-reports. Anxiety researchers also use self-reports but in addition have a practical operational definition based on behavior: **Anxiety** is *an increase in the startle reflex*. The startle reflex is the quick, automatic response that almost any animal makes after a sudden loud noise. Within a fifth of a second after the noise, you tense your muscles, especially your neck muscles, close your eyes, and mobilize your sympathetic nervous system to prepare your body to run away if necessary. The startle reflex itself is automatic, but it can be increased or decreased by experiences and context.

For example, imagine yourself sitting with friends in a familiar place on a nice, sunny day when suddenly you hear a loud noise. You startle, but probably not very strongly. Now imagine yourself walking alone at night through a graveyard when you think you see someone walking toward you . . . and then you hear a loud noise. The noise could be the same as when sitting with friends, but your startle response will be much greater. That increase in the startle reflex is a reliable, objective measurement of your anxiety. As you would expect, the startle reflex is enhanced for people with anxiety disorders, especially posttraumatic stress disorder (Grillon, Morgan, Davis, & Southwick, 1998; Pole, Neylan, Best, Orr, & Marmar, 2003).

Learned associations can also alter the startle reflex in laboratory animals. Suppose a rat frequently sees a "danger" stimulus—say, a light—before receiving a shock. Now that danger stimulus followed by a loud noise produces a bigger than usual startle reflex to the noise. The increase in the startle reflex is taken as a measure of anxiety, and research based on this measure has identified the brain areas responsible for anxiety. The amygdala (uh-MIG-duh-luh), as shown in Figure 12.19, appears to be the key area. The figure shows a human brain, although much of the research has been conducted with rodents. For example, rats with damage to the amygdala still show a startle reflex, but a danger signal does not increase it (R. G. Phillips & LeDoux, 1992). In fact, even after many pairings of the danger signal with shock, rats with an impaired amygdala show little response of any kind to the danger signal (Schafe et al., 2000).

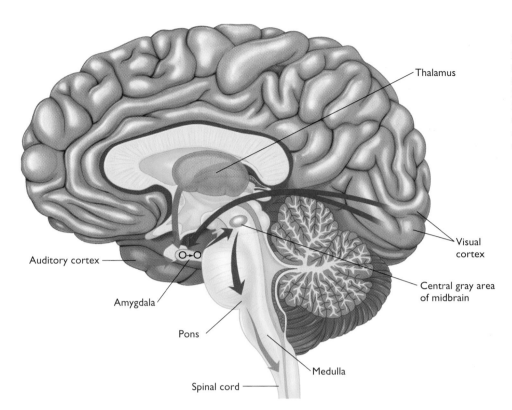

FIGURE 12.19 Structures in the pons and medulla control the startle response to a sudden loud sound. The amygdala sends information that modifies activity in the pons and medulla. This drawing is of a human brain, although the key research was conducted with rats.

People with amygdala damage report that they still feel fear and other emotions (Anderson & Phelps, 2002). However, they no longer respond quickly the way other people do to subtle or complicated signals about emotions (Baxter & Murray, 2002; Whalen, 1998). For example, they are impaired at recognizing facial expressions of emotion (Anderson & Phelps, 2000) and have trouble inferring other people's emotions from their tone of voice (Scott et al., 1997). They rate all faces about equally trustworthy (Adolphs, Tranel, & Damasio, 1998) and almost all drawings about equally attractive (Adolphs & Tranel, 1999).

CONCEPT CHECK ☑

12. What method could one use to compare anxiety levels of nonhuman animals, preverbal children, or others who cannot answer in words? (Check your answer on page 475.)

Anxiety, Arousal, and Lie Detection

Unfortunately, although most people think they know when someone is lying, most people detect lies at no better than chance rates (Etcoff, Ekman, Magee, & Frank, 2000). In one study a well-known British political commentator gave two consecutive interviews about his favorite films. In one he told the truth; in the other he lied on every question. Both interviews were broadcast on radio and television and printed in a newspaper. Members of the public were invited to guess which was the honest interview and which one was full of lies. Of the more than 41,000 people who responded, only 53% answered correctly (Wiseman, 1995). Curiously, the television viewers, who had the most information available to consider, were the least accurate.

One of the best-known methods of trying to detect lying is the **polygraph,** *an instrument that simultaneously records several indications of sympathetic nervous system arousal, such as blood pressure, heart rate, breathing rate, and electrical conduction of the skin* (Figure 12.20). (Slight sweating increases electrical conduction of the skin.) The assumption is that when people lie, they feel nervous and therefore increase their sympathetic nervous system arousal.

The polygraph sometimes accomplishes its goal simply because an accused person hooked up to a polygraph confesses, "Oh, what's the use. You're going to figure it out now anyway, so I may as well tell you. . . ." But if people do not confess, how effectively does a polygraph detect lying?

In one study investigators selected 50 criminal cases where two suspects had taken a polygraph test and one suspect had later confessed to the crime (Kleinmuntz & Szucko, 1984). Thus, they had data from 100 people who were considered equally plausible

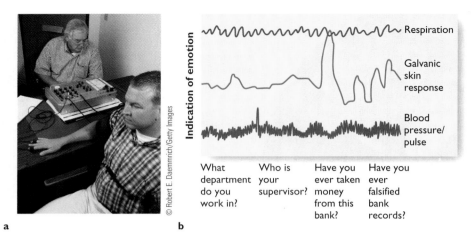

a   b

FIGURE 12.20 The polygraph, a method for detecting nervous arousal, is the basis for the so-called "lie detector" test. The polygraph operator (a) asks a series of nonthreatening questions to establish base-line readings of the subject's autonomic responses (b), and then asks questions relevant to an investigation.

suspects at the time, of whom 50 were later shown to be guilty and 50 shown to be innocent. Six professional polygraph administrators examined all the polygraph results and judged which suspects appeared to be lying. Figure 12.21 shows the results. The polygraph administrators identified 76% of the guilty suspects as liars but also classified 37% of the innocent suspects as liars.

Other research on the polygraph has produced varying results. In an ideal study, some suspects are innocent and others are guilty, all are seriously worried about being convicted, and the investigators eventually determine for certain who was guilty. Such studies are difficult, so most of the research has used much weaker

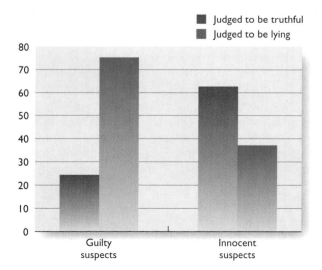

FIGURE 12.21 Polygraph examiners correctly identified 76% of guilty suspects as lying. However, they also identified 37% of innocent suspects as lying. (*Based on data of Kleinmuntz & Szucko, 1984*)

methods (Iacono & Patrick, 1999).

Although many police officers continue to believe in polygraph testing, most researchers regard the accuracy as either too low or too uncertain to make important decisions (Fiedler, Schmid, & Stahl, 2002). Therefore, polygraph results are almost never admissible as evidence in U.S. or European courts (Fiedler et al., 2002; Saxe & Ben-Shakhar, 1999). The U.S. Congress passed a law in 1988 prohibiting private employers from giving polygraph tests to employees or job applicants, except under special circumstances (Camara, 1988), and a commission of the U.S. National Academy of Sciences in 2002 concluded that polygraphs should not be used for national security clearances.

Alternative Methods of Detecting Lies

If polygraphs are unsatisfactory, what would work better? Researchers have reported that when people are nervous about telling a lie, they usually have increased blood flow to the face, thereby radiating heat that a thermal camera can detect, as shown in Figure 12.22. This technique has the advantage that it can be used without attaching any instruments to the person's body—in fact, except for laws and ethics, it could be used without even telling someone. Preliminary results suggest this procedure would work at least as accurately as a polygraph (Pavlidis, Eberhardt, & Levine, 2002). However, just doing as well as a polygraph is not a great recommendation.

The **guilty-knowledge test,** *a modified version of the polygraph test,* produces more accurate results by *asking questions that should be threatening only to someone who knows the facts of a crime that have not been publicized* (Lykken, 1979). Instead of asking, "Did you rob the gas station?" the interrogator asks, "Was the gas station robbed at 8 P.M.? At 10:30? At midnight? At 1:30 in the morning? Did the robber carry a gun? A knife? A club? Was the getaway car green? Red? Blue?" Someone who shows heightened arousal only in response to the correct details of the crime is presumed to have "guilty knowledge" that only the guilty person or someone who had talked to the guilty person would

a   b

FIGURE 12.22 Thermal images show ordinary blood flow to the face (a) and increased blood flow just after the person lied to an interviewer (b). *(Pavlidis, I., Eberhardt, N.L., and Levine, J.A., "Seeing through the face of deception," Nature, 415, 35. Reprinted with permission.)*

possess. The guilty-knowledge test, when properly administered, identifies most guilty people and only rarely classifies an innocent person as guilty (Iacono & Patrick, 1999).

CRITICAL THINKING:
A STEP FURTHER
The Guilty-Knowledge Test

How might the results of the guilty-knowledge test be biased by a questioner who knows the correct details of the crime? How should the test be administered to minimize that bias?

Another approach is to avoid technology and simply improve the way we observe others. Paul Ekman (2001) conducted extensive research to see how people react when they are lying. For example, he asked people to watch either a pleasant movie or a disturbing documentary about burns and amputations and then, regardless of the content of the movie, to say they found the movie pleasant. So they all said the same words, but some were lying. Based on this and similar designs, Ekman found that people who are lying usually try to maintain a calm, happy expression but occasionally show microexpressions (brief involuntary emotional expressions), such as slight expressions of fear or a brief, partial shrug of the shoulders.

One final comment: Note that all these methods of detecting lying, from the polygraph to microexpressions, assume that the person is nervous about lying or getting caught. They work poorly with experienced, confident liars or people who have come to believe their own lies.

CONCEPT CHECK ☑

13. What does a polygraph measure?
14. What is the main objection to polygraph tests? (Check your answers on page 475.)

Anger and Aggressive Behavior

During World War II, nearly all the industrialized nations were at war, the Nazis were exterminating the Jews, and the United States was preparing a nuclear bomb that it later dropped on Japan. Meanwhile, Mohandas K. Gandhi was in jail for leading a nonviolent protest march against British rule in India. The charge against Gandhi was, ironically, "disturbing the peace." Someone asked Gandhi what he thought of Western civilization. He replied that he thought it might be a good idea.

Human beings are capable of ghastly acts of cruelty, but also of nobility, heroism, and courageous opposition to violence. The struggle to understand violence is among the most important goals facing humanity in general and psychology in particular.

Relationship of Anger to Aggression

Anger is an emotion associated with a desire to harm someone or drive that person away. Aggressive behavior is easy to observe in nonhuman animals—or in little boys on a playground—but most adults learn to restrain their physical aggression. Surveys across a variety of cultures have found that people experience anger frequently but seldom even consider striking anyone (Ramirez, Santisteban, Fujihara, & Van Goozen, 2002).

Participants in one study kept an "anger diary" for a week (Averill, 1983). A typical entry was, "My roommate locked me out of the room when I went to the shower." They also described how they reacted, such as, "I talked to my roommate about it," or "I did nothing about it." Very few admitted to threatening violence, much less actually attacking.

Causes of Anger

According to the **frustration-aggression hypothesis,** *the main cause of anger (and therefore aggression) is frustration—an obstacle that stands in the way of doing something or obtaining some expected reinforcer* (Dollard, Miller, Doob, Mowrer, & Sears, 1939). Many instances of anger easily fit this description. However, frustration makes you angry only when you believe the other person acted intentionally. For example, you might feel angry at someone who ran down the hall and bumped into you but probably not at someone who slipped on a wet spot and bumped into you.

Leonard Berkowitz (1983, 1989) proposed a more comprehensive theory: Any unpleasant event—frustration, pain, heat, foul odors, bad news, whatever—excites both the impulse to fight and the impulse to flee. That is, it excites the sympathetic nervous system and its fight-or-flight response. Your choice between fight and flight depends on the circumstances, especially the expected result of attacking. If you have won many fights, have seldom been punished, and think the person who just spilled coffee on you looks easy to beat, you may threaten or even strike. If you think you have little chance of winning a fight, you suppress your anger. And if the one who bumped into you is your boss or the loan and scholarship officer at your college, you smile and apologize for being in the way.

Many people make threatening gestures and shout angry insults while driving. Two explanations stand out: First, frustrations are common; other drivers block you from reaching your destination. Second, the probability of retaliation is low. You can threaten without much risk of harm.

Individual Differences in Anger and Aggression

Why are some people angry or aggressive more often than others? One hypothesis that used to be popular was that low self-esteem led to violence. According to this idea, people who thought little of themselves tried to build themselves up by tearing someone else down. Perhaps that hypothesis works in certain cases of group violence. Some outbreaks of ethnic violence have occurred when one group suffered defeats and humiliations and then blamed another group for their problems (Staub, 1996).

For individuals, however, the research finds little link between violence and low self-esteem. *Victims* certainly report low self-esteem, but aggressors tend to be arrogant, egotistical, and self-confident. One study found that most aggressive children believe they are very popular among their classmates (David & Kistner, 2000). (Many were wrong in that belief.) At most it may be that violence results when something threatens someone's high self-esteem, and that person then strikes out against someone to reaffirm a sense of superiority (Baumeister, Smart, & Boden, 1996).

Another hypothesis not consistently supported is any strong link between violence and mental illness. Drug and alcohol abuse are highly associated with violence, and many mental patients abuse alcohol or other drugs. However, those without drug or alcohol abuse are, on the average, no more likely than other people to be violent (Hodgins, Mednick, Brennan, Schulsinger, & Engberg, 1996).

If low self-esteem and mental illness do not predict violence, what does? Genetic factors make some contribution, as to almost anything in behavior. Studies of twins and adopted children imply that genetic factors account for about 40% of the variance in aggressive and criminal behaviors (Rhee & Waldman, 2002). However, researchers do not know the route by which any genes act, and no one gene by itself appears to be decisive.

People who were physically abused as children and who witnessed violence between their parents are more likely than others to commit repeated acts of violence, including murder (Malinosky-Rummell & Hansen, 1993). The physical pain of being beaten may provoke future violence, and a violent parent provides a model for the child to imitate. (Recall the principles of social learning from Chapter 6.) Even this predictor is far from foolproof, however; only about one third of abused children become abusive parents (Widom, 1989).

Several other factors are associated with a tendency toward violent behavior (Davidson, Putnam, & Larson, 2000; Lewis et al., 1985; Lynam, 1996; Osofsky, 1995; Raine, Lencz, Bihrle, LaCasse, & Colletti, 2000):

- Growing up in a violent neighborhood
- Not feeling guilty after hurting someone
- Weaker-than-normal physiological responses to arousal
- Smaller-than-average prefrontal cortex and decreased release of serotonin to this area
- A history of suicide attempts
- Frequently watching violence on television

Also, two studies have found that the more cigarettes a woman smoked during pregnancy, the greater the probability that her son would be arrested for violent crimes in adolescence or early adulthood, especially if the woman also had complications during delivery (Brennan, Grekin, & Mednick, 1999; Fergusson, Woodward, & Horwood, 1998). Figure 12.23 shows the link between smoking in pregnancy and violent crimes by the woman's son decades later. These are correlational data, so as always we should beware of cause-and-effect conclusions. Some women who smoked during pregnancy may have provided poor care for their sons after birth (Silberg et al., 2003).

FIGURE 12.23 The more cigarettes the mother of a male baby smoked during pregnancy, the more likely her son was to be arrested for a crime during late adolescence or early adulthood. The top graph shows results for all women; the bottom graph shows only those women who also had complications during delivery. *(From "Maternal Smoking During Pregnancy and Adult Male Criminal Outcomes," by P. A. Brennan, E. R. Grekin, and S. A. Mednick,* Archives of General Psychiatry, *1999, 56, 215–219. Copyright © 1999 American Medical Association. Reprinted by permission.)*

If a psychologist wants to predict how violent someone will be—perhaps to make recommendations to a court about sentencing—the best predictor of future behavior is past behavior. People with a long history of violent acts are likely to commit more, whereas those who committed only a single violent act are less dangerous. Someone's history of violence is far from a perfect predictor of future behavior, but it is the best predictor we have (Borum, 1996; Grisso & Tomkins, 1996; Monahan & Steadman, 1996).

CONCEPT CHECK ✓

15. Is low self-esteem a good predictor of violent behavior? Is mental illness? What is? (Check your answers on page 475.)

Sexual Aggression and Violence in Relationships

Most acts of violence occur between people who know each other well, including romantic couples. A review of the extensive research within heterosexual couples reported that women commit *more* acts of violence against men than men do against women (Archer, 2000). Almost everyone finds that result surprising. After all, we have heard of battered women's clinics but not battered men's clinics. The explanation is that most of the researchers defined violence to include slaps, pushes, and other minor acts. Men commit more serious attacks, inflict more injuries, and are certainly more likely to kill their partners than women are. Ordinarily, the men who most frequently and severely attack their romantic partners have a long history of criminal and violent behavior toward other people as well (Holtzworth-Munroe, 2000).

Rape is *sexual activity without the consent of the partner.* It of course includes cases in which a stranger grabs a woman and uses violence or threats of violence to force her into submission. However, rape also includes cases in which someone was unable to resist because of the influence of alcohol or other drugs. In one survey about 10% of adult women reported that they had been forcibly raped, and another 10% said they had involuntary sex while incapacitated by alcohol or other drugs (Testa, Livingston, Vanzile-Tamsen, & Frone, 2003). However, the statistics vary considerably from one study to another. Recall from Chapter 2 that slight changes in the wording of a survey question can enormously influence people's answers. Surveys that ask about "unwanted" sex report very high numbers because many people interpret "unwanted" to include unexpected, unplanned events or times when one person wasn't in the mood but agreed to sex to please a partner (Hamby & Koss, 2003). Not only most women but also most men say they have sometimes had sex when they did not want to (Struckman-Johnson, Struckman-Johnson, & Anderson, 2003).

However, even with a narrowly worded definition, surveys find rape to be far more widespread than the crime statistics indicate. Of all sexual assaults that would legally qualify as rape, only about half the victims call the experience rape, and far fewer report the event to the police (Fisher, Daigle, Cullen, & Turner, 2003). Generally, women who had involuntary sex with a boyfriend or other acquaintance were unlikely to call the event rape, especially if alcohol was involved (Kahn, Jackson, Kully, Badger, & Halvorsen, 2003). In some cases the man does not even realize that the woman considered his behavior abusive.

What kind of man commits rape? Most who commit violent rape have a history of other violent acts against both men and women (Hanson, 2000). Unlike most other men, rapists find the idea of forcible sex appealing and are likely to enjoy violent pornography (Donnerstein & Malamuth, 1997). That is, they display hostility toward women. One survey of admitted "date rapists" or "acquaintance rapists" found that they too reported anger against women and a wish to dominate them (Lisak & Roth, 1988).

Another element in rape is extreme self-centeredness, or lack of concern for others (Dean & Malamuth, 1997). Also, sexually aggressive men tend not to believe women who say they do not want to have sex (Malamuth & Brown, 1994).

Controlling Anger and Violence

Animals that live in social groups cannot let two individuals continue to fight. If two male birds fight during the breeding season, one can drive the other out of his territory, but if two members of a chimpanzee troop fight, they try to patch up their relationship afterward, and if they don't, another chimpanzee drags them together (de Waal, 2000). After one of these reconciliation ceremonies, they become less likely to fight. People also frequently reconcile with each other after a fight, especially if they know they will continue to see each other or work together.

If someone too frequently gets angry at others, psychologists have worked out methods of **anger management training,** *which are techniques for decreasing or restraining displays of anger.* Typical methods include relaxation, distraction, improved communication with others, and learning to reinterpret other people's actions as less threatening or insulting (Dahlen & Deffenbacher, 2001).

CONCEPT CHECK ☑

16. Psychologists often study the causes of aggression by putting one person at a time in a laboratory and testing the effects of some experience on that person's willingness to flip a switch that supposedly shocks another person. Which aspect of aggression will that procedure probably overlook? (Check your answer on page 475.)

Other Emotions

As mentioned in the previous module, psychologists have no consensus on how many types of emotion people have. Indeed, they may not form an enumerable list. We can list all the elements of chemistry, but not everything comes in distinct elements. Here, very briefly, let us consider a few other important emotional experiences.

Many psychologists list surprise among the emotions. It occurs when events do not match expectations. However, frankly, it is hard to say much more. Almost no research or theory has focused on surprise as an emotion.

Anger, disgust, and contempt are reactions to different kinds of offenses. Anger occurs when someone interferes with your rights or expectations. Disgust is literally *dis* (bad) + *gust* (taste). In the English language, we use the term loosely to refer to almost anything displeasing (Royzman & Sabini, 2001), but narrowly speaking, **disgust** refers to *a reaction to something that would make you feel contaminated if it got into your mouth* (Rozin, Lowery, et al., 1999). For most people the idea of eating feces or insects is highly disgusting. In contrast **contempt** is *a reaction to a violation of community standards,* such as our reaction when someone fails to do a fair share of the work or claims credit for something that another person did (Rozin, Lowery, et al., 1999).

Embarrassment, shame, guilt, and pride are regarded as "self-conscious" emotions because they occur when you think about how other people regard you or might regard you if they knew what you had done. The distinctions among embarrassment, shame, and guilt are not sharp, and different cultures draw the distinctions in different ways. For example, the Japanese use a word we translate as *shame* far more often than the word we translate as *embarrassment* (Imahori & Cupach, 1994). For English speakers most causes of **embarrassment** fall into three categories (Sabini, Siepmann, Stein, & Meyerowitz, 2000):

- *mistakes,* such as wearing casual clothes to a formal event or thinking someone was flirting with you when in fact they were flirting with the person right behind you.
- *being the center of attention,* such as having people sing "Happy Birthday" to you.
- *sticky situations,* such as having to ask someone for a major favor.

Sometimes people also feel embarrassed out of sympathy for someone else who is in an embarrassing situation (Shearn, Spellman, Straley, Meirick, & Stryker, 1999). Simply imagining how the other person feels causes you embarrassment too.

Emotions and the Richness of Life

We try to feel happy as much as possible and try to avoid feeling sad, angry, or frightened, right? Well, usually, but not entirely. People voluntarily go to movies that they know will make them sad. They ride roller coasters that advertise how scary they are. Some people seem to enjoy being angry. Alcoholics and drug abusers experience wild swings of emotion, and many who quit say that although life is better since they quit, they miss the emotional swings. Mostly they miss the highs, but to some extent they miss the low spots too.

Obviously, there are limits. Severe sadness (depression) and severe fear (panic) are miserable experiences to be avoided as much as possible. The point is that all of our emotions, within limits, provide richness to our experiences.

Summary

- *Happiness and joy.* Most studies of happiness rely on questionnaires and self-ratings. Unfortunately, a given rating may mean something different to one person than another, so it is hard to compare one person's happiness to another's. Happiness level appears to be a fairly stable aspect of personality despite changes in people's lives. (page 465)

- *Sadness.* Sadness is a reaction to a loss. Crying is a way of communicating sadness or distress to others. (page 467)

- *"Depressive realism."* Whereas most people are overconfident of their own success and popularity, sad people tend to be more accurate. They also tend to evaluate evidence more patiently before making a decision. (page 468)

- *Fear and anxiety.* Anxiety can be measured objectively by variations in the startle reflex after a loud noise. Processing of emotional information, including that related to anxiety, depends on a brain area called the amygdala. (page 468)

- *Polygraph.* The polygraph measures the activity of the sympathetic nervous system through such variables as heart rate, breathing rate, blood pressure, and electrical conductance of the skin. The polygraph is sometimes used as a "lie detector." However, because the responses of honest people overlap those of liars, the polygraph makes many mistakes. (page 469)

- *Anger.* People experience anger frequently, although it seldom leads to violence. Anger arises when we perceive that someone has done something intentionally that blocks our intended actions. A situation can evoke either anger or fear depending on the probable consequences of fighting or fleeing. (page 471)

- *Individual differences in anger and aggression.* Many factors correlate with violence, including genetic predisposition, drug and alcohol abuse, living in a violent neighborhood, a history of being abused as a child, several physiological indicators, and having a mother who smoked heavily during pregnancy. The best predictor of future violent behavior is previous violent behavior. (page 472)

- *Other emotions.* Anger, disgust, and contempt are reactions to different types of offenses. Embarrassment, shame, guilt, and pride arise in social contexts based on how we believe others will react to our actions. (page 474)

Answers to Concept Checks

9. One possibility is that climate makes less difference to people's happiness than they think it will. The other is that students in each state rate themselves compared to how happy they usually are or think they could be. (page 466)
10. No. While people are crying, they have increased signs of tension. Even after they stop, their tension is no lower than normal, and they may report feeling worse than those who suppressed crying. (page 468)
11. In some regards sad people are more realistic and more likely to consider evidence slowly and carefully before making a decision. (page 468)
12. One could measure the strength of the startle reflex. (page 469)
13. The polygraph measures several aspects of sympathetic nervous system activity, such as heart rate, breathing rate, and sweating. (page 471)
14. A polygraph will too often identify an innocent person as lying. (page 471)
15. The best predictor of violent behavior is the person's history of previous violent behavior. Low self-esteem is not a good predictor, and neither is mental illness. (page 473)
16. It would overlook reconciliation. (page 474)

Stress, Coping, and Health

What is stress and how does it affect health?

How can we learn to deal more effectively with stress?

Imagine you meet a man suffering from, say, multiple sclerosis. Would you say, "It's his own fault he's sick; he's being punished for his sins"? I presume not. However, many people in previous times believed just that. We congratulate ourselves today on having learned not to blame the victim.

Or have we? We think that cigarette smokers are at least partly at fault if they develop lung cancer. We note that AIDS is usually contracted by people with a history of intravenous drug use or unsafe sex. If women drink alcohol during pregnancy, we hold them partly responsible if their infants have deformities or mental retardation. As we learn more and more about the causes of various illnesses, we expect people to accept more responsibility for their own health.

However, we can easily overstate how much people's behavior influences their health. Even if you are as careful as possible about your diet, exercise regularly, and have healthy habits, you could become ill anyway. **Health psychology** *is concerned with how people's behavior can enhance health and prevent illness and how behavior contributes to recovery from illness.* It deals with such issues as why people smoke, why they sometimes ignore their physician's advice, and how to reduce pain. In this module we focus on stress, methods of coping with stress, and the effects of stress on health.

Stress

Have you ever gone without sleep several nights in a row trying to meet a deadline? Or waited in a dangerous area for someone who was supposed to pick you up? Or had a close friend suddenly not want to see you anymore? Or tried to explain why you no longer want to date someone? An enormous variety of experiences can cause stress.

Selye's Concept of Stress

According to Hans Selye (1979), an Austrian-born physician who worked at McGill University in Montreal, **stress** is *the nonspecific response of the body to any demand made upon it.* Every demand on the body evokes certain specific responses as well. The body responds in one way to the loss of blood and in another way to the lack of sleep. But all demands on the body evoke generalized re-

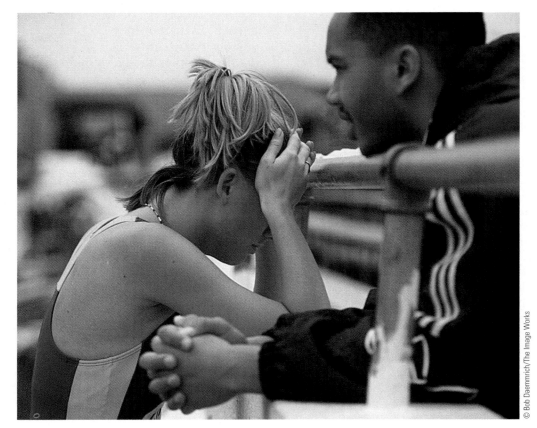

▮ Our emotions affect physiological processes and thereby influence health.

476

sponses such as increased response of the sympathetic nervous system, increased release of the hormone epinephrine, and impaired concentration.

When people say, "I've been under a lot of stress lately," they usually refer to unpleasant experiences. Selye's concept of stress is broader, including any experience that brings about change in a person's life. For example, getting married and being promoted are presumably pleasant experiences, but they also require changes in your life, so in Selye's sense they produce stress. Note, however, that by Selye's definition, the effects of poverty, racism, or a lifelong disability would *not* count as a stress because they are unchanging over time. In that sense Selye's definition is too limited. For example, the experience of African Americans of being insulted, avoided, excluded from opportunities, and so on certainly appears to be stressful, and it aggravates the medical problems associated with stress (Clark, Anderson, Clark, & Williams, 1999; Contrada et al., 2000).

Selye believed that the body goes through three stages in its response to a stressor: The first is **alarm**, *a brief period of high arousal of the sympathetic nervous system, readying the body for vigorous activity.* Some stressors last longer than the body can maintain this high state of arousal, however. If you have a high-stress job or live near the runway of a busy airport, you cannot overcome your problem with a brief burst of intense activity. You enter **resistance**, *a stage of prolonged but moderate arousal.* Your epinephrine levels remain high day after day, week after week. Your adrenal cortex secretes cortisol, a hormone that elevates blood sugar and enhances metabolism. The increased fuel supply to the cells enables them to sustain a high, steady level of activity to endure prolonged stress. However, you no longer feel ready for vigorous activity; you feel withdrawn and inactive much of the time, your performance deteriorates, and you complain of a decreased quality of life (Evans, Bullinger, & Hygge, 1998). The body often treats prolonged, inescapable problems the same way it treats an illness: You develop a fever, sleep more, eat less, and lose much of your sex drive (Maier & Watkins, 1988). Also, the elevated cortisol level impairs memory retrieval (deQuervain, Roozendaal, Nitsch, McGaugh, & Hock, 2000).

With even more intense and long-lasting stress, the body enters the third stage, **exhaustion**. *As cortisol and other hormones shift energy toward increasing blood sugar and metabolism, they shift it away from synthesis of proteins, including the proteins necessary for the immune system.* In the short term, that shift may not be a problem; however, severe stress over months can leave an individual vulnerable to a variety of illnesses (S. Cohen, 1996). The end result is characterized by weakness, fatigue, loss of appetite, and a general lack of interest.

CONCEPT CHECK ✓

17. According to Selye's definition of stress, would getting married be stressful? Would constant quarreling with your family be stressful? (Check your answers on page 485.)

Posttraumatic Stress Disorder

A profound result of severe stress is **posttraumatic stress disorder (PTSD)**. *People who have endured extreme stress feel prolonged anxiety and depression.* This condition has been recognized in postwar periods throughout history and given such names as "battle fatigue" or "shell shock." It also occurs in rape or assault victims, torture victims, survivors of an airplane crash or a severe automobile crash, and witnesses to a murder.

People with posttraumatic stress disorder suffer from frequent nightmares, outbursts of anger, unhappiness, and guilt. A brief reminder of the tragic experience can trigger a flashback that borders on panic. Mild problems seem unduly stressful, even years after the original event (Solomon, Mikulincer, & Flum, 1988).

However, most people who suffer severely traumatic events do not develop PTSD. Most suffer badly for the first few weeks and then gradually recover (McFarlane, 1997). Many psychologists have assumed that the more intense the initial reaction to a stressful event, the more likely the person is to develop PTSD. If so, then an immediate intervention, such as talking to a therapist right after a traumatic event, should help reduce the likelihood of PTSD. However, although this idea sounds reasonable, the evidence does not support it. The intensity of someone's response in the first week or so after a trauma is a poor predictor of PTSD (Harvey & Bryant, 2002), and most studies find that talking to a therapist right after a traumatic event has no measurable effect on the development of PTSD (McNally, Bryant, & Ehlers, 2003).

One possibility is that some people are simply more vulnerable than others. Most PTSD victims have a smaller than average hippocampus, and their brains differ on the average from those of other people in several other ways (Stein, Hanna, Koverola, Torchia, & McClarty, 1997; Yehuda, 1997). At first the results were ambiguous as to whether these brain abnormalities were causes or results of PTSD. However, one study compared identical male twins in which one twin had developed PTSD after combat experiences in war and the other had not been in battle and had not developed PTSD. The results: The more severe the symptoms of

PTSD, the smaller the hippocampus of *both* the twin with PTSD and the twin without it (Gilbertson et al., 2002). These results imply that the hippocampus was already small before the combat trauma, perhaps for genetic reasons. In other words some people are more vulnerable than others to PTSD.

Measuring Stress

Most investigators agree that severe stress can endanger a person's health. For example, people have increased risk of both major and minor illnesses during the months just after the death of a husband or wife (Hugoson, Ljungquist, & Breivik, 2002; Lillberg et al., 2003). People also report increased illness during periods of job stress, academic stress, and so forth.

How much stress is injurious to one's health? Is it true that the more stress a person experiences, the more that person's health suffers? To answer such questions, we need to measure both stress and health. Measuring health is difficult enough; measuring stress is harder yet. One approach is to give people a checklist of presumably stressful experiences. For example, the Social Readjustment Rating Scale lists 43 life-change events (Holmes & Rahe, 1967). The authors of this test asked a group of people to rate how stressful each event would be, and on that basis they assigned each event a certain number of points, such as 100 for death of a spouse and 11 for a traffic ticket. If you answered this questionnaire, you would check each event you have experienced recently, and then the psychologist administering the test would total your points to determine how stressful your life has been.

A later revision of this checklist changed and clarified many of these items (Hobson et al., 1998; Hobson & Delunas, 2001). However, checklists of this sort have serious problems. One is the assumption that a series of small stressors adds to the same as one large stressor. For example, graduating from college, getting unexpected money, moving to a new address, and starting a new job are all considered stressors worth a moderate number of points each. Combined, those four constitute almost twice as many points as you would get from a divorce. That assumption has not been tested, but it appears implausible. Another problem is the ambiguity of many items. You can get 44 points for "change in health of a family member." You would certainly check that item if you discovered that your 5-year-old son or daughter had diabetes and 44 points would underestimate your stress. Might someone else check that item because his aunt, whom he seldom sees, recovered nicely from a bout of influenza?

Moreover, a given event has different meanings for different people depending on how they interpret the event and what they can do about it (Lazarus, 1977). Becoming pregnant is not equally stressful to a 27-year-old married woman as to an unmarried 16-year-old. Losing a job may be a disaster to a 50-year-old, a minor annoyance to a 17-year-old with a summer job, and a nonevent for an actor who works in many plays each year and never expects any one of them to last long.

According to Lazarus (1977) *a stressful situation is one that someone regards as threatening and as possibly exceeding his or her resources* (see Figure 12.24). For example, if a snake bites you, you might remain calm if you recognize the snake as nonpoisonous. If your boss criticizes your work, you might shrug off the insult if you know your boss had reason to be in a bad mood.

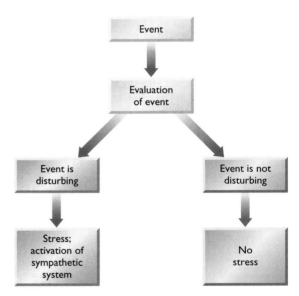

FIGURE 12.24 Lazarus stated that evaluation of some kind, conscious or unconscious, always precedes emotion. Thus, a given event can be highly stressful for one person yet only slightly stressful or not at all for someone else.

People can learn to deal with events actively instead of feeling threatened by them. Given this view the proper measure of stress would include not only the unpleasant events ("hassles") that we have to deal with but also the pleasant events ("uplifts") that brighten our day and help to cancel out the unpleasant events (Kanner, Coyne, Schaefer, & Lazarus, 1981). Table 12.1 presents one example of this approach. Given that the stressfulness of an event depends on our interpretation of the event, the best way to measure someone's stress is through a careful, well-structured interview that can evaluate all the pluses and minuses in someone's life (Brown, 1989).

TABLE 12.1   Ten Most Frequent Hassles and Uplifts

Hassles	Uplifts
1. Concerns about weight	1. Relating well with your spouse or lover
2. Health of a family member	2. Relating well with friends
3. Rising prices of common goods	3. Completing task
4. Home maintenance	4. Feeling healthy
5. Too many things to do	5. Getting enough sleep
6. Misplacing or losing things	6. Eating out
7. Yard work or outside home maintenance	7. Meeting your responsibilities
8. Property, investment, or taxes	8. Visiting, phoning, or writing someone
9. Crime	9. Spending time with family
10. Physical appearance	10. Home (inside) pleasing to you

Source: Adapted from "Comparison of Two Modes of Stress Measurement: Daily Hassles and Uplifts Versus Major Life Events," by A. D. Kanner, J. C. Coyne, C. Schaefer, and R. S. Lazarus, *Journal of Behavioral Medicine*, 1981, *4*, 14. Copyright © 1981 Plenum Publishing Corporation. Reprinted by permission.

CONCEPT CHECK

18. Why are checklists an unsatisfactory way to measure stress? (Check your answer on page 485.)

are devastated by minor setbacks. Coping with stress is the process of developing ways to decrease its effects and to get through difficult tasks despite the stress.

People cope with stress in many ways. Most coping methods can be grouped into two categories. One category is **problem-based coping** (or **monitoring**), *in which people attend carefully to the stressful event and try to take effective actions.* The other category is **emotion-based coping** (or **blunting**), *in which people try to weaken their emotional reaction.* For example, if you are nervous about an upcoming test, studying harder for it would be a problem-based method of coping, whereas deep breathing exercises would be an emotion-based method. The problem-based methods are generally more effective (Gross, 2001), but if you are dealing with problems beyond your control, emotion-based methods are the only choice.

The distinction is not a firm one, however (Skinner, Edge, Altman, & Sherwood, 2003). For example, one way of coping is to seek help and support from friends. Their support helps calm emotions (emotion-based) but also may help deal with the problem itself (problem-based). Actually, *giving* social support to others improves health even more than getting it (Brown, Nesse, Vinokur, & Smith, 2003). Various other coping techniques also blur the distinction between problem-based and emotion-based.

Coping with Stress

How you react to an event depends not only on the event itself but also on how you interpret it (Frijda, 1988; Lazarus, Averill, & Opton, 1970). Was it better or worse than you had expected? Better or worse than what happened to other people? Was it a one-time event or the start of a trend? How you feel about an event also depends on your personality. Some people manage to keep their spirits high even in the face of tragedy; others

© Wally Macnamee/CORBIS

▌ The stressfulness of an event depends on how we interpret it. For example, most people would be delighted to finish second or third in an Olympic event, but someone who was expecting to finish first may consider any lesser result a defeat.

❚ People who devote a short time each day to deliberate relaxation report diminished stress. Exercise can work off excess energy, allowing greater relaxation.

Problem-Based (Monitoring) Strategies

Gaining any sense of control over a situation makes it less stressful. Consider two hypothetical situations. First, imagine that some torturer is keeping you awake 24 hours per day. You have no way of escaping and no way of knowing how long the torture will last, but in fact it lasts 3 days until someone liberates you. Contrast that experience with an experiment in which you agree to go without sleep for 3 days. You could quit if you wanted, but in fact you don't.

Another comparison: A huge snowstorm has trapped you in a small cabin. You have enough food and fuel, but you have no idea how long you will be stuck. The snow melts 5 days later, enabling you to leave. Contrast a case where you decide to isolate yourself in a cabin for 5 days so you can finish a painting.

In both cases the physical circumstances are the same—3 days without sleep or 5 days without leaving a cabin. But if you are doing something voluntarily, you know what to expect, you know that you can quit, and there is much less stress.

When hospital patients or nursing-home residents are told what to expect and are given the chance to make some decisions for themselves, they feel better, their alertness and memory improve, and on the average they live longer (Rodin, 1986; D. H. Shapiro, Schwartz, & Astin, 1996). Many people find that religious faith helps them to cope with stress by giving them some sense of control over matters that are otherwise uncontrollable.

Why does a predictable or controllable event produce less stress than an unpredictable or uncontrollable event? One reason is that we fear an unpredictable, uncontrollable event may grow so intense that it will eventually become unbearable. If we have some control, we tell ourselves that we can do something if the situation becomes unbearable. A second reason is that, when an event is predictable, we can prepare for it at the appropriate time and relax at other times.

People can gain a sense of control over a future problem by rehearsing it in their imagination. For example, you might imagine what someone else might say or do and then what you might say or do in response (Sanna, 2000). Of course, the better you can predict the situation, the more easily you can rehearse your responses to it.

Many self-help books advise you to "visualize yourself succeeding" at something. The research says that visualizing yourself getting good grades, winning a prize, or receiving honors does little or no good. What does help is to visualize yourself doing the work that will achieve the prize. You might visualize yourself performing some athletic feat because visualizing the act is a kind of practice. As a student you might visualize yourself studying in the library or writing a long research paper. By imagining the work, you get started on it sooner, organize your time better, and finish sooner (S. E. Taylor, Pham, Rivkin, & Armor, 1998). You also gain a feeling of control, which makes the task less stressful.

CONCEPT CHECK ☑️

19. Which would disrupt your studying more, your own radio or your roommate's radio? Why? (Check your answers on page 485.)

A stressful experience is less disturbing if you know what to expect, but it is hard to know what to expect if you have not been through the experience before. Sometimes a good solution is to get a small-scale preview of a stressful experience that you may face later. In other words you can "inoculate" or immunize yourself against stressful experiences.

One way to **inoculate** yourself against stressful events is *by exposing yourself to small amounts of such events beforehand* (Janis, 1983; Meichenbaum, 1985; Meichenbaum & Cameron, 1983). For example,

Practicing self-defense serves as a kind of inoculation against fear. The thought of being attacked is less frightening when we have some idea of how to handle a situation.

many armies have soldiers practice combat skills under realistic conditions, even under actual gunfire. Another way is through role-playing. A police trainee might pretend to intervene while two people act like a husband and wife having a violent quarrel. If you are nervous about going to your landlord with a complaint, you might get a friend to play the part of the landlord and then practice what you plan to say.

Inoculation has proved successful with young people suffering from "dating anxiety." Some young people are so nervous about saying or doing the wrong thing that they avoid all opportunities to go out on a date. By means of role-playing, they can practice dating behaviors with assigned partners and thus feel less apprehensive about dating (Jaremko, 1983).

CONCEPT CHECK ☑

20. Suppose you are nervous about giving a speech before a group of 200 strangers. How could you inoculate yourself to reduce the stress? (Check your answer on page 485.)

Emotion-Based (Blunting) Strategies

Emotion-based strategies do not attempt to solve the underlying problems, but they help us manage our reactions to them. Four common examples are reinterpretation, relaxation, exercise, and distraction.

To reinterpret the situation is to find a different meaning. For example, when people look at a series of pictures of injured people, they ordinarily find them very upsetting. However, some tell themselves, "This soldier's battle is over and now he will get medical help," or "Someone will come to comfort this crying child." Seeing the photos in a hopeful light decreases the tension (Jackson, Malmstadt, Larson, & Davidson, 2000). Similarly, many religious people tell themselves that even tragic events are part of God's plan, and in the process they calm their tensions.

Relaxation is another emotion-based coping method. Sometimes people have a real problem, such as an impending medical operation, that they cannot control. At other times they get nervous even when they have no real problem (Manuck, Cohen, Rabin, Muldoon, & Bachen, 1991). In such situations it is helpful to try to relax. Here are some suggestions (Benson, 1985):

- Find a quiet place. Do not insist on absolute silence; just find a spot where the noise is least disturbing.
- Adopt a comfortable position, relaxing your muscles. If you are not sure how to do so, start with the opposite: *Tense* all your muscles so you become fully aware of how they feel. Then relax them one by one, starting from your toes and working systematically toward your head.
- Reduce sources of stimulation, including your own thoughts. Focus your eyes on a simple, unexciting object. Or repeat something over and over—a sentence, a phrase, a prayer, perhaps the Hindu syllable *om*—whatever feels comfortable to you.
- Don't worry about anything, not even about relaxing. If worrisome thoughts keep popping into your head, dismiss them with "oh, well."

Some people call this practice meditation. People who practice this technique report that they feel less stress. Many of them improve their overall health (Benson, 1977, 1985). One study found that people who went through a 12-week meditation program had a long-lasting decrease in anxiety and depression, as compared with a control group who spent the same amount of time listening to lectures about how to reduce stress (Sheppard, Staggers, & John, 1997).

Exercise also can help to reduce stress. It may seem contradictory to say that both relaxation and exercise reduce stress, but exercise does help people relax. Suppose you are tense about something that you have to do tomorrow. Your sympathetic nervous system becomes highly aroused, but you cannot actually do anything. Under those conditions your best approach may be to work off some excess energy through exercise and then relax afterward.

Also, people in good physical condition react less strongly than other people do to stressful events (Crews & Landers, 1987). An event that would elevate the heart rate enormously in other people elevates it only moderately in a person who has been exercising regularly.

A fourth powerful blunting strategy is distraction (Cioffi, 1991). For example, many people find that they can reduce dental or postsurgical pain by playing video games or by watching comedies on television. The Lamaze method teaches pregnant women to suppress the pain of childbirth by concentrating on breathing exercises. Hospitalized patients can handle their pain better if they can distract themselves with a view or pleasant music (Fauerbach, Lawrence, Haythornthwaite, & Richter, 2002). Many people report that they distract themselves from stressful events by going shopping (Hama, 2001).

The effectiveness of distraction depends partly on people's expectations. In one experiment college students were asked to hold their fingers in ice water until the sensation became too painful to endure (Melzack, Weisz, & Sprague, 1963). Some of them listened to music of their own choice and were told that listening to music would lessen the pain. Others also listened to music but were given no suggestion that it would ease the pain. Still others heard nothing but were told that a special "ultrasonic sound" was being transmitted that would lessen the pain. The group that heard music and expected it to lessen the pain tolerated the pain better than either of the other two groups. Evidently, neither the music nor the suggestion of reduced pain is as effective as both are together.

CONCEPT CHECK ☑

21. What is the difference between monitoring strategies and blunting strategies? (Check your answer on page 485.)

CRITICAL THINKING:
A STEP FURTHER
Placebos

Many experiments report that a placebo alone serves as an effective painkiller for certain patients. Why might that be true?

Stress and Illness

When stress persists or coping methods fail, the result is increased risk of illness. A **psychosomatic illness** is not imagined or pretended. Rather, it is *an illness that is influenced by someone's experiences—particularly stressful experiences—and by his or her reactions to those experiences.* That is, something about the per-

son's behavior or way of life influenced the onset and progression of the disease. Most illnesses are partly psychosomatic in this sense.

Researchers do not assume that emotions lead directly to illness. One possible route is that people with emotional difficulties are likely to overeat, smoke, have unsafe sex, and so forth. Also, prolonged stressful experiences can damage the immune system and increase a person's vulnerability to a variety of disorders, ranging from minor infections to cancer (Maier & Watkins, 1998; Tingate, Lugg, Muller, Stowe, & Pierson, 1997).

Emotions can also impair health in strange, roundabout ways: Many years ago a midwife delivered three female babies on Friday the 13th and announced that all three were hexed and would die before their 23rd birthday. The first two did die young. As the third woman approached her 23rd birthday, she checked into a hospital and informed the staff of her fears. The staff noted that she dealt with her anxiety by extreme hyperventilation (deep breathing). Shortly before her birthday, she hyperventilated to death.

How did this happen? Ordinarily, when people do not breathe voluntarily, they breathe reflexively; the reflex is triggered by carbon dioxide in the blood. By extreme hyperventilation this woman had exhaled so much carbon dioxide that she did not have enough left to trigger reflexive breathing. When she stopped breathing voluntarily, she stopped breathing altogether ("Clinicopathologic Conference," 1967). This is a clear example of a self-fulfilling prophecy: The fact that she believed the hex caused it to be fulfilled. It also illustrates the indirect influence of emotions on health.

Heart Disease

An upholsterer repairing the chairs in a physician's waiting room once noticed that the fronts of the seats wore out before the backs. To figure out why, the physician began watching patients in the waiting room. He noticed that his heart patients habitually sat on the front edges of their seats, waiting impatiently to be called in for their appointments. This observation led the physician to hypothesize a link between heart disease and an impatient, success-driven personality, now known as the Type A personality (Friedman & Rosenman, 1974).

People with **Type A personality** are *highly competitive; they believe that they must always win. They are impatient, always in a hurry, and often angry and hostile.* By contrast people with **a Type B personality** are *relatively easygoing, less hurried, and less hostile.* Are you a Type A or a Type B? Test yourself by answering the questions in Figure 12.25.

Statistically, a link does exist between heart disease and Type A behavior, especially with hostility,

Measuring the Type A Personality

_____ 1. Do you find it difficult to restrain yourself from hurrying others' speech (finishing their sentences for them)?

_____ 2. Do you often try to do more than one thing at a time (such as eat and read simultaneously)?

_____ 3. Do you often feel guilty if you use extra time to relax?

_____ 4. Do you tend to get involved in a great number of projects at once?

_____ 5. Do you find yourself racing through yellow lights when you drive?

_____ 6. Do you need to win in order to derive enjoyment from games and sports?

_____ 7. Do you generally move, walk, and eat rapidly?

_____ 8. Do you agree to take on too many responsibilities?

_____ 9. Do you detest waiting in lines?

_____ 10. Do you have an intense desire to better your position in life and impress others?

FIGURE 12.25 If you answer "yes" to most of these items, Friedman and Rosenman would say that you probably have a Type A personality. But they would also take into account how you explain your answers, so this questionnaire gives only a rough estimate of your personality. _(From_ Type A Behavior and Your Heart, _by Meyer Friedman and Ray H. Rosenman. Copyright ©_ _1974 by Meyer Friedman. Reprinted with permission.)_

but the link is weak. When hostility and high blood pressure correlate, we cannot conclude that one led to the other. A better study is to measure hostility now and high blood pressure later. Studies of that kind find a correlation of only about .08 (Rutledge & Hogan, 2002).

The strongest known psychological influence on heart disease is social support. People with strong friendships and family ties usually take better care of themselves and keep their heart rate and blood pressure under control (Uchino, Cacioppo, & Kiecolt-Glaser, 1996). People who learn techniques for managing stress also lower their blood pressure and decrease their risk of heart disease (Linden, Lenz, & Con, 2001).

Variations in the prevalence of heart disease across cultures may have behavioral influences (Levine, 1990). Some cultures have a hurried pace of life; people walk fast; they talk fast; almost everyone wears a watch; storekeepers pay prompt attention to their customers. Other cultures have a more relaxed pace of life; people are seldom in a rush; few people wear watches; the buses and trains seldom arrive on schedule but no one seems to care. As you might guess, heart disease is more common in countries with a hurried pace of life.

CONCEPT CHECK ☑

22. People with a Type A personality are likely to develop stress-related heart disease. Yet, when they fill out a stress checklist like one of those mentioned earlier, their scores are often low. Why might that scale understate the stress levels of Type A people? (Check your answer on page 485.)

Cancer

There are many kinds of cancer and many causes that are not yet well understood. Behavior can also influence the onset and spread of cancer, at least indirectly. For example, women who examine their

❚ People in some cultures (a) live at a frantic pace: People walk fast, talk fast, and push one another around. In other cultures (b), no one is sure what time it is and no one cares. The risk of heart disease is greatest in cultures and subcultures characterized by a hectic pace.

breasts regularly can detect breast cancer at an early stage, when treatment is more likely to be successful. However, most women do not conduct regular, competent self-examinations, either because they do not know how, because they are fearful, or because they doubt that a checkup would help (S. M. Miller, Shoda, & Hurley, 1996). Latina women in the United States have a higher rate of cervical cancer than other women, partly because they are less likely than other women to see doctors regularly for Pap smear tests (Meyerowitz, Richardson, Hudson, & Leedham, 1998). In many ways preventing or treating cancer requires behavioral as well as medical interventions.

Does stress contribute directly to cancer? Brief stress actually strengthens the immune system, but prolonged stress or depression robs it of resources, weakens it, and increases vulnerability to infections (S. Cohen et al., 1998).

Stress and depression probably increase the risk of cancer, but the influence is weak. For example, one study of 673 breast-cancer patients found no relationship between stressful events prior to the disease and the patients' survival time (Maunsell, Brisson, Mondor, Verreault, & Deschênes, 2001). Social support does, however, strengthen the immune system (S. Cohen, Doyle, Turner, Alper, & Skoner, 2003) and improve both the survival time and the quality of life for cancer patients. That is, even if stress is not a clear cause of cancer, decreased stress is a good weapon for fighting cancer (Fawzy, Fawzy, Arndt, & Pasnau, 1995).

IN CLOSING

Health Is Both Psycho and Somatic

In this module we have considered the ways people try to deal with stressful situations, but how well do these strategies work? The answer is that they work well for many people, but at a cost. The cost is that coping with serious stressors requires energy. Many people who have had to cope with long-lasting stressors break their diets, resume smoking and drinking habits that they had abandoned long ago, and find it difficult to concentrate on difficult cognitive tasks (Muraven & Baumeister, 2000).

Still, in spite of the costs, an amazing number of people say that the experience of battling with a chronic illness, tending to a loved one with a severe illness, or dealing with other painful experiences has brought them personal strength and an enhanced feeling of meaning in life (Folkman & Moskowitz, 2000). They found positive moments even in the midst of fear and loss. Not everyone rises to the occasion, but we should respect and admire those who do.

Summary

- *Selye's concept of stress.* According to Hans Selye, stress is "the nonspecific response of the body to any demand made upon it." Any event, pleasant or unpleasant, that brings about change in a person's life produces some measure of stress. One problem with this definition is that it omits lifelong problems, such as coping with racism. (page 476)

- *Stages of response to stress.* The body goes through three stages in response to a stressful experience: alarm, resistance, and exhaustion. In the resistance and exhaustion stages, prolonged channeling of energy toward resisting stress can weaken the immune system. (page 477)

- *Posttraumatic stress disorder.* After severe traumatic experiences, some people have long-lasting changes in experience. Some people may be more vulnerable than others to this outcome. (page 477)

- *Difficulties of measuring stress.* Stress checklists are problematic because many items are ambiguous. Also, the stressfulness of an event depends on the person's interpretation of the event and ability to cope with it. (page 478)

- *Coping styles.* Most strategies for dealing with stress fall into two major categories: trying to fix the problem and trying to control emotions. (page 479)

- *Prediction and control.* Events are generally less stressful when people think they can predict or control them. (page 480)

- *Inoculation.* Someone who has experienced a mildly stressful experience is less stressed than other people are by a later, more intense version of the same experience. (page 480)

- *Reinterpretation.* It is possible to reduce one's tension by interpreting a situation in a new, less threatening way. (page 481)

- *Relaxation and exercise.* One way of coping with stress is to find a quiet place, relax the muscles, and eliminate distracting stimuli. Exercise can help channel nervous energy. (page 481)

- *Distraction.* Distracting a person's attention from the source of stress helps to reduce the stress. (page 482)

- *Psychosomatic illness.* Stress, hostility, and other emotional experiences may increase the probability of certain illnesses. A psychosomatic illness is related to a person's experiences and reactions to them. (page 482)

- *Heart disease.* Hostility increases the risk of heart disease, although the effect is small. Having the support of friends improves health and decreases the danger of heart disease. (page 482)

- *Cancer.* Depression and stress can increase the risk of cancer, at least slightly. Social support improves people's chances of recovery from cancer and also improves their quality of life while fighting the disease. (page 483)

Answers to Concept Checks

17. By Selye's definition getting married produces stress because it requires a change in one's life. However, constant quarreling with one's family would not be stressful because it is not a change in one's life. (page 477)

18. Items on stress checklists are often ambiguous, and therefore, the results have low reliability and validity. Also, a given event can be more stressful for one person than another. (page 479)

19. Your roommate's radio would be more disruptive. You can turn your own radio on or off, switch stations, or reduce the volume. You have no such control over your roommate's radio (unless your roommate happens to be very cooperative). (page 480)

20. Practice giving your speech to a small group of friends. If possible, practice giving the speech in the room where you will ultimately deliver it. (page 481)

21. Monitoring strategies attack the cause of the problem and increase one's sense of control over it. Blunting strategies distract one from a presumably uncontrollable problem. (page 482)

22. The Social Readjustment Rating Scale measures events that change a person's life; it does not measure constant sources of stress such as the pressures of work. The scale also fails to measure people's reactions, such as impatience, competitiveness, and hostility. (page 483)

CHAPTER ENDING

Key Terms and Activities

Key Terms

alarm: the first stage of response to stress, a brief period of high arousal of the sympathetic nervous system, readying the body for vigorous activity (page 477)

anger management training: techniques for decreasing or restraining displays of anger (page 474)

anxiety (defined operationally): an increase in the startle reflex (page 468)

autonomic nervous system: a section of the nervous system that controls the functioning of the internal organs, such as the heart (page 449)

contempt: a reaction to a violation of community standards (page 474)

disgust: a reaction to something that would make you feel contaminated if it got into your mouth (page 474)

Duchenne smile: a spontaneous expression that includes movement of both the mouth muscles and certain muscles near the eyes (page 456)

embarrassment: the emotional reaction to mistakes, being the center of attention, or "sticky situations" (page 474)

emotion-based coping (or **blunting**): methods in which people try to weaken their emotional reaction (page 479)

emotional intelligence: the ability to perceive, imagine, and understand emotions and to use that information in decision making (page 462)

exhaustion: the third stage of response to stress, when the body's prolonged response to stress decreases the synthesis of proteins, including the proteins necessary for activity of the immune system (page 477)

frustration-aggression hypothesis: the theory that frustration leads to aggressive behavior (page 472)

guilty-knowledge test: a test that uses the polygraph to measure whether a person has information that should be known only by someone guilty of a certain crime or someone who talked with the guilty person (page 470)

health psychology: a field of psychology concerned with how people's behavior can enhance health and prevent illness and how behavior contributes to recovery from illness (page 476)

inoculation: protection against the harmful effects of stress by earlier exposure to smaller amounts of it (page 480)

James-Lange theory: the theory that emotion is merely our perception of autonomic changes and movements evoked directly by various stimuli (page 452)

microexpressions: very brief, involuntary expressions of fear, anger, or other emotions (page 449)

parasympathetic nervous system: a system of neurons located in the medulla and the bottom of the spinal cord; these neurons send messages to the internal organs to prepare the body for digestion and related processes (page 450)

polygraph: a machine that simultaneously measures heart rate, breathing rate, blood pressure, and electrical conduction of the skin (page 469)

positive psychology: the study of the features that enrich life, such as hope, creativity, courage, spirituality, and responsibility (page 465)

posttraumatic stress disorder (PTSD): a condition in which people who have endured extreme stress feel prolonged anxiety and depression (page 477)

problem-based coping (or monitoring): methods in which people attend carefully to the stressful event and try to take effective actions (page 479)

psychosomatic illness: an illness that is influenced by a person's experiences—particularly stressful experiences—and by his or her reactions to those experiences (page 482)

pure autonomic failure: an uncommon condition with unknown cause in which the autonomic nervous system stops regulating the organs (page 452)

rape: sexual activity without the consent of the partner (page 473)

resistance: the second stage of response to stress; a stage of prolonged but moderate arousal (page 477)

Schachter and Singer's theory of emotions: the theory that the intensity of sympathetic arousal determines the intensity of an emotion but that cognitive factors determine the type of emotion (page 453)

stress: according to Selye the nonspecific response of the body to any demands made upon it; according to Lazarus a situation that someone regards as threatening and as possibly exceeding his or her resources (page 476)

subjective well-being: a self-evaluation of one's life as pleasant, interesting, and satisfying (page 465)

sympathetic nervous system: a system composed of two chains of neuron clusters lying just to the left and right of the spinal cord; these neurons send messages to the internal organs to prepare them for a burst of vigorous activity (page 450)

Type A personality: a personality characterized by constant competitiveness, impatience, anger, and hostility (page 482)

Type B personality: a personality characterized by an easygoing attitude, with little hurry or hostility (page 482)

 ## Suggestions for Further Reading

Damasio, A. (1999). *The feeling of what happens.* New York: Harcourt Brace. Ambitious treatment of the role of emotions in thinking and consciousness.

LeDoux, J. E. (1996). *The emotional brain.* New York: Simon & Schuster. Discussion of the biological bases of emotion by a pioneering researcher.

Provine, R. (2000). *Laughter.* New York: Viking Press. Pioneering observations of who laughs, when, and why. Highly recommended.

 ## Book Companion Web Site

Need help studying? Go to

http://psychology.wadsworth.com/kalat_intro7e/

for a virtual study center. You'll find a personalized Self-Study Assessment that will provide you with a study plan based on your answers to a pretest. Also study using flash cards, quizzes, interactive art, and an online glossary.

Check out interactive **Try It Yourself** exercises on the companion site! For example, the Universal Emotions exercise ties to what you've learned in this chapter.

Your companion site also has direct links to the following Web sites. These links are checked often for changes, dead links, and new additions

Cross-Cultural Studies of Happiness

www.eur.nl/fsw/research/happiness/index.htm

This site presents survey results from many countries, as well as links to many other kinds of research on happiness.

MINCAVA: Global Links on Violence

http://www.mincava.umn.edu/

The Minnesota Center Against Violence and Abuse (MINCAVA) maintains hundreds of links to sites that provide information about all forms of violence.

Stress Assess

http://wellness.uwsp.edu/Health_Service/Services/ stress.htm

Evaluate your current stress sources, distress symptoms, and lifestyle behaviors. A personalized assessment includes strategies to counteract stress.*

*Note: Any psychological test that is readily available to the public, while entertaining and possibly informative, should not be used to make important decisions about yourself or others. The most powerful, valid, and reliable psychological assessment devices are usually kept under the tight control of their creators or copyright holders.

Try It Yourself CD-ROM
with Critical Thinking Video Exercises

Use your CD to access **videos** related to activities designed to help you think critically about the important topics discussed. For example, the video about health and stress ties to what you've learned in this chapter. You'll also find an easy portal link to the book companion site where you can access your personalized **Self-Study Assessments** and interactive **Try It Yourself** exercises.

PsychNow! 2.0

PsychNow! is a fun interactive CD designed to help you with the difficult concepts in psychology. Check out the Motivation & Emotion section for the following topics that relate to this chapter:

Emotion: match emotions to faces and show different emotions by building faces.

Coping with Emotion: how to change stressful situations, explore coping styles, and take a quiz.

Stress and Health: play a stress-level game, learn the components of health, and take an undergraduate stress questionnaire.

InteractNOW! Online Collaborative Lab: Emotion and the Stroop test

Personality

Several thousand people have the task of assembling the world's largest jigsaw puzzle, which contains more than a trillion pieces. Connie Conclusionjumper examines 20 pieces very closely, stares off into space, and announces, "When the puzzle is fully assembled, it will be a picture of the Sydney Opera House!" Prudence Plodder says, "Well, I don't know what the whole puzzle will look like, but I think I've found two little pieces that fit together."

Which of the two has made the greater contribution to completing the puzzle? We could argue either way. Clearly, the task requires an enormous number of little, unglamorous accomplishments like Prudence's. But if Connie is right, her flash of insight will be extremely valuable for assembling all the pieces. Of course, if the puzzle turns out to be a picture of a sailboat at sunset, then Connie will have misled us and wasted our time.

Some psychologists have offered grand theories about the nature of personality. Others have tried to classify personality types and understand why people act differently in specific situations. In this chapter we explore several methods of approaching personality, ranging from large-scale theories to small-scale descriptions. In the first module, we survey some of the most famous and influential theories of personality, such as that of Sigmund Freud. The second module concerns descriptions of personality. Any description is, of course, a theory, but it is a different kind of theory. The final module deals with measurements of personality.

This three-dimensional jigsaw puzzle of the ocean liner *Titanic* consists of 26,000 pieces. Assembling all the pieces is an overwhelming task, but at least people know how the final product should look. Understanding personality is an even more complex puzzle, and we do not know the overall structure before we start investigating.

Personality Theories

How can we best describe the overall structure of personality?

> Every individual is virtually an enemy of civilization. . . . Thus civilization has to be defended against the individual. . . . For the masses are lazy and unintelligent . . . and the individuals composing them support one another in giving free rein to their indiscipline.
> —Sigmund Freud (1927/1961)

> It has been my experience that persons have a basically positive direction. In my deepest contacts with individuals in therapy, even those whose troubles are most disturbing, whose behavior has been most antisocial, whose feelings seem most abnormal, I find this to be true.
> —Carl Rogers (1961)

What is human nature? The 17th-century philosopher Thomas Hobbes argued that humans are by nature selfish. Life in a state of nature, he said, is "nasty, brutish, and short." If we are to protect ourselves from one another, the government must restrain us. The 18th-century political philosopher Jean-Jacques Rousseau disagreed, maintaining that people are naturally good and that governments are the problem, not the solution. Rational people acting freely, he maintained, would advance the welfare of all.

The debate between those two viewpoints survives in modern theories of personality (Figure 13.1). Some theorists, including Sigmund Freud, have held that people are born with sexual and destructive impulses that must be held in check if civilization is to survive. Others, including Carl Rogers, believed that people will achieve good and noble goals once they have been freed from unnecessary restraints.

Which point of view is correct? Way down deep, are we good, bad, both, or neither? We cannot expect a firm scientific answer, but psychologists have developed many approaches to exploring personality.

The term *personality* comes from the Latin word *persona,* meaning "mask." In the plays of ancient Greece and Rome, actors wore masks to indicate whether they were comic or tragic characters. Unlike a mask that one can either put on or take off, however, the term *personality* implies something stable. **Personality consists of** *all the consistent ways in which the behavior of one person differs from that of others, especially in social situations.* (Differences in learning, memory, sensation, or muscle control are generally not considered personality.)

Of course, in any one aspect of your personality, you resemble many other people. For example, you might be about as cheerful as many others. Nevertheless, your particular combination of behavior tendencies and mental processes sets you apart.

In this module we concentrate largely on the theory of Sigmund Freud because it has been so influential outside psychology as well as within. However, you should evaluate it carefully before you decide how seriously to take it.

Sigmund Freud and the Psychodynamic Approach

Sigmund Freud (1856–1939), an Austrian physician, developed the first psychodynamic theory. *A* **psychodynamic theory** *relates personality to the interplay of conflicting forces within the individual, including some that the individual may not consciously recognize.* That is, we are being pushed and pulled by internal forces that we do not fully understand.

Freud's influence extends into sociology, literature, art, religion, and politics. And yet, here we are, about three fourths of the way through this text on psychology, and until now I have barely mentioned Freud. Why?

The reason is that Freud's influence within psychology has declined substantially. According to one

Hobbes	Rousseau
Government is required for protection	Humans are good
Humans are selfish	Government is a corrupting influence
Freud	**Rogers**
Natural impulses are detrimental to society	Natural impulses are noble and good

FIGURE 13.1 Sigmund Freud, like the philosopher Thomas Hobbes, stressed the more destructive aspects of human nature. Carl Rogers, like Jean-Jacques Rousseau, emphasized the more favorable aspects.

▌ Sigmund Freud interpreted dreams, slips of the tongue, and so forth to infer unconscious thoughts and motivations. Most researchers today, however, are skeptical of Freud's interpretations.

psychologist, Frederick Crews (1996, p. 63), "independent studies have begun to converge toward a verdict that was once considered a sign of extremism or even of neurosis: that there is literally nothing to be said, scientifically or therapeutically, to the advantage of the entire Freudian system or any of its constituent dogmas." Think about that: *nothing* to be said in favor of *any* of Freud's theories. Needless to say, not everyone agrees with that statement. Still, the decline of Freud's influence is striking.

▌ The fame of Sigmund Freud far exceeds that of any other psychologist. His picture has even appeared on the Austrian 50-schilling bill and bimetal millennial coin.

Freud's Search for the Unconscious

Freud would have preferred to be a professor of cultural history or anthropology; he wrote several books and articles about those topics in his later years. In Austria at the time, however, few university positions were offered to Jews. The only professions readily open to him were law, business, and medicine. Freud chose medicine, but without much commitment to healing people. His interests were almost purely theoretical.

Early in his career, Freud worked with the psychiatrist Josef Breuer, who had been treating a young woman with a fluctuating variety of physical complaints. As she talked with Breuer about her past, she remembered various traumatic, or emotionally damaging, experiences. Breuer, and later Freud also, said that remembering these experiences produced catharsis, *a release of pent-up emotional tension,* thereby relieving her illness. However, later scholars who reexamined the medical records found that this woman who was so famous in the history of psychoanalysis was not cured at all. She may not even have benefited from the treatment (Ellenberger, 1972).

Regardless of whether the "talking cure" had been successful, Freud began applying it to his own emotionally disturbed patients. He referred to *his method of explaining and dealing with personality, based on the interplay of conscious and unconscious forces,* as psychoanalysis. To this day psychoanalysts remain loyal to some version of Freud's methods and theories, although their views have of course evolved over the decades.

Psychoanalysis started out as a fairly simple theory: Each of us has an unconscious mind as well as a conscious mind (Figure 13.2). The unconscious is *the*

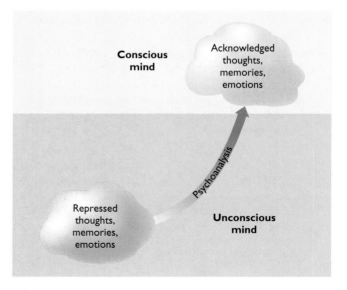

FIGURE 13.2 Freud believed that psychoanalysis could bring parts of the unconscious into the conscious mind, where the client could deal with them.

repository of memories, emotions, and thoughts, many of them illogical, that affect our behavior even though we cannot talk about them. Traumatic experiences force thoughts and emotions into the unconscious (theoretically), and the goal of psychoanalysts is to bring those memories back to consciousness. Doing so produces catharsis and enables the person to confront irrational and self-defeating impulses.

As Freud listened to his patients, however, he became convinced that the traumatic events they recalled could not account for their abnormal behavior. Some patients reacted strongly to events that others took in stride. Why? At first, in the early 1890s, Freud attributed their overreactions to sexual difficulties (Macmillan, 1997). For a while Freud claimed that increased sexual activity would cure anxiety problems, although he soon abandoned this view, and since then no one has found any reason to revive it.

People suffering from nervous exhaustion, he said, were suffering from the results of masturbation. His evidence for this idea was that all his patients who were suffering from nervous exhaustion had masturbated (!). You can see the problem: Freud boldly asserted that mentally healthy people do not masturbate. Suppose you were in his audience. Would you raise your hand and say, "Wait a minute, Dr. Freud, I think I'm mentally healthy, and I masturbate . . ."? You probably wouldn't, and neither did anyone else, so Freud concluded that he was right.

A few years later, however, Freud abandoned these hypotheses and suggested instead that the ultimate cause of psychological disorders was traumatic childhood sexual experiences, either seduction by other children or sexual abuse by adults. Freud's patients did not report any such memories, but Freud put together parts of the patients' dream reports, slips of the tongue, and so forth and claimed that they pointed to early sexual abuse.

At this point Freud's problems with evidence became serious. His ideas about inadequate sex or too much masturbation may sound ridiculous, but at least they were testable. But how was anyone to determine whether the childhood events that Freud inferred from dreams and so forth had actually happened?

A few years later, he abandoned the idea that psychological disorders resulted from childhood sexual abuse. According to Freud's own description of these events, he decided that his patients had "misled" him into believing they were sexually abused in early childhood, whereas in fact, Freud said, their claims were wishes and fantasies (Freud, 1925). Although he never fully developed his views of girls' early sexual development, he was more explicit about boys: During early childhood every boy goes through an **Oedipus complex,** *when he develops a sexual interest in his mother and competitive aggression toward his father.* (Oedipus—

EHD-ah-puhs—in the ancient Greek play by Sophocles unknowingly murdered his father and married his mother.) In short, Freud said people become psychologically disturbed not because their parents sexually molested them but because as children they wanted to have sex with their parents and couldn't.

Why did Freud switch from his idea about sexual abuse to a theory about sexual fantasies? According to one view (Masson, 1984), Freud was right the first time, and he simply lost the courage to defend his theory. According to other scholars, however, Freud never had any evidence for either theory (Esterson, 2001; Powell & Boer, 1994; Schatzman, 1992). In his earliest writings, Freud inferred his patients' sexual abuse from their symptoms and dreams despite their own denials of abuse. It was hardly fair, therefore, to complain that the patients had misled him into believing they had been abused. When he switched to saying that the patients had childhood sexual fantasies, he was again drawing inferences that his patients denied. (Freud considered his patients' protests to be signs of emotional resistance and therefore confirmation that his interpretations were correct.)

Apparently, Freud's main evidence for his interpretations was simply that he could construct a coherent story linking a patient's symptoms, dreams, and so forth to the sexual fantasies that Freud inferred (Esterson, 1993). In short, he did not distinguish between his results and his interpretations.

Consider another example of Freud's use of evidence: A patient described as "Dora" came to Freud at the insistence of her father, an acquaintance of Freud's. Since about age 8, Dora had suffered from headaches, coughing, and shortness of breath, all of which Freud interpreted as psychological in nature. She had also avoided a certain friend of her father, Mr. K, ever since she was 14, when he grabbed her and kissed her on her lips.

Freud wrote that Dora surely experienced sexual pleasure at this time because K's presumably erect penis must have rubbed up against her clitoris and excited it. Freud described Dora's disgust as "entirely and completely hysterical" (Freud, 1905/1963, p. 44). He then proceeded to try to trace Dora's behavior to her presumed love for both K and her father and her homosexual attraction to Mrs. K. As one reads Freud's elaborate discussion, one wonders what was wrong with Dora's simpler explanation—that she found the sexual advances of this middle-aged man repulsive.

Stages of Psychosexual Development in Freud's Theory of Personality

Right or wrong, Freud's theory is so well known that you should learn what his terms mean. One of his central points was that psychosexual interest and pleasure

TABLE 13.1 Freud's Stages of Psychosexual Development

Stage (approximate ages)	Sexual Interests	Effects of Fixation at This Stage
Oral stage (birth to 1 year)	Sucking, swallowing, biting	Lasting concerns with dependence and independence; pleasure from eating, drinking, and other oral activities
Anal stage (1 to 3 years)	Expelling feces, retaining feces	Orderliness or sloppiness, stinginess or wastefulness, stubbornness
Phallic stage (3 to 5 or 6 years)	Touching penis or clitoris; Oedipus complex	Difficulty feeling closeness. Males: fear of castration Females: penis envy
Latent period (5 or 6 to puberty)	Sexual interests suppressed	—
Genital stage (puberty onward)	Sexual contact with other people	—

begin in infancy. He used the term **psychosexual pleasure** broadly to include *all strong, pleasant excitement arising from body stimulation.* He maintained that how we deal with our psychosexual development influences nearly all aspects of our personality. According to Freud, just as nonhuman mammals respond sexually to sounds and smells, children respond sexually to stimulation of the mouth, anus, and other body zones that do not greatly excite human adults. Freud based his views on his patients' reconstructions of childhood; he did not systematically observe children himself.

According to Freud (1905/1925), people have a *psychosexual energy,* which he called **libido** (lih-BEE-doh), from a Latin word meaning "desire." Normally, libido is focused in an infant's mouth and "flows" to other body parts as the child grows older. Children go through five stages of psychosexual development, each with a characteristic sexual focus that leaves its mark on the adult personality. If normal sexual development is blocked or frustrated at any stage, Freud said, part of the libido becomes **fixated** at that stage; that is, *it continues to be preoccupied with the pleasure*

area associated with that stage. Table 13.1 summarizes these stages.

The Oral Stage

In the **oral stage,** from birth to about age 2—Freud was vague about the age limits—*the infant derives intense psychosexual pleasure from stimulation of the mouth, particularly while sucking at the mother's breast.* According to Freud someone fixated at this

■ According to Freud, if normal sexual development is blocked at the oral stage, the child will seek pleasure from drinking and eating and later from kissing and smoking. Perhaps this cigarette smoker's mother weaned him too quickly—or let him nurse too long. Like most of Freud's ideas, this one is difficult to test.

stage continues to receive great pleasure from eating, drinking, and smoking and may also have lasting concerns with dependence and independence.

The Anal Stage

At about 2 years of age, children enter the anal stage, when *they get psychosexual pleasure from stimulation of the sensations of bowel movements.* A person fixated at this stage goes through life "holding things back"—being orderly, stingy, and stubborn—or less commonly, may go to the opposite extreme and become messy and wasteful.

The Phallic Stage

Beginning at about age 3, in the phallic stage, children begin to *play with their genitals* and according to Freud become sexually attracted to the opposite-sex parent. Freud claimed that boys with a phallic fixation are afraid of being castrated; girls with such a fixation develop "penis envy." These ideas have always been controversial. Some girls report fantasies about what it would be like to be a boy (Linday, 1994), but calling these fantasies "penis envy" is a stretch, and assuming that they play a major role in personality development is even more of a stretch. Similarly, few boys show clear signs of castration fears.

The Latent Period

From about age 5 or 6 until adolescence, Freud said, most children enter a latent period in which they *suppress their psychosexual interest.* At this time they play mostly with peers of their own sex. The latent period is evidently a product of European culture and is not apparent in all societies.

The Genital Stage

Beginning at puberty young people *take a strong sexual interest in other people.* This is known as the genital stage. According to Freud anyone who has fixated a great deal of libido in an earlier stage has little libido left for the genital stage. But people who have successfully negotiated the earlier stages can now derive primary satisfaction from sexual intercourse.

Evaluation of Freud's Stages

Freud's theory is vague and difficult to test (Grünbaum, 1986; Popper, 1986). When it has been tested, the results have been mostly inconclusive. For example, the characteristics of being orderly, stingy, and stubborn, which Freud described as due to anal fixation, tend to correlate with one another, suggesting that they are part of a single personality trait. However, we have no evidence that these attributes result from toilet training (Fisher & Greenberg, 1977).

Freud's Description of the Structure of Personality

Personality, Freud claimed, consists of three aspects: id, ego, and superego. (Actually, he used German words that mean *it, I,* and *over-I.* A translator used Latin equivalents instead of English words.) The id consists of *all our biological drives,* such as sex and hunger, that demand immediate gratification. The ego is *the rational, decision-making aspect of the personality.* The superego contains *the memory of rules and prohibitions we learned from our parents and the rest of society,* such as, "Nice little boys and girls don't do that." Sometimes the id produces sexual or other motivations that the superego considers repugnant, thus evoking feelings of guilt. However, most psychologists today find it difficult to imagine the mind in terms of three warring factions and therefore regard Freud's description as only a metaphor.

CONCEPT CHECK ☑

1. If someone has persistent problems with independence and dependence, Freud would suggest a fixation at which psychosexual stage?
2. What kind of behavior would Freud expect of someone with a strong id and a weak superego? What behavior would Freud expect of someone with an unusually strong superego? (Check your answers on page 505.)

Defense Mechanisms Against Anxiety

According to Freud *the ego defends itself against conflicts and anxieties by relegating unpleasant thoughts and impulses to the unconscious.* Among the defense mechanisms that the ego employs are repression, denial, rationalization, displacement, regression, projection, reaction formation, and sublimation (Figure 13.3). He saw these as normal processes that sometimes went to extremes. Descriptions of these mechanisms were largely developed and elaborated by his daughter, Anna.

Repression

The defense mechanism of repression is *motivated forgetting*—rejecting unacceptable thoughts, desires, and memories and banishing them to the unconscious. One example would be someone who sees a murder and later cannot remember it. Another example: Someone has an unacceptable sexual or aggressive impulse and represses it so thoroughly as to be unaware of it.

Researchers have struggled to find clear evidence of repression. As discussed in Chapter 7, most people who endure miserable experiences remember them well. Laboratory investigators have exposed participants to

FIGURE 13.3 The ego, or "rational I," has numerous ways of defending itself against anxiety, that apprehensive state named for the Latin word meaning "to strangle." We use defense mechanisms to avoid unpleasant realities. They are part of an internal battle that you fight against yourself.

various unpleasant or threatening experiences in the expectation that repression would interfere with their memories. Even in the cases where people did forget, alternative explanations were available that did not include repression (Holmes, 1990). If repression occurs at all, it occurs rarely or under very special circumstances.

Denial

The refusal to believe information that provokes anxiety ("This can't be happening") is called denial. Whereas repression is the motivated forgetting of certain information, denial is an assertion that the information is incorrect. For example, someone with a serious alcohol problem may insist, "I'm not an alcoholic. I can take it or leave it." A patient who is told that he or she has a fatal illness may refuse to accept the diagnosis.

Rationalization

When people *attempt to prove that their actions are rational and justifiable and thus worthy of approval,* they are using rationalization. For example, a student who wants to go to the movies says, "More studying

won't do me any good anyway." Someone who misses a deadline to apply for a job says, "I didn't really want that job."

Displacement

By diverting a behavior or thought away from its natural target toward a less threatening target, displacement lets people engage in the behavior more safely or with less anxiety. For example, someone who is angry with a boss or professor might yell at a friend instead. The person is angry but feels inhibited about yelling at someone who could retaliate.

Regression

A return to a more immature level of functioning, regression is an effort to avoid the anxiety of facing one's current role in life. By adopting a childish role, a person can escape responsibility and return to an earlier, perhaps more secure, way of life. For example, after a new sibling is born, an older child may cry or pout. Adults who have just gone through a divorce or business loss may sometimes move in with their parents and depend on them.

Projection

The attribution of one's own undesirable characteristics to other people is known as **projection.** In theory, by suggesting that other people have those faults, the faults become more acceptable and less anxiety provoking. For example, someone who secretly enjoys pornography might accuse other people of enjoying it. However, the research finds that people using projection do not ordinarily decrease their anxiety or their awareness of their own faults (Holmes, 1978; Sherwood, 1981). If so, projection is not an effective defense.

Reaction Formation

To keep undesirable characteristics repressed, people may use **reaction formation** to *present themselves as the opposite of what they really are to hide the unpleasant truth either from themselves or others.* For example, a man troubled by doubts about his religious faith may try to convert others to the faith. Someone with unacceptable aggressive tendencies may join a group dedicated to preventing violence. (Not everyone who proselytizes for a faith has deep doubts about it, of course, and not everyone who tries to prevent violence is secretly a violent person. Different people have different reasons for the same actions.)

Sublimation

The transformation of sexual or aggressive energies into culturally acceptable, even admirable, behaviors is **sublimation.** According to Freud sublimation enables a person to express the impulse without admitting its existence. For example, painting and sculpture may represent a sublimation of sexual impulses. Someone may sublimate aggressive impulses by becoming a surgeon. However, if the true motives of a painter are sexual, as Freud proposed, they are well hidden indeed. Sublimation is the one proposed defense mechanism that is associated with socially constructive behavior.

CONCEPT CHECK ☑

3. Match the Freudian defense mechanisms in this list with the situations that follow: Repression, Regression, Denial, Projection, Rationalization, Reaction formation, Displacement, Sublimation.
   a. A man who is angry with his neighbor goes hunting and kills a deer.
   b. Someone with a smoking habit insists there is no convincing evidence that smoking impairs health.
   c. A woman with doubts about her religious faith tries to convert others to her religion.
   d. A man who beats his wife writes a book arguing that people have an instinctive need for aggressive behavior.
   e. A woman forgets a doctor's appointment for a test for cancer.
   f. Someone who has difficulty dealing with certain people resorts to pouting, crying, and throwing tantrums.
   g. A boss takes credit for a good idea suggested by an employee because "It's better for me to take the credit so that our department will look good and all the employees will benefit."
   h. Someone with an unacceptable impulse to shout obscenities becomes a writer of novels. (Check your answers on page 505.)

Freud's Legacy

Undeniably, Freud was a great pioneer in identifying new questions. The validity of his answers is less certain, however. He based his conclusions on inferences he drew from what his patients said and did, without testing the validity of his inferences. A growing number of psychologists today contend that Freud imposed theories onto his data instead of drawing conclusions from the data.

It is conceivable, of course, that someone might draw correct conclusions even from worthless data. If later data support a theory, the weakness of the original evidence does not matter. One reviewer of the literature (Westen, 1998) identifies the following ideas as among Freud's enduring contributions to psychology:

- Much of mental life is unconscious. We don't always know why we're doing something.
- People often have conflicting motives.
- Childhood experiences are important for the development of personality and social behavior.
- Our relationships with other people can resemble the relationships we had with other people in the past, such as our parents.

▌ Freud's own couch is now part of our history. What is the future of the psychoanalytic couch?

- People develop through stages of psychosexual interest and relationships with the social world.

However, a critic can reply that these comments are "damning with faint praise." That is, Freud's goal was not to make generalizations such as "people often have conflicting motives" or "childhood is important"—ideas that were hardly original to Freud! Freud thought he had found a way to probe and reveal people's unconscious thoughts and motives. Furthermore, the kinds of unconscious processes that current data support are very different from Freud's concepts. For example, implicit memory (Chapter 7) and priming (Chapter 8) are unconscious in the sense that people are unaware of certain influences on their behavior. However, these processes are unconscious only because the stimulus was presented briefly, not because the person repressed offensive ideas. What Freud said about the unconscious did not lead to research on implicit memory or priming; if anything, it may have deterred and delayed research on unconscious processes. In short, how much credit we should give Freud is a matter of opinion.

Neo-Freudians

Some psychologists, known as **neo-Freudians, remained faithful to parts of Freud's theory while modifying other parts.** One of the most influential neo-Freudians was the German physician Karen Horney (HOR-nigh; 1885–1952), who believed that Freud exaggerated the role of the sex drive in human behavior and misunderstood women's sexual motivations. She believed, for example, that the conflict between a child and parents was a reaction to parental hostility and intimidation, not a manifestation of sexual desires. Horney emphasized the social and cultural influences on personality that give rise to anxiety. Still, she maintained many Freudian concepts such as repression and the attempt to understand people's inner conflicts. Her views were more a revision than a rejection of Freud's theories.

Other theorists, including Carl Jung and Alfred Adler, broke more sharply with Freud. Although Jung and Adler were at one point associates of Freud, each broke with Freud's theory in substantial ways and should not be classified as neo-Freudians.

Carl Jung and the Collective Unconscious

Carl G. Jung (YOONG; 1875–1961), a Swiss physician, was an early member of Freud's inner circle. Freud regarded Jung like a son, the "heir apparent" or "crown prince" of the psychoanalytic movement, until their father–son relationship deteriorated (Alexander, 1982).

Jung's own theory of personality emphasized people's search for a spiritual meaning in life and the continuity of human experience, past and present. Jung believed that every person has not only a conscious mind and a "personal unconscious" (equivalent to Freud's unconscious) but also a collective unconscious. You could think of it as a "group mind." The personal unconscious results from each person's own experience. The **collective unconscious**, present at birth, represents *the cumulative experience of preceding generations*. Because all humans share common ancestors, all have the same collective unconscious. The collective unconscious contains **archetypes,** which are *vague images that we inherited from the experiences of our ancestors*. As evidence for this view, Jung pointed out that similar images emerge in the art of cultures throughout the world (Figure 13.4) and that similar themes emerge in various religions, myths, and folklore.

Those images and themes also appear in dreams and hallucinations. So, for example, if you dream about a beetle, Jung might relate your dream to the important role that beetles have played in human mythology dating back at least to the ancient Egyptians. Given modern views of genetics, Jung's ideas are hard to defend. Having an experience does

Karen Horney, a major neo-Freudian, revised some of Freud's theories and paid greater attention to cultural influences. She was a pioneer in the development of feminine psychology.

Carl G. Jung rejected Freud's concept that dreams hide their meaning from the conscious mind: "To me dreams are a part of nature, which harbors no intention to deceive, but expresses something as best it can" (Jung, 1965).

FIGURE 13.4 Carl Jung was fascinated that similar images appear in the artwork of different cultures. One recurring image is the circular mandala, a symbol of unity and wholeness. These mandalas are: (a) a Hindu painting from Bhutan; (b) a mosaic from Beth Alpha Synagogue, Israel; (c) a tie-dye tapestry created in California; and (d) a Navajo sand painting from the southwestern United States.

not change anyone's genes, and you cannot inherit a representation of your ancestors' memories. Jung's alternative to a genetic explanation was that perhaps archetypes exist on their own, independent of time, space, and brains. That idea is difficult even to understand, much less test. In short, Jung's views of the collective unconscious and archetypes are mystical (Neher, 1996).

CRITICAL THINKING:
A STEP FURTHER
Archetypes

Jung believed that the similarities in artworks throughout the world—such as the drawings he called mandalas—indicated that people inherited images or archetypes for those shapes. Can you suggest a simpler, more parsimonious explanation?

CONCEPT CHECK

4. How does Jung's idea of the collective unconscious differ from Freud's idea of the unconscious? (Check your answer on page 505.)

Alfred Adler and Individual Psychology

Alfred Adler (1870–1937), an Austrian physician who, like Jung, had been one of Freud's early associates, broke with Freud because he believed Freud overemphasized the sex drive and neglected other more important influences on personality. They parted company in 1911, with Freud insisting that women experience "penis envy" and with Adler contending that women were more likely to envy men's status and power.

Adler founded a rival school of thought, which he called **individual psychology**. To Adler, this term did not mean "psychology of the individual." Rather, it meant *"indivisible psychology," a psychology of the person as a whole rather than a psychology of parts,* such as id, ego, and superego. Adler emphasized the importance of conscious, goal-directed behavior and deemphasized (but did not deny) unconscious influences.

Adler's Description of Personality

Several of Adler's early patients were acrobats who had had an arm or a leg damaged by a childhood illness or injury. As they worked to overcome their disabilities, they continued until they developed the needed strength and coordination to perform as acrobats. Perhaps, Adler surmised, people in general try to overcome their weaknesses and to transform them into strengths (Adler, 1932/1964).

As infants, Adler noted, we are small, dependent creatures who strive to overcome our inferiority. Normal experiences with failure goad people to try harder. However, persistent failures or overcritical parents and others can produce an **inferiority complex**, *an exaggerated feeling of weakness, inadequacy, and helplessness.*

▌ Alfred Adler emphasized the ways in which personality depended on people's goals, especially their way of striving for a sense of superiority.

According to Adler everyone has a natural **striving for superiority**, *a desire to seek personal excellence and fulfillment.* Each person creates a **style of life**, or *master plan for achieving a sense of superiority.* That style of life may be directed toward success in business, sports, or any other competitive activity. People can also strive for success in other ways. For example, someone who withdraws from life may gain a sense of accomplishment or superiority from being uncommonly self-sacrificing. Someone who constantly complains about illnesses or disabilities may win a measure of control over friends and family. Or someone may commit crimes to savor the attention that they bring. People also sometimes get a feeling of superiority by making excuses for their lack of achievements (and thereby imaging how great they would have been if these impediments hadn't blocked their way).

If you marry someone who is likely to thwart your ambitions, perhaps your underlying motivation is to maintain an illusion: "I could have been a great success if my spouse hadn't prevented me." Failure to study can have a similar motivation: "I could have done well on this test, but my friends talked me into going to a party the night before." Adler recognized that people are not always aware of their own style of life and the assumptions behind it and may fail to understand that the real motive behind a word or action is to manipulate others. They may engage in self-defeating behavior because they have not admitted to themselves what their goals really are.

Adler tried to determine people's real motives. For example, he would ask someone who complained of a backache, "How would your life be different if you could get rid of your backache?" Those who said they would become more active were presumably suffering from physical ailments that they were trying to overcome. Those who said they could not imagine how their life would change, or said only that they would get less sympathy from others, were presumably suffering from psychologically caused ailments or, at least, were exaggerating their discomfort.

CONCEPT CHECK

5. In Adler's theory what is the relationship between striving for superiority and style of life? (Check your answer on page 505.)

Adler's View of Psychological Disorders

Any personality based on a selfish style of life is unhealthy, Adler (1928/1964) said. People's needs for one another require a **social interest**, *a sense of solidarity and identification with other people.* Note that social interest does not mean a desire to socialize; it means an interest in the welfare of society. People with a strong social interest strive for superiority and welfare of a large group of people or all of humanity. They want to cooperate with other people, not to compete. In equating mental health with a strong social interest, Adler saw mental health as a positive state, not just the absence of impairments. In Adler's view people with excessive anxieties are not suffering from an "illness." Rather, they have set immature goals, are following a faulty style of life, and show little social interest. Their response to new opportunity is "Yes, but . . ." (Adler, 1932/1964). They strive for superiority in useless ways.

For example, one of Adler's patients was a man who lived in conflict with his wife because he was constantly trying to impress and dominate her (Adler, 1927). When discussing his problems, the man revealed that he had been very slow to mature physically and had not reached puberty until he was 17 years old. Other teenagers had ignored him and had treated him like a child. He was now a physically normal adult, but he was overcompensating for those years of feeling inferior by trying to seem bigger and more important than he really was.

Adler tried to get patients to understand their own style of life and to correct the faulty assumptions on which they had based their lives. He urged them to strengthen their social interest and to strive for superiority in ways that would benefit both themselves and others.

Adler's Legacy

Adler's influence exceeds his fame, and he probably would be glad for that. His concept of the "inferiority complex" has become part of the common culture. He was the first to talk about mental health as a positive state rather than as merely the absence of impairments. Many later forms of therapy drew upon Adler's emphasis on understanding the assumptions that people make and how those assumptions influence behavior. Many psychologists also followed Adler by urging people to take responsibility for their own behavior. According to Adler the key to a healthy personality was not just freedom from disorders but "social interest," a desire for the welfare of other people.

The Learning Approach

How did you develop your personality? At least part of the answer surely depends on how you have learned to behave in certain situations. Indeed, some psychologists have argued that the whole concept of personality is overrated and that most of what we call personality is learned on a situation-by-situation basis (Mischel, 1973, 1981). For example, you might be honest about returning a lost wallet to its owner; yet you lie to your professor about why your paper is late.

So how useful is it to say that you are an honest person or even that you are "more honest than 80% of other people"? It might be more useful to describe what you do in particular situations (Mischel & Shoda, 1995). Presumably, you learned these behaviors, and different people learn different behaviors. The fact that learning is specific to a situation helps explain both variations among individuals and variations among situations for a given individual.

The Social Learning section of Chapter 6 described several ways in which we learn our personality. We learn much by imitation or by vicarious reinforcement and punishment. That is, we copy behaviors that were successful for other people and avoid behaviors that failed for others. We behave like the people that we respect and want to resemble.

Let's illustrate this idea by applying the approach to masculine and feminine personality tendencies. Part of learning how we are expected to act is developing a **gender role,** *the pattern of behavior that each person is expected to follow because of being male or*

▍Children learn gender roles partly by imitating adults, but they probably learn more from other children.

FIGURE 13.5 Gender roles vary greatly from one culture to another and even from one time period to another within a single culture. Here a Palestinian man (a) and a Vietnamese woman (b) plow the fields. Men in Bangladesh (c) and women in Thailand (d) do the wash.

female. A gender role is the psychological aspect of being male or female, as opposed to sex, which is the biological aspect. We know that gender role is at least partly learned because certain aspects vary strikingly among cultures (Figure 13.5). For example, some cultures define cooking as "women's work" and others define it as "men's work." Men wear their hair short in some cultures and long in others.

To say that children learn their gender role does not mean that anyone teaches it intentionally. People teach mainly by example. Boys tend to imitate men, and girls tend to imitate women. In one experiment children watched adults choose between an apple and a banana. If all the men chose one fruit and all the women chose the other, the boys wanted what the men had and the girls wanted what the women had (Perry & Bussey, 1979). The choice of fruit is in itself trivial, but the study shows the potential for influence on more important behaviors. Even more powerfully, boys and girls learn their gender roles from older children. In short, the learning approach focuses on specific behaviors and attempts to relate them to specific experiences.

Humanistic Psychology

Another general perspective on personality, **humanistic psychology,** *deals with consciousness, values, and abstract beliefs, including spiritual experiences and the beliefs that people live by and die for.* According to humanistic psychologists, personality depends on what people believe and how they perceive the world. If you *believe* that a particular experience was highly meaningful, then it *was* highly meaningful. A psychologist can understand your behavior only by asking you for your own evaluations and interpretations of the events in your life. (In theology a *humanist* glorifies human potentials, generally denying or paying little attention to a Supreme Being. The term *humanistic psychologist* implies nothing about religious beliefs.)

Humanistic psychology emerged in the 1950s and 1960s as a protest against both behaviorism and psychoanalysis, the dominant viewpoints in psychology at that time (Berlyne, 1981). Behaviorists and psychoanalysts often emphasize the less noble, or at least morally neutral, aspects of people's thoughts and actions, whereas humanistic psychologists see people as essentially good and striving to achieve their best potential. Also, behaviorism and psychoanalysis, despite their many differences, are both rooted in *determinism* (the belief that every behavior has a cause) and in *reductionism* (the attempt to explain behavior in terms of its component elements).

Humanistic psychologists do not try to explain behavior in terms of its parts or hidden causes. They claim that people make deliberate, conscious decisions about what to do. For example, people might decide to devote themselves to a great cause, to sacrifice their own well-being, or to risk their lives. To the humanistic psychologist, it is fruitless to ascribe such behavior to past rewards and punishments or to unconscious thought processes.

Humanistic psychologists generally study the special qualities of a given individual, as opposed to seeking means or medians for large representative groups. Their research consists mostly of recording narratives of individuals' lives, more like a biographer than like a scientist in the usual sense. Therefore, their data are qualitative, not quantitative, and often difficult to evaluate scientifically.

Carl Rogers and the Goal of Self-Actualization

Carl Rogers, an American psychologist, studied theology before turning to psychology, and the influence of those early studies is apparent in his view of human nature. Rogers became probably the most influential humanistic psychologist.

Rogers (1980) regarded human nature as basically good. He said people have a natural drive toward **self-actualization,** *the achievement of one's full potential.* According to Rogers it is as natural for people to strive for excellence as it is for a plant to grow. The drive for self-actualization is the basic drive behind the development of personality. (Rogers's concept of self-actualization is similar to Adler's concept of striving for superiority. Adler was a forerunner of humanistic psychology.)

Children evaluate themselves and their actions beginning at an early age. They learn that what they do is sometimes good and sometimes bad. They develop a **self-concept,** *an image of what they really are,* and an **ideal self,** *an image of what they would like to be.* Rogers measured a person's self-concept and ideal self by handing the person a stack of cards containing statements such as "I am honest" and "I am suspicious of others." The person would then sort the statements into piles representing *true of me* and *not true of me* or arrange them in a continuum from *most true of me* to *least true of me.* (This method is known as a *Q-sort.*) Then Rogers would provide an identical stack of cards and ask the person to sort them into two piles: *true of my ideal self* and *not true of my ideal self.* In this manner he could determine whether someone's self-concept was similar to his or her ideal self; people who perceive a great discrepancy between the two generally feel distress. Humanistic psychologists try to help people overcome this distress either by improving their self-concept or by revising their ideal self.

To promote human welfare, Rogers maintained that people should relate to one another with **unconditional positive regard,** a relationship that Thomas Harris (1967) described as "I'm OK—You're OK." Unconditional positive regard is *the complete, unqualified acceptance of another person as he or she is,* much like the love of a parent for a child. If you feel unconditional positive regard, you might disapprove of someone's actions or intentions, but you would still accept and love that person. (This view resembles the Christian admonition to "hate the sin but love the sinner.") The alternative is *conditional positive regard,* the attitude that "I shall like you only if . . . ." People who are treated this way may feel restrained about opening themselves to new ideas or activities for fear of losing someone else's support.

Abraham Maslow and the Self-Actualized Personality

Abraham Maslow, another founder of humanistic psychology, complained that most psychologists concentrate on disordered personalities, assuming that all personality is either "normal" or worse than normal. Maslow insisted that personality can differ from normal

▮ Carl Rogers maintained that people naturally strive toward positive goals and that they do not need special urging. He recommended that people relate to one another with "unconditional positive regard."

▮ Abraham Maslow, one of the founders of humanistic psychology, introduced the concept of a "self-actualized personality," a personality associated with high productivity and enjoyment of life.

Harriet Tubman (1823–1913)
© CORBIS

■ Harriet Tubman, identified by Maslow as having a self-actualized personality, was a leader of the Underground Railroad, a system for helping slaves escape from the southern states before the Civil War. Maslow defined the self-actualized personality by first identifying highly admirable people, such as Tubman, and then determining which personality features they shared.

in positive, desirable ways. He proposed that people's highest need is *self-actualization,* the fulfillment of an individual's potential. That is, of course, a difficult concept, as we have no way to know what someone's potential is or whether he or she has achieved it, but we can recognize people who seem to be coming closer than others are.

As a first step toward describing the self-actualized personality, Maslow (1962, 1971) made a list of people who in his opinion were approaching their full potential. His list included people he knew personally as well as some from history. He then sought to discover what, if anything, they had in common.

According to Maslow (1962, 1971), people with a self-actualized (or self-actualizing) personality show the following characteristics:

- An accurate perception of reality: They perceive the world as it is, not as they would like it to be. They are willing to accept uncertainty and ambiguity.
- Independence, creativity, and spontaneity: They make their own decisions, even if others disagree.
- Acceptance of themselves and others: They treat people with unconditional positive regard.

- A problem-centered outlook rather than a self-centered outlook: They think about how to solve a problem, not how to make themselves look good. They also concentrate on significant problems, such as philosophical or political issues, not just the petty issues of getting through the day.
- Enjoyment of life: They are open to positive experiences, including "peak experiences" when they feel truly fulfilled and content.
- A good sense of humor.

Critics have attacked Maslow's description on the ground that, because it is based on his own choice of examples, it may simply reflect the characteristics that he himself admired. That is, his reasoning was circular: He defined certain people as self-actualized and then inquired what they had in common to figure out what "self-actualized" means (Neher, 1991). In any case Maslow paved the way for other attempts to define a healthy personality as something more than a personality without disorder.

CONCEPT CHECK ☑

6. According to humanistic psychologists, is developing a self-actualized personality a way to achieve another person's unconditional positive regard? (Check your answer on page 505.)

IN CLOSING

In Search of Human Nature

Most psychologists would list as the three most comprehensive personality theorists Freud, Jung, and Adler, who all lived and worked in Austria in the early 1900s. Here we are, close to a century later, and most specialists in personality research neither accept any of those three theories nor attempt to replace them with something better. The whole idea of a single theory of personality seems either wrong or at best premature. These theories have been historically influential, however, and they have produced both the questions and the hypotheses that have guided much of later research.

Recall from Chapter 1 that a good research question is interesting and answerable. Fundamental questions about human nature are extraordinarily interesting, but answering them is extraordinarily difficult. Most researchers today try to answer smaller questions about specific, measurable aspects of behavior, as the next two modules will describe. If and when researchers answer a long series of simpler questions, it may make more sense to return to the big questions of "what makes people tick?"

Summary

- *Personality theories as views of human nature.* Personality consists of the stable, consistent ways in which the behavior of one person differs from that of others. Theories of personality are closely related to conceptions of human nature. Some observers believe that human beings are basically hostile and need to be restrained (Hobbes, Freud). Others believe that humans are basically good (Rousseau, Rogers). (page 491)
- *Psychodynamic theories.* Several historically influential theories have described personality as the outcome of internal forces of which people are not fully conscious. (page 491)
- *Freud.* Sigmund Freud, the founder of psychoanalysis, proposed that human behavior is greatly influenced by unconscious thoughts and motives and that much of what we do and say has hidden meanings. Critics say he twisted his evidence to fit his theories instead of deriving theories from the evidence itself. (page 492)
- *Freud's psychosexual stages.* Freud believed that many unconscious thoughts and motives are sexual in nature. He proposed that people progress through stages or periods of psychosexual development—oral, anal, phallic, latent, and genital—and that frustration at any stage fixates the libido at that stage. (page 493)
- *Defense mechanisms.* Freud and his followers argued that people defend themselves against anxiety by such mechanisms as denial, repression, projection, and reaction formation. (page 495)
- *Jung.* Carl Jung believed that all people share a "collective unconscious" that represents the entire experience of humanity. (page 498)
- *Adler.* Alfred Adler proposed that people's primary motivation is a striving for superiority. Each person adopts his or her own "style of life," or method of striving. (page 500)
- *Adler's view of a healthy personality.* According to Adler the healthiest style of life is one that emphasizes "social interest"—that is, concern for the welfare of others. (page 500)
- *The learning approach.* The behaviors that constitute personality can be learned through individual experience, or by vicarious reinforcement and punishment. Different people develop different behavior patterns ("personalities") at least partly because of different experiences. (page 501)
- *Humanistic psychology.* Humanistic psychologists emphasize conscious, deliberate decision making. (page 502)

Answers to Concept Checks

1. Freud would interpret this behavior as a fixation at the oral stage. (page 495)
2. Someone with a strong id and a weak superego could be expected to give in to a variety of sexual and other impulses that other people would inhibit. Someone with an unusually strong superego would be unusually inhibited and dominated by feelings of guilt. (page 495)
3. **a.** displacement; **b.** denial; **c.** reaction formation; **d.** projection; **e.** repression; **f.** regression; **g.** rationalization; **h.** sublimation. (page 497)
4. Jung's collective unconscious is the same for all people and is present at birth. Freud believed the unconscious developed from repressed experiences. (page 500)
5. In Adler's theory a person's style of life is a method of striving for superiority. (page 500)
6. No. People strive for self-actualization because of their own intrinsic desire for it, not for any external reward. Unconditional positive regard is like the love of a parent for a child, independent of what the other person does. (page 504)

What traits provide the best description of personality?

Why do people differ in their personalities?

With regard to human personality, which would you say?

a. Every person is different from every other.
b. Way down deep, we're all the same.
c. It depends.

I vote for "it depends." The answer depends on our purposes. By analogy, in some ways every rock is unique. If you want to know the fair market value of a rock, you cannot treat diamonds the same as granite, and if you want to predict how well a rock will conduct electricity or how easily you could break it, you need to know a good deal about the content of the rock. However, if you want to predict how fast a rock will fall if you drop it or what will happen when you throw it against a window, one kind of rock is about the same as another.

■ Like this man playing the role of a woman in Japanese Kabuki theater, actors can present personalities that are very different from their private ones. All of us occasionally display temporary personalities that are different from our usual selves.

Similarly, people resemble one another in some ways but not others. Psychologists study personalities in two ways, called the nomothetic and the idiographic approaches. The word *nomothetic* (NAHM-uh-THEHT-ick) comes from the Greek *nomothetes,* meaning "legislator," and the **nomothetic approach** *seeks general laws about various aspects of personality,* based on studies of large groups of people. For example, we might make the nomothetic statement that people vary in a trait called *extraversion,* and the more extraverted someone is, the more likely that person will introduce himself or herself to a stranger.

In contrast the word *idiographic* is based on the root *idio-,* meaning "individual." The **idiographic approach** concentrates on *intensive studies of individuals* (Allport, 1961). For example, a psychologist might study one person in detail, trying to understand that person's goals, moods, and reactions. The conclusions would apply only to this person and anyone else who is very similar.

Personality Traits and States

Meteorologists distinguish between climate (the usual conditions) and weather (the current conditions). For example, the climate in Scotland is moister and cooler than the climate in Texas, but on a given day, the weather could be warm in Scotland and cool in Texas. Similarly, psychologists distinguish between long-lasting personality conditions and temporary fluctuations.

A *consistent, long-lasting tendency in behavior, such as shyness, hostility, or talkativeness,* is known as a **trait.** In contrast a **state** is *a temporary activation of a particular behavior.* For example, being afraid at a particular moment is a state; being nervous most of the time is a trait. Being quiet in a library is a state; being quiet habitually is a trait. A trait, like a climate condition, manifests itself as an average over time, though not at every moment. For example, someone who is usually quiet will have an occasional talkative moment, and someone who is usually outgoing may be shy in special circumstances.

Note that both traits and states are descriptions of behavior, not explanations. To say that someone is nervous and quiet does not explain anything; it merely tells us what we are trying to explain.

7. Suppose someone becomes nervous as soon as he sits down in a dentist's chair. Is this experience "trait anxiety" or "state anxiety"? (Check your answer on page 514.)

The Search for Broad Personality Traits

The point of the **trait approach to personality** is the idea that *people have consistent personality characteristics that can be measured and studied.* Psychologists have described, studied, and measured a great many personality traits, such as honesty, friendliness, authoritarianism, and nervousness.

Some of the research deals with traits that are not familiar descriptions in everyday life. For example, people who *believe they are largely in control of their lives* are said to have an **internal locus of control.** Those who *believe they are controlled mostly by external forces* are said to have an **external locus of control** (Rotter, 1966). Table 13.2 lists some items from a questionnaire designed to measure locus of control. After you complete these items, check answer A on page 514. Generally, people with an internal locus of control like to choose tasks where they believe they can control the outcome, and then they persist at these tasks. At the end they take the credit or blame for the outcome.

TABLE 13.2   Sample Items from the Internal–External Scale

For each item, choose the statement you agree with more.
1. a. Without the right breaks, one cannot be an effective leader. b. Capable people who fail to become leaders have not taken advantage of their opportunities.
2. a. Becoming a success is a matter of hard work; luck has little or nothing to do with it. b. Getting a good job depends mainly on being in the right place at the right time.
3. a. As far as world affairs are concerned, most of us are the victims of forces we can neither understand nor control. b. By taking an active part in political and social affairs, people can control world events.
4. a. Many times I feel that I have little influence over the things that happen to me. b. It is impossible for me to believe that chance or luck plays an important role in my life.

Source: Rotter, 1966, pp. 11–12.

8. Who would be more likely to buy lottery tickets—someone with an internal or external locus of control? (Check your answer on page 514.)

Issues in Personality Measurement

In past chapters, particularly in the discussions of intelligence and emotion, we have dealt with difficulties of measurement. Progress in any field depends on good measurement, and in personality research measurement is particularly difficult. The problem is that we care about how someone acts *in general* (the person's traits), but behavior fluctuates substantially from one moment to another. The same is true to some extent for any aspect of psychology: Your memory varies from one time to another, and so do your intelligence and even your vision and hearing. But those fluctuations are small compared to fluctuations in personality: You might be very friendly and outgoing at one time or in one situation but much less so an hour later. Theoretically, a researcher could observe your behavior nonstop for days or weeks to get an adequate sample, but by far the most common procedure is to ask you, or someone who knows you well, to report about your personality with a questionnaire.

Devising and evaluating a useful questionnaire are more difficult than you might think. Recall the discussion of reliability and validity from Chapter 9. Reliability means repeatability or consistency of scores; validity means usefulness of the scores for predicting something else. Determining the reliability of a personality questionnaire is the first step; if the reliability is low, then some of the questions may be unclear or confusing, or different questions may be measuring different aspects of personality. Validity is more difficult. When people rate their own personality, can we trust them to be accurate? For example, most Americans describe their own intelligence as well above average, whereas the British are more modest, and the Japanese are still more modest, although on actual IQ tests the British do at least as well as Americans and the Japanese usually do better (Furnham, Hosoe, & Tang, 2002). On personality questionnaires also, presumably people vary in how accurately they describe themselves.

One way to check the validity of a personality questionnaire is to compare questionnaire results to behaviors recorded in diary form. In one study 170 college students filled out questionnaires about several personality dimensions including aggressiveness and spontaneity. Then they kept daily records of such behaviors as yelling at someone (aggression) and buying something on the spur of the moment (spontaneous behavior). Both kinds of data rely on self-reports, but the daily behavior records are more detailed, closer in time to the actual events, and presumably more accurate. The questionnaire results correlated about .4 with reports of aggressive behavior, but less well with reports of spontaneous acts (Wu & Clark, 2003). That is, the questionnaire results were moderately accurate measurements.

In another study 10- to 11-year-old girls filled out a questionnaire about conscientiousness (tendency to follow the rules and keep one's promises), and a year later reported whether they had engaged in any risky sexual behaviors. Conscientiousness correlated –.42 with risky sexual behaviors; that is, those girls low in conscientiousness were the most likely to engage in risky sexual activities (Markey, Markey, & Tinsley, 2003). Again, it appears that the personality questionnaire is measuring an important aspect of behavior—not perfectly, but moderately well.

An Example of Measurement Problems: Self-Esteem

For some years a popular goal among both psychologists and the general public was to raise people's self-esteem. The belief was that low self-esteem led to self-destructive activities and violence toward others, whereas high self-esteem led to satisfaction, productivity, and a host of other good outcomes. That belief was only a hypothesis, however, and researchers needed data to test it. Psychologists developed several questionnaires to measure self-esteem and devised programs to help people raise their self-esteem. However, research results were mixed and often disappointing. On the plus side, as people increase their self-esteem, they are less likely to feel depressed (Watson, Suls, & Haig, 2002). However, raising people's self-esteem generally has little effect on aggressive behavior and in many cases leads to *decreased* performance in school or on the job (Baumeister, Campbell, Krueger, & Vohs, 2003). Evidently, if we convince people that "you're doing great," they see little need to try harder!

Part of the problem is that self-esteem means many things, and different questionnaires measure it differently. Consider some example questions on self-esteem questionnaires (Blascovich & Tomaka, 1991). Here is one set of examples:

- I feel that I have a number of good qualities.
- I am able to do things as well as most other people.
- At times I think I'm no good at all.
- I'm a failure.

An answer of "true" to the first two or "false" to the second two would count as points toward a high self-esteem score. Contrast those to the following items from a different self-esteem questionnaire, on which you are to answer from 1 (rarely or never) to 5 (usually or always):

- I feel that I am a beautiful person.
- I think that I make a good impression on others.
- I think that I have a good sense of humor.
- I feel that people really like me very much.

Would you call those items "self-esteem" or "self-evaluation"? Certainly, they highlight a different aspect of self-regard. For example, you might think you have "a number of good qualities" as in the first set of items but not describe yourself as "beautiful."

Now consider these additional true–false items:

- There are lots of things about myself I'd change if I could.
- I'm often sorry for the things I do.
- I'm not doing as well in school as I'd like.
- I wish I could change my physical appearance.

A "true" answer on any of those items would count as a point toward low self-esteem. But do the answers really indicate low self-esteem or high goals? Someone who says "true" is presumably striving for self-improvement. Someone who says "false" is satisfied with current performance, whatever that might be. In short, a self-esteem questionnaire might not be measuring what we want to measure.

Here is an additional problem: Most Americans rate themselves above average in intelligence, personality, and self-esteem. Therefore, if you rate yourself "average," you are considered to have *below-average* self-esteem! Next a survey asks what you think of minority groups or foreigners. Most Americans claim to have a "very high" opinion of minority groups and foreigners, so if you rate them "about average," you are considered to have a *below-average* opinion of them. Using these methods some studies have reported that "people with low self-esteem tend to be prejudiced," when a better statement of the data would be "people who rate themselves average rate other people average too" (Baumeister et al., 2003). As emphasized before, to evaluate anyone's conclusions, we need to examine the evidence carefully, especially the measurement methods.

CONCEPT CHECK ☑

9. If someone's questionnaire results indicate "low self-esteem," what else might the results actually mean, other than low self-esteem? (Check your answer on page 514.)

The Big Five Model of Personality

Psychologists have devised questionnaires to measure locus of control, self-esteem, aggressiveness, and hundreds of other traits. Measuring hundreds of traits is impractical; the goal should be a simple system listing no more traits than necessary. Remember the principle of parsimony from Chapter 2: If we can adequately describe personality with, say, five or ten traits, we do not need to measure more.

One way to begin is by examining our language. Many psychologists assume that any human language probably has a word for every important personality trait. Although this assumption is not a logical necessity, it seems reasonable considering how much attention people pay to other people's personalities.

Gordon Allport and H. S. Odbert (1936) plodded through an English dictionary and found almost 18,000 words that might be used to describe personality. They deleted from this list words that were merely evaluations, such as *nasty*, and terms referring to temporary states, such as *confused*. (At least we hope that being confused is temporary.) In the remaining list, they looked for clusters of synonyms, such as *affectionate, warm,* and *loving,* and kept only one of these terms. When they found opposites, such as *honest* and *dishonest,* they also kept just one of them. (*Honesty* and *dishonesty* are different extremes of one dimension, not separate traits.) After eliminating synonyms and antonyms, Raymond Cattell (1965) narrowed the original list to 35 traits.

Derivation of the Big Five Personality Traits

Although some of the 35 personality traits that Cattell identified are not exactly synonyms or antonyms of one another, many of them overlapped. To determine which traits correlate with one another, psychologists use a method called *factor analysis.* For example, if measurements of warmth, gregariousness, and assertiveness correlate strongly with one another, we can cluster them together as a single trait. But if this combined trait does not correlate highly with self-discipline, then self-discipline (and anything that correlates strongly with it) is a separate trait.

Using this approach researchers found major clusters of personality traits, which they call the **big five personality traits:** *neuroticism, extraversion, agreeableness, conscientiousness, and openness to new experience* (McCrae & Costa, 1987). The case for these five traits is that (a) each correlates with many personality dimensions for which our language has a word and (b) none of these five traits correlates highly with any of the other five, so they are not measuring the same thing.

The big five dimensions are described in the following list (Costa, McCrae, & Dye, 1991). Note that the first two, neuroticism and extraversion, are the "biggest" of the big five. Even psychologists who are skeptical of the big five model agree that neuroticism

and extraversion are powerful traits that influence much of human behavior (Block, 1995).

Neuroticism is *a tendency to experience unpleasant emotions relatively easily.* Neuroticism correlates positively with anxiety, hostility, depression, and self-consciousness. In one study college students kept a diary in which they recorded the most stressful event of the day. Students who scored high on a neuroticism questionnaire were more likely than other students to identify their most stressful event as some conflict they had with another person. They were also more likely than other students to rate the experience as highly distressing, and they were less likely than others to deal effectively with their stressful events (Gunthert, Cohen, & Armeli, 1999).

Extraversion is *a tendency to seek stimulation and to enjoy the company of other people.* The opposite of extraversion is introversion. Extraversion is associated with warmth, gregariousness, assertiveness, impulsiveness, and a need for excitement. Extraverted people tend to be risk-takers, and the unpleasant side of extraversion is an increased risk of alcohol abuse and similar problems (Martsh & Miller, 1997). The pleasant side is that extraverts tend to be happy most of the time (Francis, Brown, Lester, & Philipchalk, 1998). In one study participants reported five times a day for 2 weeks what they had been doing and how they were feeling. Generally, they reported feeling happy at the same times when they had been talkative, energetic, and adventuresome. Furthermore, when people were *instructed* to act in an extraverted way, they reported feeling happier afterward, and when instructed to act in an introverted way, they reported decreased happiness, regardless of whether they were usually extraverted or introverted (Fleeson, Malanos, & Achille, 2002). These results imply that active, outgoing behavior leads to happiness, although it is also likely that happiness leads to active, outgoing behavior.

Active, outgoing behavior   Happy feelings

Agreeableness is *a tendency to be compassionate toward others.* It implies a concern for the welfare of other people and is closely related to Adler's concept of social interest. People high in agreeableness generally trust other people and expect other people to trust them.

Conscientiousness is *a tendency to show self-discipline, to be dutiful, and to strive for achievement and competence.* People high in conscientiousness tend to show a strong work motivation (Judge & Ilies, 2002). They are likely to complete the tasks they say they will perform. If you were giving a speech or making some other kind of performance, would you prefer to have your performance rated by someone high in agreeableness or conscientiousness? As you might guess, people high in conscientiousness generally give lower, presumably more honest, ratings, whereas people high in agreeableness give higher, more generous ratings (Bernardin, Cooke, & Villanova, 2000).

Openness to experience, the big five trait that is usually the least variable and hardest to observe, is *a tendency to enjoy new intellectual experiences and new ideas.* Someone high in this trait would be likely to enjoy modern art, unusual music, thought-provoking films and plays, and so forth. People open to experience enjoy meeting different kinds of people and exploring new ideas and opinions (McCrae, 1996).

CONCEPT CHECK ☑

10. Some psychologists suggest that we should divide extraversion into two traits—which they call *ambition* and *sociability*—changing the big five

Courtesy of Morimura Yasumasa

▌ The Japanese artist Morimura Yasumasa re-creates famous paintings, substituting his own face for the original. Some people love his work; others dislike it or object to the whole idea. People high in "openness to experience" delight in new, unusual forms of art, literature, and music.

into the big six. How should psychologists determine whether to do so? (Check your answer on page 514.)

Criticisms and Problems

You may already have thought about one peculiarity of the research so far: Almost none of the research behind the big five model depended on observing people's behavior. The research was based entirely on a study of personality words in the English language and people's answers to questionnaires. Questionnaire results are moderately good predictors of real behavior, but they are far from perfect.

The research methods could overlook certain personality traits just because of quirks of the English language. For example, we identify extraversion–introversion as a big factor because it relates to so many words in the English language—sociability, warmth, friendliness, adventuresomeness, gregariousness, happiness, and so forth. Religiousness would not emerge as a major personality trait because the language has few synonyms for it. Critics of the big five approach have identified nine personality dimensions that the big five model seems to have overlooked (Paunonen & Jackson, 2000). These nine are religiousness, manipulativeness, honesty, sexiness, thriftiness, conservativeness, masculinity–femininity, snobbishness, and sense of humor. None of these correlates very strongly with any of the others or with the big five.

Other critics raise the opposite objection that five is more traits than we need. Openness to experience has a modest positive correlation with extraversion, and conscientiousness correlates negatively with neuroticism, so perhaps we could get by with just three factors: neuroticism, extraversion, and agreeableness (Eysenck, 1992).

Cross-cultural studies offer partial, but only partial, support to the big five approach. Some studies have used translations of English words or an array of personality descriptions from other languages. Others have shown pictures of people in various activities and asked, "How likely would you be to do this?" The picture approach makes it easy to test people of various cultures without first thoroughly studying their language (Paunonen, Zeidner, Engvik, Oosterveld, & Maliphant, 2000). Many studies have found results approximately consistent with the big five model (McCrae & Costa, 1997).

However, some studies did find important cross-cultural differences. For example, in many traditional cultures, almost everyone is low in what Westerners call "openness to experience" (Mastor & Cooper, 2000; Saggino, 2000; Silverthorne, 2001). A study in China identified four big traits corresponding approximately to extraversion, neuroticism, conscientiousness, and "loyalty to Chinese traditions" (Cheung et al., 1996).

Overall, how should we evaluate the five-factor description? The answer depends on our purposes. If we are interested in a theoretical understanding of personality, it is premature at best to call the five-factor description a fact of nature (as some have done). The five-factor description accounts for enough of the variability in human behavior to be useful, although for some purposes three factors may be enough and for other purposes more may be necessary. It depends on how much precision we want in describing and predicting people's behavior.

The Origins of Personality

A description of personality differences is not an explanation. What makes some people more extraverted, neurotic, agreeable, conscientious, or open to experience than other people are?

Heredity and Environment

If you want evidence that heredity can influence personality, you need look no further than the nearest pet dog. For centuries people have selectively bred dogs for the personalities they desired, ranging from the tamest and friendliest lap dogs to those that are capable of attacking ferociously.

To measure the influences of heredity and environment on human personality, researchers have relied mostly on the same kinds of data as in other areas of psychology (Bouchard & McGue, 2003). First, they compare the similarities between identical twins and fraternal twins. As Figure 13.6 shows, five studies conducted in separate locations indicated much greater similarities in extraversion between identical pairs than fraternal pairs (Loehlin, 1992). Studies in Australia and the United States found a similar pattern for neuroticism, with identical twins resembling each other much more than fraternal twins, who resembled each other no more than brothers or sisters born at different times (Lake, Eaves, Maes, Heath, & Martin, 2000).

Modern methods make it possible to search for specific genes linked to particular personality traits. Several studies have identi-fied genes apparently linked to neuroticism or to the specific aspect of neuroticism known as *harm avoidance* or anxiety-proneness (Fullerton et al., 2003; Zohar et al., 2003). However, each of the genes identified so far makes only a small contribution, and researchers have not yet established the route by which any gene acts.

Second, researchers compare the personalities of parents, their biological children, and their adopted children. As Figure 13.7 shows, parents' extraversion levels correlate moderately with those of their biological children but hardly at all with their adopted children. Similarly, biologically related brothers or sisters growing up together resemble each other moderately in personality, and unrelated children adopted into the same family do not (Loehlin, 1992). The results shown in Figures 13.6 and 13.7 pertain to extraversion; similar studies provide a largely similar pattern for neuroticism and other personality traits (Heath, Neale, Kessler, Eaves, & Kendler, 1992; Loehlin, 1992; Viken, Rose, Kaprio, & Koskenvuo, 1994).

The low correlations between adopted children and adoptive parents imply that children learn rather little of their personalities by imitating their parents.

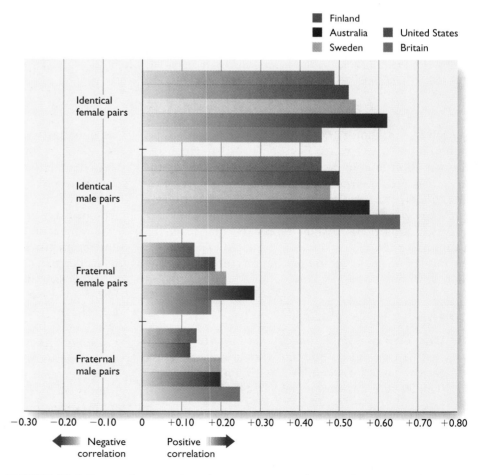

FIGURE 13.6 Five studies—conducted in Great Britain, the United States, Sweden, Australia, and Finland—found larger correlations between the extraversion levels of identical (monozygotic) twins than those of fraternal (dizygotic) twins. *(Based on data summarized by Loehlin, 1992)*

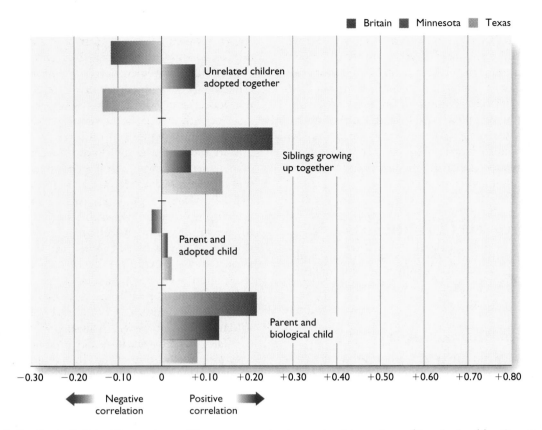

FIGURE 13.7 Studies in Britain, Minnesota, and Texas measured extraversion in members of hundreds of families. Each found moderate positive correlations between parents and their biological children and between pairs of biologically related brothers and sisters. However, all found low or even negative correlations between parents and adopted children and among adopted children living in the same family. *(Based on data summarized by Loehlin, 1992)*

(Recall from Chapter 10 that Judith Harris made this same point.) Many researchers believe that much of the variation among people's personalities relates to the **unshared environment,** *the aspects of environment that differ from one individual to another, even within a family.* Unshared environment includes the effects of a particular playmate, a particular teacher, an injury or illness, or any other isolated experience. Because of its idiosyncratic nature, unshared environment is difficult to investigate.

CONCEPT CHECK ☑

11. What evidence would indicate an important role of the *shared environment*—the influences that are the same for all children within a family? (Check your answer on page 514.)

Influences of Age and Historical Era

Do you think your personality now resembles what it was in childhood? In some aspects it probably does. In one study investigators observed the behavior of 3-year-

old children and followed them longitudinally until age 26. Children who were fearful and easily upset at age 3 were more nervous and inhibited than others at age 26. Those who were impulsive and restless at age 3 tended to have been in trouble with others from then on and to feel alienated from society. On the other hand, those who were confident, friendly, and eager to explore their environment at 3 tended to be confident adults, eager to take charge of events (Caspi, Harrington, et al., 2003).

Will your personality change much in the next few years? According to the research, the older people get, the more consistent their personalities remain over time. In childhood, answers on a personality questionnaire correlate a modest .34 between two tests given 6 or 7 years apart. By college age the correlation is .54. It increases to .64 at age 30 and .74 at age 60 (Roberts & DelVecchio, 2000). Why personality becomes more fixed as we grow older is not known, but you can probably imagine a few hypotheses.

The differences that occur over age are not large, but they are fairly predictable, and many are consistent across cultures. One trend is that as people grow older, they become more conscientious. In every culture that has been studied throughout the world, middle-aged people are more likely to be highly conscientious—that is, to do what they promise they will do—than are teenagers (McCrae et al., 2000). A simple explanation is that adults are forced, whether they like it or not, to hold a job, pay the bills, repair the house, care for children, and take responsibility in other ways.

As people age, they also tend to become less extraverted, especially less sensation seeking. Again this trend is found cross-culturally (Labouvie-Vief, Diehl, Tarnowksi, & Shen, 2000). Older people also tend to be less neurotic—that is, less prone to anxieties and unpleasant mood swings—and slightly more agreeable (Cramer, 2003; McCrae et al., 2000). In the United States, young people on the average score higher on openness to new experience than older people. This trend is no surprise; we see that young people enjoy new types of music, new kinds of food, new styles of clothing, and so forth (Sapolsky, 1998), whereas older people stay with old habits. In some other cultures, however, openness to experience shows no clear trend over age (McCrae et al., 2000).

Finally, does personality change from one generation to the next? Remember the Flynn effect from Chapter 9: Over the years people's performance on IQ tests has gradually increased so that each generation does better on the tests than the previous generation. Researchers have also found generational differences in personality. For example, over the years, beginning in the 1950s, measurements of anxiety have steadily increased (Twenge, 2000). On the Child Manifest Anxiety Scale, the mean score in the 1950s was 15.1, and the mean for children in mental hospitals was 20.1. By the 1980s the mean for *all* children was 23.3! Do we really have that much more anxiety than in past generations? It is possible that people's answers do not mean exactly the same as what they used to. The more disturbing possibility is that we really do live in an age of anxiety despite our increases in health and wealth and the decreased probability of nuclear war. Compared to past generations, more children today have to live through their parents' divorce, and fewer live in a neighborhood with many friends and relatives. Might those social changes have raised the average anxiety level to what used to characterize the top 10%? The answer is uncertain, but now researchers need to worry about why people worry so much.

IN CLOSING

The Challenges of Classifying Personality

Personality descriptions refer to averages over time. We don't expect anyone to be equally extraverted at all times or equally neurotic, conscientious, agreeable, open to experience, or anything else. What you do at any moment depends largely on the situation. In a sufficiently novel situation, you may be surprised by the actions of people you know well, and even by your own behavior.

The dimensions of personality apply best in familiar situations that apply few constraints on us, allowing personality differences to emerge clearly. The first step is for researchers to describe those differences. Later, they can better address the causes of the differences—the issues of "what makes us tick" that we addressed in the first module.

Summary

- *Nomothetic and idiographic research.* Nomothetic studies examine large numbers of people briefly, whereas idiographic studies examine one or a few individuals intensively. (page 506)

- *Traits and states.* Traits are personality characteristics that persist over time; states are temporary tendencies in response to particular situations. (page 506)

- *Measurement problems.* Personality researchers rely mostly on self-reports, which are not entirely accurate. Many people misrepresent themselves, either knowingly or unintentionally. (page 507)

- *Five major traits.* Much of personality can be explained by these five traits: neuroticism, extraversion, openness to new experience, agreeableness, and conscientiousness. However, several other important dimensions may have been overlooked. (page 508)

- *Determinants of personality.* Studies of twins and adopted children indicate that heredity contributes to the observed differences in personality. Family environment evidently contributes rather little. Much of the variation in personality may be due to unshared environment, the special experiences that vary from one person to another even within a family. (page 511)

- *Changes over time.* Compared to younger people, older people tend to be higher in conscientiousness and agreeableness. They are somewhat lower in extraversion and neuroticism. Openness to experience decreases with age in the United States, but several other countries do not show this trend. (page 512)

- *Changes over historical era.* Measurements of anxiety have gradually increased over the decades so that normal people now report anxiety levels that used to characterize people in mental hospitals. (page 513)

Answers to Concept Checks

7. This nervousness is state anxiety because it is evoked by a particular situation. Trait anxiety is a tendency to become nervous in many situations. (page 507)

8. People with an external locus of control would be more likely to buy lottery tickets. Those with an internal locus of control prefer tasks where they can control the outcome. (page 507)

9. Depending on the questionnaire items, what appears to be low self-esteem might indicate high goals and therefore lack of satisfaction with one's current performance. Also, rating one's intelligence and personality as "average" could simply mean that the person tends to use the middle part of the rating scale. (page 508)

10. They should determine whether measures of ambition correlate strongly with measures of sociability. If so, then ambition and sociability can be considered two aspects of a single trait, extraversion. If not, then they are indeed separate personality traits. (page 510)

11. If the personalities of adopted children within a family correlated highly with one another, we would conclude that the similarity reflected the shared environment. The weakness of such correlations is the main evidence for the importance of the unshared environment. (page 512)

Answer to Other Question in the Module

A. Choices 1b, 2a, 3b, and 4b indicate internal locus of control; the other choices indicate external locus of control. Your answers to a longer list of such items could more accurately assess your locus of control. (page 507)

Personality Assessment

What inferences can we safely draw from the results of a personality test?

A new P. T. Barnum Psychology Clinic has just opened at your local shopping mall and is offering a grand opening special on personality tests. You have always wanted to know more about yourself, so you sign up. Here is Barnum's true–false test:

Questionnaire for Universal Assessment of Zealous Youth (QUAZY)

1. I have never met a cannibal I didn't like.	T	F
2. Robbery is the only felony I have ever committed.	T	F
3. I eat "funny mushrooms" less frequently than I used to.	T	F
4. I don't care what people say about my nose-picking habit.	T	F
5. Sex with vegetables no longer disgusts me.	T	F
6. This time I am quitting glue-sniffing for good.	T	F
7. I generally lie on questions like this one.	T	F
8. I spent much of my childhood sucking on telephone cords.	T	F
9. I find it impossible to sleep if I think my bed might be clean.	T	F
10. Naked bus drivers make me nervous.	T	F
11. I spend my spare time playing strip solitaire.	T	F

You turn in your answers. A few minutes later, a computer prints out your individual personality profile:

> You have a need for other people to like and admire you, and yet you tend to be critical of yourself. While you have some personality weaknesses, you are generally able to compensate for them. You have considerable unused capacity that you have not turned to your advantage. Disciplined and self-controlled on the outside, you tend to be worrisome and insecure on the inside. At times, you have serious doubts as to whether you have made the right decision or done the right thing. You prefer a certain amount of change and variety and become dissatisfied when hemmed in by restrictions and limitations. You also pride yourself as an independent thinker and do not accept others' statements without satisfac-

tory proof. But you have found it unwise to be too frank in revealing yourself to others. At times you are extraverted, affable, and sociable, while at other times you are introverted, wary, and reserved. Some of your aspirations tend to be rather unrealistic. (Forer, 1949, p. 120)

Do you agree with this assessment? Several experiments have been conducted along these lines with psychology classes (Forer, 1949; Marks & Kammann, 1980; Ulrich, Stachnik, & Stainton, 1963). Students started by filling out a questionnaire that looked fairly reasonable, not something as preposterous as the QUAZY. Several days later, each student received a sealed envelope with his or her name on it. Inside was a "personality profile," supposedly based on the student's answers to the questionnaire. The students were asked, "How accurately does this profile describe you?" About 90% rated it as good or excellent. Some expressed amazement at its accuracy: "I didn't realize until now that psychology was an exact science." None of them realized that everyone had received exactly the same personality profile—the same one you just read.

The students accepted this personality profile partly because it vaguely describes almost everyone, much like newspaper horoscopes do, and partly because people tend to accept almost *any* statement that a psychologist makes about them (Marks & Kammann, 1980). *This tendency to accept and praise vague statements about our personality is known as the* **Barnum effect,** named after P. T. Barnum, the circus

▌ People tend to accept almost any personality assessment that someone offers them, especially if it is stated in vague, general terms that each person can interpret to fit himself or herself.

owner who specialized in fooling people out of their money.

The conclusion: Psychological testing must be done carefully. If we want to know whether a particular test measures a particular person's personality, we cannot simply ask that person's opinion. Many people will praise as "highly accurate" even the results of a worthless test. To devise a psychological test that not only *appears* to work but also actually *does* work, psychologists need to design the test carefully and determine its reliability and validity.

Standardized Personality Tests

Psychologists have devised a great variety of personality tests. A **standardized test** is *one that is administered according to exact rules that specify how to interpret the results.* One important step for standardizing a test is to determine the distribution of scores. We need to know the mean score and the range of scores for a representative sample of the population and how they differ for special populations, such as people with severe depression. Given such information, we can determine whether a particular score on a personality test is within the normal range or whether it is more typical of people with some disorder.

Most of the tests published in popular magazines have never been standardized. A magazine may herald an article: "Test Yourself: How Good Is Your Marriage?" or "Test Yourself: How Well Do You Control the Stress in Your Life?" After you take the test and compare your answers to the scoring key, the article may tell you that "if your score is greater than 80, you are doing very well . . . if it is below 20, you need to work on improving yourself!"—or some such nonsense. Unless the magazine states otherwise, you can safely assume that the author pulled the scoring norms out of thin air and never even bothered to make sure that the test items were clearly stated.

Over the years psychologists have developed an enormous variety of tests to measure both normal and abnormal personality. We shall examine a few prominent examples and explore some creative possibilities for future personality measurement.

An Objective Personality Test: The Minnesota Multiphasic Personality Inventory

Some of the most widely used personality tests are based on simple pencil-and-paper responses. We now consider in detail the MMPI, the most widely used of all personality tests (Piotrowski & Keller, 1989).

The **Minnesota Multiphasic Personality Inventory** (mercifully abbreviated MMPI) consists of *a series of true–false questions intended to measure certain personality dimensions and clinical conditions such as depression.* The original MMPI, developed in the 1940s and still in use, has 550 items; *the second edition,* **MMPI-2**, published in 1990, has 567. Typical items are "my mother never loved me" and "I think I would like the work of a pharmacist." (The items stated in this text are rewordings of the actual items.)

The MMPI was devised *empirically*—that is, based on evidence rather than theory (Hathaway & McKinley, 1940). The authors wrote hundreds of true–false questions that they thought might be useful for measuring personality. They put these questions to people who were known to be suffering from various psychological disorders and to a group of hospital visitors, who were assumed to be psychologically normal. The researchers selected those items that most of the people in a given clinical group answered differently from most of the normal people. They assumed, for example, that if you answer many questions as most people with depression do, you probably are depressed also. The MMPI had scales for reporting depression, paranoia, schizophrenia, and others. The result was a test that worked, and still works, moderately well in practice. For example, most people with scores above a certain level on the Depression scale are in fact depressed.

Some of the items on the MMPI made sense theoretically; others did not. For example, some items on the Depression scale asked about feelings of helplessness or worthlessness, which are an important part of depression. But two other items were "I attend religious services frequently" and "occasionally I tease animals." If you answered *false* to either of those items, you would get a point on the Depression scale! These items were included simply because more depressed people than others answered *false.* Why is not obvious. (Perhaps people with depression do not tease animals because they do hardly anything just for fun.)

Revisions of the Test

The MMPI was standardized in the 1940s. As time passed the meaning of certain items, or at least of certain answers, changed. For example, how would you respond to the following item?

I believe I am important.   T F

In the 1940s fewer than 10% of all people marked this item *true.* At the time the word "important" meant about the same thing as "famous," and people who called themselves important were thought to have an inflated view of themselves. Today, we stress that every person is important.

TABLE 13.3 The Ten MMPI-2 Clinical Scales

Scale	Typical Item
Hypochondria (Hs)	I have chest pains several times a week. (T)
Depression (D)	I am glad that I am alive. (F)
Hysteria (Hy)	My heart frequently pounds so hard I can hear it. (T)
Psychopathic Deviation (Pd)	I get a fair deal from most people. (F)
Masculinity–Femininity (Mf)	I like to arrange flowers. (T = female)
Paranoia (Pa)	There are evil people trying to influence my mind. (T)
Psychasthenia (Obsessive–Compulsive) (Pt)	I save nearly everything I buy, even after I have no use for it. (T)
Schizophrenia (Sc)	I see, hear, and smell things that no one else knows about. (T)
Hypomania (Ma)	When things are dull I try to get some excitement started. (T)
Social Introversion (Si)	I have the time of my life at parties. (F)

What about this item?

I like to play drop the handkerchief.   T F

Drop the handkerchief, a game similar to tag, dropped out of popularity in the 1950s. Most people born since then have never even heard of it, much less played it.

To bring the MMPI up to date, a group of psychologists rephrased some of the items, eliminated some, and added others to deal with drug abuse, suicidal thoughts, and other issues that did not concern psychologists in the 1940s (Butcher, Graham, Williams, & Ben-Porath, 1990). Then they tried out the new MMPI–2 on a large representative sample of the U.S. population. In other words they restandardized the test. (You may recall the discussion in Chapter 9 about the need to restandardize IQ tests.) Psychologists also developed a new form, the MMPI–A, intended for use with adolescents.

The MMPI–2 has 10 clinical scales, as shown in Table 13.3. The various scales have 32 to 78 items each, scattered throughout the test rather than clustered. Most people get at least a few points on each scale; a score above a certain level indicates a probable difficulty. Figure 13.8 shows how MMPI–2 scores are plotted.

Generalizability of the MMPI

Can a single test measure personality for all kinds of people? In particular, is the MMPI (or MMPI–2 or MMPI–A) a fair measure of personality for people of different ethnic and cultural backgrounds?

This is a difficult question to answer. In general, the means and ranges on each scale are about the same for many ethnic groups, even after translation into different languages (Negy, Leal-Puente, Trainor, & Carlson, 1997). However, differences do occur. For example, Mexicans are more likely than U.S. people to say *true* to "Life is a constant strain for me." Presumably, the reason is that life really is more difficult for many people who live in Mexico. On several scales of the MMPI–2, the means for Mexicans differ from the U.S. means (Lucio, Ampudia, Durán, León, & Butcher, 2001). Consequently, the scoring standards for a personality test should differ from one country to another. Even within a country, psychologists need to be

FIGURE 13.8 For the MMPI–2's 10 clinical scales, a score is plotted to profile an individual. This is the profile of a middle-aged man with no psychological problems. A person with a disorder such as hypochondria or paranoia would have scores in the range of 65 or higher on those scales. *(Minnesota Multiphasic Personality Inventory–2, © by the Regents of the University of Minnesota. Data courtesy of R. J. Huber.)*

cautious in interpreting scores for ethnic minorities (Gynther, 1989).

Detection of Deception

If you were taking the MMPI or another personality test, could you lie to make yourself look mentally healthier than you really are? Yes. Could someone catch your lies? Probably.

The designers of the MMPI and MMPI–2 included items designed to identify lying (Woychyshyn, McElheran, & Romney, 1992). For example, consider the items "I like every person I have ever met" and "occasionally I get angry at someone." If you answer *true* to the first question and *false* to the second, you are either a saint or a liar. The test authors, convinced that liars outnumber saints, would give you 1 point for each of these answers on a scale to measure lies. If you get too many points on that scale, a psychologist will distrust your answers to the other items. Strangely enough, some people lie on the test to try to make themselves look bad. The MMPI includes items to detect that kind of faking also.

A similar method detects deception on other questionnaires. For example, many employers ask job applicants about their experience with job-related skills. Suppose some employer's questionnaire asked you how much experience you have had at "determining myopic weights for periodic tables." You're not sure what that means, but you really want the job. Do you claim to have had extensive experience? If so, your claimed expertise will count *against* you because "determining myopic weights for periodic tables" is nonsense. The employer asked about it just to see whether you were exaggerating your qualifications on other items. According to the results of one study, almost half of all job applicants claimed to have experience with one or more nonexistent tasks (Anderson, Warner, & Spencer, 1984). Some claimed they had not only performed these tasks but had also trained others! The more skill an applicant claims to have on nonexistent tasks, the more the employer discounts that applicant's claims about real tasks.

CRITICAL THINKING:
A STEP FURTHER
Assessing Honesty

Could you use this strategy in other situations? Suppose a political candidate promises to increase aid to college students. You are skeptical. How could you use the candidate's statements on other issues to help you decide whether to believe this promise?

Uses of the MMPI

The MMPI is useful for personality assessment and for research on personality. It also helps clinical psychologists learn something about a client before therapy or measure a client's personality changes during therapy. The MMPI has better reliability and validity than many other personality tests (Garb, Florio, & Grove, 1998). However, to a client, the MMPI results are seldom surprising. For example, suppose you gave the following answers:

I doubt that I will ever be successful.	True
I am glad that I am alive.	False
I have thoughts about suicide.	True
I am helpless to control the important events in my life.	True

A psychologist analyzes your answer sheet and tells you that your results show indications of depression. Yes, of course. You already knew that. But even in a case like this, the results can be useful for comparing *how* depressed you are now and later.

CONCEPT CHECK ☑

12. Suppose a person thinks "True or false, black is my favorite color" would be a good item for the Depression scale of the MMPI. How would a researcher decide whether to include it?
13. Why does the MMPI include some items that ask about common flaws, such as, "Sometimes I think more about my own welfare than that of others"? (Check your answers on page 526.)

Projective Techniques

The MMPI and similar personality tests are easy to score and easy to handle statistically, but they restrict how a person can respond to a question. In hopes of learning more, psychologists ask open-ended questions that permit an unlimited range of responses.

However, to the inquiry "tell me about yourself," many people are reluctant to confide embarrassing information. Many people find it easier to discuss their problems in the abstract than in the first person. For instance, they might say, "I have a friend with this problem. Let me tell you my friend's problem and ask what my friend should do." They then describe their own problem. They are "projecting" their problem onto someone else, in Freud's sense of the word—that is, attributing it to someone else.

Rather than discouraging projection, psychologists often make use of it. They use **projective techniques,** which are *designed to encourage people to project their personality characteristics onto ambiguous* *stimuli.* This strategy helps people reveal themselves more fully than they normally would. Let's consider the best-known projective techniques: the Rorschach Inkblots and the Thematic Apperception Test.

CONCEPT CHECK

14. Which of the following is a projective technique?
    a. A psychologist gives a child a set of puppets with instructions to act out a story about a family.
    b. A psychologist hands you a stack of cards, each containing one word, such as *tolerant,* with instructions to sort the cards into a stack of cards that apply to you and a stack of cards that do not. (Check your answers on page 526.)

The Rorschach Inkblots

The **Rorschach Inkblots,** *a projective technique based on people's interpretations of 10 ambiguous inkblots,* is the most famous and most widely used projective personality technique. It was created by Hermann Rorschach (ROAR-shock), a Swiss psychiatrist, who showed people inkblots and asked them to say whatever came to mind (Pichot, 1984). Rorschach was impressed that his patients' interpretations of the blots differed from his own. In a book published in 1921 (English translation 1942), he presented the 10 symmetrical inkblots that still constitute the Rorschach Inkblot Technique. (Originally, he had used a larger number, but the publisher insisted on cutting the number to 10 to reduce printing costs.) As other psychiatrists and psychologists began using these blots, they gradually developed the Rorschach into the projective technique we know today.

Administering the Rorschach

The Rorschach Inkblot Technique consists of cards similar to the one in Figure 13.9. Five are in black and white and five are in color. A psychologist administering this procedure hands you a card and asks, "What might this be?" The instructions are intentionally

FIGURE 13.9 In the Rorschach Inkblot Technique, people study an abstract pattern and say what it looks like. The idea is that in an ambiguous situation personality will be revealed by anything that someone does and says.

vague on the assumption that everything you do in an ill-defined situation reveals something significant about your personality.

Sometimes people's answers are revealing, either immediately or in response to a psychologist's probes. Here is an example (Aronow, Reznikoff, & Moreland, 1995):

Client: (looking at Card 5) Some kind of insect; it's not pretty enough to be a butterfly.

Psychologist: Any association to that?

Client: It's an ugly black butterfly, no colors.

Psychologist: What does that make you think of in your own life?

Client: You probably want me to say "myself." Well, that's probably how I thought of myself when I was younger—I never thought of myself as attractive—my sister was the attractive one. I was the ugly duckling—I did get more attractive as I got older.

Evaluation of the Rorschach

It is true that personality makes a bigger difference in an ill-defined, ambiguous situation than in one where everyone is asked to do something specific. The question is how accurately a psychologist can interpret the responses in that ambiguous situation. When I describe what I see in a picture, I sometimes see how my answer relates to a past experience or current concern. But would anyone else guess the connection?

In the 1950s and 1960s, certain psychologists made exaggerated claims, even calling the Rorschach "an x-ray of the mind." Those claims provoked vigorous criticism. The main problem was that different psychologists drew different conclusions from the same answer depending on their theoretical expectations. For example, a man with depression described one blot, "It looks like a bat that has been squashed on the pavement under the heel of a giant's boot" (Dawes, 1994, p. 149). Psychologist Robyn Dawes initially was impressed with how the Rorschach had revealed the client's sense of being overwhelmed and crushed by powers beyond his control. However, Dawes later realized that he had already known the client was depressed. If a client with a history of violence had made the same response, he would have focused on the aggressive nature of the giant's foot stomp. For a hallucinating or paranoid client, he would have made still other interpretations. Psychologists often believe the Rorschach gave them some insight, when in fact they already knew it before administering the test (Wood, Nezworski, Lilienfeld, & Garb, 2003).

James Exner (1986) developed methods for interpreting Rorschach responses that were intended to standardize the interpretations. Using Exner's system, a psychologist counts the number of times a client mentions certain kinds of themes, such as aggression, how often the response refers to the whole blot or just part of it, and several other reasonably objective measurements. From comparison to standards that presumably represent normal people, a psychologist derives measures of certain kinds of mental disturbance.

However, serious problems with the Rorschach remain (Lilienfeld, Wood, & Garb, 2000; Wood et al., 2003):

- The standardization sample must have been strange because the test identifies *most* people as psychologically disturbed.
- People are asked to give as many answers as they wish on each blot, but psychologists count the *total number* of aggressive, depressive, or otherwise pathological answers. Highly intelligent or talkative people give more answers than other people do, and the more total answers you give, the more likely you are to say something that counts as "disturbed."
- Different ethnic groups have certain characteristic ways of responding that differ from the standardization group, and the test may be inappropriate for use with some groups.
- The interrater reliability of the test is only about .85. That is, different psychologists listening to the same answers do not fully agree on their counts of aggressive themes, depressive themes, and so forth. A reliability around .85 is acceptable for research purposes but is risky for making decisions about an individual.
- Many of the individual scales have doubtful validity. For example, the supposed measures of depression, anxiety, and hostility have low correlations with depressive, anxious, or hostile behavior.
- Finally and most important, the Rorschach rarely gives information that could not be obtained more easily in other ways. For example, psychologists who are given biographical and MMPI information about someone usually make the same personality judgments as psychologists who are given the same information plus the Rorschach results. In fact adding the Rorschach results sometimes makes their judgments *less* accurate.

Critics of the Rorschach stop short of calling it completely invalid. Their point is that it is not valid enough to make decisions about an individual and that it seldom provides information that a psychologist could not get more easily in other ways. For example, Rorschach results are reasonably valid for determining that someone's thinking is severely disturbed (schizophrenic), but psychologists can usually recognize a severe disturbance from a brief conversation with the person. In its defense some users of the Rorschach say they use it not for diagnosis or decisions but only as a way of starting a conversation and getting clients to

talk more freely about topics they might be reluctant to discuss (Aronow et al., 1995). Of course, if used in that way, it is no longer a personality test, and its results should not be reported. Some psychologists continue to use Rorschach results to recommend to the courts which parent should get custody of a child, which prisoners should get parole, and so forth. Using the results for those purposes should require solid evidence of validity, and that evidence is lacking (Wood et al., 2003).

CONCEPT CHECK

15. Why are highly talkative people more likely than others to have their Rorschach answers considered disturbed? (Check your answer on page 526.)

The Thematic Apperception Test

The **Thematic Apperception Test (TAT)** consists of pictures like the one shown in Figure 13.10. *The person is asked to make up a story for each picture, describing what is happening, what events led up to the scene, and what will happen in the future.* The test was devised by Christiana Morgan and Henry Murray as a means of measuring people's needs; it was revised and published by Murray (1943) and later revised by others. It includes 31 pictures in all, including some showing women, some showing men, some with both or neither, and one that is totally blank. Originally, it was intended that a psychologist would select 20 cards for use with a given client, but in actual practice most psychologists use fewer (Lilienfeld et al., 2000).

The assumption behind the TAT is that when you tell a story about a person in the drawing, you probably identify with the person and so the story is really about yourself. You might describe events and concerns in your own life, including some that you might

FIGURE 13.10 In the Thematic Apperception Test, people tell a story about what is going on in a picture such as this one. Most people include material that relates to current concerns in their lives.

be reluctant to discuss openly. For example, one young man told the following story about a picture of a man clinging to a rope:

> This man is escaping. Several months ago he was beat up and shanghaied and taken aboard ship. Since then, he has been mistreated and unhappy and has been looking for a way to escape. Now the ship is anchored near a tropical island and he is climbing down a rope to the water. He will get away successfully and swim to shore. When he gets there, he will be met by a group of beautiful native women with whom he will live the rest of his life in luxury and never tell anyone what happened. Sometimes he will feel that he should go back to his old life; but he will never do it. (Kimble & Garmezy, 1968, pp. 582–583)

This young man had entered divinity school, mainly to please his parents, but was unhappy there. He was wrestling with a secret desire to escape to a new life with greater worldly pleasures. In his story he described someone doing what he wanted to do.

Psychologists use the TAT in several ways. Many therapists use it unsystematically. They use different cards and different numbers of cards with different clients, and they interpret the results according to their "clinical judgment," without any clear rules. The results may be reasonable in some cases, but under these circumstances it is impossible to collect adequate data to estimate the reliability or validity of the test.

If you took the TAT with two psychologists, they might reach different conclusions about you. As with the Rorschach, the interrater reliability is about .85— good enough for research purposes but not for making important decisions about an individual (Cramer, 1996). When someone retakes the test a few weeks later, the test–retest reliability is generally lower, usually less than .5 (Cramer, 1996). As with the Rorschach, one criticism is that the test seldom provides information that goes beyond what we could get in other ways (Lilienfeld et al., 2000).

On the other hand, the TAT is sometimes used to measure people's need for achievement by counting all the times that they mention achievement. The test is similarly used to measure power and affiliation needs. These results are useful for many research purposes, although not necessarily for making decisions about an individual (Lilienfeld et al., 2000).

Handwriting as a Projective Technique

Based on the theory that your personality affects everything you do, some psychologists (and others) have tried analyzing people's handwriting. For example, perhaps people who dot their i's with a dash—

i—are especially energetic, or perhaps people who draw large loops above the line—as in *allow*—are highly idealistic. Carefully collected data, however, show only random relationships between handwriting and personality (Tett & Palmer, 1997).

Possible Implicit Personality Tests

The research has failed to support any of the projective tests, but the motivation behind them remains: Psychologists would like to measure personality aspects that people cannot or will not discuss openly. So the search for another kind of personality test continues.

Recall from Chapter 7 the distinction between explicit and implicit memory. If you listen to a list of words and then try to repeat them, what you recall is explicit memory. If you unknowingly use words from the list in your later conversation, your use of those words constitutes implicit memory. Implicit memory occurs even when you are not aware of remembering something.

Many researchers are trying to develop an implicit personality test—that is, one that measures some aspect of your personality without your awareness. No one knows yet whether these methods will succeed. We shall consider two examples: the Emotional Stroop Test and the Implicit Association Test.

The Emotional Stroop Test

Recall the Stroop effect from Chapter 8: People are asked to look at a display like this and read the color of the ink instead of reading the words:

purple brown green blue yellow purple yellow red brown

In the **Emotional Stroop Test,** *someone examines a list of words, some of which relate to a possible source of worry or concern to the person, and tries to say the color of the ink of each word.* For example, in the following display, say the color of the ink of each word as fast as possible:

cancer venom defeat hospital rattler failure fangs blood loser slither nurses bite jobless cobra inadequate disease

If you had a snake phobia, might you pause longer when you try to read the color of snake-related words— *venom, rattler, fangs, slither, bite, cobra?* You can collect results for yourself. Go to http://psychology.wadsworth.com/kalat_intro7e. Navigate to the student Web site, then to Online Try it Yourself, and click on Emotional Stroop Test.

Let's examine a representative study.

The Emotional Stroop Test is sometimes called the Personal Stroop Test because the items are individualized to concerns that some person might have. In this case the research dealt with people who had attempted suicide (Becker, Strohbach, & Rinck, 1999).

Hypothesis   It is always somewhat difficult to look at a word and say the color of ink instead of reading the word. It may be especially difficult if the word has a strong emotional meaning. In this case the hypothesis is that people who have attempted suicide will be slower than other people to read the color of words that relate to suicide.

Method   The experimenters asked 31 suicide attempters and 31 other people to look at four cards with 12 words each and say the color of ink for each word. One card had words with *positive* connotations, such as *talent* and *love*. Another card had words with *negative* connotations, such as *jail* and *stupidity*. A third card had words with *neutral* connotations, such as *ankle bone* and *square*. The final card had *suicide-related* words such as *grave, coldness,* and *darkness.* Different people looked at the cards in different orders. The experimenters timed how long each person took to say the ink colors of words on each card.

Results   Previous suicide attempters took slightly longer to read the suicide-related words. Other people took about equal times with all four cards. Here are the means for the two groups:

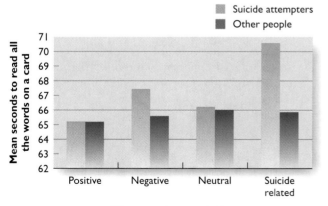

Interpretation   The previous suicide attempters apparently were distracted by the suicide-related words. The difference was not large, however. In its present form, the Emotional Stroop Test can report differences between groups, but it is not accurate enough to make decisions about any individual.

The Emotional Stroop Test has similarly shown that violent offenders have long delays on words like *anger*

and *hate* (P. Smith & Waterman, 2003), that pain sufferers respond slowly for words related to pain (Crombez, Hermans, & Adriaensen, 2000), and so forth. However, an extra delay on a word does not necessarily mean that the word reflects a fear or worry. In one study pessimistic people were slow to read the colors of unpleasant words like *germ, loser,* and *failure,* whereas optimistic people were slower with pleasant words like *joy, smile,* and *accomplish* (Segerstrom, 2001). Evidently, people were slow with words that grabbed their attention for whatever reason.

The Implicit Association Test

Recall from Chapter 9 the idea of priming: Immediately after reading or hearing a word, such as *red,* you are quicker than usual to identify a related word, such as *cherry.* The fact that you are quicker indicates that you see the two words as related. Similarly, the **Implicit Association Test** *measures whether you respond faster to a category that combines some topic with pleasant words or with unpleasant words.* The results have implications for whether you find that category pleasant or unpleasant.

To illustrate, imagine this example: You rest your left and right forefingers on a computer keyboard. When the experimenter reads a word, you are to press with your left finger if it is an unpleasant word, such as *blunder, fail,* or *shame,* and press with your right finger if it is a pleasant word, such as *joy, nice,* or *success.* Once you have mastered this procedure, we change the instructions. Now you should press the left key if you hear either an unpleasant word or a word relating to insects, and the right key if you hear either a pleasant word or one relating to flowers. Some other people have the reverse instructions: The left key means either an unpleasant word or a flower; the right key means either a pleasant word or an insect. Most people respond faster if they pair flowers with pleasant and insects with unpleasant than if they have to pair flowers with unpleasant and insects with pleasant. The conclusion is that most people like flowers and dislike insects. In this case the procedure seems more trouble than it is worth, as people could readily tell us that they like flowers more than insects. However, we can use the method to measure preferences that people did not want to admit, perhaps not even to themselves.

For example, people in one study were given the following instructions: When they saw a word in UP-PERCASE letters, they should press one key if the word was pleasant (like *FRIEND*) and another key if it was unpleasant (like *UGLY*). When they saw a word in lowercase letters, they should press one key for violent words (like *kill*) and the other key for nonviolent words (like *clock*). The rule periodically changed so that sometimes pleasant was paired with violent (and unpleasant with nonviolent), and sometimes pleasant was paired with nonviolent (and unpleasant with violent). Most people responded faster when the key for pleasant words was the same as the key for nonviolent words, implying that they considered violence unpleasant. However, a group of 13 murderers responded equally fast under both conditions, implying that for them, violence was neither pleasant nor unpleasant (Gray, MacCulloch, Smith, Morris, & Snowden, 2003).

Unfortunately, the Implicit Association Test, like the Emotional Stroop Test, produces measures accurate enough for research purposes but not for classifying individuals. Research on implicit personality tests continues, though, because of the potential advantages. Mainly, it is hard for people to "fake" their results. They can try to conceal their personalities in an interview or on the MMPI, but they cannot accurately control their reaction times on the Stroop test or an association test.

CONCEPT CHECK ☑

16. On the preceding sample items of an emotional Stroop test, if you had the greatest delay in naming the ink color for *cancer, hospital, blood, nurses,* and *disease,* what would these results imply about your emotions? (Check your answer on page 526.)

Uses and Misuses of Personality Tests

Before any drug company can market a new drug in the United States, the Food and Drug Administration (FDA) requires that it be carefully tested. If the FDA

finds the drug safe and effective, it approves the drug for certain purposes but requires a warning label stating how it is to be used. After the drug is approved, however, the FDA cannot prevent a physician from prescribing it for unapproved purposes.

Personality tests are a little like prescription drugs: They should be used with caution and only for the purposes for which they have demonstrable usefulness. They are, at a minimum, helpful to psychologists as an interviewing technique to help "break the ice" and begin a good conversation. Tests can also be useful as an aid in personality assessment by a clinical psychologist. However, a test score by itself can be misleading if it is interpreted without caution. For example, suppose someone has an MMPI personality profile that resembles the profile typical for schizophrenia. Identifying schizophrenia or any other unusual condition is a signal-detection problem, as we discussed in Chapter 4—a problem of reporting a stimulus when it is present without falsely reporting it when it is absent. Suppose (realistically) that people without schizophrenia outnumber people with schizophrenia by 100 to 1. Suppose further that a particular personality profile on the MMPI–2 is characteristic of 95% of people with schizophrenia and only 5% of other people. As Figure 13.11 shows, 5% of the normal population is a *larger* group than 95% of the schizophrenic population. Thus, if we labeled as "schizophrenic" everyone with a high score, we would be wrong more often than right. (Recall the representativeness heuristic and the issue of base-rate information, discussed in Chapter 8: Someone who seems "representative" of people in a rare category does not necessarily belong to that category.) Therefore, a conscientious psychologist will look for other evidence beyond the test score before drawing

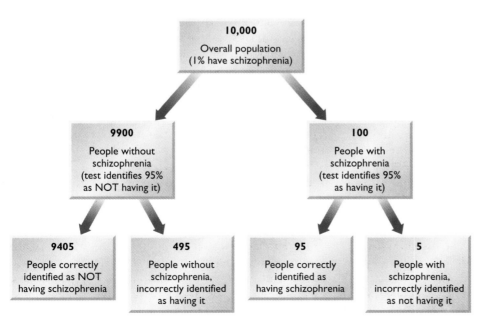

FIGURE 13.11 Assume that a certain profile occurs in 95% of people with schizophrenia and 5% of other people. If we relied entirely on this test, we would correctly identify 95 schizophrenic people, but we would also misidentify 495 normal people.

a firm conclusion. The same, of course, should be said of any test, including IQ tests.

Personality Tests in Action: Criminal Profiling

Although you might not have thought of it this way, psychological profiling of criminals is an application of personality testing. The idea is that a psychologist or experienced police investigator examines the crime scene and other information about a crime and then surmises the personality, emotions, and motivations of whoever committed the crime. Constructing such a profile presupposes that someone who commits a crime has nearly the same personality as other people who have committed similar crimes in the past.

Many movies and popular television shows have featured psychological profilers almost as super-heroes. In 2003, a colleague and I informally surveyed our university's freshman psychology majors about their career plans and discovered to our amazement that about one fourth said they aspired to become forensic psychologists who would construct criminal profiles to help the police. We tried to explain that the number of freshmen at this university aspiring to be criminal profilers was probably greater than the number of people currently employed as profilers in the entire country.

How accurate are criminal profiles? Can a psychologist look at the evidence of a crime and infer the criminal's personality and background in enough detail to aid a police investigation? If so, we should be amazed, even stunned. As you have seen in this chapter, personality testing is far from an exact science, even when psychologists spend hours testing and interviewing the most cooperative people.

Even skeptics do concede the possibility of a limited degree of criminal profiling (Alison, Bennell, & Mokros, 2002; Scott, Lambie, Henwood, & Lamb, 2003). For example, most criminals live or work near the location of their crimes. Also, obviously, a rapist is more likely to be a young man than a child or an old man. Less obviously, but also less consistently, a rapist who removes all trace of his semen from the scene of the crime evidently knows something about police investigative techniques and may have been arrested for similar crimes in the past. The question is whether profilers can go beyond such general statements to infer anything about a specific individual who committed a specific crime.

A few studies have tried to collect data about the relationship between the crime and the criminal. For example, one study of sex-related murders categorized some crimes as deliberate and cruel, some as motivated more by sex than violence, others as "furious"

and possibly revenge-based, and still others as antisocial and perverse. The kinds of people who committed one kind of murder differed on the average from those who committed other kinds. However, most of the crimes the researchers examined did not fit neatly into any of these categories, and those that did fit were so few that the apparent links to personal characteristics could have been due to chance (Kocsis, Cooksey, & Irwin, 2002).

Another study examined 100 cases of stranger rape (as opposed to acquaintance rape). Researchers rated the degree of similarity among crimes and also the degree of similarity among convicted offenders. They found no consistent relationship. That is, men who had committed apparently similar crimes were no more likely than others to be similar in age, ethnic group, education, marital status, employment records, or criminal records (Mokros & Alison, 2002). If, indeed, people who commit similar crimes do not resemble one another, the prospects for criminal profiling are limited.

A few studies have directly measured the ability of profilers to infer the characteristics of people who committed specific crimes. Unfortunately, sample sizes have been small because most profilers have declined to be tested. In one study five professional profilers as well as larger numbers of police officers, psychologists, college students, and self-declared psychics were given extensive details about a murder case, including photos of the crime scene, information about the victim, and various laboratory reports. Then they were asked 30 multiple-choice questions about the probable criminal—sex, height, weight, age, marital status, religion, violent fantasies, and so forth. The results were compared to what was known about the actual murderer (who had in fact been caught, although the participants did not know about him). The number of choices per multiple-choice item varied from 2 to 9; overall, random guessing would produce 8.1 correct answers out of the 30 items. However, even an uninformed person should do better than chance, just by knowing, for example, that more crimes are committed by men than women and by guessing some common religion instead of a rare one. Of the tested groups, the profilers in fact did the best, at 13.8 correct, and the psychics did the worst, at 11.3, but the differences were small and none of the groups did well (Kocsis, Irwin, Hayes, & Nunn, 2000). Even for this modest success, we do not know that the profilers based their guesses on any information about the crime. Maybe they just have more accurate stereotypes of the "average criminal" than other people do.

A similar study compared police officers with varying levels of experience and college students with no relevant experience at all. In this case the college students outperformed the police officers, although

▌ When two snipers shot a series of people in the Washington, D.C., area, psychological profilers said to look for a White man acting alone. That description fit most previous serial killers but was wrong this time. John Allen Muhammad (a) and Lee Boyd Malvo (b) were convicted of the killings.

even the students averaged only 12.4 correct out of 30. Again, the differences among groups were small (Kocsis, Hayes, & Irwin, 2002).

We should not conclude that criminal profiling is impossible. However, as it is currently practiced, the results are certainly unimpressive. After all, 13.8 correct answers out of a possible 30, where 8.1 is random, means that profilers would give the police mostly wrong information.

Why, then, do so many police investigators insist that they find criminal profiles useful? Recall the Barnum effect mentioned in the introduction to this module: People tend to accept almost any statement about their own personality, especially vague statements that can be interpreted to fit the facts. A similar process applies here. Most actual (as opposed to television) profiles of criminals include vague or untestable statements that would apply to many people: The criminal is about the same age as the victim . . . average appearance . . . does not look out of context in the area . . . possibly unemployed . . . has a pornography collection . . . probably a very confused person . . . (Alison, Smith, & Morgan, 2003). In one study researchers gave police officers a criminal profile that an FBI profiler had prepared for the investigation of a particular murder, plus a description of the actual murderer (who had been caught), and asked the officers how well the profile fit the actual criminal. Most called it a good fit, rating it between 5 and 6 on a 1-to-7 scale. The researchers then gave a different group of police officers the same profile, plus a completely different, fictional description of the murderer, changing his age, relationship to the

victim, childhood history, and everything else. Most of this group also called the profile a good fit, again rating it between 5 and 6 (Alison et al., 2003). In short, the actual facts about the criminal made little difference to how highly the police rated the profile.

CONCEPT CHECK ☑

17. In what way does criminal profiling illustrate the representativeness heuristic, as described in Chapter 8? (Check your answer on page 526.)

IN CLOSING

Possibilities and Limits of Personality Tests

One of most people's main topics of conversation could be described uncharitably as "gossip" or more kindly as "other people's personalities." Knowing about other people is important. You need to know whom to trust and whom to distrust.

Given this focus on personality, most of us tend to believe that personality is highly stable and governs a great deal of behavior. If so, someone should be able to look at a crime scene and discern the personality of the perpetrator. Psychologists should be able to listen to a client's answers to the Rorschach Inkblots and figure out his or her innermost secrets. So it might seem, but the research says otherwise. Personality is somewhat consistent over time and situations, but (as stated at the start of the second module) it is like climate—a trend over a long period of time but not always a good guide to what is happening at the moment.

The problem is that psychologists seldom want to watch and record anyone's behavior over months to get an accurate reading. Instead, they ask people for self-reports, using the MMPI or something similar. Such tests are useful within limits. However, we should remember those limits and avoid overconfident conclusions.

Our personalities depend on the situations at least as much as they do on consistent tendencies within us. In the next chapter, we take up the influence of social situations.

Summary

- *People's tendency to accept personality test results.* Because most people accept almost any interpretation of their personality based on a personality test, tests must be carefully scrutinized to ensure that they are measuring what they claim to measure. (page 515)
- *Standardized personality tests.* A standardized test is administered according to explicit rules, and its results are interpreted in a prescribed fashion based on the norms for the population. (page 516)
- *The MMPI.* The MMPI, a widely used personality test, consists of a series of true–false questions selected in an effort to distinguish among various personality types. The MMPI–2 is a modern version. (page 516)
- *Detection of lying.* The MMPI and certain other tests guard against lying by including items on which most people admit common faults or deny rare virtues. Denying common faults or claiming rare virtues is probably a lie. An unusual number of lying answers will invalidate the results. (page 518)
- *Projective techniques.* A projective technique, such as the Rorschach Inkblots or the Thematic Apperception Test, lets people describe their concerns indirectly while talking about the person in the picture or about other ambiguous stimuli. The results from projective techniques are difficult to interpret and have unimpressive validity for making decisions about any individual. (page 518)
- *Implicit personality tests.* The Emotional Stroop Test measures people's delays in naming the color of ink on the assumption that they will pause longer if the word has emotional meaning to them. The Implicit Association Test asks people to give one re-

sponse to a particular combination of categories (e.g., social words and happy outcomes) and a different response to a different combination (e.g., nonsocial words and unhappy outcomes). So far, such tests are useful for research but not for decisions about an individual. (page 521)
- *Uses and misuses of personality tests.* Personality tests can be used as an aid for assessing personality, but their results should be interpreted cautiously and in conjunction with other evidence. (page 523)
- *Criminal profiling.* Some psychologists and police officers try to aid police investigations by constructing personality profiles of the kind of person who would probably commit a certain crime. There has been little research, but what has been conducted casts doubt on the accuracy of these profiles. (page 524)

Answers to Concept Checks

12. Researchers would determine whether people with depression were more likely than other people to answer *true.* If so, the item could be included. If people with depression answer about the same as others, the item would be discarded. (page 518)
13. Such items are intended to detect lying. If you answered *false,* you would get a point on a lying scale. (page 518)
14. **a.** The puppet activity could be a projective technique because the child is likely to project his or her own family concerns onto the puppets, using them to enact various problems. (page 519)
15. The psychologist administering the test counts the total number of answers that are considered abnormal or disturbed. The more answers someone gives, the greater the probability of saying something that seems disturbed. (On the other hand, if you give very few answers, you will be considered unimaginative and dull-witted.) (page 520)
16. The results would suggest that you are especially worried about health-related matters. (page 523)
17. The representativeness heuristic is the assumption that if something resembles category A, then it is a member of category A. In this case the idea is that if someone resembles people who have committed a particular type of crime, then he or she is a likely suspect to have committed that crime. This reasoning is risky if many people fit that description. (page 525)

Key Terms and Activities

Key Terms

agreeableness: the tendency to be compassionate toward others and not antagonistic (page 509)

anal stage: Freud's second stage of psychosexual development; here, psychosexual pleasure is focused on the anus (page 495)

archetypes: according to Jung vague images inherited from our ancestors and contained in the collective unconscious (page 498)

Barnum effect: the tendency to accept and praise vague statements about our personality (page 515)

big five personality traits: five traits that account for a great deal of human personality differences: neuroticism, extraversion, agreeableness, conscientiousness, and openness to new experience (page 509)

catharsis: the release of pent-up emotions associated with unconscious thoughts and memories (page 492)

collective unconscious: according to Jung an inborn level of the unconscious that symbolizes the collective experience of the human species (page 498)

conscientiousness: the tendency to show self-discipline, to be dutiful, and to strive for achievement and competence (page 509)

defense mechanism: a method employed by the ego to protect itself against anxiety caused by the conflict between the id's demands and the super-ego's constraints (page 495)

denial: the refusal to believe information that provokes anxiety (page 496)

displacement: the diversion of a thought or behavior away from its natural target toward a less threatening target (page 496)

ego: according to Freud the rational, decision-making aspect of personality (page 495)

Emotional Stroop Test: a procedure in which someone tries to say the color of ink for a number of words, some of which might pertain to a source of worry or concern (page 521)

external locus of control: the belief that external forces are largely in control of the events of one's life (page 507)

extraversion: the tendency to seek stimulation and to enjoy the company of other people (page 509)

fixation: in Freud's theory a persisting preoccupation with an immature psychosexual interest as a result of frustration at that stage of psychosexual development (page 494)

gender role: the pattern of behavior that each person is expected to follow because of being male or female (page 501)

genital stage: Freud's final stage of psychosexual development, in which sexual pleasure is focused on sexual intimacy with others (page 495)

humanistic psychology: a field that is concerned with consciousness, values, and abstract beliefs, including spiritual experiences and the beliefs that people live by and die for (page 502)

id: according to Freud the aspect of personality that consists of all our biological drives and demands for immediate gratification (page 495)

ideal self: an image of what one would like to be (page 503)

idiographic approach: an approach to the study of personality differences that concentrates on intensive studies of individuals (page 506)

Implicit Association Test: a procedure that measures how fast someone responds to a category that combines a topic with pleasant words or with unpleasant words (page 522)

individual psychology: the psychology of the person as an indivisible whole, as formulated by Adler (page 500)

inferiority complex: an exaggerated feeling of weakness, inadequacy, and helplessness (page 500)

internal locus of control: the belief that one is largely in control of the events of one's life (page 507)

latent period: according to Freud a period in which psychosexual interest is suppressed or dormant (page 495)

libido: in Freud's theory psychosexual energy (page 494)

Minnesota Multiphasic Personality Inventory (MMPI): a standardized test consisting of true–false items and intended to measure various personality dimensions and clinical conditions such as depression (page 516)

MMPI–2: the modernized edition of the MMPI (page 516)

neo-Freudians: personality theorists who have remained faithful to parts of Freud's theory while modifying other parts (page 498)

neuroticism: the tendency to experience unpleasant emotions relatively easily (page 509)

nomothetic approach: an approach to the study of individual differences that seeks general laws about how an aspect of personality affects behavior (page 506)

Oedipus complex: according to Freud a young boy's sexual interest in his mother accompanied by competitive aggression toward his father (page 493)

openness to experience: the tendency to enjoy new intellectual experiences, the arts, fantasies, and anything that exposes a person to new ideas (page 510)

oral stage: Freud's first stage of psychosexual development; here, psychosexual pleasure is focused on the mouth (page 494)

personality: all the consistent ways in which the behavior of one person differs from that of others, especially in social situations (page 491)

phallic stage: Freud's third stage of psychosexual development; here, psychosexual interest is focused on the penis or clitoris (page 495)

projection: the attribution of one's own undesirable characteristics to other people (page 497)

projective techniques: procedures designed to encourage people to project their personality characteristics onto ambiguous stimuli (page 518)

psychoanalysis: an approach to personality and psychotherapy developed by Sigmund Freud, based on identifying unconscious thoughts and emotions and bringing them to consciousness (page 492)

psychodynamic theory: a system that relates personality to the interplay of conflicting forces within the individual, including some that the individual may not consciously recognize (page 491)

psychosexual pleasure: according to Freud any strong, pleasant enjoyment arising from body stimulation (page 494)

rationalization: attempting to prove that one's actions are rational and justifiable and thus worthy of approval (page 496)

reaction formation: presenting oneself as the opposite of what one really is in an effort to reduce anxiety (page 497)

regression: the return to a more juvenile level of functioning as a means of reducing anxiety or in response to emotionally trying circumstances (page 496)

repression: according to Freudian theory, motivated forgetting, the process of moving an unacceptable memory, motivation, or emotion from the conscious mind to the unconscious mind (page 495)

Rorschach Inkblots: a projective personality technique; people are shown 10 inkblots and asked what each might be depicting (page 519)

self-actualization: the achievement of one's full potential (page 503)

self-concept: an image of what one really is (page 503)

social interest: a sense of solidarity and identification with other people (page 500)

standardized test: a test that is administered according to specified rules and its scores are interpreted in a prescribed fashion (page 516)

state: a temporary activation of a particular behavior (page 506)

striving for superiority: according to Adler a universal desire to seek personal excellence and fulfillment (page 500)

style of life: according to Adler a person's master plan for achieving a sense of superiority (page 500)

sublimation: the transformation of sexual or aggressive energies into culturally acceptable, even admirable, behaviors (page 497)

superego: according to Freud the aspect of personality that consists of memories of rules put forth by one's parents (page 495)

Thematic Apperception Test (TAT): a projective personality technique; a person is asked to tell a story about each of 20 pictures (page 520)

trait: a consistent, long-lasting tendency in behavior (page 506)

trait approach to personality: the study and measure of consistent personality characteristics (page 507)

unconditional positive regard: the complete, unqualified acceptance of another person as he or she is (page 503)

unconscious: according to Freud the repository of memories, emotions, and thoughts—often illogical thoughts—that affect our behavior even though we cannot talk about them (page 492)

unshared environment: the aspects of environment that differ from one individual to another, even within a family (page 512)

Suggestions for Further Reading

Crews, F. C. (1998). *Unauthorized Freud.* New York: Viking Press. Devastating criticisms of Sigmund Freud's use and misuse of evidence.

Freud, S. (1924). *Introductory lectures on psycho-analysis.* New York: Boni and Liveright. Read Freud's own words and form your own opinion.

 ## Book Companion Web Site

Need help studying? Go to

http://psychology.wadsworth.com/kalat_intro7e/

for a virtual study center. You'll find a personalized Self-Study Assessment that will provide you with a study plan based on your answers to a pretest. Also study using flash cards, quizzes, interactive art, and an online glossary.

Check out interactive **Try It Yourself** exercises on the companion site! These exercises will help you put what you've learned into action.

Your companion site also has direct links to the following Web sites. These links are checked often for changes, dead links, and new additions.

Personality Measures and the Big Five

personality-project.org/personality.html

This site offers a wealth of information about personality traits and research, including links to many research sites.

 ## Try It Yourself CD-ROM
with Critical Thinking Video Exercises

Use your CD to access **videos** related to activities designed to help you think critically about the important topics discussed. You'll also find an easy portal link to the book companion site where you can access your personalized **Self-Study Assessments** and interactive **Try It Yourself** exercises.

PsychNow! 2.0

PsychNow! is a fun interactive CD designed to help you with the difficult concepts in psychology. Check out the Personality and Abnormal Psychology section for the following topics that relate to this chapter:

Theories of Personality: explore a self-image checklist, learn about personality theories, and take a test.

InteractNOW! Online Collaborative Lab: Personality and the Rorschach Inkblot Test

Social Psychology

In the *Communist Manifesto*, Karl Marx and Friedrich Engels wrote, "Mankind are more disposed to suffer, while evils are sufferable, than to right themselves by abolishing the forms to which they are accustomed. But when a long train of abuses and usurpations, pursuing invariably the same object, evinces a design to reduce them under absolute despotism, it is their right, it is their duty, to throw off such government." Fidel Castro wrote, "A little rebellion, now and then, is a good thing." Do you agree with those statements? Why or why not? Can you think of anything that would change your mind?

▌ Influence depends not only on what someone says but also on what listeners think of the person who says it. Arnold Schwarzenegger, now governor of California, has advantages based on appearance and acting skills; however, some people discount his ideas because of his lack of political experience.

Oh, pardon me. . . . That first statement is not from the *Communist Manifesto*. It is from the United States' Declaration of Independence. Sorry. And that second statement is a quotation from Thomas Jefferson, not Castro. Do you agree more with these statements now that you know they came from democratic revolutionaries instead of communist revolutionaries?

What kinds of influences alter your opinions? This question is one example of the issues that interest **social psychologists**—*the psychologists who study social behavior and how individuals influence other people and are influenced by other people.* Social psychology can be described as a broad field because it includes the study of attitudes, persuasion, self-understanding, and almost all everyday behaviors of relatively normal people in their relationships with others. It can also be criticized as a narrow field because so much of its research deals with North American college students in laboratory settings (Rozin, 2001). As you will see, social psychologists have studied some very interesting phenomena, but much more remains to be learned.

Social Perception and Cognition

What factors influence our judgments of others?

How can we measure stereotypes that people do not want to admit?

How do we explain the causes of our own behavior and that of others?

People generally measure their own success by comparing themselves to others. To decide whether you are satisfied with your grades in school, your salary on the job, or even the morality of your behavior, you compare yourself to other people similar to yourself. You cheer yourself up by noting that you are doing better than some of your friends; you motivate yourself to try harder by comparing yourself to someone more successful (Suls, Martin, & Wheeler, 2002).

To make these comparisons, we need accurate information about other people. We also need that information to form expectations about how others will act, whom we can trust, and so forth. **Social perception and cognition** are *the processes we use to gather and remember information about others and to make inferences from that information.* Social perception and cognition, like any other perception and cognition, influence our observations, memory, and thinking.

First Impressions

Other things being equal, *the first information we learn about someone influences us more than later information does* (Belmore, 1987; E. E. Jones & Goethals, 1972). This tendency is known as the **primacy effect.** For example, if a professor makes a good impression on the first day of class, your favorable attitude helps you discount a lackluster performance later in the semester. A professor who seems dull at first will have a hard time impressing you later. Similarly, your professor's early impression of you can have lasting effects.

Why are first impressions so influential? If your first impression of someone is unfavorable, you may not spend enough time with that person to change your view. Also, once you have formed an impression, it alters your interpretation of later experiences. Suppose your first impression of someone is that he talks about himself too much. Later, whenever he talks about himself, you take his comments as supporting your initial impression.

Our first impressions can become **self-fulfilling prophecies,** *expectations that change one's own behavior in such a way as to increase the probability of the predicted event.* Suppose a psychologist hands you a telephone receiver and asks you to have a conversation with someone, while handing you a photo supposedly of that person. It is not actually of that person at all. Unknown to you and to the person you are talking to, the psychologist hands some people a photo of a very attractive member of the opposite sex and hands other people a much less attractive photo. Not surprisingly, you act friendlier to someone you regard as attractive. More interesting, if you think you are talking to someone attractive, that person reacts to you by becoming more cheerful and talkative. In short, your first impression changes how you act and influences the other person to live up to (or down to) your expectations (Snyder, Tanke, & Berscheid, 1977).

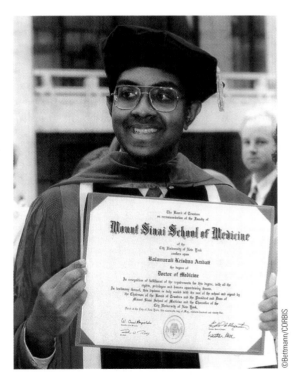

If you were a new patient of Dr. Balamurali Ambati, the world's youngest doctor (at age 17), what would your first impression probably be? An impression based only on his youthful appearance could be greatly mistaken.

In a criminal trial, the prosecution presents its evidence first. Might that give the jury an unfavorable first impression of the defendant and increase the probability of a conviction?

CONCEPT CHECK ☑

I. Why do some professors avoid looking at students' names when they grade essay exams? Why is it more important for them to avoid looking at the names on tests given later in the semester than on the first test? (Check your answers on page 542.)

Stereotypes and Prejudices

A **stereotype** is *a generalized belief or expectation about a group of people.* It is possible to develop false stereotypes because of our tendency to remember the unusual. If we see an unusual person doing something unusual, the event is doubly memorable. For example, you might remember one left-handed redhead who cheated you and then form a false stereotype about left-handed redheads—an illusory correlation, as discussed in Chapter 2.

Stereotypes can also be based on exaggerations of correct observations. In particular, people tend to perceive and describe their political opponents as being far more extreme than they really are (Keltner & Robinson, 1996; Robinson & Keltner, 1996).

However, researchers have also come to admit that many stereotypes are correct. For example, who do you think gets into more fistfights on the average—men or women? If you answered "men," you are supporting a stereotype, but you are correct. Similarly, who do you think is more likely to be sensitive to the subtle social connotations of what people say—a liberal-arts major or an engineering major? Again, if you said "liberal-arts major," you are endorsing a stereotype, but the research supports you (Ottati & Lee, 1995).

Indeed, whenever we say that members of two cultures behave differently, we are endorsing a stereotype. In some cases members of both cultures agree on those stereotypes but express them in different words. For example, many Americans describe the Chinese as "inhibited," whereas Chinese call themselves "self-controlled." U.S. businesspeople complain that Mexicans "don't show up on time," whereas Mex-

icans complain that people from the United States "are always in a rush" (Lee & Duenas, 1995). People even form stereotypes about their own group, such as "we Americans are patriotic," "people in my town are very conservative," or "students at my college drink a lot of alcohol" (Prentice & Miller, 2002).

However, agreeing that some stereotype is correct on the average does not mean that it fits all individuals (Banaji & Bhaskar, 2000). For example, most 20-year-olds are more athletic than most 80-year-olds, but some 80-year-olds are in better shape than some 20-year-olds. Also, believing that a stereotype is usually correct does not mean that we have to let it influence the way we treat people. Ideally, we should strive to know people as individuals and treat them accordingly.

Aversive Racism

A **prejudice** is *an unfavorable attitude toward a group of people.* It is usually associated with **discrimination**, which is *unequal treatment of different groups,* such as minority groups, women, the physically disabled, obese people, or gays and lesbians. Decades ago many Americans admitted their prejudices and discriminated openly. Today, although some people are more prejudiced than others (Duckitt,

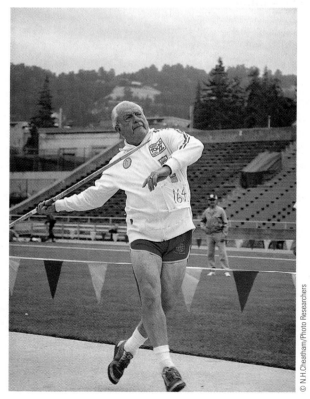

■ The usual stereotype of old people as inactive is largely correct on the average, but almost every stereotype has exceptions.

2001), most prejudices are subtle and not expressed openly. People may be ashamed of having such feelings, or they may not even be aware of them. In either case people *consciously express the idea that all people are equal, but nevertheless harbor negative feelings or unintentionally discriminate.* When these conflicting feelings pertain to race, psychologists use the term **aversive racism,** also known as subtle prejudice, modern racism, symbolic racism, racial ambivalence, or other similar terms (Sears & Henry, 2003). This kind of racism is called "aversive" because it is unpleasant to the person who acts this way. In a similar way, many people have **ambivalent sexism,** *an overt belief in equal treatment of the sexes joined with a lingering, often unstated belief that women should be treated differently* (Glick & Fiske, 2001).

Subtle, unstated prejudices are less harmful than the overt hostility of previous eras, but they can take their toll nevertheless. For example, if you are a victim of prejudice, you might be excluded from conversations among fellow students or workers (S. T. Fiske, 2002). People might smile at you less, offer you less help, and give you less benefit of the doubt in an uncertain situation (Crandall & Eshleman, 2003). If they see you frowning slightly, they may overestimate your hostility (Hugenberg & Bodenhausen, 2003). When you fail to get a job, promotion, or other opportunity, you may not know whether you were rejected because of something you did wrong or because of prejudices against your group (Major, Quinton, & McCoy, 2002).

Stereotypes and prejudices can also become self-fulfilling prophecies. Recall the idea of *stereotype threat* from Chapter 9 (p. 342): African American students' test performance is impaired if they are told that the test measures intelligence. In a variety of other situations and with many types of people, a general principle has emerged: People who are told "your group usually doesn't do well on this test" fail to perform as well as they could, especially if the task is difficult (Steele, Spencer, & Aronson, 2002). Perhaps they simply don't try very hard, or maybe they are distracted from the task.

Researchers have tried to measure aversive racism (unintentional, unconscious discrimination). Here is an example (Dovidio & Gaertner, 2000): Each European American college student was asked to evaluate the folder for one person applying for a job as a peer counselor. One third of the applications described strong experience and qualifications for the job, one third were marginal, and one third had weak qualifications. Of each kind of application (strong, marginal, or weak), half mentioned membership in a nearly all-White fraternity and the other half mentioned membership in the Black Student Union. So each student read what appeared to be a strong White, strong Black, marginal White, marginal Black, weak White, or weak Black application. The following graph shows the mean results: Note that the students were slightly more generous with well-qualified or poorly qualified Black applicants than with equally qualified Whites. The big difference, however, was for the marginal applications.

The students favorably recommended 77% of the marginal White applicants but only 40% of the marginal Black applicants (Dovidio & Gaertner, 2000). Without realizing it, the students evaluated the ambiguous qualifications more positively if they thought they applied to White applicants.

Implicit Measures of Stereotypes and Prejudice

Most people in the United States believe in fair treatment for everyone, or so we say. But if we are all as unprejudiced as we claim we are, where do all the racism, sexism, and so forth come from? Researchers have sought methods of measuring subtle prejudices that people do not want to admit, not even to themselves.

One method uses the Implicit Association Test described in Chapter 13. Recall the idea: A participant might be asked to press the left key after hearing either a pleasant word or the name of a flower and to press the right key after either an unpleasant word or the name of an insect. At another time the participant might be asked to press the left key for pleasant or insect and the right key for unpleasant or flower. The fact that "unpleasant or insect" is easier than "pleasant or insect" indicates that most people find insects unpleasant. The effect is not huge, but it has some advantages over just asking people what they like and dislike. (People often say what they think they are supposed to say instead of what they really think.)

The same strategy can be used for measuring prejudices (Greenwald, Nosek, & Banaji, 2003). Imagine yourself in the following experiment: You are seated in front of a computer screen that will sometimes show a

FIGURE 14.1 Procedures for an Implicit Association Test to measure prejudices.

photo and sometimes a word. If it is a photo of a Black person or a pleasant word (e.g., *peace, joy,* or *love*), press the left key. If it is a photo of a White person or an unpleasant word (e.g., *evil, failure,* or *death*), press the right key. After you have done it that way for a while, the rule will switch to the opposite pairing.

Figure 14.1 illustrates the procedures and Figure 14.2 summarizes the results of one study using White college students. Most of them responded faster if the responses were for *Black or unpleasant* and *White or pleasant.* They responded slower if the responses were for *Black or pleasant* and *White or unpleasant.* That is, even though most of the participants in this study claimed to have no racial stereotypes or prejudices, they evaluated White faces more favorably than Black faces (Phelps et al., 2000). A similar study reported that White students found it easier to pair pleasant words with White names, such as *Andrew* and *Brandon,* and unpleasant words with Black names, such as *Lamar* and *Jamal* (Dasgupta, McGhee, Greenwald, & Banaji, 2000).

Researchers made available a simplified version of the Implicit Association Test on a Web site, which you can try yourself:

Online Try It Yourself

https://implicit.harvard.edu/implicit/demo/

They have analyzed the results for more than 600,000 people who have visited this Web site over the years (Nosek, Banaji, & Greenwald, 2002). People who visit a Web site are, of course, not a representa-

tive sample of the population, but neither are the college students in a usual study. The Web site participants are, at least, a huge number of people varying in age, geographical region, and so forth. The results were that White participants on the average linked White-pleasant, Black-unpleasant more easily than White-unpleasant, Black-pleasant, in spite of the fact that most of them claimed to have little or no racial prejudice. The implicit prejudice was slightly stronger among political conservatives. Black participants showed an interesting pattern: Although most stated that their explicit attitude was more favorable to Blacks than to Whites, the Implicit Association Test results indicated a slight implicit attitude favoring Whites over Blacks. That is, they too linked White-pleasant, Black-unpleasant more readily than White-unpleasant, Black-pleasant, at least to a small extent. The Web site made other kinds of tests available also. For example, most participants showed an implicit attitude favoring young over old, linking young-pleasant, old-unpleasant more easily than the reverse.

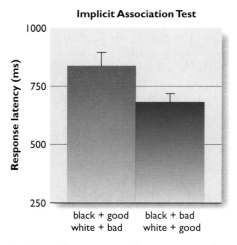

FIGURE 14.2 On the average, White students who claimed to have no racial prejudice responded faster if they had to make one response for "Black face or unpleasant word" and a different response for "White face or pleasant word" than if the pairings were reversed—Black and pleasant, White and unpleasant. *(From "Performance on Indirect Measures of Race Evaluation Predicts Amygdala Activation" by E. A. Phelps, K. J. O'Connor, W. A. Cunningham, E. S. Funayama, J. C. Gatenby, J. C. Gore, and M. R. Banaji, Journal of Cognitive Neuroscience, 2000, 12, 729–738. Copyright © 2000 MIT Press. Reprinted by permission.)*

All these results are important for showing that even well-meaning people can have prejudices that operate without their awareness (Greenwald & Banaji, 1995). That result is important to remember when people insist that we should evaluate college applicants or job applicants "entirely on the basis of their qualifications." The problem is that we may be influenced by stereotypes and prejudices that we do not even recognize, especially when the qualifications are hard to evaluate (Crosby, Iyer, Clayton, & Downing, 2003). Perhaps it is better to recognize that we have stereotypes and try to take them into account, instead of denying their existence.

On the other hand, it may also be that the Implicit Association Test overstates people's prejudices. In a related task, called the **bona fide pipeline**, *people alternate between looking at different kinds of faces, such as Black and White, and reading words that they need to classify as pleasant or unpleasant.* The assumption is that someone who is prejudiced against Black people will answer "unpleasant" faster after seeing a Black face than after seeing a White face. However, the results depend on the instructions. If White students just look at the faces with the expectation of trying to recognize them later, then seeing a Black or White face has little effect on how fast they say "pleasant" or "unpleasant" to the next word. If, however, they have to count the number of Black faces so that they are forced to pay attention to race, then the predicted results do occur, with faster "unpleasant" responses after seeing Black faces (Olson & Fazio, 2003). In other words the bona fide pipeline, and presumably also the Implicit Association Test, show implicit prejudice if the instructions ask people to pay attention to race. Without such urging people may react to the faces as individuals without showing clear evidence of prejudice.

CONCEPT CHECK ☑

2. What is the advantage of the Implicit Association Test over simply asking people about their racial prejudices?
3. Under what condition are the Implicit Association Test and bona fide pipeline most likely to show evidence of implicit prejudice? (Check your answers on page 542.)

Overcoming Prejudice

After prejudices and hostility have arisen between two groups, what can anyone do to break down those barriers? Simply getting to know each other better helps sometimes, but not always. A more effective technique is to get the two groups to work toward a common goal, to think of themselves as part of a larger, combined group (Dovidio & Gaertner, 1999).

Many years ago psychologists demonstrated the power of this technique using two arbitrarily chosen groups (Sherif, 1966). At a summer camp at Robbers' Cave, Oklahoma, 11- to 12-year-old boys were divided into two groups in separate cabins. The groups competed for prizes in sports, treasure hunts, and other activities. With each competition the antagonism between the two groups grew more intense. The boys made threatening posters, shouted insults, and engaged in food fights. Each group had clearly developed prejudice and hostility toward the other.

Up to a point, the "counselors" (the experimenters) allowed the hostility to take its course, neither encouraging nor prohibiting it. Then, they tried to reverse it by stopping the competitions and setting common goals. First, they asked the two groups to work together to find and repair a leak in the water pipe that supplied the camp. Later, they had the two groups pool their treasuries to rent a movie that both groups wanted to see. Still later, they had the boys pull together to get a truck out of a rut. Gradually, hostility turned into friendship—except for a few holdouts who nursed their hatred to the bitter end! The point of this study is that competition leads to hostility; cooperation leads to friendship.

People who work together for a common goal can overcome prejudices that initially divide them.

Attribution

We often try to figure out why the people we observe behave as they do. Yesterday, you won $1 million in the state lottery, and today, some classmates who previously ignored you want to be your friends. You draw inferences about their reasons. **Attribution** is *the set of thought processes we use to assign causes to our own behavior and to the behavior of others.*

Internal Versus External Causes

Fritz Heider, the founder of attribution theory, emphasized the distinction between internal and external causes of behavior (Heider, 1958). **Internal attributions** are *explanations based on someone's individual characteristics, such as attitudes, personality traits, or abilities.* **External attributions** are *explanations based on the situation, including events that presumably would influence almost anyone.* An example of an internal attribution is that your brother walked to work this morning "because he likes the exercise." An external attribution would be that he walked "because his car wouldn't start." Internal attributions are also known as *dispositional* (i.e., something about the person's disposition led to the behavior); external attributions are also known as *situational* (i.e., something about the situation led to the behavior).

You make internal attributions when someone does something that you think most people would not do. For example, if I tell you I would like to visit Hawaii, you probably draw no conclusions about me. However, if I say I would like to visit northern Norway in midwinter, you would seek an attribution to something special about my personality or interests (Krull & Anderson, 1997).

This tendency sometimes leads to misunderstandings between members of different cultures. Each person views the other's behavior as "something I would not have done" and therefore as grounds for making an attribution about the other one's personality. In fact such behavior may actually be what the other culture dictates. For example, some cultures expect people to cry loudly at funerals, whereas others expect people to be more restrained. People who are unfamiliar with other cultures may inappropriately attribute a behavior to someone's personality.

Harold Kelley (1967) proposed that we rely on three types of information when deciding whether to make an internal or an external attribution for someone's behavior:

- **Consensus information** *(how the person's behavior compares with other people's behavior).* If someone behaves the same way you believe other people would in the same situation, then you make an external attribution. If someone's behavior seems unusual, you look for an internal attribution pertaining to something about the person instead of the situation. (You can easily be wrong if you misunderstand the situation.)
- **Consistency information** *(how the person's behavior varies from one time to the next).* If someone almost always seems friendly, for example, you would make an internal attribution ("a friendly person"). If someone's friendliness varies, you look for an external attribution, such as an event that elicited a good or bad mood.
- **Distinctiveness** *(how the person's behavior varies from one situation to another).* For example, if your friend is pleasant to most people but consistently unfriendly to one particular person, you assume that person has done something to irritate your friend (an external attribution).

▌ We are sometimes surprised by people's behavior and attribute an internal cause when in fact the people are acting according to the customs of their culture. In the United States, a funeral usually calls for reserved behavior; in many other places, the opposite is true.

4. Classify the following as either internal or external attributions:
   a. She contributed money to charity because she is generous.
   b. She contributed money to charity because she wanted to impress her boss, who was watching.
   c. She contributed money to charity because she owed a favor to the man who was asking for contributions.

5. Juanita returns from watching *The Return of the Son of Sequel Strikes Back Again Part 2* and says it was excellent. Most other people that you know disliked the movie. Will you make an internal or external attribution for Juanita's opinion? Why? (Distinctiveness, consensus, or consistency?) (Check your answers on page 542.)

The Fundamental Attribution Error

A common error is *to make internal attributions for people's behavior even when we see evidence for an external influence on behavior*. This tendency is known as the **fundamental attribution error** (Ross, 1977). It is also known as the *correspondence bias,* meaning a tendency to assume a strong similarity between someone's current actions and his or her dispositions.

Imagine yourself in a classic study demonstrating this phenomenon. You are told that U.S. college students were randomly assigned to write essays praising or condemning Fidel Castro, the Communist leader of Cuba. You read an essay that defends Castro, criticizes the United States for its long embargo against Cuba, and compares Cuba favorably to other Latin American countries. Now what's your guess about the actual attitude of the student who wrote this essay?

very anti-Castro   neutral   very pro-Castro

Most U.S. students in one study guessed that the author of a pro-Castro essay was at least mildly pro-Castro, even though they were informed, as you were, that the author had been told to praise Castro (E. E. Jones & Harris, 1967). In a later study, experimenters explained that one student in a creative writing class had been assigned to write a pro-Castro essay and an anti-Castro essay at different times in the course. Then the participants read the two essays and estimated the writer's true beliefs. Most thought that the writer had changed attitudes between the two essays (Allison, Mackie, Muller, &

Worth, 1993). That is, even when people are told of a powerful external reason for someone's behavior, they apparently believe the person probably had internal reasons as well (McClure, 1998).

6. Would people who believe they control their own destinies in life (internal locus of control) be more likely or less likely than others to make the fundamental attribution error? (Check your answer on page 542.)

Cultural Differences in Attribution and Related Matters

The fundamental attribution error is partly due to culture. In general, people of Western cultures tend to rely on internal (personality) attributions in situations where people in China, Korea, and other nearby Asian cultures tend to rely more on external (situational) attributions. For example, how would you explain the behavior of the fish designated with an arrow in this drawing? Most Americans say this fish is leading the others, whereas many Chinese say the other fish are chasing it (Hong, Morris, Chiu, & Benet-Martinez, 2000). That is, the cultures differ in whether they think the fish controls its own behavior or obeys the influence of the others.

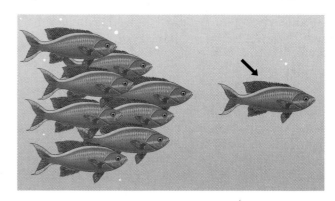

Richard Nisbett and his colleagues have noted other cases in which Chinese and Korean people tend to focus more on the situation, and less on individual personality, than do most people in Western cultures (Nisbett, Peng, Choi, & Norenzayan, 2001). As a result they expect more change and less consistency in people's behavior from one situation to another. The Chinese and Koreans are also more likely to accept contradictions and look for compromises, instead of viewing one position as correct and another as incorrect. Here are a few examples:

- When given a description of a conflict, such as one between mother and daughter, Chinese students are more likely than Americans to see merit in both arguments, instead of siding with one or the other (Peng & Nisbett, 1999).
- Far more Chinese than English-language proverbs include apparent self-contradictions, such as "beware of your friends, not your enemies" and "too humble is half proud" (Peng & Nisbett, 1999).
- Chinese people are more likely than Americans to expect events to change and to predict that current trends—whatever they might be—will reverse themselves. For example, if life seems to have been getting better lately, most Americans predict that things will continue getting better, whereas Chinese predict that things will get worse (Ji, Nisbett, & Su, 2001).
- In one study people were told about some event and then told the final outcome. Americans often expressed surprise when Koreans said the outcome was to be expected. That is, in this study the Koreans showed a stronger hindsight bias (Chapter 7)—the tendency to say, "I knew it all along" (Choi & Nisbett, 2000).

The reported differences are interesting. Still, an important question remains: To the extent that Chinese people respond differently from Western-culture people, is that difference due to ancient traditions within the two cultures or to social, political, and economic pressures of the current time? Unfortunately, cross-cultural research is as difficult as it is important. Questionnaire studies are often misleading, as people from different cultures interpret the questions and answers differently. It is important to take cultural differences seriously but also important to avoid overstating them.

The Actor-Observer Effect

Here is another common bias related to the fundamental attribution error: *People are more likely to make internal attributions for other people's behavior and more likely to make external attributions for their own* (E. E. Jones & Nisbett, 1972). This tendency is called the **actor-observer effect**. You are an "actor" when you try to explain the causes of your own behavior and an "observer" when you try to explain someone else's behavior.

In one study investigators asked college students to rate themselves, their fathers, their best friends, and Walter Cronkite (a television news announcer at the time) on several personality traits. For each trait (e.g., "leniency"), the participants were given three choices: (a) the person possesses the trait, (b) the person possesses the opposite trait, and (c) the person's behavior "depends on the situation." Participants checked "depends on the situation"—an external at-

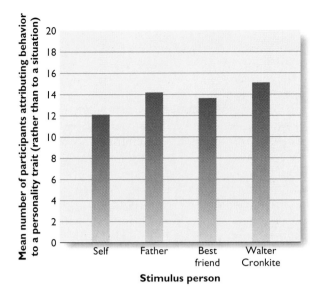

FIGURE 14.3 Participants were asked whether certain people had certain traits, the opposite traits, or whether "it depended on the situation." They were most likely to say that their own behavior depended on the situation and least likely to say "it depends" for Walter Cronkite, the person they knew the least. *(Based on data of Nisbett, Caputo, Legant, & Marecek, 1973)*

tribution—most frequently for themselves, less frequently for their fathers and friends, and least often for Walter Cronkite (Nisbett, Caputo, Legant, & Marecek, 1973). Figure 14.3 shows the results.

Why do we tend to explain our own behavior differently from that of others? First, we are aware of how our own behavior varies from one situation to another. The less well we know someone else, the less aware we are of variations from situation to situation. Second, we tend to attribute unexpected, surprising behavior to internal causes. Our own behavior seldom surprises us, so we do not attribute it to internal causes.

The third reason is perceptual. We see other people as objects in our visual field, and we tend to think that whatever we are watching is the cause of the action. The perceptual explanation for the actor-observer effect has an interesting implication: If you became an object in your own visual field, you might explain your own behavior in terms of internal traits, as you do with others. Researchers have found that if you watch a videotape of your own behavior, you do tend to explain your behavior in terms of personality factors more than situational factors (Storms, 1973).

A further application of this idea: Suppose you watch a videotape of a conversation between two people. The actual conversation is planned so that both people participate equally. However, you are randomly given one of two versions of the videotape, with the camera focused on one person or the other. You will tend to perceive the person you are watching as the one who dominated the conversation and influenced the other person. Similarly, if you watch a videotape of an interrogation between a detective and a suspect, you will judge the suspect's confession to be more voluntary if the camera is focused on the suspect and more coerced if the camera is focused on the detective (Lassiter, Geers, Munhall, Ploutz-Snyder, & Breitenbecher, 2002).

CRITICAL THINKING:
A STEP FURTHER
Attributions

Try to explain these examples of behavior:

- Why did you choose to go to the college you are attending?
- Why did your roommate choose this college?
- Why are you reading this book right now?
- Why does your roommate study so much (or so little)?

Did you attribute internal causes or external causes for these behaviors? Did you rely more on external causes to explain other people's behavior or to explain your own?

Using Attributions to Manage Perceptions of Ourselves

Even if you generally attribute your own behavior largely to external causes, you probably vary your attributions to try to present yourself in a favorable light. For example, you might credit your good grades to your intelligence and hard work (an internal attribution) but blame your bad grades on unfair tests (an external attribution). *Attributions that we adopt to maximize our credit for our success and minimize our blame for our failure* are called **self-serving biases** (D. T. Miller & Ross, 1975; van der Pligt & Eiser, 1983).

People can also protect their images with **self-handicapping strategies,** in which they *intentionally put themselves at a disadvantage to provide an excuse for a possible failure.* Suppose you fear you will do poorly on a test. You go to a party the night before and stay out late. Now you can blame your low score on your lack of sleep without admitting that you might have done poorly anyway.

In an experiment on self-handicapping strategies, Steven Berglas and Edward Jones (1978) asked some college students to work on solvable problems and asked others to work on a mixture of solvable and unsolvable problems. (The students did not know that some of the problems were impossible.) Then the experimenters told all the students that they had done well. The students who had been given solvable problems (and had solved them) felt good about their success. Those who had worked on many unsolvable problems were unsure in what way they had "done well." They certainly had no confidence that they could continue to do well.

Next the experimenters told the participants that the purpose of the experiment was to investigate the effects of drugs on problem solving and that they were now going to hand out another set of problems. The participants could choose between taking a drug that supposedly impaired problem-solving abilities and another drug that supposedly improved them. The participants who had worked on unsolvable problems the first time were more likely than the others to choose the drug that supposedly impaired performance. Because they did not expect to do well on the second set of problems anyway, they provided themselves with a convenient excuse.

CONCEPT CHECK ☑

7. Who is more likely to make the fundamental attribution error, people from Western cultures or Chinese?
8. If, instead of watching someone, you close your eyes and imagine yourself in that person's position, will you be more likely to explain the behavior with internal or external attributions? Why?
9. Why would people sometimes intentionally do something likely to harm their own performance? (Check your answers on page 542.)

IN CLOSING

How Social Perceptions Affect Behavior

We are seldom fully aware of the reasons for our own behavior, much less someone else's, but we make our best guesses. If someone you know passes by without saying hello, you might attribute that person's behavior to absent-mindedness, indifference, or outright hostility. You might attribute someone's friendly response to your own personal charm, the other person's extraverted personality, or that person's devious and manipulative personality. Whatever attributions you make are sure to influence your own social behaviors.

Summary

- *First impressions.* Other things being equal, we pay more attention to the first information we learn about someone than to later information. (page 533)

- *Stereotypes.* Stereotypes are generalized beliefs about groups of people. Even if a stereotype is true on the average, it does not apply to all individuals. (page 534)
- *Prejudice.* A prejudice is an unfavorable stereotype. Many people will not admit their prejudices, even to themselves. Through indirect measures, researchers have found ways to demonstrate subtle effects of stereotypes and prejudices even in people who deny having them. (page 534)
- *Attribution.* Attribution is the set of thought processes by which we assign internal or external causes to behavior. According to Harold Kelley, we are likely to attribute behavior to an internal cause if it is consistent over time, different from most other people's behavior, and directed toward a variety of other people or objects. (page 537)
- *Fundamental attribution error.* People frequently attribute people's behavior to internal causes, even when they see evidence of external influences. (page 539)
- *Cultural differences.* People in China and Korea are less likely than those in Western cultures to attribute behavior to consistent personality traits and more likely to attribute it to the situation. (page 539)
- *Actor-observer effect.* We are more likely to attribute internal causes to other people's behavior than to our own. (page 540)
- *Self-serving bias and self-handicapping.* People sometimes try to protect their self-esteem by attributing their successes to skill and their failures to outside influences. They can also intentionally place themselves at a disadvantage to provide an excuse for their expected failure. (page 541)

Answers to Concept Checks

1. They want to avoid being biased by their first impressions of the students. This procedure is less important with the first test because they have not yet formed strong impressions. (page 534)
2. The Implicit Association Test can reveal prejudices that people don't want to admit, perhaps even to themselves. (page 537)
3. They are most likely to show evidence of implicit prejudice if the instructions ask people to pay attention to the race of the people in the photos. (page 537)
4. **a.** internal; **b.** and **c.** external. An internal attribution relates to a stable aspect of personality or attitudes; an external attribution relates to the current situation. (page 539)
5. You probably will make an internal attribution because of *consensus.* When one person's behavior differs from others', we make an internal attribution. (page 539)
6. They would be more likely to make the fundamental attribution error because they tend to attribute behaviors to internal causes instead of situations. (page 539)
7. Westerners are more likely to make the fundamental attribution error because the Chinese tend to attribute behavior more to situational factors than do Westerners. (page 541)
8. You will be more likely to give an external attribution because you will become more like an actor and less an observer. (page 541)
9. People sometimes do something to harm their own performance to give themselves an excuse for doing poorly, especially if they thought they might do poorly anyway. (page 541)

Attitudes and Persuasion

What are some effective ways of influencing people's attitudes?

"If you want to change people's behavior, you have to change their attitudes first." Do you agree? Suppose you say "yes." Now answer two more questions: (a) What is your attitude about paying higher taxes? (b) If the government raises taxes, will you pay the higher taxes?

I assume you said that you have an unfavorable attitude about paying higher taxes, but if the taxes are raised, you will pay them. In other words, by changing the law, the government could change your behavior without changing your attitude. In fact it is often easier to change behaviors than attitudes.

So what effects do attitudes have on behavior? And what leads people to change their attitudes?

Attitudes and Their Influence

An **attitude** is *a like or dislike that influences our behavior toward someone or something* (Allport, 1935; Petty & Cacioppo, 1981). Your attitudes include an evaluative or emotional component (how you feel about something), a cognitive component (what you know or believe), and a behavioral component (what you are likely to do). *Persuasion* is an attempt to alter your attitudes or behavior.

One common way of measuring attitudes (and thus the effectiveness of persuasion) is through the use of attitude scales, such as Likert scales, also known as summated rating scales (Dawes & Smith, 1985). On a Likert scale (named after psychologist Rensis Likert), a person checks a point along a line ranging from 1, meaning "strongly disagree," to 7, meaning "strongly agree," for each of several statements about a topic, as illustrated in Figure 14.4.

The attitudes that people report sometimes relate closely to their behaviors but often do not. For example, many people report attitudes about cigarettes, alcohol, safe sex, wearing seat belts in a car, studying hard for tests, and so forth that do not match their behavior. Why? One reason is that people sometimes answer attitude questionnaires impulsively, especially on questions that are not important to them (van der Pligt, de Vries, Manstead, & van Harreveld, 2000). Recall that the same idea arose in Chapter 2 concerning surveys. A second reason is that people's answers to an attitude question fluctuate because of momentary influences (Lord & Lepper, 1999). For example, what is your attitude toward politicians on a scale from 1 (very unfavorable) to 7 (very favorable)? If you are thinking about the public servants you admire most, you might rate politicians favorably. At a later time, however, you might be thinking about corrupt or incompetent politicians, and you would answer differently.

A third reason, which overlaps the other two, is that people sometimes maintain mixed or contradictory attitudes (T. D. Wilson, Lindsey, & Schooler, 2000). For example, you might have long held an unfavorable attitude toward homosexuals. More recently,

---

Indicate your level of agreement with the items below, using the following scale:

	Strongly disagree		Neutral			Strongly agree
1. Labor unions are necessary to protect the rights of workers.	1 2	3	4	5	6	7
2. Labor union leaders have too much power.	1 2	3	4	5	6	7
3. If I worked for a company with a union, I would join the union.	1 2	3	4	5	6	7
4. I would never cross a picket line of striking workers.	1 2	3	4	5	6	7
5. Striking workers hurt their company and unfairly raise prices for the consumer.	1 2	3	4	5	6	7
6. Labor unions should not be permitted to engage in political activity.	1 2	3	4	5	6	7
7. America is a better place for today's workers because of the efforts by labor unions in the past.	1 2	3	4	5	6	7

Note: Items 2, 5, and 6 are scored the opposite of 1, 3, 4, and 7.

FIGURE 14.4 Likert scales, such as this one assessing attitudes toward labor unions, are commonly used in attitude research. Participants rate their agreement or disagreement with each statement.

you have been persuaded that this attitude was unfair, and you now express a more positive attitude. You state your new explicit attitude on questionnaires, but your old attitude emerges in your nonverbal behaviors and emotional reactions.

CONCEPT CHECK ☑

10. What test or method mentioned in the first module of this chapter could demonstrate mixed or contradictory attitudes? (Check your answer on page 551.)

Central and Peripheral Routes of Attitude Change and Persuasion

Sometimes people ponder the evidence carefully and develop a thoughtfully reasoned attitude, and sometimes they form attitudes with only a superficial basis. Richard Petty and John Cacioppo (1981, 1986) proposed the following distinction: *When people take a decision seriously, they invest the necessary time and effort to evaluate the evidence and logic behind each message.* Petty and Cacioppo call this logical approach the **central route to persuasion.** In contrast, *when people listen to a message on a topic they consider unimportant, they attend to such factors as the speaker's appearance and reputation or the sheer number of arguments presented, regardless of their quality.* This superficial approach is the **peripheral route to persuasion.**

CONCEPT CHECK ☑

11. You listen to a debate about raising tuition at Santa Enigma Junior College. Later, you listen to a debate about raising tuition at your own college. In which case will you follow the central route to persuasion? (Check your answer on page 551.)

Delayed Influence

Some messages have no apparent influence at first but an important effect later. A message can have a delayed effect for many reasons; we consider two examples.

The Sleeper Effect

Suppose you reject a message because of peripheral route influences. For example, you quickly reject some idea because of your low opinion of the person who suggested it. Weeks or months later, you may forget where you heard the idea (*source amnesia*) and remember only the idea itself. At that time you evaluate it on its merits and perhaps decide it was a good idea (Hovland & Weiss, 1951; Pratkanis, Greenwald, Leippe, & Baumgardner, 1988). If you completely forget the source, you might even claim it as your own idea! Psychologists use the term **sleeper effect** to describe *delayed persuasion by an initially rejected message.*

Minority Influence

Delayed influence also occurs when a minority group, especially one that is not widely respected, proposes a worthwhile idea: The majority rejects the idea at first but reconsiders it later. By "minority group," I do not necessarily mean an ethnic minority; it could be a political minority or any other outnumbered group.

If a minority group continually repeats a single simple message and its members seem united, it has a good chance of eventually influencing the majority's decision. The minority's united, uncompromising stance forces the majority to wonder, "Why won't they conform? Maybe their idea is better than we thought." The minority's influence often increases gradually, even if the majority hesitates to admit that the minority has swayed them (Wood, Lundgren, Ouellette, Busceme, & Blackstone, 1994). A minority, by expressing its views, can also prompt the majority to generate new ideas of its own (Nemeth, 1986). That is, by demonstrating the possibility of disagreement, the minority opens the way for other people to offer new suggestions different from the original views of both the majority and the minority.

One powerful example of minority influence is that of the Socialist party of the United States, which ran candidates for elective offices from 1900 through the 1950s. The party never received more than 6% of the vote in any presidential election. No Socialist candidate was ever elected senator or governor, and only a few were elected to the House of Representatives (Shannon, 1955). Beginning in the 1930s, the party's membership and support dwindled, until eventually the party stopped nominating candidates. Was that because they had failed? No! Most of the major proposals of the party had been enacted into law (see Table 14.1). Of course, the Democrats and Republicans who voted for these changes claimed credit for the ideas. Still, the Socialist party, without winning elections, had exerted an enormous influence.

CONCEPT CHECK ☑

12. At a meeting of your student government, you suggest a new method of testing and grading students. The other members immediately reject your plan. Should you become discouraged and give up? If not, what should you do? (Check your answers on page 551.)

TABLE 14.1 Political Proposals of the U.S. Socialist Party, Around 1900

Proposal	Eventual Fate of Proposal
Women's right to vote	Established by 19th Amendment to U.S. Constitution; ratified in 1920
Old-age pensions	Included in the Social Security Act of 1935
Unemployment insurance	Included in the Social Security Act of 1935; also guaranteed by the other state and federal legislation
Health and accident insurance	Included in part in the Social Security Act of 1935 and in the Medicare Act of 1965
Increased wages, including minimum wage	First minimum-wage law passed in 1938; periodically updated since then
Reduction of working hours	Maximum 40-hour workweek (with exceptions) established by the Fair Labor Standards Act of 1938
Public ownership of electric, gas, and other utilities and of the means of transportation and communication	Utilities not owned by government but heavily regulated by federal and state government since the 1930s
Initiative, referendum, and recall (mechanisms for private citizens to push for changes in legislation and for removal of elected officials)	Adopted by most state governments

Sources: Foster, 1968; and Leuchtenburg, 1963.

Ways of Presenting Persuasive Messages

The influence of an attempt at persuasion can depend on many factors that we hardly notice. For example, a television ad may become more effective because of the pleasant music in the background. Often, we are influenced by some factor that we would insist did not affect us. Advertisers, politicians, and many others attend closely to the details of how they present their messages.

The Role of Fear

Most persuasive messages fall into one of two categories: (a) Do this to accomplish something good, and (b) do this to avoid something bad. Either approach can be effective depending on the circumstances. Figure 14.5 shows the "St. Jude" chain letter that has circulated throughout the world for decades. It has been called a "mind virus" because it inspires people to duplicate and spread the letter (Goodenough & Dawkins, 1994). Many people who receive this letter cannot resist its command to make copies and send them to others, even if they regard the message as a silly superstition. Why? The letter claims to be offering "good luck" and "love," but it follows those promises with an implied threat: Allegedly, people who have failed to follow the instructions have lost their job, lost a loved one, died, or had car problems! The threat makes people feel nervous and uneasy if they decline to follow the instructions.

Fear messages are effective in some cases, as in the St. Jude letter, but not always. Appeals for money are often accompanied by implied threats, such as "If you don't send enough money to support our cause, then our political opponents will gain power and do terrible things." According to the research, messages that appeal to fear are effective only if they can convince people that the danger is real (Leventhal, 1970). People tend to disbelieve an organization that exaggerates the threats or sends "emergency" appeals too often.

Moreover, a fear message is effective only if people believe they can easily reduce the danger. For example, most people will visit a physician for an immunization against a contagious disease or for an x-ray to test for cancer. Many people, but not all, will change their sex habits to avoid herpes or AIDS. Even fewer people consistently change their behavior to conserve natural resources or to avoid damaging the

FIGURE 14.5 If you received a copy of this chain letter, would you copy it and send it to other people, as it requests? Why or why not?

world's climate because most people doubt that their behavior will make much difference.

Fear messages sometimes backfire. To motivate action against a problem, an organization might try to describe the danger as severe. For example, an antidrug campaign might say that drug use is spreading wildly, or a conservation organization might say that pollution and destruction of the environment are out of control. The intended message is, "Take this problem seriously and act now." The unintended message that people sometimes receive is, "Drug use, pollution, etc. are normal." If the problem seems extremely widespread, people see no point in fighting it (Cialdini, 2003).

Influence of Similarity

Other things being equal, a persuasive message is more effective if the speaker conveys the message, "I resemble you." In one striking illustration of the influence of similarity, students were asked to read a very unflattering description of Grigory Rasputin, the "mad monk of Russia," and then rate Rasputin on several scales such as pleasant to unpleasant, effective to ineffective, and strong to weak. All students read the same description except for Rasputin's birth date: In some cases Rasputin's birth date had been changed to match the student's own birth date. Students who thought Rasputin had the same birth date as their own

© Hulton-Deutsch Collection/CORBIS

▌ Grigory Rasputin was a contemptible person whose unsavory influence on the czar of Russia led to the Communist revolution. However, people who are told Rasputin resembled them, even in trivial ways, soften their criticisms.

were more likely than others to rate him as "strong" and "effective" (Finch & Cialdini, 1989).

Influence of Group Endorsement

Imagine some preposterous idea that you reject vigorously. Now imagine that some group you respect endorses the idea. Would you suddenly think it was a good idea?

In one study psychologists used a questionnaire to identify the most politically liberal students and the most conservative ones. Then they gave each student one of two versions of what they said was a proposed law about welfare for the unemployed. One version offered extraordinarily generous benefits, including $800 per month for up to 8 years, plus full medical care, $2,000 in food stamps, subsidies for housing and day care, job training, full tuition at a community college, and more. Although this policy goes well beyond what the U.S.'s most liberal politicians have recommended, if students were told that the Republicans (the more conservative party) endorsed it, conservative students said they supported it too, while liberal students opposed it. Other students were told about a much stingier proposed law, which provided only $250 per month, with an 18-month limit, and no other benefits. Ordinarily, almost anyone would consider this policy inadequate, but if students were told that the Democrats (the more liberal party) endorsed it, liberal students supported it while conservatives did not. When students were asked the reasons for their decisions, almost none admitted that endorsement by one party or the other was a significant influence. They insisted that they decided on their own (G. L. Cohen, 2003).

CONCEPT CHECK

13. A salesperson calls at your door and says that several of your neighbors (whom the salesperson names) have bought the product and recommended you as another possible customer. What techniques of persuasion is this salesperson using? (Check your answer on page 551.)

Audience Variables

Some people are more easily persuaded than others are, and someone may be more easily influenced at some times than at others. The ease of persuading someone depends on both the person and the situation.

Intelligence and Interest

Who would you guess would be persuaded more easily—more intelligent or less intelligent people? It depends. The peripheral route to persuasion is more likely to persuade less intelligent people of an illogical or poorly supported idea (Eagly & Warren, 1976). The central route to persuasion is generally more effective with highly intelligent people, who are better able to understand complicated evidence.

However, the effectiveness of the central or peripheral route also depends on people's level of interest. A clever salesperson gauges a client's interests and concentrates on personally relevant issues. For example, some customers have more patience than others for listening to a series of facts. Today, it is possible to tailor Internet ads to the individual; computers store information about you and change the emphasis of an ad depending on what kinds of information are most likely to interest and persuade you (Kreutzer & Holt, 2001).

Heightened Resistance

Psychologists long assumed that people avoided reading or listening to arguments with which they disagree. Researchers have found, however, that people do expose themselves to ideas they dislike, and they remember the arguments surprisingly well. However, they argue against them and resist any major change in their attitudes (Eagly, Kulesa, Chen, & Chaiken, 2001).

Simply informing people that they are about to hear a persuasive speech activates their resistance and weakens the effect of the talk on their attitudes (Petty & Cacioppo, 1977). This tendency is called the **forewarning effect**. Actually, the effects are somewhat complex. Suppose you have a strongly unfavorable attitude toward something—higher tuition at your college, for example. Now someone tells you that a well-informed person is going to try to persuade you in favor of higher tuition. At once, before the speech even begins, your attitudes shift slightly in that direction, toward favoring higher tuition! Exactly why is unclear; perhaps you are telling yourself, "I guess there must be some good reason for that opinion." Then when you hear the speech itself, it does have some influence, and your attitudes will shift still further toward favoring it (or at least toward neutrality), but your attitudes do not shift as much as those of someone who had not been forewarned. The warning alerts you to resist the persuasion, to criticize weak arguments, and to reject weak evidence (Wood & Quinn, 2003).

In the closely related **inoculation effect**, *people first hear a weak argument and then a stronger argument supporting the same conclusion.* After they have rejected the first argument, they are likely to reject the second one also. In one experiment people listened to speeches *against* brushing their teeth after every meal. Some of them heard just a strong argument (e.g., "Brushing your teeth too frequently wears away tooth enamel, leading to serious disease"). Others first heard a weak argument and then the strong

argument 2 days later. Still others first heard an argument *for* tooth-brushing and then the strong argument against it. Only those who heard the weak antibrushing argument before the strong one resisted its influence; the other two groups found it highly persuasive (McGuire & Papageorgis, 1961). So if you want to convince people, start with your strong evidence, not with evidence that they may consider faulty.

CONCEPT CHECK ☑

14. If you want your children to preserve the beliefs and attitudes you try to teach them, should you give them only arguments that support those beliefs or should you also expose them to attacks on those beliefs? Why? (Check your answers on page 551.)

Strategies of Persuasion

People representing anything from worthless products to noble charities will sometimes ask you to give more of your time or money than you would rationally choose to spend. You should understand several of their techniques so that you can resist these appeals.

One technique is to start with a modest request, which the person accepts, and then follow it with a larger request. This procedure is called the **foot-in-the-door technique**. When Jonathan Freedman and Scott Fraser (1966) asked suburban residents in Palo Alto, California, to put a small "Drive Safely" sign in their windows, most of them agreed to do so. A couple of weeks later, other researchers asked the same residents to let them set up a large, unsightly "Drive Safely" billboard in their front yards for 10 days. They also made the request to some residents who had not been approached by the first researchers. Of those who had already agreed to display the small sign, 76% agreed to the billboard. Only 17% of the others agreed. Even agreeing to make as small a commitment as signing a petition to support a cause significantly increases the probability that people will later donate money to that cause (Schwarzwald, Bizman, & Raz, 1983).

In another approach, called the **door-in-the-face technique** (Cialdini et al., 1975), *someone follows an outrageous initial request with a more reasonable second one,* implying that if you refused the first request, you should agree to the second. For example, I once received a telephone call from a college alumni association asking me to show my loyalty by contributing $1,000. When I apologetically declined, the caller acted sympathetic (as if to say, "It's too bad you don't have a high-paying job like all our other alumni . . .") and then asked whether I could contribute $500. And if not $500, how about $200? The implication was that, if I had refused the original request, I should "compromise" by donating a smaller amount.

Robert Cialdini and his colleagues (1975) demonstrated the power of the door-in-the-face technique with a clever experiment. They asked one group of college students, chosen randomly, whether they would be willing to chaperone a group from the juvenile detention center on a trip to the zoo. Only 17% said they would. They asked other students to spend 2 hours per week for 2 years working as counselors with juvenile delinquents. Not surprisingly, all of them refused. But then the researchers asked them, "If you won't do that, would you chaperone a group from the juvenile detention center on one trip to the zoo?" Half of them said they would. Apparently, they felt that the researchers were conceding a great deal and that it was only fair to meet them halfway.

Someone using the **bait-and-switch technique** *first offers an extremely favorable deal, gets the other person to commit to the deal, and then makes additional demands.* Alternatively, the person might offer a product at a very low price to get customers to the store but then claim to be out of the product and try to sell them something else. For example, a car dealer offers you an exceptionally good price on a new car and a generous price for the trade-in of your old car. You weren't sure you wanted this make of car, but the deal is too good to resist. After you have committed yourself to buying this car, the dealer checks with the boss, who rejects the deal. Your salesperson comes back saying, "I'm so sorry. I forgot that this car has some special features that raise the value. If we sold it for the price I originally quoted, we'd lose money." So you agree to a higher price. Then the company's used car specialist looks at your old car and "corrects" the trade-in value to a lower amount. Still, you have already committed yourself, so you don't back out. Eventually, you leave with a deal that you would not have accepted at the start.

In the **that's-not-all technique,** *someone makes an offer and then improves the offer before you have a chance to reply.* The television announcer says, "Here's your chance to buy this amazing combination paper shredder and coffeemaker for only $39.95. But wait, there's more! We'll throw in a can of dog deodorant! Also this handy windshield wiper cleaner and a solar-powered flashlight and a subscription to *Modern Lobotomist!* If you call now, you can get this amazing offer, which usually costs $39.95, for only $19.95! Call this number!" People who hear the first offer and then the "improved" offer are more likely to comply than are people who hear the "improved" offer from the start (Burger, 1986).

CONCEPT CHECK ☑

15. Identify each of the following as an example of the foot-in-the-door technique, the door-in-the-face technique, or the that's-not-all technique.
   a. Your boss says, "We need to cut costs drastically. I'm afraid I'm going to have to cut your salary in half." You protest vigorously. Your boss replies, "Well, I suppose we could cut expenses some other way. Maybe I can give you just a 5% cut." "Thanks," you reply. "I can live with that."
   b. A store marks its prices "25% off" and then scratches that out and marks them "50% off!"
   c. A friend asks you to help carry some supplies over to the elementary school for an afternoon tutoring program. When you get there, the principal says that one of the tutors is late and asks whether you could take her place until she arrives. You agree and spend the rest of the afternoon tutoring. The principal then talks you into coming back every week as a tutor. (Check your answers on page 551.)

Cognitive Dissonance

Much research asks whether people's attitudes change their behavior. The theory of cognitive dissonance reverses the direction: It holds that a change in people's behavior alters their attitudes (Festinger, 1957). **Cognitive dissonance** is *a state of unpleasant tension that people experience when they hold contradictory attitudes or when their behavior is inconsistent with their attitudes, especially if they are distressed about the inconsistency.*

For example, if you pride yourself on honesty and find yourself saying something you do not believe, you feel tension. You can reduce that tension in three ways: You can change what you are saying to match your attitudes, change your attitude to match what you are saying, or find an explanation that justifies your behavior under the circumstances (Wicklund & Brehm, 1976) (see Figure 14.6). Although you might adopt any of these options, most of the existing research has focused on how cognitive dissonance changes people's attitudes.

Imagine yourself as one of the participants in this classic experiment on cognitive dissonance (Festinger & Carlsmith, 1959). The experimenters explain that they are studying motor behavior. They show you a board full of pegs. Your task is to take each peg out of the board, rotate it one fourth of a turn, and return it to the board. When you finish all the pegs, you start over from the top, rotating all the pegs again as quickly and accurately as possible for an hour. As you

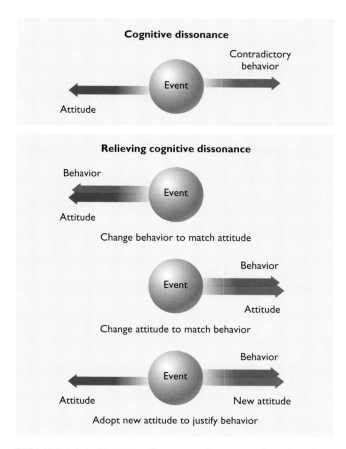

Cognitive dissonance

Attitude ← Event → Contradictory behavior

Relieving cognitive dissonance

Behavior ← Event
Attitude

Change behavior to match attitude

Event → Behavior
Attitude

Change attitude to match behavior

Attitude ← Event → Behavior
New attitude

Adopt new attitude to justify behavior

FIGURE 14.6 Cognitive dissonance is a state of tension that arises when people perceive that their attitudes do not match their behavior. They can resolve this discrepancy by changing either their attitudes or their behavior or by developing a new attitude or excuse to explain the discrepancy.

proceed an experimenter silently takes notes. You find your task tedious and boring. (In fact the researchers intentionally chose this task because it was so boring.)

At the end of the hour, the experimenter thanks you for participating and "explains" to you (falsely) that the study's purpose was to determine whether people's performances are influenced by their attitudes toward the task. You were in the neutral-attitude group, but those in the positive-attitude group are told before they start that they will enjoy this interesting experience.

In fact, the experimenter continues, right now the research assistant is supposed to give that instruction to the next participant, a young woman waiting in the next room. The experimenter excuses himself to find the research assistant and then returns distraught. The assistant is nowhere to be found, he says. He turns to you and asks, "Would you be willing to tell the next partic-

ipant that you thought this was an interesting, enjoyable experiment? If so, I will pay you." Assume that you consent, as most students in the study did. After you tell that woman in the next room that you enjoyed the study, what would you actually think of the study, assuming the experimenter paid you $1? What if he paid you $20? (This study occurred in the 1950s, before decades of inflation. In today's money that $20 would be worth more than $100.)

In this study, after participants told the woman how much fun the experiment was, they left, believing the study was over. As they walked down the hall, a representative of the psychology department greeted them and explained that the department wanted to find out what kinds of experiments were being conducted and whether they were educationally worthwhile. (The answers to these questions were the real point of the experiment.) Participants were asked how enjoyable they considered the experiment and whether they would be willing to participate in a similar experiment later.

The students who received $20 said they thought the experiment was boring and that they wanted nothing to do with another such experiment. However, contrary to what you might guess, those who received $1 said they enjoyed the experiment and would be willing to participate again (Figure 14.7).

Why? According to the theory of cognitive dissonance, those who accepted $20 to tell a lie experienced little conflict. They knew they were lying, but they also knew why: for the $20. They had no reason to change their original low opinion of the experiment. However, the students who had told a lie for only $1 felt a conflict between their true attitude and what they had said about the experiment. The small payment provided little reason for lying, so they experienced cognitive dissonance—an unpleasant tension. They did not want to feel bad about telling a lie, so the only way they could reduce their tension was to change their attitude, deciding that the experiment really had been interesting after all. ("I learned a lot of

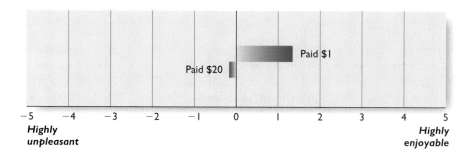

Paid $20   Paid $1

−5   −4   −3   −2   −1   0   1   2   3   4   5
Highly unpleasant   *Highly enjoyable*

FIGURE 14.7 In a classic experiment demonstrating cognitive dissonance, participants were paid either $1 or $20 for telling another subject that they enjoyed an experiment (which was actually boring). Later, they were asked for their real opinions. Participants who were paid the smaller amount said that they enjoyed the study more than the others. *(Based on data from Festinger & Carlsmith, 1959)* interesting things about myself, like . . . uh . . . how good I am at rotating pegs.")

The idea of cognitive dissonance attracted much attention and inspired a great deal of research (Aronson, 1997). Here are two examples:

- An experimenter left a child in a room with toys but forbade the child to play with one particular toy. If the experimenter threatened the child with severe punishment for playing with the toy, the child avoided it but still regarded it as desirable. However, if the experimenter merely said that he or she would be unhappy or disappointed if the child played with that toy, the child avoided the toy and said (even weeks later) that it was not a good toy (Aronson & Carlsmith, 1963).
- The experimenter asked college students to write an essay defending a position that the experimenter knew, from previous information, was contrary to the students' beliefs. For example, college students who favored freer access to alcohol might be asked to write essays on why the college should increase restrictions on alcohol. Those who were told they must write the essays did not change their views significantly, but those who were asked to "please" write the essay and were also reminded that they did so voluntarily generally came to agree with what they wrote (Croyle & Cooper, 1983).

The general principle is that, if you entice people to do something by means of a minimum reward or a tiny threat so that they are acting almost voluntarily, they change their attitudes to defend what they are doing and reduce cognitive dissonance. This procedure is a powerful way of changing attitudes because people are actively participating, not just quietly listening to someone.

This module began with the statement, "If you want to change people's behavior, you have to change their attitudes first." The results of cognitive dissonance experiments tell us quite the opposite: If you start by changing people's behavior, their attitudes will change too.

CONCEPT CHECK ☑

16. Suppose your parents pay you to get a good grade in a course that you consider boring. According to cognitive dissonance theory, are you more likely to develop a positive attitude toward your studies if your parents pay you $10 or $100?

17. The effort to avoid cognitive dissonance leads to consistency in behavior. Use that principle to explain the foot-in-the-door technique. (Check your answers on page 551.)

Persuasion and Manipulation

Broadly defined, attitudes influence almost everything we do. The stereotypes, prejudices, and so forth that we considered in the first module are attitudes about people or groups of people. You also have attitudes about political issues, the value of various products, and various ethical questions.

When you form an attitude about something of little consequence to you, it is understandable that you will follow the peripheral route, paying little attention to the complexities of the evidence. When you are dealing with important matters, however, such as how you will spend your time and money, you will almost certainly follow the central route, examining the facts as carefully as you can. It is important to be alert to some of the influences that might throw you off course, such as the foot-in-the-door technique, bait-and-switch, and cognitive dissonance. Advertisers, politicians, and vast numbers of others try to polish their techniques of persuasion, and not everyone has your best interest at heart.

Summary

- *Attitudes.* An attitude is a like or dislike of something or somebody that influences our behavior toward that thing or person. (page 543)
- *Two routes to persuasion.* When people consider a topic of little importance to them, they are easily persuaded by the speaker's appearance and other superficial factors. When people care about the topic, they pay more attention to logic and to the quality of the evidence. (page 544)
- *Sleeper effect.* When people reject a message because of their low regard for the person who proposed it, they sometimes forget where they heard the idea and later come to accept it. (page 544)
- *Minority influence.* Although a minority may have little influence at first, it can, through persistent repetition of its message, eventually persuade the majority to adopt its position or consider other alternatives. (page 544)
- *Influence of fear-inducing messages.* Messages that appeal to fear are effective if people perceive the danger as real and think they can do something about it. (page 545)
- *Influence of group endorsement.* People tend to accept a position endorsed by a political party or other group they favor, even if they would ordinarily doubt that position. (page 546)
- *Forewarning and inoculation effects.* If people have been warned that someone will try to persuade them of something, or if they have previously

heard a weak version of the persuasive argument, they tend to resist the argument. (page 547)

* *Strategies of persuasion.* Several procedures can influence people to do something they would not have done otherwise. These include starting with a tiny request and then increasing it, starting with an enormous request and offering to compromise, offering a generous deal and then demanding more, and offering a moderate deal and then adding inducements. (page 547)

* *Cognitive dissonance.* Cognitive dissonance is a state of unpleasant tension that arises from contradictory attitudes or from behavior that conflicts with a person's attitudes. When people's behavior does not match their attitudes, they try to eliminate the inconsistency by changing either their behavior or their attitudes. (page 548)

Answers to Concept Checks

10. Some people express one attitude openly but demonstrate another attitude on the Implicit Association Test. (page 544)

11. You will pay more attention to the evidence and logic, following the central route to persuasion, for the debate about your own college because it is worth your effort to evaluate the evidence carefully. (page 544)

12. The fact that your idea was overwhelmingly rejected does not mean that you should give up. If you and a few allies continue to present this plan in a simple way, showing apparent agreement among yourselves, the majority may eventually endorse a similar plan—but probably without giving you credit for it. (page 544)

13. The salesperson is relying on endorsement by a group that you presumably like and trust. Also you are likely to be persuaded by people similar to yourself. (page 546)

14. You should expose them to weak attacks on their beliefs so that they will learn how to resist such attacks. (page 547)

15. a. door-in-the-face technique; b. that's-not-all technique; c. foot-in-the-door technique. (page 548)

16. You will come to like your studies more if you are paid $10 than if you are paid $100. If you are paid only $10, you won't be able to tell yourself that you are studying harder only for the money. Instead, you will tell yourself that you must be really interested.

The theory of intrinsic and extrinsic motivation leads to the same prediction: If you study hard in the absence of any strong external reason, you will perceive that you have internal reasons for studying. (page 550)

17. Once you have agreed to a small request, you can maintain consistency (decrease dissonance) by agreeing to similar requests in the future. (page 550)

How do we choose our partners? Do men and women choose for the same reasons?

William Proxmire, a former U.S. senator, used to give Golden Fleece Awards to those who, in his opinion, most flagrantly wasted the taxpayers' money. He once bestowed an award on some psychologists who had received a federal grant to study how people fall in love. According to Proxmire the research was pointless because people do not want to understand love. They prefer, he said, to let such matters remain a mystery.

This module presents the information Senator Proxmire thought you did not want to know.

Establishing Lasting Relationships

Of all the people you meet, how do you choose those few who become your friends? (Or how do they choose you?) Here we consider factors relevant to both friendships and romantic relationships; later, we specifically discuss dating and marriage.

Proximity and Familiarity

Proximity means *closeness.* (It comes from the same root as *approximate.*) Not surprisingly, *we are most likely to become friends with people who live or work in close proximity and become familiar to us.* At the start of a school year, Robert Hays (1985) asked college students to name two other students with whom they thought they might become friends. After 3 months he found that more of the potential friends who lived close together had become friends than had those who lived farther apart.

One reason proximity is important is that people who live nearby have frequent opportunities to discover what they have in common. Another reason is the **mere exposure effect,** the principle that *the more often we come in contact with someone or something, the more we tend to like that person or object* (Saegert, Swap, & Zajonc, 1973; Zajonc, 1968). You can think of exceptions, of course; for example, frequent contact with a disease will not make you like it. However, mere exposure can elevate something from "neutral" to "liked." (Exactly why is not obvious.)

Similarity

Here's another finding that will hardly surprise you: Most close friends resemble one another in age, physical attractiveness, political and religious beliefs, intelligence, academic interests, religion, and attitudes (Laumann, 1969).

Choice of friends can be difficult for members of minorities. If your ethnic or religious group is greatly outnumbered where you live, your potential friends or romantic partners may be limited to individuals within your group who do not share your interests or members of other groups who do (Hamm, 2000).

Do you like people better when you learn that their beliefs and attitudes resemble yours? This question turns out to be more complex than it sounds. You probably like most of the people you meet until you have a reason to alter your judgment. If you think at all about a new acquaintance's beliefs and attitudes, you probably assume that he or she shares your own beliefs and attitudes . . . because most people do, don't they? After all, you believe your opinions and actions

▌ Behavior is guided by external forces, such as waves, and by forces within the individual. According to the determinist view, even those internal forces follow physical laws.

are normal and correct (Alicke & Largo, 1995). Therefore, finding a disagreement with someone *lowers* your regard for them more than finding an agreement *increases* your regard (Rosenbaum, 1986).

Confirmation of Self-Concept

You might well be saying, "Big deal. People make friends with others who live nearby and resemble them. Psychologists needed research to demonstrate *that?*" It is worthwhile to test the obvious because occasionally what seems obvious might be wrong. For example, suppose you are in a research study. First you are asked to describe yourself. Then two other people tell you their reactions. The first says, "You seem a pleasant, honest person. You're intelligent and you have some interesting ideas and a nice sense of humor." The second says, "I hate to be rude, but frankly you seem superficial. You're trying to make a good impression, but for me, you're failing. You drift aimlessly; you can't even organize your thoughts." Which one would you choose as a possible partner or friend?

The obvious answer is "the first one." However, many people with unusually low self-esteem choose the person who gave them a low evaluation (Swann, 1997). Evidently, people who think little of themselves find it satisfying to be with others who share that low opinion. You can see the potential harm. Someone with a low self-evaluation chooses friends and perhaps even a spouse who constantly criticizes. The result is even lower self-esteem.

The Equity Principle

According to **exchange** or **equity theories**, *social relationships are transactions in which partners exchange goods and services.* In some cases the businesslike nature of a romantic relationship is fairly blatant. In the Singles' Ads of many newspapers, those seeking a relationship describe what they have to offer and what they expect in return. Generally, women who describe themselves as attractive and men who describe themselves as wealthy set high demands on what they are seeking in a mate. People who have less to offer make fewer demands (Waynforth & Dunbar, 1995).

As in business, a relationship is most stable if both partners believe the deal is fair. It is easiest to establish a fair deal if the partners are about equally attractive and intelligent, contribute about equally to the finances and the chores, and so forth. With many couples one partner contributes more in one way and the other contributes more in another way. Those arrangements can also seem fair, although it is more difficult to be sure.

The equity principle readily applies while people are forming friendships or romances, but it is less applicable later. For example, you might nurse your spouse or lifelong friend through a long illness without worrying about whether you are still getting a fair deal.

CONCEPT CHECK ☑

18. Someone your own age from another country moves next door. Neither of you speaks the other's language. What factors will tend to strengthen the likelihood of your becoming friends? What factors will tend to weaken it? (Check your answers on page 560.)

Special Concerns in Selecting a Mate

Choosing a partner for marriage or long-term partnership has special features because of the extra dimension of raising children. Yes, I know, not everyone wants to get married, not all married couples want children, and many unmarried people rear children. The following discussion does not apply to everyone—almost nothing in psychology does!—but it applies to those who hope to marry and have children.

Physical Attractiveness

What characteristics do you look for in someone you might date and eventually marry? You probably reply that you want "someone who is intelligent, honest, easy to talk to, with a good sense of humor." Now imagine a friend says, "Hey, you're not doing anything this weekend, right? How about going on a blind date with my cousin who is visiting for the weekend?" "Well, I don't know. Tell me about your cousin." "My cousin is intelligent, honest, easy to talk to, and has a good sense of humor." That description matches what you said you wanted, but you are skeptical. Your friend did not mention the cousin's appearance, so you assume the worst. Were you being dishonest when you said you wanted someone intelligent, honest, and easy to talk to? Not really. You did not mention appearance because you assumed anyone would take that for granted. (You also didn't say that you hope your date speaks English. You don't mention the obvious.)

In one study social psychologists arranged blind dates for 332 freshman couples for a dance before the start of classes. They asked participants to fill out questionnaires, but then the experimenters ignored the questionnaires and paired students at random. Midway through the dance, the experimenters separated the men and women and asked them to rate how much they liked their dates. The only factor that influenced the ratings was physical attractiveness (Walster, Aronson, Abrahams, & Rottman, 1966). Similarities of attitudes, personality, and intelligence counted for almost nothing. Surprising? Hardly. During the brief time they had spent together at the dance, the couples had little opportunity to learn about each other. Intelligence, honesty, and other character values do become important in a lasting relationship, but not on the first date or two, and certainly not in the first hour (Keller, Thiessen, & Young, 1996).

On the average, attractive people are judged more favorably than other people. They have more friends and they are treated better. The usual result is a self-fulfilling prophecy: Because people expect to like attractive people, they treat them better, and the attractive people therefore become more friendly and outgoing (Langlois et al., 2000).

The Possible Biological Value of Attractiveness

Why do we care about physical appearance? We take its importance so much for granted that we don't even understand why there is a question, so for a moment let's consider other species.

In many bird species, early in the mating season, females shop around and choose a brilliantly colored male that sings vigorously from the treetops. In several species, females also prefer males with especially long tails (Figure 14.8). From an evolutionary standpoint, aren't these choices foolish? The most "popular" males risk their lives by singing loudly from the treetops, where they call the attention of hawks and eagles. They also seemingly waste enormous energy on bright feathers. (It takes more energy to produce bright colors than dull ones.) A long tail may look pretty, but it interferes with flying. Why does the female prefer a mate who wastes energy and endangers his life?

FIGURE 14.8 In some bird species, males with long tails attract more mates. However, they pay a price: The long tail impairs their flying abilities. Only healthy males can afford this handicap.

Biologists eventually decided that wasting energy and risking life were precisely the point (Zahavi & Zahavi, 1997). Only a healthy, vigorous male has enough energy to make bright, colorful feathers (Blount, Metcalfe, Birkhead, & Surai, 2003; Faivre, Grégoire, Préault, Cézilly, & Sorci, 2003). Only a strong male can fly despite a long tail, and only a strong male would risk predation by singing from an exposed perch. In effect a col-

orful, singing male is showing off: "Look at me! I am so healthy and vigorous that I can afford to take crazy risks and waste energy frivolously!" The female, we presume, does not understand why she is attracted to colorful, loud, active males. She just is because, throughout her evolutionary history, most females who chose such partners reproduced more successfully than those who chose dull-colored, inactive males.

So it would seem, theoretically. The problem is that although a male's bright colors and vigorous singing do indicate health, his health depends more on his luck in finding a good feeding place than on his genes. The same is true for fish as well as birds (Brooks, 2000; Cunningham & Russell, 2000).

Now back to humans: Are attractive people more likely than others to be healthy and fertile? Theoretically, they should be. Certainly, many illnesses decrease people's attractiveness. Also, *good-looking* is in many regards similar to *normal,* which probably indicates *good genetics.* Suppose a computer takes photographs of many people and averages their faces. The resulting composite face has about an average nose, average distance between the eyes, and so forth, and most people rate this face "highly attractive" (Langlois & Roggman, 1990; Langlois, Roggman, & Musselman, 1994; Rhodes, Sumich, & Byatt, 1999) (see Figure 14.9). This is not to say that the average person is highly attractive, but a highly attractive person does have approximately average features. If we note anything "unusual" about an attractive face, it is the absence of irregularities—no crooked teeth, skin blemishes, or asymmetries, and no facial hair on women (Fink & Penton-Voak, 2002).

Why is normal attractive? One hypothesis is that normal means healthy. Presumably, the genes for an average face have spread in the population because they are linked to success. Any face far different from the average might indicate a genetic mutation. Researchers have found that even infants prefer to look at the same faces that adults consider attractive and that judgments of facial attractiveness are fairly consistent from one culture to another (Berry, 2000). A competing hypothesis, however, is that we like the normal, average face only because it is familiar, and we like anything that is familiar. Research has found that people tend to think that "average-looking" dogs, birds, and wristwatches are attractive (Halberstadt & Rhodes, 2000). Also, if you have recently seen many faces that are thinner than usual, fatter than usual, or in some other way distorted, your judgment of "attractive" is shifted slightly in the direction of the faces you have just seen (Rhodes, Jeffery, Watson, Clifford, & Nakayama, 2003). So our preference for normal faces might be unrelated to advantageous genes.

The best way to settle this issue is to see whether attractive people tend to be healthier or more fertile than others. In one study researchers

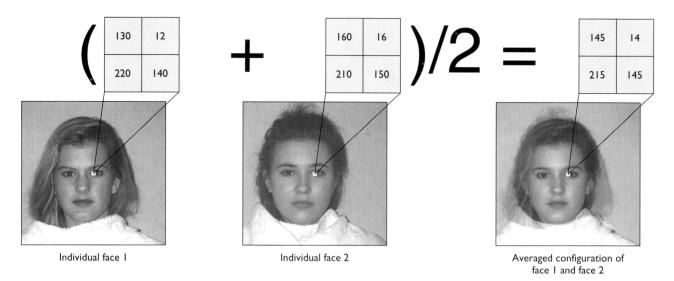

FIGURE 14.9 A computer measured the gray value of each point on each picture. It then produced a new picture with the average of the grays at each point. This set of photos illustrates the procedure for two original faces. The numbers are for illustrative purposes only. Most people rate the resulting face as highly attractive. (© *Langlois, Roggman, & Musselman, "Average Faces,"* Psychological Science, *Vol. 5, no.4.*)

obtained photos of hundreds of teenagers from long ago. They asked other people to rate the faces for attractiveness; they also obtained extensive medical records for the people in the photos. The ratings of attractiveness did not correlate reliably with health. People who were rated attractive were more likely to marry, and especially to marry early, but unattractive people who did marry were just as likely to have children as the more attractive people (Kalick, Zebrowitz, Langlois, & Johnson, 1998). Evidently, at least for this sample, attractiveness had nothing to do with health or fertility.

If facial attractiveness is a poor cue to health, what about the rest of the body? According to one theory, men should prefer women with a narrow waist and wide hips—a waist-to-hip ratio of about 0.7—because medical researchers believe women with that ratio are most likely to be healthy and fertile. Examine the drawings of women's figures in Figure 14.10. Which one do you consider most attractive? In the United States, both men and women rated thinner women as the most attractive (Tassinary & Hansen, 1998). In non-Westernized cultures of Tanzania and southeastern Peru, most men regarded heavier women as the most attractive (Marlowe

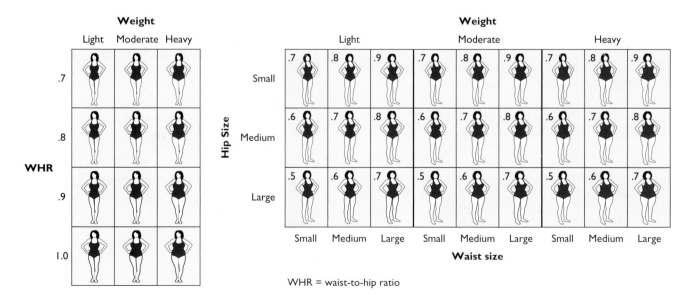

FIGURE 14.10 Which of these female figures do you find most attractive? Most fertile? Average ratings vary across cultures. (*From "A Critical Test of the Waist-to-Hip-Ratio Hypothesis of Female Physical Attractiveness" by L. G. Tassinary and K. A. Hansen,* Psychological Science, *1998, 9, 150-155. Copyright © 1998 Blackwell Publishers. Reprinted by permission.*)

& Wetsman, 2001; Yu & Shepard, 1998). In short, preferences for female shape vary somewhat across cultures and do not necessarily match what researchers consider healthy or fertile.

Where do all these studies leave us? Theoretically, it would make sense for good appearance to represent "truthful advertising" of healthful genes. However, so far researchers have not found a strong link between good appearance and healthful genes. Until we have more extensive research, we cannot be sure.

CONCEPT CHECK ☑

19. According to the evolutionary theory, attractiveness is a sign of good health. Why would it be difficult for an unhealthy individual to produce "counterfeit" attractiveness? (Check your answer on page 560.)

Men's and Women's Preferences

Imagine that two people have expressed a desire to date you, and you have reason to believe the date could lead to a long-term relationship and eventual marriage. You have to choose between the two; you cannot date both. Here are the descriptions. The choice for women: Man A is extraordinarily good-looking. He works as a waiter at a small restaurant and has no ambition to do anything more. Man B is about average looking. He patented an invention and sold it for a fortune. He was recently accepted to a prestigious medical school, and he is said to have an outstanding career ahead as a medical researcher.

The choice for men: Woman A is extraordinarily good-looking. She works as a waitress at a small restaurant and has no ambition to do anything more. Woman B is about average looking. She patented an invention and sold it for a fortune. She was recently accepted to a prestigious medical school, and she is said to have an outstanding career ahead as a medical researcher.

I have offered these choices to my own classes, and you probably can guess the results: Nearly all of the women chose man B. The men were divided, but most chose woman A. (Curiously, secret ballots gave different results from a show of hands, but the trend was in the same direction.)

The same trends occur in all cultures for which we have data (Buss, 2000). Both men and women prefer a physically attractive

partner, if possible, but women have the additional concern of preferring a partner who can be a good provider. Most men are less concerned about a woman's potential job success.

Another trend found worldwide is that many men will accept almost any partner for a short-term sexual relationship, whereas most women either refuse a short-term sexual relationship or accept only a very appealing partner (Buss, 2000). Another is that men are more interested in sexual variety. As shown in Figure 14.11, in all of the 52 nations that were surveyed, men were more likely than women to want more than one sexual partner in the near future and in the long term (Schmitt et al., 2003). Still another trend pertains to jealousy: In most cultures men insist that women be sexually faithful more than women require fidelity from men. In some cultures, such as China, men and women are equally

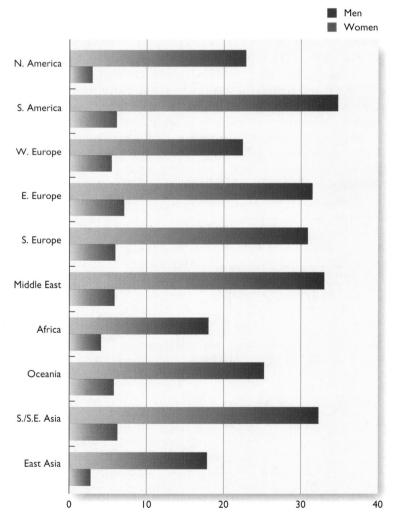

FIGURE 14.11 More than 16,000 people in 52 nations throughout the world were asked how many sexual partners they hoped to have in the next month. In all countries a higher percentage of men than women wanted more than one. *(Based on data of Schmitt et al., 2003)*

insistent on the other's sexual fidelity, and in Sweden both seem equally unconcerned, but in no culture do women demand more fidelity from men than men demand from women (Buss, Larsen, Westen, & Semmelroth, 1992; Buunk, Angleitner, Oubaid, & Buss, 1996).

All of those trends are well confirmed, but the explanation is not. One hypothesis is that we have evolved to act this way (Bjorklund & Shackelford, 1999; Buss, 2000; Gangestad, 2000; Geary, 2000). The argument goes as follows. First, consider short-term sexual relationships: A man who has a quick sexual relationship has some chance of spreading his genes if the woman becomes pregnant and manages to rear the child successfully. Therefore, a hypothetical gene that caused men to act this way would spread in the population. For a woman, having sex with many partners cannot give her more babies than sex with one partner. So a gene causing her to have sex with many partners would provide no advantage.

A man's other way of spreading his genes is to devote his energies to supporting one woman and her children (presumably his, too). However, this strategy succeeds only if the woman he marries is fertile. A young woman will be fertile for a long time, and an attractive woman is (perhaps) more likely to be fertile. So men increase their probable contribution to the gene pool if they marry young, attractive women. In contrast a woman can be less concerned about the age of her partner because men remain fertile into old age. However, she should prefer a man who can provide food and other resources while she is pregnant and caring for young children.

Theoretically, the reported difference in sexual jealousy might relate to the nature of human reproduction. If a man is going to pair with just one woman for life and help rear her children, he should make sure that she is sexually faithful; otherwise, he could be spreading another man's genes and not his own. A woman does not need to be equally jealous if her husband has a brief sexual affair because she doesn't have to worry about whether she is the mother of her child. She would, however, suffer a disadvantage if her husband stopped supporting her and shifted his attentions to another woman.

However, even if we accept these descriptions of male and female behavior, it is not necessary to agree that they are products of genetics and natural selection. The alternative view is that people throughout the world learn these preferences (Eagly & Wood, 1999). Yes, of course, the brain is subject to natural selection just as much as any other organ, but we need not assume that evolution has "micromanaged" our behavior with specific mechanisms for each decision.

Furthermore, many psychologists question the generalized descriptions of male and female behavior just discussed. For example, the strength of women's preference for financially secure men varies from culture to culture, largely dependent on women's ability to earn money and control resources of their own (Kasser & Sharma, 1999). Much of the evidence that men have stronger sexual jealousy than women rests on two kinds of studies—surveys of college students and crime records showing more jealousy-related violence by men. Surveys of older, more experienced people show less difference between men and women (Harris, 2002), and the crime records are indecisive because men commit more of almost *all* kinds of crime (Harris, 2003).

Finally, is it really true that women gain nothing from having sex with multiple partners? Sarah Hrdy (2000) has pointed out a number of potential benefits, including the following:

- Her husband might be infertile.
- Another man might have better genes than her husband and give her better children.
- The other man may provide her with additional resources and protection.
- If she has sex with many men, all of them may provide a modest amount of care and protection for her children.
- She might be able to "trade up," leaving her husband and joining the new partner.

A general point is that we cannot reconstruct the social life of our ancestors with great confidence. Mating customs vary from one human culture to another and even from one chimpanzee troop to another (Parish & deWaal, 2000). So reconstructing the evolution of human social behavior is uncertain. The case for evolutionary influence on mate choices would be stronger if someone found a gene that produces variations in preferences. (For example, imagine genes that caused men to prefer older women or women to prefer impoverished men.) Without evidence of genetic variation in mate choice, discussions of the evolution of social behavior will remain speculative.

CONCEPT CHECK ☑

20. Suppose astronauts discover humanlike beings on another planet, whose biology and culture resemble ours except that all men have exactly the same wealth and women remain fertile all their lives instead of losing their fertility at menopause. What would an evolutionary theorist predict about the mate preferences of men and women on this planet? (Check your answer on page 560.)

Marriage

A couple that decides to marry pledges that they will stay together as long as they both shall live, and yet a distressing percentage of marriages end in divorce. What went wrong?

Many couples date each other for a long time before exploring some of the issues that would become critical during a life together. Questionnaire studies have found that, as couples continue to date, their estimates of each other's sexual histories, activity preferences, and so forth become more *confident* without becoming more *accurate* (Swann & Gill, 1997). Answer the following questions, first for yourself and second *as you think your dating partner would answer them.* (Several questions assume a heterosexual relationship; disregard any items that do not apply to you.)

1. After you marry or establish another long-term relationship, how often would you want to visit your parents? Your in-laws?
2. How many children do you want to have? How soon?
3. If you have children, should one partner stay home with the children while they are young? Should both partners share the responsibility for child care? Should the children be placed in a day-care center as soon as possible?
4. Suppose the two of you are offered good jobs in cities far apart. Neither of you can find a satisfactory job in the other's city. How would you decide where to live?
5. Suppose a sudden financial crisis strikes. Where would you cut expenses to balance the budget? Clothes? Food? Housing? Entertainment?
6. How often do you plan to attend religious services?
7. How and where do you like to spend your vacations?
8. How often would you expect to spend an evening with friends, apart from your partner?

Were you uncertain about how your dating partner would answer any of these questions? If so, you are in the majority. Disagreements about such questions are common reasons for relationship conflicts. I do not suggest that you ask every person you date to fill out this questionnaire. However, before you get far into a relationship, you should discuss anything that is important to you.

Sometimes couples change in ways they could not have foreseen, but many breakups are predictable. Psychologists have studied recently married couples and related the observations to how the marriages developed later. Most of the problems and hostilities that eventually led to divorce were present early in the marriage. If a marriage ended in divorce within 7 years, in most cases the couple showed mixed feelings toward each other even before marriage and made frequent negative comments about each other. Apparently, they married in hopes they could work out their problems, but matters just grew worse. Couples that divorced after more than 7 years started on stronger terms but became disillusioned and less affectionate within the first 2 years or so. Although they did not express overt hostility early in their marriage, they also did not show as much love and affection as most other couples whose marriages were going to last (Gottman & Levenson, 2000; Huston, Niehuis, & Smith, 2001).

There are probably some additional subtle cues, hard to quantify, that distinguish successful marriages from less successful ones. In one fascinating study, various kinds of people watched 3-minute videotaped conversations between 10 married couples and estimated how satisfied each couple was. Their estimates were then compared to reports by the couples themselves. People who reported that their own marriages were either highly satisfying or highly unsatisfying were the best at judging the quality of other couples' marriages. Marriage counselors and marriage researchers lagged behind, as did unmarried people (Ebling & Levenson, 2003).

Marriages That Last

When you hear about how many marriages end in divorce, it is easy to despair, but many marriages remain strong for a lifetime. Most characteristics of successful marriages are what you would probably expect (Howard & Dawes, 1976; Karney & Bradbury, 1995; Thornton, 1977). The following list is based on studies mainly in the United States in the late 20th century, so we do not know how they might differ for other times and places:

- The husband and wife have similar attitudes and personalities.
- They have sexual relations frequently and arguments infrequently.
- They have an adequate income.
- The husband has a good enough job to maintain self-respect.
- The wife was not pregnant before they married.
- The couple's parents also had successful marriages.

A successful marriage changes over the years, just as individual lives do. At first the couple has the intense excitement of learning about each other and doing new things together. Years later, although they do not arouse each other's emotions as intensely as before (Berscheid, 1983), they still love each other, perhaps even more deeply. If one of them becomes ill or dies, the emotion inherent in the mature relationship becomes vividly apparent.

© PhotoDisc.

▌ In a mature, lasting relationship, a couple can count on each other for care and affection through both good and bad times.

Trying to Save a Marriage

Many couples with troubled marriages seek help from a marriage counselor. The results of marriage counseling are, unfortunately, not very encouraging. Of the couples receiving help, only about one third report improving their relationship during counseling, and even of those, half deteriorate later, leaving only about 15 to 20% that show any lasting improvement (Gottman, 1999). Even that 15 to 20% may overstate the success of marriage counseling, as some of those couples might have solved their own problems without counseling.

One reason for the disappointing results is, of course, that it takes two to save a marriage, and sometimes one partner has already given up before meeting the marriage counselor. Another reason, however, is that many marriage counselors have offered well-meaning but unhelpful advice. In particular, many counselors emphasize extremely open communication, including full expression of emotions. "Open communication" sounds like a good thing—after all, who is opposed to communication?—but venting hostile emotions toward your spouse is almost always harmful. The other person feels hurt and retaliates with equally insulting remarks (Fincham, 2003). The result is further deterioration of the relationship.

The distinction is this: If you have a complaint against your partner—an annoying habit, for example—yes, of course you should state it. However, state it politely, not angrily. And if the other person expresses hostile emotions, you are better off if you restrain your reaction.

In several studies dating or married couples recorded their emotional reactions toward each other

during a single conversation or on a daily basis; then each person reported what emotions they thought their partner had expressed. Happy couples expressed negative emotions only occasionally, and even then, the other usually did not report perceiving the negativity (Gable, Reis, & Downey, 2003; Simpson, Oriña, & Ickes, 2003). In other words successful couples limit both their expression and perception of negative emotions.

CONCEPT CHECK ☑

21. Why does the advice to "fully express your emotions" sometimes backfire in marriage counseling? (Check your answer on page 560.)

IN CLOSING

Choosing Your Partners Carefully

Few people enjoy living as a hermit, isolated from others. In prisons one of the harshest forms of punishment is solitary confinement. Almost any social contact is better than none at all. However, many people may choose their friends and their spouses poorly. In the first module of this chapter, we considered social perception—how we form impressions of other people. Finding friends and romantic partners is a special case, where more is at stake, but the processes are the same. In some regards forming impressions of romantic partners is especially difficult. A person you date is probably trying to make a good impression, and you *hope* to like the person. As the relationship progresses, another factor kicks in: Remember from the section on persuasion that anyone you like tends to be highly persuasive.

Life is like a roller-coaster ride in the dark: It has lots of ups and downs, and you never know what is going to happen next. Be sure you are riding with someone you like and trust.

Summary

* *Friendship choices.* People generally choose friends and romantic partners who live near them, resemble them, and confirm their self-esteem. Relationships are most likely to survive and grow if each person believes that he or she is getting about as good a deal as the other person is. (page 552)
* *Marriage and similar attachments.* People have special considerations when choosing a potential marriage partner because marriage usually implies a commitment to rearing children together. (page 553)

- *Physical attractiveness.* In many nonhuman species, physical attractiveness is a reliable cue to the individual's health, vigor, and therefore desirability as a mate. However, the relationship to genetics is unclear. In humans attractiveness is a powerful determinant of mate choice but has not been demonstrably linked to health. (page 553)

- *Men's and women's preferences in marriage partners.* In every human culture, men prefer young, attractive women and women prefer men who are good providers. Men tend to be more upset about possible sexual infidelity by their wives. Evolutionary theorists believe humans evolved to have these preferences to improve chances of reproducing. However, it is also plausible that people in different societies have learned these preferences. (page 556)

- *Marriage.* Marriage and similar relationships often break up because of problems that were present from the start. Marriages are successful when the partners have much in common and find ways to satisfy each other's needs. They are unsuccessful if the partners express too much hostility. (page 558)

Answers to Concept Checks

18. Proximity and familiarity will strengthen the likelihood of your becoming friends. The similarity principle will weaken it. Because of the difference in languages, you will have little chance, at least at first, to discover any similarities in interests or attitudes. In fact proximity will probably not be as a potent force as usual, because it serves largely as a means of enabling people to discover what they have in common. (page 553)

19. Attractive features such as bright feathers in a bird or large muscles in a man require much energy. It would be difficult for an unhealthy individual to devote enough energy to produce such features. (page 556)

20. If all men are equally wealthy, women would select men on some other basis, such as appearance. If women's fertility lasts as late in life as men's does, then the men on this planet should not have a strong preference for younger women. (page 557)

21. If the spouses exchange hostile comments, their relationship deteriorates. Better advice would be to discuss complaints or difficulties calmly. (page 559)

Interpersonal Influence

How are we influenced by other people's actions or inactions?

People tend to imitate one another, even when they have no apparent motive for doing so (Dijksterhuis & Bargh, 2001). If you see someone smile or frown, you briefly start to smile or frown also. Your expression may be just a quick, involuntary twitch, and an observer may have to watch carefully to see it, but it does occur. Similarly, people tend to copy the hand gestures they see. (You can demonstrate this tendency by telling someone, "Please wave your hands" while you in fact clap your hands. Many people copy your actions instead of following your verbal directions.)

Try It Yourself

Here is an even more surprising kind of imitation: Young adults performed a task in which different groups read different lists of words. After the study appeared to be over, the experimenters timed how fast the participants walked out of the room. Those who had just been reading a list of words like *gray, forgetful,* and *retired* that presumably reminded them of old people walked out of the room more slowly than the other participants (Bargh, Chen, & Burrows, 1996). In a similar study, students who had just been thinking about old people before filling out an attitude questionnaire expressed attitudes more consistent with their stereotypes of old people, such as supporting more government support for health care and opposing nudity on television (Kawakami, Dovidio, & Dijksterhuis, 2003). In effect the students conformed to the stereotype of the old people they had been thinking about!

In short, other people influence us constantly, even in ways we do not recognize. They influence us in two major ways: First, they provide us with *information* (or misinformation). For example, if almost everyone else is moving in the same direction, they might know something we don't. Second, people set *norms* that define the expectations of a situation. In much of our social behavior, we follow rules of politeness, such as "do not interrupt," "raise your hand if you want to speak," and "wait in line." In this module we encounter many examples of both informational and normative influences.

Conformity

Conformity means *maintaining or changing one's behavior to match the behavior or expectations of others.* The pressure to conform often exerts an over-

whelming normative influence. For example, Koversada is a small, totally nudist city on the coast of the Adriatic (although people there sometimes dress for dinner at an elegant restaurant). If a first-time visitor walks around the city wearing clothes, other people stop and stare, shaking their heads with disapproval. The visitor feels as awkward and self-conscious as a naked person would be in a city of clothed people. Most visitors quickly undress (Newman, 1988).

If you exclaim, "I wouldn't conform," compare your own clothing right now to what others around you are wearing. Professors have sometimes reported the irony of watching a class full of students in blue jeans insisting that they do not conform to other people's style of dress (Snyder, 2003).

Conformity also serves informational functions, especially when we are not quite sure what we are seeing or hearing. One example is an illusion known as the **autokinetic effect:** *If you sit in a darkened room and stare at a small, stationary point of light, the point will eventually seem to move,* partly because of small involuntary eye movements that occur almost constantly. If some-

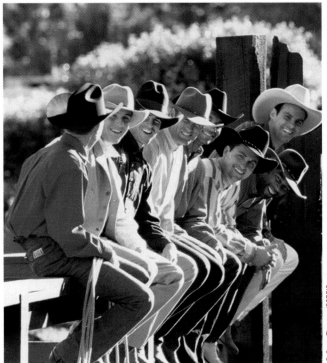

■ People conform to one another in their clothing and other customs.

561

one says, "I see it moving in a zigzag manner" or "I see it moving slowly in a counterclockwise direction," you are likely to perceive it the same way.

Conformity to an Obviously Wrong Majority

Early research suggested that people are most likely to conform their opinions in ambiguous situations that make it difficult to be sure of our own judgment (Sherif, 1935). For example, there are no absolutely right or wrong styles of clothing. In matters such as politics, religion, or the movement of a single point of light in a darkened room, the information we have is ambiguous, and we rely on other people's opinions to help form our own.

Would we also conform to opinions that were obviously wrong? To answer that question, Solomon Asch (1951, 1956) carried out a now-famous series of experiments. Asch assembled groups of students and asked them to look at a vertical bar, as shown in Figure 14.12, which was defined as the model. He also showed them three other vertical bars (right half of Figure 14.12) and asked them which bar was the same length as the model. As you can see, the task is simple. Asch asked the students to give their answers aloud. He repeated the procedure with 18 sets of bars.

FIGURE 1.2 More than one third of psychologists work in academic institutions; the remainder find positions in a variety of settings. *(Based on data of Chamberlin, 2000)*

Only one student in each group was a real participant. All the others were confederates who had been instructed to give incorrect answers on 12 of the 18 trials. Asch arranged for the real participant to be the next-to-last person in the group to announce his answer so that he would hear most of the confederates' incorrect responses before giving his own (Figure 14.13). Would he go along with the crowd?

To Asch's surprise, 37 of the 50 participants conformed to the majority at least once, and 14 conformed on most of the trials. When faced with a unanimous wrong answer by the other group members, the mean participant conformed on 4 of the 12 trials. Asch (1955) was disturbed by these results: "That we have found the tendency to conformity in our society so strong . . . is a matter of concern. It raises questions about our ways of education and about the values that guide our conduct" (p. 34).

FIGURE 14.13 Three of the eight participants in one of Asch's experiments on conformity. The one in the middle looking uncomfortable is the real participant; the others are the experimenter's confederates. *(From Asch, 1951)*

Why did people conform so readily? When they were interviewed after the experiment, some said they thought the rest of the group was correct or they guessed that an optical illusion was influencing the appearance of the bars. Others said they knew their "conforming" answers were wrong but went along with the group for fear of ridicule. That is, they were subject to a normative influence even without any informational influence. The nonconformists were interesting too. Some were nervous but felt duty bound to say how the bars looked to them. A few seemed socially withdrawn. Still others were supremely self-confident, as if to say, "I'm right and everyone else is wrong. It happens all the time." Asch (1951, 1955) found that the amount of conforming influence depended on the size of the opposing majority. In a series of studies, he varied the number of confederates who gave incorrect answers from 1 to 15. He found that people conformed to a group of 3 or 4 just as readily as to a larger group (Figure 14.14). However, a participant conformed much less if he or she had an

FIGURE 14.14 Asch (1955) found that conformity became more frequent as group size increased to about three, and then it leveled off. *(Adapted from "Opinion and Social Pressure" by Soloman Asch, Scientific American, November 1955. Copyright © 1955 by Scientific American, Inc. Reprinted with permission of the Asch estate.)*

FIGURE 14.15 In Asch's experiments participants who were faced with a unanimous incorrect majority conformed on 32% of trials. Participants who had one "ally" giving the correct answer were less likely to conform.

"ally." Being a minority of one is painful, but being in a minority of two is not as bad (Figure 14.15).

CONCEPT CHECK ☑

22. Are you more likely to conform to a group when you are outnumbered 5 to 1, 10 to 1, or 10 to 2? (Check your answer on page 567.)

Cultural Differences in Conformity

Over the years since Asch's experiments, similar studies have been conducted in many countries. In the United States, most studies show a slight decrease in the amount of conformity since the 1950s. In most Asian cultures, the percentage of conforming answers tends to be relatively high, partly because people are trying to be polite and not embarrass the others by pointing out their error (Bond & Smith, 1996). That is, when researchers use the same procedure in different cultures, they may not be testing the same psychological processes.

Are people in certain cultures, particularly in southern Asia, in fact more prone to conformity as a general rule? The cultures of southern Asia, including China and Japan, are often described as more "collectivist" in contrast to the "individualist" cultures of the United States, Canada, Australia, and most of Europe. According to this view, Western culture encourages originality, competition, and individual freedom, whereas Eastern culture favors subordination of the individual to the welfare of the family or society. Originally, this contrast was based on observations of the Japanese during and shortly after World War II. However, Japan is a far different place today from what it was then. Acting collectively is a common response of any country when under attack or recovering from at-

Table 14.2 Examples of Questions to Measure Collectivist Versus Individualist Attitudes

T	F	I take pride in accomplishing what no one else can accomplish.
T	F	It is important to me that I perform better than others on a task.
T	F	I am unique—different from others in many respects.
T	F	I like my privacy.
T	F	To understand who I am, you must see me with members of my group.
T	F	I would help, within my means, if a relative were in financial difficulty.
T	F	Before making a decision, I always consult with others.
T	F	I have respect for the authority figures with whom I interact.

Note: The first four items measure individualism; the second four measure collectivist attitudes.
Source: From Oyserman, Coon, & Kemmelmeier, 2002.

tack (Takano & Osaka, 1999). After all, shortly after terrorists crashed four passenger planes on September 11, 2001, U.S. citizens showed a strong collectivist "we're all in this together" attitude.

Many studies have contrasted Japanese and U.S. attitudes, mostly using college students and relying on questions like those in Table 14.2. A few investigators have directly observed conformist, cooperative, and competitive behaviors in various countries. Most studies have found no significant difference between Japanese and American attitudes, and some have even found Japanese students to be slightly *more* individualistic than Americans (Bond, 2002; Oyserman, Coon, & Kemmelmeier, 2002; Takano & Osaka, 1999).

Some researchers therefore suggest that the "collectivist" notion is wrong, at least with regard to modern-day Japan (Takano & Osaka, 1999). Others point out that each country has multiple subcultures, and no generalization holds for an entire country (A. P. Fiske, 2002). Also, we need to measure collectivism or individualism more carefully and distinguish different aspects of each (Bond, 2002). For example, you can probably find fault with some of the items in Table 14.2. It is difficult to write questionnaire items that adequately measure cultural attitudes. In any case we should discard the simple, unqualified generalization that some cultures are more collectivist or conformist than others.

CONCEPT CHECK ☑

23. What is one possible explanation for why collectivism may have been a more prominent aspect of Japanese thinking in the past than it is today? (Check your answer on page 567.)

Accepting or Denying Responsibility Toward Others

Other people can encourage us to do something we would not have done on our own, as in Asch's studies. Other people can also inhibit us from doing something that we would have done on our own. We look around to see what others are doing—or *not* doing—and we say, "Okay, I'll do that too." Why do people sometimes work together to help one another and sometimes ignore the needs of others?

Bystander Helpfulness and Apathy

Suppose while you are waiting at a bus stop, you see me trip and fall down, just 10 meters away. I am not screaming in agony, but I don't get up right away either, so you are not sure whether I need help. Would you come over and offer to help? Or would you stand there and ignore me? Before you answer, try imagining the situation in two ways: First, you and I are the only people in sight. Second, there are many other people nearby, none of them rushing to my aid. Does the presence of those other people make any difference to you? (It doesn't to me. I am in the same pain, regardless of how many people ignore me.)

Late one night in March 1964, Kitty Genovese was stabbed to death near her apartment in Queens, New York. For 30 minutes, at least 38 of her neighbors listened to her screams. A few stood at their windows watching, but none called the police or helped in any other way. When interviewed later, several said they thought at first that it might be a lovers' quarrel. By the time they were sure it was a real attack, they assumed someone else must have called the police already. For detailed information, see:

> **www.crimelibrary.com/serial_killers/**
> **predators/kitty_genovese/**

Are we less likely to act just because we know that another person could act on the same information? Bibb Latané and John Darley (1969) proposed that being in a crowd decreases our probability of action because of **diffusion of responsibility:** *We tend to feel less responsibility to act when other people nearby are equally able to act.* Latané and Darley suggested that people ignored Kitty Genovese's distress because everyone knew that many other people *could* help her.

In an experiment designed to test this hypothesis, a young woman ushered one or two students into a room and asked them to wait for the start of a market research study (Latané & Darley, 1968, 1969). She went into the next room, closing the door behind her. There she played a tape recording that sounded as though she had climbed onto a chair and fallen off. For about 2 minutes, she could be heard crying and moaning, "Oh . . . my foot . . . I can't move it. Oh . . .

my ankle . . ." Of the participants who were waiting alone, 70% went next door and offered to help. Of the participants who were waiting with someone else, only 13% offered to help.

In a more recent study, investigators entered 400 Internet chat groups of different sizes and in each one asked, "Can anyone tell me how to look at someone's profile?" (That is, how can I check the biographical sketch that each chat room user posts?) The researchers found that the more people in a chat room at the time, the longer the wait before anyone answered the question. In large groups the researchers sometimes had to post the same question repeatedly (Markey, 2000).

▌ People watch other people's responses to help decide how they should respond. When a group of sidewalk Santas—who had gathered in Manhattan to promote a back-rub business—came to the aid of an injured cyclist, a few Santas made the first move and the others followed.

Diffusion of responsibility is one possible explanation. Each person thinks, "It's not my responsibility to help any more than someone else's." A second possible explanation is that the presence of other people who are also doing nothing provides information (or misinformation). At first the situation is ambiguous: "Do I need to act or not?" Other people's inaction implies that the situation requires no action. In fact the others are just as uncertain as you are, and they draw conclusions from *your* inaction. Social psychologists use the term **pluralistic ignorance** to describe *a situation in which people say nothing and each person falsely assumes that everyone else has a different, perhaps better informed, opinion.* Notice that the presence of other people exerts both normative and informational influences: Their inactivity implies that doing nothing is acceptable (a norm) and that the situation is not an emergency (information).

Social Loafing

When you take a test, you are required to work alone, and your success depends entirely on your own effort. In many other cases, however, you work as part of a team. For example, if you work for a company that gives workers a share of the profits, your rewards depend on other workers' productivity as well as your own. Do you work as hard when the rewards depend on the group's productivity as when they depend on your own efforts alone?

In many cases the answer is "no." In one experiment students were told to scream, clap, and make as much noise as possible, like cheerleaders at a sports event. Sometimes each student screamed and clapped alone; sometimes students acted in groups; and sometimes they acted alone but *thought* that other people were screaming and clapping too. (They wore headphones so they could not hear anyone else.) Most of the students who screamed and clapped alone made more noise than those who were or thought they were part of a group (Latané, Williams, & Harkins, 1979). Social psychologists call this phenomenon **social loafing**—*the tendency to "loaf" (or work less hard) when sharing work with other people.*

Social loafing has been demonstrated in many situations. For example, suppose you were asked to "name all the uses you can think of for a brick" (e.g., crack nuts, anchor a boat, or use as a doorstop) and write each one on a card. You would probably fill many cards by yourself but fewer if you were tossing cards into a pile along with other people's suggestions to be evaluated as a group (Harkins & Jackson, 1985). You probably wouldn't bother submitting ideas that you assume other people had already suggested.

At this point you may be thinking, "Wait a minute. When I'm playing basketball or soccer, I try as hard as

■ During a catastrophe people abandon their usual tendencies toward bystander apathy and social loafing.

I can. I don't think I loaf." You are right; social loafing is rare in team sports. The reason is that observers, including teammates, watch your performance. People work hard in groups if they expect other people to notice their effort or if they think they can contribute something that other group members cannot (Shepperd, 1993; K. D. Williams & Karau, 1991). People also give full effort if it appears that the benefit to the group will be large compared to the cost to themselves (Goren, Kurzban, & Rapoport, 2003).

CONCEPT CHECK

24. Given what we have learned about social loafing, why are most people unlikely to work hard to clean the environment?
25. In a typical family, one or two members have jobs, but their wages benefit all. Why do those wage earners *not* engage in social loafing? (Check your answers on page 567.)

Group Decision Making

An organization that needs to reach a decision will frequently set up a committee to look into the issues and make recommendations. A committee has more time, more total information, and fewer peculiarities and biases than any individual has. Research finds that a group generally makes better decisions than the average individual. However, the advantage of a group over an individual is often not as great as we might expect (Sorkin, Hays, & West, 2001). Groups sometimes rush to a decision, and many groups show social loafing. Some individuals conform to the majority opinion and discard their own, possibly better, opinions.

Group Polarization

If nearly all the people who compose a group lean in the same direction on a particular issue, then a group discussion will move the group as a whole even further in that direction. This phenomenon is known as **group polarization.** Note that it requires a fairly homogeneous group to begin with. If the group has several factions that disagree at the start, the effects are less predictable and harder to interpret (Rodrigo & Ato, 2002).

The term *polarization* does not mean that the group breaks up into fragments favoring different positions. Rather, it means that the members of a group move *together* toward one pole (extreme position) or the other. For example, a group of people who are opposed to abortion or in favor of animal rights or opposed to gun regulations will, after discussing the issue among themselves, generally become more extreme in their views than they had been at the start (Lamm & Myers, 1978).

Group polarization demonstrates both informational and normative influences (Isenberg, 1986). During the discussion, if most of the members were already leaning in the same direction, they hear new arguments favoring that side of the issue and few or none for the opposition (Kuhn & Lao, 1996). Also, as the members of the group become aware of the consensus during the discussion, the pressure to conform is especially powerful for those who do not feel fully accepted by the group (Noel, Wann, & Branscombe, 1995).

CONCEPT CHECK ☑

26. Is a jury more likely to reach a biased or extreme decision than a single individual would be? (Check your answer on page 567.)

Groupthink

One extreme form of group polarization is known as **groupthink**, when *the members of a group suppress their doubts about a group's poorly thought-out decision for fear of making a bad impression or disrupting group harmony* (Janis, 1972, 1985). The main elements leading to groupthink are overconfidence by the leadership, underestimation of the competitors or problems, and pressure to conform. Sometimes dissenters conform on their own; sometimes the leadership actively urges them to conform.

One dramatic example of groupthink led to the Bay of Pigs fiasco of 1962. President John F. Kennedy and his advisers were considering a plan to support a small-scale invasion of Cuba at the Bay of Pigs. They assumed that a small group of Cuban exiles could overwhelm the Cuban army and trigger a spontaneous rebellion of the Cuban people against their government. Most of the advisers who doubted this assumption kept quiet. The one who did express his doubts was told that he should loyally support the president. Within a few hours after the invasion began, all the invaders were killed or captured. The decision makers then wondered how they could have made such a stupid decision.

Groupthink often occurs in business decisions, especially in highly prosperous and successful companies. The leaders become overconfident and their critics become hesitant to speak up. For example, British Airways at one point discovered that 60% of its passengers were non-British. Its leaders therefore decided that it made sense to remove the British flag from the tailfins of the planes. This decision not only irritated the British public far more than the company expected but also outraged the employees who resented what seemed a pointless expense of £60 million to change

Many organizations try to resist the tendency toward groupthink, which stifles dissenting views. During the Renaissance, European kings sometimes called on a "fool" (or court jester) to describe some proposal in a fresh and possibly amusing light. In a court composed largely of yes-men, the fool sometimes was the only one who could openly point out the folly of a proposed action without fear of reprisals.

the company's logo at the same time the company was firing workers to save costs. By itself this decision was a small mistake, but it was part of a series of mistakes by British Airways executives at the time, who seemed to dismiss all criticism (Easton, 2001).

Groupthink is not easy to avoid. We generally admire government or business leaders who are bold, decisive, and confident. Groupthink occurs when they become *too* bold, decisive, and confident, failing to consider everything that could go wrong or failing to take the risks seriously. One strategy is for a leader to consult the advisers individually so they are not influenced by what they hear other advisers saying. A message for all of us is to be concerned when anyone in a position of power starts becoming too confident of success.

IN CLOSING

To Conform or Not?

Conforming to what others do is a good idea more often than not. For example, when we are on the road, it is safe to be surrounded by conformists who are willing to drive at the same speed as everyone else and on the same side of the road. Conformity is dangerous only when the group is doing something risky. However, even when we recognize a danger, for example, when people urge us to try drugs, it is seldom easy to resist the pressure to conform.

Summary

- *Types of social influence.* People influence our behavior by offering information (right or wrong) and by setting norms of expected conduct. (page 561)
- *Conformity.* Many people conform to the majority view even when they are confident that the majority is wrong. An individual is as likely to conform to a group of three as to a larger group, but an individual with an ally is less likely to conform. (page 561)
- *Diffusion of responsibility.* People in groups are less likely than an isolated individual to come to someone's aid because they experience a diffusion of responsibility. (page 564)
- *Social loafing.* People working together on a task tend to exert less effort than people working independently. However, people will work just as hard on the group task if they are evaluated on their individual performances or if they believe their contributions will make a big difference. (page 565)
- *Group polarization.* Groups of people who lean mostly in the same direction on a given issue often make more extreme decisions than most people would have made on their own. (page 565)
- *Groupthink.* Groupthink occurs when members of a cohesive group fail to express their opposition to a decision for fear of making a bad impression or harming the cohesive spirit of the group. (page 566)

Answers to Concept Checks

22. You would be about equally likely to conform when outnumbered 5 to 1 or 10 to 1. Any group of 3 or more produces about the same urge to conform. However, having even one ally decreases the pressure, so you would be less likely to conform when outnumbered 10 to 2. (page 563)
23. During and shortly after World War II, the people of Japan were under attack or recovering from attack. In that situation people of any country are motivated to work collectively. (page 563)
24. Social loafing is likely because many one-person contributions, such as picking up litter, would not earn individual credit or recognition. Also, each person thinks, "What good could one person do with such a gigantic problem?" (page 565)
25. The main reason is that the wage earners see they can make a special contribution that the others (children, injured, or retired) cannot. Also, their contributions are easily observed by the others. (page 565)
26. It depends. Group polarization would probably move a nearly unanimous jury toward a unanimous verdict. However, a jury that starts out divided would not experience group polarization. Most research has found that juries and similar groups are no more extreme than the average individual (Kerr, MacCoun, & Kramer, 1996). (page 566)

Why do people sometimes engage in self-defeating behavior?

In the 1960s world problems seemed to threaten the very future of civilization. The Vietnam War seemed to go on forever, the nations of the world were preparing for global nuclear war, racial injustice and other forms of discrimination were widespread, and we were beginning to recognize how terribly people were damaging the environment. As a high school and college student at the time, I had grandiose dreams of saving the world. I wasn't sure how, but I thought psychological research was a possibility. I hoped to somehow change human nature so that people would stop being so cruel and selfish.

Decades later, I reflect on the people who really did make the world a better place. Some made their impact through moral leadership, such as Martin Luther King Jr., Mother Teresa, Alexander Solzhenitsyn, and Nelson Mandela. However, many advanced the causes of peace and justice through technology—a route that I never even contemplated during my youthful "save the world" fantasies. For example, the engineers who devised spy satellites made possible the international treaties banning tests of nuclear weapons. (Without the capacity to watch one another, competing countries would never have agreed to the treaties.) The engineers who developed computers, printers, and modems spread freedom of the press, even in countries whose leaders did not want it. DNA testing has increased the accuracy of our criminal prosecutions and freed many people who were falsely accused. These technological advances changed human *behavior* without changing human *nature*.

The general point is that much of our behavior is controlled by the situation—sometimes the technological situation, sometimes the social situation. A situation can almost compel us to behave either in constructive ways or in uncooperative and self-defeating ways. We need to recognize the power of these situations so that we can avoid or change the most harmful ones.

What would you think of someone who knowingly paid a great deal more for something than it

was worth? Or someone who confessed to a crime even though the police admitted they did not have enough evidence for a conviction? Or someone who used all the available resources instead of saving some for later? You would probably question that person's intelligence or sanity. And yet, under certain circumstances, you would probably do the same. We can easily fall into a **behavior trap**—*a situation that coerces us into self-defeating behaviors.* We call such situations "traps" because people wander into them without realizing the danger. A simple example is being in a crowded theater when someone shouts "fire!" We all know we should file out calmly because a panic would jam the exits and no one could escape. In a real situation, though, we might decide that it is better to be among the first to panic than among the last! Therefore, a panic is

❚ A crowd of rock music fans can trample one another while trying to get close to the stage. Sometimes a situation becomes dangerous before people recognize the risk.

likely, no matter how many times we have been warned against it (Helbing, Farkes, & Vicsek, 2000). If you want to prevent panics in crowded theaters, don't tell people not to panic; build more exits. We shall consider four situations: escalation of conflict, the prisoner's dilemma, the commons dilemma, and obedience to authority.

Escalation of Conflict

Imagine that you, I, and a few other people are at an auction. The auctioneer explains that the next item up for bids is a dollar bill, to be sold to the highest bidder, even if the highest bid is only a few cents. There is one catch, however; at the end, when someone finally buys the dollar bill, the second highest bidder must pay his or her bid to the auctioneer also, receiving nothing in return. So, for example, if I bid 5 cents, you bid 10 cents, and the bidding stops there, you would buy the dollar bill for 10 cents and I would simply lose my 5 cents.

Suppose we plunge right in. I bid 5 cents, you bid 10, I bid 15, and so forth. Eventually, you bid 90 cents and I bid 95. Now what do you do? If you let me have the dollar bill for 95 cents, you lose 90 cents. So you bid $1, hoping to break even. What do I do? If I stop bidding, I lose 95 cents, but if I buy the dollar for $1.05, I sustain a net loss of only 5 cents. So I bid $1.05. Then you bid $1.10 because you would rather lose 10 cents than lose a whole dollar. The bidding continues. After a while, we start to become angry with each other. After all, as soon as one of us quits bidding, the other one will "win." Psychologists conducting such auctions usually manage to sell their dollar bills in the range of $3 to $5 and sometimes much more (Brockner & Rubin, 1985). As soon as the bidding goes over $1, bidders become increasingly distressed—sweating, trembling, sometimes even crying. (At the end of the experiment, the psychologists always return the money, although they had not promised to do so.)

The point of this study is *not,* "Here's a good scam you can use to make some quick money." The point is that if you get into a situation like this, it is hard to escape. Similar situations do arise in real life. For example, from the end of World War II until the Soviet Union collapsed in 1991, the United States and the Soviet Union devoted enormous sums of money to a weapons race. Critics often wondered whether the expenditures made sense. The reply was, "Having spent as much as we have already, we can't quit now and let the other side have more weapons than we do." Similarly, a manager who has already spent a fortune developing and advertising a product feels a need to continue developing the product because quitting would mean that the whole investment was wasted (Lant & Hurley, 1999). Perhaps you can think of additional examples. Note also the similarity of these examples to the sunk cost effect, mentioned in Chapter 8.

The Prisoner's Dilemma

Sometimes you have a choice between the action that seems best for you and one that seems best for your group. The most widely studied example is the pris-oner's dilemma, *a situation where people must choose between a cooperative act and a competitive act that could benefit themselves but hurt others.* Let's start with the original version of this dilemma: You and a partner are arrested and charged with armed robbery. The police take each of you into separate rooms and ask you to confess. If neither of you confesses, the police do not have enough evidence to convict you of armed robbery, but they can convict you of a lesser offense with a sentence of 1 year in prison. If either of you confesses and testifies against the other, the confessor goes free and the other gets 20 years in prison. If you both confess, you each get 5 years in prison. Each of you knows that the other person has the same options. Figure 14.16 illustrates your choices.

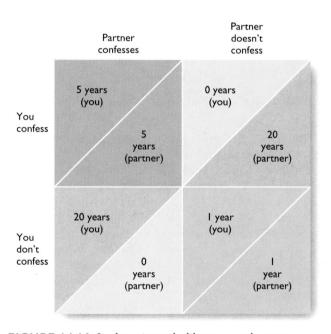

FIGURE 14.16 In the prisoner's dilemma, each person considering the choice alone finds it beneficial to confess. But when both people confess, they suffer worse consequences than if both had refused to confess.

If your partner does not confess, you gain by confessing because you will go free. (Your partner will get 20 years in prison, but let's assume you care mostly about yourself.) If your partner does confess, it is still to your advantage to confess because you will get only 5 years in prison instead of 20. So, you confess. Your partner, reasoning the same way, also confesses, and you both get 5 years in prison. If you had both kept quiet, you would each have served only 1 year in prison. The situation led you both to uncooperative, self-defeating behavior.

If you and your partner could have discussed your strategy, you would have agreed not to confess. Then, when the police took you to separate rooms, you would each hope that the other would keep the bargain. But can you be sure? Maybe your partner will double-cross you and confess. If so, you should too. And if your partner does keep the bargain, what should you do? Confess, of course! We're back where we started.

The two of you are most likely to cooperate if you can stay in constant communication with each other (Nemeth, 1972). If each hears what the other one says, you know that, if one confesses, the other will retaliate immediately.

The prisoner's dilemma can also be stated in terms of gains. Suppose you and another person have a choice between two moves, which we call *cooperate* and *compete*. Depending on your choices, here are the payoffs:

Here are the payoffs:

	Other person cooperates	Other person competes
You cooperate	Both win $1	Other person gains $2; you lose $2
You compete	You gain $2; other person loses $2	Both lose $1

Suppose you will play this game only once. The other person will answer by telephone, and the two of you will never meet. Which move do you choose? If the other person cooperates, your winning choice is *compete* because you will get $2 instead of $1. If the other person competes, again you gain by competing because you will lose just $1 instead of $2. Logically, you should choose to compete, and so should the other person, so you both lose $1. Here we encounter a classic behavior trap in which the situation logically leads people into self-defeating behaviors (Axelrod & Dion, 1988).

The strategy changes drastically if the two of you are going to play repeatedly. Unless you know what the other person will do, the recommended strategy is reciprocity, also called "tit-for-tat": Start with the *cooperate* move. If the other person cooperates too, then you continue to cooperate on later moves. If the other person makes a *compete* move, you retaliate with a *compete* move on your next turn. (Your retaliation should teach the other person not to try to take advantage of you.) You should refuse to play with anyone who is known to make mostly *compete* moves (D. S. Wilson, Near, & Miller, 1996). You can try this strategy and others at this Web site, where you compete against a computer opponent:

http://serendip.brynmawr.edu/bb/pd.html

This game is much more than a laboratory curiosity. First, it is a pretty good model of what happens in business deals, in which each person has to cooperate or the other person will retaliate. Second, it has implications for how human social behavior developed. From a biological standpoint, why should you ever cooperate with a nonrelative? A reasonable answer is **reciprocal altruism:** *You cooperate with someone who cooperates with you, or you help someone who may repay the favor later.* However, reciprocal altruism works only if you can keep track of who "cheats" by not helping in return. Therefore, reciprocal altruism and cooperative behavior in general require individual recognition. Otherwise, we could not distinguish between cooperators and cheaters. Reciprocal altruism—that is, cooperation—occurs mainly when people deal repeatedly with the same individuals and establish a reputation for cooperating or cheating. However, it also varies from one culture to another in ways that require further research to understand (Fehr & Fischbacher, 2003).

In species in which individuals cannot recognize other individuals, theoretically, reciprocal altruism should not develop. In fact altruism is rare in nonhuman animals.

CONCEPT CHECK ☑

27. Suppose you have been playing the prisoner's dilemma game as described, using the tit-for-tat strategy, and the other person has been cooperating on every move. When you get to the last move (so there will be no further chance to retaliate), what move would be best? Why? (Check your answers on page 574.)

The Commons Dilemma

Here is another case where people hurt themselves and others by considering only their own short-term interests (Hardin, 1968): In the **commons dilemma,** *people who share a common resource tend to overuse it and therefore make it unavailable in the long run.* The commons dilemma takes its name from this parable: You are a shepherd in a small village. Everyone shares one piece of land, called the commons. Ordinarily, your sheep graze on your own land, but when a few of them need a little extra grass, you can take them to the commons.

The village has 50 shepherds, and the commons can support about 50 sheep a day. So if each shepherd takes an average of one sheep per day to the commons, everything works out. Suppose a few shepherds decide to take several sheep per day to the commons to save the grass on their own land. Not to be outdone, other shepherds do the same. Soon the commons is barren and useless.

Social psychologists have simulated the commons dilemma in laboratory games. In one study college students were asked to sit around a bowl that contained 10 nuts (Edney, 1979). They were told that they could take as many nuts as they wanted whenever they chose. Every 10 seconds the number of nuts remaining in the bowl would double. The object of the game was to collect as many nuts as possible. The rational strategy is to let the nuts double every 10 seconds for a while and then let each participant occasionally harvest some. But most of the groups never made it past the first 10 seconds. The students simply plunged in and grabbed as many nuts as they could, immediately exhausting the resources.

Obedience to Authority

Another example of a self-defeating situation arises when people obey an authority who gives bad orders. Ordinarily, if a stranger ordered you to hurt another person, you probably would refuse. However, some situations can induce you to do something voluntarily that later leaves you feeling ashamed.

Decades ago psychologist Philip Zimbardo and his colleagues paid college students to play the roles of guards and prisoners for 2 weeks during a vacation period. The researchers set up the basement of a university building as a prison but gave the students only minimal instructions on how to conduct themselves. In this case the researchers gave no orders at all, although assigning people roles of prisoner or guard does have clear implications about how they were expected to behave. Within 6 days the researchers had to cancel the study because many of "guards" had become severely abusive toward the "prisoners," bullying them physically and emotionally (Haney, Banks, & Zimbardo, 1973). Why? None of these students were habitually cruel to others in everyday life. However, in this situation they could get away with cruelty, without any penalties or retaliation. Also, the students presumably inferred that cruelty was expected. After all, what would be the point of "playing prison" for 2 weeks while behaving politely? Although this is an interesting demonstration, beware of drawing strong conclusions, as no one has ever replicated the prison study. The results might be different with slight changes in instructions or procedure.

CRITICAL THINKING:
WHAT'S THE EVIDENCE?
The Milgram Experiment

A more extensive series of studies examined how people would react if an experimenter asked them to deliver shocks to another person, starting with weak shocks and progressing to stronger ones. At what point, if any,

would they refuse? This research by Stanley Milgram (1974) was inspired by reports of atrocities in the Nazi concentration camps during World War II. People who had committed the atrocities defended themselves by saying that they were only obeying orders. International courts rejected that defense, and outraged people throughout the world told themselves, "If I had been there, I would have refused to follow such orders" and "It couldn't happen here." What do you think? Could it happen here?

Hypothesis   When an authority figure gives normal people instructions to do something that might hurt another person, at least some of them will obey.

Method   Two adult male participants arrived at the experimental room—the real participant and a confederate of the experimenter pretending to be a participant. (They were not college students. The experimenters wanted results that would generalize to a broad population. They also wanted to minimize the risk that the participants would guess the true purpose of the experiment.) The experimenter told the participants that in this study on learning, one participant would be the "teacher" and the other the "learner." The teacher would read lists of words through a microphone to the learner, who would sit in a nearby room. The teacher would then test the learner's memory for the words. Whenever the learner made a mistake, the teacher was to deliver an electric shock as punishment.

The experiment was rigged so that the real participant was always the teacher and the confederate was always the learner. The teacher watched as the learner was strapped into the escape-proof shock device (Figure 14.17). The learner never received any shocks, but the teacher was led to believe that he did. In fact, be-

FIGURE 14.17 In Milgram's experiment a rigged drawing selected a confederate of the experimenter to be the "learner." Here the learner is strapped to a device that supposedly delivers shocks.

fore the start of the study, the experimenter had the teacher feel a "sample shock" from the machine.

At the start of the experiment, the teacher read the words and the learner made many mistakes. The teacher sat at a shock generator that had levers to deliver shocks ranging from 15 volts to 450 volts in 15-volt increments (Figure 14.18). The experimenter instructed the teacher to deliver a shock every time the learner made a mistake, beginning with the 15-volt switch and increasing by 15 volts for each successive mistake.

FIGURE 14.18 The "teacher" in Milgram's experiment flipped switches on this box, apparently delivering stronger and stronger shocks for each successive error that the "learner" made. The situation was designed to appear realistic, although the device did not shock the learner.

As the voltage went up, the learner in the next room cried out in pain and even kicked the wall. In one version of the experiment, the learner complained that he had a heart condition. If a teacher asked who would take responsibility for any harm done to the learner, the experimenter replied that he, the experimenter, would take responsibility but insisted, "while the shocks may be painful, they are not dangerous." When the shocks reached 150 volts, the learner called out in pain and begged to be let out of the experiment, complaining that his heart was bothering him. Beginning at 270 volts, he responded to shocks with agonized screams. At 300 volts, he shouted that he would no longer answer any questions. After 330 volts, he made no response at all. Still, the experimenter ordered the teacher to continue asking questions and delivering shocks. (Remember, the learner was not really being shocked. The screams of pain came from a tape recording.)

Results Of 40 participants, 25 continued to deliver shocks all the way to 450 volts. The people who did so were not sadists but normal adults recruited from the community through newspaper ads. They were paid a few dollars for their services, and those who asked were told that they could keep the money even if they quit. (Not many asked.) People from all walks of life obeyed the experimenter's orders, including blue-col-

lar workers, white-collar workers, and professionals. Most of them grew quite upset and agitated while they were supposedly delivering shocks to the screaming learner, but they kept right on.

Interpretation The level of obedience Milgram observed depended on certain factors that he injected into the situation. One was that the experimenter agreed to take responsibility. (Remember the diffusion of responsibility principle.) Another influence was that the experimenter started with a small request, asking the participant to press the lever for a 15-volt shock, and then gradually progressed to stronger shocks.

Figures 14.19 and 14.20 illustrate the results of a few variations in procedure that Milgram tried. For example, participants were more obedient to an experimenter who remained in the same room than to one who left. They were less obedient if they needed to force the learner's hand back onto the shock plate. If additional "teachers" divided the task—the other "teachers" also being confederates of the experimenter—a participant was very likely to obey if the others obeyed, but unlikely if the others did not.

FIGURE 14.19 In one variation of Milgram's standard procedure, he asked the teacher to hold the learner's hand on the shock electrode. This close contact with the learner decreased obedience to less than half its usual level; still, some teachers continued following orders to deliver shocks.

Still, the remarkable conclusion remains that, under a variety of conditions, many normal people followed orders from an experimenter they had just met, even though they thought they might hurt or even kill someone. Imagine how much stronger the pressure to obey orders from a government or military leader would be.

Ethical Issues Milgram's experiment told us something about ourselves that we did not want to hear. No longer could we say, "What happened in Nazi Germany could never happen here." We found that most of us do follow orders, even quite offensive orders. We

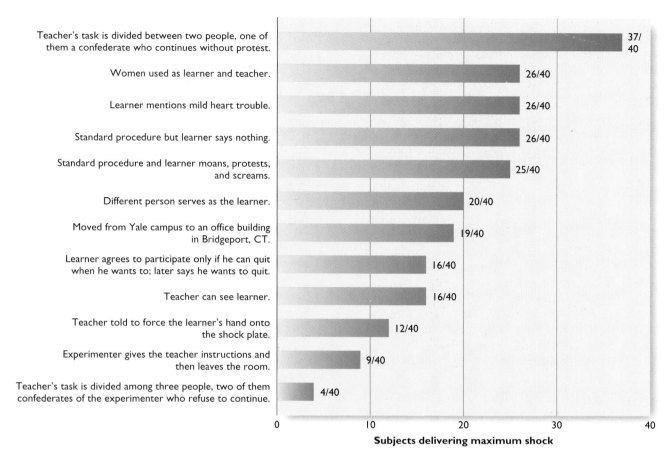

Teacher's task is divided between two people, one of them a confederate who continues without protest.   **37/40**

Women used as learner and teacher.   **26/40**

Learner mentions mild heart trouble.   **26/40**

Standard procedure but learner says nothing.   **26/40**

Standard procedure and learner moans, protests, and screams.   **25/40**

Different person serves as the learner.   **20/40**

Moved from Yale campus to an office building in Bridgeport, CT.   **19/40**

Learner agrees to participate only if he can quit when he wants to; later says he wants to quit.   **16/40**

Teacher can see learner.   **16/40**

Teacher told to force the learner's hand onto the shock plate.   **12/40**

Experimenter gives the teacher instructions and then leaves the room.   **9/40**

Teacher's task is divided among three people, two of them confederates of the experimenter who refuse to continue.   **4/40**

0   10   20   30   40

Subjects delivering maximum shock

FIGURE 14.20 Milgram varied his procedure in many ways to find out what elements promoted or inhibited obedience. Division of responsibility increased obedience; an implication of personal responsibility decreased obedience.

are indebted to Milgram's study for this important, if unwelcome, information.

However, although I am glad to know about Milgram's results, I doubt that I would have enjoyed participating in his experiment. Most people were emotionally drained, and some were visibly upset to discover how readily they had obeyed orders to deliver dangerous shocks to another person. ▬

Milgram's study prompted psychology researchers to establish much clearer and stricter rules about what an experimenter can ethically ask someone to do. Today, before the start of any psychological experiment—even the simplest and most innocuous—the experimenter is required to submit a plan to an institutional committee that can either approve or reject the ethics of the experiment.

If anyone today submitted a proposal to conduct research similar to Milgram's study, the local institutional committee would presumably refuse permission or require some changes in procedure. However, if the same rules had been in place *at the time* of Milgram's study, a committee might not have objected. Before the research, almost no one expected his results to

turn out as they did. Milgram asked various psychologists and psychiatrists to predict the results, and nearly all replied that only a rare psychopathic weirdo would press levers to deliver severe shocks. The distress experienced by so many participants underscores just how surprising Milgram's results were.

CONCEPT CHECK ☑

28. In what way did the obedience in Milgram's experiment resemble the foot-in-the-door procedure? How did it resemble Skinner's shaping procedure? (Check your answers on page 574.)

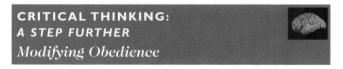

CRITICAL THINKING:
A STEP FURTHER
Modifying Obedience

Here is one version of the experiment that Milgram never tried: At the start of the experiment, we announce that the teacher and the learner will trade places halfway through the experiment so that the previous learner will start delivering shocks to the teacher. How do you think the teachers would behave then? What other changes in procedure can you imagine that might influence the degree of obedience?

Fix the Situation, Not Human Nature

If we want to prevent people from panicking when a fire breaks out in a crowded theater, the best solution is to build more exits. Similarly, it is difficult to teach people to behave productively in any of the behavior traps presented in this chapter. For example, the more shocks you have already given someone in Milgram's obedience study, the harder it is to quit. (As soon as you quit, you are taking responsibility for your actions, and you can no longer excuse what you have already done by saying, "I was just following orders.") In short, instead of just finding the right action to take in each situation, it is important to choose one's situations.

Summary

- *Behavior traps.* Certain situations pressure even intelligent people into self-defeating behaviors. (page 568)
- *Escalation of conflict.* In the dollar auction, the second highest bidder must pay the amount bid and receives nothing in return. If two people start bidding, it is difficult to stop. (page 569)

- *The prisoner's dilemma.* In the prisoner's dilemma, two people can choose to cooperate or compete. The compete move seems best from the individual's point of view, but it is harmful to the group. (page 569)
- *The commons dilemma.* If people can withdraw resources from a common pool while saving their individual resources, it is tempting to take as much as possible and therefore ruin the common pool. (page 570)
- *Obedience.* Many people obey the orders of a person in authority even if they believe their actions will injure someone else. They are less likely to obey if they can see the person who would be injured. They are more likely to obey if other people are following orders without protest. (page 571)

Answers to Concept Checks

27. If your identity is completely anonymous, you have something to gain and nothing to lose by choosing to *compete* on the final move—leaving aside issues of morality. However, if anyone will know your identity, it may be better to cooperate to protect your reputation as a cooperator. That reputation could help you the next time you play. (page 570)

28. In all three cases—Milgram's experiment, the foot-in-the-door procedure, and Skinner's shaping procedure—someone starts with a small, hard-to-refuse request and gradually builds up to bigger requests. (page 573)

Key Terms and Activities

Key Terms

actor-observer effect: the tendency to attribute internal causes more often for other people's behavior and external attributions more often for one's own behavior (page 540)

ambivalent sexism: an overt belief in equal treatment of the sexes joined with a lingering, often unstated belief that women should be treated differently (page 535)

attitude: a like or dislike that influences our behavior toward a person or thing (page 543)

attribution: the set of thought processes we use to assign causes to our own behavior and to the behavior of others (page 538)

autokinetic effect: the illusory perception that a point of light in a darkened room is in motion (page 561)

aversive racism: consciously expressing the idea that all people are equal, but nevertheless unintentionally discriminating against some groups (page 535)

bait-and-switch technique: the procedure of first offering an extremely favorable deal and then making additional demands after the other person has committed to the deal (page 548)

behavior trap: a situation that almost forces people into self-defeating behaviors (page 568)

bona fide pipeline: a task on which people alternate between looking at different kinds of faces, such as Black and White, and reading words that they need to classify as pleasant or unpleasant; investigators measure whether they respond "pleasant" faster after one kind of face or the other (page 537)

central route to persuasion: a method of persuasion based on careful evaluation of evidence and logic (page 544)

cognitive dissonance: a state of unpleasant tension that people experience when they hold contradictory attitudes or when their behavior is inconsistent with their attitudes, especially if they are displeased with this inconsistency (page 548)

commons dilemma: a situation where people who share a common resource tend to overuse it and therefore make it unavailable in the long run (page 570)

conformity: maintaining or changing one's behavior to match the behavior or expectations of others (page 561)

consensus information: comparisons of one person's behavior with that of others (page 538)

consistency information: observations of how a person's behavior varies from one time to another (page 538)

diffusion of responsibility: the tendency to feel less responsibility for helping when other people are around than when we know that no one else can help (page 564)

discrimination: in social behavior unequal treatment of different groups of people (page 534)

distinctiveness: observations of how a person's behavior varies from one object or social partner to another (page 538)

door-in-the-face technique: a method of eliciting compliance by first making an outrageous request and then replying to the refusal with a more reasonable request (page 547)

exchange (or equity) theories: theories maintaining that social relationships are transactions in which partners exchange goods and services (page 553)

external attribution: an explanation for someone's behavior based on the current situation, including events that presumably would influence almost anyone (page 538)

foot-in-the-door technique: a method of eliciting compliance by first making a modest request and then following it with a larger request (page 547)

forewarning effect: the tendency of a brief preview of a message to decrease its persuasiveness (page 547)

fundamental attribution error: the tendency to make internal attributions for people's behavior, even

when an observer sees evidence for an external influence (page 539)

group polarization: the tendency of a group whose members lean in the same direction on a particular issue to become more extreme in its views after discussing the issue as a group (page 565)

groupthink: a process by which the members of a group suppress their doubts about a group's poorly thought-out decision for fear of making a bad impression or disrupting the harmony of the group (page 566)

inoculation effect: the tendency of a persuasive message to be weakened if people first hear a weak argument supporting the same conclusion (page 547)

internal attribution: an explanation based on someone's individual characteristics, such as attitudes, personality traits, or abilities (page 538)

mere exposure effect: the tendency to increase our liking for everything and everyone that has become familiar (page 552)

peripheral route to persuasion: a method of persuasion based on such superficial factors as the speaker's appearance and reputation or the sheer number of arguments presented, regardless of their quality (page 544)

pluralistic ignorance: a situation where people say nothing and each person falsely assumes that everyone else has a different, perhaps better informed opinion. (page 564)

prejudice: an unfavorable stereotype; a negative attitude toward a group of people (page 534)

primacy effect: the tendency to be more influenced by the first information learned about someone than by later information about the same person (page 533)

prisoner's dilemma: a situation where people must choose between an act that is beneficial to themselves but harmful to others and an act that is moderately beneficial to all (page 569)

proximity: in social psychology the tendency to choose as friends people with whom we come in frequent contact (page 552)

reciprocal altruism: helping someone in the expectation that the other person will repay the favor, either now or later (page 570)

self-fulfilling prophecy: an expectation that alters one's behavior in such a way as to increase the probability of the predicted event (page 533)

self-handicapping strategies: techniques for intentionally putting oneself at a disadvantage to provide an excuse for an expected failure (page 541)

self-serving biases: attributions that people adopt to maximize their credit for their successes and to minimize their blame for their failures (page 541)

sleeper effect: delayed persuasion by an initially rejected message (page 544)

social loafing: the tendency to "loaf" (or work less hard) when sharing work with other people (page 565)

social perception and cognition: the process of gathering and remembering information about others and making inferences based on that information (page 533)

social psychologists: the psychologists who study social behavior and how individuals influence other people and are influenced by other people (page 532)

stereotypes: the overgeneralization of either positive or negative attitudes toward a group of people (page 534)

that's-not-all technique: a method of eliciting compliance whereby someone makes an offer and then improves the offer before anyone has a chance to reply (page 548)

Suggestions for Further Reading

Cialdini, R. B. (1993). *Influence: Science and practice* (Rev. ed.). New York: William Morrow. One of the most enjoyable and entertaining books in psychology. Take a copy with you for vacation reading.

Milgram, S. (1975). *Obedience to authority.* New York: Harper & Row. Describes Milgram's classic experiments on obedience.

Book Companion Web Site

Need help studying? Go to

http://psychology.wadsworth.com/kalat_intro7e/

for a virtual study center. You'll find a personalized Self-Study Assessment that will provide you with a study plan based on your answers to a pretest. Also study using flash cards, quizzes, interactive art, and an online glossary.

Check out interactive exercises on the companion site! These exercises will help you put what you've learned into action.

Your companion site also has direct links to the following Web sites. These links are checked often for changes, dead links, and new additions.

Implicit Association Test

https://implicit.harvard.edu/implicit/demo/

Test your own responses on the Implicit Association Test.

Groupthink: Theoretical Framework

choo.fis.utoronto.ca/FIS/Courses/LIS2149/Groupthink.html

This three-page series by Chun Wei Choo of the University of Toronto begins with an elaborate diagram showing the antecedent conditions and observable consequences of groupthink; pages 2 and 3 provide steps to minimize its development.

Social Psychology Network

www.socialpsychology.org/

This huge database includes more than 5,000 links to resources about social behavior.

Cross-Cultural Psychology

www.vanguard.edu/faculty/ddegelman/amoebaweb/index.cfm?doc_id=857

This page contains links to worldwide studies of cultural influences and culture differences.

Interpersonal Perception

nw3.nai.net/dakenny/interp.htm

David A. Kenny of the University of Connecticut, author of *Interpersonal Perception: A Social Relations Analysis,* offers an outstanding tutorial on the judgments that one person makes about another.

Prisoner's Dilemma

serendip.brynmawr.edu/bb/pd.html

Play the prisoner's dilemma game with a computer opponent. Try different strategies to see which works best.

 Try It Yourself CD-ROM
with Critical Thinking Video Exercises

Use your CD to access **videos** related to activities designed to help you think critically about the important topics discussed. For example, the video about implicit association relates to what you've learned in this chapter. You'll also find an easy portal link to the book companion site where you can access your personalized **Self-Study Assessments** and interactive **Try It Yourself** exercises.

PsychNow! 2.0

PsychNow! is a fun interactive CD designed to help you with the difficult concepts in psychology. Check out the Social Psychology section for the following topics that relate to this chapter:

Helping Others: the Kitty Genovese scenario, process of deciding whether or not to help, and scenarios of person getting/not getting help.

Attribution: choose reactions to situations, the attribution theory explained, and rate woman's and man's attributions.t know; didn't write this.>

Social Influence: moon/star exercise, watch a video of Milgram's experiment on obedience to authority, explore conformity in terms of the Asch experiment, and apply personal action decisions.

Attitudes and Prejudice: test your own beliefs, imagine people's responses, define attitudes, cognitive dissonance, prejudice, and stereotypes, and identify statements as representing belief, emotion, or action.

Aggression: take a contextual behavior quiz, explore an interactive analysis of "aggressive" behavior, and apply three perspectives on aggression to the Gulf War.

Environmental Psychology: casino environment and gambling behavior, six environments that determine behavior, and desk arrangements for different situations.

Abnormality, Therapy, and Social Issues

Over the past 4 months, George has injured several dozen people, most of whom he hardly knew. Two of them had to be sent to the hospital. George expresses no guilt, no regrets. He says he would hit every one of them again if he got the chance. What should society do with George?

1. Send him to jail.

2. Commit him to a mental hospital.

3. Give him an award for being the best defensive player in the league.

You cannot answer the question unless you know the context of George's behavior. Behavior that seems normal at a party might seem bizarre in a business meeting. Behavior that earns millions for a rock singer might earn a trip to the mental hospital for a college professor. Behavior that is routine in one culture might be criminal in another.

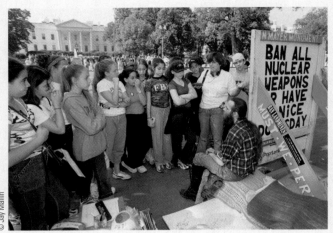

■ A protestor who spends years of his life picketing the White House in search of peace is statistically abnormal and puts himself at risk of harm. Still, most of us would not call him psychologically abnormal. Abnormality is hard to define.

Even knowing the context of someone's behavior may not tell us whether it is normal. Suppose your rich Aunt Tillie starts passing out money to strangers on the street corner and plans to continue until she has exhausted her fortune. Should the court commit her to a mental hospital and make you the trustee of her estate?

A man claims to be Jesus Christ and asks permission to appear before the United Nations to announce God's message to the world. A psychiatrist is sure that he can relieve this man of his disordered thinking by giving him antipsychotic drugs, but the man insists that he is perfectly sane. Should we force him to take the drugs, ignore him, or place his address on the agenda of the United Nations?

Abnormal Behavior: An Overview

What do we mean by "abnormal" behavior and how can we distinguish it from normal?

Students in medical school often contract what is known as "medical students' disease." Imagine that you are just beginning your training in medicine. One of your textbooks describes "Cryptic Ruminating Umbilicus Disorder": "The symptoms are hardly noticeable until the condition becomes hopeless. The first symptom is a pale tongue." (You go to the mirror. You can't remember what your tongue is supposed to look like, but it *does* look a little pale.) "Later, a hard spot forms in the neck." (You feel your neck. "Wait! I never felt *this* before! I think it's something hard!") "Just before the arms and legs fall off, there is shortness of breath, increased heart rate, and sweating." (Already distressed, you *do* have shortness of breath, your heart *is* racing, and you *are* sweating profusely.)

Sooner or later, most medical students misunderstand the description of some disease and confuse it with their own normal condition. When my brother was in medical school, he diagnosed himself as having a rare, fatal illness, checked himself into a hospital, and wrote out his will. (He finished medical school and is still doing fine today, decades later.)

"Medical students' disease" is even more common among students of psychological disorders. As you read this chapter and the next one, you may decide that you are suffering from one of the disorders you read about. Perhaps you are, but recognizing a little of yourself in the description of a psychological disorder does not mean that you have the disorder. All of us feel sad, nervous, or angry occasionally, and many of us have mood swings, bad habits, or beliefs that strike other people as odd. *A diagnosis of a psychological disorder should be reserved for people whose problems seriously interfere with their lives.*

Defining Abnormal Behavior

How should we define abnormal behavior? To try to be completely objective, we might define *abnormal behavior* as any behavior significantly different from the average. However, by that definition, unusually happy or successful people are abnormal, and severe depression would be normal if it became common enough. When we say "abnormal," we don't mean just "different"; we mean different in an undesirable way.

Another way to define abnormal would be to let people decide for themselves whether they are troubled. For example, someone who complains of feeling miserable has a problem, even if it is not apparent to anyone else. Fair enough, but what about certain people who insist that they do *not* have a problem? Imagine a woman who babbles incoherently, urinates and defecates in the street, insults strangers, begs for $1 bills and then sets them on fire, while claiming to be obeying messages from another planet. She reports feeling fine and does not

a

b

▐ What we consider normal or abnormal depends on the context. (a) People dressed as witches ski down a mountain as part of an annual festival in Belalp, Switzerland, in which dressing as witches is supposed to chase away evil spirits. (b) A woman walks through a public park carrying a large snake. We don't know why but "unusual" behavior is not necessarily a sign of psychological disorder.

▌ Edvard Munch (1864–1944), *Self Portrait, The Night Wanderer,* 1923–24, Munch Museum, Oslo, Norway. The uncurtained windows and the bare room emphasize the feeling of loneliness and isolation.

regard herself as troubled, although most people would think she needs help.

The American Psychiatric Association (1994) defined abnormal behavior as any behavior that leads to distress (including distress to others), disability (impaired functioning), or an increased risk of death, pain, or loss of freedom. This definition presumably includes the woman just described. Its weakness is that it may be too inclusive. For example, when Dr. Martin Luther King Jr. fought for the rights of African Americans, he risked death, pain, and loss of freedom, but we regard his acts as heroic, not abnormal. Again, presumably, we want to limit our concept of "abnormal behavior" to conditions that are clearly undesirable.

CRITICAL THINKING:
A STEP FURTHER
What Is Abnormal?

How would *you* define abnormal behavior?

Cultural Influences on Abnormality

Each time and place has interpreted abnormal behavior according to its own worldview. People in the Middle Ages, for example, regarded peculiar behavior as a sign of demon possession that needed treatment with religious rituals.

In one culture in Sudan some years ago, women had low status and very limited rights; if a woman's husband mistreated her, she had no defense. However, people in this society believed that a woman could be possessed by a demon who caused her to lose control and scream all sorts of "crazy" things that she "could not possibly believe," including insults against her own husband (!). Her husband could not scold or punish her because, after all, it was not really she, but only the demon who was speaking. The standard way to remove the demon was to provide the woman with luxurious food, new clothing, an opportunity to spend much time with other women, and almost anything else she demanded until the demon departed. You can imagine how common demon possession became (Constantinides, 1977).

More examples: *Brain fag syndrome* is a psychiatric condition marked by headache, dizziness, eye fatigue, and inability to concentrate—a common complaint among high school and college students in sub-Saharan Africa (Morakinyo & Peltzer, 2002). You might ask your own professor to excuse you from a test tomorrow because of brain fag syndrome, but unless you live in sub-Saharan Africa, I doubt that your explanation will do you much good.

You have probably heard the expression "to run amok." *Running amok* is a type of abnormal behavior recognized in parts of Southeast Asia, where someone (usually a young man) runs around engaging in indiscriminate violent behavior (Berry, Poortinga, Segal, & Dasen, 1992). Such behavior is considered an understandable reaction to psychological stress, not a criminal offense. Does running amok remind you of anything common in North America or Europe? How about the celebrations that occur after a sports team wins a major championship? Like running amok, people often regard such wild displays as temporary responses to overwhelming emotion.

I do not mean to imply that brain fag, running amok, and demon possession are pretended. Presumably, those people are reacting to genuine stresses and problems. The point is that their way of reacting was

▌ Fans sometimes celebrate a major sports victory with a destructive rampage. In some ways this behavior is like "running amok"—it is an abnormal behavior copied from other people's example.

modeled on suggestions from others. For a Western-culture example, one Australian psychiatrist found three mental patients in one hospital who had cut off one of their ears. Assuming that this behavior must be a common symptom of mental illness, he contacted other psychiatrists to ask how often they had seen the same thing. They reported it was almost unheard-of. Apparently, when one patient in this hospital cut off his ear, the other two copied (Alroe & Gunda, 1995). (Why they copied is, of course, an interesting question.)

Suggestion is probably also a major influence in **dissociative identity disorder (DID)**, previously known as **multiple personality disorder**, in which *a person alternates among two or more distinct personalities, each with its own behavioral patterns, memories, and even name, almost as if each personality were really a different person.* Note that alternating among different personalities is *not* schizophrenia, although the media often mislabel it as such. We consider schizophrenia in Chapter 16, which treats in some detail four major categories of psychological disorders and the specific ways in which therapists treat them. Dissociative identity disorder was extremely rare before the 1950s, when a few cases received much publicity. Chris Costner White Sizemore was featured in the book and movie *The Three Faces of Eve,* written by her psychiatrists (Thigpen & Cleckley, 1957). Sizemore ("Eve") eventually told her own story, which was very different from her psychiatrists' version (Sizemore & Huber, 1988; Sizemore & Pittillo, 1977). A few other cases of dissociative identity disorder also received extensive publicity, such as the celebrated case *Sybil,* although one of the psychiatrists associated with that case later said he thought the author of the book about Sybil had greatly distorted the fact to improve sales of the book (Borch-Jacobsen, 1997). By the early 1990s, some ther-

apists were reporting many such cases. Why was this condition becoming so common?

A likely hypothesis is that overeager therapists notice minor symptoms and then through well-meaning questions, sometimes using hypnosis, suggest that the person might have an additional personality. At first, the person may have had only a small tendency toward different personalities at different times, but after a few therapy sessions, the dissociation becomes more severe (Lilienfeld et al., 1999). As mentioned in the last chapter, people often conform to the expectations of others, and an expectation of abnormal behavior can produce that abnormality in vulnerable people.

▌ Chris Sizemore, whose story was told in *The Three Faces of Eve,* exhibited a total of 22 personalities, including her final, permanent identity.

CONCEPT CHECK ☑

1. In what way might dissociative identity disorder resemble brain fag syndrome and running amok? (Check your answer on page 589.)

The Biopsychosocial Model

In Western cultures today, the predominant view is the **biopsychosocial model,** which emphasizes that *abnormal behavior has three major aspects: biological, psychological, and sociological.* Many researchers and therapists focus more on one aspect than another, but few deny that all three are important.

The *biological* roots of abnormal behavior include genetic factors, which can lead to abnormal brain development, excesses or deficiencies in the activity of various neurotransmitters or hormones, and so forth. Behavior can also be affected by brain damage, infectious diseases, brain tumors, poor nutrition, inadequate sleep, and the overuse of drugs, including nonprescription medications.

The *psychological* component of abnormality includes a person's vulnerability to stressful events. For example, people who are known to have been physically or sexually abused in childhood are more likely than others to develop psychological problems in adulthood (Johnson, Cohen, Brown, Smailes, & Bernstein, 1999).

Finally, the behavior must be understood in a *social* and cultural context. People are greatly influenced by how other people act toward them and what other people expect of them. Many people with strange behavior have disordered families or social networks.

Unfortunately, the agreement that abnormality depends on biological, psychological, and social influences doesn't tell us much about an individual case. For example, suppose you are a therapist and you meet someone who cries almost constantly. Before you begin treatment for depression, you need to rule out other possibilities, ranging from the recent death of a loved one to the presence of a brain tumor. Different people with apparently the same symptoms can have different underlying problems.

CONCEPT CHECK

2. Of the three aspects of the biopsychosocial model, which one would be most prominent in explanations of brain fag syndrome and running amok? (Check your answer on page 589.)

Classifying Psychological Disorders

Any scientific study requires agreed standards for classifying information. If different psychologists conducting research on depression defined depression differently, chaos would result. That kind of chaos *has* sometimes occurred in psychology, and as a result psychologists have worked hard to establish uniform definitions and standards for diagnosis. One result is *a reference book called the* **Diagnostic and Statistical Manual of Mental Disorders (DSM)**— now in its fourth edition and therefore known as *DSM-IV*[1]—which *lists the acceptable labels for all psychological disorders* (alcohol intoxication, exhibitionism, pathological gambling, anorexia nervosa, sleepwalking disorder, stuttering, and hundreds of others), including a description of each disorder and an explanation of how to distinguish it from similar disorders.

DSM-IV Classifications

The clinicians and researchers who use *DSM-IV* classify each client along five separate *axes* (lists). A person may have one disorder, several, or none at all. The axis that gets the most attention is *Axis I, clinical disorders.* Table 15.1 lists the major categories of disorder on Axis I.

Axis II, personality disorders and mental retardation, lists disorders that generally persist throughout life. *Axis III, general medical conditions,* lists physical disorders, such as diabetes, head trauma, or alcoholic cirrhosis of the liver. A psychotherapist does not provide treatment for Axis III disorders but needs to know about them because they influence behavior. *Axis IV, psychosocial and environmental problems,* indicates how much stress the person has had to endure. Stress can intensify a psychological disorder and thus affect the course of treatment. *Axis V, global assessment of functioning,* evaluates a person's overall level of functioning on a scale from 1 (serious attempt at suicide or complete inability to take care of oneself) to 100 (happy, productive, with many interests). Some people with a psychological disorder are able to proceed with their normal work and social activities; others are not.

Axis I Disorders

Most psychological disorders that are listed on Axis I have their onset after infancy and represent in some way a deterioration of functioning. Eating disorders and sleep disorders, which are listed on Axis I, have been mentioned in previous chapters. In Chapter 16 we shall concentrate on the most common Axis I disorders—anxiety disorders, substance-abuse disorders, and depression—as well as schizophrenia, a less common but often disabling condition.

As an example of an Axis I disorder, let's briefly discuss one that we haven't already considered and that we won't have occasion to discuss in Chapter 16: **attention-deficit disorder (ADD)**, which is characterized by *easy distraction from important tasks, impulsiveness, moodiness, and failure to follow through on plans* (Wender, Wolf, & Wasserstein, 2001). **Attention-deficit hyperactivity disorder (ADHD)** is *the same except with excessive activity and "fidgetiness."* Both are obviously a matter of degree, and it is often difficult to distinguish ADD or ADHD from normal high energy (Panksepp, 1998). (After all, how normal is it for a 6-year-old to sit still in school for hours at a time?) On the average, people diagnosed with ADD or ADHD have some minor abnormalities on brain scans, but no therapist relies on those to make the diagnosis (Giedd, Blumenthal, Molloy, & Castellanos, 2001; Ravizza & Ivry, 2001; Stefanatos & Wasserstein, 2001). For example, a well-behaved child with those brain abnormalities would not be labeled ADD.

---

[1]A revised version is the *Diagnostic and Statistical Manual,* Fourth Edition, Text Revision, or DSM-IV-TR. The general principles are the same.

TABLE 15.1 Some Major Categories of Psychological Disorders According to Axis I of *DSM-IV*

Category	Examples and Descriptions
Disorder usually first evident in childhood	*Attention deficit hyperactivity disorder:* impulsivity, impaired attention *Tourette's disorder:* repetitive movements such as blinking, twitching, chanting sounds or words *Elimination disorders:* bedwetting, urinating or defecating in one's clothes *Stuttering:* frequent repetition or prolongation of sounds while trying to speak
Substance-related disorders	*Abuse of alcohol, cocaine, opiates, or other drugs*
Schizophrenia	Deterioration of daily functioning along with a combination of hallucinations, delusions, or other symptoms
Delusional (paranoid) disorder	Unjustifiable beliefs, such as "everyone is talking about me behind my back"
Mood disorders	*Major depressive disorder:* Repeated episodes of depressed mood and lack of energy *Bipolar disorder:* Alternation between periods of depression and mania
Anxiety disorders	*Panic disorder:* Repeated attacks of intense terror *Phobia:* Severe anxiety and avoidance of a particular object or situation
Somatoform disorders	*Conversion disorder:* Physical ailments caused partly by psychological factors but not faked *Hypochondriasis:* Exaggerated complaints of illness *Somatization disorder:* Complaints of pain or other ailments without any physical disorder
Dissociative disorders	Loss of personal identity or memory without brain damage
Sexual disorders	*Pedophilia:* Sexual attraction to children *Voyeurism:* Sexual arousal primarily from watching others undress or have sexual relations *Exhibitionism:* Sexual arousal from exposing one's genitals in public
Eating disorders	*Anorexia nervosa:* Refusal to eat, fear of fatness *Bulimia nervosa:* Binge eating alternating with severe dieting
Sleep disorders	*Sleep terror disorder:* Repeated sudden awakenings in a state of panic *Insomnia:* Frequently not getting enough sleep to feel well rested the next day
Impulse control disorders	Frequently acting on impulses that others would inhibit, such as stealing, gambling foolishly, or hitting people

In the United States, the ADD or ADHD diagnosis is applied to an estimated 3 to 10% of children, about 70% of them boys. Some of them "outgrow" the problem, but many have problems that persist into adulthood, impairing social behavior and job performance (Mannuzza, Klein, Bessler, Malloy, & LaPadula, 1998).

The causes are not known. Researchers have tentatively linked several genes to this disorder, but no one gene appears to have a strong relationship (Bakker et al., 2003; Faraone, Doyle, Mick, & Biederman, 2001; Ogdie et al., 2003). The environmental causes include fetal alcohol exposure, lead poisoning, epilepsy, sleep deprivation, emotional stress, and several kinds of mild brain damage (Pearl, Weiss, & Stein, 2001). In most cases the causes are unknown.

The most common treatment is stimulant drugs such as methylphenidate (Ritalin) (Elia, Ambrosini, & Rapoport, 1999). Stimulant drugs improve school performance and everyday behaviors (de Wit, Crean, & Richards, 2000; Jerome & Segal, 2001). However, the fact that stimulant drugs appear to help a given child should not be taken as evidence to confirm a diagnosis of ADD/ADHD. One study found that stimulant drugs increase the attention span even of normal children (Zahn, Rapoport, & Thompson, 1980).

Is it a good idea to prescribe drugs for so many young people? Psychologists disagree on this point. The idea of giving strong drugs to so many children is worrisome. In addition to or instead of drugs, psychologists recommend behavioral approaches to controlling ADD, such as controlling stress and distraction (Sohlberg & Mateer, 2001).

Researchers are trying to clarify exactly what they mean by "attention deficit." The problem is *not* simply a short attention span. Many ADD/ADHD children or teens can pay attention to a video game for hours. The problem lies more with controlling attention. Everyone, of course, has trouble paying attention to something that seems uninteresting, but people with ADD/ADHD have more trouble than others. They also have trouble restraining impulses, and following an impulse can interfere with controlling attention. Here are two tasks that measure impulsivity:

- **The Choice-Delay Task** Which would you prefer, a small reward now or a bigger reward later? Obviously, your answer depends on *how much* bigger and *how much* later. Most people with ADD or ADHD need a larger than usual incentive to choose the delayed reward (Solanto et al., 2001).
- **The Stop Signal Task** Suppose your task is to press a button whenever you see a circle on the screen, as fast as possible, but if you hear a "beep" shortly after you see the circle, then you should not press. If the circle and beep occur simultaneously, you can inhibit your urge to press the button. If the beep occurs after you have already started to press, it's too late. The interesting results are with short delays: After how long a delay could you still manage to stop your finger from pressing the button? Most people with ADD or ADHD have trouble inhibiting their response, even after short delays (Rubia, Oosterlaan, Sergeant, Brandeis, & v. Leeuwen, 1998; Solanto et al., 2001). To see for yourself go to http://psychology. wadsworth.com/kalat_intro7e, go to the student Web site, then to Online Try It Yourself, and click on Stop Signal Task.

For links to many kinds of information about ADHD, visit this Web site:

www.add-adhd.org/

CONCEPT CHECK ☑

3. What are some possible causes of attention-deficit disorder?
4. Describe one of the behavioral tests used to measure deficits of attention or impulse control. (Check your answers on page 589.)

Axis II Disorders

Axis II of *DSM-IV* includes mental retardation and personality disorders, as listed in Table 15.2. If there is a distinction between Axis I and Axis II disorders, it is that Axis II disorders tend to be lifelong, whereas most Axis I disorders represent a deterioration of functioning. However, that rule has many exceptions. The main reason for distinguishing Axis II from Axis I is that Axis II disorders are generally less spectacular and less likely to be the main reason someone came to a therapist. By listing Axis II disorders separately, *DSM-IV* encourages the therapist to notice them. That is, a therapist fills out a diagnosis on Axis I and then comes to the question of what, if anything, to list on Axis II. It is possible to list "no diagnosis," but at least the therapist has to pause to consider the possibilities.

A **personality disorder** is *a maladaptive, inflexible way of dealing with the environment and other people,* such as being unusually self-centered. Some personality disorders are widespread; for example, one survey found that 5% of people had avoidant personality disorder, and about 2% each had paranoid and histrionic personality disorders (Torgerson, Kringlen, & Cramer, 2001). Most people with personality disorders do not complain about them or seek treatment, except when other people insist on it. Treatment is usually slow and difficult, as it implies changing someone's personality.

The Importance of Differential Diagnosis

In abnormal psychology, as in medicine, any diagnosis (identification) of a disorder requires ruling out other possibilities. For example, suppose someone says, "I feel unenergetic and pessimistic; I awaken often during the night; I don't have much appetite; and nothing brings me pleasure anymore." That description sounds very much like depression, but the same symptoms could be the result of a malfunctioning thyroid gland, a stroke, the side effects from certain medications, drug withdrawal, a grief reaction following the death of a loved one, nutritional deficiencies, or fatigue. Psychiatrists and clinical psychologists must learn to make a **differential diagnosis**—that is, *a determination of what problem a person has in contrast to all the other possible problems that might produce similar symptoms.* Only a therapist who understands the problem well can choose the best treatment.

Criticisms of DSM-IV

DSM-IV has helped standardize psychiatric diagnoses, but even its most loyal defenders admit it has flaws. Problems include the difficulty of distinguishing normal from abnormal and the question of whether *DSM-IV* is treating reactions to difficult situations as if they were mental illnesses.

Distinguishing Normal from Abnormal

Consider the sexual disorders such as *pedophilia* (sexual interest in children), *voyeurism* (sexual excitement from secretly watching others undress or have sexual relations), and *sexual masochism* (sexual pleasure from receiving pain). *DSM-IV* classifies each of these as a mental illness if it continues for at least 6 months. Obviously, it is arbitrary to say that 5 months of pedophilia is not a disorder but 6 months is. A more difficult question is whether an unacceptable sexual desire implies mental illness (Widiger & Clark, 2000). We can disapprove of something without calling it a mental illness. For example, we do not assume that all murderers are mentally ill.

TABLE 15.2 Some Major Categories of Psychological Disorders According to Axis II of *DSM-IV*

Category and Examples	Descriptions
Mental Retardation	Intellectual functioning significantly below average; inability to function effectively and independently
Personality Disorders	
Paranoid personality disorder	Suspiciousness, habitual interpretation of others' acts as threatening
Schizoid personality disorder	Impaired social relations and emotional responses
Schizotypal personality disorder	Poor relationships with other people; odd thinking; neglect of normal grooming. (Similar to schizophrenia but less severe.)
Antisocial personality disorder	Lack of affection for others; high probability of harming others without feeling guilty; apparent weakness of most emotions
Borderline personality disorder	Lack of stable self-image; trouble establishing lasting relationships or maintaining lasting decisions; repeated self-endangering behaviors
Histrionic personality disorder	Excessive emotionality and attention seeking
Narcissistic personality disorder	Exaggerated opinion of one's own importance and disregard for others. (Narcissus was a figure in Greek mythology who fell in love with his own image.)
Avoidant personality disorder	Avoidance of social contact; lack of friends
Dependent personality disorder	Preference for letting other people make decisions; lack of initiative and self-confidence
Obsessive-compulsive personality disorder	Preoccupation with orderliness and perfectionism. (Similar to obsessive-compulsive disorder, but less severe.)

Furthermore, every disorder varies in degree from mild to severe. Psychologists and psychiatrists do their best to make consistent diagnoses, but marginal cases call for difficult judgments. Therefore, any statistics about the prevalence of psychological disorders are somewhat uncertain. In one survey of a random sample of about 20,000 people in three U.S. cities, trained interviewers reported that about one fifth of all adults were suffering from a psychological disorder of some sort (as defined by *DSM*) and that close to one third had suffered from such a disorder at some point (Myers et al., 1984; Robins et al., 1984). A similar study 10 years later yielded somewhat higher numbers (Kessler et al., 1994), and a still later study found somewhat lower numbers (Narrow, Rae, Robins, & Regier, 2002). The discrepancies depend mostly on where the researchers draw the line between disordered and not disordered—that is, how many marginal cases are labeled as

problems. All the surveys agree that the most common disorders are anxiety disorders, alcohol or drug abuse, and mood disorders (e.g., depression), as shown in Figure 15.1.

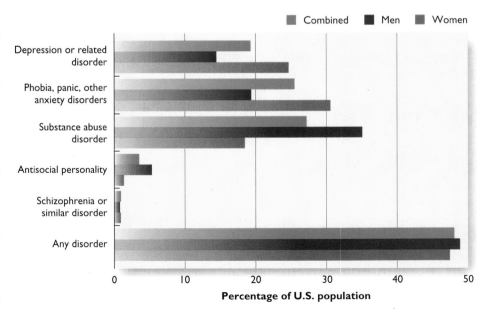

FIGURE 15.1 According to one extensive survey, about half the people in the United States will suffer at least one psychological disorder at some time. (The figures for the individual conditions do not add up to the total percentage for "any disorder" because some people have more than one disorder.) However, the exact percentages depend on where one draws the dividing line between "normal" and "abnormal." *(Based on data of Kessler et al., 1994)*

▌ Almost everyone has an unpleasant mood or behaves strangely once in a while. Many people who qualify for a *DSM-IV* diagnosis are not very different from other people.

Is Abnormal Behavior in the Person or the Situation?

Another major criticism is that *DSM-IV* classifies understandable responses to difficult situations as if they were mental illnesses (Kutchins & Kirk, 1997). Suppose a child who is frequently bullied starts protesting vehemently against going to school, sometimes even vomiting on school mornings. Imagine a woman who has left an abusive relationship and is trying to restore her damaged self-esteem. It would seem pointless or harmful to give either of them the stigma of a psychiatric diagnosis. However, if a therapist diagnoses them as having anxiety disorders, the insurance company will pay for the treatment. Therefore, the authors of *DSM-IV* broadened the definitions of many disorders and described new disorders so that if you go to a therapist for almost any problem, you can receive a psychiatric diagnosis and your insurance company will pay for at least a few sessions of treatment.

CONCEPT CHECK ☑

5. Why should we be somewhat skeptical of all statistics about the prevalence of psychological disorders? (Check your answer on page 589.)

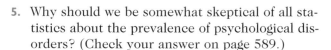

IN CLOSING

Is Anyone Normal?

DSM-IV gives both psychotherapists and researchers a way to use terms like *depression* or *phobia* in as consistent a way as possible. On the negative side, it encourages therapists to apply a psychiatric diagnosis, with its potential stigma, to almost anyone who seeks

help. Even someone who does not qualify for depression, anxiety disorders, schizophrenia, or substance abuse may qualify for a diagnosis of a personality disorder under Axis II.

According to the studies described in this module, about one third to one half of all people in the United States will have a *DSM-IV* disorder at some point in life. If those statistics are even close to accurate, the implication is obvious: Most of the people who qualify for a psychological diagnosis are not much different from everyone else. At some point in your life, you may have a bout of some kind of psychological distress. If so, remember that you have plenty of company.

Summary

- *Normal and abnormal behavior.* The American Psychiatric Association defines abnormal behavior as behavior that leads to distress, disability, or increased risk of harm. However, any definition of abnormal behavior has difficulties. (page 581)

- *Cultural influences on abnormality.* Every culture provides examples not only of how to behave normally but also of how to behave abnormally. (page 582)

- *Multiple causes of abnormal behavior.* Abnormal behavior is the result of various combinations of biological factors, early experiences, and learned responses to a stressful or unsupportive environment. (page 583)

- *The Diagnostic and Statistical Manual.* Psychological disorders are classified in the *Diagnostic and Statistical Manual of Mental Disorders, Fourth Edition (DSM-IV)*. This manual classifies disorders along five axes. Axes I and II contain psychological disorders; Axis III lists physical ailments that can affect behavior; Axes IV and V provide the means of evaluating a person's stress level and overall functioning. (page 584)

- *Axis I disorders.* Axis I of *DSM-IV* lists a wide variety of disorders, including anxiety disorders, substance abuse, and depression. (page 584)

- *Attention-deficit disorder (ADD) and attention-deficit hyperactivity disorder (ADHD).* ADD and ADHD are common diagnoses of a condition with a variety of causes, although usually the cause is unknown. Researchers have been trying to measure the attention and impulse-control problems to better specify the nature of the problem. (page 584)

- *Axis II disorders.* Axis II of *DSM-IV* lists mental retardation and various personality disorders. (page 586)

- *Personality disorders.* Personality disorders are stable characteristics that impair a person's effectiveness or ability to get along with others. Examples of personality disorders are excessive dependence on others and excessive self-centeredness. (page 586)

- *Differential diagnosis.* Psychiatrists and clinical psychologists need to learn to consider all the possible diagnoses of a given set of symptoms and to identify the correct one by eliminating all the other possibilities. (page 586)

- *Criticisms of DSM-IV.* In spite of the efforts of *DSM-IV* to provide clear guidelines, it remains difficult to distinguish between normal and abnormal. Also, *DSM-IV* has been criticized for labeling many people as psychologically disordered, when in fact they are reacting normally to an abnormal situation. (page 586)

Answers to Concept Checks

1. In each case people are reacting to real problems, but the way they react follows suggestions or expectations from other people. (page 583)

2. The social aspect would certainly be prominent because these disorders occur only in cultures that have made them seem like options. However, the people showing these symptoms may have biological and psychological problems as well. (page 584)

3. Possible causes include genetics, fetal alcohol exposure, lead poisoning, epilepsy, sleep deprivation, emotional stress, and mild brain damage. (page 586)

4. In the Choice Delay Task, the question is under what conditions someone will sacrifice a reward now for a larger one later. In the Stop Signal Task, one signal calls for a response and a second signal cancels the first signal; the question is under what circumstances a person can inhibit the response. (page 586)

5. Each disorder occurs in varying degrees, and the apparent prevalence of a disorder depends on how many marginal cases we include. (page 588)

What methods are used to combat psychological disorders, and how effective are they?

Observation
If I don't drive around the park, I'm pretty sure to make my mark.
If I'm in bed each night by ten, I may get back my looks again.
If I abstain from fun and such, I'll probably amount to much.
But I shall stay the way I am, Because I do not give a damn.
—Dorothy Parker (1944)[1]

Psychotherapy is *a treatment of psychological disorders by methods that include a personal relationship between a trained therapist and a client.* But psychotherapy does little good unless the client gives the proverbial damn.

Psychotherapy is used for many well-defined disorders that are listed in *DSM-IV* and also for adjustment and coping problems. Some psychotherapy clients are virtually incapacitated by their problems, but others are reasonably happy, successful people who would like to function even more successfully.

Historical Trends in Psychotherapy

Psychotherapy has changed greatly since the mid-1900s for both scientific and economic reasons (Sanchez & Turner, 2003). Before World War II, almost all psychotherapists were psychiatrists. In the 1940s and 1950s, most therapists used Freudian methods and expected to see each patient frequently, perhaps even daily, for months or years. People who wanted therapy had to pay for it themselves, as almost no one had health insurance that covered psychiatric visits. (Most didn't have health insurance at all.) Therefore, few other than the wealthy received psychotherapy. At this time almost no research had been done concerning the effectiveness of psychotherapy, so clients had little choice but to trust whatever their therapists claimed. Some clients received a diagnosis such as depressed or schizophrenic, but many were given either no diagnosis at all or a vague, almost undefined diagnosis like "neurotic."

Today all of that has changed, largely because health maintenance organizations (HMOs) and other health insurance programs will pay for mental health care, but only under certain conditions. HMOs try to restrain costs and make sure that money is spent effectively. If the man down the street pays for his own treatment, no one will object if he sees his therapist every day for the rest of his life. However, if his health insurance pays for the treatment, and you and I are under the same insurance program that he is, then we are helping to pay his fees. Suddenly, we and our insurance company want to know whether he needs that much treatment and whether the treatment is effective. Generally, insurance companies will pay for more treatment if someone has a diagnosed mental disorder. They limit the treatment to a moderate number of sessions and support only therapies that appear to be effective according to the best available evidence. The consequences have been, as you might guess:

- Therapists have listed more and more diagnoses of mental disorder so that more clients can qualify for insurance help. The previous module mentioned the huge number of diagnoses listed in *DSM-IV*, and now you understand why.
- Therapists have found ways to provide briefer and cheaper treatments, as we shall consider later in this module.
- Psychologists have conducted extensive research on the effectiveness of psychotherapy. Again, you will read about that research later in this module.
- Psychologists have made their treatment more systematic. Many follow published manuals that specify exactly how to treat various disorders.

Psychotherapists today employ a great variety of methods. Different therapists treating the same problem approach it in strikingly different ways. We shall review some of the most common types of therapy, exploring what they have in common as well as how they differ.

CONCEPT CHECK ☑

6. What is one major reason psychotherapists have added so many diagnoses to *DSM-IV*? (Check your answer on page 603.)

---

[1] Quote from "Observation" by Dorothy Parker, copyright 1928, renewed © 1956 by Dorothy Parker from *The Portable Dorothy Parker*, by Dorothy Parker, introduction by Brendan Gill. Used by permission of Viking Penguin, a division of Penguin Books USA, Inc.

Psychoanalysis

Psychodynamic therapies *attempt to relate personality to the interplay of conflicting impulses within the individual, including some that the individual may not consciously recognize.* For example, both Sigmund Freud's procedure (looking for sexual motives) and Alfred Adler's procedure (looking for power and superiority motives) are considered psychodynamic despite the differences between them. Here we focus on the procedure developed by Freud, although its practitioners have modified and developed it further since Freud's time.

Psychoanalysis, the first of the "talk" therapies, is *a method based on identifying unconscious thoughts and emotions and bringing them to consciousness to help people understand their thoughts and actions.* Psychoanalysis is therefore described as an "insight-oriented therapy" in contrast to therapies that focus on changing thoughts and behaviors (Figure 15.2). Psychoanalysis was the dominant form of psychotherapy in the United States in the mid-1900s. Over the years it has declined in popularity and influence in the United States, although it remains more widespread in several European countries.

Freud believed that psychological problems result from unconscious thought processes and that the way to control self-defeating behavior is to make those processes conscious. Bringing them to consciousness, he thought, would produce **catharsis,** *a release of pent-up emotions associated with unconscious thoughts and memories.* Among Freud's methods of

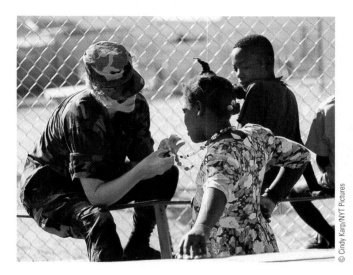

▌ A psychotherapist, like this military psychologist in a Haitian refugee camp, tries to help people overcome problems.

bringing unconscious material to consciousness were free association and transference. He also used dream analysis, as discussed in Chapter 5.

Free Association

In **free association** *the client starts thinking about a particular symptom or problem and then reports everything that comes to mind—a word, a phrase, a visual image.* The client is instructed not to omit or censor anything or even try to speak in complete sentences. The psychoanalyst listens for links and themes that might tie the patient's fragmentary remarks together. The assumption is that nothing happens without a cause, and every jump from one thought to another reveals a relationship between them.

Here is a paraphrased excerpt from a session of free-association:

> A man begins by describing a conference he had with his boss the previous day. He did not like the boss's policy, but he was in no position to contradict the boss. He dreamed something about an ironing board, but that was all he remembered of the dream. He comments that his wife has been complaining about the way their maid irons. He thinks his wife is being unfair; he hopes she does not fire the maid. He complains that his boss did not give him credit for some work he did recently. He recalls a childhood episode: He jumped off a cupboard and bounced off his mother's behind while she was leaning over to do some ironing. She told his father, who gave him a spanking. His father never let him explain; he was always too strict. (Munroe, 1955, p. 39)

To a psychoanalyst, the links in this story suggest that the man is associating his wife with his mother. His wife was unfair to the maid about the ironing, just as his mother had been unfair to him. Moreover, his

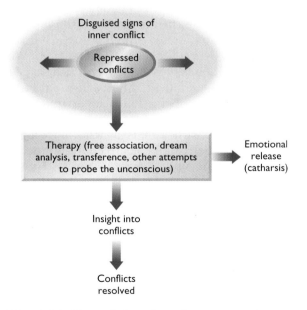

FIGURE 15.2 The goal of psychoanalysis is to resolve psychological problems by bringing to awareness the unconscious thought processes that created the difficulty. *Analysis* literally means "to loosen or break up, to look at the parts."

boss is like his father, never giving him a chance to explain his errors and never giving him credit for what he did well.

Transference

Some clients express love or hatred for their therapist because he or she reminds them of someone else. Psychoanalysts call this inappropriate reaction **transference**; they mean that clients are *transferring onto the therapist the behaviors and feelings they originally established toward their father, mother, or other important person in their lives.* Transference often provides clues to the client's feelings about that person.

Psychoanalysts offer **interpretations** of what the client says—that is, they *explain the underlying meaning*—and may even argue with the client about interpretations. They may regard the client's disagreement as resistance. For example, a client who has begun to touch on an extremely anxiety-provoking topic may turn the conversation to something trivial or may simply "forget" to come to the next session.

Psychoanalysts today modify Freud's approach in many ways. The goal is still to bring about a major reorganization of the personality, changing a person from the inside out, by helping people understand the hidden reasons behind their actions.

CONCEPT CHECK ☑

7. Name at least two methods psychoanalysts use to try to gain access to the unconscious mind. (Check your answer on page 603.)

Behavior Therapy

Behavior therapists assume that human behavior is learned and that someone can extinguish the learned response or learn a competing response. They identify the behavior that needs to be changed, such as a phobia or an addiction, and then set about changing it through reinforcement and other principles of learning. They may try to understand the causes of the behavior as a first step toward changing it, but unlike psychoanalysts, they are more interested in changing behaviors than in understanding their hidden meanings.

Behavior therapy *begins with clear, well-defined behavioral goals, such as eliminating test anxiety or breaking a bad habit, and then attempts to achieve those goals through learning.* Setting clear goals enables the therapist to judge whether the therapy is succeeding. If the client shows no im-

provement after a few sessions, the therapist tries a different procedure.

One example of behavior therapy is for children who wet the bed long after the usual age of toilet training. Most of them outgrow the problem, but it occasionally lingers to age 5, 10, or even into the teens. Many bedwetters have small bladders and thus have difficulty getting through the night without urinating. Also, many are unusually deep sleepers who do not wake up when they need to urinate (Stegat, 1975).

The most effective procedure uses classical conditioning to train the child to wake up at night when the bladder is full (Houts, Berman, & Abramson, 1994). A small battery-powered device is attached to the child's underwear at night (Figure 15.3). When the child urinates, the device detects the moisture and produces a pulsing vibration that awakens the child. (Alternative

FIGURE 15.3 A small device called a Potty Pager fits into a child's underwear and produces a vibration when it becomes moist. This awakens the child, who then learns to awaken when the bladder is full.

devices work on the same principle but produce loud noises.) The vibration acts as an unconditioned stimulus (UCS) that evokes the unconditioned response (UCR) of waking up. In this instance the body itself generates the conditioned stimulus (CS): the sensation produced by a full bladder (Figure 15.4). Whenever that sensation is present, it serves as a signal that the vibration is imminent. After a few pairings (or more), the sensation of a full bladder is enough to wake the child.

Actually, the situation is a little more complicated because the child is positively reinforced with praise for waking up to use the toilet. Thus, the process includes both classical and operant conditioning. Training with an alarm or vibration eliminates bedwetting in most children, sometimes after as little as one night.

CONCEPT CHECK ☑

8. Contrast the goals and methods of behavior therapy with those of psychoanalysis. (Check your answer on page 603.)

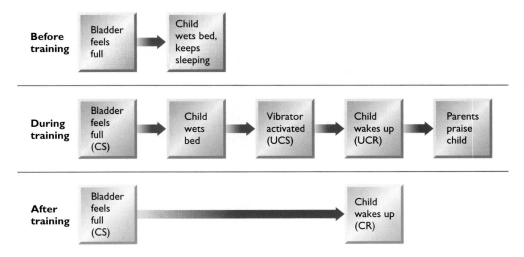

FIGURE 15.4 A child can be trained not to wet the bed by using classical conditioning techniques. At first, the sensation of a full bladder (the CS) produces no response, and the child wets the bed. This causes a vibration or other alarm (the UCS), and the child wakes up (the UCR). By associating the sensation of a full bladder with a vibration, the child soon begins waking up to the sensation of a full bladder alone and will not wet the bed.

Therapies That Focus on Thoughts and Beliefs

Suppose someone asks for your opinion on something and then asks someone else also. How do you react? You might think, "It's perfectly reasonable to get several opinions." Or you might feel hurt by the implication that your opinion wasn't trusted, wasn't good enough. Suppose someone invites several of your friends to a party but not you. Do you shrug your shoulders or do you take it as an insult? Your emotions depend not just on the events of life but on how you interpret them. Some therapists focus on the thoughts and beliefs that underlie emotional reactions. Unlike psychoanalysts, these therapists are more concerned about what their clients are thinking right now than about the early experiences that led to those thoughts.

Cognitive Therapies

Cognitive therapy *seeks to improve people's psychological well-being by changing their thoughts and beliefs—their cognitions* (Beck, 1976; Hollon & Beck, 1979). A cognitive therapist works to identify distressing thoughts and encourages the client to explore the evidence behind them. Usually, the client discovers that the beliefs are unjustified. Cognitive therapy also encourages people to monitor their daily activities and determine which ones provide opportunities for pleasure or a sense of accomplishment. The therapist helps the client overcome specific problems, such as poor social skills, and take a more active role in life.

(We shall discuss cognitive therapy for depression in Chapter 16.)

A related approach, **rational-emotive behavior therapy,** *assumes that thoughts (rationality) lead to emotions. The problem therefore is not the unpleasant emotions themselves, but the irrational thoughts that lead to them.* Rational-emotive therapists believe that abnormal behavior often results from irrational "internal sentences" such as these (Ellis, 1987):

- I must perform certain tasks successfully.
- I must perform well at all times.
- I must have the approval of certain people at all times.
- Others must treat me fairly and with consideration.
- I must live under easy, gratifying conditions.

The word *must* makes these beliefs irrational. Rational-emotive therapists try to identify irrational beliefs (which people may never have verbalized) and then contradict them. They urge clients to substitute other more realistic internal sentences. Here is an excerpt from a rational-emotive therapy session with a 25-year-old physicist:

Client: The whole trouble is that I am really a phony. I am living under false pretenses. And the longer it goes on, the more people praise me and make a fuss over my accomplishments, the worse I feel.

Therapist: What do you mean you are a phony? I thought that you told me, during our last session, that your work has been examined at another laboratory and that some of the people there think your ideas are of revolutionary importance.

Client: But I have wasted so much time. I could be doing very much better. . . . Remember that book I told you I was writing . . . it's been three weeks now since I've spent any time on it. And this is simple stuff that I should be able to do with my left hand while I am writing a technical paper with my right. I have heard Bob Oppenheimer reel off stuff extemporaneously to a bunch of newspaper reporters that is twice as good as what I am mightily laboring on in this damned book!

Therapist: Perhaps so. And perhaps you're not quite as good—yet—as Oppenheimer or a few other outstanding people in your field. But the real point, it seems to me, is that . . . here you are, at just twenty-five, with a Ph.D. in a most difficult field, with an excellent job, much good work in process, and what well may be a fine professional paper and a good popular book also in progress. And just because you're not another Oppenheimer or Einstein quite yet, you're savagely berating yourself.

Client: Well, shouldn't I be doing much better than I am?

Therapist: No, why the devil should you? As far as I can see, you are not doing badly at all. But your major difficulty—the main cause of your present unhappiness—is your utterly perfectionistic criteria for judging your performance. (Ellis & Harper, 1961, pp. 99–100)

CONCEPT CHECK ☑

9. How does the concept behind rational-emotive therapy compare to the James-Lange theory of emotions discussed in Chapter 12? (Check your answer on page 603.)

Cognitive-Behavior Therapy

Many therapists combine important features of both behavior therapy and cognitive therapy to form **cognitive-behavior therapy.** Cognitive-behavior therapists *set explicit goals for changing people's behavior, but they place more emphasis than most behavior therapists do on changing people's interpretation of their situation.* For example, most of us become very upset if we see a video news report showing a fatal automobile accident; we would be much less upset if someone told us that the film was a special-effects simulation (Meichenbaum, 1995). Similarly, cognitive-behavior therapists try to help clients distinguish between serious problems and imagined or exaggerated problems. They help clients change their interpretations of past events, current concerns, and future possibilities. Cognitive-behavior therapy has become one of

▌ Fictional tragedies in films, like the one in *Con Air*, are far less disturbing than real ones. The impact of any event depends not just on the event itself but also on its context and how we interpret it.

the most widespread forms of therapy in the United States.

Humanistic Therapy

As we saw in Chapter 13, humanistic psychologists believe that people can decide deliberately what kind of person to be and that we naturally strive to achieve our full potential. However, people sometimes learn to dislike themselves because others criticize and reject them. They become distressed by the **incongruence** *(mismatch) between their perceptions of their real self and their ideal self.* According to humanistic therapists, once people are freed from the inhibiting influences of a rejecting society, they can solve their own problems.

The best-known version of humanistic therapy is **person-centered therapy,** pioneered by Carl Rogers, which is also known as *nondirective* or *client-centered* therapy. *The therapist listens to the client with total acceptance and unconditional positive regard.* Most of the time, the therapist paraphrases what the client has said to clarify it, thus conveying the message, "I'm trying to understand your experience from your point of view." The therapist strives to be genuine, empathic, and caring, rarely offering any interpretation or advice. Here is an example (shortened from Rogers, 1951, pp. 46–47):

Client: I've never said this before to anyone. This is a terrible thing to say, but if I could just find some glorious cause that I could give my life for I would be happy. I guess maybe I haven't the guts—or the strength—to kill myself—and I just don't want to live.

Counselor: At the present time things look so black to you that you can't see much point in living.

Client: Yes. I wish people hated me, because then I could turn away from them and could blame them. But no, it is all in my hands. I either fight whatever it is that holds me in this terrible conflict, or retreat clear back to the security of my dream world where I could do things, have clever friends, be a pretty wonderful sort of person.

Counselor: It's really a tough struggle, digging into this like you are, and at times the shelter of your dream world looks more attractive and comfortable.

Client: My dream world or suicide.

Counselor: Your dream world or something more permanent than dreams.

Client: Yes. (A long pause. Complete change of voice.) So I don't see why I should waste your time. I'm not worth it. What do you think?

Counselor: It's up to you, Gil. It isn't wasting my time. I'd be glad to see you, whenever you come, but it's how you feel about it. If you want to come twice a week, once a week, it's up to you.

Client: You're not going to suggest that I come in oftener? You're not alarmed and think I ought to come in every day until I get out of this?

Counselor: I believe you are able to make your own decision. I'll see you whenever you want to come.

Client: I don't believe you are alarmed about . . . I see. I may be afraid of myself, but you aren't afraid for me.

The therapist provides an atmosphere in which the client can freely explore feelings of guilt, anxiety, and hostility. By accepting the client's feelings, the therapist conveys the message, "You can make your own decisions. Now that you are more aware of certain problems, you can deal with them constructively yourself." Few therapists today rely purely on person-centered therapy, but most users of other therapy methods have adopted its emphasis on the close, caring, honest relationship between therapist and client (Hill & Nakayama, 2000).

CONCEPT CHECK ☑

10. Answer the following questions with reference to psychoanalysis, cognitive therapy, humanistic therapy, and behavior therapy.
    a. With which type of therapy is the therapist least likely to offer advice and interpretations of behavior?
    b. Which type focuses more on changing what people do than on exploring what they think?

c. Which two types of therapy try to change what people think? (Check your answers on page 603.)

Family Systems Therapy

In **family systems therapy,** *the guiding assumptions are that most people's problems develop in a family setting and that the best way to deal with them is to improve family relationships and communication.* Family systems therapy is not an alternative to other forms of therapy; a family therapist can use behavior therapy, cognitive therapy, or other techniques. What distinguishes family therapists is that they prefer to talk with two or more members of a family together. Even when they do talk with just one person, they focus on how that individual fits into the family and how other family members react to him or her. Solving the problem requires changing the family dynamics as well as any individual's behavior (Clarkin & Carpenter, 1995; Rohrbaugh, Shoham, Spungen, & Steinglass, 1995).

For example, a young woman with anorexia nervosa (as described in Chapter 10) may have excessively demanding parents or other family difficulties. Treating only the woman with anorexia would be pointless. A therapist needs to enlist her parents' help to monitor her eating without blame, criticism, or dominance (Eisler et al., 2000).

© Express Newspapers/Archive Photos

▌ Family therapists treat anorexia nervosa by trying to get the parents to supervise the patient's feeding, but without criticism or blame.

For another example, a young man who had been caught stealing a car was taken to a family therapist who asked to talk with the parents as well. As it turned out, the father had been a heavy drinker until his boss pressured him to quit drinking and join Alcoholics Anonymous. Until then the mother had made most of the family decisions in close consultation with her son, who had become almost a substitute husband. When the father quit drinking, he began to resume his authority within the family, and his son came to resent him. The mother felt less needed and grew depressed. Each member of the family had problems that they could not resolve separately. The therapist worked to help the father improve his relationship with both his son and his wife and to help all three find satisfying roles within the family (Foley, 1984).

Other Trends in Psychotherapy

Hundreds of types of therapy are available, including some that are quite different from the five discussed thus far (see Table 15.3). About half of all U.S. psychotherapists profess no strong allegiance to any single form of therapy. Instead, they practice **eclectic therapy,** meaning that they *use a combination of methods and approaches.* An eclectic therapist might use behavior therapy with one client and rational-emotive therapy with another or else start with one therapy and then shift to another if the first is inef-

fective. The therapist would probably borrow insights from several approaches, including person-centered therapy's emphasis on a caring relationship between therapist and client. Today, most therapists regard themselves as eclectic (Wachtel, 2000).

Because health insurance companies insist on limiting costs, psychotherapists have sought methods for quick and inexpensive help, such as brief therapy and group therapy. Self-help groups provide a no-cost alternative.

Brief Therapy

Some types of psychotherapy require a major commitment of time and money. You might see a therapist for a 50-minute session once a week, perhaps three to five times a week with psychoanalysis. The cost of each session varies, but it is seldom cheap. A physician who sees many patients per hour—a dermatologist, for example—might charge a moderate amount per visit, but a therapist who sees just one person per hour charges more. If the therapy will continue "as long as necessary," it might drag on for years.

However, most clients do not need such prolonged treatment. About half of all people who enter psychotherapy show significant improvement within 8 sessions, and three fourths improve within 26 sessions (Howard, Kopta, Krause, & Orlinsky, 1986). Insurance companies will pay for only a limited number of sessions.

TABLE 15.3 Comparison of Five Types of Psychotherapy

Type of Psychotherapy	Theory of What Causes Psychological Disorders	Goal of Treatment	Therapeutic Methods	Role of Therapist
Psychoanalysis	Unconscious thoughts and motivations	To bring unconscious thoughts to consciousness to achieve insight	Free association, dream analysis, and other methods of probing the unconscious mind	To interpret associations
Cognitive therapies	Irrational beliefs and unrealistic goals	To establish realistic goals, expectations, and interpretations of a situation	Dialog with the therapist	To help the client reexamine assumptions
Humanistic (person-centered) therapy	Reactions to a rejecting society; incongruence between self-concept and ideal self	To enable client to make personal decisions; to promote self-acceptance	Client-centered interviews	To focus the client's attention; to provide unconditional positive regard
Behavior therapy	Learned inappropriate maladaptive behaviors	To change behaviors	Positive reinforcement and other learning techniques	To develop, direct, and evaluate the behavior therapy program
Family system therapy	Distorted communication and confused roles within a family	To improve the life of each individual by improving functioning of the family	Counseling sessions with the whole family or with the individual talking about life in the family	To promote better family communication and understanding

As a result many therapists place limits on the duration of therapy. At the start of **brief therapy,** or *time-limited therapy, the therapist and client reach an agreement about what they can expect from each other and how long the treatment will last*—such as once per week for 2 months (Koss & Butcher, 1986). The therapy focuses on using the client's existing strengths to overcome difficulties. As the deadline approaches, both therapist and client are strongly motivated to reach a successful conclusion. (The same issue arose in the motivation chapter. Without deadlines, few people apply themselves diligently.)

Moreover, with a deadline that's agreed on in advance, clients do not feel deserted or rejected when the therapy ends. They may return for an occasional extra session months later, but for a time they must get along without help. Any client who fails to make progress by the deadline should consider going to a different therapist. Most clients with mild problems respond well to brief therapy.

Unfortunately, however, many HMOs have insisted on extremely brief therapy, in some cases as few as three sessions. Even a few sessions can be better than none, so the HMOs do make help available for many distressed people (Hoyt & Austad, 1992). However, many need more help than their insurance provides. Economically speaking, it is of course impossible to maximize the quality of care and minimize the cost at the same time. Working out a cost-effective solution is a serious challenge.

Group Therapy

The pioneers of psychotherapy saw their clients individually. Individual psychotherapy has advantages, such as privacy. However, therapists today frequently treat clients in groups. **Group therapy** is *administered to a group of people all at once.* It first became popular

as a method of providing help to people who could not afford individual sessions. (Spreading the costs among five to ten people reduces the cost for each.) Eventually, therapists found that group therapy has other advantages as well. Just meeting other people with similar problems can be reassuring. People learn, "I am not so odd after all." Also, many clients seek help because of failed relationships or because they have trouble dealing with other people. A group therapy session enables them to examine how they relate to others, to practice better social skills, and to receive feedback from a variety of people (Ballinger & Yalom, 1995).

(Consider an analogy to education. Would you prefer your professor to teach you privately instead of in a large class? Perhaps so, but the cost of your tuition would sky-rocket. Besides, discussions with your fellow students are a valuable part of your education.)

Self-Help Groups

A **self-help group,** such as Alcoholics Anonymous, *operates much like group therapy, except without a therapist.* Each participant both gives and receives help. People who have experienced a problem themselves can offer special insights to others with the same problem. They are especially well prepared when someone says, "You just don't understand." They reply, "Oh, yes, we do!" Self-help groups have another advantage: The members are available whenever someone needs help, without an appointment and without charge.

Some self-help groups are composed of current or former mental patients. The members feel a need to talk to others who have gone through a similar experience, either in addition to or instead of seeing a therapist. For example, the Mental Patients' Association in Canada consists of former patients who were frustrated about their treatment (or lack of treatment) in mental hospitals (Chamberlin, 1978). Members share

a

b

▌ (a) Individual therapy offers complete privacy and the opportunity to pursue individual problems in depth. (b) In group therapy participants can explore their ways of relating to other people.

experiences, provide support, and work together to defend the rights and welfare of mental patients.

The ultimate in self-help is to deal with your own problems without any therapist or group. In a series of studies, James Pennebaker and his colleagues have found that people with mild problems can do themselves an amazing amount of good just by organizing their thoughts about their emotional difficulties. Research participants have been randomly assigned to two groups. One group writes about their intense and difficult emotional experiences for 15 minutes on 3 or more days; the other group spends the same time writing about unemotional events. The people writing about their emotions consistently show improved mental and physical health over the next few months, especially those with much variation and flexibility in what they write (Campbell & Pennebaker, 2003; Pennebaker & Seagal, 1999). Apparently, writing about a difficult experience helps people to make sense of it and eventually put it behind them. In many cases writing about emotions prompts people to make decisions and change their way of life. In short, for mild problems you might be a good therapist for yourself.

CONCEPT CHECK ✓

11. Brief therapy is a goal or policy for many therapists. Why would it be less important in self-help groups? (Check your answer on page 603.)

CRITICAL THINKING:
WHAT'S THE EVIDENCE?
How Effective Is Psychotherapy?

The rise of HMOs and other insurance programs heightened interest in measuring the effectiveness of psychotherapy. Hans Eysenck (1952) pointed out that most of the people who receive no therapy neverthe-

less improve in a year or two. (Most psychological crises are temporary.) *Improvement without therapy* is called **spontaneous remission.** Psychotherapy is effective only if it does better than what we could expect by spontaneous remission.

In other chapters each What's the Evidence? section has highlighted a particular study. Here the section highlights a general research approach. Hundreds of research studies similar to this have been conducted, although they vary in their details (Kazdin, 1995).

Hypothesis Psychologically troubled people who receive psychotherapy will show greater improvements in their condition than similar people who do not receive therapy.

Method For the results to be meaningful, participants must be randomly assigned to the therapy and nontherapy groups. Comparing people who sought therapy to those who did not seek it would be unfair because the two groups might differ in the severity of their problems or their motivation for overcoming them. In the best studies, people who contact a clinic about receiving therapy are all given a preliminary examination and then randomly assigned to receive therapy at once or to be placed on a waiting list for therapy later. A few months later, the investigators compare the amount of improvement shown by the therapy group and the waiting-list group.

How should the investigators measure the amount of improvement? Researchers cannot rely on the judgments of the therapists; after all, they want to demonstrate the effectiveness of their procedures. For similar reasons researchers cannot ask the clients for an unbiased opinion; most clients exaggerate how much they improved (Safer & Keuler, 2002). Therefore, the researchers may ask a "blind" observer (see Chapter 2) to evaluate each client without knowing who has received therapy and who has been on the waiting list. Or they may ask each person to take a

▌ Because everyone's moods and effectiveness fluctuate over time, an apparent improvement between (a) the start of therapy and (b) the end is hard to interpret. How much of the improvement is due to the therapy and how much would have occurred even without it?

a

b

standardized personality test, such as the MMPI. None of these measures are perfect, of course, and they probably overlook some kinds of improvement.

Many experiments compare a group that received therapy to a control group that was on the waiting list. Other experiments, however, have compared groups receiving different kinds of therapy or different frequencies of therapy.

Results Here we do not focus on the results of any one study. Most experiments have included only a modest number of people, such as 10 or 20 receiving therapy and a similar number on the waiting list. To draw a conclusion, we need to pool the results from a great many similar experiments. Psychologists use a method called **meta-analysis,** *taking the results of many experiments, weighting each one in proportion to the number of participants, and determining the overall average effect.* According to one meta-analysis that pooled the results of 475 experiments, the average person in therapy shows greater improvement than 80% of similarly troubled people who do not receive therapy (M. L. Smith, Glass, & Miller, 1980). Figure 15.5 illustrates this effect.

Interpretation Every study has limitations, and even a collection of 475 studies has limitations. In particular, most research has dealt with relatively mild disorders, mainly because it seems unethical to assign anyone suffering from severe problems to a waiting list. Most research deals with fairly brief treatments, again largely because it is hard to keep anyone in a waiting-list control group for more than a few months. Also, most of the research has examined behavior therapy or cognitive therapy because these methods use consistent methods and set specific goals. It is more difficult to evaluate psychoanalysis or person-centered therapy.

FIGURE 15.5 According to one review of 475 studies, the average person receiving psychotherapy shows more improvement than do 80% of similar, randomly assigned people who are not in therapy. This comparison lumps together all kinds of therapy and all kinds of disorders. *(From* The Benefits of Psychotherapy, *by M. L. Smith, G. V. Glass, and T. I. Miller. Copyright © 1980. The Johns Hopkins University Press. Reprinted by permission.)*

One could easily complain that investigators have invested a great deal of effort for rather little payoff. After 475 experiments, we can confidently say that therapy is usually better than no therapy for relatively mild psychological disorders. This conclusion is like saying that, if you are ill, medicine is usually better than no medicine. However, even if this conclusion seems unimpressive, it does pave the way for further, more detailed studies about how therapy produces its benefits and so forth. It also tells us something about the magnitude of psychotherapy's effects: The effects are real but usually not huge. Most clients benefit but perhaps not as much as they had hoped.

CONCEPT CHECK ☑

12. Although well-designed experiments on psychotherapy use a blind observer to rate clients' mental health, double-blind studies are difficult or impossible. Why? (Check your answer on page 603.)

Comparing Therapies and Therapists

Next we would like to know which kinds of therapy are most effective for which disorders. The practical problem for researchers is that therapists use hundreds of types of therapy for hundreds of psychological disorders. To test each form of therapy on each possible disorder would require tens of thousands of experiments, not counting replications. Furthermore, many clients have several problems, not just one, and most therapists use an eclectic trial-and-error approach instead of a single well-defined therapy (Goldfried & Wolfe, 1996).

Many studies have proceeded despite these difficulties, and they lead to a stunningly simple conclusion: For the disorders studied, researchers find only small differences in effectiveness between one type of therapy and another (Leichsenring & Leibing, 2003; Lipsey & Wilson, 1993; Stiles, Shapiro, & Elliott, 1986; Wampold et al., 1997). Even those differences are sometimes hard to interpret. For example, in some studies one kind of treatment produced better immediate benefits and another produced greater long-term benefits, so the apparent advantage depended on the time of measurement (Sandell et al., 1999). We should view this research with some caution, as it has dealt mainly with mild to moderate disorders suitable for brief therapy and mostly with behavioral and cognitive therapies. The effectiveness of psychoanalysis, for example, remains more controversial.

Furthermore, in Chapter 16 we shall encounter examples in which one type of therapy appears to have the advantage, such as behavior therapy for phobias and cognitive therapy for depression. However, even in these cases, the differences between one form of therapy and another are small, and the interesting point remains that therapies differing widely in their assumptions and methods produce results far more similar than most psychologists had expected.

Researchers also have compared the effectiveness of therapists with different kinds of training. The U.S. magazine *Consumer Reports* (1995) surveyed its readers about their mental health and their contact with psychotherapy. Of the thousands who said they had sought help for a mental-health problem within the previous 3 years, most said they were satisfied with the treatment and thought it had helped them. For measuring the effectiveness of psychotherapy, this study has some obvious problems: the lack of a random sample, the lack of a control group, and reliance on clients to evaluate their own improvement (Jacobson & Christensen, 1996). Nevertheless, the results indicated that people reported about equal satisfaction and benefits from talking with a psychiatrist, a psychologist, or a social worker (Seligman, 1995). They reported somewhat less satisfaction from consulting a marriage counselor or a general-practice physician (see Figure 15.6). A later survey of psychotherapy clients in Germany yielded similar results (Hartmann & Zepf, 2003).

The same general pattern emerged in a variety of other studies with different research methods: The type of therapist is not critical to the amount of improvement. Even the amount of therapist experience makes little difference in most studies (Christensen & Jacobson, 1994; Dawes, 1994).

▌ Just talking to a sympathetic listener, even someone without training, is helpful for many people with mild to moderate problems.

Is the conclusion, then, that if you are psychologically troubled, you may as well talk to your next-door neighbor as to a psychotherapist? No, for several reasons:

* The research comparing inexperienced to experienced therapists has examined clients with mild problems. We cannot assume that the same results would hold for more disabling conditions.
* Few of us know someone with enough patience to listen to hours of our personal ramblings.
* Conversation with a professional psychotherapist is confidential (except under special circumstances, such as if you tell your therapist you are planning to kill someone). You are less sure that a friend will keep your secrets.
* A well-trained psychotherapist can recognize symptoms of a brain tumor or other medical disorder and can refer you to an appropriate medical specialist.
* Clinical psychologists know enough about therapy research to avoid untested "fad" treatments (Maki & Syman, 1997).

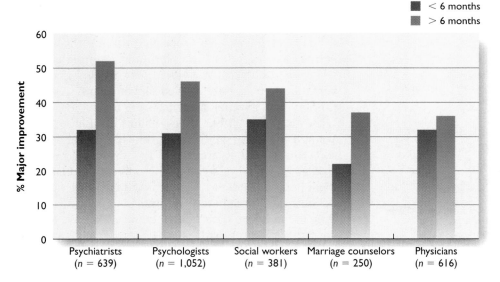

FIGURE 15.6 The percentage of *Consumer Reports* respondents who said they experienced great improvement in the problem that led them to treatment. *(From "The Effectiveness of Psychotherapy: The Consumer Reports Study," by M. E. P. Seligman,* American Psychologist, *1995, 50, 965–974. Copyright © 1995 by the American Psychological Association. Reprinted by permission.)*

In short, although you would probably benefit by talking to almost any sympathetic listener, there are important advantages to seeing a professional psychotherapist (Strupp, 1996).

Is More Treatment Better?

If seeing a therapist once per week for 3 months is helpful, would meeting twice per week for a year help even more? How much is the right amount?

Respondents in the *Consumer Reports* (1995) study were asked how much treatment they received and how much it helped them. Generally, those who received longer treatment reported that it helped them more. However, perhaps those who stayed in treatment the longest were those with the greatest problems at the start and therefore had the greatest room for improvement.

A somewhat better research design examines a single group of clients repeatedly as all of them progress through a given number of therapy sessions. Figure 15.7 shows the results of one such study. According to both the researchers and the clients themselves, most clients showed fairly rapid progress at first and then gradual additional progress (Howard et al., 1986). Evidently, prolonged treatment is at least somewhat more beneficial than brief treatment on the average.

An elaborate study of this issue was a 5-year study conducted at Fort Bragg, North Carolina. A government-supported program provided free clinical services for every teenager or child who needed psychological help and who had a parent in the military. Each client had a case manager who determined what treatment plan was best, made sure that the client received every necessary type of help, and coordinated all the service providers to make sure that each one knew what the others were doing. The goal was to demonstrate that a well-planned, integrated program would be highly effective and perhaps even inexpensive because it would avoid wasteful overlap of services. Results were compared to those in a similar community that offered the usual, less coordinated services. The result? The integrated program at Fort Bragg was no more beneficial, just more expensive (Bickman, 1996). We should not draw too strong a conclusion from this study or from any other single study. Still, most people had expected the integrated program to show clear advantages, and the results seem to imply that more therapy is not always better.

Similarities Among Psychotherapeutic Methods

What should we conclude from the observation that different forms of psychotherapy seem to be similar in their effectiveness? Consider an analogy to education: Suppose researchers found that, on the average, students learn about equally from lecture courses as from discussion classes, from experienced professors as from first-time instructors, and from one textbook as another. I, personally, would not be happy about that finding. As a professor and textbook author, I like to think that students learn *way* more from my lectures and textbook than from anyone else's! However, I should not be terribly surprised by those results. How much a student learns depends mainly on the student. A better lecture, a better class organization, or a better textbook presumably makes some difference, but it is surely a small difference compared to the difference between one student and another. Similarly, how much a client benefits from psychotherapy varies enormously depending on the client, and the difference between one therapist and another is relatively small and hard to measure (Bohart, 2000).

The similarity in outcomes among different forms of psychotherapy implies that they have much in common despite the differences in their assumptions, methods, and goals. One feature is that all rely on a "therapeutic alliance"—a relationship between therapist and client characterized by acceptance, caring, respect, and attention. This relationship provides social support that helps clients deal with their problems and acquire social skills that they can apply to other relationships (Krupnick et al., 1994).

Moreover, in nearly all forms of therapy, clients talk openly and honestly about their beliefs and emotions,

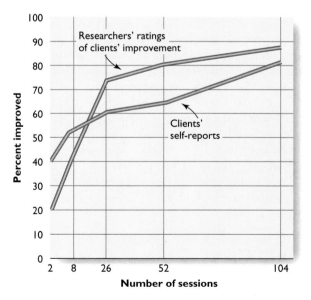

FIGURE 15.7 The relationship of the number of psychotherapy sessions to the percentage of clients who improved. *(From "The Dose-Effect Relationship in Psychotherapy," by K. I. Howard et al., American Psychologist, 1986, 41, 159–164. Copyright © 1986 by the American Psychological Association. Reprinted by permission of the author.)*

relationships with family members, and other issues that people ordinarily keep secret. They examine aspects of themselves that they usually take for granted; in so doing they gain self-understanding. Because of the expectation of self-disclosure, psychotherapy as practiced in North America and Europe does not transplant readily into other cultures. For example, most Chinese would consider it shameful to discuss personal or family matters with a stranger (Bond, 1991).

The mere fact of entering therapy, whatever the method, improves clients' morale. The therapist conveys the message "you are going to get better." Clients gain confidence in their ability to cope with and overcome their problems. The expectation of improvement can lead to improvement.

Finally, every form of therapy requires clients to commit themselves to changes in their lifestyle. Simply by coming to the therapy session, they reaffirm their commitment to feel less depressed, to overcome their fears, or to conquer some bad habit. They work on that change between sessions so that they can report at the next session, "I've been doing a little better lately." Improvement probably depends more on what clients do between sessions than on anything in the sessions themselves.

CONCEPT CHECK ☑

13. Name four ways in which nearly all forms of psychotherapy are similar. (Check your answer on page 603.)

Advice for Potential Clients

At some point you or someone close to you may be interested in seeing a psychotherapist. If so, here are some points to remember:

- Consulting a therapist does not mean that something is wrong with you. Many people merely want to talk with someone about difficulties they are facing.
- If you live in the United States, you can look in the white pages of your telephone directory for the Mental Health Association. Call and ask for a recommendation. You can specify how much you can pay, what kind of problem you have, and even what kind of therapist you prefer.
- Other things being equal, you may do best with a therapist from your own cultural background (Sue, 1998). Therapists are trained to be sensitive to people from different backgrounds, but a communication barrier often remains nevertheless. For example, certain responses to grief or fear that are considered abnormal by many Western psychotherapists are considered normal in many other cultures.

- You might prefer a therapist who shares your religious beliefs or lack of them (Worthington, Kurusu, McCullough & Sandage, 1996).
- Be skeptical of any therapist who seems overconfident. Clinical experience does not give anyone quick access to your private thoughts.
- Expect at least some improvement within 6 to 8 weeks. If you do not seem to be making progress, ask your therapist why. If you do not receive a convincing answer, consider seeing someone else.

IN CLOSING

Trying to Understand Therapy

As you have seen, therapists differ enormously in their assumptions and methods. A psychoanalyst hopes to uncover your unconscious thoughts, memories, and motives, on the assumption that knowing about them will help solve your problems. A cognitive or behavior therapist is more interested in changing your current thoughts and actions than in dwelling on the past and is skeptical about inferring any unconscious processes. A person-centered therapist provides a warm, supportive setting, in which you can set your own goals and decide for yourself how to achieve them. Despite these major differences, different forms of therapy are all effective and in many studies are almost equally effective. It is as if researchers found that when you are sick, one kind of medicine is as good as another.

Psychotherapy began with psychiatry, a branch of medicine, and we still treat it as analogous to medicine. That is, a client comes with a "disorder" that gets a medical diagnosis, the therapist provides a "treatment," and health insurance pays the bills. In some ways this analogy fails, and therapy is more like education. A client is like a student, and the therapist is like an instructor who tries to provide direction, but the amount of progress depends on the client's own efforts. This is not to say that the therapist is irrelevant; it is hard to doubt that some do a better job than others, just as some professors do. However, the variation between one client and another is greater than the typical difference between one treatment and another.

Summary

- *Psychoanalysis.* Psychoanalysts try to uncover the unconscious reasons behind self-defeating behaviors. To bring the unconscious to consciousness, they rely on free association, dream analysis, and transference. (page 591)
- *Behavior therapy.* Behavior therapists set specific goals for changing a client's behavior and use learn-

ing techniques to help a client achieve those goals. (page 592)

- *Cognitive therapies.* Cognitive therapists try to get clients to give up their irrational beliefs and unrealistic goals and to replace defeatist thinking with more favorable views of themselves and the world. Many therapists combine features of behavior therapy and cognitive therapy, attempting to change people's behaviors by altering how they interpret the situation. (page 593)

- *Humanistic therapy.* Humanistic therapists, including person-centered therapists, assume that, if people accept themselves as they are, they can solve their own problems. Person-centered therapists listen with unconditional positive regard but seldom offer interpretations or advice. (page 594)

- *Family systems therapy.* In many cases an individual's problem is part of an overall disorder of family communications and expectations. Family systems therapists try to work with a whole family. (page 595)

- *Eclectic therapy.* About half of all psychotherapists today call themselves "eclectic." That is, they use a combination of methods depending on the circumstances. (page 596)

- *Brief therapy.* Many therapists set a time limit for the treatment, usually ranging from 2–6 months. Brief therapy is typically about as successful as long-term therapy if the goals are limited. (page 596)

- *Group therapies and self-help groups.* Psychotherapy is sometimes provided to people in groups, often composed of individuals with similar problems. Self-help groups provide sessions similar to group therapy but without a therapist. (page 597)

- *Effectiveness of psychotherapy.* The average troubled person in therapy improves more than at least 80% of the troubled people not in therapy. In general, all therapies appear effective, and the differences among them are small. Psychiatrists, psychologists, and social workers provide approximately equal benefits on the average. (page 598)

- *Similarities among therapies.* A wide variety of therapies share certain features: All rely on a caring relationship between therapist and client. All promote self-understanding. All improve clients' morale. And all require a commitment by clients to try to make changes in their lives. (page 601)

Answers to Concept Checks

6. It is possible to get health insurance to pay for treatment if someone has a diagnosed disorder. (page 590)

7. Psychoanalysts use free association and transference to infer the contents of the unconscious. They also use dream analysis, as discussed in Chapter 5. (page 592)

8. Psychoanalysts try to infer unconscious thoughts and motives and try to trace current behavior to experiences of long ago. Behavior therapists pay little attention to thoughts, conscious or unconscious. They set specific goals and try to change current behavior regardless of whether they understand how the behavior originated. (page 592)

9. Rational-emotive therapy assumes that many thoughts lead to emotions. This assumption is the reverse of the James-Lange theory, which argues that emotion-related changes in the body give rise to thoughts. (page 594)

10. **a.** humanistic therapy;
    b. behavior therapy;
    c. psychoanalysis and cognitive therapy. (page 595)

11. One of the advantages of brief therapy is that it limits the expense. Expense is not an issue for self-help groups because they charge nothing (other than a voluntary contribution toward rental of the facilities). (page 598)

12. A double-blind design requires that neither the subjects nor the observers know which subjects received the experimental treatment and which ones were in the control group. It is not possible to prevent subjects from knowing whether they have received psychotherapy. (It is, of course, possible to use a treatment believed to be ineffective and call it psychotherapy.) (page 599)

13. Nearly all forms of psychotherapy include a "therapeutic alliance" (a close relationship between client and therapist), an effort to understand oneself and discuss personal difficulties openly, an expectation of improvement, and a commitment to make changes in one's life. (page 602)

How should society deal with psychological disorders?

A group of nearsighted people lost in the woods were trying to find their way home. One of the few who wore glasses said, "I think I know the way. Follow me." The others burst into laughter. "That's ridiculous," said one. "How could anybody who needs glasses be our leader?"

In 1972 the Democratic party nominated Senator Thomas Eagleton for vice president of the United States. Shortly after his nomination, he revealed that he had once received psychiatric treatment for depression. He was ridiculed mercilessly: "How could anybody who needed a psychiatrist be our leader?"

As mentioned in the first module, about one third to one half of all people suffer from at least a mild psychological disorder at some point in life. However, many people prefer to struggle along on their own, like a nearsighted person who refuses to wear glasses, rather than seek help.

As a citizen and a voter, you should be aware of issues relating to psychological disorders and therapies: Who, if anyone, should receive psychiatric treatment involuntarily? Should mental patients have the right to refuse treatment? Under what circumstances, if any, should a criminal defendant be acquitted because of "insanity"? Can society as a whole take steps to prevent psychological disorders?

Deinstitutionalization

In the 1800s and early 1900s, growing numbers of people with severe psychological disturbances were confined in large mental hospitals supported by the government (Torrey & Miller, 2001). Most of these hospitals were understaffed and overcrowded. Residents included not only mental patients but also elderly people who could not care for themselves, probably suffering from Alzheimer's disease (Leff, 2002). Hospital attendants cooked the food, washed the laundry, and cared for the residents but did not try to teach them the skills they would need if they were ever to leave. After all, most would never leave. Some hospitals were better than others, but most were grim places.

Beginning in the 1950s and continuing since then, more and more hospitals moved toward **deinstitutionalization**, *the removal of patients from mental hospi-*

Mental hospitals of the mid-1900s were unpleasant warehouses where people received minimal care.

tals, to give them the least restrictive care possible. Only people who were dangerous to themselves or others would stay for long. Others would live at home or in group houses and receive outpatient care as needed at community mental-health centers, which are usually cheaper and more effective than large mental hospitals (Fenton, Hoch, Herrell, Mosher, & Dixon, 2002; Fenton, Mosher, Herrell, & Blyler, 1998). The idea was that troubled people should receive appropriate supervision and care but should also have as much contact as possible with the outside world. As a result of deinstitutionalization policies, as well as the advent of antidepressant and antipsychotic medications, the number of long-term mental patients declined sharply. For example, England and Wales had 130 psychiatric hospitals in 1975 but only 12 in 2000 (Leff, 2002).

Unfortunately, most governments saw deinstitutionalization mainly as a way to save money; they discharged patients from the mental hospitals without planning adequate alternatives. Many people discharged from mental hospitals became homeless, especially those who had lost contact with their relatives and those with substance-abuse problems (Odell & Commander, 2000). Some ended in nursing homes or prisons. Deinstitutionalization was and is a good idea in principle, but only if implemented well, including much supervision and good opportunities for community health care.

I Deinstitutionalization moved people out of mental hospitals, but many received little or no treatment after their release.

CONCEPT CHECK

14. Why did deinstitutionalization seem to be a good idea? For what reason has it often not worked well? (Check your answers on page 609.)

Involuntary Commitment and Treatment

In a democratic society, we treasure both freedom and security. Sometimes these values are in conflict. For example, the right of a person with a psychological disorder to be free may conflict with the right of other people to feel safe and secure.

Imagine someone who mutters incoherently, cannot keep a job, does not pay bills or take care of personal hygiene, bothers the neighbors, and refuses treatment. Should it be possible to require treatment? We can argue this question either way. On the one hand, some of the most seriously disordered people fail to recognize that they have a problem. On the other hand, some families have been known to commit annoying relatives to mental hospitals just to get them out of the way, and some psychiatrists have given strong medications to people with minor problems, doing more harm than good.

Unfortunately, it is difficult to determine who really needs help and who doesn't. In the United States, laws vary from state to state, but typically, people can be involuntarily committed if they are dangerous to

themselves or others or if they are incompetent to take care of their daily needs. In all cases a judge holds a hearing and makes the final decision (Weiner & Wettstein, 1993).

After people have been committed to a mental hospital, voluntarily or involuntarily, they still have the right to refuse treatment (Appelbaum, 1988). According to their psychiatrists, most of the people who refuse treatment are hostile, emotionally withdrawn, and prone to disorganized thinking (Marder et al., 1983). According to the patients themselves, they have good reason to be hostile and withdrawn; the hospital staff is trying to force dangerous treatments upon them. Either can be right in a given case. Studies find that the patients most likely to deny having a problem are those with the mildest problems and those with the most severe problems (Pyne, Bean, & Sullivan, 2001).

Figure 15.8 shows the results of one study that compared patients who refused drug treatment to those who accepted it. Understandably, it can be very difficult to make decisions about enforced treatment.

CRITICAL THINKING:
A STEP FURTHER
Involuntary Treatment

Thomas Szasz (1982) proposed that psychologically "normal" people write a "psychiatric will," specifying what treatments to give them, and what treatments to avoid, if they ever develop a severe psychological disorder. If you wrote such a will, what would you include? Or would you prefer to trust your judgment later, at the onset of the disorder?

The Duty to Protect

Suppose someone tells his psychotherapist that he is planning to kill his former girlfriend. The therapist doubts the threat and ignores it. However, a few days later, the client really does kill his ex-girlfriend . . . who happens to be your sister. Should your family be able to sue the therapist and collect damages?

Before you answer "yes," consider the following. First, psychotherapy is based on a trusting relationship in which the therapist promises to keep the client's comments secret. Second, therapists are seldom certain about which clients are dangerous (Monahan, 1993). Suppose you are a therapist. Over the course of a day, you see eight patients, and three of them say they are so angry they could kill somebody. How do you decide which ones, if any, to take seriously? (Have you yourself ever said you were so mad you could kill someone?)

FIGURE 15.8 (a) People with schizophrenia who refuse drug therapy impress their physicians as being seriously disturbed. High scores indicate greater ratings of disturbance. (b) Patients who refuse drugs rate themselves as dissatisfied with their physicians and their treatments. The higher scores indicate greater satisfaction with treatment. *(Based on data from Marder, et al., 1983.)*

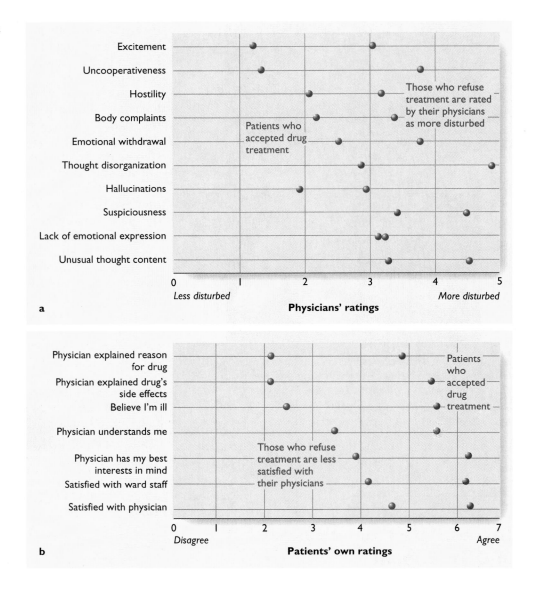

The Insanity Defense

In 1976 a California court ruled in the *Tarasoff* case that *a therapist who has reason to believe that a client is dangerous must break the pledge of confidentiality and warn the endangered person* (Weiner & Wettstein, 1993). A Canadian court made a similar ruling in the case of *Wenden v. Trikha* (Truscott & Crook, 1993). However, applying such rules in practice is difficult because of the uncertainty about dangerousness. The courts have also ruled that the duty to inform applies only if the patient is a threat to a *specific* individual. For example, a therapist is *not* obligated to warn anyone about a drug-abusing client who is an airplane pilot. The client may be a danger to a huge number of people but not to any *specific,* identifiable person (Felthous, 1993). In fact the rules on confidentiality actually prohibit the therapist from informing the pilot's employer! We can sympathize with therapists who are puzzled and confused. So far, the courts have been reluctant to hold therapists legally accountable.

Suppose that, in the midst of an epileptic seizure, you flail your arms about and accidentally knock someone down the stairs, who dies from the fall. Should you be convicted of murder? Of course not; you had no intention to do harm. Now suppose that, in the midst of severely disordered thinking and perception, you attack and kill what appears to be a giant insect but is in fact a human being. Again you intended no harm. You didn't even realize you were attacking a person. Should you be convicted of murder?

The tradition dating back to Roman times has been that you would be "not guilty by reason of insanity." Most people agree with that principle for extreme cases. The problem is where to draw the line. Under what conditions should someone be judged legally insane? *Insanity* is a legal term, not a psycho-

▌ Theodore Kaczynski (a), a brilliant mathematician who once had a promising career, became (b) a recluse who over the course of 17 years mailed bombs that killed 3 and injured 23 others. However, merely being "strange" or committing bizarre acts of violence does not qualify someone as legally insane.

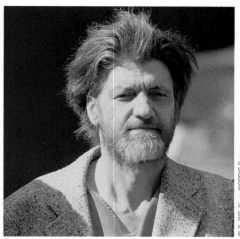

a

b

© Scott Manchester/CORBIS Sygma.

© S. O'Sullivan/CORBIS Sygma.

logical or medical one, and its definition is based on politics more than science.

One point of broad agreement is that the crime itself, no matter how atrocious, does not demonstrate insanity. Jeffrey Dahmer, who was arrested in 1991 after murdering and cannibalizing several men, was ruled sane and sentenced to prison. Theodore Kaczynski, arrested for mailing bombs over decades, refused to plead insanity and probably would not have been ruled insane anyway. Bizarre crimes do not, in themselves, demonstrate insanity. In fact each of these murderers knew what he was doing and tried to avoid getting caught.

In many cases, however, a decision about sanity or insanity is difficult; lawyers, physicians, and psychologists have long struggled to establish a clear and acceptable definition of insanity. Probably the most famous definition, the **M'Naghten rule**, written in Great Britain in 1843, states:

> To establish a defense on the ground of insanity, it must be clearly proved that, at the time of the committing of the act, the party accused was laboring under such a defect of reason, from disease of the mind, as not to know the nature and quality of the act he was doing; or if he did know it, that he did not know he was doing what was wrong. (Shapiro, 1985)

In other words, *to be regarded as insane under the M'Naghten rule, people must be so disordered that they do not understand what they are doing.* Presumably, they would continue the act even if a police officer were standing nearby. Many observers consider that rule too narrow and would like to broaden the definition, but any definition requires a difficult judgment about the defendant's state of mind at the time of the act. To help make that judgment, psychologists and psychiatrists are called as "expert witnesses" to evaluate the defendant's state

of mind. If all the experts agree that the defendant is insane, the prosecution ordinarily accepts the insanity plea. If the experts agree the defendant is not insane, the defense abandons the plea. Therefore, the only insanity cases that come to a jury trial are the difficult cases in which the experts disagree. Those cases are rare. In the United States, fewer than 1% of accused felons plead insanity, and of those, only about 25% are found not guilty (Lymburner & Roesch, 1999). However, those few cases generally receive much media attention, and because people hear about them, they assume such cases are common. (Remember the availability heuristic from Chapter 8.) The insanity defense is just as rare in other countries.

Another common misconception is that defendants found not guilty by reason of insanity simply go free, where they are apt to commit further attacks. People found not guilty by reason of insanity are almost always committed to a mental hospital, and they usually stay at least as long in the hospital as they would have in prison (Silver, 1995).

Several states in the United States have experimented with allowing a verdict of "guilty but mentally ill," intended as a compromise between guilty and not guilty. However, the defendant actually receives the same sentence as if he or she had been simply found guilty and is no more likely to receive psychiatric care in prison than any other convicted person (Lymburner & Roesch, 1999). In short, the guilty but mentally ill verdict is the same as a guilty verdict. An appealing alternative proposal is to specify that anyone found not guilty by reason of insanity must be temporarily hospitalized and, when eventually released, must abide by many conditions and restrictions, similar to those of a released prisoner on parole (Linhorst & Dirks-Linhorst, 1999).

For more information about cases using the insanity defense, as well as other legal cases relevant to psychology, visit this Web site:

bama.ua.edu/~jhooper/tableofc.html

CONCEPT CHECK ☑

15. Someone who has been involuntarily committed to a mental hospital escapes and commits a murder. Will this person be judged not guilty by reason of insanity? (Check your answer on page 609.)

Preventing Mental Illness

Traditionally, psychotherapy has been a method to relieve psychological distress. More recently, community psychologists and others have made efforts at prevention. **Community psychologists** *focus on the needs of large groups rather than those of individuals.* **Prevention** is *avoiding a disorder from the start.* For example, in one study of "pessimistic" college students and another study with children of depressed parents, half of the participants were given cognitive therapy and half were not. In both studies fewer people in the therapy group became depressed over the next 2 or 3 years (Clarke et al., 2001; Seligman, Schulman, DeRubeis, & Hollon, 1999).

Prevention is distinguished from intervention and maintenance. **Intervention** is *identifying a disorder in its early stages and relieving it,* and **maintenance** is *taking steps to keep it from becoming more serious.* For example, therapists identify people showing early signs of schizophrenia and try to stop further deterioration (McGorry et al., 2002).

Just as our society puts fluoride into drinking water to prevent tooth decay and immunizes people against contagious diseases, it can take action to prevent certain types of psychological disorders (Albee, 1986; Wandersman & Florin, 2003). Here are some examples:

- **Ban toxins.** The sale of lead-based paint has been banned because children who eat flakes of it sustain brain damage. Other toxins in the air and water have yet to be controlled.
- **Educate pregnant women about prenatal care.** For example, women need to be informed that the use of alcohol or other drugs during pregnancy damages the brain of a fetus and that bacterial and viral infections during pregnancy can impair fetal brain development and increase the risk of psychological disorders in the child.
- **Outlaw smoking in public places and educate people about the risks of smoking.** Improvements in

physical health can improve psychological well-being too, and preventing smoking by pregnant women is good for the brain development of the fetus.
- **Help people get jobs.** People who lose their jobs lose self-esteem and increase their risk of depression and substance abuse.
- **Provide child care.** Improved, affordable day-care services would relieve stress for both parents and children.
- **Improve educational opportunities.** Programs that get young people interested in their schoolwork have made notable progress in decreasing juvenile delinquency.

These techniques are aimed at prevention for the entire community. Prevention or intervention techniques can be targeted at specific individuals who are beginning to show symptoms of a particular disorder. For example, psychologists identified fifth- and sixth-grade children prone to distress and then for 12 weeks taught them how to avoid negative beliefs about themselves. These children showed fewer signs of depression over the next 2 years compared to a similarly distressed group who did not receive this training (Gillham, Reivich, Jaycox, & Seligman, 1995).

Unfortunately, prevention is often more difficult than it might seem. For example, many programs designed to teach young people to avoid illegal drugs have produced no measurable benefits. In one study adolescents with a history of aggression met in groups to discuss their problems. Over the next year, they showed an *increase* in delinquent behaviors compared to a no-treatment control group (Poulin, Dishion, & Burraston, 2001). Evidently, associating with an all-delinquent group provided bad role models and did more harm than good. In another program patients recovering from anorexia nervosa or bulimia nervosa described their struggles to college women. The women who heard this presentation had an *increase* in eating problems over the next couple of months, whereas women who did not hear the presentation remained unchanged (Mann et al., 1997).

Attempts have been made to combat suicide, especially teenage suicide, by television programs about suicide and the pain it causes to friends and relatives. These programs have never decreased the suicide rate; in fact the research controversy is about how much the programs *increase* the suicide rate (Joiner, 1999). One study compared suicidal patients receiving brief crisis intervention to others receiving more prolonged therapy. Those receiving more help had a *higher* rate of suicide (Moller, 1992). The general point is that we cannot take it for granted that a procedure intended to help will succeed. Sometimes just talking about a behavior problem makes it more likely.

CONCEPT CHECK ☑

16. Why is it important to do careful research before initiating a new program to prevent a psychological disorder? (Check your answer on this page.)

IN CLOSING

The Science and Politics of Mental Illness

Suppose you are a storekeeper. Someone dressed as Batman stands outside your store every day shouting gibberish at anyone who comes by. Your once-thriving business draws fewer and fewer customers each day. The disturbing man outside does not seem to be breaking any laws. A psychologist consults *DSM-IV* and finds a couple of possible diagnoses. However, the man is not obviously dangerous or incompetent, just annoying, and he wants nothing to do with psychologists or psychiatrists. Should he nevertheless be forced to accept treatment for his odd behavior? If not, what happens to your rights as a storekeeper?

Similarly, the insanity defense and all the other issues in this module are complicated questions that require political decisions by society as a whole, not just the opinions of psychologists or psychiatrists. Regardless of what career you enter, you will be a voter and potential juror, and you will have a voice in deciding these issues. The decisions deserve serious, informed consideration.

Summary

* *Deinstitutionalization.* Today, few patients stay very long in mental hospitals. However, many states have released patients from mental hospitals without providing adequate community mental-health facilities. (page 604)
* *Involuntary commitment.* Laws on involuntary commitment to mental hospitals vary, but typically, people can be committed if they are judged to be dangerous or incompetent. It is difficult to frame laws that ensure treatment for those who need it while also protecting the rights of those who have good reasons for refusing it. (page 605)
* *Duty to warn.* The courts have ruled that a therapist who is convinced that a client is dangerous should warn the endangered person. Applying this rule in practice is difficult, however, because judging dangerousness is difficult. (page 605)
* *The insanity defense.* Some defendants accused of a crime are acquitted for reasons of insanity, which is a legal rather than a medical or psychological concept. The criteria for establishing insanity are controversial. (page 606)
* *Prevention of psychological disorders.* Psychologists and psychiatrists are increasingly concerned about preventing psychological disorders. Many preventive measures require the cooperation of society as a whole. Methods of prevention based on good intentions do not always succeed. (page 608)

Answers to Concept Checks

14. Deinstitutionalization appears to be a good idea because treatment in a community mental health center is more effective and less costly than treatment in a mental hospital. However, many states removed people from mental hospitals without providing adequate alternative care. (page 605)
15. Not necessarily. Having a psychological disorder, even a severe one, does not automatically qualify a person as insane in the legal sense. The judge or jury must also find that the psychological disorder prevented the person from knowing what he or she was doing or made law-abiding behavior impossible. (page 608)
16. In many cases a program intended for prevention has proved to be ineffective or counterproductive. It is important to test the effectiveness of a program before setting it up on a large scale. (page 609)

Key Terms and Activities

Key Terms

attention-deficit disorder (ADD): a condition marked by easy distraction from important tasks, impulsiveness, moodiness, and failure to follow through on plans (page 584)

attention-deficit hyperactivity disorder (ADHD): a condition marked by easy distraction from important tasks, impulsiveness, moodiness, and failure to follow through on plans, plus excessive activity and fidgetiness (page 584)

behavior therapy: treatment that begins with clear, well-defined behavioral goals, such as eliminating test anxiety, and then attempts to achieve those goals through learning (page 592)

biopsychosocial model: the concept that abnormal behavior has three major aspects—biological, psychological, and sociological (page 583)

brief therapy: treatment that begins with an agreement about what the therapist and the client can expect from each other and how long the treatment will last; also known as time-limited therapy (page 597)

catharsis: the release of pent-up emotions associated with unconscious thoughts and memories (page 591)

cognitive therapy: treatment that seeks to improve people's psychological well-being by changing their cognitions (page 593)

cognitive-behavior therapy: treatment that combines important features of both behavior therapy and cognitive therapy, attempting to change people's behavior by changing their interpretation of their situation (page 594)

community psychologist: a psychologist who focuses on the needs of large groups rather than those of individuals (page 608)

deinstitutionalization: the removal of patients from mental hospitals (page 604)

Diagnostic and Statistical Manual of Mental Disorders, Fourth Edition (DSM-IV): a book that lists the acceptable labels for all psychological disorders, with a description of each and guidelines on how to distinguish it from similar disorders (page 584)

differential diagnosis: a determination of what problem a person has, in contrast to all the other possible problems that might produce similar symptoms (page 586)

dissociative identity disorder: a rare condition in which the personality separates into several identities; also known as multiple personality disorder (page 583)

eclectic therapy: treatment that uses a combination of methods and approaches (page 596)

family systems therapy: treatment based on the assumptions that most people's problems develop in a family setting and that the best way to deal with them is to improve family relationships and communication (page 595)

free association: a procedure where a client lies on a couch, starts thinking about a particular symptom or problem, and then reports everything that comes to mind (page 591)

group therapy: treatment administered to a group of people all at once (page 597)

incongruence: a mismatch between the perceptions of one's real self and ideal self (page 594)

interpretation: a therapist's explanation of the underlying meaning of what a client says (page 592)

intervention: identifying a disorder in its early stages and relieving it (page 608)

maintenance: treating a disorder to keep it from becoming more serious (p. 608)

meta-analysis: a method of taking the results of many experiments, weighting each one in proportion to the number of participants, and determining the overall average effect (page 599)

M'Naghten rule: the rule that a defendant is not criminally responsible if, at the time of committing an unlawful act, the person was laboring under such a defect of reason, from disease of the mind, as not to know the nature and quality of the act he was doing; or if he did know it, that he did not know he was doing wrong (page 607)

person-centered therapy: a procedure in which a therapist listens to the client with unconditional positive regard and offers little interpretation or advice; also known as nondirective or client-centered therapy (page 594)

personality disorder: a maladaptive, inflexible way of dealing with the environment and other people (page 586)

prevention: avoiding a disorder from the start (page 608)

psychoanalysis: an approach to personality and psychotherapy developed by Sigmund Freud, based on identifying unconscious thoughts and emotions and bringing them to consciousness (page 591)

psychodynamic therapies: treatment that attempts to uncover people's underlying drives and motivations (page 591)

psychotherapy: the treatment of psychological disorders by methods that include a personal relationship between a trained therapist and a client (page 590)

rational-emotive behavior therapy: treatment based on the assumption that thoughts (rationality) lead to emotions and that problems arise not from the unpleasant emotions themselves but from the irrational thoughts that lead to them (page 593)

self-help group: an assembly of people with similar problems, who operate much like group therapy but without a therapist (page 597)

spontaneous remission: improvement of a psychological condition without therapy (page 598)

Tarasoff: the rule that a therapist who knew, or who should have known, that a client was dangerous is obligated to break the pledge of confidentiality and warn the endangered person (page 606)

transference: the extension of a client's feelings toward a parent or other important figure onto the therapist (page 592)

 # Suggestions for Further Reading

Dawes, R. M. (1994). *House of cards: Psychology and psychotherapy built on myth.* New York: Free Press. A harsh criticism of psychotherapists who rely on their intuition and experience instead of scientific evidence.

Seligman, M. E. P. (1993). *What you can change . . . and what you can't.* New York: Fawcett Columbine. Description of both the possibilities and the limitations of psychotherapy.

Sheehan, S. (1982). *Is there no place on earth for me?* Boston: Houghton Mifflin. The story of a young woman with schizophrenia and her life in and out of mental hospitals.

 # Book Companion Web Site

Need help studying? Go to

http://psychology.wadsworth.com/kalat_intro7e/

for a virtual study center. You'll find a personalized Self-Study Assessment that will provide you with a study plan based on your answers to a pretest. Also study using flash cards, quizzes, interactive art, and an online glossary.

 Check out interactive **Try It Yourself** exercises on the companion site! For example, the Stop Signal Task exercise ties to what you've learned in this chapter.

Your companion site also has direct links to the following Web sites. These links are checked often for changes, dead links, and new additions.

Attention-Deficit Disorder

www.add-adhd.org/

This site offers a wealth of information and opinion about attention-deficit disorder, its causes, and treatment.

Landmark Cases in Forensic Psychiatry

bama.ua.edu/~jhooper/tableofc.html

In his excellent Forensic Psychiatry Resource Page, James Hooper offers brief summaries of criminal and civil cases in which mental disorders became an issue.

 # Try It Yourself CD-ROM
with Critical Thinking Video Exercises

Use your CD to access **videos** related to activities designed to help you think critically about the important topics discussed. You'll also find an easy portal link to the book companion site where you can access your personalized **Self-Study Assessments** and interactive **Try It Yourself** exercises.

PsychNow! 2.0

PsychNow! is a fun interactive CD designed to help you with the difficult concepts in psychology. Check out the Personality and Abnormal Psychology section for the following topics that relate to this chapter:

Abnormality and Psychopathology: six portraits—decide who looks normal, explore the biographies of the six people and the case histories of two men.

Nonpsychotic, Psychotic, and Affective Disorders: eight famous people with disorders, *DSM-IV* categories with examples, and case studies to review and diagnose.

Major Psychological Theories: five kinds of therapy with details and case studies and treatment.

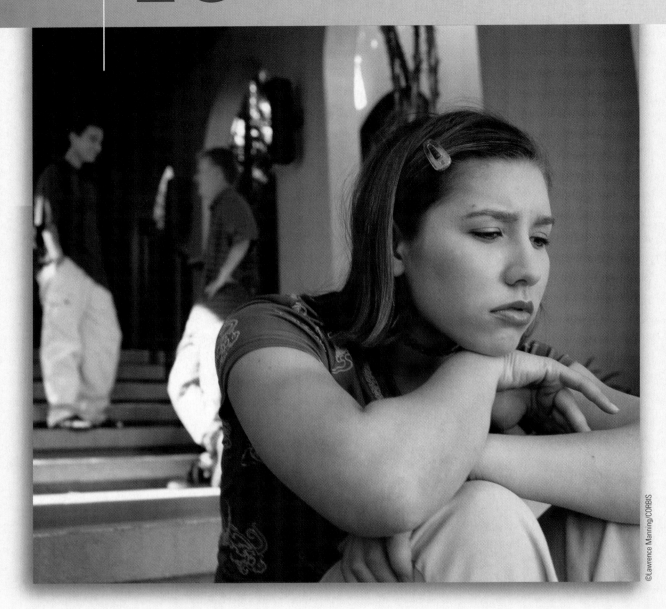

Specific Disorders and Treatments

In the 1700s and 1800s, medical science was primitive by today's standards. Most physicians did not even try to distinguish one illness from another. Regardless of the symptoms, physicians recommended general all-purpose "tonics," suggested bed rest, sometimes applied leeches to withdraw blood, and so forth. Medical progress since then has been marked by an increasing ability to apply specific treatments aimed at specific disorders.

Psychotherapy has been trying to move in the same direction. Instead of just providing general-purpose counseling, therapists would like to distinguish one disorder from another and apply specific treatments aimed at particular disorders. However, not everyone is convinced that we can or should. As discussed in the previous chapter, for mild to moderate disorders, researchers find that many types of therapy are similar in their effectiveness. If the type of therapy doesn't matter, then carefully diagnosing someone's disorder may not be important either (Messer & Wampold, 2002).

Furthermore, the various psychological disorders listed in *DSM-IV* are not altogether distinct from one another (Widiger & Clark, 2000). For example, poor prenatal nutrition or other prenatal difficulties increase the risk of almost any psychological disorder (Huizink, Mulder, & Buitelaar, 2004), and some genetic influences predispose to a variety of disorders also (Fu et al., 2002). Furthermore, most people with any one psychiatric diagnosis qualify for others. For example, many people with anxiety disorders have depression also and perhaps alcohol abuse as well.

The distinctiveness of each psychological disorder is an empirical question—that is, one to be decided by the evidence. In the first three modules of this chapter, we consider research on the most commonly diagnosed psychological disorders: anxiety disorders, substance abuse, and depression. The final module is about schizophrenia, which is less common but often disabling. As you will see, each disorder has its own special features, but each overlaps with the others as well.

▌ In the early days of medicine, physicians provided the same treatments for all diseases (e.g., applying leeches as a means of letting blood, as shown). Progress depended on differentiating particular disorders and developing individual treatments for each. Clinical psychology, likewise, is trying to determine the right treatment for different types of psychological disorders.

Anxiety and Avoidance Disorders

Why do some people develop exaggerated fears?

Why do some people develop strange habits of thought and action?

You go to the beach, looking forward to an afternoon of swimming and surfing. Will you go in the water if someone tells you that a shark attacked two swimmers yesterday? What if the shark attack was a month ago? What if someone saw a small shark a few days ago, but it did not attack anyone?

How much fear and caution are normal? Staying out of the water because you see a large shark is perfectly reasonable. Staying out because a small shark was present a few days ago is less sensible. If you refuse even to look at photographs of the ocean because they might *remind* you of sharks, you have a serious problem indeed. Excessive fear and caution are linked to some relatively common psychological disorders.

Disorders with Excessive Anxiety

Many psychological disorders are marked by anxiety and attempts to avoid anxiety. Anxiety, unlike fear, is not generally associated with a specific situation. You might be afraid of a growling dog, but your fear subsides when you get away from the dog. Anxiety is an apprehensive feeling that something might go wrong. We also talk of anxieties about dying or anxieties about some personal deficiency. The key is that you

▍ Many situations evoke temporay anxiety or tension in almost anyone. Anxiety becomes a problem only if it is frequently more intense than the situation justifies.

cannot escape from anxieties as easily as you could from the growling dog.

Some degree of anxiety is normal; anxiety becomes a problem only when it interferes with our ability to cope with everyday life. The people most prone to severe anxiety are those who feel helpless to control the major events of their lives (Chorpita & Barlow, 1998). Recall from Chapter 12 that shock, noise, and all sorts of other unpleasant events are more stressful when people cannot predict or control them.

We have already considered one example of an anxiety disorder, posttraumatic stress disorder, in Chapter 12. Here let's consider additional anxiety disorders.

Generalized Anxiety Disorder (GAD)

People with **generalized anxiety disorder (GAD)** are *almost constantly plagued by exaggerated worries.* They worry that "I might get sick," "My daughter might get sick," "I might lose my job," or "I might not be able to pay my bills." Although they have no more reason for worry than anyone else, they grow so tense, irritable, and fatigued that they have trouble working or enjoying life. Sometimes they are not even sure what they are worried about. About 5% of all people experience generalized anxiety disorder at some point in life (Wittchen, Zhao, Kessler, & Eaton, 1994). Very few have GAD by itself; because anxiety is a common symptom of so many other disorders, most people with GAD have (or have had or will have) other disorders too, such as depression, panic disorder, or phobia (Bruce, Machan, Dyck, & Keller, 2001).

GAD responds fairly well to antidepressant drugs (Rivas-Vazquez, 2001). Another effective treatment is relaxation training, in which people are taught how to relax their muscles quickly in stressful situations (Öst & Breitholtz, 2000). The drug treatment shows benefits more quickly, but the relaxation training is more likely to produce long-lasting benefits.

Panic Disorder (PD)

People with **panic disorder (PD)** *have frequent periods of anxiety and occasional attacks of panic— rapid breathing, increased heart rate, chest pains, sweating, faintness, and trembling.* A panic attack usually lasts only minutes, although it can last an hour or more. Both during and after an attack, people worry about fainting, having a heart attack, dying, or going crazy.

Panic disorder occurs in 1 to 3% of adults at some time during their lives throughout the world. It is more common in women than men (Weissman, Warner, Wickramaratne, Moreau, & Olfson, 1997) and more common in young adults than older ones. Indeed, the whole tendency toward anxiety tends to weaken with age. One study found that 8 of 24 people with panic disorder recovered completely within 11 years, while all of the others had less frequent panic attacks than before (Swoboda, Amering, Windhaber, & Katschnig, 2003).

Several studies have indicated a genetic contribution, although the results do not point strongly to any one gene (Crowe et al., 2001; Hamilton et al., 2003; Hettema, Neale, & Kendler, 2001). A study of Spanish people with panic disorder found a high overlap between panic disorder and *joint laxity* (the ability to bend fingers farther than usual, popularly called "double-jointedness"). The authors reported that both panic disorder and joint laxity were linked to an extra copy of one segment of human chromosome 15 (Gratacòs et al., 2001). However, other investigators have been unable to replicate this finding (Benjamin et al., 2001; Schumacher et al., 2003; Tabiner, 2003).

One key symptom of panic disorder is **hyperventilation,** *rapid deep breathing.* People who are prone to hyperventilation for any reason, including cigarette smoking, allergies, asthma, and gluten intolerance, are more likely than others to develop panic disorder (Carta et al., 2002; Isensee, Wittchen, Stein, Höfler, & Lieb, 2003; Kovalenko et al., 2001; Perna, Bertani, Politi, Colombo, & Bellodi, 1997). Almost anything that causes hyperventilation makes the body react as if it were suffocating, thereby triggering other sympathetic nervous system responses such as sweating and increased heart rate (Coplan et al., 1998; Klein, 1993). If this arousal occurs after exercise, people do not react emotionally because they attribute their arousal to the exercise. In fact, even if the arousal was caused by something else, people assume the exercise was responsible and think no more about it (Esquivel, Schruers, Kuipers, & Griez, 2002). However, suppose you suddenly increase your breathing rate, heart rate, and sweating and don't know why. The reason could be stress, something you ate, a high level of carbon dioxide in the room, or some other temporary problem, but the cause isn't apparent to you. If you are surprised by your sudden arousal, your interpretation of it becomes critical. If you shrug it off, you have a

panic attack without developing panic disorder. However, if you worry about the next attack, worry that it may embarrass you in public, and so forth, your worry increases the risk of further attacks (McNally, 2002).

People who have repeated panic attacks start to associate them with places, events, activities, or even internal states. Any situation that resembles those of previous panic attacks may trigger a new panic attack as a conditioned response (Bouton, Mineka, & Barlow, 2001). They may also interpret any onset of hyperventilation as the start of a panic attack (Battaglia, Bertella, Ogliari, Bellodi, & Smeraldi, 2001; Gorman et al., 2001). Figure 16.1 summarizes the processes of panic attack.

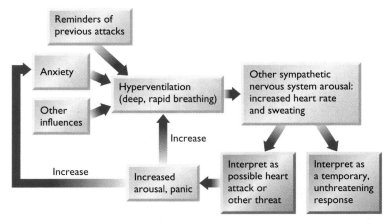

FIGURE 16.1 Many people experience an episode of hyperventilation leading to increased arousal. If they interpret it as nonthreatening, the episode passes. However, if they interpret it as threatening, their worry heightens the arousal, magnifies the symptoms, and increases the constant anxiety level.

Panic attack has been treated with psychotherapy as well as antidepressant drugs with varying degrees of benefit. Any learned fear can be unlearned, and behavior therapy is often effective. Part of any treatment is based on rather simple advice: A panic attack is not going to kill you, and it probably won't last very long. If you feel an attack coming on, say, "Excuse me, but I feel a breathing problem starting." Sit down, wait it out, and then go back to your activities. Of course, it is not easy to take that advice.

Many people with panic disorder also have **social phobia,** *a severe avoidance of other people and a fear of doing anything in public,* where they might become embarrassed. Common types of social phobia include fear of talking to strangers or large groups and fear of feeling rejected or ridiculed by others (Stein, Torgrud, & Walker, 2000). Many also have **agoraphobia** (from *agora,* the Greek word for "marketplace"), *an excessive fear of open or public places,* although it is also possible to have agoraphobia without panic disorder (Wittchen, Reed, & Kessler, 1998). Most psychologists believe that people with panic disorder develop their social phobia or agoraphobia because they are afraid of being incapacitated or embarrassed by a panic attack in a public place. In a sense they are afraid of their own anxiety (McNally, 1990). To avoid the prospect of a public panic attack, they stay home as much as possible and seldom go out alone.

CONCEPT CHECK

1. Some psychologists advise people with panic attacks to adopt the attitude, "If it happens, it happens." Why would they make this recommendation? (Check your answer on page 625.)

Disorders with Exaggerated Avoidance

People learn to avoid punishment, as we saw in Chapter 6. In some cases their efforts become so extreme and persistent that they interfere with daily activities.

Let's begin with some general observations on avoidance learning, which is relevant to the later discussion of phobias (extreme fears) and compulsions (rituals designed to avoid unpleasant thoughts or events). If you learn to do something for positive reinforcement, your responses will extinguish when reinforcements cease. Avoidance behaviors are different. Suppose you learn to press a lever to avoid electric shocks. Soon you are responding so consistently that you receive no shocks. Now the experimenter disconnects the shock generator without telling you. The extinction procedure has begun; you no longer need to press the lever.

What will you do? You will continue pressing, of course. As far as you can tell, nothing has changed; the response still works. *Avoidance behaviors are highly resistant to extinction;* once someone learns a response to avoid mishap, the response continues long after it ceases to be necessary.

You can see how this tendency would support superstitions. Suppose you believe that Friday the 13th is dangerous. Every Friday the 13th, you

are cautious, and if nothing goes wrong, your cautious behavior seemed to work. If a misfortune happens anyway, it confirms your belief that Friday the 13th is dangerous. In other words, as long as you continue an avoidance behavior, you never learn whether it is useful or not!

CONCEPT CHECK

2. Suppose you are an experimenter, and you have trained someone to press a lever to avoid shocks. Now you disconnect the shock generator. Other than telling the person what you have done, what procedure could you use to facilitate extinction of the lever pressing? (Check your answer on page 625.)

Phobias

Terror is the only thing that comes close to how I feel when I think of moths. Their willowy, see-through wings always seem filthy. I remember being stuck in a car with a huge moth and my date, not knowing how terrified I was of moths, thought I was kidding when I told him I was afraid. It was terrible! I can feel it right now . . . feeling trapped and the moth with its ugly body flitting around so quickly, I couldn't anticipate where it would go next. Finally that creature hit me in the arm and I screamed—it felt dirty and sleazy and then it hit me in the face and I began to scream uncontrollably. I had the terrible feeling it was going to fly into my mouth while I was screaming, but I couldn't stop. (Phobia patient quoted by Duke & Nowicki, 1979, p. 244)

A **phobia** is best defined as *a persistent fear that is extreme enough to interfere with normal living.* A phobia is often described as an irrational fear. However,

❚ Many people who watched the famous shower scene in the movie *Psycho* became afraid to take showers. Actress Janet Leigh, who portrayed the woman killed in that scene, subsequently avoided showers herself.

fearing snakes is not irrational because some snakes are dangerous, as are most other objects of phobias. What is irrational is the excessive degree of the fear, which leads to avoidance behaviors—avoiding the object itself (e.g., a snake), places where it might be lurking, and even reminders of snakes. Confronting the object of a phobia can lead to sweating, trembling, rapid breathing, and elevated heart rate. In most cases people with phobias are not so much afraid of the object itself but of their own reactions (Beck & Emery, 1985). They fear that they will have a heart attack or that they will embarrass themselves by trembling or fainting. In many ways phobias are like panic disorder, but phobias are aroused by a specific kind of object or situation, whereas panic attacks occur less predictably.

Prevalence

According to an extensive study of U.S. adults, about 11% of people suffer a phobia at some time in life, and 5 to 6% have a phobia at any given time (Magee, Eaton, Wittchen, McGonagle, & Kessler, 1996). However, phobias vary from mild to extreme, so their apparent prevalence depends on how many marginal cases we include. As with other anxiety disorders, phobias are more common in women than men and usually fade away as people grow older (Burke, Burke, Regier, & Rae, 1990).

Here is a list of some common objects of phobias (Cox, McWilliams, Clara, & Stein, 2003):

- Open, public places (*agoraphobia*)
- Public speaking
- Heights (including elevators, being on a high floor of a building)
- Not being on solid ground (being in the air or on the water)
- Being with or being observed by strangers (*social phobia*)
- Being alone
- Threats or reminders of threats (snakes, spiders, other animals, blood, injections, storms, etc.)

Figure 16.2 shows the prevalence of phobias by age. As with panic disorder, phobias are most common in young adults and less common with age.

Acquiring Phobias

Like almost everything else in psychology, phobias show a genetic predisposition. The more closely related you are to someone with a phobia or similar disorders, the more likely you are to develop a phobia yourself (Kendler, Myers, Prescott, & Neale, 2001; Skre, Onstad, Torgerson, Lygren, & Kringlen, 2000).

However, no one is born with a phobia. People are born with the fear of sudden loud noises, but most fears are learned, and so are phobias. Indeed, some phobias can be traced to a specific event; for example,

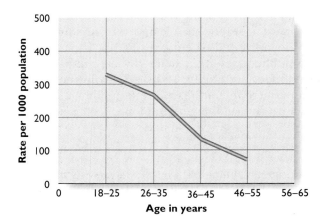

FIGURE 16.2 Most phobias do not last a lifetime. Young people with phobias often lose them by middle age. *(Based on the data of Burke, Burke, Regier, & Rae, 1990)*

one child got locked in a trunk and developed a phobia of closed spaces. Another person developed a phobia of water after diving into a lake and discovering a corpse (Kendler et al., 1995). Other things being equal, people with a history of terrible experiences, such as abuse during childhood, are more likely than others to acquire phobias (Friedman et al., 2002).

John B. Watson, one of the founders of behaviorism, was the first to demonstrate that people learn fears (Watson & Rayner, 1920). Today, we would consider it unethical to try to teach a child a fear, but in 1920 researchers felt less restraint. Watson and Rosalie Rayner studied an 11-month-old child, "Albert B.," who had previously shown no fear of white rats or other animals (Figure 16.3). They set a white rat

FIGURE 16.3 John B. Watson first demonstrated that Little Albert showed little fear of small animals. Then Watson paired a white rat with a loud, frightening noise. Little Albert became afraid of the white rat, as well as other small animals and odd-looking masks.

down in front of him and then struck a large steel bar behind him with a hammer. The sound made Albert whimper and cover his face. After a few repetitions, the mere sight of the rat made Albert cry and crawl away. Watson and Rayner declared that they had created a strong fear and that phobias in general might develop along similar lines. (Unfortunately, they made no attempt to extinguish Albert's fear.)

Watson and Rayner's explanation of phobias ignored some important questions: Why do people develop phobias toward objects that have never injured them? Why are some phobias much more common than others? And why are phobias so persistent? Although Watson and Rayner's study was unsatisfactory in many ways (B. Harris, 1979; Samelson, 1980), it led the way for later studies of phobias as learned responses.

CONCEPT CHECK ☑️

3. In classical conditioning terms, what was the CS in Watson and Rayner's experiment? The UCS? The CR? The UCR? (Check your answers on page 625.)

CRITICAL THINKING: *WHAT'S THE EVIDENCE?*
Learning Fear by Observation

Contrary to Watson and Rayner's explanation, almost half of all people with phobias have never had a painful experience with the object they fear (Öst & Hugdahl, 1981). As noted in the discussion of social learning in Chapter 6, we learn much by watching or listening to others. Perhaps we learn our fears and phobias from other people.

That hypothesis sounds reasonable, but how can we test it? Susan Mineka and her colleagues demonstrated that monkeys learn fears by observing other monkeys (Mineka, 1987; Mineka, Davidson, Cook, & Keir, 1984). Her research shows how animal studies can shed light on important human issues.

EXPERIMENT I

Hypothesis Monkeys that have seen other monkeys avoid a snake will develop a similar fear themselves.

Method Nearly all monkeys in the wild develop a fear of snakes, but laboratory monkeys do not. Mineka put a laboratory-reared monkey with a wild-born monkey and let them both see a snake (Figure 16.4a). The lab monkey watched the wild monkey show signs of fear. Later, Mineka tested the lab monkey by itself to see its response to a snake.

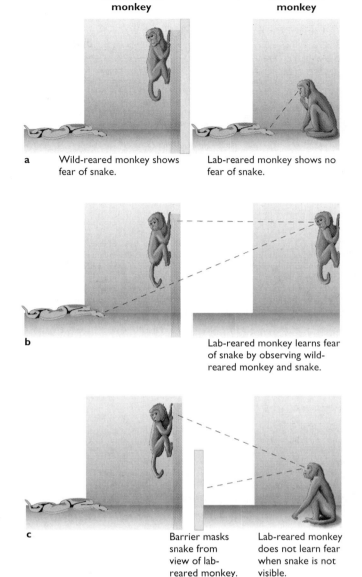

Wild-reared monkey | **Lab-reared monkey**

a Wild-reared monkey shows fear of snake. | Lab-reared monkey shows no fear of snake.

b Lab-reared monkey learns fear of snake by observing wild-reared monkey and snake.

c Barrier masks snake from view of lab-reared monkey. | Lab-reared monkey does not learn fear when snake is not visible.

FIGURE 16.4 A lab-reared monkey learns to fear snakes from the reactions of a wild-reared monkey. But if the snake is not visible, the lab-reared monkey learns no fear.

Results When the lab monkey saw how frightened its partner was of the snake, it became frightened too (Figure 16.4b). It continued to be afraid of the snake when tested by itself, even months later.

Interpretation The lab monkey may have learned a fear of snakes because it saw that its partner was afraid of snakes. But Mineka also considered a less likely interpretation: The lab monkey may have become fearful simply because it observed the other monkey's fear. That is, maybe it did not matter what the wild monkey was afraid of. To test this possibility, Mineka conducted a second experiment.

EXPERIMENT 2

Hypothesis   A monkey that does not see the object that another monkey fears will not develop a fear itself.

Method   A monkey reared in a lab watched a monkey reared in the wild through a plate-glass window. The wild monkey could look through another window, where it saw a snake. Thus, when the wild monkey shrieked and ran away from the snake, the lab monkey saw the wild monkey's fear but did not know what it was afraid of. Later, the lab monkey was placed close to a snake to see whether it would show fear.

Results   The lab monkey showed no fear of the snake.

Interpretation   To develop a fear of snakes, the observer monkey needed to see that the other monkey was frightened of snakes, not just that it was frightened (Figure 16.4c).

Note that, although the observer monkey had to see *what* the other monkey feared, it did not have to see *why* it was afraid. Just seeing the other monkey's fear of the snake in Experiment 1 was enough. Humans not only observe other people's fears but can also explain why.

Why Some Phobias Are More Common Than Others

Imagine that you survey your friends. (You can actually survey them, if you wish, but it's pretty easy to imagine the results.) You ask them:

- Are you afraid of snakes?
- Are you afraid of cars?
- Have you ever been bitten by a snake or seen someone else bitten?
- Have you ever been injured in a car accident or seen someone else injured?

I think you know what to expect. Far more people have been injured or seen someone injured by cars than by snakes, but far more are afraid of snakes than cars. So why do people develop some fears more readily than others?

Common phobias include open spaces, closed spaces, heights, lightning and thunder, animals, and illness. In contrast few people have phobias of cars, guns, tools, or electricity—even though they produce many injuries. When my son Sam was a toddler, at least three times he stuck his finger into an electric outlet. He even had a name for it: "Smoky got me again." (I worried about him!) But he never developed a fear of electricity or gadgets.

One explanation is that people may be evolutionarily "prepared" to learn certain phobias (Öhman & Mineka, 2003; Seligman, 1971). For millions of years, people who quickly learned to avoid snakes, heights, and lightning probably improved their chance to survive and to transmit their genes. We have not had enough time to evolve a tendency to fear cars and electricity.

Evidence supporting this view comes from both monkey and human studies. Monkeys who watch a videotape of another monkey running away from a snake learn to fear snakes; monkeys who watch another monkey running away from a flower show no fear of flowers (Mineka, 1987). People who receive electric shocks paired with pictures of snakes quickly develop a strong and persistent response to snake pictures; people who receive shocks paired with pictures of houses show a much weaker response (Öhman, Eriksson, & Olofsson, 1975).

However, there are other possible explanations for why some phobias are more common than others. For example, we have many safe experiences with cars and tools that outweigh the bad experiences. Most people have few safe experiences with snakes, spiders, or falling from high places. One study found that people who had extensive experiences with tarantulas lost their fears and sometimes even developed an interest in tarantulas as a hobby (Kleinknecht, 1982).

Another possible explanation is that people generally develop phobias of objects that they cannot predict or control. If you are afraid of spiders, for example, you must be constantly on the alert. Because you never know where those tiny little critters might be, you can never completely relax. Lightning is also unpredictable and uncontrollable. In contrast you don't have to worry that hammer, saws, or electric outlets will take you by surprise. You must be on the alert for cars when you are near a road but not at other times.

CONCEPT CHECK ☑

4. Name three explanations for why more people develop phobias of snakes and spiders than cars and guns. (Check your answer on page 625.)

▌ Many people are afraid of extreme heights, partly because the danger is hard to control and partly because we have few safe experiences with heights.

Behavior Therapy for Phobias

Well-established phobias can last a lifetime. Remembering the discussion about avoidance learning, you can see why phobias are so difficult to extinguish: If you have learned to press a lever to avoid shock, you may not stop pressing long enough to find out that such a response is no longer necessary. Similarly, if you stay away from snakes or heights or closed places, you will never learn that your fear is exaggerated. In other words you will not extinguish your fear.

Recall the concept of behavior therapy from Chapter 15: A therapist sets a specific goal and uses learning techniques to help the client achieve that goal. One common and usually successful type of behavior therapy for phobia is **systematic desensitization,** *a method of reducing fear by gradually exposing people to the object of their fear* (Wolpe, 1961). Someone with a phobia of snakes, for example, is first trained in relaxation methods and then asked to lie on a comfortable couch listening to relaxing music with the therapist nearby. When the client is fully relaxed, the therapist asks the client briefly to imagine a small black-and-white photo of a snake, then to imagine a color photo, and then to imagine a real snake. After the client has successfully visualized all of those images, the same sequence is repeated with real photos and eventually with a view of a real snake (Figure 16.5).

The process resembles Skinner's shaping procedure (see Chapter 6). The person is given time to master each step before going on to the next. The client can say "stop" if the distress becomes threatening; the therapist then goes back several steps and repeats the sequence. Some people complete the whole procedure in a single 1-hour session; others need more time. Systematic desensitization can easily be combined with so-

cial learning: The person with a phobia watches other people who display a fearless response to the object.

However, most therapists do not keep handy a supply of snakes, spiders, and so forth. Instead, a growing number use virtual reality, which proves effective in most cases (Garcia-Palacios, Hoffman, Carlin, Furness, & Botella, 2002): The client is equipped with a helmet that displays a virtual-reality scene, as shown in Figure 16.6. Then, without even leaving the office, the therapist can expose the client to the feared object or situation. For example, a client with a phobia of heights can go up a glass elevator in a hotel or cross a narrow bridge over a chasm (Rothbaum et al., 1995). This technology gives the therapist excellent control of the situation, including the option of turning off the display if the client becomes too fearful.

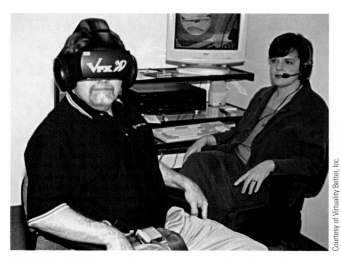

FIGURE 16.6 Some therapists use virtual reality to let a patient with a phobia of heights experience heights under carefully controlled conditions.

Flooding (or **implosion** or **intensive exposure therapy**) is *a treatment that exposes the person to the object of the phobia suddenly rather than gradually* (Hogan & Kirchner, 1967; Rachman, 1969). (This treatment is called *flooding* because the patient is flooded with fear.) If you had a phobia of rats, for example, you might be told to imagine that you were locked in a room full of rats crawling all over you and viciously attacking you. The image arouses your sympathetic nervous system enormously, and your heart and breathing rates soar (Lande, 1982). The human sympathetic nervous system cannot maintain a panic for long, however, so within a few minutes your heart and breathing rates begin to decline. A little later, you report feeling more relaxed, even though the therapist continues to suggest gory images of what rats are doing to you. Once you have reached this point, the battle is half won. People with phobias fear mainly that they will have a heart attack or other catastrophic re-

FIGURE 16.5 Systematic desensitization is an effective therapy for phobia. A therapist gradually exposes a client to the object of the phobia, first in imagination and later in reality. Exposure therapy is a similar procedure. The therapist demonstrates fearlessness in the presence of the object and encourages the client to do the same.

action. When they learn that they can withstand even the most frightening experience, they become less afraid of their own responses.

Drug Therapies for Phobias and Anxiety Disorders

Tranquilizers are among the most widely prescribed drugs in the United States. The most common tranquilizers are the *benzodiazepines* (BEN-zo-die-AZ-uh-peens), including drugs with the trade names Valium, Librium, and Xanax. Benzodiazepines relieve anxiety, induce sleep, and inhibit epileptic seizures. They act by facilitating activity at synapses using the transmitter GABA (Macdonald, Weddle, & Gross, 1986). These drugs can help relieve an occasional episode of anxiety or act as a sleeping pill. One disadvantage is that they are habit-forming, and withdrawing from them after repeated use produces increased anxiety. Another is that they suppress anxiety only temporarily. Usually, therapists treat anxiety disorders more effectively with antidepressant drugs, which we shall discuss later in this chapter.

CONCEPT CHECK ✓

5. How does systematic desensitization resemble extinction of a learned shock-avoidance response?

6. Suppose someone reports that a long-term therapy, lasting 10 years, cures many people of phobia and significantly helps the others. Should we be impressed? Why or why not?

7. How is the flooding procedure related to the James-Lange theory of emotions that was discussed in Chapter 12?

8. Alcohol facilitates transmission at GABA synapses. What effect should we expect if someone took both alcohol and a benzodiazepine tranquilizer? (Check your answers on page 625.)

Obsessive-Compulsive Disorder

People with **obsessive-compulsive disorder** have two kinds of problems. An **obsession** is a *repetitive, unwelcome stream of thought*. For example, such people might find themselves constantly imagining gruesome scenes, worrying that they are about to kill someone, dwelling on doubts about their religion, or thinking, "I hate my sister. I hate my sister." A **compulsion** is a *repetitive, almost irresistible action*. Obsessions generally lead to compulsions, as an itching sensation leads to scratching. For example, someone obsessed about dirt and disease develops compulsions of continual cleaning and washing. Someone with obsessive worries about doing something shameful develops compulsive rituals that maintain excessive self-control. That is, the compulsion is an attempt to reduce the obsession or the distress caused by the obsession.

An estimated 2 to 3% of all people in the United States suffer from obsessive-compulsive disorder at some time in life, although most cases are mild (Karno, Golding, Sorenson, & Burnam, 1988). The disorder occurs most frequently among hardworking, perfectionist people of average or above-average intelligence. It can develop either suddenly or gradually, usually beginning between the ages of 10 and 25. Nearly all people with obsessive-compulsive disorder have some insight into their own behavior and realize that their rituals are inappropriate. However, that realization does not stop the rituals.

Most people with obsessive-compulsive disorder have relatives with either obsessive-compulsive disorder or other anxiety disorders (Black, Noyes, Goldstein, & Blum, 1992). As mentioned in the introduction to this chapter, the causes of any one psychiatric disorder overlap the causes of others. Alterations of a gene controlling one brain chemical have been linked to increased risk of obsessive-compulsive disorder, especially in people with onset before age 18 (Hall, Dhilla, Charalambous, Gogos, & Karayiorgou, 2003).

DSM-IV lists obsessive-compulsive disorder with the anxiety disorders, but it is associated with guilt at least as much as with anxiety. People with obsessive-compulsive disorder say they feel guilt and anxiety over persistent frightening impulses—perhaps an impulse to engage in a sexual act that they consider shameful, an impulse to hurt someone, or an impulse to commit suicide. They decide, "Oh, what a terrible thought. I don't want to think that ever again." And so they resolve to shut the thought or impulse out of their consciousness.

However, trying to block out a thought only makes it more intrusive. As a child, the Russian novelist Leo Tolstoy once organized a club with a most unusual qualification for membership: A prospective member had to stand alone in a corner *without thinking about a white bear* (Simmons, 1949). If you think that sounds easy, try it. Ordinarily, you go months at a time between thoughts about polar bears, but when you try *not* to think about them, you can think of little else.

In one experiment college students were asked to tape-record everything that came to mind during 5 minutes but to try *not* to think about white bears. If they did, they were to mention it and ring a bell. Participants reported thinking about bears a mean of more than six times during the 5 minutes (Wegner, Schneider, Carter, & White, 1987). Afterward, they reported that almost everything in the room reminded them of white bears. Evidently, attempts to suppress a thought are likely to backfire, even with an emotionally trivial thought about something such as white bears. You can imagine how hard it is with severely upsetting thoughts.

People with obsessive-compulsive disorder have any of several kinds of compulsions. Some collect

▌ Most people seldom think about polar bears. But if you try to avoid thinking about them, you can think of little else. Many attempts to block obsessive thinking backfire in a similar way.

things. One man collected newspapers under his bed until they raised the bed so high it almost touched the ceiling. Others have odd habits, such as touching everything they see, trying to arrange objects in a completely symmetrical manner, or walking back and forth through a doorway nine times before leaving a building. One obsessive-compulsive person could not go to sleep at night until he had counted the corners of every object in the room to make sure that the total number of corners was evenly divisible by 16. If it was not, he would add or remove objects until the room had an acceptable total of corners. (The Obsessive-Compulsive Foundation produces a button that reads, "Every Member Counts"!) The most common compulsions are cleaning and checking.

Cleaning Compulsion

Obsessive-compulsive cleaning is similar to a phobia of dirt. Here is a description of a severe cleaning compulsion (Nagera, 1976): "R.," a 12-year-old boy, had a long-standing habit of prolonged bathing and hand washing, dating from a film about germs he had seen in the second grade. At about age 12, he started to complain about "being dirty" and having "bad thoughts," but he would not elaborate. His hand washing and bathing became longer and more frequent. When he bathed, he carefully washed himself with soap and washcloth all over, including the inside of his mouth and the inside of each nostril. He even opened his eyes in the soapy water and carefully washed his eyeballs. The only part he did not wash was his penis, which he covered with a washcloth as soon as he entered the tub.

In addition to his peculiar bathing habits, he developed some original superstitions. Whenever he did anything with one hand, he immediately did the same thing with the other hand. Whenever anyone mentioned a member of his family, he would mention the corresponding member of the other person's family.

He always walked to school by the same route, being careful never to step on any spot he had ever stepped on before. (You can imagine the strain on his memory.) At school he would wipe the palm of his hand on his pants after any "good" thought; at home he would wipe his hand on his pants after any "bad" thought.

R.'s problems were traced to a single event. Just before the onset of his exaggerated behaviors, R. and another boy had pulled down their pants and looked at each other. Afterward, he felt guilty and full of anxiety that he might do the same thing again. The constant bathing was apparently an attempt to wash away his feelings of "dirtiness." The superstitious rituals were an attempt to impose rigid self-control. His underlying reasoning could be described as: "If I can keep myself under perfect control at all times, I won't lose control and do something shameful."

Checking Compulsion

An obsessive-compulsive checker "double-checks" everything. Before going to bed at night, he or she makes sure that all the doors and windows are locked and that all the water faucets and gas outlets are turned off. But then the question arises, "Did I *really* check them all, or did I only imagine it?" So everything has to be checked again. And again. "After all, maybe I accidentally unlocked one of the doors while I was checking it." Obsessive-compulsive checkers can never decide when to stop checking; they may go on for hours and even then not be satisfied.

Obsessive-compulsive checkers have been known to check every door they pass to see whether anyone has been locked in, to check trash containers and bushes to see whether anyone has abandoned a baby, to call the police every day to ask whether they have committed a crime that they have forgotten, and to drive back and forth along a street to see whether they ran over any pedestrians the last time through (Pollak, 1979; Rachman & Hodgson, 1980).

Why do they go on checking? Part of the explanation is that they do not trust their own memory. In one study obsessive-compulsive patients took a memory test and estimated how many questions they answered correctly. Their actual percentage correct was as good as average, but their estimates of their own performance were considerably less than average (Dar, Rish, Hermish, Taub, & Fux, 2000). So perhaps the obsessive-compulsive patients continue checking because they do not trust their memory that they have already checked.

Why do they distrust their own memory? One study found that repeated checking makes the memories less distinct! Normal college students were asked to turn on and off the gas rings of a "virtual gas stove" on a computer. One group did it just once; the other group turned the rings on and off repeatedly. At the end both groups were asked which rings they had turned off on the most recent trial. Those who had manipulated the controls

TABLE 16.1 Obsessive-Compulsive Cleaners and Checkers

	Cleaners	Checkers
Sex distribution	Mostly female	About equally male and female
Dominant emotion	Anxiety, similar to phobia	Guilt, shame
Speed of onset	Usually rapid	More often gradual
Life disruption	Dominates life	Usually does not disrupt job and family life
Ritual length	Less than 1 hour at a time	Some go on indefinitely
Feel better after rituals?	Yes	Usually not

Source: From *Obsessions and Compulsions,* by Stanley J. Rachman and Ray J. Hodgson. Copyright © 1980 by Prentice-Hall, Inc. Reprinted by permission.

repeatedly answered as correctly as the others but expressed much less confidence in their answers. That is, the authors of this study suggest a vicious cycle: Not trusting your memory causes you to check repeatedly, and repeated checking makes the memory less distinct (van den Hout & Kindt, 2003).

Table 16.1 summarizes key differences between obsessive-compulsive cleaners and checkers. Table 16.2 lists some items from a questionnaire on obsessive-compulsive tendencies (Rachman & Hodgson, 1980). Try answering these questions yourself, or try guessing how an obsessive-compulsive person would answer them. (The few items listed here are not sufficient to diagnose someone as obsessive-compulsive. So don't obsess about it if you agreed with all the obsessive-compulsive answers.)

Therapies for Obsessive-Compulsive Disorder

Most people with obsessive-compulsive disorder improve over time, with or without treatment, and about half will become normal or nearly normal (Skoog & Skoog, 1999). Still, no one wants to wait years for spontaneous improvement if a treatment can hasten matters.

One effective treatment is *exposure therapy,* which resembles systematic desensitization for phobias: The obsessive-compulsive person is exposed to the situation in which he or she ordinarily performs certain rituals and is then prevented from performing them. For example, someone might be prevented from cleaning the house or checking the doors and windows more than once before going to sleep. The point is to demonstrate that nothing catastrophic occurs if one leaves a little mess in the house or runs a slight risk of leaving a door unlocked.

TABLE 16.2 Obsessive-Compulsive Tendencies

1. I avoid public telephones because of possible contamination.	T	F
2. I frequently get nasty thoughts and have difficulty getting rid of them.	T	F
3. I usually have serious thoughts about the simple everyday things I do.	T	F
4. Neither of my parents was very strict during my childhood.	T	F
5. I do not take a long time to dress in the morning.	T	F
6. One of my major problems is that I pay too much attention to detail.	T	F
7. I do not stick to a very strict routine when doing ordinary things.	T	F
8. I do not usually count when doing a routine task	T	F
9. Even when I do something very carefully, I often feel that it is not quite right.	T	F

Check typical answers on page 625.
Source: From *Obsessions and Compulsions,* by Stanley J. Rachman and Ray J. Hodgson. Copyright © 1980 by Prentice-Hall, Inc. Reprinted by permission.

The drug clomipramine (Anafranil) and related antidepressant drugs are also helpful for at least half of obsessive-compulsive patients (Greist, Jefferson, Kobak, Katzelnick, & Serlin, 1995). Clomipramine prolongs the effects of the neurotransmitter serotonin by preventing the presynaptic neuron from reabsorbing it. That is, after an axon releases serotonin from its terminal bouton, clomipramine prolongs serotonin's presence in the synapse, reexciting the postsynaptic neuron. Researchers do not yet understand why prolonging serotonin activity should relieve obsessive-compulsive disorder.

CONCEPT CHECK ☑

9. In what way do people with obsessive-compulsive disorder have an abnormal memory? (Check your answer on page 625.)

IN CLOSING

Emotions and Avoidance

Phobia and obsessive-compulsive disorder illustrate some of the possible links between emotions and cognitions. At the risk of seriously oversimplifying, we could say that people with phobias experience emotional attacks because of their cognitions about a particular object, whereas people with obsessive-compulsive disorder experience repetitive cognitions for emotional reasons. In both conditions most people know that their reactions are exaggerated, but mere awareness of the problem does not correct it. Dealing with such conditions requires attention to emotions, cognitions, and the links between them.

Summary

- *Anxiety disorder and panic disorder.* People with generalized anxiety disorder or panic disorder experience extreme anxiety. Panic disorder is characterized by episodes of disabling anxiety. People have periods of high heart and breathing rates, which they interpret as threatening. (page 615)
- *Persistence of avoidance behaviors.* A learned shock-avoidance response can persist long after the possibility of shock has been removed. As with shock-avoidance responses, phobias and obsessive-compulsive disorder persist because people do not discover that their avoidance behaviors are unnecessary. (page 617)
- *Phobia.* A phobia is a fear so extreme that it interferes with normal living. Phobias are learned through observation as well as through experience. (page 617)
- *Common phobias.* People are more likely to develop phobias of certain objects than of others; for example, snake phobias are more common than car phobias. The objects of the most common phobias have menaced humans throughout evolutionary history. They pose dangers that are difficult to predict or control, and they are generally objects with which we have had few safe experiences. (page 620)
- *Systematic desensitization of phobias.* A common therapy for phobia is systematic desensitization. The patient is taught to relax and is then gradually exposed to the object of the phobia. Flooding is similar, but the person is exposed to the object suddenly. (page 621)
- *Tranquilizers.* Drugs that facilitate activity at GABA synapses help to relieve anxiety. (page 622)
- *Obsessive-compulsive disorder.* People with obsessive-compulsive disorder try to avoid certain thoughts or impulses that cause anxiety or guilt. They also perform repetitive behaviors. (page 622)
- *Types of obsessive-compulsive disorder.* Two common types of compulsion are cleaning and checking. Cleaners try to avoid any type of contamination. Checkers constantly double-check themselves and invent elaborate rituals. (page 623)

Answers to Concept Checks

1. Worrying about anything—even panic attacks themselves—often prompts these people to hyperventilate, and hyperventilation can in turn lead to another panic attack. (page 617)
2. Temporarily prevent the person from pressing the lever. Only by ceasing to press it does the person discover that pressing is not necessary. (page 617)
3. The CS was the white rat. The UCS was the loud noise. The CR and the UCR were a combination of crying and other fear reactions. (page 619)
4. People may be born with a predisposition to learn fears of objects such as snakes and spiders that have been dangerous throughout our evolutionary history. We learn fears more readily of objects that we cannot predict or control. We learn fears more readily of objects with which we have few safe experiences. (page 620)
5. The method of extinguishing a learned shock-avoidance response is to prevent the response so that the individual learns that the failure to respond is not followed by shock. Similarly, with systematic desensitization the patient is prevented from fleeing the feared stimulus; he or she therefore learns that the danger is not as great as imagined. (page 622)
6. We should not be impressed. Over a 10-year period, most people recover from panic disorder on their own, either largely or completely. (page 622)
7. The flooding procedure is compatible with the James-Lange theory of emotions, which holds that emotions follow from perceptions of body arousal. In flooding, as arousal of the autonomic nervous system decreases, the person perceives, "I am calming down. I must not be as frightened of this situation as I thought I was." (page 622)
8. The combined effect of alcohol and a benzodiazepine tranquilizer would decrease anxiety, relax the muscles, and induce sleep more effectively than either alcohol or a benzodiazepine by itself. In fact the combined effect can be so strong as to be dangerous, even fatal. People given prescriptions for benzodiazepine tranquilizers are warned not to take them in conjunction with alcohol. (page 622)
9. People with obsessive-compulsive disorder do not trust their memory, although its accuracy is normal. (page 624)

Answers to Other Questions in the Module

Typical answers for obsessive-compulsive people (page 624): 1. T; 2. T; 3. T; 4. F; 5. F; 6. T; 7. F; 8. F; 9. T

Why do people abuse alcohol or other drugs?

What can be done to help people with substance-related disorders?

How would you like to volunteer for a little experiment? I want to implant into your brain a little device that will automatically lift your mood. There are still a few kinks in it, but most people who have tried say that it makes them feel good at least some of the time, and some people say they like it a great deal.

I should tell you about the possible risks. My device will endanger your health and will reduce your life expectancy by, oh, 10 years or so. Some people believe it causes brain damage, but they haven't proved that charge, so I don't think you should worry about it. Your behavior will change a good bit, though. You may have difficulty concentrating, for example. The device affects some people more than others. If you happen to be strongly affected, you will have difficulty completing your education, getting or keeping a job, and carrying on a satisfactory personal life. But if you are lucky, you can avoid all that. Anyway, you can quit the experiment anytime you decide. You should know, though, that the longer the device remains in your brain, the harder it is to remove.

I cannot pay you for taking part in this experiment. In fact *you* will have to pay *me*. But I'll give you a bargain rate: only $5 for the first week and then a little more each week as time passes. One other thing: Technically speaking, this experiment is illegal. We probably won't get caught, but if we do, we could both go to jail.

What do you say? Is it a deal? I presume you will say "no." I get very few volunteers. And yet, if I change the term *brain device* to *drug* and change *experimenter* to *drug dealer,* it is amazing how many volunteers come forward.

The effects of alcohol or other drugs range from pleasure to disaster. In Chapter 5 we examined the effects of several drugs on behavior. Instead of reviewing all the drugs again, we focus here on abuse of alcohol and opiates, with a few comments about nicotine.

Substance Dependence (Addiction)

We think of opiate drugs, such as morphine and heroin, as highly addictive. However, almost no one develops an addiction after taking morphine to con-

trol postsurgical pain. Why not? One reason is the dosage; hospital patients get only enough to control the pain. Another is the social setting; taking a drug in a hospital room is not like a party.

The main point is that simply taking a drug does not automatically produce addiction. Even people who take morphine or heroin illegally in recreational settings do not all become addicted. Two major questions are what causes occasional drug use to develop into an overwhelming craving, and why this process happens for some people and not others.

People who *find it difficult or impossible to quit a self-destructive habit* are said to have a **dependence** on it or an **addiction** to it. Someone has a physical dependence if quitting the drug produces withdrawal symptoms; a craving without such symptoms is a psychological dependence. However, that distinction is not always easy to draw, and a psychological dependence can be quite intense.

Addictions vary in many ways, and many people convince themselves that they are not addicted because they can still function. In fact many people with alcoholism or other addictions keep their jobs and even work well at times. Many go days or weeks without using the substance at all. To decide whether you are addicted, ask, "Does the substance cause troubles in my life, and do I often take more than I had decided I would?"

Nearly all the drugs that commonly produce addictions stimulate dopamine receptors in a small brain area called the *nucleus accumbens* (Koob & LeMoal, 1997). Some people have called these synapses "pleasure receptors." However, they respond to almost any unpredicted event, even an unpleasant one, but hardly at all to pleasant but expected events (Waelti, Dickinson, & Schultz, 2001; Young, Joseph, & Gray, 1993). They also become active when a person or animal starts seeking a drug, long before receiving the effects of it (Phillips, Stuber, Heien, Wightman, & Carelli, 2003). So the role of the nucleus accumbens probably relates more to attention than to pleasure. Indeed, it is reasonable to describe addiction as something that monopolizes people's attention (Robinson & Berridge, 2000).

Moreover, it is probably not helpful to imagine that something becomes addictive *because* it stimulates the nucleus accumbens. If anything, we might say that it stimulates the nucleus accumbens because it has become addictive. Gambling and even video game playing stimulate the nucleus accumbens in people who have developed strong habits (Koepp et al., 1998).

A great many substances can be addictive under certain circumstances. In a hospital ward where alcoholics were being treated, one of the patients moved his bed into the men's room (Cummings, 1979). At first the hospital staff ignored this curious behavior. Then, one by one, other patients moved their beds into the men's room. Eventually, the staff discovered what was happening.

These men, deprived of alcohol, had discovered that they could get a feeling similar to drunkenness from enormous amounts of water! By drinking about 30 liters (7.5 gallons) of water per day and urinating the same amount (which was why they moved into the men's room), they managed to alter the acid-to-base balance of their blood enough to produce a sensation that resembled drunkenness.

CONCEPT CHECK ☑

10. Why is it pointless to distinguish between substances that are and are not addictive? (Check your answer on page 633.)

What Motivates Addictive Behavior?

After someone has become addicted, what motivation sustains the repetitive and insistent drug-seeking? The motivation for trying a drug the first time is to experience something new, interesting, and presumably pleasant. If it is indeed pleasant, then the motivation for trying it a second time is to repeat the experience. However, people who have become addicted to a drug do not report great pleasure from it. So why do they continue despite the high costs and manifest risks?

One possibility is that they really are still motivated by pleasure. Even if the experience usually is not good, *sometimes* it is, and you may remember from Chapter 6 that behavior on a partial reinforcement schedule can be highly persistent. In particular, the first use of a drug after any period of abstention tends to be more intense than usual, so the user learns to return to the substance after any attempt to quit (Hoebel, Rada, Mark, & Pothos, 1999).

An alternative hypothesis, not contradictory to the first, is that the motivation is to escape unpleasant feelings. Even for someone in the early stages of becoming addicted, a brief period of abstention produces withdrawal symptoms. The symptoms are intense in the case of heroin, less so with cocaine, but always include depressed feelings. The user learns to take the drug to escape these feelings.

That explanation by itself does not explain why cravings persist so long after the end of withdrawal, so a modified hypothesis was that users learn to associate the drug with various places and other cues. Later exposure to those cues presumably triggers renewed withdrawal symptoms as a conditioned response. However, researchers found little evidence that environmental cues produce conditioned withdrawal symptoms (Drummond, Cooper, & Glautier, 1990).

Another modified hypothesis is that a drug user learns to associate the drug with relief from internal distress. That is, at first the person takes the drug to relieve withdrawal symptoms but later learns to use it to relieve other kinds of displeasure. Support for this idea comes from the observation that people who have quit drugs are most likely to relapse during a period of financial or social difficulties (Baker, Piper, McCarthy, Majeskie, & Fiore, 2004). Even nicotine, which produces a mixture of pleasant and unpleasant effects, helps relieve some kinds of distress (Kassel, Stroud, & Paronis, 2003).

The relief-from-distress explanation is plausible, so far as it goes, but leaves the question of why addiction produces such obsessive use. After all, many people deal with stress by exercising, but few continue until they collapse and lose consciousness. Many cope by shopping, but not to the point of bankruptcy. Some drug users, however, do continue to such extremes.

To account for the persistence of drug use far beyond what seems necessary for escape from distress, Terry Robinson and Kent Berridge (2000, 2001) propose that we separate the concepts of "liking" and "wanting." Addicted drug users rarely get intense pleasure ("liking") from a drug, but they continue to want it anyway. By analogy, someone who plays video games by the hour *wants* to play but probably does not feel great pleasure. The process of becoming addicted changes the organization of several brain areas, including some that are important for motivation and attention. Although some aspects of the response to the drug become weaker over time (tolerance, as discussed in Chapter 6), other aspects increase over time (sensitization) until the drug monopolizes the person's attention (Laviolette & van der Kooy, 2004; Robinson & Berridge, 2001). One remaining problem: It is easier to imagine how these changes would occur for cocaine, nicotine, or heroin than for gambling or video game playing, which can also be addictions (Griffiths & Wood, 2000).

CONCEPT CHECK ☑

11. According to one of the theories just described, how do people first learn to use drugs when they are feeling bad? (Check your answer on page 633.)

Is Substance Dependence a Disease?

You have no doubt heard people call alcoholism or drug dependence a disease. It is hard to confirm or deny that statement, however, without a clear definition of *disease*. (The medical profession assigns it no precise meaning.)

When people call alcoholism or drug dependence a disease, they apparently mean that people who abuse alcohol or other drugs should feel no guiltier about their condition than they would about having pneumonia. Although the "disease" label is reassuring, the concept has some questionable implications. For example, it implies an all or none distinction between people with the disease and those without it. The evidence suggests a continuum from no problem to severe problems (W. R. Miller & Brown, 1997; Polcin, 1997).

Also, disease implies that alcoholism or drug dependence becomes inevitably worse over time. In fact the long term varies (Hser, Hoffman, Grella, & Anglin, 2001; Vaillant, 1983). Some individuals deteriorate, some reach a steady level of abuse, and still others improve or fluctuate.

Furthermore, to regard substance dependence as a disease seems to imply a need for medical intervention. One of the most effective treatments for alcoholism or drug dependence is family therapy (Stanton & Shadish, 1997). By improving the person's family life, possibly improving the job situation, and helping the person to develop new interests, family therapy decreases the person's compulsion for alcohol or drug use.

Nicotine Dependence

Nicotine stimulates neurons that cause other neurons to release dopamine in the nucleus accumbens, the same brain area stimulated by other commonly addictive drugs (Laviolette & van der Kooy, 2004). You have no doubt heard that the cigarette smoking habit depends on nicotine addiction. One type of evidence for this conclusion is that some people find it easier to quit cigarettes if they have a replacement source of nicotine, such as a nicotine patch, nicotine chewing gum, or nicotine nasal spray (Rose, 1996).

"If so," you may have wondered, "why have so many smokers switched to low-tar, low-nicotine cigarette brands? Wouldn't those brands fail to satisfy a nicotine craving?" Yes, they would, *if* they delivered low nicotine!

Most low-tar, low-nicotine cigarettes have the same kind of tobacco as other cigarettes but have a filter with a row of little air holes, as shown at the top of Figure 16.7. The idea is that air entering these holes will dilute the tobacco smoke coming through the barrel of the cigarette. However, many smokers wrap their fingers around the air holes, either accidentally or intentionally. Some even wrap tape over the holes.

Regardless of whether people cover the holes, those who switch to low-nicotine cigarettes generally inhale more deeply than they did when smoking regular cigarettes, and they smoke more cigarettes per day. Consequently, people smoking low-nicotine cigarettes inhale about as much tar and nicotine per day as do people smoking regular cigarettes (Benowitz, 1986; Kozlowski, Frecker, Khouw, & Pope, 1980).

FIGURE 16.7 "Low-nicotine" cigarettes have a row of holes in the filter; room air is supposed to enter through those holes when the smoker inhales and therefore dilute the tobacco smoke. However, many smokers cover the holes with their fingers.

Alcoholism

Why do some people and not others develop addictions? The issue is a central concern with **alcoholism**, *the habitual overuse of alcohol.* Clearly, most alcohol users drink in moderation, but just as clearly, some let alcohol ruin their lives. Treating alcoholism is difficult and usually unsuccessful. If we could identify the problem earlier, or identify young people who are at great risk for alcoholism, perhaps we could initiate effective prevention or treatment. At least psychologists would like to try.

Genetics and Family Background

Twin studies indicate a strong genetic basis for habitual use of cigarettes (Kendler, Thornton, & Pedersen, 2000), illegal drugs (Kendler, Karkowski, Neale, & Prescott, 2000), gambling (Slutske et al., 2000), and alcoholism (True et al., 1999). Because many people have more than one addiction, the likely interpreta-

TABLE 16.3 Type I and Type II Alcoholism

	Severity	Gender Distribution	Genetics Basis	Onset
Type I (or Type A)	Generally less severe; better long-term outcome	Both males and females	Weaker genetic contribution	Gradual onset later in life
Type II (or Type B)	More severe, more likely to be associated with aggressive behavior and antisocial personality	Almost exclusively males	Strong evidence for genetic contribution	Rapid onset in teens or early 20s

tion is that some genes predispose people to excessive or addictive behaviors of many types. However, researchers have not strongly linked substance abuse to any identifiable gene (Lappalainen et al., 2002), and even people with no family history of alcoholism sometimes develop an alcohol problem.

A genetic predisposition also contributes mainly to early-onset alcoholism. Late-onset or **Type I alcoholism** *develops gradually over the years, affects about as many women as men, is generally less severe, and depends more on life experiences than genetics.* Early-onset or **Type II alcoholism** *develops rapidly, usually by age 25, is much more common in men than women, is usually more severe, and shows a strong genetic basis* (Devor, Abell, Hoffman, Tabakoff, & Cloninger, 1994; McGue, 1999). Table 16.3 summarizes this distinction. Naturally, not every alcoholic fits neatly into one category or the other.

The incidence of alcoholism is greater than average among people who grew up in families marked by conflict between parents, poor relationships between parents and children, and inadequate parental supervision of the children (Schulsinger, Knop, Goodwin, Teasdale, & Mikkelsen, 1986; Zucker & Gomberg, 1986). Women who were sexually abused in childhood are also at increased risk for alcoholism (Kendler, Bulik, et al., 2000).

Culture also plays an important role. For example, most Jewish families emphasize drinking in moderation,

▮ Italian and Jewish cultures, which stress moderation, have a fair amount of alcohol use but relatively little alcohol abuse.

and relatively few Jews develop alcoholism (Cahalan, 1978). The same conclusion holds true for Italians as well. By contrast alcoholism is more prevalent in the Irish culture, which tolerates it more (Vaillant & Milofsky, 1982).

Still, individuals differ. Not all children of alcoholic parents become alcoholics themselves, and not all children who grow up in a culture that tolerates heavy drinking become alcoholics. Can we identify people who are highly vulnerable to alcoholism?

CRITICAL THINKING: WHAT'S THE EVIDENCE?
Ways of Predicting Alcoholism

Perhaps people's early behavior might indicate who is more likely to develop alcoholism. One way to find such clues is to record the behaviors of young people and then, many years later, examine their alcohol use. However, this procedure requires decades of research and a huge sample of participants.

A more feasible approach is to compare children of an alcoholic parent with children who have no alcoholic relatives. From previous studies we know that more children of alcoholics will become alcoholics. Therefore, behaviors that are significantly more prevalent among the children of alcoholics may predict vulnerability to alcoholism.

In the first of the following studies, experimenters tested whether alcohol might be more rewarding to the sons of alcoholics than to the sons of nonalcoholics (Levenson, Oyama, & Meek, 1987). (The study focused on men because alcoholism is more common in men than women.) Alcohol is known to help people relax (Swendsen et al., 2000); the question is whether it helps some people more than others.

EXPERIMENT I

Hypothesis Drinking alcohol will provide relief for almost anyone in a stressful situation. It will provide more relief to the adult sons of alcoholic fathers than to other men of the same age.

The researchers did not study sons of alcoholic mothers because the focus was on genetics, not prenatal environment. If a mother drinks heavily during pregnancy, she increases the risk of alcohol abuse in her children regardless of genetics (Baer, Sampson, Barr, Connor, & Streissguth, 2003).

Method   Half of the participants were sons of alcoholic fathers and the others were from families with no known alcoholics. The young men were told that, at a certain time, they would receive an electric shock and later they would have to give a 3-minute speech entitled "What I Like and Dislike About My Body." (You can imagine the embarrassment and stress of that assignment.) They watched a clock tick off the waiting time. Half of each group were offered alcohol at the start of the waiting period. Everyone who was offered drank it.

Results   All of the men showed considerable stress, as measured by heart rate, restlessness, and self-reports. Those who drank alcohol showed a lower heart rate and reported less anxiety. The easing of stress was more pronounced in those with an alcoholic father (Figure 16.8).

Interpretation   Men who are genetically vulnerable to alcoholism experience greater stress-reducing effects from alcohol than other men of the same age. Why that is true, we do not know, but we might use the stress-reducing effects to predict vulnerability to alcoholism.

EXPERIMENT 2

Several other studies found that young men who are vulnerable to alcoholism have difficulty estimating their own degree of intoxication. This study tested whether young drinkers who underestimate their degree of intoxication are more likely than others to become alcoholics later in life (Schuckit & Smith, 1997).

Hypothesis   Men who underestimate their intoxication after moderate drinking will be more likely than others to become alcoholics later.

Method   This study was limited to 18- to 25-year-old men with a close relative who was alcoholic. After each of them drank a fixed amount of alcohol, they were asked to walk and describe how intoxicated they felt. Experimenters measured the stagger or sway when the men walked. Ten years later, the experimenters located as many of these men as possible, interviewed them, and determined which ones had become alcoholics.

Results   Of those who either did not sway much when walking or stated that they did not feel intoxicated, 51 of 81 (63%) became alcoholics within 10 years. Of those who clearly swayed and reported that they felt intoxicated, 9 of 52 (17%) became alcoholics.

Interpretation   Men who neither act nor feel intoxicated after a moderate amount of drinking are likely to continue drinking and to become alcoholics. By watching and interviewing young drinkers, psychologists may be able to identify a high-risk population.

Any research study has limitations, and one limitation of these studies is clear: They examined only men. Considering that more men than women become alcoholics, the research strategy was reasonable; however, someone should repeat the studies with women.

CONCEPT CHECK ☑

12. What are two ways in which sons of alcoholics differ from sons of nonalcoholics? (Check your answer on page 633.)

Treatments

> My mind is a dark place, and I should not be left alone there at night.
> —Participant at Alcoholics Anonymous Meeting

Of all the people who try to quit alcohol or other drugs on their own, an estimated 10 to 20% manage to succeed (S. Cohen et al., 1989), though not necessarily on the first try. Some people quit and relapse many times before eventual success. In many cases, however, people with a substance-abuse problem find that

FIGURE 16.8 Changes in stress over time for a typical subject: The line goes up to indicate an increase in heart rate. Alcohol suppressed the signs of stress, especially for the sons of alcoholics. (*From "Greater Reinforcement from Alcohol for Those at Risk: Parental Risk, Personality Risk, and Sex," by Levenson et al., Journal of Abnormal Psychology, 1987, 96, 242–253. Copyright © 1987 by the American Psychological Association. Reprinted by permission of the author.*)

they cannot quit on their own. Eventually, they "hit bottom," discovering that they have damaged their health, their ability to hold a job, and their relationships with friends and family. At that point they turn to others for help—either a mental-health professional or a self-help group such as Alcoholics Anonymous.

People who seek professional help improve their likelihood of long-term abstention, although there are no guarantees. Addicts who check into a hospital for treatment can be supervised 24 hours a day to ensure full abstinence. In the long run, however, most addicts respond as well to outpatient treatment as to hospital treatment (W. R. Miller & Hester, 1986).

Combating alcoholism is difficult but not hopeless. Let's consider several approaches and controversies.

Alcoholics Anonymous

The most widespread treatment for alcoholism in North America is **Alcoholics Anonymous (AA)**, *a self-help group of people who are trying to abstain from alcohol use and help others do the same.* AA meetings are held regularly in community halls, church basements, and other available spaces. The meeting format varies but often includes study of the book *Alcoholics Anonymous* (Anonymous, 1955) and discussions of participants' individual problems. Some meetings feature an invited speaker. The group has a strong spiritual focus, including a reliance on "a Power greater than ourselves," but no affiliation with any particular religion. Although AA imposes no requirements on its members other than making an effort to quit alcohol, new members are strongly encouraged to attend 90 meetings during the first 90 days. (Those who miss a day or two can compensate by attending extra meetings on another day.) The idea is to make a strong commitment. From then on, members attend as often as they like.

Millions of people have participated in the AA program in the United States and other countries. One reason for its appeal is that all its members have gone through similar experiences. If someone tries to make an excuse for drinking, saying, "You just don't understand how I feel," others can retort, "Oh, yes we do!" A member who feels the urge to take a drink can call a fellow member day or night for support. Attendance at meetings is free; members contribute what they can toward the cost of renting the meeting place. AA has inspired other "anonymous" self-help groups whose purpose is to help drug addicts, compulsive gamblers, compulsive eaters, and so forth.

Although AA members themselves have confidence in the program, research on its effectiveness has been scarce. One reason is that the organization is serious about its members' anonymity; it does not provide a list of members, and many of its meetings are closed to nonmembers. A further problem is that people cannot be assigned randomly to an AA group and a control group; AA participants are those who wish to participate, and they undoubtedly differ in many ways from those who decline to participate.

Antabuse

In addition to or instead of attendance at AA meetings, some individuals with alcoholism seek medical treatment. Many years ago investigators noticed that the workers in a certain rubber manufacturing plant drank very little alcohol. The investigators eventually linked this behavior to *disulfiram*, a chemical that was used in the manufacturing process. Ordinarily, the liver converts alcohol into a toxic substance, *acetaldehyde* (ASS-eh-TAL-de-HIDE) and then converts acetaldehyde into a harmless substance, *acetic acid.* Disulfiram, however, blocks the conversion of acetaldehyde to acetic acid. Whenever the workers exposed to disulfiram drank alcohol, they accumulated acetaldehyde and became ill. Over time they learned to avoid alcohol.

Disulfiram, available under the trade name **Antabuse,** is now sometimes used in the treatment of alcoholism, for which it is regarded as only moderately effective (Hughes & Cook, 1997). *Alcoholics who take a daily Antabuse pill become sick whenever they have a drink.* They develop headache, nausea, blurred vision, anxiety, and a sensation of heat in the face. The threat of sickness is more effective than the sickness itself (Fuller & Roth, 1979). By taking a daily Antabuse pill, a recovering alcoholic renews the decision not to drink. Those who do take a drink in spite of the threat become quite ill, at which point they decide either not to drink again or not to take the pill again!

CONCEPT CHECK ✓

13. About 50% of Southeast Asians have a gene that makes them unable to convert acetaldehyde to acetic acid. Would such people be more likely or less likely than others to become alcoholics? (Check your answer on page 633.)

Controlled Drinking

Most physicians agree with Alcoholics Anonymous that the only hope for an alcoholic is total abstinence. Drinking in moderation, they insist, is out of the question. A few psychologists doubt that abstention is always a realistic goal (Peele, 1998). Of those who fail to learn abstention, a few do manage to reduce their drinking. This is not to say that alcoholics can simply decide to drink in moderation; if they could, they would not have become alcoholics in the first place. Rather, the point is that a few people learn (with difficulty) to drink less, to stay out of legal trouble, and in general to do themselves less damage.

Psychologists have established several programs to try to teach alcoholics "controlled drinking," with at least occasional success (Rosenberg, 1993). Similarly, the **harm reduction** approach *concentrates on decreasing the frequency of drug use and minimizing the harmful consequences to health and well-being,* even if the person does not quit altogether (MacCoun, 1998). Critics charge that the idea of controlled drinking or harm reduction discourages people from making a serious effort at abstinence. Defenders reply that when people find that they cannot quit, we should not give up on helping them. This controversy is not likely to end soon.

Contingency Management

Another approach is a form of behavior therapy known as *contingency management*. Practitioners monitor alcohol use by a Breathalyzer or other drugs by urine samples. Whenever the test shows no alcohol or drugs, a therapist provides an immediate reinforcement. For example, teenagers might receive a movie pass or a voucher for a pizza (Kaminer, 2000).

A major strength of this approach is that many people who are not motivated to try other approaches do agree to receive rewards for being free of alcohol and drugs. In a way the effectiveness of contingency management is surprising, as the rewards are small. That is, people could have abstained from alcohol and drugs and then used the money they saved to give themselves the same or greater rewards. Evidently, there is something powerful about testing negative for drugs and then receiving an immediate reinforcement.

Opiate Dependence

Prior to 1900 opiate drugs such as morphine and heroin were considered less dangerous than alcohol (Siegel, 1987). In fact many doctors urged their patients with alcoholism to switch from alcohol to morphine. Then, around 1900, opiates became illegal in the United States, except by prescription to control pain. Since then research on opiate use has been limited by the fact that only lawbreakers use opiates.

Opiate dependence often has a rapid onset in contrast to alcohol and tobacco dependence, which develop more slowly. Like alcoholism, opiate abuse shows a hereditary tendency; that is, the closer your genetic relationship to an opiate abuser, the higher your probability of developing the same problem (Kendler, Karkowski, et al., 2000).

Treatments

Some users of heroin and other opiates try to break their habit by going "cold turkey"—abstaining completely and suddenly, sometimes under medical supervision. Many people, however, experience a recurring urge to take the drug, even long after the withdrawal symptoms have subsided. To combat that urge, they can turn to self-help groups, contingency management, and other treatments, which succeed sometimes but not always. For those who cannot quit, researchers have sought to find a nonaddictive substitute that would satisfy the craving for opiates without harmful side effects. (Heroin was originally introduced as a substitute for morphine, before physicians discovered that it is even more troublesome!)

The drug **methadone** (METH-uh-don) *is sometimes offered as a less dangerous substitute for opiates.* Methadone is chemically similar to morphine and heroin and can itself be addictive. (Table 16.4 compares

Heroin withdrawal resembles a severe bout of the flu, with aching limbs, intense chills, vomiting, and diarrhea; it takes a week on average to go cold turkey. Unfortunately, even after people have suffered through withdrawal, they still sometimes crave the drug.

TABLE 16.4 Comparison of Methadone with Morphine

	Morphine	Methadone By Injection	Methadone Taken Orally
Addictive?	Yes	Yes	Weakly
Onset	Rapid	Rapid	Slow
"Rush"?	Yes	Yes	No
Relieves craving?	Yes	Yes	Yes
Rapid withdrawal symptoms?	Yes	Yes	No

methadone and morphine.) When methadone is taken in pill form, however, it enters the bloodstream gradually and departs gradually (Dole, 1980). (If morphine or heroin is taken as a pill, much of the drug is broken down in the digestive system and never reaches the brain.) Thus, methadone does not produce the "rush" associated with injected opiates nor the rapid withdrawal symptoms. Although methadone satisfies the craving for opiates, it does not eliminate the addiction. If the dosage is reduced, the craving returns.

A more recent alternative to methadone is *buprenorphine,* which attaches to the same receptors as heroin and morphine but attaches to them for long times and stimulates them less strongly. Thus, it prevents heroin or similar drugs from attaching to those receptors.

CONCEPT CHECK ☑

14. Many heroin users report withdrawal symptoms when they take buprenorphine. Why? (Check your answer on this page.)

IN CLOSING

Substances, the Individual, and Society

Substance dependence is costly to society as well as to the individual. The United States and many other countries have tried to control the problem by issuing stiff prison sentences for those who use or sell certain drugs. The result? Hard to say; drug use continues to be widespread, but we do not know what it would be without the legal prohibitions. We do know that law enforcement itself is costly; prisons are crowded with those whose only offense was drug related and nonviolent, and many drug users turn to theft or violence as a way of getting drugs. The Netherlands has experimented with greatly decreased penalties against the use of marijuana and other drugs. The results are favorable in some ways but not others; overall, it is impossible to generalize about what might happen if other countries tried the same approach (MacCoun & Reuter, 1997).

Summary

* *Substance dependence.* People who find it difficult or impossible to stop using a substance are said to be dependent on it or addicted to it. (page 626)
* *Addictive substances.* Nearly all addictive substances stimulate dopamine synapses in a brain area that is apparently associated with attention. (page 626)
* *Motivations behind addiction.* Some people continue using drugs frequently despite little apparent

pleasure. One hypothesis is that they use the drugs to escape displeasure. Another is that frequent use of a drug modifies brain circuits to make the drug dominate attention. In effect the user "wants" the drug even without enormously "liking" the experience. (page 627)
* *The disease concept.* Whether or not substance abuse is considered a disease depends on what we mean by disease. (page 628)
* *Predisposition to alcoholism.* People at risk for alcoholism find that alcohol relieves their stress more than it does for other people. People who underestimate their level of intoxication are more likely than others to become alcoholics later. (page 628)
* *Alcoholics Anonymous.* The self-help group Alcoholics Anonymous provides the most common treatment for alcoholism in North America. (page 631)
* *Antabuse.* Some alcoholics are treated with Antabuse, a prescription drug that makes them ill if they drink alcohol. (page 631)
* *The controlled drinking controversy.* Whether certain alcoholics can be trained to drink in moderation is controversial. (page 631)
* *Opiate abuse.* Some opiate users quit using opiates, suffer through the withdrawal symptoms, and manage to abstain from further use. Others substitute methadone or buprenorphine under medical supervision. (page 632)

Answers to Concept Checks

10. Some people show addictions to gambling or video games, which are not substances at all. Some have managed to abuse even water. Also, not everyone who tries heroin or cocaine becomes addicted. (page 627)
11. At first, they learn to use the drug to escape withdrawal symptoms caused by abstention from the drug itself. Later, they learn to use the drug to escape from other kinds of distress. (page 627)
12. Alcohol gives them more than the average amount of relief from stress, and they do not appear or feel as drunk as other people do after a moderate amount of drinking. (page 630)
13. They are less likely than others to become alcoholics. This gene is considered the probable reason that relatively few Asians become alcoholics (Harada, Agarwal, Goedde, Tagaki, & Ishikawa, 1982; Reed, 1985). (page 631)
14. Buprenorphine attaches to the opiate receptors in the brain but excites them less than heroin or morphine would. Therefore, the user gets less than the accustomed amount of effect and enters withdrawal. (page 633)

Why do people have severe mood swings, and what can be done to help them?

For most of us, most of the time, our moods match the events of our lives. We feel happy when life is going well and sad when we experience disappointments. Some people, however, feel extremely good or extremely bad for long periods of time regardless of the events in their lives. Why?

Depression

People who say "I'm depressed," often mean "I'm sad. Life isn't going very well for me right now." In psychology **major depression** is a more *extreme condition, persisting most of each day for at least 2 weeks, usually more, during which the person experiences little interest in anything, little pleasure, and little motivation for any productive activity.* People who are depressed cannot even imagine anything that would make them happy. They have trouble concentrating. They lose interest in food and sex. Aaron Beck (1973) described one woman with depression who stood in front of an elevator for 15 minutes because she did not have enough desire to press the button. People with long-lasting depression don't even cry as much as normal after watching a sad movie, evidently because they don't even have the energy to cry (Rottenberg, Gross, Wilhelm, Najmi, & Gotlib, 2002).

Nearly all depressed people experience sleep abnormalities (Carroll, 1980; Healy & Williams, 1988)

(see Figure 16.9). They enter REM sleep within 45 minutes after falling asleep (an unusually short time for most people). Most depressed people wake up early and cannot get back to sleep. When morning comes, they feel poorly rested. In fact they usually feel most depressed early in the morning. During much of the day, they feel a little sleepy.

Depression is common from adolescence through old age. About 5% of adults are depressed within any given year (Narrow et al., 2002), and 10 to 20% are depressed at some time in life (Kessler et al., 1994). Most people with depression say they had been somewhat depressed off and on for years before they first visited a therapist (Eaton et al., 1997). Some reports indicate that depression has been growing more common over the decades, although the research is mixed on this point (Murphy, Laird, Monson, Sobol, & Leighton, 2000). It is difficult, of course, to distinguish between changes in prevalence and changes in standards of diagnosis.

The good news is that few people remain permanently depressed. Typically, people have an episode of depression that lasts a few months (less commonly for years), then recover for months or years, and then experience another episode of depression. On the average, earlier depressed episodes and recovery periods last longer than later ones (Solomon et al., 1997).

People with a special variety of depression known as **seasonal affective disorder (SAD), or depression with a seasonal pattern** (Figure 16.10), *repeatedly become depressed during a particular season of the year.* It is common in Scandinavia, which has huge differences between summer and winter (Haggarty et al., 2002), and almost universal among explorers who spend long times in Antarctica (Palinkas, 2003). Although annual winter depressions have received the most publicity, annual summer depressions also occur (Faedda et al., 1993). Unlike other depressed patients, most people with seasonal affective disorder sleep and eat excessively during their depressed periods (Jacobsen, Sack, Wehr, Rogers, & Rosenthal, 1987).

Normal sleep

← 90 minutes →

Depressed sleep

← 90 minutes →

FIGURE 16.9 When most people go to sleep at their usual time, they progress slowly to stage 4 and then back through stages 3 and 2, reaching REM sleep toward the end of their first 90-minute cycle. Depressed people enter REM more rapidly and awaken frequently during the night.

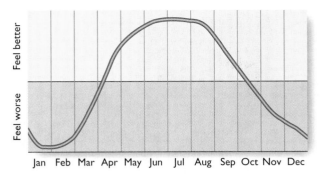

FIGURE 16.10 Most people feel slightly better during the summer than during the winter, when there are fewer hours of sunlight. The differences are even greater for people with seasonal affective disorder (SAD).

Also, they tend to fall asleep late and awaken late, in contrast to other depressed patients who generally get sleepy early and wake up early (Teicher et al., 1997).

The winter variety of seasonal affective disorder can be relieved by sitting in front of a bright light for a few hours each day, preferably in the morning. The morning light shifts the circadian rhythm forward so that the person wakes earlier and feels sleepy earlier. A strong shift in the circadian rhythm is essential to the antidepressant effect, but why that shift helps depression remains uncertain (Terman, Terman, Lo, & Cooper, 2001). Although the effects of light therapy are poorly understood, they are powerful and reliable, with relatively little cost and no side effects (Wirz-Justice, 1998).

If you have seasonal affective disorder and want to try light therapy, check "light therapy" with your Internet browser and you will find several companies that can supply the product. You can also visit this Web site:

http://www.sada.org.uk/

Bipolar disorder, previously known as *manic-depressive disorder,* is a related condition in which someone *alternates between periods of depression and periods of mania, which are opposite extremes.* We shall consider bipolar disorder in more detail later.

CONCEPT CHECK ☑

15. How does major depression differ from ordinary sadness or discouragement? (Check your answer on page 644.)

Genetic Influences

Although no one gene by itself is strongly linked to depression (Wong & Licinio, 2001), several genes increase the risk. One study examined the effects of different alleles (forms) of a gene controlling neurons'

ability to reabsorb the neurotransmitter serotonin after they release it. For young adults under little or no stress, the risk of depression was low regardless of this gene. However, for those who had undergone stressful experiences, people with the "short" allele of the gene had a greater probability of depression than those with the "long" allele, and the greater the stress, the greater the difference between people with the short and long alleles of the gene (Caspi, Sugden, et al., 2003). That is, the genetic predisposition magnified the depressive influence of stressful experiences.

Your probability of becoming depressed increases if you have close biological relatives with depression, especially if they became depressed before age 30 (Kendler, Gardner, & Prescott, 1999; Lyons et al., 1998). In that regard depression resembles many other psychological and neurological disorders: People with an early onset are more likely than those with a later onset to have relatives with the same disorder. However, probably no gene is specific to depression. People with depression are more likely than other people to have relatives with substance abuse, antisocial personality disorder, attention-deficit disorder, bulimia nervosa, migraine headaches, and a variety of other disorders (Fu et al., 2002; Hudson et al., 2003; Kendler et al., 1995). Evidently, the relevant genes magnify many risks and problems. Your risk of depression is also increased, but not as much, if you have adoptive relatives with depression (see Figure 16.11). That is, depression depends on both hereditary and family influences, as well as experiences outside the family setting.

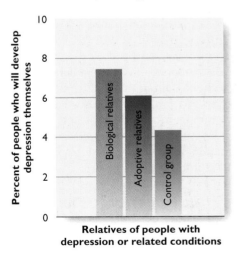

FIGURE 16.11 Blood relatives of depressed people, substance-dependent people, and suicidal people have an increased risk of depression, as do adopted relatives to a lesser extent. *(Based on data of Weissman, Kidd, & Prusoff, 1982)*

Gender Differences

Depression is uncommon before adolescence, but from adolescence on, it occurs about twice as often in women as in men, and the ratio is even higher for severe depression. Women experience depression more than men in all cultures for which we have data (Culberson, 1997; Cyranowski, Frank, Young, & Shear, 2000; Silberg et al., 1999).

Why is depression more common in women than in men? On the average, depressed women have about the same hormonal levels as other women (Roca, Schmidt, & Rubinow, 1999), so hormones are apparently not the answer. (Conceivably, hormones might magnify the effects of stressful experiences, as the genetic influences do.) One hypothesis is that females encounter more negative events than males do (Hankin & Abramson, 2001). For example, severe sexual abuse in childhood increases the risk of later depression, and more girls than boys are sexually abused. The strongest evidence for the effects of sexual abuse comes from a study that compared pairs of twins in which one reported childhood sexual abuse and the other did not. On the average, the twin reporting sexual abuse had more depression than the other twin (E. C. Nelson et al., 2002). Of course, this conclusion presumes that both twins accurately reported childhood events.

Susan Nolen-Hoeksema (1990, 1991) has suggested that the excess of depression among women relates to how people react to emotional distress: When men start to feel depressed, they generally try to distract themselves. They play basketball or watch a movie or do something else instead of thinking about how they feel. Women are more likely to ruminate—to think about why they are depressed, to talk with others about their feelings, even to have a long cry. According to Nolen-Hoeksema, ruminating about depression only makes it worse. The ruminative thoughts interfere with useful problem solving and bias a person toward a pessimistic appraisal of the situation. This explanation has the advantage of suggesting ways to help women (and men) avoid or minimize their depression. It does not, however, explain *why* women ruminate more and distract themselves less than men do. Another difficult question: Do the ruminative thoughts *lead to* depression? Or are they just an early symptom of depression?

Events That Precipitate Depression

As a rule people become depressed when bad things happen to them. Depression is particularly likely after events that leave people feeling not only sad but also humiliated and guilty, feeling that some bad event was their own fault (Kendler, Hettema, Butera, Gardner, & Prescott, 2003). However, the event itself is not the sole cause of depression; when various people have roughly the same experience, some become depressed and others do not.

One study followed students at a California university who had answered a questionnaire about their mental health 2 weeks before a major earthquake in

Depression is most common among people who have little social support.

1989. Psychologists asked the same students to fill out the questionnaires again 10 days and 7 weeks after the earthquake. The results were that students who were already somewhat depressed before the earthquake became and remained depressed; students who had not been depressed recovered rapidly (Nolen-Hoeksema & Morrow, 1991). In other words a stressful event has its strongest effects on people who were already somewhat depressed.

CONCEPT CHECK ☑

16. What is the relationship between depression and precipitating events? (Check your answer on page 644.)

Cognitive Aspects of Depression

Depression depends less on the events that transpire than on how people interpret them. For example, not being invited to a party might depress someone who regarded it as evidence of rejection (S. L. Johnson & Roberts, 1995). Instead of believing that every cloud has a silver lining, people with depression believe that every silver lining has a cloud. Perhaps their thought patterns lead to their depression.

Suppose you fail a test. Choose your probable explanation:

- The test was difficult. Probably other students did poorly too.
- I had a weaker background from my previous education than most other students in the class.

- I didn't get a good chance to study.
- I'm just stupid. I always do badly, no matter how hard I try.

Any of the first three explanations would not leave you depressed. They attribute your failure to something temporary, specific, or correctable. However, the fourth attribution applies to you always and everywhere. If you make that attribution—and if your grades are important to you—you are likely to feel depressed (Abramson, Seligman, & Teasdale, 1978; C. Peterson, Bettes, & Seligman, 1985).

In a given situation, you might have a good reason for one attribution or another. For example, if you get a low grade on a French test, perhaps you really are the only one in your class who did not take high school French. Still, everyone has an **explanatory style**, *a tendency to accept one kind of explanation for success or failure more often than others*. Recall from Chapter 14 that an *internal attribution* cites a cause within the person. ("I failed because I studied poorly.") An *external attribution* identifies causes outside the person. ("I failed because the test was so hard.") Most people are inconsistent about how they explain their successes but more consistent in how they explain their failures (Burns & Seligman, 1989).

Blaming yourself isn't always wrong, of course. However, consistently taking the blame even when the problem is not your fault constitutes a *pessimistic* explanatory style, especially if your attributions for failure are global (consistent over situations) and stable (consistent over time). People with a pessimistic style are more likely than others to have been depressed in the past and more likely to become depressed in the future (Alloy et al., 1999). Indeed, according to Aaron Beck (1973, 1987), depressed people put unfavorable interpretations on almost all their experiences. If someone walks by without comment, their likely response is, "See, people ignore me. They don't like me." After any kind of defeat, "I'm hopeless." People who are depressed exaggerate their failures, minimize their successes, and feel depressed after even mild setbacks.

Researchers have also gauged the explanatory styles of famous people, even dead people, by reading their speeches and writings to see what explanations they offered for successes and failures. Using this method psychologists have found that pessimistic political leaders tend to be cautious, indecisive, and inactive. Leaders with an optimistic explanatory style take bold, even risky actions (Satterfield & Seligman, 1994; Zullow, Oettingen, Peterson, & Seligman, 1988). Athletes with a pessimistic style tend to give up and try less after a defeat. Athletes with a more optimistic style try harder after a defeat because, after all, they believe they can overcome their defeats if they work hard enough (Seligman, Nolen-Hoeksema,

Thornton, & Thornton, 1990). (How do you react after you try something and fail? Do you try harder or do you give up?)

CONCEPT CHECK

17. Would depressed people be more or less likely than others to buy a lottery ticket? (Check your answer on page 644.)

Treatments

Several kinds of treatment are effective in combating depression, including two with no cost or side effects: One is to keep to a regular sleep schedule (Wehr et al., 1998). Depressed people have sleep problems, and sleep problems increase the risk of depression. The other method is to get some consistent aerobic exercise, such as jogging, brisk walking, or dancing. The exercise helps simply by increasing the blood flow to the brain (Leppämäki, Partonen, & Lönnqvist, 2002). Of course, this advice applies mainly to people with mild to moderate depression. Someone with severe depression has barely enough energy to get out of bed, much less exercise.

For people with major depression, the statistics are these: Of those who have no treatment or take only a placebo, about one third will improve significantly over the next few months. Of those who take antidepressant drugs, more than half will improve. Of those who get interpersonal or cognitive behavioral psychotherapy, again more than half will improve. Psychodynamic therapy, including psychoanalysis, has been tested less often but appears to be less effective (Hollon, Thase, & Markowitz, 2002). Figure 16.12 shows the results.

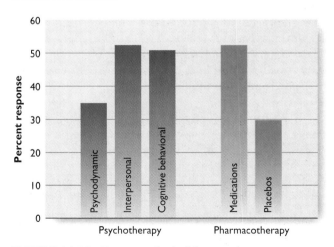

FIGURE 16.12 About one third of depressed patients recover without treatment, many others recover with treatment, and more than one third respond poorly to treatment. *(From Hollon, S. D., et al. "Treatment and Prevention of Depression," Fig. 3, pg. 53, in* Psychological Science in Public Interest, 3, *39–77. Reprinted with permission of Blackwell Publishing.)*

CRITICAL THINKING:
A STEP FURTHER
Drugs and Psychotherapy

Researchers report that the combination of drugs plus psychotherapy helps about the same percentage of people as either one alone (Thase et al., 1997). What inference can we draw about whether drugs help the same people who would have responded to psychotherapy?

Psychotherapy

Most of the research on psychotherapy for depression focuses on two methods that are frequently effective, as shown in Figure 16.12. One is **interpersonal therapy,** *which focuses on coping with difficulties someone has faced in the present or recent past, such as death of a loved one, a bad marriage, changes in life status, and lack of social skills* (Hollon et al., 2002). The therapist tries to understand the difficulties and help the client develop a strategy and skills to deal with them.

Cognitive therapy, as discussed in Chapter 15, focuses on changing people's thoughts and beliefs and on encouraging a more active life. According to Aaron Beck, a pioneer in cognitive therapy, depressed people are guided by certain thoughts or assumptions of which they are only dimly aware. He refers to the "negative cognitive triad of depression":

- I am deprived or defeated.
- The world is full of obstacles.
- The future is devoid of hope.

Based on these "automatic thoughts," people who are depressed interpret ambiguous situations to their own disadvantage. When something goes wrong, they blame themselves without even considering alternative interpretations (Beck, 1991). The therapist focuses on a belief, such as "no one likes me," points out that it is a hypothesis, and invites the client to collect evidence to test the hypothesis and if possible discard or modify it.

In addition to the focus on changing thoughts and beliefs, cognitive therapy also encourages people to become more active, to take part in more activities that might bring pleasure or a sense of accomplishment. If necessary, the therapist helps the person improve social skills or overcome any unfortunate habits that stand in the way of greater activity. Research has found that giving depressed people just this guidance toward greater activity produces about the same antidepressant effect as the complete cognitive therapy treatment (Jacobson et al., 1996). Think about a parallel finding in Chapter 12: Extraverted personality consists of friendly, active, outgoing behavior and enjoyment of life. Introverts who "pretend" to be extraverted, talking more and being more outgoing for the time being, report feeling happier. The same applies here: Just getting people to *do things* helps them overcome depression.

Antidepressant Medications

The common antidepressants include tricyclics, serotonin reuptake inhibitors, and monoamine oxidase inhibitors. **Tricyclic drugs** (e.g., imipramine, trade name Tofranil) *block the reabsorption of the neurotransmitters dopamine, norepinephrine, and serotonin after they are released by an axon's terminal* (Figure 16.13). Thus, tricyclics prolong the effect of these neurotransmitters on the receptors of the postsynaptic cell. Although they are effective for many people, they produce unpleasant side effects, including dry mouth, difficulty urinating, heart irregularities, and drowsiness (Horst & Preskorn, 1998). Many people quit the drugs or reduce the dosage because of the side effects.

Selective serotonin reuptake inhibitors (SSRIs) (e.g., fluoxetine, trade name Prozac) are similar to tricyclic drugs but more specific in their effects. They *block the reuptake of the neurotransmitter serotonin.* Their side effects are usually limited to mild nausea or headache (Feighner et al., 1991), and consequently, many people can take them in larger doses than the tricyclics. However, the selective serotonin reuptake blockers sometimes produce nervousness, so they are not recommended for people with both depression and anxiety. Other common drugs in this category are sertraline (Zoloft), fluvoxamine (Luvox), citalopram (Celexa), and paroxetine (Paxil or Seroxat).

Monoamine (MAHN-oh-ah-MEEN) **oxidase inhibitors (MAOIs)** (e.g., phenelzine, trade name Nardil) *block the metabolic breakdown of released dopamine, norepinephrine, and serotonin* by the enzyme monoamine oxidase (MAO) (Figure 16.13c). Thus, MAOIs also prolong the ability of released neurotransmitters to stimulate the postsynaptic cell. MAOIs are usually less effective than the other antidepressant drugs, but they help some people who do not respond to other drugs (Thase, Trivedi, & Rush, 1995).

Another "group" of antidepressant drugs have little in common with each other except that they do not fit into the first three groups. These **atypical antidepressants** *generally produce only mild side effects and help many patients who do not respond to the other antidepressant drugs.* The most common of these, buproprion (Wellbutrin), acts mainly by blocking the reuptake of dopamine (Horst & Preskorn, 1998).

You have probably heard about **St. John's wort,** *an herb with antidepressant effects.* It contains several chemicals that block the reuptake of dopamine and serotonin, as other antidepressant drugs do. Be-

a Normal process

Terminal bouton

1 Neurotransmitter molecules released
2 Receptor stimulated
3 Some molecules reabsorbed
4 Some molecules broken down by MAO

Postsynaptic neuron

b Effects of tricyclics and selective serotonin reuptake inhibitors (SSRIs)

Terminal bouton

5 Port of reabsorption blocked

Postsynaptic neuron

c Effects of MAOIs

Terminal bouton

6 MAO inhibitor prevents breakdown

Postsynaptic neuron

FIGURE 16.13 (a) Ordinarily, after the release of a neurotransmitter, some of the molecules are reabsorbed by the terminal bouton, and some are broken down by the enzyme monoamine oxidase (MAO). (b) Selective serotonin reuptake inhibitors (SSRIs) prevent reabsorption of serotonin. Tricyclic drugs prevent reabsorption of dopamine, norepinephrine, and serotonin. (c) MAO inhibitors (MAOIs) block the enzyme monoamine oxidase and thereby increase the availability of the neurotransmitter.

cause St. John's wort is a naturally occurring substance, it is fairly inexpensive and available without a doctor's prescription. St. John's wort is about as effective as other antidepressant drugs, but it has drawbacks. First, because the Food and Drug Administration does not regulate the sale of herbs, the purity varies from one bottle to another. Second, it has side effects, including gastrointestinal distress, drowsiness, and painful sensitivity to light (Wong, Smith, & Boon, 1998). Third, it has an additional very interesting side effect: It activates a liver enzyme that breaks down a wide variety of toxic plant chemicals. Helping to break down toxins sounds like a benefit, and indeed it can be. However, that enzyme also breaks down most medications. Therefore, taking St. John's wort decreases the effectiveness of cancer drugs, AIDS drugs, and even birth-control pills (Moore et al., 2000). How much it impairs those other drugs varies from one person to another. Thus, the advice is that people who are depressed should consider trying St. John's wort only if they take *no* other medications.

CONCEPT CHECK ☑

18. Which type of antidepressant drug has effects similar to methylphenidate (Ritalin), discussed in Chapter 5?
19. If someone takes prescription antidepressant drugs, would it help to take St. John's wort also? (Check your answers on page 644.)

The effects of antidepressant drugs develop gradually. Any benefit that people report within the first 2 weeks is a *placebo effect;* that is, it depends on the

person's expectation of feeling better (J. W. Stewart et al., 1998). The effects of the drug itself begin after 2 to 3 weeks and increase over the next 4 to 5 weeks (Blaine, Prien, & Levine, 1983). Even then, part of what appears to be a drug effect is also a placebo effect or an effect of the passage of time. That is, people taking the drugs usually improve, but many people taking no drug or an ineffective drug also improve to some extent (Kirsch & Sapirstein, 1998).

The fact that antidepressant drugs alter synaptic activity within an hour or so but need weeks to improve a patient's mood tells us that the explanation in terms of synapses must be incomplete. The most promising current hypothesis concerns cell growth. In several brain areas, neurons' cell bodies shrink visibly—well, visibly under a microscope—when people become depressed (Cotter, Mackay, Landau, Kerwin, & Everall, 2001). Antidepressants stimulate neuronal growth, which is evidently necessary for the improvement of mood (Saarelainen et al., 2003).

Choosing Between Psychotherapy and Antidepressant Drugs

Cognitive therapy produces no side effects, and its benefits generally persist longer than do those of antidepressant drugs (Robinson, Berman, & Neimeyer, 1990). That is, people who quit taking antidepressant drugs are more likely to relapse into another depressive episode months or years later than are people who had psychotherapy. Nevertheless, the use of antidepressant drugs has been increasing (Olfson et al., 1998). You might wonder why.

Two reasons are convenience and cost. If a depressed person has enough time and money (or a generous insurance program), then psychotherapy is a good idea. However, antidepressant pills are cheaper and require only a few seconds a day plus an occasional checkup at the doctor's office.

Electroconvulsive Shock Therapy

Another well-known but controversial treatment for depression is electroconvulsive therapy (ECT) (Figure 16.14): *A brief electrical shock is administered across the patient's head to induce a convulsion similar to epilepsy.* ECT was first used in the 1930s and became popular in the 1940s and 1950s as a treatment for many psychiatric disorders. It then fell out of favor, partly because of the advent of antidepressant drugs and partly because ECT had been widely abused. Some patients were subjected to ECT hundreds of times without informed consent, and sometimes ECT was used more as a punishment than as a therapy.

FIGURE 16.14 Electroconvulsive therapy is administered today only with the patient's informed consent. ECT is given in conjunction with muscle relaxants and anesthetics to minimize discomfort.

Beginning in the 1970s, ECT made a comeback in modified form, mostly for severely depressed people who fail to respond to antidepressant drugs, whose thinking is seriously disordered, or who have strong suicidal tendencies (Scovern & Kilmann, 1980). For suicidal patients ECT has the advantage of taking effect rapidly, generally within 1 week. When a life is at stake, rapid relief is important.

ECT is now used only with patients who have given their informed consent. The shock is less intense than it used to be, and the patient is given muscle relaxants to prevent injury and anesthetics to reduce discomfort. As a rule the procedure is applied every other day for about 2 weeks. Then the psychiatrist evaluates the progress and either stops the treatment or decides to repeat it a few more times.

How ECT works is uncertain (Fink, 2000). The data do not support the idea that it relieves depression by causing people to forget depressing thoughts and memories. ECT that is administered to just the frontal part of the brain or just the right hemisphere is as effective as the usual whole-brain ECT, but without significant memory loss (Lisanby, Maddox, Prudic, Devanand, & Sackeim, 2000; Sackeim et al., 2000).

Another option is to apply powerful magnetic fields over the scalp, temporarily disabling all the neurons under the magnet (George et al., 1997). This procedure has effects similar to those of ECT.

Although ECT is often effective and produces fewer side effects than drugs, its benefits are generally temporary. About half of those who show a good response will relapse into depression within 6 months unless they receive some other therapy to prevent it (Riddle & Scott, 1995).

Bipolar Disorder

People with bipolar disorder (formerly known as manic-depressive disorder) alternate between the extremes of mania and depression. In many respects mania is the *opposite of depression.* When people are in the depressed phase, they are slow, inactive, and inhibited. In the manic phase, they are *constantly active and uninhibited.* People with a mild degree of mania ("hypomania") are productive, well-liked, life-of-the-party types, but people with more severe mania are dangerous to themselves and others. Some mental hospitals have to disable the fire alarms in certain wards because manic patients impulsively pull the alarm again and again. People during a depressed phase feel helpless, guilt-ridden, and sad. When they are manic, they are either *excited* or *irritable.* In either phase they have problems with attention and memory (Quraishi & Frangou, 2002). Typically, episodes of depression alternate with briefer episodes of mania. Although most episodes last months, episodes as short as a day are possible.

Psychologists distinguish two types of bipolar disorder. People with bipolar I disorder *have had at least one episode of mania.* People with bipolar II disorder *have had episodes of major depression and hypomania, which is a milder degree of mania.* In some cases the hypomanic phases do not seem troubling to the patient, although others regard the behavior as odd. In the past about 1% of all adults in the United States have been diagnosed with bipolar disorder (Robins et al., 1984), but the diagnosis is applied more broadly today, including some people with a mixture of bipolar symptoms, attention deficit, anxiety, and sometimes even hallucinations and delusions (Hilty,

Brady, & Hales, 1999). Twin studies indicate a strong hereditary component for bipolar disorder. It does not typically show up in the same families as unipolar (noncycling) depression, so the genetic basis is different (McGuffin et al., 2003).

Many artists, writers, and composers have suffered from bipolar disorder. To test whether creative skills increase or decrease over various phases of the bipolar cycle, Robert Weisberg (1994) examined the works of the classical composer Robert Schumann, who is known to have had bipolar disorder. He found that Schumann produced more works during his manic phases than during his depressed phases. However, the compositions written during the depressed phases have been performed and recorded as often as those written during the manic phases, on average. That is, the works that Schumann composed during his depressed phases have been about as popular as those of his manic phases.

A Self-Report

Mania can become so serious that it makes normal life impossible. The theatrical director Joshua Logan has described his own experiences with depression and mania. A few excerpts follow.[1]

Depressive Phase

First, Logan describes life in his depressed phase.

> I had no faith in the work I was doing or the people I was working with. . . . It was a great burden to get up in the morning and I couldn't wait to go to bed at night, even though I started not sleeping well. . . . I thought I was well but feeling low because of a hidden personal discouragement of some sort—something I couldn't quite put my finger on. . . . I just forced myself to live through a dreary, hopeless existence that lasted for months on end. . . .
>
> My depressions actually began around the age of thirty-two. I remember I was working on a play, and I was forcing myself to work. . . . I can remember that I sat in some sort of aggravated agony as it was read aloud for the first time by the cast. It sounded so awful that I didn't want to direct it. I didn't even want to see it. I remember feeling so depressed that I wished that I were dead without having to go through the shame and defeat of suicide. I couldn't sleep well at all, and sleep meant, for me, oblivion, and that's what I longed for and couldn't get. I didn't know what to do and I felt very, very lost. (Fieve, 1975, pp. 42–43)

Manic Phase

Here Logan describes his manic experiences:

> Finally, as time passed, the depression gradually wore off and turned into something else, which I didn't understand either. But it was a much pleasanter thing to go through, at least at first. Instead of hating everything, I started liking things—liking them too much, perhaps. . . . I put out a thousand ideas a minute: things to do, plays to write, plots to write stories about. . . .
>
> I decided to get married on the spur of the moment. . . . I practically forced her to say yes. Suddenly we had a loveless marriage and that had to be broken up overnight. . . .
>
> I can only remember that I worked constantly, day and night, never even seeming to need more than a few hours of sleep. I always had a new idea or another conference. . . . It was an exhilarating time for me.
>
> It finally went too far. In the end I went over the bounds of reality, or law and order, so to say. I don't mean that I committed any crimes, but I could easily have done so if anyone had crossed me. I flew into rages if contradicted. I began to be irritable with everyone. Should a man, friend or foe, object to anything I did or said, it was quite possible that I could poke him in the jaw. I was eventually persuaded by the doctors that I was desperately ill and should go into the hospital. But it was not, even then, convincing to me that I was ill.
>
> There I was, on the sixth floor of a New York building that had special iron bars around it and an iron gate that had slid into place and locked me away from the rest of the world. . . . I looked about and saw that there was an open window. I leaped up on the sill and climbed out of the window on the ledge on the sixth floor and said, "Unless you open the door, I'm going to climb down the outside of this building." At the time, I remember feeling so powerful that I might actually be able to scale the building. . . . They immediately opened the steel door, and I climbed back in. That's where manic elation can take you. (Fieve, 1975, pp. 43–45)

CONCEPT CHECK ☑

20. What are the similarities and differences between seasonal affective disorder and bipolar disorder? (Check your answer on page 644.)

Drug Therapies

Many years ago researcher J. F. Cade proposed that uric acid might be effective for treating mania. To dissolve uric acid in water, he mixed it with lithium salts. The resulting mixture proved effective, but researchers eventually discovered that the benefits depended on the lithium salts, not the uric acid.

---

[1] Excerpts from Joshua Logan in *Moodswing* by Ronald R. Fieve. Copyright © 1975 by Ronald R. Fieve. Published by William R. Morrow & Co.

Lithium salts were adopted quickly in the Scandinavian countries but only later in the United States. One reason was that drug manufacturers had no interest in marketing lithium pills. (Lithium is a natural substance and cannot be patented.) A second reason was that the lithium dosage must be carefully monitored. A dose slightly too low does no good, and one slightly too high produces nausea, blurred vision, and tremors.

Properly regulated dosages of lithium are now a common and effective treatment for bipolar disorder (Baldessarini & Tondo, 2000). People can take the recommended doses of lithium for years without suffering unfavorable consequences (Schou, 1997).

Anticonvulsant drugs, such as valproate (Depakene, Depacote), also used for bipolar disorder, are about equal to lithium in effectiveness (Hilty et al., 1999). Researchers do not yet know how lithium or the anticonvulsant drugs alleviate bipolar disorder. One promising hypothesis is that the drugs act by blocking the synthesis of a chemical called *arachidonic acid,* which is produced mostly during times of brain inflammation (Rapoport & Bosetti, 2002). Psychotherapy is useful for helping bipolar patients cope with life difficulties and is an important supplement to the drug treatments (Hollon et al., 2002).

Mood Disorders and Suicide

Most severely depressed people and people with bipolar disorder consider suicide, and many attempt it. Suicides also occur for other reasons, though. Some people commit suicide because of feelings of guilt or disgrace. Some have committed suicide because of obedience to a cult leader (Maris, 1997). Others have a painful terminal illness and wish to hasten the end.

▌ Members of the Heaven's Gate cult in San Diego committed mass suicide in 1997 because their leader assured them that death was the route to being rescued by an alien spacecraft that tailed the comet Hale-Bopp.

Records on suicide are not fully accurate because some people disguise their suicides to look like accidents and because many physicians, when in doubt, record a cause of death other than suicide. One survey in the United States reported that more than 13% of adults had considered suicide and more than 4% had survived a suicide attempt (Kessler, Borges, & Walters, 1999). Figure 16.15 shows the recorded deaths by suicide for three countries in 1988 (Lester, 1996). Note the major differences by age, country, and gender.

FIGURE 16.15 Suicide rates differ as a function of age, gender, and culture. The rates shown here are for 1988; the rate has dropped since then for Hungary, presumably because of economic and social changes within the country. *(Based on data of Lester, 1996)*

TABLE 16.5 People Most Likely to Attempt Suicide

- People who have recently endured the death of a spouse or a child, and men who recently have been divorced or separated (Blumenthal & Kupfer, 1986; Qin & Mortensen, 2003)

- People who have had major recent setbacks in their job, finances, or social life (Hendin, Maltsberger, Lipschitz, Haas, & Kyle, 2001).

- People with depression or bipolar disorder, especially those not in treatment and those who feel hopeless (Baldessarini, Tondo, & Hennen, 2001; Beck, Steer, Beck, & Newman, 1993)

- People who have made previous suicide attempts (Beck, Steer, & Brown, 1993)

- Drug or alcohol abusers (Beck & Steer, 1989)

- People who, during their childhood or adolescence, lost a parent by death or divorce (Adam, 1986)

- People with guns in their home (Brent, 2001)

- People whose relatives committed suicide (Blumenthal & Kupfer, 1986)

Across cultures more men die by suicide, although women make more attempts (Canetto & Sakinofsky, 1998; Cross & Hirschfeld, 1986). Many people, especially women, who attempt suicide are probably crying out for help without really intending to die. Unfortunately, some do die and others become disabled.

Suicide has no dependable pattern. Some people give warning signals well in advance, but many do not, and some firmly deny they are considering suicide (Fawcett, 2001). One study found that more than half of the people who attempted suicide made the decision impulsively within 24 hours of the attempt (Peterson, Peterson, O'Shanick, & Swann, 1985). However, anyone who admits to having a plan of how to commit suicide is at serious risk. Table 16.5 lists additional risk factors. Similar patterns have been found in the United States and China, so they are apparently not culture-specific (Cheng, 1995).

If you suspect that someone you know is thinking about suicide, what should you do? Treat the person like a normal human being. Anyone contemplating suicide needs social support and friendship. Don't assume that he or she is so fragile that one wrong word will be disastrous.

IN CLOSING

Mood and Mood Disorders

In the last three modules, we have considered anxiety, substance abuse, and depression. The symptoms differ among these three categories and so do the treatments, but the disorders also have significant overlap. Many people have both anxiety and depression, both substance abuse and depression, or all three. Many who have one of these disorders have relatives with another one. Evidently, the underlying causes are similar.

The capacity to feel emotions, even negative emotions, is important. If you never felt sad under any circumstances, you might make disastrous decisions. If you never acted embarrassed or guilty, you would anger those around you. Depression can be seen as the result of normal, useful mechanisms that have gone to an extreme (Allen & Badcock, 2003). Mood disorders distort thinking and feeling so badly that people who have been depressed insist you can't really understand how miserable it is if you haven't been through it yourself. Psychologists have several kinds of drugs and psychotherapy at their disposal, but we need research to find further weapons to fight this monster.

Summary

- *Symptoms of depression.* People with depression find little interest or pleasure in life, have trouble sleeping, lose interest in sex and food, and cannot concentrate. (page 634)
- *Seasonal affective disorder.* People with seasonal affective disorder become depressed during one season of the year. Bright light in the morning usually relieves this condition. (page 634)
- *Predispositions.* Certain genes magnify the depressive effects of stressful experiences. That is, people with these genes are more likely than other people to become depressed after a stressful experience, although unlikely to become depressed in a less stressful environment. (page 635)
- *Gender differences.* Psychologists are uncertain why more women than men become depressed. One hypothesis is that women are more likely to ruminate about their depression, and therefore aggravate and prolong it, whereas men find ways to distract themselves. (page 635)
- *Cognitive factors.* People who consistently blame themselves for their failures are likely to become depressed. (page 636)
- *Treatments.* About one third of depressed patients recover on their own within a few months. Up to another third recover with either psychotherapy or antidepressant drugs. (page 637)
- *Psychotherapy.* Interpersonal therapy helps depressed people deal with current life problems, such as the death of a loved one, a bad marriage, and so forth. Cognitive therapy attempts to change people's self-defeating thoughts and encourages more active participation in life. The increased activity is a powerful antidepressant procedure by itself. (page 638)

- *Antidepressant drugs.* Several kinds of drugs prolong the activity of dopamine or serotonin at synaptic receptors. Although the drugs affect the synapses within an hour or so, their behavioral effects begin after 2 or 3 weeks of treatment. The benefits apparently depend on stimulating the growth of shrunken neurons. (page 638)
- *Advantages and disadvantages.* Psychotherapy is more likely to produce long-lasting benefits, but antidepressant drugs remain popular because of their convenience and lower cost. (page 639)
- *Electroconvulsive therapy.* Electroconvulsive therapy (ECT) has a long history of abuse; in modified form it has made a comeback and helps some depressed people who fail to respond to antidepressant drugs. (page 640)
- *Bipolar disorder.* People with bipolar disorder alternate between periods of depression and mania, when they engage in constant, uninhibited activity. Lithium salts are an effective treatment, as are certain anticonvulsant drugs. (page 640)
- *Suicide.* Although it is difficult to know who will attempt suicide, several warning signs are associated with an increased risk. (page 642)

Answers to Concept Checks

15. Major depression is more severe than mere sadness and lasts months. Also, a person with major depression can hardly even imagine anything that would be enjoyable. (page 635)

16. Unpleasant events make anyone sad, but most people recover soon. People who were already sad and predisposed to depression (because of genetics or other reasons) may go into an episode of major depression. (page 636)

17. Depressed people are less likely than others to buy a lottery ticket because they regard their chances of success as remote on any task. (page 637)

18. The effects of methylphenidate (Ritalin) resemble those of buproprion (Wellbutrin). Both block the reuptake of dopamine. Buproprion, like methylphenidate, is sometimes prescribed for attention-deficit disorder. The effects of methylphenidate also overlap those of tricyclics. (page 639)

19. Possibly, but it would be risky. Presumably, the psychiatrist recommended a certain dose of the antidepressant drug for a reason. Because St. John's wort acts by the same mechanism, adding it is like increasing the dose of the drug. Also, St. John's wort activates the enzyme that inactivates many drugs, probably including the antidepressant drug itself. (page 639)

20. Both seasonal affective disorder and bipolar disorder have repetitive cycles. However, people with bipolar disorder swing back and forth between two extremes, depression and mania, whereas most people with seasonal affective disorder alternate between depression and normal mood. (Some experience a slightly manic phase during the season opposite to the time of their depression.) (page 641)

Schizophrenia

What is schizophrenia?

What causes it and what can be done about it?

How would you like to live in a world all your own? You can be the supreme ruler, and no one will ever criticize you or tell you what to do. You can tell other people—and even inanimate objects—what to do, and they will immediately obey. Your fantasies become realities.

Perhaps that world sounds like heaven to you. I suspect it would not feel that way for long. Most of us enjoy the give and take of interactions with other people; we enjoy struggling to achieve our fantasies more than we would enjoy their immediate fulfillment.

Some people with schizophrenia live practically in a world of their own, confusing fantasy with reality. Eventually, they may retreat into a private existence and pay little attention to others.

Symptoms

The widely misunderstood term *schizophrenia* is based on Greek roots meaning "split mind." However, the term does *not* refer to a split into two minds or personalities. Many people use the term *schizophrenia* when they really mean *dissociative identity disorder* or *multiple personality*. People with dissociative identity disorder have several personalities, any one of which might be considered normal if the person had only that one personality.

The "split" in the term schizophrenia does not refer to a split between personalities but to a split between the intellectual and emotional aspects of one personality, as if the intellect were no longer in contact with the emotions (Figure 16.16). Someone suffering from schizophrenia may show emotions for no apparent reason or fail to show emotion in a situation when it seems appropriate. This separation of intellect and emotions is no longer considered the key feature of schizophrenia, but it does occur.

To be diagnosed with **schizophrenia,** according to *DSM-IV, a person must exhibit a deterioration of daily activities, including work, social relations, and self-care. He or she must also exhibit at least two of the following: hallucinations, delusions, disorganized speech, grossly disorganized behavior, or a loss of normal emotional responses and social behaviors* (American Psychiatric Association, 1994).

However, if someone's hallucinations or delusions are severe, then no other symptoms are necessary.

Finally, before assigning a diagnosis of schizophrenia, a psychologist or psychiatrist must rule out other conditions that produce similar symptoms, including depression, bipolar illness, drug abuse, brain damage, early stages of Huntington's disease, niacin deficiency, and food allergies.

Positive and Negative Symptoms

The definition of schizophrenia calls for two or more symptoms from a list of five. Consequently, it is possible for different people diagnosed with schizophrenia to have no symptoms in common with one another (Andreasen, 1999). What we have traditionally lumped together as one disorder, schizophrenia, may consist of several separate conditions.

One way of trying to separate different types of schizophrenia is to distinguish between positive and negative symptoms. In this case *positive* means *present* and *negative* means *absent;* they do not mean *good* and *bad.* **Positive symptoms** are *behaviors that are notable because of their presence,* such as hallucinations and delusions. **Negative symptoms** are *behaviors notable for their absence,* including a lack of speech and emotional

FIGURE 16.16 Although the term *schizophrenia* is derived from Greek roots meaning "split personality," it does not refer to alternation among different personalities. Rather, the term originally indicated a split between the intellectual and emotional aspects of a single personality.

Intellect

Emotions

expression, a lack of ability to feel pleasure, and a general inability to take care of oneself.

Patients with mostly negative symptoms may differ from those with mostly positive or a mixture of positive and negative symptoms (Kirkpatrick, Buchanan, Ross, & Carpenter, 2001). Their symptoms tend to be more consistent over time and more difficult to treat (Arndt, Andreasen, Flaum, Miller, & Nopoulos, 1995). People with many negative symptoms have an earlier onset of the disorder and worse performance in school and on the job (Andreasen, Flaum, Swayze, Tyrrell, & Arndt, 1990). They also have different kinds of brain abnormalities (Palmer et al., 1997).

Hallucinations

Hallucinations are *perceptions that do not correspond to anything in the objective world.* Visual hallucinations are not common, although some people with schizophrenia have distorted visual experiences. A more common hallucination is to hear voices and other sounds that no one else hears. The voices may speak nonsense, or they may direct the person to do something. Hallucinating people may think the voices are real, they may know the voices are coming from within their own head, or they may not be sure (Junginger & Frame, 1985). Auditory hallucinations occur at the same time as spontaneous activity in the auditory cortex and several related brain areas (Shergill, Brammer, Williams, Murray, & McGuire, 2000).

Have you ever heard a voice when you knew you were alone? I once asked my class this question. At first just a few people hesitantly raised their hands, and then more and more, until about one fourth of the class admitted they had heard a voice at least once. In many cases it was while lying in bed, not asleep but not fully awake either. Having auditory hallucinations on a few occasions does not mean you are losing your mind.

Delusions

Delusions are *unfounded beliefs that are strongly held despite evidence against them.* Three common types are delusions of persecution, grandeur, and reference. A **delusion of persecution** is *a belief that you are being persecuted* by dangerous enemies. A **delusion of grandeur** is *a belief that you are unusually important,* perhaps a special messenger from God or a person of central importance to the future of the world. A **delusion of reference** is *a tendency to interpret all sorts of messages as if they were meant for oneself.* For example, someone with a delusion of reference may interpret a headline in the morning newspaper as a coded message or take a television announcer's comments as personal insults.

However, it is hazardous to diagnose someone with schizophrenia if the only symptoms are delusions. For example, suppose someone constantly sees evidence of government conspiracies in everyday events. Is that belief a delusion of persecution or merely an unusual opinion? (Might it even be correct?) Many elderly people have occasional hallucinations or delusions, as do hospitalized patients receiving pain medication (Östling & Skoog, 2002). Some people who believe they have been abducted by outer-space aliens seem to be normal in other regards. Even if we confidently label their beliefs as false and unfounded, we should not consider them mentally ill (Banaji & Kihlstrom, 1996). Members of religious minorities also have beliefs that other people regard as strange. (If the truth be known, don't most of us have a belief or two that someone might consider unjustifiable?)

Disordered Thinking

Even those people with schizophrenia who have normal or above-average intelligence are impaired on tasks requiring selective attention or "executive functions," as described in Chapter 7 (Weickert et al., 2000). For example, the Wisconsin Card Sorting Task asks people to sort a stack of cards by one rule (e.g., putting them into piles according to color) and then shift to a different rule (e.g., number or shape). People with schizophrenia have trouble with this task, as do people with frontal cortex damage.

The impaired attention may relate to the tendency of patients with schizophrenia to idiosyncratic and loose associations, somewhat like the illogical leaps that occur in dreams. For example, one man used the words *Jesus, cigar,* and *sex* as synonyms. He explained that they were the same because Jesus has a halo around his head, a cigar has a band around it, and during sex people put their arms around each other.

Another characteristic of schizophrenic thought is difficulty using abstract concepts. For instance, many people with schizophrenia have trouble sorting objects into categories. Many also give strictly literal responses when asked to interpret the meaning of proverbs. Here are some examples (Krueger, 1978, pp. 196–197):

Proverb: People who live in glass houses shouldn't throw stones.
Interpretation: "It would break the glass."
Proverb: All that glitters is not gold.
Interpretation: "It might be brass."
Proverb: A stitch in time saves nine.
Interpretation: "If you take one stitch for a small tear now, it will save nine later."

People with schizophrenic thought disorder often misunderstand simple statements because of their tendency to interpret everything literally. Upon being taken to the admitting office of a hospital, one person said, "Oh, is this where people go to admit their faults?" Many schizophrenic people also use many words to say very little, as in this excerpt from a letter one man wrote to his mother:

> I am writing on paper. The pen which I am using is from a factory called "Perry & Co." This factory is in England. I assume this. Behind the name of Perry & Co. the city of London is inscribed; but not the city. The city of London is in England. I know this from my school-days. Then, I always liked geography. My last teacher in that subject was Professor August A. He was a man with black eyes. I also like black eyes. There are also blue and gray eyes and other sorts, too. I have heard it said that snakes have green eyes. All people have eyes. There are some, too, who are blind. These blind people are led about by a boy. It must be very terrible not to be able to see. There are people who can't see and, in addition, can't hear. I know some who hear too much. (Bleuler, 1911/1950, p. 17)

CONCEPT CHECK ☑️

21. If someone alternates between one personality and another, is that a case of schizophrenia?
22. What are typical "positive" and "negative" symptoms of schizophrenia? (Check your answer on page 653.)

Types and Prevalence

Depending on which symptoms are most prominent, psychiatrists and psychologists distinguish five major types of schizophrenia. These distinctions are useful for descriptive purposes, although they do not identify the underlying causes.

Types of Schizophrenia

Catatonic schizophrenia is characterized by a *prominent movement disorder, including either rigid inactivity or excessive activity.* In either case the person's movement pattern seems unrelated to events in the outside world. Periods of extremely rapid, repetitive activity may alternate with periods of total inactivity. During the inactive periods, he or she may hold a given posture without moving and may resist attempts to alter that posture (Figure 16.17). Despite the inactivity, the brain is alert and the person may complain later about comments someone said at the time. Catatonic schizophrenia

is diagnosed less often today than decades ago, although the reason is not clear (Stompe, Ortwein-Swoboda, Ritter, Schanda, & Friedmann, 2002).

Disorganized schizophrenia is characterized by *incoherent speech, extreme lack of social relationships, and "silly" or odd behavior.* Here is a conversation with someone suffering from disorganized schizophrenia (Duke & Nowicki, 1979, p. 162):

Interviewer: How does it feel to have your problems?
Patient: Who can tell me the name of my song? I don't know, but it won't be long. It won't be short, tall, none at all. My head hurts, my knees hurt—my nephew, his uncle, my aunt. My God, I'm happy . . . not a care in the world. My hair's been curled, the flag's unfurled. This is my country, land that I love, this is the country, land that I love.
Interviewer: How do you feel?
Patient: Happy! Don't you hear me? Why do you talk to me? (barks like a dog).

Paranoid schizophrenia is characterized by *elaborate hallucinations and delusions, especially delusions of persecution and delusions of grandeur.* Many people with paranoid schizophrenia are more cognitively intact than most people with other forms of schizophrenia. They can generally take care of themselves well enough to get through the activities of the day, and some manage to complete college work and take good jobs.

Undifferentiated schizophrenia is characterized by the *basic symptoms— deterioration of daily functioning plus some combination of hallucinations, delusions, inappropriate emotions, thought disorders, and so forth.* However, the person does not have any of the special features that would qualify for the catatonic, disorganized, or paranoid types.

Residual schizophrenia is a diagnosis for people *who have had an episode of schizophrenia and who are partly, but not fully, recovered.* That is, the person has some mild symptoms, but nothing severe. This is usually a temporary state on the way to either recovery or a renewed episode of more serious symptoms.

Many people fall on the margin between two or more types of schizophrenia, perhaps switching back and forth between them. Switching is especially common between undifferentiated schizophrenia and one of the other types (Kendler, Gruenberg, & Tsuang, 1985).

FIGURE 16.17 Someone with catatonic schizophrenia alternates between long periods of rigid stupor and periods of purposeless excited activity.

© Grunnitus/Photo Researchers

CONCEPT CHECK ☑

23. Why are people more likely to switch between undifferentiated schizophrenia and one of the other types than, say, between disorganized schizophrenia and another type? (Check your answer on page 653.)

Prevalence

About 1% of Americans have schizophrenia at some point in life (Kendler, Gallagher, Abelson, & Kessler, 1996). Some sources cite higher or lower figures depending on how many marginal cases they include. Incidence rates also vary from one location to another.

As well as researchers can reconstruct from historical records, the incidence of schizophrenia and severe mental illness in general began to increase in the late 1700s, especially in England and Ireland, and later in the United States. For generation after generation, people tried to convince themselves that mental illness wasn't really becoming more common but that it just appeared to increase because previous generations had not kept good records (Torrey & Miller, 2001). Nevertheless, they kept building new mental hospitals, which quickly became crowded to overflowing, despite offering the most uninviting accommodations. However, since about 1950 the incidence of schizophrenia has stopped increasing. It appears to be decreasing in some parts of the world (Suvisaari, Haukka, Tanskanen, & Lönnqvist, 1999) and increasing in others (Healy et al., 2001). Part of the fluctuation is probably due to changes in patterns of diagnosis, such that someone diagnosed with schizophrenia at one time and place might receive a different diagnosis in another (Ösby et al., 2001). However, it is also likely that the incidence really does vary from one time and place to another, and if we can understand why, we may get major clues to the causes of schizophrenia. Unfortunately, few investigators have taken the variations seriously enough even to try to investigate their causes (Torrey & Miller, 2001). Note that either an increase or decrease in incidence from one time to another implies nongenetic influences. (Evolution doesn't occur that rapidly.)

Schizophrenia occurs in all ethnic groups, but it is less common and usually less severe in Third World countries (El-Islam, 1982; Leff et al., 1987; Torrey, 1986; Wig et al., 1987). It is more common in crowded cities than in small towns and farms (Torrey, Bowler, & Clark, 1997). One explanation is that mentally ill people move from small towns and farms to big cities where they can get more help. Another is that some aspect of life in crowded and technologically advanced countries increases the risk of schizophrenia. Still another possibility is that people in small towns and

Third World countries receive more social support from nearby relatives and friends.

Schizophrenia is most frequently diagnosed in young adults in their teens or 20s. Older statistics indicated that schizophrenia was equally common in men and women, but more recent data show more men than women by a ratio of about 7 to 5. Men are also more likely to be diagnosed younger and to have more severe symptoms (Aleman, Kahn, & Selten, 2003).

Schizophrenia's onset can be sudden but is usually gradual. Most people with schizophrenia are described as having been strange children who had a short attention span, made few friends, and often disrupted their class (Arboleda & Holzman, 1985; Parnas, Schulsinger, Schulsinger, Mednick, & Teasdale, 1982). Many had less severe psychological disorders as adolescents before developing schizophrenia in young adulthood (Weiser et al., 2001).

CRITICAL THINKING:
A STEP FURTHER
Retrospective Accounts

If you try to recall the childhood behavior of someone who later developed schizophrenia, what kinds of memory errors are you likely to make and why? (Recall the issues raised in Chapters 7 and 8.)

Causes

The causes of schizophrenia are not known but probably include a combination of factors and not just one. Genetics and prenatal environment are prime candidates.

Genetics

The evidence of a genetic basis rests primarily on studies of adopted children and twins. Adopted children who eventually develop schizophrenia have more biological relatives than adoptive relatives with schizophrenia (Kety et al., 1994). If one member of a pair of monozygotic (identical) twins develops schizophrenia, there is an almost 50% chance that the other will develop it too (Cardno et al., 1999; Gottesman, 1991) (see Figure 16.18).

However, the research on adopted children is ambiguous. The child's biological mother influenced her baby's brain development not only through genes but also through prenatal environment. Women with schizophrenia tend to be impoverished and poorly educated. Many smoke and drink during pregnancy and fail to eat a good diet. Therefore, if some of their children develop schizophrenia, we cannot assume a genetic explanation.

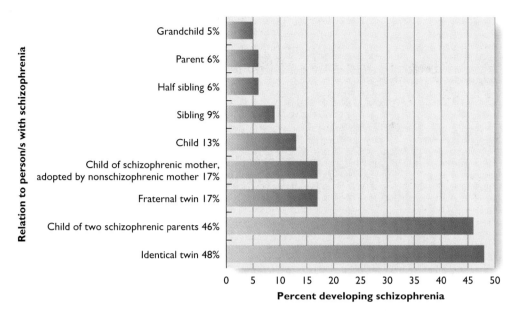

Relation to person/s with schizophrenia

Grandchild 5%
Parent 6%
Half sibling 6%
Sibling 9%
Child 13%
Child of schizophrenic mother, adopted by nonschizophrenic mother 17%
Fraternal twin 17%
Child of two schizophrenic parents 46%
Identical twin 48%

0   5   10   15   20   25   30   35   40   45   50

Percent developing schizophrenia

FIGURE 16.18 The relatives of a schizophrenic person have an increased probability of developing schizophrenia themselves. Note that children of a schizophrenic mother have a 17% risk of schizophrenia even if adopted by a family with no schizophrenic members. *(Based on data from Gottesman, 1991)*

The most persuasive evidence would be a demonstration linking schizophrenia to a specific gene. So far the results of repeated studies have been unimpressive. Identifiable genetic abnormalities have been found for childhood schizophrenia, an uncommon condition that differs from adult-onset schizophrenia in several regards (Burgess et al., 1998; Nopoulos, Giedd, Andreasen, & Rapoport, 1998). For the more common adult-onset version of schizophrenia, various researchers have found links to many different genes, but different studies point to different genes and many findings have been hard to replicate (Brzustowicz, Hodgkinson, Chow, Honer, & Bassett, 2000; Jönsson, Sedvall, Nöthen, & Cichon, 2003; Levinson et al., 2002; Maziade et al., 2001; McGinnis et al., 2001; Sklar et al., 2001; Vaswani & Kapur, 2001). Even when a gene does appear to have an effect according to the results of a particular study, the effect is small. For example, investigators found one gene to be present in 70% of people with schizophrenia and 60% of everyone else (Saleem et al., 2001).

If schizophrenia does have a genetic basis, we shall need to explain why natural selection has not eliminated the gene. People with schizophrenia are less likely than others to have children, and their unaffected brothers and sisters do not compensate by reproducing more than average (Haukka, Suvisaari, & Lönnqvist, 2003). So it is difficult to imagine how genes that lead to schizophrenia could remain common enough to affect 1% of the population. One hypothesis is that the relevant genes are mutations that occur frequently enough to balance the selective pressure against them. The one bit of evidence supporting this speculation is that schizophrenia is more common among the children of fathers over the age of 50 (Byrne, Agerbo, Ewald, Eaton, & Mortensen, 2003).

Older fathers have higher probabilities of producing mutations in their sperm. (Women over 50 almost never have babies.) Another hypothesis is that schizophrenia may reflect genes that are often advantageous but capable of producing unfavorable effects when the environment isn't quite right (Shaner, Miller, & Mintz, in press). At present the situation remains puzzling.

Brain Damage

Much evidence points to mild–brain abnormalities in many, though not all, people with schizophrenia. Brain damage is, of course, not an alternative to genetics; brain damage could occur for either genetic or nongenetic reasons.

Indications of brain abnormalities have been reported in patients in cultures as different as the United States and Nigeria (Ohaeri, Adeyinka, & Osuntokun, 1995). Brain scans indicate that the hippocampus and several areas of the cerebral cortex are a few percent smaller than normal in people with schizophrenia, especially those with the greatest behavioral deficits (Kasai et al., 2003; Velakoulis et al., 1999; Wright et al., 2000). The cerebral ventricles, which are fluid-filled cavities in the brain, are larger than normal in people with schizophrenia (Wolkin et al., 1998; Wright et al., 2000). Figure 16.19 shows an example of enlarged cerebral ventricles.

Most people with schizophrenia also have smaller than average neurons (Pierri, Volk, Auh, Sampson, & Lewis, 2001; Weinberger, 1999) and fewer than the average number of synapses, especially in the prefrontal cortex (Glantz & Lewis, 1997, 2000). They also show deficits in the amount of myelin, a material that surrounds and insulates many axons (K. L. Davis et al., 2003). One area of the cortex with consistent

FIGURE 16.19 The twin on the left has schizophrenia; the twin on the right does not. Note that the ventricles (near the center of each brain) are larger in the twin with schizophrenia. The ventricles are fluid-filled cavities; an enlargement of the ventricles implies a loss of brain tissue.

impairments, the dorsolateral prefrontal cortex, is theoretically interesting: It is important for those aspects of working memory that are consistently impaired in schizophrenia, and it is one of the slowest areas of the brain to mature. Therefore, its malformation supports the view that schizophrenia is related to impaired brain maturation (Gur et al., 2000; Pearlson, Petty, Ross, & Tien, 1996; Sowell, Thompson, Holmes, Jernigan, & Toga, 1999).

However, many of these results must be interpreted cautiously. Many people with schizophrenia abuse alcohol or other drugs, and some of the brain damage associated with schizophrenia is due to alcohol use. That is, people with both schizophrenia and alcohol abuse have greater indications of brain damage than those with schizophrenia alone (Deshmukh, Rosenbloom, Pfefferbaum, & Sullivan, 2002; Mathalon, Pfefferbaum, Lim, Rosenbloom, & Sullivan, 2003; Sullivan et al., 2000). Unfortunately, most studies have not attempted to separate the effects of schizophrenia from those of alcohol abuse.

CONCEPT CHECK ☑

24. Suppose someone argues that the brain abnormalities in schizophrenia indicate that brain damage *causes* schizophrenia. What is an alternative explanation? (Check your answer on page 653.)

The Neurodevelopmental Hypothesis

Research results conflict about the time course of the brain damage associated with schizophrenia. Many studies indicate that the brain abnormalities develop early and remain steady over the years (Benes, 1995; Heaton et al., 2001). Other studies, however, report a

small degree of gradual brain shrinkage (Cahn et al. 2002; Hulshoff et al., 2001). In either case the results do not show progressive death of neurons on a scale comparable to Parkinson's disease or other deteriorative conditions. That is, most if not all of the brain abnormality is present from the earliest time that someone is diagnosed with schizophrenia.

If the abnormalities are present in young adults, perhaps they were present from the start—that is, since infancy. Researchers therefore suggested the **neurodevelopmental hypothesis,** *the idea that schizophrenia originates with nervous system impairments that develop before or around the time of birth, possibly for genetic reasons but sometimes for other reasons* (McGrath, Féron, Burne, Mackay-Sim, & Eyles, 2003; Weinberger, 1996). For example, the probability of schizophrenia is higher than normal following these events:

- The patient's mother had a difficult pregnancy, labor, or delivery (Hultman, Öhman, Cnattingius, Wieselgren, & Lindström, 1997).
- The mother was poorly nourished during pregnancy (Dalman, Allebeck, Cullberg, Grunewald, & Köstler, 1999; Susser et al., 1996).
- The mother had an infection, and presumably a high fever, during pregnancy (Buka et al., 2001).
- The mother had an Rh-negative blood type and her baby was Rh-positive. The risk of schizophrenia is more than 2% for her second and later Rh-positive children, especially boys (Hollister, Laing, & Mednick, 1996).
- The patient was unusually small at birth (Wahlbeck, Forsén, Osmond, Barker, & Eriksson, 2001).
- The patient had a serious head injury in early childhood (AbdelMalik, Husted, Chow, & Bassett, 2003).

Furthermore, *a person born in the winter or early spring is slightly more likely to develop schizophrenia than a person born at other times* (Bradbury & Miller, 1985; Davies, Welham, Chant, Torrey, & McGrath, 2003). Investigators have clearly demonstrated this **season-of-birth effect** only in the northern climates, not near the equator. Evidently, something about the weather contributes to some people's vulnerability to schizophrenia. No other psychological disorder has this characteristic.

One possible explanation relates to the fact that influenza and other epidemics are most common in the fall and early winter. If a woman catches influenza or another infection during the second trimester of pregnancy, her illness can impair critical stages of brain development in her fetus at that time. A virus does not cross the placenta into the fetus (Taller et al., 1996), so the problem is not the virus itself but probably the mother's fever, which can impair the development of fetal neurons (Laburn, 1996). Researchers have found a small but significant increase in schizophrenia among people born 2 to 3 months after an epidemic of influenza or measles (Adams, Kendell, Hare, & Munk-Jorgensen, 1993).

You might ask, "If brain damage occurs before or near the time of birth, why do the symptoms emerge so much later?" One possible answer is that certain parts of the brain, especially the prefrontal cortex, go through a critical stage of development during the second trimester of pregnancy but do not become fully functional until adolescence. As the brain begins to rely more and more on those areas, the effects of damage become more evident (Weinberger, 1987).

Therapies

Before the discovery of effective drugs to combat schizophrenia, the outlook was bleak. Most people spent virtually their entire adult lives in mental hospitals, growing more and more disoriented. Matters are better now, although there is still enormous room for improvement. Psychotherapy helps, presumably by controlling the stress that often aggravates schizophrenia (Sensky et al., 2000). However, nearly all patients with schizophrenia receive drugs as part of their treatment.

Medications

During the 1950s researchers discovered the first effective **antipsychotic drug**—*that is, a drug that can relieve schizophrenia.* That drug was chlorpromazine (klor-PRAHM-uh-ZEEN, trade name Thorazine). Chlorpromazine and other antipsychotic drugs, including haloperidol (HAHL-o-PAIR-ih-dol, trade name Haldol), have enabled many people to escape lifelong confinement in mental hospitals. Although the drugs do not cure the disorder, a daily pill does help control it, much as insulin shots control diabetes.

Antipsychotic drugs take effect gradually and produce variable degrees of recovery. As a rule the greater someone's deterioration before drug treatment begins, the less the recovery will be. Most of the recovery emerges in about a month (Szymanski, Simon, & Gutterman, 1983). Beyond that point the drugs maintain the recovery but do not advance it much fur-

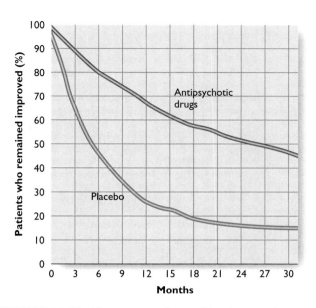

FIGURE 16.20 After recovery from schizophrenia, the percentage of schizophrenic patients who remained improved for the next 2 ½ years was higher in the group that received continuing drug treatment than in the placebo group. *(Based on Baldessarini, 1984)*

ther. When affected people stop taking the drugs, the symptoms return (Figure 16.20).

All antipsychotic drugs share one characteristic: They block dopamine synapses in the brain. In fact their therapeutic effectiveness is nearly proportional to their ability to block those synapses (Seeman & Lee, 1975). Furthermore, large doses of amphetamines, cocaine, or other drugs that stimulate dopamine activity induce a condition, sometimes long-lasting, with the positive symptoms of schizophrenia. These observations led to the **dopamine hypothesis of schizophrenia**—that *the underlying cause of schizophrenia is excessive stimulation of certain types of dopamine synapses.* People with schizophrenia do not overproduce dopamine. However, either they release it more often or it remains at the synapses longer because a higher than normal percentage of their dopamine synapses are actually occupied by dopamine at any given time (Abi-Dargham et al., 2000).

Nevertheless, dopamine may not be the entire explanation of schizophrenia. According to the **glutamate hypothesis of schizophrenia,** *schizophrenia results partly from deficient stimulation of certain glutamate synapses.* In many brain areas, dopamine inhibits glutamate activity, so drugs that block dopamine synapses would increase the activity of glutamate synapses. The glutamate hypothesis is supported by the fact that prolonged use of *phencyclidine* ("angel dust"), which inhibits glutamate receptors, produces symptoms that match schizophrenia even more closely than do cocaine and amphetamines (Olney & Farger, 1995). Drugs that stimulate certain glutamate synapses facilitate relief from the negative symptoms of schizophrenia, such as social withdrawal (Heresco-Levy & Javitt, 2004).

Side Effects

Antipsychotic drugs produce unwelcome side effects in many people. The most serious, **tardive dyskinesia** (TAHRD-eev DIS-ki-NEE-zhuh), *a condition characterized by tremors and involuntary movements,* develops gradually in many people taking antipsychotic drugs (Kiriakakis, Bhatia, Quinn, & Marsden, 1998). Presumably, tardive dyskinesia relates to the fact that antipsychotic drugs alter activity at dopamine synapses, some of which control movement. Researchers have sought new drugs that can combat schizophrenia without causing tardive dyskinesia.

Atypical antipsychotic drugs, such as risperidone, *relieve schizophrenia without causing tardive dyskinesia.* They combine moderate effects on specific types of dopamine synapses with additional effects on serotonin synapses. Atypical antipsychotic drugs have shown significant benefits without producing dyskinesia; they also relieve the negative symptoms of schizophrenia that most antipsychotic drugs fail to address (J. M. Davis, Chen, & Glick, 2003). These drugs are becoming more widely used.

CONCEPT CHECK ☑

25. Why is early diagnosis of schizophrenia important? (Check your answer on page 653.)

Family Matters

The intensity of any patient's symptoms varies from time to time, despite consistent use of antipsychotic drugs. One hypothesis to explain the fluctuation is that patients react to variations in emotional stress, especially from their own family. Many, probably most, young patients with schizophrenia live with their parents, and many parents grow understandably frustrated with an adult son or daughter who cannot hold a job, does not take care of even routine self-grooming, and seems unmotivated to change. Occasionally, a parent has an outburst of *hostile or critical comments,* known as **expressed emotion.** Many studies have found a patient exposed to frequent expressed emotion from his or her parents is likely to have frequent relapses of schizophrenic symptoms (Butzlaff & Hooley, 1998).

Most psychologists have assumed that the expressed emotion leads to the relapses. However, the evidence is correlational. Here is my last opportunity in this book to remind you yet again to beware of using correlational evidence to infer cause and effect: Perhaps the parents' high degree of expressed emotion leads the patient to frequent relapses, or perhaps the patient's fre-

quent relapses stimulate the parents to more expressed emotion. One study examined both the parents' expressed emotion and the patient's behavior repeatedly over a year and a half. The amount of expressed emotion correlated better with the patient's *previous* levels of negative symptoms (social withdrawal and so forth) than with the patient's *subsequent* levels of those symptoms (King, 2000). These results suggest that a parent's expressed emotion is more a reaction to the patient's behavior than a cause of it.

In any case the families of people with schizophrenia need help, too. They need help for their own sake, as well as for making them more patient and more helpful to their son or daughter with schizophrenia. Research has confirmed that including the parents in the therapy program magnifies the benefits to the patients (Pitschel-Walz, Leucht, Bäuml, Kissling, & Engel, 2001).

IN CLOSING

The Elusiveness of Schizophrenia

Whereas anxiety disorders, substance abuse, and depression overlap somewhat in symptoms, causes, and genetics, schizophrenia stands alone. Most of us can imagine circumstances that would drive us to excess anxiety, depression, or addictive behaviors, but it is harder to imagine developing schizophrenia, with hallucinations, delusions, and an apparent break from reality.

People with schizophrenia not only have relatively little in common with other psychiatric patients; sometimes they have little in common with one another. One patient diagnosed with schizophrenia might have hallucinations and delusions; another speaks incoherently and avoids other people. One has relatives with schizophrenia; the other doesn't. One has evidence of brain abnormalities; the other doesn't. As you can imagine, it is difficult to draw generalizations about schizophrenia, and many researchers wonder whether we are dealing with one disorder or several. We need more research to understand the disorder itself as well as its causes and treatment.

Summary

- *Symptoms of schizophrenia.* A diagnosis of schizophrenia applies if someone has deteriorated in everyday functioning and shows at least two of the following symptoms: hallucinations (mostly auditory), delusions, disorganized speech, disorganized behavior, and loss of normal emotional responses and social behaviors. (page 645)
- *Positive and negative symptoms.* Positive symptoms are behaviors that attract attention by their presence, such as hallucinations and delusions. Negative symptoms are behaviors that are notewor-

thy for their absence, such as impaired emotional expression. (page 645)

- *Thought disorder of schizophrenia.* The thought disorder of schizophrenia is characterized by loose associations, impaired use of abstract concepts, and vague, wandering speech that conveys little information. (page 646)
- *Types of schizophrenia.* Psychologists distinguish five types of schizophrenia: catatonic, disorganized, paranoid, undifferentiated, and residual. (page 647)
- *Genetic influences.* Much evidence indicates that it is possible to inherit a predisposition toward schizophrenia, although little is known about how the genes exert their influence. Researchers have not identified any single gene with a major influence. (page 648)
- *Brain abnormalities.* Many people with schizophrenia show indications of mild brain abnormalities, especially in the prefrontal cortex. However, some of the damage may be due to alcohol abuse. (page 649)
- *Neurodevelopmental hypothesis.* Many researchers believe that schizophrenia originates with abnormal brain development before or around the time of birth, sometimes for genetic reasons but sometimes for other reasons, such as the mother's fever during pregnancy. (page 650)
- *Antipsychotic drugs.* Drugs that alleviate schizophrenia block dopamine synapses. Results are best if treatment begins before someone has suffered serious deterioration. (page 651)
- *Neurotransmitters.* The effectiveness of dopamine blockers in alleviating schizophrenia has suggested that the underlying problem might be excessive dopamine activity. An alternative hypothesis is that part of the problem relates to a deficiency of glutamate. (page 651)
- *Family therapy.* Reducing the family's expressed emotion (hostile comments) improves the patient's chances for lasting recovery. (page 652)

Answers to Concept Checks

21. No, that would be dissociative identity disorder (multiple personality). (page 647)
22. Positive symptoms include hallucinations, delusions, and thought disorder. Negative symptoms include lack of (or weak) emotions, speech, and social contact. (page 647)
23. Whenever any of the special symptoms of catatonic, disorganized, or paranoid schizophrenia become less severe, the person is left with undifferentiated or residual schizophrenia. To shift between any two of the other types, a person would have to lose the symptoms of one type and gain the symptoms of the other type. (page 648)
24. Perhaps schizophrenia leads to alcohol abuse, which in turn leads to brain abnormalities. As always, we should beware of drawing cause-and-effect conclusions from correlational data. (page 650)
25. Antipsychotic drugs are more helpful to people in the early stages of schizophrenia than to those who have deteriorated severely. However, psychiatrists do not want to administer drugs to people who do not need them. Consequently, early and accurate diagnosis of schizophrenia is helpful. (page 652)

CHAPTER ENDING
Key Terms and Activities

Key Terms

agoraphobia: an excessive fear of open or public places (page 616)

Alcoholics Anonymous (AA): a self-help group of people who are trying to abstain from alcohol use and to help others do the same (page 631)

alcoholism: the habitual overuse of alcohol (page 628)

Antabuse: the trade name for disulfiram, a drug used in the treatment of alcoholism (page 631)

antipsychotic drugs: drugs that relieve schizophrenia (page 651)

atypical antidepressants: drugs that relieve depression for some patients who do not respond to other antidepressants, generally with only mild side effects (page 638)

atypical antipsychotic drugs: drugs such as clozapine and risperidone, which relieve schizophrenia without causing tardive dyskinesia (page 652)

bipolar disorder: a condition in which a person alternates between periods of depression and periods of mania (page 635)

bipolar I disorder: a disorder condition characterized by at least one episode of mania (page 640)

bipolar II disorder: a disorder condition characterized by episodes of major depression and hypomania, which is a milder degree of mania (page 640)

catatonic schizophrenia: a type of schizophrenia characterized by the basic symptoms plus prominent movement disorders (page 647)

compulsion: a repetitive, almost irresistible action (page 622)

delusion: an unfounded belief that is strongly held despite evidence against it (page 646)

delusion of grandeur: the belief that one is unusually important (page 646)

delusion of persecution: the belief that one is being persecuted (page 646)

delusion of reference: the tendency to interpret all sorts of messages as if they were meant for oneself (page 646)

dependence (or **addiction**): a self-destructive habit that someone finds difficult or impossible to quit (page 626)

disorganized schizophrenia: a type of schizophrenia characterized by incoherent speech, extreme lack of social relationships, and "silly" or odd behavior (page 647)

dopamine hypothesis of schizophrenia: the theory that the underlying cause of schizophrenia is excessive stimulation of certain types of dopamine synapses (page 651)

electroconvulsive therapy (ECT): a treatment using a brief electrical shock that is administered across the patient's head to induce a convulsion similar to epilepsy, sometimes used as a treatment for certain types of depression (page 640)

explanatory style: a tendency to accept one kind of explanation for success or failure more often than others (page 637)

expressed emotion: hostile or critical comments directed toward a person with a psychiatric disorder such as schizophrenia (page 652)

flooding (or **implosion** or **intensive exposure therapy**): a treatment for phobia in which the person is suddenly exposed to the object of the phobia (page 621)

generalized anxiety disorder (GAD): a disorder in which people are almost constantly plagued by exaggerated worries (page 615)

glutamate hypothesis of schizophrenia: the view that the underlying problem causing schizophrenia is deficient stimulation of certain glutamate synapses (page 651)

hallucinations: a perception not corresponding to reality, such as seeing or hearing something that is not present or failing to see or hear something that is present (page 646)

harm reduction: an approach to drug abuse that concentrates on decreasing the frequency of drug use and minimizing the harmful consequences to health and well-being (page 632)

hyperventilation: rapid deep breathing (page 616)

interpersonal therapy: a treatment that focuses on coping with difficulties someone has faced in the present or recent past, such as death of a loved one, a bad marriage, changes in life status, and lack of social skills (page 638)

major depression: a condition lasting most of the day, day after day, with a loss of interest and pleasure and a lack of productive activity (page 634)

mania: a condition in which people are constantly active, uninhibited, and either excited or irritable (page 640)

methadone: a drug commonly offered as a less dangerous substitute for opiates (page 632)

monoamine oxidase inhibitors (MAOIs): drugs that block the metabolic breakdown of released dopamine, norepinephrine, and serotonin, thus prolonging the effects of these neurotransmitters on the receptors of the postsynaptic cell (page 638)

negative symptoms: symptoms that are present in other people—such as the ability to take care of themselves—but absent in people with schizophrenia (page 645)

neurodevelopmental hypothesis: the idea that schizophrenia originates with impaired development of the nervous system before or around the time of birth, possibly but not necessarily for genetic reasons (page 650)

obsession: a repetitive, unwelcome stream of thought (page 622)

obsessive-compulsive disorder: a condition with repetitive thoughts and actions (page 622)

panic disorder (PD): a disorder characterized by frequent bouts of moderate anxiety and occasional attacks of sudden increased heart rate, chest pains, difficulty breathing, sweating, faintness, and trembling (page 615)

paranoid schizophrenia: a type of schizophrenia characterized by the basic symptoms plus strong or elaborate hallucinations and delusions (page 647)

phobia: a strong, persistent fear of a specific object, extreme enough to interfere with normal living (page 617)

positive symptoms: characteristics present in people with schizophrenia and absent in others—such as hallucinations, delusions, abnormal movements, and thought disorder (page 645)

residual schizophrenia: a condition in which someone has had an episode of schizophrenia and is now partly, but not fully, recovered (page 647)

schizophrenia: a condition marked by deterioration of daily activities over a period of at least 6 months, plus hallucinations, delusions, flat or inappropriate emotions, certain movement disorders, or thought disorders (page 645)

season-of-birth effect: the tendency for people born in the winter months to be slightly more likely than other people are to develop schizophrenia (page 650)

seasonal affective disorder (SAD) (or depression with a seasonal pattern): a condition in which people become seriously depressed in one season of the year, such as winter (page 634)

selective serotonin reuptake inhibitors (SSRIs): drugs that block the reuptake of the neurotransmitter serotonin by the terminal bouton (page 638)

social phobia: a severe avoidance of other people and an especially strong fear of doing anything in public (page 616)

St. John's wort: an herb with antidepressant effects (page 638)

systematic desensitization: a method of reducing fear by gradually exposing people to the object of their fear (page 621)

tardive dyskinesia: a disorder characterized by tremors and involuntary movements (page 652)

tricyclic drugs: drugs that block the reabsorption of the neurotransmitters dopamine, norepinephrine, and serotonin, after they are released by the terminal bouton, thus prolonging the effect of these neurotransmitters on the receptors of the postsynaptic cell (page 638)

Type I (or Type A) alcoholism: alcoholism that is generally less severe, equally common in men and women, less dependent on genetics, and likely to develop gradually, presumably in response to the difficulties of life (page 629)

Type II (or Type B) alcoholism: alcoholism that is generally more severe, more common in men, more often associated with aggressive or antisocial behavior, more dependent on genetics, and likely to begin early in life (page 629)

undifferentiated schizophrenia: a type of schizophrenia characterized by the basic symptoms but no unusual or especially prominent symptoms (page 647)

Suggestions for Further Reading

Andreasen, N. C. (1994). *Schizophrenia: From mind to molecule.* Washington, DC: American Psychiatric Press. Review of schizophrenia by one of the leading researchers.

Jamison, K. R. (1997). *An unquiet mind.* New York: Random House. A psychiatrist describes her own lifelong battle with bipolar disorder.

Book Companion Web Site

Need help studying? Go to

http://psychology.wadsworth.com/kalat_intro7e/

for a virtual study center. You'll find a personalized Self-Study Assessment that will provide you with a study plan based on your answers to a pretest. Also study using flashcards, quizzes, interactive art, and an online glossary.

Check out interactive **Try It Yourself** exercises on the companion site! These exercises will help you put what you've learned into action.

Your companion site also has direct links to the following Web sites. These links are checked often for changes, dead links, and new additions.

Psychological Disorders and More

www.psych.org/

The American Psychiatric Association offers facts about various disorders, drug therapies, how to choose a therapist, and much more.

National Clearinghouse for Alcohol and Drug Information

www.health.org/

Here is comprehensive information for those who want to overcome a drug problem.

Harbor of Refuge

www.Harbor-of-Refuge.org/

Postings by people with bipolar disorder for others with the same problem.

The Experience of Schizophrenia

http://www.chovil.com

This is the personal site of Ian Chovil, who began struggling with schizophrenia in late adolescence and suffered greatly until he began taking medication in 1990. He tells his own story in unsparing detail. He describes the biology of schizophrenia, recommends books and movies on the subject, and provides many links.

Walkers in Darkness

http://www.walkers.org/

This long-established and award-winning site is dedicated to helping people with schizophrenia, bipolar illness, and related mood disorders. Included are descriptions of each disorder, information on medication and therapy, links to a variety of resources, forums, chat rooms, and mailing lists.

Try It Yourself CD-ROM
with Critical Thinking Video Exercises

Use your CD to access **videos** related to activities designed to help you think critically about the important topics discussed. For example, the videos about reality for a schizophrenic person and virtual-reality therapy tie to what you've learned in this chapter. You'll also find an easy portal link to the book companion site where you can access your personalized **Self-Study Assessments** and interactive **Try It Yourself** exercises.

PsychNow! 2.0

PsychNow! is a fun interactive CD designed to help you with the difficult concepts in psychology. Check out the Personality and Abnormal Psychology section for the following topics that relate to this chapter:

Abnormality and Psychopathology: six portraits—decide who looks normal, explore the biographies of the six people and case histories of two men.

Nonpsychote, Psychotic, and Affective Disorders: eight famous people with disorders, *DSM-IV* categories with examples, and case studies to review and diagnose.

Major Psychological Theories: five kinds of therapy with details and case studies and treatment.

Epilogue

Here we are at the end of the book. As I have been writing and revising, I have imagined you sitting there reading. I have imagined a student much like I was in college, reading about psychology for the first time and often growing excited about it. I remember periodically telling a friend or relative, "Guess what I just learned about psychology! Isn't this interesting?" (I still do the same today.) I also remember occasionally thinking, "Hmm. The book says such-and-so, but I'm not convinced. I wonder whether psychologists ever considered a different explanation. . . ." I started thinking about research I might do if I ever became a psychologist.

I hope that you have had similar experiences yourself. I hope you have occasionally become so excited about something you read that you thought about it and told other people about it. In fact I hope you told your roommate so much about psychology that you started to become annoying. I also hope you have sometimes doubted a conclusion, imagining a research project that might test it or improve on it.

Now, as I picture you reaching the end of the course, I'm not sure how you will react. You might be thinking, "Wow, I sure have learned a lot!" Or you might be thinking, "Is that *all?*" Maybe you are reacting both ways: "Yes, I learned a lot. But it seems like there should be more. I still don't understand what conscious experience is all about, and I don't understand why I react the way I do sometimes. And this book—*wonderful as it is!*—hardly mentioned certain topics. Why do we laugh? How do we sense the passage of time? Why do people like to watch sports? Why are some people religious and others not? Why do I feel like yawning whenever I see someone else yawn?"

I have two good reasons for not answering all your questions. One is that this is an introductory text and it can't go on forever. If you want to learn more, you should take other psychology courses or do some additional reading. The other reason is that psychologists do not know all the answers.

Perhaps someday you will become a researcher yourself and add to the sum of our knowledge. If not, you can try to keep up to date on current developments in psychology by reading good books and magazine articles. One of my main goals has been to prepare you to continue learning about psychology.

Try to read critically: Is a conclusion based on good evidence? If you read about a survey, were the questions worded clearly? How reliable and valid were the measurements? Did the investigators obtain a representative or random sample? If someone draws a cause-and-effect conclusion, was the evidence based on experiments or only correlations? Even if the evidence looks solid, is the author's explanation the best one?

Above all, remember that any conclusion is tentative. Psychological researchers seldom use the word *prove;* their conclusions are almost always tentative and guarded. I once suggested to my editor, half-seriously, that we should include in the index to this book the entry "*maybe*—see pages 1–657." We did not include such an entry, partly because I doubt anyone would have noticed the humor, and partly because our understanding of psychology is not really that bad. Still, be leery of anyone who seems a little too certain about a great new insight in psychology. The route from *maybe* to *definitely* is long and arduous.

References

Numbers in parentheses indicate the chapter in which a source is cited.

AbdelMalik, P., Husted, J., Chow, E. W. C., & Bassett, A. S. (2003). Childhood head injury and expression of schizophrenia in multiply affected families. *Archives of General Psychiatry, 60*, 231–236. (16)

Abi-Dargham, A., Rodenhiser, J., Printz, D., Zea-Ponce, Y., Gil, R., Kegeles, L. S., et al. (2000). Increased baseline occupancy of D_2 receptors by dopamine in schizophrenia. *Proceedings of the National Academy of Sciences, USA, 97*, 8104–8109. (16)

Abramson, L. Y., Seligman, M. E. P., & Teasdale, J. D. (1978). Learned helplessness in humans: Critique and reformulation. *Journal of Abnormal Psychology, 87*, 49–74. (16)

Abrams, R. A., & Christ, S. E. (2003). Motion onset captures attention. *Psychological Science, 14*, 427–432. (8)

Abrams, R. L., Klinger, M. R., & Greenwald, A. G. (2002). Subliminal words activate semantic categories (not automated motor responses). *Psychonomic Bulletin and Review, 9*, 100–106. (4)

Ackil, J. K., Van Abbema, D. L., & Bauer, P. J. (2003). After the storm: Enduring differences in mother-child recollections of traumatic and nontraumatic events. *Journal of Experimental Child Psychology, 84*, 286–309. (7)

Adam, K. S. (1986). Early family influences on suicidal behavior. *Annals of the New York Academy of Sciences, 487*, 63–76. (16)

Adams, D. L., & Horton, J. C. (2002). Shadows cast by retinal blood vessels mapped in primary visual cortex. *Science, 298*, 572–576. (4)

Adams, J. S. (1963). Wage inequities, productivity, and work quality. *Industrial Relations, 3*, 9–16. (11)

Adams, R. B., & Kleck, R. E. (2003). Perceived gaze direction and the processing of facial displays of emotion. *Psychological Science, 14*, 644–647. (12)

Adams, W., Kendell, R. E., Hare, E. H., & Munk-Jorgensen, P. (1993). Epidemiological evidence that maternal influenza contributes to the aetiology of schizophrenia: An analysis of Scottish, English, and Danish data. *British Journal of Psychiatry, 163*, 522–534. (16)

Adler, A. (1927). *Understanding human nature*. New York: Greenberg. (13)

Adler, A. (1964). Brief comments on reason, intelligence, and feeble-mindedness. In H. L. Ansbacher & R. R. Ansbacher (Eds.), *Superiority and social interest* (pp. 41–49). New York: Viking Press. (Original work published 1928) (13)

Adler, A. (1964). The structure of neurosis. In H. L. Ansbacher & R. R. Ansbacher (Eds.), *Superiority and social interest* (pp. 83–95). New York: Viking Press. (Original work published 1932) (13)

Adler, E., Hoon, M. A., Mueller, K. L., Chandrashekar, J., Ryba, N. J. P., & Zuker, C. S. (2000). A novel family of mammalian taste receptors. *Cell, 100*, 693–702. (4)

Adolph, K. E. (2000). Specificity of learning: Why infants fall over a veritable cliff. *Psychological Science, 11*, 290–295. (10)

Adolphs, R., Baron-Cohen, S., & Tranel, D. (2002). Impaired recognition of social emotions following amygdala damage. *Journal of Cognitive Neuroscience, 14*, 1264–1274. (12)

Adolphs, R., Russell, J. A., & Tranel, D. (1999). A role for the human amygdala in recognizing emotional arousal from unpleasant stimuli. *Psychological Science, 10*, 167–171. (12)

Adolphs, R., & Tranel, D. (1999). Preferences for visual stimuli following amygdala damage. *Journal of Cognitive Neuroscience, 11*, 610–616. (12)

Adolphs, R, Tranel, D., & Damasio, A. R. (1998). The human amygdala in social judgment. *Nature, 393*, 470-474. (12)

Ainsworth, M. D. S. (1979). Attachment as related to mother-infant interaction. In J. S. Rosenblatt, R. A. Hinde, C. Beer, & M. Busnel (Eds.), *Advances in the study of behavior* (Vol. 9, pp. 1–51). New York: Academic Press. (10)

Ainsworth, M. D. S., Blehar, M., Waters, E., & Wall, S. (1978). *Patterns of attachment*. Hillsdale, NJ: Erlbaum. (10)

Albee, G. W. (1986). Toward a just society: Lessons from observations on the primary prevention of psychopathology. *American Psychologist, 41*, 891–898. (15)

Aleman, A., Kahn, R. S., & Selten, J.P. (2003). Sex differences in the risk of schizophrenia. *Archives of General Psychiatry, 60*, 565–571. (16)

Alexander, I. E. (1982). The Freud-Jung relationship—the other side of Oedipus

and countertransference. *American Psychologist, 37*, 1009–1018. (13)

Alicke, M. D., & Largo, E. (1995). The role of the self in the false consensus effect. *Journal of Experimental Social Psychology, 31*, 28–47. (14)

Alison, L., Bennell, C., & Mokros, A. (2002). The personality paradox in offender profiling: A theoretical review of the processes involved in deriving background characteristics from crime scene actions. *Psychology, Public Policy, and Law, 8*, 115–135. (13)

Alison, L., Smith, M. D., & Morgan, K. (2003). Interpreting the accuracy of offender profiles. *Psychology, Crime & Law, 9*, 185–195. (13)

Allen, N. B., & Badcock, P. B. T. (2003). The social risk hypothesis of depressed mood: Evolutionary, psychosocial, and neurobiological perspectives. *Psychological Bulletin, 129*, 887–913. (16)

Allison, S. T., Mackie, D. M., Muller, M. M., & Worth, L. T. (1993). Sequential correspondence biases and perceptions of change: The Castro studies revisited. *Personality and Social Psychology Bulletin, 19*, 151–157. (14)

Alloy, L. B., Abramson, L. Y., Whitehouse, W. G., Hogan, M. E., Tashman, N. A., Steinberg, D. L., et al. (1999). Depressogenic cognitive styles: Predictive validity, information processing and personality characteristics, and developmental origins. *Behaviour Research and Therapy, 37*, 503–531. (16)

Allport, G. W. (1935). Attitudes. In C. Murchison (Ed.), *A handbook of social psychology* (pp. 798–844). Worcester, MA: Clark University Press. (14)

Allport, G. W. (1961). *Pattern and growth in personality*. New York: Holt, Rinehart & Winston. (13)

Allport, G. W., & Odbert, H. S. (1936). Trait-names: A psycholexical study. *Psychological Monographs, 47*(Whole No. 211). (13)

Alpert, J. L., Brown, L. S., & Courtois, C. A. (1998). Symptomatic clients and memories of childhood abuse. *Psychology, Public Policy, and Law, 4*, 941–995. (7)

Alroe, C. J., & Gunda, V. (1995). Self-amputation of the ear. *Australian and New Zealand Journal of Psychiatry, 29*, 508–512. (15)

Altmann, E. M., & Gray, W. D., (2002). Forgetting to remember: The functional relationship of decay and interference. *Psychological Science, 13,* 27–33. (7)

Amabile, T. M. (2001). Beyond talent. *American Psychologist, 56,* 333–336. (8)

Amanzio, M., Pollo, A., Maggi, G., & Benedetti, F. (2001). Response variability to analgesics: A role for non-specific activation of endogenous opioids. *Pain, 90,* 205–215. (4)

Amato, P. R., & Keith, B. (1991). Parental divorce and the well-being of children: A meta-analysis. *Psychological Bulletin, 110,* 26–46. (10)

Ambady, N., Shih, M., Kim, A., & Pittinsky, T. L. (2001). Stereotype susceptibility in children: Effects of identity activation on quantitative performance. *Psychological Science, 12,* 385–390. (9)

American Medical Association. (1986). Council report: Scientific status of refreshing recollection by the use of hypnosis. *International Journal of Clinical and Experimental Hypnosis, 34,* 1–12. (5)

American Psychiatric Association. (1994). *Diagnostic and statistical manual of mental disorders* (4th ed.). Washington, DC: Author. (15, 16)

American Psychological Association. (1982). *Ethical principles in the conduct of research with human participants.* Washington, DC: Author. (2)

Amzica, F., & Steriade, M. (1996). Progressive cortical synchronization of ponto-geniculo-occipital potentials during rapid eye movement sleep. *Neuroscience, 72,* 309–314. (5)

Anastasi, A. (1988). *Psychological testing* (6th ed.). New York: Macmillan. (9)

Anderson, A., & Phelps, E. A. (2000). Expression without recognition: Contributions of the human amygdala to emotional communication. *Psychological Science, 11,* 106–111. (12)

Anderson, A. K., & Phelps, E. A. (2002). Is the human amygdala critical for the subjective experience of emotion? Evidence of intact dispositional affect in patients with amygdala lesions. *Journal of Cognitive Neuroscience, 14,* 709–720. (12)

Anderson, C. A., & Bushman, B. J. (2001). Effects of violent video games on aggressive behavior, aggressive cognition, aggressive affect, physiological arousal, and prosocial behavior: A meta-analytic review of the scientific literature. *Psychological Science, 12,* 353–359. (2)

Anderson, C. D., Warner, J. L., & Spencer, C. C. (1984). Inflation bias in self-assessment examinations: Implications for valid employee selection. *Journal of Applied Psychology, 69,* 574–580. (13)

Andreasen, N. C. (1999). A unitary model of schizophrenia. *Archives of General Psychiatry, 56,* 781–787. (16)

Andreasen, N. C., Flaum, M. Swayze, V. W., II, Tyrrell, G., & Arndt, S. (1990).

Positive and negative symptoms in schizophrenia. *Archives of General Psychiatry, 47,* 615–621. (16)

Andrew, D., & Craig, A. D. (2001). Spinothalamic lamina I neurons selectively sensitive to histamine: A central neural pathway for itch. *Nature Neuroscience, 4,* 72–77. (4)

Andrews, T. J., Halpern, S. D., & Purves, D. (1997). Correlated size variations in human visual cortex, lateral geniculate nucleus, and optic tract. *Journal of Neuroscience, 17,* 2859–2868. (4)

Anglin, D., Spears, K. L., & Hutson, H. R. (1997). Flunitrazepam and its involvement in date or acquaintance rape. *Academy of Emergency Medicine, 4,* 323–326. (5)

Anonymous. (1955). *Alcoholics anonymous* (2nd ed.). New York: Alcoholics Anonymous World Services. (16)

Appelbaum, P. S. (1988). The new preventive detention: Psychiatry's problematic responsibility for the control of violence. *American Journal of Psychiatry, 145,* 779–785. (15)

Appley, M. H. (1991). Motivation, equilibration, and stress. In R. Dienstbier (Ed.), *Nebraska Symposium on Motivation 1990* (pp. 1–67). Lincoln: University of Nebraska Press. (11)

Arboleda, C., & Holzman, P. S. (1985). Thought disorder in children at risk for psychosis. *Archives of General Psychiatry, 42,* 1004–1013. (16)

Archer, J. (2000). Sex differences in aggression between heterosexual partners: A meta-analytic review. *Psychological Bulletin, 126,* 651–680. (12)

Ariely, D., & Wertenbroch, K. (2002). Procrastination, deadlines, and performance: Self-control by precommitment. *Psychological Science, 13,* 219–224. (11)

Arkes, H. R. (2003). The nonuse of psychological research at two federal agencies. *Psychological Science, 14,* 1–6. (8)

Arkes, H. R., & Ayton, P. (1999). The sunk cost and Concorde effects: Are humans less rational than lower animals? *Psychological Bulletin, 125,* 591–600. (8)

Arndt, S., Andreasen, N. C., Flaum, M., Miller, D., & Nopoulos, P. (1995). A longitudinal study of symptom dimensions in schizophrenia. *Archives of General Psychiatry, 52,* 352–360. (16)

Arnett, J. (1990). Contraceptive use, sensation seeking, and adolescent egocentrism. *Journal of Youth and Adolescence, 19,* 171–180. (10)

Arnett, J. J. (1999). Adolescent storm and stress reconsidered. *American Psychologist, 54,* 317–326. (10)

Arnett, J. J. (2000). Emerging adulthood: A theory of development from the late teens through the twenties. *American Psychologist, 55,* 469–480. (10)

Arnold, H. J., & House, R. J. (1980). Methodological and substantive extensions to the job characteristics model of motivation. *Organizational Behavior and Human Performance, 25,* 161–183. (11)

Aronow, E., Reznikoff, M., & Moreland, K. L. (1995). The Rorschach: Projective technique or psychometric test? *Journal of Personality Assessment, 64,* 213–228. (13)

Aronson, E. (1997). The theory of cognitive dissonance: The evolution and vicissitudes of an idea. In C. McGarty & S. A. Haslam (Eds.), *The message of social psychology* (pp. 20–35). Cambridge, MA: Blackwell. (14)

Aronson, E., & Carlsmith, J. M. (1963). Effect of the severity of threat on the devaluation of forbidden behavior. *Journal of Abnormal and Social Psychology, 66,* 584–588. (14)

Arvey, R. D., McCall, B. P., Bouchard, T. J., Jr., Taubman, P., & Cavanaugh, M. A. (1994). Genetic influences on job satisfaction and work values. *Personality and Individual Differences, 17,* 21–33. (11)

Arvey, R. D., & 51 others. (1994, December 13). Mainstream science on intelligence. *The Wall Street Journal,* p. A18. (9)

Asch, S. E. (1951). Effects of group pressure upon the modification and distortion of judgments. In H. Guetzkow (Ed.), *Groups, leadership, and men* (pp. 177–190). Pittsburgh, PA: Carnegie Press. (14)

Asch, S. E. (1955, November). Opinions and social pressure. *Scientific American, 193*(5), 31–35. (14)

Asch, S. E. (1956). Studies of independence and conformity: I. A minority of one against a unanimous majority. *Psychological Monographs, 70*(9, Whole No. 416). (14)

Ash, R. (1986, August). An anecdote submitted by Ron Ash. *The Industrial-Organizational Psychologist, 23*(4), 8. (6)

Atkinson, R. C., & Shiffrin, R. M. (1968). Human memory: A proposed system and its control. In K. W. Spence & J. T. Spence (Eds.), *The psychology of learning and motivation* (Vol. 2, pp. 89–105). New York: Academic Press. (7)

Au, T. K., Knightly, L. M., Jun, S.-A., & Oh, J. W. (2002). Overhearing a language during childhood. *Psychological Science, 13,* 238–243. (8)

Austin, J. T., & Vancouver, J. B. (1996). Goal constructs in psychology: Structure, process, and content. *Psychological Bulletin, 120,* 338–375. (11)

Averill, J. R. (1983). Studies on anger and aggression: Implications for theories of emotion. *American Psychologist, 38,* 1145–1160. (12)

Axelrod, R., & Dion, D. (1988). The further evolution of cooperation. *Science, 242,* 1385–1390. (14)

Azrin, N. H., & Nunn, R. G. (1973). Habit-reversal: A method of eliminating nervous habits and tics. *Behaviour Research and Therapy, 11,* 619–628. (6)

Babkoff, H., Caspy, T., Mikulincer, M., & Sing, H. C. (1991). Monotonic and rhythmic influences: A challenge for sleep deprivation research. *Psychological Bulletin, 109,* 411–428. (5)

Baddeley, A. D. (2001). Is working memory still working? *American Psychologist, 56,* 851–864. (7)

Baddeley, A., Gathercole, S., & Papagno, C. (1998). The phonological loop as a language learning device. *Psychological Review, 105,* 158–173. (7)

Baddeley, A. D., & Hitch, G. (1974). Working memory. In G. H. Bower (Ed.), *Psychology of learning and motivation* (Vol. 8, pp. 47–89). New York: Academic Press. (7)

Baddeley, A., & Hitch, G. J. (1994). Developments in the concept of working memory. *Neuropsychology, 8,* 485–493. (7)

Baer, J. S., Sampson, P. D., Barr, H. M., Connor, P. D., & Streissguth, A. P. (2003). A 21-year longitudinal analysis of the effects of prenatal alcohol exposure on young adult drinking. *Archives of General Psychiatry, 60,* 377–385. (16)

Bahrick, H. (1984). Semantic memory content in permastore: 50 years of memory for Spanish learned in school. *Journal of Experimental Psychology: General, 113,* 1–29. (7)

Bahrick, H. P., Bahrick, L. E., Bahrick, A. S., & Bahrick, P. E. (1993). Maintenance of foreign language vocabulary and the spacing effect. *Psychological Science, 4,* 316–321. (7)

Bailey, J. M., & Pillard, R. C. (1991). A genetic study of male sexual orientation. *Archives of General Psychiatry, 48,* 1089–1096. (11)

Bailey, J. M., Pillard, R. C., Neale, M. C., & Agyei, Y. (1993) Heritable factors influence sexual orientation in women. *Archives of General Psychiatry, 50,* 217–223. (11)

Baillargeon, R. (1986). Representing the existence and the location of hidden objects: Object permanence in 6- and 8-month-old infants. *Cognition, 23,* 21–41. (10)

Baillargeon, R. (1987). Object permanence in 3 1/2- and 4 1/2-month-old infants. *Developmental Psychology, 23,* 655–664. (10)

Baird, J. C. (1982). The moon illusion: A reference theory. *Journal of Experimental Psychology: General, 111,* 304–315. (4)

Baker, T. B., Piper, M. E., McCarthy, D. E., Majeskie, M. R., & Fiore, M. C. (2004). Addiction motivation reformulated: An affective processing model of negative reinforcement. *Psychological Review, 111,* 33–51. (16)

Baker, T. B., & Tiffany, S. T. (1985). Morphine tolerance as habituation. *Psychological Bulletin, 92,* 78–108. (5)

Baker-Ward, L., Gordon, B. N., Ornstein, P. A., Larus, D. M., & Clubb, P. A. (1993). Young children's long-term retention of a pediatric examination. *Child Development, 64,* 1519–1533. (7)

Bakermans-Kranenburg, M. J., van IJzendoorn, M. H., & Juffer, F. (2003). Less is more: Meta-analyses of sensitivity and attachment interventions in early childhood. *Psychological Bulletin, 129,* 195–215. (10)

Bakker, S. C., van der Meulen, E. M., Buitelaar, J. K., Sandkuijl, L. A., Pauls, D. L., Monsuur, A. J., et al. (2003). A whole-genome scan in 164 Dutch sib pairs with attention-deficit/hyperactivity disorder: Suggestive evidence for linkage on chromosomes 7p and 15q. *American Journal of Human Genetics, 72,* 1251–1260. (15)

Baldessarini, R. J. (1984). Antipsychotic drugs. In T. B. Karasu (Ed.), *The psychiatric therapies: I. The somatic therapies* (pp. 119–170). Washington, DC: American Psychiatric Press. (16)

Baldessarini, R. J., & Tondo, L. (2000). Does lithium treatment still work? *Archives of General Psychiatry, 57,* 187–190. (16)

Baldessarini, R. J., Tondo, L., & Hennen, J. (2001). Treating the suicidal patient with bipolar disorder. *Annals of the New York Academy of Sciences, 932,* 24–38. (16)

Banaji, M. R., & Bhaskar, R. (2000). Implicit stereotypes and memory: The bounded rationality of social beliefs. In D. L. Schacter & E. Scarry (Eds.), *Memory, brain, and belief* (pp. 139–175). Cambridge, MA: Harvard University Press. (14)

Banaji, M. R., & Kihlstrom, J. F. (1996). The ordinary nature of alien abduction memories. *Psychological Inquiry, 7,* 132–135. (7, 16)

Bandura, A. (1977). *Social learning theory.* Upper Saddle River, NJ: Prentice Hall. (6)

Bandura, A. (1986). *Social foundations of thought and action.* Upper Saddle River, NJ: Prentice Hall. (6)

Bandura, A. (2000). Exercise of human agency through collective efficacy. *Current Directions in Psychological Science, 9,* 75–78. (6)

Bandura, A., Barbaranelli, C., Caprara, G. V., & Pastorelli, C. (2001). Self-efficacy beliefs as shapers of children's aspirations and career trajectories. *Child Development, 72,* 187–206. (6)

Bandura, A., Ross, D., & Ross, S. A. (1963). Imitation of film-mediated aggressive models. *Journal of Abnormal and Social Psychology, 66,* 3–11. (6)

Baptista, L. F., & Petrinovich, L. (1984). Social interaction, sensitive phases and the song template hypothesis in the white-crowned sparrow. *Animal Behaviour, 32,* 172–181. (6)

Bardone, A. M., Vohs, K. D., Abramson, L. Y., Heatherton, T. F., & Joiner, T. E., Jr. (2000). The confluence of perfectionism, body dissatisfaction, and low self-esteem predicts bulimic symptoms: Clinical implications. *Behavior Therapy, 31,* 265–280. (11)

Bargh, J. A., Chen, M., & Burrows, L. (1996). The automaticity of social behavior: Direct effects of trait concept and stereotype activation on action. *Journal of Personality and Social Psychology, 71,* 230–244. (14)

Barnett, R. C., & Hyde, J. S. (2001). Women, men, work, and family. *American Psychologist, 56,* 781–796. (10)

Barnett, S. M., & Ceci, S. J. (2002). When and where do we apply what we learn? A taxonomy for far transfer. *Psychological Bulletin, 128,* 612–637. (3, 8)

Barnier, A. J., & McConkey, K. M. (1998). Posthypnotic responding away from the hypnotic setting. *Psychological Science, 9,* 256–262. (5)

Baron, J. (1997). The illusion of morality as self-interest: A reason to cooperate in social dilemmas. *Psychological Science, 8,* 330–335. (14)

Baron, J., & Norman, M. F. (1992). SATs, achievement tests, and high-school class rank as predictors of college performance. *Educational and Psychological Measurement, 52,* 1047–1055. (9)

Bartlett, F. C. (1932). *Remembering.* Cambridge, England: Cambridge University Press. (7)

Bartoshuk, L. M. (1991). Taste, smell, and pleasure. In R. C. Bolles (Ed.), *The hedonics of taste* (pp. 5–28). Hillsdale, NJ: Erlbaum. (4)

Bartoshuk, L. M. (2000). Psychophysical advances aid the study of genetic variation in taste. *Appetite, 34,* 105. (12)

Bartoshuk, L. M., Duffy, V. B., Lucchina, L. B., Prutkin, J., & Fast, K. (1998). PROP (6-n-propyl-thiouracil) supertasters and the saltiness of NaCl. *Annals of the New York Academy of Sciences, 855,* 793–796. (4, 12)

Basabe, N., Paez, D., Valencia, J., Gonzalez, J. L., Rimé, B., & Diener, E. (2002). Cultural dimensions, socioeconomic development, climate, and emotional hedonic level. *Cognition and Emotion, 16,* 103–125. (12)

Bassetti, C., & Aldrich, M. S. (1997). Idiopathic hypersomnia: A series of 42 patients. *Brain, 120,* 1423–1435. (5)

Batson, C. D., & Thompson, E. R. (2001). Why don't people act morally? Motivational considerations. *Current Directions in Psychological Science, 10,* 54–57. (10)

Battaglia, M., Bertella, S., Ogliari, A., Bellodi, L., & Smeraldi, E. (2001). Modulation by muscarinic antagonists of the response to carbon dioxide challenge in panic disorder. *Archives of General Psychiatry, 58,* 114–119. (16)

Bauer, P. J. (1996). What do infants recall of their lives? *American Psychologist, 51,* 29–41. (7)

Bauer, P. J. (2002). Long-term recall memory: Behavioral and neuro-developmental changes in the first 2 years of life. *Current Directions in Psychological Science, 11*, 137–141. (7)

Baumeister, R. F. (2000). Gender differences in erotic plasticity: The female sex drive as socially flexible and responsive. *Psychological Bulletin, 126*, 347–374. (11)

Baumeister, R. F., Campbell, J. D., Krueger, J. I., & Vohs, K. D. (2003). Does high self-esteem cause better performance, interpersonal success, happiness, or healthier lifestyles? *Psychological Science in the Public Interest, 4*, 1–44. (13)

Baumeister, R. F., Smart, L., & Boden, J. M. (1996). Relation of threatened egotism to violence and aggression: The dark side of high self-esteem. *Psychological Review, 103*, 5–33. (12)

Baumrind, D. (1971). Current patterns of parental authority. *Developmental Psychology Monographs, 4*(1, Pt. 2). (10)

Baumrind, D., Larzelere, R. E., & Cowan, P. A. (2002). Ordinary physical punishment: Is it harmful? Comment on Gershoff (2002). *Psychological Bulletin, 128*, 580–589. (6)

Baxter, M. G., & Murray, E. A. (2002). The amygdala and reward. *Nature Reviews Neuroscience, 3*, 563–573. (3, 12)

Beauregard, M., Chertkow, H., Gold, D., & Bergman, S. (2001). The impact of semantic impairment on word stem completion in Alzheimer's disease. *Neuropsychologia, 39*, 302–314. (7)

Becht, M. C., & Vingerhoets, A. J. J. M. (2002). Crying and mood change: A cross-cultural study. *Cognition and Emotion, 16*, 87–101. (12)

Beck, A. T. (1973). *The diagnosis and management of depression.* Philadelphia: University of Pennsylvania Press. (16)

Beck, A. T. (1976). *Cognitive therapy and the emotional disorders.* New York: New American Library. (15)

Beck, A. T. (1987). Cognitive models of depression. *Journal of Cognitive Psychotherapy: An International Quarterly, 1*, 5–37. (16)

Beck, A. T. (1991). Cognitive therapy: A 30-year retrospective. *American Psychologist, 46*, 368–375. (16)

Beck, A. T., & Emery, G. (1985). *Anxiety disorders and phobias.* New York: Basic Books. (16)

Beck, A. T., & Steer, R. A. (1989). Clinical predictors of eventual suicide: A 5- to 10-year prospective study of suicide attempters. *Journal of Affective Disorders, 17*, 203–209. (16)

Beck, A. T., Steer, R. A., Beck, J. S., & Newman, C. F. (1993). Hopelessness, depression, suicidal ideation, and clinical diagnosis of depression. *Suicide and Life-Threatening Behavior, 23*, 139–145. (16)

Beck, A. T., Steer, R. A., & Brown, G. (1993). Dysfunctional attitudes and suicidal ideation in psychiatric outpatients. *Suicide and Life-Threatening Behavior, 23*, 11–20. (16)

Beck, K., & Wilson, C. (2000). Development of affective organizational commitment: A cross-sequential examination of change with tenure. *Journal of Vocational Behavior, 56*, 114–136. (11)

Becker, A. E., Burwell, R. A., Gilman, S. E., Herzog, D. B., & Hamburg, P. (2002). Eating behaviours and attitudes following prolonged exposure to television among ethnic Fijian adolescent girls. *British Journal of Psychiatry, 180*, 509–514. (11)

Becker, A. E., Burwell, R. A., Navara, K., & Gilman, S. E. (2003). Binge eating and binge eating disorder in a small-scale, indigenous society: The view from Fiji. *International Journal of Eating Disorders, 34*, 423–431. (11)

Becker, A. E., Franko, D. L., Speck, A., & Herzog, D. B. (2003). Ethnicity and differential access to care for eating disorder symptoms. *International Journal of Eating Disorders, 33*, 205–212. (11)

Becker, E. S., Strohbach, D., & Rinck, M. (1999). A specific attentional bias in suicide attempters. *Journal of Nervous and Mental Disease, 187*, 730–735. (13)

Becker, M. W., & Pashler, H. (2002). Volatile visual representations: Failing to detect changes in recently processed information. *Psychonomic Bulletin & Review, 9*, 744–750. (8)

Beeman, M. J., & Chiarello, C. (1998). Complementary right- and left-hemisphere language comprehension. *Current Directions in Psychological Science, 7*, 2–8. (3)

Bell, R., & Pliner, P. L. (2003). Time to eat: The relationship between the number of people eating and meal duration in three lunch settings. *Appetite, 41*, 215–218. (11)

Bellugi, U., Lichtenberger, L., Jones, W., Lai, Z., & St. George, M. (2000). I. The neurocognitive profile of Williams syndrome: A complex pattern of strengths and weaknesses. *Journal of Cognitive Neuroscience, 12*(Suppl.), 7–29. (8)

Bellugi, U., & St. George, M. (2000). Preface. *Journal of Cognitive Neuroscience, 12*(Suppl.), 1–6. (8)

Bellugi, U., Wang, P. P., & Jernigan, T. L. (1994). Williams syndrome: An unusual neuropsychological profile. In S. H. Broman & J. Grafman (Eds.), *Atypical cognitive deficits in developmental disorders* (pp. 23–56). Hillsdale, NJ: Erlbaum. (2)

Belmore, S. M. (1987). Determinants of attention during impression formation. *Journal of Experimental Psychology: Learning, Memory, and Cognition, 13*, 480–489. (14)

Belsky, J. (1996). Parent, infant, and social-contextual antecedents of father-son attachment security. *Developmental Psychology, 32*, 905–913. (10)

Bem, D. J., & Honorton, C. (1994). Does psi exist? Replicable evidence for an anomalous process of information transfer. *Psychological Bulletin, 115*, 4–18. (2)

Benbow, C. P., Lubinski, D., Shea, D. L., & Efekhari-Sanjani, H. (2000). Sex differences in mathematical reasoning at age 13: Their status 20 years later. *Psychological Science, 11*, 474–480. (10)

Benes, F. M. (1995). Is there a neuroanatomic basis for schizophrenia? An old question revisited. *The Neuroscientist, 1*, 104–115. (16)

Benjamin, J., Ben-Zion, I. Z., Dannon, P., Schreiber, S., Meiri, G., Ofek, A., et al. (2001). Lack of association between joint hyperlaxity and, I: panic disorder, and II: reactivity to carbon dioxide in healthy volunteers. *Human Psychopharmacology—Clinical and Experimental, 16*, 189–192. (16)

Benowitz, N. L. (1986). The human pharmacology of nicotine. *Research Advances in Alcohol and Drug Problems, 9*, 1–52. (16)

Benson, H. (1977). Systemic hypertension and the relaxation response. *New England Journal of Medicine, 296*, 1152–1156. (12)

Benson, H. (1985). Stress, health, and the relaxation response. In W. D. Gentry, H. Benson, & C. J. de Wolff (Eds.), *Behavioral medicine: Work, stress and health* (pp. 15–32). Dordrecht, The Netherlands: Martinus Nijhoff. (12)

Berger, R. J., & Phillips, N. H. (1995). Energy conservation and sleep. *Behavioural Brain Research, 69*, 65–73. (5)

Berglas, S., & Jones, E. E. (1978). Drug choice as a self-handicapping strategy in response to noncontingent success. *Journal of Personality and Social Psychology, 36*, 405–417. (14)

Berkowitz, L. (1983). Aversively stimulated aggression: Some parallels and differences in research with animals and humans. *American Psychologist, 38*, 1135–1144. (12)

Berkowitz, L. (1989). Frustration-aggression hypothesis: Examination and reformulation. *Psychological Bulletin, 106*, 59–73. (12)

Berlyne, D. E. (1981). Humanistic psychology as a protest movement. In J. R. Royce & L. P. Mos (Eds.), *Humanistic psychology: Concepts and criticisms* (pp. 261–293). New York: Plenum Press. (13)

Bernardin, H. J., Cooke, D. K., & Villanova, P. (2000). Conscientiousness and agreeableness as predictors of rating leniency. *Journal of Applied Psychology, 85*, 232–234. (13)

Bernstein, I. L. (1991). Aversion conditioning in response to cancer and cancer treatment. *Clinical Psychology Review, 11*, 185–191. (6)

Berntson, G. G., Cacioppo, J. T., & Quigley, K. S. (1993). Cardiac psychophysiology and autonomic space in humans: Empirical perspectives and conceptual implications. *Psychological Bulletin, 114,* 296–322. (12)

Berridge, K. C., & Robinson, T. E. (1995). The mind of an addicted brain: Neural sensitization of wanting versus liking. *Current Directions in Psychological Science, 4,* 71–76. (6)

Berridge, K. C., & Robinson, T. E. (1998). What is the role of dopamine in reward: Hedonic impact, reward learning, or incentive salience? *Brain Research Reviews, 28,* 309–369. (5)

Berry, D. S. (2000). Attractiveness, attraction, and sexual selection: Evolutionary perspectives on the form and function of physical attractiveness. *Advances in Experimental Social Psychology, 32,* 273–342. (14)

Berry, J. W., Poortinga, Y. H., Segal, H., & Dasen, P. R. (1992). *Cross-cultural psychology.* Cambridge, England: Cambridge University Press. (15)

Berscheid, E. (1983). Emotion. In H. H. Kelley, E. Berscheid, A. Christensen, J. H. Harvey, T. L. Huston, G. Levinger, et al. (Eds.), *Close relationships* (pp. 110–168). New York: W. H. Freeman. (14)

Bickman, L. (1996). A continuum of care: More is not always better. *American Psychologist, 51,* 689–701. (15)

Billy, J. O. G., Tanfer, K., Grady, W. R., & Klepinger, D. H. (1993, March/April). The sexual behavior of men in the United States. *Family Planning Perspectives, 25,* 52–60. (11)

Binet, A., & Simon, T. (1905). Méthodes nouvelles pour le diagnostic du niveau intellectuel des anormaux [New methods for the measurement of the intellectual level of the abnormal]. *L'Année Psychologique, 11,* 191–244. (9)

Birch, S. A. J., & Bloom, P. (2003). Children are cursed: An asymmetric bias in mental-state attribution. *Psychological Science, 14,* 283–286. (10)

Birnbaum, M. H. (1999). Testing critical properties of decision making on the Internet. *Psychological Science, 10,* 399–407. (8)

Bishop, E. G., Cherny, S. S., Corley, R., Plomin, R., DeFries, J. C., & Hewitt, J. K. (2003). Development genetic analysis of general cognitive ability from 1 to 12 years in a sample of adoptees, biological siblings, and twins. *Intelligence, 31,* 31–49. (9)

Bjork, R. A., & VanHuele, M. (1992). Retrieval inhibition and related adaptive peculiarities of human memory. *Advances in Consumer Research, 19,* 155–160. (7)

Bjorklund, D. F., & Shackelford, T. K. (1999). Differences in parental investment contribute to important differences between men and women. *Current Directions in Psychological Science, 8,* 86–92. (14)

Black, D. W., Noyes, R., Jr., Goldstein, R. B., & Blum, N. (1992). A family study of obsessive-compulsive disorder. *Archives of General Psychiatry, 49,* 362–368. (16)

Blackless, M., Charuvastra, A., Derryck, A., Fausto-Sterling, A., Lauzanne, K., & Lee, E. (2000). How sexually dimorphic are we? Review and synthesis. *American Journal of Human Biology, 12,* 151–166. (11)

Blackwell, A., & Bates, E. (1995). Inducing agrammatic profiles in normals: Evidence for the selective vulnerability of morphology under cognitive resource limitation. *Journal of Cognitive Neuroscience, 7,* 228–257. (8)

Blaine, J. D., Prien, R. F., & Levine, J. (1983). The role of antidepressants in the treatment of affective disorders. *American Journal of Psychotherapy, 37,* 502–520. (16)

Blake, R., & Logothetis, N. K. (2002). Visual competition. *Nature Reviews Neuroscience, 3,* 13–23. (4)

Blakemore, C., & Sutton, P. (1969). Size adaptation: A new aftereffect. *Science, 166,* 245–247. (4)

Blascovich, J., & Tomaka, J. (1991). Measures of self-esteem. In J. P. Robinson, R. R. Shaver, & L. S. Wrightsman (Eds.), *Measures of personality and social psychological attitudes* (Vol. 1, pp. 115–160). San Diego, CA: Academic Press. (13)

Bless, H., Bohner, G., Schwarz, N., & Strack, F. (1990). Mood and persuasion: A cognitive response analysis. *Personality and Social Psychology Bulletin, 16,* 331–345. (12)

Bleuler, E. (1950). *Dementia praecox, or the group of schizophrenias* (J. Zinkin, Trans.). New York: International Universities Press. (Original work published 1911) (16)

Block, J. (1995). A contrarian view of the five-factor approach to personality description. *Psychological Bulletin, 117,* 187–215. (13)

Blount, J. D., Metcalfe, N. B., Birkhead, T. R., & Surai, P. F. (2003). Carotenoid modulation of immune function and sexual attractiveness in zebra finches. *Science, 300,* 125–127. (14)

Blum, D. (1994). *The monkey wars.* New York: Oxford University Press. (2)

Blum, G. S., & Barbour, J. S. (1979). Selective inattention to anxiety-linked stimuli. *Journal of Experimental Psychology: General, 108,* 182–224. (4)

Blumenthal, S. J., & Kupfer, D. J. (1986). Generalizable treatment strategies for suicidal behavior. *Annals of the New York Academy of Sciences, 487,* 327–340. (16)

Bohart, A. C. (2000). The client is the most important common factor: Clients' self-healing capacities and psychotherapy.

Journal of Psychotherapy Integration, 10, 127–149. (15)

Bond, M. H. (1991). *Beyond the Chinese face.* New York: Oxford University Press. (15)

Bond, M. H. (2002). Reclaiming the individual from Hofstede's ecological analysis—A 20-year odyssey: Comment on Oyserman et al. (2002). *Psychological Bulletin, 128,* 73–77. (14)

Bond, R., & Smith, P. B. (1996). Culture and conformity: A meta-analysis of studies using Asch's (1952b, 1956) line judgment task. *Psychological Bulletin, 119,* 111–137. (14)

Bonnie, R. J. (1997). Research with cognitively impaired subjects: Unfinished business in the regulation of human research. *Archives of General Psychiatry, 54,* 105–111. (2)

Borch-Jacobsen, M. (1997, April 24). Sybil—The making of a disease: An interview with Dr. Herbert Spiegel. *New York Review of Books,* no. 7, 60–64. (15)

Borden, V. M. H., & Rajecki, D. W. (2000). First-year employment outcomes of psychology baccalaureates: Relatedness, preparedness, and prospects. *Teaching of Psychology, 27,* 164–168. (1)

Boring, E. G. (1930). A new ambiguous figure. *American Journal of Psychology, 42,* 444–445. (4)

Bornstein, R. F. (1989). Subliminal techniques as propaganda tools: Review and critique. *Journal of Mind and Behavior, 10,* 231–262. (4)

Borum, R. (1996). Improving the clinical practice of violence risk assessment: Technology, guidelines, and training. *American Psychologist, 51,* 945–956. (12)

Boswell, J. (1990). Sexual and ethical categories in premodern Europe. In D. P. McWhirter, S. A. Sanders, & J. M. Reinisch (Eds.), *Homosexuality/heterosexuality* (pp. 15–31). New York: Oxford University Press. (11)

Bouchard, T. J., Lykken, D. T., McGue, M., Segal, N. L., & Tellegen, A. (1990). Sources of psychological differences: The Minnesota study of twins reared apart. *Science, 250,* 223–228. (10)

Bouchard, T. J., Jr., & McGue, M. (1981). Familial studies of intelligence: A review. *Science, 212,* 1055–1059. (9)

Bouchard, T. J., Jr., & McGue, M. (2003). Genetic and environmental influences on human psychological differences. *Journal of Neurobiology, 54,* 4–45. (13)

Bouton, M. E. (1994). Context, ambiguity, and classical conditioning. *Current Directions in Psychological Science, 3,* 49–53. (6)

Bouton, M. E., Mineka, S., & Barlow, D. H. (2001). A modern learning theory perspective on the etiology of panic disorder. *Psychological Review, 108,* 4–32. (16)

Bowers, K. S., Regehr, G., Balthazard, C., & Parker, K. (1990). Intuition in the context of discovery. *Cognitive Psychology, 22,* 72–110. (8)

Bowlby, J. (1973). *Attachment and loss: Vol. II. Separation.* New York: Basic Books. (10)

Bowmaker, J. K. (1998). Visual pigments and molecular genetics of color blindness. *News in Physiological Sciences, 13,* 63–69. (4)

Bowmaker, J. K., & Dartnall, H. J. A. (1980). Visual pigments of rods and cones in a human retina. *Journal of Physiology* (London), *298,* 501–511. (4)

Bradbury, T. N., & Miller, G. A. (1985). Season of birth in schizophrenia: A review of evidence, methodology, and etiology. *Psychological Bulletin, 98,* 569–594. (16)

Brainard, M. S., & Doupe, A. J. (2000). Auditory feedback in learning and maintenance of vocal behaviour. *Nature Reviews Neuroscience, 1,* 31–40. (6)

Brainerd, C. J., & Reyna, V. F. (2002). Fuzzy-trace theory and false memory. *Current Directions in Psychological Science, 11,* 164–169. (7)

Bray, G. A., & Tartaglia, L. A. (2000). Medicinal strategies in the treatment of obesity. *Nature, 404,* 672–677. (11)

Bregman, A. S. (1981). Asking the "what for" question in auditory perception. In M. Kubovy & J. R. Pomerantz (Eds.), *Perceptual organization* (pp. 99–118). Hillsdale, NJ: Erlbaum. (4)

Brennan, P. A., Grekin, E. R., & Mednick, S. A. (1999). Maternal smoking during pregnancy and adult male criminal outcomes. *Archives of General Psychiatry, 56,* 215–219. (12)

Brent, D. A. (2001). Firearms and suicide. *Annals of the New York Academy of Sciences, 932,* 225–239. (16)

Brewin, C. R., & Beaton, A. (2002). Thought suppression, intelligence, and working memory capacity. *Behaviour Research and Therapy, 40,* 923–930. (7)

Broadbent, J., Muccino, K. J., & Cunningham, C. L. (2002). Ethanol-induced conditioned taste aversion in 15 inbred mouse strains. *Behavioral Neuroscience, 116,* 138–148. (6)

Brockner, J., & Rubin, J. Z. (1985). *Entrapment in escalating conflicts.* New York: Springer-Verlag. (14)

Brody, N. (2003). Construct validation of the Sternberg Triarchic Abilities Test: Comment and reanalysis. *Intelligence, 31,* 319–329. (9)

Brooks, R. (2000). Negative genetic correlation between male sexual attractiveness and survival. *Nature, 406,* 67–70. (14)

Brooks-Gunn, J., & Furstenberg, F. F., Jr. (1989). Adolescent sexual behavior. *American Psychologist, 44,* 249–257. (10)

Brosnan, S. F., & de Waal, F. B. M. (2003). Monkeys reject unequal pay. *Nature, 425,* 297–299. (11)

Brower, K. J., & Anglin, M. D. (1987). Adolescent cocaine use: Epidemiology, risk

factors, and prevention. *Journal of Drug Education, 17,* 163–180. (5)

Brown, G. W. (1989). Life events and measurement. In G. W. Brown & T. O. Harris (Eds.), *Life events and illness* (pp. 3–45). New York: Guilford Press. (12)

Brown, J. (1977). *Mind, brain, and consciousness.* New York: Academic Press. (8)

Brown, R., & McNeill, D. (1966). The "tip of the tongue." *Journal of Verbal Learning and Verbal Behavior, 5,* 325–337. (7)

Brown, S. L., Nesse, R. M., Vinokur, A. D., & Smith, D. M. (2003). Providing social support may be more beneficial than receiving it: Results from a prospective study of mortality. *Psychological Science, 14,* 320–327. (12)

Brownstein, A. L. (2003). Biased predecision processing. *Psychological Bulletin, 129,* 545–568. (8)

Bruce, S. E., Machan, J. T., Dyck, I., & Keller, M. B. (2001). Infrequency of "pure" GAD: Impact of psychiatric comorbidity on clinical course. *Depression and Anxiety, 14,* 219–225. (16)

Bruck, M., Cavanagh, P., & Ceci, S. J. (1991). Fortysomething: Recognizing faces at one's 25th reunion. *Memory & Cognition, 19,* 221–228. (4)

Bruner, J. S., & Potter, M. C. (1964). Interference in visual recognition. *Science, 144,* 424–425. (8)

Bryant, F. B., & Guilbault, R. L. (2002). "I knew it all along" eventually: The development of hindsight bias in the Clinton impeachment verdict. *Basic and Applied Social Psychology, 24,* 27–41. (7)

Brysbaert, M., Vitu, F., & Schroyens, W. (1996). The right visual field advantage and the optimal viewing position effect: On the relation between foveal and parafoveal word recognition. *Neuropsychology, 10,* 385–395. (8)

Brzustowica, L. M., Hodgkinson, K. A., Chow, E. W. C., Honer, W. G., & Bassett, A. S. (2000). Location of a major susceptibility locus for familial schizophrenia on chromosome 1q21-q22. *Science, 288,* 678–682. (16)

Buck, L., & Axel, R. (1991). A novel multigene family may encode odorant receptors: A molecular basis for odor recognition. *Cell, 65,* 175–187. (4)

Buck, R. (1994). Social and emotional functions in facial expression and communication: The readout hypothesis. *Biological Psychology, 38,* 95–115. (12)

Buka, S. L., Tsuang, M. T., Torrey, E. F., Klebanoff, M. A., Bernstein, D., & Yolken, R. H. (2001). Maternal infections and subsequent psychosis among offspring. *Archives of General Psychiatry, 58,* 1032–1037. (16)

Burger, J. M. (1986). Increasing compliance by improving the deal: The that's-not-all technique. *Journal of Personality and Social Psychology, 51,* 277–283. (14)

Burgess, C. E., Lindblad, K., Sigransky, E., Yuan, Q.-P., Long, R. T., Breschel, T., et al. (1998). Large CAG/CTG repeats are associated with childhood-onset schizophrenia. *Molecular Psychiatry, 3,* 321–327. (16)

Burke, K. C., Burke, J. D., Jr., Regier, D. A., & Rae, D. S. (1990). Age at onset of selected mental disorders in five community populations. *Archives of General Psychiatry, 47,* 511–518. (16)

Burns, M. O., & Seligman, M. E. P. (1989). Explanatory style across the life span: Evidence for stability over 52 years. *Journal of Personality and Social Psychology, 56,* 471–477. (16)

Burr, D. C., Morrone, M. C., & Ross, J. (1994). Selective suppression of the magnocellular visual pathway during saccadic eye movements. *Nature, 371,* 511–513. (8)

Bushman, B. J., & Anderson, C. A. (2001). Media violence and the American public: Scientific facts versus media misinformation. *American Psychologist, 56,* 477–489. (2)

Bushman, B. J., & Phillips, C. M. (2001). If the television program bleeds, memory recedes. *Current Directions in Psychological Science, 10,* 43–47. (7)

Buss, D. M. (2000). Desires in human mating. *Annals of the New York Academy of Sciences, 907,* 39–49. (1, 14)

Buss, D. M., Larsen, R. J., Westen, D., & Semmelroth, J. (1992). Sex differences in jealousy: Evolution, physiology, and psychology. *Psychological Science, 3,* 251–255. (14)

Butcher, J. N., Graham, J. R., Williams, C. L., & Ben-Porath, Y. S. (1990). *Development and use of the MMPI-2 content scales.* Minneapolis: University of Minnesota Press. (13)

Butler, L. (2002). A list of published papers is no measure of value. *Nature, 419,* 877. (11)

Butzlaff, R. L., & Hooley, J. M. (1998). Expressed emotion and psychiatric relapse. *Archives of General Psychiatry, 55,* 547–552. (16)

Buunk, B. P., Angleitner, A., Oubaid, V., & Buss, D. M. (1996). Sex differences in jealousy in evolutionary and cultural perspective: Tests from the Netherlands, Germany, and the United States. *Psychological Science, 7,* 359–363. (14)

Byne, W., Tobet, S., Mattiace, L. A., Lasco, M. S., Kemether, E., Edgar, M. A., et al. (2001). The interstitial nuclei of the human anterior hypothalamus: An investigation of variation with sex, sexual orientation, and HIV status. *Hormones and Behavior, 40,* 86–92. (11)

Byrne, M., Agerbo, E., Ewald, H., Eaton, W. W., & Mortensen, P. B. (2003). Parental age and risk of schizophrenia. *Archives of General Psychiatry, 60,* 673–678. (16)

Cacioppo, J. T., Hawkley, L. C., & Berntson, G. G. (2003). The anatomy of loneliness. *Current Directions in Psychological Science, 12,* 71–74. (12)

Cahalan, D. (1978). Subcultural differences in drinking behavior in U.S. national surveys and selected European studies. In P. E. Nathan, G. A. Marlatt, & T. Løberg (Eds.), *Alcoholism: New directions in behavioral research and treatment* (pp. 235–253). New York: Plenum Press. (16)

Cahill, L., & McGaugh, J. L. (1998). Mechanisms of emotional arousal and lasting declarative memory. *Trends in Neurosciences, 21,* 294–299. (7)

Cahn, W., Hulshoff, H. E., Lems, E. B. T. E., van Haren, N. E. M., Schnack, H. G., van der Linden, J. A., et al. (2002). Brain volume changes in first-episode schizophrenia. *Archives of General Psychiatry, 59,* 1002–1010. (16)

Calvin, W. H., & Bickerton, D. (2000). *Lingua ex machina.* Cambridge, MA: MIT Press. (8)

Camara, W. J. (1988). Reagan signs ban of polygraph testing for job applicants. *The Industrial-Organizational Psychologist, 26,* 39–41. (12)

Cameron, P., & Cameron, K. (2002). What proportion of heterosexuals is ex-homosexual? *Psychological Reports, 91,* 1087–1097. (11)

Cameron, P., Proctor, K., Coburn, W., & Forde, N. (1985). Sexual orientation and sexually transmitted disease. *Nebraska Medical Journal, 70,* 292–299. (11)

Campbell, R. S., & Pennebaker, J. W. (2003). The secret life of pronouns: Flexibility in writing style and physical health. *Psychological Science, 14,* 60–65. (15)

Campbell, S. (2000). Is there an intrinsic period of the circadian clock? *Science, 288,* 1174. (5)

Campbell, S. S., & Tobler, I. (1984). Animal sleep: A review of sleep duration across phylogeny. *Neuroscience & Biobehavioral Reviews, 8,* 269–300. (5)

Campion, M. A., & McClelland, C. L. (1991). Interdisciplinary examination of the costs and benefits of enlarged jobs: A job design quasi-experiment. *Journal of Applied Psychology, 76,* 186–198. (11)

Campion, M. A., & Thayer, P. W. (1985). Development and field evaluation of an interdisciplinary measure of job design. *Journal of Applied Psychology, 70,* 29–43. (11)

Campion, M. A., & Thayer, P. W. (1989). How do you design a job? *Personnel Journal, 68,* 43–46. (1)

Campos, J. J., Bertenthal, B. I., & Kermoian, R. (1992). Early experience and emotional development. *Psychological Science, 3,* 61–64. (10)

Canetto, S. S., & Sakinofsky, I. (1998). The gender paradox in suicide. *Suicide and Life-Threatening Behavior, 28,* 1–23. (16)

Cannon, W. B. (1929). Organization for physiological homeostasis. *Physiological Reviews, 9,* 399–431. (11)

Capaldi, E. D. (1996). Conditioned food preferences. In E. D. Capaldi (Ed.), *Why we eat what we eat* (pp. 53–80). Washington, DC: American Psychological Association. (11)

Cardno, A. G., Marshall, E. J., Coid, B., Macdonald, A. M., Ribchester, T. R., Davies, N. J., et al. (1999). Heritability estimates for psychotic disorders. *Archives of General Psychiatry, 56,* 162–168. (16)

Carey, S. (1978). The child as word learner. In M. Halle, J. Bresnan, & G. A. Miller (Eds.), *Linguistic theory and psychological reality* (pp. 264–293). Cambridge, MA: MIT Press. (8)

Carlson, V. J., & Harwood, R. L. (2003). Attachment, culture, and the caregiving system: The cultural patterning of everyday experiences among Anglo and Puerto Rican mother-infant pairs. *Infant Mental Health Journal, 24,* 53–73. (10)

Carlsson, K., Petrovic, P., Skare, S., Petersson, K. M., & Ingvar, M. (2000). Tickling expectations: Neural processing in anticipation of a sensory stimulus. *Journal of Cognitive Neuroscience, 12,* 691–703. (4)

Carney, D. R., & Harrigan, J. A. (2003). It takes one to know one: Interpersonal sensitivity is related to accurate assessment of others' interpersonal sensitivity. *Emotion, 3,* 194–200. (12)

Carney, R. N., & Levin, J. R. (1998). Coming to terms with the keyword method in introductory psychology: A "neuromnemonic" example. *Teaching of Psychology, 25,* 132–134. (7)

Carpenter, P. A., Just, M. A., & Shell, P. (1990). What one intelligence test measures: A theoretical account of the processing in the Raven Progressive Matrices test. *Psychological Review, 97,* 404–431. (9)

Carroll, B. J. (1980). Implications of biological research for the diagnosis of depression. In J. Mendlewicz (Ed.), *New advances in the diagnosis and treatment of depressive illness* (pp. 85–107). Amsterdam: Excerpta Medica. (16)

Carstensen, L. L., & Charles, S. T. (1998). Emotion in the second half of life. *Current Directions in Psychological Science, 7,* 144–149. (10)

Carta, M. G., Hardoy, M. C., Boi, M. F., Mariotti, S., Carpiniello, B., & Usai, P. (2002). Association between panic disorder, major depressive disorder and celiac disease: A possible role of thyroid autoimmunity. *Journal of Psychosomatic Research, 53,* 789–793. (16)

Carvell, C., Inglis, N. F. J., Mace, G. M., & Purvis, A. (1998). How Diana climbed the ratings at the zoo. *Nature, 395,* 213. (2)

Caspi, A., Harrington, H., Milne, B., Amell, J. W., Theodore, R. F., & Moffitt, T. E. (2003). Children's behavioral styles at age 3 are linked to their adult personality traits at age 26. *Journal of Personality, 71,* 495–513. (13)

Caspi, A., McClay, J., Moffitt, T. E., Mill, J., Martin, J., Craig, I. W., Taylor, A., & Poulton, R. (2002). Role of genotype in the cycle of violence in maltreated children. *Science, 297,* 851–854. (10)

Caspi, A., Sugden, K., Moffit, T. E., Taylor, A., Craig, I. W., Harrington, H. L., et al. (2003). Influence of life stress on depression: Moderation by a polymorphism in the 5-HTT gene. *Science, 301,* 386–389. (16)

Caterina, M. J., Rosen, T. A., Tominaga, M., Brake, A. J., & Julius, D. (1999). A capsaicin-receptor homologue with a high threshold for noxious heat. *Nature, 398,* 436–441. (4)

Cattell, R. B. (1965). *The scientific analysis of personality.* Chicago: Aldine. (13)

Cattell, R. B. (1987). *Intelligence: Its structure, growth and action.* Amsterdam: North-Holland. (9)

Ceci, S. J. (1995). False beliefs: Some developmental and clinical considerations. In D. L. Schacter (Ed.), *Memory distortion* (pp. 91–125). Cambridge, MA: Harvard University Press. (7)

Ceci, S. J., & Bruck, M. (1993). Suggestibility of the child witness: A historical review and synthesis. *Psychological Bulletin, 113,* 403–439. (7)

Chabris, C. F. (1999). Prelude or requiem for the "Mozart effect"? *Nature, 400,* 826–827. (2)

Chabris, C. F., & Hearst, E. S. (2003). Visualization, pattern recognition, and forward search: Effects of playing speed and sight of the position on grandmaster chess errors. *Cognitive Science, 27,* 637–648. (8)

Chamberlin, J. (1978). *On our own.* New York: Hawthorn. (15)

Chamberlin, J. (2000, February). Where are all these students coming from? *Monitor on Psychology, 31*(2), 32–34. (1)

Charlton, S. G. (1983). Differential conditionability: Reinforcing grooming in golden hamsters. *Animal Learning & Behavior, 11,* 27–34. (6)

Chase-Lansdale, P., Moffitt, R. A., Lohrman, B. J., Cherlin, A. J., Coley, R. L., Pittman, L. D., et al. (2003). Mothers' transitions from welfare to work and the well-being of preschoolers and adolescents. *Science, 299,* 1548–1552. (10)

Chaudhari, N., Landin, A. M., & Roper, S. D. (2000). A metabotropic glutamate receptor variant functions as a taste receptor. *Nature Neuroscience, 3,* 113–119. (4)

Cheetham, E. (1973). *The prophecies of Nostradamus.* New York: Putnam's. (2)

Chehab, F. F., Mounzih, K., Lu, R., & Lim, M. E. (1997). Early onset of reproductive function in normal female mice treated with leptin. *Science, 275,* 88–90. (11)

Chemelli, R. M., Willie, J. T., Sinton, C. M., Elmquist, J. K., Scammell, T., Lee, C., et al. (1999). Narcolepsy in orexin knockout mice: Molecular genetics of sleep regulation. *Cell, 98,* 437–451. (5)

Chen, D., & Haviland-Jones, J. (2000). Human olfactory communication of emotion. *Perceptual and Motor Skills, 91,* 771–781. (12)

Cheng, A. T. A. (1995). Mental illness and suicide. *Archives of General Psychiatry, 52,* 594–603. (16)

Cherlin, A. J., Furstenberg, F. F., Jr., Chase-Lansdale, P. L., Kiernan, K. E., Robins, P. K., Morrison, D. R., et al. (1991). Longitudinal studies of effects of divorce on children in Great Britain and the United States. *Science, 252,* 1386–1389. (10)

Cheryan, S., & Bodenhausen, G. V. (2000). When positive stereotypes threaten intellectual performance: The psychological hazards of "model minority" status. *Psychological Science, 11,* 399–402. (9)

Cheung, F. M., Leung, K., Fang, R. M., Song, W. Z., Zhang, J. X., & Zhang, J. P. (1996). Development of the Chinese Personality Assessment Inventory (CPAI). *Journal of Cross-Cultural Psychology, 27,* 181–199. (13)

Choi, I., & Nisbett, R. E. (2000). Cultural psychology of surprise: Holistic theories and recognition of contradiction. *Journal of Personality and Social Psychology, 79,* 890–905. (14)

Chomsky, N. (1980). *Rules and representations.* New York: Columbia University Press. (8)

Chorpita, B. F., & Barlow, D. H. (1998). The development of anxiety: The role of control in the early environment. *Psychological Bulletin, 124,* 3–21. (16)

Christensen, A., & Jacobson, N. S. (1994). Who (or what) can do psychotherapy: The status and challenge of nonprofessional therapies. *Psychological Science, 5,* 8–14. (15)

Cialdini, R. B. (1993). *Influence: The psychology of persuasion* (Rev. ed.). New York: Morrow. (6)

Cialdini, R. B. (2003). Crafting normative messages to protect the environment. *Current Directions in Psychological Science, 12,* 105–109. (14)

Cialdini, R. B., Vincent, J. E., Lewis, S. K., Catalan, J., Wheeler, D., & Darby, B. L. (1975). Reciprocal concessions procedure for inducing compliance: The door-in-the-face technique. *Journal of Personality and Social Psychology, 31,* 206–215. (14)

Cioffi, D. (1991). Beyond attentional strategies: A cognitive-perceptual model of somatic interpretation. *Psychological Bulletin, 109,* 25–41. (12)

Clark, D. A., Mitra, P. P., & Wang, S. S.-H. (2001). Scalable architecture in mammalian brains. *Nature, 411,* 189–193. (9)

Clark, R., Anderson, N. B., Clark, V. R., & Williams, D. R. (1999). Racism as a stressor for African Americans. *American Psychologist, 54,* 805–816. (12)

Clarke, G. N., Hornbrook, M., Lynch, F., Polen, M., Gale, J., Beardslee, W., et al. (2001). A randomized trial of a group cognitive intervention for preventing depression in adolescent offspring of depressed patients. *Archives of General Psychiatry, 58,* 1127–1134. (15)

Clarkin, J. F., & Carpenter, D. (1995). Family therapy in historical perspective. In B. Bongar & L. E. Beutler (Eds.), *Comprehensive textbook of psychotherapy: Theory and practice* (pp. 205–227). Oxford, England: Oxford University Press. (15)

Clément, K., Vaisse, C., Lahlou, N., Cabrol, S., Pelloux, V., Cassuto, D., et al. (1998). A mutation in the human leptin receptor gene causes obesity and pituitary dysfunction. *Nature, 392,* 398–401. (11)

Clinicopathologic conference. (1967). *Johns Hopkins Medical Journal, 120,* 186–199. (12)

Cocodia, E. A., Kim, J. S., Shin, H.-S., Kim, J.-W., Ee, J., Wee, M. S. W., et al. (2003). Evidence that rising population intelligence is impacting in formal education. *Personality and Individual Differences, 35,* 797–810. (9)

Cohen, B., Novick, D., & Rubinstein, M. (1996). Modulation of insulin activities by leptin. *Science, 274,* 1185–1188. (11)

Cohen, D. (2001). Cultural variation: Considerations and implications. *Psychological Bulletin, 127,* 451–471. (10)

Cohen, G. L. (2003). Party over policy: The dominating impact of group influence on political beliefs. *Journal of Personality and Social Psychology, 85,* 808–822. (14)

Cohen, J. D., Noll, D. C., & Schneider, W. (1993). Functional magnetic resonance imaging: Overview and methods for psychological research. *Behavior Research Methods, Instruments, & Computers, 25,* 101–113. (3)

Cohen, N. J., & Squire, L. R. (1980). Preserved learning and retention of pattern-analyzing skill in amnesia: Dissociation of knowing how and knowing that. *Science, 210,* 207–211. (7)

Cohen, S. (1996). Psychological stress, immunity, and upper respiratory infections. *Current Directions in Psychological Science, 5,* 86–90. (12)

Cohen, S., Doyle, W. J., Turner, R., Alper, C. M., & Skoner, D. P. (2003). Sociability and susceptibility to the common cold. *Psychological Science, 14,* 389–395. (12)

Cohen, S., Frank, E., Doyle, W. J., Skoner, D. P., Rabin, B. S., & Swaltney, J. M., Jr. (1998). Types of stressors that increase susceptibility to the common cold in healthy adults. *Health Psychology, 17,* 214–223. (12)

Cohen, S., Lichtenstein, E., Prochaska, J. O., Rossi, J. S., Gritz, E. R., Carr, C. R., et al. (1989). Debunking myths about self-quitting: Evidence from 10 prospective studies of persons who attempt to quit smoking by themselves. *American Psychologist, 44,* 1355–1365. (16)

Coie, J. D., & Dodge, K. (1983). Continuities and change in children's social status: A five-year longitudinal study. *Merrill-Palmer Quarterly, 29,* 261–282. (10)

Colantuoni, C., Rada, P., McCarthy, J., Patten, C., Avena, N. M., Chadeayne, A., et al. (2002). Evidence that intermittent, excessive sugar intake causes endogenous opioid dependence. *Obesity Research, 10,* 478–488. (11)

Colantuoni, C., Schwenker, J., McCarthy, J., Rada, P., Ladenheim, B., Cadet, J.L., et al. (2001). Excessive sugar intake alters binding to dopamine and mu-opioid receptors in the brain. *NeuroReport, 12,* 3549–3552. (11)

Colcombe, S. J., Erickson, K. I., Raz, N., Webb, A. G., Cohen, N. J., McAuley, E., et al. (2003). Aerobic fitness reduces brain tissue loss in aging humans. *Journal of Gerontology: Medical Sciences, 58A,* 176–180. (3)

Colcombe, S., & Kramer, A. F. (2003). Fitness effects on the cognitive function of older adults: A meta-analytic study. *Psychological Science, 14,* 125–130. (10)

Collins, A. M., & Loftus, E. F. (1975). A spreading-activation theory of semantic processing. *Psychological Review, 82,* 407–428. (8)

Collins, A. M., & Quillian, M. R. (1969). Retrieval time from semantic memory. *Journal of Verbal Learning and Verbal Behavior, 8,* 240–247. (8)

Collins, A. M., & Quillian, M. R. (1970). Does category size affect categorization time? *Journal of Verbal Learning and Verbal Behavior, 9,* 432–438. (8)

Collins, D. W., & Kimura, D. (1997). A large sex difference on a two-dimensional mental rotation task. *Behavioral Neuroscience, 111,* 845–849. (10)

Colom, R., & García-López, O. (2003). Secular gains in fluid intelligence: Evidence from the Culture-Fair Intelligence Test. *Journal of Biosocial Science, 35,* 33–39. (9)

Colom, R., Juan-Espinosa, M., Abad, F., & Garciá, L. F. (2000). Negligible sex differences in general intelligence. *Intelligence, 28,* 57–68. (9)

Comings, D. E., & Amromin, G. D. (1974). Autosomal dominant insensitivity to pain with hyperplastic myelinopathy and autosomal dominant indifference to pain. *Neurology, 24,* 838–848. (4)

Comuzzie, A. G., & Allison, D. B. (1998). The search for human obesity genes. *Science, 280,* 1374–1377. (11)

Conners, C. K., & Schulte, A. C. (2002). Learning disorders. In K. L. Davis, D.

Charney, J. T. Coyle, & C. Nemeroff (Eds.), *Neuropsychopharmacology* (pp. 597–612). Philadelphia: Lippincott, Williams, & Wilkins. (9)

Connine, C. M., Blasko, D. G., & Hall, M. (1991). Effects of subsequent sentence context in auditory word recognition: Temporal and linguistic constraints. *Journal of Memory and Language, 30,* 234–250. (8)

Constantinides, P. (1977). Ill at ease and sick at heart: Symbolic behavior in a Sudanese healing cult. In I. Wilson (Ed.), *Symbols and sentiments* (pp. 61–84). New York: Academic Press. (15)

Consumer Reports. (1995, November). Mental health: Does therapy help? *Consumer Reports,* pp. 734–739. (15)

Contrada, R. J., Ashmore, R. D., Gary, M. L., Coups, E., Egeth, J. D., Sewell, A., et al. (2000). Ethnicity-related sources of stress and their effects on well-being. *Current Directions in Psychological Science, 9,* 136–139. (12)

Coplan, J. D., Goetz, R., Klein, D. F., Papp, L. A., Fyer, A. J., Leibowitz, M. R., et al. (1998). Plasma cortisol concentrations preceding lactate-induced panic. *Archives of General Psychiatry, 55,* 130–136. (16)

Corkin, S. (1984). Lasting consequences of bilateral medial temporal lobectomy: Clinical course and experimental findings in H. M. *Seminars in Neurology, 4,* 249–259. (7)

Corkin, S. (2002). What's new with the amnesic patient H. M.? *Nature Reviews Neuroscience, 3,* 153–159. (7)

Cosmides, L. (1989). The logic of social exchange: Has natural selection shaped how humans reason? Studies with the Wason selection task. *Cognition, 31,* 187–276. (8)

Costa, P. T., Jr., McCrae, R. R., & Dye, D. A. (1991). Facet scales for agreeableness and conscientiousness: A revision of the NEO personality inventory. *Personality and Individual Differences, 12,* 887–898. (13)

Cotter, D., Mackay, D., Landau, S., Kerwin, R., & Everall, I. (2001). Reduced glial cell density and neuronal size in the anterior cingulate cortex in major depressive disorder. *Archives of General Psychiatry, 58,* 545–553. (16)

Courage, M. L., & Howe, M. L. (2002). From infant to child: The dynamics of cognitive change in the second year of life. *Psychological Bulletin, 128,* 250–277. (10)

Cox, B. J., McWilliams, L. A., Clara, I. P., & Stein, M. B. (2003). The structure of feared situations in a nationally representative sample. *Journal of Anxiety Disorders, 17,* 89–101. (16)

Craig, A. D., Bushnell, M. C., Zhang, E. T., & Blomqvist, A. (1994). A thalamic nucleus specific for pain and temperature sensation. *Nature, 372,* 770–773. (4)

Craig, S. B., & Gustafson, S. B. (1998). Perceived leader integrity scale: An instrument for assessing employee perceptions of leader integrity. *Leadership Quarterly, 9,* 127–145. (11)

Craik, F. I. M., & Lockhart, R. S. (1972). Levels of processing: A framework for memory research. *Journal of Verbal Learning and Verbal Behavior, 11,* 671–684. (7)

Cramer, P. (1996). *Storytelling, narrative, and the Thematic Apperception Test.* New York: Guilford Press. (13)

Cramer, P. (2003). Personality change in later adulthood is predicted by defense mechanism use in early adulthood. *Journal of Research in Personality, 37,* 76–104. (13)

Crandall, C. S., & Eshleman, A. (2003). A justification-suppression model of the expression and experience of prejudice. *Psychological Bulletin, 129,* 414–446. (14)

Crews, D. J., & Landers, D. M. (1987). A meta-analytic review of aerobic fitness and reactivity to psychosocial stressors. *Medicine & Science in Sports & Exercise, 19,* S114–S120. (12)

Crews, F. (1996). The verdict on Freud. *Psychological Science, 7,* 63–68. (13)

Crick, F., & Koch, C. (2003). A framework for consciousness. *Nature Neuroscience, 6,* 119–126. (1)

Critchley, H. D., Mathias, C. J., & Dolan, R. J. (2001). Neuroanatomical basis for first- and second-order representations of bodily states. *Nature Neuroscience, 4,* 207–212. (12)

Crombez, G., Hermans, D., & Adriaensen, H. (2000). The emotional Stroop task and chronic pain: What is threatening for chronic pain sufferers? *European Journal of Pain* (London), *4,* 37–44. (13)

Crosby, F. J., Iyer, A., Clayton, S., & Downing, R. A. (2003). Affirmative action: Psychological data and the policy debates. *American Psychologist, 58,* 93–115. (14)

Cross, C. K., & Hirschfeld, R. M. A. (1986). Psychosocial factors and suicidal behavior. *Annals of the New York Academy of Sciences, 487,* 77–89. (16)

Crowe, R. R., Goedken, R., Samuelson, S., Wilson, R., Nelson, J., & Noyes, R., Jr. (2001). Genomewide survey of panic disorder. *American Journal of Medical Genetics, 105,* 105–109. (16)

Crowley, K., Callanen, M. A., Tenenbaum, H. R., & Allen, E. (2001). Parents explain more often to boys than to girls during shared scientific thinking. *Psychological Science, 12,* 258–261. (10)

Croyle, R. T., & Cooper, J. (1983). Dissonance arousal: Physiological evidence. *Journal of Personality and Social Psychology, 45,* 782–791. (14)

Crucian, G. P., Hughes, J. D., Barrett, A. M., Williamson, D. J. G., Bauer, R. M., Bowers, D., et al. (2000). Emotional and physio-

logical responses to false feedback. *Cortex, 36,* 623–647. (12)

Crystal, S. R., Bowen, D. J., & Berstein, I. L. (1999). Morning sickness and salt intake, food cravings, and food aversions. *Physiology & Behavior, 67,* 181–187. (6)

Csikszentmihalyi, M. (1999). If we are so rich, why aren't we happy? *American Psychologist, 54,* 821–827. (12)

Culbertson, F. M. (1997). Depression and gender. *American Psychologist, 52,* 25–31. (16)

Cummings, N. A. (1979). Turning bread into stones: Our modern antimiracle. *American Psychologist, 34,* 1119–1129. (16)

Cunningham, E. J. A., & Russell, A. F. (2000). Egg investment is influenced by male attractiveness in the mallard. *Nature, 404,* 74–77. (14)

Cutler, A., Demuth, K., & McQueen, J. M. (2002). Universality versus language-specificity in listening to running speech. *Psychological Science, 13,* 258–262. (8)

Cyranowski, J. M., Frank, E., Young, E., & Shear, K. (2000). Adolescent onset of the gender difference in lifetime rates of major depression. *Archives of General Psychiatry, 57,* 21–27. (16)

Czeisler, C. A., Duffy, J. F., Shanahan, T. L., Brown, E. N., Mitchell, J. F., Rimmer, D. W., et al. (1999). Stability, precision, and near-24-hour period of the human circadian pacemaker. *Science, 284,* 2177–2181. (5)

Czeisler, C. A., Johnson, M. P., Duffy, J. F., Brown, E. N., Ronda, J. M., & Kronauer, R. E. (1990). Exposure to bright light and darkness to treat physiologic maladaptation to night work. *New England Journal of Medicine, 322,* 1353–1359. (5)

Czeisler, C. A., Moore-Ede, M. C., & Coleman, R. M. (1982). Rotating shift work schedules that disrupt sleep are improved by applying circadian principles. *Science, 217,* 460–463. (5)

Dackis, C. A., Pottash, A. L. C., Annitto, W., & Gold, M. S. (1982). Persistence of urinary marijuana levels after supervised abstinence. *American Journal of Psychiatry, 139,* 1196–1198. (5)

Dadds, M. R., Bovbjerg, D. H., Redd, W. H., & Cutmore, T. R. H. (1997). Imagery in human classical conditioning. *Psychological Bulletin, 122,* 89–103. (6)

Dahlen, E. R., & Deffenbacher, J. L. (2001). Anger management. In W. J. Lyddon & J. V. Jones, Jr. (Eds.), *Empirically supported cognitive therapies* (pp. 163–181). New York: Springer. (12)

Daley, T. C., Whaley, S. E., Sigman, M. D., Espinosa, M. P., & Neumann, C. (2003). IQ on the rise: The Flynn effect in rural Kenyan children. *Psychological Science, 14,* 215–219. (9)

Dallenbach, K. M. (1951). A puzzle picture with a new principle of concealment. *American Journal of Psychology, 64,* 431–433. (4)

Dalman, C., Allebeck, P., Cullberg, J., Grunewald, C., & Köstler, M. (1999). Obstetric complications and the risk of schizophrenia. *Archives of General Psychiatry, 56,* 234–240. (16)

Damaser, E. C., Shor, R. E., & Orne, M. E. (1963). Physiological effects during hypnotically requested emotions. *Psychosomatic Medicine, 25,* 334–343. (5)

Damasio, A. R. (1994). *Descartes' error: Emotion, reason, and the human brain.* New York: G. P. Putnam's Sons. (12)

Damasio, A. (1999). *The feeling of what happens.* New York: Harcourt Brace. (12)

Damasio, A. (2003). *Looking for Spinoza.* Orlando, FL: Harcourt. (5)

Damasio, H., Grabowski, T., Frank, R., Galaburda, A. M., & Damasio, A. R. (1994). The return of Phineas Gage: The skull of a famous patient yields clues about the brain. *Science, 264,* 1102–1105. (12)

Damron-Rodríguez, J. (1991). Commentary: Multicultural aspects of aging in the U.S.: Implications for health and human services. *Journal of Cross-Cultural Gerontology, 6,* 135–143. (10)

Daniel, M. H. (1997). Intelligence testing: Status and trends. *American Psychologist, 52,* 1038–1045. (9)

Dar, R., Rish, S., Hermish, H., Taub, M., & Fux, M. (2000). Realism of confidence in obsessive-compulsive checkers. *Journal of Abnormal Psychology, 109,* 673–678. (16)

Darwin, C. (1859). *On the origin of species by means of natural selection.* New York: D. Appleton. (1)

Darwin, C. (1871). *The descent of man.* New York: D. Appleton. (1)

Darwin, C. (1965). *The expression of emotions in man and animals.* Chicago: University of Chicago Press. (Original work published 1872) (12)

Das, J. P. (2002). A better look at intelligence. *Current Directions in Psychological Science, 11,* 28–33. (9)

Dasgupta, N., McGhee, D. E., Greenwald, A. G., & Banaji, M. R. (2000). Automatic preference for White Americans: Eliminating the familiarity explanation. *Journal of Experimental Social Psychology, 36,* 316–328. (14)

Davenport, D., & Foley, J. M. (1979). Fringe benefits of cataract surgery. *Science, 204,* 454–457. (4)

David, C. F., & Kistner, J. A. (2000). Do positive self-perceptions have a "dark side"? Examination of the link between perceptual bias and aggression. *Journal of Abnormal Child Psychology, 28,* 327–337. (12)

David, D., Brown, R., Pojoga, C., & David, A. (2000). Impact of posthypnotic amnesia and directed forgetting on implicit and explicit memory: New insights from a modified process dissociation procedure. *International Journal of Clinical and Experimental Hypnosis, 48,* 267–289. (5)

Davidson, D., Jergovic, D., Imami, Z., & Theodos, V. (1997). Monolingual and bilingual children's use of the mutual exclusivity constraint. *Journal of Child Language, 24,* 3–24. (8)

Davidson, R. J., Putnam, K. M., & Larson, C. L. (2000). Dysfunction in the neural circuitry of emotion regulation—A possible prelude to violence. *Science, 289,* 591–594. (12)

Davies, G., Welham, J., Chant, D., Torrey, E. F., & McGrath, J. (2003). A systematic review and meta-analysis of Northern Hemisphere season of birth studies in schizophrenia. *Schizophrenia Bulletin, 29,* 587–593. (16)

Davis, J. M., Chen, N., & Glick, I. D. (2003). A meta-analysis of the efficacy of second-generation antipsychotics. *Archives of General Psychiatry, 60,* 553–564. (16)

Davis, K. L., Stewart, D. G., Friedman, J. I., Buchsbaum, M., Harvey, P. D., Hof, P. R., et al. (2003). White matter changes in schizophrenia. *Archives of General Psychiatry, 60,* 443–456. (16)

Dawes, R. M. (1994). *House of cards: Psychology and psychotherapy.* New York: Free Press. (13, 15)

Dawes, R. M., & Smith, T. L. (1985). Attitude and opinion measurement. In G. Lindzey & E. Aronson (Eds.), *Handbook of social psychology* (Vol. 1, pp. 509–566). New York: Random House. (14)

Dawson, D., & Reid, K. (1997). Fatigue, alcohol, and performance impairment. *Nature, 388,* 235. (5)

Day, R. H. (1972). Visual spatial illusions: A general explanation. *Science, 175,* 1335–1340. (4)

Day, W. F., Jr., & Moore, J. (1995). On certain relations between contemporary philosophy and radical behaviorism. In J. T. Todd & E. K. Morris (Eds.), *Modern perspectives on B. F. Skinner and contemporary behaviorism* (pp. 75–84). Westport, CT: Greenwood Press. (6)

de Castro, J. M. (2000). Eating behavior: Lessons from the real world of humans. *Nutrition, 16,* 800–813. (11)

De Corte, E. (2003). Transfer as the productive use of acquired knowledge, skills, and motivation. *Current Directions in Psychological Science, 12,* 142–146. (8)

de Groot, A. D. (1966). Perception and memory versus thought: Some old ideas and recent findings. In B. Kleinmuntz (Ed.), *Problem solving* (pp. 19–50). New York: Wiley. (8)

de Waal, F. B. M. (2000). Primates—A natural heritage of conflict resolution. *Science, 289,* 586–590. (12)

de Waal, F. B. M. (2002). Evolutionary psychology: The wheat and the chaff. *Current Directions in Psychological Science, 11,* 187–191. (1)

de Wit, H., Crean, J., & Richards, J. B. (2000). Effects of *d*-amphetamine and ethanol on a measure of behavioral inhibition in humans. *Behavioral Neuroscience, 114,* 830–837. (15)

Deacon, S., & Arendt, J. (1996). Adapting to phase shifts: II. Effects of melatonin and conflicting light treatment. *Physiology & Behavior, 59,* 675–682. (5)

Deacon, T. W. (1997). *The symbolic species.* New York: Norton. (8)

Dean, K. E., & Malamuth, N. M. (1997). Characteristics of men who aggress sexually and of men who imagine aggressing: Risk and moderating variables. *Journal of Personality and Social Psychology, 72,* 449–455. (12)

Deary, I. J. (2002). g and cognitive elements of information processing: An agnostic view. In R. J. Sternberg & E. L. Grigorenko (Eds.), *The general intelligence factor: How general is it?* (pp. 151-181). Mahwah, NJ: Erlbaum. (9)

Deary, I. J., Whalley, L. J., Lemmon, H., Crawford, J. R., & Starr, J. M. (2000). The stability of individual differences in mental ability from childhood to old age: Follow-up of the 1932 Scottish mental survey. *Intelligence, 28,* 49–55. (9)

DeCasper, A. J., & Fifer, W. P. (1980). Of human bonding: Newborns prefer their mothers' voices. *Science, 208,* 1174–1177. (10)

Deci, E. L. (1971). Effects of externally mediated rewards on intrinsic motivation. *Journal of Personality and Social Psychology, 18,* 105–115. (11)

Deese, J. (1959). On the prediction of occurrence of particular verbal intrusions in immediate recall. *Journal of Experimental Psychology, 58,* 17–22. (7)

DeFelipe, C., Herrero, J. F., O'Brien, J. A., Palmer, J. A., Doyle, C. A., Smith, A. J. H., et al. (1998). Altered nociception, analgesia and aggression in mice lacking the receptor for substance P. *Nature, 392,* 394–397. (4)

DeGrandpre, R. J. (2000). A science of meaning: Can behaviorism bring meaning to psychological science? *American Psychologist, 55,* 721–739. (6)

Dehaene, S., Naccache, L., Cohen, L., LeBihan, D., Mangin, J.-F., Poline, J.B., et al. (2001). Cerebral mechanisms of word masking and unconscious repetition priming. *Nature Neuroscience, 4,* 752–758. (1)

Dehue, T. (2000). From deception trials to control agents. *American Psychologist, 55,* 264–268. (2)

DeLoache, J. S. (1989). The development of representation in young children. *Advances in Child Development and Behavior, 22,* 1–39. (10)

DeLoache, J. S., Miller, K. F., & Rosengren, K. S. (1997). The credible shrinking room: Very young children's performance with symbolic and nonsymbolic relations. *Psychological Science, 8,* 308–313. (10)

DeLuise, M., Blackburn, G. L., & Flier, J. S. (1980). Reduced activity of the red-cell sodium-potassium pump in human obesity. *New England Journal of Medicine, 303,* 1017–1022. (11)

Dement, W. (1960). The effect of dream deprivation. *Science, 131,* 1705–1707. (5)

Dement, W. C. (1972). *Some must watch while some must sleep.* Stanford, CA: Stanford Alumni Association. (5)

Dement, W., & Kleitman, N. (1957a). Cyclic variations in EEG during sleep and their relation to eye movements, body motility, and dreaming. *Electroencephalography and Clinical Neurophysiology, 9,* 673–690. (5)

Dement, W., & Kleitman, N. (1957b). The relation of eye movements during sleep to dream activity: An objective method for the study of dreaming. *Journal of Experimental Psychology, 53,* 339–346. (5)

DeNeve, K. M. (1999). Happy as an extraverted clam? The role of personality for subjective well-being. *Current Directions in Psychological Science, 8,* 141–144. (12)

DeNeve, K. M., & Cooper, H. (1998). The happy personality: A meta-analysis of 137 personality traits and subjective well-being. *Psychological Bulletin, 124,* 197–229. (12)

Dennett, D. C. (1991). *Consciousness explained.* Boston: Little, Brown. (1)

Dennett, D. C. (2003). *Freedom evolves.* New York: Viking Press. (1)

Dennis, P. M. (1998). Chills and thrills: Does radio harm our children? The controversy over program violence during the age of radio. *Journal of the History of the Behavioral Sciences, 34,* 33–50. (2)

deQuervain, D. J.-F., Roozendaal, B., Nitsch, R. M., McGaugh, J. L., & Hock, C. (2000). Acute cortisone administration impairs retrieval of long-term declarative memory in humans. *Nature Neuroscience, 3,* 313–314. (12)

Deshmukh, A., Rosenbloom, M. J., Pfefferbaum, A., & Sullivan, E. V. (2002). Clinical signs of cerebellar dysfunction in schizophrenia, alcoholism, and their comorbidity. *Schizophrenia Research, 57,* 281–291. (16)

Detterman, D. K. (1979). Detterman's laws of individual differences research. In R. J. Sternberg & D. K. Detterman (Eds.), *Human intelligence* (pp. 165–175). Norwood, NJ: Ablex. (9)

Detterman, D. K., & Thompson, L. A. (1997). What is so special about special education? *American Psychologist, 52,* 1082–1090. (9)

Deutsch, J. A., & Gonzalez, M. F. (1980). Gastric nutrient content signals satiety. *Behavioral and Neural Biology, 30,* 113–116. (11)

DeValois, R. L., & Jacobs, G. H. (1968). Primate color vision. *Science, 162,* 533–540. (4)

Devane, W. A., Hanuš, L., Breuer, A., Pertwee, R. G., Stevenson, L. A., Griffin, G., et al. (1992). Isolation and structure of a brain constituent that binds to the cannabinoid receptor. *Science, 258,* 1946–1949. (5)

Devlin, B., Daniels, M., & Roeder, K. (1997). The heritability of IQ. *Nature, 388,* 468–471. (9)

Devor, E. J., Abell, C. W., Hoffman, P. L., Tabakoff, B., & Cloninger, C. R. (1994). Platelet MAO activity in Type I and Type II alcoholism. *Annals of the New York Academy of Sciences, 708,* 119–128. (16)

Dewsbury, D. A. (1998). Celebrating E. L. Thorndike a century after *Animal Intelligence. American Psychologist, 53,* 1121–1124. (6)

Dewsbury, D. A. (2000a). Introduction: Snapshots of psychology circa 1900. *American Psychologist, 55,* 255–259. (1)

Dewsbury, D. A. (2000b). Issues in comparative psychology at the dawn of the 20th century. *American Psychologist, 55,* 750–753. (6)

Diamond, L. M. (2000). Sexual identity, attractions, and behavior among young sexual-minority women over a 2-year period. *Developmental Psychology, 36,* 241–250. (11)

Diamond, L. M. (2003a). Was it a phase? Young women's relinquishment of lesbian/bisexual identities over a 5-year period. *Journal of Personality and Social Psychology, 84,* 352–364. (11)

Diamond, L. M. (2003b). What does sexual orientation orient? A biobehavioral model distinguishing romantic love and sexual desire. *Psychological Review, 110,* 173–192. (11)

Dick, F., Bates, E., Wulfeck, B., Utman, J. A., Dronkers, N., & Gernsbacher, M. A. (2001). Language deficits, localization, and grammar: Evidence for a distributive model of language breakdown in aphasic patients and neurologically intact individuals. *Psychological Review, 108,* 759–788. (3)

Dickens, W. T., & Flynn, J. R. (2001). Heritability estimates versus large environmental effects: The IQ paradox resolved. *Psychological Review, 108,* 346–369. (9)

Dickson, N., Paul, C., & Herbison, P. (2003). Same-sex attraction in a birth cohort: Prevalence and persistence in early adulthood. *Social Science & Medicine, 56,* 1607–1615. (11)

Diener, E. (2000). Subjective well-being. *American Psychologist, 55,* 34–43. (12)

Diener, E., & Diener, C. (1996). Most people are happy. *Psychological Science, 7,* 181–185. (12)

Diener, E., & Seligman, M. E. P. (2002). Very happy people. *Psychological Science, 13,* 81–84. (12)

Diener, E., Suh, E. M., Lucas, R. E., & Smith, H. L. (1999). Subjective well-being: Three decades of progress. *Psychological Bulletin, 125,* 276–302. (12)

Dijksterhuis, A., & Aarts, H. (2003). On wildebeests and humans: The preferential detection of negative stimuli. *Psychological Science, 14,* 14–18. (4)

Dijksterhuis, A., & Bargh, J. A. (2001). The perception-behavior expressway: Automatic effects of social perception on social behavior. *Advances in Experimental Social Psychology, 33,* 1–40. (14)

DiLalla, D. L., Carey, G., Gottesman, I. I., & Bouchard, T. J., Jr. (1996). Heritability of MMPI personality indicators of psychopathology in twins reared apart. *Journal of Abnormal Psychology, 105,* 491–499. (10)

Dimberg, U., Thunberg, M., & Elmehed, K. (2000). Unconscious facial reactions to emotional facial expressions. *Psychological Science, 11,* 86–89. (4)

Dixon, M. R., Benedict, H, & Larson, T. (2001). Functional analysis and treatment of inappropriate verbal behavior. *Journal of Applied Behavior Analysis, 34,* 363. (6)

Dobelle, W. H. (2000). Artificial vision for the blind by connecting a television camera to the visual cortex. *ASAIO Journal, 46,* 3–9. (4)

Dobrzecka, C., Szwejkowska, G., & Konorski, J. (1966). Qualitative versus directional cues in two forms of differentiation. *Science, 153,* 87–89. (6)

Doi, T. (1981). *The anatomy of dependence.* Tokyo: Kodansha International. (12)

Dole, V. P. (1980). Addictive behavior. *Scientific American, 243*(6), 138–154. (16)

Dollard, J., Miller, N. E., Doob, L. W., Mowrer, O. H., & Sears, R. R. (1939). *Frustration and aggression.* New Haven, CT: Yale University Press. (12)

Domhoff, G. W. (1996). *Finding meaning in dreams: A quantitative approach.* New York: Plenum Press. (5)

Domhoff, G. W. (1999). Drawing theoretical implications from descriptive empirical findings on dream content. *Dreaming, 9,* 201–210. (5)

Domhoff, G. W. (2001). A new neurocognitive theory of dreams. *Dreaming, 11,* 13–33. (5)

Domhoff, G. W. (2003). *The scientific study of dreams.* Washington, DC: American Psychological Association. (2, 5)

Donnerstein, E., & Malamuth, N. (1997). Pornography: Its consequences on the observer. In L. B. Schlesinger & E. Revitch (Eds.), *Sexual dynamics of antisocial behavior* (2nd ed., pp. 30–49). Springfield, IL: Charles C Thomas. (12)

Dovidio, J. F., & Gaertner, S. L. (1999). Reducing prejudice: Combating intergroup biases. *Current Directions in Psychological Science, 8,* 101–105. (14)

Dovidio, J. F., & Gaertner, S. L. (2000). Aversive racism and selection decisions: 1989 and 1999. *Psychological Science, 11,* 315–319. (14)

Dreger, A. D. (1998). *Hermaphrodites and the medical invention of sex.* Cambridge, MA: Harvard University Press. (11)

Drewnowski, A., Henderson, S. A., Shore, A. B., & Barratt-Fornell, A. (1998). Sensory responses to 6-n-propylthiouracil (PROP) or sucrose solutions and food preferences in young women. *Annals of the New York Academy of Sciences, 855,* 797–801. (4)

Driver, J., & Frith, C. (2000). Shifting baselines in attention research. *Nature Reviews Neuroscience, 1,* 147–148. (8)

Drummond, D. C., Cooper, T., & Glautier, S. P. (1990). Conditioned learning in alcohol dependence: Implications for cue exposure treatment. *British Journal of Addiction, 85,* 725–743. (16)

Duckitt, J. (2001). A dual-process cognitive-motivational theory of ideology and prejudice. *Advances in Experimental Social Psychology, 33,* 41–113. (14)

Duke, M., & Nowicki, S., Jr. (1979). *Abnormal psychology: Perspectives on being different.* Monterey, CA: Brooks/Cole. (16)

Duncan, J., Seitz, R. J., Kolodny, J., Bor, D., Herzog, H., Ahmed, A., et al. (2000). A neural basis for general intelligence. *Science, 289,* 457–460. (9)

Dunning, D., Johnson, K., Ehrlinger, J., & Kruger, J. (2003). Why people fail to recognize their own incompetence. *Current Directions in Psychological Science, 12,* 83–87. (7)

Durgin, F. H. (2000). The reverse Stroop effect. *Psychonomic Bulletin & Review, 7,* 121–125. (8)

Dywan, J., & Bowers, K. (1983). The use of hypnosis to enhance recall. *Science, 22,* 184–185. (5)

Eagly, A. H., & Crowley, M. (1986). Gender and helping behavior: A meta-analytic review of the social psychological literature. *Psychological Bulletin, 100,* 283–308. (10)

Eagly, A. H., Johannesen-Schmidt, M. C., & van Engen, M. L. (2003). Transformational, transactional, and laissez-faire leadership styles: A meta-analysis comparing women and men. *Psychological Bulletin, 129,* 569–591. (10)

Eagly, A. H., Karau, S. J., & Makhigani, M. G. (1995). Gender and the effectiveness of leaders: A meta-analysis. *Psychological Bulletin, 117,* 125–145. (11)

Eagly, A. H., Kulesa, P., Chen, S., & Chaiken, S. (2001). Do attitudes affect memory? Tests of the congeniality hypothesis. *Current Directions in Psychological Science, 10,* 5–9. (14)

Eagly, A. H., & Warren, R. (1976). Intelligence, comprehension, and opinion change. *Journal of Personality, 44,* 226–242. (14)

Eagly, A. H., & Wood, W. (1999). The origins of sex differences in human behavior. *American Psychologist, 54,* 408–423. (14)

Earnest, D. J., Liang, F.-Q., Ratcliff, M., & Cassone, V. M. (1999). Immortal time: Circadian clock properties of rat suprachiasmatic cell lines. *Science, 283,* 693–695. (5)

Eaton, J. (2001). Management communication: The threat of groupthink. *Corporate Communications, 6,* 183–192. (14)

Eaton, W. W., Anthony, J. C., Gallo, J., Cai, G., Tien, A., Romanoski, A., et al. (1997). Natural history of diagnostic interview schedule/*DSM-IV* major depression. *Archives of General Psychiatry, 54,* 993–999. (16)

Ebbinghaus, H. (1913). *Memory.* New York: Teachers College Press. (Original work published 1885) (7)

Ebling, R., & Levenson, R. W. (2003). Who are the marital experts? *Journal of Marriage and the Family, 65,* 130–142. (14)

Edelman, B. (1981). Binge eating in normal weight and overweight individuals. *Psychological Reports, 49,* 739–746. (11)

Edney, J. J. (1979). The nuts game: A concise commons dilemma analog. *Environmental Psychology and Nonverbal Behavior, 3,* 252–254. (14)

Educational Testing Service. (1994). *GRE 1994–95 guide.* Princeton, NJ: Author. (9)

Edwards, J., Jackson, H. J., & Pattison, P. E. (2002). Emotion recognition via facial expression and affective prosody in schizophrenia: A methodological review. *Clinical Psychology Review, 22,* 789–832. (12)

Edwards, K. (1998). The face of time: Temporal cues in facial expressions of emotion. *Psychological Science, 9,* 270–276. (12)

Eibl-Eibesfeldt, I. (1973). *Der vorprogrammierte Mensch* [The preprogrammed human]. Vienna: Verlag Fritz Molden. (12)

Eibl-Eibesfeldt, I. (1974). *Love and hate.* New York: Schocken Books. (12)

Eich, E. (1995). Searching for mood dependent memory. *Psychological Science, 6,* 67–75. (7)

Eich, E., & Macaulay, D. (2000). Are real moods required to reveal mood-congruent and mood-dependent memory? *Psychological Science, 11,* 244–248. (7)

Eichenbaum, H. (2002). *The cognitive neuroscience of memory.* New York: Oxford University Press. (7)

Eimas, P. D., Siqueland, E. R., Jusczyk, P., & Vigorito, J. (1971). Speech perception in infants. *Science, 171,* 303–306. (10)

Einstein, G. O., & Hunt, R. R. (1980). Levels of processing and organization: Additive effects of individual item and relational processing. *Journal of Experimental Psychology: Human Learning and Memory, 6,* 588–598. (7)

Eisenberger, N. I., Lieberman, M. D., & Williams, K. D. (2003). Does rejection hurt? An fMRI study of social exclusion. *Science, 302,* 290–292. (4)

Eisenberger, R., & Cameron, J. (1996). Detrimental effects of reward: Reality or myth? *American Psychologist, 51,* 1153–1166. (11)

Eisler, I., Dare, C., Hodes, M., Russell, G., Dodge, E., & LeGrange, D. (2000). Family

therapy for adolescent anorexia nervosa: The results of a controlled comparison of two family interventions. *Journal of Child Psychology and Psychiatry and Allied Disciplines, 41,* 727–736. (15)

Ekman, P. (1992). Facial expressions of emotion: New findings, new questions. *Psychological Science, 3,* 34–38. (12)

Ekman, P. (1994). Strong evidence for universals in facial expressions: A reply to Russell's mistaken critique. *Psychological Science, 3,* 34–38. (12)

Ekman, P. (2001). *Telling lies* (3rd ed.). New York: Norton. (12)

Ekman, P., & Davidson, R. J. (1993). Voluntary smiling changes regional brain activity. *Psychological Science, 4,* 342–345. (12)

Ekman, P., & Friesen, W. V. (1984). *Unmasking the face* (2nd ed.). Palo Alto, CA: Consulting Psychologists Press. (12)

El-Islam, M. F. (1982). Rehabilitation of schizophrenics by the extended family. *Acta Psychiatrica Scandinavica, 65,* 112–119. (16)

Elia, J., Ambrosini, P. J., & Rapoport, J. L. (1999). Treatment of attention-deficit hyperactivity disorder. *New England Journal of Medicine, 340,* 780–788. (15)

Elicker, J., Englund, M., & Sroufe, L. A. (1992). Predicting peer competence and peer relationships in childhood from early parent-child relationships. In R. D. Parke & G. W. Ladd (Eds.), *Family-peer relationships* (pp. 77–106). Hillsdale, NJ: Erlbaum. (10)

Elkind, D. (1984). *All grown up and no place to go.* Reading, MA: Addison-Wesley. (10)

Ellenberger, H. F. (1972). The story of "Anna O": A critical review with new data. *Journal of the History of the Behavioral Sciences, 8,* 267–279. (13)

Elliott, C. (1997). Caring about risks: Are severely depressed patients competent to consent to research? *Archives of General Psychiatry, 54,* 113–116. (2)

Ellis, A., & Harper, R. A. (1961). *A guide to rational living.* Upper Saddle River, NJ: Prentice Hall. (15)

Ellis, N. C., & Hennelley, R. A. (1980). A bilingual word-length effect: Implications for intelligence testing and the relative ease of mental calculation in Welsh and English. *British Journal of Psychology, 71,* 43–52. (7)

Emery, C. E., Jr. (1997, November/December). UFO survey yields conflicting conclusions. *Skeptical Inquirer, 21,* 9. (2)

Engel, S. A. (1999). Using neuroimaging to measure mental representations: Finding color-opponent neurons in visual cortex. *Current Directions in Psychological Science, 8,* 23–27. (4)

Engle, R. W., Tuholski, S. W., Laughlin, J. E., & Conway, A. R. A. (1999). Working memory, short-term memory, and general fluid intelligence: A latent-variable approach. *Journal of Experimental Psychology: General, 128,* 309–331. (7)

Enns, J. T., & Rensink, R. A. (1990). Sensitivity to three-dimensional orientation in visual search. *Psychological Science, 1,* 323–326. (7)

Erel, O., & Burman, B. (1995). Interrelatedness of marital relations and parent-child relations: A meta-analytic review. *Psychological Bulletin, 118,* 108–132. (10)

Erel, O., Oberman, Y., & Yirmiya, N. (2000). Maternal versus nonmaternal care and seven domains of children's development. *Psychological Bulletin, 126,* 727–747. (10)

Erev, I., Wallsten, T. S., & Budescu, D. V. (1994). Simultaneous over- and underconfidence: The role of error in judgment processes. *Psychological Review, 101,* 519–527. (8)

Ericsson, K. A., & Charness, N. (1994). Expert performance: Its structure and acquisition. *American Psychologist, 49,* 725–747. (8)

Ericsson, K. A., Chase, W. G., & Faloon, S. (1980). Acquisition of a memory skill. *Science, 208,* 1181–1182. (7)

Ericsson, K. A., Krampe, R. T., & Tesch-Römer, C. (1993). The role of deliberate practice in the acquisition of expert performance. *Psychological Review, 100,* 363–406. (8)

Erikson, E. H. (1963). *Childhood and society* (2nd ed.). New York: Norton. (10)

Eriksson, P. S., Perfilieva, E., Björk-Eriksson, T., Alborn, A.-M., Nordborg, C., Peterson, D. A., et al. (1998). Neurogenesis in the adult human hippocampus. *Nature Medicine, 4,* 1313–1317. (3)

Ernhart, C. B., Sokol, R. J., Martier, S., Moron, P., Nadler, D., Ager, J. W., & et al. (1987). Alcohol teratogenicity in the human: A detailed assessment of specificity, critical period, and threshold. *American Journal of Obstetrics and Gynecology, 156,* 33–39. (10)

Ernst, C., & Angst, J. (1983). *Birth order: Its influence on personality.* New York: Springer-Verlag. (10)

Esquivel, G., Schruers, K., Kuipers, H., & Griez, E. (2002). The effects of acute exercise and high lactate levels on 35% CO_2 challenge in healthy volunteers. *Acta Psychiatrica Scandinavica, 106,* 394–397. (16)

Esterson, A. (1993). *Seductive mirage.* Chicago: Open Court. (5, 13)

Esterson, A. (2001). The mythologizing of psychoanalytic history: Deception and self-deception in Freud's accounts of the seduction theory episode. *History of Psychology, 12,* 329–352. (13)

Etcoff, N. L., Ekman, P., Magee, J. J., & Frank, M. G. (2000). Lie detection and language comprehension. *Nature, 405,* 139. (3, 12)

Evans, G. W., Bullinger, M., & Hygge, S. (1998). Chronic noise exposure and physiological response: A prospective study of children living under environmental stress. *Psychological Science, 9,* 75–77. (12)

Evans, J. S. B. T. (2002). Logic and human reasoning: An assessment of the deduction paradigm. *Psychological Bulletin, 128,* 978–996. (8)

Everson, C. A. (1995). Functional consequences of sustained sleep deprivation in the rat. *Behavioural Brain Research, 69,* 43–54. (5)

Exner, J. E., Jr. (1986). *The Rorschach: A comprehensive system* (2nd ed.). New York: Wiley. (13)

Eysenck, H. J. (1952). The effects of psychotherapy: An evaluation. *Journal of Consulting Psychology, 16,* 319–324. (15)

Eysenck, H. J. (1992). Four ways five factors are not basic. *Personality and Individual Differences, 13,* 667–673. (13)

Faedda, G. L., Tondo, L., Teicher, M. H., Baldessarini, R. J., Gelbard, H. A., & Floris, G. F. (1993). Seasonal mood disorders: patterns of seasonal recurrence in mania and depression. *Archives of General Psychiatry, 50,* 17–23. (16)

Fairburn, C. G., Welch, S. L., Doll, H. A., Davies, B. A., & O'Connor, M. E. (1997). Risk factors for bulimia nervosa. *Archives of General Psychiatry, 54,* 509–517. (11)

Faivre, R., Grégoire, A., Préault, M., Cézilly, F., & Sorci, G. (2003). Immune activation rapidly mirrored in a secondary sexual trait. *Science, 300,* 103. (14)

Fallon, A. E., & Rozin, P. (1985). Sex differences in perceptions of desirable body shape. *Journal of Abnormal Psychology, 94,* 102–105. (11)

Fantz, R. L. (1963). Pattern vision in newborn infants. *Science, 140,* 296–297. (10)

Farah, M. J. (1992). Is an object an object an object? Cognitive and neuropsychological investigations of domain specificity in visual object recognition. *Current Directions in Psychological Science, 1,* 164–169. (4)

Faraone, S. V., & Biederman, J. (1998). Neurobiology of attention-deficit hyperactivity disorder. *Biological Psychiatry, 44,* 951–958. (3)

Faraone, S. V., Doyle, A. E., Mick, E., & Biederman, J. (2001). Meta-analysis of the association between the 7-repeat allele of the dopamine D_4 receptor gene and attention deficit hyperactivity disorder. *American Journal of Psychiatry, 158,* 1052–1057. (15)

Farber, S. L. (1981). *Identical twins reared apart: A reanalysis.* New York: Basic Books. (9)

Farmer-Dougan, V. (1998). A disequilibrium analysis of incidental teaching. *Behavior Modification, 22,* 78–95. (6)

Farooqi, I. S., Keogh, J. M., Kamath, S., Jones, S., Gibson, W. T., Trussell, R., et al. (2001). Partial leptin deficiency and human adiposity. *Nature, 414,* 34–35. (11)

Fauerbach, J. A., Lawrence, J. W., Haythornthwaite, J. A., & Richter, L. (2002). Coping with the stress of a painful medical procedure. *Behaviour Research and Therapy, 40,* 1003–1015. (12)

Faust, M., Kravetz, S., & Babkoff, H. (1993). Hemispheric specialization or reading habits: Evidence from lexical decision research with Hebrew words and sentences. *Brain and Language, 44,* 254–263. (8)

Fawcett, J. (2001). Treating impulsivity and anxiety in the suicidal patient. *Annals of the New York Academy of Sciences, 932,* 94–102. (16)

Fawzy, F. I., Fawzy, N. W., Arndt, L. A., & Pasnau, R. O. (1995). Critical review of psychosocial interventions in cancer care. *Archives of General Psychiatry, 52,* 100–113. (12)

Fay, R. E., Turner, C. F., Klassen, A. D., & Gagnon, J. H. (1989). Prevalence and patterns of same-gender sexual contact among men. *Science, 243,* 338–348. (11)

Feeney, D. M. (1987). Human rights and animal welfare. *American Psychologist, 42,* 593–599. (2)

Fehr, E., & Fischbacher, U. (2003). The nature of human altruism. *Nature, 425,* 785–791. (14)

Feighner, J. P., Gardner, E. A., Johnston, J. A., Batey, S. R., Khayrallah, M. A., Ascher, J. A., et al. (1991). Double-blind comparison of buproprion and fluoxetine in depressed outpatients. *Journal of Clinical Psychiatry, 52,* 329–335. (16)

Feingold, A., & Mazzella, R. (1998). Gender differences in body image are increasing. *Psychological Science, 9,* 190–195. (11)

Felthous, A. R. (1993). Substance abuse and the duty to protect. *Bulletin of the American Academy of Psychiatry and the Law, 21,* 419–426. (15)

Fenn, K. M., Nusbaum, H. C., & Margoliash, D. (2003). Consolidation during sleep of perceptual learning of spoken language. *Nature, 425,* 614–616. (5)

Fenton, W. S., Hoch, J. S., Herrell, J. M., Mosher, L., & Dixon, L. (2002). Cost and cost-effectiveness of hospital vs. residential crisis care for patients who have serious mental illness. *Archives of General Psychiatry, 59,* 357–364. (15)

Fenton, W. S., Mosher, L. R., Herrell, J. M., & Blyler, C. R. (1998). Randomized trial of general hospital and residential alternative care for patients with severe and persistent mental illness. *American Journal of Psychiatry, 155,* 516–522. (15)

Ferguson, C. P., & Pigott, T. A. (2000). Anorexia and bulimia nervosa: Neurobiology and pharmacotherapy. *Behavior Therapy, 31,* 237–263. (11)

Fergusson, D. M., Woodward, L. J., & Horwood, J. (1998). Maternal smoking during pregnancy and psychiatric adjustment in late adolescence. *Archives of General Psychiatry, 55,* 721–727. (12)

Fernald, D. (1984). *The Hans legacy: A story of science.* Hillsdale, NJ: Erlbaum. (2)

Fernandez, E., & Turk, D. C. (1992). Sensory and affective components of pain: Separation and synthesis. *Psychological Bulletin, 112,* 205–217. (4)

Fernández-Dols, J. M., & Ruiz-Belda, M. A. (1997). Spontaneous facial behavior during intense emotional episodes: Artistic truth and optical truth. In J. A. Russell & J. M. Fernández-Dols (Eds.), *The psychology of facial expression* (pp. 255–274). Cambridge, England: Cambridge University Press. (12)

Ferreira, F., Bailey, K. G. D., & Ferraro, V. (2002). Good-enough representations in language comprehension. *Current Directions in Psychological Science, 11,* 11–15. (8)

Festinger, L. (1957). *A theory of cognitive dissonance.* Stanford, CA: Stanford University Press. (14)

Festinger, L., & Carlsmith, J. M. (1959). Cognitive consequences of forced compliance. *Journal of Abnormal and Social Psychology, 58,* 203–210. (14)

Fichter, M. M., & Quadflieg, N. (1997). Six-year course of bulimia nervosa. *International Journal of Eating Disorders, 22,* 361–384. (11)

Fiedler, K., Schmid, J., & Stahl, T. (2002). What is the current truth about polygraph lie detection? *Basic and Applied Social Psychology, 24,* 313–324. (12)

Fieve, R. R. (1975). *Moodswing.* New York: Morrow. (16)

Finch, J. F., & Cialdini, R. B. (1989). Another indirect tactic of (self-) image imagement: Boosting. *Personality and Social Psychology Bulletin, 15,* 222–232. (14)

Fincham, F. D. (2003). Marital conflict: Correlates, structure, and context. *Current Directions in Psychological Science, 12,* 23–27. (14)

Fine, M. A., & Schwebel, A. I. (1987). An emergent explanation of differing racial reactions to single parenthood. *Journal of Divorce, 11,* 1–15. (10)

Fink, B., & Penton-Voak, I. (2002). Evolutionary psychology of facial attractiveness. *Current Directions in Psychological Science, 11,* 154–158. (14)

Fink, M. (2000). Electroshock revisited. *American Scientist, 88,* 162–167. (16)

Fischhoff, B. (1975). Hindsight ≠ foresight: The effect of outcome knowledge on judgment under uncertainty. *Journal of Experimental Psychology: Human Perception and Performance, 1,* 288–299. (7)

Fisher, B. S., Daigle, L. E., Cullen, F. T., & Turner, M. G. (2003). Acknowledging sexual victimization as rape: Results from a national-level survey. *Justice Quarterly, 20,* 535–574. (12)

Fisher, S., & Greenberg, R. P. (1977). *The scientific credibility of Freud's theories and therapy.* New York: Basic Books. (13)

Fisher, S. E., Vargha-Khadem, F., Watkins, K. E., Monaco, A. P., & Pembrey, M. E. (1998). Localisation of a gene implicated in a severe speech and language disorder. *Nature Genetics, 18,* 168–170. (8)

Fiske, A. P. (2002). Using individualism and collectivism to compare cultures—A critique of the validity and measurement of the constructs: Comment on Oyserman et al. (2002). *Psychological Bulletin, 128,* 78–88. (14)

Fiske, S. T. (2002). What we know now about bias and intergroup conflict, the problem of the century. *Current Directions in Psychological Science, 11,* 123–128. (14)

Flack, W. F., Jr., Laird, J. D., & Cavallaro, L. A. (1999). Separate and combined effects of facial expressions and bodily postures on emotional feelings. *European Journal of Social Psychology, 29,* 203–217. (12)

Flatz, G. (1987). Genetics of lactose digestion in humans. *Advances in Human Genetics, 16,* 1–77. (10)

Flavell, J. (1986). The development of children's knowledge about the appearance-reality distinction. *American Psychologist, 41,* 418–425. (10)

Fleeson, W., Malanos, A. B., & Achille, N. M. (2002). An intraindividual process approach to the relationship between extraversion and positive affect: Is acting extraverted as "good" as being extraverted? *Journal of Personality and Social Psychology, 83,* 1409–1422. (13)

Fletcher, R., & Voke, J. (1985). *Defective colour vision.* Bristol, England: Hilger. (4)

Fligstein, D., Barabasz, A., Barabasz, M., Trevisan, M. S., & Warner, D. (1998). Hypnosis enhances recall memory: A test of forced and non-forced conditions. *American Journal of Clinical Hypnosis, 40,* 297–305. (5)

Flor, H., Elbert, T., Knecht, S., Wienbruch, C., Pantev, C., Birbaumer, N., et al. (1995). Phantom-limb pain as a perceptual correlate of cortical reorganization following arm amputation. *Nature, 375,* 482–484. (4)

Flynn, J. R. (1984). The mean IQ of Americans: Massive gains 1932 to 1978. *Psychological Bulletin, 95,* 29–51. (9)

Flynn, J. R. (1998). IQ gains over time: Toward finding the causes. In U. Neisser (Ed.), *The rising curve* (pp. 25–66). Washington, DC: American Psychological Association. (9)

Flynn, J. R. (1999). Searching for justice: The discovery of IQ gains over time. *American Psychologist, 54,* 5–20. (9)

Fodor, J. (1998). When is a dog a DOG? *Nature, 396,* 325–327. (8)

Foley, V. D. (1984). Family therapy. In R. J. Corini (Ed.), *Current psychotherapies* (3rd ed., pp. 447–490). Itasca, IL: Peacock. (15)

Folkman, S., & Moskowitz, J. T. (2000). Positive affect and the other side of coping. *American Psychologist, 55,* 647–654. (12)

Forer, B. R. (1949). The fallacy of personal validation: A classroom demonstration of gullibility. *Journal of Abnormal and Social Psychology, 44,* 118–123. (13)

Foster, W. Z. (1968). *History of the Communist party of the United States.* New York: Greenwood Press. (16)

Foulkes, D. (1999). *Children's dreaming and the development of consciousness.* Cambridge, MA: Harvard University Press. (5)

Fox, C. R., & Rottenstreich, Y. (2003). Partition priming in judgment under uncertainty. *Psychological Science, 14,* 195–200. (8)

Francis, L. J., Brown, L. B., Lester, D., & Philipchalk, R. (1998). Happiness as stable extraversion: A cross-cultural examination of the reliability and validity of the Oxford Happiness Inventory among students in the U.K., U.S.A., Australia, and Canada. *Personality and Individual Differences, 24,* 167–171. (13)

Francis, W. S. (1999). Cognitive integration of language and memory in bilinguals: Semantic representation. *Psychological Bulletin, 125,* 193–222. (8)

Franz, E. A., Waldie, K. E., & Smith, M. J. (2000). The effect of callosotomy on novel versus familiar bimanual actions: A neural dissociation between controlled and automatic processes? *Psychological Science, 11,* 82–85. (3)

Freedland, R. L., & Bertenthal, B. I. (1994). Developmental changes in interlimb coordination: Transition to hands-and-knees crawling. *Psychological Science, 5,* 26–32. (10)

Freedman, J. L., & Fraser, S. C. (1966). Compliance without pressure: The foot in the door technique. *Journal of Personality and Social Psychology, 4,* 195–202. (14)

French, A. R. (1988). The patterns of mammalian hibernation. *American Scientist, 76,* 568–575. (5)

Frensch, P. A., & Rünger, D. (2003). Implicit learning. *Current Directions in Psychological Science, 12,* 13–18. (7)

Freud, S. (1925). An autobiographical study. In J. Strachey, A. Freud, A. Strachey, & A. Tyson (Eds.), *The standard edition of the complete psychological works of Sigmund Freud* (Vol. XX, pp. 7–70). London: Hogarth Press and the Institute of Psycho-Analysis. (13)

Freud, S. (1925). *Three contributions to the theory of sex* (A. A. Brill, Trans.). New York: Nervous and Mental Disease Publishing (Original work published 1905) (13)

Freud, S. (1935). *A general introduction to psychoanalysis* (Rev. ed.). New York: Liveright. (5)

Freud, S. (1955). *The interpretation of dreams* (J. Strachey, Trans.). New York: Basic Books. (Original work published 1900) (5)

Freud, S. (1961). *The future of an illusion* (J. Strachey, Trans.). New York: Norton. (Original work published 1927) (13)

Freud, S. (1963). *Dora: An analysis of a case of hysteria.* New York: Collier Books. (Original work published 1905) (13)

Freud, S. (1973). *New introductory lectures on psychoanalysis.* In *The standard edition of the complete psychological works of Sigmund Freud* (Vol. 22). London: Hogarth Press. (Original work published 1933) (2)

Friedman, J. M. (2000). Obesity in the new millennium. *Nature, 404,* 632–634. (11)

Friedman, M., & Rosenman, R. H. (1974). *Type-A behavior and your heart.* New York: Knopf. (12)

Friedman, M. A., & Brownell, K. D. (1996). A comprehensive treatment manual for the management of obesity. In V. B. Van Hasselt & M. Hersen (Eds.), *Sourcebook of psychological treatment manuals for adult disorders* (pp. 375–422). New York: Plenum Press. (11)

Friedman, S., Smith, L., Fogel, D., Paradis, C., Viswanathan, R., Ackerman, R., et al. (2002). The incidence and influence of early traumatic life events in patients with panic disorder: A comparison with other psychiatric outpatients. *Journal of Anxiety Disorders, 16,* 259–272. (16)

Frijda, N. H. (1988). The laws of emotion. *American Psychologist, 45,* 349–358. (12)

Fritz, C. O., Morris, P. E., Bjork, R. A., Gelman, R., & Wickens, T. D. (2000). When further learning fails: Stability and change following repeated presentation of text. *British Journal of Psychology, 91,* 493–511. (7)

Fu, Q., Heath, A. C., Bucholz, K. K., Nelson, E., Goldberg, J., Lyons, M. J., et al. (2002). Shared genetic risk of major depression, alcohol dependence, and marijuana dependence. *Archives of General Psychiatry, 59,* 1125–1132. (16)

Fuligni, A. J. (1998). The adjustment of children from immigrant families. *Current Directions in Psychological Science, 7,* 99–103. (10)

Fuller, R. K., & Roth, H. P. (1979). Disulfiram for the treatment of alcoholism: An evaluation in 128 men. *Annals of Internal Medicine, 90,* 901–904. (16)

Fullerton, J., Cubin, M., Tiwari, H., Wang, C., Bomhra, A., Davidson, S., et al. (2003). Linkage analysis of extremely discordant and concordant sibling pairs identifies quantitative-trait loci that influence variation in the human personality trait neuroticism. *American Journal of Human Genetics, 72,* 879–890. (13)

Furman, W. (2002). The emerging field of adolescent romantic relationships. *Current Directions in Psychological Science, 11,* 177–180. (10)

Furnham, A., Hosoe, T., & Tang, T. L.-P. (2002). Male hubris and female humility? A crosscultural study of ratings of self, parental, and sibling multiple intelligence in America, Britain, and Japan. *Intelligence, 30,* 101–115. (13)

Furukawa, T. (1997). Cultural distance and its relationship to psychological adjustment of international exchange students. *Psychiatry and Clinical Neurosciences, 51,* 87–91. (11)

Gable, S. L., Reis, H. T., & Downey, G. (2003). He said, she said: A quasi-signal detection analysis of daily interactions between close relationship partners. *Psychological Science, 14,* 100–105. (14)

Gabrieli, J. D. E., Cohen, N. J., & Corkin, S. (1988). The impaired learning of semantic knowledge following bilateral medial temporal-lobe resection. *Brain and Cognition, 7,* 157–177. (7)

Gabrieli, J. D. E., Corkin, S., Mickel, S. F., & Growdon, J. H. (1993). Intact acquisition of mirror-tracing skill in Alzheimer's disease and in global amnesia. *Behavioral Neuroscience, 107,* 899–910. (7)

Gage, F. H. (2000). Mammalian neural stem cells. *Science, 287,* 1433–1438. (3)

Galef, B. G., Jr. (1998). Edward Thorndike: Revolutionary psychologist, ambiguous biologist. *American Psychologist, 53,* 1128–1134. (6)

Gallistel, C. R., & Gibbon, J. (2000). Time, rate, and conditioning. *Psychological Review, 107,* 289–344. (6)

Galton, F. (1978). *Hereditary genius.* New York: St. Martin's Press. (Original work published 1869) (1, 9)

Gangestad, S. W. (2000). Human sexual selection, good genes, and special design. *Annals of the New York Academy of Sciences, 907,* 50–61. (14)

Garb, H. N., Florio, C. M., & Grove, W. M. (1998). The validity of the Rorschach and the Minnesota Multiphasic Personality Inventory: Results from meta-analyses. *Psychological Science, 9,* 402–404. (13)

Garcia, J. (1990). Learning without memory. *Journal of Cognitive Neuroscience, 2,* 287–305. (6)

Garcia, J., Ervin, F. R., & Koelling, R. A. (1966). Learning with prolonged delay of reinforcement. *Psychonomic Science, 5,* 121–122. (6)

Garcia, J., & Koelling, R. A. (1966). Relation of cue to consequence in avoidance learning. *Psychonomic Science, 4,* 123–124. (6)

Garcia-Andrade, C., Wall, T. L., & Ehlers, C. L. (1997). The firewater myth and response to alcohol in Mission Indians. *American Journal of Psychiatry, 154,* 983–988. (5)

Garcia Coll, C. T. (1990). Developmental outcome of minority infants: A process-oriented look into our beginnings. *Child Development, 61,* 270–289. (10)

Garcia-Palacios, A., Hoffman, H., Carlin, A., Furness, T. A., III, & Botella, C. (2002). Virtual reality in the treatment of spider phobia: A controlled study. *Behaviour Research and Therapy, 40,* 983–993. (16)

Gardner, H. (1985). *Frames of mind.* New York: Basic Books. (9)

Gardner, H. (1993). *Creating minds.* New York: Basic Books. (8)

Gardner, H. (1995). Why would anyone become an expert? *American Psychologist, 50,* 802–803. (8)

Gardner, M. (1978). Mathematical games. *Scientific American, 239*(5), 22–32. (8)

Gardner, M. (1994). Notes of a fringe watcher: The tragedies of false memories. *Skeptical Inquirer, 18,* 464–470. (7)

Gardner, R. A., & Gardner, B. T. (1969). Teaching sign language to a chimpanzee. *Science, 165,* 664–672. (9)

Garlick, D. (2003). Integrating brain science research with intelligence research. *Current Directions in Psychological Science, 12,* 185–189. (9)

Gaser, C., & Schlaug, G. (2003). Brain structures differ between musicians and non-musicians. *Journal of Neuroscience, 23,* 9240–9245. (3)

Gawin, F. H. (1991). Cocaine addiction: Psychology and neurophysiology. *Science, 251,* 1580–1586. (5)

Geary, D. C. (2000). Evolution and proximate expression of human paternal investment. *Psychological Bulletin, 126,* 55–77. (14)

Gegenfurtner, K. R. (2003). Cortical mechanisms of colour vision. *Nature Reviews Neuroscience, 4,* 563–572. (3)

Gelman, R. (1982). Accessing one-to-one correspondence: Still another paper about conservation. *British Journal of Psychology, 73,* 209–220. (10)

Genoux, D., Haditsch, U., Knobloch, M., Michalon, A., Storm, D., & Mansuy, I. M. (2002). Protein phosphatase 1 is a molecular constraint on learning and memory. *Nature, 418,* 970–975. (7)

George, M. S., Wasserman, E. M., Kimbrell, T. A., Little, J. T., Williams, W. E., Danielson, A. L., et al. (1997). Mood improvement following daily left prefrontal repetitive transcranial magnetic stimulation in patients with depression: A placebo-controlled crossover trial. *American Journal of Psychiatry, 154,* 1752–1756. (16)

Gershoff, E. T. (2002). Corporal punishment by parents and associated child behaviors and experiences: A meta-analytic and theoretical review. *Psychological Bulletin, 128,* 539–579. (6)

Geschwind, N. (1970). The organization of language and the brain. *Science, 170,* 940–944. (3)

Geschwind, N. (1979). Specializations of the human brain. In *Scientific American* (Ed.), *The brain: A Scientific American book.* San Francisco: W. H. Freeman. (8)

Gibson, J. J. (1968). What gives rise to the perception of movement? *Psychological Review, 75,* 335–346. (4)

Gick, M. L., & Holyoak, K. J. (1983). Schema induction and analogical transfer. *Cognitive Psychology, 15,* 1–38. (8)

Giebel, H. D. (1958). Visuelles Lernvermögen bei Einhufern [Visual learning capacity in hoofed animals]. *Zoologische Jahrbücher Abteilung für Allgemeine Zoologie, 67,* 487–520. (1)

Giedd, J. N., Blumenthal, J., Molloy, E., & Castellanos, F. X. (2001). Brain imaging of attention deficit/hyperactivity disorder. *Annals of the New York Academy of Sciences, 931,* 33–49. (15)

Gilbertson, M. W., Shenton, M. E., Ciszewski, A., Kasai, K., Lasko, N. B., Orr, S. P., et al. (2002). Smaller hippocampal volume predicts pathological vulnerability to psychological trauma. *Nature Neuroscience, 5,* 1242–1247. (12)

Gilbreth, F. B. (1911). *Motion study.* London: Constable. (11)

Gillham, J. E., Reivich, K. J., Jaycox, L. H., & Seligman, M. E. P. (1995). Prevention of depressive symptoms in schoolchildren: Two year follow-up. *Psychological Science, 6,* 343–351. (15)

Gilligan, C. (1977). In a different voice: Women's conceptions of self and morality. *Harvard Educational Review, 47,* 481–517. (10)

Gilligan, C. (1979). Woman's place in man's life cycle. *Harvard Educational Review, 49,* 431–446. (10)

Gingell, C., Nicolosi, A., Glasser, D. B., Brock, G., & Buvat, J., for the GSSAB Investigators' Group. (2002). *Sexual behaviors and functioning in mature men: Results of an international survey.* Paper presented at the second World Congress of Men's Health, Vienna. Retrieved from http://www.pfizerglobalstudy.com/public/publications.asp (11)

Giros, B., Jaber, M., Jones, S. R., Wightman, R. M., & Caron, M. G. (1996). Hyperlocomotion and indifference to cocaine and amphetamine in mice lacking the dopamine transporter. *Nature, 379,* 606–612. (3, 5)

Giurfa, M., Zhang, S., Jennett, A., Menzel, R., & Srinivasan, M. V. (2001). The concepts of "sameness" and "difference" in an insect. *Nature, 410,* 930–933. (6)

Glantz, L. A., & Lewis, D. A. (1997). Reduction of synaptophysin immunoreactivity in the prefrontal cortex of subjects with schizophrenia. *Archives of General Psychiatry, 54,* 660–669. (16)

Glantz, L. A., & Lewis, D. A. (2000). Decreased dendritic spine density on prefrontal cortical pyramidal neurons in schizophrenia. *Archives of General Psychiatry, 57,* 65–73. (16)

Glass, M. (2001). The role of cannabinoids in neurodegenerative diseases. *Progress in Neuro-Psychopharmacology & Biological Psychiatry, 25,* 743–765. (5)

Glick, P., & Fiske, S. T. (2001). Ambivalent sexism. *Advances in Experimental Social Psychology, 33,* 115–188. (14)

Goate, A., Chartier-Harlin, M. C., Mullan, M., Brown, J., Crawford, F., Fidani, L., et al. (1991). Segregation of a missense mutation in the amyloid precursor protein gene with familial Alzheimer's disease. *Nature, 349,* 704–706. (7)

Gold, P. E., Cahill, L., & Wenk, G. L. (2002). Gingko biloba: A cognitive enhancer? *Psychological Science in the Public Interest, 3,* 2–11. (7)

Goldberg, T. E., Egan, M. F., Gscheidle, T., Coppola, R., Weickert, T., Kolachana, B. S., et al. (2003). Executive subprocesses in working memory. *Archives of General Psychiatry, 60,* 889–896. (9)

Goldfried, M. R., & Wolfe, B. E. (1996). Psychotherapy practice and research: Repairing a strained alliance. *American Psychologist, 51,* 1007–1016. (15)

Goldin-Meadow, S., McNeill, D., & Singleton, J. (1996). Silence is liberating: Removing the handcuffs on grammatical expression in the manual modality. *Psychological Review, 103,* 34–55. (8)

Goldin-Meadow, S., & Mylander, C. (1998). Spontaneous sign systems created by deaf children in two cultures. *Nature, 391,* 279–281. (8)

Goldstein, A. (1980). Thrills in response to music and other stimuli. *Physiological Psychology, 8,* 126–129. (4)

Goldstein, D. G., & Gigerenzer, G. (2002). Models of ecological rationality: The recognition heuristic. *Psychological Review, 109,* 75–90. (8)

Goldstein, E. B. (1989). *Sensation and perception* (3rd ed.). Belmont, CA: Wadsworth. (4)

Golombok, S., Perry, B., Burston, A., Murray, C., Mooney-Somers, J., Stevens, M., et al. (2003). Children with lesbian parents: A community study. *Developmental Psychology, 39,* 20–33. (10)

Goodall, J. (1971). *In the shadow of man.* Boston: Houghton Mifflin. (2)

Goodenough, O. R., & Dawkins, R. (1994). The "St Jude" mind virus. *Nature, 371,* 23–24. (14)

Goodman, G. S., Ghetti, S., Quas, J. A., Edelstein, R. S., Alexander, K. W., Redlich, A. D., et al. (2003). A prospective study of memory for child sexual abuse: New findings relevant to the repressed-memory controversy. *Psychological Science, 14,* 113–118. (7)

Goodwin, C. J. (1991). Misportraying Pavlov's apparatus. *American Journal of Psychology, 104,* 135–141. (6)

Gordon, P. C., Hendrick, R., & Levine, W. H. (2002). Memory-load interference in syntactic processing. *Psychological Science, 13,* 425–430. (8)

Goren, H., Kurzban, R., & Rapoport, A. (2003). Social loafing vs. social enhancement: Public goods provisioning in real-time with irrevocable commitments. *Organizational Behavior and Human Decision Processes, 90,* 277–290. (14)

Gorman, J. M., Kent, J., Martinez, J., Browne, S., Coplan, J., & Papp, L. A. (2001). Physiological changes during carbon dioxide inhalation in patients with panic disorder, major depression, and premenstrual dysphoric disorder. *Archives of General Psychiatry, 58,* 125–131. (16)

Gottesman, I. I. (1991). *Schizophrenia genesis.* New York: W. H. Freeman. (16)

Gottfredson, L. S. (2002a). *g*: Highly general and highly practical. In R. J. Sternberg & E. L. Grigorenko (Eds.), *The general intelligence factor: How general is it?* (pp. 331–380). Mahwah, NJ: Erlbaum. (9)

Gottfredson, L. S. (2002b). Where and why *g* matters: Not a mystery. *Human Performance, 15,* 25–46. (9)

Gottfredson, L. S. (2003). Dissecting practical intelligence theory: Its claims and evidence. *Intelligence, 31,* 343–397. (9)

Gottman, J. M. (1999). *The marriage clinic.* New York: Norton. (14)

Gottman, J. M., & Levenson, R. W. (2000). The timing of divorce: Predicting when a couple will divorce over a 14-year period. *Journal of Marriage and the Family, 62,* 737–745. (14)

Graf, P., & Mandler, G. (1984). Activation makes words more accessible, but not necessarily more retrievable. *Journal of Verbal Learning and Verbal Behavior, 23,* 553–568. (7)

Gratacòs, M., Nadalm M., Martín-Santos, R., Pujana, M. A., Gago, J., Peral, B., et al. (2001). A polymorphic genomic duplication on human chromosome 15 is a susceptibility factor for panic and phobic disorders. *Cell, 106,* 306–379. (16)

Gray, J. R., Chabris, C. F., & Braver, T. S. (2003). Neural mechanisms of general fluid intelligence. *Nature Neuroscience, 6,* 316–322. (9)

Gray, N. S., MacCulloch, M. J., Smith, J., Morris, M., & Snowden, R. J. (2003). Violence viewed by psychopathic murderers. *Nature, 423,* 497–498. (13)

Graziadei, P. P. C., & deHan, R. S. (1973). Neuronal regeneration in the frog olfactory system. *Journal of Cell Biology, 59,* 525–530. (3)

Green, B. G. (1996). Rapid recovery from capsaicin desensitization during recurrent stimulation. *Pain, 68,* 245–253. (4)

Green, C. S., & Bavelier, D. (2003). Action video game modifies visual selective attention. *Nature, 423,* 534–537. (8)

Green, D. M., & Swets, J. A. (1966). *Signal detection theory and psychophysics.* New York: Wiley. (4)

Green, J. P., & Lynn, S. J. (2000). Hypnosis and suggestion-based approaches to smoking cessation: An examination of the evidence. *International Journal of Clinical and Experimental Hypnosis, 48,* 195–224. (5)

Green, L., Myerson, J., & Ostraszewski, P. (1999). Discounting of delayed rewards across the life span: Age differences in individual discounting functions. *Behavioural Processes, 46,* 89–96. (11)

Greene, J. D., Sommerville, R. B., Nystrom, L. E., Darley, J. M., & Cohen, J. D. (2001). An fMRI investigation of emotional engagement in moral judgment. *Science, 293,* 2105–2108. (12)

Greenfield, P. M. (1997). You can't take it with you: Why ability assessments don't cross cultures. *American Psychologist, 52,* 1115–1124. (9)

Greenhoot, A. F., Ornstein, P. A., Gordon, B. N., & Baker-Ward, L. (1999). Acting out the details of a pediatric check-up: The impact of interview condition and behavioral style on children's memory reports. *Child Development, 70,* 363–380. (7)

Greeno, C. G., & Wing, R. R. (1994). Stress-induced eating. *Psychological Bulletin, 115,* 444–464. (11)

Greenough, W. T. (1975). Experiential modification of the developing brain. *American Scientist, 63,* 37–46. (3)

Greenwald, A. G., & Banaji, M. R. (1995). Implicit social cognition: Attitudes, self-esteem, and stereotypes. *Psychological Review, 102,* 4–27. (14)

Greenwald, A. G., & Draine, S. C. (1997). Do subliminal stimuli enter the brain unnoticed? Tests with a new method. In J. D. Cohen & J. W. Schooler (Eds.), *Scientific approaches to consciousness* (pp. 83–108). Mahwah, NJ: Erlbaum. (4)

Greenwald, A. G., Nosek, B. A., & Banaji, M. R. (2003). Understanding and using the Implicit Association Test: I. An improved scoring algorithm. *Journal of Personality and Social Psychology, 85,* 197–216. (14)

Greenwald, A. G., Spangenberg, E. R., Pratkanis, A. R., & Eskanazi, J. (1991). Double-blind tests of subliminal self-help audiotapes. *Psychological Science, 2,* 119–122. (4)

Greist, J. H., Jefferson, J. W., Kobak, K. A., Katzelnick, D. J., & Serlin, R. C. (1995). Efficacy and tolerability of serotonin transport inhibitors in obsessive-compulsive disorder. *Archives of General Psychiatry, 52,* 53–60. (16)

Griffith, R. M., Miyagi, O., & Tago, A. (1958). The universality of typical dreams: Japanese vs. Americans. *American Anthropologist, 60,* 1173–1179. (5)

Griffiths, M., & Wood, R. T. A. (2000). Risk factors in adolescence: The case of gambling, videogame playing, and the Internet. *Journal of Gambling Studies, 16,* 199–225. (16)

Grillon, C., Morgan, C. A., III, Davis, M., & Southwick, S. M. (1998). Effects of darkness on acoustic startle in Vietnam veterans with PTSD. *American Journal of Psychiatry, 155,* 812–817. (12)

Grissmer, D. W., Williamson, S., Kirby, S. N., & Berends, M. (1998). Exploring the rapid rise in the Black achievement scores in the United States (1970–1990). In U. Neisser (Ed.), *The rising curve* (pp. 251–285). Washington, DC: American Psychological Association. (9)

Grisso, T., & Tomkins, A. J. (1996). Communicating violence risk assessments. *American Psychologist, 51,* 928–930. (12)

Gross, J. J. (2001). Emotion regulation in adulthood: Timing is everything. *Current Directions in Psychological Science, 10,* 214–219. (12)

Gross, J. J., Fredrickson, B. L., & Levenson, R. W. (1994). The psychophysiology of crying. *Psychophysiology, 31,* 460–468. (12)

Gross, J. J., & Levenson, R. W. (1993). Emotional suppression: Physiology, self-report, and expressive behavior. *Journal of Personality and Social Psychology, 64,* 970–986. (12)

Grünbaum, A. (1986). Précis of *The foundations of psychoanalysis:* A philosophical critique. *Behavioral and Brain Sciences, 9,* 217–284. (13)

Grutzendler, J., Kasthuri, N., & Gan, W.B. (2002). Long-term dendritic spine stability in the adult cortex. *Nature, 420,* 812–816. (3)

Guilleminault, C., Heinzer, R., Mignot, E., & Black, J. (1998). Investigations into the neurologic basis of narcolepsy. *Neurology, 50*(Suppl. 1), S8–S15. (5)

Guisinger, S. (2003). Adapted to flee famine: Adding an evolutionary perspective on anorexia nervosa. *Psychological Review, 110,* 745–761. (11)

Gunthert, K. C., Cohen, L. H., & Armeli, S. (1999). The role of neuroticism in daily stress and coping. *Journal of Personality and Social Psychology, 77,* 1087–1100. (13)

Gur, R. E., Cowell, P. E., Latshaw, A., Turetsky, B. I., Grossman, R. I., Arnold, S. E., et al. (2000). Reduced dorsal and orbital prefrontal gray matter volumes in schizophrenia. *Archives of General Psychiatry, 57,* 761–768. (16)

Gusella, J. F., & MacDonald, M. E. (2000). Molecular genetics: Unmasking polyglutamine triggers in neurodegenerative disease. *Nature Reviews Neuroscience, 1,* 109–115. (10)

Gustavson, C. R., Kelly, D. J., Sweeney, M., & Garcia, J. (1976). Prey-lithium aversions: I. Coyotes and wolves. *Behavioral Biology, 17,* 61–72. (6)

Gusterson, H. (1992, May/June). Coming of age in a weapons lab. *The Sciences, 32,* 16–22. (10)

Gynther, M. D. (1989). MMPI comparisons of Blacks and Whites: A review and commentary. *Journal of Clinical Psychology, 45,* 878–883. (13)

Haarmeier, T., Thier, P., Repnow, M., & Petersen, D. (1997). False perception of motion in a patient who cannot compensate for eye movements. *Nature, 389,* 849–852. (4)

Habermas, T., & Bluck, S. (2000). Getting a life: The emergence of the life story in adolescence. *Psychological Bulletin, 126,* 748–769. (10)

Hackman, J. R., & Lawler, E. E., III (1971). Employee reactions to job characteristics. *Journal of Applied Psychology, 55,* 259–286. (11)

Haggarty, J. M., Cernovsky, Z., Husni, M., Minor, K., Kermean, P., & Merskey, H. (2002). Seasonal affective disorder in an arctic community. *Acta Psychiatrica Scandinavica, 105,* 378–384. (16)

Haidt, J. (2001). The emotional dog and its rational tail: A social intuitionist approach to moral judgment. *Psychological Review, 108,* 814–834. (12)

Hakuta, K., Bialystok, E., & Wiley, E. (2003). Critical evidence: A test of the critical-period hypothesis for second-language acquisition. *Psychological Science, 14,* 31–38. (8)

Halberstadt, J., & Rhodes, G. (2000). The attractiveness of nonface averages: Implications for an evolutionary explanation of the attractiveness of average faces. *Psychological Science, 11,* 285–289. (14)

Hale, S., Myerson, J., Rhee, S. H., Weiss, C. S., & Abrams, R. A. (1996). Selective interference with the maintenance of location information in working memory. *Neuropsychology, 10,* 228–240. (7)

Hall, C. S., & Van de Castle, R. L. (1966). *The content analysis of dreams.* New York: Appleton-Century-Crofts. (5)

Hall, D., Dhilla, A., Charalambous, A., Gogos, J. A., & Karayiorgou, M. (2003). Sequence variants of the brain-derived neurotrophic factor (BDNF) gene are strongly associated with obsessive-compulsive disorder. *American Journal of Human Genetics, 73,* 370–376. (16)

Hall, J. A., & Halberstadt, A. G. (1994). "Subordination" and sensitivity to nonverbal cues: A study of married working women. *Sex Roles, 31,* 149–165. (12)

Hall, L. J., & McGregor, J. A. (2000). A follow-up study of the peer relationships of children with disabilities in an inclusive school. *Journal of Special Education, 34,* 114–126. (9)

Halmi, K. A., Sunday, S. R., Strober, M., Kaplan, A., Woodside, D. B., Fichter, M., et al. (2000). Perfectionism in anorexia nervosa: Variation by clinical subtype, obsessionality, and pathological eating behavior. *American Journal of Psychiatry, 157,* 1799–1805. (11)

Halpern, D. F. (1997). Sex differences in intelligence. *American Psychologist, 52,* 1091–1102. (9)

Halpern, S. D., Andrews, T. J., & Purves, D. (1999). Interindividual variation in human visual performance. *Journal of Cognitive Neuroscience, 11,* 521–534. (4)

Hama, Y. (2001). Shopping as a coping behavior for stress. *Japanese Psychological Research, 43,* 218–224. (12)

Hamann, S. B., & Squire, L. R. (1997). Intact perceptual memory in the absence of conscious memory. *Behavioral Neuroscience, 111,* 850–854. (7)

Hambrick, D. Z., & Engle, R. W. (2002). Effects of domain knowledge, working memory capacity, and age on cognitive performance: An investigation of the knowledge-is-power hypothesis. *Cognitive Psychology, 44,* 339–387. (7)

Hamby, S. L., & Koss, M. P., (2003). Shades of gray: A qualitative study of terms used in the measurement of sexual victimization. *Psychology of Women Quarterly, 27,* 243–255. (12)

Hamilton, S. P., Fyer, A. J., Durner, M., Heiman, G. A., Baisre de Leon, A., Hodge, S. E., et al. (2003). Further genetic evidence for a panic disorder syndrome mapping to chromosome 13q. *Proceedings of the National Academy of Sciences, USA, 100,* 2550–2555. (16)

Hamm, J. V. (2000). Do birds of a feather flock together? The variable bases for African American, Asian American, and European American adolescents' selection of similar friends. *Developmental Psychology, 36,* 209–219. (14)

Haney, C., Banks, C., & Zimbardo, P. (1973). Interpersonal dynamics in a simulated prison. *International Journal of Criminology and Penology, 1,* 69–97. (14)

Hankin, B. L., & Abramson, L. Y. (2001). Development of gender differences in depression: An elaborated cognitive vulnerability-transactional stress theory. *Psychological Bulletin, 127,* 773–796. (16)

Hanson, R. K. (2000). Will they do it again? Predicting sex-offense recidivism. *Current Directions in Psychological Science, 9,* 106–109. (12)

Harada, S., Agarwal, D. P. Goedde, H. W., Tagaki, S., & Ishikawa, B. (1982). Possible protective role against alcoholism for aldehyde dehydrogenase isozyme deficiency in Japan. *Lancet, ii,* 827. (16)

Hardin, G. (1968). The tragedy of the commons. *Science, 162,* 1243–1248. (14)

Harker, L. A., & Keltner, D. (2001). Expressions of positive emotion in women's college yearbook pictures and their relationship to personality and life outcomes across adulthood. *Journal of Personality and Social Psychology, 80,* 112–124. (12)

Harkins, S. G., & Jackson, J. M. (1985). The role of evaluation in eliminating social loafing. *Journal of Personality and Social Psychology, 11,* 457–465. (14)

Harley, B., & Wang, W. (1997). The critical period hypothesis: Where are we now? In A. M. B. deGroot & J. F. Knoll (Eds.), *Tutorials in bilingualism* (pp. 19–51). Mahwah, NJ: Erlbaum. (8)

Harlow, H. F., Harlow, M. K., & Meyer, D. R. (1950). Learning motivated by a manipulative drive. *Journal of Experimental Psychology, 40,* 228–234. (11)

Harris, B. (1979). What ever happened to Little Albert? *American Psychologist, 34,* 151–160. (16)

Harris, C. R. (2002). Sexual and romantic jealousy in heterosexual and homosexual adults. *Psychological Science, 13,* 7–12. (14)

Harris, C. R. (2003). The evolution of jealousy. *American Scientist, 92*(1), 62–71. (14)

Harris, J. R. (1995). Where is the child's environment? A group socialization theory of development. *Psychological Review, 102,* 458–489. (10)

Harris, J. R. (1998). *The nurture assumption.* New York: Free Press. (10)

Harris, J. R. (2000). Context-specific learning, personality, and birth order. *Current Directions in Psychological Science, 9,* 174–177. (10)

Harris, R. J., Schoen, L. M., & Hensley, D. L. (1992). A cross-cultural study of story memory. *Journal of Cross-Cultural Psychology, 23,* 133–147. (7)

Harris, T. (1967). *I'm OK—You're OK.* New York: Avon. (13)

Harrison, A. O., Wilson, M. N., Pine, C. J., Chan, S. Q., & Buriel, R. (1990). Family ecologies of ethnic minority children. *Child Development, 61,* 347–362. (10)

Harrison, Y., & Horne, J. A. (2000). The impact of sleep deprivation on decision making: A review. *Journal of Experimental Psychology: Applied, 6,* 236–249. (5)

Hartmann, S., & Zepf, S. (2003). Effectiveness of psychotherapy in Germany: A replication of the *Consumer Reports* study. *Psychotherapy Research, 13,* 235–242. (15)

Hartshorn, K., Rovee-Collier, C., Gerhardstein, P., Bhatt, R. S., Klein, P. J., Aaron, F., et al. (1998). Developmental changes in the specificity of memory over the first year of life. *Developmental Psychobiology, 33,* 61–78. (10)

Harvey, A. G., & Bryant, R. A. (2002). Acute stress disorder: A synthesis and critique. *Psychological Bulletin, 128,* 886–902. (12)

Hathaway, S. R., & McKinley, J. C. (1940). A multiphasic personality schedule (Minnesota): I. Construction of the schedule. *Journal of Psychology, 10,* 249–254. (13)

Haukka, J., Suvisaari, J., & Lönnqvist, J. (2003). Fertility of patients with schizophrenia, their siblings, and the general population: A cohort study from 1950 to 1959 in Finland. *American Journal of Psychiatry, 160,* 460–463. (16)

Hauri, P. (1982). *The sleep disorders.* Kalamazoo, MI: Upjohn. (5)

Hauser, R. M. (1998). Trends in Black–White test-score differentials: I. Uses and misuses of NAEP/SAT data. In U. Neisser (Ed.), *The rising curve* (pp. 219–249). Washington, DC: American Psychological Association. (9)

Hays, R. B. (1985). A longitudinal study of friendship development. *Journal of Personality and Social Psychology, 48,* 909–924. (14)

Healy, D., Savage, M., Michael, P., Marris, M., Hirst, D., Carter, M., et al. (2001). Psychiatric bed utilization: 1896 and 1996 compared. *Psychological Medicine, 31,* 779–790. (16)

Healy, D., & Williams, J. M. G. (1988). Dysrhythmia, dysphoria, and depression: The interaction of learned helplessness and circadian dysrhythmia in the pathogenesis of depression. *Psychological Bulletin, 103,* 163–178. (16)

Heath, A. C., Neale, M. C., Kessler, R. C., Eaves, L. J., & Kendler, K. S. (1992). Evidence for genetic influences on personality from self-reports and informant ratings. *Journal of Personality and Social Psychology, 63,* 85–96. (10, 13)

Heatherton, T. G., & Baumeister, R. F. (1991). Binge eating as escape from self-awareness. *Psychological Bulletin, 110,* 86–108. (11)

Heaton, R. K., Gladsjo, J. A., Palmer, B. W., Kuck, J., Marcotte, T. D., & Jeste, D. V. (2001). Stability and course of neuropsychological deficits in schizophrenia. *Archives of General Psychiatry, 58,* 24–32. (16)

Heck, A., Collins, J., & Peterson, L. (2001). Decreasing children's risk taking on the playground. *Journal of Applied Behavior Analysis, 34,* 349–352. (6)

Hedges, L. V., & Nowell, A. (1995). Sex differences in mental test scores, variability, and numbers of high-scoring individuals. *Science, 269,* 41–45. (9)

Heider, F. (1958). *The psychology of interpersonal relations.* New York: Wiley. (14)

Heine, S. J., Lehman, D. R., Markus, H. R., & Kitayama, S. (1999). Is there a universal need for positive self-regard? *Psychological Review, 106,* 766–794. (12)

Heit, E. (1993). Modeling the effects of expectations on recognition memory. *Psychological Science, 4,* 244–251. (7)

Hejmadi, A., Davidson, R. J., & Rozin, P. (2000). Exploring Hindu Indian emotion expressions. *Psychological Science, 11*, 183–187. (12)

Helbing, D., Farkes, I., & Vicsek, T. (2000). Simulating dynamical features of escape panic. *Nature, 407*, 487–490. (14)

Henderlong, J., & Lepper, M. R. (2002). The effects of praise on children's intrinsic motivation: A review and synthesis. *Psychological Bulletin, 128*, 774–795. (11)

Henderson, J. M., & Hollingworth, A. (2003a). Eye movements and visual memory: Detecting changes to saccade targets in scenes. *Perception & Psychophysics, 65*, 58–71. (8)

Henderson, J. M., & Hollingworth, A. (2003b). Global transsaccadic change blindness during scene perception. *Psychological Science, 14*, 493–497. (8)

Hendin, H., Maltsberger, J. T., Lipschitz, A., Haas, A. P., & Kyle, J. (2001). Recognizing and responding to a suicide crisis. *Annals of the New York Academy of Sciences, 932*, 169–186. (16)

Hendrie, H. C. (2001). Exploration of environmental and genetic risk factors for Alzheimer's disease: The value of cross-cultural studies. *Current Directions in Psychological Science, 10*, 98–101. (7)

Heresco-Levy, U., & Javitt, D. C. (2004). Comparative effects of glycine and D-cycloserine on persistent negative symptoms in schizophrenia: A retrospective analysis. *Schizophrenia Research, 66*, 89–96. (16)

Hergenhahn, B. R. (1992). *An introduction to the history of psychology* (2nd ed.). Belmont, CA: Wadsworth. (1)

Herkenham, M., Lynn, A. B., deCosta, B. R., & Richfield, E. K. (1991). Neuronal localization of cannabinoid receptors in the basal ganglia of the rat. *Brain Research, 547*, 267–274. (5)

Herkenham, M., Lynn, A. B., Little, M. D., Johnson, M. R., Melvin, L. S., deCosta, B. R., et al. (1990). Cannabinoid receptor localization in brain. *Proceedings of the National Academy of Sciences, USA, 87*, 1932–1936. (5)

Herman, J., Roffwarg, H., & Tauber, E. S. (1968). Color and other perceptual qualities of REM and NREM sleep. *Psychophysiology, 5*, 223. (5)

Hernandez, L., Murzi, E., Schwartz, D. H., & Hoebel, B. G. (1992). Electrophysiological and neurochemical approach to a hierarchical feeding organization. In P. Bjorntorp & B. N. Brodoff (Eds.), *Obesity* (pp. 171–183). Philadelphia: Lippincott. (11)

Herrnstein, R. J., & Murray, C. (1994). *The bell curve*. New York: Free Press. (9)

Hertenstein, M. J. (2002). Touch: Its communicative functions in infancy. *Human Development, 45*, 70–94. (10)

Hetherington, E. M. (1989). Coping with family transitions. Winners, losers, and survivors. *Child Development, 60*, 1–14. (10)

Hetherington, E. M., Bridges, M., & Insabella, G. M. (1998). What matters? What does not? *American Psychologist, 53*, 167–184. (10)

Hetherington, E. M., Henderson, S. H., & Reiss, D. (1999). Adolescent siblings in stepfamilies: Family functioning and adolescent adjustment. *Monographs of the Society for Research in Child Development*(Serial No. 259). (10)

Hetherington, E. M., Stanley-Hagan, M., & Anderson, E. R. (1989). Marital transitions: A child's perspective. *American Psychologist, 44*, 303–312. (10)

Hettema, J. M., Neale, M. C., & Kendler, K. S. (2001). A review and meta-analysis of the genetic epidemiology of anxiety disorders. *American Journal of Psychiatry, 158*, 1568–1578. (16)

Hildreth, K., Sweeney, B., & Rovee-Collier, C. (2003). Differential memory-preserving effects of reminders at 6 months. *Journal of Experimental Child Psychology, 84*, 41–62. (10)

Hilgard, E. R. (1971). Hypnotic phenomena: The struggle for scientific acceptance. *American Scientist, 59*, 567–577. (5)

Hilgard, E. R. (1973). A neodissociation interpretation of pain reduction in hypnosis. *Psychological Review, 80*, 396–411. (5)

Hill, C. E., & Nakayama, E. Y. (2000). Client-centered therapy: Where has it been and where is it going? A comment on Hathaway (1948). *Journal of Clinical Psychology, 56*, 861–875. (15)

Hill, W. D., Blake, M., & Clark, J. E. (1998). Ball court design dates back 3,400 years. *Nature, 392*, 878–879. (11)

Hilty, D. M., Brady, K. T., & Hales, R. E. (1999). A review of bipolar disorder among adults. *Psychiatric Services, 50*, 201–213. (16)

Hinson, J. M., Jameson, T. L., & Whitney, P. (2003). Impulsive decision making and working memory. *Journal of Experimental Psychology: Learning, Memory, and Cognition, 29*, 298–306. (7)

Hinton, G. (1979). Some demonstrations of the effects of structural descriptions in mental imagery. *Cognitive Science, 3*, 231–250. (8)

Hobson, C. J., & Delunas, L. (2001). National norms and life-event frequencies for the revised social readjustment rating scale. *International Journal of Stress Management, 8*, 299–314. (12)

Hobson, C. J., Kamen, J., Szostek, J., Neithercut, C. M., Tidemann, J. W., & Wojnarowicz, S. (1998). Stressful life events: A revision and update of the social readjustment rating scale. *International Journal of Stress Management, 5*, 1–23. (12)

Hobson, J. A., & McCarley, R. W. (1977). The brain as a dream state generator: An activation-synthesis hypothesis of the dream process. *American Journal of Psychiatry, 134*, 1335–1348. (5)

Hodgins, S., Mednick, S. A., Brennan, P. A., Schulsinger, F., & Engberg, M. (1996). Mental disorder and crime. *Archives of General Psychiatry, 53*, 489–496. (12)

Hoebel, B. G., & Hernandez, L. (1993). Basic neural mechanisms of feeding and weight regulation. In A. J. Stunkard & T. A. Wadden (Eds.), *Obesity: Theory and therapy* (2nd ed., pp. 43–62). New York: Raven Press. (11)

Hoebel, B. G., Rada, P. V., Mark, G. P., & Pothos, E. (1999). Neural systems for reinforcement and inhibition of behavior: Relevance to eating, addiction, and depression. In D. Kahneman, E. Diener, & N. Schwartz (Eds.), *Well-being: Foundations of hedonic psychology* (pp. 560–574). New York: Russell Sage Foundation. (11)

Hoek, H. W., & van Hoeken, D. (2003). Review of the prevalence and incidence of eating disorders. *International Journal of Eating Disorders, 34*, 383–396. (11)

Hoffrage, U., Hertwig, R., & Gigerenzer, G. (2000). Hindsight bias: A by-product of knowledge updating? *Journal of Experimental Psychology: Learning, Memory, and Cognition, 26*, 566–581. (7)

Hogan, R. A., & Kirchner, J. H. (1967). Preliminary report of the extinction of learned fears via short-term implosive therapy. *Journal of Abnormal Psychology, 72*, 106–109. (16)

Holcombe, A. O., & Cavanagh, P. (2001). Early binding of feature pairs for visual perception. *Nature Neuroscience, 4*, 127–128. (3)

Holden, G. W., & Miller, P. C. (1999). Enduring and different: A meta-analysis of the similarity in parents' child rearing. *Psychological Bulletin, 125*, 223–254. (10)

Hollingsworth, D. E., McAuliffe, S. P., & Knowlton, B. J. (2001). Temporal allocation of visual attention in adult attention deficit hyperactivity disorder. *Journal of Cognitive Neuroscience, 13*, 298–305. (8)

Hollister, J. M., Laing, P., & Mednick, S. A. (1996). Rhesus incompatibility as a risk factor for schizophrenia in male adults. *Archives of General Psychiatry, 53*, 19–24. (16)

Hollon, S. D., & Beck, A. T. (1979). Cognitive therapy of depression. In P. C. Kendall & S. D. Hollon (Eds.), *Cognitive-behavioral interventions* (pp. 153–203). New York: Academic Press. (15)

Hollon, S. D., Thase, M. E., & Markowitz, J. C. (2002). Treatment and prevention of depression. *Psychological Science in the Public Interest, 3*, 39-77. (16)

Holmes, D. S. (1978). Projection as a defense mechanism. *Psychological Bulletin, 85*, 677–688. (13)

Holmes, D. S. (1987). The influence of meditation versus rest on physiological arousal: A second examination. In M. A. West (Ed.), *The psychology of meditation* (pp. 81–103). Oxford, England: Clarendon Press. (5)

Holmes, D. S. (1990). The evidence for repression: An examination of sixty years of research. In J. L. Singer (Ed.), *Repression and dissociation* (pp. 85–102). New York: Wiley. (7, 13)

Holmes, T., & Rahe, R. (1967). The social readjustment rating scale. *Journal of Psychosomatic Research, 11,* 213–218. (12)

Holtzworth-Munroe, A. (2000). A typology of men who are violent toward their female partners: Making sense of the heterogeneity in husband violence. *Current Directions in Psychological Science, 9,* 140–143. (12)

Homa, D. (1983). An assessment of two extraordinary speed-readers. *Bulletin of the Psychonomic Society, 21,* 123–126. (8)

Hong, Y., Morris, M. W., Chiu, C., & Benet-Martinez, V. (2000). Multicultural minds: A dynamic constructivist approach to culture and cognition. *American Psychologist, 55,* 709–720. (14)

Honzik, M. P. (1974). The development of intelligence. In B. B. Wolman (Ed.), *Handbook of general psychology* (pp. 644–655). Upper Saddle River, NJ: Prentice Hall. (9)

Hoover, D. W., & Milich, R. (1994). Effects of sugar ingestion expectancies on mother-child interactions. *Journal of Abnormal Child Psychology, 22,* 501–515. (2)

Horn, J. L. (1968). Organization of abilities and the development of intelligence. *Psychological Review, 75,* 242–259. (9)

Horn, J. L., & Donaldson, G. (1976). On the myth of intellectual decline in adulthood. *American Psychologist, 31,* 701–719. (9)

Horne, J. A. (1988). *Why we sleep.* Oxford, England: Oxford University Press. (5)

Horne, J. A., Brass, C. G., & Pettitt, A. N. (1980). Circadian performance differences between morning and evening "types." *Ergonomics, 23,* 29–36. (5)

Horne, J. A., & Minard, A. (1985). Sleep and sleepiness following a behaviorally "active" day. *Ergonomics, 28,* 567–575. (5)

Horst, W. D., & Preskorn, S. H. (1998). Mechanisms of action and clinical characteristics of three atypical antidepressants: Venlafaxine, nefazodone, bupropion. *Journal of Affective Disorders, 51,* 237–254. (16)

Houkes, I., Janssen, P. P. M., de Jonge, J., & Nijhuis, F. J. N. (2001). Work and individual determinants of intrinsic work motivation, emotional exhaustion, and turnover intention: A multi-sample analysis. *International Journal of Stress Management, 8,* 257–283. (11)

Houts, A. C., Berman, J. S., & Abramson, H. (1994). Effectiveness of psychological and pharmacological treatments for nocturnal enuresis. *Journal of Consulting and Clinical Psychology, 62,* 737–745. (15)

Hovland, C. I., & Weiss, W. (1951). The influences of source credibility on communication effectiveness. *Public Opinion Quarterly, 15,* 635–650. (14)

Howard, G. S. (2000). Adapting human lifestyles for the 21st century. *American Psychologist, 55,* 509–515. (1)

Howard, J. W., & Dawes, R. M. (1976). Linear prediction of marital happiness. *Personality and Social Psychology Bulletin, 2,* 478–480. (14)

Howard, K. I., Cornille, T. A., Lyons, J. S., Vessey, J. T., Lueger, R. J., & Saunders, S. M. (1996). Patterns of mental health service utilization. *Archives of General Psychiatry, 53,* 696–703. (15)

Howard, K. I., Kopta, S. M., Krause, M. S., & Orlinsky, D. E. (1986). The dose-effect relationship in psychotherapy. *American Psychologist, 41,* 159–164. (15)

Howard, R. W. (1999). Preliminary real-world evidence that average human intelligence really is rising. *Intelligence, 27,* 235–250. (9)

Howe, M. L., & Courage, M. L. (1993). On resolving the enigma of infantile amnesia. *Psychological Bulletin, 113,* 305–326. (7)

Howe, M. L., & Courage, M. L. (1997). The emergence and early development of autobiographical memory. *Psychological Review, 104,* 499–523. (7)

Hoyt, M. F., & Austad, C. S. (1992). Psychotherapy in a staff model health maintenance organization: Providing and assuring quality care in the future. *Psychotherapy, 29,* 119–129. (15)

Hrdy, S. B. (2000). The optimal number of fathers. *Annals of the New York Academy of Sciences, 907,* 75–96. (14)

Hróbjartsson, A., & Gøtzsche, P. C. (2001). Is the placebo powerless? *New England Journal of Medicine, 344,* 1594–1602. (4)

Hser, Y.-I., Hoffman, V., Grella, C. E., & Anglin, D. (2001). A 33-year follow-up of narcotics addicts. *Archives of General Psychiatry, 58,* 503–508. (16)

Huang, M.-H., & Hauser, R. M. (1998). Trends in Black–White test-score differentials: II. The WORDSUM vocabulary test. In U. Neisser (Ed.), *The rising curve* (pp. 303–332). Washington, DC: American Psychological Association. (9)

Hubel, D. H., & Wiesel, T. N. (1968). Receptive fields and functional architecture of monkey striate cortex. *Journal of Physiology* (London), *195,* 215–243. (4)

Hudson, J. I., Mangweth, B., Pope, H. G., Jr., De Col, C., Hausmann, A., Gutweniger, S., et al. (2003). Family study of affective spectrum disorder. *Archives of General Psychiatry, 60,* 170–177. (16)

Hudson, W. (1960). Pictorial depth perception in sub-cultural groups in Africa. *Journal of Social Psychology, 52,* 183–208. (4)

Huesmann, L. R., Moise-Titus, J., Podolski, C.-L., & Eron, L. D. (2003). Longitudinal relations between children's exposure to TV violence and their aggressive and violent behavior in young adulthood: 1977–1992. *Developmental Psychology, 39,* 201–221. (2)

Huff, D. (1954). *How to lie with statistics.* New York: Norton. (2)

Hugenberg, K., & Bodenhausen, G. V. (2003). Facing prejudice: Implicit prejudice and the perception of facial threat. *Psychological Science, 14,* 640–643. (14)

Hughes, J. C., & Cook, C. C. H. (1997). The efficacy of disulfiram: A review of outcome studies. *Addiction, 92,* 381–395. (16)

Hughes, J., Smith, T. W., Kosterlitz, H. W., Fothergill, L. A., Morgan, B. A., & Morris, H. R. (1975). Identification of two related pentapeptides from the brain with potent opiate antagonist activity. *Nature, 258,* 577–579. (5)

Hughes, J. R., Higgins, S. T., Bickel, W. K., Hunt, W. K., Fenwick, J. W., Gulliver, S. B., et al. (1991). Caffeine self-administration, withdrawal, and adverse effects among coffee drinkers. *Archives of General Psychiatry, 48,* 611–617. (5)

Hugoson, A., Ljungquist, B., & Breivik, T. (2002). The relationship of some negative events and psychological factors to periodontal disease in an adult Swedish population 50 to 80 years of age. *Journal of Clinical Periodontology, 29,* 247–253. (12)

Huizink, A. C., Mulder, E. J. H., & Buitelaar, J. K. (2004). Prenatal stress and risk for psychopathology: Specific effects or induction of general susceptibility? *Psychological Bulletin, 130,* 115–142. (16)

Hull, C. L. (1932). The goal gradient hypothesis and maze learning. *Psychological Review, 39,* 25–43. (1)

Hull, C. L. (1943). *Principles of behavior: An introduction to behavior theory.* New York: D. Appleton. (11)

Hulshoff, H. E., Schnack, H. G., Mandl, R. C. W., van Haren, N. E. M., Koning, H., Collins, L., et al. (2001). Focal gray matter density changes in schizophrenia. *Archives of General Psychiatry, 58,* 1118–1125. (16)

Hultman, C. M., Öhman, A., Cnattingius, S., Wieselgren, I.-M., & Lindström, L. H. (1997). Prenatal and neonatal risk factors for schizophrenia. *British Journal of Psychiatry, 170,* 128–133. (16)

Humphreys, L. G., & Stark, S. (2002). General intelligence: Measurement, correlates, and interpretations of the cultural-genetic construct. In R. J. Sternberg & E. L. Grigorenko (Eds.), *The general intelligence factor: How general is it?* (pp. 87–115). Mahwah, NJ: Erlbaum. (9)

Hunter, J. E. (1997). Needed: A ban on the significance test. *Psychological Science, 8,* 3–7. (2)

Hur, Y.-M., Bouchard, T. J., Jr., & Eckert, E. (1998). Genetic and environmental influences on self-reported diet: A reared-apart twin study. *Physiology & Behavior, 64,* 629–636. (10)

Hur, Y.-M., Bouchard, T. J., Jr., & Lykken, D. T. (1998). Genetic and environmental influence on morningness–eveningness. *Personality and Individual Differences, 25*, 917–925. (10)

Hurovitz, C. S., Dunn, S., Domhoff, G. W., & Fiss, H. (1999). The dreams of blind men and women: A replication and extension of previous findings. *Dreaming, 9*, 183–193. (5)

Huston, T. L., Niehuis, S., & Smith, S. E. (2001). The early marital roots of conjugal distress and divorce. *Current Directions in Psychological Science, 10*, 116–119. (14)

Iacono, W. G., & Patrick, C. J. (1999). Polygraph ("lie detector") testing: The state of the art. In A. K. Hess & I. B. Weiner (Eds.), *The handbook of forensic psychology* (pp. 440–473). New York: Wiley. (12)

Iggo, A., & Andres, K. H. (1982). Morphology of cutaneous receptors. *Annual Review of Neuroscience, 5*, 1–31. (4)

Ikonomidou, C., Bittigau, P., Ishimaru, M. J., Wozniak, D. F., Koch, C., Genz, K., et al. (2000). Ethanol-induced apoptotic neurodegeneration and fetal alcohol syndrome. *Science, 287*, 1056–1060. (10)

Ilies, R., & Judge, T. A. (2003). On the heritability of job satisfaction: The mediating role of personality. *Journal of Applied Psychology, 88*, 750–759. (11)

Imahori, T. T., & Cupach, W. R. (1994). A cross-cultural comparison of the interpretation and management of face: U.S. American and Japanese responses to embarrassing predicaments. *International Journal of Intercultural Relations, 18*, 193–219. (12)

Imhoff, M. C., & Baker-Ward, L. (1999). Preschoolers' suggestibility: Effects of developmentally appropriate language and interviewer supportiveness. *Journal of Applied Developmental Psychology, 20*, 407–429. (7)

Inglehart, R. (1997). *Modernization and postmodernization.* Princeton, NJ: Princeton University Press. (12)

Inhoff, A. W. (1989). Lexical access during eye fixations in sentence reading: Are word access codes used to integrate lexical information across interword fixations? *Journal of Memory and Language, 28*, 444–461. (8)

Inhoff, A. W., Radach, R., Eiter, B. M., & Juhasz, B. (2003). Distinct subsystems for the parafoveal processing of spatial and linguistic information during eye fixations in reading. *Quarterly Journal of Experimental Psychology, 56A*, 803–827. (8)

Inouye, S. T., & Kawamura, H. (1979). Persistence of circadian rhythmicity in a mammalian hypothalamic "island" containing the suprachiasmatic nucleus. *Proceedings of the National Academy of Sciences, USA, 76*, 5962–5966. (5)

Isaacs, E. A., & Clark, H. H. (1987). References in conversation between experts and novices. *Journal of Experimental Psychology: General, 116*, 26–37. (1)

Isenberg, D. J. (1986). Group polarization: A critical review and meta-analysis. *Journal of Personality and Social Psychology, 50*, 1141–1151. (14)

Isensee, B., Wittchen, H.-U., Stein, M. B., Höfler, M., & Lieb, R. (2003). Smoking increases the risk of panic. *Archives of General Psychiatry, 60*, 692–700. (16)

Ivry, R. B., & Diener, H. C. (1991). Impaired velocity perception in patients with lesions of the cerebellum. *Journal of Cognitive Neuroscience, 3*, 355–366. (3)

Izazola-Licea, J. A., Gortmaker, S. L., Tolbert, K., De Gruttola, V., & Mann, J. (2000). Prevalence of same-gender sexual behavior and HIV in a probability household survey of Mexican men. *Journal of Sex Research, 37*, 37–43. (11)

Jackson, D. C., Malmstadt, J. R., Larson, C. L., & Davidson, R. J. (2000). Suppression and enhancement of emotional responses to unpleasant pictures. *Psychophysiology, 37*, 515–522. (12)

Jacobs, B., Schall, M., & Scheibel, A. B. (1993). A quantitative dendritic analysis of Wernicke's area in humans: II. Gender, hemispheric, and environmental factors. *Journal of Comparative Neurology, 327*, 97–111. (3)

Jacobs, B. L. (1987). How hallucinogenic drugs work. *American Scientist, 75*, 386–392. (5)

Jacobs, K. M., Mark, G. P., & Scott, T. R. (1988). Taste responses in the nucleus tractus solitarius of sodium-deprived rats. *Journal of Physiology, 406*, 393–410. (11)

Jacobsen, F. M., Sack, D. A., Wehr, T. A., Rogers, S., & Rosenthal, N. E. (1987). Neuroendocrine 5-hydroxytryptophan in seasonal affective disorder. *Archives of General Psychiatry, 44*, 1086–1091. (16)

Jacobson, N. S., & Christensen, A. (1996). Studying the effectiveness of psychotherapy: How well can clinical trials do the job? *American Psychologist, 51*, 1031–1039. (15)

Jacobson, N. S., Dobson, K. S., Truax, P. A., Addis, M. E., Koerner, K., Gollan, J. K., et al. (1996). A component analysis of cognitive-behavior therapy for depression. *Journal of Consulting and Clinical Psychology, 64*, 295–304. (16)

Jaffee, S., & Hyde, J. S. (2000). Gender differences in moral orientation: A meta-analysis. *Psychological Bulletin, 126*, 703–726. (10)

James, L. E., & McKay, D. G. (2001). H. M., word knowledge, and aging: Support for a new theory of long-term retrograde amnesia. *Psychological Science, 12*, 485–492. (7)

James, W. (1884). What is an emotion? *Mind, 9*, 188–205. (12)

James, W. (1890). *The principles of psychology.* New York: Henry Holt. (1)

James, W. (1894). The physical basis of emotion. *Psychological Review, 1*, 516–529. (12)

James, W. (1961). *Psychology: The briefer course.* New York: Harper. (Original work published 1892). (5)

Janis, I. L. (1972). *Victims of groupthink.* Boston: Houghton Mifflin. (14)

Janis, I. L. (1983). Stress inoculation in health care. In D. Meichenbaum & M. E. Jaremko (Eds.), *Stress reduction and prevention* (pp. 67–99). New York: Plenum Press. (12)

Janis, I. L. (1985). Sources of error in strategic decision making. In J. M. Pennings and associates (Eds.), *Organizational strategy and change* (pp. 157–197). San Francisco: Jossey-Bass. (14)

Jaremko, M. E. (1983). Stress inoculation training for social anxiety, with emphasis on dating anxiety. In D. Meichenbaum & M. E. Jaremko (Eds.), *Stress reduction and prevention* (pp. 419–450). New York: Plenum Press. (12)

Jensen, A. R. (1980). *Bias in mental testing.* New York: Free Press. (9)

Jerome, L., & Segal, A. (2001). Benefit of long-term stimulants on driving in adults with ADHD. *Journal of Nervous and Mental Disease, 189*, 63–64. (15)

Ji, L-J., Nisbett, R. E., & Su, Y. (2001). Culture, change, and prediction. *Psychological Science, 12*, 450–456. (14)

Johnson, J. G., Cohen, P., Brown, J., Smailes, E. M., & Bernstein, D. P. (1999). Childhood maltreatment increases risk for personality disorders during early adulthood. *Archives of General Psychiatry, 56*, 600–606. (15)

Johnson, J. G., Cohen, P., Smailes, E. M., Kasen, S., & Brook, J. S. (2002). Television viewing and aggressive behavior during adolescence and adulthood. *Science, 295*, 2468–2471. (2)

Johnson, M. K., Hashtroudi, S., & Lindsay, D. S. (1993). Source monitoring. *Psychological Bulletin, 114*, 3–28. (7)

Johnson, S. L., & Roberts, J. E. (1995). Life events and bipolar disorders: Implications from biological theories. *Psychological Bulletin, 117*, 434–449. (16)

Johnston, J. C., & McClelland, J. L. (1974). Perception of letters in words: Seek not and ye shall find. *Science, 184*, 1192–1194. (8)

Johnston, J. J. (1975). Sticking with first responses on multiple-choice exams: For better or for worse? *Teaching of Psychology, 2*, 178–179. (Preface)

Johnstone, H. (1994, August 8). Prince of memory says victory was on the cards. *The Times* (London), p. 2. (7)

Joiner, T. E., Jr. (1999). The clustering and contagion of suicide. *Current Directions in Psychological Science, 8*, 89–92. (15)

Jones, E. E., & Goethals, G. R. (1972). Order effects in impression formation: Attribution context and the nature of the entity. In E. Jones, D. Kanouse, H. Kelley, R. Nisbett, S. Valins, & B. Wiener (Eds.), *Attribution: Perceiving the causes of behavior* (pp. 27–46). Morristown, NJ: General Learning Press. (14)

Jones, E. E., & Harris, V. A. (1967). The attribution of attitudes. *Journal of Experimental Social Psychology, 13,* 1–24. (14)

Jones, E. E., & Nisbett, R. E. (1972). The actor and the observer: Divergent perception of the causes of behavior. In E. Jones, D. Kanouse, H. Kelley, R. Nisbett, S. Valins, & B. Wiener (Eds.), *Attribution: Perceiving the causes of behavior* (pp. 79–94). Morristown, NJ: General Learning Press. (14)

Jones, S. S., Collins, K., & Hong, H. W. (1991). An audience effect on smile production in 10-month-old infants. *Psychological Science, 2,* 45–49. (12)

Jönsson, E. G., Sedvall, G. C., Nöthen, M. M., & Cichon, S. (2003). Dopamine D4 receptor gene (DRD4) variants and schizophrenia: Meta-analyses. *Schizophrenia Research, 61,* 111–119. (16)

Joseph, R. (2000). Fetal brain behavior and cognitive development. *Developmental Review, 20,* 81–98. (10)

Jouvet, M., Michel, F., & Courjon, J. (1959). Sur un stade d'activité électrique cérébrale rapide au cours du sommeil physiologique [On a state of rapid electrical cerebral activity during physiological sleep]. *Comptes Rendus des Séances de la Société de Biologie, 153,* 1024–1028. (5)

Judge, T. A., & Ilies, R. (2002). Relationship of personality to performance motivation: A meta-analytic review. *Journal of Applied Psychology, 87,* 797–807. (13)

Judge, T. A., & Laarsen, R. J. (2001). Dispositional affect and job satisfaction: A review and theoretical extension. *Organizational Behavior and Human Decision Processes, 86,* 67–98. (11)

Judge, T. A., Thoresen, C. J., Bono, J. E., & Patton, G. K. (2001). The job satisfaction–job performance relationship: A qualitative and quantitative review. *Psychological Bulletin, 127,* 376–407. (11)

Jung, C. G. (1965). *Memories, dreams, reflections* (A. Jaffe, Ed.). New York: Random House. (13)

Junginger, J., & Frame, C. L. (1985). Self-report of the frequency and phenomenology of verbal hallucinations. *Journal of Nervous and Mental Disease, 173,* 149–155. (16)

Jusczyk, P. W. (2002). How infants adapt speech-processing capacities to native-language structure. *Current Directions in Psychological Science, 11,* 15–18. (10)

Juslin, P., Winman, A., & Olsson, H. (2000). Naive empiricism and dogmatism in confidence research: A critical examination of the hard–easy effect. *Psychological Review, 107,* 384–396. (8)

Just, M. A., & Carpenter, P. A. (1987). *The psychology of reading and language comprehension.* Boston: Allyn & Bacon. (8)

Just, M. A., Carpenter, P. A., Keller, T. A., Eddy, W. F., & Thulborn, K. R. (1996). Brain activation modulated by sentence comprehension. *Science, 274,* 114–116. (8)

Kagan, J. (1989). Temperamental contributions to social behavior. *American Psychologist, 44,* 668–674. (10)

Kagan, J., Reznick, J. S., & Snidman, N. (1988). Biological bases of childhood shyness. *Science, 240,* 167–171. (10)

Kagan, J., & Snidman, N. (1991). Infant predictors of inhibited and uninhibited profiles. *Psychological Science, 2,* 40–44. (10)

Kahn, A. S., Jackson, J., Kully, C., Badger, K., & Halvorsen, J. (2003). Calling it rape: Differences in experiences of women who do or do not label their sexual assault as rape. *Psychology of Women Quarterly, 27,* 233–242. (12)

Kahneman, D., & Tversky, A. (1973). On the psychology of prediction. *Psychological Review, 80,* 237–251. (8)

Kaiser, M. K., Jonides, J., & Alexander, J. (1986). Intuitive reasoning about abstract and familiar physics problems. *Memory & Cognition, 14,* 308–312. (8)

Kalick, S. M., Zebrowitz, L. A., Langlois, J. H., & Johnson, R. M. (1998). Does human facial attractiveness honestly advertise health? *Psychological Science, 9,* 8–13. (14)

Kamin, L. J. (1969). Predictability, surprise, attention, and conditioning. In B. A. Campbell & R. M. Church (Eds.), *Punishment and aversive behavior* (pp. 279–296). New York: Appleton-Century-Crofts. (6)

Kaminer, Y. (2000). Contingency management reinforcement procedures for adolescent substance abuse. *Journal of the American Academy of Child & Adolescent Psychiatry, 39,* 1324–1326. (16)

Kanaya, T., Scullin, M. H., & Ceci, S. J. (2003). The Flynn effect and U.S. policies. *American Psychologist, 58,* 778–790. (9)

Kane, M. J., & Engle, R. W. (2000). Working-memory capacity, proactive interference, and divided attention: Limits on long-term memory retrieval. *Journal of Experimental Psychology: Learning, Memory, and Cognition, 26,* 336–358. (7)

Kanizsa, G. (1979). *Organization in vision.* New York: Praeger. (4)

Kanner, A. D., Coyne, J. C., Schaefer, C., & Lazarus, R. S. (1981). Comparison of two modes of stress measurement: Daily hassles and uplifts versus major life events. *Journal of Behavioral Medicine, 4,* 1–39. (12)

Kanwisher, N. (2000). Domain specificity in face perception. *Nature Neuroscience, 3,* 759–763. (4)

Karlin, R. A. (1997). Illusory safeguards: Legitimizing distortion in recall with guidelines for forensic hypnosis—two case reports. *International Journal of Clinical and Experimental Hypnosis, 45,* 18–40. (5)

Karney, B. R., & Bradbury, T. N. (1995). The longitudinal course of marital quality and stability: A review of theory, method, and research. *Psychological Review, 118,* 3–34. (14)

Karno, M., Golding, J. M., Sorenson, S. B., & Burnam, A. (1988). The epidemiology of obsessive-compulsive disorder in five U.S. communities. *Archives of General Psychiatry, 45,* 1094–1099. (16)

Kasai, K., Shenton, M. E., Salisbury, D. F., Hirayasu, Y., Onitsuka, T., Spencer, M. H., et al. (2003). Progressive decrease of left Heschl gyrus and planum temporale gray matter volume in first-episode schizophrenia. *Archives of General Psychiatry, 60,* 766–775. (16)

Kassel, J. D., Stroud, L. R., & Paronis, C. A. (2003). Smoking, stress, and negative affect: Correlation, causation, and context across stages of smoking. *Psychological Bulletin, 129,* 270–304. (16)

Kasser, T., & Sharma, Y. S. (1999). Reproductive freedom, educational equality, and females' preference for resource-acquisition characteristics in mates. *Psychological Science, 10,* 374–377. (14)

Kasser, T., & Sheldon, K. M. (2000). Of wealth and death. Materialism, mortality salience, and consumption behavior. *Psychological Science, 11,* 348–351. (10)

Katkin, E. S., Wiens, S., & Öhman, A. (2001). Nonconscious fear conditioning, visceral perception, and the development of gut feelings. *Psychological Science, 12,* 366–370. (6)

Kaufman, A. S. (2001). WAIS-III IQs, Horn's theory, and generational changes from young adulthood to old age. *Intelligence, 29,* 131–167. (9)

Kaufman, L., & Rock, I. (1989). The moon illusion thirty years later. In M. Hershenson (Ed.), *The moon illusion* (pp. 193–234). Hillsdale, NJ: Erlbaum. (4)

Kawakami, K., Dovidio, J. F., & Dijksterhuis, A. (2003). Effect of social category priming on personal attitudes. *Psychological Science, 14,* 315–319. (14)

Kazdin, A. E. (1995). Methods of psychotherapy research. In B. Bongar & L. E. Beutler (Eds.), *Comprehensive textbook of psychotherapy: Theory and practice* (pp. 405–433). Oxford, England: Oxford University Press. (15)

Keel, P. K., & Klump, K. L. (2003). Are eating disorders culture-bound syndromes? Implications for conceptualizing their etiology. *Psychological Bulletin, 129,* 747–769. (11)

Keele, S. W., & Ivry, R. B. (1990). Does the cerebellum provide a common computation for diverse tasks? *Annals of the New York Academy of Sciences, 608,* 179–207. (3)

Keller, M. C., Thiessen, D., & Young, R. K. (1996). Mate assortment in dating and married couples. *Personality and Individual Differences, 21*, 217–221. (14)

Kelley, H. H. (1967). Attribution theory in social psychology. In D. Levine (Ed.), *Nebraska Symposium on Motivation* (Vol. 15, pp. 192–238). Lincoln: University of Nebraska Press. (14)

Keltner, D., & Buswell, B. N. (1997). Embarrassment: Its distinct form and appeasement functions. *Psychological Bulletin, 122*, 250–270. (12)

Keltner, D., & Robinson, R. J. (1996). Extremism, power, and the imagined basis of social conflict. *Current Directions in Psychological Science, 5*, 101–105. (14)

Keltner, D., & Shiota, M. N. (2003). New displays and new emotions: A commentary on Rozin and Cohen (2003). *Emotion, 3*, 86–91. (12)

Kendler, K. S., Bulik, C. M., Silberg, J., Hettema, J. M., Myers, J., & Prescott, C. A. (2000). Childhood sexual abuse and adult psychiatric and substance abuse disorders in women. *Archives of General Psychiatry, 57*, 953–959. (16)

Kendler, K. S., Gallagher, T. J., Abelson, J. M., & Kessler, R. C. (1996). Lifetime prevalence, demographic risk factors, and diagnostic validity of nonaffective psychosis as assessed in a U.S. community sample. *Archives of General Psychiatry, 53*, 1022–1031. (16)

Kendler, K. S., Gardner, C. O., & Prescott, C. A. (1999). Clinical characteristics of major depression that predict risk of depression in relatives. *Archives of General Psychiatry, 56*, 322–327. (16)

Kendler, K. S., Gruenberg, A. M., & Tsuang, M. T. (1985). Subtype stability in schizophrenia. *American Journal of Psychiatry, 142*, 827–832. (16)

Kendler, K. S., Hettema, J. M., Butera, F., Gardner, C. O., & Prescott, C. A. (2003). Life event dimensions of loss, humiliation, entrapment, and danger in the prediction of onsets of major depression and generalized anxiety. *Archives of General Psychiatry, 60*, 789–796. (16)

Kendler, K. S., Karkowski, L. M., Neale, M. C., & Prescott, C. A. (2000). Illicit psychoactive substance use, heavy use, abuse, and dependence in a US population-based sample of male twins. *Archives of General Psychiatry, 57*, 261–269. (16)

Kendler, K. S., MacLean, C., Neale, M., Kessler, R., Heath, A., & Eaves, L. (1991). The genetic epidemiology of bulimia nervosa. *American Journal of Psychiatry, 148*, 1627–1637. (11)

Kendler, K. S., Myers, J., Prescott, C. A., & Neale, M. C. (2001). The genetic epidemiology of irrational fears and phobias in men. *Archives of General Psychiatry, 58*, 257–265. (16)

Kendler, K. S., Thornton, L. M., Gilman, S. E., & Kessler, R. C. (2000). Sexual orientation in a U.S. sample of twin and non-twin sibling pairs. *American Journal of Psychiatry, 157*, 1843–1846. (11)

Kendler, K. S., Thornton, L. M., & Pedersen, N. L. (2000). Tobacco consumption in Swedish twins reared apart and reared together. *Archives of General Psychiatry, 57*, 886–892. (16)

Kendler, K. S., Walters, E. E., Neale, M. C., Kessler, R. C., Heath, A. C., & Eaves, L. J. (1995). The structure of the genetic and environmental risk factors for six major psychiatric disorders in women. *Archives of General Psychiatry, 52*, 374–383. (16)

Keppel, G., & Underwood, B. J. (1962). Proactive inhibition in short-term retention of single items. *Journal of Verbal Learning and Verbal Behavior, 1*, 153–161. (7)

Kerr, N. L., MacCoun, R. J., & Kramer, G. P. (1996). Bias in judgment: Comparing individuals and groups. *Psychological Review, 103*, 687–719. (14)

Kerr, R., & Booth, B. (1978). Specific and varied practice of motor skill. *Perceptual and Motor Skills, 46*, 395–401. (7)

Kessler, R. C., Borges, G., & Walters, E. E. (1999). Prevalence of and risk factors for lifetime suicide attempts in the national comorbidity survey. *Archives of General Psychiatry, 56*, 617–626. (16)

Kessler, R. C., McGonagle, K. A., Zhao, S., Nelson, C. B., Hughes, E., Eshleman, S., et al. (1994). Lifetime and 12-month prevalence of *DSM-III-R* psychiatric disorders in the United States. *Archives of General Psychiatry, 51*, 8–19. (15, 16)

Kety, S. S., Wendler, P. H., Jacobsen, B., Ingraham, L. J., Jansson, L., Faber, B., et al. (1994). Mental illness in the biological and adoptive relatives of schizophrenic adoptees. *Archives of General Psychiatry, 51*, 442–455. (16)

Keysar, B., Barr, D. J., & Horton, W. S. (1998). The egocentric basis of language use: Insights from a processing approach. *Current Directions in Psychological Science, 7*, 46–50. (10)

Keysar, B., & Henly, A. S. (2002). Speakers' overestimation of their effectiveness. *Psychological Science, 13*, 207–212. (8)

Kihlstrom, J. F., Barnhardt, T. M., & Tataryn, D. J. (1992). The psychological unconscious. *American Psychologist, 47*, 788–791. (8)

Kim, H., Baydar, N., & Greek, A. (2003). Testing conditions influence the race gap in cognition and achievement estimated by household survey data. *Journal of Applied Developmental Psychology, 23*, 567–582. (9)

Kim, J. E., & Moen, P. (2001). Is retirement good or bad for subjective well-being? *Current Directions in Psychological Science, 10*, 83–86. (10)

Kim, S. (1989). *Inversions*. San Francisco: W. H. Freeman. (4)

Kim, U., Jorgenson, E., Coon, H., Leppert, M., Risch, N., & Drayna, D. (2003). Positional cloning of the human quantitative trait locus underlying taste sensitivity to phenylthiocarbamide. *Science, 299*, 1221–1225. (4)

Kimble, G. A. (1961). *Hilgard and Marquis' conditioning and learning* (2nd ed.). New York: Appleton-Century-Crofts. (6)

Kimble, G. A. (1993). A modest proposal for a minor revolution in the language of psychology. *Psychological Science, 4*, 253–255. (6)

Kimble, G. A., & Garmezy, N. (1968). *Principles of general psychology* (3rd ed.). New York: Ronald Press. (13)

King, M. L., Jr. (1964, November 13). Speech at Duke University, Durham, NC. (10)

King, S. (2000). Is expressed emotion cause or effect in the mothers of schizophrenic young adults? *Schizophrenia Research, 45*, 65–78. (16)

Kinsey, A. C., Pomeroy, W. B., & Martin, C. E. (1948). *Sexual behavior in the human male*. Philadelphia: Saunders. (11)

Kinsey, A. C., Pomeroy, W. B., Martin, C. E., & Gebhard, P. H. (1953). *Sexual behavior in the human female*. Philadelphia: Saunders. (11)

Kiriakakis, V., Bhatia, K. P., Quinn, N. P., & Marsden, C. D. (1998). The natural history of tardive dyskinesia: A long-term follow-up of 107 cases. *Brain, 121*, 2053–2066. (16)

Kirkpatrick, B., Buchanan, R. W., Ross, D. E., & Carpenter, W. T., Jr. (2001). A separate disease within the syndrome of schizophrenia. *Archives of General Psychiatry, 58*, 165–171. (16)

Kirsch, I., & Lynn, S. J. (1998). Dissociation theories of hypnosis. *Psychological Bulletin, 123*, 100–115. (5)

Kirsch, I., & Sapirstein, G. (1998). Listening to Prozac but hearing placebo: A meta-analysis of antidepressant medication. *Prevention and Treatment, 1*, article 2a. (16)

Kirsch, J., & Braffman, W. (2001). Imaginative suggestibility and hypnotizability. *Current Directions in Psychological Science, 10*, 57-61. (5)

Kitigawa, N., & Ichihara, S. (2002). Hearing visual motion in depth. *Nature, 416*, 172–174. (4)

Klahr, D., & Simon, H. A. (2001). What have psychologists (and others) discovered about the process of scientific discovery? *Current Directions in Psychological Science, 10*, 75–79. (2)

Klein, D. F. (1993). False suffocation alarms, spontaneous panics, and related conditions. *Archives of General Psychiatry, 50*, 306–317. (16)

Kleinknecht, R. A. (1982). The origins and remission of fear in a group of tarantula enthusiasts. *Behaviour Research & Therapy, 20*, 437–443. (16)

Kleinmuntz, B., & Szucko, J. J. (1984). A field study of the fallibility of polygraphic lie detection. *Nature, 308,* 449–450. (12)

Kleitman, N. (1963). *Sleep and wakefulness* (Rev. and enlarged ed.). Chicago: University of Chicago Press. (5)

Kluger, A. N., & Tikochinsky, J. (2001). The error of accepting the "theoretical" null hypothesis: The rise, fall, and resurrection of commonsense hypotheses in psychology. *Psychological Bulletin, 127,* 408–423. (2)

Klump, K. L., Miller, K. B., Keel, P. K., McGue, M., & Iacono, W. G. (2001). Genetic and environmental influences on anorexia nervosa syndromes in a population-based twin sample. *Psychological Medicine, 31,* 737–740. (11)

Knuttinen, M.-G., Power, J. M., Preston, A. R., & Disterhoft, J. F. (2001). Awareness in classical differential eyeblink conditioning in young and aging humans. *Behavioral Neuroscience, 115,* 747–757. (6)

Kocsis, R. N., Cooksey, R. W., & Irwin, H. J. (2002). Psychological profiling of sexual murders: An empirical model. *International Journal of Offender Therapy and Comparative Criminology, 46,* 532–554. (13)

Kocsis, R. N., Hayes, A. F., & Irwin, H. J. (2002). Investigative experience and accuracy in psychological profiling of a violent crime. *Journal of Interpersonal Violence, 17,* 811–823. (13)

Kocsis, R. N., Irwin, H. J., Hayes, A. F., & Nunn, R. (2000). Expertise in psychological profiling: A comparative assessment. *Journal of Interpersonal Violence, 15,* 311–331. (13)

Koepp, M. J., Gunn, R. N., Lawrence, A. D., Cunningham, V. J., Dagher, A., Jones, T., et al. (1998). Evidence for striatal dopamine release during a video game. *Nature, 393,* 266–268. (5, 16)

Kohlberg, L. (1969). Stage and sequence: The cognitive-developmental approach to socialization. In D. A. Goslin (Ed.), *Handbook of socialization theory and research* (pp. 347–480). Chicago: Rand McNally (10)

Kohlberg, L., & Hersh, R. H. (1977). Moral development: A review of the theory. *Theory into Practice, 16,* 53–59. (10)

Koob, G. F., & LeMoal, M. (1997). Drug abuse: Hedonic homeostatic dysregulation. *Science, 278,* 52–58. (16)

Koocher, G. P., Goodman, G. S., White, C. S., Friedrich, W. N., Sivan, A. B., & Reynolds, C. R. (1995). Psychological science and the use of anatomically detailed dolls in child sexual-abuse assessments. *Psychological Bulletin, 118,* 199–222. (7)

Kopelman, M. D. (2000). Focal retrograde amnesia and the attribution of causality: An exceptionally critical review. *Cognitive Neuropsychology, 17,* 585–621. (7)

Kopelman, P. G. (2000). Obesity as a medical problem. *Nature, 404,* 635–643. (11)

Kopp, C. B. (1990). Risks in infancy: Appraising the research. *Merrill-Palmer Quarterly, 36,* 117–139. (10)

Koppenaal, R. J. (1963). Time changes in the strengths of A-B, A-C lists: Spontaneous recovery? *Journal of Verbal Learning and Verbal Behavior, 2,* 310–319. (7)

Kornreich, C., Blairy, S., Philippot, P., Hess, U., Noel, X., Streel, E., et al. (2001). Deficits in recognition of emotional facial expression are still present in alcoholics after mid- to long-term abstinence. *Journal of Studies on Alcohol, 62,* 533–542. (12)

Koss, M. P., & Butcher, J. N. (1986). Research on brief psychotherapy. In S. L. Garfield & A. E. Bergin (Eds.), *Handbook of psychotherapy and behavior change* (pp. 627–670). New York: Wiley. (15)

Kovalenko, P. A., Hoven, C. W., Ping, W., Wicks, J., Mandell, D. J., & Tiet, Q. (2001). Associations between allergy and anxiety disorders in youth. *Australian and New Zealand Journal of Psychiatry, 35,* 815–821. (16)

Koyano, W. (1991). Japanese attitudes toward the elderly: A review of research findings. *Journal of Cross-Cultural Gerontology, 4,* 335–345. (10)

Kozel, N. J., & Adams, E. H. (1986). Epidemiology of drug abuse: An overview. *Science, 234,* 970–974. (5)

Kozlowski, L. T., Frecker, R. C., Khouw, V., & Pope, M. A. (1980). The misuse of "less hazardous" cigarettes and its detection: Hole blocking of ventilated filters. *American Journal of Public Health, 70,* 1202–1203. (16)

Kraemer, D. L., & Hastrup, J. L. (1988). Crying in adults: Self-control and autonomic correlates. *Journal of Social and Clinical Psychology, 6,* 53–68. (12)

Krauss, S., & Wang, X. T. (2003). The psychology of the Monty Hall problem: Discovering psychological mechanisms for solving a tenacious brain teaser. *Journal of Experimental Psychology: General, 132,* 3–22. (8)

Kray, J., & Frensch, P. A. (2002). A view from cognitive psychology: g—(G)host in the correlation matrix? In R. J. Sternberg & E. L. Grigorenko (Eds.), *The general intelligence factor: How general is it?* (pp. 183–220). Mahwah, NJ: Erlbaum. (9)

Krebs, D. L. (2000). The evolution of moral dispositions in the human species. *Annals of the New York Academy of Sciences, 907,* 132–148. (10)

Kreitzer, A. C., & Regehr, W. G. (2001). Retrograde inhibition of presynaptic calcium influx by endogenous cannabinoids at excitatory synapses onto Purkinje cells. *Neuron, 29,* 717–727. (5)

Kreskin. (1991). *Secrets of The Amazing Kreskin.* Buffalo, NY: Prometheus. (2)

Kreutzer, M. W., & Holt, C. L. (2001). How do people process health information? Applications in an age of individualized communication. *Current Directions in Psychological Science, 10,* 206–209. (14)

Kripke, D. F., Garfinkel, L., Wingard, D. L., Klauber, M. R., & Marler, M. R. (2002). Mortality associated with sleep duration and insomnia. *Archives of General Psychiatry, 59,* 131–136. (2)

Krueger, D. W. (1978). The differential diagnosis of proverb interpretation. In W. E. Fann, I. Karacan, A. D. Pokorny, & R. L. Williams (Eds.), *Phenomenology and treatment of schizophrenia* (pp. 193–201). New York: Spectrum. (16)

Krull, D. S., & Anderson, C. A. (1997). The process of explanation. *Current Directions in Psychological Science, 6,* 1–5. (14)

Krupa, D. J., Thompson, J. K., & Thompson, R. F. (1993). Localization of a memory trace in the mammalian brain. *Science, 260,* 989–991. (3)

Krupnick, J. L., Elkin, I., Collins, J., Simmens, S., Sotsky, S. M., Pilkonis, P. A., et al. (1994). Therapeutic alliance and clinical outcome in the NIMH Treatment of Depression Collaborative Research Program: Preliminary findings. *Psychotherapy, 31,* 28–35. (15)

Kübler, A., Kotchoubey, B., Kaiser, J., Wolpaw, J. R., & Birbaumer, N. (2001). Brain-computer communication: Unlocking the locked-in. *Psychological Bulletin, 127,* 358–375. (12)

Kübler-Ross, E. (1969). *On death and dying.* New York: Macmillan. (10)

Kuhl, P. K., Andruski, J. E., Chistovich, I. A., Chistovich, L. A., Kozhevnikova, E. V., Ryskina, V. L., et al. (1997). Cross-language analysis of phonetic units in language addressed to infants. *Science, 277,* 684–686. (8)

Kuhlmeier, V. A., & Boysen, S. T. (2002). Chimpanzees (*Pan troglodytes*) recognize spatial and object correspondences between a scale model and its referent. *Psychological Science, 13,* 60–63. (10)

Kuhn, D., & Lao, J. (1996). Effects of evidence on attitudes: Is polarization the norm? *Psychological Science, 7,* 115–120. (14)

Kurihara, K., & Kashiwayanagi, M. (1998). Introductory remarks on umami taste. *Annals of the New York Academy of Sciences, 855,* 393–397. (4)

Kutchins, H., & Kirk, S. A. (1997). *Making us crazy.* New York: Free Press. (15)

Labouvie-Vief, G., Diehl, M., Tarnowski, A., & Shen, J. (2000). Age differences in adult personality: Findings from the United States and China. *Journal of Gerontology: Psychological Sciences, 55B,* P4–P17. (13)

Laburn, H. P. (1996). How does the fetus cope with thermal challenges? *News in Physiological Sciences, 11,* 96–100. (16)

Lackner, J. R. (1993). Orientation and movement in unusual force environments. *Psychological Science, 4,* 134–142. (4)

LaFromboise, T., Coleman, H. L. K., & Gerton, J. (1993). Psychological impact of biculturalism: Evidence and theory. *Psychological Bulletin, 114,* 395–412. (10)

Lai, C. S. L., Fisher, S. E., Hurst, J. A., Vargha-Khadem, F., & Monaco, A. P. (2001). A forkhead-domain gene is mutated in a severe speech and language disorder. *Nature, 413,* 519–523. (8)

Laing, D. G., Prescott, J., Bell, G. A., Gillmore, R., James, C., Best, D. J., et al. (1993). A cross-cultural study of taste discrimination with Australians and Japanese. *Chemical Senses, 18,* 161–168. (11)

Lake, R. I. E., Eaves, L. J., Maes, H. H. M., Heath, A. C., & Martin, N. G. (2000). Further evidence against the environmental transmission of individual differences in neuroticism from a collaborative study of 45,850 twins and relatives on two continents. *Behavior Genetics, 30,* 223–233. (10, 13)

Lalumière, M. L., Blanchard, R., & Zucker, K. J. (2000). Sexual orientation and handedness in men and women: A meta-analysis. *Psychological Bulletin, 126,* 575–592. (11)

LaLumiere, R. T., Buen, T.-V., & McGaugh, J. L. (2003). Post-training intra-basolateral amygdala infusions of norepinephrine enhance consolidation of memory for contextual fear conditioning. *Journal of Neuroscience, 23,* 6754–6758. (7)

Lamb, M. E., & Fauchier, A. (2001). The effects of question type on self-contradictions by children in the course of forensic interviews. *Applied Cognitive Psychology, 15,* 483–491. (7)

Lambie, J. A., & Marcel, A. J. (2002). Consciousness and the varieties of emotion experience: A theoretical framework. *Psychological Review, 109,* 219–259. (12)

Lamm, H., & Myers, D. G. (1978). Group-induced polarization of attitudes and behavior. *Advances in Experimental Social Psychology, 11,* 145–195. (14)

Land, E. H., Hubel, D. H., Livingstone, M. S., Perry, S. H., & Burns, M. M. (1983). Colour-generating interactions across the corpus callosum. *Nature, 303,* 616–618. (4)

Land, E. H., & McCann, J. J. (1971). Lightness and retinex theory. *Journal of the Optical Society of America, 61,* 1–11. (4)

Lande, S. D. (1982). Physiological and subjective measures of anxiety during flooding. *Behaviour Research and Therapy, 20,* 81–88. (16)

Lang, A. J., Craske, M. G., Brown, M., & Ghaneian, A. (2001). Fear-related state dependent memory. *Cognition, 15,* 695–703. (7)

Lang, P. J. (1994). The varieties of emotional experience: A meditation on James-Lange theory. *Psychological Review, 101,* 211–221. (12)

Langer, E. J. (1975). The illusion of control. *Journal of Personality and Social Psychology, 32,* 311–328. (10)

Langlois, J. H., Kalakanis, L., Rubenstein, A. J., Larson, A., Hallam, M., & Smoot, M. (2000). Maxims or myths of beauty? A meta-analytic and theoretical review. *Psychological Bulletin, 126,* 390–423. (14)

Langlois, J. H., & Roggman, L. A. (1990). Attractive faces are only average. *Psychological Science, 1,* 115–121. (14)

Langlois, J. H., Roggman, L. A., & Musselman, L. (1994). What is average and what is not average about average faces? *Psychological Science, 5,* 214–220. (14)

Langworthy, R. A., & Jennings, J. W. (1972). Oddball, abstract olfactory learning in laboratory rats. *Psychological Record, 22,* 487–490. (1)

Lant, T. K., & Hurley, A. E. (1999). A contingency model of response to performance feedback. *Group & Organization Management, 24,* 421–437. (14)

Lappalainen, J., Kranzler, H. R., Malison, R., Price, L. H., Van Dyck, C., Rosenheck, R. A., et al. (2002). A functional neuropeptide Y *Leu 7 Pro* polymorphism associated with alcohol dependence in a large population sample from the United States. *Archives of General Psychiatry, 59,* 825–831. (16)

Larson, R. W. (2001). How U.S. children and adolescents spend time: What it does (and doesn't) tell us about their development. *Current Directions in Psychological Science, 10,* 160–164. (10)

Larson, S. J., & Siegel, S. (1998). Learning and tolerance to the ataxic effect of ethanol. *Pharmacology Biochemistry and Behavior, 61,* 131–142. (6)

Lashley, K. S. (1951). The problem of serial order in behavior. In L. A. Jeffress (Ed.), *Cerebral mechanisms in behavior* (pp. 112–146). New York: Wiley. (8)

Lassiter, G. D., Geers, A. L., Munhall, P. J., Ploutz-Snyder, R. J., & Breitenbecher, D. L. (2002). Illusory causation: Why it occurs. *Psychological Science, 13,* 299–305. (14)

Latané, B., & Darley, J. M. (1968). Group inhibition of bystander intervention in emergencies. *Journal of Personality and Social Psychology, 10,* 215–221. (14)

Latané, B., & Darley, J. M. (1969). Bystander "apathy." *American Scientist, 57,* 244–268. (14)

Latané, B., Williams, K., & Harkins, S. (1979). Many hands make light the work: The causes and consequences of social loafing. *Journal of Personality and Social Psychology, 37,* 823–832. (14)

Latner, J. D. (2003). Macronutrient effects on satiety and binge eating in bulimia nervosa and binge eating disorder. *Appetite, 40,* 309–311. (11)

Laumann, E. O. (1969). Friends of urban men: An assessment of accuracy in reporting their socio-economic attributes, mutual choice, and attitude development. *Sociometry, 32,* 54–69. (14)

Laumann, E. O., Gagnon, J. H., Michael, R. T., & Michaels, S. (1994). *The social organization of sexuality: Sexual practices in the United States.* Chicago: University of Chicago Press. (11)

Laumann, E. O., Nicolosi, A., Glasser, D. B., Paik, A., Buvat, J., Gingell, C., et al. for the GSSAB Investigators' Group. (2003). *Prevalence of sexual problems among men and women aged 40 to 80 years: Results of an international survey.* Paper presented at the second international consultation on erectile and sexual dysfunctions, Paris. Retrieved from http://www.pfizerglobalstudy.com/public/publications.asp (11)

Lavin, J. H., Wittert, G., Sun, W. M., Horowitz, M., Morley, J. E., & Read, N. W. (1996). Appetite regulation by carbohydrate: Role of blood glucose and gastrointestinal hormones. *American Journal of Physiology, 271,* E209–E214. (11)

Laviolette, S. R., & van der Kooy, D. (2004). The neurobiology of nicotine addiction: Bridging the gap from molecules to behaviour. *Nature Reviews Neuroscience, 5,* 55–65. (16)

Lawlor, S., Richman, S., & Richman, C. L. (1997). The validity of using the SAT as a criterion for Black and White students' admission to college. *College Student Journal, 31,* 507–515. (9)

Laws, G., Byrne, A., & Buckley, S. (2000). Language and memory development in children with Down syndrome at mainstream schools and special schools: A comparison. *Educational Psychology, 20,* 447–457. (9)

Lazarus, R. S. (1977). Cognitive and coping processes in emotion. In A. Monat & R. S. Lazarus (Eds.), *Stress and coping* (pp. 145–158). New York: Columbia University Press. (12)

Lazarus, R. S., Averill, J. R., & Opton, E. M., Jr. (1970). Towards a cognitive theory of emotion. In M. B. Arnold (Ed.), *Feelings and emotions* (pp. 207–232). New York: Academic Press. (12)

Leaper, C., Anderson, K. J., & Sanders, P. (1998). Moderators of gender effects on parents' talk to their children: A meta-analysis. *Developmental Psychology, 34,* 3–27. (10)

Lee, J. E., Wong, C. M. T., Day, J. D., Maxwell, S. E., & Thorpe, P. (2000). Social and academic intelligences: A multitrait-multimethod study of their crystallized and fluid characteristics. *Personality and Individual Differences, 29,* 539–553. (9)

Lee, Y.T., & Duenas, G. (1995). Stereotype accuracy in multicultural business. In Y. T. Lee, L. J. Jussim, & C. R. McCauley (Eds.), *Stereotype accuracy* (pp. 157–186). Washington, DC: American Psychological Association. (14)

Leff, J. (2002). The psychiatric revolution: Care in the community. *Nature Reviews Neuroscience, 3,* 821–824. (15)

Leff, J., Wig, N. N., Ghosh, A., Bedi, H., Menon, D. K., Kuipers, L., et al. (1987). Expressed emotion and schizophrenia in North India: III. Influence of relatives' expressed emotion on the course of schizophrenia in Changigarh. *British Journal of Psychiatry, 151,* 166–173. (16)

Legge, G. E., Ahn, S. J., Klitz, T. S., & Luebker, A. (1997). Psychophysics of reading: XVI. The visual span in normal and low vision. *Vision Research, 37,* 1999–2010. (8)

Leibowitz, S. F., & Alexander, J. T. (1991). Analysis of neuropeptide Y-induced feeding: Dissociation of Y1 and Y2 receptor effects on natural meal patterns. *Peptides, 12,* 1251–1260. (11)

Leibowitz, S. F., Hammer, N. J., & Chang, K. (1981). Hypothalamic paraventricular nucleus lesions produce overeating and obesity in the rat. *Physiology & Behavior, 27,* 1031–1040. (11)

Leichsenring, F., & Leibing, E. (2003). The effectiveness of psychodynamic therapy and cognitive behavior therapy in the treatment of personality disorders: A meta-analysis. *American Journal of Psychiatry, 160,* 1223–1232. (15)

Leinders-Zufall, T., Lane, A. P., Puche, A. C., Ma, W., Novotny, M. V., Shipley, M. T., et al. (2000). Ultrasensitive pheromone detection by mammalian vomeronasal neurons. *Nature, 405,* 792–796. (4)

Lekeu, F., Wojtasik, V., Van der Linden, M., & Salmon, E. (2002). Training early Alzheimer patients to use a mobile phone. *Acta Neurologica Belgica, 102,* 114–121. (7)

LeMagnen, J. (1981). The metabolic basis of dual periodicity of feeding in rats. *Behavioral and Brain Sciences, 4,* 561–607. (11)

Lenneberg, E. H. (1967). *Biological foundations of language.* New York: Wiley. (8)

Lenneberg, E. H. (1969). On explaining language. *Science, 164,* 635–643. (8)

Leppämäki, S., Partonen, T., & Lönnqvist, J. (2002). Bright-light exposure combined with physical exercise elevates mood. *Journal of Affective Disorders, 72,* 139–144. (16)

Lester, D. (1996). *Patterns of suicide and homicide in the world.* Commack, NY: Nova Science. (16)

Lett, B. T., Grant, V. L., Koh, M. T., & Smith, J. F. (2001). Wheel running simultaneously produces conditioned taste aversion and conditioned place preference in rats. *Learning and Motivation, 32,* 129–136. (6)

Leuchtenburg, W. E. (1963). *Franklin D. Roosevelt and the New Deal 1932–1940.* New York: Harper & Row. (14)

LeVay, S. (1991). A difference in hypothalamic structure between heterosexual and homosexual men. *Science, 253,* 1034–1037. (11)

Levenson, R. W., Oyama, O. N., & Meek, P. S. (1987). Greater reinforcement from alcohol for those at risk: Parental risk, personality risk, and sex. *Journal of Abnormal Psychology, 96,* 242–253. (16)

Leventhal, H. (1970). Findings and theory in the study of fear communication. In L. Berkowitz (Ed.), *Advances in experimental social psychology* (Vol. 5, pp. 119–186). New York: Academic Press. (14)

Levin, M. (1994). Comment on the Minnesota transracial adoption study. *Intelligence, 19,* 13–20. (9)

Levine, R. V. (1990). The pace of life. *American Scientist, 78,* 450–459. (12)

Levinson, D. F., Holmans, P. A., Leurent, C., Riley, B., Pulver, A. E., Gejman, P. V., et al. (2002). No major schizophrenia locus detected on chromosome 1q in a large multicenter sample. *Science, 296,* 739–741. (16)

Lewis, D. O., Moy, E., Jackson, L. D., Aaronson, R., Restifo, N., Serra, S., et al. (1985). Biopsychosocial characteristics of children who later murder: A prospective study. *American Journal of Psychiatry, 142,* 1161–1167. (12)

Lewis, M. (1995). Self-conscious emotions. *American Scientist, 83,* 68–78. (12)

Lewis, M., Sullivan, M. W., Stanger, C., & Weiss, M. (1991). Self development and self-conscious emotions. In S. Chess & M. E. Hertzig (Eds.), *Annual progress in child psychiatry and child development 1990* (pp. 34–51). New York: Brunner/Mazel. (10)

Lewis, M., Thomas, D. A., & Worobey, J. (1990). Developmental organization, stress, and illness. *Psychological Science, 1,* 316–318. (10)

Lickliter, R., & Bahrick, L. E. (2000). The development of infant intersensory perception: Advantages of a comparative convergent-operations approach. *Psychological Bulletin, 126,* 260–280. (10)

Lilie, J. K., & Rosenberg, R. P. (1990). Behavioral treatment of insomnia. *Progress in Behavior Modification, 25,* 152–177. (5)

Lilienfeld, S. O., Lynn, S. J., Kirsch, I., Chaves, J. F., Sarbin, T. R., Ganaway, G. K., et al. (1999). Dissociative identity disorder and the sociocognitive model: Recalling the lessons of the past. *Psychological Bulletin, 125,* 507–523. (15)

Lilienfeld, S. O., Wood, J. M., & Garb, H. N. (2000). The scientific status of projective tests. *Psychological Science in the Public Interest, 1,* 27–66. (13)

Lillberg, K., Verkasalo, P. K., Kaprio, J., Teppo, L., Helenius, H., & Koskenvuo, M. (2003). Stressful life events and risk of breast cancer in 10,808 women: A cohort study. *American Journal of Epidemiology, 157,* 415–423. (12)

Lin, L., Faraco, J., Li, R., Kadotani, H., Rogers, W., Lin, X., et al. (1999). The sleep disorder canine narcolepsy is caused by a mutation in the hypocretin (orexin) receptor 2 gene. *Cell, 98,* 365–376. (5)

Linday, L. A. (1994). Maternal reports of pregnancy, genital, and related fantasies in preschool and kindergarten children. *Journal of the American Academy of Child and Adolescent Psychiatry, 33,* 416–423. (13)

Lindberg, L., & Hjern, A. (2003). Risk factors for anorexia nervosa: A national cohort study. *International Journal of Eating Disorders, 34,* 397–408. (11)

Lindberg, N. O., Coburn, C., & Stricker, E. M. (1984). Increased feeding by rats after subdiabetogenic streptozotocin treatment: A role for insulin in satiety. *Behavioral Neuroscience, 98,* 138–145. (11)

Lindemann, B. (1996). Taste reception. *Physiological Reviews, 76,* 719–766. (4)

Linden, W., Lenz, J. W., & Con, A. H. (2001). Individualized stress management for primary hypertension: A randomized trial. *Archives of Internal Medicine, 161,* 1071–1080. (12)

Lindsay, D. S., Hagen, L., Read, J. D., Wade, K. A., & Garry, M. (2004). True photographs and false memories. *Psychological Science, 15,* 149–154. (7)

Lindsay, D. S., & Read, J. D. (1994). Psychotherapy and memories of childhood sexual abuse: A cognitive perspective. *Applied Cognitive Psychology, 8,* 281–338. (7)

Lindsey, D. T., & Brown, A. M. (2002). Color naming and the phototoxic effects of sunlight on the eye. *Psychological Science, 13,* 506–512. (4)

Linhorst, D. M., & Dirks-Linhorst, P. A. (1999). A critical assessment of disposition options for mentally ill offenders. *Social Science Review, 73,* 65–81. (15)

Linn, R., & Gilligan, C. (1990). One action, two moral orientations—The tension between justice and care voices in Israeli selective conscientious objectors. *New Ideas in Psychology, 8,* 189–203. (10)

Lipsey, M. W., & Wilson, D. B. (1993). The efficacy of psychological, educational, and behavioral treatment. *American Psychologist, 48,* 1181–1209. (15)

Lisak, D., & Roth, S. (1988). Motivational factors in nonincarcerated sexually aggressive men. *Journal of Personality and Social Psychology, 55,* 795–802. (12)

Lisanby, S. H., Maddox, J. H., Prudic, J., Devanand, D. P., & Sackeim, H. A. (2000). The effects of electroconvulsive therapy on memory of autobiographical and public events. *Archives of General Psychiatry, 57,* 581–590. (16)

Liston, C., & Kagan, J. (2002). Memory enhancement in early childhood. *Nature, 419,* 896. (7)

Locke, E. A., & Latham, G. P. (2002). Building a practically useful theory of goal setting and task motivation. *American Psychologist, 57,* 705–717. (11)

Locke, J. L. (1994). Phases in the child's development of language. *American Scientist, 82,* 436–445. (8)

Loeb, J. (1973). *Forced movements, tropisms, and animal conduct.* New York: Dover. (Original work published 1918) (6)

Loehlin, J. C. (1992). *Genes and environment in personality development.* Newbury Park, CA: Sage. (10, 13)

Loehlin, J. C., Horn, J. M., & Willerman, L. (1989). Modeling IQ change: Evidence from the Texas adoption project. *Child Development, 60,* 993–1004. (9)

Loewenstein, G. (1987). Anticipation and the valuation of delayed consumption. *The Economic Journal, 97,* 666–684. (11)

Loewi, O. (1960). An autobiographic sketch. *Perspectives in Biology, 4,* 3–25. (3)

Loftus, E. F. (1975). Leading questions and the eyewitness report. *Cognitive Psychology, 7,* 560–572. (7)

Loftus, E. F. (1993). The reality of repressed memories. *American Psychologist, 48,* 518–537. (7)

Loftus, E. (2003). Our changeable memories: Legal and practical implications. *Nature Reviews Neuroscience, 4,* 231–234. (7)

Loftus, E. F., Feldman, J., & Dashiell, R. (1995). The reality of illusory memories. In D. L. Schacter (Ed.), *Memory distortion* (pp. 47–68). Cambridge, MA: Harvard University Press. (7)

Loftus, G. R. (1996). Psychology will be a much better science when we change the way we analyze data. *Current Directions in Psychological Science, 5,* 161–171. (2)

Logan, G. D. (2003). Executive control of thought and action: In search of the wild homunculus. *Current Directions in Psychological Science, 12,* 45–48. (7)

Longstreth, L. E. (1981). Revisiting Skeels' final study: A critique. *Developmental Psychology, 17,* 620–625. (9)

Lord, C. G., & Lepper, M. R. (1999). Attitude representation theory. *Advances in Experimental Social Psychology, 31,* 265–343. (14)

Lorenz, K. (1950). The comparative method in studying innate behaviour patterns. *Symposia of the Society for Experimental Biology, 4,* 221–268. (11)

Lotto, R. B., & Purves, D. (1999). The effects of color on brightness. *Nature Neuroscience, 2,* 1010–1014. (4)

Lotto, R. B., & Purves, D. (2002). The empirical basis of color perception. *Consciousness and Cognition, 11,* 609–629. (4)

Lotze, M., Grodd, W., Birbaumer, N., Erb, M., Huse, E., & Flor, H. (1999). Does use of a myoelectric prosthesis prevent cortical reorganization and phantom limb pain? *Nature Neuroscience, 2,* 501–502. (4)

Lovallo, D., & Kahneman, D. (2000). Living with uncertainty: Attractiveness and resolution timing. *Journal of Behavioral Decision Making, 13,* 179–190. (11)

Lövdén, M. (2003). The episodic memory and inhibition accounts of age-related increases in false memory: A consistency check. *Journal of Memory and Language, 49,* 268–283. (7)

Lowe, K. B., Kroeck, K. G., & Sivasubramaniam, N. (1996). Effectiveness correlates of transformational and transactional leadership: A meta-analytic review of the MLQ literature. *Leadership Quarterly, 7,* 385–425. (11)

Lucas, R. E., Clark, A. E., Georgellis, Y., & Diener, E. (2004). Unemployment alters the set point for life satisfaction. *Psychological Science, 15,* 8–13. (12)

Luciano, M., Wright, M. J., Smith, G. A., Geffen, G. M., Geffen, L. B., & Martin, N. G. (2001). Genetic covariance among measures of information processing speed, working memory, and IQ. *Behavior Genetics, 31,* 581–592. (9)

Lucio, E., Ampudia, A., Durán, C., León, I., & Butcher, J. N. (2001). Comparison of the Mexican and American norms of the MMPI-2. *Journal of Clinical Psychology, 57,* 1459–1468. (13)

Luck, S. J., & Vogel, E. K. (1997). The capacity of visual working memory for features and conjunctions. *Nature, 390,* 279–281. (7)

Lüer, G., Becker, D., Lass, U., Yunqiu, F., Guopeng, C., & Zhongming, W. (1998). Memory span in German and Chinese: Evidence for the phonological loop. *European Psychologist, 3,* 102–112. (7)

Luo, D., Thompson, L. A., & Detterman, D. K. (2003). The causal factor underlying the correlation between psychometric *g* and scholastic performance. *Intelligence, 31,* 67–83. (9)

Luthar, S. S., Cicchetti, D., & Becker, B. (2000). The construct of resilience: A critical evaluation and guidelines for future work. *Child Development, 71,* 543–562. (10)

Lykken, D. T. (1979). The detection of deception. *Psychological Bulletin, 86,* 47–53. (12)

Lykken, D. T., Bouchard, T. J., Jr., McGue, M., & Tellegen, A. (1993). Heritability of interests: A twin study. *Journal of Applied Psychology, 78,* 649–661. (10)

Lykken, D. T., McGue, M., Tellegen, A., & Bouchard, T. J. (1992). Emergenesis: Genetic traits that may not run in families. *American Psychologist, 47,* 1565–1577. (10)

Lykken, D., & Tellegen, A. (1996). Happiness is a stochastic phenomenon. *Psychological Science, 7,* 186–189. (12)

Lymburner, J. A., & Roesch, R. (1999). The insanity defense: Five years of research (1993–1999). *International Journal of Law and Psychiatry, 22,* 213–240. (15)

Lynam, D. R. (1996). Early identification of chronic offenders: Who is the fledgling psychopath? *Psychological Bulletin, 120,* 209–234. (12)

Lynn, R. (1998). In support of the nutrition theory. In U. Neisser (Ed.), *The rising curve* (pp. 207–215). Washington, DC: American Psychological Association. (9)

Lyons, M. J., Eisen, S. A., Goldberg, J., True, W., Lin, N., Meyer, J. M., et al. (1998). A registry-based twin study of depression in men. *Archives of General Psychiatry, 55,* 468–472. (16)

Maccoby, E. E. (1990). Gender and relationships. *American Psychologist, 45,* 513–520. (10)

Maccoby, E. E., & Jacklin, C. N. (1974). *The psychology of sex differences.* Stanford, CA: Stanford University Press. (10)

MacCoun, R. J. (1998). Toward a psychology of harm reduction. *American Psychologist, 53,* 1199–1208. (16)

MacCoun, R., & Reuter, P. (1997). Interpreting Dutch cannabis policy: Reasoning by analogy in the legalization debate. *Science, 278,* 47–52. (16)

Macdonald, R. L., Weddle, M. G., & Gross, R. A. (1986). Benzodiazepine, beta-carboline, and barbiturate actions on GABA responses. *Advances in Biochemical Psychopharmacology, 41,* 67–78. (16)

Macmillan, M. (1997). *Freud evaluated.* Cambridge, MA: MIT Press. (13)

MacQuitty, J. (1996, August 1). Lily the stink loses its 33-year reputation by a nose. *The Times* (London), pp. 1–2. (11)

Magee, W. J., Eaton, W. W., Wittchen, H. -U., McGonagle, K. A., & Kessler, R. C. (1996). Agoraphobia, simple phobia, and social phobia in the National Comorbidity Survey. *Archives of General Psychiatry, 53,* 159–168. (16)

Maguire, E. A., & Frith, C. D. (2003). Lateral asymmetry in the hippocampal response to the remoteness of autobiographical memories. *Journal of Neuroscience, 23,* 5302–5307. (7)

Maguire, E. A., Gadian, D. G., Johnsrude, I. S., Good, C. D., Ashburner, J., Frackowiak, R. S. J., et al. (2000). Navigation-related structural change in the hippocampi of taxi drivers. *Proceedings of the National Academy of Sciences, USA, 97,* 4398–4403. (3)

Maguire, E. A., Valentine, E. R., Wilding, J. M., & Kapur, N. (2003). Routes to remembering: The brains behind superior memory. *Nature Neuroscience, 6,* 90-95. (8, 9)

Maier, S. F., & Watkins, L. R. (1998). Cytokines for psychologists: Implications of bidirectional immune-to-brain communication for understanding behavior, mood, and cognition. *Psychological Review, 105,* 83–107. (12)

Major, B., Quinton, W. J., & McCoy, S. K. (2002). Antecedents and consequences of attributions to discrimination: Theoretical and empirical advances. *Advances in Experimental Social Psychology, 34,* 251–330. (14)

Maki, R. H. (1990). Memory for script actions: Effects of relevance and detail expectancy. *Memory & Cognition, 18,* 5–14. (7)

Maki, R. H., & Serra, M. (1992). The basis of test predictions for text material. *Journal of Experimental Psychology: Learning, Memory, and Cognition, 18,* 116–126. (7)

Maki, R. H., & Syman, E. M. (1997). Teaching of controversial and empirically validated treatments in APA-accredited clinical and counseling psychology programs. *Psychotherapy, 34,* 44–57. (15)

Malamed, F., & Zaidel, E. (1993). Language and task effects on lateralized word recognition. *Brain and Language, 45,* 70–85. (8)

Malamuth, N. M., & Brown, L. M. (1994). Sexually aggressive men's perceptions of women's communications: Testing three explanations. *Journal of Personality and Social Psychology, 67,* 699–712. (12)

Maldonado, R., Saiardi, A., Valverde, O., Samad, T. A., Roques, B. P., & Borrelli, E. (1997). Absence of opiate rewarding effects in mice lacking dopamine D2 receptors. *Nature, 388,* 586–589. (5)

Malinosky-Rummell, R., & Hansen, D. J. (1993). Long-term consequences of childhood physical abuse. *Psychological Bulletin, 114,* 68–79. (12)

Malmberg, A. B., Chen, C., Tonegawa, S., & Basbaum, A. I. (1997). Preserved acute pain and reduced neuropathic pain in mice lacking PKC. *Science, 278,* 179–283. (4)

Malmquist, C. P. (1986). Children who witness parental murder: Posttraumatic aspects. *Journal of the American Academy of Child Psychiatry, 25,* 320–325. (7)

Malt, B. C., Sloman, S. A., & Gennari, S. P. (2003). Universality and language specificity in object naming. *Journal of Memory and Language, 49,* 20–42. (8)

Malt, B. C., Sloman, S. A., Gennari, S., Shi, M., & Wang, Y. (1999). Knowing versus naming: Similarity and the linguistic categorization of artifacts. *Journal of Memory and Language, 40,* 230–262. (8)

Mann, T., Nolen-Hoeksema, S., Huang, K., Burgard, D., Wright, A., & Hanson, K. (1997). Are two interventions worse than none? Joint primary and secondary prevention of eating disorders in college females. *Health Psychology, 16,* 215–225. (15)

Mannuzza, S., Klein, R. G., Bessler, A., Malloy, P., & LaPadula, M. (1998). Adult psychiatric status of hyperactive boys grown up. *American Journal of Psychiatry, 155,* 493–498. (15)

Mansky, P. A. (1978). Opiates: Human psychopharmacology. In L. L. Iversen, S. D. Iversen, & S. H. Snyder (Eds.), *Handbook of psychopharmacology: Vol. 12. Drugs of abuse* (pp. 95–185). New York: Plenum Press. (5)

Manuck, S. B., Cohen, S., Rabin, B. S., Muldoon, M. F., & Bachen, E. A. (1991). Individual differences in cellular immune response to stress. *Psychological Science, 2,* 111–115. (12)

Maquet, P., Laureys, S., Peigneux, P., Fuchs, S., Petiau, C., Phillips, C., et al. (2000). Experience-dependent changes in cerebral activation during human REM sleep. *Nature Neuroscience, 3,* 831–836. (5)

Maquet, P., Peters, J. M., Aerts, J., Delfiore, G., Degueldre, C., Luxen, A., et al. (1996). Functional neuroanatomy of human rapid-eye-movement sleep and dreaming. *Nature, 383,* 163–166. (5)

Marcia, J. E. (1980). Identity in adolescence. In J. Adelson (Ed.), *Handbook of adolescent psychology* (pp. 159–187). New York: Wiley. (10)

Marcus, G. F., Vijayan, S., Rao, S. B., & Vishton, P. M. (1999). Rule learning by seven-month-old infants. *Science, 283,* 77–80. (8)

Marder, S. R., Mebane, A., Chien, C., Winslade, W. J., Swann, E., & Van Putten, T. (1983). A comparison of patients who refuse and consent to neuroleptic treatment. *American Journal of Psychiatry, 140,* 470–472. (15)

Marian, V., & Neisser, U. (2000). Language-dependent recall of autobiographical memories. *Journal of Experimental Psychology: General, 129,* 361–368. (7)

Marin, R. H., Perez, M. F., Duero, D. G., & Ramirez, O. A. (1999). Preexposure to drug administration context blocks the development of tolerance to sedative effects of diazepam. *Pharmacology Biochemistry and Behavior, 64,* 473–477. (6)

Maris, R. W. (1997). Social suicide. *Suicide and Life-Threatening Behavior, 27,* 41–49. (16)

Markey, C. N., Markey, P. M., & Tinsley, B. J. (2003). Personality, puberty, and preadolescent girls' risky behaviors: Examining the predictive value of the five-factor model of personality. *Journal of Research in Personality, 37,* 405–419. (13)

Markey, P. M. (2000). Bystander intervention in computer-mediated intervention. *Computers in Human Behavior, 16,* 183–188. (14)

Marks, D., & Kammann, R. (1980). *The psychology of the psychic.* Buffalo, NY: Prometheus. (2, 13)

Marler, P. (1997). Three models of song learning: Evidence from behavior. *Journal of Neurobiology, 33,* 501–516. (6)

Marler, P., & Peters, S. (1981). Sparrows learn adult song and more from memory. *Science, 213,* 780–782. (6)

Marler, P., & Peters, S. (1982). Long-term storage of learned birdsongs prior to production. *Animal Behaviour, 30,* 479–482. (6)

Marler, P., & Peters, S. (1987). A sensitive period for song acquisition in the song sparrow, *Melospiza melodia:* A case of age-limited learning. *Ethology, 76,* 89–100. (6)

Marler, P., & Peters, S. (1988). Sensitive periods for song acquisition from tape recordings and live tutors in the swamp sparrow, *Melospiza georgiana. Ethology, 77,* 76–84. (6)

Marlowe, F., & Wetsman, A. (2001). Preferred waist-to-hip ratio and ecology. *Personality and Individual Differences, 30,* 481–489. (14)

Marriott, F. H. C. (1976). Abnormal colour vision. In H. Davson (Ed.), *The eye* (2nd ed., pp. 533–547). New York: Academic Press. (4)

Marsh, A. A., Elfenbein, H. A., & Ambady, N. (2003). Nonverbal "accents": Cultural differences in facial expressions of emotion. *Psychological Science, 14,* 373–376. (12)

Martin, D. J., & Lynn, S. J. (1996). The hypnotic simulation index: Successful discrimination of real versus simulating participants. *International Journal of Clinical and Experimental Hypnosis, 44,* 338–353. (5)

Martindale, C. (2001). Oscillations and analogies: Thomas Young, MD, FRS, genius. *American Psychologist, 56,* 342–345. (4, 8)

Martorell, R. (1998). Nutrition and the worldwide rise in IQ scores. In U. Neisser (Ed.), *The rising curve* (pp. 183–206). Washington, DC: American Psychological Association. (9)

Martsh, C. T., & Miller, W. R. (1997). Extraversion predicts heavy drinking in college students. *Personality and Individual Differences, 23,* 153–155. (13)

Marx, J. (2003). Cellular warriors at the battle of the bulge. *Science, 299,* 846–849. (11)

Maslach, C. (2003). Job burnout: New directions in research and intervention. *Current Directions in Psychological Science, 12,* 189–192. (11)

Maslow, A. H. (1962). *Toward a psychology of being.* Princeton, NJ: Van Nostrand. (13)

Maslow, A. H. (1971). *The farther reaches of human nature.* New York: Viking Press. (13)

Masson, J. M. (1984). *The assault on truth.* New York: Farrar, Straus and Giroux. (13)

Masten, A. S., & Coatsworth, J. D. (1998). The development of competence in favorable and unfavorable environments. *American Psychologist, 53,* 205–220. (10)

Masters, W. H., & Johnson, V. E. (1966). *Human sexual response.* Boston: Little, Brown. (11)

Mastor, K. A., Jin, P., & Cooper, M. (2000). Malay culture and personality: A big five perspective. *American Behavioral Scientist, 44,* 95–111. (13)

Mastropieri, D., & Turkewitz, G. (1999). Prenatal experience and neonatal responsiveness to vocal expressions of emotion. *Developmental Psychobiology, 35,* 204–214. (12)

Mathalon, D. H., Pfefferbaum, A., Lim, K. O., Rosenbloom, M. J., & Sullivan, E. V. (2003). Compounded brain volume deficits in schizophrenia-alcoholism co-morbidity. *Archives of General Psychiatry, 60,* 245–252. (16)

Matheny, A. P., Jr. (1989). Children's behavioral inhibition over age and across situations: Genetic similarity for a trait to change. *Journal of Personality, 57,* 215–235. (10)

Matin, E., Clymer, A. B., & Matin, L. (1972). Metacontrast and saccadic suppression. *Science, 178,* 179–182. (8)

Matsunami, H., Montmayeur, J.-P., & Buck, L. B. (2000). A family of candidate taste receptors in human and mouse. *Nature, 404,* 601–604. (4)

Matsumoto, D. (1994). *People: Psychology from a cultural perspective.* Pacific Grove, CA: Brooks/Cole. (2)

Mattson, S. N., Riley, E. P., Grambling, L., Delis, D. C., & Jones, K. L. (1998). Neuropsychological comparison of alcohol-exposed children with or without physical features of fetal alcohol syndrome. *Neuropsychology, 12,* 146–153. (10)

Matzel, L. D., Han, Y. R., Grossman, H., Karnik, M. S., Patel, D., Scott, N., et al. (2003). Individual differences in the expression of a "general" learning ability in mice. *Journal of Neuroscience, 23,* 6423–6433. (9)

Maunsell, E., Brisson, J., Mondor, M., Verreault, R., & Deschênes, L. (2001). Stressful life events and survival after breast cancer. *Psychosomatic Medicine, 63,* 306–315. (12)

Maurice, D. M. (1998). The Von Sallman lecture of 1996: An ophthalmological explanation of REM sleep. *Experimental Eye Research, 66,* 139–145. (5)

May, C. P., Hasher, L., & Stoltzfus, E. R. (1993). Optimal time of day and the magnitude of age differences in memory. *Psychological Science, 4,* 326–330. (5)

May, M. (1999, January/February). Speed demons. *The Sciences, 39*(1), 16–18. (8)

Mayberry, R. I., Lock, E., & Kazmi, H. (2002). Linguistic ability and early language exposure. *Nature, 415,* 1026–1029. (8)

Mayer, J. D. (2001). Emotion, intelligence, and emotional intelligence. In J. P. Forgas (Ed.), *Handbook of affect and social cognition* (pp. 410–431). Mahwah, NJ: Erlbaum. (12)

Mayer, J. D., Caruso, D. R., & Salovey, P. (2000). Emotional intelligence meets traditional standards for an intelligence. *Intelligence, 27,* 267–298. (12)

Mayer, J. D., & Salovey, P. (1995). Emotional intelligence and the construction and regulation of feelings. *Applied & Preventive Psychology, 4,* 197–208. (12)

Mayer, J. D., & Salovey, P. (1997). What is emotional intelligence? In P. Salovey & D. J. Sluyter (Eds.). *Emotional development and emotional intelligence* (pp. 3–34). New York: Basic Books. (12)

Mayer, J. D., Salovey, P., Caruso, D. R., & Sitarenios, G. (2001). Emotional intelligence as a standard intelligence. *Emotion, 1,* 232–242. (12)

Maziade, M., Roy, M.-A., Rouillard, É., Bissonnette, L., Fournier, J.-P., Roy, A., et al. (2001). A search for specific and common susceptibility loci for schizophrenia and bipolar disorder: A linkage study in 13 target chromosomes. *Molecular Psychiatry, 6,* 684–693. (16)

Mazzoni, G., & Memon, A. (2003). Imagination can create false autobiographical memories. *Psychological Science, 14,* 186–188. (7)

McCall, V. W., Yates, B., Hendricks, S., Turner, K., & McNabb, B. (1989). Comparison between the Stanford-Binet: L-M and the Stanford-Binet: Fourth edition with a group of gifted children. *Contemporary Educational Psychology, 114,* 93–96. (9)

McCann, U. D., Lowe, K. A., & Ricaurte, G. A. (1997). Long-lasting effects of recreational drugs of abuse on the central nervous system. *The Neuroscientist, 3,* 399–411. (5)

McClelland, J. L. (1988). Connectionist models and psychological evidence. *Journal of Memory and Language, 27,* 107–123. (8)

McClelland, J. L., & Rumelhart, D. E. (1981). An interactive activation model of context effects in letter perception: Part 1. An account of basic findings. *Psychological Review, 88,* 375–407. (8)

McClintock, M. K. (1971). Menstrual synchrony and suppression. *Nature, 229,* 244–245. (4)

McClure, E. B. (2000). A meta-analytic review of sex differences in facial expression processing and their development in infants, children, and adolescents. *Psychological Bulletin, 126,* 424–453. (12)

McClure, J. (1998). Discounting causes of behavior: Are two reasons better than one? *Journal of Personality and Social Psychology, 74,* 7–20. (14)

McCormick, M. C. (1985). The contribution of low birth weight to infant mortality and childhood morbidity. *New England Journal of Medicine, 312,* 82–90. (10)

McCornack, R. L. (1983). Bias in the validity of predicted college grades in four ethnic minority groups. *Educational & Psychological Measurement, 43,* 517–522. (9)

McCourt, K., Bouchard, T. J., Jr., Lykken, D. T., Tellegen, A., & Keyes, M. (1999). Authoritarianism revisited: Genetic and environmental influences examined in twins reared apart and together. *Personality and Individual Differences, 27,* 985–1014. (10)

McCrae, R. R. (1996). Social consequences of experiential openness. *Psychological Bulletin, 120,* 323–337. (13)

McCrae, R. R., & Costa, P. T., Jr. (1987). Validation of the five-factor model of personality across instruments and observers. *Journal of Personality and Social Psychology, 52,* 81–90. (13)

McCrae, R. R., & Costa, P. T., Jr. (1997). Personality trait structure as a human universal. *American Psychologist, 52,* 509–516. (13)

McCrae, R. R., Costa, P. T., Jr., Ostendorf, F., Angleitner, A., Hrebíčková, M., Avia, M. D., et al. (2000). Nature over nurture: Temperament, personality, and life span development. *Journal of Personality and Social Psychology, 78,* 173–186. (13)

McDaniel, M. A., Einstein, G. O., & Lollis, T. (1988). Qualitative and quantitative considerations in encoding difficulty effects. *Memory & Cognition, 16,* 8–14. (7)

McDaniel, M. A., Maier, S. F., & Einstein, G. O. (2002). "Brain-specific" nutrients: A memory cure? *Psychological Science in the Public Interest, 3,* 12–38. (7)

McFarlane, A. C. (1997). The prevalence and longitudinal course of PTSD. *Annals of the New York Academy of Sciences, 821,* 10–23. (12)

McGeorge, P., Taylor, L., Della Sala, S., & Shanks, M. F. (2002). Word stem completion in young adults, elderly adults, and patients with Alzheimer's disease. *Archives of Clinical Neuropsychology, 17,* 389–398. (7)

McGinnis, R. E., Fox, H., Yates, P., Cameron, L.-A., Barnes, M. R., Gray, I. C., et al. (2001). Failure to confirm *NOTCH4* association with schizophrenia in a large population-based sample from Scotland. *Nature Genetics, 28,* 128–129. (16)

McGorry, P. D., Yung, A. R., Phillips, L. J., Yuen, H. P., Francey, S., Cosgrave, E. M., et al. (2002). Randomized controlled trial of interventions designed to reduce the risk of progression to first-episode psychosis in a clinical sample with sub-threshold symptoms. *Archives of General Psychiatry, 59,* 921–928. (15)

McGovern, P. E., Glusker, D. L., Exner, L. J., & Voigt, M. M. (1996). Neolithic resinated wine. *Nature, 381,* 480–481. (5)

McGrath, J. J., Féron, F. P., Burne, T. H. J., Mackay-Sim, A., & Eylees, D. W. (2003). The neurodevelopmental hypothesis of schizophrenia: A review of recent developments. *Annals of Medicine, 35,* 86–93. (16)

McGregor, D. M. (1960). *The human side of enterprise.* New York: McGraw-Hill. (11)

McGue, M. (1999). The behavioral genetics of alcoholism. *Current Directions in Psychological Science, 8,* 109–115. (16)

McGue, M., & Bouchard, T. J., Jr. (1998). Genetic and environmental influences on human behavioral differences. *Annual Review of Neuroscience, 21,* 1–24. (9)

McGuffin, P., Rijsdijk, F., Andrew, M., Sham, P., Katz, R., & Cardno, A. (2003). The heritability of bipolar affective disorder and the genetic relationship to unipolar disorder. *Archives of General Psychiatry, 60,* 497–502. (16)

McGuire, S., & Clifford, J. (2000). Genetic and environmental contributions to loneliness in children. *Psychological Science, 11,* 487–491. (10)

McGuire, S., Clifford, J., Fink, J., Basho, S., & McDonnell, A. (2003). Children's reactions to the unfamiliar in middle childhood and adolescence: An observational twin/sibling study. *Personality and Individual Differences, 35,* 339–354. (10)

McGuire, W. J., & Papageorgis, D. (1961). The relative efficacy of various types of prior belief-defense in producing immunity against persuasion. *Journal of Abnormal and Social Psychology, 62,* 327–337. (14)

McGurk, H., Caplan, M., Hennessy, E., & Moss, P. (1993). Controversy, theory, and social context in contemporary day care research. *Journal of Child Psychology, 34,* 3–23. (10)

McGurk, H., & MacDonald, J. (1976). Hearing lips and seeing voices. *Nature, 264,* 746–748. (8)

McMurtry, P. L., & Mershon, D. H. (1985). Auditory distance judgments in noise, with and without hearing protection. *Proceedings of the Human Factors Society* (Baltimore), pp. 811–813. (4)

McNally, R. J. (1990). Psychological approaches to panic disorder: A review. *Psychological Bulletin, 108,* 403–419. (16)

McNally, R. J. (2002). Anxiety sensitivity and panic disorder. *Biological Psychiatry, 52,* 938–946. (16)

McNally, R. J., Bryant, R. A., & Ehlers, A. (2003). Does early psychological intervention promote recovery from posttraumatic stress? *Psychological Science in the Public Interest, 4,* 45–77. (12)

Meddis, R., Pearson, A. J. D., & Langford, G. (1973). An extreme case of healthy insomnia. *EEG and Clinical Neurophysiology, 35,* 213–214. (5)

Mednick, S. C., Nakayama, K., Cantero, J. L., Atienza, M., Levin, A. A., Pathak, N., et al. (2002). The restorative effect of naps on perceptual deterioration. *Nature Neuroscience, 5,* 677–681. (5)

Mednick, S., Nakayama, K., & Stickgold, R. (2003). Sleep-dependent learning: A nap is as good as a night. *Nature Neuroscience, 6,* 697–700. (5)

Meichenbaum, D. (1985). *Stress inoculation training.* New York: Pergamon Press. (12)

Meichenbaum, D., & Cameron, R. (1983). Stress inoculation training. In D. Meichenbaum & M. E. Jaremko (Eds.), *Stress reduction and prevention* (pp. 115–154). New York: Plenum Press. (12)

Meichenbaum, D. H. (1995). Cognitive-behavioral therapy in historical perspective. In B. Bongar & L. E. Beutler (Eds.), *Comprehensive textbook of psychotherapy: Theory and practice* (pp. 140–158). Oxford, England: Oxford University Press. (15)

Mellers, B. A., Schwartz, A., Ho, K., & Ritov, I. (1997). Decision affect theory: Emotional reactions to the outcomes of risky options. *Psychological Science, 8,* 423–429. (8)

Mello, N. K., & Mendelson, J. H. (1978). Behavioral pharmacology of human alcohol, heroin and marihuana use. In J. Fishman (Ed.), *The bases of addiction* (pp. 133–158). Berlin, Germany: Dahlem Konferenzen. (5)

Melzack, R., & Wall, P. D. (1965). Pain mechanisms: A new theory. *Science, 150,* 971–979. (4)

Melzack, R., Weisz, A. Z., & Sprague, L. T. (1963). Stratagems for controlling pain: Contributions of auditory stimulation and suggestion. *Experimental Neurology, 8,* 239–247. (12)

Merckelbach, H, Dekkers, T., Wessel, I., & Roefs, A. (2003). Dissociative symptoms and amnesia in Dutch concentration camp survivors. *Comprehensive Psychiatry, 44,* 65–69. (7)

Mershon, D. H., Desaulniers, D. H., Kiefer, S. A., Amerson, T. L., Jr., & Mills, J. T. (1981). Perceived loudness and visually determined auditory distance. *Perception, 10,* 531–543. (4)

Mershon, D. H., & King, L. E. (1975). Intensity and reverberation as factors in the auditory perception of egocentric distance. *Perception & Psychophysics, 18,* 409–415. (4)

Mesmer, F. A. (1980). *Mesmerism: A translation of the original medical and scientific writings of F. A. Mesmer.* Los Altos, CA: Kaufmann. (5)

Messer, S. B., & Wampold, B. E. (2002). Let's face facts: Common factors are more potent than specific therapy ingredients. *Clinical Psychology: Science and Practice, 9,* 21–25. (16)

Messick, S. (1995). Validity of psychological assessment. *American Psychologist, 50,* 741–749. (9)

Messinger, D. S. (2002). Positive and negative: Infant facial expressions and emotions. *Current Directions in Psychological Science, 11,* 1–6. (12)

Metcalfe, J., & Wiebe, D. (1987). Intuition in insight and noninsight problem solving. *Memory & Cognition, 15,* 238–246. (8)

Meyer, I. H. (2003). Prejudice, social stress, and mental health in lesbian, gay, and bisexual populations: Conceptual issues and research evidence. *Psychological Bulletin, 129,* 674–697. (11)

Meyerowitz, B. E., Richardson, J., Hudson, S., & Leedham, B. (1998). Ethnicity and cancer outcomes: Behavioral and psychosocial considerations. *Psychological Bulletin, 123,* 47–70. (12)

Mezzanotte, W. S., Tangel, D. J., & White, D. P. (1992). Waking genioglossal electromyogram in sleep apnea patients versus normal controls (a neuromuscular compensatory mechanism). *Journal of Clinical Investigation, 89,* 1571–1579. (5)

Michener, W., Rozin, P., Freeman, E., & Gale, L. (1999). The role of low progesterone and tension as triggers of perimenstrual chocolate and sweets cravings: Some negative experimental evidence. *Physiology & Behavior, 67,* 417–420. (11)

Mikulincer, M., Shaver, P. R., & Pereg, D. (2003). Attachment theory and affect regulation: The dynamics, development, and cognitive consequences of attachment-related strategies. *Motivation and Emotion, 27,* 77–102. (10)

Milar, K. S. (2000). The first generation of women psychologists and the psychology of women. *American Psychologist, 55,* 616–619. (1)

Milgram, S. (1974). *Obedience to authority.* New York: Harper & Row. (14)

Milich, R., Wolraich, M., & Lindgren, S. (1986). Sugar and hyperactivity: A critical review of empirical findings. *Clinical Psychology Review, 6,* 493–513. (2)

Miller, C. T., Dibble, E., & Hauser, M. D. (2001). Amodal completion of acoustic signals by a nonhuman primate. *Nature Neuroscience, 4,* 783–784. (4)

Miller, D. T., & Ross, M. (1975). Self-serving biases in the attribution of causality: Fact or fiction? *Psychological Bulletin, 82,* 213–225. (14)

Miller, G. A. (1956). The magical number seven, plus or minus two: Some limits on our capacity for processing information. *Psychological Review, 63,* 81–97. (7)

Miller, L. C., & Fishkin, S. A. (1997). On the dynamics of human bonding and reproductive success: Seeking windows on the adapted-for human-environmental interface. In J. A. Simpson & D. T. Kenrick (Eds.), *Evolutionary social psychology* (pp. 197–235). Mahwah, NJ: Erlbaum. (2)

Miller, R. J., Hennessy, R. T., & Leibowitz, H. W. (1973). The effect of hypnotic ablation of the background on the magnitude of the Ponzo perspective illusion. *International Journal of Clinical and Experimental Hypnosis, 21,* 180–191. (5)

Miller, S. M., Shoda, Y., & Hurley, K. (1996). Applying cognitive-social theory to health-protective behavior: Breast self-examination in cancer screening. *Psychological Bulletin, 119,* 70–94. (12)

Miller, W. R., & Brown, S. A. (1997). Why psychologists should treat alcohol and drug problems. *American Psychologist, 52,* 1269–1279. (16)

Miller, W. R., & Hester, R. K. (1986). Inpatient alcohol treatment: Who benefits? *American Psychologist, 41,* 794–805. (16)

Milner, B. (1959). The memory defect in bilateral hippocampal lesions. *Psychiatric Research Reports, 11,* 43–52. (7)

Milton, J., & Wiseman, R. (1999). Does psi exist? Lack of replication of an anomalous process of information. *Psychological Bulletin, 125,* 387–391. (2)

Mineka, S. (1987). A primate model of phobic fears. In H. Eysenck & I. Martin (Eds.), *Theoretical foundations of behav-*

ior therapy (pp. 81–111). New York: Plenum Press. (16)

Mineka, S., Davidson, M., Cook, M., & Keir, R. (1984). Observational conditioning of snake fear in rhesus monkeys. *Journal of Abnormal Psychology, 93,* 355–372. (16)

Mischel, W. (1973). Toward a cognitive social learning reconceptualization of personality. *Psychological Review, 80,* 252–283. (13)

Mischel, W. (1981). Current issues and challenges in personality. In L. T. Benjamin, Jr. (Ed.), *The G. Stanley Hall Lecture Series* (Vol. 1, pp. 81–99). Washington, DC: American Psychological Association. (13)

Mischel, W., & Shoda, Y. (1995). A cognitive-affective system theory of personality: Reconceptualizing situations, dispositions, dynamics, and invariance in personality structure. *Psychological Review, 102,* 246–268. (13)

Misrahi, M., Meduri, G., Pissard, S., Bouvattier, C., Beau, I., Loosfelt, H., et al. (1997). Comparison of immunocytochemical and molecular features with the phenotype in a case of incomplete male pseudohermaphroditism associated with a mutation of the luteinizing hormone receptor. *Journal of Clinical Endocrinology and Metabolism, 82,* 2159–2165. (11)

Mokros, A., & Alison, L. J. (2002). Is offender profiling possible? Testing the predicted homology of crime scene actions and background characteristics in a sample of rapists. *Legal and Criminological Psychology, 7,* 25–43. (13)

Moller, H. J. (1992). Attempted suicide: Efficacy of different aftercare strategies. *International Clinical Psychopharmacology, 6*(Suppl. 6), 58–59. (15)

Monahan, J. (1993). Limiting therapist exposure to *Tarasoff* liability: Guidelines for risk containment. *American Psychologist, 48,* 242–250. (15)

Monahan, J., & Steadman, H. J. (1996). Violent storms and violent people. *American Psychologist, 51,* 931–938. (12)

Money, J., & Ehrhardt, A. A. (1972). *Man and woman, boy and girl.* Baltimore, MD: Johns Hopkins University Press. (11)

Montgomery, G., & Kirsch, I. (1996). Mechanisms of placebo pain reduction: An empirical investigation. *Psychological Science, 7,* 174–176. (4)

Monti-Bloch, L., Jennings-White, C., Dolberg, D. S., & Berliner, D. L. (1994). The human vomeronasal system. *Psychoneuroendocrinology, 19,* 673–686. (4)

Moorcroft, W. (1993). *Sleep, dreaming, and sleep disorders: An introduction* (2nd ed.). Lanham, MD: University Press of America. (5)

Moorcroft, W. H. (2003). *Understanding sleep and dreaming.* New York: Kluwer. (5)

Moore, B. C. J. (1989). *An introduction to the psychology of hearing* (3rd ed.). London: Academic Press. (4)

Moore, J. (1995). Some historical and conceptual relations among logical positivism, behaviorism, and cognitive psychology. In J. T. Todd & E. K. Morris (Eds.), *Modern perspectives on B. F. Skinner and contemporary behaviorism* (pp. 51–74). Westport, CT: Greenwood Press. (6)

Moore, L. B., Goodwin, B., Jones, S. A., Wisely, G. B., Serabjit-Singh, C. J., Willson, T. M., et al. (2000). St. John's wort induces hepatic drug metabolism through activation of the pregnane X receptor. *Proceedings of the National Academy of Sciences, USA, 97,* 7500–7502. (16)

Morakinyo, O., & Peltzer, K. (2002). "Brain fag" symptoms in apprentices in Nigeria. *Psychopathology, 35,* 362–366. (15)

Morley, K. I., & Montgomery, G. W. (2001). The genetics of cognitive processes: Candidate genes in humans and animals. *Behavior Genetics, 31,* 511–531. (9)

Morrow, R. S., & Morrow, S. (1974). The measurement of intelligence. In B. B. Wolman (Ed.), *Handbook of general psychology* (pp. 656–670). Upper Saddle River, NJ: Prentice Hall. (9)

Moscovitch, M. (1985). Memory from infancy to old age: Implications for theories of normal and pathological memory. *Annals of the New York Academy of Sciences, 444,* 78–96. (7)

Moscovitch, M. (1989). Confabulation and the frontal systems: Strategic versus associative retrieval in neuropsychological theories of memory. In H. L. Roediger, III, & F. I. M. Craik (Eds.), *Varieties of memory and consciousness: Essays in honour of Endel Tulving* (pp. 133–160). Hillsdale, NJ: Erlbaum. (7)

Moscovitch, M. (1992). Memory and working-with-memory: A component process model based on modules and central systems. *Journal of Cognitive Neuroscience, 4,* 257–267. (7)

Moskowitz, B. A. (1978). The acquisition of language. *Scientific American, 239*(5), 92–108. (8)

Müller, M. M., Malinowski, P., Gruber, T., & Hillyard, S. A. (2003). Sustained division of the attentional spotlight. *Nature, 424,* 309–312. (8)

Munakata, Y., McClelland, J. L., Johnson, M. H., & Siegler, R. S. (1997). Rethinking infant knowledge: Toward an adaptive process account of successes and failures in object permanence tasks. *Psychological Review, 104,* 686–713. (10)

Munroe, R. (1955). *Schools of psychoanalytic thought.* New York: Dryden Press. (15)

Muraven, M., & Baumeister, R. F. (2000). Self-regulation and depletion of limited resources: Does self-control resemble a muscle? *Psychological Bulletin, 126,* 247–259. (12)

Murphy, G. L., & Medin, D. L. (1985). The role of theories in conceptual coherence. *Psychological Review, 92,* 289–316. (8)

Murphy, J. M., Laird, N. M., Monson, R. R., Sobol, A. M., & Leighton, A. H. (2000). A 40-year perspective on the prevalence of depression. *Archives of General Psychiatry, 57,* 209–215. (16)

Murray, H. A. (1943). *Thematic Apperception Test manual.* Cambridge, MA: Harvard University Press. (13)

Murray, J. P. (1998). Studying television violence. A research agenda for the 21st century. In J. K. Asamen & G. L. Berry (Eds.), *Research paradigms, television, and social behavior* (pp. 369–410). Thousand Oaks, CA: Sage. (2)

Murrell, J., Farlow, M., Ghetti, B., & Benson, M. D. (1991). A mutation in the amyloid precursor protein associated with hereditary Alzheimer's disease. *Science, 254,* 97–99. (7)

Musso, M., Moro, A., Glaucho, V., Rijntjes, M., Reichenbach, J., Büchel, C., et al. (2003). Broca's area and the language instinct. *Nature Neuroscience, 6,* 774–781. (8)

Myers, D. G. (2000). The funds, friends, and faith of happy people. *American Psychologist, 55,* 56–67. (12)

Myers, J. K., Weissman, M. M., Tischler, G. L., Holzer, C. E., III, Leaf, P. J., Orvaschel, H., et al. (1984). Six-month prevalence of psychiatric disorders in three communities. *Archives of General Psychiatry, 41,* 959–967. (15)

Nachson, I., & Zelig, A. (2003). Flashbulb and factual memories: The case of Rabin's assassination. *Applied Cognitive Psychology, 17,* 59–531. (7)

Nadig, A. S., & Sedivy, J. C. (2002). Evidence of perspective-taking constraints in children's on-line reference resolution. *Psychological Science, 13,* 329–336. (10)

Nagera, H. (1976). *Obsessional neuroses.* New York: Aronson. (16)

Nantais, K. M., & Schellenberg, E. G. (1999). The Mozart effect: An artifact of preference. *Psychological Science, 10,* 370–373. (2)

Narrow, W. E., Rae, D. S., Robins, L. N., & Regier, D. A. (2002). Revised prevalence estimates of mental disorders in the United States. *Archives of General Psychiatry, 59,* 115–123. (15, 16)

Nash, M. (1987). What, if anything, is regressed about hypnotic age regression? A review of the empirical literature. *Psychological Bulletin, 102,* 42–52. (5)

Nash, M. R., Johnson, L. S., & Tipton, R. D. (1979). Hypnotic age regression and the occurrence of transitional object relationships. *Journal of Abnormal Psychology, 88,* 547–555. (5)

National Institutes of Health. (2000). *The practical guide: Identification, evaluation, and treatment of overweight and obesity in adults* (NIH Publication No. 00-4084). Washington, DC: Author. (11)

Nebes, R. D. (1974). Hemispheric specialization in commissurotomized man. *Psychological Bulletin, 81,* 1–14. (3)

Nedjam, Z., Dalla Barba, G., & Pillon, B. (2000). Confabulation in a patient with fronto-temporal dementia and a patient with Alzheimer's disease. *Cortex, 36,* 561–577. (7)

Negy, C., Leal-Puente, L., Trainor, D. J., & Carlson, R. (1997). Mexican American adolescents' performance on the MMPIA. *Journal of Personality Assessment, 69,* 205–214. (13)

Neher, A. (1991). Maslow's theory of motivation: A critique. *Journal of Humanistic Psychology, 31,* 89–112. (13)

Neher, A. (1996). Jung's theory of archetypes: A critique. *Journal of Humanistic Psychology, 36,* 61–91. (13)

Neisser, U. (1997). Rising scores on intelligence tests. *American Scientist, 85,* 440–447. (9)

Neisser, U., Boodoo, G., Bouchard, T. J., Jr., Boykin, A. W., Brody, N., Ceci, S. J., et al. (1996). Intelligence: Knowns and unknowns. *American Psychologist, 51,* 77–101. (9)

Nelson, D. L., & Goodmon, L. B. (2003). Disrupting attention: The need for retrieval cues in working memory theories. *Memory & Cognition, 31,* 65–76. (7)

Nelson, E. C., Heath, A. C., Madden, P. A. F., Cooper, L., Dinwiddie, S. H., Bucholz, K. K., et al. (2002). Association between self-reported childhood sexual abuse and adverse psychosocial outcomes: Results from a twin study. *Archives of General Psychiatry, 59,* 139–145. (16)

Nelson, T. O., & Leonesio, R. J. (1988). Allocation of self-paced study time and the "labor-in-vain effect." *Journal of Experimental Psychology: Learning, Memory, and Cognition, 14,* 676–686. (7)

Nemeth, C. (1972). A critical analysis of research utilizing the prisoner's dilemma paradigm for the study of bargaining. In L. Berkowitz (Ed.), *Advances in experimental social psychology* (Vol. 6, pp. 203–234). New York: Academic Press. (14)

Nemeth, C. J. (1986). Differential contributions of majority and minority influence. *Psychological Review, 93,* 23–32. (14)

Newman, B. (1988, September 9). Dressing for dinner remains an issue in the naked city. *The Wall Street Journal,* p. 1. (14)

Newstead, S. E., & Makinen, S. (1997). Psychology teaching in Europe. *European Psychologist, 2,* 3–10. (1)

Nickerson, C., Schwarz, N., Diener, E., & Kahneman, D. (2003). Zeroing in on the dark side of the American Dream: A closer look at the negative consequences of the goal for financial success. *Psychological Science, 14,* 531–536. (12)

Nickerson, R. S., & Adams, M. J. (1979). Long-term memory for a common object. *Cognitive Psychology, 11,* 287–307. (7)

Nikles, C. D., II, Brecht, D. L., Klinger, E., & Bursell, A. L. (1998). The effects of current-concern and nonconcern-related waking suggestions on nocturnal dream content. *Journal of Personality and Social Psychology, 75,* 242–255. (5)

Nisbett, R. E., Caputo, C., Legant, P., & Marecek, J. (1973). Behavior as seen by the actor and as seen by the observer. *Journal of Personality and Social Psychology, 27,* 154–164. (14)

Nisbett, R. E., Peng, K., Choi, I., & Norenzayan, A. (2001). Culture and systems of thought: Holistic versus analytic cognition. *Psychological Review, 108,* 291–310. (1, 14)

Noble, E. P., Ozkaragoz, T. Z., Ritchie, T. L., Zhang, X., Belin, T. R., & Sparkes, R. S. (1998). D2 and D4 dopamine receptor polymorphisms and personality. *American Journal of Medical Genetics, 81,* 257–267. (13)

Noel, J. G., Wann, D. L., & Branscombe, N. R. (1995). Peripheral ingroup membership status and public negativity toward outgroups. *Journal of Personality and Social Psychology, 68,* 127–137. (14)

Nolen-Hoeksema, S. (1990). *Sex differences in depression.* Stanford, CA: Stanford University Press. (16)

Nolen-Hoeksema, S. (1991). Responses to depression and their effects on the duration of depressive episodes. *Journal of Abnormal Psychology, 100,* 569–582. (16)

Nolen-Hoeksema, S., & Morrow, J. (1991). A prospective study of depression and post-traumatic stress symptoms after a natural disaster: The Loma Prieta earthquake. *Journal of Personality and Social Psychology, 61,* 115–121. (16)

Nopoulos, P. C., Giedd, J. N., Andreasen, N. C., & Rapoport, J. L. (1998). Frequency and severity of enlarged cavum septi pellucidi in childhood-onset schizophrenia. *American Journal of Psychiatry, 155,* 1074–1079. (16)

Norman, D. A. (1988). *The psychology of everyday things.* New York: Basic Books. (1)

Norman, R. A., Tataranni, P. A., Pratley, R., Thompson, D. B., Hanson, R. L., Prochazka, M., et al. (1998). Autosomal genomic scan for loci linked to obesity and energy metabolism in Pima Indians. *American Journal of Human Genetics, 62,* 659–668. (11)

North, R. A. (1992). Cellular actions of opiates and cocaine. *Annals of the New York Academy of Sciences, 654,* 1–6. (5)

Nosek, B. A., Banaji, M. R., & Greenwald, A. G. (2002). Harvesting implicit group attitudes and beliefs from a demonstration Web site. *Group Dynamics: Theory, Research, and Practice, 6,* 101–115. (14)

Oberauer, K., Süss, H.-M., Wilhelm, O., & Wittman, W. W. (2003). The multiple faces of working memory. *Intelligence, 31,* 167–193. (7)

O'Connor, T. G., Marvin, R. S., Rutter, M., Olrick, J. T., Britner, P. A., & the English and Romanian adoptees study team. (2003). Child-parent attachment following early institutional deprivation. *Development and Psychopathology, 15,* 19–38. (10)

Odell, S. M., & Commander, M. J. (2000). Risk factors for homelessness among people with psychotic disorders. *Social Psychiatry and Psychiatric Epidemiology, 35,* 396–401. (15)

O'Donohue, W., & Kitchener, R. F. (1999). Introduction: The behaviorisms. In W. O'Donohue & R. Kitchener (Eds.), *Handbook of behaviorism* (pp. 1–13). San Diego, CA: Academic Press. (6)

Ogdie, M. N., Macphie, I. L., Minassian, S. L., Yang, M., Fisher, S. E., Francks, C., et al. (2003). A genomewide scan for attention-deficit/hyperactivity disorder in an extended sample: Suggestive linkage on 17p11. *American Journal of Human Genetics, 72,* 1268–1279. (13)

Ohaeri, J. U., Adeyinka, A. O., & Osuntokun, B. O. (1995). Computed tomographic density changes in schizophrenic and manic Nigerian subjects. *Behavioural Neurology, 8,* 31–37. (16)

Ohayon, M. M. (1997). Prevalence of *DSM-IV* diagnostic criteria of insomnia: Distinguishing insomnia related to mental disorders from sleep disorders. *Journal of Psychiatric Research, 31,* 333–346. (5)

Öhman, A., Eriksson, A., & Olofsson, C. (1975). One-trial learning and superior resistance to extinction of autonomic responses conditioned to potentially phobic objects. *Journal of Comparative and Physiological Psychology, 88,* 619–627. (16)

Öhman, A., & Mineka, S. (2003). The malicious serpent: Snakes as a prototypical stimulus for an evolved module of fear. *Current Directions in Psychological Science, 12,* 5–9. (16)

Okasha, M., McCarron, P., McEwen, J., & Smith, G. D. (2001). Age at menarche: Secular trends and association with adult anthropometric measures. *Annals of Human Biology, 28,* 68–78. (10)

Olausson, H., Lamarre, Y., Backlund, H., Morin, C., Wallin, B. G., Starck, G., et al. (2002). Unmyelinated tactile afferents signal touch and project to insular cortex. *Nature Neuroscience, 5,* 900–904. (4)

Olfson, M., Marcus, S. C., Pincus, H. A., Zito, J. M., Thompson, J. W., & Zarin, D. A. (1998). Antidepressant prescribing practices of outpatient psychiatrists. *Archives of General Psychiatry, 55,* 310–316. (16)

Oliver, M. B., & Hyde, J. S. (1993). Gender differences in sexuality: A meta-analysis. *Psychological Bulletin, 114,* 29–51. (11)

Olney, J. W., & Farger, N. B. (1995). Glutamate receptor dysfunction and schizophrenia. *Archives of General Psychiatry, 52,* 998–1007. (16)

Olson, M. A., & Fazio, R. H. (2001). Implicit attitude formation through classical conditioning. *Psychological Science, 12,* 413–417. (6)

Olson, M. A., & Fazio, R. H. (2003). Relations between implicit measures of prejudice: What are we measuring? *Psychological Science, 14,* 636–639. (14)

Orne, M. T. (1951). The mechanisms of hypnotic age regression: An experimental study. *Journal of Abnormal and Social Psychology, 46,* 213–225. (5)

Orne, M. T. (1959). The nature of hypnosis: Artifact and essence. *Journal of Abnormal and Social Psychology, 58,* 277–299. (5)

Orne, M. T. (1969). Demand characteristics and the concept of quasi-controls. In R. Rosenthal & R. L. Rosnow (Eds.), *Artifact in behavioral research* (pp. 143–179). New York: Academic Press. (2)

Orne, M. T. (1979). On the simulating subject as a quasi-control group in hypnosis research: What, why, and how. In E. Fromm & R. E. Shor (Eds.), *Hypnosis: Developments in research and new perspectives* (2nd ed., pp. 519–565). New York: Aldine. (5)

Orne, M. T., & Evans, F. J. (1965). Social control in the psychological experiment: Antisocial behavior and hypnosis. *Journal of Personality and Social Psychology, 1,* 189–200. (5)

Orne, M. T., & Scheibe, K. E. (1964). The contribution of nondeprivation factors in the production of sensory deprivation effects: The psychology of the "panic button." *Journal of Abnormal and Social Psychology, 68,* 3–12. (2)

Ornstein, P. A., Ceci, S. J., & Loftus, E. F. (1998). Adult recollections of childhood abuse. *Psychology, Public Policy, and Law, 4,* 1025–1051. (7)

Ornstein, P. A., Merritt, K. A., Baker-Ward, L., Furtado, E., Gordon, B., & Principe, G. (1998). Children's knowledge, expectation, and long-term retention. *Applied Cognitive Psychology, 12,* 387–405. (7)

Ortony, A., & Turner, T. J. (1990). What's basic about basic emotions? *Psychological Review, 97,* 315–331. (12)

Ösby, U., Hammar, N., Brandt, L., Wicks, S., Thinsz, Z., Ekbom, A., et al. (2001). Time trends in first admissions for schizophrenia and paranoid psychosis in Stockholm county, Sweden. *Schizophrenia Research, 47,* 247–254. (16)

Osofsky, J. D. (1995). The effects of exposure to violence on young children. *American Psychologist, 50,* 782–788. (12)

Öst, L.-G., & Breitholtz, E. (2000). Applied relaxation vs. cognitive therapy in the treatment of generalized anxiety disorder. *Behaviour Research and Therapy, 38,* 777–790. (16)

Öst, L.-G., & Hugdahl, K. (1981). Acquisition of phobias and anxiety response patterns in clinical patients. *Behaviour Research and Therapy, 19,* 439–447. (16)

Östling, S., & Skoog, J. (2002). Psychotic symptoms and paranoid ideation in a nondemented population-based sample of the very old. *Archives of General Psychiatry, 59,* 53–59. (16)

O'Toole, B. I. (1990). Intelligence and behaviour and motor vehicle accident mortality. *Accident Analysis and Prevention, 22,* 211–221. (9)

Ottati, V., & Lee, Y. T. (1995). Accuracy: A neglected component of stereotype research. In Y. T. Lee, L. J. Jussim, & C. R. McCauley (Eds.), *Stereotype accuracy* (pp. 29–59). Washington, DC: American Psychological Association. (14)

Otto, R. K., & Heilbrun, K. (2002). The practice of forensic psychology. *American Psychologist, 57,* 5–18. (1)

Oyserman, D., Coon, H. M., & Kemmelmeier, M. (2002). Rethinking individualism and collectivism: Evaluation of theoretical assumptions and meta-analyses. *Psychological Bulletin, 128,* 3–72. (14)

Padgham, C. A. (1975). Colours experienced in dreams. *British Journal of Psychology, 66,* 25–28. (5)

Paladini, C. A., Fiorillo, C. D., Morikawa, H., & Williams, J. T. (2001). Amphetamine selectively blocks inhibitory glutamate transmission in dopamine neurons. *Nature Neuroscience, 4,* 275–281. (5)

Palinkas, L. A. (2003). The psychology of isolated and confined environments. *American Psychologist, 58,* 353–363. (5, 16)

Palmer, B. W., Heaton, R. K., Paulsen, J. S., Kuck, J., Braff, D., Harris, M. J., et al. (1997). Is it possible to be schizophrenic yet neuropsychologically normal? *Neuropsychology, 11,* 437–446. (16)

Panikashvili, D., Simeonidou, C., Ben-Shabat, S., Hanuš, L. Breuer, A., Mechoulam, R., et al. (2001). An endogenous cannabinoid (2-AG) is neuroprotective after brain injury. *Nature, 413,* 527–531. (5)

Panksepp, J. (1998). Attention deficit hyperactivity disorders, psychostimulants, and intolerance of childhood playfulness: A tragedy in the making? *Current Directions in Psychological Science, 7,* 91–98. (15)

Papini, M. R. (2002). Pattern and process in the evolution of learning. *Psychological Review, 109,* 186–201. (1)

Paradis, M. (1990). Language lateralization in bilinguals: Enough already! *Brain and Language, 39,* 576–586. (8)

Parent, M. B., Habib, M. K., & Baker, G. B. (1999). Task-dependent effects of the antidepressant/antipanic drug phenelzine on memory. *Psychopharmacology, 142,* 280–288. (5)

Parish, A. R., & deWaal, F. B. M. (2000). The other "closest living relative." *Annals of the New York Academy of Sciences, 907,* 97–113. (14)

Park, J., & Banaji, M. R. (2000). Mood and heuristics: The influence of happy and sad states on sensitivity and bias in stereotyping. *Journal of Personality and Social Psychology, 78,* 1005–1023. (12)

Parke, R. D. (1995). Fathers and families. In M. H. Bornstein (Ed.), *Handbook of parenting* (Vol. 3, pp. 27–63). Mahwah, NJ: Erlbaum. (10)

Parke, R. D., Berkowitz, L., Leyens, J. P., West, S. G., & Sebastian, R. J. (1977). Some effects of violent and nonviolent movies on the behavior of juvenile delinquents. In L. Berkowitz (Ed.), *Advances in experimental social psychology* (Vol. 10, pp. 135–172). New York: Academic Press. (2)

Parker, D. (1944). *The portable Dorothy Parker.* New York: Viking Press. (15)

Parmeggiani, P. L. (1982). Regulation of physiological functions during sleep in mammals. *Experientia, 38,* 1405–1408. (5)

Parnas, J., Schulsinger, F., Schulsinger, H., Mednick, S. A., & Teasdale, T. W. (1982). Behavioral precursors of schizophrenia spectrum. *Archives of General Psychiatry, 39,* 658–664. (16)

Parrott, A. C. (1999). Does cigarette smoking cause stress? *American Psychologist, 54,* 817–820. (5)

Pascual-Leone, A., Wasserman, E. M., Sadato, N., & Hallett, M. (1995). The role of reading activity on the modulation of motor control outputs to the reading hand in Braille readers. *Annals of Neurology, 38,* 910–915. (3)

Pashler, H. (1994). Dual-task interference in simple tasks: Data and theory. *Psychological Bulletin, 116,* 220–244. (8)

Pashler, H., & Harris, C. R. (2001). Spontaneous allocation of visual attention: Dominant role of uniqueness. *Psychonomic Bulletin & Review, 8,* 747–752. (8)

Pate, J. L., & Rumbaugh, D. M. (1983). The language-like behavior of Lana chimpanzee: Is it merely discrimination and paired-associate learning? *Animal Learning & Behavior, 11,* 134–138. (8)

Patel, A. D. (2003). Language, music, syntax and the brain. *Nature Neuroscience, 6,* 674–681. (8)

Patterson, C. J. (1994). Lesbian and gay families. *Current Directions in Psychological Science, 3,* 62–64. (10)

Patterson, D. R., & Jensen, M. P. (2003). Hypnosis and clinical pain. *Psychological Bulletin, 129,* 495–521. (5)

Paulhus, D. L., Trapnell, P. D., & Chen, D. (1999). Birth order effects on personality and achievement within families. *Psychological Science, 10,* 482–488. (10)

Paunonen, S. V., & Jackson, D. N. (2000). What is beyond the big five? Plenty! *Journal of Personality, 68,* 821–835. (13)

Paunonen, S. V., Zeidner, M., Engvik, H. A., Oosterveld, P., & Maliphant, R. (2000). The nonverbal assessment of personality in five cultures. *Journal of Cross-Cultural Psychology, 31,* 220–239. (13)

Paus, T., Marrett, S., Worsley, K. J., & Evans, A. C. (1995). Extraretinal modulation of cerebral blood flow in the human visual cortex: Implications for saccadic suppression. *Journal of Neurophysiology, 74,* 2179–2183. (8)

Pavlidis, I., Eberhardt, N. I., & Levine, J. A. (2002). Seeing through the face of deception. *Nature, 415,* 35. (12)

Pavlov, I. P. (1960). *Conditioned reflexes.* New York: Dover. (Original work published 1927) (6)

Pavot, W., & Diener, E. (1993). Review of the satisfaction with life scale. *Psychological Assessment, 5,* 164–172. (12)

Pearce, J. M. (1994). Similarity and discrimination: A selective review and a connectionist model. *Psychological Review, 101,* 587–607. (6)

Pearl, P. L., Weiss, R. E., & Stein, M. A. (2001). Medical mimics. *Annals of the New York Academy of Sciences, 931,* 97–112. (15)

Pearlson, G. D., Petty, R. G., Ross, C. A., & Tien, A. Y. (1996). Schizophrenia—a disease of heteromodal association cortex. *Neuropsychopharmacology, 14,* 1–17. (16)

Peele, S. (1998, March/April). All wet. *The Sciences, 38*(2), 17–21. (16)

Penfield, W., & Rasmussen, T. (1950). *The cerebral cortex of man.* New York: Macmillan. (3)

Peng, K., & Nisbett, R. E. (1999). Culture dialectics, and reasoning about contradiction. *American Psychologist, 54,* 741–754. (14)

Pennebaker, J. W., & Seagal, J. D. (1999). Forming a story: The health benefits of narrative. *Journal of Clinical Psychology, 55,* 1243–1254. (15)

Peplau, L. A. (2003). Human sexuality: How do men and women differ? *Current Directions in Psychological Science, 12,* 37–40. (11)

Peretz, I., Ayotte, J., Zatorre, R. J., Mehler, J., Ahad, P., Penhune, V. B., et al. (2002). Congenital amusia: A disorder of fine-grained pitch discrimination. *Neuron, 33,* 185–191. (4)

Perez, E. A. (1995). Review of the preclinical pharmacology and comparative efficacy of 5-hydroxytryptamine-3 receptor antagonists for chemotherapy-induced emesis. *Journal of Clinical Oncology, 13,* 1036–1043. (3)

Perna, G., Bertani, A., Politi, E., Colombo, G., & Bellodi, L. (1997). Asthma and panic attacks. *Biological Psychiatry, 42,* 625–630. (16)

Perry, D. G., & Bussey, K. (1979). The social learning theory of sex differences: Imitation is alive and well. *Journal of Personality and Social Psychology, 37,* 1699–1712. (13)

Pert, C. B., & Snyder, S. H. (1973). The opiate receptor: Demonstration in nervous tissue. *Science, 179,* 1011–1014. (4, 5)

Peterson, C., Bettes, B. A., & Seligman, M. E. P. (1985). Depressive symptoms and unprompted causal attributions: Content

analysis. *Behaviour Research and Therapy, 23,* 379–382. (16)

Peterson, L. G., Peterson, M., O'Shanick, G. J., & Swann, A. (1985). Self-inflicted gunshot wounds: Lethality of method versus intent. *American Journal of Psychiatry, 142,* 228–231. (16)

Peterson, L. R., & Peterson, M. J. (1959). Short-term retention of individual verbal items. *Journal of Experimental Psychology, 58,* 193–198. (7)

Petitto, L. A., Holowka, S., Sergio, L. E., & Ostry, D. (2001). Language rhythms in baby hand movements. *Nature, 413,* 35–36. (8)

Petrill, S. A., Luo, D., Thompson, L. A., & Detterman, D. K. (1996). The independent prediction of general intelligence by elementary cognitive tasks: Genetic and environmental influences. *Behavior Genetics, 26,* 135–147. (9)

Petrill, S. A., Plomin, R., Berg, S., Johansson, B., Pedersen, N. L., Ahern, F., et al. (1998). The genetic and environmental relationship between general and specific cognitive abilities in twins age 80 and older. *Psychological Science, 9,* 183–189. (9)

Petty, R. E., & Cacioppo, J. T. (1977). Effects of forewarning of persuasive intent and involvement on cognitive responses and persuasion. *Personality and Social Psychology Bulletin, 5,* 173–176. (14)

Petty, R. E., & Cacioppo, J. T. (1981). *Attitudes and persuasion: Classic and contemporary approaches.* Dubuque, IA: William C. Brown. (14)

Petty, R. E., & Cacioppo, J. T. (1986). *Communication and persuasion: Central and peripheral routes to attitude change.* New York: Springer-Verlag. (14)

Pezze, M. A., Bast, T., & Feldon, J. (2003). Significance of dopamine transmission in the rat medial prefrontal cortex for conditioned fear. *Cerebral Cortex, 13,* 371–380. (6)

Pfungst, O. (1911). *Clever Hans.* New York: Holt. (2)

Phan, K. L., Wager, T., Taylor, S. F., & Liberzon, I. (2002). Functional neuroanatomy of emotion: A meta-analysis of emotion activation studies in PET and fMRI. *NeuroImage, 16,* 331–348. (12)

Phelps, E. A., O'Connor, K. J., Cunningham, W. A., Funayama, E. S., Gatenby, J. C., Gore, J. C., et al. (2000). Performance on indirect measures of race evaluation predicts amygdala activation. *Journal of Cognitive Neuroscience, 12,* 729–738. (14)

Phelps, J. A., Davis, J. O., & Schwartz, K. M. (1997). Nature, nurture, and twin research strategies. *Current Directions in Psychological Science, 6,* 117–121. (10)

Phelps, M. E., & Mazziotta, J. C. (1985). Positron emission tomography: Human brain function and biochemistry. *Science, 228,* 799–809. (1, 3)

Philippot, P., Chapelle, G., & Blairy, S. (2002). Respiratory feedback in the gen-

eration of emotions. *Cognition and Emotion, 16,* 605–627. (12)

Phillips, P. E. M., Stuber, G. D., Heien, M. L. A. V., Wightman, R. M., & Carelli, R. M. (2003). Subsecond dopamine release promotes cocaine seeking. *Nature, 422,* 614–618. (16)

Phillips, R. G., & LeDoux, J. E. (1992). Differential contribution of amygdala and hippocampus to cued and contextual fear conditioning. *Behavioral Neuroscience, 106,* 274–285. (12)

Phillips, R. T., & Alcebo, A. M. (1986). The effects of divorce on Black children and adolescents. *American Journal of Social Psychology, 6,* 69–73. (10)

Piaget, J. (1954). *The construction of reality in the child* (M. Cook, Trans.). New York: Basic Books. (Original work published 1937) (10)

Pich, E. M., Pagliusi, S. R., Tessari, M., Talabot-Ayer, D., van Huijsduijnen, R. H., & Chiamuera, C. (1997). Common neural substrates for the addictive properties of nicotine and cocaine. *Science, 275,* 83–86. (5)

Pichot, P. (1984). Centenary of the birth of Hermann Rorschach. *Journal of Personality Assessment, 48,* 591–596. (13)

Pierri, J. N., Volk, C. L. E., Auh, S., Sampson, A., & Lewis, D. A. (2001). Decreased somal size of deep layer 3 pyramidal neurons in the prefrontal cortex of subjects with schizophrenia. *Archives of General Psychiatry, 58,* 466–473. (16)

Pigliucci, M. (2003, May/June). "Elementary, dear Watson." *Skeptical Inquirer, 27,* 18-19. (2)

Pind, J., Gunnarsdóttir, E. K., & Jóhannesson, H. S. (2003). Raven's standard progressive matrices: New school age norms and a study of the test's validity. *Personality and Individual Differences, 34,* 375–386. (9)

Pinel, J. P. J., Assanand, S., & Lehman, D. R. (2000). Hunger, eating, and ill health. *American Psychologist, 55,* 1105–1116. (11)

Pinker, S. (1994). *The language instinct.* New York: Morrow. (8)

Piolino, P., Desgranges, B., Benali, K., & Eustache, F. (2002). Episodic and semantic remote autobiographical memory in ageing. *Memory, 10,* 239–257. (7)

Piotrowski, C., & Keller, J. W. (1989). Psychological testing in outpatient mental health facilities: A national study. *Professional Psychology: Research and Practice, 20,* 423–425. (13)

Pitschel-Walz, G., Leucht, S., Bäuml, J., Kissling, W., & Engel, R. R. (2001). The effect of family interventions on relapse and rehospitalization in schizophrenia—A meta-analysis. *Schizophrenia Bulletin, 27,* 73–92. (16)

Plaut, D. C., & Booth, J. R. (2000). Individual and developmental differences in semantic priming: Empirical and computational support for a single-mechanism account of lexical priming. *Psychological Review, 107,* 786–823. (8)

Ploghaus, A., Tracey, I., Gati, J. S., Clare, S., Menon, R. S., Matthews, P. M., et al. (1999). Dissociating pain from its anticipation in the human brain. *Science, 284,* 1979–1981. (4)

Plomin, R., Corley, R., DeFries, J. C., & Fulker, D. W. (1990). Individual differences in television viewing in early childhood: Nature as well as nurture. *Psychological Science, 1,* 371–377. (10)

Plomin, R., Fulker, D. W., Corley, R., & DeFries, J. C. (1997). Nature, nurture, and cognitive development from 1 to 16 years: A parent-offspring adoption study. *Psychological Science, 8,* 442–447. (9)

Plomin, R., Hill, L., Craig, I. W., McGuffin, P., Purcell, S., Sham, P., et al. (2001). A genome-wide scan of 1842 DNA markers for allelic associations with general cognitive ability: A five-stage design using DNA pooling and extreme selected groups. *Behavior Genetics, 31,* 497–509. (9)

Plous, S. (1993). *The psychology of judgment and decision making.* Philadelphia: Temple University Press. (8)

Plous, S. (1996). Attitudes toward the use of animals in psychological research and education. *American Psychologist, 51,* 1167–1180. (2)

Plutchik, R., & Ax, A. F. (1967). A critique of "determinants of emotional state" by Schachter and Singer (1962). *Psychophysiology, 4,* 79–82. (12)

Polcin, D. L. (1997). The etiology and diagnosis of alcohol dependence: Differences in the professional literature. *Psychotherapy, 34,* 297–306. (16)

Pole, N., Neylan, T. C., Best, S. R., Orr, S. P., & Marmar, C. R. (2003). Fear-potentiated startle and posttraumatic stress symptoms in urban police officers. *Journal of Traumatic Stress, 16,* 471–479. (12)

Polivy, J., & Herman, C. P. (1985). Dieting and binging: A causal analysis. *American Psychologist, 40,* 193–201. (11)

Polivy, J., & Herman, C. P. (2002). If at first you don't succeed. *American Psychologist, 57,* 677–689. (11)

Pollak, J. M. (1979). Obsessive-compulsive personality: A review. *Psychological Bulletin, 86,* 225–241. (16)

Polya, G. (1957). *How to solve it.* Garden City, NY: Doubleday Anchor. (8)

Pond, S. B., III, & Geyer, P. D. (1991). Differences in the relation between job satisfaction and perceived work alternatives among older and younger blue-collar workers. *Journal of Vocational Behavior, 39,* 251–262. (10)

Poole, D. A., & White, L. T. (1993). Two years later: Effect of question repetition and retention interval on the eyewitness testimony of children and adults. *Developmental Psychology, 29,* 844–853. (7)

Poole, D. A., & White, L. T. (1995). Tell me again and again: Stability and change in the repeated testimonies of children and adults. In M. S. Zaragoza, J. R. Graham, G. C. N. Hall, R. Hirschman, & Y. S. Ben-Porath (Eds.), *Memory and testimony in the child witness* (pp. 24–43). Thousand Oaks, CA: Sage. (7)

Pope, H. G., Jr., Gruber, A. J., Hudson, J. I., Huestis, M. A., & Yurgelun-Todd, D. (2001). Neuropsychological performance in long-term cannabis users. *Archives of General Psychiatry, 58,* 909–915. (5)

Pope, H. G., Jr., Hudson, J. I., Bodkin, J. A., & Oliva, P. (1998). Questionable validity of "dissociative amnesia" in trauma victims. *British Journal of Psychology, 172,* 210–215. (7)

Pope, K. S. (1996). Memory, abuse, and science: Questioning claims about the false memory syndrome epidemic. *American Psychologist, 51,* 957–974. (7)

Popper, K. (1986). Predicting overt behavior versus predicting hidden states. *Behavioral and Brain Sciences, 9,* 254–255. (13)

Porter, S., Birt, A. R., Yuille, J. C., & Lehman, D. R. (2000). Negotiating false memories: Interviewer and rememberer characteristics relate to memory distortion. *Psychological Science, 11,* 507–510. (7)

Posthuma, D., Neale, M. C., Boomsma, D. I., & de Geus, E. J. C. (2001). Are smarter brains running faster? Heritability of alpha peak frequency, IQ, and their interrelation. *Behavior Genetics, 31,* 567–597. (9)

Poulin, F., Dishion, T. J., & Burraston, B. (2001). 3-year iatrogenic effects associated with aggregating high-risk adolescents in cognitive-behavioral preventive interventions. *Applied Developmental Science, 5,* 214–224. (15)

Povinelli, D. J., & deBlois, S. (1992). Young children's *(Homo sapiens)* understanding of knowledge formation in themselves and others. *Journal of Comparative Psychology, 106,* 228–238. (10)

Powell, R. A., & Boer, D. P. (1994). Did Freud mislead patients to confabulate memories of abuse? *Psychological Reports, 74,* 1283–1298. (13)

Powlishta, K. K., & Maccoby, E. E. (1990). Resource utilization in mixed-sex dyads: The influence of adult presence and task type. *Sex Roles, 23,* 223–240. (10)

Pratkanis, A. R., Greenwald, A. G., Leippe, M. R., & Baumgardner, M. H. (1988). In search of reliable persuasion effects: III. The sleeper effect is dead. Long live the sleeper effect. *Journal of Personality and Social Psychology, 54,* 203–218. (14)

Premack, D. (1965). Reinforcement theory. In D. Levine (Ed.), *Nebraska Symposium on Motivation* (pp. 123–188). Lincoln: University of Nebraska Press. (6)

Prentice, D. A., & Miller, D. T. (2002). The emergence of homegrown stereotypes. *American Psychologist, 57,* 352–359. (14)

Proctor, R. W., & Capaldi, E. J. (2001). Empirical evaluation and justification of methodologies in psychological science. *Psychological Bulletin, 127,* 759–772. (2)

Proffitt, J. B., Coley, J. D., & Medin, D. L. (2000). Expertise and category-based induction. *Journal of Experimental Psychology: Learning, Memory, and Cognition, 26,* 811–828. (8)

Provine, R. (2000). *Laughter.* New York: Viking Press. (2, 12)

Prutkin, J., Duffy, V. B., Etter, L., Fast, K., Gardner, E., Lucchina, L. A., et al. (2000). Genetic variation and inferences about perceived taste intensity in mice and men. *Physiology & Behavior, 69,* 161–173. (4)

Public Agenda. (2001). *Medical research: Red flags.* Downloaded from this Web site: www.publicagenda.org/issues/red_flags_detail.cfm?issue_type=medical_research&list=5&area=1 (2)

Purves, D., & Lotto, R. B. (2003). *Why we see what we do: An empirical theory of vision.* Sunderland, MA: Sinauer Associates. (4)

Pyne, J. M., Bean, D., & Sullivan, G. (2001). Characteristics of patients with schizophrenia who do not believe they are mentally ill. *Journal of Nervous and Mental Disease, 189,* 146–153. (15)

Pyszczynski, T., Greenberg, J., & Solomon, S. (2000). Proximal and distal defense: A new perspective on unconscious motivation. *Current Directions in Psychological Science, 9,* 156–160. (10)

Qin, P., & Mortensen, P. B. (2003). The impact of parental status on the risk of completed suicide. *Archives of General Psychiatry, 60,* 797–802. (16)

Quadrel, M. J., Fischhoff, B., & Davis, W. (1993). Adolescent (in)vulnerability. *American Psychologist, 48,* 102–116. (10)

Quraishi, S., & Frangou, S. (2002). Neuropsychology of bipolar disorder: A review. *Journal of Affective Disorders, 72,* 209–226. (16)

Rachlin, H. (1990). Why do people gamble and keep gambling despite heavy losses? *Psychological Science, 1,* 294–297. (8)

Rachlin, H., Siegel, E., & Cross, D. (1994). Lotteries and the time horizon. *Psychological Science, 5,* 390–393. (8)

Rachman, S. (1969). Treatment by prolonged exposure to high intensity stimulation. *Behaviour Research and Therapy, 7,* 295–302. (16)

Rachman, S. J., & Hodgson, R. J. (1980). *Obsessions and compulsions.* Upper Saddle River, NJ: Prentice Hall. (16)

Raine, A., Lencz, T., Bihrle, S., LaCasse, L., & Colletti, P. (2000). Reduced prefrontal gray matter volume and reduced autonomic activity in antisocial personality disorder. *Archives of General Psychiatry, 57,* 119–127. (12)

Rainville, P., Duncan, G. H., Price, D. D., Carrier, B., & Bushnell, M. C. (1997).

Pain affect encoded in human anterior cingulate but not somatosensory cortex. *Science, 277,* 968–971. (5)

Rainville, P., Hofbauer, R. K., Bushnell, M. C., Duncan, G. H., & Price, D. D. (2002). Hypnosis modulates activity in brain structures involved in the regulation of consciousness. *Journal of Cognitive Neuroscience, 14,* 887–901. (5)

Raison, C. L., Klein, H. M., & Steckler, M. (1999). The moon and madness reconsidered. *Journal of Affective Disorders, 53,* 99–106. (2)

Rakic, P. (2002). Neurogenesis in adult primate neocortex: An evaluation of the evidence. *Nature Reviews Neuroscience, 3,* 65–71. (3)

Ramachandran, V. S., & Blakeslee, S. (1998). *Phantoms in the brain.* New York: Morrow. (4)

Ramachandran, V. S., & Hirstein, W. (1998). The perception of phantom limbs: The D. O. Hebb lecture. *Brain, 121,* 1603–1630. (4)

Ramirez, J. M., Santisteban, C., Fujihara, T., & Van Goozen, S. (2002). Differences between experience of anger and readiness to angry action: A study of Japanese and Spanish students. *Aggressive Behavior, 28,* 429–438. (12)

Ransley, J. K., Donnelly, J. K., Botham, H., Khara, T. N., Greenwood, D. C., & Cade, J. E. (2003). Use of supermarket receipts to estimate energy and fat content of food purchased by lean and overweight families. *Appetite, 41,* 141–148. (11)

Rapoport, S. I., & Bosetti, F. (2002). Do lithium and anticonvulsants target the brain arachidonic acid cascade in bipolar patients? *Archives of General Psychiatry, 59,* 592–596. (16)

Rattenborg, N. C., Lima, S. L., & Amlaner, C. J. (1999). Half-awake to the risk of predation. *Nature, 397,* 397–398. (5)

Rauscher, F. H., Shaw, G. L., & Ky, K. N. (1993). Music and spatial task performance. *Nature, 365,* 611. (2)

Raven, J. (2000). The Raven's Progressive Matrices: Change and stability over culture and time. *Cognitive Psychology, 41,* 1–48. (9)

Ravizza, S. M., & Ivry, R. B. (2001). Comparison of the basal ganglia and cerebellum in shifting attention. *Journal of Cognitive Neuroscience, 13,* 285–297. (15)

Ravussin, E., Lillioja, S., Knowler, W. C., Christin, L., Freymona, D., Abbott, W. G. H., et al. (1988). Reduced rate of energy expenditure as a risk factor for body-weight gain. *New England Journal of Medicine, 318,* 467–472. (11)

Raymond, J. E. (2003). New objects, not new features, trigger the attentional blink. *Psychological Science, 14,* 54–59. (8)

Rayner, K. (1998). Eye movements in reading and information processing: 20 years of research. *Psychological Bulletin, 124,* 372–422. (8)

Rayner, K., Foorman, B. R., Perfetti, C. A., Pesetsky, D., & Seidenberg, M. S. (2001). How psychological science informs the teaching of reading. *Psychological Science in the Public Interest, 2,* 31–74. (8)

Rechtschaffen, A., & Bergmann, B. M. (1995). Sleep deprivation in the rat by the disk-over-water method. *Behavioural Brain Research, 69,* 55–63. (5)

Redding, R. E. (2001). Sociopolitical diversity in psychology. *American Psychologist, 56,* 205–215. (10)

Redican, W. K. (1982). An evolutionary perspective on human facial displays. In P. Ekman (Ed.), *Emotion in the human face* (pp. 212–280). Cambridge, England: Cambridge University Press. (12)

Reed, J. M., & Squire, L. R. (1999). Impaired transverse patterning in human amnesia is a special case of impaired memory for two-choice discrimination tasks. *Behavioral Neuroscience, 113,* 3–9. (7)

Reed, T. E. (1985). Ethnic differences in alcohol use, abuse, and sensitivity: A review with genetic interpretation. *Social Biology, 32,* 195–209. (16)

Reeves, A. G., & Plum, F. (1969). Hyperphagia, rage, and dementia accompanying a ventromedial hypothalamic neoplasm. *Archives of Neurology, 20,* 616–624. (11)

Reicher, G. M. (1969). Perceptual recognition as a function of meaningfulness of stimulus material. *Journal of Experimental Psychology, 81,* 275–280. (8)

Reisenzein, R. (1983). The Schachter theory of emotions: Two decades later. *Psychological Bulletin, 94,* 239–264. (12)

Reiss, M. J. (2000). The ethics of genetic research on intelligence. *Bioethics, 14,* 1–15. (9)

Reneman, L., Lavalaye, J., Schmand, B., de Wolff, F. A., van den Brink, W., den Heeten, G. J., et al. (2001). Cortical serotonin transporter density and verbal memory in individuals who stopped using 3,4-methylenedioxymethamphetamine (MDMA or "ecstasy"). *Archives of General Psychiatry, 58,* 901–906. (5)

Rensink, R. A., O'Regan, J. K., & Clark, J. J. (1997). To see or not to see: The need for attention to perceive changes in scenes. *Psychological Science, 8,* 368–373. (8)

Rescorla, R. A. (1968). Probability of shock in the presence and absence of CS in fear conditioning. *Journal of Comparative and Physiological Psychology, 66,* 1–5. (6)

Rescorla, R. A. (1988). Pavlovian conditioning: It's not what you think it is. *American Psychologist, 43,* 151–160. (6)

Restle, F. (1970). Moon illusion explained on the basis of relative size. *Science, 167,* 1092–1096. (4)

Rhee, S. H., & Waldman, I. D. (2002). Genetic and environmental influences on antisocial behavior: A meta-analysis of twin and adoption studies. *Psychological Bulletin, 128,* 490–529. (12)

Rhodes, G., Jeffery, L., Watson, T. L, Clifford, C. W. G., & Nakayama, K. (2003). Fitting the mind to the world: Face adaptation and attractiveness aftereffects. *Psychological Science, 14,* 558–566. (14)

Rhodes, G., Sumich, A., & Byatt, G. (1999). Are average facial configurations attractive only because of their symmetry? *Psychological Science, 10,* 52–58. (14)

Riccio, D. C. (1994). Memory: When less is more. *American Psychologist, 49,* 917–926. (7)

Riccio, D. C., Millin, P. M., & Gisquet-Verrier, P. (2003). Retrograde amnesia: Forgetting back. *Current Directions in Psychological Science, 12,* 41–44. (7)

Riddle, W. J. R., & Scott, A. I. F. (1995). Relapse after successful electroconvulsive therapy: The use and impact of continuation antidepressant drug treatment. *Human Psychopharmacology, 10,* 201–205. (16)

Rivera, P. A., Rose, J. M., Futterman, A., Lovett, S. B., & Gallagher- Thompson, D. (1991). Dimensions of perceived social support in clinically depressed and nondepressed female caregivers. *Psychology and Aging, 6,* 232–237. (16)

Rivers, P. C. (1994). *Alcohol and human behavior.* Upper Saddle River, NJ: Prentice Hall. (5)

Roberts, B. W., & DelVecchio, W. F. (2000). The rank-order consistency of personality traits from childhood to old age: A quantitative review of longitudinal studies. *Psychological Bulletin, 126,* 3–25. (13)

Roberts, R. D., Zeidner, M., & Matthews, G. (2001). Does emotional intelligence meet traditional standards for an intelligence? Some new data and conclusions. *Emotion, 1,* 196–231. (12)

Roberts, S. B., Savage, J., Coward, W. A., Chew, B., & Lucas, A. (1988). Energy expenditure and intake in infants born to lean and overweight mothers. *New England Journal of Medicine, 318,* 461–466. (11)

Robertson, L. C. (2003). Binding, spatial attention and perceptual awareness. *Nature Reviews Neuroscience, 4,* 93–102. (3)

Robins, L. N., Helzer, J. E., Weissman, M. M., Orvaschel, H., Gruenberg, E., Burke, J. D., Jr., et al. (1984). Lifetime prevalence of specific psychiatric disorders in three sites. *Archives of General Psychiatry, 41,* 949–958. (15, 16)

Robins, R. W., & Beer, J. S. (2001). Positive illusions about the self: Short-term benefits and long-term costs. *Journal of Personality and Social Psychology, 80,* 340–352. (12)

Robins, R. W., Gosling, S. D., & Craik, K. H. (1999). An empirical analysis of trends in psychology. *American Psychologist, 54,* 117–128. (1)

Robinson, L. A., Berman, J. S., & Neimeyer, R. A. (1990). Psychotherapy for the treatment of depression: A comprehensive review of controlled outcome research. *Psychological Bulletin, 108,* 30–49. (16)

Robinson, R. J., & Keltner, D. (1996). Much ado about nothing? Revisionists and traditionalists choose an introductory English syllabus. *Psychological Science, 7,* 18–24. (14)

Robinson, T. E., & Berridge, K. C. (2000). The psychology and neurobiology of addiction: An incentive-sensitization view. *Addiction, 95*(Suppl. 2), S91–S117. (16)

Robinson, T. E., & Berridge, K. C. (2001). Incentive-sensitization and addiction. *Addiction, 96,* 103–114. (16)

Roca, C. A., Schmidt, P. J., & Rubinow, D. R. (1999). Gonadal steroids and affective illness. *Neuroscientist, 5,* 227–237. (16)

Rock, I., & Kaufman, L. (1962). The moon illusion, II. *Science, 136,* 1023–1031. (4)

Rodd, J., Gaskell, G., & Marslen-Wilson, W. (2002). Making sense of semantic ambiguity: Semantic competition in lexical access. *Journal of Memory and Language, 46,* 245–266. (8)

Rodgers, J. L. (2001). What causes birth order-intelligence patterns? *American Psychologist, 56,* 505–510. (10)

Rodgers, J. L., Cleveland, H. H., van den Oord, E., & Rowe, D. C. (2000). Resolving the debate over birth order, family size, and intelligence. *American Psychologist, 55,* 599–612. (10)

Rodin, J. (1986). Aging and health: Effects of the sense of control. *Science, 233,* 1271–1276. (10, 12)

Rodrigo, M. F., & Ato, M. (2002). Testing the group polarization hypothesis by using logit models. *European Journal of Social Psychology, 32,* 3–18. (14)

Roediger, H. L., III, & McDermott, K. B. (1995). Creating false memories: Remembering words not presented in lists. *Journal of Experimental Psychology: Learning, Memory, and Cognition, 21,* 803–814. (7)

Roediger, H. L., III, & McDermott, K. B. (2000). Tricks of memory. *Current Directions in Psychological Science, 9,* 123–127. (7)

Rogers, C. R. (1951). *Client-centered therapy.* Boston: Houghton Mifflin. (15)

Rogers, C. R. (1961). *On becoming a person.* Boston: Houghton Mifflin. (13)

Rogers, C. R. (1980). *A way of being.* Boston: Houghton Mifflin. (13)

Rogers, T. B. (1995). *The psychological testing enterprise: An introduction.* Pacific Grove, CA: Brooks/Cole. (9)

Rogler, L. H. (2002). Historical generations and psychology. *American Psychologist, 57,* 1013–1023. (10)

Rohrbaugh, M., Shoham, V., Spungen, C., & Steinglass, P. (1995). Family systems therapy in practice: A systemic couples therapy for problem drinking. In B. Bongar & L. E. Beutler (Eds.), *Comprehensive textbook of psychotherapy: Theory and practice* (pp. 228–253). Oxford, England: Oxford University Press. (15)

Rolls, E. T. (1997). Taste and olfactory processing in the brain and its relation to the control of eating. *Critical Reviews in Neurobiology, 11,* 263–287. (4)

Ronen, T., & Rosenbaum, M. (2001). Helping children to help themselves: A case study of enuresis and nail biting. *Research on Social Work Practice, 11,* 338–356. (6)

Rosch, E. (1978). Principles of categorization. In E. Rosch & B. B. Lloyd (Eds.), *Cognition and categorization* (pp. 27–48). Hillsdale, NJ: Erlbaum. (8)

Rosch, E., & Mervis, C. B. (1975). Family resemblances: Studies in the internal structure of categories. *Cognitive Psychology, 7,* 573–605. (8)

Rose, J. E. (1996). Nicotine addiction and treatment. *Annual Review of Medicine, 47,* 493–507. (16)

Rose, J. E., Brugge, J. F., Anderson, D. J., & Hind, J. E. (1967). Phase-locked response to low-frequency tones in single auditory nerve fibers of the squirrel monkey. *Journal of Neurophysiology, 30,* 769–793. (4)

Rose, R. J., Viken, R. J., Dick, D. M., Bates, J. E., Pulkkinen, L., & Kaprio, J. (2003). It *does* take a village: Nonfamilial environments and children's behavior. *Psychological Science, 14,* 273–277. (10)

Rosen, H. J., Perry, R. J., Murphy, J., Kramer, J. H., Mychack, P., Schuff, N., et al. (2002). Emotion comprehension in the temporal variant of frontotemporal dementia. *Brain, 125,* 2286–2295. (12)

Rosen, V. M., & Engle, R. W. (1997). The role of working memory capacity in retrieval. *Journal of Experimental Psychology: General, 126,* 211–227. (7)

Rosenbaum, M. E. (1986). The repulsion hypothesis: on the nondevelopment of relationships. *Journal of Personality and Social Psychology, 51,* 1156–1166. (14)

Rosenbaum, R. S., Priselac, S., Köhler, S., Black, S. E., Gao, F., Nadel, L., et al. (2000). Remote spatial memory in an amnesic person with extensive bilateral hippocampal lesions. *Nature Neuroscience, 3,* 1044–1048. (7)

Rosenberg, H. (1993). Prediction of controlled drinking by alcoholics and problem drinkers. *Psychological Bulletin, 113,* 129–139. (16)

Ross, L. (1977). The intuitive psychologist and his shortcomings: Distortions in the attribution process. In L. Berkowitz (Ed.), *Advances in experimental social psychology* (Vol. 10, pp. 173–220). New York: Academic Press. (14)

Rosselli, M., & Ardila, A. (2003). The impact of culture and education on non-verbal neuropsychological measurements: A critical review. *Brain and Cognition, 52,* 326–333. (9)

Roth, B. L., Lopez, E., & Kroeze, W. K. (2000). The multiplicity of serotonin receptors: Uselessly diverse molecules or an embarrassment of riches? *The Neuroscientist, 6,* 252–262. (3)

Rothbaum, B. O., Hodges, L. F., Kooper, R., Opdyke, D., Williford, J. S., & North, M. (1995). Effectiveness of computer-generated (virtual reality) graded exposure in the treatment of acrophobia. *American Journal of Psychiatry, 152,* 626–628. (16)

Rothbaum, F., Weisz, J., Pott, M., Miyake, K., & Morelli, G. (2000). Attachment and culture: Security in the United States and Japan. *American Psychologist, 55,* 1093–1104. (10)

Rottenberg, J., Gross, J. J., Wilhelm, F. H., Najmi, S., & Gotlib, I. H. (2002). Crying threshold and intensity in major depressive disorder. *Journal of Abnormal Psychology, 111,* 302–312. (16)

Rotter, J. B. (1966). Generalized expectancies for internal versus external control of reinforcement. *Psychological Monographs, 80*(Whole No. 603). (13)

Rotton, J., & Kelly, I. W. (1985). Much ado about the full moon: A meta-analysis of lunar-lunacy research. *Psychological Bulletin, 97,* 286–306. (2)

Routh, D. K. (2000). Clinical psychology training: A history of ideas and practices prior to 1946. *American Psychologist, 55,* 236–241. (1)

Rovee-Collier, C. (1997). Dissociations in infant memory: Rethinking the development of explicit and implicit memory. *Psychological Review, 104,* 467–498. (10)

Rovee-Collier, C. (1999). The development of infant memory. *Current Directions in Psychological Science, 8,* 80–85. (10)

Rowe, J. W., & Kahn, R. L. (1987). Human aging: Usual and successful. *Science, 237,* 143–149. (10)

Rowland, D. L., & Burnett, A. L. (2000). Pharmacotherapy in the treatment of male sexual dysfunction. *Journal of Sex Research, 37,* 226–243. (11)

Royzman, E. B., & Sabini, J. (2001). Something it takes to be an emotion: The interesting case of disgust. *Journal for the Theory of Social Behavior, 31,* 29–59. (12)

Rozenblit, L., & Keil, F. (2002). The misunderstood limits of folk science: An illusion of explanatory depth. *Cognitive Science, 26,* 521–562. (8)

Rozin, P. (1996). Sociocultural influences on human food selection. In E. D. Capaldi (Ed.), *Why we eat what we eat* (pp. 233–263). Washington, DC: American Psychological Association. (11)

Rozin, P. (2001). Social psychology and science: Some lessons from Solomon Asch. *Personality and Social Psychology Review, 5,* 2–14. (14)

Rozin, P., & Cohen, A. B. (2003). High frequency of facial expressions corresponding to confusion, concentration, and worry in an analysis of naturally occurring facial expressions of Americans. *Emotion, 3,* 68–75. (12)

Rozin, P., & Fallon, A. E. (1987). A perspective on disgust. *Psychological Review, 94,* 23–41. (11)

Rozin, P., Fallon, A., & Augustoni-Ziskind, M. L. (1986). The child's conception of food: The development of categories of acceptable and rejected substances. *Journal of Nutrition Education, 18,* 75–81. (11)

Rozin, P., Fischler, C., Imada, S., Sarubin, A., & Wrzesniewski, A. (1999). Attitudes to food and the role of food in life in the U.S.A., Japan, Flemish Belgium and France: Possible implications for the diet-health debate. *Appetite, 33,* 163–180. (11)

Rozin, P., Kabnick, K., Pete, E., Fischler, C., & Shields, C. (2003). The ecology of eating: Smaller portion sizes in France than in the United States help explain the French paradox. *Psychological Science, 14,* 450–454. (11)

Rozin, P., & Kalat, J. W. (1971). Specific hungers and poison avoidance as adaptive specializations of learning. *Psychological Review, 78,* 459–486. (6, 11)

Rozin, P., Lowery, L., Imada, S., & Haidt, J. (1999). The CAD triad hypothesis: A mapping between three moral emotions (contempt, anger, disgust) and three moral codes (community, autonomy, divinity). *Journal of Personality and Social Psychology, 76,* 574–586. (12)

Rozin, P., Markwith, M., & Ross, B. (1990). The sympathetic magical law of similarity, nominal realism and neglect of negatives in response to negative labels. *Psychological Science, 1,* 383–384. (8)

Rozin, P., Markwith, M., & Stoess, C. (1997). Moralization and becoming a vegetarian: The transformation of preferences into values and the recruitment of disgust. *Psychological Science, 8,* 67–73. (11)

Rozin, P., Millman, L., & Nemeroff, C. (1986). Operation of the laws of sympathetic magic in disgust and other domains. *Journal of Personality and Social Psychology, 50,* 703–712. (11)

Rozin, P., & Pelchat, M. L. (1988). Memories of mammaries: Adaptations to weaning from milk. *Progress in Psychobiology and Physiological Psychology, 13,* 1–29. (10)

Rubenstein, R., & Newman, R. (1954). The living out of "future" experiences under hypnosis. *Science, 119,* 472–473. (5)

Rubia, K., Oosterlaan, J., Sergeant, J. A., Brandeis, D., & v. Leeuwen, T. (1998). Inhibitory dysfunction in hyperactive boys. *Behavioural Brain Research, 94,* 25–32. (15)

Ruch, J. (1984). *Psychology: The personal science.* Belmont, CA: Wadsworth. (10)

Rumbaugh, D. M., & Washburn, D. A. (2003). *Intelligence of apes and other rational beings.* New Haven, CT: Yale University Press. (6)

Rumelhart, D. E., & McClelland, J. L. (1982). An interactive activation model of context effects in letter perception: Part 2. The contextual enhancement effect and some tests and extensions of the model. *Psychological Review, 89,* 60–94. (8)

Rumelhart, D. E., McClelland, J. L., & the PDP Research Group. (1986). *Parallel distributed processing.* Cambridge, MA: MIT Press. (8)

Rusak, B. (1977). The role of the suprachiasmatic nuclei in the generation of circadian rhythms in the golden hamster, *Mesocricetus auratus. Journal of Comparative Physiology A, 118,* 145–164. (5)

Ruscio, J. (2000, March/April). Risky business: Vividness, availability, and the media paradox. *Skeptical Inquirer, 24*(2), 22–26. (8)

Russell, J. A. (1994). Is there universal recognition of emotion from facial expression? A review of the cross-cultural studies. *Psychological Bulletin, 115,* 102–141. (12)

Russell, J. A. (1997). Reading emotions from and into faces: Resurrecting a dimensional-contextual perspective. In J. A. Russell & J. M. Fernández-Dols (Eds.), *The psychology of facial expression* (pp. 295–320). Cambridge, England: Cambridge University Press. (12)

Russell, J. A. (2003). Core affect and the psychological construction of emotion. *Psychological Review, 110,* 145–172. (12)

Ruthruff, E., Pashler, H. E., & Hazeltine, E. (2003). Dual-task interference with equal task emphasis: Graded capacity sharing or central postponement? *Perception & Psychophysics, 65,* 801–816. (8)

Ruthruff, E., Pashler, H. E., & Klaassen, A. (2001). Processing bottlenecks in dual-task performance: Structural limitations or strategic postponement? *Psychonomic Bulletin and Review, 8,* 73–80. (8)

Rutledge, T., & Hogan, B. E. (2002). A quantitative review of prospective evidence linking psychological factors with hypertension development. *Psychosomatic Medicine, 64,* 758–766. (12)

Ryan, J. D., Althoff, R. R., Whitlow, S., & Cohen, N. J. (2000). Amnesia is a deficit in relational memory. *Psychological Science, 11,* 454–461. (7)

Ryan, L., Hatfield, C., & Hofstetter, M. (2002). Caffeine reduces time-of-day effects on memory performance in older adults. *Psychological Science, 13,* 68–71. (5)

Ryan, R. M., & Deci, E. L. (2000). Self-determination theory and the facilitation of intrinsic motivation, social development, and well-being. *American Psychologist, 55,* 68–78. (11)

Saarelainen, T., Hendolin, P., Lucas, G., Koponen, E., Sairanen, M., MacDonald, E., et al. (2003). Activation of the TrkB neurotrophin receptor is induced by antidepressant drugs and is required for antidepressant-induced behavioral effects. *Journal of Neuroscience, 23,* 349–357. (16)

Sabini, J., Siepmann, M., Stein, J., & Meyerowitz, M. (2000). Who is embarrassed by what? *Cognition and Emotion, 14,* 213–240. (12)

Sackeim, H. A., Prudic, J., Devanand, D. P., Nobler, M. S., Lisanby, S. H., Peyser, S., et al. (2000). A prospective, randomized, double-blind comparison of bilateral and right unilateral electroconvulsive therapy at different stimulus intensities. *Archives of General Psychiatry, 57,* 425–434. (16)

Sackett, P. R., Schmitt, N., Ellingson, J. E., & Kabin, M. B. (2001). High-stakes testing in employment, credentialing, and higher education. *American Psychologist, 56,* 302–318. (9)

Saegert, S., Swap, W., & Zajonc, R. B. (1973). Exposure, context, and interpersonal attraction. *Journal of Personality and Social Psychology, 25,* 234–242. (14)

Safer, M. A., & Keuler, D. J. (2002). Individual differences in misremembering pre-psychotherapy distress: Personality and memory distortion. *Emotion, 2,* 162–178. (15)

Saffran, J. R. (2003). Statistical language learning: Mechanisms and constraints. *Current Directions in Psychological Science, 12,* 110–114. (8)

Saffran, J. R., Aslin, R. N., & Newport, E. L. (1996). Statistical learning by 8-month-old infants. *Science, 274,* 1926–1928. (8)

Saggino, A. (2000). The big three or the big five? A replication study. *Personality and Individual Differences, 28,* 879–886. (13)

Saleem, Q., Dash, D., Gandhi, C., Kishore, A., Benegal, V., Sherrin, T., et al. (2001). Association of CAG repeat loci on chromosome 22 with schizophrenia and bipolar disorder. *Molecular Psychiatry, 6,* 694–700. (16)

Salovey, P., & Birnbaum, D. (1989). Influence of mood on health-relevant cognitions. *Journal of Personality and Social Psychology, 57,* 539–551. (12)

Salzarulo, P., & Chevalier, A. (1983). Sleep problems in children and their relationship with early disturbances of the waking–sleeping rhythms. *Sleep, 6,* 47–51. (5)

Samelson, F. (1980). J. B. Watson's Little Albert, Cyril Burt's twins, and the need for a critical science. *American Scientist, 35,* 619–625. (16)

Samuel, A. G. (2001). Knowing a word affects the fundamental perception of the sounds within it. *Psychological Science, 12,* 348–351. (8)

Sanchez, L. M., & Turner, S. M. (2003). Practicing psychology in the era of managed care. *American Psychologist, 58,* 116–129. (15)

Sandell, R., Blomberg, J., Lazar, A., Schubert, J., Carlsson, J., & Broberg, J. (1999). Wie die Zeit vergeht: Langzeitergebnisse von Psychoanalysen und analytischen Psychotherapien. [As time goes by: Long-term outcomes of psychoanalysis and long-term psychotherapy.] *Forum der Psychoanalyse, 15,* 327–347. (15)

Sanders, R. E., Gonzalez, D. J., Murphy, M. D., Pesta, B. J., & Bucur, B. (2002). Training content variability and the effectiveness of learning: An adult age assessment. *Aging, Neuropsychology, and Cognition, 9,* 157–174. (7)

Sanderson, A., & Dugoni, B. (1999). *Summary report 1997: Doctorate recipients from United States institutions.* Chicago: National Opinion Research Council. (1)

Sandfort, T. G. M., de Graaf, R., Bijl, R. V., & Schnabel, P. (2001). Same-sex sexual behavior and psychiatric disorders. *Archives of General Psychiatry, 58,* 85–91. (11)

Sanna, L. J. (2000). Mental simulation, affect, and personality: A conceptual framework. *Current Directions in Psychological Science, 9,* 168–173. (12)

Sapolsky, R. M. (1998, March 30). Open season. *The New Yorker, 74*(6), 57–58, 71–72. (13)

Sapp, F., Lee, K., & Muir, D. (2000). Three-year-olds' difficulty with the appearance–reality distinction: Is it real or is it apparent? *Developmental Psychology, 36,* 547–560. (10)

Satterfield, J. M., & Seligman, M. E. P. (1994). Military aggression and risk predicted by explanatory style. *Psychological Science, 5,* 77–82. (16)

Saucier, D. M., Green, S. M., Leason, J., MacFadden, A., Bell, S., & Elias, L. J. (2002). Are sex differences in navigation caused by sexually dimorphic strategies or by differences in the ability to use the strategies? *Behavioral Neuroscience, 116,* 403–410. (10)

Savage-Rumbaugh, E. S. (1990). Language acquisition in a nonhuman species: Implications for the innateness debate. *Developmental Psychology, 23,* 599–620. (8)

Savage-Rumbaugh, E. S., Murphy, J., Sevcik, R. A., Brakke, K. E., Williams, S. L., & Rumbaugh, D. M. (1993). Language comprehension in ape and child. *Monographs of the Society for Research in Child Development, 58*(Serial no. 233). (8)

Savage-Rumbaugh, E. S., Sevcik, R. A., Brakke, K. E., & Rumbaugh, D. M. (1992). Symbols: Their communicative use, communication, and combination by bonobos *(Pan paniscus).* In L. P. Lipsitt & C. Rovee-Collier (Eds.), *Advances in infancy research* (Vol. 7, pp. 221–278). Norwood, NJ: Ablex. (8)

Saxe, L., & Ben-Shakhar, G. (1999). Admissibility of polygraph tests: The application of scientific standards post-Daubert. *Psychology, Public Policy, and Law, 5,* 203–223. (12)

Scarborough, E., & Furomoto, L. (1987). *Untold lives: The first generation of American women psychologists.* New York: Columbia University Press. (1)

Scarr, S. (1997). Rules of evidence: A larger context for the statistical debate. *Psychological Science, 8,* 16–17. (2)

Scarr, S. (1998). American child care today. *American Psychologist, 53,* 95–108. (10)

Scarr, S., Pakstis, A. J., Katz, S. H., & Barker, W. B. (1977). The absence of a relationship between degree of White ancestry and intellectual skills within a Black population. *Human Genetics, 39,* 69–86. (9)

Scarr, S., Phillips, D., & McCartney, K. (1990). Facts, fantasies and the future of child care in the United States. *Psychological Science, 1,* 26–35. (10)

Scarr, S., & Weinberg, R. A. (1976). IQ test performance of Black children adopted by White families. *American Psychologist, 31,* 726–739. (9)

Schachter, D. L. (1987). Implicit memory: History and current status. *Journal of Experimental Psychology: Learning, Memory, and Cognition, 13,* 501–518. (7)

Schacter, D. L. (1999). The seven sins of memory. *American Psychologist, 54,* 182–203. (7)

Schacter, D. L., & Badgaiyan, R. D. (2001). Neuroimaging of priming: New perspectives on implicit and explicit memory. *Current Directions in Psychological Science, 10,* 1–4. (7)

Schacter, D. L., Verfaellie, M., Anes, M. D., & Racine, C. (1998). When true recognition suppresses false recognition: Evidence from amnesic patients. *Journal of Cognitive Neuroscience, 10,* 668–679. (7)

Schachter, S. (1982). Recidivism and self-cure of smoking and obesity. *American Psychologist, 37,* 436–444. (11)

Schachter, S., & Singer, J. (1962). Cognitive, social, and physiological determinants of emotional state. *Psychological Review, 69,* 379–399. (12)

Schafe, G. E., Atkins, C. M., Swank, M. W., Bauer, E. P., Sweatt, J. D., & LeDoux, J. E. (2000). Activation of ERK/MAP kinase in the amygdala is required for memory consolidation of Pavlovian fear conditioning. *Journal of Neuroscience, 20,* 8177–8187. (12)

Schatzman, M. (1992, March 21). Freud: Who seduced whom? *New Scientist,* pp. 34–37. (13)

Schellenberg, E. G., & Trehub, S. E. (2003). Good pitch memory is widespread. *Psychological Science, 14,* 262–266. (4)

Schellenberg, G. D., Bird, T. D., Wijsman, E. M., Orr, H. T., Anderson, L., Nemens, E., et al. (1992). Genetic linkage evidence for a familial Alzheimer's disease locus on chromosome 14. *Science, 258,* 668–671. (7)

Schenck, C. H., & Mahowald, M. W. (1996). Long-term, nightly benzodiazepine treatment of injurious parasomnias and other disorders of disrupted nocturnal sleep in 170 adults. *American Journal of Medicine, 100,* 333–337. (5)

Schiffman, S. S., & Erickson, R. P. (1971). A psychophysical model for gustatory quality. *Physiology & Behavior, 7,* 617–633. (4)

Schkade, D. A., & Kahneman, D. (1998). Does living in California make people happy? *Psychological Science, 9,* 340–346. (12)

Schlesier-Stropp, B. (1984). Bulimia: A review of the literature. *Psychological Review, 95,* 247–257. (11)

Schmidt, F. L., & Hunter, J. E. (1981). Employment testing: Old theories and new research findings. *American Psychologist, 36,* 1128–1137. (9)

Schmidt, F. L., & Hunter, J. E. (1998). The validity and utility of selection methods in personnel psychology: Practical and theoretical implications of 85 years of research findings. *Psychological Bulletin, 124,* 262–274. (9)

Schmidt, R. A., & Bjork, R. A. (1992). New conceptualizations of practice: Common principles in three paradigms suggest new concepts for training. *Psychological Science, 3,* 207–217. (7)

Schmitt, A. P., & Dorans, N. J. (1990). Differential item functioning for minority examinees on the SAT. *Journal of Educational Measurement, 27,* 67–81. (9)

Schmitt, D. P., and 118 members of the International Sexuality Description Project. (2003). Universal sex differences in the desire for sexual variety: Tests from 52 nations, 6 continents, and 13 islands. *Journal of Personality and Social Psychology, 85,* 85–104. (14)

Schmolck, H., Buffalo, E. A., & Squire, L. R. (2000). Memory distortions develop over time. *Psychological Science, 11,* 39–45. (7)

Schneider, P., Scherg, M., Dosch, G., Specht, H. J., Gutschalk, A., & Rupp, A. (2002). Morphology of Heschl's gyrus reflects enhanced activation in the auditory cortex of musicians. *Nature Neuroscience, 5,* 688–694. (3)

Schnider, A. (2003). Spontaneous confabulation and the adaptation of thought to ongoing reality. *Nature Reviews Neuroscience, 4,* 662–671. (7)

Schooler, C. (1972). Birth order effects: Not here, not now! *Psychological Bulletin, 78,* 161–175. (10)

Schooler, C. (1998). Environmental complexity and the Flynn effect. In U. Neisser (Ed.), *The rising curve* (pp. 67–79). Washington, DC: American Psychological Association. (9)

Schou, M. (1997). Forty years of lithium treatment. *Archives of General Psychiatry, 54,* 9–13. (16)

Schredl, M. (2000). Continuity between waking life and dreaming: Are all waking activities reflected equally often in dreams? *Perceptual and Motor Skills, 90,* 844–846. (5)

Schriesheim, C. A., Castro, S. L., & Cogliser, C. C. (1999). Leader-member exchange

(LMX) research: A comprehensive review of theory, measurement, and data-analytic practices. *Leadership Quarterly, 10,* 63–113. (11)

Schuckit, M. C., & Smith, T. L. (1997). Assessing the risk for alcoholism among sons of alcoholics. *Journal of Studies on Alcohol, 58,* 141–145. (16)

Schulsinger, F., Knop, J., Goodwin, D. W., Teasdale, T. W., & Mikkelsen, U. (1986). A prospective study of young men at high risk for alcoholism. *Archives of General Psychiatry, 43,* 755–760. (16)

Schumacher, J., Otte, A. C. J., Becker, T., Sun, Y., Wienker, T. F., Wirth, B., et al. (2003). No evidence for DUP25 in patients with panic disorder using a quantitative real-time PCR approach. *Human Genetics, 1114,* 115–117. (16)

Schwartz, C. E., Wright, C. I., Shin, L. M., Kagan, J., & Rauch, S. L. (2003). Inhibited and uninhibited infants "grown up": Adult amygdalar response to novelty. *Science, 300,* 1952–1953. (10)

Schwartz, M. B., & Brownell, K. D. (1995). Matching individuals to weight loss treatments: A survey of obesity experts. *Journal of Consulting and Clinical Psychology, 63,* 149–153. (11)

Schwarz, N. (1999). Self-reports: How the questions shape the answers. *American Psychologist, 54,* 93–105. (2)

Schwarzwald, J., Bizman, A., & Raz, M. (1983). The foot-in-the-door paradigm: Effects of second request size on donation probability and donor generosity. *Personality and Social Psychology Bulletin, 9,* 443–450. (14)

Scoboria, A., Mazzoni, G., Kirsch, I., & Milling, L. S. (2002). Immediate and persisting effects of misleading questions and hypnosis on memory reports. *Journal of Experimental Psychology: Applied, 8,* 26–32. (5)

Scott, D., Lambie, I., Henwood, D., & Lamb, R. (2003). Profiling stranger rapists: It's not so elementary, Doctor Watson. *American Journal of Forensic Psychology, 21,* 31–49. (13)

Scott, S. K., Young, A. W., Calder, A. J., Hellawell, D. J., Aggleton, J. P., & Johnson, M. (1997). Impaired auditory recognition of fear and anger following bilateral amygdala lesions. *Nature, 385,* 254–257. (12)

Scott, T. R., & Verhagen, J. V. (2000). Taste as a factor in the management of nutrition. *Nutrition, 16,* 874–885. (11)

Scovern, A. W., & Kilmann, P. R. (1980). Status of electroconvulsive therapy: Review of the outcome literature. *Psychological Bulletin, 87,* 260–303. (16)

Scribner, S. (1974). Developmental aspects of categorized recall in a West African society. *Cognitive Psychology, 6,* 475–494. (7)

Scripture, E. W. (1907). *Thinking, feeling, doing* (2nd ed.). New York: G. P. Putnam's Sons. (1)

Seamon, J. G., Lee, I. A., Toner, S. K., Wheeler, R. H., Goodkind, M. S., & Birch, A. D. (2002). Thinking of critical words during study is unnecessary for false memory in the Deese, Roediger, and McDermott procedure. *Psychological Science, 13,* 526–531. (7)

Sears, D. O., & Henry, P. J. (2003). The origins of symbolic racism. *Journal of Personality and Social Psychology, 85,* 259–275. (14)

Seeley, R. J., Kaplan, J. M., & Grill, H. J. (1995). Effect of occluding the pylorus on intraoral intake: A test of the gastric hypothesis of meal termination. *Physiology & Behavior, 58,* 245–249. (11)

Seeman, P., & Lee, T. (1975). Antipsychotic drugs: Direct correlation between clinical potency and presynaptic action on dopamine neurons. *Science, 188,* 1217–1219. (16)

Segal, N. (1993). Twin, sibling, and adoption methods: Tests of evolutionary hypotheses. *American Psychologist, 48,* 943–956. (10)

Segerstrom, S. C. (2001). Optimism and attentional bias for negative and positive symptoms. *Personality and Social Psychology Bulletin, 27,* 1334–1343. (13)

Seidenberg, M. S. (1997). Language acquisition and use: Learning and applying probabilistic constraints. *Science, 275,* 1599–1603. (8)

Sekuler, A. B., & Bennett, P. J. (2001). Generalized common fate: Grouping by common luminance changes. *Psychological Science, 12,* 437–444. (4)

Seligman, M. E. P. (1970). On the generality of the laws of learning. *Psychological Review, 77,* 406–418. (6)

Seligman, M. E. P. (1971). Phobias and preparedness. *Behavior Therapy, 2,* 307–320. (16)

Seligman, M. E. P. (1995). The effectiveness of psychotherapy: The *Consumer Reports* study. *American Psychologist, 50,* 965–974. (15)

Seligman, M. E. P., & Csikszentmihalyi, M. (2000). Positive psychology. *American Psychologist, 55,* 5–14. (12)

Seligman, M. E. P., Nolen-Hoeksema, S., Thornton, N., & Thornton, K. M. (1990). Explanatory style as a mechanism of disappointing athletic performance. *Psychological Science, 1,* 143–146. (16)

Seligman, M. E. P., Schulman, P., DeRubeis, R. J., & Hollon, S. D. (1999). The prevention of depression and anxiety. *Prevention and Treatment, 2,* article 8. (16)

Selye, H. (1979). Stress, cancer, and the mind. In J. Taché, H. Selye, & S. B. Day (Eds.), *Cancer, stress, and death* (pp. 11–27). New York: Plenum Press. (12)

Senghas, A., & Coppola, M. (2001). Children creating language: How Nicaraguan sign language acquired a spatial grammar. *Psychological Science, 12,* 323–328. (8)

Sensky, T., Turkington, D., Kingdon, D., Scott, J. L., Scott, J., Siddle, R., et al. (2000). A randomized controlled trial of cognitive-behavioral therapy for persistent symptoms in schizophrenia resistant to medication. *Archives of General Psychiatry, 57,* 165–172. (16)

Shafir, E. B., Smith, E. E., & Osheron, D. N. (1990). Typicality and reasoning fallacies. *Memory & Cognition, 18,* 229–239. (8)

Shafto, M., & MacKay, D. G. (2000). The Moses, mega-Moses, and Armstrong illusions: Integrating language comprehension and semantic memory. *Psychological Science, 11,* 372–378. (8)

Shaner, A., Miller, G., & Mintz, J. (in press). Schizophrenia as one extreme of a sexually selected fitness indicator. *Schizophrenia Research.* (16)

Shannon, D. A. (1955). *The Socialist party of America.* New York: Macmillan. (14)

Shapiro, D. H., Jr., Schwartz, C. E., & Astin, J. A. (1996). Controlling ourselves, controlling our world. *American Psychologist, 51,* 1213–1230. (12)

Shapiro, D. L. (1985). Insanity and the assessment of criminal responsibility. In C. P. Ewing (Ed.), *Psychology, psychiatry, and the law: A clinical and forensic handbook* (pp. 67–94). Sarasota, FL: Professional Resource Exchange. (15)

Shapiro, K. L., Caldwell, J., & Sorensen, R. E. (1997). Personal names and the attentional blink: A visual "cocktail party" effect. *Journal of Experimental Psychology: Human Perception and Performance, 23,* 504–514. (8)

Shearn, D., Spellman, L., Straley, B., Meirick, J., & Stryker, K. (1999). Empathic blushing in friends and strangers. *Motivation and Emotion, 23,* 307–316. (12)

Shepard, R. N. (1990). *Mind sights.* New York: W. H. Freeman. (4)

Shepard, R. N., & Metzler, J. N. (1971). Mental rotation of three-dimensional objects. *Science, 171,* 701–703. (8)

Sheppard, W. D., II, Staggers, F. J., Jr., & John, L. (1997). The effects of a stress management program in a high security government agency. *Anxiety, Stress, and Coping, 10,* 341–350. (12)

Shepperd, J. A. (1993). Productivity loss in performance groups: A motivation analysis. *Psychological Bulletin, 113,* 67–81. (14)

Shergill, S. S., Brammer, M. J., Williams, S. C. R., Murray, R. M., & McGuire, P. K. (2000). Mapping auditory hallucinations in schizophrenia using functional magnetic resonance imaging. *Archives of General Psychiatry, 57,* 1033–1038. (16)

Sherif, M. (1935). A study of some social factors in perception. *Archives of Psychology, 27,* 1–60. (14)

Sherif, M. (1966). In common predicament. Boston: Houghton Mifflin. (14)

Sherrington, R., Rogaev, E. I., Liang, Y., Rogaeva, E. A., Levesque, G., Ikeda, M., et al. (1995). Cloning of a gene bearing missense mutations in early-onset familial Alzheimer's disease. *Nature, 375,* 754–760. (7)

Sherwood, G. G. (1981). Self-serving biases in person perception: A reexamination of projection as a mechanism of defense. *Psychological Bulletin, 90,* 445–459. (13)

Shih, M., Pittinsky, T. L., & Ambady, N. (1999). Stereotype susceptibility: Identity salience and shifts in quantitative performance. *Psychological Science, 10,* 80–83. (9)

Shimaya, A. (1997). Perception of complex line drawings. *Journal of Experimental Psychology: Human Perception and Performance, 23,* 25–50. (4)

Shogren, E. (1993, June 2). Survey finds 4 in 5 suffer sex harassment at school. *Los Angeles Times,* p. A10. (2)

Shweder, R., Mahapatra, M., & Miller, J. G. (1987). Culture and moral development. In J. Kagan & S. Lamb (Eds.), *The emergence of morality in young children* (pp. 1–83). Chicago: University of Chicago Press. (10)

Siegel, J. M. (2001). The REM sleep-memory consolidation hypothesis. *Science, 294,* 1058–1063. (5)

Siegel, S. (1977). Morphine tolerance as an associative process. *Journal of Experimental Psychology: Animal Behavior Processes, 3,* 1–13. (6)

Siegel, S. (1983). Classical conditioning, drug tolerance, and drug dependence. *Research Advances in Alcohol and Drug Problems, 7,* 207–246. (6)

Siegel, S. (1987). Alcohol and opiate dependence: Reevaluation of the Victorian perspective. *Research Advances in Alcohol and Drug Problems, 9,* 279–314. (16)

Siegelman, M. (1974). Parental background of male homosexuals and heterosexuals. *Archives of Sexual Behavior, 3,* 3–18. (11)

Siegler, R. S. (2000). Unconscious insights. *Current Directions in Psychological Science, 9,* 79–83. (8)

Siegler, R. S., & Richards, D. D. (1982). The development of intelligence. In R. J. Sternberg (Ed.), *Handbook of human intelligence* (pp. 897–971). Cambridge, England: Cambridge University Press. (9)

Sigman, M., & Whaley, S. E. (1998). The role of nutrition in the development of intelligence. In U. Neisser (Ed.), *The rising curve* (pp. 155–182). Washington, DC: American Psychological Association. (9)

Silberg, J. L., Parr, T., Neale, M. C., Rutter, M., Angold, A., & Eaves, L. J. (2003). Maternal smoking during pregnancy and risk to boys' conduct disturbance: An examination of the causal hypothesis. *Biological Psychiatry, 53,* 130–135. (12)

Silberg, J., Pickles, A., Rutter, M., Hewitt, J., Simonoff, E., Maes, H., et al. (1999). The influence of genetic factors and life stress on depression among adolescent girls.

Archives of General Psychiatry, 56, 225–232. (16)

Silver, E. (1995). Punishment or treatment? Comparing the lengths of confinement of successful and unsuccessful insanity defendants. *Law and Human Behavior, 19,* 375–388. (15)

Silverman, I., Choi, J., Mackewn, A., Fisher, M., Moro, J., & Olshansky, E. (2000). Evolved mechanisms underlying wayfinding: Further studies on the hunter-gatherer theory of spatial sex differences. *Evolution and Human Behavior, 21,* 201–213. (10)

Silverstein, L. B., & Auerbach, C. F. (1999). Deconstructing the essential father. *American Psychologist, 54,* 397–407. (10)

Silverthorne, C. (2001). Leadership effectiveness and personality: A crosscultural evaluation. *Personality and Individual Differences, 30,* 303–309. (13)

Simcock, G., & Hayne, H. (2002). Breaking the barrier? Children fail to translate their preverbal memories into language. *Psychological Science, 13,* 225–231. (7)

Simmons, E. J. (1949). *Leo Tolstoy.* London: Lehmann. (16)

Simon, R. I. (1994). The law and psychiatry. In R. E. Hales, S. C. Yudofsky, & J. A. Talbott (Eds.), *Textbook of psychiatry* (2nd ed., pp. 1297–1340). Washington, DC: American Psychiatric Press. (15)

Simons, D. J., & Levin, D. T. (2003). What makes change blindness interesting? *The Psychology of Learning and Motivation, 42,* 295–322. (8)

Simons, T., & Roberson, Q. (2003). Why managers should care about fairness: The effects of aggregate justice perceptions on organizational outcomes. *Journal of Applied Psychology, 88,* 432–443. (11)

Simonton, D. K. (1997). Creative productivity: A predictive and explanatory model of career trajectories and landmarks. *Psychological Review, 104,* 66–89. (8)

Simonton, D. K. (2000). Creativity: Cognitive, personal, developmental, and social aspects. *American Psychologist, 55,* 151–158. (8)

Simpson, C. A., & Vuchinich, R. E. (2000). Reliability of a measure of temporal discounting. *Psychological Record, 50,* 3–16. (11)

Simpson, J. A., Oriña, M. M., & Ickes, W. (2003). When accuracy hurts, and when it helps: A test of the empathic accuracy model in marital interactions. *Journal of Personality and Social Psychology, 85,* 881–893. (14)

Singh, M., Hoffman, D. D., & Albert, M. K. (1999). Contour completion and relative depth: Petter's rule and support ratio. *Psychological Science, 10,* 423–428. (4)

Sinha, P., & Poggio, T. (1996). I think I know that face . . . *Nature, 384,* 404. (15)

Sizemore, C. C., & Huber, R. J. (1988). The twenty-two faces of Eve. *Individual Psychology, 44,* 53–62. (15)

Sizemore, C. C., & Pittillo, E. S. (1977). *I'm Eve.* Garden City, NY: Doubleday. (15)

Skeels, H. M. (1966). Adult status of children with contrasting early life experiences. *Monographs of the Society for Research in Child Development, 31,* 1–65. (9)

Skinner, B. F. (1938). *The behavior of organisms.* New York: D. Appleton-Century. (6)

Skinner, B. F. (1990). Can psychology be a science of mind? *American Psychologist, 45,* 1206–1210. (6)

Skinner, E. A., Edge, K., Altman, J., & Sherwood, H. (2003). Searching for the structure of coping: A review and critique of category systems for classifying ways of coping. *Psychological Bulletin, 129,* 216–269. (12)

Sklar, P., Schwab, S. G., Williams, N. M., Daly, M., Schaffner, S., Maier, W., et al. (2001). Association analysis of *NOTCH4* loci in schizophrenia using family and population-based controls. *Nature Genetics, 28,* 126–128. (16)

Skoog, G., & Skoog, I. (1999). A 40-year follow-up of patients with obsessive-compulsive disorder. *Archives of General Psychiatry, 56,* 121–127. (16)

Skre, I., Onstad, S., Torgerson, S., Lygren, S., & Kringlen, E. (2000). The heritability of common phobic fear: A twin study of a clinical sample. *Journal of Anxiety Disorders, 14,* 549–562. (16)

Slutske, W. S., Eisen, S., True, W. R., Lyons, M. J., Goldberg, J., & Tsuang, M. (2000). Common genetic vulnerability for pathological gambling and alcohol dependence in men. *Archives of General Psychiatry, 57,* 666–673. (16)

Smith, L. B., Jones, S. S., Landau, B., Gershkoff-Stowe, L., & Samuelson, L. (2002). Object name learning provides on-the-job training for attention. *Psychological Science, 13,* 13–19. (8)

Smith, L. D. (1995). Inquiry nearer the source: Bacon, Mach, and *The Behavior of Organisms.* In J. T. Todd & E. K. Morris (Eds.), *Modern perspectives on B. F. Skinner and contemporary behaviorism* (pp. 39–50). Westport, CT: Greenwood Press. (6)

Smith, M. L. (1988). Recall of spatial location by the amnesic patient H. M. *Brain and Cognition, 7,* 178–183. (7)

Smith, M. L., Glass, G. V., & Miller, T. I. (1980). *The benefits of psychotherapy.* Baltimore, MD: Johns Hopkins University Press. (15)

Smith, M. W. (1974). Alfred Binet's remarkable questions: A cross-national and cross-temporal analysis of the cultural biases built into the Stanford-Binet intelligence scale and other Binet tests. *Genetic Psychology Monographs, 89,* 307–334. (9)

Smith, P., & Waterman, M. (2003). Processing bias for aggression words in forensic and nonforensic samples. *Cognition and Emotion, 17,* 681–701. (13)

Snyder, C. R. (2003). "Me conform? No way": Classroom demonstrations for sensitizing students to their conformity. *Teaching of Psychology, 30,* 59–61. (14)

Snyder, M., Tanke, E. D., & Bersheid, E. (1977). Social perception and interpersonal behavior: On the self-fulfilling nature of social stereotypes. *Journal of Personality and Social Psychology, 35,* 656–666. (14)

Sohlberg, M. M., & Mateer, C. A. (2001). Improving attention and managing attentional problems. *Annals of the New York Academy of Sciences, 931,* 359–375. (15)

Solanto, M. V., Abikoff, H., Sonuga-Barke, E., Schachar, R., Logan, G. D., Wigal, T., et al. (2001). The ecological validity of delay aversion and response inhibition as measures of impulsivity in AD/HD: A supplement to the NIMH multimodal treatment study of AD/HD. *Journal of Abnormal Child Psychology, 29,* 215–228. (15)

Solin, D. (1989). The systematic misrepresentation of bilingual-crossed aphasia data and its consequences. *Brain and Language, 36,* 92–116. (8)

Solms, M. (1997). *The neuropsychology of dreams.* Mahwah, NJ: Erlbaum. (5)

Solms, M. (2000). Dreaming and REM sleep are controlled by different brain mechanisms. *Behavioral and Brain Sciences, 23,* 843–850. (5)

Solomon, D. A., Keller, M. B., Leon, A. C., Mueller, T. I., Shea, T., Warshaw, M., et al. (1997). Recovery from major depression. *Archives of General Psychiatry, 54,* 1001–1006. (16)

Solomon, Z., Mikulincer, M., & Flum, H. (1988). Negative life events, coping responses, and combat-related psychopathology: A prospective study. *Journal of Abnormal Psychology, 97,* 302–307. (16)

Song, H., Stevens, C. F., & Gage, F. H. (2002). Neural stem cells from adult hippocampus develop essential properties of functional CNS neurons. *Nature Neuroscience, 5,* 438–445. (3)

Sorkin, R. D., Hays, C. J., & West, R. (2001). Signal-detection analysis of group decision making. *Psychological Review, 108,* 183–203. (14)

Sowell, E.. R., Peterson, B. S., Thompson, P. M., Welcome, S. E., Henkenius, A. L., & Toga, A. W. (2003). Mapping cortical change across the human life span. *Nature Neuroscience, 6,* 309–315. (3)

Sowell, E. R., Thompson, P. M., Holmes, C. J., Jernigan, T. L., & Toga, A. W. (1999). *In vivo* evidence for post-adolescent brain maturation in frontal and striatal regions. *Nature Neuroscience, 2,* 859–861. (16)

Spanos, N. P. (1987–88). Past-life hypnotic regression: A critical view. *Skeptical Inquirer, 12,* 174–180. (5)

Spear, L. P. (2000). Neurobehavioral changes in adolescence. *Current Directions in Psychological Science, 9,* 111–114. (10)

Spearman, C. (1904). "General intelligence," objectively determined and measured. *American Journal of Psychology, 15,* 201–293. (9)

Speer, J. R. (1989). Detection of plastic explosives. *Science, 243,* 1651. (8)

Spehar, B., & Gillam, B. (2002). Modal completion in the Poggendorff illusion: Support for the depth-processing theory. *Psychological Science, 13,* 306–312. (4)

Spence, C., & Read, L. (2003). Speech shadowing while driving: On the difficulty of splitting attention between eye and ear. *Psychological Science, 14,* 251–256. (8)

Sperling, G. (1960). The information available in brief visual presentations. *Psychological Monographs, 74*(11, Whole No. 498). (7)

Sperry, R. W. (1967). Split-brain approach to learning problems. In G. C. Quarton, T. Melnechuk, & F. O. Schmitt (Eds.), *The neurosciences: A study program* (pp. 714–722). New York: Rockefeller University Press. (3)

Spira, A., et al. (1993). *Les comportements sexuels en France.* Paris: La documentation Française. (11)

Squire, L. R., Haist, F., & Shimamura, A. P. (1989). The neurology of memory: Quantitative assessment of retrograde amnesia in two groups of amnesic patients. *Journal of Neuroscience, 9,* 828–839. (7)

Staddon, J. (1993). *Behaviorism.* London: Duckworth. (6)

Staddon, J. E. R. (1999). Theoretical behaviorism. In W. O'Donohue & R. Kitchener (Eds.), *Handbook of behaviorism* (pp. 217–241). San Diego, CA: Academic Press. (6)

Stanton, M. D., & Shadish, W. R. (1997). Outcome, attrition, and family-couples treatment for drug abuse: A meta-analysis and review of the controlled, comparative studies. *Psychological Bulletin, 122,* 170–191. (16)

Starr, C., & Taggart, R. (1992). *Biology: The unity and diversity of life* (6th ed.). Belmont, CA: Wadsworth. (3)

Staub, E. (1996). Cultural-societal roots of violence. *American Psychologist, 51,* 117–132. (12)

Stayer, D. L., Drews, F. A., & Johnston, W. A. (2003). Cell phone-induced failures of visual attention during simulated driving. *Journal of Experimental Psychology: Applied, 9,* 23–32. (8)

Ste-Marie, D. M. (1999). Expert–novice differences in gymnastic judging: An information-processing perspective. *Applied Cognitive Psychology, 13,* 269–281. (8)

Steblay, N. M., & Bothwell, R. K. (1994). Evidence for hypnotically refreshed testimony. *Law and Human Behavior, 18,* 635–651. (5)

Steele, C. M., & Aronson, J. (1995). Stereotype threat and the intellectual test performance of African Americans. *Journal of Personality and Social Psychology, 69,* 797–811. (9)

Steele, C. M., Spencer, S. J., & Aronson, J. (2002). Contending with group image: The psychology of stereotype and social identity threat. *Advances in Experimental Social Psychology, 34,* 379–440. (14)

Steele, K. M., Bass, K. E., & Crook, M. D. (1999). The mystery of the Mozart effect: Failure to replicate. *Psychological Science, 10,* 366–369. (2)

Stefanatos, G. A., & Wasserstein, J. (2001). Attention deficit/hyperactivity disorder as a right hemisphere syndrome. *Annals of the New York Academy of Sciences, 931,* 172–195. (15)

Stegat, H. (1975). Die Verhaltenstherapie der Enuresis und Enkopresis [Behavior therapy for enuresis and encopresis]. *Zeitschrift für Kinder- und Jugendpsychiatrie, 3,* 149–173. (15)

Stein, M. B., Torgrud, L. J., & Walker, J. R. (2000). Social phobia symptoms, subtypes, and severity. *Archives of General Psychiatry, 57,* 1046–1052. (16)

Stella, N., Schweitzer, P., & Piomelli, D. (1997). A second endogenous cannabinoid that modulates long-term potentiation. *Nature, 382,* 677–678. (5)

Sternberg, R. J. (1985). *Beyond IQ.* Cambridge, England: Cambridge University Press. (9)

Sternberg, R. J. (1997). The concept of intelligence and its role in lifelong learning and success. *American Psychologist, 52,* 1030–1037. (9)

Sternberg, R. J. (2002). Beyond *g*: The theory of successful intelligence. In R. J. Sternberg & E. L. Grigorenko (Eds.), *The general intelligence factor: How general is it?* (pp. 447–479). Mahwah, NJ: Erlbaum.(9)

Sternberg, R. J., Nokes, C., Geissler, P. W., Prince, R., Okatcha, F., Bundy, D. A., et al. (2001). The relationship between academic and practical intelligence: A case study in Kenya. *Intelligence, 29,* 401–418. (9)

Stevens, S. S. (1961). To honor Fechner and repeal his law. *Science, 133,* 80–86. (1)

Stevenson, R. J., & Boakes, R. A. (2003). A mnemonic theory of odor perception. *Psychological Review, 110,* 340–364. (4)

Stewart, A. J., & Ostrove, J. M. (1998). Women's personality in middle age. *American Psychologist, 53,* 1185–1194. (10)

Stewart, I. (1987). Are mathematicians logical? *Nature, 325,* 386–387. (9)

Stewart, J. W., Quitkin, F. M., McGrath, P. J., Amsterdam, J., Fava, M., Fawcett, J., et al. (1998). Use of pattern analysis to predict differential relapse of remitted patients with major depression during 1 year of treatment with fluoxetine or placebo. *Archives of General Psychiatry, 55,* 334–343. (16)

Stice, E. (2002). Risk and maintenance factors for eating pathology: A meta-analytic review. *Psychological Bulletin, 128,* 825–848. (11)

Stickgold, R., Malia, A., Maguire, D., Roddenberry, D., & O'Connor, M. (2000). Replaying the game: Hypnagogic images in normals and amnesics. *Science, 290,* 350–353. (7)

Stickgold, R., Whidbee, D., Schirmer, B., Patel, V., & Hobson, J. A. (2000). Visual discrimination task improvement: A multi-step process occurring during sleep. *Journal of Cognitive Neuroscience, 12,* 246–254. (5)

Stiles, W. B., Shapiro, D. A., & Elliott, R. (1986). "Are all psychotherapies equivalent?" *American Psychologist, 41,* 165–180. (15)

Stokes, P. D. (2001). Variability, constraints, and creativity. *American Psychologist, 56,* 355–359. (8)

Stompe, T., Ortwein-Swoboda, G., Ritter, K., Schanda, H., & Friedmann, A. (2002). Are we witnessing the disappearance of catatonic schizophrenia? *Comprehensive Psychiatry, 43,* 167–174. (16)

Stone, E. R., Dodrill, C. L., & Johnson, N. (2001). Depressive cognition: A test of depressive realism versus negativity using general knowledge items. *Journal of Psychology, 135,* 583–602. (9)

Stone, V. E., Nisenson, L., Eliassen, J. C., & Gazzaniga, M. S. (1996). Left hemisphere representations of emotional facial expressions. *Neuropsychologia, 34,* 23–29. (3)

Stoolmiller, M. (1999). Implications of the restricted range of family environments for estimates of heritability and non-shared environment in behavior-genetic adoption studies. *Psychological Bulletin, 125,* 392–409. (10)

Storms, M. D. (1973). Videotape and the attribution process: Reversing actors' and observers' points of view. *Journal of Personality and Social Psychology, 27,* 165–175. (14)

Strack, F., Martin, L. L., & Stepper, S. (1988). Inhibiting and facilitating conditions of the human smile: A nonobtrusive test of the facial feedback hypothesis. *Journal of Personality and Social Psychology, 54,* 768–777. (12)

Strauch, I., & Lederbogen, S. (1999). The home dreams and waking fantasies of boys and girls between ages 9 and 15: A longitudinal study. *Dreaming, 9,* 153–161. (5)

Streissguth, A. P., Sampson, P. D., & Barr, H. M. (1989). Neurobehavioral dose-response effects of prenatal alcohol exposure in humans from infancy to adulthood. *Annals of the New York Academy of Sciences, 562,* 145–158. (10)

Struckman-Johnson, C., Struckman-Johnson, D., & Anderson, P. B. (2003). Tactics of sexual coercion: When men and women won't take no for an answer. *Journal of Sex Research, 40,* 76–86. (12)

Strupp, H. H. (1996). The tripartite model and the *Consumer Reports* study. *American Psychologist, 51,* 1017–1024. (15)

Stuss, D. T., Alexander, M. P., Palumbo, C. L., Buckle, L., Sayer, L., & Pogue, J. (1994). Organizational strategies of patients with unilateral or bilateral frontal lobe injury in word list learning tasks. *Neuropsychology, 8,* 355–373. (7)

Sudzak, P. D., Glowa, J. R., Crawley, J. N., Schwartz, R. D., Skolnick, P., & Paul, S. M. (1986). A selective imidazobenzodiazepine antagonist of ethanol in the rat. *Science, 234,* 1243–1247. (5)

Sue, S. (1998). In search of cultural competence in psychotherapy and counseling. *American Psychologist, 53,* 440–448. (15)

Sullivan, E. V., Deshmukh, A., Desmond, J. E., Mathalon, D. H., Rosenbloom, M. J., Lim, K. O., et al. (2000). Contribution of alcohol abuse to cerebellar volume deficits in men with schizophrenia. *Archives of General Psychiatry, 57,* 894–902. (16)

Suls, J., Martin, R., & Wheeler, L. (2002). Social comparisons: Why, with whom, and with what effect? *Current Directions in Psychological Science, 11,* 159–163. (14)

Süss, H. M., Oberauer, K., Wittman, W. W., Wilhelm, O., & Schulze, R. (2002). Working memory capacity explains reasoning ability—and a little bit more. *Intelligence, 30,* 261–288. (7, 9)

Susser, E., Neugebauer, R., Hoek, H. W., Brown, A. S., Lin, S., Labovitz, D., et al. (1996). Schizophrenia after prenatal famine. *Archives of General Psychiatry, 53,* 25–31. (16)

Suvisaari, J. M., Haukka, J. K., Tanskanen, A. J., & Lönnqvist, J. K. (1999). Decline in the incidence of schizophrenia in Finnish cohorts born from 1954 to 1965. *Archives of General Psychiatry, 56,* 733–740. (16)

Suzuki, L. A., & Valencia, R. R. (1997). Race-ethnicity and measured intelligence. *American Psychologist, 52,* 1103–1114. (9)

Swann, W. B., Jr. (1997). The trouble with change: Self-verification and allegiance to the self. *Psychological Science, 8,* 177–180. (14)

Swann, W. B., Jr., & Gill, M. J. (1997). Confidence and accuracy in person perception: Do we know what we think we know about our relationship partners? *Journal of Personality and Social Psychology, 73,* 747–757. (14)

Swanson, J. M., Flodman, P., Kennedy, J., Spence, M. A., Moyzis, R., Schuck, S., et al. (2000). Dopamine genes and ADHD. *Neuroscience and Biobehavioral Reviews, 24,* 21–25. (3)

Sweet, S. S., & Pianka, E. R. (2003, November). The lizard kings. *Natural History, 112*(9), 40–45. (6)

Swendsen, J. D., Tennen, H., Carney, M. A., Affleck, G., Willard, A., & Hromi, A. (2000). Mood and alcohol consumption: An experience sampling test of the self-medication hypothesis. *Journal of Abnormal Psychology, 109,* 198–204. (16)

Swinkels, A., & Giuliano, T. A. (1995). The measurement and conceptualization of mood awareness: Monitoring and labeling one's mood states. *Personality and Social Psychology Bulletin, 21,* 934–949. (12)

Swinton, S. S. (1987). *The predictive validity of the restructured GRE with particular attention to older students* (GRE Board Professional Rep. No. 83-25P. ETS Research Rep. 87-22). Princeton, NJ: Educational Testing Service. (9)

Swoboda, H., Amering, M., Windhaber, J., & Katschnig, H. (2003). The long-term course of panic disorder—an 11 year follow-up. *Journal of Anxiety Disorders, 17,* 223–232. (16)

Symons, C. S., & Johnson, B. T. (1997). The self-reference effect in memory: A meta-analysis. *Psychological Bulletin, 121,* 371–394. (7)

Szasz, T. S. (1982). The psychiatric will. *American Psychologist, 37,* 762–770. (15)

Szechtman, H., Woody, E., Bowers, K. S., & Nahmias, C. (1998). Where the imagined appears real: A positron emission tomography study of auditory hallucinations. *Proceedings of the National Academy of Sciences, USA, 95,* 1956–1960. (5)

Szymanski, H. V., Simon, J. C., & Gutterman, N. (1983). Recovery from schizophrenic psychosis. *American Journal of Psychiatry, 140,* 335–338. (16)

Tabiner, M., Youings, S., Dennis, N., Baldwin, D., Buis, C., Mayers, A., et al. (2003). Failure to find DUP25 in patients with anxiety disorders, in control individuals, or in previously reported positive control cell lines. *American Journal of Human Genetics, 72,* 535–538. (16)

Takano, Y., & Osaka, E. (1999). An unsupported common view: Comparing Japan and the U.S. on individualism/collectivism. *Asian Journal of Social Psychology, 2,* 311–341. (14)

Takeuchi, A. H., & Hulse, S. H. (1993). Absolute pitch. *Psychological Bulletin, 113,* 345–361. (4)

Talarico, J. M., & Rubin, D. C. (2003). Confidence, not consistency, characterizes flashbulb memories. *Psychological Science, 14,* 455–461. (7)

Taller, A. M., Asher, D. M., Pomeroy, K. L., Eldadah, B. A., Godec, M. S., Falkai, P. G., et al. (1996). Search for viral nucleic acid sequences in brain tissues of patients with schizophrenia using nested polymerase chain reaction. *Archives of General Psychiatry, 53,* 32–40. (16)

Tannen, D. (1990). *You just don't understand.* New York: Morrow. (10)

Tarr, M. J., & Gauthier, I. (2000). FFA: A flexible fusiform area for subordinate-level visual processing automatized by experience. *Nature Neuroscience, 3,* 764–769. (3)

Tassinary, L. G., & Hansen, K. A. (1998). A critical test of the waist-to-hip-ratio hypothesis of female physical attractiveness. *Psychological Science, 9,* 150–155. (14)

Tatler, B. W., Gilchrist, I. D., & Rusted, J. (2003). The time course of abstract visual representation. *Perception, 32,* 579–592. (8)

Taylor, S. E., Pham, L. B., Rivkin, I. D., & Armor, D. A. (1998). Harnessing the imagination: Mental simulation, self-regulation, and coping. *American Psychologist, 53,* 429–439. (12)

Teicher, M. H., Glod, C. A., Magnus, E., Harper, D., Benson, G., Krueger, K., et al. (1997). Circadian rest–activity disturbances in seasonal affective disorder. *Archives of General Psychiatry, 54,* 124–130. (16)

Terman, J. S., Terman, M., Lo, E.-S., & Cooper, T. B. (2001). Circadian time of morning light administration and therapeutic response in winter depression. *Archives of General Psychiatry, 58,* 69–75. (16)

Terr, L. (1988). What happens to early memories of trauma? A study of twenty children under age five at the time of documented traumatic events. *Journal of the American Academy of Child and Adolescent Psychiatry, 27,* 96–104. (7)

Terrace, H. S., Petitto, L. A., Sanders, R. J., & Bever, T. G. (1979). Can an ape create a sentence? *Science, 206,* 891–902. (8)

Testa, M., Livingston, J. A., Vanzile-Tamsen, C., & Frone, M. R. (2003). The role of women's substance use in vulnerability to forcible and incapacitated rape. *Journal of Studies on Alcohol, 64,* 756–764. (12)

Tetlock, P. E. (1994, July 2). *Good judgment in world politics: Who gets what right, when and why?* Address presented at the sixth annual convention of the American Psychological Society. (8)

Tett, R. P., & Burnett, D. D. (2003). A personality trait-based interactionist model of job performance. *Journal of Applied Psychology, 88,* 500–517. (11)

Tett, R. P., & Palmer, C. A. (1997). The validity of handwriting elements in relation to self-report personality trait measures. *Personality and Individual Differences, 22,* 11–18. (13)

Thanickal, T. C., Moore, R. Y., Nienhuis, R., Ramanathan, L., Gulyani, S., Aldrich, M., et al. (2000). Reduced number of hypocretin neurons in human narcolepsy. *Neuron, 27,* 469–474. (5)

Thase, M. E., Greenhouse, J. B., Frank, E., Reynolds, C. F., III, Pilkonis, P. A., Hurley, K., et al. (1997). Treatment of major depression with psychotherapy or psychotherapy-pharmacotherapy combinations. *Archives of General Psychiatry, 54,* 1009–1015. (16)

Thase, M. E., Trivedi, M. H., & Rush, A. J. (1995). MAOIs in the contemporary treatment of depression. *Neuropsychopharmacology, 12,* 185–219. (16)

Thieman, T. J. (1984). A classroom demonstration of encoding specificity. *Teaching of Psychology, 11,* 101–102. (7)

Thigpen, C., & Cleckley, H. (1957). *The three faces of Eve.* New York: McGraw-Hill. (15)

Thomas, A., & Chess, S. (1980). *The dynamics of psychological development.* New York: Brunner/Mazel. (10)

Thomas, A., Chess, S., & Birch, H. G. (1968). *Temperament and behavior disorders in children.* New York: New York University Press. (10)

Thompson, C. (2001, September). The know-it-all machine. *Lingua Franca, 11*(6), 26–35. (8)

Thompson, C. R., & Church, R. M. (1980). An explanation of the language of a chimpanzee. *Science, 208,* 313–314. (8)

Thompson, W. F., Schellenberg, E. G., & Husain, G. (2001). Arousal, mood, and the Mozart effect. *Psychological Science, 12,* 248–251. (2)

Thoresen, C. J., Kaplan, S. A., Barsky, A. P., Warren, C. R., & de Chermont, K. (2003). The affective underpinnings of job perceptions and attitudes: A meta-analytic review and integration. *Psychological Bulletin, 129,* 914–945. (11)

Thorndike, E. L. (1970). *Animal intelligence.* Darien, CT: Hafner. (Original work published 1911) (6)

Thornton, B. (1977). Toward a linear prediction model of marital happiness. *Personality and Social Psychology Bulletin, 3,* 674–676. (14)

Tiedens, L. Z., & Linton, S. (2001). Judgment under emotional certainty and uncertainty: The effects of specific emotions on information processing. *Journal of Personality and Social Psychology, 81,* 973–988. (12)

Timberlake, W., & Farmer-Dougan, V. A. (1991). Reinforcement in applied settings: Figuring out ahead of time what will work. *Psychological Bulletin, 110,* 379–391. (6)

Tingate, T. R., Lugg, D. J., Muller, H. K., Stowe, R. P., & Pierson, D. L. (1997). Antarctic isolation: Immune and viral studies. *Immunology and Cell Biology, 75,* 275–283. (12)

Titchener, E. B. (1910). *A textbook of psychology.* New York: Macmillan. (1)

Tiedens, L. Z., & Linton, S. (2001). Judgment under emotional certainty and uncertainty: The effects of specific emotions on information processing. *Journal of Personality and Social Psychology, 81,* 973–988. (12)

Todes, D. P. (1997). From the machine to the ghost within. *American Psychologist, 52,* 947–955. (6)

Toh, K. L., Jones, C. R., He, Y., Eide, E. J., Hinz, W. A., Virshup, D. M., et al. (2001). An h*Per2* phosphorylation site mutation in familial advanced sleep phase syndrome. *Science, 291,* 1040–1043. (5)

Tolman, E. C. (1938). The determinants of behavior at a choice point. *Psychological Review, 45,* 1–41. (1)

Tolstoy, L. (1978). *Tolstoy's letters: Vol. I. 1828–1879.* New York: Charles Scribner's Sons. (Original works written 1828–1879) (10)

Tombaugh, C. W. (1980). *Out of the darkness, the planet Pluto.* Harrisburg, PA: Stackpole. (4)

Torgerson, S., Kringlen, E., & Cramer, V. (2001). The prevalence of personality disorders in a community sample. *Archives of General Psychiatry, 58,* 590–596. (15)

Torrey, E. F. (1986). Geographic variations in schizophrenia. In C. Shagass, R. C. Josiassen, W. H. Bridger, K. J. Weiss, D. Stoff, & G. M. Simpson (Eds.), *Biological psychiatry 1985* (pp. 1080–1082). New York: Elsevier. (16)

Torrey, E. F., Bowler, A. E., & Clark, K. (1997). Urban birth and residence as risk factors for psychoses: An analysis of 1880 data. *Schizophrenia Research, 28,* 1–38. (16)

Torrey, E. F., & Miller, J. (2001). *The invisible plague: The rise of mental illness from 1750 to the present.* New Brunswick, NJ: Rutgers University Press. (15, 16)

Townshend, J. M., & Duka, T. (2003). Mixed emotions: Alcoholics' impairments in the recognition of specific emotional facial expressions. *Neuropsychologia, 41,* 773–782. (12)

Treisman, A. (1999). Feature binding, attention and object perception. In G. W. Humphreys, Duncan, J., & Treisman, A. (Eds.), *Attention, space and action* (pp. 91–111). Oxford, England: Oxford University Press. (3)

Treisman, A., & Souther, J. (1985). Search asymmetry: A diagnostic for preattentive processing of separable features. *Journal of Experimental Psychology: General, 114,* 285–310. (8)

Tronick, E. Z., Morelli, G. A., & Ivey, P. K. (1992). The Efe forager infant and toddler's pattern of social relationships: Multiple and simultaneous. *Developmental Psychology, 28,* 568–577. (10)

Trope, Y., & Liberman, N. (2003). Temporal construal. *Psychological Review, 110,* 403–421. (11)

True, W. R., Xian, H., Scherer, J. F., Madden, P. A. F., Bucholz, K. K., Heath, A. C., et al. (1999). Common genetic vulnerability for nicotine and alcohol dependence in men. *Archives of General Psychiatry, 56,* 655–661. (16)

Truscott, D., & Crook, K. H. (1993). *Tarasoff* in the Canadian context: *Wenden* and the duty to protect. *Canadian Journal of Psychiatry, 38,* 84–89. (15)

Tschann, J. M., Johnston, J. R., Kline, M., & Wallerstein, J. S. (1990). Conflict, loss, change and parent-child relationships: Predicting children's adjustment during divorce. *Journal of Divorce, 13,* 1–22. (10)

Tu, G. C., & Israel, Y. (1995). Alcohol consumption by Orientals in North America is predicted largely by a single gene. *Behavior Genetics, 25,* 59–65. (6)

Tuiten, A., Van Honk, J., Koppeschaar, H., Bernaards, C., Thijssen, J., & Verbaten, R. (2000). Time course of effects of testosterone administration on sexual arousal in women. *Archives of General Psychiatry, 57,* 149–153. (11)

Tulving, E. (1989). Remembering and knowing the past. *American Scientist, 77,* 361–367. (7)

Tulving, E., & Thomson, D. M. (1973). Encoding specificity and retrieval processes in episodic memory. *Psychological Review, 80,* 352–373. (7)

Turkheimer, E., Haley, A., Waldron, M., D'Onofrio, B., & Gottesman, I. I. (2003). Socioeconomic status modifies heritability of IQ in young children. *Psychological Science, 14,* 623–628. (9)

Turner, C. F., Ku, L., Rogers, S. M., Lindberg, L. D., Pleck, J. H., & Sonenstein, F. L. (1998). Adolescent sexual behavior, drug use, and violence: Increased reporting with computer survey technology. *Science, 280,* 867–873. (11)

Tversky, A., & Kahneman, D. (1981). The framing of decisions and the psychology of choice. *Science, 211,* 453–458. (8)

Tversky, A., & Kahneman, D. (1983). Extensional versus intuitive reasoning: The conjunctional fallacy in probability judgment. *Psychological Review, 90,* 293–315. (8)

Tversky, B. (1981). Distortions in memory for maps. *Cognitive Psychology, 13,* 407–433. (8)

Twenge, J. M. (2000). The age of anxiety? Birth cohort change in anxiety and neuroticism, 1952–1993. *Journal of Personality and Social Psychology, 79,* 1007–1021. (13)

Twenge, J. M. (2002). Birth cohort, social change, and personality. In D. Cervone & W. Mischel (Eds.), *Advances in personality science* (pp. 196–218). New York: Guilford Press. (10)

Tyler, L. K., deMornay-Davies, P., Anokhina, R., Longworth, C., Randall, B., & Marslen-Wilson, W. D. (2002). Dissociations in processing past tense morphology: Neuropathology and behavioral studies. *Journal of Cognitive Neuroscience, 14,* 79–94. (8)

Uchino, B. N., Cacioppo, J. T., & Kiecolt-Glaser, J. K. (1996). The relationship between social support and physiological processes: A review with emphasis on underlying mechanisms and implications for health. *Psychological Bulletin, 119,* 488–531. (12)

Udolf, R. (1981). *Handbook of hypnosis for professionals.* New York: Van Nostrand Reinhold. (5)

Ulrich, R. E., Stachnik, T. J., & Stainton, N. R. (1963). Student acceptance of generalized personality interpretations. *Psychological Reports, 13,* 831–834. (13)

Ulrich, R. S. (1984). View through a window may influence recovery from surgery. *Science, 224,* 420–421. (4)

Vaillant, G. E. (1983). *The natural history of alcoholism.* Cambridge, MA: Harvard University Press. (16)

Vaillant, G. E., & Milofsky, E. S. (1982). The etiology of alcoholism: A prospective viewpoint. *American Psychologist, 37,* 494–503. (16)

van den Hout, M., & Kindt, M. (2003). Repeated checking causes memory distrust. *Behaviour Research and Therapy, 41,* 301–316. (16)

van den Pol, A. N. (1999). Hypothalamic hypocretin (orexin): Robust innervation of the spinal cord. *Journal of Neuroscience, 19,* 3171–3182. (11)

van der Pligt, J., de Vries, N. K., Manstead, A. S. R., & van Harreveld, F. (2000). The importance of being selective: Weighing the role of attribute importance in attitudinal judgment. *Advances in Experimental Social Psychology, 32,* 135–200. (14)

van der Pligt, J., & Eiser, J. R. (1983). Actors' and observers' attributions, self-serving bias, and positivity. *European Journal of Social Psychology, 13,* 95–104. (14)

van Praag, H., Kempermann, G., & Gage, F. H. (2000). Neural consequences of environmental enrichment. *Nature Reviews Neuroscience, 1,* 191–198. (3)

Vandell, D. L. (2000). Parents, peer groups, and other socializing influences. *Developmental Psychology, 36,* 699–710. (10)

Vasta, R., & Liben, L. S. (1996). The water-level task: An intriguing puzzle. *Current Directions in Psychological Science, 5,* 171–177. (10)

Vasterling, J., Duke, L. M., Brailey, K., Constans, J. I., Allain, A. N., & Sutker, P. B. (2002). Attention, learning, and memory performances and intellectual resources in Vietnam veterans: PTSD and no disorder comparisons. *Neuropsychology, 16,* 5–14. (9)

Vaswani, M., & Kapur, S. (2001). Genetic basis of schizophrenia: Trinucleotide repeats an update. *Progress in Neuro-Psychopharmacology & Biological Psychiatry, 25,* 1187–1201. (16)

Velakoulis, D., Pantelis, C., McGorry, P. D., Dudgeon, P., Brewer, W., Cook, M., et al. (1999). Hippocampal volume in first-episode psychoses and chronic schizophrenia. *Archives of General Psychiatry, 56,* 133–140. (16)

Velluti, R. A. (1997). Interactions between sleep and sensory physiology. *Journal of Sleep Research, 6,* 61–77. (5)

Verrey, F., & Beron, J. (1996). Activation and supply of channels and pumps by aldosterone. *News in Physiological Sciences, 11,* 126–133. (11)

Viken, R. J., Rose, R. J., Kaprio, J., & Koskenvuo, M. (1994). A developmental genetic analysis of adult personality: Extraversion and neuroticism from 18 to 59 years of age. *Journal of Personality and Social Psychology, 66,* 722–730. (10, 13)

Visser, T. A. W., Bischof, W. F., & DiLollo, V. (1999). Attentional switching in spatial and nonspatial domains: Evidence from the attentional blink. *Psychological Bulletin, 125,* 458–469. (8)

Vitevitch, M. S. (2003). Change deafness: The inability to detect changes between two voices. *Journal of Experimental Psychology: Human Perception and Performance, 29,* 333–342. (8)

Vohs, K. D., & Heatherton, T. F. (2000). Self-regulatory failure: A resource-depletion approach. *Psychological Science, 11,* 249–254. (11)

Vokey, J. R., & Read, J. D. (1985). Subliminal messages: Between the devil and the media. *American Psychologist, 40,* 1231–1239. (4)

Volkow, N. D., Wang, G.-J., & Fowler, J. S. (1997). Imaging studies of cocaine in the human brain and studies of the cocaine addict. *Annals of the New York Academy of Sciences, 820,* 41–55. (5)

Volkow, N. D., Wang, G.-J., Fowler, J., Gatley, S. J., Logan, J., Ding, Y.-S., et al. (1998). Dopamine transporter occupancies in the human brain induced by therapeutic doses of oral methylphenidate. *American Journal of Psychiatry, 155,* 1325–1331. (3, 5)

Vygotsky, L. S. (1978). *Mind in society.* Cambridge, MA: Harvard University Press. (10)

Wachtel, P. L. (2000). Psychotherapy in the twenty-first century. *American Journal of Psychotherapy, 54,* 441–450. (15)

Wadden, T. A., & Stunkard, A. J. (1987). Psychopathology and obesity. *Annals of the New York Academy of Sciences, 499,* 55–65. (11)

Waelti, P., Dickinson, A., & Schultz, W. (2001). Dopamine responses comply with basic assumptions of formal learning theory. *Nature, 412,* 43–48. (16)

Wagner, A. D., Desmond, J. E., Demb, J. B., Glover, G. H., & Gabrieli, J. D. E. (1997). Semantic repetition priming for verbal and pictorial knowledge: A functional MRI study of left inferior prefrontal cortex. *Journal of Cognitive Neuroscience, 9,* 714–726. (3)

Wagner, R. K. (1997). Intelligence, training, and employment. *American Psychologist, 52,* 1059–1069. (9)

Wagner, U., Gais, S., Haider, H., Verleger, R., & Born, J. (2004). Sleep inspires insight. *Nature, 427,* 352–355. (5)

Wahlbeck, K., Forsén, T., Osmond, C., Barker, D. J. P., & Eriksson, J. G. (2001). Association of schizophrenia with low maternal body mass index, small size at birth, and thinness during childhood. *Archives of General Psychiatry, 58,* 48–52. (16)

Wakschlag, L. S., Lahey, B. B., Loeber, R., Green, S. M., Gordon, R. A., & Leventhal, B. L. (1997). Maternal smoking during pregnancy and the risk of conduct disorder in boys. *Archives of General Psychiatry, 54,* 670–676. (10)

Wald, G. (1968). Molecular basis of visual excitation. *Science, 162,* 230–239. (4)

Waldman, I. D., Weinberg, R. A., & Scarr, S. (1994). Racial-group differences in IQ in the Minnesota transracial adoption study: A reply to Levin and Lynn. *Intelligence, 19,* 29–44. (9)

Waller, N. G., Kojetin, B. A., Bouchard, T. J., Jr., Lykken, D. T., & Tellegen, A. (1990). Genetic and environmental influences on religious interests, attitudes, and values: A study of twins reared apart and together. *Psychological Science, 1,* 138–142. (10)

Walster, E., Aronson, E., Abrahams, D., & Rottman, L. (1966). Importance of physical attractiveness in dating behavior. *Journal of Personality and Social Psychology, 4,* 508–516. (14)

Wampold, B. E., Mondin, G. W., Moody, M., Stich, F., Benson, K., & Ahn, H. (1997). A meta-analysis of outcome studies comparing bona fide psychotherapies: Empirically, "All must have prizes." *Psychological Bulletin, 122,* 203–215. (15)

Wandersman, A., & Florin, P. (2003). Community interventions and effective prevention. *American Psychologist, 58,* 441–448. (15)

Warren, R. M. (1970). Perceptual restoration of missing speech sounds. *Science, 167,* 392–393. (4, 8)

Warren, R. M. (1999). *Auditory perception.* Cambridge, England: Cambridge University Press. (4)

Wason, P. C. (1960). On the failure to eliminate hypotheses in a conceptual task. *Quarterly Journal of Experimental Psychology, 12,* 129–140. (8)

Waters, E., Merrick, S., Treboux, D., Crowell, J., & Albersheim, L. (2000). Attachment security in infancy and early adulthood: A twenty-year longitudinal study. *Child Development, 71,* 684–689. (10)

Watson, D., Suls, J., & Haig, J. (2002). Global self-esteem in relation to structural models of personality and affectivity. *Journal of Personality and Social Psychology, 83,* 185–197. (13)

Watson, D., Wiese, D., Vaidya, J., & Tellegen, A. (1999). The two general activation systems of affect: Structural findings, evolutionary considerations, and psychobiological evidence. *Journal of Personality and Social Psychology, 76,* 820–838. (12)

Watson, J. B. (1913). Psychology as the behaviorist views it. *Psychological Review, 20,* 158–177. (1)

Watson, J. B. (1919). *Psychology from the standpoint of a behaviorist.* Philadelphia: Lippincott. (1)

Watson, J. B. (1925). *Behaviorism.* New York: Norton. (1, 6)

Watson, J. B., & Rayner, R. (1920). Conditioned emotional reactions. *Journal of Experimental Psychology, 3,* 1–14. (16)

Watson, J. M., Balota, D. A., & Roediger, H. L., III (2003). Creating false memories with hybrid lists of semantic and phonological associates: Over-additive false memories produced by converging associative networks. *Journal of Memory and Language, 49,* 95–118. (7)

Waynforth, D., & Dunbar, R. I. M. (1995). Conditional mate choice strategies in humans: Evidence from "lonely hearts" advertisements. *Behaviour, 132,* 755–779. (14)

Weaver, C. A., III, & Kelemen, W. L. (1997). Judgments of learning at delays: Shifts in response patterns or increased metamemory accuracy? *Psychological Science, 8,* 318–321. (7)

Webb, W. B. (1979). Theories of sleep functions and some clinical implications. In R. Drucker-Colín, M. Shkurovich, & M. B. Sterman (Eds.), *The functions of sleep* (pp. 19–35). New York: Academic Press. (5)

Wechsler, D. (1991). *Wechsler Intelligence Scale for Children-III.* San Antonio, TX: Psychological Corporation. (9)

Wegner, D. M. (2002). *The illusion of conscious will.* Cambridge, MA: MIT Press. (1)

Wegner, D. M., Schneider, D. J., Carter, S. R., III, & White, T. L. (1987). Paradoxical effects of thought suppression. *Journal of Personality and Social Psychology, 53,* 5–13. (16)

Wehr, T. A., Turner, E. H., Shimada, J. M., Lowe, C. H., Barker, C., & Leibenluft, E. (1998). Treatment of a rapidly cycling bipolar patient by using extended bed rest and darkness to stabilize the timing and duration of sleep. *Biological Psychiatry, 43,* 822–828. (16)

Weickert, T. W., Goldberg, T. E., Gold, J. M., Bigelow, L. B., Egan, M. F., & Weinberger, D. R. (2000). Cognitive impairments in patients with schizophrenia displaying preserved and compromised intellect. *Archives of General Psychiatry, 57,* 907–913. (16)

Weinberg, R. A., Scarr, S., & Waldman, I. D. (1992). The Minnesota transracial adoption study: A follow-up of IQ test performances at adolescence. *Intelligence, 16,* 117–135. (9)

Weinberger, D. R. (1987). Implications of normal brain development for the pathogenesis of schizophrenia. *Archives of General Psychiatry, 44,* 660–669. (16)

Weinberger, D. R. (1996). On the plausibility of "the neurodevelopmental hypothesis" of schizophrenia. *Neuropsychopharmacology, 14,* 1S–11S. (16)

Weinberger, D. R. (1999). Cell biology of the hippocampal formation in schizophrenia. *Biological Psychiatry, 45,* 395–402. (16)

Weiner, B. A., & Wettstein, R. M. (1993). *Legal issues in mental health care.* New York: Plenum Press. (15)

Weisberg, R. W. (1994). Genius and madness: A quasi-experimental test of the hypothesis that manic-depression increases creativity. *Psychological Science, 5,* 361–367. (16)

Weiser, M., Reichenberg, A., Rabinowitz, J., Kaplan, Z., Mark, M., Bodner, E., et al. (2001). Association between nonpsychotic psychiatric diagnoses in adolescent males and subsequent onset of schizophrenia. *Archives of General Psychiatry, 58,* 959–964. (16)

Weissman, M. M., Kidd, K. K., & Prusoff, B. A. (1982). Variability in rates of affective disorders in relatives of depressed and normal probands. *Archives of General Psychiatry, 39,* 1397–1403. (16)

Weissman, M. M., Leaf, P. J., & Bruce, M. L. (1987). Single parent women: A community study. *Social Psychiatry, 22,* 29–36. (10)

Weissman, M. M., Warner, V., Wickramaratne, P., Moreau, D., & Olfson, M. (1997). Offspring of depressed parents. *Archives of General Psychiatry, 54,* 932–940. (16)

Weller, A., & Weller, L. (1997). Menstrual synchrony under optimal conditions: Bedouin families. *Journal of Comparative Psychology, 111,* 143–151. (4)

Wellings, K., Field, J., Johnson, A., & Wadsworth, J. (1994). *Sexual behavior in Britain: The national survey of sexual attitudes and lifestyles.* New York: Penguin. (11)

Wells, G. L., Malpass, R. S., Lindsay, R. C. L., Fisher, R. P., Turtle, J. W., & Fulero, S. M. (2000). From the lab to the police station. *American Psychologist, 55,* 581–598. (7)

Wells, G. L., Olson, E. A., & Charman, S. D. (2002). The confidence of eyewitnesses in their identifications from lineups. *Current Directions in Psychological Science, 11,* 151–154. (7)

Wells, G. L., Olson, E. A., & Charman, S. D. (2003). Distorted retrospective eyewitness reports as functions of feedback and delay. *Journal of Experimental Psychology: General, 9,* 42–52. (7)

Wender, P. H., Wolf, L. E., & Wasserstein, J. (2001). Adults with ADHD. *Annals of the New York Academy of Sciences, 931,* 1–16. (15)

Wenger, J. R., Tiffany, T. M., Bombardier, C., Nicholls, K., & Woods, S. C. (1981). Ethanol tolerance in the rat is learned. *Science, 213,* 575–576. (5)

Weston, D. (1998). The scientific legacy of Sigmund Freud: Toward a psychodynamically informed psychological science. *Psychological Bulletin, 124,* 333–371. (13)

Whalen, P. J. (1998). Fear, vigilance, and ambiguity: Initial neuroimaging studies of the human amygdala. *Current Directions in Psychological Science, 7,* 177–188. (12)

Wheeler, D. D. (1970). Processes in word recognition. *Cognitive Psychology, 1,* 59–85. (8)

Wheeler, M. E., & Treisman, A. M. (2002). Binding in short-term visual memory. *Journal of Experimental Psychology: General, 131,* 48–64. (3)

Wicklund, R. A., & Brehm, J. W. (1976). *Perspectives on cognitive dissonance.* Hillsdale, NJ: Erlbaum. (14)

Widiger, T. A., & Clark, L. A. (2000). Toward DSM-V and the classification of psychopathology. *Psychological Bulletin, 126,* 946–963. (15, 16)

Widom, C. S. (1989). Does violence beget violence? A critical examination of the literature. *Psychological Bulletin, 106,* 3–28. (12)

Wig, N. N., Menon, D. K., Bedi, H., Leff, J., Kuipers, L., Ghosh, A., et al. (1987). Expressed emotion and schizophrenia in North India: II. Distribution of expressed emotion components among relatives of schizophrenic patients in Aarhus and Chandigarh. *British Journal of Psychiatry, 151,* 160–165. (16)

Wilkins, L., & Richter, C. P. (1940). A great craving for salt by a child with corticoadrenal insufficiency. *Journal of the American Medical Association, 114,* 866–868. (11)

Williams, C. L., Men, D., Clayton, E. C., & Gold, P. E. (1998). Norepinephrine release in the amygdala after systemic injection of epinephrine or escapable footshock: Contribution of the nucleus of the solitary tract. *Behavioral Neuroscience, 122,* 1414–1422. (7)

Williams, K. D., & Karau, S. J. (1991). Social loafing and social compensation: The effects of expectations of co-worker performance. *Journal of Personality and Social Psychology, 61,* 570–581. (14)

Williams, L. M. (1994). Recall of childhood trauma: A prospective study of women's memories of child sexual abuse. *Journal of Consulting and Clinical Psychology, 61,* 1167–1176. (7)

Williams, R. W., & Herrup, K. (1988). The control of neuron number. *Annual Review of Neuroscience, 11,* 423–453. (3)

Williams, W. M. (1998). Are we raising smarter children today? School- and home-related influences on IQ. In U. Neisser (Ed.), *The rising curve* (pp. 125–154). Washington, DC: American Psychological Association. (9)

Wilson, D. S., Near, D., & Miller, R. R. (1996). Machiavellianism: A synthesis of the evolutionary and psychological literatures. *Psychological Bulletin, 119,* 285–299. (14)

Wilson, J. R., & the editors of *Life.* (1964). *The mind.* New York: Time. (4)

Wilson, R. I., & Nicoll, R. A. (2001). Endogenous cannabinoids mediate retrograde signalling at hippocampal synapses. *Nature, 410,* 588–592. (5)

Wilson, R. I., & Nicoll, R. A. (2002). Endocannabinoid signaling in the brain. *Science, 296,* 678–682. (5)

Wilson, R. S. (1987). Risk and resilience in early mental development. In S. Chess & A. Thomas (Eds.), *Annual progress in child psychiatry and child development 1986* (pp. 69–85). New York: Brunner/Mazel. (10)

Wilson, T. D., Lindsey, S., & Schooler, T. Y. (2000). A model of dual attitudes. *Psychological Review, 107,* 101–126. (14)

Wimmer, H., & Perner, J. (1983). Beliefs about beliefs: Representation and constraining function of wrong beliefs in young children's understanding of deception. *Cognition, 13,* 103–128. (10)

Winer, G. A., & Cottrell, J. E. (1996). Does anything leave the eye when we see? Extramission beliefs of children and adults. *Current Directions in Psychological Science, 5,* 137–142. (4)

Winer, G. A., Cottrell, J. E., Gregg, V., Fournier, J. S., & Bica, L. A. (2002). Fundamentally misunderstanding visual perception: Adults' belief in visual emissions. *American Psychologist, 57,* 417–424. (4)

Winner, E. (1986, August). Where pelicans kiss seals. *Psychology Today,* 24–35. (10)

Winner, E. (2000). Giftedness: Current theory and research. *Current Directions in Psychological Science, 9,* 153–156. (9)

Winocur, G., & Hasher, L. (1999). Aging and time-of-day effects on cognition in rats. *Behavioral Neuroscience, 113,* 991–997. (5)

Wirz-Justice, A. (1998). Beginning to see the light. *Archives of General Psychiatry, 55,* 861–862. (16)

Wiseman, R. (1995). The megalab truth test. *Nature, 373,* 391. (12)

Wittchen, H.-U., Reed, V., & Kessler, R. C. (1998). The relationship of agoraphobia and panic in a community sample of adolescents and young adults. *Archives of General Psychiatry, 55,* 1017–1024. (16)

Wittchen, H.-U., Zhao, S., Kessler, R. C., & Eaton, W. W. (1994). DSM-III-R generalized anxiety disorder in the National Comorbidity Survey. *Archives of General Psychiatry, 51,* 355–364. (16)

Wolkin, A., Rusinek, H., Vaid, G., Arena, L., Lafargue, T., Sanfilipo, M., et al. (1998). Structural magnetic resonance image averaging in schizophrenia. *American Journal of Psychiatry, 155,* 1064–1073. (16)

Wolman, B. B. (1989). *Dictionary of behavioral science* (2nd ed.). San Diego, CA: Academic Press. (9)

Wolpe, J. (1961). The systematic desensitization treatment of neuroses. *Journal of Nervous and Mental Disease, 132,* 189–203. (16)

Wolraich, M. L., Lindgren, S. D., Stumbo, P. J., Stegink, L. D., Appelbaum, M. I., & Kiritsy, M. C. (1994). Effects of diets high in sucrose or aspartame on the behavior and cognitive performance of children. *New England Journal of Medicine, 330,* 301–307. (2)

Wong, A. H. C., Smith, M., & Boon, H. S. (1998). Herbal remedies in psychiatric practice. *Archives of General Psychiatry, 55,* 1033–1044. (16)

Wong, M.-L., & Licinio, J. (2001). Research and treatment approaches to depression. *Nature Reviews Neuroscience, 2,* 343–351. (16)

Wood, J. M., Nezworski, T., Lilienfeld, S. O., & Garb, H. N. (2003). *What's wrong with the Rorschach?* San Francisco: Jossey-Bass. (13)

Wood, W., & Eagly, A. H. (2002). A cross-cultural model of the behavior of women and men: Implications for the origins of sex differences. *Psychological Bulletin, 128,* 699–727. (2, 10)

Wood, W., Lundgren, S., Ouellette, J. A., Busceme, S., & Blackstone, T. (1994). Minority influence: A meta-analytic review of social influence processes. *Psychological Bulletin, 115,* 323–345. (14)

Wood, W., & Quinn, J. M. (2003). Forewarned and forearmed? Two meta-analytic syntheses of forewarnings of influence appeals. *Psychological Bulletin, 129,* 119–138. (14)

Woodman, G. F., & Luck, S. J. (2003). Serial deployment of attention during visual search. *Journal of Experimental Psychology: Human Perception and Performance, 29,* 121–138. (8)

Woods, J. H., & Winger, G. (1997). Abuse liability of flunitrazepam. *Journal of Clinical Psychopharmacology, 17*(Suppl. 3), S1–S57. (5)

Woods, S. C. (1991). The eating paradox: How we tolerate food. *Psychological Review, 98,* 488–505. (11)

Woodson, J. C., & Gorski, R. A. (2000). Structural sex differences in the mammalian brain: Reconsidering the male/female dichotomy. In A. Matsumoto (Ed.), *Sexual differentiation of the brain* (pp. 229–255). Boca Raton, FL: CRC Press. (11)

Woodward, E. L. (1938). *The age of reform.* London: Oxford University Press. (7)

Woodworth, R. S. (1934). *Psychology* (3rd ed.). New York: Henry Holt. (1)

Worthington, E. L., Jr., Kurusu, T. A., McCullough, M. E., & Sandage, S. J. (1996). Empirical research on religion and psychotherapeutic processes and outcomes: A 10-year review and research prospectus. *Psychological Bulletin, 119,* 448–487. (15)

Woychyshyn, C. A., McElheran, W. G., & Romney, D. M. (1992). MMPI validity measures: A comparative study of original with alternative indices. *Journal of Personality Assessment, 58,* 138–148. (13)

Wright, I. C., Rabe-Hesketh, S., Woodruff, P. W. R., David, A. S., Murray, R. M., & Bullmore, E. T. (2000). Meta-analysis of regional brain volumes in schizophrenia. *American Journal of Psychiatry, 157,* 16–25. (16)

Wright, L. (1994). *Remembering Satan.* New York: Knopf. (7)

Wu, K. D., & Clark, L. A. (2003). Relations between personality traits and self-reports of daily behavior. *Journal of Research in Personality, 37,* 231–256. (13)

Wundt, W. (1902). *Outlines of psychology* (C. H. Judd, Trans.). New York: Gustav Sechert. (Original work published 1896) (1)

Wundt, W. (1961). Contributions to the theory of sensory perception. In T. Shipley (Ed.), *Classics in psychology* (pp. 51–78). New York: Philosophical Library. (Original work published 1862) (1)

Yamauchi, Y., Endo, S., & Yoshimura, I. (2002). A new whole-mouth gustatory test procedure: II. Effects of aging, gender and smoking. *Acta Otolaryngologica, 133*(Suppl. 546), 49–59. (4)

Yarsh, T. L., Farb, D. H., Leeman, S. E., & Jessell, T. M. (1979). Intrathecal capsaicin depletes substance P in the rat spinal cord and produces prolonged thermal analgesia. *Science, 206,* 481–483. (4)

Yehuda, R. (1997). Sensitization of the hypothalamic-pituitary-adrenal axis in posttraumatic stress disorder. *Annals of the New York Academy of Sciences, 821,* 57–75. (12)

Yirmiya, N., Erel, O., Shaked, M., & Solomonica-Levi, D. (1998). Meta-analyses comparing theory of mind abilities of individuals with autism, individuals with mental retardation, and normally developing individuals. *Psychological Bulletin, 124,* 283–307. (10)

Young, A. M. J., Joseph, M. H., & Gray, J. A. (1993). Latent inhibition of conditioned dopamine release in rat nucleus accumbens. *Neuroscience, 54,* 5–9. (16)

Young, G. B., & Pigott, S. E. (1999). Neurobiological basis of consciousness. *Archives of Neurology, 56,* 153–157. (3)

Yu, D. W., & Shepard, G. H., Jr. (1998). Is beauty in the eye of the beholder? *Nature, 396,* 321–322. (14)

Zadra, A. L., Nielsen, T. A., & Donderi, D. C. (1998). Prevalence of auditory, olfactory, and gustatory experiences in home dreams. *Perceptual and Motor Skills, 87,* 819–826. (5)

Zahavi, A., & Zahavi, A. (1997). *The handicap principle.* New York: Oxford University Press. (14)

Zahn, T. P. Rapoport, J. L., & Thompson, C. L. (1980). Autonomic and behavioral effects of dextroamphetamine and placebo in normal and hyperactive prepubertal boys. *Journal of Abnormal Child Psychology, 8,* 145–160. (3, 15)

Zajonc, R. B. (1968). Attitudinal effects of mere exposure. *Journal of Personality and Social Psychology, 9*(Monograph Suppl. 2, Pt. 2). (14)

Zaragoza, M. S., Payment, K. E., Ackil, J. K., Drivdahl, S. B., & Beck, M. (2001). Interviewing witnesses: Forced confabulation and confirmatory feedback increase false memories. *Psychological Science, 12,* 473–477. (7)

Zarinpoush, F., Cooper, M., & Moylan, S. (2000). The effects of happiness and sadness on moral reasoning. *Journal of Moral Education, 29,* 397–412. (12)

Zeanah, C. H., Boris, N. W., & Larrieu, J. A. (1997). Infant development and developmental risk: A review of the past 10 years. *Journal of the American Academy of Child & Adolescent Psychiatry, 36,* 165–178. (10)

Zehr, D. (2000). Portrayals of Wundt and Titchener in introductory psychology texts: A context analysis. *Teaching of Psychology, 27,* 122–126. (1)

Zepelin, H., & Rechtschaffen, A. (1974). Mammalian sleep, longevity, and energy metabolism. *Brain, Behavior, and Evolution, 10,* 425–470. (5)

Zhang, X., & Firestein, S. (2002). The olfactory receptor gene superfamily of the mouse. *Nature Neuroscience, 5,* 124–133. (4)

Zihl, J., von Cramon, D., & Mai, N. (1983). Selective disturbance of movement vision after bilateral brain damage. *Brain, 106,* 313–340. (3)

Zillman, D., & Weaver, J. B., III (1999). Effects of prolonged exposure to gratuitous media violence on provoked and unprovoked hostile behavior. *Journal of Applied Social Psychology, 29,* 145–165. (2)

Zucker, R. A., & Gomberg, E. S. L. (1986). Etiology of alcoholism reconsidered. *American Psychologist, 41,* 783–793. (16)

Zullow, H. M., Oettingen, G., Peterson, C., & Seligman, M. E. P. (1988). Pessimistic explanatory style in the historical record. *American Psychologist, 43,* 673–682. (16)

Zuriff, G. E. (1995). Continuity over change within the experimental analysis of behavior. In J. T. Todd & E. K. Morris (Eds.), *Modern perspectives on B. F. Skinner and contemporary behaviorism* (pp. 171–178). Westport, CT: Greenwood Press. (6)

Photo Credits

Chapter 1.
0: © SuperStock/SuperStock/PictureQuest 2: center left, © AP/Wide World Photos 2: center right, © AP/Wide World Photos 2: center, © Francoise de Mulder/CORBIS 2: top left, © Galen Rowell/CORBIS 2: top right, © Mitchell Gerber/CORBIS 2: bottom left, © Richard Ellis/NEWSMAKERS/Liaison 5: © Rick Doyle/CORBIS 6: (All) Courtesy of Michael E. Phelps and John C. Mazziotta, University of California, Los Angeles, School of Medicine 7: right, © David Young Wolff/PhotoEdit 7: left, © Royalty-Free/CORBIS 9: © Michael & Patricia Fogden/Minden Pictures 10: © Michael Heron/Woodfin Camp & Associates 13: © Firefly Productions/CORBIS 18: right, © The Walt Disney Company 19: left, © Tom Rosenthal/Superstock 20: right, © Glenn Rileyno 23: © Dario Perla/International Stock 24: top, Courtesy Wellesley College Archives © Notman 24: bottom left, © Bob Daemmrich/Stock Boston 24: bottom right, © Kersten Geier/Gallo Images/CORBIS

Chapter 2.
28: © Pete Saloutos/CORBIS 30: © Frans Lanting/Minden Pictures 36: After Pfungst, 1911, in Fernald, 1984 37: top, © AP/Wide World Photos 37: © Palace of Versailles, France/ET Archive, London/SuperStock 38: © Dr. Elmar R. Gruber 42: left, © Paul Chesley/Tony Stone/Getty Images 42: right, © Tannen Maury/The Image Works 44: © Penelope Breese/Liaison Agency 48: © Herman Eisenbeis/Photo Researchers Inc. 50: © FoodPix/Getty Images 54: © 1995 David Madison

Chapter 3.
66: © Alfred Pasteka/Science Photo Library/Photo Researchers, Inc. 68: © T. Dickinson/The Image Works 70: © Custom Medical Stock Photos 71: © Manfred Kage/Peter Arnold 73: © Omikron /Photo Researchers, Inc. 76: left, © Bettmann/CORBIS 76: right, © Reuters New Media Inc./CORBIS 80: bottom left, Courtesy of Dr. Dana Copeland 80: top, © Dr. Colin Chumbley/Science Photo Library/Photo Researcher, Inc. 80: center, © Dr. Colin Chumbley/Science Photo Library/Photo Researchers, Inc. 80: bottom right, © Manfred Kage/Peter Arnold 85: left, © Richard T. Nowitz /Photo Researchers, Inc. 85: right, © Wellcome Dept. of Cognitive Neurology /Science Photo Library/Photo Researchers 86: bottom, Courtesy of Drs. Scott T. Grafton and John D.Van Horn, Dartmouth Brain Imaging Center, Dartmouth College 86: top, © Wagner, Desmond, Demp, Glover & Gabrielli 87: © Bettmann/CORBIS

Chapter 4.
94: © Lynn Rogers 96: © A. Gragera/Latin Stock/Photo Researchers 99: © Swift Photography/Chase Swift 100: bottom, © E.R. Lewis, F.S. Werb, & Y.Y. Zeevi 100: center, Glenn Rileyno 104: bottom, © Reuters New Media Inc./CORBIS 106: © AP/Wide World Photos 114: © ICM Artists, NY 116: © Julie Lemberger/CORBIS 120: © Richard T. Nowitz/Photo Researchers 123: © Louis Psihoyos/Contact Press Images/Colorific! 125: © Louis Psihoyos/Contact Press Images/Colorific! 130: top, From M.Bruck, P. Cavanaugh & S.J. Ceci "Fortysomething: Recognizing Faces at One's 25th Reunion," In Memory & Cognition,19:221-228.1991. Reprinted by permission of M. Bruck. 130: bottom, © San Francisco Exploratorium 133: top, © Courtesy of McDonnell Douglass 138: top left, © Lowell Observatory, Photo by Clyde Tombaugh 138: top right, © Lowell Observatory, Photo by Clyde Tombaugh 138: bottom, © Richard T. Nowitz/Photo Researchers 139: © Steve McGurry/Magnum Photos 141: © Andrew Brilliant 142: © The Exploratorium/S. Schwartzenberg 143: bottom left, © Mark Antman/The Image Works 143: bottom right, © Mark Antman/The Image Works 136-137: bottom, © Stock Market/Globus Bros./ZEFA

Chapter 5.
© David Young Wolff/PhotoEdit 152: © Craig Aurness/CORBIS 153: © Jeff Greenberg/The Image Works 157: © San Diego Historical Society 158: top center, © Cliff Frith/Bruce Coleman Inc. 158: bottom, © Photodisc 158: center, © Wayne Lankinen/Bruce Coleman Inc. 159: © Richard Nowitz 162: © Tony Hutchings/Getty Images 164: © Patrick Coughlin/Getty Images 169: © Mary Evans Picture Library 170: left, © AP/Wide World Photos 170: right, © AP/Wide World Photos 172: © AP/Wide World Photos 175: © Michael A. Schwartz/The Image Works 176: © Nevada Wier/CORBIS 180: © Roy Morsch/CORBIS 181: © University of Pennsylvania Museum 182: © Ted Soqui/CORBIS Sygma 183: © Archives for Research in Archetypical symbolism, San Francisco

Chapter 6.
188: © Charles Gupton/CORBIS 190: © Mark Stack/Tom Stack & Associates 192: top, © Owen Franken/CORBIS 192: bottom, © Warnher Krutein/Liaison Agency/Getty Images 193: © Peter Turnley/CORBIS 195: © Sovfoto/Eastfoto 208: right, © Michael Justice/The Image Works 208: right, © Russell D. Curtis/Photo Researchers 209: © R. Derek Smith/The Image Bank/Getty Images 213: © TIME Inc./Nina Leen, Life Magazine 214: © TIME Inc./Robert Kelly, Life Magazine 216: right, © Jose Azel/Aurora 216: left, © L. Marescot/Liaison Agency/Getty Images 220: © Stuart Ellins 222: © Joe McDonald/CORBIS 223: © Lindsay Hebberd/CORBIS 223: bottom left, © Sonda Dawes/The Image Works 224: bottom, © AP/Wide World Photos 224: top, © Courtesy of Dr. Albert Bandura 225: top right, © Shoot/photolibrary/PictureQuest 225: bottom left, © Tommy Hindley/Professional Sport/Topham/The Image Works.

Chapter 7.
230: © Lawrence Midgale/Photo Researchers 232: © AP/Wide World Photos 233: © Rupert Watts 234: Courtesy of James Kalat 237: © Joe McDonald/CORBIS 239: top, © Ann Dowie 239: bottom, © Fans Lanting/Minden Pictures 240: © David Young Wolff/PhotoEdit 245: © Spencer Grant/Stock Boston 247: © Paul A. Souders/CORBIS 249: © John Chumack/Galactic Images/Photo Researchers 252: © Wellcome Institute Library, London 254: bottom, © Remi Benali/Liaison Agency/Getty Images 254: top, © UPI/Bettmann/CORBIS 263: © Suzanne Corkin, Psychology Dept., MIT 265: Courtesy of Blue Planet Software,Inc. Tetris © Elorg 1987-2002

Chapter 8.
270: © Walter Hodges/CORBIS 272: © Owen Frankin/CORBIS 278: From Malt, Sloman, Gennari, Shi, & Wang, "Knowing vs. Naming: Similarity and the Linguistic Categorization of Artifacts", Journal of Memory and Language,40,230-262, (1999). Photo reprinted with the permission of the author. 279: top, © Michael Forsberg/www.michaelforsberg.com 279: bottom, © Wendy Shattil and Bob Rozinski 281: © GPU Nuclear Corp. 282: From Rensink, O'Regan & Clark, Science, vol.8 number 5,368-373. Photo reprinted with permission from the publisher and the author. 284: © Glenn Riley 285: © David Burnett/Contact Press Images 286: © Chip Hires/Liaison Agency/Getty Images 287: © Ann Dowie 288: left, © AP/Wide World Photos 288: right, © Porterfield/Chickering/Photo Researchers. 289: © Stephen McBrady 290: right, © HP

Name Index

Subject Index/Glossary

External locus of control the belief that external forces are largely in control of the events of one's life, 507, *507*

Extinction (1) in classical conditioning the dying out of the conditioned response after repeated presentations of the conditioned stimulus without the unconditioned stimulus; (2) in operant conditioning the weakening of a response after a period without reinforcement, 198, 211

    classical conditioning and, 198, *198*

    operant conditioning and, 211, 216

Extrasensory perception (ESP) the alleged ability of certain people to acquire information without using any sense organ and without receiving any form of physical energy, 36

    experiments for testing, 38–39

    professional psychics and, 37–38

Extraterrestrials, 34–35

Extraversion the tendency to seek stimulation and to enjoy the company of other people, 509, 511, *511*, *512*

Extrinsic motivation a motivation based on the rewards and punishments that an act may bring, 409–410, *409*

Eye-blink response, 198, *199*

Eyes

    brain hemispheres and, 88, *89*

    color vision and, 104–110

    dark adaptation of, 101–102, *102*

    disorders of, 99, *100*

    pathway of impulses from, 102–104, *103*

    structure and function of, 98–99, *98*, *99*

    visual receptors of, 99–101, *100*, *101*

    See also Vision

Eyewitness testimony, 260–261

F

Facial expressions

    cultural differences and, 457–458, *457*

    emotions and, 449, 452–453, *453*, 456–460, *456*, *460*

    lie detection and, 471

    producing, 456, *457*

    understanding, 457–459, *457*, *458*, *460*

Facial features

    physical attractiveness and, 554–555, *555*

    recognition of, 129, *130*

Factor analysis, 509

False memory a report that someone believes to be a memory but that does not actually correspond to real events, 258–260, *260*

Falsifiable (with reference to a theory) making sufficiently precise predictions that we can at least imagine evidence that would contradict the theory (if anyone had obtained such evidence), 31

Families

    alcoholism in, 628–629

    birth order in, 392–393, *392*

    conflict and divorce in, 395–396

    day care and, 394–395, *394*

    nontraditional, 395, *395*

    parenting styles in, 393–394

    personality traits in, 511–512, *511*, *512*

    schizophrenia in, 648–649, *649*, 652

    size of, 392–393, *392*

Family systems therapy treatment based on the assumptions that most people's problems develop in a family setting

and that the best way to deal with them is to improve family relationships and communication, 595–596, *595*, *596*

Farsightedness, 99, *100*

Fear, 468

    anxiety and, 468–471

    facial expressions and, 458, *458*

    learning by observation, 619–620, *619*

    persuasive messages and, 545–546, *545*

    See also Phobias

Feature detector a neuron in the visual system of the brain that responds to the presence of a certain simple feature, such as a horizontal line, 129–132, *131*, *132*

    evidence of, 130–132

    Gestalt psychology and, 136

    perception and, 132, *132*

Fetal alcohol syndrome a condition marked by stunted growth of the head and body; malformations of the face, heart, and ears; and nervous system damage, including seizures, hyperactivity, learning disabilities, and mental retardation, 359, *359*

Fetus an organism more developed than an embryo but not yet born (from about 8 weeks after conception until birth in humans), 358

Figure and ground an object and its background, 133, *133*

First impressions, 533–534, *533*

Fixation (a) in vision a period when the eyes are steady; (b) in Freud's theory a persisting preoccupation with an immature psychosexual interest as a result of frustration at that stage of psychosexual development, 314–315, 494

Fixed-interval schedule a rule for delivering reinforcement for the first response that the subject makes after a specified period of time has passed, 215

Fixed-ratio schedule a rule for delivering reinforcement only after the subject has made a specific number of correct responses, 215

Flavor, 123

Flooding (or **implosion** or **intensive exposure therapy**) a treatment for phobia in which the person is suddenly exposed to the object of the phobia, 621

Fluid intelligence the basic power of reasoning and using information, including the ability to perceive relationships, solve unfamiliar problems, and gain new types of knowledge, 328

Flynn effect the tendency for people's performance on IQ tests to improve from one decade or generation to the next, 333–334

fMRI. *See* Functional magnetic resonance imaging

Folk psychology, 3

Food

    cultural cuisines and, 423–424, *424*

    dairy product consumption, 358, *358*

    dieting and, 419–420

    genetics and, 358, *358*

    learned associations with, 424, *424*

    selection motives relative to, 422–424, *423*, *424*

    taste preferences and, 423

    See also Nutrition

Food and Drug Administration (FDA), 523

Footbridge Dilemma, 460, *460*

Foot-in-the-door technique a method of eliciting compliance by first making a modest request and then following it with a larger request, 547

Forebrain, 78–82, *79*, *82*

Forensic psychiatry, 611

Forensic psychologist one who provides advice and consultation to police, lawyers, courts, or other parts of the criminal justice system, 12

Forewarning effect the tendency of a brief preview of a message to decrease its persuasiveness, 547

Forgetting

    brain damage and, 263–266

    infant amnesia and, 266–267

    interference and, 253

    See also Amnesia; Memory

Formal operations stage, 375

Fovea the central part of the retina that has a greater density of receptors, especially cones, than any other part of the retina, 98, *98*

Framing effect the tendency to answer a question differently when it is framed (phrased) differently, 298

Framing questions, 297–298, *298*, 299

Fraternal twins are twins who develop from two eggs fertilized by two different sperm; they are no more closely related than are any other children born to the same parents, 353–354, *353*

    See also Twin studies

Free association a procedure where a client lies on a couch, starts thinking about a particular symptom or problem, and then reports everything that comes to mind, 591–592

Freebase cocaine, 180

Free recall a method of testing memory by asking someone to produce a certain item (e.g., a word) without substantial hints, as on an essay or short-answer test, 234, *235*

Free will the doctrine that behavior is caused by a person's independent decisions, not by external determinants, 5–6

Frequency principle the identification of pitch by the frequency of action potentials in neurons along the basilar membrane of the cochlea, synchronized with the frequency of sound waves, 114

Freudian personality theories, 491–498

Friendships, 552–553

Frontal lobe a portion of each cerebral hemisphere at the anterior pole, with sections that control movement and certain aspects of memory, 81–82, *81*

Frustration-aggression hypothesis the theory that frustration leads to aggressive behavior, 472

Functional fixedness the tendency to adhere to a single approach to a problem or a single way of using an item, 297

Functionalism an attempt to understand how mental processes produce useful behaviors, 20

Functional magnetic resonance imaging (fMRI) a technique that uses magnetic detectors outside the head to measure the amounts of hemoglobin, with and without oxygen, in different parts of the brain and thereby provides an indication of current activity levels in various brain areas, 84, 86

Fundamental attribution error the tendency to make internal attributions for people's behavior, even when an observer sees evidence for an external influence, 539

G

g factor Spearman's "general" factor which all IQ tests and all parts of an IQ test are believed to have in common, 326–328, *327*

GAD. *See* Generalized anxiety disorder

Gambling psychology, 296

Ganglion cells neurons in the eye that receive input from bipolar cells, which in turn receive their input from the visual receptors, 102

Ganzfield procedure, 38, *38*

Gate theory the proposal that pain messages must pass through a gate, probably in the spinal cord, that can block these messages, 117–118, *118*

Gay men, 432–436

Gender differences

cognition and, 397

depression and, 635–636

emotional intelligence and, 463

explanations for, 398

homosexual experiences and, 433–434, *433*, *434*

human development and, 396–398

intelligence tests and, 339–340, 341, *342*

learning and, 501–502

mate selection and, 556–557, *556*

schizophrenia and, 648

sexual behavior and, 427, *428*, 433–434, *433*, *434*

social development and, 397–398, *397*

Gender identity the sex that a person regards him- or herself as being, 430

Gender role the pattern of behavior that each person is expected to follow because of being male or female, 501–502, *501*, *502*

Generalized anxiety disorder (GAD) a disorder in which people are almost constantly plagued by exaggerated worries, 615

Generalizing solutions to problems, 289–291, *290*

General medical conditions, 584

Genes segments of chromosomes that control chemical reactions that ultimately direct the development of the organism, 354–355, *354*, *355*

dominant vs. recessive, 355, *355*

identifying and locating, 356

sex-linked and sex-limited, 355–356, *356*

Genetics, 353–358

behavior and, 357–358

environmental factors and, 337–339

ethnic differences and, 342–343, 344–345

heritability and, 356–357

IQ test scores and, 337–339, *338*, *339*, 342–343, 344–345

nutrition and, 358, *358*

principles of, 354–357

sexual orientation and, 434, *435*

temperament and, 392

twin studies and, 353–354, 356–357, *357*

Web resources on, 402

See also Heredity

Genital stage Freud's final stage of psychosexual development, in which sexual pleasure is focused on sexual intimacy with others, 495

Gestalt psychology an approach to psychology that seeks to explain how we perceive overall patterns, 133

feature detectors and, 136

perception and, 133–136, *133*, *134*, *135*, *136*

Glaucoma a condition characterized by increased pressure within the eyeball, resulting in damage to the optic nerve and therefore a loss of vision, 99

Glia a cell of the nervous system that insulates neurons, removes waste materials (e.g., dead cells), and performs other supportive functions, 69

Global assessment of functioning, 584

Glucagon a hormone that the pancreas releases to convert stored energy supplies back into blood glucose, 413, *413*

Glucose the most abundant sugar in the blood, 413

Glutamate hypothesis of schizophrenia the view that the underlying problem causing schizophrenia is deficient stimulation of certain glutamate synapses, 651–652

Goals, 438–440

conditions for setting, 439, *439*

deadlines and, 438–439

high and low, 439–440

Good figure in Gestalt psychology the tendency to perceive simple, symmetrical figures, 135, *135*

Graduate Record Examination (GRE), 336

Gray matter, 79, *80*

Group endorsement, 546

Group polarization the tendency of a group whose members lean in the same direction on a particular issue to become more extreme in its views after discussing the issue as a group, 565–566

Groups

decision making in, 565–566, *566*

experimental vs. control, 50–51

Group therapy treatment administered to a group of people all at once, 597, *597*

Groupthink a process by which the members of a group suppress their doubts about a group's poorly thought-out decision for fear of making a bad impression or disrupting the harmony of the group, 566, *566*, 576

Guilty-knowledge test a test that uses the polygraph to measure whether a person has information that should be known only by someone guilty of a certain crime or someone who talked with the guilty person, 470–471

H

Habits, breaking, 217–218, 225–226

Habituation a decrease in a person's response to a stimulus after it has been presented repeatedly, 361

Hallucination a sensory experience not corresponding to reality, such as seeing or hearing something that is not present or failing to see or hear something that is present, 171, 646

Hallucinogens drugs that induce sensory distortions, *179*, 183, *183*

Handwriting analysis, 521

Happiness, 465–467

factors correlated with, 466–467

influence of wealth on, 465–466, *466*

Web resources on, 487

Harm avoidance, 511

Harm reduction an approach to drug abuse that concentrates on decreasing the frequency of drug use and minimizing the harmful consequences to health and well-being, 632

Hassles, 478, *479*

Health maintenance organizations (HMOs), 590, 597

Health psychologists, 24

Health psychology a field of psychology concerned with how people's behavior can enhance health and prevent illness and how behavior contributes to recovery from illness, 476

Hearing, 112–115

anatomy of, 112–113, *113*

Gestalt principles in, 135, 136

infants and, 361, *361*

localization of sounds in, 115, *115*

loss of, 113

pitch perception and, 114–115, *114*

sound waves and, 112, *112*

See also Ears

Heart disease, 482–483

Hemisphere the left or right half of the brain; each hemisphere is responsible for sensation and motor control on the opposite side of the body, 79, *80*, 88–90, *89*

Heredity

alcoholism and, 628–629

behavior and, 357–358

depression and, 635, *635*

environmental factors and, 337–339

ethnic differences and, 342–343, 344–345

human achievement and, 22

IQ test scores and, 337–339, *338*, *339*, 342–343, 344–345

obesity and, 417

personality traits and, 511–512, *511*, *512*

schizophrenia and, 648–649, *649*

See also Genetics

Heritability an estimate of the variance within a population that is due to heredity, 356

behavior and, 357–358

estimating in humans, 356–357

Heroin, *179*, 182, 632, *632*

Hertz (Hz) a unit of frequency representing one cycle (vibration) per second, 112

Heterosexual orientation, 433

Heuristics strategies for simplifying a problem or for guiding an investigation, 288

algorithms vs., 289

availability, 294–295, *294*

reasoning by, 293–295

representativeness, 293–294, *294*

Hindbrain, 78, *79*

Hindsight bias the tendency to mold our recollection of the past to fit how events later turned out, 256, *257*

Hippocampus a forebrain structure in the interior of the temporal lobe that is important for storing certain kinds of memory, 263–264, *263*

TO THE OWNER OF THIS BOOK:

I hope that you have found *Introduction to Psychology,* 7th Edition, useful. So that this book can be improved in a future edition, would you take the time to complete this sheet and return it? Thank you.

School and address: _____

_____

Department: _____

Instructor's name: _____

1. What I like most about this book is: _____

_____

_____

2. What I like least about this book is: _____

_____

_____

3. My general reaction to this book is: _____

_____

_____

4. The name of the course in which I used this book is: _____

_____

5. Were all of the chapters of the book assigned for you to read? _____

    If not, which ones weren't? _____

6. In the space below, or on a separate sheet of paper, please write specific suggestions for improving this book and anything else you'd care to share about your experience in using this book.

_____

_____

_____

_____

_____

_____

_____

FOLD HERE

THOMSON

WADSWORTH

NO POSTAGE
NECESSARY
IF MAILED
IN THE
UNITED STATES

BUSINESS REPLY MAIL
FIRST-CLASS MAIL   PERMIT NO. 102   MONTEREY CA

POSTAGE WILL BE PAID BY ADDRESSEE

Attn: *Vicki Knight, Psychology*

Wadsworth/Thomson Learning
60 Garden Ct Ste 205
Monterey CA 93940-9967

FOLD HERE

OPTIONAL:

Your name: _____ Date: _____

May we quote you, either in promotion for *Introduction to Psychology,* 7th Edition, or in
future publishing ventures?

Yes: _____ No: _____

Sincerely yours,

James Kalat